THE VOCABULARY OF LUKE

BIBLICAL TOOLS AND STUDIES

Edited by

B. DOYLE, G. VAN BELLE, J. VERHEYDEN
K.U.Leuven

Associate Editors

C.T. BEGG, Washington DC – U. BERGES, Münster – J. FREY, München
C.M. TUCKETT, Oxford – G. VAN OYEN, Louvain-La-Neuve

Biblical Tools and Studies – Volume 10

THE VOCABULARY OF LUKE

AN ALPHABETICAL PRESENTATION AND A SURVEY OF CHARACTERISTIC AND NOTEWORTHY WORDS AND WORD GROUPS IN LUKE'S GOSPEL

BY

ADELBERT DENAUX & RITA CORSTJENS
in collaboration with HELLEN MARDAGA

PEETERS
LEUVEN – PARIS – WALPOLE, MA

2009

Cover:
Τῆς καινῆς Διαθήκης ἅπαντα. Εὐαγγέλιον
Novum Iesu Christi D.N. Testamentum ex bibliotheca regia.
Lutetiae: ex officina Roberti Stephani, 1550. in-folio
KULeuven, Maurits Sabbebibliotheek, P225.042/F°

Mt 5,3-12

A catalogue record for this book is available from the Library of Congress.

ISBN 978-90-429-2348-5
D/2009/0602/154

© 2009, Peeters, Bondgenotenlaan 153, B-3000 Leuven (Belgium)

PREFACE

"The Vocabulary of Luke" is a linguistic tool intended to help students of the Greek text of Luke and the Book of Acts. It offers a full alphabetical list of the vocabulary of the Gospel of Luke. For each lemma it gives (1) a comparative statistical survey of the occurrences in Luke and Acts, Matthew and Mark; (2) the various possible meanings (with references, based on the lexica of Louw-Nida and Bauer); (3) a comparative list of word groups (based on the concordances of Aland and Hoffmann as well as our own research); (4) a comparative list of words and word groups that have been considered to be characteristic of Luke. (This is based on research into Luke's language during the 19th and 20th centuries with systematic references to the authors who have considered them characteristic as well as our own evaluation of the results, offering our own list of characteristics); (5) the relevant linguistic literature concerning each lemma.

Our introduction gives a historical and critical survey of the research of the last two centuries and an appendix with a list of words and word groups that only occur in Luke and/or Acts.

This publication is the result of careful collecting and assessing of all the available data. It took several years of labour to finalise it and was realised by the team of the research project (1999-2003): "Het hellenistisch-Griekse taaleigen van het Lucasevangelie en de Handelingen van de Apostelen" (A Comparative Study of the Language of Luke-Acts), sponsored by the Research Council of the K.U. Leuven and by the Fonds Wetenschappelijk Onderzoek-Vlaanderen. Our sincere thanks go to the sponsors, and especially to the scientific collaborators of the research team: Rita Corstjens, who played a major role in collecting and organising the data; Inge Van Wiele, Laurens Geeraert and Beate Kowalski. Our collaborator, Dr. Hellen Mardaga, finalised the project by checking all of the data (2007-2008).

To our knowledge, there is no linguistic tool that gathers so many data in such a conveniently arranged way. All data can be verified, because references are given for each linguistic feature that occurs in Luke and Acts as well as the scholars involved in the discussion. Given the fact that thousands of data had to be collected and checked, we expect that some errors are still there, for which we take full responsibility. Over time, the tool will be perfected. Nevertheless, our efforts will be rewarded when students of Luke's language and Gospel will feel relieved when they no longer have to do the painstaking work that we have done, and when they use this tool as a basis for further linguistic and exegetical research.

Leuven, April 4, 2009   Adelbert DENAUX
                                                       Rita CORSTJENS

TABLE OF CONTENTS

INTRODUCTION

The scientific study of the language and style of Luke goes back at least to the beginning of the nineteenth century. In 1816 at Leipzig, a German pastor Christoph Gotthelf GERSDORF published his observations on the language of several NT authors. He entitled the work: "Beiträge zur Sprach-Characteristik der Schriftsteller des Neuen Testament" ('Contributions to the Characteristic Language of the Authors of the New Testament'). Aware that his contribution introduced something new to the field of NT study, he added the subtitle: "Eine Sammlung meist neuer Bemerkungen" ('A Collection of mostly unedited Remarks')[1]. For more than 30 years, he had patiently formulated his observations with the help of Griesbach's successive editions of the NT text (1775-77, [2]1796-1806, [3]1803-1807) and the concordance of Erasmus Schmid, edited at Wittenberg in 1638. During the French invasion of 1806, he almost lost all of his notes. Afterwards, it appears that he tried to get his work printed with several publishers, but in vain. But in 1816, the "Weidmannische Buchhandlung" agreed to publish it. The publisher probably accepted it based on the support of J.J. Griesbach himself as well as the help of the Leipzig professors: D. Tzschirner, D. Keil and Schäfer. In his preface, C.H. Gersdorf quotes a letter from J.J. Griesbach, dated 22 October 1803. Therein, the latter expresses his approval of Gersdorf's careful work on the characteristic language of some NT authors, work which is to be recommended for its newness and usefulness: "Die Resultate Ihres Scharfsinns und ausserordentlichen Fleisses müssen bei dem gründlichen Studium des N.T. sehr bedeutende Vortheile gewähren, die um so höher zu schätzen sind, weil bis jetzt noch viel zu wenig dieser Seite der Sache ins Auge gefasst worden ist ... Ihr Werk empfielt sich also durch Neuheit eben sowohl, als durch Nutzbarkeit, und wünsche ich daher seine baldige Vollendung und Bekanntmachung"[2].

Moreover, J.J. Griesbach considers such a study of the language of the NT to be an important tool for anyone aiming at a better knowledge and a more profound critique of the NT writings. He enumerates the aims that can be pursued with such a philological tool: "1. to judge the authenticity or inauthenticity of NT writings or passages; 2. to decide on disputes about the origin and nature of the Gospels, by which some easy yet highly praised hypotheses can be proved unreliable; 3. to correct the text in specific cases; 4. to define the value of manuscripts, which have been

---

1. Christoph Gotthelf GERSDORF, *Beiträge zur Sprach-Characteristik der Schriftsteller des Neuen Testaments: Eine Sammlung meist neuer Bemerkungen.* Erster Theil, Leipzig: Weidmannische Buchhandlung, 1816, XXXVI-579 p.

2. *Ibid.*, p. v.

judged quite diversely; and 5. to correct or confirm the usual sense given to many passages of the NT"[3]. Hence, according to Griesbach, the study of the language and vocabulary of the NT writings is not taken as an end in itself, but as a means to other ends, namely, to decide on questions of authenticity (nr. 1), text criticism (nrs. 3 and 4), literary criticism (nr. 2) and exegesis (nr. 5).

In fact, Gersdorf's study does not cover the NT Greek in all its aspects. It is limited to the idiolect of certain NT authors and hence a study of their style rather than their language[4]. In a broad sense, his expression 'Sprach-Charakteristik' (which we translate as 'characteristic language') has to do with form ("Ausdruck") as well as with content ("Vorstellungen und Ideen")[5]. In a narrow sense, 'characteristic language' has to do with an author's distinctive use or non-use of words, word forms or phrases, and with their specific meaning, position, mutual relation and order in the author's writing[6]. Gersdorf was also aware that the study of characteristic language is by definition a comparative enterprise: the student compares a NT author with non-biblical authors, OT authors or, most preferably, with other NT authors[7]. More

3. *Ibid.*, p. vi: "Jedem, dem es um genauere Kenntniss und gründliche Beurhteilung der neutestamentlichen Schriften zu thun ist, wird Ihr Werk willkommen seyn, als wichtiges Hülfsmittel 1) zu Beurtheilung der Aechtheit oder Unächtheit ganzer Bücher und einzelner Stellen derselben; 2) zur Entscheidung der so streitigen Fragen über das Entstehen und die ursprüngliche Beschaffenheit unsrer Evangelien, indem dadurch manche luftige, obgleich hochgepriesene Hypothese in ihrer Unstatthaftigkeit deutlicher dargestellt werden kann; 3) zur Berichtigung des Textes in einzelnen Stellen; 4) zur Bestimmung des Werths alter Handschriften, über die man so verschieden geurtheilt hat, und 5) zu Berichtigung oder Bestätigung des gewöhnlich angenommenen Sinnes mancher Stellen des N.T.".

4. Gersdorf is clearly aware of the distinction between language and style: "Wenn gleich in den Sprachen überhaupt, und in jeder einzelnen insbesondere, Regeln und Gesetze gelten, von welchen der Sprechende und Schreibende, ohne den Vorwurf der Denk- und Sprachwidrigkeit aus sich zu laden, durchaus nicht abweichen darf: so bleibet doch noch Vieles freigelassen, wie in der Darstellung, und Belebung der Gedanken, also auch im Gebrauche und der Verbindung der Wörter und Redensarten" (see his "Einleitung", *ibid.*, p. 1).

5. *Ibid.*, p. 3: "Sprach-Charakteristik ... umfasset im weiteren Sinne nicht nur den Ausdruck, der etwas das Individuum Bezeichnendes enthält, sowohl einzeln als in Verbindung gesetzt, sondern auch, wiefern der Ausdruck mit dem Auszudrückenden und Vorgestellten innig verbunden ist, das Unterscheidende der Vorstellingen und Ideen".

6. In his "Einleitung", Gersdorf gives a description of what he means by 'characteristic language': "Bei der *Sprach-Characteristik* aber, in engeren Sinne des Wortes, und zwar insbesondere neutestamentlichen Schriftsteller unter einander, wird auf das gesehen, was den Einen von dem Anderen unterscheidet im Gebrauche oder Nichtgebrauche gewisser Wörter, Wortformen und Phrasen, und in der Bedeutung, Stellung, Verbindung und Aufeinanderfolge derselben" (*ibid.*, p. 9).

7. *Ibid.*, p. 3: "die Sache der *Sprach-Characteristik* ... geht vergleichend zu Werke, hält mehrere oder wenigere in ihrer Sprache gegen einander, z.B. die neutestamentlichen

specifically, he tries to describe the characteristic language of Matthew and Luke in order to establish the original text (in the case of Matthew) and in order to prove that their respective infancy narratives were as authentic as the rest of their Gospel. Indeed, half of his study was devoted to the study of the characteristic vocabulary of Mt 1–2 (and parts of Mt 27–28) and Lk 1–2 (pp. 38-272). The second half was devoted to questions of word order (syntax), but again with the intention to describe the language use characteristic of the different NT authors (pp. 272-526)[8].

Until recently, the study of the characteristic language of NT writers has been undertaken within the same framework. The reason for studying the characteristic language of an author was to prove the authenticity or in-authenticity of (part of) the book or letter that was traditionally ascribed to him; to establish the text (M.-É. Boismard); to distinguish between tradition/sources and redaction (literary criticism) (e.g. H. Schürmann; F. Neirynck); finally, to establish the precise meaning of a text (the main purpose of exegesis). It is only with the rise of linguistic approaches towards the language of the NT that the study of the language itself has become a primary focus of research[9]. This does not mean, however, that the numerous philological observations made by exegetes during the last two centuries on the language or vocabulary of the NT writers – within the framework of their varied interests – cease to be valuable. They contain a treasure of judicious observations and remarks that should not be neglected by students of the language of the NT.

Our tool compiles all of the results of this type of research and presents it in a systematic way for the reader. In what follows, we survey the most important contributions to the study of Luke's characteristic vocabulary since Gersdorf. Our focus will deal primarily with a description of the criteria used by scholars to establish what they consider to be the characteristic vocabulary of Luke, coupled with an evaluation of the whole enterprise.

---

gegen die Profanscribenten, oder gegen die alttestamentlichen, oder auch, was besonders zu empfelen ist, bloss die einzelnen neutestamentlichen unter einander, trennet das Besondere und Individuelle vom Allgemeinen".

8. The remaining chapters respectively deal with: Χριστός and Ἰησοῦς and their link with κύριος, in Paul and Peter (ch. 3); the position of substantives with substantives in the genitive (ch. 4); the position of adjectives, especially of quality (ch. 5); the position of adjectives of quantity and numerals (ch. 6); the position of adjectives of relation and pronouns (ch. 7); the position of adverbs (ch. 8); something about the word order of participles and verbs (ch. 9).

9. See the studies of Stanley Porter and others. Moreover, in the past, renowned classical philologists have made substantial contributions to the study of the Greek of the NT or of NT authors, e.g. Friedrich Blass (1896), Albert Debrunner (1913), Sophie Antoniadis (1930), Édouard Delebecque (1976).

The way C.G. Gersdorf organised his study of Luke's characteristic vocabulary amounted to a continuous philological commentary on Luke 1–2. The study comprised more than 100 pages. Until recently, this approach has been followed or continued by others. Scholars like A. von Harnack (1906: Lk 1,5-15.39-56.68-79; 2,15-20.41-53; Acts 16,10-17; 28,1-16; and the "we"-sections)[10]; H. Schürmann (1953, 1955, 1957: Lk 22,7-38)[11]; G. Schneider (1969: Lk 22,54-71)[12]; J. Jeremias (1980: the non-Markan material in Luke)[13]; and R. von Bendemann (2001: Lk 8,21– 21,38)[14] take a section of Luke-Acts as the basis of their study and attempt to recover the words or phrases, which they consider to be characteristic of Luke. Or, to put it into literary-critical terms, they try to recover his 'redactional' language. This is to be distinguished from the 'traditional' language taken over from his sources or traditions[15].

However, as early as 1836, another organisational principle was used to describe Luke's characteristic vocabulary. In his "Einleitung in das Neue Testament"[16], Karl August CREDNER devoted a paragraph to the language and authenticity of Luke in which he offers a list of no less than 64 characteristic features of Luke's language. He considers these features to be Lukan because of their relative frequency in comparison with the other NT writings, especially the Gospels. His list's main purpose is to ascertain the authenticity of the parts of the Gospel considered

10. A. HARNACK, *Lukas der Arzt, der Verfasser des dritten Evangeliums und der Apostelgeschichte*, Leipzig, 1906. ET: *New Testament Studies. I: Luke the Physician: The Author of the Third Gospel and the Acts of the Apostles* (Crown Theological Library), trans. J.R. Wilkinson. Ed. W.D. Morrison, London: Williams & Norgate; New York: G.P. Putnam's Sons, 1907.

11. H. SCHÜRMANN, *Die Paschamahlbericht Lk 22,(7-14.)15-18. I. Teil einer quellenkritischen Untersuchung des lukanischen Abendmahlsberichtes Lk 22,7-38* (NTAbh, 19/5), Münster: Aschendorff, 1953; *Die Einsetzungsbericht Lk 22,19-20. II. Teil einer quellenkritischen Untersuchung des lukanischen Abendmahlsberichtes Lk 22,7-38* (NTAbh, 20/4), Münster: Aschendorff, 1955; *Jesu Abschiedsrede Lk 22,21-38. III. Teil einer quellenkritischen Untersuchung des lukanischen Abendmahlsberichtes Lk 22,7-38* (NTAbh, 20/5), Münster: Aschendorff, 1957.

12. G. SCHNEIDER, *Verleugnung, Verspottung und Verhör Jesu nach Lukas 22,54-71: Studien zur lukanischen Darstellung der Passion* (SANT, 22), München, 1969.

13. J. JEREMIAS, *Die Sprache des Lukasevangeliums. Redaktion und Tradition im Nicht-Markusstoff des dritten Evangeliums* (KEK), Göttingen, 1980.

14. R. VON BENDEMANN, *Zwischen δόξα und σταυρός: Eine exegetische Untersuchung der Texte des sogenannten Reiseberichts im Lukasevangelium* (BZNW, 101), Berlin – New York: de Gruyter, 2001.

15. This way of organising data makes it difficult to consult the monographs referred to in this paragraph. Our "Vocabulary" now solves this difficulty by offering an alphabetic list or index of all phenomena described in these monographs.

16. K.A. CREDNER, *Einleitung in das Neue Testament. Erster Theil. Erste-Zweite Abtheilung*, Halle: Verlag der Buchhandlung des Waisenhauses, 1836, X-754 p. Esp. 130-142: "Sprache und Aechtheit".

inauthentic by a number of scholars (mainly Lk 1–2). The point is that Lukan features occur in Lk 1–2 as well as in the rest of the Gospel. To our knowledge, Credner's attempt is the first of its kind. His list is not arranged in alphabetical order, but randomly arranged. It contains words (nr. 5), word groups (nrs. 1-3), word combinations (nrs. 15, 16, 27, 28), word forms (nrs. 19, 33), semantic observations (e.g. meanings of exclusively Lukan words, e.g. 8, 25), and even some tendencies (like strong affections 57, indicating the idea of fullness 60) having lexicological consequences. Since Credner, we have found at least ten works listing Lukan characteristics in alphabetical order, sometimes with subdivisions. In our bibliography we list them under a separate subtitle: "Works listing Lukan Characteristics". They are, in chronological order: Plummer (1896; [4]1922); T. Vogel (1897, [2]1899); J.C. Hawkins (1898; [2]1909); R. Morgenthaler (1958); L. Gaston (1973); F.J.G. Collison (1977); M.-É. Boismard (1984); F. Neirynck (1985); W.M.A. Hendriks (1986) and M.D. Goulder (1989).

A comparison of these lists shows that scholars get different results in both number and nature, which will become clear in the following survey. For each author, we give the number of characteristic words/lexemes (1); word forms (2); semantic peculiarities (3); word groups/phrases (4) and total (5).

Author	1	2	3	4	5
CREDNER (1836)	59	26	10	37	132
PLUMMER (1896; [4]1922)	247	6	7	91	351
VOGEL ([2]1899)	95	4	26	34	159
HAWKINS (1898; [2]1909)	136	12	10	54	212
MORGENTHALER (1958)	62				62
GASTON (1973)	63+36?	1			64+36?
COLLISON (1977)	56	11	32	67	166
BOISMARD-NEIRYNCK (1984-85)	236	39	26	314	615
HENDRIKS 1986 166-169	91		2		93
HENDRIKS 1986 428, 433, 434, 441, 448, 466	35	7	2	1	45
GOULDER (1989)	184	42	25	133	384

There are several reasons for these differences: the nature of the linguistic phenomena that are listed (only words or also other phenomena), the texts that are compared (Lk and Mt+Mk; Lk+Acts and Mt+Mk; Lk+Acts and other NT writings), the percentage of deviation needed to be considered 'characteristic', the distribution of the phenomenon, minimum occurrences needed, etc. They will be discussed in the following overview.

The first person to be mentioned is Alfred PLUMMER. He is the author of the still valuable "Critical and Exegetical Commentary on the Gospel

According to S. Luke" in the ICC series (1896)[17]. In his Preface, he
mentions one of the special features of his commentary as being "the
attention which has been paid, both in the Introduction and throughout the
Notes, to the marks of S. Luke's style"[18]. He finds a study of Luke's style to
be a matter of great interest and importance because it proves that the writer
of the Third Gospel is identical with the writer of Acts, confirming the old
tradition that the writer of these two books was Luke, the beloved
physician[19]. Paragraph six of the Introduction is devoted to Luke's
"Characteristics, Style, and Language"[20]. As to Luke's style and language,
Plummer is struck by two apparently opposite features: "his great *command
of Greek* and his very un-Greek *use of Hebrew phrases and constructions*",
which makes Luke the most versatile of all NT writers: "He can be as
Hebraistic as the LXX, and as free from Hebraisms as Plutarch"[21]. Luke's
command of Greek is abundantly clear in the freedom of his constructions
and also in the richness of his vocabulary. The richness is seen in the high
number of words which occur in Luke's two writings and nowhere else in
the NT[22]. Plummer gives a list of the most remarkable examples (list P*)[23].
Nevertheless, he considers that expressions and constructions, which Luke
frequently uses – or more frequently than any other writer of the NT – are
still more characteristic of his style than the words that are peculiar to Luke-
Acts or Luke alone[24]. In order to be more useful, he classifies them in eight
different categories:

(P[1])   Expressions peculiar to Luke and Paul in the NT (pp. liv-lvii);
(P[2])   Expressions peculiar to Luke and Paul and Hebrews (p. lix);
(P[3])   Expressions peculiar to Luke and Hebrews (p. lix);

---

17. A. PLUMMER, *The Gospel According to St. Luke* (ICC), Edinburgh: T.&T. Clark,
1896; [2]1898; [3]1900; [5]1922 (= 1964). We use the fifth edition.
    18. *Ibid.*, p. iii.
    19. *Ibid.*, p. iv.
    20. *Ibid.*, pp. xli-lxvii.
    21. *Ibid.*, pp. xlvii-xlix.
    22. *Ibid.*, p. lii: Plummer estimates them at 750 or (including doubtful cases) 851, of
which 26 occur in quotations from the LXX. "In the Gospel the words peculiar to Luke are
312; of which 52 are doubtful, and 11 occur in quotations". These numbers can now be
improved with the help of the concordances of Morgenthaler and Aland.
    23. *Ibid.*, pp. lii-liii. He notes 1 case 30× in Lk-Acts, 1 case 9× in Lk-Acts and 1 case
9× in Lk, 1 case 8× in Lk, 3 cases 7× in Lk-Acts, 2 cases 6× in Lk-Acts and 2 cases 6× in
Lk, 6 cases 5× in L-Acts and 5 cases 5× in Lk, 13 cases 4× in Lk-Acts and 4 cases 4× in
Lk, 21 cases 3× in L-Acts and 7 cases 3× in Lk, 34 cases 2× in Lk-Acts and 26 cases in
Lk. This makes altogether a list of 128 items. Moreover, there are more than 200 words in
Lk that are hapax legomena in the NT, of which Plummer only gives an exemplary list. In
the appendix, we give a survey of words and phrases that are only in Lk-Acts and
nowhere else in the NT, based on the concordances of Morgenthaler (see n. 34) and Aland
as well as on the work of Boismard and Lamouille (see n. 45).
    24. *Ibid.*, p. liii.

(P^4) Expressions not found in the other Gospels, but more frequently in St.
        Luke's writings than in all the rest of NT (p. lix);
(P^5) Expressions found in one or more of the other Gospels, but more frequent in
        St. Luke's writings than in all the rest of NT (pp. lix-lx);
(P^6) Expressions frequent in St. Luke's writings and probably due to Hebrew
        influence (pp. lx-lxi);
(P^7) Miscellaneous expressions and constructions, which are especially frequent
        in St. Luke's writings (pp. lxii-lxiii);
(P^8) Expressions that are probably or possibly medical (pp. lxiii-lxvi).

Considering that the concordance of Moulton-Geden did not yet exist
when the first edition of his commentary was published, Plummer's lists
represent an enormous amount of meticulous work. They offer quite a
complete survey of characteristic words and phrases in Luke. Contemporary
scholarship has, of course, lost its interest in list P^8. Other lists may
eventually point to some sort of relation between Luke and other NT writers
(lists P^{1-3}). The remaining lists are still useful for a study of Luke's
characteristic language (P^* and P^{4-7}), which is the focus of our study. List P^6
also touches the question of Semitisms in Luke and has some overlaps with
other lists. We note that the implicit criteria behind the lists marking Luke's
style are comparative and numerical: Luke or Luke-Acts are compared to
the rest of the NT, including the other Gospels (or not, when the word or
expression does not occur in them); words or expressions are deemed
characteristic when they occur in greater frequency than in the rest of the
NT. There is little awareness of the need for a minimal number of
occurrences required for a reliable description of Luke's characteristic
vocabulary, except for the hapax legomena[25].

At approximately the same time (1897), the German Dr. theol. and phil.
Theodor VOGEL published what he called "a philological study of a
layperson, which is the result of being engaged with the NT for many years"
about the characteristic language and style of Luke[26]. From a
methodological point of view, Vogel is very reluctant to use statistics,
especially in the field of lexicography. Using merely lexical statistics in
language studies could lead to the absurd conclusion that undoubtedly
authentic works of Horace, Schiller and Goethe might be inauthentic.
Grammatical-stylistic statistics are more reliable, although also in this field
prudence is required. Finally one should ponder each individual case in
order to avoid apparent rather than real conclusions. "Let us thank God that

---

25. *Ibid.*, p. liii: "It is not worth to make a complete list of the words (over 200 in
number) which occur *once* in the Third Gospel and nowhere else in N.T.".

26. T. VOGEL, *Zur Charakteristik des Lukas nach Sprache und Stil. Eine
philologische Laienstudie*, Leipzig: Verlag der Dürrschen Buchhandlung, 1897; [2]1899, p.
5. We use the second edition.

the spiritual has a nature which is too difficult to grasp, that it could be registered like the number of fire seats or chickens"[27]. Consequently, the main body of this study is descriptive, not statistical in nature. However, in spite of his fundamental aversion to statistics, in Appendix F, Vogel makes four comparative lists of the vocabulary of Luke and Acts: words or phrases that occur only in Lk-Acts (57 items); words and phrases that, except for Lk-Acts, occur only rarely in the rest of the NT (42 items); expressions that are especially characteristic of Lk-Acts (33 items) and favoured expressions of Lk-Acts (27 items)[28]. Vogel's study raises a fundamental question in stylistic research: how can such a qualitative and personal reality like "style" be described in an objective and scientific way, including the use of quantitative, statistical methods. The fact, however, that even Vogel offers four lists, which are based on quantitative observations, shows that a 'quantitative approach' maybe useful in stylistic studies, even when it does not in itself prove much. Hence, quantitative approaches should be used with prudence and in conjunction with other approaches.

One year later (1898), on the other side of the Channel, Sir John C. HAWKINS published the first edition of his *Horae Synopticae*, which became a classic tool for studying the language of the Synoptic Gospels[29]. In his Preface, he foresees the possible objection that his materials are not very solid or trustworthy because they are to a large extent statistical: "Statistics are proverbially misleading, and proverbially liable to be made to 'prove anything' that is wished"[30]. As a compiler, he is aware of this danger, especially "when the field from which the statistics are collected is so small as it is in the present case". Hawkins states that, first, he has done his best to guard against this danger in various ways (e.g. words that are inserted in the lists on statistical grounds are bracketed for various reasons). Secondly, "however misleading statistics may be, conjectures unsupported

---

27. *Ibid.*, p. 10: "Danken wir Gott, dass das Geistige denn doch schwerer fassbarer Natur ist, als dass er einfach registriert werden könnte wie die Zahl der Feuerstätten oder Hühner. Jeder Menschengeist darf den Anspruch erheben, in seiner Ganzheit gewürdigt zu werden, d.h. immer zugleich nach der Seite der Mannigfaltigkeit seiner Lebensäusserungen wie nach der seinen bleibenden Eigenart. Diesen Dienst leistet aber eine Statistik nicht, die vor allem darauf bedacht sein muss, Gleichartiges unsträflich zu summieren".

28. *Ibid.*, pp. 61-68: "Vergleichung des Wortschatzes von E und A"; VOGEL 1899A (pp. 61-63: "Nur bei EA im N.T. Vorkommendes" = Va); VOGEL 1899B (pp. 63-65: "Außer bei EA im N.T. nur vereinzelt Vorkommendes" = Vb); VOGEL 1899C (pp. 65-66: "Für EA besonders charakteristische Ausdrücke" = Vc); VOGEL 1899D (pp. 66-68: "Lieblingsausdrücke von EA" = Vd).

29. J.C. HAWKINS, *Horae Synopticae. Contributions to the Study of the Synoptic Problem*, Oxford: Clarendon Press, 1898; [2]1909 (= 1968). We use the second edition. The author was preparing a third edition, see F. NEIRYNCK, *Hawkins's Additional Notes to his "Horae Synopticae"*, in *ETL* 46 (1970) 78-111.

30. *Ibid.*, p. vi.

by statistics are likely to be still more so, unless they are supported by evidence of other kinds". And thirdly, "some confidence in the statistical method, as here used, may be inspired by the general accordance of its results with such intimations as we gather from the words of St. Luke and Papias, and with the general probabilities of the case"[31]. In presenting a list of words and phrases characteristic of St. Luke's Gospel (pp. 15-23), Hawkins is the first author who explicitly formulates the criterion he uses to compile the list: "I take as 'characteristic' the words and phrases which *occur at least four times* in this Gospel, and which either (*a*) *are not found at all in Matthew or Mark*, or (*b*) *are found in Luke at least twice as often as in Matthew and Mark together*"[32] (e.g. 0/0/4 or 1/2/6). We note that a minimum number of four occurrences is required, obviously to avoid arbitrary cases. We also note that "proper names and numerals are omitted, because they prove nothing as to a vocabulary and style"[33].

Moreover, Hawkins' criteria are based on comparative statistics: the number of occurrences in Luke should exceed at least twice the number of occurrences in Matthew and Mark. The application of a quantitative or numerical criterion results in a list of 151 characteristic words and phrases. Not all of them, however, have the same value: eight of them are bracketed as being less important than the rest, "because they are mainly or entirely accounted for by the subject-matter, and therefore give little or no indication of the author's style"; eleven are marked "†" because, "for various reasons, but little stress can be laid" upon them; and twenty-one are marked "*" as being "the most distinctive and important instances" (p. 2). These additional qualifications show that Hawkins is aware that statistics cannot be the only criterion for defining characteristic language use. It should sometimes be complemented by other kinds of criteria. On p. 24, he gives an additional list of words and phrases, which are "more or less characteristic of Luke," although they do not quite fall under the above-mentioned rules. Moreover, he gives two subsidiary lists, which again are based on numerical criteria, although less strict than the one used for the main list: "Subsidiary list A: words and phrases occurring upwards of four times in Luke's Gospel, which do not occur there *twice as often* as in Matthew and Mark together, but which are found *in Luke and Acts together four times as often as in Matthew and Mark together*" (p. 27: only 5 cases, HAWKINS 1909A). And "Subsidiary list B: words and phrases which are found only two or three times in Luke's Gospel, but which either (*a*) occur *at least six times in Luke and Acts taken together* while not occurring at all in Matthew and Mark (Lk+Acts = 6× [Mt+Mk=0], or else (*b*) occur in Luke and Acts together *at*

---

31. *Ibid.*, p. vii.
32. *Ibid.*, p. 15.
33. *Ibid.*, p. 175, n. 1.

least 4 times as often as in Matthew and Mark together" (Lk+Acts = 4×
[Mt+Mk= at least 1]) (pp. 28-29: 28 cases, HAWKINS 1909B). It is striking
that in each of the last list's cases, Luke has a word or phrase two or three
times, and Acts three or more times (e.g. 0/0/2+4; 0/0/3+3; but also
1/0/2+19). Hawkins does not give examples of the type 1/0/2+2, but
computer programs show that they exist. In that case, it seems strange that
the case 1/0/2+2 is accepted, whereas the case 0/0/2+2 is not. Finally,
Hawkins gives a list of "words found both in Luke and Acts, but peculiar to
them" (p. 203 HAWKINS 1909LA; cf. p. 175). In the subsidiary lists, new
evidence is adduced from a different writing, the book of Acts, which has
been added to that of Luke. The unexpressed assumption is that both books
are written by the same author, and that what is characteristic of Acts, may
give supplementary evidence for items that are not occurring in sufficient
number in Luke. Here, the question arises whether 'characteristic' language
use should be ascribed to a text or to its author.

Robert MORGENTHALER[34] (1958) also adopts a quantitative criterion: "A
word must come at least ten times to get on his list of 62 (single words
only), but it is only required to come more frequently than in proportion to
the Gospel's length. If it fulfils these requirements, it is taken to be the
preferred word of the 'Schriftsteller' himself"[35]. Morgenthaler's list
contains less than half the number of characteristic items found in
Hawkins's main list (62 in stead of 151). There are several reasons for this:
(i) the required minimum number of occurrences is much higher than
Hawkins' (10 instead of 4). Below this minimum, no reliable numerical
comparisons can be made or conclusions concerning the style of an author
or a text can be allowed[36]. (ii) Within the scope of his tool, a "Statistic of the
NT vocabulary", he limits his survey to words only. This is, of course, a
serious limitation because characteristic language use cannot be limited to
words only, but covers a whole range of infra- and supra-lexical linguistic
phenomena. An important feature of Morgenthaler's criterion is that he
takes the relation between the comparative frequency of a word (e.g. in Mt,
Mk, and Lk) and the length of the Gospels into account, that is, its total

---

34. R. MORGENTHALER, *Statistik des neutestamentlichen Wortschatzes*, Zürich/Frankfurt
am Main, 1958; [4]1992.

35. Quoted from M.D. GOULDER, *Luke. A New Paradigm* (JSNT SS, 20), Sheffield,
1989-1994 (repr. 1994), p. 80.

36. *Ibid.* p. 49 observes that out of the 5500 words of the NT, only 1000 have a
frequency above 10 occurrences. He adds: "Bei den 4500 Vokabeln, die zehnmahl und
weniger erscheinen, werden keinerlei Zahlenverhältnisse bestehen, die an sich für den Stil
eines einzelnen Schriftstellers oder einer Schiftengruppe und den Zusammenhang
zwischen verschiedenen Schriften sehr aufschlussreich sein könnten".

number of words[37]. Moreover, he is aware that in some cases editorial considerations can supplement the lack of statistical data[38].

In 1973, the computer entered the field of word statistics with the publication of Lloyd GASTON's *Horae Synopticae Electronicae*[39]. The title shows that he builds on the work of Hawkins, wanting to complete it with the help of the computer. He also wanted to improve it by assigning each word to a source (Mk, Q, Q^{Mt}, Q^{Lk}, M, L, Mt add, Lk add) and a literary form (Editorial [Q ed, Mk ed, Mt ed, Lk ed], Legend, Apothegm, Miracle Story, Parable, Prophetic Saying, Rule and Law, Wisdom Saying, Christological Saying, Old Testament Quotation, Hymn). Differing from Hawkins, Gaston chose the so-called z-score as criterion. He lists "all words which appear in a given source or form in a proportion which exceeds 2.33 standard deviations. This number was chosen because it is equivalent to a probability of .01 (1 out of 100)"[40]. Words which appear less than four times in a given category are automatically excluded. He lists 28 words (of which one is a proper name) that exceed the standard deviation (Lked) and 36 words (of which two are proper names) that do not meet this standard (Lked?)[41]. Gaston's concordance only lists isolated words. Characteristic phrases are not listed, although Gaston concedes that "usage in terms of characteristic phrases is perhaps even more important"[42].

Franklin J.C. COLLISON (1977), a student of Farmer, works within the framework of the Griesbach hypothesis (Lk knows Mt, and Mk knows both Mt and Lk). He qualifies the characteristic Lukan linguistic use or disuse of words and phrases as 'certain', 'probable' and 'likely', thereby indicating the probability in descending order of certainty. He states that the choice of the appropriate expression for a phenomenon is made on the basis of a

---

37. *Ibid.*, p. 50: "Wann aber liegt nun bei einen einzelnen Schreiber ein Vorzugswort vor? Offenbar dann, wenn dieses Wort bei ihm im Vergleich mit anderen Schreibern der neutestamentlichen Schriften im Verhältniss zum Umfang seiner Schrift besonders oft vorkommt". By "Umfang" he means "Wortbestand", that is, the total number of words (p. 164: Mt 18278, Mk 11229, Lk 19404, Acts 18374). This should be distinguished from "Wortschatz", that is, the vocabulary of each text (p. 164: Mt 1691, Mk 1345, Lk 2055, and Acts, 2038).

38. *Ibid.*, p. 50: "Je kleiner die Zahlen ind die Zahldifferenzen sind, um so unsicherer ist das Resultat. Bei Markus kann eine Vorzugsvokabel schon dann vorliegen, wenn ein Wort im zweiten Evangelium nur wenig öfter vorkommt als bei Mathäus und Lukas. Wir dürfen hier unsere Kenntnisse in der synoptischen Frage ruhig einsetzen. Matthäus und Lukas werden das betreffende Wort aller Wahrscheinlichkeit nach von Markus übernommen haben, und wir stehen also sehr wahrscheinlich vor einen Vorzugswort des zweiten Evangelisten usw.".

39. L. GASTON, *Horae Synopticae Electronicae. Word Statistics of the Synoptic Gospels* (SBL SBS, 3), Missoula, MT: University of Montana, 1973.

40. *Ibid.*, p. 13.

41. *Ibid.*, pp. 64-66.

42. *Ibid.*, p. 12.

synthetic judgment that defies precise definition and reduction to a set of rules[43]. Nevertheless, in general, seven factors have been kept in mind:

1. The purpose has been to produce a list of Luke's linguistic usages, which are more or less independent of a source theory. Hence, the location of the occurrences is of decisive importance.

2. Some importance has been given to Lukan omissions and alterations and of the occurrence of the phenomenon in the text of Matthew.

3. The 'frequency' of the phenomenon's occurrences. A phenomenon has to occur a 'reasonable' number of times in passages that are considered to be of primary importance.

4. The 'distribution' of the phenomenon in different sections and/or different types of sections in the Gospels.

5. The 'distinctiveness' of the phenomenon. If a phenomenon is somewhat uncommon with respect to either the Biblical Greek or Hellenistic Greek, then, this has been taken into consideration.

6. Some weight is given to the 'interlacing' of the different phenomena. If a phenomenon is located among what seems to be other Lukan linguistic usages, then, the probability of it being Lukan increases.

7. The evidence of the book of Acts must be considered[44].

Points 1 and 2 of this set of factors seem to contradict each other in some sense: independence from a source theory on the one side (point 1) and some preference for Luke's dependence on Matthew on the other (point 2). If dependence on source theories is needed to supply the lack of statistical data, it seems more prudent to start from the most common theory of literary dependence, Markan priority and hence, Luke's possible dependence on Mark. Points 3 and 4 are essential to build a sound quantitative approach. The exact meaning of point 5 is less clear. Factor 6 can help to define the 'characteristic' nature of smaller phenomena, which are difficult to assess in isolation. Point 7 again presupposes the same authorship of both Luke and Acts, but it cannot automatically be applied.

In 1984 Marie-Émile BOISMARD and A. LAMOUILLE published a two-volume study in which they attempted to reconstruct the Western text of the Acts of the Apostles and to demonstrate that it was written by the author of the Third Gospel. They attempted to prove Luke's authorship of the Western text of the Acts of the Apostles by thoroughly analyzing of its vocabulary and style[45]. The second volume interests us here. It contains a

---

43. F.J.G. COLLISON, *Linguistic Usages in the Gospel of Luke.* Diss. Southern Methodist University, 1977, p. 23.

44. *Ibid.*, pp. 24-28.

45. M.-É. BOISMARD – A. LAMOUILLE, *Le Texte Occidentale des Actes des Apôtres. Reconstruction et réhabilitation. Tome I. Introduction et textes. Tome II. Apparat critique,*

list of 913 stylistic characteristics (words, phrases, expressions) occurring in the Book of Acts (or 947 in the Western text), which is then divided into five categories[46]. In the first three categories (A, B, C), the characteristics of Acts or Acts+Luke are established in reference to the entire NT (A = 100%; B = between 99,99 and 80%; C = between 79,99 and 60%). In the final two categories (D, E), the characteristics of Acts and Acts+Luke are fixed in reference to the Gospels of Mk, Mt and Jn (D = 100%; E = 99,99 - 75%). These characteristics are first given in alphabetical order and then in the order of frequency (per category). For each characteristic, the authors give the frequency of occurrences in Acts and in Acts-Luke, with reference to the chapter and verse where they occur. In his review, J. Murphy-O'Connor rightly states: "This is an extraordinary exegetical tool, which in both scope and detail surpasses all previous efforts to tabulate Lukan style. Its value is entirely independent of the use the authors make of it, and it is manifest that it will be indispensable for all future critical study of both Luke and Acts ... This work will stand as a permanent bench-mark in Lukan studies, and as a model for the stylistic analysis of other sacred authors"[47]. It should be noted, however, that Boismard & Lamouille primarily want to establish a list of the linguistic characteristics of Acts, while Luke is only considered when it corresponds to Acts. This means that the characteristic linguistic features that occur only in Luke, but not in Acts, are not listed. Nevertheless, the vocabulary they cover is already so large that scholars of Luke cannot neglect their contribution. In his review on Boismard & Lamouille's study, Frans NEIRYNCK has selected an alphabetical list of 615 Lukan characteristics occurring in Acts and Luke[48]. Moreover, it should be noted that Boismard and Lamouille themselves admit that their qualification "stylistic characteristic" is not quite exact. This is because it is difficult to determine from the frequency of a word- or an expression-usage what is "characteristic" of one author or another. In order to avoid any arbitrary

---

index des caractéristiques stylistiques, index des citations patristiques, Paris: Éditions Recherche sur les Civilisations, 1984 (= 1985).

46. We give the categories followed by the number of items in the Alexandrian and the Western text: Aa (167/181) and Ab (208/219), Ba (18/26) and Bb (119/117), Ca (79/70) and Cb (175/170), Da (24/31) and Db (46/48), Ea (10/11) and Eb (67/74). The addition "a" after the capital means: Acts only; the addition "b" after the capital means: Acts and Luke.

47. Review in *RB* 93 (1986) 598-601, esp. p. 600.

48. F. NEIRYNCK, *Le texte des Actes des Apôtres et les caractéristiques stylistiques lucaniennes*, in *ETL* 61 (1985) 304-334, esp. 315-330 (= ID., *Evangelica II* [BETL, 99], 1991, pp. 243-278, esp. 254-271). Neirynck rightly points to some limitations and lacunae (e.g. words or expressions occurring in OT quotations are not listed) in Boismard & Lamouille's list. He also thinks that the more precise descriptions of J. Jeremias (see n. 12) allow for the completion of the lists of Boismard & Lamouille.

decision, they have made an inventory of *all* frequencies exceeding a certain proportion[49].

According to Willem M.A. HENDRIKS (1986), a scientific study of linguistic phenomena requires the qualities of clarity, completeness and reliability. By clarity he means a precise definition of which linguistic phenomena (e.g. vocabulary, parts of speech, connection of sentences, the tense-system, the syntax of the verb, etc.) will be studied and which texts (or corpus of texts) will be studied (e.g. which text or corpus represents the 'norm' with which the language usage or disuse of the text under study is compared; the latter is called the reference text or corpus). By completeness, he means that all phenomena of a chosen group should be investigated in all of the texts of the chosen corpus. By reliability he means that he wants reliable ('safe') criteria for investigating the characteristic use and disuse of linguistic phenomena in the Synoptic Gospels[50]. He observes that in previously published literature on the language of the Synoptic Gospels, research into the Synoptic vocabulary has been the clearest and most complete. This is unlike non-lexical research, which seldom meets the three requirements just mentioned. Vocabulary research is the only area of investigation where the criteria for evaluating the characteristic use of linguistic phenomena have been formulated and appropriated, even when the criteria have not always been sufficiently reliable and coherently applied[51]. According to Hendriks, a "linguistic phenomenon is said to be characteristic of a given text, if the frequency in which it appears in the text 'deviates' from a chosen norm. Since this 'deviation' does not concern small or coincidental discrepancies, we say that phenomena are said to be characteristic of a given text only when their frequency of occurrence or absence exceeds the probability of chance occurrence. This means that a criterion for a language phenomenon to be considered characteristic is that it must meet the requirement that the absolute value of the deviation has been taken into account"[52]. This is an interesting attempt to give a definition of a characteristic linguistic phenomenon. However, his (statistical) observations do not clarify what he precisely means by 'the absolute value of the deviation' and how he implements it. Moreover, the results of applying these criteria are very limited: only 45 linguistic usages are deemed characteristic.

---

49. BOISMARD – LAMOUILLE, *Texte occidental* (n. 45), Vol. 2, p. 195. For the sake of completeness, we also integrate in our "Vocabulary" (in the Second Frame "Word Groups") Boismard-Lamouille's "stylistic characteristics" that only occur in Acts.

50. W.M.A. HENDRICKS, *Karakteristiek woordgebruik in de synoptische evangelies*, 3 vols., Diss. Nijmegen, 1986, pp. 39-42.

51. *Ibid.*, pp. 30-38.

52. *Ibid.*, p. 587.

Michael GOULDER (1989) considers his list of words and word groups to be Lukan in two senses: either "they are introduced by Luke redactorally", or "they occur with a marked greater frequency in Luke than in Mark and Matthew, and in at least three different contexts". "Expressions marked * pass Hawkins' criteria: at least four uses in different contexts, and at least twice the combined number of uses in Mark and Matthew"[53]. Goulder rightly applies two kinds of criteria in order to establish characteristic Lukan language use, namely 'redactoral' and numerical criteria, but he is less strict than Hawkins as to the proportion needed between Luke and the compared text unit.

Conclusion

Our survey of the most important studies of Luke's language use has pointed to some recurrent problems involved in the task of establishing characteristic language use. The fundamental problem is: what are reliable criteria of characteristic language use?

Before attempting to give a scientifically reliable set of criteria, we should first answer the question whether characteristic linguistic use is primarily a property of a given *text* or of an *author*. The unexpressed assumption of many Luke-Acts language studies is that characteristic language use is a property of the *writer* or *author* of the two books. However, it seems that in order to describe the phenomenon of characteristic language use or 'style', one should first consider it at the level of the text, clearly distinguishing the text of the Third Gospel (= Luke) from the text of the Book of Acts. Indeed, when a word is characteristic of Acts (= the book of Acts), it does not automatically follow that it is also characteristic of Luke. Compare, for example, the word μαρτυρέω (1/0/1+11, i.e. the frequency of Mt/Mk/Lk + Acts), and the linguistic phenomenon καὶ αὐτός/αὐτή/αὐτοί/αὐταί nom. (with a frequency 4/5/45+8). With respect to the first example, the only occurrence in Luke might eventually be editorial or 'redactional', but it is not characteristic of Luke's text. It is potentially characteristic of the *author* (supposing that the author of Luke and Acts is the same). J. Jeremias rightly distinguishes between "Redaktion" and "Vorzugs-wort", between a word or an expression that can be qualified as "editorial" in a certain context, and a word or expression that is "characteristic" of Luke or Luke-Acts as texts. In our tool, we primarily

---

53. GOULDER, *Luke* (n. 17), p. 800. Goulder gives a statistical survey of the number of occurrences of 384 linguistic features (e.g. ἔτι: 8/5/16+5) and only some references (e.g. ἔτι: Lk 9,42; 20,36). This is a serious limitation. In our "Vocabulary," we have tried to give all references.

want to describe the characteristic or noteworthy language use of a specific text corpus, the Gospel of Luke. But in view of the common opinion that the Gospel of Luke and the Book of Acts are written by the same author, we not only list all the references of words and word groups in Luke, but also of those in Acts.

Secondly, characteristic language use can be situated in the field of vocabulary (words), morphology (word forms), syntax (word groups), and semantics (meanings of words). It would be unjustified to limit the study of characteristic language use of Luke to the lexical level. Proper names and numbers are not listed, because these are not normally indicative of an author's style.

Once there is agreement on these preliminary issues, we think that the phenomenon of Lukan style or characteristic language use cannot be described on the basis of statistical data only, nor can it be done without taking the statistical evidence into account. The most balanced way of describing Luke's style would seem to be a combination of numerical and editorial criteria. In other words, the student can reap the benefits from the research done in the field of statistics (e.g. the studies of Hawkins, Boismard & Lamouille) and in the field of literary criticism (more specifically the attempt to distinguish traditional and 'redactional' language in Luke-Acts, e.g. Harnack, Schürmann, Jeremias).

Numerical criteria can be situated on three levels: quantity, distribution and required minimum.

– Quantity: a linguistic use is characteristic of a given text if its frequency deviates from a chosen norm (e.g. the frequency in another text). According to this approach, the given text under study is the Third Gospel (= Lk) or Luke and Acts taken together (Lk-Acts). The compared text may be the rest of the NT or the Gospels of Mark and Matthew (Mk+Mt). The proportion or deviation should be defined by taking into account the total length (*Wortbestand*) of the given text (Lk or Lk-Acts) and of the compared text (rest NT; Mt+Mk).

– Distribution: the word must occur in at least three different contexts to be relevant for eventual characteristic language use. When a word, phrase or expression occurs a number of times in the same context, its frequency does not point to characteristic use, even when it meets the standard deviation norm.

– Required minimum of occurrences: the frequency of occurrence or absence of a linguistic phenomenon should exceed the probability of chance occurrence. Small or accidental discrepancies cannot be termed as a "deviation." In our approach, the required minimum occurrences in Luke should be at least four and have at least a proportion of 2× [Mt+Mk] or 4× [Mt+Mk=0].

Editorial criteria: confirming evidence may be collected on the basis of the following observations:

– As to the threefold tradition (Mt=Mk=Lk, or Mk=Lk), Luke's redaction of Mark points to his characteristic language use: additions may point to positive Lukan characteristics, changes or omissions to negative Lukan characteristics (called *Meidewort*); a common underlying presumption is the theory of Markan priority and Luke's use of Mark.

– As to the twofold tradition (Mt=Lk), Luke's deviation from parallel texts in Matthew may, by analogy to Luke's redaction of Mk, point to characteristic language use of Luke: additions may point to positive Lukan characteristics; however, changes or omissions may point to negative Lukan characteristics (called *Meidewort*). A common assumption is the Q-hypothesis, which accepts a common Greek source used by Matthew and Luke.

– Language use in editorial passages (introductions, summaries, etc.) may also point to characteristic language use.

In fact these data can be found in a "Synoptic Concordance"[54] and are evaluated in studies following the line of Gersdorf (A. von Harnack, H. Schürmann, G. Schneider, J. Jeremias and R. von Bendemann)[55]. In our tool, we note the evaluation of these authors, so that editorial considerations eventually confirm the statistical data. When the results of the two sets of criteria converge, they have indeed a greater degree of certainty.

The tool we offer covers the entire vocabulary of the text of Luke's Gospel in alphabetical order. It makes an inventory of the results of two centuries of research on his language and style, with the exception of the question of semitisms. All the alleged characteristic linguistic features of Luke's Gospel are listed. However, readers might expect us to give our own evaluation of the long history of research. Therefore, we indicate what *we* consider to be characteristic language use in the Gospel of Luke on the basis of the criteria just given. Our own evaluation will be indicated by DENAUX 2009 (this is the year we finished the analysis of applying the criteria which are set out below), followed by the qualification we give to the linguistic feature. Thus, we will make a distinction between (i) characteristic and (ii) noteworthy linguistic

---

54. See Paul HOFFMANN, Thomas HIEKE, and Ulrich BAUER, *Synoptic Concordance: A Greek Concordance to the First Three Gospels in Synoptic Arrangement, Statistically Evaluated, Including Occurrences in Acts – Griechische Konkordanz zu den ersten drei Evangelien in synoptischer Darstellung, statistisch ausgewertet, mit Berücksichtigung der Apostelgeschichte*. Volume 1: *Introduction – Einführung, A–Δ*, Berlin – New York, Walter de Gruyter, 1999, LXXIII-1032 p.; Vol. II: *E–I*, 2000, XVIII-957 p.; Vol. III: *K–O*, 2000, XVII-997 p.; Vol. IV: *Π–Ω*, 2000, XIX-1066 p. We are preparing a "Synoptic Concordance of Luke".

55. See footnotes 10-14.

features in the Gospel of Luke. The words and expressions mentioned in the latter category do not meet the numerical criteria needed to establish a Lukan characteristic language use, but are nevertheless noteworthy, because they somehow qualify the style of Luke's Gospel.

In line with Hawkins, we distinguish three subgroups of *Lukan characteristics* as certain (A), probable (B) and likely (C):

A. When a word or a word group occurs at least four times or more in Luke (of which at least 3 times are in a different context) and never in Mattthew and Mark, or two times more in Luke than in Matthew-Mark, we consider it to definitively be characteristic[56]. Such a certain characteristic feature is indicated by L***.

   In short, L***: Lk//Mt+Mk, at least 4 occurrences in Luke (of which at least 3 in different contexts): Lk = 4× (or more) [Mt+Mk=0]; or Lk = 2× [Mt+Mk].

B. When a word or a word group occurs at least four times in Luke and four times more in Luke-Acts than in Matthew-Mark, we consider it to be probably characteristic[57]. Such a probable characteristic feature is indicated by lA** (when it occurs less in Luke than in Acts) or La** (when it occurs more in Luke than in Acts).

   In short, lA** or La**: Lk-Acts//Mt+Mk, at least 4 occurrences in Luke: Lk-Acts = 4× [Mt+Mk].

C. When a word or a word group occurs at least two or three times in Luke and in Luke-Acts six times and not in Matthew-Mark or four times more in Luke-Acts than in Matthew-Mark, we consider it likely to be characteristic. Such a likely characteristic linguistic feature is indicated lA* (when it occurs less in Luke than in Acts), La* (when it occurs more in Luke than in Acts) or LA* (when the number of occurrences is the same in Luke and in Acts).

---

56. In Category A the book of Acts is not taken into consideration, although the linguistic feature may be present there. The feature is considered characteristic in the Gospel of Luke because it outnumbers significantly the number of occurrences in the Gospels of Matthew and Mark taken together and can therefore be considered characteristic of Luke's Gospel.

57. In the categories B and C the number of occurrences of a linguistic feature in Luke does not meet the criterion required in category A. But when one extends the text corpus to Luke and Acts, taken together, and compares it with the text corpus of Matthew-Mark, and the number of occurrences in Luke-Acts sufficiently outnumbers that of Matthew-Mark, then one can consider it probably or likely characteristic. This extension to Luke-Acts makes sense on the current assumption that both books are written by the same author.

In short, $1A^*$, La^* or LA^*: Lk-Acts//Mt+Mk, at least 2 or 3 occurrences in Luke: Lk-Acts = 6× [Mt+Mk=0]: e.g. 0/0/2+4; 0/0/3+3; 0/0/4+2; Lk-Acts = 4× [Mt+Mk]: e.g. 1/0/2+2; 0/1/3+1; 2/0/3+5; 1/1/3+6.

Noteworthy linguistic phenomena are subdivided as follows:

The first category of noteworthy linguistic features in Luke-Acts or Acts are words or word groups which occur never in Matthew-Mark and at least two times up to five times in Luke-Acts (noteworthy in Luke-Acts) or once in Luke and four times or more in Acts (noteworthy or even characteristic in Acts). This category is indicated LA^n (when the number of occurrences in Luke and Acts is the same), $1A^n$ (when the number of occurrences in Luke is less than in Acts), La^n (when the number of occurrences in more in Luke than in Acts).

In short: LA^n, $1A^n$, La^n: noteworthy phenomenon in Luke-Acts (e.g. 0/0/1+1; 0/0/1+2; 0/0/2+1; 0/0/2+2; 0/0/1+3; 0/0/3+1; 0/0/2+3; 0/0/3+2; 0/0/1+4 – 0/0/1+28).

The second category of noteworthy linguistic features in Luke-Acts is when a word or word group occurs considerably more in Luke-Acts than in Matthew-Mark but less than four times more. This category is indicated by LAn (when the number of occurrences in Luke and Acts is the same), 1An (when the number of occurrences are less in Luke than in Acts), Lan (when the number of occurrences are more in Luke than in Acts).

In short: LAn, 1An, Lan: noteworthy phenomenon in Luke-Acts (e.g. 3/2/9+9; 5/3/15+10).

The third category of noteworthy linguistic features in Luke are words or word groups which neither occur in Matthew-Mark nor in Acts, but two or three times in Luke. This category is indicated by L^n.

In short: L^n noteworthy of Luke only (not in Mt, Mk or Acts) (e.g. 0/0/2+0; 0/0/3+0).

The fourth category of noteworthy linguistic features in Luke are words or word groups in Luke which do not occur in Acts and almost two times more in Luke than in Matthew-Mark. This category is indicated by Ln.

In short: Ln: noteworthy of Luke only (present in Mt and/or Mk, but not in Acts) (e.g. 5/3/15+0).

Adelbert DENAUX

APPENDIX

LIST OF WORDS AND WORD GROUPS ONLY IN LUKE AND/OR ACTS IN THE NT

15× in Lk/Acts: (καὶ) ἰδού + (ὁ) ἀνήρ (8+7)

14× in Lk/Acts: ἀνάγω = embark (1+13)

13× in Lk/Acts: noun + δέ τις (5+8)

12× in Lk/Acts: αὐτὸς ὁ καιρός/ἡμέρα/ ὥρα (9+3), ὑποστρέφω without complement (11+1)

11× in Lk/Acts: εἴη, optat. (7+4), ἱκανός concerning time (3+8), πάντων/πᾶσιν (pron.) + attraction of relative (4+7)

10× in Lk/Acts: στρατηγός (2+8), μάρτυς (εἰμι/γίνομαι) + genitive (1+9)

9× in Lk/Acts: ἄν + optat. (4+5), σταθείς/σταθέντες (3+6), παραχρῆμα at the beginning of a sentence (6+3), noun + τις + adjective/participle (5+4)

8× in Lk/Acts: πάντες οἱ ἀκούοντες/-σαντες (1+7), ἀναστὰς/ ἀναστάντες δέ (2 + 6), ἀναστάς + imperative (2+6), (καὶ) παραγενόμενος (δέ), in the beginning of a sentence (2+6), ἐπλήσθην πνεύματος ἁγίου (3+5), εἰμι/γίνομαι ἐν τῇ πόλει (5+3), ὑποστρέφω εἰς Ἱεροσόλυμα/ Ἱερουσαλήμ (3+5)

7× in Lk/Acts: ἀκούω τὸν λόγον τοῦ θεοῦ/κυρίου (4+3), ἀποδέχομαι (2+5), ἐπιστρέφω ἐπὶ (τὸν) θεόν/κύριον (1+6), ἐν ταῖς ἡμέραις ταύταις (4+3), κελεύω + (ἀπ/εἰσ)άγειν (1+6), οὗ ἦν/ἦσαν + participle (3+4), ἄπαν/πᾶν τὸ πλῆθος (4+3), ἀναστάς + πορεύομαι (3+4), τὰ ῥήματα ταῦτα (3+4)

6× in Lk/Acts: αἰνέω τὸν θεόν (3+3), ἀτενίζω dat. (2+4), αὐξάνω + verb (climax) (3+3), καθότι (2+4), (καὶ) ἰδού … καί + verb (same subject) (5+1), κατέρχομαι ἀπό (1+5), ῥῆμα in the meaning of "thing" (4+2), συμβάλλω (2+4), αἴρω/ἐπαίρω φωνήν (2+4)

5× in Lk/Acts: ἀκούων δέ (2+3), ἀναιρέω of Christ (2+3), οἱ ἄρχοντες + genitive pronoun (1+4), participle + δὲ καί + participle (1+4), ἐναντίον (3+2), εἰσπορευόμενοι (οἱ) (3+2) ἐξῆς (2+3), ἐπιλαμβάνομαι + accusative (person) (2+3), θαυμάζω ἐπί + dative (4+1), καθεξῆς (2+3), διὰ νυκτός (1+4), κατὰ τὴν ὁδόν (1+4), καθ' ὅλης (2+3), οὐ μετά / μετ' οὐ (1+4), ὄχλος + genitive (3+2), πνεῦμα + verb of movement + ἐπί + accusative (person) (1+4), προσέχετε ἑαυτοῖς (3+2), πάντα τὰ ῥήματα (4+1), τις/τινες τῶν + preposition + noun/pronoun (1+4), (ὁ) ὕψιστος absolute (= God) (4+1)

4× in Lk/Acts: αἴτιος (3+1), ἀνέστη/ἐξανέστη + participle (1+3), ἅπτω λύχνον/πῦρ/πυράν (3+1), περὶ τῆς βασιλείας τοῦ θεοῦ (1+3), κατὰ τὸ αὐτό / τὰ αὐτά (3 + 1), δέομαί σου (2+2), διαμαρτύρομαι + dat. (1+3), διαπορέω (1+3), τὰ διαταχθέντα/ τὸ διατεταγμένον (3+1), διέρχομαι ἕως (1+3), ἐγένετο θάμβος/φόβος ἐπί + accusative (2+2), ἔμφοβος γενόμενος (2+2), ἐπιφωνέω (1+3), εὐλαβής (1+3), ὅλη ἡ Ἰουδαία (2+2), καθίημι (1+3), κηρύσσειν *τὴν βασιλείαν (τοῦ θεοῦ) (2+2), κράτιστος (1+3), ἐστιν μέγας, said of someone (1+3), νηστεία/ νηστεύω+ praying (2+2), ὀδυνάομαι (3+1), ὁμιλέω (2+2), ὀρθρινός, ὀρθρίζω, ὄρθρος (3+1), παραγγέλλω μηδενί + verb of saying (3+1), παραγενόμενος + ἀπαγγέλλω (1+3), παραλύω (2+2), πλῆθος (πολὺ) τοῦ λαοῦ (3+1), πλήρης πνεύματος ἁγίου (1+3), ποιέω μετά + genitive (0/0/2+2), πορεύομαι εἰς (τὸν) τόπον (2+2), μηδὲν/οὐδὲν/τι ἄξιον θανάτου πράσσω (1+3), στάσις γίνεται/γενομένη (1+3), συναρπάζω (1+3), τελέω τὸ γεγραμμένον / τὰ γεγραμμένα (2+2), φημί (ʼέφη) πρός + accusative (person) (1+3), ψαλμός in quotations (2+2), ὡσεί + expression of time (3+1)

3× in Lk/Act: ἀπ᾽ αἰῶνος (1+2), ἀναζητέω (2+1), ἀπαγγέλλω ταῦτα (2+1), ἀπῆλθεν ὁ ἄγγελος (angel) (2+1), ἀρξάμενος ἀπό place (2+1), γίνομαι κατά + accusative of place (2+1), γέγραπται ἐν βίβλῳ (1+2), διδάσκω + εὐαγγελίζομαι (1+2), διδάσκω τὸν λαόν (1+2), διῖστημι (2+1), δούλη (2+1), δυνατὸς ἐν (1+2), ἑβδομήκοντα (2+1), ἐκδίκησιν (ποιέω) (2+1), *ἔλαιων (2+1), ἐξίστημι transitive (1+2), ἐξίσταντο δὲ πάντες (1+2), ἐπέρχομαι ἐπί + accusative (1+2), ἐπιβιβάζω (2+1), ἐπιχειρέω (1+2), ἔρχομαι κατά + accusative (2+1), ἐρωτάω + ὅπως (2+1), ἑσπέρα (1+2), τῇ ἐχομένῃ (ἡμέρᾳ) (1+2), θάμβος (2+1), ἴασις (1+2), ἵστημι ἐν μέσῳ (τινῶν) (1+2), καταβαίνω μετά + genitive (2+1), καταπίπτω (1+2), κρεμάννυμι (crucify) (1+2), λόγος τῆς χάριτος (1+2), μένω σύν + person (2+1), μετανοέω + ἐπιστρέφω (1+2), ὅπως ἄν (1+2), παραδίδωμι εἰς φυλακήν (1+2), παρελθών (2+1), ἐπλήσθησαν πάντες (2+1), πολίτης (2+1), πορεύου εἰς εἰρήνην / πορεύεσθε ἐν εἰρήνῃ (2+1), imperative of movement + καί + πορεύου (1+2), προστίθημι + infinitive (2+1), πρόσωπον τῆς γῆς (2+1), πυνθάνομαι τίς/τί εἴη (2+1), συγγένεια (1+2), συγκαλέω τοὺς φίλους (2+1), συμπληρόω (2+1), τί ὅτι (1+2), τίθεμαι/τίθημι ἐν τῇ καρδίᾳ (2+1), ἐπὶ τὸν τράχηλον (1+2), φοβέομαι τὸν λαόν (2+1), χαίρων at the end of a sentence (2+1), χεὶρ κυρίου (1+2)

2× in Lk/Acts: ἀναδείκνυμι (1+1), ἀνακαθίζω (1+1), ἀνασπάω (1+1), ἀνάστασις (τῶν) δικαίων (καὶ ἀδίκων) (1+1), ἡ ἀνάστασις ἡ ἐκ νεκρῶν (1+1), ἀναφαίνω (1+1), ἀνευρίσκω (1+1), *ἀντειπειν (1+1), ἀπαλλάσσομαι ἀπό (1+1), ἀπογραφή (1+1), ἀποκρίνομαι + infinitive (1+1), ἀπολύω ἀπό (1+1), ἀποτινάσσω (1+1), ἐπὶ τὴν αὔριον (1+1), διαγγέλλω (1+1), διατηρέω (1+1), διϊσχυρίζομαι (1+1), διοδεύω (1+1), μήτι δύναται + infinitive (1+1), τὸ εἰωθός (1+1), ἐκβάλλω ἔξω τῆς πόλεως (1+1), ἔναντι (1+1), ἐνεδρεύω (1+1), ἐνισχύω (1+1), ἐξίσταντο δὲ πάντες οἱ ἀκούοντες (1+1), ἐπαγγελία τοῦ πατρός (1+1), *ἔπιδειν (1+1), ἐπὶ ἔτη (1+1), εἰσελθὼν absolute ... εὑρίσκω (1+1), εὐτόνως (1+1), ὁ δὲ ... ἰδὼν ἐθαύμασεν (1+1), κατακλείω (1+1), κατακολουθέω (1+1), κλάσις (1+1), ἡ λιμός (1+1), λοιμός (1+1), μήποτε καί (1+1), ἡμέρας/σαββάτου ὁδός (1+1), ὀμνύω ὅρκον/ὅρκῳ (1+1), ὄρθρος (1+1), παραβιάζομαι (1+1), παραγγέλλω + ἐξελθεῖν (1+1), παρίστημι ἐνώπιον (1+1), περιλάμπω (1+1), μηδὲν πλέον (1+1), πλῆθος τῶν μαθητῶν (1+1), ποιέω περί + genitive (1+1), μέλλω πράσσειν (1+1), πρεσβυτέριον (1+1), προβάλλω (1+1), προδότης γίνομαι (1+1), προπορεύομαι (1+1), προσδοκία (1+1), προϋπάρχω (1+1), στρατιά (1+1), σύνειμι (1+1), τραυματίζω (1+1), τραχύς (1+1), εἶπον φωνῇ μεγαλῇ (1+1), ἀπὸ τῆς χαρᾶς without determinative (1+1).

Words that appear only twice in Luke and nowhere else in the NT (37 cases, of which 6 are proper names)
ἀνάπειρος, ἄγρα, ἀπαιτέω, ἀποπνίγω, ἀστράπτω, ἄτεκνος, ἄτερ, αὐστηρός, βουνός, Γαβριήλ, γελάω, διαγογγύζω, διαλαλέω, δοχή, ἐκμυκτηρίζω, ἐκτελέω, ἐπαιτέω, ἐπανέρχομαι, ἐφημερία, ζεῦγος, ἡγεμονεύω, τὸ καθ' ἡμέραν, Ἰωάννα, Καϊνάμ, Ματθάτ, Μελχί, μίσθιος, ὀρεινός, οὐσία, ἡ παῖς, πράκτωρ, πρεσβεία, προσρήγνυμι, προφέρω, Σαλά, σπαργανόω, συκοφαντέω, ὑποχωρέω.

Words that appear only once in Luke (Hapax legomena in the NT)
(occurrences: Mt 102; Mk 74; Lk 284, of which 55 are proper names)
Ἀβιληνή, ἀγκάλη, ἀγραυλέω, ἀγωνία, Ἀδδί, Ἀδμίν, ἀθροίζω, αἰσθάνομαι, αἰχμάλωτος, ἀλλογενής, ἀμπελουργός, ἀμφιέζω, ἀνάβλεψις, ἀνάδειξις, ἀνάθημα, ἀναίδεια, ἀνάλημψις, ἀναπτύσσω, ἀνατάσσομαι, ἀναφωνέω, ἀνέκλειπτος, ἀνένδεκτος, ἀνθομολογέομαι, Ἄννα, ἀντιβάλλω, ἀντικαλέω, ἀντιμετρέω, ἀντιπέρα, ἀπαρτισμός, ἀπελπίζω, ἀποθλίβω, ἀποκλείω, ἀπομάσσομαι, ἀπορία, ἀποστοματίζω, ἀποψύχω, ἀρήν, Ἀρνί, ἄροτρον, Ἀρφαξάδ, ἀρχιτελώνης, ἀσώτως, Αὐγοῦστος, αὐτόπτης, ἄφαντος, ἀφρός, ἀφυπνόω, βαθύνω, βάτος, βελόνη, *βλητεος, βολή, *Βόος, βρώσιμος, βύσσος, γαμίσκω, γῆρας, δακτύλιος, δαν(ε)ιστής, δαπάνη, *δεκακαιοκτώ, διαβάλλω, διαγρηγορέω, διακαθαίρω, διαλείπω, διαμερισμός, διανεύω, διανόημα, διανυκτερεύω, διαπραγματεύομαι, διασείω, διαταράσσω, διαφυλάσσω, διαχωρίζω, διήγησις, ἔα, Ἔβερ, ἐγκάθετος, ἔγκυος, ἐδαφίζω, ἐθίζω, ἐκκομίζω, ἐκκρεμάννυμι, ἐκχωρέω, Ἐλιέζερ, Ἐλισαῖος, ἑλκόομαι, Ἐλμαδάμ, ἐμβάλλω, Ἐμμαοῦς, ἐνδέχεται, ἔνειμι, *ἐννέα, ἐννεύω, Ἐνώς, ἐξαιτέομαι, ἐξαστράπτω, ἐπαθροίζω, ἐπειδήπερ, ἐπεισέρχομαι, ἐπικρίνω, ἐπιλείχω, ἐπιμελῶς, ἐπιπορεύομαι, ἐπισιτισμός, ἐπισχύω, ἐπιχέω, Ἐσλί, εὐεργέτης, εὐφορέω, ἡγεμονία, Ἡλί, ἡμιθανής, Ἤρ, Θάρα, θεωρία, θηρεύω, θορυβάζω, θραύω, θρόμβος, θυμιάω, Ἰανναί, Ἰάρετ, ἱδρώς, ἱερατεύω, ἰκμάς, ἰσάγγελος, ἴσως, Ἰτουραῖος, Ἰωανάν, Ἰωδά, Ἰωνάμ, Ἰωρίμ, Ἰωσήχ, καθοπλίζω, κατάβασις, καταδέω, κατακρημνίζω, καταλιθάζω, κατανεύω, καταπλέω, κατασύρω, κατασφάζω, καταψύχω, κέραμος, κεράτιον, κίχρημι, Κλεοπᾶς, κλισία, κοπρία, κόρπιον, κόραξ, κόρος, κραιπάλη, κρύπτη, Κυρήνιος, Κωσάμ, Λάμεχ, λαμπρῶς, λαξευτός, λεῖος, λῆρος, Λυσανίας, λυσιτελέω,

Μάαθ, Μαθουσαλά, Μαλελεήλ, Ματταθά, Μελεά, Μεννά, μενοῦν, μεριστής, μετεωρίζομαι, μόγις, μυλικός, Ναγγαί, Ναθάμ, Ναιμάν, Ναΐν, Ναούμ, Ναχώρ, Νηρί, νοσσία, νοσσός, ὀγδοήκοντα, *ὀγδοήκοντα τεσσαρες, ὁδεύω, οἰκονομέω, ὄμβρος, ὄνειδος, ὀπτός, ὀρθρίζω, ὀρθρινός, ὀφρύς, παμπληθεί, πανδοχεῖον, πανδοχεύς, παράδοξος, παρακαθέζομαι, παρακαλύπτω, παράλιος, παρατήρησις, παρεμβάλλω, παρθενία, πεδινός, πενιχρός, πεντεκαιδέκατος, περιάπτω, περικρύβω, περικυκλόω, περιοικέω, περίοικος, περισπάομαι, πήγανον, πιέζω, πινακίδιον, πλήμμυρα, πολλαπλασίων, πραγματεύομαι, προμελετάω, προσαναβαίνω, προσαναλόω, προσδαπανάω, προσεργάζομαι, προσποιέομαι, προσψαύω, πτύσσω, Ῥαγαύ, ῥῆγμα, Ῥησά, σάλος, Σάρεπτα, Σεμεΐν, Σερούχ, Σήθ, Σήμ, σίκερα, σινιάζω, σιτομέτριον, σκῦλον, σορός, Σουσάννα, στιγμή, στρατόπεδον, συγγενίς, συγκαλύπτω, συγκατατίθεμαι, συγκύπτω, συγκυρία, συκάμινος, συκομορέα, συλλογίζομαι, συμπαραγίνομαι, συμπίπτω, συμφύομαι, συμφωνία, σύνειμι, συνοδία, συντυγχάνω, Σύρος, τελεσφορέω, τετραπλοῦς, Τιβέριος, τραῦμα, Τραχωνῖτις, τρῆμα, τρυγών, ὑγρός, ὑδρωπικός, ὑπερεκχύννομαι, ὑποκρίνομαι, ὑποστρωννύω, Φάλεκ, Φανουήλ, φάραγξ, φιλονεικία, φόβητρον, φρονίμως, χάραξ, χάσμα, χορός, Χουζᾶς, ψώχω, ᾦόν.

BIBLIOGRAPHY

ABBREVIATIONS

AnBib	Analecta Biblica (Roma)
ANRW	Aufstieg und Niedergang der Römischen Welt: Geschichte und Kultur Roms im Spiegel der neueren Forschung (Berlin – New York)
Antonianum	Antonianum (Roma)
AusBibRev	Australian Biblical Review (Melbourne)
BDAG	DANKER, F.W. (ed.), *A Greek-English Lexicon of the New Testament and Other Early Christian Literature. Third Edition (BDAG)*, revised and edited by Frederik William Danker, based on Walter Bauer's *Griechisch-Deutsches Wörterbuch zu den Schriften des Neuen Testaments und den übrigen urchristlichen Literatur*, sixth edition, ed. Kurt and Barbara Aland, with Viktor Reichmann and on previous English editions by W.F. Arndt, F.W. Gingrich, and F.W. Danker, Chicago, IL – London: The University of Chicago Press, 2000.
BDR	BLASS, Friedrich – DEBRUNNER, Albert, *Grammatik des neutestamentlichen Griechisch*. Bearbeitet von Friedrich REHKOPF. Göttingen: Vandenhoeck & Ruprecht, [14]1976; 15. durchgesehene Auflage, 1979, XXI-511 p.
BDF	*A Greek Grammar of the New Testament and Other Early Christian Literature*. A translation and revision of the ninth-tenth German edition incorporating supplementary notes of A. Debrunner by Robert W. FUNK. Cambridge: University Press; Chicago, IL: University Press, 1961, XXXVIII-325 p.
BBB	Bonner Biblische Beiträge (Bonn)
BETL	Bibliotheca Ephemeridum Theologicarum Lovaniensium (Leuven)
Bib	Biblica (Roma)
BibLeb	Bibel und Leben (Düsseldorf)
BibNot	Biblische Notizen (München)
BibOr	Bibbia e Oriente (Genova)
BiTod	The Bible Today (Collegeville, MN)
BTB	Biblical Theology Bulletin (Wilmington, DE)
BTrans	The Bible Translator (Aberdeen)
BWANT	Beiträge zur Wissenschaft vom Alten und Neuen Testament (Stuttgart)
BZ	Biblische Zeitschrift (Freiburg)
BZ NF	Biblische Zeitschrift. Neue Folge (Paderborn)
BZNW	Beihefte zur Zeitschrift für die neutestamentliche Wissenschaft und die Kunde der älteren Kirche (Gießen)
CBQ	The Catholic Biblical Quarterly (Washington, DC)
Claretianum	Claretianum (Roma)
Coniectanea Neotestamentica	Coniectanea Neotestamentica (Lund)
EHS	Europäische Hochschulschriften (Bern–Frankfurt/M)
EstBíb	Estudios Bíblicos (Madrid)
EstE	Estudios Eclesiásticos (Madrid)

ETL	Ephemerides Theologicae Lovanienses (Leuven)
Études Bibliques	Études Bibliques (Paris)
ExpT	The Expository Times (Edinburgh)
FilolNT	Filología Neotestamentaria (Córdoba)
FRLANT	Forschungen zur Religion und Literatur des Alten und Neuen Testaments (Göttingen)
Greg	Gregorianum (Roma)
HTR	The Harvard Theological Review (Cambridge, MA)
HTS	Hervormde Teologiese Studies (Pretoria)
JBL	Journal of Biblical Literature (Dallas, TX)
JEvTS	Journal of the Evangelical Theological Society (Wheaton, IL)
JSNT	Journal for the Study of the New Testament (Sheffield)
JSNT SS	Journal for the Study of the New Testament. Supplement Series (Sheffield)
JTS	The Journal of Theological Studies (Oxford)
JTS NS	The Journal of Theological Studies. New Series (Oxford)
Lectio Divina	Lectio Divina (Paris)
LN	LOUW, J.P. – E.A. NIDA, *Greek-English Lexicon of the Greek New Testament based on Semantic Domains*, 2 vols., New York: United Bible Societies, 1988.
Lumen Vitae	Lumen Vitae (Bruxelles)
Lumière et Vie	Lumière et Vie (Lyon)
MGM	MARSHALL, I. Howard (ed.), *Moulton and Geden Concordance to the Greek New Testament*, Sixth Edition Fully Revised, London – New York, 2002.
MüTZ	Münchener Theologische Zeitschrift (München)
Neotestamentica	Neotestamentica (Pretoria)
New Blackfriars	New Blackfriars (Oxford)
Nicolaus	Nicolaus (Bari)
NRT	Nouvelle Revue Théologique (Tournai)
NT	Novum Testamentum (Leiden)
NTAbh	Neutestamentliche Abhandlungen (Münster)
NTS	New Testament Studies (Cambridge)
NTTS	New Testament Tools and Studies (Leiden)
RB	Revue Biblique (Paris)
RechSR	Recherches de science religieuse (Paris)
RevistCatTeol	Revista Catalana de Teologia (Barcelona)
RevSR	Revue de Sciences Religieuses (Strasbourg)
RicBibRel	Ricerche Bibliche e Religiose (Genova)
RivBib	Rivista Biblica (Bologna)
RoczTK	Roczniki Teologiczno-Kanoniczne (Lublin)
RSPT	Revue des sciences philosophiques et théologiques (Paris)
Sal	Salesianum (Roma)
SANT	Studien zum Alten und Neuen Testament (München)
SBB	Stuttgarter Biblische Beiträge (Stuttgart)
SBF/LA	Studium Biblicum Franciscanum: Liber Annuus
SBL	Society of Biblical Literature (Missoula, MT; Atlanta, GA)
SBL DS	Society of Biblical Literature. Dissertation Series (Missoula, MT; Atlanta, GA)

SBL MS	Society of Biblical Literature. Monograph Series (Missoula, MT; Atlanta, GA)
SBL SP	Society of Biblical Literature. Seminar Papers (Missoula, MT; Atlanta, GA)
SC	HOFFMANN, Paul –HIEKE, Thomas – BAUER, Ulrich, *Synoptic Concordance: A Greek Concordance to the First Three Gospels in Synoptic Arrangement, Statistically Evaluated, Including Occurrences in Acts – Griechische Konkordanz zu den ersten drei Evangelien in synoptischer Darstellung, statistisch ausgewertet, mit Berücksichtigung der Apostelgeschichte.* Volume 1: *Introduction B Einführung*, A–Δ. Berlin - New York, Walter de Gruyter, 1999, LXXIII-1032 p.; Vol. II: E–I. 2000, XVIII-957 p.; Vol. III: K–O, 2000, XVII-997 p.; Vol. III: Π–Ω, 2000, XIX-1066 p.
Science et Esprit	Science et Esprit (Montréal) → Sciences Ecclésiastiques
Sciences Ecclésiastiques	Sciences Ecclésiastiques (Montréal) → Science et Esprit
ScotJT	Scottish Journal of Theology (Edinburgh)
Scripta Classica Israelica	Scripta Classica Israelica (Jerusalem)
SEÅ	Svensk Exegetisk Årsbok (Uppsala)
SNTG	Studies in New Testament Greek (Sheffield)
SNTS MS	Society for New Testament Studies. Monograph Series (Cambridge)
SNTU	Studien zum Neuen Testament und seiner Umwelt (Linz)
Sources bibliques	Sources bibliques (Paris)
Studien zum NT	Studien zum Neuen Testament (Gütersloh)
StudTheol	Studia Theologica (Oslo)
SUNT	Studien zur Umwelt des Neuen Testaments (Göttingen)
SupplNT	Supplements to Novum Testamentum (Leiden)
TPQ	Theologisch-praktische Quartalschrift (Linz)
TZ	Theologische Zeitschrift (Basel)
VD	Verbum Domini (Roma)
VK	ALAND, Kurt, *Vollständige Konkordanz zum Griechischen Neuen Testament: Unter Zugrundelegung aller modernen kritischen Textausgaben und des Textus Receptus in Verbindung mit H. Riesenfeld, H.-U. Rosenbaum, Chr. Hannick, B. Bonsack neu zusammengestellt under der Leitung von K. Aland.* Band I (Arbeiten zur neutestamentlichen Textforschung, 4/1). Berlin – New York: de Gruyter, 2 vols., 1983, pp. I-XIX, 1-752 and 753-1252.
VT	Vetus Testamentum (Leiden)
WestTJ	The Westminster Theological Journal (Philadelphia, PA)
WMANT	Wissenschaftliche Monographien zum Alten und Neuen Testament (Neukirchen)
WUNT	Wissenschaftliche Untersuchungen zum Neuen Testament (Tübingen)
ZAW	Zeitschrift für die alttestamentliche Wissenschaft (Berlin)
ZNW	Zeitschrift für die neutestamentliche Wissenschaft (Berlin)

BOISMARD 1984

BOISMARD, Marie-Émile – LAMOUILLE, Arnaud, *Le Texte Occidental des Actes des Apôtres. Reconstruction et réhabilitation.* Tome I: *Introduction et textes.* Tome II: *Apparat critique, Index des caractéristiques stylistiques, Index des citations patristiques* (Synthèse, 17). Paris: Éditions Recherche sur les Civilisations, 1984, XI-232 + V-356 p. Esp. II, 195-335: "Index des caractéristiques stylistiques"; 197-209: "Caractéristiques stylistiques par ordre alphabétique"; 209-277: "Caractéristiques stylistiques par ordre de fréquence"; 278-335: "Répartition par versets".

"Les caractéristiques sont classées en cinq catégories majeures désignées par les cinq premières lettres majuscules de l'alphabet. Dans les catégories A, B et C, elles sont établies en référence à l'ensemble du NT. Les proportions sont à 100% dans la catégorie A; de 99,99 à 80% dans la catégorie B; de 79,99 à 60 % dans la catégorie C. Quant aux deux dernières catégories, les caractéristiques y sont établies en référence aux évangiles et aux Actes. Les proportions seront de 100% dans la catégorie D, de 99,99 à 75% dans la catégorie E. — Chaque catégorie est subdivisée en deux sections, distinguées par les lettres minuscules a et b accolées à la lettre majuscule principale, selon l'occurrence des caractéristiques dans l'œuvre lucanienne: soit dans les Actes seuls (lettre a), soit dans les Actes et l'évangile (lettre b)" (195-196).

CADBURY 1919/20

CADBURY, Henry J., *Style and Literary Method of Luke.* I: *The Diction of Luke and Acts.* II: *The Treatment of Sources in the Gospel* (Harvard Theological Studies, 6). Cambridge: Harvard University Press, 1919/20; New York: Kraus Reprint, 1969, XI-205 p. Esp. 4-39: "Literary standard of Luke's vocabulary".
10-17: "Word lists. A. Common Attic words or word occurring in several Attic writers";
18-19: "B. Words from the vocabulary of individual Attic writers before Aristotle";
19-24: "C. Poetic expressions";
24-35: "D. Expressions used by later writers";
35-36: "E. "Expressions used first or only by Luke";
39-64: "The alleged medical language of Luke".

CREDNER 1836

CREDNER, Karl August, *Einleitung in das Neue Testament.* Erster Theil. Erste-Zweite Abtheilung. Halle: Verlag der Buchhandlung des Waisen-hauses, 1836, X-754 p. Esp. 130-142: "Sprache und Aechtheit"(A list of 65 "Spracheigentümlichkeiten").

GASTON 1973

GASTON, Lloyd, *Horae Synopticae Electronicae: Word Statistics of the Synoptic Gospels* (SBL Sources for Biblical Study, 3). Missoula, MT: Society of Biblical Literature, 1973, III-101 p. Esp. 64-66: "Luke editorial"; 68-84: "Luke editorial?"

GOULDER 1989

GOULDER, Michael D., *Luke: A New Paradigm* (JSNT SS, 20). Sheffield: Sheffield Academic Press, 1989 (repr. 1994), 2 vols., XI-824 p.. Esp. II, 800-809: "A Lucan Vocabulary".

GOULDER 1989 ("The expressions are 'Lucan' either in the sense that they are introduced by Luke redactorally, or in the sense that they occur with a markedly greater frequency in Luke than in Mark and Matthew, and in at least three different contexts").

GOULDER 1989* ("Expressions marked * pass Hawkins' criteria at least four uses in different contexts, and at least twice the combined number of uses in Mark and Matthew").

HAWKINS 1909

HAWKINS, John C., *Horae Synopticae: Contributions to the Study of the Synoptic Problem* [1898]. Oxford: Clarendon, second edition, revised and supplemented, 1909; reprint 1968, XVI-223 p.

HAWKINS 1909L (pp. 15-23: "Words and phrases characteristic of St. Luke's Gospel"; "I take as 'characteristic' the words and phrases which *occur at least four times* in this Gospel, and which either (*a*) *are not found at all in Matthew or Mark*, or (*b*) *are found in Luke at least twice as often as in Matthew and Mark together*").

HAWKINS 1909add. (p. 24: "More or less characteristic of Luke").

HAWKINS 1909A (p. 27: "Subsidiary list A: words and phrases occurring upwards of four times in Luke's Gospel, which do not occur there *twice as often* as in Matthew and Mark together, but which are found *in Luke and Acts together four times as often as in Matthew and Mark together*").

HAWKINS 1909B (pp. 28-29: "Subsidiary list B: words and phrases which are found only two or three times in Luke's Gospel, but which either (*a*) occur *at least six times in Luke and Acts taken together* while not occurring at all in Matthew and Mark, or else (*b*) occur in Luke and Acts together *at least 4 times as often* as in Matthew and Mark together").

HAWKINS 1909LA (p. 203: "Words found both in Luke and Acts, but peculiar to them" , cf. p. 175).

HENDRIKS 1986

HENDRIKS, Wilhelmus M.A., *Karakteristiek woordgebruik in de synoptische evangelies*. Nijmegen: Universitaire pers, 1986, 3 vols., 596 p. — Diss. Nijmegen, 1986 (B. van Iersel).

Esp. III, 422-435: "Karakteristieke lexemen";

428: "Tabel 3.2.5: positief karakteristiek woordgebruik in Lk TOT NAR CIT PAR L+D LOG";

433: "Tabel 3.2.11: positief karakteristiek woordgebruik in Lk CIT";

434: "Tabel 3.2.12: positief karakteristiek woordgebruik in Lk NAR";

440-449: "Karakteristieke woordvormen";

441: "Tabel 3.2.16: positief en negatief karakteristieke woordvormen in Lk NAR en CIT";

448: "Tabel 3.2.21: positief karakteristiek woordgebruik in Lk";

466: "Tabel 3.3.1: positief karakteristiek woordgebruik in resp Mt Mk Lk";

468: "Tabel 3.3.3: positief karakteristiek woordgebruik in Ac".

MORGENTHALER 1958

MORGENTHALER, Robert, *Statistik des neutestamentlichen Wortschatzes.*
Zürich–Frankfurt/M: Gotthelf, 1958; [4]1992, 188 p.

Esp. 44-48: "Statistik über die neutestamentlichen Vokabeln, die im vorchristlischen Griechisch
nirgends (I), nur ausserhalb (II) oder nur innerhalb der Septuaginta (III) belegt sind". Listen der
Vokabeln zu I, II und III; 175-180: "Statistik über den Zusammenhang des neutestamentlichen
Wortschatzes mit dem griechischen Wortschatz der vorchristlichen Zeit".
I (p. 177): "Lk Vokabeln, die im vorchristlichen Griechisch nirgends belegt sind" (19 cases,
marked with **);
II (p. 178): "Lk Vokablen, die im vorchristlischen Griechisch nur ausserhalb der Septuaginta
belegt sind" (51 cases, marked with*);
III (p. 180): "Lk Vokablen, die im vorchristlichen Griechisch nu innerhalb der Septuaginta
belegt sind" (8 cases, marked with ***).

Esp. 51-52: "Statistische Listen von Vorzugswörtern: Lukas" (cf. p. 181, L: "38 von den 62
Vorzugsvokabeln des Lukasevangeliums erscheinen auch in Acta als solche" (cf. p. 181, LA);
52: "Statistische Listen von Vorzugswörtern: Apostelgeschichte": "Was die Vorzugswörter der
Apostelgeschichte anbelangt, so ist die Liste um diejenigen Wörter die schon zum
Lukasevangelium als Vorzugsvokabeln vermerkt wurden, zu ergänzen" (cf. p. 182-183, A).

MORGENTHALER 1958* (p. 172: "Vokabelntabellen zu den Kombinationen Lk-Act").
MORGENTHALER 1958L (p. 181: "Statistische Listen von Vorzugswörtern: Lukas").
MORGENTHALER 1958LA (p. 181: "Statistische Listen von Vorzugswörtern: Lukas"; words marked
    with Ac).
MORGENTHALER 1958A (pp. 182-183: "Statistische Listen von Vorzugswörtern: Apostel-
    geschichte").

NEIRYNCK 1985

NEIRYNCK, Frans, Le texte des Actes des Apôtres et les caractéristiques
stylistiques lucaniennes. — *ETL* 61 (1985) 304-339. Esp. 317-330: "Caractéristiques lucaniennes. Actes – Luc" (615 cases); = ID., *Evangelica II*, 1991, 243-278.
Esp. 256-269.

PLUMMER 1922

PLUMMER, Alfred, *A Critical and Exegetical Commentary to the Gospel*
According to S. Luke (The International Critical Commentary). Edinburgh: T.
& T. Clark, 1896, LXXXVIII-592 p.; [5]1922 (= 1964).
Esp. xli-lxvii: "Characteristics, style and language";
lii-liii: "The most remarkable words and expressions which occur either in both his
writings and nowhere else in N.T., or in his Gospel and nowhere else in N.T.";
lix: "(4) Expressions not found in the other Gospels and more frequent in S. Luke's
Writings than in all the rest of N.T.";
lix-lx: "(5) Expressions found in one or more of the other Gospels, but more frequent
in S. Luke's Writings than in all the rest of N.T.";
lx-lxi: "(6) Expressions frequent in S. Luke's Writings and probably due to Hebrew
Influence" (we do not take all expressions, because some of them have already been
taken in previous lists or are not relevant in terms of frequency);
lxii-lxiii: "(7) Miscellaneous expressions and constructions which are specially
frequent in S. Luke's Writings" (we do not take all expressions, because some of
them have already been taken in previous lists or are not relevant in terms of
frequency).

VOGEL 1899

VOGEL, Theodor, *Zur Charakteristik des Lukas nach Sprache und Stil. Eine philologische Laienstudie.* Leipzig: Verlag der Dürr'schen Buchhandlung, [2]1899, 70 p. Esp. 61-68: "Vergleichung des Wortschatzes von E und A".

VOGEL 1899A (pp. 61-63: "Nur bei EA im N.T. Vorkommendes").
VOGEL 1899B (pp. 63-65: "Außer bei EA im N.T. nur vereinzelt Vorkommendes").
VOGEL 1899C (pp. 65-66: "Für EA besonders charakteristische Ausdrücke").
VOGEL 1899D (pp. 66-68: "Lieblingsausdrücke von EA").

SPECIFIC LUKAN BIBLIOGRAPHY, CITED IN ABBREVIATED FORM

VON BENDEMANN 2001

VON BENDEMANN, Reinhard, *Zwischen δόξα und σταυρός: Eine exegetische Untersuchung der Texte des sogenannten Reiseberichts im Lukasevangelium* (BZNW, 101). Berlin – New York: de Gruyter, 2001, XVI-512 p.
Esp. 413-439: "Inventar redaktioneller Anteile in Lk 8,1–21,38";
440-450: "Inventar des 'Sondergutes' innerhalb von Lk 8,1–21,38".

BDR

BLASS, Friedrich – DEBRUNNER, Albert, *Grammatik des neutestamentlichen Griechisch*. Bearbeitet von Friedrich REHKOPF. Göttingen: Vandenhoeck & Ruprecht, [14]1976; 15. durchgesehene Auflage, 1979, XXI-511 p.
A Greek Grammar of the New Testament and Other Early Christian Literature. A translation and revision of the ninth-tenth German edition incorporating supplementary notes of A. Debrunner by Robert W. FUNK. Cambridge: University Press; Chicago, IL: University Press, 1961, XXXVIII-325 p.

COLLISON 1977

COLLISON, Franklyn J.G., *Linguistic Usages in the Gospel of Luke*. Diss. Southern Methodist University, 1977, V-375 p.
Esp. 369-371: "A. Linguistic usages of Luke";
371-373: "B. Linguistic usages of Luke's 'other source-material'";
373-375: "Noteworthy phenomena";
*** indicating a "certain usage"; ** indicating a "probable" usage and * indicating a "likely" usage.

EASTON 1910

EASTON, Burton Scott, Linguistic Evidence for the Lucan Source L. – *JBL* 29 (1910) 139-180.
Esp. 145-149: "Words and phrases especially characteristic of L";
150-158: "Words and phrases probably characteristic of L";
158-166: "Words and phrases cited by Weiss as characteristic of L, and possibly corroborative";
167: "Words and phrases cited by Weiss as characteristic of L on insufficient(?) evidence";
175-178: "Possible Hebraisms in the Lucan writings, as classed by Dalman".

GERSDORF 1816

GERSDORF, Christoph Gotthelf, *Beiträge zur Sprach-Characteristik der Schriftsteller des Neuen Testaments: Eine Sammlung meist neuer Bemerkungen*. Erster Theil. Leipzig: Weidmannische Buchhandlung, 1816, XXXVI-579 p.
Esp. 160-212: "Zu Lucae Cap. 1";
212-272: "Zu Lucae Cap. 2".

HARNACK 1906

HARNACK, Adolf, *Beiträge zur Einleitung in das Neue Testament*.

I: *Lukas der Arzt: Der Verfasser des dritten Evangeliums und der Apostelgeschichte*. Leipzig: J.C. Hinrichs'sche Buchhandlung, 1906, VII-160 p. Esp. 29-46 [Acts 16,10-17; 28,1-16]; 51-54 ["Wirstücken"]; 69-72 [Lk 1,5-15]; 138-152: "Sprachlich-lexikalische Untersuchung von Luk. 1,39-56.68-79; 2,15-20.41-52".

II: *Sprüche und Reden Jesu. Die zweite Quelle des Matthäus und Lukas*. Leipzig: J.C. Hinrichs'sche Buchhandlung, 1907, IV-220 p. Esp. 6-87.

New Testament Studies. I: *Luke the Physician: The Author of the Third Gospel and the Acts of the Apostles* (Crown Theological Library), trans. J.R. Wilkinson. Ed. W.D. Morrison. London: Williams & Norgate; New York: G.P. Putnam's Sons, 1907, XI-231 p. Esp. 40-65 [Acts 16,10-17; 28,1-16]; 72-77 ["We"-sections]; 97-101 [Lk 1,5-15]; 199-218: "Investigation of the linguistic relations of St. Luke I.39-56, 68-79, II. 15-20, 41-52".

II: *The Sayings of Jesus. The Second Source of St. Matthew and St. Luke*, trans. J.R. Wilkinson. London: Williams & Norgate; New York: G.P. Putnam's Sons, 1908, XVI-316 p. Esp. 1-117.

HAUCK 1934

HAUCK, D. Friedrich, *Das Evangelium des Lukas (Synoptiker II)* (Theologischer Handkommentar zum Neuen Testament mit Text und Paraphrase, 3). Leipzig: A. Deichertsche Verlagsbuchhandlung D. Werner Scholl, 1934, XII-303 p. Esp. 9-10: "Sprache und Stil"; 14: "Synoptische Stilvergleichung" [Vorzugswort; häufiges/seltenes Alleinwort; Stileigentümlichkeit; Vorzugsverbindung].

JEREMIAS 1980

JEREMIAS, Joachim, *Die Sprache des Lukasevangeliums: Redaktion und Tradition im Nicht-Markusstoff des dritten Evangeliums* (Kritisch-exegetischer Kommentar über das Neue Testament. Sonderband). Göttingen: Vandenhoeck & Ruprecht, 1980, 323 p.

PAFFENROTH 1997

PAFFENROTH, Kim, *The Story of Jesus According to L* (JSNT SS, 147). Sheffield: Sheffield Academic Press, 1997, 200 p. Esp. 66-95: "Vocabulary and Style".

RADL 1975

RADL, Walter, *Paulus und Jesus im lukanischen Doppelwerk: Untersuchungen zu Parallelmotiven im Lukasevangelium und in der Apostelgeschichte* (Europäische Hochschulschriften, XXIII/49). Bern–Frankfurt/M, 1975, IV-460 p. Esp. 396-435: "Anhang zur Stilkritik".

SCHNEIDER 1969

SCHNEIDER, Gerhard, *Verleugnung, Verspottung und Verhör Jesu nach Lukas 22,54-71: Studien zur lukanischen Darstellung der Passion* (SANT, 22). München: Kösel, 1969, 245 p. Esp. 73-134: "Literarkritische Einzeluntersuchungen: 1. Lk 22,54-62 (Verleugnung); 2. Lk 22,63-65 (Verspottung); 3. Lk 22,66-71 (Verhör)"; 163-165: "Sprachlich-stilistische Beobachtungen: a. Vorzugswörter und –ausdrücke des Luk; b. Bei Luk beliebte Konstruktionen; c.

Vermeidung von mk Vokabeln und Konstruktionen; d. Un-luk Sprachgebrauch; e. Besonderheiten der luk Darstellung".

SCHÜRMANN 1953

SCHÜRMANN, Heinz, *Der Paschamahlbericht Lk 22,(7-14).15-18. I. Teil einer quellenkritischen Untersuchung des lukanischen Abendmahlsberichtes Lk 22,7-38* (NTAbh, 20/5). Münster: Aschendorff, 1953, XXX-123 p. Esp. 3-46 [22,15-18]; 76-104 [22-7-13]; 104-110 [22,14].

SCHÜRMANN 1955

SCHÜRMANN, Heinz, *Die Einsetzungsbericht Lk 22,19-20. II. Teil einer quellenkritischen Untersuchung des lukanischen Abendmahlsberichtes Lk 22,7-38* (NTAbh, 20/4). Münster: Aschendorff, 1955, XII-153 p.; [2]1970; [3]1986.

SCHÜRMANN 1957

SCHÜRMANN, Heinz, *Jesu Abschiedsrede Lk 22,21-38. III. Teil einer quellenkritischen Untersuchung des lukanischen Abendmahlsberichtes Lk 22,7-38* (NTAbh, 20/5). Münster: Aschendorff, 1957, XI-160 p.; [2]1977, XX-170 p. Esp. 37-54: "Scheidung von vorlukanischer Tradition und lukanischer Redaktion in Lk 22,28-30"; 64-92: "Lk 22,24-27 als lukanische Redaktion einer vorlukanischen Nicht/Markus-Tradition"; 99-112: "Lk 22,31-32 als lukanische Redaktion einer vorlukanischen Tradition"; 116-134: "Lk 22,35-38 als lukanische Redaktion einer vorlukanischen Tradition"; 148-154: "Sachregister zum lukanischen (und neutestamentlichen) Sprachgebrauch"; 154-160: "Griechisches Wortregister".

SCHÜRMANN 1961

SCHÜRMANN, Heinz, Umschau und Kritik: Protolukanische Spracheigentümlichkeiten? Zu Fr. Rehkopf, Die lukanische Sonderquelle. Ihr Umfang und Sprachgebrauch. — *BZ* NF 5 (1961) 266-286.

GENERAL BIBLIOGRAPHY

The works marked with asterisk are also cited (in abbreviated form) under specific lemmata.

ALAND, Kurt, *Vollständige Konkordanz zum Griechischen Neuen Testament: Unter Zugrundelegung aller modernen kritischen Textausgaben und des Textus Receptus in Verbindung mit H. Riesenfeld, H.-U. Rosenbaum, Chr. Hannick, B. Bonsack neu zusammengestellt under der Leitung von K. Aland.* Band I (Arbeiten zur neutestamentlichen Textforschung, 4/1). Berlin – New York: de Gruyter, 2 vols., 1983, pp. I-XIX, 1-752 and 753-1252. Band II: *Spezialübersichten* (Arbeiten zur neutestamentlichen Textforschung, 4/2). Berlin – New York: de Gruyter, 1978, VII-557 p.

ALEXANDER, Loveday, Luke's Preface in the Context of Greek Preface-Writing. — *NT* 28 (1986) 48-74.

*—, *The Preface to Luke's Gospel: Literary Convention and Social Context in Luke 1.1-4 and Acts 1.1* (SNTS MS, 78). Cambridge: University Press, 1993, XV-250 p. Esp. 67-101: "Scientific prefaces: structure, content and style".

—, *Septuaginta, Fachprosa, Imitatio*: Albert Wifstrand and the Language of Luke-Acts. — BREYTENBACH, C., et al. (eds.), *Die Apostelgeschichte und die hellenistische Geschichtsschreibung.* FS E. Plümacher, 2004, 1-26.

AMPHOUX, Christian-Bernard, Le chapitre 24 de *Luc* et l'origine de la tradition textuelle du *Codex de Bèze* (D.05 du NT). — *FilolNT* 4 (1991) 21-50.

—, Les premières éditions de Luc. II: L'histoire du texte au IIe siècle. — *ETL* 68 (1992) 38-48.

ANTONIADIS, Sophie, *L'évangile de Luc: Esquisse de grammaire et de style* (Collection de l'Institut néo-hellénique de l'Université de Paris, 7). Paris: Les Belles Lettres, 1930, XII-456 p.

ARGYLE, A.W., The Greek of Luke and Acts. — *NTS* 20 (1973-74) 441-445.

ÅSBERG, Christer, Om språk och stil i NT 1981. — *SEÅ* 47 (1982) 115-150.

*BACHMANN, Michael, *Jerusalem und der Tempel: Die geographisch-theologischen Elemente in der lukanischen Sicht des jüdischen Kultzentrums* (BWANT, 109). Stuttgart: Kohlhammer, 1980, X-402 p.

*BARR, James, *The Semantics of Biblical Language.* Oxford: University Press, 1961, X-313 p.

BARRETT, C.K., The Imperatival Participle. — *ExpT* 59 (1947-48) 165-166.

*BARTH, Eugene Howard – COCROFT, Ronald Edwin, *Festschrift to Honor F. Wilbur Gingrich: Lexicographer, Scholar, Teacher, and Committed Christian Layman.* Leiden: Brill, 1972, VII-226 p.

*BAUER, Johannes B., *Scholia Biblica et Patristica.* Graz: Akademische Druck- u. Verlagsanstalt, 1972, VII-293 p.

BENOIT, Pierre, L'enfance de Jean-Baptiste selon Luc I. — *NTS* 3 (1956-57) 169-194. Esp. 169-176: "La langue".

BETORI, Giuseppe, Confermare le Chiese con la parola dell'esortazione: ἐπιστηρίζειν nel libro degli Atti. — FABRIS, Rinaldo (ed.), *La parola di Dio cresceva (At 12,24): Scritti in onore di Carlo Maria Martini nel suo 70°*

compleanno (Supplementi alla Rivista Biblica, 33). Bologna: Dehoniane, 1998, 345-356.

BEUTLER, Johannes, Lk 6,16: Punkt oder Komma? — *BZ* NF 35 (1991) 231-233.

*BEYER, Klaus, *Semitische Syntax im Neuen Testament*. Band I: *Satzlehre Teil 1* (SUNT, 1). Göttingen: Vandenhoeck & Ruprecht, 1962, 324 p.

BLACK, David Alan, New Testament Semitisms. — *BTrans* 39 (1988) 215-223.

*BLACK, Matthew, *An Aramaic Approach to the Gospels and Acts*. Oxford: Clarendon, [3]1967, X-359 p.

BLASS, Friedrich — DEBRUNNER, Albert, *Grammatik des neutestamentlichen Griechisch*. Bearbeitet von Friedrich REHKOPF. Göttingen: Vandenhoeck & Ruprecht, [14]1976; 15. durchgesehene Auflage, 1979.

*BLINZLER, J. — KUSS, O. — MUßNER, F. (eds.), *Neutestamentliche Aufsätze: Festschrift für Prof. Josef Schmid zum 70. Geburtstag*. Pustet: Regensburg, 1963, X-340 p.

*BÖCHER, Otto — HAACKER, Klaus (eds.), *Verborum Veritas: Festschrift für Gustav Stählin zum 70. Geburtstag*. Wuppertal: Brockhaus, 1970, XII-384 p.

*BORMANN, Lukas, *Recht, Gerechtigkeit und Religion im Lukasevangelium* (SUNT, 24). Göttingen: Vandenhoeck & Ruprecht, 2001, 420 p. Esp. 103-216: "Rechtsterminologie im Lukasevangelium".

BOTHA, J. Eugene, Style in the New Testament: The Need for Serious Reconsideration. — *JSNT* 43 (1991) 71-87.

—, Style, Stylistics and the Study of the New Testament. — *Neotestamentica* 24 (1990) 173-184.

BOYER, J.L., First Class Conditions: What Do They Mean?.— *Grace Theological Journal* 2 (1981) 76-114.

—, Second Class Conditions in New Testament Greek. — *Grace Theological Journal* 3 (1982) 81-88.

—, Third (and Fourth) Class Conditions. — *Grace Theological Journal* 3 (1982) 163-175.

—, Other Conditional Elements in New Testament Greek. — *Grace Theological Journal* 3 (1983) 173-188.

—, The Classification of Participles: A Statistical Study. — *Grace Theological Journal* 5 (1984) 163-179.

—, The Classification of Infinitives: A Statistical Study. — *Grace Theological Journal* 6 (1985) 3-27.

—, The Classification of Imperatives: A Statistical Study. — *Grace Theological Journal* 8 (1987) 35-54.

—, The Classification of Optatives: A Statistical Study. — *Grace Theological Journal* 9 (1988) 129-140.

BRAUN, Willi, *Feasting and Social Rhetoric in Luke 14* (SNTS MS, 85). Cambridge: University Press, 1995, XII-221 p.

*BREYTENBACH, Cilliers — SCHRÖTER, Jens — DU TOIT, David S. (eds.), *Die Apostelgeschichte und die hellenistische Geschichtsschreibung: Festschrift für Eckhard Plümacher zu seinem 65. Geburtstag* (Ancient Judaism & Early Christianity, 57). Leiden — Boston: Brill, 2004, XII-385 p.

BROCK, Sebastian P., The Treatment of Greek Particles in the Old Syriac Gospels, with Special Reference to Luke. — ELLIOTT, J.K. (ed.), *Studies in New Testament Language and Text*. FS G.D. Kilpatrick, 1976, 80-86.

*BURCHARD, Christoph, Fußnoten zum neutestamentlichen Griechisch. — *ZNW* 61 (1970) 157-171.

*—, Fußnoten zum neutestamentlichen Griechisch II. — *ZNW* 69 (1978) 147-157.

*CADBURY, Henry J., Commentary on the Preface of Luke. — JACKSON, F.J. Foakes — LAKE, Kirsop (eds.), *The Beginning of Christianity*. Part I: *The Acts of the Apostles*. Vol. II: *Prolegomena*. II: *Criticism*. London: Macmillan, 1922, 480-510.

*—, Lexical Notes on Luke-Acts. II. Recent Arguments for Medical Language. — *JBL* 45 (1926) 190-209.

*—, Lexical Notes on Luke-Acts. III. Luke's Interest in Lodging. — *JBL* 45 (1926) 305-322.

*—, Lexical Notes on Luke-Acts. IV. On Direct Quotation, with Some Uses of ὅτι and εἰ. — *JBL* 48 (1929) 412-425.

*—, Lexical Notes on Luke-Acts. V. Luke and the Horse-Doctors. — *JBL* 52 (1933) 55-65.

—, Four Features of Lucan Style. — KECK, L.E. — MARTYN, J.L. (eds.), *Studies in Luke-Acts*. FS P. Schubert, 1966, ^{3}1978, 87-102.

—, Litotes in Acts. — BARTH, E.H. — COCROFT, R.E. (eds.), *Festschrift to Honor F. Wilbur Gingrich*, 1972, 70-84. Esp. 59-61 [οὐκ ἄσημος]; 61-62 [οὐ μετρίως]; 62-63 [οὐκ ὀλιγός]; 63-64 [οὐχ ὁ τύχων]; 64 [οὐ πολύς]; 64-65 [οὐ ἀμάρτυρον]; 65-66 [οὐ μακράν].

CANCIK, Hubert, The History of Culture, Religion, and Institutions in Ancient Historiography: Philological Observations concerning Luke's History. — *JBL* 116 (1997) 673-695. [ἐκκλησία and αἵρεσις]

*CARAGOUNIS, Chrys C., *The Development of Greek and the New Testament: Morphology, Syntax, Phonology, and Textual Transmission* (WUNT, 167). Tübingen: Mohr Siebeck, 2004, XX-732 p.

*CAZELLES, Henri (ed.), *La vie de la Parole: De l'Ancien au Nouveau Testament. Études d'exégèse et d'herméneutique bibliques offertes à Pierre Grelot professeur à l'Institut Catholique de Paris*. Paris: Desclée, 1987, XLV-486 p.

*CHILTON, Bruce, Announcement in Nazara: An Analysis of Luke 4:16-21. — FRANCE, R.T. — WENHAM, D. (eds.), *Gospel Perspectives*, II, 1981, 147-172.

CIGNAC, Francis T., Morphological Phenomena in the Greek Papyri Significant for theText and Language of the New Testament. — *CBQ* 48 (1986) 499-511.

CIGNELLI, Lino — BOTTINI, G.C., L'articolo nel Greco biblico. — *SBF/LA* 41 (1991) 159-199.

*— — PIERRI, Rosario, *Sintassi di Greco biblico (LXX e NT)*. Quaderno I.A: *Le concordanze* (Studium Biblicum Franciscanum. Analecta, 61). Jerusalem: Franciscan Printing Press, 2003, 134 p.

CLARK, D.J., A Not Infrequent Construction: Litotes in the Book of Acts. — *BTrans* 55 (2004) 433-440.

*CLAUSSEN, Carsten, *Versammlung, Gemeinde, Synagoge: Das hellenistisch-jüdische Umfeld der frühchristlichen Gemeinden* (SUNT, 27). Göttingen: Vandenhoeck & Ruprecht, 2002, 368 p.

Co, Maria Anicia, The Major Summaries in Acts: Acts 2,42-47; 4,32-35; 5,12-16: Linguistic and Literary Relationship. — *ETL* 68 (1992) 49-85.

CREED, John Martin, *The Gospel according to St. Luke: The Greek Text with Introduction, Notes, and Indices*. London: Macmillan; New York: St. Martin's Press, 1930; repr. 1965, XC-340 p. Esp. LXXVI-LXXXIV: "Language, style, and vocabulary".

DANKER, F.W. (ed.), *A Greek-English Lexicon of the New Testament and Other Early Christian Literature. Third Edition (BDAG)*, revised and edited by Frederik William Danker, based on Walter Bauer's *Griechisch-Deutsches Wörterbuch zu den Schriften des Neuen Testaments und den übrigen urchristlichen Literatur*, sixth edition, ed. Kurt and Barbara Aland, with Viktor Reichmann and on previous English editions by W.F. Arndt, F.W. Gingrich, and F.W. Danker, Chicago, IL – London: The University of Chicago Press, 2000.

* DANOVE, Paul, Verbs of Experience: Toward a Lexicon Detailing the Argument Structures Assigned by Verbs. — PORTER, S.E. – CARSON, D.A. (eds.), *Linguistics and the New Testament: Critical Junctures* (JSNT SS, 168; SNTG, 5). Sheffield: Academic Press, 1999, 144-205.

DAVIES, David, The Position of Adverbs in Luke. — ELLIOTT, J.K. (ed.), *Studies in New Testament Language and Text*. FS G.D. Kilpatrick, 1976, 106-121.

DAWSEY, J., The Literary Unity of Luke-Acts: Questions of Style – A Task for Literary Critics. — *NTS* 35 (1989) 48-66.

*DELEBECQUE, Édouard, *Études grecques sur l'Évangile de Luc* (Collection d'études anciennes). Paris: Les Belles Lettres, 1976, VI-183 p.

*DELOBEL, Joël (ed.), *Logia: Les paroles de Jésus – The Sayings of Jesus. Mémorial Joseph Coppens* (BETL, 59). Leuven: University Press – Peeters, 1982, 644 p.

DELORME, Jean, Le magnificat: La forme et le sens. — CAZELLES, H. (ed.), *La vie de la Parole*. FS P. Grelot, 1987, 175-194. Esp. 177-179: "Forme linguistique"; 179-182: "Parallélismes lexicaux".

*DENAUX, A., L'hypocrisie des pharisiens et le dessein de Dieu: Analyse de *Lc.*, XIII, 31-33. — NEIRYNCK, F. (ed.), *L'Évangile de Luc*, 1973, 245-285. Esp. 258-261: "La terminologie"; [2]1989, 155-195 (316-323: note additionnelle). Esp. 168-171.

—, The Delineation of the Lukan Travel Narrative within the Overall Structure of the Gospel of Luke. — FOCANT, C. (ed.), *The Synoptic Gospels. Source Criticism and the New Literary Criticism* (BETL, 110), Leuven, University Press – Peeters, 1993, 359-392.

—, The theme of Divine Visits and Human (In)hospitality in Luke-Acts: Its Old Testament and Graeco-Roman Antecedents. — VERHEYDEN, J. (ed.), *The Unity of Luke-Acts*, 1999, 255-279.

* — (ed.), *New Testament Textual Criticism and Exegesis: Festschrift J. Delobel* (BETL, 161). Leuven: University Press – Peeters, 2002, XVIII-391 p.

*DERRETT, J. Duncan M., *Studies in the New Testament*. Volume two: *Midrash in Action and as a Literary Device*. Leiden: Brill, 1978, X-229 p.

* —, *Studies in the New Testament*. Volume three: *Midrash, Haggadah, and the Character of the Community*. Leiden: Brill, 1982, XII-261 p.

*—, *Studies in the New Testament*. Volume five: *The Sea-Change of the Old Testament in the New*. Leiden: Brill, 1989, XII-245 p.

*—, *Studies in the New Testament*. Volume six: *Jesus among Biblical Exegetes*. Leiden: Brill, 1995, X-251 p.

*DESCAMPS, Albert – DE HALLEUX, André (eds.), *Mélanges bibliques en hommage au R.P. Béda Rigaux*. Gembloux: Duculot, 1970, XXVIII-618 p.

DE VILLIERS, Pieter G.R., The Medium is the Message: Luke and the Language of the New Testament against a Graeco-Roman Background. — *Neotestamentica* 24 (1990) 247-256. [ἀγράμματοὶ ... καὶ ἰδιῶται in Acts 4,13]

*DICKERSON, Patrick L., The New Character Narrative in Luke-Acts and the Synoptic Problem. — *JBL* 116 (1997) 291-312.

DIEFENBACH, Manfred, Das Lukasevangelium und die antike Rhetorik. — *SNTU* 18 (1993) 151-161.

*DOBLE, Peter, *The Paradox of Salvation: Luke's Theology of the Cross* (SNTS MS, 87). Cambridge: University Press, 1996, XIV-272 p.

*DONALDSON, Amy M. – SAILORS, Timothy B. (eds.), *New Testament Greek and Exegesis: Essays in Honor of Gerald F. Hawthorne*. Grand Rapids, MI – Cambridge: Eerdmans, 2003, XIV-262 p.

DUPLACY, Jean, Le véritable disciple: Un essai d'analyse sémantique de Luc 6,43-49. — *RechSR* 69 (1981) 71-86.

*DUPONT, Jacques, *Les Béatitudes*. [Tome I:] *Le problème littéraire: Les deux versions du Sermon sur la montagne et des Béatitudes*. Brugge: St. Andriesabdij; Leuven: Nauwelaerts, ²1958 (new ed.), 387 p.; (Études Bibliques). Paris: Gabalda, 1969, 387 p. Esp. 43-59: "Les matériaux propres à Luc"; 189-203: "Le discours de Luc"; 265-298: "Les béatitudes de Luc"; 299-342: "Les malédictions".

*—, *Le discours de Milet: Testament pastoral de Saint Paul (Actes 20,18-36)* (Lectio Divina, 32). Paris: Cerf, 1962, 407 p.

*—, *Les Béatitudes*. Tome II: *La bonne nouvelle* (Études Bibliques). Paris: Gabalda, 1969, 426 p. Esp. 19-34: "Le vocabulaire de la pauvreté"; 320-322: "'Se réjouir', 'exulter'"; 324: "Μακάριοι".

*—, *Les Béatitudes*. Tome III: *Les Évangélistes* (Études Bibliques). Paris: Gabalda, 1973, 743 p. Esp. 21-203: "La version de Luc".

*—, *Études sur les évangiles synoptiques*. Présentées par F. Neirynck (BETL, 70/A-B). Leuven: University Press – Peeters, 1985, pp. I-XXI, 1-526 + I-IX, 527-1210.

*ELLIOTT, J.K. (ed.), *Studies in New Testament Language and Text: Essays in Honour of George D. Kilpatrick on the Occasion of His Sixty-Fifth Birthday* (SupplNT, 44). Leiden: Brill, 1976, X-400 p.

*—, The Two Forms of the Third Declension Comparative Adjectives in the New Testament. — *NT* 19 (1977) 234-239.

*—, Textual Variation Involving the Augment in the Greek New Testament. — *ZNW* 69 (1978) 247-252.

—, Temporal Augment in Verbs with Initial Diphthong in the Greek New Testament. — *NT* 22 (1980) 1-11.

* —, New Testament Linguistic Usage. — BLACK, David Alan (ed.), *New Testament Essays in Honor of J. Harold Greenlee*. Winona Lake, IN: Eisenbrauns, 1992, 41-48.

—, The Greek Manuscript Heritage of the Book of Acts — *FilolNT* 9 (1996) 37-50.

ELLIS, E. Earle, Midrashic Features in the Speeches of Acts. — DESCAMPS, A. – DE HALLEUX, A. (eds.), *Mélanges bibliques en hommage au R.P. Béda Rigaux*, 1970, 303-312.

* — – GRÄSSER, Erich (eds.), *Jesus und Paulus: Festschrift für Werner Georg Kümmel zum 70. Geburtstag*. Göttingen: Vandenhoeck & Ruprecht, 1975, 411 p.

ELLUL, Danielle, Antioche de Pisidie: Une prédication ... trois credos? (Acts 13,13-43). — *FilolNT* 5 (1992) 3-14.

EVANS, C.F., "Speeches" in Acts. — DESCAMPS, A. – DE HALLEUX, A. (eds.), *Mélanges bibliques en hommage au R.P. Béda Rigaux*, 1970, 287-302.

* FANNING, Buist M., *Verbal Aspect in New Testament Greek* (Oxford Theological Monographs). Oxford: Clarendon Press, 1990, XIV-471 p.

FARMER, William R., Notes on a Literary and Form-Critical Analysis of Some of the Synoptic Material Peculiar to Luke. — *NTS* 8 (1961-62) 301-316.

FARRIS, Stephen C., On Discerning Semitic Sources in Luke 1–2. — FRANCE, R.T. – WENHAM, D. (eds.), *Gospel Perspectives*, II, 1981, 201-237.

* FITZMYER, Joseph A., *The Gospel according to Luke I-IX. Introduction, Translation and Notes* (AB, 28), Garden City, NY: Doubleday, 1981, XXVI-837 p. Esp. 107-127 [Lukan Language].

* —, *To Advance the Gospel: New Testament Studies*. New York: Crossroad, 1981, XIII-265 p.

* FRANCE, R.T. – WENHAM, David (eds.), *Gospel Perspectives: Studies of History and Tradition in the Four Gospels*. Volume II. Sheffield: JSOT Press, 1981, 375 p.

* FUCHS, Albert, *Sprachliche Untersuchungen zu Mattäus und Lukas: Ein Beitrag zur Quellenkritik* (AnBib, 49). Roma: Biblical Institute Press, 1971, X-217 p.

FUNK, T.W., *A Greek Grammar of the New Testament and Other Early Christian Literature*. A translation and revision of the ninth-tenth German edition incorporating supplementary notes of A. Debrunner by Robert W. Funk. Cambridge: University Press; Chicago, IL: University Press, 1961.

* GARCÍA PÉREZ, José Miguel, El Endemoniado de Gerasa (Lc 8,26-39). — *EstBíb* 44 (1986) 117-146.

* —, El relato del Buen Ladrón (Lc 23,39-43). — *EstBíb* 44 (1986) 263-304.

GATES, John Edward, *An Analysis of the Lexicographic Resources Used by American Biblical Scholars Today* (SBL DS, 8). Missoula, MT: Scholars, 1972, XXI-175 p.

* GEORGE, Augustin, *Études sur l'œuvre de Luc* (Sources bibliques). Paris: Gabalda, 1978, 487 p.

GIBSON, Arthur, *Biblical Semantic Logic: A Preliminary Analysis*. Oxford: Blackwell, 1981, XI-244 p.

GINGRICH, F. Wilbur, The Contributions of Professor Walter Bauer to New Testament Lexicography. — *NTS* 9 (1962-63) 3-10.

*GLÖCKNER, Richard, *Die Verkündigung des Heils beim Evangelisten Lukas* (Walberberger Studien. Theologische Reihe, 9). Mainz: Grünewald, 1975, XXII-246 p.

GRAMAGLIA, Pier Angelo, Analisi linguistica di Lc XXII,24-27: Ministero di presidenza ed eucaristia. — *Archivio Teologico Torinese* (Torino) 6/2 (2000) 25-57.

—, Analisi linguistica di Lc XXII,28-30: Eucaristia ed escatologia. — *Archivio Teologico Torinese* 7 (2001) 255-298.

*GUERRA GÓMEZ, Manuel, Análisis filológico-teológico y traducción del himno de los ángeles en Belén. — *Burgense* 30 (1989) 31-86.

HAENCHEN, Ernst, The Book of Acts as Source Material for the History of Early Christianity. — KECK, L.E. – MARTYN, J.L. (eds.), *Studies in Luke-Acts.* FS P. Schubert, 1966, [3]1978, 258-278. Esp. 260-261: "An example of Lucan style".

*HAGENE, Sylvia, *Zeiten der Wiederherstellung: Studien zur lukanischen Geschichtstheologie als Soteriologie* (NTAbh, 42). Münster: Aschendorff, 2003, IX-366 p.

*HAHN, Ferdinand, *Christologische Hoheitstitel: Ihre Geschichte im frühen Christentum* (FRLANT, 83). Göttingen: Vandenhoeck & Ruprecht, 1963, 442 p.

*HARTMAN, Lars, *Testimonium linguae: Participial Constructions in the Synoptic Gospels. A Linguistic Examination of Luke 21,13* (Coniectanea Neotestamentica, 19). Lund: Gleerup, 1963, 75 p. Esp. 36-45: "The Gospel of St. Luke"; 57-75: "Ἀποβήσεται ὑμῖν εἰς μαρτύριον".

*HATCH, Edwin, *Essays in Biblical Greek.* Oxford: Clarendon, 1889, X-293 p.

HAUBECK, Wilfrid – VON SIEBENTHAL, Heinrich, *Neuer sprachlicher Schlüssel zum Griechischen Neuen Testament: Matthäus bis Apostelgeschichte.* Gießen–Basel: Brunnen, 1997, XXXVI-899 p. Esp. 350-518: "Lukas"; 609-891: "Apostelgeschichte".

HEIMERDINGER, Jenny – LEVINSOHN, Stephen, The Use of the Definite Article before Names of People in the Greek Text of Acts with Particular Reference to Codex Bezae. — *FilolNT* 5 (1992) 15-44; = READ-HEIMERDINGER, J., *The Bezan Text of Acts*, 2002, 116-144.

—, Word Order in Koine Greek: Using a Text-Critical Approach to Study Word Order Patterns in the Greek Text of Acts. — *FilolNT* 9 (1996) 139-180; = READ-HEIMERDINGER, J., *The Bezan Text of Acts*, 2002, 62-115.

*HEITMÜLLER, Wilhelm, *"Im Namen Jesu": Eine sprach- und religionsgeschichtliche Untersuchung zum Neuen Testament, speziell zur altchristlichen Taufe* (FRLANT, 2). Göttingen: Vandenhoeck & Ruprecht, 1903, X-347 p.

*HILL, David, *Greek Words and Hebrew Meanings: Studies in the Semantics of Soteriological Terms* (SNTS MS, 5). Cambridge: University Press, 1967, XV-333 p.

*HOFFMANN, Paul – BROX, Norbert – PESCH, Wilhelm (eds.), *Orientierung an Jesus: Zur Theologie der Synoptiker. Für Josef Schmid.* Freiburg-Basel-Wien: Herder, 1973, 431 p.

HOFFMANN, Paul –HIEKE, Thomas – BAUER, Ulrich, *Synoptic Concordance: A Greek Concordance to the First Three Gospels in Synoptic Arrangement,*

Statistically Evaluated, Including Occurrences in Acts – Griechische Konkordanz zu den ersten drei Evangelien in synoptischer Darstellung, statistisch ausgewertet, mit Berücksichtigung der Apostelgeschichte. Volume 1: *Introduction B Einführung*, A–Δ. Berlin - New York, Walter de Gruyter, 1999, LXXIII-1032 p.; Vol. II: E–I. 2000, XVIII-957 p.; Vol. III: K–O, 2000, XVII-997 p.; Vol. III: Π–Ω, 2000, XIX-1066 p.

HORSLEY, G.H.R., Divergent Views on the Nature of the Greek of the Bible. — *Bib* 65 (1984) 393-403.

* — – LEE, John A.L., A Lexicon of the New Testament with Documentary Parallels: Some Interim Entries, 1. — *FilolNT* 10 (1997) 55-84.

HUNDESHAGEN, Frank, *"Wenn doch auch du erkannt hättest, was dir zum Frieden dient...": Das "Kommen Jesu" nach Jerusalem in Lk 19,28-48 als Zeichen des Heils und Ansage des Gerichts* (Erfurter theologische Studien, 85). Leipzig: Benno Verlag, 2002, XXXVII-227 p. Esp. 15-51: "Sprachlich-syntaktische Analyse"; 52-98: "Semantische Analyse".

JEREMIAS, Joachim, Perikopen-Umstellungen bei Lukas? — *NTS* 4 (1957-58) 115-119.

*JUNG, Chang-Wook, *The Original Language of the Lukan Infancy Narrative* (JSNT SS, 267). London – New York: T&T Clark International, 2004, XI-249 p.

*KECK, Leander E. – MARTYN, J. Louis (eds.), *Studies in Luke-Acts: Essays Presented in Honor of Paul Schubert.* Nashville, TN: Abingdon, 1966; London: SPCK, ³1978, 316 p.

KENNY, Anthony, *A Stylometric Study of the New Testament.* Oxford: Clarendon, 1986, 127 p.

KILPATRICK, G.D., The Order of Some Noun and Adjective Phrases in the New Testament. — *NT* 5 (1962) 111-115; = *BTrans* 16 (1965) 117-119; = ID., *Principles and Practice*, 1990, 163-166.

—, Atticism and the Text of the Greek New Testament. — BLINZLER, J. – KUSS, O. – MUSSNER, F. (eds.), *Neutestamentliche Aufsätze.* FS J. Schmid, 1963, 125-137.

* —, Style and Text in the Greek New Testament. — DANIELS, Boyd L. – SUGGS, M. Jack (eds.), *Studies in the History and Text of the New Testament in Honor of Kenneth Willis Clark* (Studies and Documents, 29). Salt Lake City: University of Utah Press, 1967, 153-160; = ID., *Principles and Practice*, 1990, 153-160.

—, The Historic Present in the Gospels and Acts. — *ZNW* 68 (1977) 258-262; = ID., *Principles and Practice*, 1990, 169-176.

* —, *The Principles and Practice of New Testament Textual Criticism: Collected Essays* (BETL, 96). Leuven: University Press – Peeters, 1990, XXXVIII-489 p.

KLIJN, A.F.J., A Survey of the Research into the Western Text of the Gospels and Acts (1949-1959). — *NT* 3 (1959) 1-27, 161-173.

KOFFI, Ettien N., *Language and Society in Biblical Times.* International Scholars Publications, s.d., XVI-254 p.

KOHLENBERGER, John R., III – GOODRICK, Edward W. – SWANSON, James A., *The Greek English Concordance to the New Testament with the New International Version.* Grand Rapids, MI: Zondervan, 1997, XX-1131 p.

KOWALSKI, Beate, Forschungsgeschichtlicher Überblick: Sprache und Stil des Lukasevangeliums. — *SNTU* 27 (2002) 41-84; 28 (2003) 27-64.

KRÄMER, Helmut, Zur explikativen Redeweise im neutestamentlichen Griechisch. — SCHRAGE, Wolfgang (ed.), *Studien zum Text und zur Ethik des Neuen Testaments: Festschrift zum 80. Geburtstag von Heinrich Greeven.*(BZNW, 47). Berlin – New York: de Gruyter, 1986, 212-216.

KRAUS, Thomas J., "Uneducated", "Ignorant", or Even "Illiterate"? Aspects and Background for an Understanding of ἀγράμματοι (and ἰδιῶται) in Acts 4.13. — *NTS* 45 (1999) 434-449.

LAGRANGE, M.-J., *Évangile selon Saint Luc* (Études Bibliques). Paris: Gabalda, 1921, CLXVII-631 p.; [7]1948, CLXVII-635 p. Esp. XCV-CXXVII: "La langue de Luc".

LAVERGNE, R.P., *L'expression biblique*. Paris: Vrin, 1946, 136 p.

LEANEY, Robert, The Resurrection Narratives in Luke (XXIV. 12-53). — *NTS* 2 (1955-56) 110-114.

LEE, John A.L., The United Bible Societies' Lexicon and Its Analysis of Meanings. — *FilolNT* 5 (1992) 167-190.

*— – HORSLEY, G.H.R., A Lexicon of the New Testament with Documentary Parallels: Some Interim Entries, 2. — *FilolNT* 11 (1998) 57-84. [NTA 44, 808]

*—, A History of New Testament Lexicography (Studies in Biblical Greek, 8). New York – Washington, DC: Lang, 2003, XIV-414 p.

*LEONARDI, Giovanni – TROLESE, Francesco G.B. (eds.), *San Luca Evangelista: Testimone della fede che unisce. Atti del Congresso Internazionale Padova, 16-21 Ottobre 2000. I: L'unità letteraria e teologica dell'opera di Luca (Vangelo e Atti degli apostoli)* (Fonti e ricerche di storia ecclesiastica padovana, 28). Padova: Istituto per la storia ecclesiastica padovana, 2000, 637 p.

*LEVISOHN, Stephen H., *Textual Connections in Acts* (SBL MS, 31). Atlanta, GA: Scholars, 1987, XVIII-187 p.

*LOSS, Nicolò Maria, Amore d'amicizia nel Nuovo Testamento: Contributo ad uno studio lessicologico e religioso sull'uso neotestamentario di φίλος, φιλέω e loro composti. — *Sal* 39 (1977) 3-55.

LOUW, Johannes P., Discourse Analysis and the Greek New Testament. — *BTrans* 24 (1973) 101-118.

—, Semantics of New Testament Greek (SBL Semeia Studies). Philadelphia, PA: Scholars; Chico, CA: Scholars, 1982, IX-166 p.

—, A Semiotic Approach to Discourse Analysis with Reference to Translation Theory. — *BTrans* 36 (1985) 101-107.

—, How Do Words Mean – If They Do? — *FilolNT* 4 (1991) 125-142.

—, The Analysis of Meaning in Lexicography. — *FilolNT* 6 (1993) 139-148.

*MAHFOUZ, Hady, *La fonction littéraire et théologique de Lc 3,1-20 dans Luc-Actes* (Faculté pontificale de théologie, 11). Kaslik, Liban: Université Saint-Esprit de Kaslik, 2003, VI-486 p.

MAKUJINA, John, Modal Possibilities for the Elliptical Verb in the Imperative-Comparative Clause in NT Greek. — *FilolNT* 11 (1998) 43-55.

MARGUERAT, Daniel, Luc-Actes entre Jérusalem et Rome: Un procédé lucanien de double signification. — *NTS* 45 (1999) 70-87. Esp. 73-79: "L'ambivalence sémantique: un procédé rhétorique lucanien".

MARSHALL (ed.), I. Howard, *Moulton and Geden Concordance to the Greek New Testament*, Sixth Edition Fully Revised, London – New York, 2002,

*MARTIN, Raymond A., Syntactical Evidence of Aramaic Sources in Acts I–XV. — *NTS* 11 (1964-65) 38-59.

—, *Syntactical Evidence of Semitic Sources in Greek Documents* (Septuagint and Cognate Studies, 3). Cambridge, MA: Society of Biblical Literature, 1974, VI-165 p.

—, *Syntax Criticism of the Synoptic Gospels* (Studies in the Bible and Early Christianity, 10). Lewiston, NY – Queenston, Ont.: The Edwin Mellen Press, 1987, IX-219 p.

MARUCCI, Corrado, Influssi latini sul greco del Nuovo Testamento. — *FilolNT* 6 (1993) 3-30.

*MARYKS, Robert A., I latinismi del Nuovo Testamento in relazione alle Letterature Greca e alle Iscrizioni (II sec. aC-IIsec.dC.) . — *FilolNT* 13 (25-26, 2000) 23-33.

MATEOS, Juan – ALEPUZ, Miguel, El imperfecto sucesivo en el Nuevo Testamento. — URBÁN, A. – MATEOS, J. – ALEPUZ, M., *Estudios de Nuevo Testamento*. II, 1977, 65-101.

*MCKAY, K.L., On the Perfect and Other Aspects in New Testament Greek. — *NT* 23 (1981) 289-329.

—, Aspect in Imperatival Constructions in New Testament Greek. — *NT* 27 (1985) 201-226.

MEALAND, D.L., The Close of Acts and Its Hellenistic Greek Vocabulary. — *NTS* 36 (1990) 583-597.

—, Luke-Acts and the Verbs of Dionysius of Halicarnassus. — *JSNT* 63 (1996) 63-86.

MEECHAM, H.G., The Use of the Participle for the Imperative in the New Testament. — *ExpT* 58 (1946-47) 207-208.

MINEAR, Paul S., Luke's Use of the Birth Stories. — KECK, L.E. – MARTYN, J.L. (eds.), *Studies in Luke-Acts*. FS P. Schubert, 1966, [3]1978, 111-130. Esp. 112-118: "The integrity of Luke-Acts".

MONTGOMERY, James A., Some Aramaisms in the Gospels and Acts. — *JBL* 46 (1927) 69-73.

Moulton and Geden Concordance to the Greek New Testament. Sixth edition, fully revised. Edited by I. Howard MARSHALL. London – New York: T&T Clark, 2002.

MUSSIES, Gerard, Variation in the Book of Acts. — *FilolNT* 4 (1991) 165-182; 8 (1995) 23-62.

NAVONE, John, Three Aspects of the Lucan Theology of History. — *BTB* 3 (1973) 115-132.

NEIRYNCK, Frans, Hawkins's Additional Notes to His "Horae Synopticae". — *ETL* 46 (1970) 78-111.

*— (ed.), *L'évangile de Luc: Problèmes littéraires et théologiques. Mémorial Lucien Cerfaux* (BETL, 32). Gembloux: Duculot, 1973, 385 p.

L'évangile de Luc – The Gospel of Luke. Revised and Enlarged Edition (BETL, 32). Leuven: University Press – Peeters, 1989, x-590 p.

*—, La matière marcienne dans l'évangile de Luc. — *Ibid.*, 1973, 157-201. Esp.
167-179: "Les éléments propres de Luc"; 179-193: "Les sémitismes"; [2]1989, 67-111.
Esp. 77-89; 89-103; = ID., *Evangelica*, 1982, 37-81 (81-82: note additionnelle;
Appendix, *Evangelica II*, 1991, 793-794). Esp. 47-59; 59-73.

*—, *Evangelica: Gospel Studies – Études d'évangile. Collected Essays.* Edited by
F. Van Segbroeck (BETL, 60). Leuven: Peeters – University Press, 1982, XIX-
1033 p.

— – VAN SEGBROECK, Frans, with the collaboration of Henri LECLERCQ, *New
Testament Vocabulary: A Companion Volume to the Concordance* (BETL,
65). Leuven: University Press – Peeters, 1984, XVI-494 p.

—, New Testament Vocabulary: Corrections and Supplement. — *ETL* 62 (1986)
134-140.

—, Le lexique de Bauer-Aland. — *ETL* 64 (1988) 450-454; = ID., *Evangelica II*,
1991, 785-790.

*—, *Evangelica II: 1982-1991. Collected Essays.* Edited by F. Van Segbroeck
(BETL, 99). Leuven: University Press – Peeters, 1991, XIX-874 p.

*—, *Evangelica III: 1992-2000. Collected Essays* (BETL, 150). Leuven: University Press – Peeters, 2001, XVII-666 p.

NEW, David S., The Injunctive Future and Existential Injunctions in the New
Testament. — *JSNT* 44 (1991) 113-127.

NIDA, Eugene A., Implications of Contemporary Linguistics for Biblical
Scholarship. — *JBL* 91 (1972) 73-89.

— – LOUW, J.P. – SNYMAN, A.H. – CRONJE, J.v.W., *Style and Discourse: With
Special Reference to the Text of the Greek New Testament.* Cape Town: Bible
Society, 1983, II-199 p.

PASQUALETTI, Tito, Note sulle determinazioni temporali del Vangelo secondo
Luca. — *RivBib* 23 (1975) 399-412.

PAX, Elpidius, Beobachtungen zum biblischen Sprachtabu. — *SBF/LA* 11 (1960-
61) 66-112.

—, Die syntaktischen Semitismen in Neuen Testament: Eine grundsätzliche
Erwägung. — *SBF/LA* 13 (1962-63) 136-162.

—, Spuren sog. "erlebter Rede" im Neuen Testament. — *SBF/LA* 14 (1963-64)
339-354.

—, Stilistische Beobachtungen an neutralen Redewendungen im Neuen
Testament. — *SBF/LA* 17 (1967) 335-347.

—, Probleme des neutestamentlichen Griechisch. — *Bib* 53 (1972) 557-564.

*PERNOT, Hubert, *Études sur la langue des Évangiles* (Collection de l'Institut
Néo-Hellénique de l'Université de Paris, 6). Paris: Les Belles Lettres, 1927,
XI-225 p.

*PETZER, Kobus, Style and Text in the Lucan Narrative of the Institution of the
Lord's Supper (Luke 22.19b-20). — *NTS* 37 (1991) 113-129.

PLÜMACHER, Eckhard, *Lukas als hellenistischer Schriftsteller: Studien zur
Apostelgeschichte* (SUNT, 9). Göttingen: Vandenhoeck & Ruprecht, 1972,
164 p.

—, Cicero und Lukas: Bemerkungen zu Stil und Zweck der historischen Mono-
graphie. — VERHEYDEN, J. (ed.), *The Unity of Luke-Acts*, 1999, 759-775.

PORTER, Stanley E., *Verbal Aspect in the Greek of the New Testament, with Reference to Tense and Mood* (Studies in Biblical Greek, 1). New York – Bern – Frankfurt/M: Lang, 1989, XII-582 p.

—, Studying Ancient Languages from a Modern Linguistic Perspective: Essential Terms and Terminology. — *FilolNT* 2 (1989) 147-172.

— (ed.), *The Language of the New Testament: Classic Essays* (JSNT SS, 60). Sheffield: Academic Press, 1991, 238 p.

— – REED, Jeffrey T., Greek Grammar Since BDF: A Retrospective Analysis. — *FilolNT* 4 (1991) 143-164.

—, Keeping Up with Recent Studies: 17. Greek Language and Linguistics. — *ExpT* 103 (1991-92) 202-208.

— – CARSON, D.A. (eds.), *Biblical Greek Language and Linguistics: Open Questions in Current Research* (JSNT SS, 80). Sheffield: Academic Press, 1993, 217 p.

— – CARSON, D.A. (eds.), *Discourse Analysis and Other Topics in Biblical Greek* (JSNT SS, 113). Sheffield: Academic Press, 1995, 227 p.

*—, *Studies in the Greek New Testament. Theory and Practice* (Studies in Biblical Greek, 6). New York – Washington, DC: Lang, 1996, VII-290 p.

*— – CARSON, D.A. (eds.), *Linguistics and the New Testament: Critical Junctures* (JSNT SS, 168; SNTG, 5). Sheffield: Academic Press, 1999, 297 p.

— (ed.), *Diglossia and Other Topics in New Testament Linguistics* (JSNT SS, 193; SNTG, 6). Sheffield: Academic Press, 2000, 305 p.

PRETE, Benedetto, Il racconto dei discepoli di Emmaus e le sue prospettive eucaristiche (*Lc* 24,12-35). — *L'Eucaristia nella Comunità locale: XVIII Congresso Eucaristico Nazionale, Udine*. Udine: Arti Graffiche Friulane, 1972, 47-70; = ID., *L'Opera di Luca*, 1986, 307-327. Esp. 308-311: "Rilievi filologici e letterari".

—, Il sommario di *Atti* 1,13-14 e suo apporto per la conoscenza della Chiesa delle origini. — *Sacra Doctrina* 18 (1973) 65-124; = ID., *L'opera di Luca*, 1986, 453-493. Esp. 457-463: "Rilievi filologici e critici".

*—, *L'opera di Luca: Contenuti e prospettive*. Torino: Elle Di Ci, 1986, 591 p.

—, L'insegnamento di Gesù sulla risurrezione dei morti nella formulazione di Lc 20,27-40. — *RivBib* 41 (1993) 429-451. Esp. 429-435: "Rilievi filologici e critici".

RAEYMAEKERS, C., *Het evangelie van Lucas: Met inleiding, aantekeningen en woordenlijst*. Turnhout: Brepols, 1949, XLVIII-215 p. Esp. XXIX-XXI: "Taal en stijl"; XXI-XLI: "Grammaticale aanmerkingen".

READ-HEIMERDINGER, Jenny, Variation in the Use of Prepositions between Codex Bezae and the Alexandrian Uncials. — AMPHOUX, C.-B. – ELLIOTT, J.K. (eds.), *The New Testament Text in Early Christianity*, Lausanne: Éditions du Zèbre, 2003, 275-287; = ID., *The Bezan Text of Acts*, 2002, 173-201.

*—, *The Bezan Text of Acts: A Contribution of Discourse Analysis to Textual Criticism* (JSNT SS, 236). Sheffield: Academic Press, 2002, XI-379 p.

REED, Jeffrey T., The Infinitive with Two Substantival Accusatives: An Ambiguous Construction? — *NT* 33 (1991) 1-27.

*RESE, Martin, *Alttestamentliche Motive in der Christologie des Lukas* (Studien zum NT, 1). Gütersloh: Gütersloher Verlagshaus Gerd Mohn, 1969, 227 p.

RICHARD, Earl, *Acts 6:1–8:4: The Author's Method of Composition* (SBL DS, 41). Missoula, MT: Scholars, 1978, XIII-379 p. Esp. 157-242: "Functional character of stylistic data".

RIENECKER, Fritz, *Sprachlicher Schlüssel zum Griechischen Neuen Testament nach der Ausgabe von D. Eberhard Nestle* (Urtextstudium, 1). Neumünster: Ihloff, 1938, XLII-793 p. Esp. 158-241: "Evangelium des Lukas"; 312-392: "Die Apostelgeschichte des Lukas"; Gießen: Brunnen, 1950, XLII-793 p.; [10]1960, XXX-636 p.

A Linguistic Key to the Greek New Testament. Translated, with additions and revisions, from the German *Sprachlicher Schlüssel zum Griechischen Neuen Testament.* Edited by Cleon L. Rogers, Jr.. Volume I: *Matthew through Acts.* Grand Rapids, MI: Zondervan, 1977, XIV-345 p. Esp. 137-216: "The Gospel of Luke"; 263-345: "Acts".

RIUS-CAMPS, Josep, ¿Constituye Lc 3,21-38 un solo período? Propuesta de un cambio de puntuación. — *Bib* 65 (1984) 189-209.

—, Las variantes de la recensión occidental de los Hechos de los Apostoles (I-XI) (Hch 1,1-3.4-14.15-26; 2,1-13.14-40.41-47; 3,1-26; 4,1-22.23-31; 4,32–5,16; 5,17-42; 6,1–7,22). — *FilolNT* 6 (1993) 59-68, 219-230; 7 (1994) 53-64, 197-208; 8 (1995) 63-78, 199-208; 9 (1996) 61-76, 201-216; 10 (1997) 99-104; 11 (1998) 107-122; 12 (1999) 107-121; 13 (2000) 89-109.

ROBERTSON, A.T., The Aorist Participle for Purpose in the κοινή. — *JTS* 25 (1923-24) 286-289.

*RODRÍGUEZ, Isidoro, Consideración filologica sobre el mensaje de la anunciación (Lc. 1,26-38). — *Generos literarios en los evangelios. Otros estudios. XVII Semana Biblica Española (24-28 sept. 1956).* Madrid: Consejo Superior de Investigaciones Cientificas, 1958, 223-249.

ROHRBAUGH, Richard L., Semiotic Behavior in Luke and John. — *HTS* 58 (2002) 746-766.

*ROTH, S. John, *The Blind, the Lame and the Poor. Character Types in Luke-Acts* (JSNT SS, 144). Sheffield: Sheffield Academic Press, 1997, 253 p.

*RYDBECK, Lars, *Fachprosa, vermeintliche Volkssprache und Neues Testament: Zur Beurteilung der sprachlichen Niveauunterschiede im nachklassischen Griechisch* (Acta Universitatis Upsaliensis: Studia Graeca Upsaliensia, 5). Uppsala: Universitas Upsaliensis, 1967, 221 p.

*SCHNEIDER, Gerhard, *Lukas, Theologe der Heilsgeschichte: Aufsätze zum lukanischen Doppelwerk* (BBB, 59). Bonn: Hanstein, 1985, 328 p.

SCHWARZ, Günther, Lukas 6,22a.23c.26: Emendation, Rückübersetzung, Interpretation. — *ZNW* 66 (1975) 269-274.

SCHWEIZER, Eduard, Eine hebraisierende Sonderquelle des Lukas? — *TZ* 6 (1950) 161-185.

SILVA, Moisés, *Biblical Words and Their Meaning: An Introduction to Lexical Semantics.* Grand Rapids, MI: Zondervan, 1983, 201 p.

SMIT SIBINGA, J., The Function of Verbal Forms in Luke-Acts. — *FilolNT* 6 (1993) 31-50.

*SOISALON-SOININEN, Ilmari, *Die Infinitive in der Septuaginta* (Annales Academiae Scientiarum Fennicae. Series B, 132,1). Helsinki: Suomalainen Tiedeakatemia, 1965, 229 p.

SPARKS, H.F.D., The Semitisms of Luke's Gospel. — *JTS* 44 (1943) 129-138.
—, The Semitisms of the Acts. — *JTS* NS 1 (1950) 16-28.
—, St Luke's Transpositions. — *NTS* 3 (1956-57) 219-223.
STEYN, G.J., Intertextual Similarities between Septuagint Pretexts and Luke's Gospel. — *Neotestamentica* 24 (1990) 229-246.
—, Notes on the *Vorlage* of the Amos Quotations in Acts. — BREYTENBACH, C., et al. (eds.), *Die Apostelgeschichte und die hellenistische Geschichtsschreibung*. FS E. Plümacher, 2004, 59-81.
*Studia Evangelica 1 (1959): ALAND, Kurt – CROSS, F.L. – DANIELOU, Jean – RIESENFELD, Harald – VAN UNNIK, W.C.. (eds.), *Studia Evangelica: Papers Presented to the International Congress on "The Four Gospels in 1957" Held at Christ Church, Oxford, 1957* (TU, 73). Berlin: Akademie-Verlag, 1959, XI-813 p.
*Studia Evangelica 2 (1964): CROSS, F.L. (ed.), *Studia Evangelica*. Vol. II: *Papers Presented to the Second International Congress on New Testament Studies Held at Christ Church, Oxford, 1961*. Part I: *The New Testament Scriptures* (TU, 87). Berlin: Akademie-Verlag, 1964, XIII-680 p.
*Studia Evangelica 3 (1964): CROSS, F.L. (ed.), *Studia Evangelica*. Vol. III: *Papers Presented to the Second International Congress on New Testament Studies Held at Christ Church, Oxford, 1961*. Part II: *The New Testament Message* (TU, 88). Berlin: Akademie-Verlag, 1964, XI-498 p.
*Studia Evangelica 6 (1973): LIVINGSTONE, Elizabeth A. (ed.), *Studia Evangelica*. Vol. VI: *Papers Presented to the Fourth International Congress on New Testament Studies Held at Oxford, 1969* (TU, 112). Berlin: Akademie-Verlag, 1973, X-676 p.
*Studia Evangelica 7 (1982): LIVINGSTONE, Elizabeth A. (ed.), *Studia Evangelica*. Vol. VII: *Papers Presented to the Fifth International Congress on Biblical Studies Held at Oxford, 1973* (TU, 126). Berlin: Akademie-Verlag, 1982, XI-570 p.
SWEETLAND, Dennis M., Discipleship and Persecution: A Study of Luke 12,1-12. — *Bib* 65 (1984) 61-79. Esp. 63: "Vocabulary".
TABER, Charles R., Exegesis and Linguistics. — *BTrans* 20 (1969) 150-153.
**TAEGER, Jens-W., *Der Mensch und sein Heil: Studien zum Bild des Menschen und zur Sicht der Bekehrung bei Lukas* (Studien zum NT, 14). Gütersloh: Gütersloher Verlaghaus Mohn, 1982, 244 p.
TALBERT, Charles H., *Literary Patterns, Theological Themes, and the Genre of Luke-Acts* (SBL MS, 20). Missoula, MT: Scholars, 1974, IX-159 p.
TAYLOR, Bernard A. – LEE, John A.L. – BURTON, Peter R. – WHITAKER, Richard E. (eds.), *Biblical Greek Language and Lexicography. Essays in Honor of Frederick W. Danker*. Grand Rapids, MI – Cambridge: Eerdmans, 2004, XXI-266 p
**THRALL, Margaret E., *Greek Particles in the New Testament: Linguistic and Exegetical Studies* (NTTS, 3). Leiden: Brill, 1962, IX-107 p.
**TRITES, Allison A., *The New Testament Concept of Witness* (SNTS MS, 31). Cambridge: University Press, 1977, X-294 p. Esp. 66-76: "The witness terminology of the New Testament".

TURNER, Nigel, The Relation of Luke I and II to Hebraic Sources and to the Rest of Luke-Acts. — *NTS* 2 (1955-56) 100-109.

—, The Literary Character of New Testament Greek. — *NTS* 20 (1973-74) 107-114.

—, The Quality of the Greek of Luke-Acts. — ELLIOTT, J.K. (ed.), *Studies in New Testament Language and Text*. FS G.D. Kilpatrick, 1976, 387-400. Esp. 387-390: "The alleged secularism of St. Luke's style"; 390-397: "The integrity of the Lucan style"; 397-399: "The presence of Aramaisms".

—, Biblical Greek – The Peculiar Language of a Peculiar People. — *Studia Evangelica* 7 (1982) 505-512.

*URBÁN, Angel – MATEOS, Juan – ALEPUZ, Miguel, *Estudios de Nuevo Testamento*. II: *Cuestiones de gramatica y lexico* (Institución San Jeronimo para la investigación bíblica: Estudios y monografias, 2). Madrid: Cristiandad, 1977, 150 p.

VAN DER HORST, Pieter W., Hellenistic Parallels to the Acts of the Apostles (2.1-47). — *JSNT* 25 (1985) 49-60.

VAN IERSEL, Bastiaan Martinus Franciscus, *"Der Sohn" in den synoptischen Jesusworten: Christusbezeichnung der Gemeinde oder Selbstbezeichnung Jesu?* Leiden: Brill, 1961, XXIII-195 p. Esp. 34-40: "Der Quellenwert von Apg. 1–13: Der Wortschatz".

VAN SEGBROECK, Frans, *The Gospel of Luke: A Cumulative Bibliography 1973-1988* (BETL, 88; Collectanea Biblica et Religiosa Antiqua, 2). Leuven: University Press – Peeters; Brussel: Koninklijke Academie voor Weten-schappen, Letteren en Schone Kunsten van België, 1989, 243 p. Esp. 217: "Style and language".

*— – TUCKETT, C.M. – VAN BELLE, G. – VERHEYDEN, J. (eds.), *The Four Gospels 1992: Festschrift Frans Neirynck* (BETL, 100). Leuven: University Press – Peeters, 1992, vol. I, XVIII-690 p.; vol. II, X-691-1720 p. Esp. II, 1451-1716: "The Gospel of Luke".

*VAN UNNIK, W.C., *Sparsa Collecta: The Collected Essays of W.C. van Unnik*. Part One: *Evangelia – Paulina – Acta* (SupplNT, 29). Leiden: Brill, 1973, X-409 p.

*VERHEYDEN, J. (ed.), *The Unity of Luke-Acts* (BETL, 142). Leuven: University Press – Peeters, 1999, XXV-828 p.

VICTOR, Ulrich, Der Wechsel der Tempora in griechischen erzählenden Texten mit besonderer Berücksichtigung der Apostelgeschichte. — BREYTENBACH, C., et al. (eds.), *Die Apostelgeschichte und die hellenistische Geschichtsschreibung*. FS E. Plümacher, 2004, 27-57.

VOELZ, James W., The Language of the New Testament. — *ANRW* II.25.2 (1984) 893-977.

*VOS, Gerhard, *Die Christologie der lukanischen Schriften in Grundzügen* (Studia Neotestamentica, 2). Paris-Brugge: Desclée de Brouwer, 1965, 219 p.

WALLACE, Daniel B., The Relation of Adjective to Noun in Anarthrous Constructions in the New Testament. — *NT* 26 (1984) 128-167.

WALSER, Georg, *The Greek of the Ancient Synagogue: An Investigation of the Greek of the Septuagint, Pseudepigrapha and the New Testament* (Studia Graeca et Latina Lundensia, 8). Lund: Almqvist & Wiksell International, 2001, XXV-197 p.

WATT, Jonathan M., *Code-Switching in Luke and Acts* (Berkeley Insights in Linguistics and Semiotics, 31). New York – Washington, DC – Baltimore, MD: Lang, 1997, VIII-307 p.

WEIßENGRUBER, Franz, Zum Verbalaspekt im griechischen des Neuen Testaments. — *SNTU* 16 (1991) 169-177.

*WEISSENRIEDER, Annette, *Images of Illness in the Gospel of Luke: Insights of Ancient Medical Texts* (WUNT, II/164). Tübingen: Mohr Siebeck, 2003, XIV-429 p.

*WELLS, Louise, *The Greek Language of Healing from Homer to New Testament Times* (BZNW, 83), Berlin – New York: de Gruyter, 1998, XVIII-489 p.

*WILCOX, Max, *The Semitisms of Acts*. Oxford: Clarendon, 1965, XIV-206 p.

*—, Semitisms in the New Testament. — *ANRW* II.25.2 (1984) 978-1029.

—, Semitisms in Luke-Acts in the Light of the Tobit Mss from Qumran and the Babatha Archive (P. Yadin). — LEONARDI, G. – TROLESE, F.G.B. (eds.), *San Luca Evangelista*, 2000, 555-565.

WILSON, Mark, Greek Vocabulary Acquisition Using Semantic Domains. — *JevTS* 46 (2003) 193-204.

WINEDT, M.D., *A Relevance-Theoretical Approach to Translation and Discourse Markers: With Special Reference to the Greek Text of the Gospel of Luke*. Diss. Amsterdam, 1999, 326 p. (dir. J. de Waard).

*WINK, Walter, *Naming the Powers: The Language of Power in the New Testament* (The Powers, 1). Philadelphia, PA: Fortress, 1984, [2]1986, XI-181 p.

WINTER, Paul, Some Observations on the Language in the Birth and Infancy Stories of the Third Gospel. — *NTS* 1 (1954-55) 111-121.

—, On Luke and Lukan Sources: A Reply to the Reverend N. Turner. — *ZNW* 47 (1956) 217-242.

WOOTTON, R.W.F., The Implied Agent in Greek Passive Verbs in Mark, Luke and John. — *BTrans* 19 (1968) 159-164.

ZWECK, Dean, The *Exordium* of the Areopagus Speech, Acts 17.22, 23. — *NTS* 35 (1989) 94-103.

GUIDE TO THE USE OF "THE VOCABULARY OF LUKE"

This study of the vocabulary of Luke is based on the text of NA^{27} and is organised in alphabetical order.

1. First Frame

ἄγω 13/14 + 26/28 (Mt 4/5, Mk 3/4)	
1. bring (Lk 19,27); 2. carry (Lk 4,40); 3. go away; 4. guide (Lk 4,9); 5. function (Acts 19,38); 6. occur (Lk 24,21); 7. spend time (Lk 24,21); 8. BDAG 2000: lead away, arrest (Lk 22,54; Acts 6,12, 18,12)	

At the top of the frame, each lemma is printed in bold. The word is followed by the number of occurrences in Luke and Acts, and (between parentheses) in Matthew and Mark respectively. The variant readings, which are marked with an asterisk in the *Vollständige Konkordanz* of Aland, have been totaled and then mentioned for each evangelist after the slash ("/").

Lukan lemmata that are attested in pre-Christian Greek, but which occur only outside of the LXX, are marked with an asterisk (*) (51 cases, see MORGENTHALER 1958 178); lemmata that are never attested in pre-Christian Greek are marked with two asterisks (**) (19 cases, see MORGENTHALER 1958 177); lemmata that are only attested in the LXX and not in other witnesses of pre-Christian Greek are marked with three asterisks (***) (8 cases, see MORGENTHALER 1958 180). This division does not necessarily assume that the text of the LXX, which we have, is clear evidence of the usage of "Pre-Christian" Greek, given that almost all existing LXX manuscripts are Christian.

If the word has only one meaning, the English translation is given directly after the Greek word and its frequency. Otherwise, the various meanings denoted by the word are enumerated, i.e. a series of English glosses or translation equivalents are given (Arabic numerals) that represent the possible meanings of the Greek word proposed by J.P. Louw & E.A. Nida (LN) (*Greek-English Lexicon of the New Testament, based on Semantic Domains*, 1989). In some cases LN is supplemented with additional possibilities given by BDAG. When possible, a reference is given for each meaning. References to various meanings are normally taken from LN, and complemented by those in BDAG and our own findings. Not all references are given for each meaning, except when the word occurs less than six times. By indicating how many of the possible meanings of a word Luke has used, we just want to give an indication of the semantic richness of his vocabulary. When one particular meaning is "characteristic" or "noteworthy", references are given in the "word group" box (e.g. ἄγγελος of human beings in the second frame).

2. Second Frame

Word groups	Lk	Acts	Mt	Mk
ἀκοῇ ἀκούω (*LN*: listen carefully; *VK*e)		28,26	1	0
ἀκούσας (+) ἀποκρίνομαι/λέγω/ εἶπον → **ἀκούων** + λέγω/εἶπον; cf. παρακούσας + λέγω Mk 5,36	1,66; 7,9; 8,50; 14,15; 18,22.26; 20,16	2,37; 4,24; 11,18; 17,32; 19,28; 21,20; 22,26	7	6
ἀκούω + genitive (*VK*a) → **ἀκούω** αὐτοῦ / αὐτῶν / τῶν λόγων / τινὸς λαλοῦντος	2,46.47; 6,18.47; 9,35; 10,16[1.2]; 15,1.25; 16,29.31; 18,36; 19,48; 21,38	1,4; 2,6.11; 3,22.23; 4,19; 6,11.14; 7,34.37*; 8,30; 9,7; 10,46; 11,7; 14,9; 15,12.13; 17,32; 18,26; 22,1.7.22; 24,4.24; 25,22[1.2]; 26,3.29	3	9
ἀκούω (+) ἀπό/παρά + genitive (*VK*c) DENAUX 2009 1A[n]	22,71	9,13; 10,22; 28,22	0	0
ἀκούω (+) αὐτοῦ → **ἀκούω** αὐτῶν DENAUX 2009 1An	2,47; 6,18; 9,35; 15,1; 19,48; 21,38	3,22; 6,11.14; 7,37*; 8,30; 18,26; 22,22; 24,24; 25,22[2]	0	4
ἀκούω + βλέπω / θεωρέω / ὁράω/εἶδον → **ἀκούω** + συνίημι	2,20; 7,22[1]; 8,10.18; 10,24[1.2.3]; 23,8	2,33; 4,20; 7,34; 8,6; 19,26; 22,14.15; 28,26.27[2]	8	4
ἀκούω + δέχομαι	8,13	8,14; 11,1	1	1
ἀκούω + εἰς τὸ οὖς / τὰ ὦτα (*LN*: hear in secret)		11,22	1	0
ἀκούω (+) θαυμάζω → **(ὁράω/)εἶδον** + θαυμάζω	2,18; 7,9		2	0
ἀκούω κωφός	7,22[2]		1	1
ἀκούω τινὸς λαλοῦντος; cf. Jn 1,37 BOISMARD 1984 Ba10		2,6.11; 6,11; 10,46; 14,9	0	0
ἀκούω (+) τὸν λόγον / τοὺς λόγους / ῥήματα → **ἀκούω** τὸν λόγον; **ἀκούω** τὸν λόγον τοῦ θεοῦ/ κυρίου; **αἴρω/(ἀπο)δέχομαι** (τὸν) λόγον/λόγια; cf. ἠκούσθη + ὁ λόγος Acts 11,22; παρακούω τὸν λόγον Mk 5,36	5,1; 8,15.21; 10,39; 11,28	2,22; 4,4; 5,5[1].24; 10,22.44; 13,7.44; 15,7; 19,10	9	3
ἀκούω + τῶν λόγων	6,47		0	0
ἀκούω (+) οὖς	8,8[1]; 12,3; 14,35[1]	11,22; 28,27[1.2]	7	3/4
ἀκούω + συνίημι → **ἀκούω** + βλέπω / θεωρέω / ὁράω/εἶδον	8,10	28,26.27[2]	6	2
ἀκούω τι περί τινος DENAUX 2009 L[n]	9,9;16,2		0	0
ἀκούων + λέγω/εἶπον → **ἀκούσας** + ἀποκρίνομαι / λέγω/εἶπον	19,11; 20,45	9,21	0	1
τοῖς ὠσὶν βαρέως ἀκούω (*LN*: be mentally dull)		28,27[1]	1	0
ὦτα ἀκούειν ἀκουέτω (*SC*b; *VK*d)	8,8[1.2]; 14,35[1.2]		0/3	2/3
ἀκούων in genitive absolute DENAUX 2009 L[n]	19,11; 20,45		0	0
ἀκούομαι passive (*VK*b)	12,3	11,22	2	1

A second frame gives a list of "word groups". This title normally indicates (i) that several words form a grammatical group (e.g. verb + case: ἀκούω + genitive; verb + object: ἀκούω (+) τὸν λόγον; verb + participle: ἀκούσας (+) ἀποκρίνομαι/λέγω/εἶπον; verb + preposition: ἀκούω (+) ἀπό/παρά + genitive; noun + genitive; preposition + cases, etc.). In some instances a plus sign ("+") is used. When the words that form a word group are always interrupted by other words, then, a plus sign is put between them (e.g. ἀκούω + συνίημι). When the words that form a word group are sometimes interrupted by other words, then a plus sign enclosed in parentheses is put between them (e.g. ἀκούω (+) ἀπό/παρά + genitive). When the words that form a word group are never interrupted by other words, then, a plus sign is omitted (e.g. ὦτα ἀκούειν ἀκουέτω). The title "word groups" can also point to (ii) a combination of words in a phrase or a sentence, mainly having a semantic interest (not necessarily having a grammatical connection) (e.g. ἀκούω + δέχομαι). When this category is listed, the words are linked by a "+." This indicates that a grammatical connection does not necessarily exist between them and that they do not necessarily follow each other. The general title "word groups" can be even extended to (iii) a single form of a lemma, which is noteworthy for its grammatical or semantic features (e.g. ἀκούομαι passive; ἀκούων in genitive absolute; a verb having a specific meaning, etc.). This category is listed at the end of the frame after a blank space.

The word groups are based on those indicated in Aland's *Vollständige Konkordanz* (recognisable by the references *VK*a, *VK*b, *VK*c, etc.), Hoffmann's *Synoptic Concordance* (*SC*a, *SC*b, *SC*c, etc.), the "units", i.e. the idiomatic expressions that J.P. Louw & E.A. Nida list (LN), and for the article, in Marshall's *Moulton and Geden Concordance* (MGM). They are harmonised and supplemented by other relevant word combinations. Some of these are the result of our own research and noted in Denaux 2009 Ln, etc. Others are word groups, even characteristic ones, which are found in Acts but are lacking in Luke. These are taken from the list of Boismard-Lamouille or, exceptionally, from other authors. A word group is often completed with references to other (slightly different) word groups, quoted after an arrow (the word group is treated under the bold Lukan lemma). A "cf." can refer to other New Testament writings, or can indicate expressions that differ from Lukan vocabulary. In that case, the references are given after the "cf. text".

All the instances of each word group found in Luke and Acts are given in the second and third column. Variant readings, which add the referenced word, are marked with an asterisk. Those that concern another word in the word group or a different grammatical form of the referenced word are indicated by *v.l.* We only recognised those variant readings that are marked with an asterisk in the *Vollständige Konkordanz* of Aland.

The number of occurrences in Matthew and Mark is given (with the total number, variant readings included, after the slash; brackets are only used for the ending of Mark) in the last two columns.

All the word groups are listed alphabetically except for αὐτός/ ἐγώ/ἡμεῖς/σύ and ὑμεῖς. These are arranged according to case forms. Prepositions governed by particular cases, are also arranged according to case. The word groups of λέγω and ὁράω are listed in three groups (λέγω/εἶπον/ἐρῶ and ὁράω/εἶδον/ὄψομαι).

→ **αἴρω** ἀπό; **αἰτέω** ἀπό; **ἀκούω** ἀπό; **ἀνάγομαι** ἀπό; ἀπὸ **ἀνατολῶν**; **ἀνὴρ** ἀπὸ τοῦ ὄχλου; **ἀπαίρομαι** ἀπό; **ἀπαιτέω** ἀπό; **ἀπέρχομαι** ἀπό; **ἀπέχω** οὐ μακρὰν ἀπό; **ἀποβαίνω** ἀπό; **ἀποκρύπτω** ἀπό; **ἀπολύομαι** ἀπὸ ἀνδρός; **ἀποχωρέω** ἀπό; Ἰωσὴφ ἀπὸ **Ἀριμαθαίας**; ἀπ' **ἀρχῆς**; **ἀφαιρέω** ἀπό; **βλέπω** ἀπό; ἀπὸ **βορρᾶ**; **διαχωρίζομαι** ἀπό; ἀπὸ **δυσμῶν**; **εἰμι** + ἀπό; **εἰς** + ἀπό; **ἐκ** + ἀπό; **ἐκβάλλω** ἀπό; **ἐκζητέω** ἀπό; **ἐξέρχομαι** ἀπό + place; **ἐπανάγω** ἀπό; **ἐπέρχομαι** ἀπό; **ἔρχομαι** ἀπό; **ἥκω** ἀπό; ἀφ' **ἡμερῶν** ἀρχαίων; **ἰάομαι** ἀπό; **καθαιρέω** ἀπό; **καθαρὸς** ἀπό; ἀπὸ τοῦ **καρποῦ** δίδωμι; **καταβαίνω** ἀπό (Ἱεροσολύμων); ἀπὸ **καταβολῆς** κόσμου; **κατέρχομαι** ἀπὸ Ἱεροσολύμων/τῆς Ἰουδαίας/τοῦ ὄρους; **κρύπτω** ἀπό; **κωλύω** ἀπό; **λύω** ἀπό; **μετανοέω** ἀπό; Ἰησοῦς (ὁ) ἀπὸ **Ναζαρέθ**; ἀπὸ (τῶν) **νεκρῶν**; ἀπὸ **νότου**; ἀπὸ (τοῦ) **οὐρανοῦ**; **παρακαλύπτω** ἀπό; **παραφέρω** τὸ ποτήριον ἀπό; **πίπτω** ἀπό; **προσέχω** ἀπό; **ῥύομαι** ἀπό; **σῴζω** ἀπό; **ὑπάρχω** οὐ μακρὰν ἀπό; **καταφέρομαι** ἀπὸ τοῦ **ὕπνου**; **ὑποστρέφω** ἀπό; **φεύγω** ἀπό; **φοβέομαι** ἀπό; ἀπὸ τοῦ **φόβου**; **φυλάσσω** ἀπό; **χορτάζομαι** ἀπό

Sometimes the word group is followed by a list of expressions that contain the Lukan lemma, but are fully treated under the bold word. This is often the case with prepositions and pronouns.

3. Third Frame

Characteristic of Luke

GASTON 1973 65 [Lked?]; HENDRIKS 1986 468; MORGENTHALER 1958A; PLUMMER 1922 lix

	Lk	Acts	Mt	Mk
ἀναστάς + imperative; cf. ἀνάστηθι + imper. Acts 8,26; 9,6.34[1]; 26,16 BOISMARD 1984 Ab18; DENAUX 2009 IA*; NEIRYNCK 1985	17,19; 22,46	9,11; 10,13.20; 11,7; 22,10.16	0	0
ἀναστάς/ἀναστάντες BOISMARD 1984 Bb56; CREDNER 1836 139; DENAUX 2009 L***; GOULDER 1989*; HARNACK 1906 138; HAWKINS 1909L; NEIRYNCK 1985; PLUMMER 1922 lxii	1,39; 4,29.38.39; 5,25.28; 6,8; 11,7.8; 15,18.20; 17,19; 22,45.46; 23,1; 24,12.33	1,15; 5,6.17.34; 8,27; 9,11.18.39; 10,13.20.23; 11,7.28; 13,16; 14,20; 15,7; 22,10.16; 23,9	2	6[7]/8
ἀναστάς/ἀναστάντες δέ BOISMARD 1984 Ab17; DENAUX 2009 IA*; NEIRYNCK 1985	1,39; 4,38	5,6.17.34; 9,39; 11,28; 13,16	0	0[1]
ἀναστάς ἔστη HARNACK 1906 43	6,8		0	0
ἀναστάς + πορεύομαι; cf. ἀνάστηθι + πορεύου Acts 8,26 BOISMARD 1984 Ab40; DENAUX 2009 IA*; HARNACK 1906 138; NEIRYNCK 1985	1,39; 15,18; 17,19	8,27; 9,11; 10,20; 22,10	0	0

ἀνέστη/ἀνέστησεν/ἀνέστησαν; cf. Jn 11,31; 1 Cor 10,7; 1 Thess 4,14; ἐξανέστησαν Acts 15,5 DENAUX 2009 1A**	4,16; 8,55; 9,8.19; 10,25; 17,12*	2,24.32; 5,36.37; 6,9; 7,18; 9,34².41; 13,34; 15,5; 26,30	0	3
ἀνέστη and cognate ἐξανέστη + participle → ἐξανέστη + part. BOISMARD 1984 Ab68; NEIRYNCK 1985	10,25	5,36; 6,9; 15,5	0	0

If the word is considered characteristic of Luke, the names of authors doing so are mentioned in a third frame ("Characteristic of Luke"). Characteristic word groups are also listed in this frame. Here, we follow the same method as in the word groups frames, except that we indicate the name of the authors who consider this word group or expression to be "characteristic". The word groups mentioned in the third frame are not listed in the second frame. Here, thirteen authors are taken into account because they give clear criteria why the listed words or word groups should be considered characteristic: Boismard-Lamouille 1984, Cadbury 1920, Credner 1836, Denaux 2009, Gaston 1963, Goulder 1989, Hawkins 1909, Hendriks 1986, Morgenthaler 1958, Neirynck 1985, Plummer 1922, Vogel 1899 (in some cases also Harnack and Schürmann). Full bibliographical references to these authors are given in the first list of the bibliography, pp. XIII-XV.

4. Fourth Frame

Literature

DENAUX 2009 1Aⁿ [λαλέω with an angel as speaker]; Laⁿ [ἄγγελος/ἄγγελοι τοῦ θεοῦ]; LA [ἀπέστη/ἀπῆλθεν ὁ ἄγγελος (angel)]; EASTON 1910 150 [probably characteristic of L]; GERSDORF 1816 168 [ὁ ἄγγελος Γαβριήλ].193 [ὁ ἄγγελος Γαβριήλ]; 198 [ἀπῆλθεν ἀπ' αὐτῆς ὁ ἄγγελος]; 232 [καὶ ἐγένετο ὡς ἀπῆλθον ἀπ' αὐτῶν εἰς τὸν οὐρανὸν οἱ ἄγγελοι]; JEREMIAS 1980 54-55 [ἀπῆλθεν ὁ ἄγγελος: red.]; 208 [ἄγγελος/ἄγγελοι τοῦ θεοῦ: red.]; RADL 1975 397 [ἄγγελος; ἄγγελος singular].

BRUN, Lyder, Engel und Blutschweiß Lc 22,43-44. — ZNW 32 (1933) 265-276.
GEORGE, Augustin, Les anges. — ID., Études, 1978, 149-183. Esp. 150-151: "Dénominations des anges"; 178-183: "Quelques données sur les anges".
SCHNEIDER, Gerhard, Engel und Blutschweiß (Lk 22,43-44): "Redaktionsgeschichte" im Dienste der Textkritik. — BZ NF 20 (1976) 112-116. Esp. 113-115: "Vokabular und Stil von Lk 22,43.44"; = ID., Lukas, Theologe der Heilsgeschichte, 1985, 153-157. Esp. 154-156.
TUCKETT, Christopher M., Luke 22,43-44: The "Agony" in the Garden and Luke's Gospel. — DENAUX, A. (ed.), New Testament Textual Criticism and Exegesis. FS J. Delobel, 2002, 131-144. Esp. 133-135: "Vocabulary and style".
WALLS, A.F., "In the Presence of the Angels" (Luke xv 10). — NT 3 (1959) 314-316.
WINK, Walter, Naming the Powers, 1984. Esp. 22-23.

In a fourth frame, the relevant linguistic literature that concerns the Lukan lemma is provided.

A first block gives a list of Lukan scholars (specific Lukan studies and commentaries) in abbreviated form (only name and date of the publication is given, with the specific page numbers): von Bendemann 2001, BDR,

Collison 1977, Denaux 2009, Easton 1910, Gersdorf 1816, Hauck 1934, Jeremias 1980, Paffenroth 1997, Radl 1975, Schneider 1969, Schürmann 1953, 1955, 1957, 1961. List 2 of the general bibliography provides full bibliographical references to these works (pp. XVI-XVII).

The second block lists specific studies on the referenced word. Either the full bibliographical reference is given here, or a shortened form (author, short title, date, and specific page numbers). The shortened titles are fully cited in the general bibliography (marked with an asterisk).

A

Ἀαρών 1 + 1	Aaron (Lk 1,5)			
Word groups	Lk	Acts	Mt	Mk
θυγάτηρ Ἀαρών	1,5		0	0

Ἄβελ 1 (Mt 1)	Abel (Lk 11,51)			
Word groups	Lk	Acts	Mt	Mk
αἷμα Ἄβελ	11,51		1	0

Literature

JEREMIAS 1980 210 [αἷμα Ἄβελ: trad.]: "Artikellose Genitivverbindungen übernahm Lukas aus der Überlieferung".

Ἀβιά 1 (Mt 2)	Abijah (Lk 1,5)			
Word groups	Lk	Acts	Mt	Mk
from the course of Abia (VKb)	1,5		0	0

Literature

JEREMIAS 1980 (18-)20 [ἐκ ἐφημερίας Ἀβιά: trad.]: "artikellosen Genitivverbindungen … wir es nicht mit alltäglicher Sprache, sondern mit einer biblizistischen Konstruktion zu tun haben ".

SCHWARZ, Günther, εξ εφημεριας Αβια? (Lukas 1,5). — *BibNot* 53 (1990) 30-31.

Ἀβιληνή 1	Abilene (Lk 3,1)

Ἀβραάμ 15 + 7 (Mt 7, Mk 1)	Abraham			
Word groups	Lk	Acts	Mt	Mk
Ἀβραάμ (+) θυγάτηρ/τέκνον/υίός → **Ἀβραάμ** + σπέρμα	3,8[2]; 13,16; 16,25; 19,9		2	0
Ἀβραάμ + Ἰσαάκ + Ἰακώβ	3,34; 13,28; 20,37	3,13; 7,32	2	1
Ἀβραάμ + πατήρ → πάτερ **Ἀβραάμ**	1,55.73; 3,8[1]	3,13.25; 7,2.32	1	0
Ἀβραάμ + σπέρμα (VKa) → **Ἀβραάμ** (+) θυγάτηρ/τέκνον/υίός; **Δαυίδ** + σπέρμα DENAUX 2009 LAⁿ	1,55	3,25	0	0
γένος Ἀβραάμ		13,26	0	0
ὁ θεὸς Ἀβραάμ (SCb; VKb) → θεὸς **Ἰακώβ/ Ἰσαάκ**	20,37	3,13; 7,32	1	1
κόλπος + Ἀβραάμ (LN: heaven)	16,22.23		0	0
πάτερ Ἀβραάμ (SCa) → **Ἀβραάμ** + πατήρ DENAUX 2009 LAⁿ	16,24.30		0	0

Characteristic of Luke

GOULDER 1989; HENDRIKS 1986 433; MORGENTHALER 1958L

Literature

DENAUX 2009 Lan; JEREMIAS 1980 19 [γένος Ἀβραάμ: trad.]; 230 [θυγάτηρ Ἀβραάμ: trad.].

ἄβυσσος 1 | very deep place (Lk 8,31)

Literature

HAUCK 1934 [Vorzugswort].

GARCÍA PÉREZ, José Miguel, El Endemoniado de Gerasa (Lc 8,26-39), 1986. Esp. 137-140.

ἀγαθοποιέω 4 + 0/1 (Mk 0/1) | do good (Lk 6,9.33$^{1.2}$.35)

Characteristic of Luke

DENAUX 2009 L***; HAWKINS 1909 16

Literature

COLLISON 1977 88 [noteworthy phenomena]; HAUCK 1934 [Vorzugswort]; JEREMIAS 1980 145 [trad.]: "Von sich aus schrieb Lukas ἀγαθουργέω Apg 14,17. Wo er der Überlieferung folgt, greift er das ihm angebotene ἀγαθοποιέω auf".

VAN UNNIK, Willem C., Die Motivierung der Feindesliebe in Lukas VI 32-35. — NT 8 (1966) 284-300; = ID., Sparsa Collecta, I, 1973, 111-126.

ἀγαθός 16 + 3 (Mt 16/17, Mk 4)

1. good (moral) (Lk 23,50; Acts 11,24); 2. good (value) (Lk 8,8; 16,25); 3. generous

Word groups	Lk	Acts	Mt	Mk
τὸ ἀγαθόν / τὰ ἀγαθά (μου/σου) (LN: possessions; VKa) → τὰ κακά	6,45^3; 12,18; 16,25		1/2	0
ἀγαθός + κακός	16,25		0	0
ἀγαθὸς ἄνθρωπος → ἀνὴρ ἀγαθός; ἄνθρωπος δίκαιος/ εὐλαβής	6,45^1		1	0
ἀγαθὸς δοῦλος → δοῦλος πονηρός; cf. δοῦλος κακός Mt 24,48	19,17		2	0
ἀνὴρ ἀγαθός → ἄνθρωπος ἀγαθός; ἀνὴρ δίκαιος/ εὐλαβής DENAUX 2009 LA^n	23,50	11,24	0	0
διδάσκαλος ἀγαθός	18,18		0/1	1
ἔργα ἀγαθά; cf. ἔργα καλά Mt 5,16		9,36		
καλὸς καὶ ἀγαθός	8,15			
συνείδησις ἀγαθός		23,1	0	0

Literature

PAFFENROTH 1997 83 [τὸ ἀγαθόν/τὰ ἀγαθά: pre-Lukan]; REHKOPF 1959 91 [τὸ ἀγαθόν/τὰ ἀγαθά: vorlukanisch]; 98 [ἀγαθὲ/πονηρὲ δοῦλε: "Substantiva in Anrede bei den Synoptikern"]; SCHÜRMANN 1961 278 [τὸ ἀγαθόν/τὰ ἀγαθά: protoluk R weniger wahrscheinlich].

BORMANN, Lukas, *Recht, Gerechtigkeit und Religion*, 2001. Esp. 145 [τὰ ἀγαθά].

ἀγαλλίασις 2 + 1   extreme joy

Word groups	Lk	Acts	Mt	Mk
ἀγαλλίασις + χαρά; cf. ἀγαλλιάω (+) χαρά/χαίρω Mt 5,12; Jn 8,56; 1 Pe 1,8; 4,13; Rev 19,7	1,14		0	0
ἐν ἀγαλλιάσει; cf. Jud 1,24 DENAUX 2009 LAⁿ	1,44	2,46	0	0

Characteristic of Luke

BOISMARD 1984 cb13; HARNACK 1906 72.140; NEIRYNCK 1985; PLUMMER 1922 lix

	Lk	Acts	Mt	Mk
ἀγαλλίασις and cognate ἀγαλλιάω DENAUX 2009 L***; GOULDER 1989	1,14.44(.47; 10,21)	2,(26).46; (16,34)	0	0

Literature

DENAUX 2009 Laⁿ

ἀγαλλιάω 2 + 2 (Mt 1)   be extremely joyful

Characteristic of Luke

DENAUX 2009 LA**; HARNACK 1906 72.140.151

	Lk	Acts	Mt	Mk
ἀγαλλιάομαι middle; cf. Jn 8,56; 1 Pet 1,6.8; 4,16 GOULDER 1989 [ἀγαλλιάσθαι/-ις]	10,21	2,26; 16,34	1	0
ἀγαλλιάω and cognate ἀγαλλίασις DENAUX 2009 L***; GOULDER 1989	1,(14.44).47; 10,21)	2,26.(46); 16,34	0	0

Literature

COLLISON 1977 88 [noteworthy phenomena].

DUPONT, Jacques, *Les Béatitudes*, II, 1969. Esp. 320-322: "'Se réjouir', 'exulter'".

ἀγανακτέω 1 (Mt 3, Mk 3)   be indignant (Lk 13,14)

ἀγαπάω 13 (Mt 8, Mk 5)
1. love (Lk 16,13); 2. show love (Lk 7,47¹); 3. take pleasure in (Lk 11,43)

Word groups	Lk	Acts	Mt	Mk
ἀγαπάω + δουλεύω → μισέω + δουλεύω	16,13		1	0
ἀγαπάω + ἐχθρός → μισέω + ἐχθρός	6,27.35		1	0
ἀγαπάω + θεός/κύριος → ἀγάπη τοῦ θεοῦ	10,27		1	1
ἀγαπάω + μισέω	6,27; 16,13		2	0
ἀγαπάω + πλησίον	10,27		3	2
ἀγαπάω absolute (VKa) DENAUX 2009 Lⁿ	7,47¹·²		0	0

Characteristic of Luke
GOULDER 1989

Literature
COLLISON 1977 88-89 [noteworthy phenomena]; JEREMIAS 1980 141(-142) [6,27-28: trad.]: "Das LkEv liebt den Gebrauch der Wortgruppe ἀγαπάω κτλ im profanen Sinn"; "ἀγαπᾶτε … ποιεῖτε … εὐλογεῖτε … προσεύχεσθε: Die asyndetische Aufreihung von Imperativen wird von Lukas in dem von ihm übernommenen Markusstoff konsequent beseitigt"; REHKOPF 1959 91 [vorlukanisch]; SCHÜRMANN 1961 275.

GREENLEE, J.Harold, "Love" in the New Testament. — *Notes on Translation* 14 (2000) 49-53. [NTA 46, 73]

JOLY, Robert, *Le vocabulaire chrétien de l'amour est-il original? Φιλεῖν et ἀγαπᾶν dans le grec antique* (Institut d'histoire du christianisme). Bruxelles: Presses universitaires de Bruxelles, 1968, 63 p.

LOSS, Nicolò Maria, *Amore d'amicizia nel Nuovo Testamento*, 1977. Esp. 7-20: "Breve esame comparativo della frequenza di ἀγαπάω e φιλέω e dei loro gruppi negli scritti del NT".

MOFFATT, James, *Love in the New Testament*. London: Hodder and Stoughton, 1929, XV-333 p. Esp. 35-40: "Need for studying NT language about love"; 44-48: "The verbs ἀγαπᾶν and φιλεῖν"; 48-51: "Three special senses of ἀγαπᾶν in NT Greek".

SCHWARZ, Günther, αγαπατε τους εχθρους υμων Mt 5,44a / Lk 6,27a(35a). Jesu Forderung *kat' exochen*. — *BibNot* 12 (1980) 32-34.

SEGALLA, Giuseppe, La predicazione dell'amore nella tradizione presinottica. — *RivBib* 20 (1972) 481-528. Esp. 486: "Agapân e filein".

SÖDING, Thomas, Das Wortfeld der Liebe im paganen und biblischen Griechisch: Philologische Beobachtungen an der Wurzel ἀγαπ-. — *ETL* 68 (1992) 284-330.

SPICQ, Ceslaus, Le verbe ἀγαπάω et set dérivés dans le grec classique. — *RB* 60 (1953) 372-397.

—, *Agapè dans le Nouveau Testament. Analyse des textes*, I (Études bibliques). Paris: Gabalda, 1958, 334 p. Esp. 98-155: "La charité dans l'évangile de saint Luc"; 187-207: "L'épitre de saint Jacques et les Actes des Apôtres".

—, *Agape in the New Testament*. I: *Agape in the Synoptic Gospels*. II: *Agape in the Epistles of St. Paul, the Acts of the Apostles and the Epistles of St. James, St. Peter, and St. Jude*, trans. Marie Aquinas McNamara and Mary Honoria Richter. St. Louis, MO – London: B. Herder Book Co., 1963, XIV-153 + X-450 p. Esp. I, 75-125: "Agape in the Gospel of St. Luke"; II, 1-14: "St. James and the Acts of the Apostles".

VAN UNNIK, Willem C., Die Motivierung der Feindesliebe in Lukas VI 32-35. — *NT* 8 (1966) 284-300; = ID., *Sparsa Collecta*, I, 1973, 111-126.

VOORWINDE, S., Ἀγαπάω and φιλέω — Is There a Difference? — *Reformed Theological Review* [Doncaster, Australia] 64 (2005) 76-90.

WISCHMEYER, Oda, Vorkommen und Bedeutung von Agape in der außerchristlichen Antike. — *ZNW* 69 (1978) 212-238.

WOOD, Herbert Geoffry, The Use of ἀγαπάω in Luke viii.42, 47. — *ExpT* 66 (1954-55) 319-320.

ἀγάπη 1 (Mt 1)
1. love (Lk 11,42); 2. fellowship meal

Word groups	Lk	Acts	Mt	Mk
ἀγάπη τοῦ θεοῦ (VKa) → **ἀγαπάω** + θεός/κύριος	11,42		0	0

Literature

PHIPPS, William E., The Sensuousness of *Agape*. — *Theology Today* 29 (1973) 370-379.
[NTA 17, 844]
SEGALLA, Giuseppe, La predicazione dell'amore nella tradizione presinottica. — *RivBib* 20
(1972) 481-528. Esp. 484-486: "Agápê redazionale".
SPICQ, Ceslaus, Charity in the Synoptic Gospels. — *BiTod* 17 (1965) 1137-1143.
TARELLI, C.C., ἀγάπη. — *JTS* NS 1 (1950) 64-67.
WARNACH, Viktor, *Agape: Die Liebe als Grundmotiv der neutestamentlichen Theologie*.
Düsseldorf: Patmos, 1951, 756 p. Esp. 173-179: "Bedeutungsfülle und Sprachfeld des
neutestamentlichen Wortes 'Agape'".
See also ἀγαπάω

ἀγαπητός 2/3 + 1 (Mt 3, Mk 3)

1. beloved (Acts 15,25); 2. only dear (Lk 3,22)

Word groups	Lk	Acts	Mt	Mk
υἱός + (ὁ) ἀγαπητός (*VK*b) → υἱὸς (ὁ) ἐκλελεγμένος	3,22; 9,35*; 20,13		2	3

Literature

ἀγαπητός. — *JTS* 20 (1919) 339-344.
DAWSEY, James M., What's in a Name? Characterization in Luke. — *BTB* 16 (1986) 143-
147. Esp. 146-147: "Luke's use of 'son of God'".
LEE, John A.L., *A History of New Testament Lexicography*, 2003. Esp. 193-211.
SCATTOLON, Alfredo, L'ἀγαπητός sinottico nella luce della tradizione giudaica. —
RivBib 26 (1978) 3-32.
SEGALLA, Giuseppe, La predicazione dell'amore nella tradizione presinottica. — *RivBib* 20
(1972) 481-528. Esp. 487-493: "Il figlio: ὁ ἀγαπητός".
VOSS, Gerhard, *Die Christologie der lukanischen Schriften in Grundzügen*, 1965. Esp. 84-
95: "Υἱὸς ἀγαπητός".
See also ἀγαπάω

ἄγγελος 25/26 + 21 (Mt 20, Mk 6)

1. messenger (Lk 7,24); 2. angel (Lk 1,26)

Word groups	Lk	Acts	Mt	Mk
ἄγγελος subject of λέγω/εῖπον + μὴ φοβοῦ/φοβεῖσθε	1,13.30; 2,10	27,23(-24)	2	0
ἄγγελος (+) ἀπ/εἰσέρχομαι → ἀπέστη/ἀπῆλθεν ὁ **ἄγγελος**; cf. ἄγγελος (+) ἀναβαίνω Jn 1,51; Rev 7,2; ἄγγελος ἐξέρχομαι Mt 13,49; ἄγγελος (+) καταβαίνω Mt 28,2; Jn 1,51; Rev 10,1; 18,1; 20,1; ἄγγελος (+) προσέρχομαι Mt 4,11; 28,2 DENAUX 2009 La[n]	7,24; 9,52	10,3	0	0
ἄγγελος + (ἐξ)ἀποστέλλω	1,19.26; 7,27; 9,52	7,35; 12,11	3	2
ὁ ἄγγελος Γαβριήλ; cf. ἄγγελος + Γαβριήλ Lk 1,19	1,26		0	0
ἄγγελος + δόξα	2,9; 9,26	12,23	2	1
ἄγγελος + εὐαγγελίζομαι; cf. Gal 1,8 DENAUX 2009 L[n]	1,19; 2,10		0	0

ἄγγελος (+) κυρίου/αὐτοῦ/μου (SCa; VKa) → **ἄγγελος κυρίου; ἄγγελος/ἄγγελοι** τοῦ θεοῦ	1,11; 2,9; 4,10; 7,27	5,19; 7,30 v.l; 8,26; 12,7.11.23	7	1/2
ἄγγελος + ὀπτασία → **ἄγγελος** object of ὁράω DENAUX 2009 Lⁿ	1,19(-22); 24,23		0	0
ἅγιος ἄγγελος	9,26	10,22	0/1	1
ἔμπροσθεν τῶν ἀγγέλων τοῦ θεοῦ → ἐνώπιον τῶν **ἀγγέλων** τοῦ θεοῦ ἔμπροσθεν/ ἐναντίον/ἐνώπιον τῶν **ἀνθρώπων**/(τοῦ) **θεοῦ/κυρίου**	12,8		0	0
ἐνώπιον τῶν ἀγγέλων τοῦ θεοῦ → ἔμπροσθεν τῶν **ἀγγέλων** τοῦ θεοῦ; ἔμπροσθεν/ ἐναντίον/ἐνώπιον τῶν **ἀνθρώπων**/(τοῦ) **θεοῦ/κυρίου** DENAUX 2009 Lⁿ	12,9; 15,10		0	0
ἄγγελος of human beings (VKc) DENAUX 2009 Lⁿ	7,24; 9,52		0	0

Characteristic of Luke

HENDRIKS 1986 434

	Lk	Acts	Mt	Mk
ἄγγελος object of ὁράω / ἄγγελος ὤφθη → **ἄγγελος** + ὀπτασία; cf. ἄγγελος object of θεωρέω Jn 20,12; ἄγγελος + ὅραμα Acts 10,3 DENAUX 2009 lA*	1,11; 22,43; 24,23	7,30.35; 10,3; 11,13	0	0
ἄγγελος subject of λέγω/εἶπον → **ἄγγελος** subject of λαλέω DENAUX 2009 lA*	1,13.19.28*.30. 35; 2,10; 24,23	5,19; 8,26; 10,3; 11,13; 12,7.8; 27,23(-24)	3	0
ἄγγελος singular; cf. Jn 12,29 BOISMARD 1984 Eb40; DENAUX 2009 lA**; NEIRYNCK 1985	1,11.13.18.19.26. 28*.30.34.35.38; 2,9.10.13.21; 7,27; 22,43	5,19; 6,15; 7,30.35.38; 8,26; 10,3.7.22; 11,13; 12,7.8.9.10.11.15. 23; 23,8.9; 27,23	7	1
ἄγγελος subject of λαλέω → **ἄγγελος** subject of λέγω/εἶπον; cf. Jn 12,29 BOISMARD 1984 Eb37; NEIRYNCK 1985	1,19	7,38; 8,26; 10,7; 23,9	0	0
ἄγγελος + θεός → **ἄγγελος/ἄγγελοι** τοῦ θεοῦ DENAUX 2009 L***	1,26; 2,13; 12.8.9; 15,10	7,35; 10,3; 12,23; 27,23	0/1	0
ἄγγελος/ἄγγελοι τοῦ θεοῦ (SCa; VKa) → **ἄγγελος** + θεός; **ἄγγελος** κυρίου BOISMARD 1984 cb72; NEIRYNCK 1985	12.8.9; 15,10	10,3; 27,23	0/1	0
ἄγγελος + (ἐφ/παρ)ἵστημι→ ἀπέστη/ ἀπῆλθεν ὁ **ἄγγελος**; ἀπέστη ὁ **διάβολος** DENAUX 2009 LA*	1.11.19; 2,9	11,13; 12,7; 27,23	1	0
ἄγγελος κυρίου → **ἄγγελος** κυρίου/ αὐτοῦ/ μου; **ἄγγελος/ἄγγελοι** τοῦ θεοῦ HARNACK 1906 71	1,11; 2,9	5,19; 7,30 v.l; 8,26; 12,7.23	5	0
ἀπέστη/ἀπῆλθεν ὁ ἄγγελος (angel) → **ἄγγελος** + ἀπ/εἰσέρχομαι; **ἄγγελος** + (ἐφ/παρ)ἵστημι; ἀπέστη ὁ **διάβολος** BOISMARD 1984 Ab66; HARNACK 1906 146; NEIRYNCK 1985	1,38; 2,15	10,7; 12,10	0	0

Literature

DENAUX 2009 lAⁿ [λαλέω with an angel as speaker]; Lⁿ [ἄγγελος/ἄγγελοι τοῦ θεοῦ]; LA

[ἀπέστη/ἀπῆλθεν ὁ ἄγγελος (angel)]; EASTON 1910 150 [probably characteristic of L];
GERSDORF 1816 168 [ὁ ἄγγελος Γαβριήλ].193 [ὁ ἄγγελος Γαβριήλ]; 198 [ἀπῆλθεν ἀπ᾽
αὐτῆς ὁ ἄγγελος]; 232 [καὶ ἐγένετο ὡς ἀπῆλθον ἀπ᾽ αὐτῶν εἰς τὸν οὐρανὸν οἱ ἄγγελοι];
JEREMIAS 1980 54-55 [ἀπῆλθεν ὁ ἄγγελος: red.]; 208 [ἄγγελος/ἄγγελοι τοῦ θεοῦ: red.];
RADL 1975 397 [ἄγγελος; ἄγγελος singular].

BRUN, Lyder, Engel und Blutschweiß Lc 22,43-44. — ZNW 32 (1933) 265-276.
GEORGE, Augustin, Les anges. — ID., Études, 1978, 149-183. Esp. 150-151: "Dénominations
   des anges"; 178-183: "Quelques données sur les anges".
SCHNEIDER, Gerhard, Engel und Blutschweiß (Lk 22,43-44): "Redaktionsgeschichte" im
   Dienste der Textkritik. — BZ NF 20 (1976) 112-116. Esp. 113-115: "Vokabular und Stil von
   Lk 22,43.44"; = ID., Lukas, Theologe der Heilsgeschichte, 1985, 153-157. Esp. 154-156.
TUCKETT, Christopher M., Luke 22,43-44: The "Agony" in the Garden and Luke's Gospel.
   — DENAUX, A. (ed.), New Testament Textual Criticism and Exegesis. FS J. Delobel,
   2002, 131-144. Esp. 133-135: "Vocabulary and style".
WALLS, A.F., "In the Presence of the Angels" (Luke XV 10). — NT 3 (1959) 314-316.
WINK, Walter, Naming the Powers, 1984. Esp. 22-23.

ἀγέλη 2 (Mt 3/4, Mk 2)   herd (Lk 8,32.33)

Word groups	Lk	Acts	Mt	Mk
ἀγέλη χοίρων	8,32		3/4	1

ἀγιάζω 1 + 2 (Mt 3)

1. dedicate (Acts 20,32; 26,18); 2. make holy (Lk 11,2); 3. honor as holy

Word groups	Lk	Acts	Mt	Mk
ἀγιάζω τὸ ὄνομα → ἅγιον ὄνομα	11,2		1	0

Literature
PRETE, Benedetto, Il senso della formula "coloro che sono stati santificati per la fede in
   me" (At 26,18c). — RivBib 35 (1987) 313-320. Esp. 314-316: "Motivi di carattere
   filologico".

ἅγιος 20 + 53/55 (Mt 10/11, Mk 7)

1. holy (Lk 1,15); 2. dedicated (Lk 1,70; 2,23)

Word groups	Lk	Acts	Mt	Mk
ἁγία γῆ / ἅγιος (+) τόπος		6,13; 7,33; 21,28	1	0
ἁγία διαθήκη	1,72		0	0
ἅγιον τὸ ὄνομα → ἁγιάζω τὸ ὄνομα	1,49		0	0
ἅγιος ἄγγελος	9,26	10,22	0/1	1
ἅγιος παῖς		4,27.30	0	0
ἅγιος προφήτης	1,70	3,21	0	0
DENAUX 2009 LA[n]				
ὁ ἅγιος → (οἱ) ἅγιοι		3,14	0	0
ὁ ἅγιος τοῦ θεοῦ (VKd)	4,34		0	1
(οἱ) ἅγιοι (LN: God's people; VKb) → ὁ ἅγιος		9,13.32.41; 26,10	1	0
BOISMARD 1984 Ea4				

βαπτίζω ἐν πνεύματι ἁγίῳ	3,16	1,5; 11,16	1	1
διὰ πνεύματος ἁγίου		1,2; 4,25	0	0
ἐκχέω/ἐκχύννω + ἅγιον + πνεῦμα		2,33; 10,44	0	0

Characteristic of Luke

DENAUX 2009 1A**; GOULDER 1989; HARNACK 1906 144; HAWKINS 1909A; HENDRIKS 1986 468; MORGENTHALER 1958LA

	Lk	Acts	Mt	Mk
(τὸ) πνεῦμα (τὸ) ἅγιον (SCa; VKa) BOISMARD 1984 cb162; DENAUX 2009 1A**; GOULDER 1989; NEIRYNCK 1985	1,15.35[1].41.67; 2,25.26; 3,16.22; 4,1; 10,21; 11,13; 12,10.12	1,2.5.8.16; 2,4.33.38; 4,8.25.31; 5,3.32; 6,3*.5; 7,51.55; 8,15.17.18*.19; 9,17.31; 10,38.44.45.47; 11,15.16.24; 13,2.4.9.52; 15,8.28; 16,6; 19,2[12].6; 20,23.28; 21,11; 28,25	5	4

→ ἐπιπίπτει τὸ πνεῦμα τὸ ἅγιον; λαμβάνω πνεῦμα (ἅγιον); ἐπλήσθην πνεύματος ἁγίου; πλήρης πνεύματος ἁγίου; τὸ πνεῦμα (τὸ ἅγιον) εἶπεν + dat.

Literature

COLLISON 1977 176 [πνεῦμα ἅγιον: linguistic usage of Luke: certain]; HAUCK 1934 [Vorzugswort; Vorzugsverbindung: πνεῦμα (τὸ) ἅγιον]; 55-56: "Exk 6: Der heilige Geist bei Lk".

BAER, Heinrich VON, *Der Heilige Geist in den Lukasschriften* (BWANT, 39). Stuttgart: Kohlhammer, 1926, VII-220 p. Esp. 20-38: "Die Abgrenzung des Heiligen Geistes, in seinem speziellen Sinne, vom Pneuma im allgemeinen (kosmischen, psychologischen usw.) Gebrauch dieses Wortes im N.T."; 38-43: "Das Pneuma Hagion und andere Korrelatbegriffe an den Lukasschriften".

BOVER, José M., "Quod nascetur (ex te) sanctum vocabitur filius Dei" (Lc. 1,35). — *Bib* 1 (1920) 92-94.

—, "Quod nascetur (ex te) sanctum vocabitur filius Dei" (Lc., 1,35). — *EstE* 8 (1929) 381-392.

MARÍN HEREDIA, H Francesco, Difícil equilibrio en Lc 1,35b. — *Carthaginensia* 5 (1989) 19-30.

MUÑOZ IGLESIAS, Salvador, Lucas 1,35b. — *La idea de Dios en la Biblia. XXVIII Semana Biblica Española (Madrid 23-27 sept. 1968)*. Madrid: Consejo Superior de Investigaciones Cientificas, 1971, 303-324.

READ-HEIMERDINGER, Jenny, *The Bezan Text of Acts*, 2002. Esp. 145-172: "The Holy Spirit".

RESE, Martin, *Alttestamentliche Motive in der Christologie des Lukas*, 1969. Esp. 131-133: "Προφήτης, ἅγιος, δίκαιος, ἀρχηγός, σωτήρ und υἱὸς θεοῦ in der Apostelgeschichte"; 204: ""Ἅγιος im Lukasevangelium".

SCHNEIDER, Gerhard, Lk 1,34. 35 als redaktionelle Einheit. — *BZ* NF 15 (1971) 255-259. Esp. 256-257: "Lk 1,35 ist nach Wortschatz, Stil und Theologie 'lukanisch'".

—, Jesu geistgewirkte Empfängnis (Lk 1,34f): Zur Interpretation einer christologischen Aussage. — *TPQ* 119 (1971) 105-116. Esp. 109.110; = ID., *Lukas, Theologe der Heilsgeschichte*, 1985, 86-97. Esp. 90.91.

ἀγκάλη 1	bent arm (Lk 2,28)

Literature

HAUCK 1934 [seltenes Alleinwort].

ἀγνοέω 1 + 2 (Mk 1)	
1. not know (Acts 13,27; 17,23); 2. ignore; 3. fail to understand (Lk 9,45)	

Literature
DANOVE, Paul, Verbs of Experience, 1999. Esp. 160.174-175.

ἀγορά 3 + 2 (Mt 3, Mk 3) | market

Word groups	Lk	Acts	Mt	Mk
ἀγορά + συναγωγή	11,43; 20,46	17,17	1	1
ἀγορά with article	11,43; 20,46	16,19; 17,17	3	2
ἀγορά without article	7,32		0	1

Literature
JEREMIAS 1980 166: "das artikellose formelhafte ἐν ἀγορᾷ wird vorlukanisch sein".

BORMANN, Lukas, Recht, Gerechtigkeit und Religion, 2001. Esp. 145-146.

ἀγοράζω 5/6 (Mt 7, Mk 5)
1. buy (Lk 9,13; 14,18.19; 17,28; 22,36); 2. redeem

Word groups	Lk	Acts	Mt	Mk
ἀγοράζω + πωλέω	17,28; 19,45*; 22,36		3	1

Literature
JEREMIAS 1980 240 [trad.]; SCHÜRMANN 1957 123-124.

BORMANN, Lukas, Recht, Gerechtigkeit und Religion, 2001. Esp. 146.

ἄγρα* 2 | catch (Lk 5,4.9)

Characteristic of Luke
PLUMMER 1922 liii

Literature
DENAUX 2009 L^n; HAUCK 1934 [seltenes Alleinwort].

LEE, John A.L. – HORSLEY, G.H.R., A Lexicon of the New Testament, 2, 1998. Esp. 59-60.

ἀγραυλέω* 1 | remain outdoors (Lk 2,8)

Literature
HAUCK 1934 [seltenes Alleinwort].

ἀγρός 9 + 1 (Mt 17, Mk 8[9])
1. field (Lk 14,18); 2. countryside (Lk 8,34); 3. farm settlement (Lk 15,15)

Word groups	Lk	Acts	Mt	Mk
ἀγρός + κώμη/πόλις	8,34; 9,12		0	3

ἀγρός + οἰκία; cf. χωρίον + οἰκία Acts 4,34	17,31	2	3		
ἐν ἀγρῷ DENAUX 2009 Lⁿ	12,28; 15,25; 17,31	0	0		
ἀγροί plural (VKa)	8,34; 9,12; 15,15			1	6
ἀγρός with article	8,34; 9,12 v.l.; 12,28 v.l.; 15,15; 17,7; 17,31 v.l.			15	4
ἀγρός without article	9,12; 12,28; 14,18; 15,25; 17,31; 23,26	4,37	2		4[5]

Literature

JEREMIAS 1980 218 [ἐν ἀγρῷ: trad.].

ἀγρυπνέω 1 (Mk 1)

1. be alert (Lk 21,36); 2. take care of

Word groups	Lk	Acts	Mt	Mk
ἀγρυπνεῖτε imperative → γρηγορεῖτε imper.	21,36		0	0

Literature

CADBURY 1920A

DUPONT, Jacques, Le discours de Milet, 1962. Esp. 223-224.363.

ἄγω 13/14 + 26/28 (Mt 4/5, Mk 3/4)

1. bring (Lk 19,27); 2. carry (Lk 4,40); 3. go away; 4. guide (Lk 4,9); 5. function (Acts 19,38); 6. occur (Lk 24,21); 7. spend time (Lk 24,21); 8. BDAG 2000: lead away, arrest (Lk 22,54; Acts 6,12, 18,12)

Word groups	Lk	Acts	Mt	Mk
ἄγει ἡμέραν (VKb) DENAUX 2009 Lⁿ	4,1(-2); 24,21		0/1	0
ἀγοραῖοι ἄγονται		19,38	0	0
ἄγω ἐν + place → συνάγω ἐν + place	4,1		0	0
ἄγω + ἕως → ἐξάγω ἕως	4,29		0	0
ἄγω temporal DENAUX 2009 LAⁿ	24,21	19,38	0/1	0

Characteristic of Luke

DENAUX 2009 IA**; GOULDER 1989; HAWKINS 1909A; HENDRIKS 1986 434; MORGENTHALER 1958LA; PLUMMER 1922 lix

	Lk	Acts	Mt	Mk
ἄγομαι passive → ἀν/ἀπ/εἰσ/ἐπισυν/ κατ/συνάγομαι passive DENAUX 2009 IA*	4,1; 18,40; 21,12*; 23,32	5,21; 8,32; 19,38; 21,34; 22,24*; 25,6.17.23	1	0
ἄγω transitive → ἀν/ἀπ/εἰσ/ἐξ/ἐπισυν/ κατ/προ/προσ/συνάγω transitive; cf. Jn 1,42; 7,45; 9,13; 10,16; 18,13.28; 19,4.13; Rom 2,4; 8,14; 1 Cor 12,2; Gal 5,18; 1 Thess 4,14; 2 Tim 3,6; 4,11; Heb 2,10; ἐπάγω trans. Acts 5,28 BOISMARD 1984 cb131; DENAUX 2009 L***; NEIRYNCK 1985	4,1.9.29.40; 10,34; 18,40; 19,27.30.35; 21,12*; 22,54; 23,1.32; 24,21	5,21.26.27; 6,12; 8,32; 9,2.21.27; 11,26; 13,23; 17,5*.15.19; 18,12; 19,37.38; 20,12; 21,16.34; 22,5.24*; 23,10.18¹·².31; 25,6.17.23	3	1/2

ἄγω + εἰς + place → ἀν/ἀπ/εἰσ/ἐξ/ἐπαν/ κατ/προ/συν/ὑπάγω εἰς + place BOISMARD 1984 Ab12; DENAUX 2009 lA*; NEIRYNCK 1985	4,9; 10,34	6,12; 9,2; 11,26; 17,5*; 21,34; 22,5.24*; 23,10.31	0	1
ἄγω (and cognate ἀπάγω) ἐπί + accusative → ἄγω πρός + acc. (person); ἀν/κατάγω ἐπί + acc. (place); ἀπ/συν/ὑπάγω ἐπί + acc. (person); προάγω ἐπί + gen. (person); προσάγω + dat.; cf. ἐπάγω ἐπί + acc. Acts 5,28 BOISMARD 1984 Bb60; NEIRYNCK 1985	21,12*; 23,1	8,32; 9,21; 17,19; 18,12	1	0
ἄγω + πρός + accusative (person) → ἄγω ἐπί + acc.; ἀπάγω/ἐξάγω πρός + acc.; προσάγω + dat. DENAUX 2009 LA*	4,40; 18,40; 19,35	9,27; 23,18[1.2]	0	0/1
ἤγαγον → ἀν/ἀπ/εἰσ/κατήγαγον; cf. συνήγαγον Mt 22,10; 27,27 DENAUX 2009 lA*	4,29.40; 19,35; 22,54; 23,1	6,12; 17,15.19; 18,12; 20,12; 23,31	1	0
κελεύω and cognates εἰσ/ἀπ/ ἄγειν → κελεύω + ἀπάγειν/ εἰσάγειν BOISMARD 1984 Ab26; NEIRYNCK 1985	18,40	12,19; 21,34; 22,24*; 23,10; 25,6.17	0	0

→ ἡμέρα + ὁ υἱὸς τοῦ ἀνθρώπου

Literature

COLLISON 1977 35 [linguistic usage of Luke: certain]; DENAUX 2009 [lA[n]: κελεύω + ἄγειν]; HAUCK 1934 [Vorzugswort]; JEREMIAS 1980 84 [ἄγω ἕως: red.]; 316 [ἄγω temporal: red.]; RADL 1975 397 [ἄγω; ἤγαγον; ἄγω ἐπί + acc.]; 415 [κελεύω + ἄγειν]; SCHNEIDER 1969 64.163: "Luk zeigt eine Vorliebe für ἄγω" [Vorzugswörter und -ausdrücke des Luk].

FITZMYER, Joseph A., The Use of *agein* and *ferein* in the Synoptic Gospels. — BARTH, E.H. – COCROFT, R.E. (eds.), *Festschrift to Honor F. Wilbur Gingrich*, 1972, 147-160.

ἀγωνία 1	intense sorrow (Lk 22,44)

Literature

HAUCK 1934 [seltenes Alleinwort].

BRUN, Lyder, Engel und Blutschweiß Lc 22,43-44. — *ZNW* 32 (1933) 265-276.
SCHNEIDER, Gerhard, Engel und Blutschweiß (Lk 22,43-44): "Redaktionsgeschichte" im Dienste der Textkritik. — *BZ* NF 20 (1976) 112-116. Esp. 113-115: "Vokabular und Stil von Lk 22,43.44"; = ID., *Lukas, Theologe der Heilsgeschichte*, 1985, 153-157. Esp. 154-156.
TUCKETT, Christopher M., Luke 22,43-44: The "Agony" in the Garden and Luke's Gospel. — DENAUX, A. (ed.), *New Testament Textual Criticism and Exegesis*. FS J. Delobel, 2002, 131-144. Esp. 133-135: "Vocabulary and style".

ἀγωνίζομαι 1

1. fight; 2. compete; 3. make effort (Lk 13,24)

Literature

HAUCK 1934 [seltenes Alleinwort]; JEREMIAS 1980 93 [red.].

DODD, Charles H., Some Problems of New Testament Translation. — *BTrans* 13 (1962) 145-157. Esp. 148-149: "*agônizomenos*".

Ἀδάμ 1	Adam (Lk 3,38)

Ἀδδί 1	Addi (Lk 3,28)

ἀδελφή 3 + 1 (Mt 3, Mk 5)
1. sister (Lk 10,39.40; 14,26; Acts 23,16); 2. fellow believer

Word groups	Lk	Acts	Mt	Mk
ἀδελφή + ἀδελφός	14,26		2	4
ἀδελφή + μήτηρ → ἀδελφός + μήτηρ	14,26		2	4

Literature

ARTZ-GRABNER, P., 'Brothers' and 'Sisters' in Documentary Papyri and in Early
Christianity. — *RivistBib* 50 (2002) 185-204.

ἀδελφός 24 + 57/58 (Mt 39, Mk 20)
1. brother (Lk 6,14); 2. fellow believer (Lk 22,32; Acts 15,1); 3. fellow Jew (Acts
22,1); 4. fellow countryman (Acts 7,23); 5. neighbor (Lk 6,41)

Word groups	Lk	Acts	Mt	Mk
ἀδελφός + ἀδελφή	14,26		2	4
ἀδελφός + μήτηρ → ἀδελφή + μήτηρ	8,19.20.21; 14,26	1,14	7	7
ἀδελφός + συγγενής + γείτων/γονεῖς + φιλός DENAUX 2009 L^n	14,12; 21,16		0	0
ἄνδρες ἀδελφοί (καὶ πατέρες) (SCa; VKb) → ἄνδρες voc.		1,16; 2,29.37; 7,2; 13,15.26.38; 15,7.13; 22,1; 23,1.6; 28,17	0	0
ἀδελφοί brothers of Jesus (VKa)	8,19.20.21	1,14	6	5

Characteristic of Luke

HENDRIKS 1986 468; MORGENTHALER 1958A

	Lk	Acts	Mt	Mk
ἀδελφέ singular; cf. Phm 7.20 BOISMARD 1984 cb99; NEIRYNCK 1985	6,42^2	9,17; 21,20; 22,13	0	0

Literature

VON BENDEMANN 2001 427: "Die Verbindung von φίλος mit 'Verwandten' und 'Nachbarn' ist
lukanisch'"; DENAUX 2009 lA^n [ἀδελφέ singular]; EASTON 1910 150 [ἀδελφοὶ καὶ συγγενεῖς
καὶ γείτονες: probably characteristic of L]; JEREMIAS 1980 107 [πέντε ἀδελφοί: trad.]: "Lukas
bevorzugt die Nachstellung der Kardinalzahl".147; RADL 1975 397 [ἀδελφός]; 399 [ἄνδρες
ἀδελφοί]; REHKOPF 1959 98 [ἀδελφέ: "Substantiva in Anrede bei den Synoptikern"];
SCHÜRMANN 1957 110-112.

ARTZ-GRABNER, P., 'Brothers' and 'Sisters' in Documentary Papyri and in Early
Christianity. — *RivistBib* 50 (2002) 185-204.

BAUCKHAM, R.J., The Brothers and Sisters of Jesus: An Epiphanian Response to John P.
Meier. —*JBL* 56 (1994) 686-700.

ἄδηλος 1	not evident, unmarked (Lk 11,44)

Literature

HAUCK 1934 [seltenes Alleinwort].

SCHWARZ, Günther, "Unkenntliche Gräber" (Lukas xi.44). — *NTS* 23 (1976-77) 345-346.
Esp. 345: "Fehlübersetzung bei Lukas" [of the aramaic ṭuš]. [NTA 21, 764]

ᾄδης 2 + 2 (Mt 2)	
1. world of the dead (Lk 10,15; 16,23; Acts 2,27.31); 2. death	

ἀδικέω 1 + 5 (Mt 1)	
1. hurt (Lk 10,19); 2. act unjustly (Acts 25,10); 3. mistreat (Acts 7,27)	

Word groups	Lk	Acts	Mt	Mk
ἀδικέω + double accusative	10,19	7,26; 25,10	1	0
ἀδικέομαι passive (*VK*a); cf. 1 Cor 6,7; 2 Cor 7,12; Rev 2,11		7,24	0	0

Characteristic of Luke	Lk	Acts	Mt	Mk
ἀδικέω and cognates ἀδικία, ἄδικος, ἀδίκημα; → ἀδικία, ἄδικος BOISMARD 1984 Eb26; DENAUX 2009 L***; GOULDER 1989*; NEIRYNCK 1985	10,19; (13,27; 16,8.9.10$^{1.2}$.11; 18,6.11)	(1,18); 7,24.26. 27; (8,23); (18,14); (24,15. 20); 25,10.11	1	0

Literature

DENAUX 2009 lAn; RADL 1975 397 [ἀδικέω; ἀδικέω + double acc.].

BORMANN, Lukas, *Recht, Gerechtigkeit und Religion*, 2001. Esp. 170.

ἀδικία 4 + 2	unjust deed

Word groups	Lk	Acts	Mt	Mk
οἰκονόμος τῆς ἀδικίας	16,8		0	0
πάντες ἐργάται ἀδικίας	13,27		0	0

Characteristic of Luke

CREDNER 1836 134 "in der Bedeutung Schlechtigkeit"; DENAUX 2009 L***; HAWKINS 1909 16

	Lk	Acts	Mt	Mk
(τῆς) ἀδικίας; cf. Rom 6,13; 2 Thess 2,10; Jam 3,6; 2 Pet 2,13.15 DENAUX 2009 L***; VOGEL 1899C	13,27; 16,8.9; 18,6	1,18; 8,23	0	0
ἀδικία and cognates ἀδικέω, ἄδικος, ἀδίκημα; → ἀδικέω, ἄδικος BOISMARD 1984 Eb26; DENAUX 2009 L***; GOULDER 1989*; NEIRYNCK 1985	(10,19); 13,27; 16,8.9.(10$^{1.2}$.11); 18,6.(11)	1,18; (7,24.26.27); 8,23; (18,14); (24,15.20); (25,10.11)	0	0

Literature

VON BENDEMANN 2001 430 [lukanisch]; COLLISON 1977 180 [noteworthy phenomena]; HAUCK 1934 [Vorzugswort]; JEREMIAS 1980 232 [πάντες ἐργάται ἀδικίας: semitisierende

Genitivverbindung red.; cit. Ψ 6,9 πάντες οἱ ἐργαζόμενοι τὴν ἀνομίαν]: "ἀδικία ist eine der zahlreichen lukanischen Korrekturen an einem Schriftzitat". 233 "semitisierende Gebrauch des Genitivs (τῆς) ἀδικίας als Ersatz für das Adjektiv bzw. Objektsakkusativ ist ein eingebürgerter Sprachgebrauch, den Lukas bereits vorfand" [trad.]; REHKOPF 1959 91 [(τῆς) ἀδικίας: vorlukanisch]; SCHÜRMANN 1961 271 [τῆς ἀδικίας: semitisch das Adj. ersetzend].

BORMANN, Lukas, *Recht, Gerechtigkeit und Religion*, 2001. Esp. 170.
CAMPS, Guiu M. – UBACH, B.M., Un sentido bíblico de ἄδικος, ἀδικία y la interpretación de Lc 16,1-13. — *EstBíb* 25 (1966) 75-82. [OT background].
TAEGER, Jens-Wilhelm, *Der Mensch und sein Heil*, 1982. Esp. 33-34: "Verwandte Begriffe (πονηρία, ἀδικία, κακία)".

ἄδικος 4 + 1 (Mt 1)
1. unbeliever; 2. unjust (Lk 16,10[1.2].12; 18,11)

Word groups	Lk	Acts	Mt	Mk
ἄδικος + δίκαιος → ἁμαρτωλός + δίκαιος		24,15	1	0

Characteristic of Luke → ἀδικέω, ἀδικία; cf. ἀδίκημα Acts 18,14; 24,20

BOISMARD 1984 Eb26; DENAUX 2009 L***; HAWKINS 1909 16; NEIRYNCK 1985; VOGEL 1899C

	Lk	Acts	Mt	Mk
ἄδικος and cognates ἀδικία, ἀδικέω, ἀδίκημα; → ἀδικία, ἀδικέω BOISMARD 1984 Eb26; DENAUX 2009 L***; GOULDER 1989*; NEIRYNCK 1985	(10,19;13,27); 16,(8.9.)10[1.2].1; 18,(6).11	(1,18; 7,24.26.27; 8,23; 18,14); 24,15.(20; 25,10.11)	1	0
→ ἀνάστασις (τῶν) δικαίων (καὶ ἀδίκων)				

Literature
COLLISON 1977 183 [linguistic usage of Luke's "other source-material": probable]; HAUCK 1934 [Vorzugswort].

BORMANN, Lukas, *Recht, Gerechtigkeit und Religion*, 2001. Esp. 171-172.
CAMPS, G.M. – UBACH, B.M., Un sentido bíblico de ἄδικος, ἀδικία y la interpretación de Lc 16,1-13. — *EstBíb* 25 (1966) 75-82. [OT background].

Ἀδμίν 1
Admin (Lk 3,33)

ἀδυνατέω 1 (Mt 1)
impersonal: it is impossible (Lk 1,37)

Literature
JEREMIAS 1980 54 [1,37 red.]: "οὐκ ἀδυνατήσει παρὰ τοῦ θεοῦ πᾶν ῥῆμα: ist ein freies Zitat von Gen 18,14 LXX: μὴ ἀδυνατεῖ παρὰ τῷ θεῷ ῥῆμα; Lukas hat ein πᾶν zugefügt und παρά mit dem Genitiv (LXX: Dativ) konstruiert. Sowohl das stilistische Feilen am LXX-Text wie die Verstärkung durch πᾶς ist typisch lukanisch".

ἀδύνατος 1 + 1 (Mt 1, Mk 1)
1. incapable (Acts 14,8); 2. impossible (Lk 18,27)

Word groups	Lk	Acts	Mt	Mk
ἀδύνατος noun (VKa)	18,27		0	0

ἀετός 1 (Mt 1)

eagle, vulture (Lk 17,37)

Literature

BRIDGE, Steven L., *"Where the Eagles Are Gathered": The Deliverance of the Elect in Lukan Eschatology* (JSNT SS, 240). Sheffield: Academic Press, 2003, xix-193 p. Esp. 58-60: "The meaning of ἀετός".

TOPEL, John, What Kind of a Sign Are Vultures? Luke 17,37b. — *Bib* 84 (2003) 403-411.

ἄζυμος 2 + 2 (Mt 1, Mk 2)

without yeast

Word groups	Lk	Acts	Mt	Mk
ἑορτὴ τῶν ἀζύμων	22,1		0	0
ἡμέρα τῶν ἀζύμων	22,7	12,3; 20,6	0	1
πάσχα + ἄζυμος	22,1.7		1	2

ἀθετέω 5 (Mk 2)

1. reject (Lk 10,16$^{1-4}$); 2. regard as invalid (Lk 7,30)

Characteristic of Luke

DENAUX 2009 L***†; HAWKINS 1909 16

Literature

HAUCK 1934 [Vorzugswort].

BORMANN, Lukas, *Recht, Gerechtigkeit und Religion*, 2001. Esp. 129-130.

ἀθροίζω 1

come together (Lk 24,33)

Literature

HAUCK 1934 [seltenes Alleinwort].

αἷμα 8 + 11/12 (Mt 11/12, Mk 3)

1. blood (Lk 8,43); 2. death; 3. killing

Word groups	Lk	Acts	Mt	Mk
αἷμα ῞Αβελ/Ζαχαρίου	11,51$^{1.2}$		2	0
αἷμα + διαθήκη	22,20		1	1
αἷμα + ἐκχέω/ἐκχύννω (LN: kill; SCa; VKa)	11,50; 22,20	22,20	1	1
ἅπτομαι + ῥύσις τοῦ αἵματος; cf. Mk 5,28-29 ἅπτομαι + πηγὴ αἵματος	8,44		0	0
ῥύσις (τοῦ) αἵματος (LN: menstrual flow)	8,43.44		0	1

Literature

JEREMIAS 1980 210 [αἷμα ῞Αβελ/Ζαχαρίου: trad.]: "Artikellosen Genitivverbindungen übernahm Lukas aus der Überlieferung".

DOLFE, Karl Gustav, The Greek Word of "Blood" and the Interpretation of Acts 20:28. — *SEÅ* 55 (1990) 64-70.

MORRIS, Leon, The Biblical Use of the Term "Blood". — *JTS* 53 (1952) 216-227.

SCHNEIDER, Gerhard, Engel und Blutschweiß (Lk 22,43-44): "Redaktionsgeschichte" im Dienste der Textkritik. — *BZ* NF 20 (1976) 112-116. Esp. 113-115: "Vokabular und Stil von Lk 22,43.44"; = ID., *Lukas, Theologe der Heilsgeschichte*, 1985, 153-157. Esp. 154-156.

WEISSENRIEDER, Annette, The Plague of Uncleanness? The Ancient Illness Construct "Issue of Blood" in Luke 8:43-48. — STEGEMANN, Wolfgang – MALINA, Bruce J. – THEISSEN, Gerd (eds.), *The Social Setting of Jesus and the Gospels*. Minneapolis, MN: Fortress, 2002, 207-222.

αἰνέω 3/4 + 3   praise

Word groups

	Lk	Acts	Mt	Mk
αἰνέω τὸν θεόν + verb of saying → δοξάζω/εὐλογέω τὸν θεόν + verb of saying DENAUX 2009 L[n]	2,13; 19,37(-38)		0	0
αἰνέω + λέγων	2,13		0	0
χαίρω αἰνέω→ εὐλογέω + χαρά	19,37		0	0

Characteristic of Luke

DENAUX 2009 LA*; HARNACK 1906 148; HAWKINS 1909B; PLUMMER 1922 lix

	Lk	Acts	Mt	Mk
αἰνέω τὸν θεόν → αἶνος τῷ θεῷ; δοξάζω/εὐλογέω τὸν θεόν; cf. αἰνέω τῷ θεῷ Rev 19,5 BOISMARD 1984 Ab30; DENAUX 2009 LA*; GOULDER 1989; NEIRYNCK 1985	2,13.20; 19,37; 24,53*	2,47; 3,8.9	0	0

Literature

VON BENDEMANN 2001 436: "αἰνέω τὸν θεόν findet sich im Neuen Testament nur beim auctor ad Theophilum"; COLLISON 1977 89 [noteworthy phenomena]; EASTON 1910 150 [probably characteristic of L]; GERSDORF 1816 230-232 [καὶ ἐξαίφνης ἐγένετο σὺν τῷ ἀγγέλῳ πλῆθος στρατιᾶς οὐρανίου αἰνούντων τὸν θεόν]; HAUCK 1934 [häufiges Alleinwort]; JEREMIAS 1980 68 [αἰνέω + λέγων: red.]; 83 [αἰνέω τὸν θεόν: red.]; REHKOPF 1959 91 [vorlukanisch]; SCHÜRMANN 1961 273.

GEORGE, Augustin, La prière. — ID., *Études*, 1978, 395-427. Esp. 402-405: "Le vocabulaire lucanien de la prière".

αἶνος 1 (Mt 1)   praise

Word groups

	Lk	Acts	Mt	Mk
αἶνος τῷ θεῷ → αἰνέω τὸν θεόν; δόξα θεῷ; εὐλογητός + θεός	18,43		0	0

Literature

EASTON 1910 150 [probably characteristic of L].

GEORGE, Augustin, La prière. — ID., *Études*, 1978, 395-427. Esp. 402-405: "Le vocabulaire lucanien de la prière".

αἴρω 20 + 9 (Mt 19/20, Mk 19[20]/21)

1. carry (Lk 5,24); 2. destroy; 3. execute (Lk 23,18); 4. withdraw (Lk 19,21)

Word groups	Lk	Acts	Mt	Mk
αἴρω (+) ἀπό (*LN*: cause to no longer experience; *SC*a; *VK*a) → **ἀπαίρομαι** ἀπό	8,12.18; 19,24.26	8,33[2]; 22,22	5	2
αἴρω τὸν λόγον → **ἀκούω/(ἀπο)δέχομαι** τὸν λόγον; cf. συναίρω λόγον Mt 18,23; 25,19	8,12		0	1
αἴρω + τὸν σταυρόν (*LN*: suffer unto death) → **βαστάζω** τὸν σταυρόν; cf. λαμβάνω τὸν σταυρόν Mt 10,38	9,23		2	2/3
αἴρω + τίθημι	19,21.22		0	1
αἴρω φωνήν λέγων	17,13		0	0
αἶρε DENAUX 2009 1A[n]	23,18	21,36; 22,22	0	0
αἴρομαι passive (*VK*b)	8,18; 9,17; 19,26	8,33[2]; 20,9	4	4

Characteristic of Luke	Lk	Acts	Mt	Mk
αἴρω (and cognate ἐπαίρω) φωνήν (*LN*: speak loudly) → **ἐπαίρω** τὴν φωνήν BOISMARD 1984 Ab45; NEIRYNCK 1985;	17,13	4,24	0	0

Literature

COLLISON 1977 36 [linguistic usage of Luke: certain]; DENAUX 2009 LA[n] [αἴρω φωνήν (*LN*: speak loudly)] ; EASTON 1910 166 [αἴρω φωνήν: cited by Weiss as characteristic of L, and possibly corroborative]; JEREMIAS 1980 68 [αἴρω φωνήν + λέγων: red.]; 303 [αἶρε: red.]; SCHÜRMANN 1957 122.

WILCOX, Max, *The Semitisms of Acts*, 1965. Esp. 67-68 [Lk 23,18; Acts 22,22].

αἰσθάνομαι 1   able to understand (Lk 9,45)

Literature

HAUCK 1934 [seltenes Alleinwort].

αἰσχύνη 1

1. shame (Lk 14,9); 2. what causes shame; 3. indecent behavior

Literature

PAFFENROTH 1997 79 [αἰσχύνη/αἰσχύνομαι/καταισχύνω: prelukan].

αἰσχύνομαι 1   be ashamed (Lk 16,3)

Literature

JEREMIAS 1980 256 [trad.]: "In den Geschichtsbüchern des NT nur hier"; PAFFENROTH 1997 79 [αἰσχύνη/αἰσχύνομαι/καταισχύνω: prelukan].

VORSTER, Willem S., Aischunomai *en stamverwante woorde in die Nuwe Testament*. Pretoria: Universiteit van Suid-Africa, 1979, XVIII-299 p. Esp. 67-87: "Αἰσχύνομαι"; 87-100: "ἐπαισχύνομαι"; 100-121: "καταισχύνω".

αἰτέω 11/12 + 10 (Mt 14, Mk 9/10)   ask for

Word groups	Lk	Acts	Mt	Mk
αἰτέομαι + ὅπως		9,2; 25,3	0	0
αἰτέω ἀπό → **αἰτέω/ζητέω** παρά + gen.;	12,20*		1	0
ἀπαιτέω/ἐκζητέω/κωλύω ἀπό				
αἰτέω + ἀποκρίνομαι → **(ἐπ)ἐρωτάω** +		25,3(-4).15(-16)	2	1
ἀποκρίνομαι				
αἰτέω + (ἐπι)δίδωμι→ **αἰτέω** + λαμβάνω/	6,30;	13,21	6	2
παρατίθημι; **δίδωμι** + ζητέω; **εὑρίσκω** + (ἀνα/	11,9.11.			
ἐπι)ζητέω; cf. αἰτέω + ἀποδίδωμι Mt 27,58	12.13			
αἰτέω λαμβάνω → **αἰτέω** +	11,10		3	1
(ἐπι)δίδωμι/παρατίθημι				
αἰτέω + παρά + genitive → **αἰτέω** ἀπό		3,2; 9,2	0	0
αἰτέω + παρατίθημι → **αἰτέω** +	12,48		0	0
(ἐπι)δίδωμι/λαμβάνω				
αἰτία θανάτου → **αἴτιος/ἄξιος** θανάτου		13,28; 28,18	0	0
ἐλεημοσύνην αἰτέω → ἐλεημοσύνην		3,2		
δίδωμι/ποιέω				
VOGEL 1899C				
αἰτέομαι middle (*VK*a)	23,23.25.	3,14; 7,46; 9,2; 12,20;	5	6/7
	52	13,21.28; 25,3.15		

Characteristic of Luke	Lk	Acts	Mt	Mk
αἰτέομαι + infinitive; cf. Jn 4,9; Eph 3,13	23,23	3,14; 7,46;	0	0
BOISMARD 1984 Bb92; NEIRYNCK 1985		13,28		

Literature

CADBURY 1920A; DENAUX 2009 1A[n] [αἰτέομαι + infinitive]; JEREMIAS 1980 304 [αἰτέομαι + inf.: red.]; SCHÜRMANN 1957 103 [αἰτέω and composita].

GEORGE, Augustin, La prière. — ID., *Études*, 1978, 395-427. Esp. 402-405: "Le vocabulaire lucanien de la prière".

αἴτημα 1	request (Lk 23,24)

Literature

BORMANN, Lukas, *Recht, Gerechtigkeit und Religion*, 2001. Esp. 172.

αἰτία 1 + 8 (Mt 3, Mk 1)	

1. reason (Lk 8,47; Acts 28,20); 2. reason for accusation (Acts 13,28); 3. accusation (Acts 25,18); 4. guilt; 5. relation

Word groups	Lk	Acts	Mt	Mk
αἰτία θανάτου → **αἴτιος/ἄξιος** θανάτου		13,28; 28,18	0	0
BOISMARD 1984 Aa113				
δι' ἣν αἰτίαν/ ἡ αἰτία δι' ἥν; cf. 2 Tim 1,6.12; Tit 1,13; Heb 2,11	8,47	10,21; 22,24;	0	0
DENAUX 2009 1A[n]		23,28		

Literature

RADL 1975 397 [αἰτία; δι' ἣν αἰτίαν / ἡ αἰτία δι' ἥν].

BORMANN, Lukas, *Recht, Gerechtigkeit und Religion*, 2001. Esp. 172-173.

αἴτιος 3 + 1
1. reason (Acts 19,40); 2. guilt (Lk 23,4.14.22)

Characteristic of Luke
BOISMARD 1984 Ab67; HAWKINS 1909LA; MORGENTHALER 1958*; NEIRYNCK 1985; PLUMMER 1922 lii; VOGEL 1899A

	Lk	Acts	Mt	Mk
αἴτιος θανάτου → αἰτία/ἄξιος θανάτου VOGEL 1899C	23,22		0	0
μηδὲν/οὐδὲν/οὐθὲν αἴτιον (no guilt) GOULDER 1989; VOGEL 1899A	23,4.14.22	19,40	0	0

Literature
CADBURY 1920A; DENAUX 2009 Lan; Lan [μηδὲν/οὐδὲν/οὐθὲν αἴτιον (no guilt)]; HAUCK 1934 [seltenes Alleinwort]; JEREMIAS 1980 300-301 [οὐδὲν ... αἴτιον: red.].

BORMANN, Lukas, *Recht, Gerechtigkeit und Religion*, 2001. Esp. 173.

αἰφνίδιος 1   immediately (Lk 21,34)

Literature
HAUCK 1934 [seltenes Alleinwort].

DAUBE, David, *The Sudden in the Scriptures*. Leiden: Brill, 1964, VII-86 p. Esp. 28-29.

αἰχμαλωτίζω 1
1. take captive (Lk 21,24); 2. get control of

αἰχμάλωτος 1   captive (Lk 4,18)

Literature
HAUCK 1934 [seltenes Alleinwort].

αἰών 7 + 2 (Mt 8/9, Mk 4)
1. era (Lk 20,34); 2. universe (Lk 16,8); 3. world system

Word groups	Lk	Acts	Mt	Mk
ὁ αἰὼν ἐκεῖνος/ὁ ἐρχόμενος (*SC*d; *VK*b) → ὁ αἰὼν οὗτος; ἡ ἡμέρα ἐκείνη; αἱ ἡμέραι ἐκεῖναι; ὁ ἐκεῖνος καιρός; νὺξ ἐκείνη; ἐν ἐκείνῃ τῇ ὥρᾳ / τῇ ὥρᾳ ἐκείνῃ; cf. ὁ αἰὼν ὁ (+) μέλλων Mt 12,32; Heb 6,5	18,30; 20,35		0	1
ὁ αἰὼν οὗτος (*SC*a; *VK*a) → ὁ αἰὼν ἐκεῖνος; ἡ ἡμέρα αὕτη; αἱ ἡμέραι αὗται; οὗτος καιρός; αὕτη ἡ νύξ	16,8; 20,34		1/3	0/1
εἰς τὸν αἰῶνα / τοὺς αἰῶνας (*LN*: forever; *SC*c; *VK*c-d) → βασιλεύω εἰς τοὺς αἰῶνας	1,33.55		1/2	2
υἱοὶ τοῦ αἰῶνος τούτου (*LN*: non-religious people) DENAUX 2009 Ln	16,8; 20,34		0	0

Characteristic of Luke	Lk	Acts	Mt	Mk
ἀπ' αἰῶνος (*LN*: long ago; *SC*b; *VK*e); cf. ἀπὸ τῶν αἰώνων Eph 3,9; Col 1,26; ἐκ τοῦ αἰῶνος Jn 9,32; Gal 1,4 BOISMARD 1984 Ab105; HARNACK 1906 144; NEIRYNCK 1985; PLUMMER 1922 lii	1,70	3,21; 15,18	0	0

Literature

DENAUX 2009 lA[n] [ἀπ' αἰῶνος]; JEREMIAS 1980 74 [ἀπ' αἰῶνος: red.]: "Apg 15,18 cit. Am 9,11 … Wir haben einen der zahlreichen Fälle vor uns, in denen Lukas den Bibeltext ungenau zitiert bzw. an ihm feilt".

FAU, G., Sur le sens divers du mot grec *'aiôn*. — *Cahiers du Cercle Ernest-Renan* 20 (1977) 15-16. [NTA 17, 438]
JASIŃSKI, Andrzej S., Ἀιών w Nowym Testamencie. — *RoczTK* 33/1 (1986) 79-99.
JENNINGS, G.E., *A Survey of αἰών and αἰώνιος and Their Meaning in the New Testament*. Diss. Southern Baptist Theological Seminary, 1948.
LYS, D., Des ères du Nouveau Testament. — *Études Théologiques et Religieuses* (Montpellier) 72 (1997) 515-542.
PRETE, Benedetto, Valore dell'espressione ἀφ' ἡμερῶν ἀρχαίων in *Atti* 15,7: Nesso cronologico, oppure istanza teologica della Chiesa delle origini? — *BibOr* 13 (1971) 119-133; = ID., *L'opera di Luca*, 1986, 494-508. Esp. 500-503: "L'uso dell'espressione ἀπ' αἰῶνος negli scritti di Luca"; 503-504: "Le espressioni ἀπ' ἀρχῆς e ἐν ἀρχῇ negli scritti di Luca"; 504-506: "La formula ἀφ' ἡμερῶν ἀρχαίων nel contesto di Atti 15,1-35"; 506-508: "La formula ἀφ' ἡμερῶν ἀρχαίων: espressione di un'istanza della Chiesa primitiva".

αἰώνιος 4 + 2 (Mt 6, Mk 3[4]) — eternal (Lk 16,9)

Word groups	Lk	Acts	Mt	Mk
ζωή (+) αἰώνιος (*SC*a; *VK*a)	10,25; 18,18.30	13,46.48	3	2
ζωὴν αἰώνιον κληρονομέω; cf. βασιλείαν + κληρονομέω Mt 25,34	10,25; 18,18		1	1

Literature

HILL, David, *Greek Words and Hebrew Meanings*, 1967. Esp. 191-192: "The use of ζωὴ αἰώνιος in the New Testament: The Synoptic Gospels".

ἀκάθαρτος 6 + 5 (Mt 2, Mk 11) — defiled (religiously)

Word groups	Lk	Acts	Mt	Mk
ἀκάθαρτον (+) πνεῦμα (*LN*: unclean spirit; *SC*a) → τὸ πνεῦμα (τὸ) πονηρόν	4,36; 6,18; 8,29; 9,42; 11,24	5,16; 8,7	2	11
ἀκάθαρτος + πνεῦμα + δαιμόνιον; cf. Rev 18,2[1-3] DENAUX 2009 L[n]	4,33; 8,29; 9,42		0	0
δαιμόνιον ἀκάθαρτον	4,33		0	0
(τὸ) ἀκάθαρτον / τὰ ἀκάθαρτα (*VK*a)		10,14; 11,8	0	0
ἀκάθαρτος unclean person		10,28	0	0

Literature

COLLISON 1977 171 [πνεῦμα ἀκάθαρτον: linguistic usage of Luke: likely]; JEREMIAS 1980 202 [ἀκάθαρτον πνεῦμα: trad.].

ἄκανθα 4 (Mt 5, Mk 3)	thorn plant (Lk 6,44; 8,7[1.2].14)

ἀκαταστασία 1

1. rebellion (Lk 21,9); 2. riot

Literature

HAUCK 1934 [seltenes Alleinwort].
BORMANN, Lukas, *Recht, Gerechtigkeit und Religion*, 2001. Esp. 112.

ἀκοή 1 + 2 (Mt 4, Mk 3)

1. hearing (Lk 7,1?); 2. ability to hear; 3. what is heard; 4. news; 5. pay attention to;
BDAG: 6. "the organ with which one hears, ear" (Lk 7,1: εἰς τὰς ἀκοή τινος)

Word groups	Lk	Acts	Mt	Mk
ἀκοῇ ἀκούω (*LN*: listen carefully; *VK*a)		28,26	1	0
εἰσφέρω εἰς τὰς ἀκοάς (*LN*: [a]cause to hear; [b]speak about)		17,[a]20	0	0

Literature

CADBURY 1920A; PLUMMER 1922 lxii [In the use of certain *prepositions* he has some characteristic expressions: εἰς τὰ ὦτα (i.44, ix.44) and εἰς τὰς ἀκοάς (vii.1), ἐν τοῖς ὠσίν (iv.21)...].

ἀκολουθέω 17 + 4 (Mt 25, Mk 18/20[21])

1. go/come behind (Lk 22,54; Acts 21,36); 2. accompany as follower (Lk 7,9); 3. be a disciple (Lk 9,23)

Word groups	Lk	Acts	Mt	Mk
ἀκολούθει/ἀκολουθείτω μοι	5,27; 9,23.59; 18,22	12,8	4	3
ἀκολουθέω + to leave (ἀφίημι/ἀπέρχομαι/ ἀποτάσσομαι/καταλείπω/ πωλέω) somebody/ something	5,11.28; 9,59.61; 18,22.28		5	3
ἀκολουθέω μετά + genitive (*VK*b)	9,49		0	0
ἀκολουθέω + ὄχλος/πλῆθος → **συμπαραγίνομαι/συμπνίγω/συμπορεύομαι/ συνάγω/συναντάω/σύνειμι/συνέρχομαι/ συνέχω** + ὄχλος/πλῆθος	7,9; 9,11; 23,27	21,36	7	3
ἀκολουθέω absolute (*VK*a)	22,54	12,9; 21,36	2	3
ἠκολούθει; cf. Jn 6,2; 18,15; Rev 6,8; 19,14; συνηκολούθει Mk 14,51	5,28; 18,43; 22,54; 23,27	12,9; 21,36	1	3

Literature

JEREMIAS 1980 155 [τῷ ἀκολουθοῦντι αὐτῷ ὄχλῳ: red.]: "Lukas setzt gelegentlich das Partizip zwischen Artikel und Substantiv"; RADL 1975 398 [ἀκολουθέω; ἠκολούθει]; SCHNEIDER 1969 76 [ἠκολούθει].

GONZÁLEZ SILVA, Santiago, El seguimiento de Cristo en los logia ἀκολουθεῖν. — *Claretianum* 14 (1974) 115-162.
GREGER, Barbara, *Hlk 'hry* und die Folgen. — *BibNot* 111 (2002) 23.
TAEGER, Jens-Wilhelm, *Der Mensch und sein Heil*, 1982. Esp. 151-152.

ἀκούω 65 + 89/91 (Mt 63/64, Mk 43[44]/47)

1. hear (Lk 1,41); 2. be able to hear (Lk 8,8[1]); 3. receive news (Lk 9,7); 4. pay attention to (Acts 28,28); 5. obey (Lk 9,35); 6. understand (Lk 8,8[2]); 7. hear legal case (Acts 25,22)

Word groups	Lk	Acts	Mt	Mk
ἀκοῇ ἀκούω (*LN*: listen carefully; *VK*e)		28,26	1	0
ἀκούσας (+) ἀποκρίνομαι/λέγω/ εἶπον → ἀκούων + λέγω/εἶπον; cf. παρακούσας + λέγω Mk 5,36	1,66; 7,9; 8,50; 14,15; 18,22.26; 20,16	2,37; 4,24; 11,18; 17,32; 19,28; 21,20; 22,26	7	6
ἀκούω + genitive (*VK*a) → ἀκούω αὐτοῦ / αὐτῶν / τῶν λόγων / τινὸς λαλοῦντος	2,46.47; 6,18.47; 9,35; 10,16[1.2]; 15,1.25; 16,29.31; 18,36; 19,48; 21,38	1,4; 2,6.11; 3,22.23; 4,19; 6,11.14; 7,34.37*; 8,30; 9,7; 10,46; 11,7; 14,9; 15,12.13; 17,32; 18,26; 22,1.7.22; 24,4.24; 25,22[1.2]; 26,3.29	3	9
ἀκούω (+) ἀπό/παρά + genitive (*VK*c) DENAUX 2009 1A[n]	22,71	9,13; 10,22; 28,22	0	0
ἀκούω (+) αὐτοῦ → ἀκούω αὐτῶν DENAUX 2009 1An	2,47; 6,18; 9,35; 15,1; 19,48; 21,38	3,22; 6,11.14; 7,37*; 8,30; 18,26; 22,22; 24,24; 25,22[2]	0	4
ἀκούω + βλέπω / θεωρέω / ὁράω/εἶδον → ἀκούω + συνίημι	2,20; 7,22[1]; 8,10.18; 10,24[1.2.3]; 23,8	2,33; 4,20; 7,34; 8,6; 19,26; 22,14.15; 28,26.27[2]	8	4
ἀκούω + δέχομαι	8,13	8,14; 11,1	1	1
ἀκούω + εἰς τὸ οὖς / τὰ ὦτα (*LN*: hear in secret)		11,22	1	0
ἀκούω (+) θαυμάζω → (ὁράω/)εἶδον + θαυμάζω	2,18; 7,9		2	0
ἀκούω κωφός	7,22[2]		1	1
ἀκούω τινὸς λαλοῦντος; cf. Jn 1,37 BOISMARD 1984 Ba10		2,6.11; 6,11; 10,46; 14,9	0	0
ἀκούω (+) τὸν λόγον / τοὺς λόγους / ῥήματα → ἀκούω τὸν λόγον; ἀκούω τὸν λόγον τοῦ θεοῦ/ κυρίου; αἴρω/(ἀπο)δέχομαι (τὸν) λόγον/λόγια; cf. ἠκούσθη + ὁ λόγος Acts 11,22; παρακούω τὸν λόγον Mk 5,36	5,1; 8,15.21; 10,39; 11,28	2,22; 4,4; 5,5[1].24; 10,22.44; 13,7.44; 15,7; 19,10	9	3
ἀκούω + τῶν λόγων	6,47		0	0
ἀκούω (+) οὖς	8,8[1]; 12,3; 14,35[1]	11,22; 28,27[1.2]	7	3/4
ἀκούω + συνίημι → ἀκούω + βλέπω / θεωρέω / ὁράω/εἶδον	8,10	28,26.27[2]	6	2
ἀκούω τι περί τινος DENAUX 2009 L[n]	9,9;16,2		0	0
ἀκούων + λέγω/εἶπον → ἀκούσας + ἀποκρίνομαι / λέγω/εἶπον	19,11; 20,45	9,21	0	1
τοῖς ὠσὶν βαρέως ἀκούω (*LN*: be mentally dull)		28,27[1]	1	0
ὦτα ἀκούειν ἀκουέτω (*SC*b; *VK*d)	8,8[1.2]; 14,35[1.2]		0/3	2/3
ἀκούων in genitive absolute DENAUX 2009 L[n]	19,11; 20,45		0	0
ἀκούομαι passive (*VK*b)	12,3	11,22	2	1

Characteristic of Luke

GASTON 1973 65 [Lked?]; MORGENTHALER 1958A

	Lk	Acts	Mt	Mk
verb of movement + ἀκούειν/ ἀκοῦσαι → verb of movement + ὑπακοῦσαι DENAUX 2009 L***	5,15; 6,18; 11,31; 15,1	13,44	0	0
ἀκούομεν/ἠκούσαμεν 1st person plural DENAUX 2009 1A*	4,23; 22,71	2,8.11; 4,20; 6,11.14; 15,24; 17,32²; 19,2; 21,12	0	1
ἀκούσας δέ → ἀκούων δέ; cf. Jn 11,4 BOISMARD 1984 cb98; GOULDER 1989; NEIRYNCK 1985	7,3.9; 14,15; 18,22.36; 20,16	2,37; 5,21; 7,12; 8,14; 11,18; 14,14; 17,32; 18,26; 19,5.28; 22,2.26; 23,16; 24,22*	7/8	1
ἀκούω + predicative participle DENAUX 2009 1A*	4,23; 18,36	6,14; 7,12; 8,30; 9,4; 10,33; 11,7; 22,7; 26,14	0	0
ἀκούω (+) αὐτῶν → ἀκούω αὐτοῦ DENAUX 2009 LA*	2,46; 16,29	2,6.11; 10,46	0	1
ἀκούω τὸν λόγον / τοὺς λόγους / ῥήματα; ἀκούω τὸν λόγον τοῦ θεοῦ/κυρίου; αἴρω/(ἀπο) δέχομαι (τὸν) λόγον/λόγια; cf. ἠκούσθη ὁ λόγος Acts 11,22; παρακούω τὸν λόγον Mk 5,36 HAWKINS 1909add	5,1; 8,15.21; 10,39; 11,28	4,4; 10,44; 13,7.44; 15,7; 19,10	6	3
ἀκούω τὸν λόγον τοῦ θεοῦ/κυρίου → ἀκούω τὸν λόγον / τοὺς λόγους / ῥήμα BOISMARD 1984 Ab31; DENAUX 2009 LA*; GOULDER 1989; NEIRYNCK 1985	5,1; 8,21; 10,39 (αὐτοῦ); 11,28	13,7.44; 19,10	0	0
ἀκούω ταῦτα; cf. Jn 9,40; Rev 22,8 BOISMARD 1984 Bb59; DENAUX 2009 L ***; NEIRYNCK 1985	4,28; 7,9; 14,15; 16,14; 18,23; 19,11	5,5 v.l.11; 7,54; 11,18; 17,8; 21,12; 24,22*	0	0
ἀκούω περί + genitive BOISMARD 1984 Bb25; DENAUX 2009 L***; GOULDER 1989; NEIRYNCK 1985	7,3; 9,9; 16,2; 23,8	9,13; 11,22; 17,32; 24,24	0	2
ἀκούω δέ → ἀκούσας δέ BOISMARD 1984 Ab46; GOULDER 1989; NEIRYNCK 1985	19,11; 20,45	5,5; 7,54; 13,48	0	0
ὁ δὲ ἀκούων/ἀκούσας; cf. Jn 8,9; ὁ δὲ Ἰησοῦς ἀκούσας Lk 8,50 BOISMARD 1984 cb142; NEIRYNCK 1985	6,49; 18,23	4,24; 5,33; 21,20	2	1
ἤκουεν/ἤκουον → ὑπήκουεν/ὑπήκουον HARNACK 1906 33	10,39; 16,14	2,6; 10,46; 15,12; 16,14; 22,22	0	4
πάντες οἱ ἀκούοντες/ἀκούσαντες → πᾶς ὁ + part. BOISMARD 1984 Ab16; DENAUX 2009 1A*; HARNACK 1906 147; NEIRYNCK 1985;	1,66; 2,18.47	5,5.11; 9,21; 10,44; 26,29	0	0

Literature

VON BENDEMANN 2001 435: "ἀκούειν im gen. abs. findet sich im Neuen Testament nur zweimal"; DENAUX 2009 1Aⁿ [ἀκούων δέ]; GERSDORF 1816 240 [καὶ πάντες οἱ ἀκούσαντες ἐθαύμασεν περὶ τῶν λαληθέντων]; JEREMIAS 1980 72 [πάντες οἱ ἀκούοντες/ἀκούσαντες: red.]; 124 [ἀκούω + pred. part.: red.]; 255 [ἀκούω τι περί + gen.: red.]; 258 [ἤκουον δέ: red.]; 277 [ἀκούων in gen. abs.: red.]; RADL 1975 398 [ἀκούω; ἀκούω + gen.; ἀκούω αὐτοῦ; ἀκούω ταῦτα; ἀκούομεν 1st pers. pl.; ἀκούσας δέ; ἠκούσαμεν]; 416 [ἀκούω τὸν λόγον]; SCHNEIDER 1969 131: "Beachtet man Formen von ἀκούω in der ersten Person plural, so zeigt sich ein deutliches luk Übergewicht".

DANOVE, Paul, The Grammatical Uses of ἀκούω: In the Septuagint & the New Testament.
— *Forum* 2 (1999) 239-260.
—,Verbs of Experience, 1999. Esp. 153-154.171-172.
—, A Comparison of the Usage of ἀκούω and ἀκούω-Compounds in the Septuagint and
New Testament. — *FilolNT* 14 (2001) 65-85.
MOEHRING, Horst R., The Verb ἀκούειν in Acts IX 7 and XXII 9. — *NT* 3 (1959) 80-99.
STEUERNAGEL, Gert, Ἀκούοντες μὲν τῆς φωνῆς (Apg 9.7): Ein Genitiv in der
Apostelgeschichte. — *NTS* 35 (1989) 625-627.
TAEGER, Jens-Wilhelm, *Der Mensch und sein Heil*, 1982. Esp. 153-155.

ἀκριβῶς 1 + 5 (Mt 1)   accurately (Lk 1,3; Acts 18,25)

Word groups	Lk	Acts	Mt	Mk
ἀκριβέστερον comparative (*VK*a) BOISMARD 1984 Aa36		18,26; 23,15.20; 24,22	0	0

Characteristic of Luke
PLUMMER 1922 lix

Literature
DENAUX 2009 lAn; GERSDORF 1816 162 [παρηκολουθηκότι ἀκριβῶς]: "ἀκριβῶς und
ἀκριβέστερον ist auch sonst dem Lucas nicht ungewöhlich"; RADL 1975 398 [ἀκριβῶς;
ἀκριβέστερον].

ALEXANDER, Loveday, *The Preface to Luke's Gospel*, 1993. Esp. 131.
CADBURY, Henry J., Commentary on the Preface of Luke, 1922. Esp. 504.
KÜRZINGER, Joseph, Lk 1,3: ... ἀκριβῶς καθεξῆς σοι γράψαι. — *BZ* NF 18 (1974)
249-255. [NTA 19, 575]

ἄκρον 1 (Mt 2, Mk 2)
1. extreme boundary; 2. tip, top (Lk 16,24)

ἀλάβαστρος/ον 1 (Mt 1, Mk 2)   alabaster jar (Lk 7,37)

ἅλας 2 (Mt 2, Mk 3/4)   salt (Lk 14,34$^{1.2}$)

Literature
HUTTON, W.R., The Salt Sections. — *ExpT* 58 (1946-47) 166-168.
SHILLINGTON, George, W., Salt of the Earth? (Mt 5:13/Lk14:34f) . — *ExpT* 112 (2001)
120-121.
SCHWARZ, Günther, Καλον το αλας. — *BibNot* 7 (1978) 32-35.

ἀλείφω 3 (Mt 1, Mk 2)   anoint

Word groups	Lk	Acts	Mt	Mk
ἀλείφω + ἔλαιον; cf. χρίω + ἔλαιον Heb 1,9	7,46[1]		0	1
ἀλείφω (τῷ) μύρῳ DENAUX 2009 L^n	7,38.46[2]		0	0

Literature

COLLISON 1977 36 [linguistic usage of Luke's "other source-material": likely]

RAVENS, David A.S., The Setting of Luke's Account of the Anointing: Luke 7.2–8.3. — *NTS* 34 (1988) 282-292.

ἀλέκτωρ 3 (Mt 3, Mk 4)	rooster (Lk 22,34.60.61)

ἄλευρον 1 (Mt 1)	wheat flour (Lk 13,21)

Literature

CADBURY 1920A

ἀλήθεια 3 + 3 (Mt 1, Mk 3)	truth (Acts 26,25)			
Characteristic of Luke	Lk	Acts	Mt	Mk
ἐπ' ἀληθείας (*LN*: really; *S*Ca; *VK*a)	4,25; 20,21;	4,27;	0	2
BOISMARD 1984 cb73; NEIRYNCK 1985; PLUMMER 1922 lix	22,59	10,34		

Literature

COLLISON 1977 136 [ἐπ' ἀληθείας: linguistic usage of Luke: probable]; JEREMIAS 1980 126 [ἐπ' ἀληθείας: trad.].

ἀληθινός 1	
1. real; 2. true (Lk 16,11); 3. genuine	

Word groups	Lk	Acts	Mt	Mk
τὸ ἀληθινόν (*VK*b); cf. ὁ ἀληθινός 1 Jn 5,20[1.2]; Rev 3,7	16,11		0	0

ἀλήθω 1 (Mt 1)	grind grain (Lk 17,35)

Literature

JEREMIAS 1980 270 [ἔσονται ... ἀλήθουσαι: red.].

ἀληθῶς 3 + 1 (Mt 3, Mk 2)	really (Acts 12,11)			
Characteristic of Luke				
CREDNER 1836 134				
	Lk	Acts	Mt	Mk
ἀληθῶς λέγω ὑμῖν → ἀμὴν/ναὶ λέγω ὑμῖν	9,27; 12,44; 21,3		0	0
GOULDER 1989; HAWKINS 1909add				

Literature

COLLISON 1977 149 [noteworthy phenomena]; DENAUX 2009 L[n] [ἀληθῶς λέγω ὑμῖν]; HAUCK 1934 [häufiges Alleinwort; Vorzugsverbindung: ἀληθῶς λέγω ὑμῖν]; JEREMIAS 1980 221 [red.]; SCHNEIDER 1969 88.163 [ἀληθῶς im Munde Jesu: Vorzugswörter und -ausdrücke des Luk].

ἁλιεύς 1 (Mt 2, Mk 2)	fisherman (Lk 5,2)

ἀλλά 35/38 + 30 (Mt 37, Mk 45)

1. but (Lk 1,60); 2. and; 3. yet (Lk 6,27); 4. certainly

Word groups	Lk	Acts	Mt	Mk
ἀλλά γε (VKe); cf. ἀλλὰ μενοῦνγε Phil 3,8	24,21		0	0
ἀλλ᾽ ἐάν (SCa)	13,3.5; 16,30		1	0/1
ἀλλ᾽ ἤ (LN: but; VKd)	12,51		0	0
ἀλλ᾽ ἰδού → ἤ/πλὴν ἰδού		13,25	0	0
ἀλλ᾽ ἵνα (VKc)		4,17	0	2
ἀλλ᾽ ὅταν DENAUX 2009 Lⁿ	14,10.13		0	0
ἀλλὰ νῦν → νῦν δέ	22,36		0	0
ἀλλ᾽ οὐ/οὐδέ/οὐχί (SCb; VKb)	17,8; 21,9; 23,15	7,48; 19,2	0	4
ἀλλὰ οὐαί → πλὴν οὐαί	11,42		0	0
δοκεῖτε ὅτι ...; οὐχί, λέγω ὑμῖν, ἀλλ᾽... DENAUX 2009 Lⁿ	12,51; 13,(2-)3.(4-)5		0	0
οὐ/οὐδὲ/οὐδεὶς ... ἀλλά	4,4*; 5,31.32; 7,7; 8,16.27.52; 9,56*; 11,33; 18,13; 20,21.38; 22,26.53; 24,6	1,(7-)8; 2,(15-)16; 4,(16-)17.32; 5,4.13; 7,39; 10,(34-)35.41; 13,25; 16,37; 18,(20-)21; 19,26.27; 21,13.24; 26,(19-)20.25.29; 27,10	27	24
οὐ μόνον (δὲ) ... ἀλλά / οὐ ... μόνος ... ἀλλά	4,4*	19,26.27; 21,13; 26,29; 27,10	2	0

Characteristic of Luke	Lk	Acts	Mt	Mk
ἀλλὰ καί (VKa); cf. ἀλλά γε καί Lk 24,21; ἀλλὰ κἄν Mt 21,21 DENAUX 2009 IA*; GOULDER 1989	12,7; 16,21; 24,22	19,27; 21,13; 26,29; 27,10	0	0
οὐχὶ ... ἀλλά DENAUX 2009 L***; GOULDER 1989*; HAWKINS 1909L	1,60; 12,51; 13,3.5; 16,30		0	0

Literature

COLLISON 1977 100 [ἀλλὰ καί: noteworthy phenomena]; 120 [οὐχὶ ἀλλά: linguistic usage of Luke's "other source-material": certain]; EASTON 1910 149 [οὐχί, ἀλλά: especially characteristic of L]; GERSDORF 1816 204 [οὐχί ... ἀλλά]: "so schreibt nur Lucas und Paulus"; RADL 1975 398 [ἀλλά; ἀλλὰ καί]; 421 [οὐ μόνον ... ἀλλὰ καί]; REHKOPF 1959 96 [οὐχὶ ... ἀλλά (ἀλλ᾽ οὐχί): vorlukanisch]; SCHÜRMANN 1957 121 [ἀλλὰ νῦν: luk R unwahrscheinlich]; 1961 283-284 [οὐχὶ ... ἀλλά (ἀλλ᾽ οὐχί): protoluk R nicht beweisbar].

MINEAR, Paul S., A Note on Luke XXII,36. — NT 7 (1964-65) 128-134. Esp. 133-134 [ἀλλὰ νῦν]: "To Luke it was on the very night (and at the very *table* where) Jesus took bread *that he was betrayed*. It is this betrayal, set over against Jesus' intercession, that marks for Luke the extent and the limit of 'the power of darkness' (vs. 53), and the boundary between the two kingdoms (vs.24-30)".

THRALL, Margaret E., *Greek Particles in the New Testament*, 1962. Esp. 11-16 [ἀλλά γε καί, ἀλλὰ μενοῦν γε καί]; 16-20 [ἀλλ᾽ ἤ for ἀλλά].

WILSON, W.A.A., "But me no Buts". — BTrans 15 (1964) 173-180.

ἀλλήλων 11 + 8/9 (Mt 3, Mk 5) — each other

Word groups	Lk	Acts	Mt	Mk
ἀλλήλων + ἐκεῖνος		21,6	0	0
διαλογίζομαι πρὸς ἀλλήλους	20,14		0	1
εἰμί + ἀσύμφωνος + πρὸς ἀλλήλους		28,25	0	0
(δια/συλ)λαλέω πρὸς ἀλλήλους	2,15; 4,36; 6,11	26,31	0	0
DENAUX 2009 Laⁿ				
λέγω πρὸς ἀλλήλους; cf. διαλέγομαι +	8,25; 24,32	28,4	0	1
πρὸς ἀλλήλους Mk 9,34				
λόγους + ἀντιβάλλω πρὸς ἀλλήλους	24,17		0	0
μετ᾽ ἀλλήλων (VKc)	23,12		0	0
ὁμιλέω πρὸς ἀλλήλους	24,14		0	0
συμβάλλω πρὸς ἀλλήλους		4,15	0	0

Characteristic of Luke

GASTON 1973 65 [Lked?]; GOULDER 1989; SCHÜRMANN 1957 11, n. 45.

	Lk	Acts	Mt	Mk
πρὸς ἀλλήλους (SCa; VKa) → πρὸς αὐτόν/ αὐτούς/ἑαυτόν/ἑαυτούς DENAUX 2009 L***	2,15; 4,36; 6,11; 8,25; 20,14; 24,14.17.32	2,7*; 4,15; 26,31; 28,4.25	0	4

Literature

COLLISON 1977 201 [linguistic usage of Luke: certain]; 202 [πρὸς ἀλλήλους: linguistic usage of Luke: certain]; DENAUX 2009 Lan; JEREMIAS 1980 84 [πρὸς ἀλλήλους; (δια/συλ)λαλέω/διελάλουν/ συνελάλουν + πρὸς ἀλλήλους: red.]; RADL 1975 398 [ἀλλήλων; πρὸς ἀλλήλους]; SCHÜRMANN 1957 11 [πρὸς ἀλλήλους], n. 45.

HOLMBERG, B., Reciprocitetnyanser ἀλλήλων. — SEÅ 51-52 (1986-87) 90-99.
TILLER, Patrick A., Reflexive Pronouns in the New Testament. — FilolNT 15 (29-30, 2002) 43-63.

ἀλλογενής*** 1 — foreigner (Lk 17,18)

Literature

HAUCK 1934 [seltenes Alleinwort].

WEISSENRIEDER, Annette, Images of Illness in the Gospel of Luke, 2003. Esp. 195-209: "On the linguistic tradition of ἀλλογενής".

ἄλλος 11/12 + 8 (Mt 29/32, Mk 22/25)
1. different; 2. another (Lk 23,35)

Word groups	Lk	Acts	Mt	Mk
ἄλλοι ... ἄλλο τι		19,32[1.2]; 21,34[1.2]	0	0
BOISMARD 1984 Aa115				
ἄλλοι δέ (SCa; VKa); cf. ἄλλος δέ Mt 27,49*; 1 Cor 3,10; 12,8.9.10[1.2.3.4]; 15,39[2.3.4]	9,8.19[1.2]	21,34[1]	5	5
ὁ ἄλλος (SCb; VKb); cf. οἱ ἄλλοι Jn 20,25; 21,8; 1 Cor 14,29	6,10*.29		4/6	0/1

		4,12	1	0
ἄλλος ... ἕτερος		4,12	1	0
ἄλλος + οὗτος → ἐκεῖνος/ἕτερος/κἀκεῖνος + οὗτος	7,8; 20,16		1/2	3
οὐ + ἄλλος; cf. οὐ + ἑαυτοῦ Mt 27,42; Mk 15,31		4,12	0	2
οὐδεὶς ἄλλος → οὐδεὶς ἕτερος		4,12	0	0

Characteristic of Luke	Lk	Acts	Mt	Mk
ἄλλος τις / ἄλλο τι (VKc) → ἕτερός τις; cf. 1 Cor 1,16 BOISMARD 1984 Db29; NEIRYNCK 1985	22,59	15,2; 19,32[2]; 21,34[2]	0	0

Literature

COLLISON 1977 185 [noteworthy phenomena]; DENAUX 2009 IA[n] [ἄλλος τις / ἄλλο τι]; RADL 1975 398 [ἄλλος; ἄλλο τι].

SANDIYAGU, Virginia R., Ἕτερός and ἄλλος in Luke. — NT 48 (2006) 105-131.

ἀλλότριος 1 + 1 (Mt 2)

1. belonging to another (Lk 16,12); 2. foreigner (Acts 7,6); 3. be enemy of

ἄλυσις 1 + 4 (Mk 3)

1. chain (Lk 8,29); 2. imprisonment

Ἀλφαῖος 1 + 1 (Mt 1, Mk 2)   Alphaeus

Word groups	Lk	Acts	Mt	Mk
Ἀλφαῖος father of James the less (VKa)	6,15	1,13	1	1

ἄλων 1 (Mt 1)

1. threshing floor (Lk 3,17); 2. threshed grain

ἀλώπηξ 2 (Mt 1)

1. fox (Lk 9,58); 2. wicked person (Lk 13,32)

Literature

BUTH, Randall, That Small-fry Herod Antipas, or When a Fox Is Not a Fox. — Jerusalem Perspective 40 (1993) 7-9.
CASEY, Maurice, The Jackals and the Son of Man (Matt. 8.20 // Lk 9.58). — JSNT 23 (1985) 3-22.

ἁμαρτάνω 4 + 1 (Mt 3)   sin (Lk 17,3)

Word groups	Lk	Acts	Mt	Mk
ἁμαρτάνω + ἐνώπιον (VKa)	15,18.21		0	0

Characteristic of Luke	Lk	Acts	Mt	Mk
ἁμαρτάνω εἰς (SCa; VKa) BOISMARD 1984 Eb62; NEIRYNCK 1985	15,18.21; 17,4	25,8	2	0

Literature

GRAYSTON, Kenneth, A Study of the Word "Sin": With Its Correlatives *Sinner, Err, Fault, Guilt, Iniquity, Offence, Malefactor, Mischief, Perverse, Transgress, Trespass, Wicked, Wrong.* Part II: New Testament. — *BTrans* 4 (1953) 149-152.

TAEGER, Jens-Wilhelm, *Der Mensch und sein Heil*, 1982. Esp. 36-43.

ἁμαρτία 11 + 8 (Mt 7, Mk 6)

1. sin (Acts 7,60); 2. being evil; 3. guilt (Lk 1,77)

Word groups	Lk	Acts	Mt	Mk
ἁμαρτία (+) αφίημι (*VK*a) → ἄφεσις (τῶν) ἁμαρτιῶν;	5,20.21.23.24;		4	4
cf. ἐξαλείφω/ἀπολούω + ἁμαρτία Acts 3,19; 22,16	7,47.48.49; 11,4			
ἄφεσις ἁμαρτιῶν + μετάνοια	3,3; 24,47	5,31	0	1
ἀφέωνται + αἱ ἁμαρτίαι τινός	5,20.23; 7,47.48		0/2	0
εἰς ἄφεσιν / ἐν ἀφέσει (τῶν) ἁμαρτιῶν	1,77; 3,3; 24,47	2,38	1	1
λαμβάνω ἄφεσιν ἁμαρτιῶν		10,43;	0	0
BOISMARD 1984 Aa141		26,18		

Characteristic of Luke

GOULDER 1989

	Lk	Acts	Mt	Mk
ἄφεσις (τῶν) ἁμαρτιῶν (*SC*b; *VK*a) → ἁμαρτία + ἀφίημι;	1,77; 3,3;	2,38; 5,31;	1	1
cf. Col 1,14	24,47	10,43; 13,38;		
BOISMARD 1984 cb63; DENAUX 2009 IA*; GOULDER 1989;		26,18		
HARNACK 1906 145; NEIRYNCK 1985; PLUMMER 1922 lix				

Literature

GERSDORF 1816 212 [ἐν ἀφέσει ἁμαρτιῶν]; JEREMIAS 1980 322 [μετάνοια ἀφέσει ἁμαρτιῶν red.].

GRAYSTON, Kenneth, A Study of the Word "Sin". With Its Correlatives *Sinner, Err, Fault, Guilt, Iniquity, Offence, Malefactor, Mischief, Perverse, Transgress, Trespass, Wicked, Wrong.* Part II: New Testament. — *BTrans* 4 (1953) 149-152.

MAHFOUZ, Hady, *La fonction littéraire et théologique de Lc 3,1-20*, 2003. Esp. 133-137.168-174 [ἄφεσις ἁμαρτιῶν].

TAEGER, Jens.-Wilhelm, *Der Mensch und sein Heil*, 1982. Esp. 31-33.

ἁμαρτωλός 18 (Mt 5, Mk 6)

1. sinner (Lk 15,2); 2. sinful (Lk 19,7)

Word groups	Lk	Acts	Mt	Mk
ἁμαρτωλός + δίκαιος → ἄδικος + δίκαιος	5,32; 15,7		1	1
ἀνήρ/ἄνθρωπος ἁμαρτωλός; γυνή + ἁμαρτωλός	5,8; 7,37.39; 19,7; 24,7		0	0
DENAUX 2009 L[n]				
τελῶναι καὶ ἁμαρτωλοί; cf. τελώνης + ἁμαρτωλός	5,30; 7,34; 15,1		3	3
Lk 18,13; ἀρχιτελώνης + ἁμαρτωλός Lk 19,(2-)7				
ἁμαρτωλός attributive adjective (*VK*a)	5,8; 19,7; 24,7		0	1

Characteristic of Luke

GOULDER 1989; HAWKINS 1909add; MORGENTHALER 1958L

Literature

EASTON 1910 145 [not in Weiss; especially characteristic of L]; HAUCK 1934 [Vorzugswort]; SCHÜRMANN 1957 128, n. 447.

GRAYSTON, Kenneth, A Study of the Word "Sin". With Its Correlatives *Sinner, Err, Fault, Guilt, Iniquity, Offence, Malefactor, Mischief, Perverse, Transgress, Trespass, Wicked, Wrong*. Part II: New Testament. — *BTrans* 4 (1953) 149-152.

ἄμεμπτος 1 | blameless (Lk 1,6)

Literature
CADBURY 1920A; HARNACK 1906 70

ἀμήν 6/8 (Mt 31/33, Mk 13[14]/15[16]) | truly

Word groups	Lk	Acts	Mt	Mk
ἀμὴν λέγω δὲ ὑμῖν; cf. ἀμὴν δὲ λέγω ὑμῖν Mk 14,9	13,35*		0	0
ἀμὴν λέγω ὑμῖν (*SC*a) → ἀληθῶς/ναὶ λέγω ὑμῖν; cf. ἀμὴν γὰρ λέγω ὑμῖν Mt 5,18; 10,23; 13,17; 17,20	4,24; 12,37; 18,17.29; 21,32		25	11/12
ἀμὴν λέγω ὑμῖν ὅτι	4,24; 12,37; 13,35* *v.l.*; 18,29; 21,32		10	8
ἀμὴν λέγω (δὲ) ὑμῖν / σοι λέγω without ὅτι	18,17; 13,35*; 23,43		15	3/4
ἀμήν σοι λέγω (*SC*e); cf. ἀμὴν λέγω σοι Mt 5,26; 26,34; Mk 14,30	23,43		0	0
ἀμήν at the beginning (*VK*a)	4,24; 12,37; 13,35*; 18,17.29; 21,32; 23,43		31	13/14
ἀμήν at the end (*VK*c)	24,53*		0/2	[1]/[2]

Literature
COLLISON 1977 149 [noteworthy phenomena]; EASTON 1910 150 [probably characteristic of L; not in Weiss]; SCHÜRMANN 1953 14-16 [luk beseitigt manchmal ein mit λέγω verbundenes ἀμήν].

CHILTON, Bruce, "Amen": An Approach through Syriac Gospels. — *ZNW* 69 (1978) 203-211.
JANNARIS, A.N., Does ἀμήν Mean "Verily"? — *ExpT* 13 (1901-02) 563-565.
JEREMIAS, Joachim, Zum nicht-responsorischen Amen. — *ZNW* 64 (1973) 122-123. [NTA 18, 401]
ROSS, J.M., Amen. — *ExpT* 102 (1990-91) 166-171.

Ἀμιναδάβ 1 (Mt 2) | Amminadab (Lk 3,33)

ἄμπελος 1 (Mt 1, Mk 1) | grapevine

Word groups	Lk	Acts	Mt	Mk
ἄμπελος literally (*VK*a)	22,18		1	1

Literature
PETZER, Kobus H. (= Kobus) Hendrik, *Style and Text in the Lucan Narrative of the Institution of the Lord's Supper*, 1991. Esp. 122.

ἀμπελουργός 1 | vinedresser (Lk 13,7)

Literature
HAUCK 1934 [seltenes Alleinwort].

ἀμπελών 7 (Mt 10, Mk 5) | vineyard

Word groups	Lk	Acts	Mt	Mk
ἀμπελών (+) φυτεύω	13,6; 20,9		1	1

ἀμφιέζω 1

1. clothe (Lk 12,28); 2. adorn (Lk 12,28)

Literature
HAUCK 1934 [seltenes Alleinwort].

ἀμφιέννυμι 1/2 (Mt 2)

1. clothe (Lk 7,25); 2. adorn (Lk 7,25)

ἀμφότεροι 5/6 + 3 (Mt 3)

1. both (Lk 1,6.7; 5,7; 6,39; 7,42); 2. all (Acts 19,16)

Characteristic of Luke
PLUMMER 1922 lix

Literature
HARNACK 1906 70 (ET 97); RADL 1975 398.

Ἀμώς 1 (Mt 2) | Amos

Word groups	Lk	Acts	Mt	Mk
Ἀμώς son of Nahum (*VK*b)	3,25		0	0

ἄν 32/39 + 15/22 (Mt 42/51, Mk 20/27)

1. would (Lk 7,39); 2. ever (Lk 9,4)

Word groups	Lk	Acts	Mt	Mk
ἄν + aorist or imperfect indicative (iterative force) (*SC*a)		2,45; 4,35	0	2

ἄν + indicative (*VK*c) → ἐάν + indic.	7,39; 10,13; 12,8 v.l.39*.39; 13,35*; 17,6¹·².33 v.l.; 19,23	2,12* v.l.45; 4,35; 7,7*; 18,14; 26,29 v.l.	8	4
ἄν καί → ἐάν/εἰ/ὅταν (δὲ) καί	12,39*		1	0
ἄν ... οὐ → ἐάν/εἰ ... οὐ; cf. κἂν ... οὐ Mt 26,35; Mk [16,18]	18,17		0	0
ἀφ' οὗ ἄν (*SC*d) → ὅπως/πρὶν ἄν	13,25		0	0
ἕως ἄν + subjunctive (*SC*d; *VK*b)	9,27; 13,35*; 20,43; 21,32	2,35	11	3
καθότι ἄν		2,45; 4,35	0	0
καθότι ἄν τις → ἐάν + τις		2,45; 4,35	0	0
ὅπου ἄν → ὅπου ἐάν	9,57*		0	1/3
ὅς + ἄν (*SC*c; *VK*a) → ὃς ἐάν	4,6*; 8,18¹·²; 9,4.24¹·².26. 48*.48; 10,5.8.10.22*; 12,8; 13,25; 17,33; 18,17; 20,18	2,21; 7,3.7*; 8,19*	20/25	14/17
ὅσος ἄν (*SC*c); cf. ὅσος ἐάν Mt 7,12; 18,18¹·²; 22,9; 23,3; Mk 3,28; Rev 3,19; 13,15	9,5	2,39; 3,22	1/4	1/3
ὅστις ἄν (*SC*c; *VK*a) → ὅστις ἐάν	10,35	3,23*	2	0
ὅς/ὅσος/ὅστις + ἄν ... μή → ὅς/ὅσος/ὅστις ἐάν ... μή	8,18²; 9,5; 10,10; 18,17	3,23*	2/3	3
οὐκ ἄν	12,39		4	1
πᾶς (...) ὅσος ἄν; cf. πᾶς (...) ὅσος ἐάν Mt 7,12; 23,3; Mk 3,28		2,39; 3,22	1/3	0/2
πρὶν ἄν (*SC*d) → ἀφ' οὗ / ὅπως ἄν	2,26		0	0
ἄν "unreal" apodosis (*SC*b)	7,39; 10,13; 12,39*.39; 17,6¹·²; 19,23	18,14	8	1

Characteristic of Luke	Lk	Acts	Mt	Mk
ἄν + optative (*SC*e; *VK*d) BOISMARD 1984 Ab13; DENAUX 2009 L***; GOULDER 1989*; HAWKINS 1909L; NEIRYNCK 1985	1,62; 6,11; 9,46; 15,26; 18,36*	2,12*; 5,24; 8,31; 10,17; 17,18.20*; 21,33*; 26,29	0	0
ὅπως ἄν (*SC*d) → ἀφ' οὗ/πρὶν ἄν BOISMARD 1984 Ab189; NEIRYNCK 1985	2,35	3,20; 9,2*; 15,17	0/1	0
(τὸ) τί(ς) ἄν + optative; cf. Jn 13,24 DENAUX 2009 L***	1,62; 6,11; 9,46; 15,26; 18,36*	2,12*; 5,24; 10,17; 17,18.20*; 21,33*		

Literature

VON BENDEMANN 2001 429: "Der optativus potentialis mit ἄν findet sich im Neuen Testament nur bei Lukas"; BDR § 385: "Der Potentialis (Opt. mit ἄν) zur Bezeichnung des lediglich Gedachten ist in der Volkssprache ganz abhanden gekommen, im NT nur noch selten und nur in Lk und Apg"; COLLISON 1977 101 [ἄν + optative: linguistic usage of Luke: certain]; DENAUX 2009 IAⁿ [ὅπως ἄν]; HAUCK 1934 [Vorzugsverbindung: τί ἄν + opt.]; JEREMIAS 1980 48 [ἄν + opt.]: "spezifisch lukanisch".97 [ὅπως ἄν: red]: "begegnet im NT, abgesehen von einem paulinischen Bibelzitat, nur in den beiden Teilen des Doppelwerks".

ἀνά 3 (Mt 3, Mk 1/3)	each			

Word groups	Lk	Acts	Mt	Mk
ἀνά ... εἰς	10,1		0	1

Characteristic of Luke	Lk	Acts	Mt	Mk
ἀνά + numbers (*VK*a) GOULDER 1989		9,3.14; 10,1	0	0/2

Literature

DENAUX 2009 L[n] [ἀνά + numbers]; JEREMIAS 1980 183: [ἀνὰ δύο: red.] "Lukas meidet die aramaisierende distributive Verdoppelung ... Er schreibt klassisch ἀνά + Kardinalzahl".

ἀναβαίνω 9 + 19/20 (Mt 9, Mk 9)

1. go up (Lk 18,10); 2. go aboard (Acts 21,6); 3. sprout and grow; 4. grow up

Word groups	Lk	Acts	Mt	Mk
ἀναβαίνω to a city	2,4.(41-)42; 18,31; 19,28	11,2; 15,2; 18,22; 21,4*.12.15; 24,11; 25,1.9	2	2
ἀναβαίνω (+) εἰς (SCa; VKa) → ἀπο/δια/ἐμ/κατα/μεταβαίνω εἰς; cf. ἐπιβαίνω εἰς Acts 21,6*	2,4; 9,28; 18,10.31; 19,28	1,13; 2,34; 3,1; 10,4; 11,2; 15,2; 21,4*.6.12. 15; 24,11; 25,1.9	6	3
ἀναβαίνω εἰς τὸ ἱερόν → εἰσάγω/εἰσπορεύομαι/(εἰσ)ἔρχομαι εἰς τὸ ἱερόν; cf. εἴσειμι εἰς τὸ ἱερόν Acts 3,3; 21,26 DENAUX LA[n]	18,10	3,1	0	0
ἀναβαίνω (+) εἰς Ἱεροσόλυμα/Ἱερουσαλήμ → καταβαίνω ἀπὸ Ἱεροσολύμων/Ἱερουσαλήμ; cf. ἀνέρχομαι Gal 1,17.18; ἐπιβαίνω Acts 21,4; συναναβαίνω Mk 15,41; Acts 13,31	2,42 v.l.; 18,31; 19,28	11,2; 15,2; 21,4*.12.15; 24,11; 25,1.9	2	2
ἀναβαίνω + εἰς τὴν Ἰουδαίαν → κατέρχομαι ἀπὸ τῆς Ἰουδαίας	2,4		0	0
ἀναβαίνω εἰς τὸ ὄρος → ἐξέρχομαι/πορεύομαι εἰς τὸ ὄρος; κατέρχομαι ἀπὸ τοῦ ὄρους; cf. καταβαίνω ἀπὸ τοῦ ὄρους Mt 8,1; καταβαίνω ἐκ τοῦ ὄρους Mt 17,9; Mk 9,9	9,28		3	1
ἀναβαίνω εἰς τὸ πλοῖον → ἐμβαίνω εἰς (τὸ) πλοῖον; cf. ἐπιβαίνω εἰς τὸ πλοῖον Acts 21,6*		21,6	1	1
ἀναβαίνω ἐκ → κατα/μεταβαίνω ἐκ		8,39	0	1
ἀναβαίνω ἐν καρδίᾳ	24,38		0	0
ἀναβαίνω (+) ἐπί + accusative (SCb; VKb) → καταβαίνω ἐπί + acc. DENAUX 2009 LA[n]	5,19; 19,4	7,23; 10,9		
ἀναβαίνω ἐπὶ καρδίαν (LN: begin to think)		7,23	0	0
ἀναβαίνω + ἵνα	19,4		0	0
ἀναβαίνω + προσευχή → ἀναβαίνω + προσεύξασθαι		3,1; 10,4	0	0

Characteristic of Luke

VOGEL 1899B

	Lk	Acts	Mt	Mk
ἀναβαίνω + infinitive of purpose → συνέβη + inf. DENAUX La*	2,4(-5); 9,28; 18,10	7,23; 10,9	1	0
ἀναβαίνω + προσεύξασθαι → ἀναβαίνω + προσευχή BOISMARD 1984 cb14; NEIRYNCK 1985	9,28; 18,10	10,9	1	0

Literature

BDAG 2000 58 [semitism ἀ. ἐπὶ καρδίαν 'to arise in the heart' enter one's mind; cp. Lk 24,38];

GERSDORF 1816 217 [ἀνέβη δὲ καὶ Ἰωσὴφ - εἰς πόλιν Δαυίδ - ἀπογράψασθαι]: "wie πορεύεσθαι im Lucas mit dem Infinitive construiert wird, so auch ἀναβαῖνειν"; JEREMIAS 1980 78-79 [ἀναβαίνω + inf. of purpose: red.]; RADL 1975 398-399 [ἀναβαίνω; ἀναβαίνω "mit Jerusalem als Ziel"].

EPP, Eldon Jay, The Ascension in the Textual Tradition of Luke-Acts. — ID. – FEE, G.D. (eds.), *New Testament Textual Criticism*. FS B.M. Metzger, 1981, 131-145.

ἀναβλέπω 7 + 5 (Mt 3, Mk 6/7)

1. look up (Lk 21,1); 2. gain sight (Lk 7,22)

Word groups	Lk	Acts	Mt	Mk
ἀναβλέπω εἰς τὸν οὐρανόν (*S*Ca; *VK*a)	9,16		1	2
ἀναβλέπω + (ὁράω/)εἶδον → **ἀτενίζω/βλέπω/θεάομαι/θεωρέω** + (ὁράω/)εἶδον; cf. βλέπω + ὁράω Mk 8,15.24; ἐμβλέπω + εἶδον Mk 14,67; περιβλέπω + εἶδον Mk 5,32; 9,8	19,5 *v.l.*; 21,1		0	0
ἀναβλέπω + ὀφθαλμός → **ἀτενίζω/(δια)βλέπω/ὁράω/εἶδον** + ὀφθαλμός		9,18	0/1	0
ἀναβλέψας (+) εἶδεν; cf. ἀναβλέψας + θεωρέω Mk 16,4	21,1		0	0
τυφλός ἀναβλέπω → τυφλός + **βλέπω**	7,22		1	1

ἀνάβλεψις 1   gaining sight (Lk 4,18)

Literature

HAUCK 1934 [seltenes Alleinwort].

ἀνάγαιον 1 (Mk 1)   upstairs room

Word groups	Lk	Acts	Mt	Mk
ἀνάγαιον + ἐστρωμένον	22,12		0	1

ἀναγινώσκω 3 + 8 (Mt 7, Mk 4)   read (Lk 4,16; 6,3)

Word groups	Lk	Acts	Mt	Mk
ἀναγινώσκω + γινώσκω; cf. 2 Cor 3,2; ἀναγινώσκω + νοέω Mt 24,15; Mk 13,14		8,30[2]	0	0
ἀναγινώσκω + νόμος; cf. ἀνάγνωσις + νόμος Acts 13,15	10,26		1	0

Literature

BDAG 2000 60 [read aloud for public hearing: Lk 4,16; Acts 15,21; cp. 13,27].

CHILTON, Bruce, *Announcement in Nazara*, 1981. Esp. 155.

ἀναγκάζω 1 + 2 (Mt 1, Mk 1)   compel (Acts 26,11; 28,19)

Word groups	Lk	Acts	Mt	Mk
ἀναγκάζω εἰσέρχομαι → **παραβιάζομαι/παρακαλέω** + εἰσέρχομαι	14,23		0	0

Literature

BDAG 2000 60 [strongly urge/invite: Lk 14,23]; HAUCK 1934 [seltenes Alleinwort].

KREUZER, Siegfried, Der Zwang des Boten – Beobachtungen zu Lk 14,23 und 1 Kor 9,16. — *ZNW* 76(1985) 123-128.

ἀνάγκη 2 (Mt 1)

1. trouble (Lk 21,23); 2. complete obligation (Lk 14,18); 3. inevitability

Word groups	Lk	Acts	Mt	Mk
ἀνάγκην ἔχω (VKb)	14,18; 23,17*		0	0

Literature

HAUCK 1934 [Vorzugswort].

BORMANN, Lukas, *Recht, Gerechtigkeit und Religion*, 2001. Esp. 146-147.

ἀνάγω 3/4 + 17 (Mt 1, Mk 0/1)

1. lead up (Lk 2,22; 4,5); 2. offer to (Acts 7,41); 3. ἀνάγομαι: set sail (Lk 8,22)

Word groups	Lk	Acts	Mt	Mk
ἀνάγομαι (+) ἀπό + place → ἐπανάγω ἀπό; cf. ἐκπλέω ἀπό Acts 20,6		13,13; 16,11; 18,21; 27,21	0	0
ἀνάγομαι + πλοῖον DENAUX 2009 1Aⁿ	8,22	20,13; 21,2; 27,2; 28,11	0	0
ἀνάγω (+) εἰς + place → (ἀπ/εἰσ/ἐξ/ ἐπαν/κατ/προ/συν/ὑπ)ἄγω εἰς + place	2,22; 22,66*	9,39; 16,11.34; 20,3	1	0
ἀνάγω ἐπί + accusative (place) → (ἀπ/συν/ὑπ)ἄγω ἐπί + acc. (person); (κατ)ἄγω ἐπί + acc. (place); προάγω ἐπί + gen. (person)		20,13		
ἀνάγομαι passive → (ἀπ/εἰσ/ἐπισυν/ κατ/συν) ἄγομαι passive	8,22	13,13; 16,11; 18,21; 20,3.13; 21,1.2; 27,2.4.12.21; 28,10.11	1	0
ἀνήγαγον → (ἀπ/εἰσ/κατ)ήγαγον; cf. συνήγαγον Mt 22,10; 27,27 DENAUX 2009 1Aⁿ	2,22; 22,66*	7,41; 9,39	0	0

Characteristic of Luke

DENAUX 2009 1A*†; HAWKINS 1909B; MORGENTHALER 1958A; PLUMMER 1922 lix

	Lk	Acts	Mt	Mk
ἀνάγω transitive → (ἀπ/εἰσ/ἐξ/ ἐπισυν/κατ/προ/προσ/συν)ἄγω transitive DENAUX 2009 1A*	2,22; 4,5; 8,22; 22,66*	7,41; 9,39; 12,4; 13,13; 16,11.34; 18,21; 20,3.13; 21,1.2; 27,2.4.12.21; 28,10.11	1	0/1
ἀνάγομαι set sail, launching forth (VKa) BOISMARD 1984 Ab1; HARNACK 1906 30.51; HAWKINS 1909B; NEIRYNCK 1985	8,22	13,13; 16,11; 18,21; 20,3.13; 21,1.2; 27,2.4.12.21; 28,10.11	0	0

Literature

BDAG 2000 61 [bring up for judicial purpose: Acts 12,4]; DENAUX 2009 1Aⁿ [ἀνάγω = set sail, launching fort]; JEREMIAS 1980 90: "ἀνάγω ist lk Vorzugswort (…). Kennzeichnend für Lukas ist der Gebrauch von ἀνάγομαι (Pass.) als nautischer Terminus technicus 'auslaufen'".

ἀναδείκνυμι 1 + 1
1. make known (Acts 1,24); 2. give a task (Lk 10,1)

Word groups	Lk	Acts	Mt	Mk
ἀναδείκνυμι imperative → (ἐπι)δείκνυμι imperative		1,24	0	0

Characteristic of Luke
BOISMARD 1984 Ab154; HAWKINS 1909LA; MORGENTHALER 1958*; NEIRYNCK 1985; PLUMMER 1922 liii; VOGEL 1899A

Literature
DENAUX 2009 LA[n]; EASTON 1910 158 [cited by Weiss as characteristic of L, and possibly corroborative]; HAUCK 1934 [seltenes Alleinwort]; JEREMIAS 1980 77 [ἀναδείκνυμι, ἀναδείξεως red.] "Die Wortgruppe erscheint im NT nur im lk Doppelwerk".

BORMANN, Lukas, *Recht, Gerechtigkeit und Religion*, 2001. Esp. 130.

ἀνάδειξις 1   revelation (Lk 1,80)

Literature
EASTON 1910 158 [cited by Weiss as characteristic of L, and possibly corroborative]; GERSDORF 1816 212 [ἕως ἡμέρας ἀναδείξεως]; HAUCK 1934 [seltenes Alleinwort]; JEREMIAS 1980 77 [ἀναδείκνυμι, ἀναδείξεως red.; ἡμέρας ἀναδείξεως: "Artikellose Genitivverbindung": trad.].

BORMANN, Lukas, *Recht, Gerechtigkeit und Religion*, 2001. Esp. 130.

ἀναζάω 1/2
1. live again (Lk 15,24); 2. begin to function

Word groups	Lk	Acts	Mt	Mk
ἀναζάω+ νεκρός → ζῶ + νεκρός	15,24.32*		0	0

ἀναζητέω 2 + 1   try to find out

Word groups	Lk	Acts	Mt	Mk
ἀναζητέω + direct object → ζητέω + direct obj. DENAUX 2009 La[n]	2,44.45	11,25	0	0
ἀναζητέω + εὑρίσκω → αἰτέω + (ἐπι)δίδωμι/λαμβάνω; ζητέω + δίδωμι; (ἐπι)ζητέω + εὑρίσκω DENAUX 2009 LA[n]	2,45	11,25(-26)	0	0

Characteristic of Luke
BOISMARD 1984 Ab106; HARNACK 1906 149; HAWKINS 1909LA; MORGENTHALER 1958*; NEIRYNCK 1985; PLUMMER 1922 lii; VOGEL 1899A

Literature
DENAUX 2009 La[n]; HAUCK 1934 [seltenes Alleinwort]; GERSDORF 1816 265 [ἦλθον ἡμέρας ʽ

ὁδὸν καὶ ἀνεζήτουν αὐτόν]; JEREMIAS 1980 100 [red.]: "ἀναζητεῖν τινα ('jemanden aufsuchen', 'nach jemanden suchen') im NT nur im lk Doppelwerk".

BURCHARD, Christoph, *Fußnoten zum neutestamentlichen Griechisch II*, 1978. Esp. 153-155: "Act 11,25 ἀναζητῆσαι Σαῦλον".
DELEBECQUE, Édouard, *Études grecques*, 1976. Esp. 48-50 [2,41-52].

ἀνάθημα 1	offering (Lk 21,5)

Literature
HAUCK 1934 [seltenes Alleinwort].

ἀναίδεια 1	insolence (Lk 11,8)

Literature
HAUCK 1934 [seltenes Alleinwort].

JOHNSON, Alan F., Assurance for Man: The Fallacy of Translating *Anaideia* by "Persistence" in Luke 11,5-8. — *JEvTS* 22 (1979) 123-131.
SNODGRASS, Klyne, *Anaideia* and the Friend at Midnight (Luke 11:8). — *JBL* 116 (1997) 505-513.

ἀναιρέω 2 + 19 (Mt 1)	

1. kill (Lk 23,32; Acts 22,20); 2. do away with (Lk 22,2); 3. ἀναιρέομαι: adopt (Acts 7,21)

Word groups	Lk	Acts	Mt	Mk
ἀναιρέω αὐτόν/αὐτούς DENAUX 2009 1A[n]	22,2	5,33; 7,21; 9,23.24.29; 13,28; 22,20; 23,15.21; 25,3	0	0
ἀναιρέομαι middle (*VK*b)		7,21	0	0
ἀναιρέομαι passive (*VK*a) DENAUX 2009 1A[n]	23,32	5,36; 13,28; 23,27; 26,10	0	0
ἀνέλωσιν DENAUX 2009 1A[n]	22,2	9,24; 23,21	0	0

Characteristic of Luke
BOISMARD 1984 Bb37; DENAUX 2009 1A*; HAWKINS 1909B; MORGENTHALER 1958A; NEIRYNCK 1985; PLUMMER 1922 lix

	Lk	Acts	Mt	Mk
ἀναιρέω (and cognate ἀναίρεσις) of Christ BOISMARD 1984 Ab32; NEIRYNCK 1985	22,2; 23,32	2,23; (8,1); 10,39; 13,28; (22,20*)	0	0

Literature
COLLISON 1977 91 [noteworthy phenomena]; DENAUX 2009 1A[n] [ἀναιρέω of Christ]; HAUCK 1934 [Vorzugswort]; JEREMIAS 1980 305: "lukanisches Vorzugswort"; RADL 1975 399 [ἀναιρέω; ἀναιρέω + αὐτόν/αὐτούς; ἀνέλωσιν].

BORMANN, Lukas, *Recht, Gerechtigkeit und Religion*, 2001. Esp. 174.
GOLDSMITH, G.P., Acts ii:23. — *ExpT* 9 (1897-98) 237. [προσπήξαντες ἀνείλατε]

ἀνακαθίζω 1 + 1   sit up (Lk 7,15; Acts 9,40)

Characteristic of Luke
BOISMARD 1984 Ab155; HAWKINS 1909LA; MORGENTHALER 1958*; NEIRYNCK 1985; PLUMMER 1922 liii; VOGEL 1899A

Literature
DENAUX 2009 LA[n]; HAUCK 1934 [seltenes Alleinwort]; JEREMIAS 1980 159 [trad.].

CADBURY, Henry J., Lexical Notes on Luke-Acts, V, 1933. Esp. 58.

ἀνακάμπτω 1 + 1 (Mt 1)
1. return (Lk 10,6; Acts 18,21); 2. change to former belief

ἀνάκειμαι 2/3 (Mt 5, Mk 2[3]/4)
1. recline to eat (Lk 22,27[1.2]); 2. eat a meal (Lk 7,37 v.l.)

Literature
COLLISON 1977 90 [noteworthy phenomena]; SCHÜRMANN 1953 107; 1957 81-82.

ἀνακλίνω 3/5 (Mt 2, Mk 1)
1. cause to lie down (Lk 2,7); 2. cause to recline to eat (Lk 12,37); 3. ἀνακλίνομαι: recline to eat (Lk 13,29)

Word groups	Lk	Acts	Mt	Mk
ἀνακλίνω active (VKa)	2,7; 9,15*; 12,37		0	1

Literature
COLLISON 1977 90 [noteworthy phenomena]; EASTON 1910 150 [probably characteristic of L; not in Weiss]; GERSDORF 1816 220-222 [ἀνέκλινεν αὐτὸν ἐν τῇ φάτνῃ]; REHKOPF 1959 91 [vorlukanisch]; SCHÜRMANN 1961 273.

ἀνακράζω 3 (Mk 2)   shout

Word groups	Lk	Acts	Mt	Mk
ἀνακράζω + λέγω/εἶπον → **κράζω/κραύγαζω** + λέγω/εἶπον	4,33 v.l.; 8,28; 23,18		0	1
ἀνακράζω + λέγων → **κράζω** + λέγων	23,18		0	0
ἀνακράζω (+) φωνῇ μεγαλῇ → **βοάω/κράζω/(ἀνα)φωνέω** + φωνῇ μεγαλῇ; cf. ἀναβοάω + φωνῇ μεγαλῇ Mt 27,46 DENAUX 2009 L[n]	4,33; 8,28		0	0

Literature
JEREMIAS 1980 68 [ἀνακράζω + λέγων: red].

ἀνακρίνω 1 + 5
1. study thoroughly (Acts 17,11); 2. investigate (Lk 23,14); 3. criticize; 4. evaluate carefully

Word groups	Lk	Acts	Mt	Mk
ἀνακρίνας DENAUX 2009 1A[n]	23,14	12,19; 24,8; 28,18	0	0

Characteristic of Luke
BOISMARD 1984 Db10; NEIRYNCK 1985; PLUMMER 1922 lii

Literature
DENAUX 2009 1A[n]; JEREMIAS 1980 303: "sowohl ἐνώπιον wie ἀνακρίνω sind lukanische Vorzugswörter"; RADL 1975 399 [ἀνακρίνω; ἀνακρίνας].

ἀνακύπτω 2	straighten up (Lk 13,11; 21,28)

Literature
DENAUX 2009 L[n]; EASTON 1910 150 [probably characteristic of L]; HAUCK 1934 [seltenes Alleinwort].

NEIRYNCK, Frans, Παρακύψας βλέπει: Lc 24,12 et Jn 20,5. — *ETL* 53 (1977) 113-152. Esp. 117-129: "Κύπτω et composés dans la LXX". [NTA 22, 130]; = Id., *Evangelica*, 1982, 401-440 (Appendix, *Evangelica II*, 1991, 799). Esp. 405-417.

ἀνάλημψις* 1	ascension (Lk 9,51)

Characteristic of Luke	Lk	Acts	Mt	Mk
ἀνάλημψις of Christ → ἀναφέρω; ὑπολαμβάνω; cf. ἀναλαμβάνω Mk [16,19]; Acts 1,2.11.22 VOGEL 1899B	9,51		0	0

Literature
HAUCK 1934 [seltenes Alleinwort]; JEREMIAS 1980 179 [red.].

DAVIES, J.H., The Purpose of the Central Section of St. Luke's Gospel. — *Studia Evangelica* 2 (1964) 164-169. Esp. 164-165.
DENAUX, Adelbert, The Delineation of the Lukan Travel Narrative within the Overall Structure of the Gospel of Luke. — FOCANT, Camille (ed.), *The Synoptic Gospels: Source Criticism and the New Literary Criticism* (BETL, 110). Leuven: Leuven University Press – Uitgeverij Peeters, 1993, 357-392. Esp. 372-377: "The ἀνάλημψις motif".
EPP, Eldon Jay, The Ascension in the Textual Tradition of Luke-Acts. — ID. – FEE, G.D. (eds.), *New Testament Textual Criticism*. FS B.M. Metzger, 1981, 131-145.
FRIEDRICH, Gerhard, Lk 9,51 und die Entrückungschristologie des Lukas. — HOFFMANN, P. – BROX, N. – PESCH, W. (eds.), *Orientierung an Christus*. FS J. Schmid, 1973, 48-77.

ἀναλίσκω 1	destroy (Lk 9,54)

Literature
HAUCK 1934 [seltenes Alleinwort].

ἀναλύω 1	

1. return (Lk 12,36); 2. die

Literature

HAUCK 1934 [seltenes Alleinwort].

| ἀνάμνησις 1 | reminder (Lk 22,19) |

Literature

HAUCK 1934 [seltenes Alleinwort].

PETZER, Kobus H., Style and Text in the Lucan Narrative of the Institution of the Lord's Supper, 1991. Esp. 116-117.

| ἀνάπαυσις 1 (Mt 2) | |

1. stop; 2. rest; 3. place to rest (Lk 11,24); 4. relief

| ἀναπαύω 1 (Mt 2, Mk 2) | |

1. cause to rest; 2. ἀναπαύομαι: rest (Lk 12,19); 3. ἀναπαύομαι: abide; 4. ἀναπαύομαι: remain

| ἀνάπειρος 2 | maimed (Lk 14,13.21) |

Characteristic of Luke

PLUMMER 1922 liii

Literature

DENAUX 2009 L[n]; HAUCK 1934 [seltenes Alleinwort].

LEE, John A.L. – HORSLEY, G.H.R., A Lexicon of the New Testament, 2, 1998. Esp. 62.

| ἀναπέμπω 3 + 1 | |

1. send back (Lk 23,11.15); 2. send on (Lk 23,7; Acts 25,21)

Word groups	Lk	Acts	Mt	Mk
ἀναπέμπω + πρός + accusative → πέμπω πρός + acc. DENAUX 2009 La[n]	23,7.15	25,21	0	0

Characteristic of Luke

BOISMARD 1984 Bb93; NEIRYNCK 1985; PLUMMER 1922 lix; VOGEL 1899B

Literature

DENAUX 2009 La[n]; JEREMIAS 1980 301 [red.] : "ἀναπέμπω kommt außer Phlm 12 ('senden') nur im Doppelwerk vor und ist hier an allen vier Stellen … juristischer t.t. mit der Bedeutung '(einen Angeklagten dem zuständigen Gericht) überstellen'".

| ἀναπίπτω 4 (Mt 1, Mk 2) | recline to eat |

Characteristic of Luke	Lk	Acts	Mt	Mk
ἀναπίπτω aorist → (ἐμ/ἐπι/κατα/περι/προσ/συμ)πίπτω aorist; cf. ἀποπίπτω Acts 9,18; ἐκπίπτω Acts 12,7; 27,17.26.29.32 DENAUX 2009 L***; GOULDER 1989	11,37; 14,10; 17,7; 22,14		1	2

Literature

COLLISON 1977 91 [linguistic usage of Luke: likely]; EASTON 1910 145 [especially characteristic of L]; REHKOPF 1959 91 [vorlukanisch]; SCHÜRMANN 1961 278 [protoluk R weniger wahrscheinlich].

ἀναπτύσσω 1   unroll

Word groups	Lk	Acts	Mt	Mk
ἀναπτύσσω τὸ βιβλίον → ἀνοίγω/πτύσσω τὸ βιβλίον; διανοίγω/ συνίημι τὰς γραφάς	4,17		0	0

Literature

CHILTON, Bruce, Announcement in Nazara, 1981. Esp. 156.

VAN MINNEN, P., Luke 4:17-20 and the Handling of Ancient Books. — *JTS* 52 (2001) 689-690.

ἀνάπτω 1 + 0/1   start fire

Word groups	Lk	Acts	Mt	Mk
ἀνάπτω πῦρ/πυράν → (περι)ᾶπτω λύχνον/πῦρ	12,49	28,2*	0	0

Characteristic of Luke

VOGEL 1899B

Literature

HAUCK 1934 [seltenes Alleinwort].

ἀνασείω 1 (Mk 1)   cause an uproar (Lk 23,5)

ἀνασπάω 1 + 1   pull up (Lk 14,5; Acts 11,10)

Characteristic of Luke

BOISMARD 1984 Ab156; HAWKINS 1909LA; MORGENTHALER 1958*; NEIRYNCK 1985; PLUMMER 1922 liii; VOGEL 1899A

Literature

VON BENDEMANN 2001 427; DENAUX 2009 LAⁿ; HAUCK 1934 [seltenes Alleinwort].

ἀνάστασις 6 + 11 (Mt 4, Mk 2)

1. resurrection (Lk 14,14); 2. rising up (status) (Lk 2,34); 3. rising up (change) (Lk 2,34)

Word groups	Lk	Acts	Mt	Mk
ἀνάστασιν μὴ εἶναι (SCb; VKb)	20,27	23,8	1	1
ἀνάστασις νεκρῶν without article		17,32; 23,6; 24,15 v.l.21; 26,23	0	0
BOISMARD 1984 Da6				
ἀνάστασις τοῦ Χριστοῦ		2,31	0	0
ἐν τῇ ἀναστάσει	14,14; 20,33		2	1

Characteristic of Luke
GOULDER 1989

	Lk	Acts	Mt	Mk
ἀνάστασις (τῶν) δικαίων (καὶ ἀδίκων)	14,14	24,15	0	0
BOISMARD 1984 Ab157; NEIRYNCK 1985				
ἡ ἀνάστασις ἡ ἐκ νεκρῶν (SCa; VKa); cf. ἡ ἀνάστασις ἡ ἐκ	20,35	4,2	0	0
τῶν νεκρῶν Mt 22,31 → ἀνίστημι/ἐγείρω ἐκ (τῶν) νεκρῶν				
BOISMARD 1984 Ab158; NEIRYNCK 1985				

Literature
DENAUX 2009 LAⁿ [ἀνάστασις (τῶν) δικαίων (καὶ ἀδίκων)/ἡ ἀνάστασις ἡ ἐκ νεκρῶν];
HAUCK 1934 [häufiges Alleinwort; Vorzugsverbindung: ἀνάστασις (τῶν) δικαίων]; JEREMIAS
1980 239: "ἐν τῇ ἀναστάσει (20,33) + τῶν δικαίων (14,14) + καὶ (τῶν) ἀδίκων (Apg 24,15)
sind Termini der jüdischen Eschatologie" [trad.]; RADL 1975 399 [ἀνάστασις (ἡ) (ἐκ) (τῶν)
νεκρῶν].

SCHWARZ, Günther, ανιστημι und αναστασις in den Evangelien. — BibNot 10 (1979)
35-39.

ἀνατάσσομαι* 1   compile (Lk 1,1)

Literature
HAUCK 1934 [seltenes Alleinwort].

ALEXANDER, Loveday, The Preface to Luke's Gospel, 1993. Esp. 110.
CADBURY, Henry J., Commentary on the Preface of Luke, 1922. Esp. 494-495.
—, Lexical Notes on Luke-Acts, V, 1933. Esp. 56-58.
HEAD, Peter M., Papyrological Perspectives on Luke's Predecessors (Luke 1,1). — P.J.
  WILLIAMS – A.D. CLARKE – P.M. HEAD – D. INSTONE-BREWER (eds.), The New
  Testament in Its First Century Setting: Essays on Context and Background in Honour of
  B.W. Winter on His 65th Birthday, Grand Rapids, MI – Cambridge, UK, Eerdmans,
  2004, 30-45. Esp. 38-40.
LEE, John A.L. – HORSLEY, G.H.R., A Lexicon of the New Testament, 2, 1998. Esp. 62-63.79.
LEE, John A.L., A History of New Testament Lexicography, 2003. Esp. 225-237.

ἀνατέλλω 1 (Mt 3, Mk 2)
1. rise (Lk 12,54); 2. dawn; 3. be a descendant

Word groups	Lk	Acts	Mt	Mk
ἀνατέλλω ἐπὶ δυσμῶν	12,54		0	0

ἀνατολή 2 (Mt 5, Mk 0[1])
1. rising (Lk 1,78); 2. east (Lk 13,29)

Word groups	Lk	Acts	Mt	Mk
ἀνατολὴ ἐξ ὕψους (LN: the dawn from on high)	1,78		0	0
ἀπὸ ἀνατολῶν (SCa; VKa) → ἀπὸ βορρᾶ/δυσμῶν/νότου	13,29		3	0

Literature

HAUCK 1934 [Vorzugswort].

JACOBY, A., Ἀνατολὴ ἐξ ὕψους. — ZNW 20 (1921) 205-214. [ἀνατολὴ ἐξ ὕψους Lk
1,78 = sprout or scion of God]

ἀναφαίνω 1 + 1   ἀναφαίνομαι: come into view, appear

Word groups	Lk	Acts	Mt	Mk
ἀναφαίνω βασιλεία τοῦ θεοῦ → ἔρχομαι/φθάνω + βασιλεία τοῦ θεοῦ	19,11		0	0

Characteristic of Luke

BOISMARD 1984 Ab159; HARNACK 1906 54; HAWKINS 1909LA; MORGENTHALER 1958*;
NEIRYNCK 1985; PLUMMER 1922 liii; VOGEL 1899A

Literature

DENAUX 2009 LAⁿ; HAUCK 1934 [seltenes Alleinwort]; JEREMIAS 1980 278 [red.].

ἀναφέρω 1 (Mt 1, Mk 1)

1. lead up; 2. carry up (Lk 24,51); 3. offer up

Word groups	Lk	Acts	Mt	Mk
ἀναφέρω of Christ → ἀνάλημψις; ὑπολαμβάνω; cf. ἀναλαμβάνω Mk [[16,19]]; Acts 1,2.11.22	24,51		0	0
ἀναφέρω εἰς → (ἀπο/ἐκ)φέρω εἰς	24,51		1	1

Literature

LOHFINK, Gerhard, Die Himmelfahrt Jesu (SANT, 26). München: Kösel, 1971, 315 p. Esp.
171: "Bei der Beschreibung von Himmelsreisen und Entrückungen ist ἀναφέρομαι im
hellenistischen Bereich durchaus geläufig" [Cp. p. 42, n. 72]

ἀναφωνέω 1   cry out

Word groups	Lk	Acts	Mt	Mk
ἀναφωνέω κραυγῇ/φωνῇ μεγαλῇ → βοάω/(ἀνα)κράζω/φωνέω + φωνῇ μεγαλῇ; cf. ἀναβοάω + φωνῇ μεγαλῇ Mt 27,46	1,42		0	0
ἀναφωνέω + (λέγω/)εῖπον→ (ἐπι/προσ)φωνέω + λέγω/εῖπον	1,42		0	0

Literature

GERSDORF 1816 198-199 [ἀνεφώνησεν κραυγῇ μεγαλῇ]; HAUCK 1934 [seltenes Alleinwort];
JEREMIAS 1980 57 "Lukas hat eine Vorliebe für Worte der Stammsilbe -φων".

Ἀνδρέας 1 + 1 (Mt 2, Mk 4)   Andrew

Word groups	Lk	Acts	Mt	Mk
Πέτρος + Ἀνδρέας	6,14	1,13	2	1

ἀνέκλειπτος* 1   unfailing (Lk 12,33)

Literature
HAUCK 1934 [seltenes Alleinwort]; SCHÜRMANN 1957 106-107.

ἀνεκτότερος 2 (Mt 3, Mk 0/1)   ἀνέκτος: endurable (Lk 10,12.14)

ἄνεμος 4 + 4 (Mt 9, Mk 7)   wind

Word groups	Lk	Acts	Mt	Mk
ἄνεμος + ὕδωρ DENAUX 2009 Lⁿ	8,24.25		0	0
λαῖλαψ ἀνέμου	8,23		0	1

ἀνένδεκτος* 1   impossible (Lk 17,1)

Literature
HAUCK 1934 [seltenes Alleinwort]; JEREMIAS 1980 262: "ἀνένδεκτος scheint im Unterschied zu οὐκ ἐνδέχεται redaktionell zu sein".

ἀνευρίσκω 1 + 1   find by searching

Word groups	Lk	Acts	Mt	Mk
ἀνευρίσκω + ἔρχομαι → εὑρίσκω + (ἀπ/δι/εἰσ/ἐξ/κατ)ἔρχομαι / (εἰσ)πορεύομαι	2,16		0	0

Characteristic of Luke
BOISMARD 1984 Ab160; HARNACK 1906 54.73.147; HAWKINS 1909LA; MORGENTHALER 1958*; NEIRYNCK 1985; PLUMMER 1922 liii; VOGEL 1899A

Literature
DENAUX 2009 LAⁿ; GERSDORF 1816 239-240 [καὶ ἀνεῦραν τήν τε Μαριάμ]; HAUCK 1934 [seltenes Alleinwort]; JEREMIAS 1980 85 [red.].

ἀνέχομαι 1 + 1 (Mt 1, Mk 1)
1. be patient with (Lk 9,41); 2. accept (Acts 18,4)

Word groups	Lk	Acts	Mt	Mk
κατὰ λόγον + ἀνέχομαι (LN: accept a complaint)		18,14	0	0

ἀνήρ 27 + 100/101 (Mt 8, Mk 4)
1. man (Lk 9,14); 2. human being (Lk 5,8); 3. husband (Lk 1,27)

Word groups	Lk	Acts	Mt	Mk
ἄνδρες ἀδελφοί (καὶ πατέρες) (SCa; VKa) → ἄνδρες voc.		1,16; 2,29.37; 7,2; 13,15.26.38; 15,7.13; 22,1; 23,1.6; 28,17	0	0
ἄνδρες τῆς γενεᾶς ταύτης → ἄνθρωποι τῆς γενεᾶς ταύτης	11,31		0	0
ἄνδρες Ἰουδαῖοι → ἀνὴρ Ἰουδαῖος		2,14	0	0
ἄνδρες Ἰσραηλῖται (SCb)		2,22[1]; 3,12; 5,35; 13,16; 21,28	0	0
ἄνδρες (τε) καὶ γυναῖκες (SCc) → ἀνὴρ + γυνή; cf. ἄνδρες χωρὶς γυναικῶν Mt 14,21; 15,38 BOISMARD 1984 Aa13		5,14; 8,3.12; 9,2; 17,12; 22,4	0	0
ἀνήρ + geographic origin	11,32	1,11; 2,14.22[1]; 3,12; 5,35; 8,27; 10,28; 11,20; 13,16; 16,9; 17,22; 19,35; 21,28; 22,3	1	0
ἀνήρ + numeral → ἄνθρωπος + numeral	9,14.30.32; 17,12; 24,4	1,10; 4,4; 5,36; 6,3; 9,38; 10,19; 11,11; 19,7; 21,23.38; 23,21	2	1
ἀνὴρ ἀγαθός/εὐλαβής → ἀνὴρ δίκαιος; ἄνθρωπος + ἀγαθός/δίκαιος/εὐλαβής DENAUX 2009 1A[n]	23,50[2]	2,5; 8,2; 11,24; 22,12	0	0
ἀνὴρ ἁμαρτωλός → ἄνθρωπος ἁμαρτωλός; γυνή + ἁμαρτωλός DENAUX 2009 L[n]	5,8; 19,7		0	0
ἀνὴρ ἀπὸ τοῦ ὄχλου → γυνὴ/τις ἐκ τοῦ ὄχλου	9,38		0	0
ἀνήρ + γυνή → ἄνδρες (τε) καὶ γυναῖκες; cf. ἄνθρωπος + γυνή Mt 19,3.5.10; Mk 10,7	16,18	5,1.14; 8,3.12; 9,2; 17,12.34; 22,4	2	1
ἀνὴρ δέ τις ὀνόματι + proper name BOISMARD 1984 Aa71		5,1; 8,9; 10,1		
ὁ ἀνὴρ ἐκεῖνος → ὁ ἀνὴρ οὗτος; ὁ ἄνθρωπος ἐκεῖνος/οὗτος; γυνὴ αὕτη	14,24		0	0
ἀνὴρ (+) Ἰουδαῖος → ἄνδρες Ἰουδαῖοι; ἄνθρωπος Ἰουδαῖος; γυνὴ Ἰουδαία		10,28; 13,6; 22,3	0	0
ὁ ἀνὴρ οὗτος → ὁ ἀνὴρ ἐκεῖνος; ὁ ἄνθρωπος ἐκεῖνος/οὗτος; γυνὴ αὕτη BOISMARD 1984 Aa37		9,13; 19,37; 23,27; 24,5; 25,5 v.l.	0	0
ἀνὴρ προφήτης	24,19		0	0
ἀπολύομαι ἀπὸ ἀνδρός; cf. ἀπολύω ἄνδρα Mk 10,12	16,18		0	0
(καὶ) (ἰδοὺ) ἄνδρες δύο DENAUX 2009 La[n]	9,30.32; 24,4	1,10; 9,38; 10,19 v.l.	0	0
πάντες ἄνδρες → πάντες (οἱ) ἄνθρωποι		19,7	0	0
ἄνδρες vocative (VKA) → ἄνδρες ἀδελφοί; ἄνθρωπε/γύνη voc. BOISMARD 1984 Aa1		1,11.16; 2,14.221.29.37; 3,12; 5,35; 7,2.26; 13,15.16.26.38; 14,15; 15,7.13; 17,22; 19,25.35; 21,28; 22,1; 23,1.6; 27,10.21.25; 28,17	0	0
ἀνήρ a supernatural being DENAUX 2009 La[n]	9,30.32; 24,4	1,10	0	0

Characteristic of Luke

BOISMARD 1984 Eb20; CADBURY 1920 189; CREDNER 1836 142; DENAUX 2009 L***;
GASTON 1973 65 [Lked?]; GOULDER 1989*; HAWKINS 1909 16; HENDRIKS 1986 434.468;
MORGENTHALER 1958LA; NEIRYNCK 1985; PLUMMER 1922 lx

	Lk	Acts	Mt	Mk
ἀνήρ/γυνή + geographic origin (VKb) → **ἄνθρωπος/γυνή** + geographic origin; cf. ἀνὴρ ἐκ φυλῆς Βενιαμίν Acts 13,21 BOISMARD 1984 Ba7;	11,32	1,11; 2,14.22[1]; 3,12; 5,35; 8,27; 10,28; 11,20; 13,16; 16,9; 17,22; 19,35; 21,28; 22,3	2	0
ἀνήρ (ὀνόματι/ᾧ ὄνομα) + proper name → **ἄνθρωπος/γυνή** (ὀνόματι/ᾧ ὄνομα) + proper name BOISMARD 1984 Bb14; DENAUX 2009 L***; NEIRYNCK 1985	1,27; 8,41; 19,2; 23,50[1]	2,22[2]; 5,1; 6,5; 8,9; 9,12; 10,1.22; 13,6.7.21.22; 15,22[2]; 18,24; 22,12	0	0
ἀνὴρ δίκαιος (epitethon) (VKc) → **ἀνήρ** + ἀγαθός/εὐλαβής; **ἄνθρωπος** + ἀγαθός/δίκαιος/εὐλαβής BOISMARD 1984 Cb100; NEIRYNCK 1985	23,50[2]	10,22	0	1
ἀνήρ τις → **ἄνθρωπός/γυνή** τις HARNACK 1906 32	8,27	3,2; 5,1; 8,9; 10,1; 11,20; 13,6; 14,8; 16,9; 17,5.34; 25,14	0	0
(καὶ) ἰδού + (ὁ) ἀνήρ → (καὶ) ἰδού + **ἄνθρωπος/γυνή** BOISMARD 1984 Ab2; CADBURY 1920 178; DENAUX 2009 L***; NEIRYNCK 1985	5,12.18; 8,41; 9,30.38; 19,2; 23,50[1]; 24,4	1,10; 5,25; 8,27; 10,17.19.30; 11,11	0	0
καὶ ἰδοὺ ἀνήρ + ὄνομα → καὶ ἰδοὺ **ἄνθρωπος** + ὄνομα DENAUX 2009 L***	8,41; 19,2; 23,50[1]		0	0
οἱ ἄνδρες nominative → **γυναῖκες** nom. DENAUX 2009 lA*	7,20; 22,63	5,25; 9,7; 10,17; 19,7	1	0

Literature

VON BENDEMANN 2001 414: "ἀνήρ τις entspricht lukanischer Vorliebe für ἀνήρ"; 428 [τῶν ἀνδρῶν in Lk 14,24]; BDR §242: "Adjektivierung von Substantiva durch ἀνήρ und ἄνθρωπος: Nur Lk und Apg mit ἀνήρ"; COLLISON 1977 167 [linguistic usage of Luke: certain]; DENAUX 2009 lAn [ἀνήρ/γυνή + geographic origin], lA[n] [ἀνήρ τις] ; HAUCK 1934 [Vorzugswort; Vorzugsverbindung: ἀνήρ τις]; JEREMIAS 1980 134-135: "erst so wird man erkennen, daß wir es mit einem ausgesprochenen Vorzugswort des Doppelwerks zu tun haben. An unserer Stelle [5,8] ist neben der Häufigkeit des Vorkommens noch ein weiteres Indiz für den spezifisch lukanischen Gebrauch von ἀνήρ zu notieren: die klassischem Vorbild folgende "Adjektivierung" von Substantiven durch ἀνήρ: Lk 5,8 (ἀνὴρ ἁμαρτωλός); 11,32 (ἄνδρες Νινευῖται par. Mt 12,41); 17,12 (λεπροὶ ἄνδρες); 19,7 (ἁμαρτωλῷ ἀνδρί); 24,19 (ἀνὴρ προφήτης), ein Phänomen, das sich im NT sonst nur in der Apg findet. (Dabei 14mal in der Anrede ἄνδρες ἀδελφοί, 16mal in Verbindung mit Gentilicien). Darüber hinaus ist zweierlei kennzeichnend für den lk Sprachgebrauch von ἀνήρ: 1. die Verwendung von ἀνήρ als Ersatz für indefinites τις …; 2. die Wendung καὶ ἰδοὺ ἀνήρ, die im NT ebenfalls nur im lk Doppelwerk vorkommt"; RADL 1975 399 [ἀνήρ; "ἀνήρ im Sinne von 'Mensch' ist ein Lieblingswort des Lukas"; "häufiger gebrauch von ἀνήρ in Anreden und vor Substantiven"; ἀνήρ τις; οἱ ἄνδρες; ἄνδρες ἀδελφοί; ἄνδρες Ἰσραηλῖται]; SCHNEIDER 1969 97.163 [οἱ ἄνδρες in der Erzählung: Vorzugswörter und -ausdrücke des Luk].

BAUER, Johannes Baptist, Monstra te esse matrem, Virgo singularis! Zur Diskussion um Lk 1,34. — MüTZ 9 (1958) 124-135. [ἄνδρα οὐ γινώσκω]
—, Philologische Bemerkungen zu Lk 1,34. — Bib 45 (1964) 535-540. [ἄνδρα οὐ γινώσκω]

BRINKMANN, B., Die Jungfrauengeburt und das Lukasevangelium. — *Bib* 34 (1953) 327-332. [ἄνδρα οὐ γινώσκω]

CRAGHAN, John F., A Redactional Study of Lk 7,21 in the Light of Dt 19,15. — *CBQ* 29 (1967) 353-367. Esp. 52-56: "The redactor's hand" [ἄνδρες δύο].

DICKERSON, Patrick L., The New Character Narrative in Luke-Acts, 1997. Esp. 293-298: "The elements of the Lukan new character narrative" [τις/ἰδοὺ ἀνὴρ/γυνὴ ὀνόματι]; 303-305: "The use of ἀνήρ in the introduction".

GEWIEß, Josef, Die Marienfrage, Lk 1,34. — *BZ* NF 5 (1961) 221-254. [ἄνδρα οὐ γινώσκω]

QUECKE, Hans, Lk 1,34 in den alten Übersetzungen und im Protevangelium des Jakobus. — *Bib* 44 (1963) 499-520. [ἄνδρα οὐ γινώσκω]

ZERWICK, Maximilian, "… quoniam virum non cognosco" (Lc 1,34) (Conspectus criticus de opinionibus recentioribus). — *VD* 37 (1959) 212-224, 276-288. [ἄνδρα οὐ γινώσκω]

ἀνθίστημι 1 + 2 (Mt 1)

1. be hostile toward; 2. resist (Lk 21,15)

Word groups	Lk	Acts	Mt	Mk
ἀνθίσταμαι middle (*VK*a)		13,8	0	0

Literature
BORMANN, Lukas, *Recht, Gerechtigkeit und Religion*, 2001. Esp. 174.
FUCHS, Albert, *Sprachliche Untersuchungen zu Mattäus und Lukas*, 1971. Esp. 180.

ἀνθομολογέομαι 1

give thanks (Lk 2,38)

Literature
HAUCK 1934 [seltenes Alleinwort].

GEORGE, Augustin, La prière. — ID., *Études*, 1978, 395-427. Esp. 402-405: "Le vocabulaire lucanien de la prière".

ἄνθρωπος 95/101 + 46/47 (Mt 115/118, Mk 56)

1. human being (Lk 1,25); 2. man (Lk 2,25); 3. husband

Word groups	Lk	Acts	Mt	Mk
ἄνθρωποι (plural) + θεός/κύριος → ἄνθρωπος sing. + θεός/κύριος DENAUX 2009 lAn	1,25; 2,14.52; 12,8¹.9.36; 16,15¹·²; 18,11.27	5,4.29.38²(-39); 14,11.15; 15,17.26; 16,17; 17,30; 18,13; 24,16	3	3
ἄνθρωποι τῆς γενεᾶς ταύτης → ἀνήρ τῆς γενεᾶς ταύτης	7,31		0	0
ἄνθρωποι εὐδοκίας	2,14		0	0
ἄνθρωπος + numeral → ἀνήρ + numeral	18,10		0	0
ἄνθρωπος + ἀγαθός/δίκαιος/εὐλαβής → ἀνήρ + ἀγαθός/δίκαιος/εὐλαβής	2,25²; 6,45; 23,47		2	0
ἄνθρωπος ἁμαρτωλός → ἀνήρ ἁμαρτωλός; γυνή + ἁμαρτωλός	24,7²		0	0

	Lk	Acts	Mt	Mk
ὁ ἄνθρωπος ἐκεῖνος (SCb; VKb) → ὁ ἄνθρωπος οὗτος; ὁ ἀνὴρ ἐκεῖνος/ οὗτος; γυνὴ αὕτη	11,26; 22,22[2]	16,35	3/4	2
ἄνθρωπος + θεός	2,14.52; 4,4 v.l.; 12,8[1].9; 16,15[1.2]; 18,2.4.11.27; 22,69; 23,47	5,4.29.38[2](-3 9); 7,56; 10,28; 12,22; 14,11.15; 16,17; 17,30; 18,13; 24,16	5	5
ἄνθρωπος (singular) + θεός/κύριος → ἄνθρωποι plural + θεός/κύριος	4,4 v.l.; 6,5; 18,2.4; 22,69; 23,47	7,56; 10,28; 12,22	4	3
ἄνθρωπος Ἰουδαῖος → ἀνὴρ Ἰουδαῖος; γυνὴ Ἰουδαία		21,39	0	0
ἄνθρωπος + ὀνόματι/ᾧ ὄνομα + proper name → ἀνήρ/γυνή (ὀνόματι/ᾧ ὄνομα) + proper name	2,25[1]	9,33	1	1
εἰρήνη ἐν ἀνθρώποις εὐδοκίας	2,14		0	0
ἔμπροσθεν τῶν ἀνθρώπων (SCc; VKd) → ἐνώπιον τῶν ἀνθρώπων; ἔμπροσθεν/ἐναντίον/ ἐνώπιον τῶν ἀγγέλων τοῦ θεοῦ / (τοῦ) θεοῦ / κυρίου	12,8[1]		5	0
ἐν ἀνθρώποις DENAUX 2009 La[n]	1,25; 2,14; 16,15[2]	4,12	0	0
ἐνώπιον τῶν ἀνθρώπων (SCc; VKd) → ἔμπροσθεν τῶν ἀνθρώπων; ἔμπροσ- θεν/ἐναντίον/ ἐνώπιον τῶν ἀγγέλων τοῦ θεοῦ / (τοῦ) θεοῦ / κυρίου DENAUX 2009 L[n]	12,9; 16,15[1]		0	0
(καὶ) ἰδοὺ ἄνθρωπος → (καὶ) ἰδού + ἀνήρ/γυνή	2,25[1]; 7,34[2]; 14,2		2	0
καὶ ἰδοὺ ἄνθρωπος + ὄνομα → καὶ ἰδοὺ ἀνήρ + ὄνομα	2,25[1]		0	0
οὐαὶ τῷ ἀνθρώπῳ δι᾽ οὗ	22,22[2]		2	1
πάντες (οἱ) ἄνθρωποι → πάντες ἄνδρες DENAUX 2009 La[n]	6,26; 13,4	22,15	0	0
ὁ υἱὸς τοῦ ἀνθρώπου (LN: Son of Man; SCa; VKa)	5,24; 6,5.22[2]; 7,34[1]; 9,22.26.44[1].56[1]*.58; 11,30; 12,8[2].10.40; 17,22.24.26.30; 18,8.31; 19,10; 21,27.36; 22,22[1].48.69; 24,7[1]	7,56	30/32	14
ὁ υἱὸς τοῦ ἀνθρώπου + ἔρχομαι	7,34[1]; 9,56[1]*; 12,40; 18,8; 19,10; 21,27		7/9	3
ὁ υἱὸς τοῦ ἀνθρώπου + ἡμέρα/ὥρα	12,40; 17,22.24.26.30		2	1
ὁ υἱὸς + τοῦ ἀνθρώπου ἑστὼς/ καθήμενος ἐκ δεξιῶν (τοῦ θεοῦ)	22,69	7,56	1	1
ὁ υἱὸς τοῦ ἀνθρώπου + κύριος	6,5		1	1
ὁ υἱὸς τοῦ ἀνθρώπου + παραδίδωμι	9,44[1]; 18,31(-32); 22,22[1].48; 24,7[1]		5	4
χεῖρες ἀνθρώπων	9,44[2]; 24,7[2]	17,25*	1	1

Characteristic of Luke	Lk	Acts	Mt	Mk
ἄνθρωπε vocative (VKc) → ἄνδρες voc.; γύναι voc.; cf. ὦ ἄνθρωπε Rom 2,1.3; 9,20; 1 Tim 6,11; Jam 2,20 DENAUX 2009 L***; GOULDER 1989*; HAWKINS 1909L	5,20; 12,14; 22,58.60		0	0

ἄνθρωπος + geographic origin (*VK*e) → ἀνήρ/γυνή + geografic origin BOISMARD 1984 Bb94; NEIRYNCK 1985	23,6	16,37; 21,39; 22,25.26	1	0
ὁ ἄνθρωπος οὗτος (*SC*b; *VK*b) → ὁ ἄνθρωπος ἐκεῖνος; ὁ ἀνὴρ ἐκεῖνος/οὗτος; γυνὴ αὕτη; cf. Jn 18,17.29 BOISMARD 1984 Bb61; DENAUX 2009 L***; GOULDER 1989*; HARNACK 1906 36; NEIRYNCK 1985	2,25[2]; 14,30; 23,4.14[1.2].47	4,16; 5,28.35.38[1]; 6,13; 16,17.20; 22,26; 23,9; 26,31.32; 28,4	0	2
ἄνθρωπός τις → ἀνήρ/γυνή τις DENAUX 2009 L***; GOULDER 1989*	10,30; 12,16; 14,2.16; 15,11; 16,1.19; 19,12; 20,9	9,33; 25,16	0	0
ἄνθρωπός (+) τις (ἦν) εὐγενής/πλούσιος DENAUX 2009 L***	12,16; 16,1.19; 19,12		0	0

Literature

COLLISON 1977 166 [noteworthy phenomena]; 168 [ἄνθρωπε vocative: linguistic usage of Luke: likely]; 212 [ἄνθρωπός τις: linguistic usage of Luke's "other source-material": certain]; DENAUX 2009 lAn [ἄνθρωπος + geographic origin]; GERSDORF 1816 193 [ἐν ἀνθρώποις]; 245 [καὶ ἰδοὺ ἄνθρωπος ἦν]; HAUCK 1934 [ἄνθρωπε: seltenes Alleinwort; Vorzugsverbindung: τίς ἄνθρωπος ἐξ; ἄνθρωπός (δέ) τις]; PAFFENROTH 1997 79 [ἄνθρωπός τις]; RADL 1975 421 [ὁ ἄνθρωπος οὗτος]; REHKOPF 1959 91 [ἄνθρωπός τις: vorlukanisch]; 97 [υἱὸς τοῦ ἀνθρώπου: vorlukanisch]; 98 [ἄνθρωπε:"Substantiva in Anrede bei den Synoptikern"]; SCHÜRMANN 1961 276 [υἱὸς τοῦ ἀνθρώπου]; 278 [ἄνθρωπός τις; protoluk R weniger wahrscheinlich].

BAUCKHAM, Richard, The Son of Man: "A Man in My Position" or "Someone"? — *JSNT* 23 (1985) 23-33.

BERGER, Paul-Richard, Lk 2,14: ἄνθρωποι εὐδοκίας: Die auf Gottes Weisung mit Wohlgefallen beschenkten Menschen. — *ZNW* 74 (1983) 129-144.

—, Menschen ohne "Gottes Wohlgefallen" Lk 2,14? — *ZNW* 76 (1985) 119-122.

BIETENHARD, Hans, "Der Menschensohn" – ὁ υἱὸς τοῦ ἀνθρώπου: Sprachliche und religionsgeschichtliche Untersuchungen zu einem Begriff der synoptischen Evangelien. I: Sprachlicher und religionsgeschichtlicher Teil. — *ANRW* II.25.1 (1982) 265-350.

CASEY, P. Maurice, The Son of Man Problem. — *ZNW* 67 (1976) 147-154.

—, The Jackals and the Son of Man (Matt. 8.20 // Lk 9.58). — *JSNT* 23 (1985) 3-22.

DAWSEY, James M., What's in a Name? Characterization in Luke. — *BTB* 16 (1986) 143-147. Esp. 143-144: "Luke's use of 'son of man'".

DEICHGRÄBER, Reinhard, Lk 2,14: ἄνθρωποι εὐδοκίας. — *ZNW* 51 (1960) 132.

DELEBECQUE, Édouard, *Études grecques*, 1976. Esp. 25-38: "Le 'gloria' des anges (2,14)".

DERRETT, J. Duncan M., ῎Ανθρωποι εὐδοκίας (Lk 2:14b). — *FilolNT* 11 (1998) 101-106. Esp. 101-102: "The problem"; 102-103: "A Greek word with a Hebrew meaning"; 103-105: "The angelic host". [NTA 44, 971]

FITZMYER, Joseph A., "Peace Upon Earth Among Men of His Good Will" (Lk 2:14). — *TS* 19 (1958) 225-227; = ID., *Essays on the Semitic Background of the New Testament*, London: Chapman, 1971, 101-104.

GUERRA GÓMEZ, Manuel, Análisis filológico-teológico y traducción del himno de los ángeles en Belén, 1989. Esp. 53-55: "ἐν ἀνθρώποις (in) hominibus, entre-en (para) los hombres".

HAHN, Ferdinand, *Christologische Hoheitstitel*, 1963. Esp. 13-23: "Menschensohn: Philologische und religionsgeschichtliche Probleme".

HUNZINGER, Claus-Hunno, Neues Licht auf Lc 2,14 ἄνθρωποι εὐδοκίας. — *ZNW* 44 (1952-53) 85-90.

—, Ein weiterer Beleg zu Lc 2,14 ἄνθρωποι εὐδοκίας. — *ZNW* 49 (1958) 129-130.

50 ἄνθρωπος – ἀνίστημι

JEREMIAS, Joachim, ῎Ανθρωποι εὐδοκίας (Lk 2,14). — ZNW 28 (1929) 13-20.
KILPATRICK, Ross S., The Greek Syntax of Luke 2.14. — NTS 34 (1988) 472-475.
KUHNERT, E., Ὁ υἱὸς τοῦ ἀνθρώπου. — ZNW 18 (1917) 165-176.
MÜLLER, Theodore, Observations on Some New Testament Texts Based on Generative-Transformational Grammar. — BTrans 29 (1978) 117-120. Esp. 117: "Luke 2.14b καὶ ἐπὶ γῆς εἰρήνη ἐν ἀνθρώποις εὐδοκίας". [NTA 22, 712]
RAD, Gerhard VON, Noch einmal Lc 4,14 ἄνθρωποι εὐδοκίας. — ZNW 29 (1930) 111-115.
ROPES, James H., "Good Will Toward Men" (Luke 2,14). — HTR 10 (1917) 52-56.
SCHWARZ, Günther, Der Lobgesang der Engel (Lukas 2,14): Emendation und Rückübersetzung. — BZ NF 15 (1971) 260-264.
—, "…ἄνθρωποι εὐδοκίας"? (Lk 2,14). — ZNW 75 (1984) 136-137. [NTA 26, 143]
SMOTHERS, Edgar R., ἐν ἀνθρώποις εὐδοκίας. — RechSR 24 (1934) 86-93.
WILLIAMS, A. Lukyn, "Glory to God in the Highest, and on Earth Peace among Men of Good-will" (Luke ii.14). — ExpT 50 (1938-39) 283-284.
WOBBE, Joseph, Das Gloria (Lk 2,14). — BZ 22 (1934) 118-152.224-245; 23 (1936) 358-364.

ἀνίστημι 27/28 + 45/46 (Mt 4/6, Mk 16[17]/18)

1. cause to stand up (Acts 9,41); 2. raise to life (Acts 2,24); 3. ἀνίσταμαι: stand up (Lk 4,16); 4. ἀνίσταμαι: go away (Lk 4,38); 5. ἀνίσταμαι: appear (Acts 5,36); 6. ἀνίσταμαι: live again (Lk 9,8); 7. ἀνίσταμαι: rebel against

Word groups	Lk	Acts	Mt	Mk
ἀναστάς + verb of movement	1,39; 4,38; 5,25.28; 6,8; 15,18.20; 17,19; 24,12.33	8,27; 9,11; 10,20.23; 14,20; 22,10	1	4/5
ἀναστάς + (λέγω/)εἶπεν BOISMARD 1984 Ca5		1,15; 13,16; 15,7	1	0
ἀνέστη + participle DENAUX 2009 1A[n]	10,25	5,36; 6,9	0	0
ἀνίστημι (+) ἐκ νεκρῶν → (ἡ) ἀνάστασις (ἡ) (ἐκ) (τῶν) νεκρῶν; ἐγείρω ἐκ (τῶν) νεκρῶν	16,31; 24,46	10,41; 13,34; 17,3.31	0/1	3
ἀνίστημι + εὐθέως/παραχρῆμα; cf. ἀνίστημι + εὐθύς Mk 5,42; ἐγείρω + εὐθύς Mk 2,12 DENAUX 2009 La[n]	4,39; 5,25; 8,55	9,34[2]	0	0/1
ἀνίστημι + καθεύδω; cf. Eph 5,14; ἐγείρω + καθεύδω Mt 8,(24-)25; 9,(24-)25; 25,(5-)7; 26,(45-)46; Mk 4,27.38; 14,(41-)42	22,46		0	0
ἀνίστημι (+) τῇ τρίτῃ ἡμέρᾳ / τῇ ἡμέρᾳ τῇ τρίτῃ → ἐγείρω τῇ τρίτῃ ἡμέρᾳ; cf. ἀνίστημι μετὰ τρεῖς ἡμέρας Mk 8,31; 9,31; 10,34 DENAUX 2009 L[n]	18,33; 24,7.46		0/1	0/1
ἀνάστηθι imperative BOISMARD 1984 Aa11		8,26; 9,6.34[1].40; 10,26; 14,10; 26,16	0	0
ἀνίστημι resurrection (VKb) → ἐγείρω	8,55; 9,8.19; 16,31; 18,33; 24,7.46	2,24.30*.32; 9,40.41; 10,41; 13,33.34; 17,3.31	0/2	9

ἀνίστημι resurrection of Jesus (SCa) → ἐγείρω	18,33; 24,7.46	2,24.30*.32; 3,26; 10,41; 13,33.34; 17,3.31	0/2	5
ἀνίστημι transitive (VKa)		2,24.30*.32; 3,22.26; 7,37; 9,41; 13,33.34; 17,31	1	0
ἀνίστημι transitive, said of Christ BOISMARD 1984 Aa14		2,24.30*.32; 3,26; 13,33.34; 17,31	0	0

Characteristic of Luke

GASTON 1973 65 [Lked?]; HENDRIKS 1986 468; MORGENTHALER 1958A; PLUMMER 1922 lix

	Lk	Acts	Mt	Mk
ἀναστάς + imperative; cf. ἀνάστηθι + imper. Acts 8,26; 9,6.34[1]; 26,16 BOISMARD 1984 Ab18; DENAUX 2009 lA*; NEIRYNCK 1985	17,19; 22,46	9,11; 10,13.20; 11,7; 22,10.16	0	0
ἀναστάς/ἀναστάντες BOISMARD 1984 Bb56; CREDNER 1836 139; DENAUX 2009 L***; GOULDER 1989*; HARNACK 1906 138; HAWKINS 1909L; NEIRYNCK 1985; PLUMMER 1922 lxii	1,39; 4,29.38.39; 5,25.28; 6,8; 11,7.8; 15,18.20; 17,19; 22,45.46; 23,1; 24,12.33	1,15; 5,6.17.34; 8,27; 9,11.18.39; 10,13.20.23; 11,7.28; 13,16; 14,20; 15,7; 22,10.16; 23,9	2	6[7]/8
ἀναστάς/ἀναστάντες δέ BOISMARD 1984 Ab17; DENAUX 2009 lA*; NEIRYNCK 1985	1,39; 4,38	5,6.17.34; 9,39; 11,28; 13,16	0	0[1]
ἀναστὰς ἔστη HARNACK 1906 43	6,8		0	0
ἀναστάς + πορεύομαι; cf. ἀνάστηθι + πορεύου Acts 8,26 BOISMARD 1984 Ab40; DENAUX 2009 lA*; HARNACK 1906 138; NEIRYNCK 1985	1,39; 15,18; 17,19	8,27; 9,11; 10,20; 22,10	0	0
ἀνέστη/ἀνέστησεν/ἀνέστησαν; cf. Jn 11,31; 1 Cor 10,7; 1 Thess 4,14; ἐξανέστησαν Acts 15,5 DENAUX 2009 lA**	4,16; 8,55; 9,8.19; 10,25; 17,12*	2,24.32; 5,36.37; 6,9; 7,18; 9,34[2].41; 13,34; 15,5; 26,30	0	3
ἀνέστη and cognate ἐξανέστη + participle → ἐξανέστη + part. BOISMARD 1984 Ab68; NEIRYNCK 1985	10,25	5,36; 6,9; 15,5	0	0

Literature

VON BENDEMANN 2001 418: "lukanische Vorzugsvokabel ist ἀνιστάναι"; 419: "charakteristisch lukanisch ist das Partizip ἀναστάς"; COLLISON 1977 37 [linguistic usage of Luke: certain]; DENAUX 2009 lA[n] [ἀνέστη and cognate ἐξανέστη+ participle]; EASTON 1910 176 [ἀναστάς: possible Hebraisms in the Lucan Writings, as classed by Dalman]; GERSDORF 1816 198 [ἀναστᾶσα - ἐπορεύθη; ἀναστᾶσα δὲ Μαριὰμ ἐν ταῖς ἡμέραις ταύταις]; HAUCK 1934 [Vorzugswort]; JEREMIAS 1980 55 [ἀνίστημι intransitive; ἀναστάς; ἀναστάς + imper.]; RADL 1975 399 [ἀνίστημι; ἀναστάς; ἀνέστη/ἀνέστησαν].

CHILTON, Bruce, Announcement in Nazara, 1981. Esp. 155.
DAUER, Anton, Lk 24,12 – Ein Produkt lukanischer Redaktion? — F. VAN SEGBROECK, et al. (eds.), The Four Gospels 1992. FS F. Neirynck, 1992, II, 1697-1716.
—, Zur Authentizität von Lk 24,12. — ETL 70 (1994) 294-318.
MUDDIMAN, John, A Note on Reading Luke XXIV.12. — ETL 48 (1972) 542-548.
NEIRYNCK, Frans, The Uncorrected Historic Present in Lk XXIV.12. — ETL 48 (1972) 548-553; = ID., Evangelica, 1982, 329-334 (334: additional note; Appendix, Evangelica II, 1991, 798).

—, Once More Lk 24,12. — *ETL* 70 (1994) 319-340; = ID., *Evangelica III*, 2001, 549-571.

—, A Supplementary Note on Lk 24,12. — *ETL* 72 (1996) 425-430; = ID., *Evangelica III*, 2001, 572-578.

—, Luke 24,12: An Anti-Docetic Interpolation? — DENAUX, A. (ed.), *New Testament Textual Criticism and Exegesis*. FS J. Delobel, 2002, 145-158. Esp. 146-148.

REYNOLDS, S.M., The Word *Again* in Creeds and Bible. — *WestTJ* 35 (1972) 28-35. [NTA 17, 445: *ana* in *anistēmi*: for clarity "again" should be dropped from all references to rising from the dead]

RODRÍGUEZ CARMONA, Antonio, Origen de las fórmulas neotestamentarias de resurrección con anistánai y egeírein. — *EstE* 55 (1980) 27-58.

SABUGAL, Santos, *Anástasis. Resucitó y resucitaremos* (BAC), Madrid, 1993. 712 pp.

SCHWARZ, Günther, ανιστημι und αναστασις in den Evangelien. — *BibNot* 10 (1979) 35-39.

WILCOX, Max, Semitisms in the New Testament, 1984. Esp. 1008-1009: "ἀνάστηθι ἐπὶ τοὺς πόδας σου (Acts 14:10)".

"Αννα 1	Anna (Lk 2,36)

Literature
GERSDORF 1816 258 [καὶ ἦν "Αννα προφῆτις - αὕτη προβεβηκυῖα].

"Αννας 1 + 1	Annas (Lk 3,2; Acts 4,6)

ἀνόητος 1	without understanding (Lk 24,25)

Literature
LEE, John A.L. – HORSLEY, G.H.R., A Lexicon of the New Testament, 2, 1998. Esp. 64.

ἄνοια 1	
1. lack of understanding; 2. extreme fury (Lk 6,11)	

Literature
LEE, John A.L. – HORSLEY, G.H.R., A Lexicon of the New Testament, 2, 1998. Esp. 64-65.80.

ἀνοίγω 6/7 + 16/17 (Mt 11, Mk 1)		open		
Word groups	Lk	Acts	Mt	Mk
ἀνοίγω τὸ βιβλίον → (ἀνα)πτύσσω τὸ βιβλίον; διανοίγω/συνίημι τὰς γραφάς	4,17*		0	0
ἀνοίγω + θύραν (*LN*: make possible)		14,27	0	0
ἀνοίγω (+) τὴν θύραν / τὴν πύλην / τὸν πυλῶνα → (ἀπο)κλείω/κρούω τὴν θύραν DENAUX 2009 1Aⁿ	13,25	5,19.23; 12,10.14; 14,27; 16,26.27	0	0
ἀνοίγω + (ἀπο)κλείω→ ἀνοίγω + κρούω DENAUX 2009 LAⁿ	13,25	5,23	0	0

ἀνοίγω + κρούω → **ἀνοίγω** + (ἀπο)κλείω	11,9.10; 12,36; 13,25	12,16	2	0
ἀνοίγω τὸν οὐρανόν → **διανοίγω/κλείω** τὸν οὐρανόν	3,21	7,56*; 10,11	1	0
ἀνοίγω (+) (τοὺς) ὀφθαλμούς (*LN*: cause to be able to see; *SC*b; *VK*b) → **διανοίγω/ἐπαίρω** τοὺς ὀφθαλμούς; cf. ἀνοίγω τὰς ἀκοάς Mk 7,35		9,8.40; 26,18	2	0
ἀνοίγω (+) τὸ στόμα (*LN*: start speaking; *SC*a; *VK*a)	1,64	8,32.35; 10,34; 18,14	3	0

ἄνομος 1 + 1 (Mk 0/1)

1. lawless (Lk 22,37; Acts 2,23); 2. without the Law; 3. heathen

Literature

SCHÜRMANN 1957 128.

BORMANN, Lukas, *Recht, Gerechtigkeit und Religion*, 2001. Esp. 119.
MINEAR, Paul S., A Note on Luke XXII,36. — *NT* 7 (1964-65) 128-134. Esp. 133 [ἄνομοι]:
"*Now* it is clear that the apostles without exception are the ἄνομοι with whom Jesus is to be 'reckoned' in his arrest, trial and death".

ἀνορθόω 1 + 1

1. build up again (Acts 15,16); 2. straighten up (Lk 13,13)

Literature

DENAUX 2009 LA[n].

ἀνταποδίδωμι 2

1. pay back (Lk 14,14[1.2]); 2. repay

Literature

DENAUX 2009 L[n]; Hauck 1934 [seltenes Alleinwort].

BORMANN, Lukas, *Recht, Gerechtigkeit und Religion*, 2001. Esp. 147.

ἀνταπόδομα 1

1. repayment (Lk 14,12); 2. recompense

Literature

HAUCK 1934 [seltenes Alleinwort].

BORMANN, Lukas, *Recht, Gerechtigkeit und Religion*, 2001. Esp. 147.

ἀνταποκρίνομαι 1

1. answer (Lk 14,16); 2. criticize in return

Word groups	Lk	Acts	Mt	Mk
ἀνταποκρίνομαι πρὸς ταῦτα	14,6		0	0

Literature
BORMANN, Lukas, *Recht, Gerechtigkeit und Religion*, 2001. Esp. 174.

ἀντέχομαι 1 (Mt 1)	
1. adhere to (Lk 16,13); 2. cling to a belief; 3. help	

ἀντί 4 + 1 (Mt 5, Mk 1)	
1. instead (Lk 11,11); 2. on behalf of; 3. for this reason, because (Lk 1,20; 19,44); 4. so then (Lk 12,3); 5. in place of	

Characteristic of Luke	Lk	Acts	Mt	Mk
ἀνθ' ὧν (*VK*a); cf. 2 Thess 2,10 BOISMARD 1984 Bb95; GOULDER 1989; HAWKINS 1909add; NEIRYNCK 1985; PLUMMER 1922 lix	1,20; 12,3; 19,44	12,23	0	0

Literature
COLLISON 1977 123 [ἀνθ' ὧν: noteworthy phenomena]; DENAUX 2009 La[n] [ἀνθ' ὧν]; EASTON 1910 158-159 [ἀνθ' ὧν: cited by Weiss as characteristic of L, and possibly corroborative]; GERSDORF 1816 188 [ἀνθ' ὧν]; JEREMIAS 1980 43 [ἀνθ' ὧν: red.] ; REHKOPF 1959 91 [ἀνθ' ὧν: vorlukanisch]; SCHÜRMANN 1961 273 [ἀνθ' ὧν].

ἀντιβάλλω 1	discuss

Word groups	Lk	Acts	Mt	Mk
λόγους + ἀντιβάλλω + πρὸς ἀλλήλους	24,17		0	0

Characteristic of Luke	Lk	Acts	Mt	Mk
ἀντιβάλλω πρός + accusative → verb of saying πρός + acc. CREDNER 1836 138	24,17		0	0

Literature
HAUCK 1934 [seltenes Alleinwort].

ἀντίδικος 2 (Mt 2)	
1. accuser (Lk 12,58; 18,3); 2. adversary	

Literature
BORMANN, Lukas, *Recht, Gerechtigkeit und Religion*, 2001. Esp. 174.

ἀντικαλέω* 1	invite back (Lk 14,12)

Literature
HAUCK 1934 [seltenes Alleinwort].

ἀντίκειμαι 2	be hostile toward

Word groups	Lk	Acts	Mt	Mk
οἱ ἀντικείμενοι + dative (person) DENAUX 2009 L[n]	13,17; 21,15		0	0

Literature

DENAUX 2009 L[n]; EASTON 1910 150 [probably characteristic of L]; HAUCK 1934 [seltenes Alleinwort]; JEREMIAS 1980 230 [οἱ ἀντικείμενοι + dat. of person: red.].

BARTELINK, Gerhardus J.M., Ἀντικείμενος (Widersacher) als Teufels- und Dämonenbezeichnung. — *Sacris Erudiri* (Steenbrugge) 30 (1987-88) 205-224.
BORMANN, Lukas., *Recht, Gerechtigkeit und Religion*, 2001. Esp. 174.
FUCHS, Albert, *Sprachliche Untersuchungen zu Mattäus und Lukas*, 1971. Esp. 184.

ἀντιλαμβάνομαι 1 + 1

1. help (Lk 1,54); 2. devote oneself to; 3. enjoy benefit

Characteristic of Luke	Lk	Acts	Mt	Mk
ἀντιλαμβάνομαι help HARNACK 1906 73.142; VOGEL 1899B	1,54	20,35	0	0

Literature

DENAUX 2009 LA[n] [ἀντιλαμβάνομαι help]; GERSDORF 1816 200-201 [ἀντελάβετο Ἰσραὴλ παιδὸς αὐτοῦ].

DUPONT, Jacques, *Le discours de Milet*, 1962. Esp. 308-319.

ἀντιλέγω 3 + 4/5   oppose (Lk 2,34; 20,27; 21,5)

Characteristic of Luke

BOISMARD 1984 cb143; DENAUX 2009 IA*; NEIRYNCK 1985; PLUMMER 1922 lix

	Lk	Acts	Mt	Mk
ἀντειπεῖν (and cognate ἀντιλέγω) BOISMARD 1984 Ab161; GOULDER 1989; HAWKINS 1909LA; MORGENTHALER 1958*; NEIRYNCK 1985; PLUMMER 1922 liii; VOGEL 1899A	21,15	4,14	0	0

Literature

DENAUX 2009 LA[n] [ἀντειπεῖν (and cognate ἀντιλέγω)];GERSDORF 1816 257 [εἰς σημεῖον ἀντιλεγόμενον]; HAUCK 1934 [seltenes Alleinwort]; JEREMIAS 1980 97 [red.]; RADL 1975 399.

BORMANN, Lukas, *Recht, Gerechtigkeit und Religion*, 2001. Esp. 174-175.
DERRETT, J. Duncan M., Ἀντιλεγόμενον, ῥομφαία, διαλογισμοί (Lk 2:34-35): The Hidden Context. — *FilolNT* 6 (1993) 207-218. ["the author examines the meaning and significance of the main terms used in Lk 2:34-35, by studying their double context, the obvious one and the one based on Genesis and Deuteronomy. The choice of vocabulary is part of a great scheme of Luke's to demonstrate the new religion as a renewal of the pristine worship of YHWH"]; = ID., *Studies in the New Testament*, VI, 1995, 64-75.
FUCHS, Albert, *Sprachliche Untersuchungen zu Mattäus und Lukas*, 1971. Esp. 183 [ἀντειπεῖν-ἀντιλέγειν].

ἀντιμετρέω** 1 (Mt 0/1)	repay (Lk 6,38)

Literature
HAUCK 1934 [seltenes Alleinwort].

ἀντιπαρέρχομαι*** 2	pass by on opposite side (Lk 10,31.32)

Characteristic of Luke
PLUMMER 1922 liii

Literature
DENAUX 2009 Lⁿ; HAUCK 1934 [seltenes Alleinwort].

BURCHARD, Christoph, Fußnoten zum neutestamentlichen Griechisch II, 1978. Esp. 149-151: "Lk 10,31.32 ἀντιπαρῆλθεν".

ἀντιπέρα* 1	across from

Word groups	Lk	Acts	Mt	Mk
εἰμι ἀντιπέρα	8,26		0	0

Literature
HAUCK 1934 [seltenes Alleinwort].

ELLINGTON, John, Where Is the Other Side? — *BTrans* 38 (1987) 221-226.

ἄνυδρος 1 (Mt 1)	waterless (Lk 11,24)

ἄνωθεν 1 + 1 (Mt 1, Mk 1)	
1. from above; 2. again; 3. for a long time (Lk 1,3); 4. BDAG 2000: from the beginning (Acts 26,5)	

Literature
ALEXANDER, Loveday, *The Preface to Luke's Gospel*, 1993. Esp. 130.
RINALDI, Giovanni, Risalendo alle più lontane origini della tradizione (*Luca* 1,3). — *BibOr* 7 (1965) 252-258.

ἀνώτερον 1	
1. preceding; 2. higher status (Lk 14,10)	

ἀξίνη 1 (Mt 1)	axe (Lk 3,9)

ἄξιος 8 + 7 (Mt 9)	
1. worthy (Lk 10,7); 2. proper (Lk 3,8)	

Characteristic of Luke	Lk	Acts	Mt	Mk
ἄξιος + genitive (thing) BOISMARD 1984 Eb43; DENAUX 2009 lA**; NEIRYNCK 1985	3,8; 10,7; 12,48; 23,15.41	13,46; 23,29; 25,11.25; 26,20.31	2	0
ἄξιος + infinitive (*VK*a) → (κατ)ἀξιόω + inf. BOISMARD 1984 Db31; NEIRYNCK 1985	15,19.21	13,25	0	0
ἄξιος θανάτου → αἰτία/αἴτιος θανάτου VOGEL 1899C	23,15	23,29; 25,11.25; 26,31	0	0
πράσσω τι/οὐδὲν ἄξιον θανάτου; cf. Rom 1,32 BOISMARD 1984 Ab100; NEIRYNCK 1985	23,15	25,11.25; 26,31	0	0

Literature
VON BENDEMANN 2001 424 [ἄξιος + gen.]; BDR § 393,3: "Der Infinitiv bei unpersönlichen Ausdrücken und bei Nomina: ἄξιος mit Infinitiv Lk 15,19.21"; COLLISON 1977 183 [linguistic usage of Luke's "other source-material": probable]; DENAUX 2009 La[n] [ἄξιος + infinitive], lA[n] [ἄξιος θανάτου; πράσσω τι/ οὐδὲν ἄξιον θανάτου]; RADL 1975 400 [ἄξιος; ἄξιον θανάτου πράσσω]; 412 [θανάτου ἄξιον]; REHKOPF 1959 92 [vorlukanisch]; SCHÜRMANN 1961 275. BORMANN, Lukas, *Recht, Gerechtigkeit und Religion*, 2001. Esp. 197. KLEIST, James A., "Axios" in the Gospels. — *CBQ* 6 (1944) 342-346.

ἀξιόω 1 + 2

1. regard worthy (Lk 7,7); 2. choose; 3. desire (Acts 28,22)

Word groups	Lk	Acts	Mt	Mk
ἀξιόω = to ask BOISMARD 1984 Aa72		15,38; 28,22	0	0

Characteristic of Luke	Lk	Acts	Mt	Mk
ἀξιόω + infinitive → ἄξιος/καταξιόω + inf. PLUMMER 1922 lii	7,7	15,38; 28,22	0	0

Literature
DENAUX 2009 lA[n], lA[n] [ἀξιόω + infinitive]; HAUCK 1934 [seltenes Alleinwort]; JEREMIAS 1980 154 [ἀξιόω + inf.: red.]. BORMANN, Lukas, *Recht, Gerechtigkeit und Religion*, 2001. Esp. 191.

ἀπαγγέλλω 11 + 15/16 (Mt 8/9, Mk 3[5])

1. inform (Lk 14,21); 2. command

Word groups	Lk	Acts	Mt	Mk
ἀνα/ὑποστρέφω / εἰστρέχω / (ἀπ/εἰσ/προσ) ἔρχομαι / πορεύομαι / φεύγω + ἀπαγγέλλω → ἀπέρχομαι + διαγγέλλω; ὑποστρέφω + διηγέομαι; ἀποστέλλω / εἰσπορεύομαι / (ἀπ/δι/κατ)ἔρχομαι + κηρύσσω; cf. συνάγω/ τρέχω/ὑπάγω + ἀπαγγέλλω Mt 28,8.10; Mk 5,19; 6,30	7,22; 8,34; 24,9	4,23; 5,22; 11,(12-)13; 12,14; 22,26; 23,16	5/6	1[3]

ἀπαγγέλλω + accusative	7,22; 9,36; 14,21; 24,9	4,23; 12,17; 15,27; 16,36.38; 17,30*; 23,17; 28,21	4	2
ἀπαγγέλλω + infinitive		12,14; 17,30*; 26,20	0	0
BOISMARD 1984 Aa73				
ἀπαγγέλλω τὰ αὐτά → **ἀπαγγέλλω** ταῦτα		15,27	0	0
ἀπαγγέλλω εἰς (VKa)	8,34		0	1
ἀπαγγέλλω (+) λέγω/εἶπον → **ἐπιτιμάω**/	8,20 v.l.	4,23; 5,22(-23).25	0	0
παραγγέλλω + λέγω/εἶπον; cf. διαστέλλομαι		v.l.; 22,26		
+ λέγω Mk 8,15; ἐντέλλομαι + λέγω Mt 17,9				
ἀπαγγέλλω (+) λέγων		5,22(-23); 22,26	0	0
ἀπαγγέλλω + τοὺς λόγους τούτους / τὰ ῥήματα		16,36.38	0	0
ταῦτα → **ἀπαγγέλλω** ταῦτα				
ἀπαγγέλλω + πάντα / περὶ πάντων τούτων; cf.	7,18; 24,9		1	0
ἀπαγγέλλω ἅπαντα Mt 28,11				
ἀπαγγέλλω + περί + genitive	7,18; 13,1		0	0
DENAUX 2009 Lⁿ				
ἀπαγγέλλω πρός + accusative → verb of saying		16,36	0	0
πρός + acc.				
CREDNER 1836 138				

Characteristic of Luke

BOISMARD 1984 cb128; GASTON 1973 65 [Lked?]; MORGENTHALER 1958A; NEIRYNCK 1985; PLUMMER 1922 lix

	Lk	Acts	Mt	Mk
participle + ἀν/ἀπαγγέλλω	7,22; 8,34;	4,23; 5,22.25;	4	0
BOISMARD 1984 cb61; NEIRYNCK 1985	14,21; 24,9	12,14; 14,27; 22,26; 23,16; 28,21		
ἀπαγγέλλω + (ὁράω/)εἶδον; cf. ἀπαγγέλλω +	7,22;	11,13	0	1
ἑώρακα Lk 9,36; ἀπαγγέλλω + ὄψομαι Mt 28,10	8,34.36.47			
DENAUX 2009 La*				
ἀπαγγέλλω ταῦτα → **ἀπαγγέλλω** τὰ αὐτά / τοὺς	14,21; 24,9	12,17		
λόγους τούτους / τὰ ῥήματα ταῦτα; cf.				
καταγγέλλω τοῦτο Acts 17,23				
BOISMARD 1984 Ab107; NEIRYNCK 1985				
παραγενόμενος ... ἀπαγγέλλω; cf. παραγίνομαι +	14,21	5,25; 23,16; 28,21	0	0
ἀπαγγέλλω Lk 8,(19-)20; Acts 5,22; παραγίνομαι				
+ ἀναγγέλλω Acts 14,27; 15,4				
BOISMARD 1984 Ab94; NEIRYNCK 1985				

Literature

VON BENDEMANN 2001 424: "Sodann ist ἀπαγγέλλειν lukanisches Vorzugsverb"; COLLISON 1977 184 [linguistic usage of Luke: certain]; DENAUX 2009 lAⁿ [παραγενόμενος ... ἀπαγγέλλω], Laⁿ [ἀπαγγέλλω ταῦτα]; JEREMIAS 1980 68 [ἀπαγγέλλω + λέγων: red.]; 160: "ἀπαγγέλλω gibt sich schon von der Statistik her als von Lukas gern gebrauchte Vokabel zu erkennen"; RADL 1975 400.

ἀπάγω 4 + 2/3 (Mt 5, Mk 3)

1. lead away (Lk 13,15); 2. lead off to punishment (Lk 21,12; 22,66; 23,26); 3. execute (Acts 12,19); 4. deceive; 5. extend to

Word groups	Lk	Acts	Mt	Mk
ἀπάγω εἰς + place → (ἀν/εἰσ/ἐξ/ἐπαν/κατ/προ/συν/ὑπ)ἄγω	22,66		0	0
+ place				

		23,17	1	1
ἀπάγω πρός + accusative (person) → **ἀπάγω** ἐπί + acc. (person); **ἄγω** πρός + acc. (person); **προσάγω** + dat.				
ἀπάγομαι passive → (**ἀν/εἰσ/ἐπισυν/κατ/συν)ἄγομαι** passive DENAUX 2009 LA[n]	21,12	12,19	0	0
ἀπάγω transitive → (**ἀν/εἰσ/ἐξ/ἐπισυν/κατ/προ/προσ/συν**) **ἄγω** transitive	13,15; 21,12; 22,66; 23,26	12,19; 23,17	3	3
ἀπήγαγον → (**ἀν/εἰσ/κατ)ἤγαγον**; cf. συνήγαγον Mt 22,10; 27,27	22,66; 23,26		3	2

Characteristic of Luke	Lk	Acts	Mt	Mk
ἀπάγω (and cognate ἄγειν) ἐπί + accusative (person) → **ἀπάγω** πρός + acc. (person); (**συν/ὑπ)ἄγω** ἐπί + acc. (person); **προάγω** ἐπί + gen. (person); (**ἀν/κατ)ἄγω** ἐπί + acc. (place); cf. ἐπάγω ἐπί + acc. Acts 5,28 BOISMARD 1984 Bb60; NEIRYNCK 1985	21,12*; 23,1	8,32; 9,21; 17,19; 18,12	1	0
κελεύω and cognates εἰσ/ἀπ/άγειν → **κελεύω +** (**εἰσ)ἄγειν** BOISMARD 1984 Ab26; NEIRYNCK 1985	18,40	12,19; 21,34; 22,24*; 23,10; 25,6.17	0	0

Literature

DENAUX 2009 lA[n] [κελεύω and cognates εἰσ/ἀπ/άγειν].

BORMANN, Lukas, *Recht, Gerechtigkeit und Religion*, 2001. Esp. 175.

ἀπαίρομαι 1 (Mt 1, Mk 1) ἀπαίρω: lead away

Word groups	Lk	Acts	Mt	Mk
ἀπαίρομαι ἀπό → **αἴρω** ἀπό	5,35		1	1

ἀπαιτέω 2 ask back

Word groups	Lk	Acts	Mt	Mk
ἀπαιτέω (+) ἀπό → **αἰτέω** ἀπό/παρά; **ζητέω** παρά; **κωλύω** ἀπό DENAUX 2009 L[n]	6,30; 12,20		0	0

Literature

VON BENDEMANN 2001 423: "ἀπαιτέω findet sich im Neuen Testament nur hier sowie Lk 6,30 diff Mt 5,42; damit dürfte es redaktionell sein"; DENAUX 2009 L[n]; HAUCK 1934 [Vorzugswort]; SCHÜRMANN 1957 103.

BORMANN, Lukas, *Recht, Gerechtigkeit und Religion*, 2001. Esp. 147-148.
SCHWARZ, Günther, ταυτη τη νυκτι την ψυχην σου απαιτουσιν απο σου? — *BibNot* 25 (1984) 36-41. [NTA 29, 983]

ἀπαλλάσσω 1 + 1

1. set free; 2. ἀπαλλάσσομαι: settle with (Lk 12,58); 3. cease; 4. BDAG: ἀπαλλάσσομαι intr.: leave (Acts 19,12)

Characteristic of Luke	Lk	Acts	Mt	Mk
ἀπαλλάσσομαι ἀπό BOISMARD 1984 Ab162; NEIRYNCK 1985	12,58	19,12	0	0

Literature
DENAUX 2009 LAⁿ [ἀπαλλάσσομαι ἀπό]; HAUCK 1934 [seltenes Alleinwort].

ἀπαντάω 1/2 + 0/1 (Mt 0/1, Mk 1/2) | meet up with (Lk 17,12)

ἀπαρνέομαι 3/4 (Mt 4, Mk 4)

1. deny (Lk 9,23; 22,34); 2. disregard; 3. reject (Lk 12,9)

Word groups	Lk	Acts	Mt	Mk
ἀπαρνέομαι ἑαυτόν (VKa) → ἀρνέομαι ἑαυτόν	9,23*		1	1

Literature
SCHÜRMANN 1957 26 [Lk 22,34: luk R sehr wahrscheinlich].

ἀπαρτισμός* 1 | completion (Lk 14,28)

Literature
HAUCK 1934 [seltenes Alleinwort].

ἅπας 11/25 + 12/18 (Mt 3, Mk 3[4]/5) | all

Word groups	Lk	Acts	Mt	Mk
ἅπαν τὸ πλῆθος → ἅπας/ὅλος/πᾶς ὁ λαός; πᾶν τὸ πλῆθος; πάντα τὰ ἔθνη; πᾶς ὁ ὄχλος; πλῆθος πολύ DENAUX 2009 Laⁿ	8,37; 19,37; 23,1	25,24	0	0
ἅπαντες (...) ὅσοι → πάντες (...) ὅσοι	4,40		0	0
ἅπας followed by an adjective	11,41*	2,44; 4,32	0	0
ἅπας followed by a pronoun → πᾶς followed by a demonstrative or personal pronoun DENAUX 2009 LAⁿ	21,4¹	2,7	0	0
ἅπας following a noun → πᾶς following a noun DENAUX 2009 Lⁿ	2,51*; 4,6; 19,48; 20,6		0	0[1]
ἅπας following a participle → πᾶς following a part.		2,14*	0	0
ἅπας following a pronoun → πᾶς following a demonstrative or personal pronoun	4,6; 21,12*	16,33*	1	0
ἅπας ὁ + participle → πᾶς ὁ + part.	21,15	6,15*; 13,29*	1	0
ἅπας ὁ λαός → ἅπαν/πᾶν τὸ πλῆθος; ὅλος/πᾶς ὁ λαός; πάντα τὰ ἔθνη; πᾶς ὁ ὄχλος DENAUX 2009 Lⁿ	3,21; 19,48; 20,6		0	0

ἅπας γάρ → **πᾶς** γάρ	21,4[1]*	16,28	0	1
οὐ + ἅπας → οὐ + **πᾶς**	21,15		0	0
τὰ ῥήματα ἅπαντα → **πάντα** τὰ ῥήματα	2,51*		0	0
ἅπαντα without article/noun	5,11*.28*; 11,41*; 15,13*; 21,12*	2,44; 4,32; 10,8; 11,10	2	1
ἅπαντες without article/noun	3,16*; 4,40; 5,26; 7,16*; 9,15; 17,27*.29*; 19,7*; 21,4[1]*	2,1*.4*; 2,7; 4,31; 5,12.16; 16,3; 16,28; 27,33	1	2/3

Characteristic of Luke

BOISMARD 1984 cb92; CADBURY 1920 115.195; CREDNER 1836 136; GASTON 1973 64 [Lked]; GOULDER 1989; HAWKINS 1909add.187; MORGENTHALER 1958LA; NEIRYNCK 1985; PLUMMER 1922 lxii

	Lk	Acts	Mt	Mk
ἅπαν (and cognate πᾶν) τὸ πλῆθος → **ἅπας/ὅλος/πᾶς** ὁ λαός; **πᾶν** τὸ πλῆθος; **πάντα** τὰ ἔθνη; **πᾶς** ὁ ὄχλος; πλῆθος **πολύ** BOISMARD 1984 Ab28; CREDNER 1836 141; DENAUX 2009 L***; GOULDER 1989*; HARNACK 1906 71; NEIRYNCK 1985	1,10; 8,37; 19,37; 23,1	6,5; 15,12; 25,24	0	0
ἅπας followed by a noun DENAUX 2009 L***;	3,21; 8,37; 19,37; 21,4[2]*; 23,1	25,24	0	0
ἅπας + article → **πᾶς** + article; cf. 1 Tim 1,16 BOISMARD 1984 Bb62; DENAUX 2009 L***; NEIRYNCK 1985	2,39*.51*; 3,21; 4,6; 8,37; 19,37.48; 20,6; 21,4[2]*.15; 23,1	2,14*; 6,15*; 13,29*; 16,33*; 25,24	1	0
ἅπας/πᾶς/ὅλος ὁ λαός → **ἅπαν/πᾶν** τὸ πλῆθος; **ὅλος/πᾶς** ὁ λαός; **πάντα** τὰ ἔθνη; **πᾶς** ὁ ὄχλος BOISMARD 1984 Bb36; DENAUX 2009 L***; GOULDER 1989; HAWKINS 1909L; NEIRYNCK 1985; PLUMMER 1922 lx	2,10.31; 3,21; 7,29; 8,47; 9,13; 18,43; 19,48; 20,6.45; 21,38; 24,19	2,47; 3,9.11; 4,10; 5,34; 10,41; 13,24	1	0
ὡς (δὲ) ἐτέλεσαν ἅπαντα → ὡς (δὲ) ἐτέλεσαν **πάντα** VOGEL 1899C	2,39*	13,29*	0	0

Literature

VON BENDEMANN 2001 436: "vorangestelltes ἅπας ... entspricht ebenso wie περὶ πασῶν lukanischem Stil"; COLLISON 1977 174 [ἅπας/πᾶς ὁ λαός: linguistic usage of Luke: certain]; 176 [ἅπαν τὸ πλῆθος: noteworthy phenomena]; DENAUX 2009 lAn; GERSDORF 1816 261 [ὡς ἐτέλεσαν ἅπαντα]; 262 [ἅπαντα τὰ κατὰ τὸν νόμον]; HAUCK 1934 [Vorzugswort]; JEREMIAS 1980 113: "ἅπας wird ebenfalls von Lukas mit Vorliebe gebraucht ... Kennzeichnend für Lukas ist besonders die Wendung ἅπας ὁ λαός ... und ἅπαν τὸ πλῆθος"; RADL 1975 400; 424 [ἅπαν(πᾶν) τὸ πλῆθος].

FUCHS, Albert, *Sprachliche Untersuchungen zu Mattäus und Lukas*, 1971. Esp. 185-189.

ἀπειθής 1 + 1	disobedient (Lk 1,17; Acts 26,19)

Characteristic of Luke

BOISMARD 1984 Db38; HARNACK 1906 74; NEIRYNCK 1985

Literature

DENAUX 2009 LAⁿ; HAUCK 1934 [seltenes Alleinwort].

SCHWARZ, Günther, Μηδὲν ἀπελπίζοντες. — *ZNW* 71 (1980) 133-135. [NTA 26, 521]

ἀπελπίζω 1	expect (Lk 6,35)

Literature

HAUCK 1934 [seltenes Alleinwort].

SCHWARZ, Günther, Μηδὲν ἀπελπίζοντες. — *ZNW* 71 (1980) 133-135. [NTA 26, 521]

ἀπέρχομαι 20/23 + 6/7 (Mt 35/37, Mk 22[23])

1. go away (Lk 1,38); 2. pass away

Word groups	Lk	Acts	Mt	Mk
ἀπέρχομαι + infinitive → (εἰσ/ἐξ/προ/προσ/συν) ἔρχομαι + inf.	9,59		1	1
ἀπέρχομαι + ἄγγελος → ἀπῆλθεν ὁ ἄγγελος; εἰσέρχομαι + ἄγγελος; cf. ἐξέρχομαι + ἄγγελος Mt 13,49; προσέρχομαι + ἄγγελος Mt 4,11; 28,2	7,24		0	0
ἀπέρχομαι + ἀπαγγέλλω/διαγγέλλω/κηρύσσω → ἀποστέλλω / (δι/εἰσ/κατ/προσ)ἔρχομαι / (εἰσ)πορεύομαι / ὑποστρέφω / φεύγω + ἀπαγγέλλω/διηγέομαι/κηρύσσω	8,34*.39; 9,60		1	0[1]
ἀπέρχομαι ἀπό (*SC*a; *VK*c) → ἀποβαίνω / ἀποχωρέω / (ἐξ/ἐπ/κατ)ἔρχομαι / πορεύομαι / ὑποστρέφω ἀπό	1,38; 2,15; 5,13; 8,37	16,39	1	2
ἀπέρχομαι (+) εἰς (*SC*b; *VK*a) → ἀποβαίνω εἰς; ἔρχομαι + εἰς	1,23; 2,15; 5,25; 8,31; 9,12*		12/13	8
ἀπέρχομαι εἰς τὸν οἶκον → (εἰς)ἔρχομαι εἰς τὴν οἰκίαν/τὸν οἶκον	1,23; 5,25		1	1
ἀπέρχομαι + ἔξω (*SC*a; *VK*c) → ἐξέρχομαι ἔξω		4,15	0	0
ἀπέρχομαι + ἐπί + accusative (*SC*b; *VK*a) → (εἰσ/ἐξ/ἐπ)ἔρχομαι ἐπί + acc.	23,33*; 24,24		0	0
ἀπέρχομαι + εὑρίσκω → (δι/εἰσ/ἐξ/κατ)ἔρχομαι/ (εἰσ)πορεύομαι + εὑρίσκω; ἔρχομαι + ἀνευρίσκω	9,12*; 19,32; 22,13; 24,24		1	2
ἀπέρχομαι πρός + accusative (*SC*b; *VK*a) → (εἰσ/κατ)ἔρχομαι πρός + acc.	24,12		0/1	2
ἀπέρχομαι πρὸς ἑαυτόν (*LN*: go back to one's place)	24,12		0	0
διηγέομαι + ἀπέρχομαι → διηγέομαι + ἐξέρχομαι	8,39		0	0

Characteristic of Luke	Lk	Acts	Mt	Mk
ἀπῆλθεν/ἀπέστη ὁ ἄγγελος (angel) → ἀπέρχομαι + ἄγγελος; ἀπέστη + ἄγγελος BOISMARD 1984 Ab66; HARNACK 1906 146; NEIRYNCK 1985	1,38; 2,15	10,7; 12,10	0	0

Literature

DENAUX 2009 LAⁿ [ἀπῆλθεν/ἀπέστη ὁ ἄγγελος (angel)] ; GERSDORF 1816 198 [ἀπῆλθεν ἀπ' αὐτῆς ὁ ἄγγελος]; 232 [καὶ ἐγένετο ὡς ἀπῆλθον ἀπ' αὐτῶν εἰς τὸν οὐρανὸν οἱ ἄγγελοι]; JEREMIAS 1980 54-55 [ἀπῆλθεν: red.]; SCHÜRMANN 1953 90, n. 399; 102.

DAUER, Anton, Zur Authentizität von Lk 24,12. — *ETL* 70 (1994) 294-318.

GARCÍA PÉREZ, José Miguel, El Endemoniado de Gerasa (Lc 8,26-39), 1986. Esp. 142-143.
MUDDIMAN, John, A Note on Reading Luke XXIV.12. — *ETL* 48 (1972) 542-548.
NEIRYNCK, Frans, The Uncorrected Historic Present in Lk XXIV.12. — *ETL* 48 (1972) 548-553; = ID., *Evangelica*, 1982, 329-334 (334: additional note; Appendix, *Evangelica II*, 1991, 799).
—, Ἀπῆλθεν πρὸς ἑαυτόν: Lc 24,12 et Jn 20,10. — *ETL* 54 (1978) 104-118; = ID., *Evangelica*, 1982, 441-455 (455: note additionnelle; Appendix, *Evangelica II*, 1991, 799).
—, Once More Lk 24,12. — *ETL* 70 (1994) 319-340; = ID., *Evangelica III*, 2001, 549-571.

ἀπέχω 4 + 2 (Mt 5, Mk 2)

1. receive in full (Lk 6,24); 2. be away from (Lk 7,6; 15,20; 24,13); 3. be enough; 4. experience (Lk 6,24); 5. ἀπέχομαι: avoid (Acts 15,20)

Word groups	Lk	Acts	Mt	Mk
ἀπέχω οὐ μακρὰν ἀπό → **ὑπάρχω** οὐ μακρὰν ἀπό; cf. ἀπέχω μακράν Lk 15,20	7,6		0	0
ἀπέχομαι middle (*VK*a)		15,20.29	0	0
ἀπέχω intransitive (*VK*b)	7,6; 15,20; 24,13		2	1

Characteristic of Luke	Lk	Acts	Mt	Mk
ἀπέχω distance GOULDER 1989	7,6; 15,20; 24,13		1	1

Literature

EASTON 1910 150 [probably characteristic of L]; REHKOPF 1959 92 [vorlukanisch]; SCHÜRMANN 1961 278-279 [protoluk R weniger wahrscheinlich].

DUPONT, Jacques, *Les Béatitudes*, I, 1958. Esp. 308-309.

ἀπιστέω 2 + 1 (Mk 0[2])

1. not think true; 2. not trust; 3. not believe (Lk 24,11.41)

Word groups	Lk	Acts	Mt	Mk
ἀπιστέω + θαυμάζω DENAUX 2009 L[n]	24,11(-12).41		0	0

Characteristic of Luke

BOISMARD 1984 Db32; NEIRYNCK 1985

Literature

DENAUX 2009 La[n]; JEREMIAS 1980 312: "ἀπιστέω im alltäglichen, nicht spezifisch religiösen Sinn 'keinen Glauben schenken', 'nicht für möglich halten', 'sich nicht überzeugen lassen' im NT nur im Doppelwerk ... Auch die Kombination ἀπιστέω/θαυμάζω findet sich im NT nur im LkEv".

NEIRYNCK, Frans, The Uncorrected Historic Present in Lk XXIV.12. — *ETL* 48 (1972) 548-553; = ID., *Evangelica*, 1982, 329-334 (334: additional note; Appendix, *Evangelica II*, 1991, 798).

ἄπιστος 2 + 1 (Mt 1, Mk 1)

1. unbeliever (Lk 9,41; 12,46); 2. non-Christian; 3. unbelievable (Acts 26,8); 4. lack in trust

ἁπλοῦς 1 (Mt 1)

1. healthy (Lk 11,34); 2. generous

Literature
BDAG 2000 104 [literature].

ἀπό 125/134 + 114/120 (Mt 115/121, Mk 47[48]/53[54])

1. from (dissociation) (Lk 24,9); 2. from (source) (Lk 1,52); 3. from (extension) (Lk 24,47); 4. of (part-whole) (Lk 6,13); 5. of (substance); 6. by (agent) (Lk 9,22); 7. by (instrument); 8. since (time) (Lk 24,21); 9. because of (reason) (Lk 19,3); 10. upon (responsibility) (Lk 12,57)

Word groups	Lk	Acts	Mt	Mk
ἀπό + composite verb ἀπο- → ἐκ + composite verb ἀπο-	1,26.38; 2,15.37*; 4,13; 5,2.13.35; 6,30; 7,6; 8,37; 9,5².22.39; 10,21; 12,20.58; 13,12*.27; 16,3.18; 17,25; 21,26; 22,41; 24,2.13	2,22; 3,26; 5,38; 9,18; 10,21*; 11,11; 12,10; 13,13²; 15,4 v.l.20*.33.38¹.39; 16,39; 18,16; 19,9.12¹·²; 21,1; 22,29; 27,34	7/8	5/6
ἀπό + composite verb ἐκ- → ἐκ + composite verb ἐκ-	4,35¹·².41; 5,8; 6,13; 8,2².29¹.33.35.38. 46; 9,5¹; 11,24.50. 51²; 17,29¹; 18,3	2,17.18; 13,50; 16,18.40; 19,12¹·²*; 20,6; 27,(43-)44; 28,3	5/7	3/4[5]
ἀπό + composite verb κατα- → ἐκ + composite verb κατα-	1,52; 9,37.54; 10,30	8,26; 11,27; 12,19; 13,29; 15,1; 18,5; 20,9¹; 21,10; 25,7	4	3
ἀπό + composite verb συν- → ἐκ + composite verb συν-	23,49²	13,31	2	1
ἀπό ... ἄχρι/ἕως/μέχρι → ἐκ ... ἕως; cf. ἐκ ... ἄχρι Rev 14,20	11,51¹; 22,18²; 23,5	1,22¹; 8,10; 10,30; 28,23²	14	4
ἀπό ... εἰς (LN: from ... to) with the same verb	2,15; 10,30	1,11.12; 8,26; 11,27; 12,19; 13,31; 20,17; 25,1; 26,18	3	0
ἀπὸ μακρόθεν (SCb; VKd)	16,23; 23,49¹		2	5
ἀπὸ μιᾶς (LN: one by one; VKr)	14,18		0	0
ἀφ' οὗ ἄν → ὅπως/πρὶν ἄν	13,25		0	0
ἀπὸ προσώπου; cf. 2 Thess 1,9; Rev 6,16; 12,14 BOISMARD 1984 Da14		3,20; 5,41; 7,45	0	0
ἀπὸ τότε (SCc; VKb)	16,16		3	0
ἀπό cause	19,3; 21,26; 24,41	11,19; 12,14; 22,11	4	0
ἀπό time → ἐκ time	1,2.48.70; 2,36; 5,10; 7,45; 8,43¹; 11,50¹.51¹; 12,52; 13,7.25; 16,16; 22,18¹.69; 24,21	1,22¹; 3,21.24; 10,30; 15,7.18; 18,6; 20,18¹·²; 24,11; 26,4	21	2

→ αἴρω ἀπό; αἰτέω ἀπό; ἀκούω ἀπό; ἀνάγομαι ἀπό; ἀπὸ ἀνατολῶν; ἀνὴρ ἀπὸ τοῦ ὄχλου; ἀπαίρομαι ἀπό; ἀπαιτέω + ἀπό; ἀπέρχομαι ἀπό; ἀπέχω οὐ μακρὰν ἀπό; ἀποβαίνω ἀπό; ἀποδοκιμάζω ἀπό; ἀποκρύπτω ἀπό; ἀπολύομαι ἀπὸ ἀνδρός; ἀποχωρέω ἀπό; Ἰωσὴφ ἀπὸ Ἀριμαθαίας; ἀπ' ἀρχῆς; ἀφαιρέω ἀπό; βλέπω ἀπό; ἀπὸ βορρᾶ; διαχωρίζομαι ἀπό; ἀπὸ δυσμῶν; εἰμί + ἀπό; εἰς + ἀπό; ἐκ + ἀπό; ἐκβάλλω ἀπό; ἐκζητέω ἀπό; ἐξέρχομαι ἀπό + place; ἐπανάγω ἀπό; ἐπέρχομαι ἀπό; ἔρχομαι ἀπό; ἥκω ἀπό; ἀφ' ἡμερῶν ἀρχαίων; ἰάομαι ἀπό; καθαιρέω ἀπό; καθαρὸς ἀπό; ἀπὸ τοῦ καρποῦ δίδωμι; καταβαίνω ἀπό (Ἱεροσολύμων); ἀπὸ καταβολῆς κόσμου; κατέρχομαι ἀπὸ Ἱεροσολύμων/τῆς Ἰουδαίας/τοῦ ὄρους; κρύπτω ἀπό; κωλύω ἀπό; λύω ἀπό; μετανοέω ἀπό; Ἰησοῦς (ὁ) ἀπὸ Ναζαρέθ; ἀπὸ (τῶν) νεκρῶν; ἀπὸ νότου; ἀπὸ (τοῦ) οὐρανοῦ; παρακαλύπτω ἀπό; παραφέρω τὸ ποτήριον ἀπό; πίπτω ἀπό; προσέχω ἀπό; ῥύομαι ἀπό; σῴζω ἀπό; ὑπάρχω οὐ μακρὰν ἀπό; καταφέρομαι ἀπὸ τοῦ ὕπνου; ὑποστρέφω ἀπό; φεύγω ἀπό; φοβέομαι ἀπό; ἀπὸ τοῦ φόβου; φυλάσσω ἀπό; χορτάζομαι ἀπό

Characteristic of Luke

CADBURY 1920 202; GASTON 1973 65 [Lked?]

	Lk	Acts	Mt	Mk
ἀπό + composite verb ἀνα-/ἐπανα-/ συνανα- → ἐκ + composite verb ἀνα- DENAUX 2009 lA**	2,4; 4,38; 5,3; 12,54*; 22,45[1]	1,11.22[2]; 13,13[1].31; 16,11; 18,21; 25,1; 27,21	1	0/1
ἀπ' αἰῶνος (LN: long ago); cf. ἀπὸ τῶν αἰώνων Eph 3,9; Col 1,26; ἐκ τοῦ αἰῶνος Jn 9,32; Gal 1,4 BOISMARD 1984 Ab105; HARNACK 1906 144; NEIRYNCK 1985; PLUMMER 1922 lii	1,70	3,21; 15,18	0	0
ἀπὸ ... εἰς (LN: from ... to) with different verbs DENAUX 2009 lA*	4,38; 8,33; 24,51	13,13[1.2].14.29; 16,11.40 v.l.; 18,21(-22); 20,6; 21,1.7	1	0
ἀπὸ ἐτῶν → ἐξ ἐτῶν; cf. Rom 15,23 BOISMARD 1984 cb29; NEIRYNCK 1985	8,43[1]		0	0
ἀπὸ τοῦ νῦν (SCd; VKc); cf. Jn 8,11; 2 Cor 5,16 BOISMARD 1984 bb47; CREDNER 1836 134; DENAUX 2009 L***; GOULDER 1989*; HARNACK 1906 141.151; HAWKINS 1909L; NEIRYNCK 1985; PLUMMER 1922 lix	1,48; 5,10; 12,52; 22,18[1].69	18,6	0	0
ἀπὸ τοῦ ὄχλου → διὰ τὸν ὄχλον; ἐκ τοῦ ὄχλου GOULDER 1989	9,38; 19,3.39		0	2
ἀπὸ τῆς χαρᾶς without determinative BOISMARD 1984 Ab208; NEIRYNCK 1985	24,41	12,14	0	0
ἀφ' ἧς / ἀφ'οῦ since; cf. 2 Pet 3,4; Rev 16,18 BOISMARD 1984 cb42; DENAUX 2009 L***; GOULDER 1989; NEIRYNCK 1985	7,45; 13,7.25; 24,21	20,18[2]; 24,11	0	0

→ ἀπαλλάσσομαι ἀπό; ἀπολύω ἀπό; ἀποσπάομαι ἀπό; ἀποστέλλω ἀπό; ἀρξάμενος ἀπό; ἀφίστημι ἀπό; ἀφ' ἑαυτοῦ/ἑαυτῶν; ἐν + ἀπό; ἐξέρχομαι + ἀπό; ἐξέρχομαι ἀπό + person; ἐξέρχομαι ἀπό + person (exorcism); θεραπεύω ἀπό; θρὶξ ἀπὸ τῆς κεφαλῆς; οἵ/τινες ἀπό + place + Ἰουδαῖοι; ἵστημι ἀπὸ μακρόθεν; καταβαίνω ἀπὸ Ἱερουσαλήμ; κατέρχομαι ἀπό; πορεύομαι ἀπό

Literature

VON BENDEMANN 2001 436 [ἀπὸ τοῦ ὄχλου]; COLLISON 1977 123 [ἐξέρχομαι + ἀπό: linguistic usage of Luke: certain; preference for ἀπό over ἐκ: noteworthy phenomena]; 124 [ἀπό with verbs of healing when the infirmity is specified: linguistic usage of Luke: certain]; 124-125 [instead of ὑπό; for genitive of separation; ἀφ' οὗ/ἀφ' ἧς/ἀφ' ἑαυτοῦ: noteworthy phenomena]; 158-159 [ἀπὸ τοῦ νῦν: linguistic usage of Luke: likely]; DENAUX 2009 lA[n] [ἀπ' αἰῶνος]; LA[n] [ἀπὸ τῆς χαρᾶς without determinative]; EASTON 1910 145 [ἀπὸ τοῦ νῦν: especially characteristic of L]; GERSDORF 1816 200.253 [ἀπὸ τοῦ νῦν]; HAUCK 1934 [Vorzugsverbindungen: αἰτῶν-ἀπὸ δοῦναι; ἀπὸ τοῦ νῦν; ἐξερχόμαι ἀπό; θεραπεύομαι ἀπό]; JEREMIAS 1980 60 [ἀπὸ τοῦ νῦν: red.]; 74 [ἀπ' αἰῶνος: red.]; 172 [ἀφ' ἧς/ἀφ' οὗ: red.]; 275 [ἀπό causal: red.]; RADL 1975 400 [ἀπό instead of ἐκ; ἀπό "bezüglich der Vorsilbe im Kompositum"; ἐξέρχομαι + ἀπό; ἀπὸ τοῦ νῦν]; REHKOPF 1959 92 [ἀπὸ τοῦ νῦν; ἀφ' οὗ: vorlukanisch]; SCHNEIDER 1969 119.163 [ἀπὸ τοῦ νῦν: Vorzugswörter und -ausdrücke des Luk]; SCHÜRMANN 1961 271 [ἀφ' οὗ]; 279 [ἀπὸ τοῦ νῦν; protoluk R weniger wahrscheinlich].

BACHMANN, Michael, *Jerusalem und der Tempel*, 1980. Esp. 85-96 [ἀρξάμενος ἀπό].
READ-HEIMERDINGER, Jenny, *The Bezan Text of Acts*, 2002. Esp. 183-184: "ἀπό"; 184-187: "ἀπό-ὑπό"; 187-192: "ἀπό-ἐκ".
WILCOX, Max, Semitisms in the New Testament, 1984. Esp. 1009: "ἀπὸ μιᾶς (Luke 14:18)".

ἀποβαίνω 2	disembark

Word groups	Lk	Acts	Mt	Mk
ἀποβαίνω + ἀπό → ἀπέρχομαι/καταβαίνω ἀπό	5,2		0	0
ἀποβαίνω + εἰς (*LN*: result in) → ἀνα/δια/ἐμ/κατα/μεταβαίνω εἰς; ἀπέρχομαι εἰς; cf. ἐπιβαίνω εἰς Acts 21,6*	21,13		0	0

Literature
DENAUX 2009 L[n]; HAUCK 1934 [seltenes Alleinwort].

HARTMAN, Lars, *Testimonium linguae*, 1963. Esp. 57-75: "'Αποβήσεται ὑμῖν εἰς μαρτύριον".

ἀπογραφή 1 + 1	census (Lk 2,2; Acts 5,37)

Characteristic of Luke
BOISMARD 1984 Ab163; HARNACK 1906 74; HAWKINS 1909LA; MORGENTHALER 1958*; NEIRYNCK 1985; PLUMMER 1922 lii; VOGEL 1899A

Literature
DENAUX 2009 LA[n]; GERSDORF 1816 213 [αὕτη ἀπογραφὴ πρώτη ἐγένετο]; HAUCK 1934 [seltenes Alleinwort].

'Απογραφή, "censimento". — *BibOr* 24 (1982) 206.
BARNETT, Paul W., 'Απογραφή and ἀπογράφεσθαι in Luke 2,1-5. — *ExpT* 85 (1973-74) 377-380. [NTA 19, 179]
BORMANN, Lukas, *Recht, Gerechtigkeit und Religion*, 2001. Esp. 130.

ἀπογράφω 3	register

Word groups	Lk	Acts	Mt	Mk
ἀπογράφομαι middle DENAUX 2009 L[n]	2,1.3.5		0	0

Literature
DENAUX 2009 L[n].

BARNETT, Paul W., 'Απογραφή and ἀπογράφεσθαι in Luke 2,1-5. — *ExpT* 85 (1973-74) 377-380. [NTA 19, 179]
BORMANN, Lukas, *Recht, Gerechtigkeit und Religion*, 2001. Esp. 130.

ἀποδεκατόω* 2 (Mt 1)

1. give a tenth (Lk 11,42; 18,12); 2. collect tithes

Literature
HAUCK 1934 [seltenes Alleinwort].

ἀποδέχομαι 2 + 5/6

1. welcome (Lk 8,40; 9,11); 2. accept (Acts 2,41); 3. acknowledge (Acts 24,3)

Word groups	Lk	Acts	Mt	Mk
ἀποδέχομαι τὸν λόγον		2,41	0	0

Characteristic of Luke
BOISMARD 1984 Ab23; DENAUX 2009 IA*; HARNACK 1906 51; HAWKINS 1909B.LA; MORGENTHALER 1958*; NEIRYNCK 1985; PLUMMER 1922 lii; VOGEL 1899A

	Lk	Acts	Mt	Mk
ἀποδέχομαι (and cognate δέχομαι) τὸν λόγον → δέχομαι τὸν λόγον BOISMARD 1984 cb144; NEIRYNCK 1985	8,13	2,41; 8,14; 11,1; 17,11	0	0

Literature
DENAUX 2009 IAⁿ [ἀποδέχομαι(and cognate δέχομαι) τὸν λόγον]; HAUCK 1934 [Vorzugswort]; JEREMIAS 1980 193 [red.].

TAEGER, Jens-Wilhelm, *Der Mensch und sein Heil*, 1982. Esp. 125-127: "ἀποδέχεσθαι τὸν λόγον αὐτοῦ (= des Petrus)".

ἀποδημέω 2 (Mt 3, Mk 1)   leave home on a journey (Lk 15,13; 20,9)

ἀποδίδωμι 8 + 4 (Mt 18, Mk 1)

1. pay (Lk 10,35; 12,59); 2. reward; 3. cause to happen; 4. do; 5. ἀποδίδομαι: sell (Acts 7,9); 6. BDAG: give back (Lk 4,20; 9,42; 16,2; Acts 19,40)

Word groups	Lk	Acts	Mt	Mk
ἀποδίδωμι λόγον (give an account of)/μαρτύριον (SCa; VKa); cf. ἀποδίδωμι ὅρκους Mt 5,33; συναίρω λόγον Mt 18,23; 25,19	16,2	4,33; 19,40	1	0
ἀποδίδομαι middle (VKb)		5,8; 7,9	0	0

Literature
BORMANN, Lukas, *Recht, Gerechtigkeit und Religion*, 2001. Esp. 131 [ἀποδίδωμι τὸν λόγον]. MITCHELL, Alan C., Zacchaeus Revisited: Luke 19,8 as a Defense. — *Bib* 71 (1990) 153-176.

ἀποδοκιμάζω 3 (Mt 1, Mk 2)   regard as unworthy

Word groups	Lk	Acts	Mt	Mk
ἀποδοκιμάζω ἀπό; cf. (ἀπο)δοκιμάζω ὑπό Mk 8,31; 1 Thess 2,4 DENAUX 2009 Lⁿ	9,22; 17,25		0	0

Literature
VON BENDEMANN 2001 432 [ἀποδοκιμασθῆναι + ἀπό]; JEREMIAS 1980 268 [ἀποδοκιμασθῆναι + ἀπό: red.].

ἀποθήκη 3 (Mt 3)   storehouse

Word groups	Lk	Acts	Mt	Mk
ἀποθήκη + συνάγω	3,17; 12,18		3	0

ἀποθλίβω 1   crowd against (Lk 8,45)

Literature
HAUCK 1934 [seltenes Alleinwort].

ἀποθνῄσκω 10/12 + 4 (Mt 5, Mk 8)
1. die (Lk 8,42); 2. likely to die; 3. be dead to

Word groups	Lk	Acts	Mt	Mk
ἀποθνῄσκω + preposition (VKa)		21,13	2	0
ἀποθνῄσκω + ζῶ → θνῄσκω + ζῶ; cf. τελευτάω + ζῶ Mt 9,18		9,37(-41)	0	0
ἀποθνῄσκω + καθεύδω	8,52		1	1

Characteristic of Luke
GASTON 1973 64 [Lked]

	Lk	Acts	Mt	Mk
ἀποθανεῖν; cf. συναποθανεῖν Mk 14,31 DENAUX 2009 lA*	16,22[1]; 20,36	7,4; 9,37; 21,13; 25,11	1	0

Literature
RADL 1975 400 [ἀποθνῄσκω; ἀποθανεῖν].

ἀποκαθίστημι 1 + 1 (Mt 2, Mk 3)
1. restore (Lk 6,10); 2. send back

Word groups	Lk	Acts	Mt	Mk
ἀποκαθίσταμαι passive → (μεθ)ίσταμαι passive	6,10		1	1

ἀποκαλύπτω 5 (Mt 4)   reveal (Lk 2,35; 10,21.22; 12,2; 17,30)

Literature
REHKOPF 1959 92 [vorlukanisch]; SCHÜRMANN 1961 275.

ἀποκάλυψις 1   revelation (Lk 2,32)

Literature
GERSDORF 1816 256 [φῶς εἰς ἀποκάλυψιν ἐθνῶν].

ἀπόκειμαι 1

1. put away (Lk 19,20); 2. exist; 3. be necessary

Word groups	Lk	Acts	Mt	Mk
ἀπόκειμαι ἐν → κατάκειμαι/κεῖμαι ἐν; cf. ἀνάκειμαι ἐν Mt 9,10	19,20		0	0

ἀποκεφαλίζω 1 (Mt 1, Mk 2)

behead, cut head off (Lk 9,9)

ἀποκλείω 1

close

Word groups	Lk	Acts	Mt	Mk
ἀποκλείω + ἀνοίγω → κλείω/κρούω + ἀνοίγω	13,25		0	0
ἀποκλείω θύρα → ἀνοίγω/κλείω/κρούω + θύρα	13,25		0	0

ἀποκρίνομαι 46/49 + 20/21 (Mt 55/56, Mk 30/44)

1. answer (Lk 1,19); 2. speak (Lk 8,50)

Word groups	Lk	Acts	Mt	Mk
αἰτέω/(ἐπ)ἐρωτάω + ἀποκρίνομαι	3,(10-)11; 9,(18-)19; 17,20; 20,3.39(-40); 22,68; 23,3.9	5,(27-)29; 25,(3-)4.(15-)16	8	12/20
ἀκούσας ἀποκρίνομαι → ἀκούσας/ἀκούων + λέγω/εἶπον	8,50		0	1
ἀπεκρίθη + καὶ εἶπεν DENAUX 2009 Lⁿ	13,15; 17,20	21,13 v.l.	0	0
ἀποκριθεὶς δέ (SCb)	3,11; 7,43 v.l; 9,41.49; 10,41; 11,45; 13,14; 17,17; 20,3.24*.39; 22,51; 23,40; 24,18	5,29; 8,24.34.37*; 19,15	16/17	0/2
ἀποκριθεὶς δὲ (+) εἶπεν	7,43 v.l.; 9, 41.49; 10,41; 17,17; 20,3.24*.39; 22,51; 24,18	5,29; 8,24.34.37*; 19,15	16	0/1
ἀποκριθεὶς δὲ + λέγει/ἔλεγεν	3,11; 11,45; 13,14		0	0/1
ἀποκριθεὶς (+) εἶπεν; cf. ἀποκριθεὶς λέγει Mk 8,29	5,22; 7,43; 9,20; 11,7	4,19; 25,9	3/4	0/2
ἀποκριθεὶς + ἔφη	23,3.40		1	0/1
ἀποκρίνομαι + dative → ἀποκρίνομαι πρός + acc.	8,50; 13,15; 17,20; 22,68 v.l.; 23,3.9	8,34; 25,9	8	12/13
ἀποκρίνομαι (+) λέγω/εἶπον/ἐρῶ	1,19.35.60; 3,11.16; 4,4 v.l.8.12; 5,5.22.31; 6,3; 7,22.40.43; 8,21.50 v.l.; 9,19.20.41.49; 10,27.41; 11,7.45; 13,2.8.14.15.25; 14,3.5*; 15,29; 17,17.20.37; 19,40; 20,3.24*.34*.39; 22,51; 23,40 v.l.; 24,18	4,19; 5,29; 8,24.34.37*; 15,13; 19,15; 21,13 v.l.; 24,10; 25,9	50/51	18/33
ἀποκρίνομαι (+) λέγων	3,16	15,13; 21,13 v.l.	5	1
ἀποκρίνομαι + φωνή		11,9	0	0
καὶ ἀποκριθεὶς (+) εἶπεν (SCf)	1,19.35.60; 4,8.12; 5,5.31; 6,3; 7,22.40; 13,2; 14,3.5*; 19,40; 20,34*		5	3/7

καὶ ἀποκριθεὶς ἐρεῖ (SCh)	13,25	1	0
καὶ ἀποκριθεὶς λέγει (SCg); cf. καὶ ἀποκριθεὶς ἔλεγεν Mk 12,35	17,37	0	4/5
ὁ δὲ ἀποκριθεὶς εἶπεν (SCc)	8,21; 9,19; 10,27; 15,29	19	2/7
ὁ δὲ ἀποκριθεὶς λέγει (SCd); cf. ὁ δὲ ἀποκριθεὶς ἔλεγεν Mk 15,12	13,8	0	3
ὁ δὲ ἀποκριθεὶς + ἔφη (SCe); cf. καὶ ἀποκριθεὶς ἔφη Mt 8,8	23,3	0	0/1
ἀπεκρίθη → ἀπεκρίνατο	4,4; 8,50; 13,15; 17,20	5,8; 9,13; 10,46; 11,9; 15,13; 21,13; 22,28; 24,10.25; 25,4.12	2	7
ἀπεκρίνατο → ἀπεκρίθη	3,16; 23,9	3,12	1	1
ἀποκριθεὶς (SCa; VKa)	1,19.35.60; 3,11; 4,8.12; 5,5.22.31; 6,3; 7,22.40.43; 8,21; 9,19.20. 41.49; 10,27.41; 11,7.45; 13,2.8.14.25; 14,3.5*; 15,29; 17,17.37; 19,40; 20,3.24*.34*.39; 22,51; 23,3.40; 24,18	4,19; 5,29; 8,24.34.37*; 19,15; 25,9	45/46	16/28
ἀποκρίνομαι after a direct or indirect question	1,19.35; 3,11.16; 5,31; 6,3; 7,22.43; 9,19.20; 10,27; 11,7; 13,8; 14,5*; 17,20; 20,3.7.24*.34*; 22,51; 23,3; 24,18	5,29; 8,37*; 22,8	21/22	7/15

Characteristic of Luke	Lk	Acts	Mt	Mk
ἀπεκρίθη δέ/τε → (λέγω/)εἶπόν/εἶπέν τε BOISMARD 1984 Bb38; NEIRYNCK 1985	13,15	5,8; 9,13; 11,9; 22,28; 24,10	0	0
ἀποκρίνομαι + infinitive BOISMARD 1984 Ab164; NEIRYNCK 1985	20,7	25,4	0	0
ἀποκρίνομαι with direct speech without λέγω DENAUX 2009 1A*	4,4; 8,50; 20,7	3,12; 5,8; 9,13; 10,46; 11,9; 21,13; 22,8.28; 24,10.25; 25,12	0	2
ἀποκρίνομαι πρός + accusative (person) → ἀποκρίνομαι + dat.; verb of saying πρός + acc.; cf. Jn 8,33 BOISMARD 1984 Bb39; CREDNER 1836 138; NEIRYNCK 1985; PLUMMER 1922 lxii	4,4; 6,3; 14,5*	3,12; 5,8; 25,16	0	0

Literature

VON BENDEMANN 2001 415: "Die Verbindung ἀποκριθεὶς + εἶπεν kennt Lukas aus seinen Quellen … Kennzeichnend lukanisch ist dabei die Verbindung mit δέ"; COLLISON 1977 38 [ἀποκριθεὶς δέ: linguistic usage of Luke's "other source-material": probable]; DENAUX 2009 1A[n] [ἀποκρίνομαι πρός + accusative (person)], LA[n] [ἀποκρίνομαι + infinitive], IA [ἀπεκρίθη δέ/τε]; EASTON 1910 176 [ἀποκριθεὶς εἶπεν: possible Hebraisms in the Lucan Writings, as classed by Dalman]; HAUCK 1934 [Vorzugsverbindung: ἀποκρίνομαι πρός]; JEREMIAS 1980 68 [ἀποκρίνομαι + λέγων: red.]; 116 [ἀποκρίνομαι πρός: red.]; RADL 1975 400-401 [ἀποκρίνομαι; ἀπεκρίθη; ἀποκρίνομαι + δέ; ἀποκριθεὶς εἶπεν: "Septuagintismus"]; REHKOPF 1959 61-62 [ἀποκριθεὶς εἶπεν].

JOÜON, Paul, "Respondit et dixit". — Bib 13 (1932) 309-314.

PADILLA, Carmen, Sobre el verbo ἀποκρίνομαι en el Nuevo Testamento. — FilolNT 3 (1990) 67-74.

SCHNEIDER, Gerhard, Lk 1,34. 35 als redaktionelle Einheit. — *BZ* NF 15 (1971) 255-259.
Esp. 256-257: "Lk 1,35 ist nach Wortschatz, Stil und Theologie 'lukanisch'".
—, Jesu geistgewirkte Empfängnis (Lk 1,34f): Zur Interpretation einer christologischen Aussage. — *TPQ* 119 (1971) 105-116. Esp. 109; = ID., *Lukas, Theologe der Heilsgeschichte*, 1985, 86-97. Esp. 90.

ἀπόκρισις 2   answer (Lk 2,47; 20,26)

Literature
VON BENDEMANN 2001 437; COLLISON 1977 180 [noteworthy phenomena]; DENAUX 2009 L[n].

BORMANN, Lukas, *Recht, Gerechtigkeit und Religion*, 2001. Esp. 175.

ἀποκρύπτω 1 (Mt 0/2)   keep secret

Word groups	Lk	Acts	Mt	Mk
ἀποκρύπτω + ἀπό → κρύπτω/παρακαλύπτω ἀπό	10,21		0/1	0

ἀπόκρυφος 1 (Mk 1)   secret (Lk 8,17)

ἀποκτείνω 12 + 6 (Mt 13, Mk 11)
1. kill (Lk 13,4); 2. do away with

Word groups	Lk	Acts	Mt	Mk
μαστιγόω + ἀποκτείνω; cf. μαστιγόω + σταυρόω Mt 20,19; 23,34; φραγελλόω + σταυρόω Mt 27,26; Mk 15,15	18,33		1	1

ἀποκυλίω 1 (Mt 1, Mk 2)   roll away (Lk 24,2)

ἀπολαμβάνω 5/6 (Mk 1)
1. obtain from (Lk 16,25); 2. receive back (Lk 6,34; 18,30); 3. lead away; 4. welcome (Lk 15,27); 5. undergo (Lk 23,41)

Word groups	Lk	Acts	Mt	Mk
ἀπολαμβάνω + παρά + genitive → λαμβάνω παρά + gen.; cf. ἀναλαμβάνω ἀπό Acts 1,11; (ἀπο)λαμβάνω ἀπό Mt 17,25; Mk 7,33; 12,2	6,34*		0	0

Characteristic of Luke
DENAUX 2009 L***; GOULDER 1989*; HAWKINS 1909 16.

Literature
VON BENDEMANN 2001 429; COLLISON 1977 91 [noteworthy phenomena]; EASTON 1910 145 [especially characteristic of L]; HAUCK 1934 [Vorzugswort]; REHKOPF 1959 92 [vorlukanisch]; SCHÜRMANN 1961 279 [protoluk R weniger wahrscheinlich].

CARAGOUNIS, Chrys C., *The Development of Greek and the New Testament*, 2004. Esp. 279-291 [Does ἀπολαμβάνω In Lk 16:25 and Rm 1:27 Mean 'Receive' or 'Enjoy'?]

ἀπόλλυμι 27/28 + 2 (Mt 19/20, Mk 10)

1. destroy (Lk 4,34); 2. fail to get; 3. lose (Lk 15,8); 4. unaware of location (Lk 15,4); 5. ἀπόλλυμαι: die (Lk 15,17); 6. ἀπόλλυμαι: disappear; 7. ἀπόλλυμαι: be lost (Lk 5,37)

Word groups	Lk	Acts	Mt	Mk
ἀπόλλυμι lose + εὑρίσκω → ἀπόλλυμι lose + ζητέω	15,4².6.8.9².24.32;		2	0
ἀπόλλυμι lose + ζητέω → ἀπόλλυμι lose + εὑρίσκω DENAUX 2009 Lⁿ	15,8; 17,33¹; 19,10		0	0
ἀπόλλυμι (+) τὴν ψυχήν (*LN*: die; *VK*b) → **ζητέω/ζῳογονέω/σῴζω** τὴν ψυχήν; cf. εὑρίσκω τὴν ψυχήν Mt 10,39¹·²; 16,25²	6,9; 9,24¹·².56*; 17,33¹·²		5	2
ἀπόλλυμι (+) ζῳογονέω/σῴζω	6,9; 9,24¹·².56*; 17,33; 19,10		2/3	2
ἀπόλλυμαι middle (*VK*a)	5,37; 8,24; 11,51; 13,3.5.33; 15,4.6.8.17.24.32; 19,10; 21,18	5,37; 27,34	8/9	2

Characteristic of Luke
MORGENTHALER 1958L

	Lk	Acts	Mt	Mk
ἀπόλλυμι lose GOULDER 1989	9,24¹·².25; 15,4¹·².6.8.9.24.32; 17,33¹·²; 19,10		7	3
ἀπολωλός DENAUX 2009 L***; GOULDER 1989	15,4.6.24.32; 19,10		2	0

Literature
FERRARO, Giuseppe, "Oggi e domani e il terzo giorno" (osservazioni su *Luca* 13,32,33). — *RivBib* 16 (1968) 397-407. Esp. 401-407: "Considerazioni sul vocabolario di Luca 13,32.33" [ἐκβάλλειν δαιμόνια; ἰάσεις ἀποτελῶ; τελειοῦσθαι e πορεύεσθαι; ἀπολέσθαι].

ἀπολογέομαι 2 + 6   defend oneself (Lk 12,11; 21,14)

Characteristic of Luke
BOISMARD 1984 Bb96; DENAUX 2009 1A*; HAWKINS 1909B; NEIRYNCK 1985; PLUMMER 1922 lix

Literature
COLLISON 1977 91-92 [noteworthy phenomena]; HAUCK 1934 [Vorzugswort]; JEREMIAS 1980 214 [red.]; RADL 1975 401.

BORMANN, Lukas, *Recht, Gerechtigkeit und Religion*, 2001. Esp. 175-176.
FUCHS, Albert, *Sprachliche Untersuchungen zu Mattäus und Lukas*, 1971. Esp. 173.178.

ἀπολύτρωσις 1   deliverance (Lk 21,28)

Literature
EASTON 1910 149 [especially characteristic of L]; HAUCK 1934 [seltenes Alleinwort].

BORMANN, Lukas, *Recht, Gerechtigkeit und Religion*, 2001. Esp. 148.
DE LORENZI, Lorenzo, Gesù λυτρωτής: Atti 7,35. — *RivBib* 8 (1960) 31-41. Esp. 36-38.
DODD, Charles H., Some Problems of New Testament Translation. — *BTrans* 13 (1962) 145-157. Esp. 150-151: "*apolutrôsis*".
HILL, David, *Greek Words and Hebrew Meanings*, 1967. Esp. 66-81: "The λύτρον-words in the New Testament".
MARROW, Stanley B., Principles for Interpreting the New Testament Soteriological Terms. — *NTS* 36 (1990) 268-280. Esp. 272-274: "Redemption and ransom".

ἀπολύω 14/16 + 15 (Mt 19/20, Mk 12)

1. dismiss (Lk 2,29); 2. send; 3. set free (Lk 23,22); 4. divorce (Lk 16,18); 5. forgive (Lk 6;37); 6. BDAG 2000: go away (Acts 28,25)

Word groups	Lk	Acts	Mt	Mk
ἀπολύομαι ἀπὸ ἀνδρός; cf. ἀπολύω ἄνδρα Mk 10,12	$16,18^2$		0	0
ἀπολύω γυναῖκα → **ἀπολύω** divorce; **γαμέω** γυναῖκα; cf. ἀπολύω ἄνδρα Mk 10,12	$16,18^1$		5	2
ἀπολύω τὸν ὄχλον; cf. ἀπολύω τοὺς ὄχλους Mt 14,15.22.23; 15,39	9,12		0	1
ἀπολυθέντες BOISMARD 1984 Aa117		4,23; 15,30	0	0
ἀπολύω divorce (*VK*a) → **ἀπολύω** γυναῖκα	$16,18^{1.2}$		8/9	4

Characteristic of Luke	Lk	Acts	Mt	Mk
ἀπολύω ἀπό → **λύω/ῥύομαι** ἀπό BOISMARD 1984 Ab165; NEIRYNCK 1985	13,12 *v.l.*; $16,18^2$	15,33	0	0

Literature

DENAUX 2009 LAⁿ [ἀπολύω ἀπό]; EASTON 1910 159 [cited by Weiss as characteristic of L, and possibly corroborative]; GERSDORF 1816 254 [νῦν ἀπολύεις τὸν δοῦλόν σου, δέσποτα, κατὰ τὸ ῥῆμά σου ἐν εἰρήνῃ]; JEREMIAS 1980 259: "ἀπολύω wird im NT nur von Lukas mit ἀπό konstruiert".

ἀπομάσσομαι 1 wipe off (Lk 10,11)

Literature
HAUCK 1934 [seltenes Alleinwort].

ἀποπνίγω 2 (Mt 0/1)

1. choke (Lk 8,7); 2. BDAG 2000: drown (Lk 8,33)

Literature
DENAUX 2009 Lⁿ.

ἀπορέω 1 + 1 (Mk 1) be at a loss (Lk 24,4; Acts 25,20)

Literature
EASTON 1910 151 [probably characteristic of L]; JEREMIAS 1980 310 [red.].

| **ἀπορία** 1 | consternation (Lk 21,25) |

Literature

EASTON 1910 151 [probably characteristic of L]; HAUCK 1934 [seltenes Alleinwort]; JEREMIAS 1980 310 [red.].

| **ἀποσπάω** 1 + 2 (Mt 1) | |

1. pull out; 2. lure away (Acts 20,30); 3. BDAG 2000: pass. in mid. sense: withdraw (Lk 22,41)

Characteristic of Luke

HAWKINS 1909 187

	Lk	Acts	Mt	Mk
ἀποσπάομαι (ἀπό) go away from	22,41	21,1	0	0
HARNACK 1906 54; VOGEL 1899A				

Literature

DENAUX 2009 LA[n] [ἀποσπάομαι (ἀπό) go away from]; JEREMIAS 1980 294 [ἀποσπάομαι ἀπό: red.].

| **ἀποστέλλω** 26 + 24/27 (Mt 22, Mk 20/21) | | |

1. send someone (Lk 1,19); 2. send a message (Acts 16,36)

Word groups	Lk	Acts	Mt	Mk
ἀποστέλλω + infinitive → **πέμπω** + inf.	1,19; 4,18[1]. 18[2](-19); 9,2; 14,17	5,21; 26,17(-18)	2	1
ἀποστέλλω (+) ἄγγελος → **ἐξαποστέλλω** + ἄγγελος	1,19.26; 7,27; 9,52	7,35	3	2
ἀποστέλλω + ἀποστόλους	11,49		0	1
ἀποστέλλω + δοῦλον → **πέμπω** δοῦλον; cf. ἀποστέλλω δούλους Mt 21,34.36; 22,3.4	14,17; 20,10		0	2
ἀποστέλλω (+) εἰς (SCa; VKa) → **ἀποστέλλω** πρός + acc.; **ἐξαποστέλλω/πέμπω** εἰς	1,26; 10,1; 11,49	5,21; 7,34; 10,8; 11,13; 19,22; 26,17	4	1
ἀποστέλλω (+) εἰς + person → **ἀποστέλλω** πρός + acc.; **ἐξαποστέλλω** εἰς + person DENAUX 2009 LA[n]	11,49	26,17	0	0
ἀποστέλλω + εὐαγγελίζομαι DENAUX 2009 La[n]	1,19; 4,18[1]; 4,43	10,36	0	0
ἀποστέλλω + λέγων/εἰπών → **πέμπω** λέγων	7,20; 19,14.29(-30); 22,8	13,15; 16,35	6	2
ἀποστέλλω πρεσβείαν DENAUX 2009 L[n]	14,32; 19,14		0	0
ἀποστέλλω + πρὸ προσώπου (SCc); cf. προκηρύσσω πρὸ προσώπου Acts 13,24	7,27; 9,52; 10,1		1	1
ἀποστέλλω (+) πρός + accusative (SCb; VKa) → **ἀποστέλλω** εἰς; **πέμπω** πρός + acc.	1,26(-27); 7,3.20; 13,34; 20,10	8,14; 9,38; 10,21*; 11,11.30; 13,15	5	5

Characteristic of Luke

GASTON 1973 65 [Lked?]

	Lk	Acts	Mt	Mk
ἀποστέλλομαι passive (*VK*b) DENAUX 2009 L***; GOULDER 1989 ἀποστέλλω ἀπό; cf. 1 Pet 1,12 BOISMARD 1984 cb101; NEIRYNCK 1985 ἀποστέλλω + κηρύσσω → (ἀπ/δι/εἰσ/κατ/ προσ)ἔρχομαι / (εἰσ)πορεύομαι / ὑποστρέφω / φεύγω + ἀπαγγέλλω/ διαγγέλλω/διηγέομαι/κηρύσσω DENAUX 2009 L***	1,19.26; 4,43; 13,34; 19,32 1,26 4,18¹.18²(-19). 43(-44); 9,2	10,17.21*; 11,11; 13,26*; 28,28 10,21*;11,11	1 0 0	0 0 1

Literature

DENAUX 2009 LAⁿ [ἀποστέλλω ἀπό]; EASTON 1910 165 [πρεσβείαν ἀποστέλλω: cited by Weiss as characteristic of L, and possibly corroborative]; JEREMIAS 1980 68 [ἀποστέλλω + λέγων: red.]; 161 [(ἐξ)ἀποστέλλω εἰς: red.]; 209 [ἀποστέλλω εἰς + person: red.].

LOHMEYER, Monika, *Der Apostelbegriff im Neuen Testament: Eine Untersuchung auf dem Hintergrund der synoptischen Aussendungsrede* (SBB, 29). Stuttgart: Katholisches Bibelwerk, 1995, XI-472 p. Esp. 141-154: "ἀποστέλλειν und πέμπειν".

ἀπόστολος 6/7 + 28/30 (Mt 1, Mk 2)
1. apostle (Lk 24,10); 2. messenger

Word groups	Lk	Acts	Mt	Mk
ἀποστέλλω + ἀποστόλους	11,49		0	1
ἀπόστολοι καὶ πρεσβύτεροι (*SC*a; *VK*b) BOISMARD 1984 Aa15		15,2.4.6.22. 23; 16,4	0	0
δώδεκα + ἀπόστολοι (*VK*c) → ἕνδεκα **ἀπόστολοι**; δώδεκα **μαθηταί**	6,13; 9,1*; 22,14 *v.l.*		1	1
ἕνδεκα ἀπόστολοι → δώδεκα **ἀπόστολοι**; cf. ἕνδεκα μαθηταί Mt 28,16		1,26	0	0
προφῆται καὶ ἀπόστολοι	11,49		0	0

Characteristic of Luke

BOISMARD 1984 Eb6; DENAUX 2009 L***; GOULDER 1989*; HAWKINS 1909 16; HENDRIKS 1986 468; MORGENTHALER 1958A; NEIRYNCK 1985

	Lk	Acts	Mt	Mk
οἱ ἀπόστολοι nominative DENAUX 2009 IA*; GOULDER 1989*	9,10; 17,5; 22,14	4,33; 5,29; 8,14; 11,1; 14,14; 15,6.23	0	1

Literature

COLLISON 1977 168 [linguistic usage of Luke: certain]; EASTON 1910 159 [ἀπόστολοι: cited by Weiss as characteristic of L, and possibly corroborative]; HAUCK 1934 [Vorzugswort]; JEREMIAS 1980 209: "ἀπόστολος ist lk Vorzugswort"; REHKOPF 1959 92 [vorlukanisch]; SCHÜRMANN 1953 109: "οἱ ἀπόστολοι ist somit deutlichst das Vorzugswort des Paulusschülers Luk".

DUPONT, Jacques, Le nom d'apôtres: a-t-il été donné aux douze par Jésus? — *L'Orient Syrien* 'Paris) 1 (1956) 267-290, 425-444; = ID., *Études*, II, 1985, 976-1018.

FRIZZI, Giuseppe, L'ἀπόστολος delle tradizioni sinottiche (Mc, Q, Mt, Lc, e Atti). — *RivBib* 22 (1974) 3-37. Esp. 12-24: "Ἀπόστολος lucano"; 24-31: "Caratteristiche dell'

ἀπόστολος lucano"; 31-33: "Chi sono οἱ δώδεκα?"; 33-37: "Storicità della realtà sinottiche: οἱ δώδεκα/οἱ ἀπόστολοι".
GEORGE, Augustin, L'œuvre de Luc: Actes et Évangile. — DELORME, J. (ed.), *Le ministère et les ministères selon le Nouveau Testament: dossier exégétique et réflexion théologique* (Parole de Dieu, 10). Paris: Seuil, 1974, 207-240; = Les ministères. — ID., *Études*, 1978, 369-394.
HAACKER, Klaus, Verwendung und Vermeidung des Apostelbegriffs im lukanischen Werk. — *NT* 30 (1988) 9-38.
LOHMEYER, Monika, *Der Apostelbegriff im Neuen Testament: Eine Untersuchung auf dem Hintergrund der synoptischen Aussendungsrede* (SBB, 29). Stuttgart: Katholisches Bibelwerk, 1995, XI-472 p. Esp. 133-139: "ἀπόστολος".

ἀποστοματίζω* 1 — ask hostile questions (Lk 11,53)

Literature
HAUCK 1934 [seltenes Alleinwort].
HATCH, Edwin, *Essays*, 1889. Esp. 39-40.

ἀποστρέφω 1 + 1 (Mt 2/3)
1. cause to change belief (Lk 23,14); 2. lead astray (Lk 23,14); 3. put back; 4. change; 5. stop; 6. ἀποστρέφομαι: reject belief; 7. ἀποστρέφομαι: forsake; 8. ἀποστρέφομαι: refuse to help

ἀποτάσσομαι 2 + 2 (Mk 1)
1. say goodbye (Lk 9,61); 2. take leave of; 3. part with possessions (Lk 14,33)

Characteristic of Luke
BOISMARD 1984 cb102; DENAUX 2009 LA*; NEIRYNCK 1985; PLUMMER 1922 lix

Literature
HAUCK 1934 [Vorzugswort]; JEREMIAS 1980 182 [red.].

ἀποτελέω 1 — complete (Lk 13,32)

Literature
FERRARO, Giuseppe, "Oggi e domani e il terzo giorno" (osservazioni su *Luca* 13,32,33). — *RivBib* 16 (1968) 397-407. Esp. 401-407: "Considerazioni sul vocabolario di Luca 13,32.33" [ἐκβάλλειν δαιμόνια; ἰάσεις ἀποτελῶ; τελειοῦσθαι e πορεύεσθαι; ἀπολέσθαι].

ἀποτινάσσω 1 + 1 — shake off (Lk 9,5; Acts 28,5)

Characteristic of Luke
BOISMARD 1984 ab166; HARNACK 1906 40.54; HAWKINS 1909LA; MORGENTHALER 1958*; NEIRYNCK 1985; PLUMMER 1922 liii; VOGEL 1899A

Literature
DENAUX 2009 LA[n]; HAUCK 1934 [seltenes Alleinwort].

ἀποφέρω 1 + 1 (Mk 1)

1. carry away (Lk 16,22; Acts 19,12); 2. lead off

Word groups	Lk	Acts		Mt	Mk
ἀποφέρω + εἰς → (ἀνα/ἐκ)φέρω εἰς	16,22			0	0

ἀποχωρέω 1 + 1 (Mt 1) go away (Lk 9,39; Acts 13,13)

Word groups	Lk	Acts	Mt	Mk
ἀποχωρέω ἀπό (exorcism) → ἐξέρχομαι ἀπό	9,39		0	0

Characteristic of Luke

BOISMARD 1984 cb103; NEIRYNCK 1985

ἀποψύχω 1

1. faint (Lk 21,26); 2. be discouraged

Literature

HAUCK 1934 [seltenes Alleinwort].

ἅπτω 13/15 + 1 (Mt 9, Mk 11)

1. start a fire (Lk 11,33); 2. ἅπτομαι: hold on to; 3. ἅπτομαι: touch (Lk 7,14); 4. ἅπτομαι: harm

Word groups	Lk	Acts	Mt	Mk
ἅπτομαι + ῥύσις αἵματος; cf. Mk 5,27-28 ἅπτομαι + πηγὴ αἵματος	8,44		0	0
ἅπτω active (VKa) → περιάπτω; cf. ἀν/καθάπτω Acts 28,2*.3 DENAUX 2009 Laⁿ	8,16; 11,33; 15,8; 22,55*	28,2	0	0

Characteristic of Luke

PLUMMER 1922 lii

	Lk	Acts	Mt	Mk
ἅπτω λύχνον/πῦρ/πυράν → ἀν/περιάπτω πῦρ/πυράν BOISMARD 1984 Ab69; GOULDER 1989*; HARNACK 1906 54; HAWKINS 1909 186; NEIRYNCK 1985	8,16; 11,33; 15,8; 22,55*	28,2	0	0

Literature

COLLISON 1977 39 [ἅπτω active: linguistic usage of Luke: likely]; DENAUX 2009 Laⁿ [ἅπτω λύχνον/πῦρ/πυράν]; JEREMIAS 1980 204: "ἅπτω in der Bedeutung 'anzünden' findet sich im NT nur im lk Doppelwerk".

WEISSENRIEDER, Annette, The Plague of Uncleanness? The Ancient Illness Construct "Issue of Blood" in Luke 8:43-48. — STEGEMANN, Wolfgang – MALINA, Bruce J. – THEISSEN, Gerd (eds.), The Social Setting of Jesus and the Gospels. Minneapolis, MN: Fortress, 2002, 207-222.

WELLS, Louise, The Greek Language of Healing, 1998. Esp. 196-200.

ἄρα 6 + 5/6 (Mt 7, Mk 2)

1. as a result (Lk 11,20); 2. possible (Lk 22,23); 3. perhaps (Acts 8,22)

Word groups	Lk	Acts	Mt	Mk
ἄρα γε / ἄραγε (SCa; VKc)		11,18 v.l.; 17,27	2	0
ἄρα καί		11,18	0	0
εἰ ἄρα		7,1*; 8,22; 17,27	0	1
BOISMARD 1984 Ca39				
τίς/τί ἄρα (SCb; VKb)	1,66; 8,25; 12,42; 22,23	12,18	4	1

Literature

COLLISON 1977 101 [linguistic usage of Luke: probable; ἄρα following the interrogative pronoun: noteworthy phenomena]; JEREMIAS 1980 72 [τί ἄρα: red.]; REHKOPF 1959 97 [τίς/τί ἄρα: vorlukanisch]; SCHÜRMANN 1957 12 [ἄρα steht als Folgerungspartikel wie klassisch bei Fragen (außer 2× Mk; 4× Mt) im NT nur bei Luk]; 1961 273 [τίς/τί ἄρα].

CLARK, Kenneth Willis, The Meaning of αρα. — BARTH, E.H. – COCROFT, R.E. (eds.), *Festschrift to Honor F. Wilbur Gingrich*, 1972, 70-84. Esp. 75-77: "Luke-Acts".
THRALL, Margaret E., *Greek Particles in the New Testament*, 1962. Esp. 10-11 [ἄρα/οὖν]; 36-39 [ἄρα].

ἄρα 1 + 1   indeed (Lk 18,8)

Word groups	Lk	Acts	Mt	Mk
ἆρά γε (VKa)		8,30	0	0

Literature

COLLISON 1977 102 [noteworthy phenomena]; DENAUX 2009 LAⁿ; JEREMIAS 1980 272 [red.].

ἀργύριον 4 + 5 (Mt 9, Mk 1)

1. silver (Acts 3,6); 2. silver money (Lk 9,3; 19,25.23; 22,5)

Word groups	Lk	Acts	Mt	Mk
ἀργύριον ἤ/καί χρυσίον (LN: money)		3,6; 20,33	0	0

Characteristic of Luke	Lk	Acts	Mt	Mk
ἀργύριον singular; cf. 1 Cor 3,12; 1 Pet 1,18 BOISMARD 1984 cb88; DENAUX 2009 L***; NEIRYNCK 1985	9,3; 19,15.23; 22,5	3,6; 7,16; 8,20; 19,19; 20,33	1	1

Literature

EHLING, Kay, Zwei Anmerkungen zum ἀργύριον in Apg 19,19. — ZNW 94 (2003) 268-275.

ἀρήν* 1   lamb

Word groups	Lk	Acts	Mt	Mk
ἀρήν + λύκος; cf. πρόβατον + λύκος Mt 7,15; 10,16	10,3		0	0

Literature

HAUCK 1934 [seltenes Alleinwort].

ἀριθμέω 1 (Mt 1)	count (Lk 12,7)

ἀριθμός 1 + 5

1. number (Lk 22,3); 2. total (Acts 6,7)

Characteristic of Luke
BOISMARD 1984 Eb27; NEIRYNCK 1985

Literature
DENAUX 2009 IA[n].

TAEGER, Jens-Wilhelm, *Der Mensch und sein Heil*, 1982. Esp. 181-183: "περισσεύειν τῷ ἀριθμῷ / ἐγενήθη ἀριθμός".

ʿΑριμαθαία 1 (Mt 1, Mk 1)	Arimathea			
Word groups	**Lk**	**Acts**	**Mt**	**Mk**
Ἰωσὴφ + ἀπὸ ʿΑριμαθαίας	23,(50-)51		1	1

ἀριστάω 1

1. eat a meal (Lk 11,37); 2. have breakfast

Literature
EASTON 1910 151 [probably characteristic of L].

LEE, John A.L. – HORSLEY, G.H.R., A Lexicon of the New Testament, 2, 1998. Esp. 66-67.

ἀριστερός 1 (Mt 1, Mk 1)

1. left (Lk 23,33); 2. ἡ ἀριστερά: left hand

Word groups	**Lk**	**Acts**	**Mt**	**Mk**
ἀριστερός + δεξιός; cf. 2 Cor 6,7; cf. εὐώνυμος + δεξιός Mt 20,21.23; 25,33; 27,38; Mk 10,40; 15,27	23,33		1	1
ἐξ ἀριστερῶν → ἐκ **δεξιῶν**; cf. ἐξ εὐωνύμων Mt 20,21.23; 25,33.41; 27,38; Mk 10,40; 15,27	23,33			

ἄριστον 2 (Mt 1)

1. meal (Lk 11,38); 2. noon meal (Lk 14,12)

Word groups	**Lk**	**Acts**	**Mt**	**Mk**
ἄριστον ποιέω → **δεῖπνον/δοχὴν** ποιέω; cf. ποιέω γάμους Mt 22,2	14,12		0	0

Literature
BDAG 2000 131 [Lk 14,12 ἄρ. = breakfast, differentiated from δεῖπνον]; EASTON 1910 151 [probably characteristic of L].

ἀρκέω 1 (Mt 1)
1. be sufficient; 2. ἀρκέομαι: be satisfied (Lk 3,14)

ἀρνέομαι 4 + 4 (Mt 4, Mk 2)
1. deny (verbal) (Lk 8,45; 22,57); 2. deny (non-verbal) (Lk 12,9); 3. refuse to agree; 4. disregard (Lk 9,23); 5. refuse to follow; 6. be false to oneself

Word groups	Lk	Acts	Mt	Mk
ἀρνέομαι ἑαυτόν → ἀπαρνέομαι ἑαυτόν	9,23		0	0
ἀρνέομαι λέγων	22,57		1	0

Literature
JEREMIAS 1980 68 [ἀρνέομαι + λέγων: red.]; SCHÜRMANN 1957 26 [Lk 22,34: Luk Mk-R sehr wahrscheinlich].

Ἀρνί 1
Arni (Lk 3,33)

ἀροτριάω 1
plow (Lk 17,7)

Literature
EASTON 1910 159 [cited by Weiss as characteristic of L, and possibly corroborative].

ἄροτρον 1
plow (Lk 9,62)

Word groups	Lk	Acts	Mt	Mk
ἐπιβάλλω τὴν χεῖρα ἐπ' ἄροτρον καὶ βλέπω εἰς τὰ ὀπίσω (LN: start to do and then hesitate)	9,62		0	0

Literature
EASTON 1910 159 [cited by Weiss as characteristic of L, and possibly corroborative]; HAUCK 1934 [seltenes Alleinwort].

ἁρπαγή 1 (Mt 1)
1. plunder; 2. booty; 3. violent greed (Lk 11,39)

ἅρπαξ 1 (Mt 1)
1. robber (noun) (Lk 18,11); 2. vicious (adjective); 3. violently greedy (adjective)

ἄρσην 1 (Mt 1, Mk 1)
male

Word groups	Lk	Acts	Mt	Mk
ἄρσεν διανοῖγον μήτραν (LN: firstborn son)	2,23		0	0

Literature
JUNG, Chang-Wook, *Infancy Narrative*, 2004. Esp. 82-83.

ἄρτος 15/16 + 5 (Mt 21, Mk 21/22)

1. loaf of bread (Lk 9,13; 22,19); 2. food (Lk 15,17)

Word groups	Lk	Acts	Mt	Mk
ἄρτος + ἰχθύς; cf. ἄρτος + ἰχθύδιον Mt 15,34; Mk 8,6(-7)	9,13.16		4	3
ἄρτος + λίθος	4,3		2	0
ἄρτος τῆς προθέσεως (LN: consecrated bread; SCa; VKa)	6,4		1	1
ἄρτους + παρατίθημι	9,16; 11,5(-6)		0	2
(ἐπι)δίδωμι + ἄρτον	6,4; 9,16; 11,3; 22,19; 24,30		4	5
ἐσθίω (+) (τὸν) ἄρτον / (τοὺς) ἄρτους	6,4; 7,33; 9,16(-17); 14,1.15	27,35	3	7
εὐλογέω + ἄρτον → εὐχαριστέω/(κατα)κλάω ἄρτον	9,16; 24,30		2	2
εὐχαριστέω ἄρτον → εὐλογέω/(κατα)κλάω ἄρτον	22,19	27,35	1	1
ζῶ + ἐπ' ἄρτῳ	4,4		1	0
κατακλάω + ἄρτον → κλάσις τοῦ **ἄρτου**; κλάω **ἄρτον**	9,16		0	1
κλάσις τοῦ ἄρτου (SCb) → (κατα)κλάω **ἄρτον** DENAUX 2009 LAⁿ	24,35	2,42	0	0
λαμβάνω (+) ἄρτον	6,4; 9,16; 22,19; 24,30	27,35	6/7	5

Characteristic of Luke	Lk	Acts	Mt	Mk
κλάω ἄρτον singular (LN: have a meal; SCb; VKb) → κατακλάω **ἄρτον**; κλάσις τοῦ **ἄρτου**; cf. 1 Cor 10,16; 11,24 BOISMARD 1984 cb146; NEIRYNCK 1985	22,19; 24,30	2,46; 20,7.11; 27,35	1	1

Literature

DENAUX 2009 lAn [κλάω ἄρτον singular]; SCHÜRMANN 1955 90, n. 312 [ἄρτον ἐσθίειν].

BLACK, Matthew, The Aramaic of τὸν ἄρτον ἡμῶν τὸν ἐπιούσιον (Matt. vi.11 = Luke xi.3). — JTS 42 (1941) 186-189.
DELEBECQUE, Édouard, Études grecques, 1976. Esp. 167-181: "Le pain du Pater (11,3)".
DEWAILLY, Louis-Marie, "Donne-nous notre pain": Quel pain? Note sur la quatrième demande du Pater. — RSPT 64 (1980) 561-588.
TAYLOR, Justin, La fraction du pain en Luc-Actes. — VERHEYDEN, Joseph (ed.), The Unity of Luke-Acts, 1999, 281-295.

ἀρτύω 1 (Mk 1)

season (Lk 14,34)

Ἀρφαξάδ 1

Arphaxad (Lk 3,36)

ἀρχαῖος 2 + 3 (Mt 2/3)

ancient (Lk 9,8.19; Acts 15,21; 21,16)

Word groups	Lk	Acts	Mt	Mk
ἀφ' ἡμερῶν ἀρχαίων (LN: long ago)		15,7	0	0

Literature

PRETE, Benedetto, Valore dell'espressione ἀφ' ἡμερῶν ἀρχαίων in Atti 15,7: Nesso cronologico, oppure istanza teologica della Chiesa delle origini? — *BibOr* 13 (1971) 119-133; = ID., *L'opera di Luca*, 1986, 494-508. Esp. 500-503: "L'uso dell'espressione ἀπ' αἰῶνος negli scritti di Luca"; 503-504: "Le espressioni ἀπ' ἀρχῆς e ἐν ἀρχῇ negli scritti di Luca"; 504-506: "La formula ἀφ' ἡμερῶν ἀρχαίων nel contesto di Atti 15,1-35"; 506-508: "La formula ἀφ' ἡμερῶν ἀρχαίων: espressione di un'istanza della Chiesa primitiva".

ἀρχή 3 + 4 (Mt 4, Mk 4)

1. beginning (aspect); 2. beginning (time) (Lk 1,2); 3. first cause; 4. sphere of authority (Lk 20,20); 5. ruler (Lk 12,11); 6. supernatural power; 7. elementary aspect; 8. corner (Acts 10,11)

Word groups	Lk	Acts	Mt	Mk
ἀπ' ἀρχῆς (*SC*a; *VK*a)	1,2	26,4	3	2
ἀρχή + ἐξουσία (*VK*b)	12,11; 20,20		0	0
DENAUX 2009 L[n]				
ἐν ἀρχῇ		11,15	0	0

Literature

ALEXANDER, Loveday, *The Preface to Luke's Gospel*, 1993. Esp. 119-120.
BORMANN, Lukas, *Recht, Gerechtigkeit und Religion*, 2001. Esp. 131.
CADBURY, Henry J., Commentary on the Preface of Luke, 1922. Esp. 498.
CHILTON, Bruce, Announcement in Nazara, 1981. Esp. 160.
PRETE, Benedetto, Valore dell'espressione ἀφ' ἡμερῶν ἀρχαίων in Atti 15,7: Nesso cronologico, oppure istanza teologica della Chiesa delle origini? — *BibOr* 13 (1971) 119-133; = ID., *L'opera di Luca*, 1986, 494-508. Esp. 500-503: "L'uso dell'espressione ἀπ' αἰῶνος negli scritti di Luca"; 503-504: "Le espressioni ἀπ' ἀρχῆς e ἐν ἀρχῇ negli scritti di Luca"; 504-506: "La formula ἀφ' ἡμερῶν ἀρχαίων nel contesto di Atti 15,1-35"; 506-508: "La formula ἀφ' ἡμερῶν ἀρχαίων: espressione di un'istanza della Chiesa primitiva".
SAMAIN, Étienne, La notion de ἀρχή dans l'œuvre lucanienne. — NEIRYNCK, Frans (ed.), *L'Évangile de Luc*, 1973, 299-328; [2]1989, 209-238 (327: note additionnelle).
WINK, Walter, *Naming the Powers*, 1984. Esp. 13-15.151.

ἀρχιερεύς 15/16 + 22/23 (Mt 25, Mk 22)

1. chief priest (Lk 19,47); 2. high priest (Lk 22,50)

Word groups	Lk	Acts	Mt	Mk
ἀρχιερεῖς + γραμματεῖς + πρεσβυτέριον	22,66		0	0
ἀρχιερεῖς + ἱερεύς		5,24 *v.l.*	0	0
ἀρχιερεῖς + πρεσβύτεροι + στρατηγοί	22,52		0	0
ἀρχιερεῖς + στρατηγοί/ός (τοῦ ἱεροῦ) DENAUX 2009 La[n]	22,4.52	4,1*; 5,24	0	0
ἀρχιερεύς/εῖς + ἄρχων/ἄρχοντες DENAUX 2009 LA[n]	23,13.23* *v.l.*; 24,20	4,(5-)6; 23,5	0	0
ἀρχιερεύς/εῖς + γραμματεῖς	9,22; 19,47; 20,1.19; 22,2.66; 23,10		5/6	9
ἀρχιερεύς/εῖς + γραμματεῖς + πρεσβύτεροι → ἄρχοντες + γραμματεῖς + πρεσβύτεροι	9,22; 20,1		3	5
ἀρχιερεύς/εῖς + πρεσβύτεροι	9,22; 20,1; 22,52	4,23; 23,14; 24,1; 25,15	9	5
ἀρχιερεύς/εῖς + συνέδριον	22,66	5,21.27; 22,30	1	2
ἀρχιερεύς + ὑπηρέτης		5,21(-22)	1	2

ἀρχιερεύς singular (VKa)	3,2; 22,50.54	4,6; 5,17.21.27; 7,1; 9,1; 19,14; 22,5; 23,2.4.5; 24,1; 25,2 v.l.	7	8
ἀρχιερεῖς plural	9,22.47; 20,1.19; 22,2.4.52.66; 23,4.10.13.23*; 24,20	4,1*.23; 5,24; 9,14.21; 22,30; 23,14; 25,2.15; 26,10.12	18	14

Literature

COLLISON 1977 168-169 [linguistic usage of Luke: probable; ἀρχιερεύς + γραμματεύς: certain]; EASTON 1910 151 [probably characteristic of L].

BACHMANN, Michael, *Jerusalem und der Tempel*, 1980. Esp. 187-190.
BORMANN, Lukas, *Recht, Gerechtigkeit und Religion*, 2001. Esp. 211-212.
KLIJN, Albertus F.J., Scribes, Pharisees, Highpriests and Elders in the New Testament. — *NT* 3 (1959) 259-267.

ἀρχισυνάγωγος 2 + 3 (Mk 4)   leader of a synagogue (Lk 8,49; 13,14)

Characteristic of Luke
VOGEL 1899B

Literature
BDAG 2000 139 [literature].

BORMANN, Lukas, *Recht, Gerechtigkeit und Religion*, 2001. Esp. 212.
CLAUSSEN, Carsten, *Versammlung, Gemeinde, Synagoge*, 2002. Esp. 256-264: "'Ἀρχισυνάγωγος".
HORSLEY, G.H.R. – LEE, John A.L., A Lexicon of the New Testament, 1, 1997. Esp. 66-68.79-80.

ἀρχιτελώνης** 1   chief tax collector (Lk 19,2)

Literature
HAUCK 1934 [seltenes Alleinwort].

BORMANN, Lukas, *Recht, Gerechtigkeit und Religion*, 2001. Esp. 131.

ἄρχω 31 + 10 (Mt 13, Mk 27/28)
1. rule; 2. ἄρχομαι: begin (aspect) (Lk 3,23); 3. ἄρχομαι: begin (time) (Lk 9,12)

Word groups	Lk	Acts	Mt	Mk
ἄρξομαι future + infinitive → ἄρχομαι + inf. DENAUX 2009 L[n]	13,26; 14,9; 23,30		0	0
ἄρχομαι + infinitive (SCa) → ἄρξομαι future + inf.	3,8; 4,21; 5,21; 7,15.24.38.49; 9,12; 11,29.53; 12,1.45; 13,25.26; 14,9.18.29.30; 15,14.24; 19,37.45; 20,9; 21,28; 22,23; 23,2.30	1,1; 2,4; 11,15; 18,26; 24,2; 27,35	12	26/27
ἄρχομαι (+) ἀπό (VKb)	13,25; 23,5; 24,27.47	1,22; 8,35; 10,37	3	0

ἄρχομαι (+) λαλεῖν DENAUX 2009 1Aⁿ	7,15		2,4; 11,15	0	0
ἄρχομαι absolute use DENAUX 2009 LAⁿ	3,23		11,4	0	0
ἤρξατο/ἤρξαντο aorist	4,21; 5,21; 7,15.24.38.49; 9,12; 11,29.53; 12,1; 14,18.30; 15,14.24; 19,37.45; 20,9; 22,23; 23,2		1,1; 2,4; 18,26; 24,2; 27,35	9	26/27

Characteristic of Luke	Lk		Acts	Mt	Mk
ἀρξάμενος ἀπό CADBURY 1920 163; DENAUX 2009 LA*; GOULDER 1989; VOGEL 1899C	23,5; 24,27.47		1,22; 8,35; 10,37	1	0
ἀρξάμενος ἀπό + place BOISMARD 1984 Ab108; NEIRYNCK 1985	23,5; 24,47		10,37	0	0
ἄρχομαι + infinitive in direct speech DENAUX 2009 L***; HENDRIKS 1986 433	3,8; 12,45; 13,25.26; 14,9.18.29.30; 15,14.24; 21,28; 23,30			3	0
ἄρχομαι λέγειν GOULDER 1989	3,8; 4,21; 7,24.49; 11,29; 12,1; 13,26; 20,9; 23,30			3	7/8

Literature

VON BENDEMANN 2001 420 [ἄρχεσθαι + inf.]: "typisch lukanisch"; COLLISON 1977 39-40
[ἄρχομαι + infinitive (pleonastic/inceptive): linguistic usage of Luke: certain; linguistic usage of
Luke's "other source-material": nearly certain]; 40 [ἄρχομαι + inf. = future: linguistic usage of
Luke's "other source-material": likely]; 41 [ἀρξάμενος ἀπό: likely]; 125 [ἄρχω + ἀπό: likely];
DENAUX 2009 Laⁿ [ἀρξάμενος ἀπό + place]; EASTON 1910 145 [especially characteristic of L];
176 [ἤρξατο/ ἤρξαντο: possible Hebraisms in the Lucan Writings, as classed by Dalman]; HAUCK
1934 [Vorzugswort]; JEREMIAS 1980 114: "absoluter Gebrauch von medialem ἄρχεσθαι im NT ist
nur im Doppelwerk: Lk 3,23/Apg 11,4 zu finden"; 173 [7,49 ἤρξαντο: red.]; 301: "ἀρξάμενος mit
Nennung des Ausgangspunktes (ἀπό) ist lukanisch"; REHKOPF 1959 92 [ἄρξομαι fut. + inf.:
vorlukanisch]; SCHÜRMANN 1957 8, n. 28 [Lk 22,23]; 1961 277 [ἄρξομαι fut. + inf.].

BACHMANN, Michael, *Jerusalem und der Tempel*, 1980. Esp. 85-96 [ἀρξάμενος ἀπό].
CHILTON, Bruce, Announcement in Nazara, 1981. Esp. 160.
HUNKIN, J.W., "Pleonastic" ἄρχομαι in the New Testament. — *JTS* 25 (1923-24) 390-
402.
KILGALLEN, John J., Did Peter Actually Fail to Get a Word in? (Acts 11,15). — *Bib* 71
(1990) 405-410. [ἤρξατο]
MAHFOUZ, Hady, *La fonction littéraire et théologique de Lc 3,1-20*, 2003. Esp. 186
[ἄρχομαι].

ἄρχων 8 + 11 (Mt 5, Mk 1)
1. ruler (Lk 23,35); 2. judge (Lk 12,58)

Word groups	Lk	Acts	Mt	Mk
ἄρχοντες + γραμματεῖς + πρεσβύτεροι → **ἀρχιερεύς/ἀρχιερεῖς** + γραμματεῖς + πρεσβύτεροι		4,5	0	0
ἄρχοντες τῶν Φαρισαίων	14,1		0	0
ἄρχων/ἄρχοντες + ἀρχιερεύς/ἀρχιερεῖς DENAUX 2009 LAⁿ	23,13.23 v.l.; 24,20	4,5(-6); 23,5	0	0
ἄρχων τῶν δαιμονίων	11,15		2	1

| ἄρχων τοῦ λαοῦ → οἱ **πρῶτοι** τοῦ λαοῦ; cf. ἀρχιερεῖς τοῦ λαοῦ Mt 2,4; 21,23; 26,3.47; 27,1; γραμματεῖς τοῦ λαοῦ Mt 2,4; πρεσβύτεροι τοῦ λαοῦ Mt 21,23; 26,3.47; 27,1 | | 4,8; 23,5 | 0 | 0 |
| ἄρχων τῆς συναγωγῆς | 8,41 | | 0 | 0 |

Characteristic of Luke
GOULDER 1989

	Lk	Acts	Mt	Mk
οἱ ἄρχοντες (plural) (VKa) DENAUX 2009 1A*;	14,1; 23,13. 35; 24,20	3,17; 4,5.8.26; 13,27; 14,5; 16,19	1	0
οἱ ἄρχοντες leaders of the Jews; cf. Jn 7,26.48; 12,42 BOISMARD 1984 cb62; DENAUX 2009 L***; GOULDER 1989*; HAWKINS 1909L; NEIRYNCK 1985	14,1; 23,13.35; 24,20	3,17; 4,5.8; 13,27; 14,5	0	0
οἱ ἄρχοντες + genitive pronoun BOISMARD 1984 Ab47; NEIRYNCK 1985	24,20	3,17; 4,5; 13,27; 14,5	0	0

Literature
COLLISON 1977 169 [οἱ ἄρχοντες: linguistic usage of Luke's "other source-material": likely]; DENAUX 2009 1A[n] [οἱ ἄρχοντες + genitive pronoun]; EASTON 1910 159 [cited by Weiss as characteristic of L, and possibly corroborative]; HAUCK 1934 [Vorzugswort; Vorzugsverbindung: ἀρχόντων τῶν Φαρισαίων]; JEREMIAS 1980 235-236: "Der Plural von ὁ ἄρχων, auf jüdische Obrigkeiten angewendet, findet sich im NT außer dreimal bei Joh nur im Doppelwerk"; RADL 1975 401 [ἄρχων; ἄρχοντες].

BORMANN, Lukas, *Recht, Gerechtigkeit und Religion*, 2001. Esp. 131-132.
CLAUSSEN, Carsten, *Versammlung, Gemeinde, Synagoge*, 2002. Esp. 273-278: "Ἄρχων".
WINK, Walter, *Naming the Powers*, 1984. Esp. 13-15.151.

ἄρωμα 2 (Mk 1)
perfumed ointment (Lk 23,56; 24,1)

Literature
EASTON 1910 159 [cited by Weiss as characteristic of L, and possibly corroborative].

ἄσβεστος 1 (Mt 1, Mk 1/2)
unquenchable

Word groups	Lk	Acts	Mt	Mk
πῦρ ἄσβεστον; cf. τὸ πῦρ οὐ σβέννυται	3,17		1	1/2

Ἀσήρ 1
Asher (Lk 2,36)

ἀσθένεια 4 + 1 (Mt 1)
1. incapacity; 2. illness (Lk 5,15; 8,2; 13,11.12); 3. timidity

Word groups	Lk	Acts	Mt	Mk
πνεῦμα ἀσθενείας; πνεῦμα + ἀσθένεια DENAUX 2009 LA[n]	8,2; 13,11	5,16; 19,12	0	0

Characteristic of Luke
DENAUX 2009 L***; GOULDER 1989*; HARNACK 1906 43.

Literature
VON BENDEMANN 2001 413: "zu ἀσθένεια im Sinne der Krankheit"; HAUCK 1934 [Vorzugswort]; JEREMIAS 1980 176 [red.].

ἀσθενέω 1/3 + 3 (Mt 3, Mk 1)
1. be weak (Acts 20,35); 2. be ill (Lk 4,40)

Literature
BDAG 2000 142 [ἀσθ. Acts 20,35 = be in need].

DUPONT, Jacques., *Le discours de Milet*, 1962. Esp. 307-319.

ἀσθενής 2 + 3 (Mt 3/4, Mk 1)
1. unable; 2. morally weak; 3. illness (Lk 9,2: 10,9); 4. helpless condition; 5. weak

ἀσκός 4 (Mt 4, Mk 4)   wineskin (Lk 5,37$^{1.2.3}$.38)

ἀσπάζομαι 2 + 5/6 (Mt 2, Mk 2)
1. greet (Lk 1,40; 10,4); 2. be happy about; 3. welcome

Word groups	Lk	Acts	Mt	Mk
ἀσπασάμενος; cf. Heb 11,13		18,22; 20,1; 21,7.19; 25,13	0	0
BOISMARD 1984 Ba11				

Literature
HARNACK 1906 138; RADL 1975 401 [ἀσπάζομαι; ἀσπασάμενος].

ἀσπασμός 5 (Mt 1, Mk 1)   greeting (Lk 1,29.41.44; 11,43; 20,46)

Characteristic of Luke
DENAUX 2009 L***; GOULDER 1989*.

ἀσσάριον 1 (Mt 1)   penny (Lk 12,6)

Literature
MARYKS, Robert, A., Il latinismi del Nuovo Testamento, 2000. Esp. 24.

ἀστραπή 3 (Mt 2)
1. lightning (Lk 10,18; 17,24); 2. bright beam (Lk 11,36)

Literature
RÜSTOW, Alexander, Ἐντὸς ὑμῶν ἐστιν: Zur Deutung von Lukas 17,20-21. — ZNW 51

(1960) 197-224. Esp. 197-203 [παρατηρέω/παρατήρησις]; 203-204 [ἀστραπή]; 208-218 [ἐντός].

ἀστράπτω 2	glisten (Lk 17,24; 24,4)

Characteristic of Luke
PLUMMER 1922 liii

Literature
DENAUX 2009 Lⁿ; HAUCK 1934 [seltenes Alleinwort]; PLUMMER 1922 lxiii [Lk "is fond of *combinations of cognate words*, e.g. ἡ ἀστραπὴ ἀστράπτουσα (xvii.24)"].

ἄστρον 1 + 2	

1. star, planet (Lk 21,25); 2. constellation

Word groups	Lk	Acts	Mt	Mk
ἄστρον + ἥλιος → σελήνη + ἥλιος	21,25	27,20	0	0

Characteristic of Luke
HARNACK 1906 51

Literature
DENAUX 2009 IAⁿ.

ἀσφάλεια 1 + 1	

1. safety (Acts 5,23); 2. certainty (Lk 1,4)

Characteristic of Luke; cf. ἀσφαλής Acts 21,34; 22,30; 25,26; ἀσφαλῶς Acts 2,36; 16,23
BOISMARD 1984 cb134; NEIRYNCK 1985; PLUMMER 1922 lix

Literature
DENAUX 2009 LAⁿ; GERSDORF 1816 162 [ἵνα ἐπιγνῷς περὶ ὧν κατηχήθης λόγων τὴν ἀσφάλειαν]; RADL 1975 401.

BORMANN, Lukas., *Recht, Gerechtigkeit und Religion*, 2001. Esp. 132.
CADBURY, Henry J., Commentary on the Preface of Luke, 1922. Esp. 509-510.
GLÖCKNER, Richard, *Die Verkündigung des Heils beim Evangelisten Lukas*, 1975. Esp. 3-11: "Die Bedeutung des Begriffsfeldes zum Wortstamm ἀσφαλ- bei Lukas".
ROPES, James Hardy, St. Luke's Preface; ἀσφάλεια and παρακολουθεῖν. — *JTS* 25 (1923-24) 67-71.

ἀσώτως* 1	recklessly (Lk 15,13)

Literature
HAUCK 1934 [seltenes Alleinwort].

ἄτεκνος 2/3	childless (Lk 20,28.29)

Literature

DENAUX 2009 Lⁿ; HAUCK 1934 [seltenes Alleinwort].

BORMANN, Lukas, *Recht, Gerechtigkeit und Religion*, 2001. Esp. 148-149.

ἀτενίζω 2 + 10	stare at

Word groups	Lk	Acts	Mt	Mk
ἀτενίζω + (ὁράω/)εἶδον→ (ἀνα)βλέπω/ θεάομαι/θεωρέω + (ὁράω/)εἶδον; cf. βλέπω + ὁράω Mk 8,15.24; ἐμβλέπω + εἶδον Mk 14,67; περιβλέπω + εἶδον Mk 5,32; 9,8 DENAUX 2009 IAⁿ	22,56	6,15; 7,55; 11,6; 14,9	0	0
ἀτενίζω εἰς (VKa) → ἀτενίζω + dat.		1,10; 3,4; 6,15; 7,55; 11,6; 13,9	0	0
ἀτενίζω + ὀφθαλμός → (ἀνα/δια)βλέπω/ὁράω/εἶδον + ὀφθαλμός	4,20		0	0

Characteristic of Luke

BOISMARD 1984 вb40; DENAUX 2009 IA*; HAWKINS 1909B; MORGENTHALER 1958A; NEIRYNCK 1985; PLUMMER 1922 lix

	Lk	Acts	Mt	Mk
ἀτενίζω + dative (person) → ἀτενίζω εἰς; cf. ἀτενίζω + acc. (person) 2 Cor 3,7.13 BOISMARD 1984 ʌb33; CREDNER 1836 137; DENAUX 2009 IA*; NEIRYNCK 1985; VOGEL 1899D	4,20; 22,56	3,12; 10,4; 14,9; 23,1	0	0

Literature

COLLISON 1977 92 [noteworthy phenomena]; HAUCK 1934 [Vorzugswort]; JEREMIAS 1980 122: "lk Vorzugswort … die an unserer Stelle [4,20] vorliegende Verbindung mit dem Dativ der Person (statt des üblichen εἰς τινα) ist kennzeichnend für Lukas"; RADL 1975 401 [ἀτενίζω; ἀτενίζω + dat.]; SCHNEIDER 1969 79-80.163: "Vorliebe des Luk für ἀτενίζω" [Vorzugswörter und -ausdrücke des Luk].

CHILTON, Bruce, *Announcement in Nazara*, 1981. Esp. 158-159.
STRELAN, Rick, *Strange Stares: ἀτενίζειν in Acts. — NT* 41 (1999) 235-255.
—, Recognizing the Gods (Acts 14.8-10). — *NTS* 46 (2000) 488-503. Esp. 490-493: "The stare"; 493-501: "The loud voice".

ἄτερ 2	without (Lk 22,6.35)

Word groups	Lk	Acts	Mt	Mk
ἄτερ ὄχλου	22,6		0	0

Characteristic of Luke

PLUMMER 1922 liii

Literature

COLLISON 1977 147 [noteworthy phenomena]; DENAUX 2009 Lⁿ; HAUCK 1934 [seltenes Alleinwort]; JEREMIAS 1980 292 [red.]; SCHÜRMANN 1957 117: "wahrscheinlich luk R".

ἀτιμάζω 1 + 1 (Mk 1)	
1. treat shamefully (Lk 20,11); 2. cause to be dishonored	

ἄτοπος 1 + 2

1. bad (Lk 23,41); 2. unusual (Acts 28,6)

Characteristic of Luke
BOISMARD 1984 cb15; HARNACK 1906 41.51; HAWKINS 1909 187; NEIRYNCK 1985; PLUMMER 1922 lix

Literature
DENAUX 2009 lAⁿ; HAUCK 1934 [seltenes Alleinwort]; JEREMIAS 1980 307 [red.]; RADL 1975 401.

BORMANN, Lukas, *Recht, Gerechtigkeit und Religion*, 2001. Esp. 198.
TAEGER, Jens-Wilhelm, *Der Mensch und sein Heil*, 1982. Esp. 43-44: "Verwandte Begriffe (πονηρός, κακός, ἄτοπος)".

Αὔγουστος 1   Augustus (Lk 2,1)

Literature
MORRIS, Royce L.B., Why Ἀύγουστος? A Note to Luke 2.1. — *NTS* 38 (1992) 142-144.

αὐλέω 1 (Mt 1)   play the flute (Lk 7,32)

αὐλή 2 (Mt 3, Mk 3)	
1. courtyard (Lk 22,55); 2. dwelling (Lk 11,21)	

αὐλίζομαι 1 (Mt 1)   spend the night

Word groups	Lk	Acts	Mt	Mk
αὐλίζομαι εἰς	21,37		0	0

Literature
JEREMIAS 1980 284 [αὐλίζομαι εἰς: red.].

αὐξάνω 4 + 4 (Mt 2, Mk 1)

1. increase; 2. cause to increase; 3. grow (Lk 1,80; 2,40; 12,27; 13,19); 4. enjoy greater respect

Word groups	Lk	Acts	Mt	Mk
ὁ λόγος ηὔξανεν BOISMARD 1984 Ab98		6,7; 12,24; 19,20	0	0

Characteristic of Luke
CREDNER 1836 141; GOULDER 1989; VOGEL 1899D

	Lk	Acts	Mt	Mk
αὐξάνω intransitive (increase, grow) DENAUX 2009 L***; VOGEL 1899D	1,80; 2,40; 12,27; 13,19	6,7; 7,17; 12,24; 19,20	1	1
αὐξάνω + verb (climax) BOISMARD 1984 Ab48; DENAUX 2009 LA*; NEIRYNCK 1985	1,80; 2,40; 13,19	7,17; 12,24; 19,20	0	0

Literature

JEREMIAS 1980 76 [intransitive αὐξάνω: red.].

KODELL, Jerome, "The Word of God Grew": The Ecclesial Tendency of λόγος in Acts 1,7; 12,24; 19,20. — Bib 55 (1974) 505-519.

TAEGER, Jens-Wilhelm, Der Mensch und sein Heil, 1982. Esp. 163-177: "ὁ λόγος τοῦ θεοῦ / τοῦ κυρίου) ηὔξανεν".

αὔριον 4 + 4/5 (Mt 3)

1. tomorrow (Lk 10,35; 12,28; 13,32.33); 2. soon

Word groups	Lk	Acts	Mt	Mk
ἡ αὔριον (VKa)	10,35	4,3.5	2	0
σήμερον καὶ αὔριον	12,28; 13,32.33		1	0

Characteristic of Luke

PLUMMER 1922 lix

	Lk	Acts	Mt	Mk
ἐπὶ τὴν αὔριον BOISMARD 1984 Ab167; NEIRYNCK 1985	10,35	4,5	0	0

Literature

COLLISON 1977 151 [linguistic usage of Luke's "other source-material": likely]; 162 [σήμερον + αὔριον: noteworthy phenomena]; DENAUX 2009 LAⁿ [ἐπὶ τὴν αὔριον]; JEREMIAS 1980 192 [ἐπὶ τὴν αὔριον]: "ἐπί c. acc. de tempore ist lukanisch".

αὐστηρός 2   exacting (Lk 19,21.22)

Characteristic of Luke

PLUMMER 1922 liii

Literature

DENAUX 2009 Lⁿ; HAUCK 1934 [seltenes Alleinwort].

αὐτόπτης* 1   eyewitness (Lk 1,2)

Literature

HAUCK 1934 [seltenes Alleinwort].

ALEXANDER, Loveday, The Preface to Luke's Gospel, 1993. Esp. 120-123.

CADBURY, Henry J., Commentary on the Preface of Luke, 1922. Esp. 498-500.

KUHN, Karl A., Beginning the Witness: The αὐτόπται καὶ ὑπηρέται of Luke's Infancy Narrative. — NTS 49 (2003) 237-255.

αὐτός 1086/1156 + 703/754 (Mt 922/991, Mk 749[760]/804)
1. same (Lk 6,33); 2. he, she, it (Lk 1,36); 3. self (Lk 2,35)

Word groups

αὐτός	Lk		Acts	Mt	Mk
ἐγὼ αὐτός (VKc)	24,39 v.l.		10,26	0	0
καὶ ἐν τῷ + infinitive / ἐν δὲ τῷ + infinitive + καὶ αὐτός	2,(27-)28¹; 10,38 v.l.			0	0

αὐτοῦ	Lk	Acts	Mt	Mk
ἀκούω (+) αὐτοῦ → ἀκούω **αὐτῶν**	2,47¹; 6,18¹; 9,35; 15,1²; 19,48; 21,38²	3,22; 6,11.14; 7,37*; 8,30; 18,26¹; 22,22¹; 24,24; 25,22²	0	4
αὐτοῦ object of verb with the genitive (SCc)	2,47¹; 5,12².13¹; 6,7².18¹.19¹; 7,39²; 8,38¹.47².53; 9,35; 10,34⁴.35; 15,1²; 19,31.34.48; 20,20¹.26¹; 21,38²; 23,2.10	3,22; 6,11.14; 7,37*; 8,30; 17,19; 18,26¹; 21,33; 22,22¹; 24,8².24; 25,5.22²	5/6	11
ἔτι αὐτοῦ λαλοῦντος	8,49; 22,47¹.60		3	2
οἱ μετ' αὐτοῦ → οἱ σὺν αὐτῷ/αὐτοῖς	6,3³.4; 8,45*		3	3[4]
αὐτοῦ after a preposition (VKa)	1,17².66².75; 2,27².33².38²; 3,7.19¹; 4,13.14.35²·⁴.37.42²; 5,13². 15*·¹.18³; 6,3³.4.19²; 7,17.30.36²; 8,18².45*; 9,7*.33².39³; 10,37¹; 11,16; 12,48¹.58; 13,17³; 14,2.8; 19,14³.24.26*; 22,16 v.l.59; 23,8²·³.14²	2,22¹.24²; 3,16³; 5,37¹; 7,9; 9,2; 10,38²; 12,5.10²; 13,29; 22,29¹; 23,15².20; 25,3¹.15.27	29	31[32]/33
αὐτοῦ before a noun (SCa; VKc)	20,20¹.26¹.44²; 22,64*	3,21; 5,32*; 9,18; 12,7²; 23,2²	9/10	6
αὐτοῦ absolute genitive (SCb; VKb)	7,6²; 8,49; 9,34¹.42¹; 11,53¹; 13,17¹; 14,29¹.32; 15,14¹.20¹; 17,12¹; 18,40³; 19,36¹.37; 20,1; 22,47¹.60	1,10¹; 3,11¹; 7,21¹.31; 12,13; 18,27¹; 21,14.34¹.40; 23,7; 24,2.25; 25,7¹.8*.25²; 26,24.30*; 28,29*	16	12/13
αὐτοῦ neuter (SCd)	1,59².60.66².67; 2,21².27².33¹·².34².38².41; 13,19		9	3/4

→ προστίθημι πρὸς τοὺς **πατέρας** αὐτοῦ; τὴν ψυχὴν αὐτοῦ **περιποιέομαι**; πρὸ **προσώπου** αὐτοῦ

αὐτῆς	Lk	Acts	Mt	Mk
σοῦ αὐτῆς → ὑμῶν **αὐτῶν**	2,35		0	0
αὐτῆς after a preposition (VKa)	1,38.58³; 4,38².39¹; 10,42 v.l.	13,17²; 16,18¹; 27,14	2	2[3]
αὐτῆς before a noun (SCa; VKc)	2,35		0	0
αὐτῆς of her own (VKb)	2,35		0	0/1

αὐτῷ	Lk	Acts	Mt	Mk
τῷ αὐτῷ (VKb)	6,38*; 23,40²		0	0
αὐτῷ after a preposition (VKa)	5,9²; 8,1².38².45*.51; 9,32¹; 11,37²; 12,8; 19,45*; 22,14.56³; 23,22².32.38	5,17.21¹; 8,2.31; 16,3¹; 17,16³.24.28; 18,18; 19,38; 20,10³; 21,8.29; 23,32	10	4/5
αὐτῷ + verb of saying (SCa)	1,19; 4,3.6¹.8¹.9².12.35¹; 5,14².20*.27; 6,10²; 7,6³.43; 8,20.47*.49*.50; 9,10¹.12.30.58.60; 10,28.35*.37²; 11,5³.27².45; 12,13.14.20.41*;	7,33.38; 8,35²; 9,4.27³.34; 10,3².4².7¹.19; 11,13*; 12,8²; 16,32¹; 21,20; 22,27; 23,9.17	77/87	61/63

	Lk	Acts	Mt	Mk
	13,1².8¹.15¹.23¹.31²; 14,6*.15.16.18¹; 15,18.21.27¹.31; 16,2².6.7.29*.31; 17,3¹.7.8.19.37¹; 18,7².19.22.37.39¹.42; 19,17.22.25.31*; 22,9.33.48.49*.61; 23,3².9³.40¹.43; 24,19²			
αὐτῷ μόνῳ; cf. αὐτὸς μονός Mk 6,47; αὐτοῦ μόνου Mt 18,15²	4,8²		1	0
ἐστὶν αὐτῷ → ἐστὶν αὐταῖς	2,26; 7,2; 8,42¹	7,5⁷; 19,31¹	2	0
ὑπάρχω αὐτῷ → ὑπάρχω αὐταῖς DENAUX 2009 1Aⁿ	12,15³	4,32¹.37	0	0
αὐτῷ neuter (SCb)	23,40²		3	1

αὐτῇ	Lk	Acts	Mt	Mk
τῇ αὐτῇ (VKa)	2,8¹		0	0
αὐτῇ + verb of saying (SCa)	1,30.35.45; 7,13³.48; 8,48; 10,40.41; 13,12²		4	5
αὐτῇ after a preposition (VKc)	1,56¹; 7,12³.13²; 10,9¹; 13,6²; 19,41 v.l.; 24,18²	1,20²; 5,8* v.l.; 7,5²; 9,38¹; 20,22	3	1/2

αὐτό	Lk	Acts	Mt	Mk
τὸ αὐτό (SCa; VKa) → ἐπὶ/κατὰ τὸ αὐτό	6,33	14,1¹	3	0
εἰς αὐτό → εἰς οὐδέν/τοῦτο/τί		27,6	0	0

αὐτόν	Lk	Acts	Mt	Mk
αὐτόν after a preposition (VKc)	1,12.13¹; 2,25.48²; 3,12.22; 4,4.40²; 5,33; 7,3¹.6*.20.40; 8,4.19¹.30²; 9,50.57².62; 10,6.26.33; 11,1³.5².39; 14,31; 18,3.7² v.l.40²; 19,5.9¹.39; 20,2.19¹; 21,38¹; 22,49.52.65; 24,18¹	2,25; 3,4; 6,15¹; 7,3.5⁶.31*.54².57²; 8,20; 9,6*.10.11.15.17.38²; 10,3¹.10².11*.13.15.21*. 43²; 11,2; 12,8¹.20¹; 13,9.11; 17,15; 19,2².4.31²; 20,18¹; 21,27²; 22,13²; 23,3.30; 25,19; 28,6³.21.23².30	11	25/28
→ ἀναιρέω + αὐτόν				

αὐτήν	Lk	Acts	Mt	Mk
verb of saying + πρὸς αὐτήν (SCa); cf. πρὸς αὐτήν in elliptic construction Acts 5,9 DENAUX 2009 LAⁿ	1,61	5,8.9 v.l.; 12,15¹	0	0
αὐτήν after a preposition (VKc)	1,28.61; 7,13² v.l.; 13,8³.34; 16,16; 18,17; 19,41; 21,21²	5,8.9; 12,15¹	4	4

αὐτοί	Lk	Acts	Mt	Mk
αὐτοὶ δέ → αὐτὸς δέ; cf. αὐτῶν δέ Mt 9,32¹; Lk 24,31¹	6,11	13,14	1	0
αὐτοὶ οὗτοι (VKa)		24,15.20	0	0

αὐτά	Lk	Acts	Mt	Mk
τὰ αὐτά (VKa) → κατὰ τὰ αὐτά; ἀπαγγέλλω τὰ αὐτά DENAUX 2009 Laⁿ	6,23¹.26¹; 17,30	15,27²	0	0

αὐτῶν	Lk	Acts	Mt	Mk
αὐτῶν after a preposition (VKc)	2,15.51¹; 4,42⁴; 5,2.25¹.29³.34².35; 6,13².17¹; 8,37²; 9,45¹;	3,5²; 4,16; 5,24; 8,15; 9,28.38*.39³; 11,20.21.22.28; 13,13;	22	7[9]/10

	10,7[2]; 11,15.49[2]; 12,6; 15,4[1]; 17,15; 18,34[2]; 21,8; 22,23[2].41[2].50[1].58[2]; 24,11[1].13[1].30[2].31[4].43. 51[3]	14,27; 15,2[2].4.9[1].12.22.38[1]; 16,22[1]; 17,4.12; 19,9.12[2].12*.16[2]; 20,30[2]; 21,1; 23,10[1].21[3].27.30*		
αὐτῶν before a noun (SCa; VKb)	11,17[2].48*; 19,35[2]; 20,23[1]; 24,31[1].45	4,5; 12,20[2]; 16,22[2]	3/4	3
αὐτῶν object of verb with the genitive (SCc)	2,46[2]; 16,29; 18,15[2]; 22,25[2.3]	2,6.11; 10,46; 16,25	6	4
οὐδεὶς αὐτῶν DENAUX 2009 La[n]	4,26.27	8,16	0	0
(τίς/τις/τινες/numeral) (+) ἐξ (+) αὐτῶν	11,15.49[2]; 12,6; 15,4[1]; 17,15; 22,23[2].50[1].58[2]; 24,13[1]	11,20.28; 15,2[2].22; 17,4.12; 20,30[1]; 23,21[3].30*	5	0[1]
ὑμῶν αὐτῶν (VKa) → σοῦ αὐτῆς		20,30[1]	0	0
αὐτῶν absolute genitive (SCb; VKd)	2,42; 3,15[1]; 4,2; 7,42[1]; 8,23; 9,37[1].57[1]; 19,11[1].33[1]; 22,55*; 24,5[1].36[1].41[1]	1,9[1]; 4,1[1].31; 10,9*.10[1]; 13,2[1].42[1]; 18,6[1].20; 22,23; 25,17; 26,10; 28,6[2].17[2]	12/13	5

αὐτοῖς	Lk	Acts	Mt	Mk
αὐτοῖς after a preposition (VKa)	7,6[1]; 9,46[1]; 18,7[3]; 22,24[1]; 23,35*; 24,29[2].33[2]	3,8; 4,14.24.34; 10,20[1].23[2]; 14,15; 17,34[2]; 18,3.11.20*; 20,36[2]; 21,7.24[1.2].26[1]; 24,21; 25,6; 28,14	3/5	0/2
αὐτοῖς + verb of saying (SCa); cf. αὐ ταῖς + verb of saying (SCa) Mt 28,10; Mk 16,6[1]	1,22[1]; 2,10.17.50[2]; 3,11.14[2]; 6,5. 39; 7,22; 8,25[1].36.56[2]; 9,11[3].20. 21.48; 10,9[2].18; 11,2.17[3]; 13,2. 32; 15,6; 16,15; 17,14[1].20.37[2]; 18,1[1].29; 19,32.46[1]; 20,8.17.34; 21,10.29; 22,10[1].13.25[1].35.36[1]. 38.40.46.67; 23,20; 24,19[1].36[4]. 38.41[2].46	2,14[2]; 5,25; 13,42[2].43[1]; 19,15; 20,18[2]; 22,2; 27,10	75/85	91/95
ἦν αὐτοῖς → ἦν αὐτῷ DENAUX 2009 L[n]	1,7[1]; 2,7[4]		0	0

αὐταῖς	Lk	Acts	Mt	Mk
ὑπάρχω αὐταῖς → ὑπάρχω αὐτῷ	8,3		0	0

αὐτούς	Lk	Acts	Mt	Mk
αὐτούς after a preposition (VKa)	2,18.20.49; 3,13.14[2] v.l.; 4,21.23.43; 5,22[2].31.34[1].36; 6,3[1].9; 8,21.22[3]; 9,3.5.13[1]; 10,2[1]; 11,5[1].49[1].53*; 12,15[1].16; 13,23[2]; 14,5[1].7.25[2]; 15,3; 16,30; 18,31; 19,13[2].27[1].33[3]; 20,3.19[3].23[2].25.41; 22,15.70; 23,12[2].14[1].22[1]; 24,17.25[2].44	1,7; 2,38; 3,11[2]; 4,8.19.23.33; 5,35; 8,14.17; 10,28; 11,15; 12,21; 13,15.51; 15,2[1].7.17; 16,37[1]; 17,2[1]; 18,6[2]; 19,2[1].3*.6[2].16[1].17; 20,6; 21,32; 22,30[2]; 28,17[3]	2/3	11/12
→ ἀναιρέω + αὐτούς				

αὐτάς	Lk	Acts	Mt	Mk
verb of saying + πρὸς αὐτάς (SCa)	24,5[2]		0	0
αὐτάς after a preposition (VKb) DENAUX 2009 L[n]	23,28; 24,5[2]		0	0

Characteristic of Luke

CREDNER 1836 135; HENDRIKS 1986 441.448; PLUMMER 1922 lxiii

	Lk	Acts	Mt	Mk
verb of saying + πρὸς αὐτόν	1,13[1]; 2,48[2]; 3,12; 4,4;	7,3; 8,20; 9,10.15;	1	0/1

94 αὐτός

(SCa) → πρὸς ἀλλήλους; πρὸς ἑαυτόν/ἑαυτούς; cf. πρὸς αὐτόν in elliptic construction Acts 9,11; φωνὴ πρὸς αὐτόν Acts 7,31*; 10,13.15 DENAUX 2009 L***	5,33; 7,40; 9,50.57².62; 10,26; 11,1³.39; 18,7² v.l.; 19,5.9¹.39; 20,2; 24,18¹	10,21*; 11,2; 12,8¹; 19,2²; 23,3.30; 28,21		
verb of saying + πρὸς αὐτούς (SCa) DENAUX 2009 L***	2,18.20.49; 3,13.14² v.l.; 4,21.23.43; 5,22².31.34¹.36; 6,3¹.9; 8,21.22³; 9,3.13¹; 10,2¹; 11,5¹.53*; 12,15¹.16; 13,23²; 14,5¹.7.25²; 15,3; 18,31; 19,13².33³; 20,3.19³.23².25.41; 22,15.70; 23,14¹.22¹; 24,17.25².44	1,7; 2,38; 4,8.19.23; 5,35; 10,28; 12,21; 15,7; 16,37¹; 18,6²; 19,2¹.3*; 28,17³	0	1/2
ἀκούω (+) αὐτῶν → ἀκούω αὐτοῦ DENAUX 2009 LA*	2,46²; 16,29	2,6.11; 10,46	0	1
αὐτός nominative singular GOULDER 1989	1,17¹.22²; 2,28¹; 3,15².16².23; 4,15¹.30¹; 5,1².14¹.16.17¹.37; 6,3².8¹.20¹.35.42; 7,5; 8,1¹.22¹.37³.41*.54¹; 9,51²; 10,1³.38²; 11,17¹.28; 15,14²; 16,24¹; 17,11.16³; 18,39²; 19,2¹·².9²; 20,42; 22,41¹; 23,9².51*; 24,15².21.25¹.28.31³.36².39	2,34; 3,10²; 7,15; 8,13; 10,26².42*; 14,12; 16,33²; 17,25; 18,19; 19,22²; 20,13.35; 21,24³; 22,20¹; 24,8¹.16; 25,22¹	12/15	15[16]/20
αὐτὸς ὁ all cases (VKb) DENAUX 2009 L***; GOULDER 1989*; HAWKINS 1909 16	1,36³; 2,38¹; 7,21*; 10,7¹.21¹; 12,12.42; 13,1¹.31¹; 20,19²; 23,12¹; 24,13².33¹.36¹ v.l.	16,18²; 22,13¹	1	1[2]
αὐτὸς δέ nominative singular (SCa) → καὶ αὐτός; αὐτοὶ δέ; cf. αὐτὸν δέ Lk 24,24; αὐτοῦ δέ Acts 25,25²; αὐτῇ δέ Lk 7,21; 10,7¹ CADBURY 1920 150; DENAUX 2009 L***	4,30¹; 5,16; 6,8¹; 8,37³.54¹; 11,17¹.28; 18,39²; 23,9²	18,19²	2	2
αὐτὸς/αὐτοὶ δέ nominative + participle; cf. αὐτῶν δὲ ἐξερχομένων Mt 9,32¹ BOISMARD 1984 Bb41; DENAUX 2009 L***; NEIRYNCK 1985	4,30¹; 8,37³.54¹; 11,17¹	13,14; 18,19²	0	1
εἰμὶ ἐπὶ τὸ αὐτό; cf. 1 Cor 7,5 BOISMARD 1984 cb16; NEIRYNCK 1985	17,35	1,15; 2,1.44	0	0
(ἐν) αὐτῇ τῇ ἡμέρᾳ/ ὥρᾳ/τῷ καιρῷ BOISMARD 1984 Ab4; DENAUX 2009 L***; GOULDER 1989*; NEIRYNCK 1985; PLUMMER 1922 lii	2,38¹; 7,21*; 10,21¹; 12,12; 13,1¹.31¹v.l.31¹; 20,19²; 23,12¹; 24,13².33¹	16,18²; 22,13¹	0	0

(ἐν) αὐτῇ τῇ ὥρᾳ DENAUX L***	2,38¹; 10,21¹; 12,12; 13,31¹; 20,19²; 24,33	16,18²; 22,13¹	0	0
ἐπὶ τὸ αὐτό (SCb; VKc) → εἰμὶ ἐπὶ τὸ **αὐτό**; **συνάγω** ἐπὶ τὸ αὐτό BOISMARD 1984 Eb33; GOULDER 1989*; NEIRYNCK 1985	17,35	1,15; 2,1.44.47; 4,26¹	1	0
καὶ αὐτός/ἡ/οἱ (SCab;VKcd;) → **αὐτὸς** δέ; cf. Jn 4,12¹; 7,10². Rom 8,21; 16,2³ BOISMARD 1984 Eb58; DENAUX 2009 L***; GOULDER 1989*; HAWKINS 1909L; NEIRYNCK 1985;	1,17¹.22².36¹; 2, 28¹.37.50¹; 3,23; 4,15¹; 5,1².14 ¹.17¹.37; 6,20¹; 7,12²;8,1¹.[13v.l]. 22¹.41*.42²; 9,36.51²;10,38²v.l.; 11,4.46; 14,1².12²; 15,14²; 16, 24¹.28²; 17,11.13.16; 18,34¹; 19,2¹·².9²; 20,42 v.l.; 22,23¹.41¹; 23,51*; 24,14.15². 25¹.28.31³.35¹.52¹	2,22 v.l.; 8,13; 15,32; 21,24³;22,20¹; [23,25 v.l.]; 24,15.16; 25,22¹; 27,36.	4/6	5[6]/7
καὶ αὐτός/οἱ (only) CREDNER 1836 135; DENAUX 2009 L***	1,17¹.22²; 2,28¹.50¹; 3,23; 4,15¹; 5,1².14¹.17¹.37; 6,20¹; 8,1¹.[13v.l].22¹.41*; 9,36.51²; 10,38²v.l.; 11,4.46; 14,1².12²; 15,14²; 16,24¹.28²; 17,11.13.16³; 18,34¹; 19,2¹·².9²; 20,42v.l; 22,23¹.41¹; 23,51*; 24,14.15².25¹.28.31³.35¹.5 2¹.	2,22 v.l.; 8,13; 15,32; 21,24³; 22,20¹; [23,25 v.l.]; 24,15.16; 25,22¹; 27,36.	4/6	5[6]/7
καὶ αὐτός (only) CADBURY 1920 150; DENAUX 2009 L***; PLUMMER 1922 lix	1,17¹.22²; 2,28¹; 3,23; 4,15¹; 5,1².14¹.17¹.37; 6,20¹; 8,1¹.22¹.41*; 9, 51²; 10,38²v.l.; 15,14²; 16,24¹; 17,11.16³; 19,2¹·².9²; 20,42v.l;22,41¹; 23,51*;24,15².25¹.28.31³	8,13; 21,24³; 22,20¹; [23,25v.l.]; 24,16; 25,22¹.	2	5
καὶ αὐτή (only) DENAUX 2009 L***	1,36¹; 2,37; 7,12²; 8,42²		0	0
καὶ αὐτοί (only) DENAUX 2009 L***	2,50¹; 8,[13 v.l.], 9,36; 11,4.46; 14,1².12²; 16,28²; 17,13; 18,34¹; 22,23¹; 24,14.35¹.52¹	2,22v.l.; 15,32; 24,15; 27,36	2	0
καὶ αὐτός/οἱ unemphatic DENAUX 2009 L***; HAWKINS 1909L	1,17¹.22²; 2,28¹; 3,23; 4,15¹; 5,1².14¹.17¹; 6,20¹; 8,1¹; 9,51²; 15,14²; 16,24¹; 17,13; 19,2²; 24,14		0	0
καὶ αὐτὸς ἦν; cf. καὶ αὐτὸς ἤμην Acts 22,20¹; καὶ αὐτὴ ἦν Lk 7,12²; καὶ αὐτὸ ἦν Lk 11,14; καὶ αὐτοὶ ἦσαν Lk 14,1² DENAUX 2009 L***; GOULDER 1989*	1,22²; 3,23; 5,1².17¹; 17,16³; 19,2¹.2² v.l.		0	2
καὶ ἐγένετο / ἐγένετο δὲ (ἐν τῷ + infinitive) ... καὶ αὐτός/καὶ αὐτοί + finite verb DENAUX 2009 L***	5,1².17¹; 8,1¹.22¹; 9,51²; 14,1²; 17,11; 24,15²		0	0

κατὰ τὸ αὐτό / τὰ αὐτά → ἐπὶ τὸ **αὐτό** BOISMARD 1984 Ab70; GOULDER 1989*; NEIRYNCK 1985	$6,23^1.26^1$; 17,30	$14,1^1$	0	0
οἱ σὺν αὐτῷ/αὐτοῖς → **οἱ μετ᾽ αὐτοῦ** DENAUX 2009 LA*; GOULDER 1989*	$5,9^2$; 8,45*; $9,32^1$; $24,33^2$	$5.17.21^1$; 19,38	0	1
πάντες αὐτοί; cf. 1 Cor 15,10 BOISMARD 1984 cb118; NEIRYNCK 1985	$6,10^1$	4,33; 19,17; $20,36^2$	1	0
τὰ ὑπάρχοντα αὐτῷ; cf. τὰ ὑπάρχοντα αὐταῖς Lk 8,3 PLUMMER 1922 lii	$12,15^3$	$4,32^1$	0	0

Literature

BDR § 277,3: "Pronomina personalia: Für die 3. Person entspricht αὐτός = betontem 'er': besonders bei Lk"; 288,2: "Für αὐτὸς οὗτος (ἐκεῖνος) steht bei Lk in einigen Wendungen das einfache αὐτός wie ἐν αὐτῷ τῷ καιρῷ, ἐν αὐτῇ τῇ ἡμέρᾳ, ἐν αὐτῇ τῇ ὥρᾳ"; 297,1: "Die zusätzliche Hinzufügung von αὐτός zu einem Relativum ist durch das Semitische besonders nahegelegte, aber auch dem klass. und späteren Griechisch nicht ganz unbekannte Nachlässigkeit"; COLLISON 1977 135 [ἐν αὐτῇ τῇ ὥρᾳ: linguistic usage of Luke: certain]; 138 [κατὰ τὰ αὐτά: linguistic usage of Luke: probable]; 140 [περὶ αὐτοῦ of Jesus: linguistic usage of Luke: certain]; 194 [καὶ αὐτός of Jesus: linguistic usage of Luke: certain]; 195 [καὶ αὐτός unemphatic: linguistic usage of Luke's "other source-material": certain]; 196 [καὶ αὐτοί emphatic / αὐτὸς δέ: linguistic usage of Luke: certain]; 197-198 [καὶ αὐτός + ἦν + noun/verb: linguistic usage of Luke's "other source-material": certain]; 198 [αὐτός for pronoun: linguistic usage of Luke: certain]; 203 [αὐτός for οὗτος: probable]; DENAUX 2009 lA[n] [εἰμὶ ἐπὶ τὸ αὐτό]; La[n] [κατὰ τὸ αὐτό / τὰ αὐτά; (ἐν) αὐτῇ τῇ ἡμέρᾳ]; lAn [ἐπὶ τὸ αὐτό, πάντες αὐτοί]; LA[n] [τὰ ὑπάρχοντα αὐτῷ]; EASTON 1910 148 [καὶ αὐτός: especially characteristic of L]; 149 [ποιέω ἔλεος μετ᾽ αὐτοῦ: especially characteristic of L]; 157 [πρὸ προσώπου αὐτοῦ: probably characteristic of L]; GERSDORF 1816 202 [τὸ ἔλεος αὐτοῦ μετ᾽ αὐτῆς] 261 [Eigen ist dem Lucas αὐτῇ τῇ ὥρᾳ]; HARNACK 1906 155? [καὶ αὐτούς ist ein specifisches Merkmal des lukanischen Stils, wofür Beispiele unnötig], 1907 39 [τὰ αὐτά]; HAUCK 1934 [Vorzugsverbindung: κατὰ τὰ αὐτά; ἐν αὐτῇ τῇ ἡμέρα/ὥρᾳ; ἦν αὐτῷ/αὐτοῖς; καὶ αὐτός/αὐτή/αὐτοί; πρὸς αὐτοὺς εἶπεν (ἔφη)]; HAWKINS 1909L [with ἡμέρα, ὥρα or καιρός]; JEREMIAS 1980 37-38 [καὶ αὐτός: red.]; 98: "αὐτὸς ὁ, αὐτὴ ἡ, mit Substantiv der Zeit (ἡμέρα, ὥρα, καιρός) findet sich im NT nur im lk Doppelwerk"; 128: "Lukas schreibt gern αὐτὸς(-οι) δέ ... Das für den lukanischen Stil eigentlich Charakteristische ist jedoch die Häufigkeit des christologischen αὐτὸς δέ ('ER aber')"; 270 [εἰμὶ ἐπὶ τὸ αὐτό: red.]; 275 [καὶ αὐτός "nicht-emphatisch": trad.]; PLUMMER 1922 lxi [the frequent use of καὶ αὐτός/αὐτή/αὐτοί after ἐγένετο, καὶ ἰδού, and the like: due to Hebrew influence]; RADL 1975 401 [αὐτός nom. Sg.; καὶ αὐτός; αὐτή = Jerusalem]; 403 [ἐγένετο + καὶ αὐτός + finite verb]; 423 [πάντες αὐτοί]; REHKOPF 1959 92 [αὐτὸς ὁ: vorlukanisch]; 94 [καὶ αὐτός(αὐτοί) unbetont]; SCHNEIDER 1969 110: "αὐτόν ist ein lk Vorzugswort"; 130-131: "αὐτοί ist schon für sich genommen luk Vorzugswort"; 163 [αὐτοί/αὐτόν: Vorzugswörter und -ausdrücke des Luk]; SCHÜRMANN 1953 100 [das betonte (καὶ) αὐτὸς (δέ) ... sehr bevorzugt]; 1957 66 [ἐν αὐτοῖς ... Verdacht luk R]; 121 [εἶπεν δὲ αὐτοῖς: "wahrscheinlich luk R einer vorluk T"]; 1961 279 [αὐτὸς ὁ: protoluk R weniger wahrscheinlich]; 281 [καὶ αὐτός(αὐτοί) unbetont: protoluk R weniger wahrscheinlich].

CIGNELLI, Lino – Giovanni C. BOTTINI, Concordanza del pronome αὐτός nel greco biblico. – *Studium Biblicum Franciscanum Liber Annuus* 45 (1995) 143-164.
CIGNELLI, Lino. – PIERRI, Rosario, *Sintassi di Greco biblico.* I.a, 2003. Esp. 50-67.

DENAUX, Adelbert, L'hypocrisie des pharisiens et le dessein de Dieu, 1973. Esp. 258-259 [ἐν αὐτῇ τῇ ὥρᾳ]; ²1989. Esp. 168-169.

FERGUSON, E., "When You Come together": Epi To Auto in Early Christian Literature. — Restoration Quiaterly 16 (1973) 202-208.

GARCÍA PÉREZ, José Miguel, El relato del Buen Ladrón (Lc 23,39-43), 1986. Esp. 287-291: "La expresión ἐν αὐτῷ κρίματι".

JEREMIAS, Joachim, Ἐν ἐκείνῃ τῇ ὥρᾳ, (ἐν) αὐτῇ τῇ ὥρᾳ. — ZNW 42 (1949) 214-217.

MICHAELIS, Wilhelm, Das unbetonte καὶ αὐτός bei Lukas. — StudTheol 4 (1951) 86-93.

NEIRYNCK, Frans, Goulder and the Minor Agreements. — ETL 73 (1997) 84-93. Esp. 85 [Lk 6,19 πάντας; Lk 4,15 αὐτῶν]; 91-92 [τίς ἐστιν ὁ παίσας σε;]. [NTA 42, 185]; = ID., Evangelica III, 2001, 307-318. Esp. 308-309; 315-317.

RIUS-CAMPS, Josep, El καὶ αὐτός en los encabezamientos lucanos, ¿una fórmula anafórica? — FilolNT 2 (1989) 187-192.

WILCOX, Max, Semitisms in the New Testament, 1984. Esp. 1010-1011: "ἐπὶ τὸ αὐτό (Acts 2:47; cf. also 1:15; 2:44, 46 [D])".

αὐτοῦ 1 + 2/3 (Mt 1) — here, there (Lk 9,27; Acts 18,19; 21,4)

Characteristic of Luke
BOISMARD 1984 cb17; NEIRYNCK 1985

Literature
JEREMIAS 1980 275 [αὐτοῦ "zu Ortsadverbien gewordenen lokalen Genitive": red.].

ἀφαιρέω 4 (Mt 1, Mk 1)
1. put away (Lk 22,50); 2. take away from (Lk 1,25; 10,42; 16,3); 3. do away with

Word groups	Lk	Acts	Mt	Mk
ἀφαιρέω + ἀπό → καθαιρέω ἀπό	16,3		0	0

Characteristic of Luke
DENAUX 2009 L***; GOULDER 1989*; HAWKINS 1909 16

Literature
COLLISON 1977 41 [linguistic usage of Luke's "other source-material": likely]; EASTON 1910 151 [probably characteristic of L]; HAUCK 1934 [Vorzugswort]; PAFFENROTH 1997 83 [pre-lukan]; REHKOPF 1959 92 [vorlukanisch].

ἄφαντος* 1 — invisible (Lk 24,31)

Literature
HAUCK 1934 [seltenes Alleinwort]; JEREMIAS 1980 319 [ἄφαντος ἐγένετο: red.].

ἄφεσις 5 + 5 (Mt 1, Mk 2)
1. pardon (Lk 1,77; 3,3; 24,47); 2. liberty (Lk 4,18^{1.2})

Word groups	Lk	Acts	Mt	Mk
ἄφεσις (τῶν) ἁμαρτιῶν + μετάνοια	3,3; 24,47	5,31	0	1

εἰς ἄφεσιν / ἐν ἀφέσει (τῶν) ἁμαρτιῶν	1,77; 3,3; 24,47	2,38	1	1
λαμβάνω ἄφεσιν ἁμαρτιῶν BOISMARD 1984 Aa141		10,43; 26,18	0	0

Characteristic of Luke

GOULDER 1989

	Lk	Acts	Mt	Mk
ἄφεσις ἁμαρτιῶν (SCa; VKa) → ἀφίημι + ἁμαρτία; cf. Col 1,14 BOISMARD 1984 cb63; DENAUX 2009 IA*; GOULDER 1989; HARNACK 1906 145; NEIRYNCK 1985; PLUMMER 1922 lix	1,77; 3,3; 24,47	2,38; 5,31; 10,43; 13,38; 26,18	1	1

Literature

COLLISON 1977 169 [linguistic usage of Luke's "other source-material": likely]; DENAUX 2009 LAn; GERSDORF 1816 212 [ἐν ἀφέσει ἁμαρτιῶν]; HAUCK 1934 [Vorzugswort]; JEREMIAS 1980 322 [μετάνοιαν εἰς ἄφεσιν ἁμαρτιῶν: red.] [εἰς ἄφεσιν ἁμαρτιῶν: trad].

CALDUCH BENAGES, N., El término ἄφεσις en los papiros griegos en el Nuevo Testamento. — *RevistCatTeol* 14 (1989) 267-272.

MAHFOUZ, Hady, *La fonction littéraire et théologique de Lc 3,1-20*, 2003. Esp. 133-137.168-174 [ἄφεσις ἁμαρτιῶν].

ἀφίημι 31/32 + 3 (Mt 47, Mk 34/37)

1. dismiss; 2. depart from (Lk 4,39); 3. leave behind (Lk 5,11); 4. leave in peace; 5. divorce; 6. forgive (Lk 17,3); 7. cancel a debt; 8. reject; 9. stop (activity); 10. stop (state) (Lk 4,39); 11. allow (Lk 12,39); 12. produce

Word groups	Lk	Acts	Mt	Mk
ἄφες τοὺς νεκροὺς θάψαι τοὺς ἑαυτῶν νεκρούς (LN: that is not the issue)	9,60		1	0
ἀφίημι + ἀκολουθέω → καταλείπω/πωλέω + ἀκολουθέω	5,11; 18,28		4	2
ἀφίημι(+) ἁμαρτία → ἄφεσις (τῶν) ἁμαρτιῶν; cf. ἐξαλείφω/ἀπολούω + ἁμαρτία Acts 3,19; 22,16	5,20.21.23.24; 7,47^1.48.49; 11,4^1		4	4
ἀφέωνται DENAUX 2009 L^n	5,20.23;7,47^1.48	0	0	0
ἀφίημι imperative (VKc)	6,42; 9,60; 11,4^1; 13,8; 17,3; 18,16; 23,34	5,38	10	5
ἀφίημι forgive; remit (of sins or debts) (SCa; VKb)	5,20.21.23.24; 7,47$^{1.2}$.48.49; 11,4$^{1.2}$; 12,10$^{1.2}$; 17,3.4; 23,34	8,22	17	7/8
ἀφίεμαι passive (VKa)	5,20.23; 7,47$^{1.2}$.48; 12,10$^{1.2}$; 13,35; 17,34.35; 21,6	8,22	8/10	5

Literature

JEREMIAS 1980 172 [ἀφέωνται: red.].

CARAGOUNIS, Chrys C., *The Development of Greek and the New Testament*, 2004. Esp. 163-167 [The Hortative Subjunctive and the Imperative of ἀφίημι]

SCHWARZ, Günther, ἄφες τοὺς νεκροὺς θάψαι τοὺς ἑαυτῶν νεκρούς. — *ZNW* 72 (1981) 272-276.

ἀφίστημι 4 + 6

1. cause to rebel (Acts 5,37); 2. ἀφίσταμαι: depart (Lk 2,37; 4,13; 13,27); 3. ἀφίσταμαι: forsake (Lk 8,13); 4. ἀφίσταμαι: keep away from (Acts 5,38)

Word groups	Lk	Acts	Mt	Mk
ἀπέστη ὁ διάβολος → ἀπέστη ὁ ἄγγελος	4,13		0	0
ἀφίστημι transitive (VKa)		5,37	0	0

Characteristic of Luke
BOISMARD 1984 cb74; DENAUX 2009 L***; GOULDER 1989*; HAWKINS 1909 16; NEIRYNCK 1985; PLUMMER 1922 lix; VOGEL 1899D

	Lk	Acts	Mt	Mk
ἀπέστη/ἀπῆλθεν ὁ ἄγγελος → ἀπέστη ὁ διάβολος; ἀπῆλθεν ὁ ἄγγελος; (ἐφ/παρ)ἴστημι + ἄγγελος BOISMARD 1984 Ab66; NEIRYNCK 1985	1,38;2,15	10,7;12,10	0	0
ἀφίστημι ἀπό; cf. 2 Cor 12,8; 2 Tit 2,19; Heb 3,12; ἀποστασία ἀπό Acts 21,21 DENAUX 2009 IA*; GOULDER 1989*	2,37 v.l.; 4,13; 13,27	5,38; 12,10; 15,38; 19,9; 22,29	0	0

Literature
COLLISON 1977 41 [linguistic usage of Luke: likely]; DENAUX 2009 LAⁿ [ἀπέστη/ἀπῆλθεν ὁ ἄγγελος]; GERSDORF 1816 260 [ἀφίστατο τοῦ ἱεροῦ]; HAUCK 1934 [Vorzugswort]; RADL 1975 401-402 [ἀφίστημι; ἀφίσταμαι ἀπό].

BURCHARD, Christoph, Fußnoten zum neutestamentlichen Griechisch II, 1978. Esp. 151-153: "Lk 24,4 ἰδοὺ ἄνδρες δύο ἀπέστησαν αὐταῖς".

ἀφόβως 1

1. without fear (Lk 1,74); 2. disgracefully; 3. without reverence to God

ἀφορίζω 1 + 2 (Mt 3)

1. exclude (Lk 6,22); 2. appoint (Acts 13,2); 3. separate (Acts 19,9)

Word groups	Lk	Acts	Mt	Mk
ἀφορίζω + εἰς (VKa)		13,2	0	0

Literature
DUPONT, Jacques, Les Béatitudes, II, 1969. Esp. 287-289: "L'exclusion".

ἀφρός* 1   foam (Lk 9,39)

Literature
HAUCK 1934 [seltenes Alleinwort].

ἄφρων 2   foolish

Word groups	Lk	Acts	Mt	Mk
ἄφρων vocative (VKa) DENAUX 2009 Lⁿ	11,40; 12,20		0	0

Literature
DENAUX 2009 L[n]; REHKOPF 1959 98 [ἄφρων: "Substantiva in Anrede bei den Synoptikern"].

ἀφυπνόω** 1   fall asleep (Lk 8,23)

Literature
HAUCK 1934 [seltenes Alleinwort].
CADBURY, Henry.J., Lexical Notes on Luke-Acts, II, 1926. Esp. 192.

ἀχάριστος 1   ungrateful (Lk 6,35)

Literature
HAUCK 1934 [seltenes Alleinwort].

ἀχρεῖος 1 (Mt 1)

1. useless; 2. not worthy of praise (Lk 17,10)

Word groups	Lk	Acts	Mt	Mk
δοῦλος ἀχρεῖος	17,10		1	0

Literature
HOUZET, Pierre, Les serviteurs de l'évangile (Luc 17,5-10) sont-ils inutiles? Ou un
   contresens traditionnel. — *RB* 99 (1992) 335-372.
VILLAPADIERNA, Carlos de, ¿Siervos inútiles o qué?. — G. ARANDA, J. BASEVI, J. CHAPA
   (eds.), *Biblía, Exégesis y cultura. Estudios en honor del Prof. D. José María Casciaro*,
   Pamplona, 1994, 327-335.

ἄχρι 4 + 15/17 (Mt 1, Mk 0/[1])

1. until (Lk 1,20; 4,13; 17,27; 21,24; Acts 20,11); 2. later (Acts 20,6); 3. as far as
(Acts 13,6)

Word groups	Lk	Acts	Mt	Mk
ἀπό ... ἄχρι → ἀπό ... **ἕως/μέχρι**		1,22*	0	0
ἄχρι conjunctive particle without οὗ (*VK*c)	21,24 *v.l.*		0	0
ἄχρι ἧς ἡμέρας (*VK*b) → **ἄχρι** τῆς ἡμέρας ταύτης	1,20; 17,27	1,2	1	0[1]
ἄχρι τῆς ἡμέρας ταύτης → **ἄχρι** ἧς ἡμέρας		2,29; 23,1;	0	0
BOISMARD 1984 Aa76		26,22		
ἄχρι θανάτου; cf. ἕως θανάτου Mt 26,38; Mk 14,34		22,4	0	0
→ **διέρχομαι** + ἄχρι; **εἰμι** + ἄχρι; **εἰς** + ἄχρι; **ἐν** + ἄχρι; **ἐξέρχομαι** + ἄχρι; **ἔρχομαι** + ἄχρι				

Characteristic of Luke

BOISMARD 1984 Eb3; DENAUX 2009 L***; GOULDER 1989*; HARNACK 1906 45; HAWKINS
1909 16; MORGENTHALER 1958A; NEIRYNCK 1985; PLUMMER 1922 lx

	Lk	Acts	Mt	Mk
ἄχρι καιροῦ	4,13	13,11	0	0
PLUMMER 1922 liii				

ἄχρι (δὲ) οὗ (*LN*: ªbefore, ᵇuntil; *VK*a) → ἕως οὗ; cf. μέχρις οὗ Mk 13,30 HARNACK 1906 51	21,ᵇ24	7,ᵇ18; 27,ª33	0	0

Literature
COLLISON 1977 148 [noteworthy phenomena]; DENAUX 2009 LAⁿ [ἄχρι καιροῦ], lAⁿ [ἄχρι (δὲ) οὗ]; GERSDORF 1916 188 [ἄχρι ἧς ἡμέρας γένηται ταῦτα]; HAUCK 1934 [Vorzugswort]; JEREMIAS 1980 43 [ἄχρι καιροῦ; ἄχρι ἧς ἡμέρας; ἄχρι οὗ: red.]; RADL 1975 402 [ἄχρι]; 412 [ἄχρι τῆς ἡμέρας ταύτης].

ἄχυρον 1 (Mt 1)   chaff (Lk 3,17)

Literature
SCHWARZ, Günther, Τὸ δὲ ἄχυρον κατακαύσει. — *ZNW* 72 (1981) 264-271. [NTA 26, 464]

B

βάθος 1 (Mt 1, Mk 1)
1. depth; 2. deep place (Lk 5,4); 3. extremely; 4. the world below; 5. powers of world below

βαθύνω 1   make deep (Lk 6,48)

Literature
HAUCK 1934 [seltenes Alleinwort].

βαθύς 1 + 1
1. deep; 2. extremely (Lk 24,1; Acts 20,9)

Literature
DENAUX 2009 LAⁿ.

βαλλάντιον 4   money bag (Lk 10,4; 12,33; 22,35.36)

Characteristic of Luke
DENAUX 2009 L***; GOULDER 1989; HAWKINS 1909 16; PLUMMER 1922 lii

Literature
VON BENDEMANN 2001 423; COLLISON 1977 180 [linguistic usage of Luke: likely]; HAUCK 1934 [seltenes Alleinwort]; REHKOPF 1959 92 [vorlukanisch]; SCHÜRMANN 1957 118-119 [luk R unwahrscheinlich]; 1961 279 [protoluk R nicht beweisbar].

LEE, John A.L. – HORSLEY, G.H.R., A Lexicon of the New Testament, 2, 1998. Esp. 68-69.

βάλλω 19 + 5 (Mt 34/37, Mk 18/21)

1. throw (Lk 3,9); 2. let fall; 3. sweep down (Acts 27,14); 4. pour (Lk 5,37); 5. put (Lk 21,1); 6. bring about; 7. do away with; 8. deposit

Word groups	Lk	Acts	Mt	Mk
βάλλω + εἰς (τὸ) πῦρ (SCb; VKb); cf. βάλλω εἰς τὴν κάμινον τοῦ πυρός Mt 13,42.50; εἰς γέενναν Mt 5,29².30*; 18,9²; Mk 9,45.47; εἰς ὕδατα Mk 9,22	3,9		3	1/2
βάλλω + εἰς (τὴν) φυλακήν / ἐν (τῇ) φυλακῇ (SCa; VKa) → κατακλείω/παραδίδωμι/τίθημι εἰς (τὴν) φυλακήν / ἐν (τῇ) φυλακῇ	12,58; 23,19.25	16,23.24. 37	2	0
βάλλω ἔξω (SCc; VKc) → ἐκβάλλω ἔξω	14,35		2	0
βάλλω κλῆρον (VKd)	23,34		1	1
βάλλω (+) οἶνον (VKf)	5,37.38		2	1
πῦρ + βάλλω (LN: cause discord)	12,49		0	0
βλητέος (VKg)	5,38		0	0

Literature
HAUCK 1934 [βλητέος: seltenes Alleinwort].

βαπτίζω 10 + 21 (Mt 7/11, Mk 12[13])

1. wash (Lk 11,38); 2. baptize (Acts 2,38); 3. cause religious experience

Word groups	Lk	Acts	Mt	Mk
βαπτίζω (+) εἰς baptize in/into		8,16; 19,3.5	2	1
βαπτίζω (+) ἐν baptize in	3,16²	1,5²; 10,48; 11,16²	3	3
βαπτίζω ἐν πνεύματι ἁγίῳ (SCa; VKa)	3,16²	1,5²; 11,16²	1	1
βαπτίζω ἐν + πυρί	3,16²		1	0
βαπτίζω ὕδατι	3,16¹	1,5¹; 11,16¹	1	1
βαπτίζω (+) Ἰωάννης	3,16¹; 7,29	1,5¹; 11,16¹; 19,3.4	2	4
βαπτίζω (+) ὕδωρ	3,16¹	1,5¹; 8,36.38; 10,47; 11,16¹	2	2
βαπτίζω ὑπό + genitive (baptize for); cf. βαπτίζω ὑπέρ + gen. (baptize on behalf of) 1 Cor 15,29^{1.2}	3,7; 7,30		3	2
βάπτισμα βαπτίζω (LN: suffer severely; SCc; VKc)	7,29; 12,50	19,4	0/2	2
ἔχω βαπτισθῆναι	12,50		1	0
βαπτίζω according to the Law of Moses (VKe)	11,38		0	0
βαπτίζω in the name of Jesus (SCb; VKb); cf. εἰς τὸ ὄνομα τοῦ πατρός Mt 28,19; εἰς τὸ ὄνομα Παύλου 1 Cor 1,13 BOISMARD 1984 Aa39		2,38; 8,16; 10,48; 19,5	0	0

Characteristic of Luke
MORGENTHALER 1958A

Literature
COLLISON 1977 42 [linguistic usage of Luke: probable]; HAUCK 1934 [Vorzugsverbindung: ἔχω βαπτισθῆναι]; PLUMMER 1922 lxiii [Lk "is fond of *combinations of cognate words*, e.g. βαπτισθέντες τὸ βάπτισμα (vii.29)"].

MARSHALL, I. Howard, The meaning of the verb 'to baptise'. — *Evagelical Quarterly* 45 (1973) 130-140. [NTA 18, 50]

HEITMÜLLER, Wilhelm, *"Im Namen Jesu"*, 1903. Esp. 1-127.

βάπτισμα 4 + 6 (Mt 2/4, Mk 4) | baptism

Word groups	Lk	Acts	Mt	Mk
βάπτισμα (+) βαπτίζω (LN: suffer severely; VKa)	7,29; 12,50	19,4	0/2	2
βάπτισμα (+) Ἰωάννης	7,29; 20,4	1,22; 10,37; 13,24; 18,25; 19,3.4	1	2
κηρύσσω τὸ βάπτισμα	3,3	10,37	0	1

Characteristic of Luke	Lk	Acts	Mt	Mk
βάπτισμα of John the Baptist BOISMARD 1984 cb3; NEIRYNCK 1985	3,3; 7,29; 20,4	1,22; 10,37; 13,24; 18,25; 19,3.4	2	2
βάπτισμα μετανοίας (VKb) BOISMARD 1984 cb18; NEIRYNCK 1985	3,3	13,24; 19,4	0	1

Literature

BARR, James, *The Semantics of Biblical Language*, 1961. Esp. 140-144: "The word 'baptism'".
DELLING, G., Βάπτισμα βαπτιστθῆναι. — *NT* 2 (1957) 92-115. [Lk 12,50]
DUNN, James, Spirit-and-Fire Baptism. — *NT* 14 (1972) 81-92. [Lk 3,16]
MAHFOUZ, Hady, *La fonction littéraire et théologique de Lc 3,1-20*, 2003. Esp. 117-122.

βαπτιστής 3/4 (Mt 7, Mk 2/3) | baptizer

Word groups	Lk	Acts	Mt	Mk
Ἰωάννης ὁ βαπτιστής; cf. Ἰωάννης ὁ βαπτίζων Mk 1,4; 6,14.24	7,20.28*.33; 9,19		7	2/3

βάπτω 1 | dip in (Lk 16,24)

Βαραββᾶς 1 (Mt 5, Mk 3) | Barabbas (Lk 23,18)

βαρέω 2 (Mt 1, Mk 0/1) | βαρέομαι: be troubled (Lk 21,34)

Word groups	Lk	Acts	Mt	Mk
βαρέομαι ὕπνῳ (LN: be sound asleep) → καταφέρομαι ἀπὸ τοῦ ὕπνου/ὕπνῳ	9,32		0	0

Literature

SCHWARZ, Günther, μηποτε βαρηθωσιν υμων αι καρδιαι. [Lk 21,34] — *BibNot* 10 (1979) 40.

Βαρθολομαῖος 1 + 1 (Mt 1, Mk 1) | Bartholomew (Lk 6,18; Acts 1,13)

βασανίζω 1 (Mt 3, Mk 2) | torture (Lk 8,28)

βάσανος 2 (Mt 1) | torment (Lk 16,23.28)

βασιλεία 46 + 8 (Mt 55/57, Mk 20/21)

1. reign (Lk 1,33); 2. kingdom (Lk 17,20)

Word groups	Lk	Acts	Mt	Mk
βασιλεία (τοῦ) θεοῦ (SCa; VKa)	4,43; 6,20; 7,28; 8,1.10; 9,2.11.27.60.62; 10,9.11; 11,20; 12,31 v.l.; 13,18.20.28.29; 14,15; 16,16; 17,20[1.2].21; 18,16.17.24.25.29; 19,11; 21,31; 22,16.18; 23,51	1,3; 8,12; 14,22; 19,8; 20,25 v.l.; 28,23.31	5	14/15
βασιλεία τοῦ θεοῦ (+) ἀναφαίνω/ φθάνω → **βασιλεία** τοῦ θεοῦ + ἔρχομαι	11,20; 19,11		1	0
βασιλείαν + διατίθεμαι (LN: give right to rule)	22,29		0	0
διαγγέλλω τὴν βασιλείαν → εὐαγγελίζομαι/κηρύσσω τὴν **βασιλείαν**	9,60		0	0
ἐγγύς ἐστιν ἡ βασιλεία → ἤγγικεν ἡ **βασιλεία**	21,31		0	0
(εἰσ)έρχομαι/εἰσπορεύομαι (+) εἰς (+) τὴν βασιλείαν	18,17.24.25; 23,42	14,22	5/6	5
ἤγγικεν (+)ἡ βασιλεία → ἔγγυς ἐστιν ἡ **βασιλεία**	10,9.11		3	1
λαμβάνω βασιλείαν (LN: become a king) DENAUX 2009 L[n]	19,12.15		0	0
μυστήριον τῆς βασιλείας	8,10		1	1
ὁμοία ἐστὶν ἡ βασιλεία / ὁμοιόω + βασιλεία	13,18.20		10	1

Characteristic of Luke	Lk	Acts	Mt	Mk
βασιλεία + verb of saying (SCf) → εὐαγγελίζομαι/κηρύσσω τὴν **βασιλείαν** DENAUX 2009 L***	4,43; 8,1; 9,2.11.60; 16,16	1,3; 8,12; 19,8; 20,25; 28,23.31	1	0
βασιλεία τοῦ θεοῦ + ἔρχομαι → **βασιλεία** τοῦ θεοῦ + ἀναφαίνω/φθάνω DENAUX 2009 L***	11,2; 17,20[1.2]; 22,18		1	1
εὐαγγελίζομαι τὴν βασιλείαν / περὶ τῆς βασιλείας → διαγγέλλω/κηρύσσω τὴν **βασιλείαν** GOULDER 1989	4,43; 8,1; 16,16	8,12	0	0
κηρύσσω τὴν βασιλείαν → διαγγέλλω/ εὐαγγελίζομαι τὴν **βασιλείαν**; cf. κηρύσσω τὸ εὐαγγέλιον τῆς βασιλείας Mt 4,23; 9,35; 24,14; Mk 1,14 v.l.; κηρύσσω + βασιλεία Mt 3,1; 4,17; 10,7 BOISMARD 1984 Ab85; NEIRYNCK 1985	8,1; 9,2	20,25; 28,31	0	0
περὶ τῆς βασιλείας τοῦ θεοῦ BOISMARD 1984 Ab71; NEIRYNCK 1985	9,11	1,3; 8,12; 19,8	0	0

Literature

VON BENDEMANN 2001 413: "κηρύσσειν τὴν βασιλείαν τοῦ θεοῦ ... und εὐαγγελίζεσθαι τὴν βασιλείαν τοῦ θεοῦ ... sind typisch lukanisch"; 414: "lukanischen Verbindung von verbum dicendi + περὶ τῆς βασιλείας τοῦ θεοῦ"; 416: "Die Aufforderung zum διαγγέλλειν τὴν βασι-λείαν τοῦ θεοῦ entspricht der lukanischen Eigenart, die βασιλεία mit Verben der Verkündigung zu kombinieren"; COLLISON 1977 170 [ἡ βασιλεία τοῦ θεοῦ: linguistic usage of Luke: certain]; DENAUX 2009 La^n [εὐαγγελίζομαι τὴν βασιλείαν / περὶ τῆς βασιλείας], lA^n [περὶ τῆς βασιλείας τοῦ θεοῦ], LA^n [κηρύσσω τὴν βασιλείαν]; JEREMIAS 1980 176: "κηρύσσω τὴν βασιλείαν τοῦ θεοῦ ... εὐαγγελίζομαι [med.] τὴν βασιλείαν τοῦ θεοῦ ... begegnen im NT ausschließlich im lk Doppelwerk"; RADL 1975 415 [κηρύσσω τὴν βασιλείαν (τοῦ θεοῦ)".

AALEN, Sverre, "Reign" and "House" in the Kingdom of God in the Gospels. — *NTS* 8 (1961-62) 215-240.

BORMANN, Lukas, *Recht, Gerechtigkeit und Religion*, 2001. Esp. 112-113.

BROOKS, James A., The Kingdom of God in the New Testament. — *Southwestern Journal of Theology* 40 (1998) 21-37.

GARCÍA PÉREZ, José Miguel, *El relato del Buen Ladrón (Lc 23,39-43)*, 1986. Esp. 280-285: "El término βασιλεία".

GEORGE, Augustin, La royauté de Jésus. — ID., *Études*, 1978, 257-282. Esp. 258-259: "Roi (basileus, basileuein, basileia)".

—, Le règne de Dieu. — ID., *Études*, 1978, 285-306.

GLOVER, Warren W., "The Kingdom of God" in Luke. — *BTrans* 29 (1978) 231-237.

HAHN, S.R., *Βασιλεία and Its Cognates in the New Testament*. Diss. Southern Baptist Theol. Sem., Louisville, KY, 1951.

MERK, Otto, Das Reich Gottes in den lukanischen Schriften. — ELLIS, E.E. – GRÄßER, E. (eds.), *Jesus und Paulus*. FS W.G. Kümmel, 1975, 201-220.

PELÁEZ, Jesús, *Βασιλεία en el Nuevo Testamento*. Factor contextual, definición y traducción. — *FilolNT* 16 (31-32, 2003) 69-83.

PRIEUR, Alexander, *Die Verkündigung der Gottesherrschaft: Exegetische Studien zum lukanischen Verständnis von βασιλεία τοῦ θεοῦ* (WUNT, II/89). Tübingen: Mohr, 1996, VIII-336 p.

SCHLOSSER, Jacques, *Les logia du Règne: Étude sur le vocable "Basileia tou theou" dans la prédication de Jésus*. Thèse présentée devant l'Université de Strasbourg II, le 16 décembre 1978. Lille: Atelier national de reproduction des thèses, 1982, X-714 p.

βασίλειος 1	royal (Lk 7,25)

Literature

HAUCK 1934 [seltenes Alleinwort].

βασιλεύς 11 + 20 (Mt 22/23, Mk 12)	king

Word groups	Lk	Acts	Mt	Mk
βασιλεύς + proper name (*VK*e)	1,5	7,10; 12,1; 13,22; 17,7; 25,13.24.26; 26,2.19.27	3/4	1
βασιλεὺς τῆς γῆς (*SC*c; *VK*c)		4,26	1	0
βασιλεὺς τῶν Ἰουδαίων (*SC*a; *VK*a)	23,3.37.38		4	5
βασιλεύς + κύριος	19,38		0	0
ἡγεμὼν καὶ βασιλεύς (*SC*d; *VK*d)	21,12	26,30	1	1
Ἡρῴδης (ὁ) βασιλεύς	1,5	12,1	2	1

Literature

GERSDORF 1816 167 [Ἡρῴδου τοῦ βασιλέως].

BORMANN, Lukas, *Recht, Gerechtigkeit und Religion*, 2001. Esp. 113-115.

GEORGE, Augustin, La royauté de Jésus. — ID., *Études*, 1978, 257-282. Esp. 258-259: "Roi (basileus, basileuein, basileia)".

βασιλεύω 3 (Mt 1)

1. be a king (Lk 1,33; 19,14.27); 2. control completely

Word groups	Lk	Acts	Mt	Mk
βασιλεύω + εἰς τοὺς αἰῶνας (VKb) → εἰς τὸν/τοὺς αἰῶνα/αἰῶνας	1,33		0	0
βασιλεύω ἐπί + accusative (VKa)	1,33;		0	0
DENAUX 2009 L[n]	19,14.27			

Literature

EASTON 1910 151 [βασιλεύω ἐπί + acc.: probably characteristic of L].

GEORGE, Augustin, La royauté de Jésus. — ID., *Études*, 1978, 257-282. Esp. 258-259: "Roi (basileus, basileuein, basileia)".

βασίλισσα 1 + 1 (Mt 1)   Queen (Acts 8,27)

Word groups	Lk	Acts	Mt	Mk
βασίλισσα νότου	11,31		1	0

βαστάζω 5 + 4 (Mt 3, Mk 1)

1. carry (Lk 7,14; 10,4; 11,27; 14,27; 22,10); 2. remove; 3. endure (Acts 15,10); 4. provide for; 5. undergo; 6. accept

Word groups	Lk	Acts	Mt	Mk
βαστάζω τὸ ὄνομα (LN: inform)		9,15	0	0
βαστάζω τὸν σταυρόν (LN: suffer unto death) → αἴρω τὸν σταυρόν; cf. λαμβάνω τὸν σταυρόν Mt 10,38	14,27		0	0
ἡ κοιλία βαστάζει (LN: be pregnant with)	11,27		0	0

Characteristic of Luke

GOULDER 1989

Literature

VON BENDEMANN 2001 420; RADL 1975 402; REHKOPF 1959 92 [vorlukanisch]; SCHÜRMANN 1957 122 [luk R unwahrscheinlich]; 1961 279 [protoluk R weniger wahrscheinlich].

BRYAN, J. Davies, Cross-Bearing. — *ExpT* 38 (1926-27) 378-379.

LACHS, Samuel T., Hebrew Elements in the Gospels and Acts . — *The Jewish Querterly Review* 71 (1980) 31-43. Esp. 40-41: Lk 14,26-27..

MATHESON, Donald, Cross-Bearing. — *ExpT* 38 (1926-27) 188, 524-525.

NOLLAND, John, A Fresh Look at Acts 15.10. — *NTS* 27 (1981) 105-115. Esp. 113-115 [Appended note on βαστάζειν].

βάτος 2 + 2 (Mk 1)   thorn bush (Lk 6,44; 20,37; Acts 7,30.35)

Characteristic of Luke

DENAUX 2009 LA*.

Literature

JEREMIAS 1980 148 [red.].

LEE, John A.L. – HORSLEY, G.H.R., A Lexicon of the New Testament, 2, 1998. Esp. 69-70.
KATZ, P., Ἐν πυρὶ φλογός. — *ZNW* 46 (1955) 133-138. Esp. 136 [ὁ βατός hellenistic;
    ἡ βατός Attic, contra Moeris].

βάτος*** 1	bath (measure) (Lk 16,6)

Literature
HAUCK 1934 [seltenes Alleinwort].

βδέλυγμα 1 (Mt 1, Mk 1)	what is detestable (Lk 16,15)

Βεελζεβούλ 3 (Mt 3, Mk 1)	Beelzebul (Lk 11,15.18.19)

βελόνη* 1	needle (Lk 18,25)

Literature
HAUCK 1934 [Vorzugswort].
CADBURY, Henry J., Lexical Notes on Luke-Acts, V, 1933. Esp. 59-60.

Βηθανία 2 (Mt 2, Mk 4)	Bethany (Lk 19,29; 24,50)			
Word groups	Lk	Acts	Mt	Mk
Βηθανία near Jerusalem (*VK*a)	19,29; 24,50		2	4

Βηθλέεμ 2 (Mt 5)	Bethlehem (Lk 2,4.15)

Βηθσαϊδά 2 (Mt 1, Mk 2)	Bethsaida (Lk 9,10; 10,13)

Βηθφαγή 1 (Mt 1, Mk 1)	Bethphage (Lk 19,29)

βιάζομαι 1 (Mt 1)	
1. suffer violence; 2. use violence (Lk 16,16)	

Literature
DANKER, Frederick W., Luke 16,16: An Opposition Logion. — *JBL* 77 (1958) 231-243.
    Esp. 233-239 [βιάζεται *in malam partem*].
KÜMMEL, Werner Georg, "Das Gesetz und die Propheten gehen bis Johannes" – Lukas 16,16
    im Zusammenhang der heilsgeschichtlichen Theologie der Lukasschriften. — BÖCHER, O.
    – HAACKER, K. (eds.), *Verborum Veritas*. FS G. Stählin, 1970, 89-102. Esp. 96.
MENOUD, Philippe H., Le sens du verbe βιάζεται dans Lc 16,16. — DESCAMPS, A. – DE
    HALLEUX, A. (eds.), *Mélanges bibliques en hommage au R.P. Béda Rigaux*, 1970, 207-

212; = Menoud, Philippe H. (ed.), *Jésus-Christ et la foi: Recherches néotestamentaires* (Bibliothèque Théologique), Neuchâtel-Paris: Delachaux & Niestlé, 1975, 76-84.

βιβλίον 3 (Mt 1, Mk 1)

1. document; 2. book (Lk 4,17[1.2].20); 3. record

Word groups	Lk	Acts	Mt	Mk
ἀναπτύσσω/ἀνοίγω τὸ βιβλίον → πτύσσω τὸ **βιβλίον**; διανοίγω/συνίημι τὰς **γραφάς**	4,17[2]		0	0
πτύσσω τὸ βιβλίον → ἀναπτύσσω/ἀνοίγω τὸ **βιβλίον**	4,20		0	0
βιβλίον of the Old Testament (*VKc*) Denaux 2009 L[n]	4,17[1.2].20		0	0

Literature

Jeremias 1980 104: "im lk Doppelwerk ist die Bezeichnung der biblischen Schriftrolle mit βίβλος redaktionell, die mit βιβλίον traditionell".

Chilton, Bruce, Announcement in Nazara, 1981. Esp. 156.

βίβλος 2 + 3 (Mt 1, Mk 1)

1. book (object) (Acts 19,19); 2. book (content) (Lk 3,4; 20,42); 3. record

Characteristic of Luke	Lk	Acts	Mt	Mk
γέγραπται ἐν βίβλῳ; cf. ἐν τῇ βίβλῳ τῆς ζωῆς γεγραμμένος Rev 20,15 Boismard 1984 Ab109; Neirynck 1985	3,4	1,20; 7,42	0	0

Literature

Denaux 2009 IA[n] [γέγραπται ἐν βίβλῳ]; Jeremias 1980 104: "im lk Doppelwerk ist die Bezeichnung der biblischen Schriftrolle mit βίβλος redaktionell, die mit βιβλίον traditionell".

βίος 5 (Mk 1)

1. daily life (Lk 8,14); 2. possessions (Lk 8,43; 15,12.30)

Word groups	Lk	Acts	Mt	Mk
βίος that upon which one lives (*VKa*)	8,43; 15,12.30; 21,4		0	1

Characteristic of Luke; cf. βία Acts 5,26; 21,35; 24,7*; 27,41

Denaux 2009 L***; Goulder 1989*; Hawkins 1909 L.

Literature

Collison 1977 170 [noteworthy phenomena]; Hauck 1934 [Vorzugswort].

Bormann, Lukas, *Recht, Gerechtigkeit und Religion*, 2001. Esp. 149.

βιωτικός 1

daily life (Lk 21,34)

βλάπτω 1 (Mk 0[1])

injure (Lk 4,35)

βλασφημέω 3 + 4 (Mt 3, Mk 4) — blaspheme

Word groups	Lk	Acts	Mt	Mk
βλασφημέω + εἰς τὸ πνεῦμα (VKb)	12,10		0	1
βλασφημέω + λέγων	23,39		0	0
βλασφημοῦντες; cf. Lk 12,10 DENAUX 2009 1Aⁿ	22,65	13,45; 18,6; 19,37	0	0

Literature
JEREMIAS 1980 68 [βλασφημέω + λέγων: red.]; 214 [participle of βλασφημέω: red.]; RADL 1975 402 [βλασφημέω; βλασφημοῦντες].

βλασφημία 1 (Mt 4, Mk 3/4)
1. reviling; 2. blasphemy (Lk 5,21)

Literature
BORMANN, Lukas, *Recht, Gerechtigkeit und Religion*, 2001. Esp. 177-178.

βλέπω 16 + 13/14 (Mt 20, Mk 15)
1. see (Lk 7,44); 2. be able to see (Acts 9,9); 3. watch out for (Lk 21,8); 4. think about; 5. understand; 6. cause to happen; 7. facing (Acts 27,12)

Word groups	Lk	Acts	Mt	Mk
βλέπω + accusative + participle (VKe)		4,14	0	1
βλέπω + ἀκούω (VKg) → **θεωρέω / ὁράω/εἶδον / συνίημι** + ἀκούω	8,10[1.2].18; 10,24	2,33; 8,6; 28,26[1.2]	7	4
βλέπω ἀπό (VKb)	21,30		0	2
βλέπω εἰς (VKa)	9,62	1,11*; 3,4	1	1
βλέπω (+) μή (VKd) → **σκοπέω/φοβέομαι** μή; cf. ὁράω μή Mt 18,10; 24,6	21,8	13,40	1	1
βλέπω + (ὁράω/)εἶδον→ **ἀναβλέπω/ἀτενίζω/ θεάομαι/ θεωρέω** + (ὁράω/)εἶδον; cf. βλέπω + ὁράω Mk 8,15.24; ἐμβλέπω + εἶδον Mk 14,67; περιβλέπω + εἶδον Mk 5,32; 9,8	10,24	28,26[1.2]	3	2
βλέπω ὅραμα → **(ὁράω/)εἶδον/ὄψομαι** ὅραμα/ὅρασιν		12,9	0	0
βλέπω (+) ὀφθαλμός → **ἀνα/διαβλέπω / ἀτενίζω / ὁράω/εἶδον** + ὀφθαλμός	6,41.42; 10,23[1]	1,9; 9,8	1	0
ἐπιβάλλω τὴν χεῖρα ἐπ᾽ ἄροτρον καὶ βλέπω εἰς τὰ ὀπίσω (LN: start to do and then hesitate)	9,62		0	0
τυφλός + βλέπω → τυφλός + **ἀναβλέπω**	7,21	13,11	2	1
βλέπω of the blind (VKh)	7,21	9,8.9; 13,11	2/3	2

Characteristic of Luke
CADBURY 1920 172

Literature
DAUER, Anton, Lk 24,12 – Ein Produkt lukanischer Redaktion? — F. VAN SEGBROECK, et al. (eds.), *The Four Gospels 1992*. FS F. Neirynck, 1992, II, 1697-1716.

—, Zur Authentizität von Lk 24,12. — *ETL* 70 (1994) 294-318.
MUDDIMAN, John, A Note on Reading Luke XXIV.12. — *ETL* 48 (1972) 542-548.
NEIRYNCK, Frans, The Uncorrected Historic Present in Lk XXIV.12. — *ETL* 48 (1972) 548-553; = ID., *Evangelica*, 1982, 329-334 (334: additional note; Appendix, *Evangelica II*, 1991, 798).
—, Παρακύψας βλέπει: Lc 24,12 et Jn 20,5. — *ETL* 53 (1977) 113-152. [NTA 22, 130]; = Id., *Evangelica*, 1982, 401-440 (Appendix, *Evangelica II*, 1991, 799).
—, Once More Lk 24,12. — *ETL* 70 (1994) 319-340; = ID., *Evangelica III*, 2001, 549-571.
—, A Supplementary Note on Lk 24,12. — *ETL* 72 (1996) 425-430; = ID., *Evangelica III*, 2001, 572-578.
—, Luke 24,12: An Anti-Docetic Interpolation? — DENAUX, A. (ed.), *New Testament Textual Criticism and Exegesis*. FS J. Delobel, 2002, 145-158. Esp. 148.

βλητέον** 1 (Mt 1)	must be put (Lk 5,38)

βοάω 4 + 3/4 (Mt 1/2, Mk 2)	shout

Word groups	Lk	Acts	Mt	Mk
βοάω λέγω; cf. ἀναβοάω + λέγω Mt 27,46; Lk 9,38 *v.l.*	9,38; 18,38		0/1	0/1
βοάω φωνῇ μεγάλῃ (*VK*a) → (ἀνα)κράζω/(ἀνα)φωνέω φωνῇ μεγάλῃ; cf. ἀναβοάω + φωνῇ μεγάλῃ Mt 27,46		8,7	0/1	1
φωνὴ βοῶντος (*VK*b)	3,4		1	1

Characteristic of Luke

BOISMARD 1984 Bb42; GOULDER 1989*; NEIRYNCK 1985; PLUMMER 1922 lix

Literature

JEREMIAS 1980 68 [βοάω + λέγων: red.].

βόθυνος 1 (Mt 2)	pit, ditch (Lk 6,39)

βολή 1	throw (Lk 22,41)

Literature

HAUCK 1934 [seltenes Alleinwort].

Βόος 1 (Mt 2)	Boaz (Lk 3,32)

βορρᾶς 1	north

Word groups	Lk	Acts	Mt	Mk
ἀπὸ βορρᾶ → ἀπὸ ἀνατολῶν/δυσμῶν/νότου	13,29		0	0

Literature
HAUCK 1934 [seltenes Alleinwort].

βόσκω 3 (Mt 2, Mk 2)
1. feed animals (Lk 8,32); 2. herd animals (Lk 8,34; 15,15)

Word groups	Lk	Acts	Mt	Mk
βόσκω (+) χοῖρος	8,32.(33-)34; 15,15		2	2
οἱ βόσκοντες (VKa)	8,34		1	1

βουλεύομαι 1 + 1/3
1. intend (Acts 5,33 v.l.; 27,39); 2. think about carefully (Lk 14,31)

βουλευτής 1 (Mk 1)
member of council of Jews (Lk 23,50)

Literature
BORMANN, Lukas, *Recht, Gerechtigkeit und Religion*, 2001. Esp. 133.

βουλή 2 + 7
intention

Word groups	Lk	Acts	Mt	Mk
τίθημι βουλήν (LN: advise; VKb)		27,12	0	0

Characteristic of Luke
BOISMARD 1984 cb19; DENAUX 2009 lA*; HARNACK 1906 51; HAWKINS 1909B.187; NEIRYNCK 1985; PLUMMER 1922 lix

	Lk	Acts	Mt	Mk
βουλὴ τοῦ θεοῦ (SCa; VKa) PLUMMER 1922 lii	7,30	2,23; 13,36; 20,27	0	0

Literature
COLLISON 1977 180 [noteworthy phenomena]; DENAUX 2009 lAⁿ [βουλὴ τοῦ θεοῦ]; HAUCK 1934 [Vorzugswort]; JEREMIAS 1980 165: "lukanisches Vorzugswort".

BORMANN, Lukas, *Recht, Gerechtigkeit und Religion*, 2001. Esp. 133.
DUPONT, Jacques, *Le discours de Milet*, 1962. Esp. 119-125.

βούλομαι 2 + 14 (Mt 2, Mk 1)
1. desire (Lk 10,22; 22,42; Acts 25,22); 2. intend (Acts 12,4)

Word groups	Lk	Acts	Mt	Mk
βούλομαι + δύναμαι → θέλω + δύναμαι		17,(19-)20	0	0
βούλομαι (+) (ἐπι)γνῶναι; cf. Phil 1,12		17,20; 22,30; 23,28	0	0
εἰ βούλει absolute → ἐὰν θέλῃς	22,42		0	0

Characteristic of Luke
BOISMARD 1984 Eb52; DENAUX 2009 lA*; HARNACK 1906 50; MORGENTHALER 1958A; NEIRYNCK 1985

Literature
RADL 1975 402 [βούλομαι; βούλομαι (ἐπι)γνῶναι].

βουνός 2 — hill (Lk 3,5; 23,30)

Characteristic of Luke
PLUMMER 1922 liii

Literature
DENAUX 2009 Lⁿ; HAUCK 1934 [seltenes Alleinwort].

βοῦς 3 — cattle (Lk 13,15; 14,5.19)

Word groups	Lk	Acts	Mt	Mk
βοῦς + ὄνος	13,15		0	0
βοῦς + φάτνη	13,15		0	0
λύω βοῦν → λύω **πῶλον**	13,15		0	0

Characteristic of Luke
GOULDER 1989

Literature
DENAUX 2009 Lⁿ.

βραδύς 1 — slow (Lk 24,25)

βραχίων 1 + 1 — power (Lk 1,51)

Word groups	Lk	Acts	Mt	Mk
βραχίων ὑψηλός (*LN*: great power)		13,17	0	0

Characteristic of Luke
HARNACK 1906 74; VOGEL 1899A

Literature
DENAUX 2009 LAⁿ; HAUCK 1934 [seltenes Alleinwort].

βραχύς 1 + 2

1. few; 2. little (Lk 22,58; Acts 27,28)

Word Groups	Lk	Acts	Mt	Mk
βραχύς temporal DENAUX 2009 LAⁿ	22,58	5,34	0	0

Literature
DENAUX 2009 IAⁿ; SCHNEIDER 1969 82.163: "βραχύς im zeitlichen Sinn" [Vorzugswörter und -ausdrücke des Luk].

βρέφος 5 + 1
1. infant (Lk 1,41.44; 2,12.16; 18,15); 2. childhood

Word groups	Lk	Acts	Mt	Mk
σκιρτάω + τὸ βρέφος	1,41.44		0	0

Characteristic of Luke
BOISMARD 1984 cb20; DENAUX 2009 L***; GOULDER 1989*; HARNACK 1906 139.147; HAWKINS 1909L; NEIRYNCK 1985; PLUMMER 1922 lix; VOGEL 1899B

Literature
GERSDORF 1816 198 [ἐσκίρτησεν τὸ βρέφος]; HAUCK 1934 [seltenes Alleinwort].

βρέχω 3 (Mt 1)
1. rain (Lk 17,29); 2. send rain; 3. make wet (Lk 7,38.44)

Word groups	Lk	Acts	Mt	Mk
τοῖς δάκρυσιν (+) βρέχω DENAUX 2009 Lⁿ	7,38.44		0	0

Literature
PAFFENROTH 1997 74.

βρυγμός 1 (Mt 6)   gnashing

Word groups	Lk	Acts	Mt	Mk
βρυγμός + κλαυθμός; cf. ὀδυρμός + κλαυθμός Mt 2,18	13,28		6	0
βρυγμὸς τῶν ὀδόντων (LN: gnashing of teeth); cf. βρύχω τοὺς ὀδόντας Acts 7,54; τρίζω τοὺς ὀδόντας Mk 9,18	13,28		6	0

βρῶμα 2 (Mt 1, Mk 1)
1. food (Lk 3,11; 9,13); 2. meat

βρώσιμος 1   eatable (Lk 24,41)

Literature
HAUCK 1934 [seltenes Alleinwort].

βυθίζω 1
1. sink (Lk 5,7); 2. cause

Literature
HAUCK 1934 [seltenes Alleinwort].

βύσσος 1   fine linen (Lk 16,19)

Literature
HAUCK 1934 [seltenes Alleinwort].

Γ

Γαβριήλ 2   Gabriel

Word groups	Lk	Acts	Mt	Mk
ὁ ἄγγελος Γαβριήλ; cf. ἄγγελος + Γαβριήλ Lk 1,19	1,26		0	0

Literature
DENAUX 2009 L[n]; GERSDORF 1816 193 [ὁ ἄγγελος Γαβριήλ].

LAURENTIN, René., Traces d'allusions étymologiques en Luc 1–2 (I). — *Bib* 37 (1956) 435-456. Esp. 447-449: "Gabriel".

γαζοφυλάκιον 1 (Mk 3)
1. treasury; 2. offering box (Lk 21,1)

γαλήνη 1 (Mt 1, Mk 1)   calm (Lk 8,24)

Γαλιλαία 13/15 + 3 (Mt 16, Mk 12)   Galilee

Word groups	Lk	Acts	Mt	Mk
Γαλιλαίας genitive + the name of a city (VKb)	1,26; 4,31		2	1
πόλις + Γαλιλαία + Ναζαρέθ/Καφαρναούμ DENAUX 2009 L[n]	1,26; 2,4.39; 4,31		0	0

Characteristic of Luke
GASTON 1973 65 [Lked?]

Literature
MARTÍNEZ, Gabriel B., Galilea en los Evangelios de Mateo, Marcos y Lucas: La equivocidad del término Galilea. — *EstBíb* 43 (1985) 331-371. Esp. 353-363: "Galilea en el evangelio de Lucas".

Γαλιλαῖος 5 + 3 (Mt 1, Mk 1)   a Galilean

Word groups	Lk	Acts	Mt	Mk
Ἰούδας ὁ Γαλιλαῖος (VKa)		5,37	0	0

Characteristic of Luke
BOISMARD 1984 cb4; DENAUX 2009 L[***]; GOULDER 1989; NEIRYNCK 1985.

γαμέω 6 (Mt 6/7, Mk 4)   marry

Word groups	Lk	Acts	Mt	Mk
γαμέω (+) γαμίζω/γαμίσκω (VKb)	17,27; 20,34.35		2	1
γαμέω (+) γυναῖκα → ἀπολύω γυναῖκα	14,20; 16,18		1	1/2

Literature
KILPATRICK, George D., The Aorist of γαμεῖν in the New Testament. — *JTS* NS 18
(1967) 139-140. [NTA 12, 199]; = ID., *Principles and Practice*, 1990, 187-188.
VAN TILBORG, Sjef, The Meaning of the Word γαμῶ in Lk 14:20; 17:27; Mk 12:25 and in
a Number of Early Jewish and Christian Authors. — *HTS* 58 (2002) 802-810. [NTA 47,
918]

γαμίζω 2 (Mt 2, Mk 1)
1. marry; 2. give in marriage (Lk 17,27; 20,35)

Word groups	Lk	Acts	Mt	Mk
γαμίζω (+) γαμέω	17,27; 20,35		2	1

γαμίσκω* 1 (Mk 0/1)   give in marriage

Word groups	Lk	Acts	Mt	Mk
γαμίσκω + γαμέω	20,34		0	0

Literature
HAUCK 1934 [seltenes Alleinwort].

γάμος 2 (Mt 9)
1. marriage; 2. wedding (Lk 12,36; 14,8); 3. wedding hall

Word groups	Lk	Acts	Mt	Mk
καλέω + εἰς γάμον (VKb)	14,8		2	0
γάμοι (VKa)	12,36; 14,8		5	0

Literature
PAFFENROTH 1997 74.

γάρ 97/106 + 80/85 (Mt 124/131, Mk 66/78)
1. because (Lk 16,2); 2. then

Word groups	Lk	Acts	Mt	Mk
ἅπας/πᾶς γάρ	11,10; 20,38; 21,4	16,28	6	6
γάρ after interrogative (VKl)	9,25; 14,28; 22,27; 23,22	8,31; 19,35	5	3/4
γάρ after preposition (VKm)	6,45	5,36; 8,23; 28,20	5	0
γάρ after relative (+ ὅπου/ὅς/ὅσος /ὅστις/οὖ) (VKk)	6,38; 8,18; 9,24.26.50; 12,34	4,34²	6/7	6
γάρ καί → οὖν καί		17,23.28²	2	0
καθώς/ὡς/ὥσπερ γάρ (SCh; VKi)	11,30; 12,58; 17,24	23,11	5	0
μὲν γάρ (SCj; VKj); cf. Rom 7,14 v.l.; 1 Cor 5,3; 11,7.18; 12,8; 14,17; 2 Cor 9,1; 11,4; Heb 6,16 v.l.7,18.20; 8,4*.7 v.l.; 12,10		3,22*; 4,16; 13,36; 23,8; 25,11*; 28,22	0	0
οὐ γάρ (SCc; VKc)	6,43.44²; 7,6; 8,17.52; 9,50*; 16,2; 23,34	2,15¹.34; 16,37; 20,27; 22,22; 26,26³	5	6/7
οὐαὶ ... γάρ DENAUX 2009 Lⁿ	6,26; 21,23		0	0
οὐδὲ/οὐδέπω/οὔπω γάρ (SCd; VKd) DENAUX 2009 lAⁿ	20,36¹	4,12.34; 8,16	0	0
οὐδεὶς γάρ		27,34²	1	1
οὐκέτι γάρ	20,40		0	0
οὔτε γάρ	20,36¹ v.l.	4,12 v.l.	0	0
οὗτος γάρ	6,23 v.l. 26 v.l.; 12,30	26,16; 27,34¹	3/4	1
οὕτως γάρ (SCg; VKh)		13,8.47; 20,13	3	0
περὶ μὲν γάρ → περὶ δέ		28,22	0	0
ὑμῖν γάρ		2,39	0	0
→ ἐὰν (δὲ/γὰρ) μή				

Characteristic of Luke	Lk	Acts	Mt	Mk
ἦ γάρ CREDNER 1836 137	16,13; 18,14*		0	0
ἰδοὺ γάρ (SCa; VKa); cf. 2 Cor 7,11 BOISMARD 1984 Bb46; CREDNER 1836 137; DENAUX 2009 L***; GOULDER 1989*; HARNACK 1906 139; HAWKINS 1909L;; NEIRYNCK 1985; PLUMMER 1922 lx	1,44.48; 2,10; 6,23¹; 17,21	9,11		
καὶ γάρ (SCb; VKb) CADBURY 1920 145; CREDNER 1836 137; GOULDER 1989; HAWKINS 1909add	1,66; 6,32.33.33*.3 4*; 7,8; 11,4; 22,37².59	19,40	3	2/3
→ ἐγὼ γάρ				

Literature

COLLISON 1977 108 [ἰδοὺ γάρ: linguistic usage of Luke's "other source-material": certain]; 116 [καὶ γάρ: noteworthy phenomena]; GERSDORF 1816 199 [ἰδοὺ γάρ]; HAUCK 1934 [Vorzugsverbindung: κατὰ τὰ αὐτὰ γάρ; καὶ γάρ; ἰδοὺ γάρ; τίς γὰρ ἐξ]; JEREMIAS 1980 60 "ἰδοὺ γάρ findet sich im NT nur im lk Doppelwerk".72 "καὶ γάρ... Lk 1,66 Lukas liebt erläuternde Bemerkungen".144-145 "Die Partikelverbindung καὶ γάρ wird in doppelter Bedeutung gebraucht: 1. mit steigernder Funktion = nam etiam = denn auch; ja auch ... 2. mit satzverbindender Funktion = etenim = nämlich, doch, denn [trad]"; RADL 1975 402 [γάρ]; 406 [ἐγὼ γάρ]; REHKOPF 1959 94 [ἰδοὺ γάρ; καὶ γάρ: vorlukanisch]; 95 [λέγω γὰρ ὑμῖν: vorlukanisch]; SCHÜRMANN 1957 128 [καὶ γάρ: luk R nicht nachweisbar]; 1961 273 [ἰδοὺ γάρ]; 276 [καὶ γάρ; λέγω γὰρ ὑμῖν].

FUCHS, Albert, Sprachliche Untersuchungen zu Mattäus und Lukas, 1971. Esp. 180-181 [ἐγὼ γάρ ...].

KILGALLEN, John J., A Suggestion Regarding gar in Luke 10,42. — Bib 73 (1992) 255-258.

LARSEN, I., Notes on the Function of γάρ, οὖν, μέν, δέ, καί, and τέ in the Greek New Testament. — *Notes on Translation* (Dallas) 5 (1991) 35-47.
NADEN, T., *Digression, Explanation and Text Logic.* — *Bible Translator* 36 (1985) 244-247. [NTA 30,47]
READ-HEIMERDINGER, Jenny, *The Bezan Text of Acts*, 2002. Esp. 240-246: "γάρ".

γαστήρ 2 (Mt 3, Mk 1)
1. belly (Lk 1,31; 21,23); 2. glutton

Word groups	Lk	Acts	Mt	Mk
ἐν γαστρὶ ἔχω (*LN*: be pregnant)	21,23		3	1
ἐν γαστρὶ συλλαμβάνω → ἐν **γήρει/τῇ κοιλίᾳ** συλλαμβάνω	1,31		0	0

Literature
VICENT CERNUDA, Antonio, La intención de ἐν γαστρι en Lc 1,31. — *RevistCatTeol* 14 (1989) 175-184.

γε 8/9 + 4/5 (Mt 4)   indeed

Word groups	Lk	Acts	Mt	Mk
ἀλλά γε; cf. ἀλλὰ μενοῦνγε Phil 3,8	24,21		0	0
ἄρά γε		8,30	0	0
ἄρα γε / ἄραγε (*VK*c)		11,18*; 17,27[1]	2	0
γε καί → ἅμα **καί**	5,36; 24,21		0	0
DENAUX 2009 Lⁿ				
καί γε / καίγε (*VK*d)	19,42*	2,18; 14,17*; 17,27[2]	0	0

Characteristic of Luke
DENAUX 2009 L***; GOULDER 1989*; HAWKINS 1909L.

	Lk	Acts	Mt	Mk
εἰ δὲ μή γε (*SC*a; *VK*a); cf. εἰ δὲ μή Mk 2,21.22	5,36.37; 10,6; 13,9; 14,32		2	0
CREDNER 1836 137; DENAUX 2009 L***; HAWKINS 1909L; PLUMMER 1922 lx				

Literature
COLLISON 1977 102 [εἰ δὲ μή γε: linguistic usage of Luke: probable]; HAUCK 1934 [Vorzugswort; Vorzugsverbindung: εἰ δὲ μή γε]; JEREMIAS 1980 185 "alle drei Belege [10,6; 13,9; 14,32] finden sich im Nicht-Markusstoff des Lukas-Evangeliums" [trad]

THRALL, Margaret E., *Greek Particles in the New Testament*, 1962. Esp. 9-10 [εἰ δὲ μή γε]; 11-16 [ἀλλά γε καί, ἀλλὰ μενοῦν γε καί].

γέεννα 1 (Mt 7, Mk 3)   hell (Lk 12,5)

γείτων 3   neighbor

Word groups	Lk	Acts	Mt	Mk
ἀδελφός + συγγενής + γείτων	14,12		0	0
φίλος/φίλη + γείτων	14,12; 15,6.9		0	0
DENAUX 2009 Lⁿ				

Characteristic of Luke
GOULDER 1989

Literature
VON BENDEMANN 2001 427: "Die Verbindung von φίλος mit 'Verwandten' und 'Nachbarn' ist lukanisch'''; DENAUX 2009 Lⁿ; EASTON 1910 150 [ἀδελφοὶ καὶ συγγενεῖς καὶ γείτονες: probably characteristic of L]; PAFFENROTH 1997 75.

γελάω 2	laugh (Lk 6,21.25)

Characteristic of Luke
PLUMMER 1922 liii

Literature
DENAUX 2009 Lⁿ; HAUCK 1934 [seltenes Alleinwort].
DUPONT, Jacques, *Les Béatitudes*, III, 1973. Esp. 65-69: "Ceux qui rient".

γεμίζω 1/2 (Mk 2)	fill			
Word groups	Lk	Acts	Mt	Mk
γεμίζομαι passive (*VK*a)	14,23		0	1

γέμω 1 (Mt 2)	be full (Lk 11,39)

γενεά 15 + 5 (Mt 13, Mk 5)	
1. same generation (Lk 11,51); 2. people of same kind (Lk 16,8); 3. descendants (Acts 8,33); 4. age (Acts 14,16)	

Word groups	Lk		Acts	Mt	Mk
ἄνδρες/ἄνθρωποι τῆς γενεᾶς ταύτης DENAUX 2009 Lⁿ	7,31; 11,31			0	0
γενεὰ αὕτη	7,31; 11,29[1].30.31.32.50.51; 17,25; 21,32			6	4
γενεὰ πονηρά	11,29[2]			2	0
διηγέομαι + τὴν γενεάν			8,33	0	0
γενεά vocative (*VK*b)	9,41			1	1

Characteristic of Luke	Lk	Acts	Mt	Mk
γενεαί plural (*VK*a) HARNACK 1906 151	1,48.50[1.2]	14,16; 15,21	4	0

Literature
COLLISON 1977 204 [ἡ γενεὰ αὕτη: linguistic usage of Luke: certain]; JEREMIAS 1980 268 [τῆς γενεᾶς ταύτης].
MCKERRAS, R., Who is This Generation? An Alternative View. — *Notes on Translation* (Dallas, TX) 2 (1988) 57-58.

MEINERTZ, Max, "Dieses Geschlecht" im Neuen Testament. — *BZ* NF 1 (1957) 283-289.
STEINHAUSER, Michael G., Noah in His Generation: An Allusion in Luke 16 8b, "εἰς τὴν γενεὰν τὴν ἑαυτῶν" — *ZNW* 79 (1988) 152-157.

γένεσις 1 (Mt 2)

1. birth (Lk 1,14); 2. lineage; 3. history; 4. existence

γένημα 1/2 (Mt 1, Mk 1) — product (Lk 12,18*; 22,18)

Literature

PETZER, Kobus H., Style and Text in the Lucan Narrative of the Institution of the Lord's Supper, 1991. Esp. 121.

γεννάω 4 + 7 (Mt 45, Mk 1)

1. beget (Acts 13,33); 2. give birth (Lk 1,13.35.57; 23,29); 3. be born of; 4. cause to happen

Characteristic of Luke	Lk	Acts	Mt	Mk
γεννάω of the mother DENAUX 2009 L***; GOULDER 1989; HARNACK 1906 72	1,13.35.57; 23,29		0	0
τὸ γεννώμενον CREDNER 1836 134-135	1,35		0	0

Literature

GERSDORF 1816 196 [διὸ καὶ τὸ γεννώμενον].

BOVER, José M., "Quod nascetur (ex te) sanctum vocabitur filius Dei" (Lc. 1,35). — *Bib* 1 (1920) 92-94.

—, "Quod nascetur (ex te) sanctum vocabitur filius Dei" (Lc., 1,35). — *EstE* 8 (1929) 381-392.

BURCHARD, Christoph, Fußnoten zum neutestamentlichen Griechisch, 1970. Esp. 168-169: "Act 22,3" [γεγεννημένος].

JUNG, Chang-Wook, *Infancy Narrative*, 2004. Esp. 198-201 [Lk 1,13].

MUÑOZ IGLESIAS, Salvador, Lucas 1,35b. — *La idea de Dios en la Biblia. XXVIII Semana Biblica Española (Madrid 23-27 sept. 1968)*. Madrid: Consejo Superior de Investigaciones Cientificas, 1971, 303-324.

SCHNEIDER, Gerhard, Lk 1,34. 35 als redaktionelle Einheit. — *BZ* NF 15 (1971) 255-259.
Esp. 256-257: "Lk 1,35 ist nach Wortschatz, Stil und Theologie 'lukanisch'".

—, Jesu geistgewirkte Empfängnis (Lk 1,34f): Zur Interpretation einer christologischen Aussage. — *TPQ* 119 (1971) 105-116. Esp. 110; = ID., *Lukas, Theologe der Heilsgeschichte*, 1985, 86-97. Esp. 91.

VICENT CERNUDA, Antonio, El paralelismo de γεννῶ y τίκτω en Lc 1–2. — *Bib* 55 (1974) 260-264.

γέννημα 1 (Mt 3)

1. offspring (Lk 3,7); 2. kind

Word groups	Lk	Acts	Mt	Mk
γεννήματα ἐχιδνῶν	3,7		3	0

Literature

REHKOPF 1959 98 [γεννήματα ἐχιδνῶν: "Substantiva in Anrede bei den Synoptikern"].

MAHFOUZ, Hady, *La fonction littéraire et théologique de Lc 3,1-20*, 2003. Esp. 179-180
[γεννήματα ἐχιδνῶν].

Γεννησαρέτ 1 (Mt 1, Mk 1) | Gennesaret (Lk 5,1)

γεννητός 1 (Mt 1) | born (Lk 7,28)

Γερασηνός 2 (Mk 1) | Gerasene (Lk 8,26.37)

γεύομαι 2 + 3 (Mt 2, Mk 1)

1. taste (Lk 14,24; Acts 23,14); 2. eat (Acts 10,10); 3. experience (Lk 9,27)

Word groups	Lk	Acts	Mt	Mk
γεύομαι θανάτου (VKa)	9,27		1	1
γεύομαι + genitive of object	14,24	23,14	0	0
DENAUX 2009 LA[n]				

Literature

JEREMIAS 1980 241: "γεύομαι ('genießen'), im eigentlichen Sinn gebraucht, mit Genitiv der Sache findet sich im NT nur im Doppelwerk".

γεωργός 5 (Mt 6, Mk 5) | farmer (Lk 20,9.10[1.2].14.16)

γῆ 25/26 + 33/34 (Mt 43, Mk 19)

1. earth (Lk 2,14); 2. land (Lk 4,25); 3. soil (Lk 8,8); 4. region (Acts 7,3.6); 5. people (Lk 12,49.51)

Word groups	Lk	Acts	Mt	Mk
οἱ βασιλεῖς τῆς γῆς (SCc; VKc)		4,26	1	0
γῆ + a geographical name (SCd; VKd)		7,4[1].11*.29.36.40; 13,17.19[1]	7/8	0
γῆ ἁγία → **τόπος** ἅγιος		7,33	0	0
γῆ + θάλασσα	21,25	4,24; 7,36; 14,15	1	1
γῆ + οὐρανός (SCb; VKb)	4,25; 10,21; 11,2*; 12,56; 16,17; 21,33; 22,(43-)44	2,19; 4,24; 7,49; 10,12; 11,6; 14,15; 17,24	12/13	2
ἐν γῇ		7,6.29.36; 13,17.19[1]	0	0
ἐν τῇ (+) γῇ	8,15; 12,51		3	0
ἐπὶ (…) τὴν γῆν	4,25; 5,11; 6,49; 8,27; 12,49; 22,44; 23,44	9,4; 27,43.44	7	3
ἐπὶ γῆς	2,14		1	0
ἐπὶ τῆς γῆς	5,24; 18,8; 21,23.25	2,19; 10,11	10	10

κλίνω τὸ πρόσωπον εἰς τὴν γῆν (*LN*: prostrate oneself)	24,5		0	0
κυριὸς (τοῦ) οὐρανοῦ καὶ (τῆς) γῆς	10,21	17,24	1	0
ὅλη/πᾶσα ἡ γῆ (*SC*a; *VK*a) → κόσμος ὅλος	4,25; 21,35; 23,44		3	1
ὁ οὐρανὸς καὶ ἡ γῆ (*LN*: universe)	10,21; 12,56; 16,17; 21,33	4,24; 17,24	4	1

→ ἐπὶ **πρόσωπον** πάσης τῆς γῆς

Characteristic of Luke	Lk	Acts	Mt	Mk
πρόσωπον τῆς γῆς → πρόσωπον τοῦ **οὐρανοῦ** BOISMARD 1984 Ab143; NEIRYNCK 1985; VOGEL 1899C	12,56; 21,35	17,26	0	0

Literature

DENAUX 2009 La[n] [πρόσωπον τῆς γῆς]; GERSDORF 1816 232 [δόξα ἐν ὑψίστοις θεῷ καὶ ἐπὶ γῆς εἰρήνη].

BURCHARD, Christoph, Fußnoten zum neutestamentlichen Griechisch, 1970. Esp. 161-163: "Act 1,8 ἕως ἐσχάτου τῆς γῆς".

DELEBECQUE, Édouard, *Études grecques*, 1976. Esp. 25-38: "Le 'gloria' des anges (2,14)".

GUERRA GÓMEZ, Manuel, Análisis filológico-teológico y traducción del himno de los ángeles en Belén, 1989. Esp. 46-47: "Ἐπὶ γῆς = 'sobre (en) la tierra'".

PERLES, Felix, Zwei Übersetzungsfehler im Text der Evangelien. — *ZNW* 19 (1919-20) 96. [Lk 9,60; 14,35: γῆ].

SCHNEIDER, Gerhard, Engel und Blutschweiß (Lk 22,43-44): "Redaktionsgeschichte" im Dienste der Textkritik. — *BZ* NF 20 (1976) 112-116. Esp. 113-115: "Vokabular und Stil von Lk 22,43.44"; = ID., *Lukas, Theologe der Heilsgeschichte*, 1985, 153-157. Esp. 154-156.

VAN UNNIK, Willem C., Der Ausdruck ἕως ἐσχάτου τῆς γῆς (Apostelgeschichte 1:8) und sein alttestamentlicher Hintergrund. — *Studia Biblica et Semitica: Theodoro Christiano Vriezen qui munere professoris theologiae per XXV annos functus est, ab amicis, collegis, discipulis dedicata*. Wageningen: Veenman & Zonen, 1966, 335-349; = ID., *Sparsa Collecta*, I, 1973, 386-401.

γῆρας 1   old age

Word groups	Lk	Acts	Mt	Mk
ἐν γήρει + συλλαμβάνω → ἐν **γάστρι** / τῇ **κοιλίᾳ** συλλαμβάνω	1,36		0	0

γίνομαι 131/135 + 125/127 (Mt 75, Mk 54[55]/56)

1. come to exist; 2. be (Lk 1,5); 3. become (Acts 26,29); 4. happen (Lk 1,20); 5. move (Acts 25,15); 6. belong to (Lk 20,14.33); 7. behave; 8. be in a place (Acts 20,18); 9. come to be in a place (Lk 2,13); 10. there was (Lk 9,37)

Word groups	Lk	Acts	Mt	Mk
γενόμενος + ἐπὶ τοῦ τόπου / κατὰ τὸν τόπον DENAUX 2009 L[n]	10,32; 22,40		0	0
γίνεταί μοι → ἐστίν μοι DENAUX 2009 1A[n]	1,38	22,6.17[1]	0	0
γίνεταί + σοι → ἐστίν σοι	14,12		2	0

γίνομαι γνώμης (LN: make up mind)		20,3²	0	0
γίνομαι (+) εἰς replacing the predicate nominative (LN: become) → εἰμι + εἰς replacing the predicate nom.; cf. ἔχω εἰς Mt 21,46	13,19; 20,17	4,11; 5,36	1	1
γίνομαι ἐν ἑαυτῷ		12,11	0	0
γίνομαι ἵνα (SCg; VKg)		27,42	3	0
γίνομαι μετά + genitive		7,38; 9,19; 20,18	0	1
γίνομαι (+) ῥῆμα DENAUX 2009 La[n]	1,38; 2,15²; 3,2	10,37	0	0
γνωστὸν ἐγένετο → γνωστόν ἐστιν		1,19; 9,42; 19,17	0	0
γνωστόν verbal adjective + ἐγένετο/ἔστω/ἐστίν (VKa) BOISMARD 1984 Aa6		1,19; 2,14; 4,10; 9,42; 13,38; 19,17; 28,22.28	0	0
δεῖ γενέσθαι	21,9	1,(21-)22	2	1
ἐγένετο + indicative (SCa; VKa) DENAUX 2009 Lan	1,59; 2,1.46; 5,17; 7,11; 8,1.22; 9,37.57*; 11,14; 20,1	9,19	5	1
ἐγένετο λιμός → λιμὸς ἔσται / λιμοὶ ἔσονται DENAUX 2009 L[n]	4,25; 15,14		0	0
ἡμέρας γενομένης; cf. ὀψίας γενομένης Mt 8,16; 14,15.23; 16,2; 20,8; 26,20; 27,57; Mk 1,32; 4,35; 6,47; 14,17; 15,42	4,42	12,18; 16,35; 23,12	0	1
καθὼς ἐγένετο DENAUX 2009 L[n]	11,30; 17,26.28			
καὶ ἐγένετο ἐν τῷ καθεξῆς/ἑξῆς DENAUX 2009 L[n]	7,11; 8,1	0	0	0
καὶ γένηται; cf. καὶ γένησθε Mt 18,3	14,12		0	0
καὶ γενόμενος	22,44¹	12,23; 13,5; 19,28	0	3
καὶ γίνεται	11,26; 12,54.55		2	3
καὶ ἐγενήθη; cf. καὶ ἐγενήθησαν Mt 28,4		4,4	0	0
καὶ ἐγένοντο		5,36	0	0
μὴ γένοιτο (SCl; VKm)	20,16		0	0
ὁρμὴ γίνομαι (LN: make up mind)		14,5	0	0
πολὺς δέ + noun + γινόμενος BOISMARD 1984 Aa79		15,7; 21,40; 23,10	0	0
σημεῖον γίνεται διά + genitive BOISMARD 1984 Aa34		2,43²; 4,16.30; 5,12; 14,3	0	0
τοῦτο subject of γίνεσθαι BOISMARD 1984 Ca66		5,24; 10,16; 11,10; 19,10.17; 28,9	3	1
φίλος γίνομαι → φιλός εἰμι	23,12		0	0
γεγενημένος (VKk)	8,34 v.l.		0	0
γενηθήτω (SCm; VKn)	11,2*	1,20	5	0
γενόμενος (SCh; VKh)	1,2; 4,23.42; 6,48; 10,13².32; 18,24; 22,40.44¹; 23,19.47.48; 24,5.18.22.37	1,16.18; 2,6; 4,11; 7,32.38; 10,4.37; 11,19; 12,11.18¹.23;	17	12[13]

| | | 13,5.32;
15,2.7.25;
16,27.29.35;
19,28; 20,3¹;
21,17.40; 23,10
v.l.12; 24,25;
25,15.26;
26,4.6; 27,7.36;
28,9 | | |

Characteristic of Luke

GASTON 1973 65 [Lked?]; GOULDER 1989; HENDRIKS 1986 428.434.448; MORGENTHALER 1958LA

	Lk	Acts	Mt	Mk
adjective + γενόμενος (except ὀψίας (δὲ) γενόμενης); cf. Heb 11,24; Jam 1,12 BOISMARD 1984 cb21; DENAUX 2009 lA*; HARNACK 1906 41; NEIRYNCK 1985	18,24; 24,5.37	1,18; 7,32; 10,4; 16,27.29; 24,25; 27,36	0	1
τὸ γεγονός (SCk; VK1) BOISMARD 1984 Bb26; CREDNER 1836 134-135; DENAUX 2009 L***; GOULDER 1989 72; HARNACK 1906 147; HAWKINS 1909L; NEIRYNCK 1985	2,15²; 8,34.35.56; 24,12	4,21; 5,7²; 13,12	0	1
τὸ γενομένον DENAUX 2009 L***	9,7; 23,47.48; 24,18;	10,37; 12,9	1	1
γενομένης δέ + subject → παραγενόμενος δέ + subj.; cf. γενομένων δὲ ἡμῶν Acts 21,17 BOISMARD 1984 Bb63; NEIRYNCK 1985	4,42	2,6; 12,18¹; 15,2; 23,12	1	0
γίνομαι εἰς (SCe; VKe) → γίνομαι εἰς + place; γίνομαι + εἰς replacing the predicate nom. DENAUX 2009 lA*	4,23; 13,19; 20,17	4,11; 5,36; 20,16²; 21,17; 25,15	1	1
γίνομαι εἰς + place → γίνομαι εἰς BOISMARD 1984 Aa77; HARNACK 1906 41	4,23	20,16²; 21,17; 25,15	0	0
γίνομαι + ἐπί DENAUX 2009 L***; GOULDER 1989*	1,65; 3,2²; 4,25.36; 23,44;24,22	5,5.11; 8,1; 10,10²; 21,35	1	1
γίνομαι ἐπί + accusative BOISMARD 1984 Bb10; DENAUX 2009 L***; HAWKINS 1909L; NEIRYNCK 1985	1,65; 3,2²; 4,25.36; 23,44; 24,22	4,22; 5,5.11; 8,1; 10,10²; 21,35	1	1
γίνομαι/εἰμι ἐπί + genitive of time → εἰμι ἐπί + gen. of time; cf. Jude 18 BOISMARD 1984 cb22; NEIRYNCK 1985	3,2¹; 4,27	11,28	0	0
γίνομαι κατά + accusative of place BOISMARD 1984 Ab168; NEIRYNCK 1985	10,32; 15,14	27,7	0	0
γίνομαι ὑπό + genitive; cf. Eph 5,12 BOISMARD 1984 Bb97; NEIRYNCK 1985	9,7 v.l.; 13,17; 23,8	12,5; 20,3; 26,6	0	0
γινόμενος (SCj; VKj) DENAUX 2009 L***; HARNACK 1906 41	9,7; 13,17; 21,31; 23,8	8,13; 12,5.9; 19,26; 23,10; 24,2; 28,6	0/2	2/3
ἐγένετο DENAUX 2009 L***; HARNACK 1906 69.149; HENDRIKS 1986 441.448; PLUMMER 1922 lx; SCHÜRMANN 1953 106	1,5.8.23.41.44.59.65; 2,1.2.6.13.15¹.42.46; 3,2.21; 4,25.36; 5,1.12.17; 6,1.6.12. 13.16.49; 7,11;	1,19; 2,2; 4,5; 5,5.7¹.11; 6,1; 7,13.29.31.40; 8,1.8; 9,3.19.32.37.42.43; 10,10¹². 13.16.25;	13	18

	8,1.22.24; 9,18.28.29. 33.34.35.37.51; 10,21; 11,1.14.27.30; 13,19; 14,1; 15,14; 16,22; 17,11.14.26.28; 18,35; 19,9.15.29; 20,1; 22,14.24.44².66; 23,44; 24,4.15.19.21. 30.31.51	11,10.26.28; 12,18²; 14,1.5; 15,39; 16,16.26; 19,1.10. 17.23.34; 20,3².37; 21,1.5.30.35; 22,6.17¹; 23,7.9; 27,27.39.42.44; 28,8.17		
ἐγένετο + finite verb DENAUX 2009 L***; GOULDER 1989*; HAWKINS 1909L	1,8(-9).23.41.59; 2,1.6.15¹.46; 7,11; 9,18.28.33.37; 11,1.14.27; 17,14; 18,35; 19,29; 20,1; 24,30.51		5	2
ἐγένετο + genitive absolute BOISMARD 1984 Bb43; DENAUX 2009 L***; HARNACK 1906 35; NEIRYNCK 1985	2,2; 9,37; 11,14; 20,1	16,16; 22,17¹	1	0
ἐγένετο + infinitive (subject) (SCc; VKc) BOISMARD 1984 Bb3; CREDNER 1836 133; DENAUX 2009 L***; GOULDER 1989*; HARNACK 1906 35; HAWKINS 1909L; NEIRYNCK 1985	3,21; 6,1.6.12; 16,22	4,5; 9,3.32.37.43; 10,25; 11,26; 14,1; 16,16; 19,1; 21,1.5; 22,6.17¹; 27,44; 28,8.17	0	1
(καὶ) ἐγένετο (δέ) + expression of time BOISMARD 1984 Bb5; DENAUX 2009 L***; NEIRYNCK 1985	1,5.59; 2,1.46; 5,17; 6,1.6.12; 7,11; 8,1.22; 9,37; 20,1	4,5; 8,1; 9,37; 19,23; 28,17	0	1
(καὶ) ἐγένετο (δὲ) ἐν τῷ + infinitive (SCb; VKb) BOISMARD 1984 Bb2; CREDNER 1836 132; DENAUX 2009 L***; HARNACK 1906 70; NEIRYNCK 1985	1,8; 2,6; 3,21; 5,1.12; 8,40*; 9,18.29.33.51; 10,38*; 11,1.27; 14,1; 17,11.14; 18,35; 19,15; 24,4.15.30.51	19,1	0	1/2
ἐγένετο δέ → καὶ ἐγένετο; παρεγένετο δέ; cf. Jn 10,22 v.l.; 2 Pet 2,1 BOISMARD 1984 Bb4; CREDNER 1836 133; DENAUX 2009 L***; GOULDER 1989*; NEIRYNCK 1985; PLUMMER 1922 lii; SCHÜRMANN 1957 65-66	1,8; 2,1.6; 3,21; 5,1; 6,1.6.12; 8,22.40*; 9,28.37.51; 10,38*; 11,14.27; 16,22; 18,35; 22,24; 23,12	4,5; 5,7; 8,1.8; 9,19.32.37.43; 10,10; 11,26; 14,1; 15,39; 16,16; 19,1.23; 22,6.17; 23,9; 28,8.17	0	0
ἐγένετο θάμβος/φόβος ἐπί + accusative → φόβος λαμβάνει + acc.; θάμβος περιέχει + acc.; ἐπλήσθην θάμβους/ φόβου; ἐπέπεσεν φόβος ἐπί + acc. BOISMARD 1984 Ab72; NEIRYNCK 1985	1,65; 4,36	5.5.11		
ἐγένετο ..., καί DENAUX 2009 L***; GOULDER 1989*; HAWKINS 1909L	2,15 v.l.; 5,1.12.17; 8,1.22; 9,51; 14,1; 17,11; 19,15; 24,4.15	5,7	1	0
ἐγένετο ὡς temporal + finite verb (SCf; VKf) CREDNER 1836 133; DENAUX 2009 L***	1,23.41; 2,15¹; 19,29		0	0
ἔμφοβος γενόμενος; cf. ἔμφοβοι ἐγένοντο Acts 22,9* BOISMARD 1984 Ab78; NEIRYNCK 1985	24,5.37	10,4; 24,25	0	0
ἡμέρα γίνεται BOISMARD 1984 Bb19; DENAUX 2009 lA*; HARNACK 1906 52; HAWKINS 1909L.B; NEIRYNCK 1985; PLUMMER 1922 lii; VOGEL 1899C	4,42; 6,13; 22,66	12,18; 16,35; 23,12; 27,29.33.39	0	1

καὶ ἐγένετο → **ἐγένετο δέ** CREDNER 1836 133; DENAUX 2009 L***; GOULDER 1989*; HARNACK 1906 69	1,23.41.59.65; 2,15.46; 4,36; 5,12.17; 6,16 v.l.49; 7,11; 8,1.22 v.l.24; 9,18.29.33; 11,1; 13,19; 14,1; 17,11.14; 19,15.29; 20,1; 22,44²; 24,4.15.30.51	2,2; 5,5.11; 7,29; 10,13; 21,30	7	7
καὶ ἐγένετο / ἐγένετο δὲ (ἐν τῷ + infinitive) ... καὶ αὐτός/αὐτοί+ finite verb DENAUX 2009 L***	5,1.17; 9,51; 8,1.22; 14,1; 17,11; 24,15		0	0
μέλλει γίνεσθαι; cf. Rev 1,19 BOISMARD 1984 Bb114; NEIRYNCK 1985	21,7.36	26,22; 27,33	0	0

Literature

VON BENDEMANN 2001 414 [ἐγένετο δέ; καὶ ἐγένετο ἐν τῷ + inf.]; 435 [καὶ ἐγένετο ὡς ἤγγισεν]; 437 [καὶ ἐγένετο + ἐν temporale; μὴ γένοιτο]; COLLISON 1977 42 [καὶ ἐγένετο: linguistic usage of Luke: certain]; 43 [καὶ ἐγένετο prefatory: certain; ἐγένετο δέ: certain; ἐγένετο δέ prefatory: certain; + acc. inf.: certain]; 44 [τὸ γινόμενον etc.: certain]; 110 [καὶ ὅτε ἐγένετο: linguistic usage of Luke: likely]; 136 [γίνομαι + ἐπί: noteworthy phenomena]; CREDNER 1836 133 [ἐγένετο δὲ ἐν τῷ ... καί]; DENAUX 2009 lAn [γενομένης δέ + subject], Lⁿ [γίνομαι ἐπί + genitive of time; γίνομαι κατά + accusative of place], lAⁿ [γίνομαι εἰς + place; γίνομαι ὑπό + genitive], LAⁿ [ἔμφοβος γενόμενος; μέλλει γίνεσθαι; ἐγένετο θάμβος/φόβος ἐπί + accusative; γίνομαι κατά + accusative of place]; EASTON 1910 146 [ἐγένετο καί / ἐγένετο ἐν τῷ: especially characteristic of L]; 151-152 [ἐγένετο followed by a finite verb: probably characteristic of L; Note 1: ἐγένετο ἐν τῷ + inf.; Note 2: ἐγένετο ὡς; Note 3: ἐγένετο + inf.; Note 4: ἐγένετο in the Transfiguration narrative]; 163 [λιμὸς ἐγένετο: cited by Weiss as characteristic of L, and possibly corroborative]; 167 [ἔμφοβος γενόμενος: classed by Weiss as characteristic of L on insufficient (?) evidence]; 177 [καὶ ἐγένετο; ἐγένετο δέ: possible Hebraisms in the Lucan Writings, as classed by Dalman]; GERSDORF 1816 162 [ἐγένετο ἐν ταῖς ἡμέραις]; 172 [ἐγένετο δὲ ἐν τῷ ἱερατεύειν αὐτόν]; 191-192 [καὶ ἐγένετο ὡς ἐπλήσθησαν]; 198 [καὶ ἐγένετο ὡς ἤκουσεν]; 199 [ἐγένετο ἡ φωνή - εἰς τὰ ὦτά μου]; 202-203 [καὶ ἐγένετο ἐν τῇ ἡμέρᾳ τῇ ὀγδόῃ ἦλθον]; 204 [καὶ ἐγένετο ἐπὶ πάντας φόβος τοὺς περιοικοῦντας]; 212 [ἐγένετο δὲ ἐν ταῖς ἡμέραις ἐκείναις]; 219-220 [ἐγένετο δὲ ἐν τῷ εἶναι αὐτοὺς ἐκεῖ ἐπλήσθησαν]; 232 [καὶ ἐγένετο ὡς ἀπῆλθον ἀπ' αὐτῶν εἰς τὸν οὐρανὸν οἱ ἄγγελοι]; HARNACK 1906 41 [the participial use of γίνεται (except in determination of time) is also Lukan]; HAUCK 1934 [Vorzugsverbindung: τὸ γεγονός; (καὶ) ἐγένετο (δὲ) ἐν τῷ + inf.; καὶ ἐγένετο ἐν τῷ καθεξῆς/ ἑξῆς; ἐγένετο ἡ φωνή; ἐγένετο ἡμέρα; καὶ ἐγένετο ἐν μιᾷ τῶν ἡμερῶν; ἐγένετο δέ + inf.]; JEREMIAS 1980 25 [ἐγένετο δέ, καὶ ἐγένετο]; 25-27: "insbesondere liebt Lukas die dreiteilige Konstruktion: a) Eingangsformel mit ἐγένετο am Satzanfang + b) Zeitbestimmung + c) Anschlußsatz (Verbum finitum mit und ohne Vorangehen von καί)"; 29 [ἐγένετο ἐν τῷ + inf.]; 32 [ἐγένετο θάμβος/φόβος ἐπί + acc.: red.]; 85: "Attributiv gebrauchtes Partizip von γίνομαι ... begegnet im NT nur im lukanischen Doppelwerk"; 112-113: "γίνεσθαι mit folgendem Infinitiv ... lk Vorzugswendung"; 286 [ἐγένετο ἡ ὥρα: red.]; 294: "speziell die Konstruktion γίνεσθαι mit ἐν ist 'geradezu charakteristisch' für Lukas [22,44]"; 299: "Die Verbindung von ἡμέρα mit γίνομαι zur Umschreibung des Tagesanbruchs findet sich im NT nur im lk Doppelwerk"; 308 [τὸ γενόμενον - τὸ γεγονός: red.]; 311: "γενόμενος + Adj. findet sich im Doppelwerk 11mal"; 312: "Das substantivierte Part.perf. τὸ γεγονός ist lk Vorzugswendung"; PAFFENROTH 1997 82 [λιμὸς ἐγένετο]; RADL 1975 402-404 [γίνομαι; γινέσθω 3 pers. sg.; ἐγένετο; ἐγένετο δέ; καὶ ἐγένετο; ὅτε δὲ ἐγένετο; ὡς δὲ ἐγένετο; ἐγένετο + inf.; ἐγένετο "mit Akkusativ beim Infinitiv"; ἐγένετο without καί + finite verb; ἐγένετο "in Einleitungsversen"; ἐγένετο καί + finite verb; ἐγένετο + καὶ αὐτός + finite verb; ἐγένετο "mit einer präpositionalen Zeitbestimmung"; '

ἐγένετο + ἡμέρα/σάββατον/(καθ)ἑξῆς/καιρός; ἐγένετο "mit einem das Geschehen beschrei-
bende Substantiv auf -μος; γίνομαι + στάσις]; SCHÜRMANN 1957 76 [γίνεσθαι für εἶναι]; 77
[γίνεσθαι ὡς: luk R unwahrscheinlich]; 89 [εἶναι ὡς: luk R weniger wahrscheinlich]; 1961 277
[γίνεσθαι ὡς].

BEYER, Klaus, *Semitische Syntax im Neuen Testament.* I/1, 1962. Esp. 29-62:
    "Satzeinleitendes καὶ ἐγένετο mit Zeitbestimmung".
CADBURY, Henry J., Commentary on the Preface of Luke, 1922. Esp. 500 [Lk 1,2].
CIGNELLI, Lino. – PIERRI, Rosario., *Sintassi di Greco biblico.* I.a, 2003. Esp. 27-30.
DAUER, Anton, Lk 24,12 – Ein Produkt lukanischer Redaktion? — F. VAN SEGBROECK, et
    al. (eds.), *The Four Gospels 1992.* FS F. Neirynck, 1992, II, 1697-1716.
—, Zur Authentizität von Lk 24,12. — *ETL* 70 (1994) 294-318.
DELEBECQUE, Édouard, *Études grecques*, 1976. Esp. 123-165: "La vivante formule καὶ
    ἐγένετο".
DENAUX, Adelbert, The Delineation of the Lukan Travel Narrative within the Overall
    Structure of the Gospel of Luke. — FOCANT, Camille (ed.), *The Synoptic Gospels:
    Source Criticism and the New Literary Criticism* (BETL, 110). Leuven: Leuven
    University Press – Uitgeverij Peeters, 1993, 357-392. Esp. 377-382: "The structural function
    of the καὶ ἐγένετο-Formula".
ELY (= CHASE), F.H., On πρηνὴς γενόμενος in Acts 1,18. — *JTS* 13 (1911-12) 278-
    285, 415.
JOHANNESSOHN, Martin, Das biblische καὶ ἐγένετο und seine Geschichte. — *Zeitschrift
    für vergleichende Sprachforschung* 53 (1926) 161-212.
JUNG, Chang-Wook, *Infancy Narrative*, 2004. Esp. 136-149 [ἐγένετο: Lk 1,5].
KILPATRICK, George D., Three Problems of New Testament Text. — *NT* 21 (1979) 289-
    292. Esp. 290: "Luke v. 1 καὶ ἐγένετο"; = ID., *Principles and Practice*, 1990, 241-244.
    Esp. 242.
MAHFOUZ, Hady, *La fonction littéraire et théologique de Lc 3,1-20*, 2003. Esp. 54-55
    [ἐγένετο ἐπί + acc. = arriva, vint: Lk 1,65; 3,2; 4,25.36; 23,44; Acts 5,5.11; 8,1; 10,10; 21,35].
MOST, William G., Did St. Luke Imitate the Septuagint? — *JSNT* 15 (1982) 30-41. Esp.
    33-38 [καί; καὶ ἐγένετο]. [NTA 27, 128]
MUDDIMAN, John, A Note on Reading Luke XXIV.12. — *ETL* 48 (1972) 542-548.
NEIRYNCK, Frans, The Uncorrected Historic Present in Lk XXIV.12. — *ETL* 48 (1972) 548-
    553; = ID., *Evangelica*, 1982, 329-334 (334: additional note; Appendix, *Evangelica II*,
    1991, 798).
—, La matière marcienne dans l'évangile de Luc, 1973. Esp. 183-193 [καὶ ἐγένετο]; [2]1989.
    Esp. 93-103; = ID., *Evangelica*, 1982. Esp. 63-67.
—, Once More Lk 24,12. — *ETL* 70 (1994) 319-340; = ID., *Evangelica III*, 2001, 549-571.
—, A Supplementary Note on Lk 24,12. — *ETL* 72 (1996) 425-430; = ID., *Evangelica III*,
    2001, 572-578.
—, Luke 24,12: An Anti-Docetic Interpolation? — DENAUX, A. (ed.), *New Testament
    Textual Criticism and Exegesis.* FS J. Delobel, 2002, 145-158. Esp. 148.
REILING, Jannes, The Use and Translation of *kai egeneto*, "and it happened", in the New
    Testament. — *BTrans* 16 (1965) 153-163.
SCHNEIDER, Gerhard, Engel und Blutschweiß (Lk 22,43-44): "Redaktionsgeschichte" im
    Dienste der Textkritik. — *BZ* NF 20 (1976) 112-116. Esp. 113-115: "Vokabular und Stil von
    Lk 22,43.44"; = ID., *Lukas, Theologe der Heilsgeschichte*, 1985, 153-157. Esp. 154-156.

γινώσκω 28 + 16/18 (Mt 20, Mk 12/14)

1. know (Lk 16,15); 2. learn (Lk 9,11); 3. be familiar with; 4. understand (Lk 12,39);
5. acknowledge; 6. have sexual intercourse (Lk 1,34)

Word groups	Lk	Acts	Mt	Mk
βούλομαι (+) γνῶναι → βούλομαι ἐπιγνῶναι; cf. Phil 1,12		17,20; 22,30	0	0
δύναμαι (+) γνῶναι→ δύναμαι + ἐπιγνῶναι		17,19; 21,34	0	0
γινώσκω followed by interrogative (VKb)	7,39; 10,22; 16,4; 19,15	17,19.20	2	0
γινώσκω + ἀναγινώσκω; cf. 2 Cor 3,2; νοέω + ἀναγινώσκω Mt 24,15; Mk 13,4		8,30	0	0
γινώσκω (+) ὅτι (VKa) → γινώσκω ὅτι; ἐπιγινώσκω + ὅτι	10,11; 12,39; 20,19; 21,20.30.31	2,36; 17,13; 20,34; 21,24; 23,6; 24,11*	5	5
γινώσκω absolute (VKc)	2,43; 9,11		5	4/5
γινώσκω Christ (VKe)		19,15	0	0
γινώσκω sexual meaning (VKf)	1,34		1	0

Characteristic of Luke	Lk	Acts	Mt	Mk
γινώσκω ὅτι → γινώσκω + ὅτι GOULDER 1989	10,11; 12,39; 21,20.30.31	20,34	3	2
γινώσκω + τίς/τί DENAUX 2009 L***; GOULDER 1989*	7,39; 10,22; 16,4; 19,15	17,19.20	2	0[1]

Literature

RADL 1975 402 [βούλομαι (ἐπι)γνῶναι]; 406 [δύναμαι + (ἐπι)γνῶναι]; REHKOPF 1959 92 [γινώσκω + τίς/τί: vorlukanisch]; SCHÜRMANN 1961 279-280 [γινώσκω + τίς/τί; protoluk R weniger wahrscheinlich].

BAUER, Johannes Baptist, Monstra te esse matrem, Virgo singularis! Zur Diskussion um Lk 1,34. — MüTZ 9 (1958) 124-135. [ἄνδρα οὐ γινώσκω]

—, Philologische Bemerkungen zu Lk 1,34. — Bib 45 (1964) 535-540. [ἄνδρα οὐ γινώσκω]

BRINKMANN, B., Die Jungfrauengeburt und das Lukasevangelium. — Bib 34 (1953) 327-332. [ἄνδρα οὐ γινώσκω]

DANOVE, Paul, Verbs of Experience, 1999. Esp. 158-159.174.

DELEBECQUE, Édouard., Études grecques, 1976. Esp. 46-47 [2,41-52].

DICKERSON, Patrick L., The New Character Narrative in Luke-Acts, 1997. Esp. 293-298: "The elements of the Lukan new character narrative" [τις/ἰδοὺ ἀνὴρ/γυνὴ ὀνόματι]; 303-305: "The use of ἀνήρ in the introduction".

GEWIEß, Josef, Die Marienfrage, Lk 1,34. — BZ NF 5 (1961) 221-254. [ἄνδρα οὐ γινώσκω]

GRANT, Frederik Clifton, Where Form Criticism and Textual Criticism Overlap. — JBL 59 (1940) 11-21. Esp. 19-21 [Lk 1,43: γινώσκω rather than ἔγνω or ἔγνωκα against Luke's style].

MCKAY, K.L., On the Perfect and Other Aspects in New Testament Greek, 1981. Esp. 297-309: "Knowing".

QUECKE, Hans, Lk 1,34 in den alten Übersetzungen und im Protevangelium des Jakobus. — Bib 44 (1963) 499-520. [ἄνδρα οὐ γινώσκω]

ZERWICK, Maximilian., "… quoniam virum non cognosco" (Lc 1,34) (Conspectus criticus de opinionibus recentioribus). — VD 37 (1959) 212-224, 276-288. [ἄνδρα οὐ γινώσκω]

γλῶσσα 2 + 6 (Mk 2[3])

1. tongue (Lk 16,24); 2. language (Acts 2,4); 3. ecstatic language (Acts 10,46); 4. speech (activity) (Acts 2,26); 5. speech (faculty) (Lk 1,64); 6. utterance; 7. person

Word groups	Lk	Acts	Mt	Mk
γλώσσαις (+) λαλέω (VKa)		2,4.11; 10,46; 19,6	0	0[1]
γλῶσσαι BOISMARD 1984 Da4		2,3.4.11; 10,46; 19,6	0	0[1]

Characteristic of Luke
DENAUX 2009 1A*.

Literature
HESS, Harwood, A Study of *glōssa* in the New Testament. — *BTrans* 15 (1964) 93-96.
RIUS-CAMPS, Josep, Pentecostés versus Babel. Estudio crítico de Hch 2. — *FilolNT* 1
(1988) 35-61. Esp. 36-40 [structure of the text]; 40-45 [meaning of γλῶσσαι]; 45-51 [OT
background and languages in the ancient time: Gen 11,1-9].

γνωρίζω 2 + 1/2

1. know (Lk 2,17); 2. make known (Lk 2,15)

Literature
DENAUX 2009 La[n]; EASTON 1910 152 [probably characteristic of L].
DANOVE, Paul, Verbs of Experience, 1999. Esp. 165-166.176-177.

γνῶσις 2

1. acquaintance (Lk 1,77); 2. knowledge; 3. esoteric knowledge; 4. understanding (Lk
11,52)

Literature
DENAUX 2009 L[n]; EASTON 1910 152 [probably characteristic of L]; GERSDORF 1816 212 [οὖ
δοῦναι γνῶσιν]; HARNACK 1906 145.

γνωστός 2 + 10

1. what is known (Acts 15,18; 28,11); 2. well known (Lk 2,44); 3. remarkable (Acts
4,16); 4. what can be known; 5. friend (Lk 23,49); 6. extraordinary (Acts 4,16)

Word groups	Lk	Acts	Mt	Mk
οἱ γνωστοί (VKb) DENAUX 2009 L[n]	2,44; 23,49		0	0

Characteristic of Luke; cf. ἄγνωστος Acts 17,23; γνώστης Acts 26,3
BOISMARD 1984 Bb85; DENAUX 2009 1A*; HARNACK 1906 149; HAWKINS 1909B;
MORGENTHALER 1958A;

	Lk	Acts	Mt	Mk
γνωστός/-ης/ἄγνωστος BOISMARD 1984 Bb85; DENAUX 2009 1A*; NEIRYNCK 1985	2,44; 23,49	1,19; 2,14; 4,10.16; 9,42; 13,38; 15,18; 17,23; 19,17; 26,3; 28,22.28	0	0

Literature
EASTON 1910 152 [probably characteristic of L]; GERSDORF 1816 265 [ἐν τοῖς συγγενεῦσιν

καὶ τοῖς γνωστοῖς]; HAUCK 1934 [Vorzugswort]; JEREMIAS 1980 100 [γνωστός "substantivisch mit Artikel im Plural von Personen": trad.; "adjektivisch von Sachen": red.] .

γογγύζω 1 (Mt 1)   complain

Word groups	Lk	Acts	Mt	Mk
γογγύζω + λέγων	5,30		0	0
γογγύζω + πρός; cf. γογγύζω κατά (VKb) Mt 20,11	5,30		0	0

Literature
EASTON 1910 152 [probably characteristic of L]; JEREMIAS 1980 68 [γογγύζω + λέγων]; PLUMMER 1922 lxii [After verbs of speaking, answering, and the like he very often has πρός and the accusative instead of the simple dative. Thus, we have ... γογγύζειν πρός (v.30)].

γονεῖς 6 (Mt 1, Mk 1)   parents (Lk 2,41.43;8,56)

Word groups	Lk	Acts	Mt	Mk
γονεῖς + παιδίον/τέκνον	2,27; 18,29		1	1
φίλος + ἀδελφός + συγγενής + γονεῖς	21,16		0	0
γονεῖς general (VKa)	18,29; 21,16		1	1

Characteristic of Luke
DENAUX 2009 L***; GOULDER 1989*; HAWKINS 1909L.

Literature
VON BENDEMANN 2001 427: "Die Verbindung von φίλος mit 'Verwandten' und 'Nachbarn' ist lukanisch'"; HAUCK 1934 [Vorzugswort]; JEREMIAS 1980 95: "Das unsemitische γονεῖς ist lukanisch".

γόνυ 2 + 4 (Mk 1)
1. knee (Lk 5,8; 22,41); 2. person

Word groups	Lk	Acts	Mt	Mk
γόνυ (+) προσεύχομαι DENAUX 2009 1A[n]	22,41	9,40; 20,36; 21,5	0	0
προσπίπτω τοῖς γόνασιν → πίπτω ἐπὶ/παρὰ/πρὸς τοὺς πόδας; cf. γονυπετέω Mt 17,14; 27,29; Mk 1,40; 10,17	5,8		0	0

Characteristic of Luke
DENAUX 2009 1A*.

	Lk	Acts	Mt	Mk
θεὶς τὰ γόνατα (LN: kneel down; VKa); cf. τιθεὶς τὰ γόνατα Mk 15,19; κάμπτω γόνυ Rom 11,4; 14,11; Eph 3,14; Phil 2,10) BOISMARD 1984 Bb64; CREDNER 1836 139; HARNACK 1906 53; HAWKINS 1909 187; NEIRYNCK 1985; VOGEL 1899C	22,41	7,60; 9,40; 20,36; 21,5	0	0

Literature
DENAUX 2009 1A[n] [θεὶς τὰ γόνατα]; EASTON 1910 167 [classed by Weiss as characteristic of L on insufficient (?) evidence]; HAUCK 1934 [Vorzugswort; Vorzugsverbindung: θεὶς τὰ γόνατα];

JEREMIAS 1980 294: "τιθέναι τὰ γόνατα ('die Knie beugen') ist eine fest eingebürgerte, jedoch nicht klassische Wendung, die sich im NT außer Mk 15,19 nur im lk Doppelwerk findet (…), gern mit προσεύχομαι verbunden"; RADL 1975 404 [γόνυ; θεὶς τὰ γόνατα + προσεύχομαι].

γράμμα 2/3 + 2

1. letter of alphabet (Lk 23,38 v.l.); 2. a writing; 3. epistle (Acts 28,21); 4. record of debts (Lk 16,6.7)

Literature

BORMANN, Lukas, *Recht, Gerechtigkeit und Religion*, 2001. Esp. 149-150.

γραμματεύς 14/15 + 4 (Mt 22/24, Mk 21/22)

1. expert in the Law (Lk 5,21); 2. scholar; 3. town clerk (Acts 19,35)

Word groups	Lk	Acts	Mt	Mk
γραμματεῖς + ἀρχιερεῖς + πρεσβυτέριον	22,66		0	0
γραμματεῖς + ἀρχιερεύς/εῖς (SCb; VKa)	9,22; 19,47; 20,1.19; 22,2.66; 23,10		5/6	9
γραμματεῖς + ἀρχιερεύς/εῖς + πρεσβύτεροι	9,22; 20,1		3	5
γραμματεῖς + ἄρχοντες + πρεσβύτεροι		4,5	0	0
γραμματεῖς + ἱερεῖς	20,1 v.l.		0	0
γραμματεῖς καὶ Φαρισαῖοι ὑποκριταί	11,44*		6/7	0
γραμματεῖς + πρεσβύτεροι (SCc)	9,22; 20,1	4,5; 6,12	3	5
γραμματεῖς + Φαρισαῖοι (SCa; VKb)	5,21.30; 6,7; 11,44*.53; 15,2		23,9	10/11	3/4

Characteristic of Luke

GASTON 1973 65 [Lked?]

Literature

COLLISON 1977 169 [ἀρχιερεύς + γραμματεύς: linguistic usage of Luke: certain]; 171 [γραμματεῖς καὶ φαρισαῖοι: certain]; EASTON 1910 159 [Φαρισαῖοι καὶ γραμματεῖς: cited by Weiss as characteristic of L, and possibly corroborative].

CLAUSSEN, Carsten, *Versammlung, Gemeinde, Synagoge*, 2002. Esp. 280-281: "Γραμματεύς".

KILPATRICK, George D., Scribes, Lawyers and Lucan Origins. — *JTS* NS 1 (1950) 56-60; = ID., *Principles and Practice*, 1990, 245-249.

—, The Gentiles and the Strata of Luke. — BÖCHER, O. – HAACKER, K. (eds.), *Verborum Veritas*. FS G. Stählin, 1970, 83-88. Esp. 85-86; = ID., *Principles and Practice*, 1990, 313-318. Esp. 315-316.

KLIJN, Albertus F.J., Scribes, Pharisees, Highpriests and Elders in the New Testament. — *NT* 3 (1959) 259-267.

γραφή 4 + 7 (Mt 4, Mk 3/4)

1. passage (Lk 4,21); 2. Scripture (Lk 24,27.32.45; Acts 1,16)

Word groups	Lk	Acts	Mt	Mk
γραφή + πληρόω (VKc) → γεγραμμένα/λόγος/ ῥῆμα + πληρόω	4,21	1,16	2	1/2

			0	0
διανοίγω + τὰς γραφάς → (ἀνα)πτύσσω/ἀνοίγω τὸ βιβλίον	24,32		0	0
πᾶσαι αἱ γραφαί → πάντα τὰ γεγραμμένα	24,27		0	0
συνίημι τὰς γραφάς	24,45		0	0
αἱ γραφαί (SCa; VKa)	24,27.32.45	17,2.11; 18,24.28	4	2

Characteristic of Luke	Lk	Acts	Mt	Mk
ἡ γραφὴ αὕτη BOISMARD 1984 cb104; NEIRYNCK 1985	4,21	8,35	0	1

Literature

BORMANN, Lukas, *Recht, Gerechtigkeit und Religion*, 2001. Esp. 133-134.

γράφω 20/22 + 12 (Mt 10, Mk 10) write

Word groups	Lk	Acts	Mt	Mk
γεγραμμένα + πίμπλημι	21,22		0	0
γεγραμμένα + πληρόω → γραφή/λόγος/ῥῆμα + πληρόω	21,22 v.l.; 24,44		0	0
γράφω λέγων	1,63		0	0
γράφω + νόμος DENAUX 2009 La[n] (?)	2,23; 10,26; 24,44	24,14	0	0
γράφω + περί + gen.; cf. γράφω ἐπί + acc. Mk 9,12.13	7,27; 24,44	13,29; 25,26[1]	2	1
καθὼς/ὡς γέγραπται Μωϋσῆς ἔγραψεν; cf. Μωϋσῆς + γράφω Lk 24,44; Mk 10,4	2,23; 3,4 20,28	7,42; 13,33; 15,15	1 0	4/5 1
γέγραπται (SCa; VKa) → γέγραπται ἐν βίβλῳ	2,23; 3,4; 4,4.8.10; 7,27; 10,26; 19,46; 24,46	1,20; 7,42; 13,33; 15,15; 23,5	9	7

Characteristic of Luke

GOULDER 1989

	Lk	Acts	Mt	Mk
γεγραμμένος (SCb; VKb); cf. ἐπιγεγραμμένος Mk 15,26 DENAUX 2009 L***	4,17; 18,31; 20,17; 21,22; 22,37; 24,44	13,29; 24,14	1	0
γέγραπται ἐν βίβλῳ → γέγραπται; cf. ἐν τῇ βίβλῳ τῆς ζωῆς γεγραμμένος Rev 20,15 BOISMARD 1984 Ab109; NEIRYNCK 1985	3,4	1,20; 7,42	0	0
πάντα τὰ γεγραμμένα; cf. Gal 3,10[2] → πᾶσαι αἱ γραφαί BOISMARD 1984 Bb98; NEIRYNCK 1985; SCHÜRMANN 1953 11;	18,31; 21,22; 24,44	13,29; 24,14	0	0
τελέω τὸ γεγραμμένον / τὰ γεγραμμένα BOISMARD 1984 Ab147; NEIRYNCK 1985	18,31; 22,37	13,29		
τὸ γεγραμμένον/ τὰ γεγραμμένα DENAUX 2009 L***; GOULDER 1989	18,31; 20,17; 21,22; 22,37; 24,44		0	0

Literature

COLLISON 1977 92 [substantivised perfect participle: noteworthy phenomena]; DENAUX 2009 lA[n] [γέγραπται ἐν βίβλῳ], La[n] [πάντα τὰ γεγραμμένα; τελέω τὸ γεγραμμένον / τὰ γεγραμμένα]; GERSDORF 1816 160 [ἔδοξε κἀμοὶ ... γράψαι]; JEREMIAS 1980 68 [γράφω + λέγων: red.]; 103 [3,4: ὡς γέγραπται: red.; γέγραπται ἐν βίβλῳ: red.]; 292-293 [τὸ γεγραμμένον / πάντα τὰ γεγραμμένα: red.]; SCHÜRMANN 1957 124 [τὸ γεγραμμένον, τὰ γεγραμμένα: luk R sehr wahrscheinlich].

BARTSCH, Hans-Werner, Jesu Schwertwort, Lukas XXII. 35-38: Überlieferungsgeschichtliche Studie. — NTS 20 (1973-74) 190-203. Esp. 196-198: "Die Handschrift des Lukas".
BORMANN, Lukas, Recht, Gerechtigkeit und Religion, 2001. Esp. 134.
CHILTON, Bruce, Announcement in Nazara, 1981. Esp. 157-158.
JUNG, Chang-Wook, Infancy Narrative, 2004. Esp. 69.77-78 [καθὼς γέγραπται].
KÜRZINGER, Joseph, Lk 1,3: ... ἀκριβῶς καθεξῆς σοι γράψαι. — BZ NF 18 (1974) 249-255. [NTA 19, 575]

γρηγορέω 1/2 + 1 (Mt 6, Mk 6)

1. stay awake (Lk 12,37.39 v.l.); 2. be alert (Acts 20,31); 3. be alive

Word groups	Lk	Acts	Mt	Mk
γρηγορεῖτε imperative (SCa; VKa) → ἀγρυπνεῖτε		20,31	4	4

Literature
DUPONT, Jacques, Le discours de Milet, 1962. Esp. 219-222.363.

γυνή 41/44 + 19 (Mt 29/30, Mk 17/19)

1. woman (Acts 22,4); 2. wife (Lk 1,5)

Word groups	Lk	Acts	Mt	Mk
ἄνδρες (τε) καὶ γυναῖκες (SCf) → ἀνήρ + γυνή; cf. ἄνδρες χωρὶς γυναικῶν Mt 14,21; 15,38 BOISMARD 1984 Aa13		5,14; 8,3.12; 9,2; 17,12; 22,4	0	0
ἀνήρ + γυνή → ἄνδρες (τε) καὶ γυναῖκες; cf. ἄνθρωπος + γυνή Mt 19,3.5.10; Mk 10,7	16,18	5,1.14; 8,3.12; 9,2; 17,12.34; 22,4	2	1
ἀπολύω γυναῖκα (SCb; VKb); cf. ἀπολύω ἄνδρα Mk 10,12	16,18		5	2
γαμέω + γυναῖκα (SCd; VKd)	14,20; 16,18		1	1/2
γυνή + ἁμαρτωλός → ἀνήρ/ἄνθρωπος ἁμαρτωλός DENAUX 2009 Lⁿ	7,37.39		0	0
γυνὴ αὕτη → ἀνὴρ/ἄνθρωπος ἐκεῖνος/ οὗτος	7,44		0	0
γυνὴ Ἰουδαία → ἀνὴρ/ἄνθρωπος Ἰουδαῖος		16,1	0	0
γυνή + τέκνον	14,26; 18,29; 20,29(-31)	21,5	2/3	1/2
γυνὴ χήρα	4,26		0	0
εὐσχήμων γυνή		13,50; 17,12	0	0
ἔχω (+) γυναῖκα (SCe; VKe)	20,28¹.33³		0	2
καὶ ἰδοὺ γυνή → (καὶ) ἰδού + ἀνήρ/ἄνθρωπος	7,37; 13,11		2	0
λαμβάνω + γυναῖκα (SCc; VKc); cf. παραλαμβάνω γυναῖκα Mt 1,20.24	20,28².29.30*		0	2
τις + γυνὴ ἐκ τοῦ ὄχλου → ἀνὴρ/τις ἐκ τοῦ ὄχλου	11,27		0	0
γυνὴ ὀνόματι + proper name → ἀνήρ/ ἄνθρωπος (ὀνόματι / ᾧ ὄνομα) + proper name DENAUX 2009 IAⁿ	10,38	16,14; 17,34		
γύνη vocative (SCa; VKa) → ἄνδρες/ἄνθρωπε voc.	13,12; 22,57		1	0

Characteristic of Luke	Lk	Acts	Mt	Mk
ἀνήρ/γυνή + geographic origin BOISMARD 1984 BA7	11,32	1,11; 2,14.22[1]; 3,12; 5,35; 8,27; 10,28; 11,20; 13,16; 16,9; 17,22; 19,35; 21,28; 22,3	2	0
γυναῖκες nominative → οἱ ἄνδρες nom. DENAUX 2009 L***	8,2; 23,49.55; 24,22.24	8,12	1	1
γυνή τις/γυναῖκες τινες → ἀνήρ/ἄνθρωπός τις DENAUX 2009 L***	8,2; 10,38; 11,27; 24,22	16,14	0	0

Literature

DENAUX 2009 lAn [ἀνήρ/γυνή + geographic origin]; HAUCK 1934 [Vorzugsverbindung: γυνή (δέ) τις; γυναῖκες τινες]; JEREMIAS 1980 228 [γυνὴ πνεῦμα ἔχουσα ἀσθενείας: red.]; RADL 1975 404 [γυνή]; 411 [εὐσχήμων γυνή]; REHKOPF 1959 98 [γύναι: "Substantiva in Anrede bei den Synoptikern"].

DICKERSON, Patrick L., The New Character Narrative in Luke-Acts, 1997, 291-312. Esp. 293-298: "The elements of the Lukan new character narrative" [τις/ἰδοὺ ἀνὴρ/γυνὴ ὀνόματι].

γωνία 1 + 2 (Mt 2, Mk 1) | corner

Word groups	Lk	Acts	Mt	Mk
εἰς κεφαλὴν γωνίας (VKa; LN: cornerstone); cf. 1 Pet 2,7	20,17	4,11	1	1

Δ

δαιμονίζομαι 1 (Mt 7, Mk 4) | be demon possessed

Word groups	Lk	Acts	Mt	Mk
δαιμονίζομαι σῴζω	8,36		0	0
ὁ δαιμονισθείς (VKa)	8,36		0	1

δαιμόνιον 23 + 1 (Mt 11, Mk 11[13])
1. demon (Lk 4,33); 2. god (Acts 17,18)

Word groups	Lk	Acts	Mt	Mk
ἄρχων τῶν δαιμονίων (SCd; VKd)	11,15[1]		2	1
δαιμόνιον ἀκάθαρτον	4,33		0	0
δαιμόνιον ἐκβάλλω (SCa; VKa); cf. σατανᾶν ἐκβάλλω Mt 12,26; Mk 3,23	9,49; 11,14[1].15[2].18.19.20; 13,32		7	7[9]
δαιμόνιον ἔχω (SCc; VKc); cf. ἔχω πνεῦμα δαιμονίου ἀκαθάρτου Lk 4,33	7,33; 8,27		1	0
δαιμόνιον + πνεῦμα + ἀκάθαρτος; cf. Rev 18,2 DENAUX 2009 L[n]	4,33; 8,29; 9,42		0	0

Characteristic of Luke

GASTON 1973 64 [Lked]; GOULDER 1989

	Lk	Acts	Mt	Mk
δαιμόνιον ἐξέρχεται (SCb; VKb); cf. δαιμόνιον εἰσέρχεται Lk 8,30.33 DENAUX 2009 L***	4,35.41; 8,2.33.35.38; 11,14[2]		1	2

Literature

BDAG 2000 210 [literature]; VON BENDEMANN 2001 413; COLLISON 1977 171 [linguistic usage of Luke: certain]; HAUCK 1934 [Vorzugswort]; JEREMIAS 1980 177: "Kein neutestamentlicher Autor gebraucht δαιμόνιον so oft wie Lukas".

FERRARO, Giuseppe, "Oggi e domani e il terzo giorno" (osservazioni su *Luca* 13,32,33). — *RivBib* 16 (1968) 397-407. Esp. 401-407: "Considerazioni sul vocabolario di Luca 13,32.33" [ἐκβάλλειν δαιμόνια; ἰάσεις ἀποτελῶ; τελειοῦσθαι e πορεύεσθαι; ἀπολέσθαι].

δάκρυον 2 + 2 (Mk 0/1)   tear

Word groups	Lk	Acts	Mt	Mk
τοῖς δάκρυσιν βρέχω (VKa) DENAUX 2009 L[n]	7,38.44		0	0

Characteristics

DENAUX 2009 LA[n].

δακτύλιος 1   ring (Lk 15,22)

Literature

HAUCK 1934 [seltenes Alleinwort].

BORMANN, Lukas, *Recht, Gerechtigkeit und Religion*, 2001. Esp. 150.

δάκτυλος 3 (Mt 1, Mk 1)

1. finger (Lk 11,46); 2. power (Lk 11,20; 16,24)

Word groups	Lk	Acts	Mt	Mk
δάκτυλος θεοῦ (VKa)	11,20		0	0

Characteristic of Luke

GOULDER 1989

Literature

GEORGE, Augustin, Note sur quelques traits lucaniens de l'expression "Par le doigt de Dieu" (Luc XI,20). — *Sciences Ecclésiastiques* 18 (1966) 461-466; = "Par le doigt de Dieu" (Luc 11,20). — ID., *Études*, 1978, 127-132.

HAMERTON-KELLY, Robert G., A Note on Matthew XII. 28 par. Luke XI. 20. — *NTS* 11 (1964-65) 167-169.

VAN CANGH, Jean-Marie, "Par l'esprit de Dieu – par le doigt de Dieu" Mt 12,28 par. Lc 11,20. — DELOBEL, Joël (ed.), *Logia*, 1982, 337-342.

WOODS, Edward J., *The "Finger of God" and Pneumatology in Luke-Acts* (JSNT SS, 205). Sheffield: Academic Press, 2001, 305 p. Esp. 61-100: "Background to the Finger of God".

δανειστής 1   moneylender (Lk 7,41)

Literature

HAUCK 1934 [seltenes Alleinwort].

BORMANN, Lukas, *Recht, Gerechtigkeit und Religion*, 2001. Esp. 150.

δανίζω 3 (Mt 1)

1. give a loan (Lk 6,34[1.2].35); 2. δανίζομαι: borrow money

δαπανάω 1 + 1 (Mk 1)

1. spend (Acts 21,24); 2. waste (Lk 15,14?); 3. exert effort

Literature

EASTON 1910 160 [cited by Weiss as characteristic of L, and possibly corroborative]; PAFFENROTH 1997 80.

BORMANN, Lukas, *Recht, Gerechtigkeit und Religion*, 2001. Esp. 150.

δαπάνη 1   expense (Lk 14,28)

Literature

EASTON 1910 160 [cited by Weiss as characteristic of L, and possibly corroborative]; HAUCK 1934 [seltenes Alleinwort]; PAFFENROTH 1997 80.

BORMANN, Lukas, *Recht, Gerechtigkeit und Religion*, 2001. Esp. 150.

Δαυίδ 13 + 11 (Mt 17, Mk 7)   David

Word groups	Lk	Acts	Mt	Mk
οἶκος (+) Δαυίδ (VKb)	1,27.69; 2,4[2]		0	0
DENAUX 2009 L[n]				
παῖς Δαυίδ	1,69	4,25	0	0
πατριὰ Δαυίδ	2,4[2]		0	0
πόλις Δαυίδ	2,4[1].11		0	0
σκηνὴ Δαυίδ		15,16	0	0
σπέρμα + Δαυίδ → Ἀβραάμ + σπέρμα		13,22[2](-23)	0	0
υἱὸς (+) Δαυίδ (SCa; VKa) → Ἰησοῦς υἱὸς Δαυίδ	18,38.39; 20,41.44		11	4

Literature

GERSDORF 1816 206-207 [Δαυίδ (τοῦ) παιδὸς αὐτοῦ; ἐν οἴκῳ Δαυίδ]; 217 [ἀνέβη δὲ καὶ Ἰωσὴφ - εἰς πόλιν Δαυίδ - ἀπογράψασθαι]; REHKOPF 1959 99 [υἱὲ Δαυίδ: "Substantiva in Anrede bei den Synoptikern"].

FUCHS, Albert, *Sprachliche Untersuchungen zu Mattäus und Lukas*, 1971. Esp. 94-100
[υἱὸς Δαυίδ].
GEORGE, Augustin, La royauté de Jésus. — ID., *Études*, 1978, 257-282. Esp. 262-265:
"Descendant de David".
HAHN, Ferdinand, *Christologische Hoheitstitel*, 1963. Esp. 242-279: "Davidssohn".
RESE, Martin, *Alttestamentliche Motive in der Christologie des Lukas*, 1969. Esp. 204-205:
"Σωτήρ, Χριστός [υἱὸς Δαυίδ] im Lukasevangelium".

δέ 542/575 + 554/596 (Mt 494/520, Mk 155[163]/208)

1. and (Lk 7,6); 2. and then; 3. but (Lk 6,2)

Word groups	Lk	Acts	Mt	Mk
δέ after participle (except in absolute genitive) (VKh) → δέ in absolute genitive	1,22.39; 2,17.44; 3,11; 4,38[1]; 5,3[1.2].8.12.22; 6,40; 7,3.9.20. 39.43*; 8,24[1].25[2].27.28.33. 34.47.51; 9,1.6.12[2].16.32[2]. 41.49.54.55; 10,30*.34.40[2]. 41; 11,37[2].45; 13,12.14; 14,15; 17,17[1].20; 18,15[2].22. 24.31.36.40[1]; 19,8.13.32; 20,3.14.16.23.24.27.39; 21,1; 22,13.40.49.51.54[1]. 56; 23,11.28.34[2].40.47.55. 56; 24,3.18. 37	2,14.37; 3,4.12; 4,13.15. 23; 5,5.6.10[2].17.21[1.2]. 22[2].23.25.27.29.34; 6,2; 7,12.14.54.55.57.60; 8,14.18.24.30.34.35. 37[2]*; 9,8[3].25.26.30.37[2]. 39.40[1].41[1.2]; 10,21.34; 11,4.18.28; 12,3[1].7.10. 14.16[2].17; 13,6.13[1].16. 45.46[1]*.48; 14,14.23.27; 15,4.31.33; 16,6.7.8. 11[1].18[2].19.29.40; 17,1.5.6.19*.22.32[1]; 18,17.26; 19,5.8.15[1]. 22.28.34.35; 20,2.9.10. 11; 21,3.4; 22,2.26.27[1]; 23,1.6[1].16.17.19.28*.34; 24,7*.22; 25,6.20; 27,2. 29*.35.38.41[1]; 28,23	67/76	5[6]/12
δέ after preposition (VKg)	1,24.26; 5,5; 8,40.42; 10,1. 38[1]; 11,37[1]; 18,4; 19,26; 21,12	5,12; 6,1; 9,3; 11,15; 13,15; 15,13.36; 16,25[1]; 17,2.16; 18,1*; 19,33[1]; 20,1.7.17; 21,15.25; 24,1.24; 27,33; 28,7.11	16/18	7[9]
δέ opposition, without μέν (VKb) → μὲν … δέ	4,30; 5,16.33[2]; 6,30*.41[2]; 7,28.30.41.44.45.46.47; 8,10[2].12.13.14.15; 9,8[1.2]. 19[2.3].20[2].24.25.58; 10,10. 16.20.40[1].42.42*; 11,16. 20.22.34.39[2].47; 12,9.10.30. 48[1].56; 13,16.28; 15,17[2].30; 16,15.25[2.3]; 17,17[2].33.35; 18,13.14.39; 19,26.42; 20,6. 35; 21,4.33.37[2]; 22,26.28.68; 23,9[2].18[2].25[2]; 24,24	5,39[1]; 7,49; 8,7.16; 11,17*; 12,9; 14,12; 15,38; 16,1[2]; 17,18[2]; 20,6.15[1.2]; 21,1[2].6; 22,28[3]; 23,6[2].15.29; 25,19; 27,28.39[2]; 28,16*	69/70	16[17]/20
εἰ μὲν … εἰ δέ; cf. 2 Cor 11,4 BOISMARD 1984 Aa87		18,(14-)15; 19,(38-)39; 25,11	0	0
ἐπειδὴ δέ		13,46*	0	0
ἔτι δέ DENAUX 2009 La[n]	9,42[1]; 14,26*; 15,20; 22,47*; 24,41	2,26	0/1	0
ἡ δέ as pronoun (VKd)	1,29	5,8[2]; 9,40[2]; 12,15[2]	3	2/3
ἤδη δέ	3,9; 7,6[2]		1	0
ἵνα δέ	5,24	24,4	2	1

	Lk	Acts	Mt	Mk
καθὼς δέ time →ὡς δέ		7,17	0	0
μὲν ... δέ (LN: ᵃsome ... others, ᵇon the one hand ... on the other hand; VKa) → δέ opposition without μέν	3,16.17 v.l.(18-)19; 10,2^2.6 v.l.; 11,48; 13,9; 23,33.41	1,5; 2,(41-)42; 3,(13-)14; 5,23 v.l.; 8,(4-)5.(25-)26; 9,7^2.(31-)32; 11,16^2. (19-)20; 12,5; 13,(36-)37; 14,(3-)4$^{1.2}$.12 v.l.; 15,(3-)4.(30-)31; 16,(5-)6; 17,(12-)13.(17-)18^1.32^2; 18,(14-)15; 19,15^2.(38-)39; 21,39; 22,3 v.l.9^2; 23,8.(18-)19.(31-)32; 25,4.11; 27,41^2.44; 28,(5-)6^1.24	27	3[4]/7
νῦν δέ →ἀλλὰ νῦν DENAUX 2009 L^n	16,25; 19,42^2; 22,69		0	0
οἱ δέ as pronoun (VKe)	5,33^1; 7,4; 8,12.13.25^2 v.l.; 9,13^2.19^1.45; 14,4; 19,34; 20,5.11.12.24; 22,9.35.38^1. 71; 23,5.21.23; 24,19.42	4,21.24; 5,33; 7,25^2; 9,29; 10,22; 12,15$^{1.3}$; 13,51; 14,4; 16,31; 17,18.32^2; 19,2.3; 21,20.32; 28,6^1.21.24	26/27	17/21
ὁ δέ as pronoun (VKc)	3,13; 4,40^2.43; 5,34 v.l.; 6,8*.10; 7,40.43; 8,10^1.21. 24^2.30^2.48.52^2.56; 9,21. 59^2; 10,26.27.29.37^1; 11,46; 12,14; 13,8.23^2; 14,16; 15,12.27.29.31; 16,6$^{1.2}$.7^2.30; 17,37; 18,21. 23.27.29.41; 20,17.25; 21,8; 22,10.25.33. 34.36.38^2.57.70^2; 23,3^2.22	3,5; 7,2; 8,31; 9,5^2.10^2; 10,4^1; 19,3*; 21,37; 22,14.27^2; 25,22*; 26,15^2 v.l.	41/45	27/31
ὃς δέ →ὃς μέν	7,47; 9,24; 10,5.8*.10; 12,20^2; 17,29.33; 20,18; 23,33	3,6^2; 13,37; 27,44	18	5
ὅταν δέ →ὅτε δέ	12,11; 21,9.20		6	3/4
ὅτι δέ		13,34	0	0
οὐαὶ δέ	17,1*; 21,23*		3/4	2
πάλιν δέ →πάλιν οὖν	23,20	18,21*	2	0
περὶ δέ →περὶ μὲν γάρ		21,25	4	2
δέ as fourth word (VKl)	22,69	3,1 v.l.; 5,32*; 22,29; 27,14	1	0
δέ as third word (VKk)	1,76; 2,35; 3,1; 4,25; 7,21*.42*; 9,8^1; 10.5.7.8*. 10.31; 12,56; 15,17^1; 18,4 v.l.; 20,18	9,36; 11,27; 12,1; 17,6; 19,27; 21,14.34^2; 24,16*.17; 25,9; 27,7.26; 28,6^2	5/6	2/3

→ἄλλοι δέ; ἀποκριθεὶς δέ (λέγω/εἶπεν); ὁ δὲ ἀποκριθεὶς λέγει/εἶπεν/ἔφη; ἐν δὲ τῷ + inf.
... καὶ αὐτός; ἄχρι (δὲ) οὗ; ἐγένετο δὲ (ἐν τῷ + inf.) ... καὶ αὐτός/αὐτοί; ἐὰν (δὲ/γὰρ) μή;
ἐγὼ (δέ) (λέγω ὑμῖν); εἰ δέ; εἰ δέ τις/τι; εὐθέως δέ (τότε); ἡμεῖς δέ; οὐ μόνον (δέ) ... ἀλλά;
ὁμοίως (δὲ) καί; οὐ ... δέ; οὐδεὶς (...) δέ; παραγενόμενος δέ + subj.; παρεγένετο δέ;
παραχρῆμα δέ; πᾶς δέ; σὺ/σοῦ δέ; ὑμεῖς δέ; ὡσαύτως (δὲ) καί

Characteristic of Luke

CADBURY 1920 142-144; GASTON 1973 64 [Lked]; HENDRIKS 1986 428.434.448.466.468; PLUMMER 1922 lxiii [δέ in quoting sayings]; SCHÜRMANN 1953 76-77.

	Lk	Acts	Mt	Mk
participle + δὲ καί + participle BOISMARD 1984 Ab49; NEIRYNCK 1985	24,37	14,27; 19,28; 20,11; 23,34	0	0

αὐτὸς δέ →καὶ αὐτός DENAUX L***	4,30; 5,16; 6,8¹.11; 7,21*; 8,37.54; 10,7; 11,17.28; 18,39; 23,9²; 24,24.31	13,14; 18,19²; 25,25²	4	2
δέ in absolute genitive (VKj) → δέ after participle; cf. Jn 4,51; 12,37; 18,22; 21,4; 1 Cor 4,18; Gal 3,25; Heb 9,6 BOISMARD 1984 cb94; NEIRYNCK 1985	3,15; 4,40¹.42; 6,48; 7,6².24.42*; 8,4.23.45; 9,34¹.42¹. 43²; 11,29.53*; 15,14.20; 18,40²; 19,11.33.36.37; 20,45; 21,28; 22,47*.55; 24,5.36.41	2,6; 3,11; 4,1; 7,21.31²; 9,8².38; 10,10².19; 12,13.18; 13,2.42.43; 14,20; 15,2.7; 16,35; 17,16; 18,6.12.14.20.27; 19,30; 20,7; 21,10.14.17. 31*.34².40¹·²; 22,23*; 23,7.10.12.30; 24,2.25¹.27; 25,7.13.21.25²; 26,24; 27,9.12.13.15.18.20.21*. 30; 28,3.6².9.17.19	30/31	1/4
δὲ καί; cf. Jn 2,2; 3,23; 15,24; 18,2.5.18²; 19,19¹.39; 21,25; δὲ κἀκεῖνος Lk 20,11 BOISMARD 1984 Eb61; CREDNER 1836 135; DENAUX 2009 L***; GOULDER 1989*; HAWKINS 1909L; NEIRYNCK 1985; PLUMMER 1922 lxiii; SCHÜRMANN 1957 65-66	2,4; 3,9.12; 4,41; 5,10.36¹; 6,6 v.l.39; 9,61¹; 10,32; 11,18; 12,54.57; 14,12.26*.34; 15,28¹.32; 16,1.22²; 18,1 v.l.9; 19,19; 20,12.31; 21,2 v.l.16; 22,24.68 v.l.; 23,32.35.38.55 v.l.; 24,37	2,7.26; 3,1; 5,16; 9,24²; 11,7; 12,25; 13,5; 14,27; 15,32*.35; 16,1¹; 17,18¹; 19,27*.28.31; 20,11; 21,16; 22,28²; 23,34; 24,9.26*	6/8	2/3
εἰ δὲ μή γε; cf. εἰ δὲ μή γε Mk 2,21.22 CREDNER 1836 137; DENAUX 2009 L***; GOULDER 1989 HAWKINS 1909L; PLUMMER 1922 lx	5,36².37; 10,6; 13,9; 14,32		2	0
ἰδών/ἰδόντες δέ →καὶ ἰδών/ἰδόντες BOISMARD 1984 cb164; GOULDER 1989 NEIRYNCK 1985	2,17; 5,8.12; 7,39; 8,28.34.47; 9,54; 13,12; 18,15².24; 20,14; 22,49.56; 23,47	3,12; 8,18; 12,3¹; 13,45	9	3
ὅτε δέ → ὅταν δέ BOISMARD 1984 Eb66; NEIRYNCK 1985; SCHÜRMANN 1953 105	15,30	8,12.39; 11,2; 12,6; 21,5.35; 27,39¹; 28,16	3	0/2
ὡς δέ → καθὼς δέ; cf. Jn 2,9.23; 6,12.16; 7,10; 8,7 BOISMARD 1984 Bb55; DENAUX 2009 IA*; NEIRYNCK 1985	5,4; 7,12	5,24; 7,23; 8,36; 9,23; 10,7.17.25; 13,25.29; 14,5; 16,4.10.15; 17,13; 18,5; 19,9.21; 20,14.18; 21,1¹.12.27; 22,11.25; 25,14; 27,1.27; 28,4	0/1	0

→ ἀκούσας/ἀκούων δέ; ὁ δὲ ἀκούων/ἀκούσας; ἀναστὰς/ἀναστάντες δέ; ὡς (δὲ) ἐτέλεσεν ἅπαντα/πάντα; ἀπεκρίθη δέ; αὐτὸς/αὐτοὶ δέ + participle; γενομένης δέ + subj.; ἐγένετο δέ; (καὶ) ἐγένετο (δὲ) ἐν τῷ + inf.; καὶ ἐγένετο (δὲ) + expression of time; πολὺς δέ + noun + γινόμενος; ἐξίσταντο δὲ πάντες; ἐγὼ δέ without λέγω ὑμῖν; ἔλεγεν δέ / ἔλεγον δέ; εἶπεν δέ / εἶπαν δέ; ὁ δὲ ... ἰδὼν ἐθαύμασεν; (καὶ) παραγενόμενος (δέ); πολὺς δέ; πρῶτον δέ; noun + δέ τις; participle + δέ τις; ὡς (δὲ) ἐγένετο

Literature

COLLISON 1977 47 [εἶπεν δέ beginning sentences: linguistic usage of Luke: certain]; 56 [ἔλεγεν δέ: certain; ἔλεγεν δὲ καί: likely]; 57 [λέγω δὲ ὑμῖν: probable]; 102 [εἰ δὲ μή γε: probable]; 103

[δὲ καί: certain; εἶναι δέ: probable]; 116 [καί and δέ: noteworthy phenomena]; 198 [ἐγὼ δέ: noteworthy phenomena]; DENAUX 2009 1Aⁿ [participle + δὲ καί + participle], 1An [ὅτε δέ]; EASTON 1910 177 [καὶ ἐγένετο, ἐγένετο δέ: possible Hebraisms in the Lucan Writings, as classed by Dalman]; GERSDORF 1816 217 [ἀνέβη δὲ καὶ Ἰωσὴφ - εἰς πόλιν Δαυίδ - ἀπογράψασθαι]; HAUCK 1934 [Vorzugsverbindung: εἶπεν δέ; ἐγένετο δέ; δὲ καί; εἰ δὲ μή γε]; JEREMIAS 1980 45 [ὡς δέ: red.]; 78-79 [δὲ καί: red.]; 258 [ἤκουον δέ: red.]; RADL 1975 400 [ἀποκρίνομαι + δέ]; 402 [ἐγένετο δέ]; 403 [ὅτε δὲ ἐγένετο]; 403 [ὡς δὲ ἐγένετο]; 404 [δέ; δὲ καί]; 406 [ἐγὼ δέ]; 407 [ἰδὼν δέ]; 408 [εἶπεν/εἶπαν δέ]; 430 [ὡς δέ]; SCHNEIDER 1969 85.164 [ὁ δέ + name + ἔφη: Bei Luk beliebte Konstruktionen]; 89.164 [εἶπεν δέ mit folgendem Subjekt: Bei Luk beliebte Konstruktionen]; 122.163 [δὲ πάντες: Vorzugswörter und -ausdrücke des Luk]; 125.164 [ὁ δέ ... ἔφη: Bei Luk beliebte Konstruktionen]; 127.164 [οἱ δὲ εἶπαν: Bei Luk beliebte Konstruktionen]; SCHÜRMANN 1953 76 [Lk δέ instead of Mk καί: luk R]; 1957 22 [ὁ (οἱ) δὲ εἶπεν (-ον, -αν)]; 73.86-87 [pers. pronoun + δέ: ein Verdacht auf luk R]; 121 [εἶπεν δὲ αὐτοῖς].

KING, G.A., Δέ. — ExpT 16 (1904-05) 43.
LARSEN, I., Notes on the Function of γάρ, οὖν, μέν, δέ, καί, and τέ in the Greek New Testament. — Notes on Translation (Dallas) 5 (1991) 35-47.
LEVISOHN, Stephen H., Textual Connections in Acts, 1987. Esp. 86-120: "de and kai".
MARTIN, Raymond A., Syntactical Evidence of Aramaic Sources in Acts I–XV, 1964. Esp. 40-41: "Proportions of δέ to καί".
MILLER, Herbert G., The Rendering of δέ in the New Testament. — ExpT 15 (1903-04) 551-555.
NEIRYNCK, Frans, La matière marcienne dans l'évangile de Luc, 1973. Esp. 183 [δὲ καί]; ²1989. Esp. 93; = ID., Evangelica, 1982. Esp. 63.
READ-HEIMERDINGER, Jenny, The Bezan Text of Acts, 2002. Esp. 204-211: "δέ, καί and τε".
THRALL, Margaret E., Greek Particles in the New Testament, 1962. Esp. 9-10 [εἰ δὲ μή γε].
WILSON, W.A.A., "But me no Buts". — BTrans 15 (1964) 173-180.

δέησις 3 + 0/1

1. plea; 2. BDAG 2000: prayer (Lk 1,13; 2,37; 5,33)

Word groups	Lk	Acts	Mt	Mk
δεήσεις ποιέομαι (VKb)	5,33		0	0
δέησις + νηστεία/νηστεύω → προσεύχομαι + νηστεία/ νηστεύω DENAUX 2009 Lⁿ	2,37; 5,33		0	0
δέησις + προσευχή (VKa)		1,14*	0	0

Characteristic of Luke
GOULDER 1989; HARNACK 1906 72

Literature
COLLISON 1977 180 [noteworthy phenomena]; DENAUX 2009 Lⁿ; EASTON 1910 152 [probably characteristic of L]; GERSDORF 1816 261 [νηστείαις καὶ δεήσεσιν].

GEORGE, Augustin, La prière. — ID., Études, 1978, 395-427. Esp. 402-405: "Le vocabulaire lucanien de la prière".
JUNG, Chang-Wook, Infancy Narrative, 2004. Esp. 197.201.207.

δεῖ 18/19 + 22/25 (Mt 8, Mk 6)

1. be necessary (Lk 21,9); 2. should (Lk 12,12; Acts 27,21)

Word groups	Lk	Acts	Mt	Mk
δεῖ + γενέσθαι (VKc)	21,9	1,21-22	2	1
δεῖ (+) παθεῖν	9,22; 17,25; 24,26	9,16; 17,3	1	1
δεῖ of divine destiny or	4,43; 9,22; 13,33; 17,25; 21,9;	1,16; 3,21; 4,12; 9,16;	4	4
unavoidable fate (SCb)	22,37; 24,7.26.44.46*	14,22; 17,3; 23,11; 27,24		
(τὸ) δεῖν (VKd)	18,1	25,24; 26,9	0	0
DENAUX 2009 Lⁿ				
δέον (VKe)		19,36	0	0

Characteristic of Luke
GOULDER 1989; HAWKINS 1909add; MORGENTHALER 1958LA

	Lk	Acts	Mt	Mk
δεῖ ... ποιεῖν/ποιῆσαι	11,42	9,6; 16,30	1	0
BOISMARD 1984 ca40				
ἔδει (SCa; VKa)	11,42; 13,16; 15,32; 22,7;	1,16; 17,3; 24,19; 27,21	3	0
GOULDER 1989*	24,26.46*			

Literature
DENAUX 2009 Lan [ἔδει]; HAUCK 1934 [Vorzugswort]; JEREMIAS 1980 229: "Lukas benutzt δεῖ zur Beschreibung von rituellen Pflichten"; RADL 1975 404; SCHÜRMANN 1953 79-80; 1957 125 [sehr wahrscheinlich luk R].

BARTSCH, Hans-Werner, Jesu Schwertwort, Lukas XXII. 35-38: Überlieferungsgeschichtliche Studie. — NTS 20 (1973-74) 190-203. Esp. 196-198: "Die Handschrift des Lukas".
COSGROVE, Charles H., The Divine δεῖ in Luke-Acts: Investigations into the Lukan Understanding of God's Providence. — NT 26 (1984) 168-190.
DE JONGE, Henk J., Sonship, Wisdom, Infancy: Luke II.41-51a. — NTS 24 (1977-78) 317-354. Esp. 350-351: "I was bound".
DELEBECQUE, Édouard, Études grecques, 1976. Esp. 41 [2,41-52].
FASCHER, Erich, Theologische Beobachtungen zu δεῖ im Alten Testament. — ZNW 45 (1954) 244-252.
HINNEBUSCH, Paul, "In My Father's House ... About My Father's Business" (Luke 2:49). — BiTod 27 (1966) 1893-1899.
SYLVA, Dennis D., The Cryptic Clause en tois tou patros mou dei einai me in Luke 2,49b. — ZNW 78 (1987) 132-140.

δείκνυμι 5 + 2 (Mt 3, Mk 2)
1. make known, show (Lk 4,5; 5,14; 20,24; 22,12; 24,40); 2. explain (Acts 10,28)

Word groups	Lk	Acts	Mt	Mk
δείκνυμι imperative (VKb) → ἀνα/ἐπιδείκνυμι imper.	5,14; 20,24		1	1
δείκνυμι to show, to make clear (VKa) → ἐπιδείκνυμι		10,28	1	0

δεινῶς 1 (Mt 1)
terribly (Lk 11,53)

δειπνέω 2
to eat a meal (Lk 17,8; 22,20)

Literature
DENAUX 2009 Lⁿ.

PETZER, Kobus H., Style and Text in the Lucan Narrative of the Institution of the Lord's Supper, 1991. Esp. 118.

δεῖπνον 5 (Mt 1, Mk 2)

1. meal (Lk 20,46); 2. main meal (Lk 14,12.16.14.24)

Word groups	Lk	Acts	Mt	Mk
δεῖπνοι plural (VKb)	20,46		1	1
δεῖπνον ποιέω (VKa) → ἄριστον/δοχὴν ποιέω; cf. ποιέω γάμους Mt 22,2	14,12.16		0	1

Characteristic of Luke
GOULDER 1989

Literature
DENAUX 2009 Ln.

δέκα 11/13 + 1 (Mt 3, Mk 1)   ten

Word groups	Lk	Acts	Mt	Mk
δέκα καὶ ὀκτώ (VKb) → δεκαοκτώ	13,4*.11*.16		0	0
δέκα χιλιάδες	14,31		0	0

Characteristic of Luke
GOULDER 1989*; HENDRIKS 1986 433; MORGENTHALER 1958L

Literature
DENAUX 2009 L[***]; HAWKINS 1909 17.

δεκαοκτώ 2   eighteen (Lk 13,4.11)

Word groups
→ δέκα καὶ ὀκτώ; cf. δεκαδύο Acts 19,7*; 24,11*; δεκαπέντε Acts 27,28

Literature
DENAUX 2009 Ln; JEREMIAS 1980 228 [ἔτη δεκαοκτώ: red.]; PAFFENROTH 1997 75 [δεκαοκτώ/δέκα καὶ ὀκτώ].

δεκτός 2 + 1

1. pleasing (Acts 10,35); 2. welcomed (Lk 4,24); 3. appropriate (Lk 4,19)

Characteristic of Luke
VOGEL 1899B

Literature
DENAUX 2009 La[n].

BAJARD, J., La structure de la péricope de Nazareth en Lc., IV, 16-30: Proposition pour une lecture plus cohérente. — ETL 45 (1969) 165-171 [on Lk 4,24 δεκτός: the verbal adjective here does not have the passive sense 'acceptable', but the active sense 'favorable', 'salvific', cp. Lk 4,19].

δένδρον 7 (Mt 12, Mk 1/2)	tree, bush			
Word groups	Lk	Acts	Mt	Mk
δένδρον + καρπός (VKa)	3,9²; 6,43^{1.2}.44		9	0

δεξιός 6 + 7 (Mt 12, Mk 6[7])	right			
Word groups	Lk	Acts	Mt	Mk
ἡ δεξιὰ (+) (τῆς δυνάμεως) τοῦ θεοῦ / μου / αὐτοῦ (SCc) → ὁ υἱὸς τοῦ ἀνθρώπου ἑστὼς/καθήμενος ἐκ δεξιῶν (τοῦ θεοῦ)	20,42; 22,69	2,33.34; 5,31; 7,55.56	2	2
ἡ δεξιὰ (χείρ) (SCa; VKa)	6,6	2,33; 3,7; 5,31	3	0
δεξιός + ἀριστερός; cf. 2 Cor 6,7; cf. δεξιός + εὐώνυμος Mt 20,21.23; 25,33; 27,38; Mk 10,40; 15,27	23,33		1	1
ἐκ δεξιῶν (SCb; VKb) → ἐξ ἀριστερῶν; cf. ἐξ εὐωνύμων Mt 20,21.23; 25,33.41; 27,38; Mk 10,40; 15,27	1,11; 20,42; 22,69; 23,33	2,25.34; 7,55.56	7	5[6]
ἐκ δεξιῶν κάθημαι; cf. ἐκ δεξιῶν καθίζω Mt 20,21.23; Mk 10,37.40; [16,19]	20,42; 22,69	2,34	2	2

Characteristic of Luke

→ ὑψόομαι τῇ δεξιᾷ (τοῦ θεοῦ)

Literature

GERSDORF 1816 180 [ἑστὼς ἐκ δεξιῶν].

δέομαι 8 + 7 (Mt 1)	plead			
Word groups	Lk	Acts	Mt	Mk
δέομαι + direct discourse (VKa) DENAUX lA^n	8,28; 9,38 v.l.	8,34; 21,39	0	0
δέομαι + infinitive (VKd) DENAUX La^n	8,38; 9,38	26,3	0	0
δέομαι + εἰ (VKc); cf. Rom 1,10		8,22	0	0
δέομαι + λέγων	5,12		0	0

Characteristic of Luke

BOISMARD 1984 cb105; CADBURY 1920 172; DENAUX 2009 L***; GASTON 1973 64 [Lked]; GOULDER 1989*; HAWKINS 1909L; NEIRYNCK 1985; PLUMMER 1922 lix; SCHÜRMANN 1957 105; VOGEL 1899D

	Lk	Acts	Mt	Mk
δέομαί σου BOISMARD 1984 Ab73; NEIRYNCK 1985	8,28; 9,38	8,34; 21,39	0	0
δέομαι (+) ἵνα/ὅπως (VKb) DENAUX 2009 L***	9,40; 10,2; 21,36; 22,32	8,24	1	0

Literature

COLLISON 1977 44 [linguistic usage of Luke: certain]; DENAUX 2009 LA^n [δέομαί σου]; HAUCK 1934 [Vorzugswort]; JEREMIAS 1980 68 [δέομαι + λέγων: red.]; 283 [δεόμενοι ἵνα: trad.]; SCHÜRMANN 1957 105 [ἐδεήθην (22,32): sehr wahrscheinlich luk R].

GEORGE, Augustin, La prière. — ID., Études, 1978, 395-427. Esp. 402-405: "Le vocabulaire lucanien de la prière".

δέρω 5 + 3 (Mt 1, Mk 3) | whip

Word groups	Lk	Acts	Mt	Mk
δέρομαι passive (VKb)	12,47.48		0	1

Characteristic of Luke
GOULDER 1989

Literature
VON BENDEMANN 2001 423-424: "δέρειν ist Vorzugsverb des auctor ad Theophilum"; COLLISON 1977 92 [noteworthy phenomena]; SCHNEIDER 1969 99-100.163: "δέρω kommt bei Luk ohnehin häufiger vor als bei anderen ntl Schriftstellern" [Vorzugswörter und -ausdrücke des Luk].

BORMANN, Lukas, *Recht, Gerechtigkeit und Religion*, 2001. Esp. 178.

δεσμεύω 1 + 1 (Mt 1) | bind (Lk 8,29)

δεσμός 2 + 5/6 (Mk 1)
1. chains (Lk 8,29; Acts 16,26); 2. imprisonment (Acts 23,29); 3. illness (Lk 13,16)

Word groups	Lk	Acts	Mt	Mk
δεσμός + λύω → **δέω** + λύω	13,16	22,30*	0	1
δεσμός singular (VKa); cf. σύνδεσμος Acts 8,23	13,16		0	1

Characteristic of Luke
BOISMARD 1984 Eb21; DENAUX 2009 IA*; NEIRYNCK 1985.

	Lk	Acts	Mt	Mk
τὰ δεσμά PLUMMER 1922 lii	8,29	16,26; 22,30*; 26,29	0	0

Literature
COLLISON 1977 181 [noteworthy phenomena]; DENAUX 2009 IA[n] [τὰ δεσμά]; RADL 1975 404-405 [δεσμός; δεσμά]; SCHÜRMANN 1957 33 [imprisonment and death: Lk 22,33; Acts 23,29; 26,31].

SCHWARZ, Günther, λυθηναι απο του δεσμου τουτου. — *BibNot* 15 (1981) 47.

δεσπότης 1 + 1
1. ruler (Lk 2,29; Acts 4,24); 2. owner

Word groups	Lk	Acts	Mt	Mk
δεσπότης + δοῦλος → **οἰκοδεσπότης** + δοῦλος	2,29		0	0
δεσπότης + θεός		4,24 v.l.	0	0

Characteristic of Luke
HARNACK 1906 74

Literature
DENAUX 2009 LA[n]; GERSDORF 1816 254 [νῦν ἀπολύεις τὸν δοῦλόν σου, δέσποτα, κατὰ τὸ ῥῆμά σου ἐν εἰρήνῃ].

DICKEY, E., Κύριε, δέσποτα, *domine*. Greek Politeness in the Roman Empire. — *JHS* 121 (2001) 1-11.

δεῦρο 1 + 2 (Mt 1, Mk 1)

1. come here (Lk 18,22; Acts 7,34); 2. the present time

Word groups	Lk	Acts	Mt	Mk
δεῦρο absolute (*VK*a); cf. Jn 11,43		7,3	0	0

δεύτερος 3 + 5 (Mt 3/4, Mk 3)

1. second (Lk 12,38; 19,18; 20,30); 2. afterward

Word groups	Lk	Acts	Mt	Mk
δεύτερος + πάλιν (*VK*d)		10,15	1	0
δεύτερος + πρῶτος; δεύτερον + πρῶτον; cf. πρῶτον + εἶτα Mk 4,28	19,(16-)18; 20,(29-)30	7,(12-)13; 12,10	2/3	2/3
δεύτερος + τρίτος	12,38; 20,30(-31)		2	1
ἐκ δευτέρου (*VK*a)		10,15; 11,9	1	1
ἐν τῷ δευτέρῳ (*VK*c)		7,13	0	0

δέχομαι 16/17 + 8/9 (Mt 10, Mk 6)

1. receive (Lk 2,28; Acts 28,21); 2. welcome (Lk 9,5); 3. believe (Lk 8,13; Acts 8,14); 4. take hold of (Lk 22,17)

Word groups	Lk	Acts	Mt	Mk
δέχομαι + ἀκούω (*VK*b)	8,13	8,14; 11,1	1	1

Characteristic of Luke

GOULDER 1989; PLUMMER 1922 lx

	Lk	Acts	Mt	Mk
δέχομαι (τὸν) λόγον (*SC*a; *VK*a) → **ἀκούω/αἴρω/ἀποδέχομαι** τὸν λόγον/τοὺς λόγους/ῥήματα; cf. 1 Thess 1,6; 2,13; Jam 1,21; δέχομαι λόγια Acts 7,38 BOISMARD 1984 cb144; NEIRYNCK 1985	8,13	8,14; 11,1; 17,11	0	0

Literature

VON BENDEMANN 2001 414: "der auctor ad Theophilum hat eine Vorliebe für Komposita von δέχεσθαι"; DENAUX 2009 lAⁿ [δέχομαι (τὸν) λόγον]; GERSDORF 1816 252 [καὶ αὐτὸς ἐδέξατο]; SCHÜRMANN 1953 25-28 [Lk 22,17 vorluk].

DELEBECQUE, Édouard, *Études grecques*, 1976. Esp. 109-121: "Le pain et la coupe de la dernière cène (22,17-20)".

PETZER, Kobus H., Style and Text in the Lucan Narrative of the Institution of the Lord's Supper, 1991. Esp. 121.

TAEGER, Jens-Wilhelm, *Der Mensch und sein Heil*, 1982. Esp. 123-125: "δέχεσθαι τὸν λόγον (τοῦ θεοῦ)".

TAMBURRANO, Salvatore, L'uso lucano del verbo δέχομαι. — *Nicolaus* 8 (1980) 204-207.

δέω 2 + 12/13 (Mt 10, Mk 8)

1. bind (Lk 13,16); 2. imprison (Acts 9,21); 3. compel (Acts 20,22); 4. restrict; 5. prohibit; 6. cause illness (Lk 13,16)

Word groups	Lk	Acts	Mt	Mk
δέω + λύω (VKb) → δεσμός + λύω	13,16; 19,30	22,29(-30)	5	2
δεδεμένος	19,30	9,2.21; 12,6; 20,22; 22,5; 24,27	3	3
δέω metaphorically (VKa)	13,16	20,22	4	0

Literature

RADL 1975 405 [δέω; δεδεμένος].

SCHWARZ, Günther, λυϑηναι απο του δεσμου τουτου. — BibNot 15 (1981) 47.

δή 1 + 2 (Mt 1)	then (Lk 2,15; Acts 13,2; 15,36)

Literature

JEREMIAS 1980 84 [red.].

δηνάριον 3 (Mt 6, Mk 3)	coin, denarius (Lk 7,41; 10,35; 20,24)

Literature

MARYKS, Robert A., I latinismi del Nuovo Testamento, 2000. Esp. 24-25.

διά 39/42 + 74 (Mt 59/60, Mk 31[33]/34)

1. by (agent) (Acts 2,16); 2. by (instrument); 3. through (means) (Acts 20,28); 4. on behalf of (benefaction); 5. because of (reason participant) (Lk 21,17); 6. on account of (reason) (Lk 23,25; Acts 21,34); 7. through (extension) (Lk 11,24; Acts 20,3); 8. along (extension) (Lk 17,11?); 9. during (time) (Acts 5,19); 10. throughout (time) (Lk 5,5)

Word groups

διά + genitive	Lk	Acts	Mt	Mk
διά with a geographical name (SCj; VKj)		20,3	0	2/3
δι' ἐτῶν (LN: after years)		24,17	0	0
δι' ἡμερῶν (LN: few day later)		1,3	0	1
διὰ Ἰησοῦ Χριστοῦ		10,36	0	0
διὰ μέσου (SCk; VKk) → διὰ μέσον; διέρχομαι διὰ μέσου	4,30		0	0
διὰ νυκτός BOISMARD 1984 Ab57		5,19; 16,9; 17,10; 23,31	0	0
διὰ πνεύματος (ἁγίου)		1,2; 4,25; 11,28; 21,4	0	0
διὰ τοῦ προφήτου/προφητῶν	1,70; 18,31	2,16; 3,21; 28,25	13	0
διὰ χειρός / (τῶν) χειρῶν (SCg; VKg)		2,23; 5,12; 7,25; 11,30; 14,3; 15,23; 19,11.26	0	1
σημεῖον γίνεται διά + genitive BOISMARD 1984 Aa34		2,43; 4,16.30; 5,12; 14,3	0	0
διά through the prophets (SCh; VKh)	1,70; 18,31	1,16; 2,16; 3,18.21; 4,25; 28,25	12	0
διά expression of time (SCe; VKe)	5,5	1,3; 5,19; 16,9; 17,10; 23,31; 24,17	1	2
other instances with genitive	5,19*.19²; 6,1; 8,4; 11,24; 13,24; 17,1; 18,25; 19,4*; 22,22	2,22.23; 3,16; 7,25; 8,18.20; 9,25; 10,43; 12,9; 13,38.49; 14,22; 15,7.11.12.27.32; 18,9.27.28; 20,28; 21,19; 24,2¹·²	11	5/7

→ **εἰς** + διά; **εἰσέρχομαι** διά; **ἐν** + διά; **ἔρχομαι** διά; **λαμβάνω** διά; διὰ **λόγου**; δι' ὅλης **νυκτός**; **οὐαὶ** (τῷ ἀνθρώπῳ) δι' οὗ; διὰ **παραβολῆς**; **πίστις** ἡ διά; **σῴζω** διά; **ὑποστρέφω** διά

διά + accusative	Lk	Acts	Mt	Mk
διὰ μέσον (SCk; VKk) → **διὰ** μέσου; **διέρχομαι** διὰ μέσον	17,11		0	0
διὰ τό (+) **εἶναι** DENAUX 2009 Laⁿ	2,4; 11,8[1]; 19,11	18,3[1]; 27,4	0	0
διὰ τοῦτο (SCa; VKa)	11,19.49; 12,22; 14,20	2,26	10/11	3
διὰ τὸν ὄχλον → **ἀπὸ/ἐκ** τοῦ ὄχλου	5,19[1]; 8,19		0	2
διὰ τί / διατί (SCb; VKb)	5,30.33*; 19,23.31; 20,5; 24,38	5,3	7	3
διὰ τί; ὅτι	19,31		1	0
δι' ἢν αἰτίαν; ἡ αἰτία δι' ἢν DENAUX 2009 lAⁿ	8,47	10,21; 22,24; 23,28	0	0
other instances with accusative (SCd; VKd)	1,78; 11,8[2]; 21,17; 23,19.25	4,2.21; 8,11; 12,20; 16,3; 18,2.3; 21,34.35; 27,4.9; 28,2[1.2].18.20	16	13

→ **εἰς** + διά; **ἐν** + διά

Characteristic of Luke

GASTON 1973 65 [Lked?]; MORGENTHALER 1958A

	Lk	Acts	Mt	Mk
διὰ τό + infinitive (SCc; VKc) → διὰ τὸ **εἶναι**; cf. Jn 2,24; Phil 1,7; Heb 7,23.24; 10,2; Jam 4,2 BOISMARD 1984 cb163; CREDNER 1836 135; GOULDER 1989; HAWKINS 1909add; NEIRYNCK 1985; PLUMMER 1922 lxii; SCHÜRMANN 1953 13	2,4; 6,48; 8,6; 9,7; 11,8[1]; 18,5; 19,11; 23,8	4,2; 8,11; 12,20; 18,2.3; 27,4.9; 28,18	3	3
διὰ παντός (LN: [a]regularly; [b]always; SCf; VKf) CREDNER 1836 142	24,[b]53	2,[b]25; 10,[b]2; 24,[b]16	1	1
διὰ στόματός τινος; cf. διὰ τοῦ στόματός τινος Acts 15,7 BOISMARD 1984 Ab42; HARNACK 1906 144; NEIRYNCK 1985; PLUMMER 1922 lx	1,70	1,16; 3,18.21; 4,25 v.l.	1	0

→ **διέρχομαι** διὰ μέσον/μέσου; διὰ τοῦ **ὀνόματος**

Literature

VON BENDEMANN 2001 419: "διὰ τὸ εἶναι findet sich im Neuen Testament nur im lukanischem Doppelwerk"; 430 [διὰ πάντος]; 435 [διὰ τό + inf.]; BDR §402: "Der substantivierter Inf. mit Präp. im Akkusativ: 1. διὰ τό zur Bezeichnung des Grundes, häufig Lk/Apg, bei Paulus nur Phil 1,7. 2. εἰς τό zur Bezeichnung des Zwecks oder der Folge, vorwiegend bei Paulus und Hb und wohl ohne Unterschied von τοῦ mit Inf. bei Luk."; COLLISON 1977 102 [διὰ γε: noteworthy phenomena]; 126 [διὰ τό + inf.: linguistic usage of Luke: likely]; DENAUX 2009 LAn [διὰ τό + infinitive], lAn [διὰ στόματός τινος]; GERSDORF 1816 217 [διὰ τὸ εἶναι αὐτὸν ἐξ οἴκου]; HAUCK 1934 [Vorzugsverbindung: διὰ τό + inf.]; JEREMIAS 1980 70-71: "Die lukanische Redaktion hat eine ausgesprochene Vorliebe für Verbkomposita mit δια-"; 73-74: "διὰ στόματός τινος ('durch'), vom Boten gesagt, durch den Gott sein Wort verkünden läßt, ist nicht geläufiger judengriechischer Sprachgebrauch; ... Im NT findet sie sich nur im Doppelwerk"; 79: "διὰ τὸ εἶναι: Der präpositionale substantivierte Infinitiv ist ein markanter Lukanismus".

LE ROUX, L.V., Style and Text of Acts 4:25(a). — *Neotestamentica* 25 (1991) 29-32.

διαβαίνω 1 + 1   cross over

Word groups	Lk	Acts	Mt	Mk
διαβαίνω εἰς → ἀνα/ἀπο/ἐμ/κατα/μεταβαίνω εἰς; cf. ἐπιβαίνω εἰς Acts 21,6*		16,9	0	0
διαβαίνω + πρός + accusative → καταβαίνω πρός + acc.	16,26		0	0

Characteristic of Luke

VOGEL 1899B

Literature

DENAUX 2009 LAⁿ; JEREMIAS 1980 261 [red.].

διαβάλλω 1 — accuse (Lk 16,1)

Literature

HAUCK 1934 [seltenes Alleinwort].

BORMANN, Lukas, *Recht, Gerechtigkeit und Religion*, 2001. Esp. 178.
HATCH, Edwin, *Essays*, 1889. Esp. 45-47.
LYGRE, John G., Of What Charges? (Luke 16:1-2). — *BTB* 32 (2002) 21-28. Esp. 23.

διαβλέπω 1 (Mt 1, Mk 1) — see clearly

Word groups	Lk	Acts	Mt	Mk
διαβλέπω + ὀφθαλμός → ἀτενίζω/(ἀνα)βλέπω/ὁράω/εἶδον + ὀφθαλμός	6,42		1	1

διάβολος 5/6 + 2 (Mt 6)

1. Devil (Lk 4,2.3.6.13; 8,12); 2. demon; 3. slanderer; 4. wicked person

Word groups	Lk	Acts	Mt	Mk
ἀπέστη ὁ διάβολος → ἀπέστη/ἀπῆλθεν ὁ ἄγγελος	4,13		0	0
διάβολος (+) πειράζω/πειρασμός	4,2.13		1	0

Literature

HATCH, Edwin, *Essays*, 1889. Esp. 45-47.

διαγγέλλω 1 + 1

1. give notice (Acts 21,26); 2. proclaim (Lk 9,60)

Word groups	Lk	Acts	Mt	Mk
ἀπέρχομαι διαγγέλλω → ἀνα/ὑποστρέφω / εἰστρέχω / (ἀπ/εἰσ/προσ) ἔρχομαι / πορεύομαι / φεύγω + ἀπαγγέλλω; ὑποστρέφω + διηγέομαι; ἀποστέλλω / εἰσπορεύομαι / (ἀπ/δι/κατ)ἔρχομαι + κηρύσσω	9,60		0	0

Characteristic of Luke

BOISMARD 1984 Ab169; NEIRYNCK 1985; VOGEL 1899B

Literature

VON BENDEMANN 2001 416 [διαγγέλλειν τὴν βασιλείαν τοῦ θεοῦ]; DENAUX 2009 LAⁿ;
HARNACK 1907 13; HAUCK 1934 [seltenes Alleinwort]; JEREMIAS 1980 181-182 [διαγγέλλειν
τὴν βασιλείαν τοῦ θεοῦ: red.].

διαγογγύζω*** 2 | grumble

Word groups	Lk		Acts	Mt	Mk
διαγογγύζω (+) λέγων DENAUX 2009 Lⁿ	15,2; 19,7			0	0

Characteristic of Luke

CREDNER 1836 138; PLUMMER 1922 liii

Literature

VON BENDEMANN 2001 428; DENAUX 2009 Lⁿ; EASTON 1910 152 [probably characteristic of
L]; HAUCK 1934 [seltenes Alleinwort]; JEREMIAS 1980 244 [διαγγογύζω + λέγοντες ὅτι: red.].

διαγρηγορέω** 1 | become fully awake (Lk 9,32)

διαδίδωμι 2 + 1 | give out (Lk 11,22; 18,22; Acts 4,35)

Word groups	Lk	Acts	Mt	Mk
διαδίδωμι πτωχοῖς → δίδωμι πτωχοῖς	18,22		0	0

Characteristic of Luke

VOGEL 1899B

Literature

VON BENDEMANN 2001 420: "διαδιδόναι außer Joh 6,11 im Neuen Testament nur von Lukas
gebraucht"; DENAUX 2009 Laⁿ; JEREMIAS 1980 201 [red.].

διαθήκη 2 + 2 (Mt 1, Mk 1)

1. making of a covenant (Lk 1,72); 2. covenant (Lk 1,72; 22,20); 3. testament

Word groups	Lk	Acts	Mt	Mk
ἁγία διαθήκη	1,72		0	0
διαθήκη + αἷμα	22,20		1	1
διαθήκην + διατίθεμαι (VKe)		3,25	0	0
καινὴ διαθήκη (Vka)	22,20		0/1	0/1

Literature

BORMANN, Lukas, *Recht, Gerechtigkeit und Religion*, 2001. Esp. 151.
BOURGOIN, Henri, Alliance ou Testament ? . — *Cahiers du Cercle Ernest-Renan* 25
   (1977) 18-25. [NTA 22,343]
DELEBECQUE, Édouard, *Études grecques*, 1976. Esp. 109-121 : "Le pain et la (coupe de la
   dernière cène (22,17-20)".

HATCH, Edwin, *Essays*, 1889. Esp. 47-48.
HINDLEY, J.C., The Meaning and Translation of Covenant. — *Btrans* 13 (1962) 90-101.
HUGHES, J.J., Hebrews IX 15ff. and Galatians III 15ff.: A Study in Covenant Practice and Procedure. — *NT* 21 (1979) 27-96. Esp. 92-96 [extra-biblical references].
NORTON, F.O., *A Lexicographical and Historical Study of διαθήκη from the Earliest Times to the End of the Classical Period*. Chicago, IL: University of Chicago, 1908.
PETZER, Kobus H., Style and Text in the Lucan Narrative of the Institution of the Lord's Supper, 1991. Esp. 119.
SELB, W., *Diathēkē* im Neuen Testament. Randbemerkungen eines Juristen zo einem Theologenstreit. — *Journal of Jewish Studies* 25 (1974) 183-169. [NTA 18, 777]

διαιρέω 1

divide (Lk 15,12)

διακαθαίρω* 1

clean out (Lk 3,17)

Literature
HAUCK 1934 [seltenes Alleinwort].

διακονέω 8 + 2 (Mt 6, Mk 5)

1. serve (Lk 22,26); 2. take care of; 3. wait upon (Lk 17,8); 4. be a deacon

Word groups	Lk	Acts	Mt	Mk
διακονέω τραπέζαις (*LN*: handle finances)		6,2	0	0
διακονέω participle (*VK*a)	22,26.27[1.2]	19,22	1	0

Literature
EASTON 1910 152 [probably characteristic of L]; JEREMIAS 1980 178 [red.]; SCHÜRMANN 1957 78 [luk R].

BOULTON, P.H., Διακονέω and its Cognates in the Four Gospels. — *Studia Evangelica* 1 (1959) 415-422.

διακονία 1 + 8

1. service (Acts 6,4); 2. ministry (Acts 20,24); 3. provision (Acts 6,1); 4. waiting upon (Lk 10,40); 5. contribution (Acts 6,1)

Word groups	Lk	Acts	Mt	Mk
διακονία τοῦ λόγου		6,4	0	0

Characteristic of Luke
BOISMARD 1984 Db4; NEIRYNCK 1985

Literature
DENAUX 2009 IA[n]; RADL 1975 405; SCHÜRMANN 1957 78 [bei den Synoptikern nur 1× Lk und 6/2× Apg].

COLLINS, John N., *Diakonia Re-Interpreting the Ancient Sources*. — New York and Oxford: OUP, 1990.

DUPONT, Jacques, *Le discours de Milet*, 1962. Esp. 101-111.
GEORGE, Augustin, L'œuvre de Luc: Actes et Évangile. — DELORME, J. (ed.), *Le ministère et les ministères selon le Nouveau Testament: dossier exégétique et réflexion théologique* (Parole de Dieu, 10). Paris: Seuil, 1974, 207-240; = Les ministères. — ID., *Études*, 1978, 369-394.
GOODER, P., *Diakonia* in the New Testament. A Dialogue with John N. Collins. — *Ecclesiology* (London) 3 (2006) 33-56.

διαλαλέω 2 | converse

Word groups	Lk	Acts	Mt	Mk
διαλαλέω + πρὸς ἀλλήλους → verb of saying πρός + acc.	6,11		0	0
διαλαλέω + τὸ ῥῆμα → **λαλέω** (τὸ) ῥῆμα / τὸν λόγον	1,65		0	0

Characteristic of Luke

PLUMMER 1922 liii

Literature

DENAUX 2009 Lⁿ; GERSDORF 1816 205; HAUCK 1934 [seltenes Alleinwort; Vorzugsverbindung: διαλαλέω πρός] JEREMIAS 1980 84 [διαλαλέω + πρὸς ἀλλήλους: red.].

διαλείπω 1 | cease (Lk 7,45)

διαλογίζομαι 6 (Mt 3, Mk 7)

1. reason thoroughly (Lk 1,29; 12,17); 2. converse (Lk 20,14)

Word groups	Lk	Acts	Mt	Mk
διαλογίζομαι + καρδία → **διαλογισμός** + καρδία	3,15; 5,22		0	2
διαλογίζομαι + λέγω → **συλλογίζομαι** + λέγω	5,21; 12,17; 20,14		2	1/2
διαλογίζομαι πρός + accusative (*VK*a) → verb of saying πρός + acc.	20,14		0	2

Characteristic of Luke

CREDNER 1836 138

Literature

COLLISON 1977 45 [linguistic usage of Luke: likely]; JEREMIAS 1980 47: "διαλογίζομαι wird im LkEv teils mit indirekter Frage und Optativ (...), teils mit λέγων und direkter Rede (...) konstruiert"; 68 [διαλογίζομαι + λέγων: red.].

BORMANN, Lukas, *Recht, Gerechtigkeit und Religion*, 2001. Esp. 135.
KILPATRICK, George D., Διαλέγεσθαι and διαλογίζεσθαι in the New Testament. — *JTS* NS 11 (1960) 338-340; = ID., *Principles and Practice*, 1990, 189-190.
RODRÍGUEZ, I., Consideración filologica sobre el mensaje de la anunciación, 1958. Esp. 244-245: "διαλογίζομαι".

διαλογισμός 6 (Mt 1, Mk 1)

1. reasoning; 2. what is reasoned (Lk 2,35); 3. dispute (Lk 9,46); 4. doubt (Lk 24,38)

Characteristic of Luke

DENAUX 2009 L***; GASTON 1973 64 [Lked]; GOULDER 1989*; HAWKINS 1909L

	Lk	Acts	Mt	Mk
διαλογισμός + καρδία (VKa) → **διαλογίζομαι** + καρδία GOULDER 1989	2,35; 9,47; 24,38		1	1

Literature

VON BENDEMANN 2001 415; COLLISON 1977 172 [linguistic usage of Luke: probable]; DENAUX 2009 Ln [διαλογισμός + καρδία]; GERSDORF 1816 257 [ἐκ πολλῶν καρδιῶν διαλογισμοί]; HAUCK 1934 [Vorzugswort].

BORMANN, Lukas, *Recht, Gerechtigkeit und Religion*, 2001. Esp. 135.

DERRETT, J. Duncan M., Ἀντιλεγόμενον, ῥομφαία, διαλογισμοί (Lk 2:34-35): The Hidden Context. — *FilolNT* 6 (1993) 207-218. ["the author examines the meaning and significance of the main terms used in Lk 2:34-35, by studying their double context, the obvious one and the one based on Genesis and Deuteronomy. The choice of vocabulary is part of a great scheme of Luke's to demonstrate the new religion as a renewal of the pristine worship of YHWH"]; = ID., *Studies in the New Testament*, VI, 1995, 64-75.

διαμαρτύρομαι 1 + 9

1. testify (Acts 18,5); 2. insist (Acts 2,40); 3. warn (Lk 16,28)

Word groups

Word groups	Lk	Acts	Mt	Mk
διαμαρτύρομαι + direct object; cf. 2 Tim 2,14; 4,1 BOISMARD 1984 Ca9		10,42; 18,5; 20,21.24; 23,11; 28,23	0	0
διαμαρτύρομαι + λέγων		20,23	0	0

Characteristic of Luke

CREDNER 1836 138; PLUMMER 1922 lix; VOGEL 1899B.D

	Lk	Acts	Mt	Mk
διαμαρτύρομαι + dative BOISMARD 1984 Ab74; NEIRYNCK 1985	16,28	18,5; 20,21.23	0	0

Literature

DENAUX 2009 IAⁿ; IAⁿ [διαμαρτύρομαι + dative]; JEREMIAS 1980 69 [διαμαρτύρομαι + λέγων: red.]; 261: "mit Dativ der Person kommt διαμαρτύρομαι im NT nur im Doppelwerk vor"; RADL 1975 405.

BROX, Norbert, *Zeugen und Märtyrer: Untersuchungen zur frühchristlichen Zeugnis-Terminologie* (SANT, 5). München: Kösel, 1961, 250 p. Esp. 43-69: "Der technische Wortgebrauch bei Lukas".

DUPONT, Jacques, *Le discours de Milet*, 1962. Esp. 82.88.103-105.115.118.

TRITES, Allison A., *The New Testament Concept of Witness*, 1977. Esp. 74-75.

διαμένω 2

1. associate (Lk 22,28); 2. continue (Lk 1,22); 3. continue to exist

Literature

DENAUX 2009 Lⁿ; JEREMIAS 1980 290 [red.]; SCHÜRMANN 1957 38 [Lk 22,28: luk R einer vorluk T].

διαμερίζω 6 + 2 (Mt 1/2, Mk 1)

1. distribute (Lk 22,17; Acts 2,45); 2. be opposed to (Lk 12,52); 3. divide (Acts 2,3);
4. διαμερίζομαι: spread out

Word groups	Lk	Acts	Mt	Mk
διαμερίζομαι passive ἐπί + dative DENAUX 2009 L[n]	12,52.53		0	0
διαμερίζομαι passive ἐφ' ἑαυτόν DENAUX 2009 L[n]	11,17.18		0	0
διαμερίζω metaphorically (VKa) DENAUX 2009 L[n]	11,17.18; 12,52.53		0	0

Characteristic of Luke
BOISMARD 1984 Ab24; CREDNER 1836 138; DENAUX 2009 L***; GOULDER 1989*;
NEIRYNCK 1985; PLUMMER 1922 lix; VOGEL 1899D

Literature
HAUCK 1934 [Vorzugswort]; JEREMIAS 1980 200 [red.]; SCHÜRMANN 1953 31-32 [Lk 22,17: luk
R einer vorluk T].

διαμερισμός 1   division (Lk 12,51)

Literature
HAUCK 1934 [seltenes Alleinwort]; SCHÜRMANN 1953 31 [im NT nur Lk 12,51 diff Mt].

διανεύω 1   gesture (Lk 1,22)

Literature
HAUCK 1934 [seltenes Alleinwort].

διανόημα 1   thought (Lk 11,17)

Literature
HAUCK 1934 [seltenes Alleinwort].

διάνοια 2 (Mt 1, Mk 1)

1. mind (Lk 10,27); 2. way of thinking; 3. thought (Lk 1,51)

Literature
HARNACK 1906 151 [Lk 1,51: διάνοια καρδίας].

DELEBECQUE, Édouard, Études grecques, 1976. Esp. 17-23.

διανοίγω 4 + 3 (Mk 1/2)

1. make open (Lk 2,23; 24,31.45); 2. explain (Lk 24,32)

Word groups	Lk	Acts	Mt	Mk
ἄρσεν διανοῖγον μήτραν (*LN*: firstborn son)	2,23		0	0
διανοίγω + τὰς γραφάς (*VK*a) → ἀνοίγω/(ἀνα)πτύσσω τὸ βιβλίον; συνίημι τὰς γραφάς	24,32		0	0
διανοίγω τὴν καρδίαν (*LN*: cause to be open minded)		16,14	0	0
διανοίγω + τὸν νοῦν (*LN*: cause to be open minded)	24,45		0	0
διανοίγω τὸν οὐρανόν → ἀνοίγω/κλείω τὸν οὐρανόν		7,56	0	0
διανοίγω τοὺς ὀφθαλμούς → ἀνοίγω/ἐπαίρω τοὺς ὀφθαλμούς	24,31		0	0

Characteristic of Luke

BOISMARD 1984 Bb44; CREDNER 1836 138; DENAUX 2009 L***; GOULDER 1989*; HARNACK 1906 33; HAWKINS 1909L.187; NEIRYNCK 1985; PLUMMER 1922 lix; VOGEL 1899B

Literature

COLLISON 1977 93 [noteworthy phenomena]; HAUCK 1934 [Vorzugswort]; JEREMIAS 1980 318-319 [red.].

JUNG, Chang.-Wook, *Infancy Narrative*, 2004. Esp. 80-81 [διανοῖγον: Lk 2,23].

διανυκτερεύω 1 | spend the night (Lk 6,12)

Literature

HAUCK 1934 [seltenes Alleinwort].

διαπεράω 1 + 1 (Mt 2, Mk 2) | cross over (Lk 16,26; Acts 21,2)

Literature

ELLINGTON, John, Where Is the Other Side? — *BTrans* 38 (1987) 221-226.

διαπορεύομαι 3 + 1 (Mk 0/1)

1. travel through, go trough (Lk 6,1; 13,22; Acts 16,4); 2. pass by (Lk 18,36)

Word groups	Lk	Acts	Mt	Mk
διαπορεύομαι κατὰ πόλεις καὶ κώμας + participle καί participle → διέρχομαι κατὰ τὰς κώμας; διοδεύω κατὰ πόλιν καὶ κώμην	13,22		0	0

Characteristic of Luke

BOISMARD 1984 Bb99; GOULDER 1989; NEIRYNCK 1985; PLUMMER 1922 lix; VOGEL 1899B

Literature

DENAUX 2009 Lⁿ; HAUCK 1934 [Vorzugswort]; JEREMIAS 1980 175.231 [red.]; SCHÜRMANN 1953 90 [Vorliebe für πορεύεσθαι und einige seiner Komposita ... διαπορεύεσθαι].

DELEBECQUE, Édouard, *Études grecques*, 1976. Esp. 71-83: "Les moissonneurs du sabbat (6,1)".

διαπορέω 1/2 + 3 | be perplexed (Lk 9,7; Acts 2,12; 5,24; 10,17)

Characteristic of Luke

BOISMARD 1984 Ab75; CREDNER 1836 142; HAWKINS 1909LA; MORGENTHALER 1958*; NEIRYNCK 1985; PLUMMER 1922 lx; VOGEL 1899A

Literature

DENAUX 2009 IAⁿ; HAUCK 1934 [seltenes Alleinwort]; JEREMIAS 1980 310 [red.].

διαπραγματεύομαι* 1   earn (Lk 19,15)

Literature

HAUCK 1934 [seltenes Alleinwort]; JEREMIAS 1980 278-279 [red.].

BORMANN, Lukas, *Recht, Gerechtigkeit und Religion*, 2001. Esp. 161.

διαρρήσσω 2 + 1 (Mt 1, Mk 1)   rip (Lk 5,6; 8,29; Acts 14,14)

Literature

JEREMIAS 1980 132 [red.].

διασείω 1   extort (Lk 3,14)

Literature

HAUCK 1934 [seltenes Alleinwort].

BORMANN, Lukas, *Recht, Gerechtigkeit und Religion*, 2001. Esp. 178.
SWELLENGREBEL, J.L., Puzzles in Luke. — *BTrans* 17 (1966) 118-122. Esp. 119-120 [Lk 3,14 διασείω, συκοφαντέω].

διασκορπίζω 3 + 1 (Mt 3, Mk 1)
1. scatter (Lk 1,51); 2. squander (Lk 15,13; 16,1)

Word groups	Lk	Acts	Mt	Mk
συνάγω + διασκορπίζω → συνάγω + **σκορπίζω**	15,13		2	0

Literature

GERSDORF 1816 200 [διεσκόρπισεν ὑπερηφάνους]; PAFFENROTH 1997 80.

DELEBECQUE, Édouard, *Études grecques*, 1976. Esp. 15-17.
LYGRE, John G., Of What Charges? (Luke 16:1-2). — *BTB* 32 (2002) 21-28. Esp. 23-24.

διαστρέφω 2 + 3 (Mt 1)
1. mislead (Lk 23,2); 2. pervert (Lk 9,41; 23,2); 3. turn away from (Acts 13,8)

Word groups	Lk	Acts	Mt	Mk
διεστραμμένος (*VK*a)	9,41	20,30	1	0

Characteristic of Luke

BOISMARD 1984 cb106; DENAUX 2009 IA*; NEIRYNCK 1985; PLUMMER 1922 lix.

Literature

JEREMIAS 1980 300 [red.].

διασῴζω 1 + 5 (Mt 1)

1. rescue (Acts 28,4); 2. heal (Lk 7,3)

Characteristic of Luke

BOISMARD 1984 Cb23; CREDNER 1836 138; HARNACK 1906 38.51; HAWKINS 1909 187; NEIRYNCK 1985; PLUMMER 1922 lix; VOGEL 1899B

Literature

DENAUX 2009 lAn; JEREMIAS 1980 152 [red.].

GEORGE, Augustin, L'emploi chez Luc du vocabulaire de salut. — *NTS* 23 (1976-77) 308-320. [NTA 21, 759]; = ID., *Études*, 1978, 307-320.

VAN UNNIK, Willem C., L'usage de σῴζειν "sauver" et des dérivés dans les évangiles synoptiques. —*La formation des évangiles: problème synoptique et Formgeschichte* (Recherches bibliques, 2). Bruges: Desclée De Brouwer, 1957, 178-194; = ID., *Sparsa Collecta*, I, 1973, 16-34.

WAGNER, Wilhelm, Über σῴζειν und seine Derivata im Neuen Testament. — *ZNW* 6 (1905) 205-235.

WELLS, Louise, *The Greek Language of Healing*, 1998. Esp. 180-191.

See also σῴζω.

διαταράσσω* 1

διαταράσσομαι: be deeply troubled (Lk 1,29)

Literature

HAUCK 1934 [seltenes Alleinwort].

διατάσσω 4 + 5 (Mt 1)

1. command (Lk 3,13; 8,55; 17,9.10); 2. arrange for (Acts 20,13)

Word groups	Lk	Acts	Mt	Mk
τὰ διαταχθέντα (VKb) DENAUX 2009 L[n]	17,9.10		0	0

Characteristic of Luke

BOISMARD 1984 Eb12; CREDNER 1836 138; DENAUX 2009 L***; GOULDER 1989*; HARNACK 1906 51; HAWKINS 1909L; NEIRYNCK 1985; PLUMMER 1922 lix

	Lk	Acts	Mt	Mk
τὸ διατεταγμένον (VKa) BOISMARD 1984 Ab76; CREDNER 1836 134-135; NEIRYNCK 1985	3,13	23,31	0	0

Literature

COLLISON 1977 93 [substantivised neuter perfect participle]; DENAUX 2009 [LA[n]: τὸ διατεταγμένον]; EASTON 1910 160 [διατασσόμενος passive participle: cited by Weiss as characteristic of L, and possibly corroborative]; HAUCK 1934 [Vorzugswort]; JEREMIAS 1980 108 [red.]; RADL 1975 405.

BORMANN, L., *Recht, Gerechtigkeit und Religion*, 2001. Esp. 135.

MAKUJINA, John, Verbs Meaning "Command" in the New Testament: Determining the Factors Involved in the Choice of Command-Verbs. — *EstBíb* 56 (1998) 357-369. Esp. 358-359: "Παραγγέλλω"; 359-361: "Κελεύω"; 361-362: "Ἐντέλλω"; 362-364: "Διαστέλλω"; 364-366: "-τάσσω complex"; 366-367: "Λέγω". [NTA 43, 57]

διατηρέω 1 + 1   avoid

Word groups	Lk	Acts	Mt	Mk
διατηρέω + ἐν τῇ καρδίᾳ	2,51		0	0

Characteristic of Luke
BOISMARD 1984 Ab170; HARNACK 1906 73.150; HAWKINS 1909LA; MORGENTHALER 1958*; NEIRYNCK 1985; PLUMMER 1922 liii; VOGEL 1899A

Literature
BDAG 2000 238 [Lk 2,51: to keep someth. mentally with implication of duration; Acts 15,29: keep free of]; DENAUX 2009 LA[n]; GERSDORF 1816 272 [διετήρει πάντα τὰ ῥήματα ταῦτα]; HAUCK 1934 [seltenes Alleinwort]; JEREMIAS 1980 102 [red.].

MEYER, Ben F., "But Mary Kept All These Things..." (Lk 2,19.51). — CBQ 26 (1964) 31-49. Esp. 43-45: "Vocabulary of 2,19.51".

διατίθεμαι 2 + 1
1. make a will (Lk 22,29[1.2]); 2. make a covenant (Acts 3,25)

Word groups	Lk	Acts	Mt	Mk
διατίθεμαι βασιλείαν (LN: give right to rule) DENAUX 2009 L[n]	22,29[1.2]		0	0
διατίθεμαι διαθήκην (VKa)		3,25	0	0
διατίθεμαι + λέγων		3,25	0	0

Literature
DENAUX 2009 La[n]; JEREMIAS 1980 69 [διατίθεμαι + λέγων: red.]; 290-291 [red.]; SCHÜRMANN 1957 42.58 [trad.].

BORMANN, Lukas, Recht, Gerechtigkeit und Religion, 2001. Esp. 135.
TALBERT, Charles H., Succession in Mediterranean Antiquity. Part I: he Lukan Milieu; Part 2: Luke Acts. — SBL SP 37 (1998) 148-168.169-179.
TALBERT, Charles H., Reading Luke-Acts in Its Mediterranean Milieu (SupplNT, 107). Leiden-Boston: Brill, 2003, XII-255 p. Esp. 21-27: "The semantic field of succession thinking"; 43-50: "The concept of succession and Luke-Acts".

διαφέρω 2 + 2 (Mt 3, Mk 1)
1. carry through (Acts 13,49); 2. drive about (Acts 27,27); 3. be different; 4. be valuable (Lk 12,7.24)

Word groups	Lk	Acts	Mt	Mk
διαφέρω transitive (VKa)		13,49; 27,27	0	1

Literature
TAEGER, Jens-Wilhelm, Der Mensch und sein Heil, 1982. Esp. 123-125: "δέχεσθαι τὸν λόγον (τοῦ θεοῦ)"; 125-127: "ἀποδέχεσθαι τὸν λόγον αὐτοῦ (= des Petrus)"; 163-177: "ὁ λόγος τοῦ θεοῦ / τοῦ κυρίου) ηὔξανεν"; 177-178: "διεφέρετο ὁ λόγος τοῦ κυρίου".

διαφθείρω 1

1. destroy utterly (Lk 12,33) 2. deprave; 3. waste away

Literature
HAUCK 1934 [seltenes Alleinwort]; JEREMIAS 1980 218 [red.].

διαφυλάσσω 1   protect (Lk 4,10)

Literature
HAUCK 1934 [Vorzugswort].

διαχωρίζω 1   διαχωρίζομαι: depart from

Word groups	Lk	Acts	Mt	Mk
διαχωρίζομαι + ἀπό; cf. ἀποχωρίζομαι ἀπό Acts 15,39; χωρίζομαι ἀπό Acts 1,4; 18,2	9,33		0	0

Literature
HAUCK 1934 [seltenes Alleinwort].

διδάσκαλος 17 + 1 (Mt 12, Mk 12)   teacher (Acts 13,1)

Word groups	Lk	Acts	Mt	Mk
διδάσκαλε ἀγαθέ (VKb)	18,18		0/1	1
διδάσκαλος + μαθητής	6,40[1]; 19,39; 22,11		4	2
διδάσκαλος general (VKa)	6,40[1.2]		3	0
διδάσκαλος of John the Baptist (VKd)	3,12		0	0

Literature
REHKOPF 1959 98 [διδάσκαλε: "Substantiva in Anrede bei den Synoptikern"]

BACHMANN, Michael, *Jerusalem und der Tempel*, 1980. Esp. 261-289: "Lehre".
BRANDT, Pierre-Yves. & Alessandra LUKINOVICH, L'adresse à Jésus dans les évangiles synoptiques. — *Bib* 82 (2001) 17-50. Esp. 23-27.
DAWSEY, James M., What's in a Name? Characterization in Luke. — *BTB* 16 (1986) 143-147. Esp. 144-145: "Luke's use of 'teacher'".
GLOMBITZA, Otto, Die Titel διδάσκαλος und ἐπιστάτης für Jesus bei Lukas. — *ZNW* 49 (1958) 275-278.
HAHN, Ferdinand, *Christologische Hoheitstitel*, 1963. Esp. 76-81.
HORSLEY, G.H.R. – LEE, John A.L., A Lexicon of the New Testament, 1, 1997. Esp. 69-71.80-81.

διδάσκω 17 + 16 (Mt 14, Mk 17)   teach

Word groups	Lk	Acts	Mt	Mk
διδάσκω (+) ἱερόν (VKd)	19,47; 20,1; 21,37	5,21.25.42; 21,28	2	3

διδάσκω + κηρύσσω (VKa)		28,31	3	0
διδάσκω (+) λέγω; cf. λέγω ἐν τῇ διδαχῇ Mk 4,2; 12,38	20,21[1]	21,21	1	4
διδάσκω + συναγωγή → **κηρύσσω** + συναγωγή	4,15; 6,6; 13,10		3	2
διδάσκω τὰ περί BOISMARD 1984 Aa123		18,25; 28,31	0	0

Characteristic of Luke
GASTON 1973 64 [Lked]

	Lk	Acts	Mt	Mk
διδάσκω + εὐαγγελίζομαι (VKb) → **κηρύσσω** + εὐαγγελίζομαι BOISMARD 1984 Ab110; NEIRYNCK 1985	20,1	5,42; 15,35	0	0
διδάσκω τὸν λαόν BOISMARD 1984 Ab111; NEIRYNCK 1985	20,1	4,2; 5,25	0	0
ἦν + διδάσκων DENAUX 2009 L***	4,31; 5,17; 13,10; 19,47; 21,37		0	0

Literature
COLLISON 1977 45 [linguistic usage of Luke: certain]; DENAUX 2009 1A[n] [διδάσκω + εὐαγγελίζομαι; διδάσκω τὸν λαόν]; JEREMIAS 1980 176 n. 5 [διδάσκω + εὐαγγελίζομαι].

BACHMANN, Michael, *Jerusalem und der Tempel*, 1980. Esp. 261-289: "Lehre".
HORSLEY, G.H.R. – LEE, John A.L., A Lexicon of the New Testament, 1, 1997. Esp. 71-73.81.

διδαχή 1 + 4 (Mt 3, Mk 5)
1. teaching (Lk 4,32); 2. doctrine (Acts 5,28)

Word groups	Lk	Acts	Mt	Mk
διδαχή + καινή (VKa)		17,19	0	1
ἐκπλήσσομαι ἐπὶ τῇ διδαχῇ (VKc)	4,32	13,12	2	2

Literature
HORSLEY, G.H.R. – LEE, John A.L., A Lexicon of the New Testament, 1, 1997. Esp. 73-74.82.

δίδωμι 60 + 35 (Mt 56, Mk 39)
1. give (Lk 1,32); 2. produce (Acts 2,19); 3. allow (Lk 1,74); 4. put (Lk 15,22); 5. appoint (Acts 13,20); 6. pay (Lk 20,10); 7. deposit (Lk 19,23); 8. cause (Lk 1,77); 9. let experience

Word groups	Lk	Acts	Mt	Mk
ἀπὸ τοῦ καρποῦ + δίδωμι; cf. καρπὸν δίδωμι Mt 13,8; Mk 4,7.8; καρπὸν ἀποδίδωμι (LN: bear fruit) Mt 21,41	20,10		0	0
δίδωμι + αἰτέω → **δίδωμι** + ζητέω; **ἐπιδίδωμι/λαμβάνω/παρατίθημι** + αἰτέω; **εὑρίσκω** + (ἀνα/ἐπι)ζητέω; cf. ἀποδίδωμι + αἰτέω Mt 27,58	6,30; 11,9.13[2]	13,21	4	2
δίδωμι + ἄρτον → **ἐπιδίδωμι** ἄρτον	6,4; 9,16; 11,3; 22,19[1]		4	5

	Lk	Acts	Mt	Mk
δίδωμι + δόξαν (VKb; + τῷ θεῷ LN: promise to tell truth) → **δοξάζω** τὸν θεόν DENAUX 2009 La[n]	4,6[1.2]; 17,18	12,23	0	0
δίδωμι + ἐξουσίαν (SCa; VKa)	4,6[1.2]; 9,1; 10,19; 20,2	8,19	4	3
δίδωμι ἐργασίαν (LN: do one's best)	12,58		0	0
δίδωμι μετάνοιαν; cf. 2 Tim 2,25 BOISMARD 1984 Ca52		5,31; 11,18	0	0
δίδωμι + ζητέω → **(ἐπι)δίδωμι/λαμβάνω/ παρατίθημι** + αἰτέω; **εὑρίσκω** + (ἀνα/ἐπι)ζητέω; cf. δίδωμι + ἐπιζητέω Mt 12,39; 16,4	11,29; 12,48		0	1
δίδωμι ζωήν (VKc)		17,25	0	0
δίδωμι κλήρους		1,26	0	0
δίδωμι πτωχοῖς (SCd; VKk) → **διαδίδωμι** πτωχοῖς	19,8		2	2
δίδωμι (+) σημεῖον/σημεῖα (SCb; VKd); cf. Rev 13,14	11,29	2,19; 14,3	4	2
δίδωμι + σοφίαν (VKf)	21,15	7,10	0	1
δίδωμι + στόμα (LN: help to say)	21,15		0	0
δίδωμι τι/τινα + infinitive BOISMARD 1984 Aa124		10,40; 14,3	0	0
δίδωμι + τόπον	14,9		0	0
δίδωμι (+) (ἐσθίω/)φαγεῖν (SCe; VKl) → **ἐπιδίδωμι** + ἐσθίω; cf. δίδωμι + πιεῖν Mt 27,34	8,55; 9,13		3	3
δίδωμι + χάρις (VKj)		7,10	0	0
κληρονομίαν δίδωμι BOISMARD 1984 Aa140		7,5[1]; 20,32	0	0
δίδωμι absolute (SCf; VKm)	6,30.38[1.2]; 8,18; 11,9; 19,26	10,40; 20,35	6	1

Characteristic of Luke

PLUMMER 1922 lix

	Lk	Acts	Mt	Mk
δίδωμι (τὸ) πνεῦμα (SCc) → **παραδίδωμι** τὴν ψυχήν; cf. Jn 3,34 BOISMARD 1984 Eb46; NEIRYNCK 1985	11,13[2]	5,32; 8,18; 15,8	0	0
ἐλεημοσύνην δίδωμι → ἐλεημοσύνην **αἰτέω/ποιέω** VOGEL 1899C	11,41; 12,33		0	0

Literature

VON BENDEMANN 2001 421 [διδόναι ἐλεημοσύνην]; DENAUX 2009 L[n] [ἐλεημοσύνην δίδωμι], IA[n] [δίδωμι (τὸ) πνεῦμα]; GERSDORF 1816 208 [τοῦ δοῦναι ἡμῖν]; 212 [οὗ δοῦναι γνῶσιν]; HARNACK 1906 145 [δοῦναι + infinitive Lk 1,73-74; Acts 4,29]; HAUCK 1934 [Vorzugsverbindung: τοῦ δοῦναι]; SCHÜRMANN 1955 17-24 [Lk 22,19: διδόμενον trad.].

DELEBECQUE, Édouard, *Études grecques*, 1976. Esp. 109-121: "Le pain et la coupe de la dernière cène (22,17-20)".

MITCHELL, Alan C., Zacchaeus Revisited: Luke 19,8 as a Defense. — *Bib* 71 (1990) 153-176.

διεγείρω 2 (Mt 0/1; Mk 1/2)

1. wake up (Lk 8,24[1]); 2. cause; 3. διεγείρομαι: wake up (Lk 8,24[2]); 4. become stormy

Word groups	Lk	Acts	Mt	Mk
διεγερθείς (*VK*a) → ἐγερθείς	$8,24^2$		0/1	1

διερμηνεύω 1 + 1
1. translate (Acts 9,36); 2. explain (Lk 24,27)

Characteristic of Luke
BOISMARD 1984 Db39; NEIRYNCK 1985

Literature
DENAUX 2009 LA[n]; JEREMIAS 1980 317 [red.].

διέρχομαι 10 + 21 (Mt 2, Mk 2)
1. move on to (Acts 11,19); 2. travel through (Lk 9,6; Acts 13,6); 3. cross over (Lk 8,22); 4. penetrate (Lk 2,35; Acts 12,10)

Word groups	Lk	Acts	Mt	Mk
διελθών … ἔρχομαι BOISMARD 1984 Aa41		12,10; 14,24; 19,1 *v.l.*; 20,2	0	0
διέρχομαι + ἄχρι → **διέρχομαι** ἕως; (**ἐξ/παρ**)**ἔρχομαι** + ἄχρι/ἕως		13,6	0	0
διέρχομαι διὰ μέσον/μέσου (*VK*b) DENAUX 2009 L[n]	4,30; 17,11		0	0
διέρχομαι εἰς τὸ πέραν (*VK*a)	8,22		0	1
διέρχομαι + εὑρίσκω → (**ἀπ/εἰσ/ἐξ/κατ**)**ἔρχομαι**/ (**εἰσ**)**πορεύομαι** + εὑρίσκω	11,24	13,6; 17,23	1	0
διέρχομαι κατὰ τὰς κώμας + participle καί participle → **διαπορεύομαι** κατὰ πόλεις καὶ κώμας; **διοδεύω** κατὰ πόλιν καὶ κώμην	9,6		0	0
διέρχομαι + κηρύσσω → **ἀποστέλλω**/(**ἀπ/εἰσ**/ **κατ/προς**)**ἔρχομαι**/(**εἰσ**)**πορεύομαι**/ **ὑποστρέφω/φεύγω** + ἀπαγγέλλω/διαγγέλλω/ διηγέομαι/κηρύσσω		20,25		
διέρχομαι + πορεύομαι DENAUX 2009 La[n]	4,30; 17,11	19,21	0	0
διέρχομαι τὰ μέρη BOISMARD 1984 Aa125		19,1; 20,2	0	0
τὴν ψυχὴν διέρχεται ῥομφαία (*LN*: feel pain and sorrow)	2,35		0	0
διελθών DENAUX 2009 IA[n]	4,30	12,10; 13.6.14; 14,24; 19,1.21; 20,2	0	0
διέρχομαι metaphorically (*VK*c); cf. Rom 5,12	5,15		0	0

Characteristic of Luke
BOISMARD 1984 Cb68; CREDNER 1836 138; DENAUX 2009 L***; GOULDER 1989*;
HARNACK 1906 146; HAWKINS 1909L; HENDRIKS 1986 468; MORGENTHALER 1958LA;
NEIRYNCK 1985; PLUMMER 1922 lix

	Lk	Acts	Mt	Mk
διέρχομαι + accusative (region); cf. 1 Cor $16,5^{12}$; Heb 4,14 BOISMARD 1984 Bb100; DENAUX 2009 IA*; NEIRYNCK 1985	2,35; 19,1	12,10; 13,6; 14,24; 15,3.41; 16,6; 18,23; 19,1.21; 20,2	0	0

	9,6;	8,4; 10,38; 11,19;	1	0
διέρχομαι + participle BOISMARD 1984 Bb27; DENAUX 2009 IA*; NEIRYNCK 1985	11,24	15,3.41; 16,6; 20,25		
διέρχομαι ἕως → **διέρχομαι** + ἄχρι; **(ἐξ/παρ)έρχομαι** + ἄχρι/ἕως BOISMARD 1984 Ab112; HARNACK 1906 146; NEIRYNCK 1985; PLUMMER 1922 lii	2,15	9,38; 11,19.22	0	0

Literature

COLLISON 1977 45 [linguistic usage of Luke: probable]; DENAUX 2009 IA[n] [διέρχομαι ἕως]; GERSDORF 1816 236 [διέλθωμεν δὴ ἕως Βηθλέεμ]; 257 [διελεύσεται ρομφαία]; HAUCK 1934 [Vorzugswort]; JEREMIAS 1980 84 [διέλθωμεν δὴ ἕως Βηθλέεμ: red.]; 276: "διέρχομαι ist lk Vorzugswort; spezifisch lukanisch ist der an unsere Stelle [19,4] vorliegende absolute Gebrauch"; RADL 1975 405 [διέρχομαι; "Geographische Begriffe als Akkusativ-objekt von διέρχομαι"; διελθών; διέρχομαι + πορεύομαι; διέρχομαι "mit missionarischen Wendungen im Partizip"].

BENOIT, Pierre, "Et toi-même, un glaive te transpercera l'âme!" (Luc 2,35). — *CBQ* 25 (1963) 251-261.

BURCHARD, Christoph, Fußnoten zum neutestamentlichen Griechisch II, 1978. Esp. 145-146: "Lk 2,15 διέλθωμεν δὴ ἕως Βηθλέεμ".

διηγέομαι 2 + 3 (Mk 2)   tell fully

Word groups	Lk	Acts	Mt	Mk
διηγέομαι + ἀπ/ἐξέρχομαι DENAUX 2009 LA[n]	8,39	12,17	0	0
διηγέομαι πῶς BOISMARD 1984 Ca41		9,27; 12,17	0	1
διηγέομαι τὴν γενεάν (VKa)		8,33	0	0
ὑποστρέφω + διηγέομαι → ἀνα/ὑποστρέφω/εἰστρέχω/(ἀπ/εἰσ/ προσ)έρχομαι/πορεύομαι/φεύγω + **ἀπαγγέλλω**; ἀπέρχομαι + **διαγγέλλω**; ἀποστέλλω/εἰσπορεύομαι/(ἀπ/δι/κατ)έρχομαι + **κηρύσσω** DENAUX 2009 L[n]	8,39; 9,10		0	0

Characteristic of Luke

PLUMMER 1922 lix; VOGEL 1899B

διήγησις 1   narration (Lk 1,1)

Literature

HAUCK 1934 [seltenes Alleinwort].

ALEXANDER, Loveday, *The Preface to Luke's Gospel*, 1993. Esp. 111.

BORMANN, Lukas, *Recht, Gerechtigkeit und Religion*, 2001. Esp. 178.

CADBURY, Henry.J., Commentary on the Preface of Luke, 1922. Esp. 495.

GLÖCKNER, Richard, *Die Verkündigung des Heils beim Evangelisten Lukas*, 1975. Esp. 13-14: "Zum Begriff διήγησις".

HEAD, Peter M., Papyrological Perspectives on Luke's Predecessors (Luke 1,1). — P.J. WILLIAMS – A.D. CLARKE – P.M. HEAD – D. INSTONE-BREWER (eds.), *The New Testament in Its First Century Setting: Essays on Context and Background in Honour of*

B.W. *Winter on His 65th Birthday*, Grand Rapids, MI – Cambridge, Eerdmans, 2004, 30-45. Esp. 40-44.
PRETE, Benedetto, *Struttura del Vangelo di Luca*. — ID., *L'opera di Luca*, 1986, 34-79. Esp. 65-67: "Il sostantivo διήγησις".

διΐστημι 2 + 1

1. move on (Acts 27,28); 2. depart from (Lk 24,51; Acts 27,28); 3. pass (of time) (Lk 22,59)

Characteristic of Luke
BOISMARD 1984 ab113; HARNACK 1906 54; HAWKINS 1909LA; MORGENTHALER 1958*; NEIRYNCK 1985; PLUMMER 1922 lii; VOGEL 1899A

Literature
DENAUX 2009 La[n]; EASTON 1910 160 [cited by Weiss as characteristic of L, and possibly corroborative]; HAUCK 1934 [seltenes Alleinwort]; JEREMIAS 1980 297 [red.]; SCHNEIDER 1969 86.163: "διΐστημι findet sich im NT nur bei Luk" [Vorzugswörter und -ausdrücke des Luk].

διϊσχυρίζομαι 1 + 1   insist firmly (Lk 22,59; Acts 12,15)

Word groups	Lk	Acts	Mt	Mk
διϊσχυρίζομαι + λέγων	22,59		0	0

Characteristic of Luke
BOISMARD 1984 ab171; HAWKINS 1909LA; NEIRYNCK 1985; MORGENTHALER 1958*; PLUMMER 1922 liii; VOGEL 1899A

Literature
DENAUX 2009 LA[n]; HAUCK 1934 [seltenes Alleinwort]; JEREMIAS 1980 69 [διϊσχυρίζομαι + λέγων: red.]; 297 [red.].

BORMANN, Lukas, *Recht, Gerechtigkeit und Religion*, 2001. Esp. 178-179.

δίκαιος 11 + 6 (Mt 17/20, Mk 2)

1. righteous (Lk 2,25); 2. be put right with; 3. proper

Word groups	Lk	Acts	Mt	Mk
ἄνθρωπος + δίκαιος → ἀνὴρ δίκαιος; ἄνθρωπος/ἀνὴρ **ἀγαθός/εὐλαβής**	2,25; 23,47		1	0
δίκαιος + ἄδικος		24,15	1	0
δίκαιος + ἁμαρτωλός	5,32; 15,7		1	1
ὁ δίκαιος = Jesus BOISMARD 1984 Aa85		3,14; 7,52; 22,14		
(οἱ) δίκαιοι noun (*VK*a)	1,17; 5,32; 14,14; 15,7	24,15	8	1
(τὸ) δίκαιον (*VK*b)	12,57	4,19	1/2	0

Characteristic of Luke	Lk	Acts	Mt	Mk
ἀνὴρ δίκαιος → ἀνήρ + **ἀγαθός/εὐλαβής**; ἄνθρωπος + **ἀγαθός/δίκαιος/εὐλαβής** BOISMARD 1984 cb100; NEIRYNCK 1985	23,50	10,22	0	1
→ **ἀνάστασις** (τῶν) δικαίων (καὶ τῶν ἀδίκων)				

Literature

GERSDORF 1816 246 [δίκαιος καὶ εὐλαβής]; HAUCK 1934 [Vorzugsverbindung: ἀνάστασις (τῶν) δικαίων]; JEREMIAS 1980 22-23 [trad.].

BORMANN, Lukas., *Recht, Gerechtigkeit und Religion*, 2001. Esp. 198-200.
DOBLE, Peter, Luke 23.47 – The Problem of *Dikaios*. — *BTrans* 44 (1993) 320-331.
—, *The Paradox of Salvation*, 1996. Esp. 70-92: "Δίκαιος and 'innocent': Luke 23.47"; 93-126: "Δίκαιος in Luke's gospel"; 127-160: "Δίκαιος as a christological descriptor: Acts".
DODD, Charles H., Some Problems of New Testament Translation. — *BTrans* 13 (1962) 145-157. Esp. 154-155: "*dikaios, dikaiosunē*".
HILL, David, *Greek Words and Hebrew Meanings*, 1967. Esp. 120-139: "The δίκαιος-words in the usage of the New Testament: The Synoptic Gospels".
—, Δίκαιοι as a Quasi-Technical Term. — *NTS* 11 (1964-65) 296-302.
KILPATRICK, George D., A Theme of the Lucan Passion Story and Luke xxiii. 47. — *JTS* 43 (1942) 34-36; = ID., *Principles and Practice*, 1990, 327-329.
RESE, Martin, *Alttestamentliche Motive in der Christologie des Lukas*, 1969. Esp. 131-133: "Προφήτης, ἅγιος, δίκαιος, ἀρχηγός, σωτήρ und υἱὸς θεοῦ in der Apostelgeschichte".

δικαιοσύνη 1 + 4 (Mt 7)

1. righteousness (Lk 1,75); 2. be put right with; 3. religious observances; 4. charity

Word groups	Lk	Acts	Mt	Mk
δικαιοσύνην ἐργάζομαι (VKf); cf. δικαιοσύνην ποιέω Mt 6,1		10,35	0	0
ἐν (+) δικαιοσύνῃ (VKd); cf. ἐν ὁδῷ δικαιοσύνης Mt 21,32	1,75	17,31	0	0

Literature

BORMANN, Lukas, *Recht, Gerechtigkeit und Religion*, 2001. Esp. 200-201.
DODD, Charles H., Some Problems of New Testament Translation. — *BTrans* 13 (1962) 145-157. Esp. 154-155: "*dikaios, dikaiosunē*".

δικαιόω 5 + 2 (Mt 2)

1. to put right with; 2. show to be right (Lk 7,35; 10,29; 16,15; 18,14); 3. acquit (Acts 13,38); 4. set free; 5. obey righteous commands (Lk 7,29)

Word groups	Lk	Acts	Mt	Mk
δικαιόω ἑαυτόν DENAUX 2009 Lⁿ	10,29; 16,15		0	0

Characteristic of Luke

BOISMARD 1984 Eb63; DENAUX 2009 L***; GOULDER 1989*; HAWKINS 1909L; NEIRYNCK 1985

Literature

VON BENDEMANN 2001 418; HAUCK 1934 [Vorzugswort]; REHKOPF 1959 93 [vorlukanisch]; SCHÜRMANN 1961 275.

BORMANN, Lukas, *Recht, Gerechtigkeit und Religion*, 2001. Esp. 201.
DODD, Charles H., Some Problems of New Testament Translation. — *BTrans* 13 (1962) 145-157. Esp. 155-157: "*dikaioun*".

HILL, David, *Greek Words and Hebrew Meanings*, 1967. Esp. 120-139: "The δίκαιος-words in the usage of the New Testament: The Synoptic Gospels".
LÖVESTAM, Evald, Till förståelsen av Luk. 7:35. — *SEÅ* 22-23 (1957-58) 47-63.
SWELLENGREBEL, J.L., Puzzles in Luke. — *BTrans* 17 (1966) 118-122. Esp. 121-122 [Lk 7,35 ἐδικαιώθη ἡ σοφία ἀπὸ πάντων τῶν τέκνων αὐτῆς].

δικαίωμα 1

| 1. regulation (Lk 1,6); 2. righteous act; 3. acquit |

Word groups	Lk	Acts	Mt	Mk
δικαιώματα τοῦ κυρίου (*VK*a) → **νόμος** κυρίου	1,6		0	0

Literature
HARNACK 1906 70.

BORMANN, Lukas, *Recht, Gerechtigkeit und Religion*, 2001. Esp. 201.

δικαίως 1   right (Lk 23,41)

Literature
BORMANN, Lukas, *Recht, Gerechtigkeit und Religion*, 2001. Esp. 201.

δίκτυον 4 (Mt 2, Mk 2)   fishnet (Lk 5,2.4.5.6)

διό 2 + 8/10 (Mt 1)   therefore (Lk 1,35; 7,7)

Word groups	Lk	Acts	Mt	Mk
διὸ οὐδέ	7,7		0	0

Characteristic of Luke
BOISMARD 1984 Eb8; DENAUX 2009 1A*; NEIRYNCK 1985.

	Lk	Acts	Mt	Mk
διὸ καί (*VK*a) → **διότι**/(**καθ**)**ότι** καί BOISMARD 1984 Db19; NEIRYNCK 1985	1,35	10,29; 13,35*; 24,26	0	0

Literature
BDR § 451,5: "Konsekutive koordinierende Konjuktionen: Lk 1,35 steht die ... beliebte Verbindung διὸ καί, entsprechend διὸ οὐδέ Lk 7,7"; DENAUX 2009 1Aⁿ [διὸ καί]; HAUCK 1934 [Vorzugswort]; JEREMIAS 1980 51 [διὸ καί: red.]; RADL 1975 405.

MUÑOZ IGLESIAS, Salvador, Lucas 1,35b. — *La idea de Dios en la Biblia. XXVIII Semana Biblica Española (Madrid 23-27 sept. 1968)*. Madrid: Consejo Superior de Investigaciones Cientificas, 1971, 303-324.
SCHNEIDER, Gerhard, Lk 1,34. 35 als redaktionelle Einheit. — *BZ* NF 15 (1971) 255-259. Esp. 256-257: "Lk 1,35 ist nach Wortschatz, Stil und Theologie 'lukanisch'".
—, Jesu geistgewirkte Empfängnis (Lk 1,34f): Zur Interpretation einer christologischen Aussage. — *TPQ* 119 (1971) 105-116. Esp. 110; = ID., *Lukas, Theologe der Heilsgeschichte*, 1985, 86-97. Esp. 91.
VICENT, A., El valor atenuado de *dio kai* = ('por eso en cierto modo') dentro y fuera del N.T.. — *EstBib* 32 (1973) 57-76. [NTA 18, 405]

διοδεύω 1 + 1 | travel through (Lk 8,1; Acts 17,1)

Word groups	Lk	Acts	Mt	Mk
διοδεύω κατὰ πόλιν καὶ κώμην + participle καί participle → **διαπο-ρεύομαι** κατὰ πόλεις καὶ κώμας; **διέρχομαι** κατὰ τὰς κώμας	8,1		0	0

Characteristic of Luke
BOISMARD 1984 Ab172; HAWKINS 1909LA; MORGENTHALER 1958*; NEIRYNCK 1985;
PLUMMER 1922 liii; VOGEL 1899A

Literature
VON BENDEMANN 2001 413; DENAUX 2009 LA[n]; HAUCK 1934 [seltenes Alleinwort]; JEREMIAS
1980 175 [red.].

διορύσσω 1 (Mt 3) | break through

Word groups	Lk		Acts	Mt	Mk
διορύσσω + κλέπτης	12,39			3	0

διότι 3 + 5/6

1. because (Lk 1,13; 2,7; 21,28); 2. that

Word groups	Lk	Acts	Mt	Mk
διότι καί → **διό/(καθ)ότι** καί		13,35	0	0

Characteristic of Luke
BOISMARD 1984 Db8; DENAUX 2009 lA*; GOULDER 1989; HARNACK 1906 71; HAWKINS
1909B; NEIRYNCK 1985

Literature
HAUCK 1934 [Vorzugswort]; JEREMIAS 1980 33-34 [red.]; RADL 1975 405.

δίς 1 (Mk 2) | twice

Word groups	Lk	Acts	Mt	Mk
δὶς τοῦ σαββάτου	18,12		0	0

διχοτομέω 1 (Mt 1)

1. cut in two (Lk 12,46); 2. punish severely

διώκω 3 + 9 (Mt 6/7)

1. pursue (Lk 17,23); 2. press forward; 3. persecute (Lk 11,49; 21,12; Acts 22,4); 4.
strive to

Word groups	Lk	Acts	Mt	Mk
διώκω + accusative (thing) (VKa)		22,4	0	0

διώκω ἕως		26,11	0	0

Literature

JEREMIAS 1980 84 [διώκω ἕως: red.].

STEGEMANN, Wolfgang, *Zwischen Synagoge und Obrigkeit: Zur historischen Situation der lukanischen Christen* (FRLANT, 152). Göttingen: Vandenhoeck & Ruprecht, 1991, 304 p. Esp. 114-118: "Exkurs: Διώκειν und διωγμός bei Lukas".

δόγμα 1 + 2

1. law (Acts 16,4); 2. decree (Lk 2,1)

Characteristic of Luke

HARNACK 1906 74

Literature

DENAUX 2009 IA[n]; HAUCK 1934 [seltenes Alleinwort]; JEREMIAS 1980 77 [red.].

BORMANN, Lukas, *Recht, Gerechtigkeit und Religion*, 2001. Esp. 115.

δοκέω 10/11 + 8/9 (Mt 10, Mk 2)

1. suppose (Lk 13,2); 2. be disposed of; 3. choose

Word groups

Word groups	Lk	Acts	Mt	Mk
δοκεῖτε ὅτι ...; οὐχί, λέγω ὑμῖν, ἀλλ'... DENAUX 2009 L[n]	12,51; 13,2(-3).4-(5)		0	0

Characteristic of Luke

GASTON 1973 65 [Lked?]

	Lk	Acts	Mt	Mk
δοκεῖ/ἔδοξε impersonal (*VK*b); cf. Heb 12,10 BOISMARD 1984 Bb65; NEIRYNCK 1985	1,3	15,22.25.28.34*; 25,27	0	0
δοκεῖ εἶναι BOISMARD 1984 Db40; NEIRYNCK 1985	22,24	17,18	0	0
δοκεῖν = think GOULDER 1989	8,18; 12,40.51; 13,2.4; 17,9; 19,11; 24,37	12,9; 26,9; 27,13	4	1
δοκέω + inf. DENAUX 2009 L***	1,3; 8,18; 10,36; 22,24; 24,37	12,9; 15,22.25.28. 34*; 17,18; 25,27; 26,9; 27,13	1	1

Literature

VON BENDEMANN 2001 418: "lukanisch ist δοκεῖν c. inf."; DENAUX 2009 IA[n] [δοκεῖ/ἔδοξε impersonal], [LA[n]: δοκεῖ εἶναι]; EASTON 1910 153 [probably characteristic of L]; GERSDORF 1816 160 [ἔδοξε κἀμοὶ ... γράψαι]; JEREMIAS 1980 192: "δοκέω wird im lk Doppelwerk teils mit Infinitiv (...) konstruiert, teils mit ὅτι (...)" [δοκέω + inf.: red.; δοκέω + ὅτι: trad.]; RADL 1975 405-406 ["die unpersönlichen Formen δοκεῖ usw."]; SCHÜRMANN 1957 67 [das intransitive δοκεῖν unpersönlich in der Bedeutung "gut scheinen" ... ein Vorzugswort des Lk].

ALEXANDER, Loveday, *The Preface to Luke's Gospel*, 1993. Esp. 127.

δοκιμάζω 3

1. test (Lk 12,56[1.2]; 14,19); 2. regard as worthwhile; 3. judge as good

Literature

DENAUX 2009 L[n]; HAUCK 1934 [seltenes Alleinwort].

BORMANN, Lukas, *Recht, Gerechtigkeit und Religion*, 2001. Esp. 135-136.

δοκός 3 (Mt 3)	beam (of wood) (Lk 6,41.42[1.2])

δόμα 1 (Mt 1)	gift (Lk 11,13)

δόξα 13 + 4 (Mt 7/8, Mk 3)

1. splendor (Lk 4,6); 2. brightness (Acts 22,11); 3. amazing might; 4. praise (Lk 17,18); 5. honor (Lk 14,10); 6. greatness (Lk 12,27); 7. glorious being; 8. heaven; 9. pride

Word groups	Lk	Acts	Mt	Mk
δόξα + ἄγγελος	2,9; 9,26	12,23	2	1
δόξα + δύναμις (VKb)	21,27		1/2	1
δόξα ἐν ὑψίστοις; cf. ὡσαννὰ ἐν τοῖς ὑψίστοις Mt 21,9; Mk 11,10 DENAUX 2009 L[n]	2,14; 19,38		0	0
δόξα + ἐξουσία (VKe)	4,6		0	0
δόξα θεοῦ/κυρίου DENAUX 2009 LA[n]	2,9	7,55	0	0
δόξα (+) θεῷ → αἶνος τῷ θεῷ; **δοξάζω** τὸν θεόν; **εὐλογητός** + θεός DENAUX 2009 La[n]	2,14; 17,18		12,23	0	0
δόξα + τοῦ πατρός	9,26		1	1
δόξαν (+) δίδωμι (+ τῷ θεῷ LN: promise to tell truth) DENAUX 2009 La[n]	4,6; 17,18	12,23	0	0
ἐν (+) (τῇ) δόξῃ	9,26.31; 12,27		3	2

Characteristic of Luke

GOULDER 1989

Literature

EASTON 1910 153 [probably characteristic of L; not noted by Weiss]; GERSDORF 1816 232 [δόξα ἐν ὑψίστοις θεῷ καὶ ἐπὶ γῆς εἰρήνη]; 256 [δόξαν λαοῦ σου Ἰσραήλ].

BAARDA, Heinrich, Friede im Himmel: Die lukanische Redaktion von Lk 19,38 und ihre Deutung. — *ZNW* 76 (1985) 170-186. [ἐν οὐρανῷ εἰρήνη καὶ δόξα ἐν ὑψίστοις]

DECREUS, F., Doxa – Kabod: Schematische transpositie of struktuurg+lijkheid? . — *Sacris Erudiri* 22 (1974-75) 117-185. [NTA 21, 661]

DELEBECQUE, Édouard, *Études grecques*, 1976. Esp. 25-38: "Le 'gloria' des anges (2,14)".

DODD, Charles H., Some Problems of New Testament Translation. — *BTrans* 13 (1962) 145-157. Esp. 153-154: "*doxa*".

FRY, Euan, Translating "Glory" in the New Testament. — *BTrans* 27 (1976) 422-427.

GEORGE, Augustin, La prière. — ID., *Études*, 1978, 395-427. Esp. 402-405: "Le vocabulaire lucanien de la prière".

GUERRA GÓMEZ, Manuel, Análisis filológico-teológico y traducción del himno de los ángeles en Belén, 1989. Esp. 32-42.

—, "… Eudokia (bondad, benevolencia) en medio de los hombres", nombre o designación de Jesucristo en el himno de los ángeles (Lc 2,14 y comienzo del "Gloria…" de la Misa. — *RevistCatTeol* 14 (1989) 203-222.

KILGALLEN, John J., Jesus, Savior, the Glory of Your People Israel. — *Bib* 75 (1994) 305-328.

OWEN, E.C.E., Δόξα and Cognate Words. — *JTS* 33 (1931-32) 132-150, 265-279.

[patristic Greek]

δοξάζω 9 + 5 (Mt 4, Mk 1)

1. praise (Lk 5,25); 2. honor (Acts 13,48); 3. glorify (Lk 2,20); 4. δοξάζομαι be wonderful

Characteristic of Luke

GASTON 1973 65 [Lked?]; GOULDER 1989.

	Lk	Acts	Mt	Mk
δοξάζω τὸν θεόν (VKa) → αἰνέω/εὐλογέω τὸν θεόν; δόξα θεῷ; cf. δοξάζω τὸν λόγον τοῦ κυρίου Acts 13,48 DENAUX 2009 L***; GOULDER 1989*; HAWKINS 1909L; PLUMMER 1922 lxi	2,20; 5,25.26; 7,16; 13,13; 17,15; 18,43; 23,47	4,21; 11,18; 21,20	2	1
δοξάζω τὸν θεόν + verb of saying → αἰνέω/εὐλογέω τὸν θεόν + verb of saying BOISMARD 1984 cb24; DENAUX 2009 La*; NEIRYNCK 1985	5,26; 7,16; 23,47	11,18; 21,20	0	1

Literature

COLLISON 1977 46 [δοξάζω τὸν θεόν: linguistic usage of Luke: likely]; GERSDORF 1816 240 [δοξάζοντες καὶ αἰνοῦντες τὸν θεόν]; HAUCK 1934 [Vorzugswort; Vorzugsverbindung: δοξάζω τὸν θεόν]; JEREMIAS 1980 69 [δοξάζω + λέγων: red.]; 88 [δοξάζω τὸν θεόν: red.].

DOBLE, Peter, *The Paradox of Salvation*, 1996. Esp. 25-69: "Luke's use of δοξάζειν τὸν θεόν".

δουλεύω 3 + 2 (Mt 2)

1. be a slave; 2. be controlled by; 3. serve (Lk 15,29; 16,13[1.2]; Acts 20,19)

Word groups	Lk	Acts	Mt	Mk
δουλεύω + ἀγαπάω/μισέω	16,31[1]		1	0
δουλεύω θεῷ (VKa)	16,13[2]		1	0
δουλεύω τῷ κυρίῳ (VKb)		20,19	0	0

Literature

DUPONT, Jacques, *Le discours de Milet*, 1962. Esp. 51-54.101.

δούλη 2 + 1   slave woman (Lk 1,38.48)

Characteristic of Luke

HARNACK 1906 74; HAWKINS 1909LA; PLUMMER 1922 lii

Literature

DENAUX 2009 La[n]; HAUCK 1934 [seltenes Alleinwort].

RODRÍGUEZ, I., Consideración filologica sobre el mensaje de la anunciación, 1958. Esp. 247-248: "ἡ δούλη κυρίου".
WOOD, Irving F., Τῆς δούλης in the Magnificat, Luke i.48. — *JBL* 21 (1902) 48-50.

δοῦλος 26/27 + 3 (Mt 30, Mk 5) — slave

Word groups	Lk	Acts	Mt	Mk
ἀποστέλλω/πέμπω (+) δοῦλον; cf. ἀποστέλλω δούλ ους Mt 21,34.36; 22,3.4	14,17; 20,10.11		0	2
δοῦλος ἀγαθός/πονηρός; cf. δοῦλος κακός Mt 24,48	19,17.22		3	0
δοῦλος ἀχρεῖος	17,10		1	0
δοῦλος (+) κύριος/αὐτός (*VK*a) → οἰκέτης + κύριος	12,37.43.45.46.47; 14,21¹.22.23	4,29	15	0
δοῦλος + (οἰκο)δεσπότης/αὐτός (*VK*b)	2,29; 14,21²		5	0
δοῦλος (τοῦ) θεοῦ (*VK*c)		16,17	0	0

Literature
GERSDORF 1816 254 [νῦν ἀπολύεις τὸν δοῦλόν σου, δέσποτα, κατὰ τὸ ῥῆμά σου ἐν εἰρήνῃ]; HARNACK 1906 36 [δοῦλος of God Acts 16,17; see also Lk 2,29; Acts 4,29]; REHKOPF 1959 98 [ἀγαθὲ/πονηρὲ δοῦλε: "Substantiva in Anrede bei den Synoptikern"].

DODD, Charles H., Some Problems of New Testament Translation. — *BTrans* 13 (1962) 145-157. Esp. 145-146: *"doulos"*.
DUPONT, Jacques, *Le discours de Milet*, 1962. Esp. 45.52-56.102.

δοχή 2 — banquet

Word groups	Lk	Acts	Mt	Mk
δοχὴν ποιέω → ἄριστον/δεῖπνον ποιέω; cf. ποιέω γάμους Mt 22,2	5,29; 14,13		0	0

Characteristic of Luke
PLUMMER 1922 liii

Literature
VON BENDEMANN 2001 427: "δοχή findet sich im Neuen Testament nur Lk 5,29; 14,13";
DENAUX 2009 Lⁿ; HAUCK 1934 [seltenes Alleinwort]; JEREMIAS 1980 238 [ποιέω δοχήν: red.].

δραχμή 3 — coin, drachma (Lk 15,8¹·²·9)

Literature
DENAUX 2009 Lⁿ; HAUCK 1934 [seltenes Alleinwort].

δύναμαι 26 + 21 (Mt 27, Mk 33) — be able

Word groups	Lk	Acts	Mt	Mk
δύναμαι (+) (ἐπι)γνῶναι		17,19; 21,34; 24,8.11	0	0
δύναμαι (+) θέλω/βούλομαι (*VK*b)	5,12; 16,26	17,19(-20)	1	4

δύναται ὁ θεός → ὁ **δυνατός**	3,8; 5,21		1	1
μὴ δυνάμενος	1,20; 13,11	21,34; 27,15	1	1
δύναμαι participle (*VK*a)	1,20; 13,11	20,32; 21,34; 24,11; 27,15.43	3	1

Characteristic of Luke	Lk	Acts	Mt	Mk
μήτι δύναται + infinitive BOISMARD 1984 Ab173; NEIRYNCK 1985	6,39	10,47	0	0

Literature

DENAUX 2009 [LA[n]: μήτι δύναται + infinitive]; RADL 1975 406 [δύναμαι; μὴ δυνάμενος; δύναμαι + (ἐπι)γνῶναι].

DUPONT, Jacques, *Le discours de Milet*, 1962. Esp. 245-250.

ELLIOTT, James K., Textual Variation Involving the Augment in the Greek New Testament. — *ZNW* 69 (1978) 247-252.

δύναμις 15 + 10 (Mt 12/13, Mk 10)

1. ability; 2. power (Acts 1,8); 3. mighty deed (Acts 2,22); 4. ruler; 5. supernatural power; 6. meaning

Word groups	Lk	Acts	Mt	Mk
δυνάμεις τῶν οὐρανῶν (*VK*e); cf. αἱ δυνάμεις αἱ ἐν τοῖς οὐρανοῖς Mt 13,25	21,26		1	0
δύναμις + δόξα (*VK*g)	21,27		1/2	1
δύναμις + ἐξουσία (*VK*h) DENAUX 2009 L[n]	4,36; 9,1; 10,19		0	0
δύναμις ἐξ ὕψους	24,49		0	0
δύναμις τοῦ θεοῦ (*VK*a)	22,69	8,10	1	1
δύναμις κυρίου (*VK*b)	5,17		0	0
δύναμις μεγάλη		4,33; 8,10.13	0	0
δύναμις τοῦ πνεύματος (*VK*c)	4,14		0	0
δύναμις + σημεῖα/τέρατα (*VK*f)		2,22; 6,8; 8,13	0	0
δύναμις ὑψίστου	1,35		0	0
ἐν + δυνάμει (*VK*m)	1,17; 4,36		0	1
λαμβάνω δύναμιν		1,8	0	0
μετὰ δυνάμεως	21,27		1	1

Characteristic of Luke GASTON 1973 64 [Lked]				
	Lk	Acts	Mt	Mk
δύναμις, of Jesus' healing power GOULDER 1989	4,36; 5,17; 6,19; 8,46; 9,1	2,22; 10,38	1	2
δύναμις + πνεῦμα (*VK*d) DENAUX 2009 L***	1,17.35; 4,14.36	1,8; 10,38	0	0

Literature

DENAUX 2009 [Lan: δύναμις, of Jesus' healing power]; JEREMIAS 1980 208 [ἡ δύναμις τοῦ θεοῦ: red.].

GERHARDSSON, Birger, Jesu maktgärningar: Om de urkrista berättarnas val av termer. — *SEÅ* 44 (1979) 122-133.

SCHNEIDER, Gerhard, Lk 1,34. 35 als redaktionelle Einheit. — *BZ* NF 15 (1971) 255-259.
Esp. 256-257: "Lk 1,35 ist nach Wortschatz, Stil und Theologie 'lukanisch'".

—, Jesu geistgewirkte Empfängnis (Lk 1,34f): Zur Interpretation einer christologischen Aussage. — *TPQ* 119 (1971) 105-116. Esp. 110; = ID., *Lukas, Theologe der Heilsgeschichte*, 1985, 86-97. Esp. 91.
WINK, Walter, *Naming the Powers*, 1984. Esp. 17.159.

δυνάστης 1 + 1   official (Lk 1,52; Acts 8,27)

Characteristic of Luke
HARNACK 1906 74

Literature
DENAUX 2009 LAⁿ.

BORMANN, Lukas, *Recht, Gerechtigkeit und Religion*, 2001. Esp. 212.

δυνατός 4 + 6 (Mt 3, Mk 5)

1. possible (Lk 18,27); 2. be able (Lk 14,31); 3. competent (Lk 24,19; Acts 7,22; 18,24)

Word groups	Lk	Acts	Mt	Mk
δυνατόν ἐστιν (*VK*b)		2,24; 20,16	1	1
δυνατός ἐστιν + infinitive (*VK*a) → **δύναται** ὁ θεός DENAUX 2009 LAⁿ	14,31	11,17	0	0
δυνατός μεγάλα → μεγαλύνω + **θεός/κύριος**; μεγαλειότης τοῦ **θεοῦ**; cf. δυνατός + μεγαλεῖος Lk 1,49 *v.l.*	1,49		0	0
δυνατὸς παρὰ τῷ θεῷ	18,27		1	1
οἱ δυνατοί (*LN*: important people)		25,5	0	0
ὁ δυνατός (*LN*: the Mighty One)	1,49		0	0

Characteristic of Luke	Lk	Acts	Mt	Mk
δυνατός of a person DENAUX 2009 LA*; HARNACK 1906 141	1,49; 14,31; 24,19	7,22; 11,17; 28,24	0	0
δυνατὸς ἐν BOISMARD 1984 Ab114; NEIRYNCK 1985	24,19	7,22; 18,24	0	0

Literature
DENAUX 2009 lAⁿ [δυνατὸς ἐν]; EASTON 1910 160 [δυνατός masculine: cited by Weiss as characteristic of L, and possibly corroborative]; HARNACK 1906 151 [ὁ δυνατός]; JEREMIAS 1980 315 [δυνατὸς ἐν: red.].

δύνω 1 (Mk 1)   go down (Lk 4,40)

δύο 29 + 13/14 (Mt 40/41, Mk 17[18]/19)   two

Word groups	Lk	Acts	Mt	Mk
ἀνὰ δύο (*VK*f) DENAUX 2009 Lⁿ	9,3; 10,1²		0	0
δύο δύο (*VK*g)	10,1²·³		0	0

δύο (+) εἷς (VKj)	5,2(-3); 7,41; 12,6; 16,13; 17,34.35; 18,10	1,24	12	3
δύο ἰχϑύες	9,13.16		2	3
δύο μαϑηταί / δύο τῶν μαϑητῶν	7,18; 19,29		1/2	2
δύο τινές → εἷς τις DENAUX 2009 LA[n]	7,18	23,23	0	0
δύο + τρεῖς (VKk)	12,52[1.2]		2	0
ἑβδομήκοντα δύο (VKb) DENAUX 2009 L[n]	10,1[1].17		0	0
(καὶ) (ἰδοὺ) ἄνδρες δύο DENAUX 2009 La[n]	9,30.32; 24,4	1,10; 9,38; 10,19*	0	0
οἱ δύο noun (VKh)		1,24	4	1

Characteristic of luke	Lk	Acts	Mt	Mk
δύο + noun + ὁ εἷς ... ὁ ἕτερος DENAUX 2009 L***	7,41; 16,13; 17,34.35; 18,10		1	0

Literature

JEREMIAS 1980 183 [ἀνὰ δύο: red.]; SCHÜRMANN 1957 130 [δύο hinter das Nomen].

BURCHARD, Christoph, Fußnoten zum neutestamentlichen Griechisch, 1970. Esp. 167-168: "Act 19,34 ὡς ἐπὶ ὥρας δύο κράζοντες".
CRAGHAN, John F., A Redactional Study of Lk 7,21 in the Light of Dt 19,15. — CBQ 29 (1967) 353-367. Esp. 52-56: "The redactor's hand" [ἄνδρες δύο].

δυσβάστακτος 1 (Mt 1)   difficult (Lk 11,46)

Literature
HAUCK 1934 [seltenes Alleinwort].

δυσκόλως 1 (Mt 1, Mk 1)   with difficulty (Lk 18,24)

δυσμή 2 (Mt 2)   west

Word groups	Lk	Acts	Mt	Mk
ἀνατέλλω ἐπὶ δυσμῶν	12,54		0	0
ἀπό + δυσμῶν → ἀπὸ ἀνατολῶν/βορρᾶ/νότου	13,29		1	0

δώδεκα 12/13 + 4 (Mt 13, Mk 15)   twelve

Word groups	Lk	Acts	Mt	Mk
δώδεκα + ἀπόστολοι (SCc; VKc) → ἕνδεκα ἀπόστολοι	6,13; 9,1 v.l.; 22,14*		1	1
δώδεκα ἔτη	2,42; 8,42.43		1	2
δώδεκα μαϑηταί (SCb; VKb); cf. ἕνδεκα μαϑηταί Mt 28,16	9,1 v.l.		3/4	0
δώδεκα + προσκαλέομαι → μαϑηταί + προσκαλέομαι		6,2	1	2
αἱ δώδεκα φυλαί (LN: all God's people)	22,30		1	0

εἷς (ἐκ) τῶν δώδεκα → τις τῶν **μαθητῶν**; cf. εἷς τῶν μαθητῶν Mk 13,1; εἷς ἐξ ὑμῶν Mt 26,21; Mk 14,18	22,47		2	3
οἱ δώδεκα (*SC*a; *VK*a) → οἱ **ἕνδεκα**	8,1; 9,1.12; 18,31; 22,3.47	6,2	4/5	10

Literature

COLLISON 1977 168 [οἱ δώδεκα: linguistic usage of Luke: certain].

DE JONGE, Henk J., Sonship, Wisdom, Infancy: Luke II.41-51a. — *NTS* 24 (1977-78) 317-354. Esp. 317-324: "When he was twelve".

FRIZZI, Giuseppe, L'ἀπόστολος delle tradizioni sinottiche (Mc, Q, Mt, Lc, e Atti). — *RivBib* 22 (1974) 3-37. Esp. 31-33: "Chi sono οἱ δώδεκα?"; 33-37: "Storicità della realtà sinottiche: οἱ δώδεκα/οἱ ἀπόστολοι".

GEORGE, Augustin, L'œuvre de Luc: Actes et Évangile. — DELORME, J. (ed.), *Le ministère et les ministères selon le Nouveau Testament: dossier exégétique et réflexion théologique* (Parole de Dieu, 10). Paris: Seuil, 1974, 207-240; = Les ministères. — ID., *Études*, 1978, 369-394.

δῶμα 3 + 1 (Mt 2, Mk 1) housetop

Word groups	Lk	Acts	Mt	Mk
ἐπὶ τῶν δωμάτων (*LN*: in public)	12,3		1	0

δῶρον 2 (Mt 9, Mk 1)

1. gift (Lk 21,1); 2. offering box (Lk 21,4)

Word groups	Lk	Acts	Mt	Mk
(τὰ) δῶρα (*VK*a)	21,1.4		1	0
δῶρον τοῦ θεοῦ (*VK*b)	21,4 *v.l.*		0	0

E

ἔα 1 (Mk 0/1) ah (Lk 4,34)

Literature

HAUCK 1934 [seltenes Alleinwort].

ἐάν 28/33 + 10/11 (Mt 62/71, Mk 33/43)

1. if (Lk 4,7); 2. when; 3. ever (Lk 17,33)

Word groups	Lk	Acts	Mt	Mk
ἀλλ᾽ ἐάν	13,3.5; 16,30		1	0/1
ἐάν + aorist subjunctive (*SC*b)	4,7; 6,34; 7,23; 9,48.48*; 12,45; 13,5 *v.l.*; 14,34; 15,8; 16,30.31; 17,3¹·².4.33.33*; 18,17*; 19,40 *v.l.*; 20,5.6.28; 22,67.68	2,21*; 3,23; 7,7 *v.l.*; 8,19.31 *v.l.*; 9,2; 15,1; 27,31	42/49	25/36

ἐάν + indicative (*VK*m) → ἄν + ind.	11,12*; 17,33* *v.l.*; 19,40	7,7; 8,31	0/6	0/1
ἐάν + present subjunctive (*SC*a)	4,6; 5,12; 6,33; 9,24*.57; 10,6.22; 11,12*; 13,3.5; 19,31	5,38; 13,41; 26,5	16/17	7/9
ἐάν (δὲ) καί (*SC*e; *VK*c) → ἄν/εἰ/ὅταν (δὲ) καί	14,34; 22,68 *v.l.*		1	0
ἐὰν μέν → εἰ/κἄν μέν (οὖν)	10,6*		1	0
ἐὰν μή (*SC*c; *VK*a) → εἰ μή	13,3.5	3,23; 8,31; 15,1; 27,31	8	5
ἐὰν … οὐ → ἄν/εἰ … οὐ; cf. κἄν … οὐ Mt 26,35; Mk [16,18]	22,67.68	13,41; 15,1; 27,31	3	5
ἐὰν … οὕτως	19,31		0	0
ἐὰν … οὐχί	15,8		2	0
ἐάν τις → καθότι ἄν + τις	16,30.31; 19,31; 20,28	9,2; 13,41	5	3
καὶ ἐάν → καὶ εἰ; κἄν	6,33 *v.l.*34; 10,6; 11,12*; 12,38*; 17,3.4; 19,31		6/7	8
ὅπου ἐάν (*SC*j; *VK*j)	9,57		3	4/5
ὅπως ἐάν → ὅπως ἄν		9,2	0	0
ὃς ἐάν (*SC*f; *VK*f) → ὅς + ἄν	4,6; 7,23; 9,24*.48.48*; 10,22; 17,33.33*; 18,17*	2,21*; 7,7; 8,19	15/23	6/13
ὃς/ὅστις ἐὰν μή → ὅς/ὅσος/ὅστις ἄν … μή; cf. ὅσος ἐάν … μή Mt 23,3	7,23; 18,17*	3,23	1/2	0/2
ὅστις ἐάν (*SC*g; *VK*h) → ὅστις ἄν		3,23	0	1
ἐάν instead of ἄν (*VK*l)	4,6; 9,24*.48.48*.57; 10,22; 17,33*; 18,17*	2,21*; 3,23; 7,7; 8,19; 9,2	7/12	5/11

→ ἐὰν **θέλῃς**

Literature

COLLISON 1977 113 [ἐάν for ἄν resisted: linguistic usage of Luke: likely].

BOYER, James L., Third (and Fourth) Class Conditions. — *Grace Theological Journal* 3 (1982) 163-175.

—, Other Conditional Elements in New Testament Greek. — *Grace Theological Journal* 3 (1983) 173-188.

ROBERTS, J.W., Some Aspects of Conditional Sentences in the Greek New Testament. — *BTrans* 15 (1964) 70-76.

ἑαυτοῦ 57/68 + 20/24 (Mt 32/35, Mk 24/31)   himself, herself, itself

Word groups	Lk	Acts	Mt	Mk
ἀπέρχομαι πρὸς ἑαυτόν (*LN*: go back to one's place)	24,12		0	0
ἀφ' ἑαυτοῦ/ἑαυτῶν (*VK*c) DENAUX 2009 L[n]	12,57; 21,30	21,23 *v.l.*	0	0
ἄφες τοὺς νεκροὺς θάψαι τοὺς ἑαυτῶν νεκρούς (*LN*: that is not the issue)	9,60		1	0
γίνομαι ἐν ἑαυτῷ VOGEL 1899C		12,11	0	0
δικαιόω ἑαυτόν DENAUX 2009 L[n]	10,29; 16,15		0	0

εἰς ἑαυτόν/ἑαυτούς (VKe) DENAUX 2009 Lⁿ	7,30; 15,17; 22,17		0	0
ἐν ἑαυτῷ/ἑαυτοῖς (SCa; VKf)	3,8; 7,39.49; 12,17; 16,3; 18,4	10,17; 12,11; 28,29*	8	5
ἐφ' ἑαυτοῖς (VKj)	18,9		0	0
ἐφ' ἑαυτόν/ἑαυτούς (VKk) → διαμερίζομαι ἐφ' ἑαυτόν	11,17.18; 23,28		1	3
ἐφ' ἑαυτοῦ/ἑαυτῶν (VKh)		21,23	0	0
καθ' ἑαυτόν (VKm)		28,16	0	0
λέγω/εἶπον (δὲ) ἐν ἑαυτῷ (LN: think to oneself) / ἐν ἑαυτοῖς	3,8; 7,39.49; 16,3; 18,4		6	1
ὀπίσω ἑαυτῶν (VKp)		20,30*	0	0
παρ' ἑαυτῷ (VKr)	9,47		0/1	0
περὶ ἑαυτοῦ (VKs)	24,27	8,34	0	0
ποιήσατε ἑαυτοῖς DENAUX 2009 Lⁿ	12,33; 16,9		0	0
πρὸς ἑαυτόν/ούς (VKt) → πρὸς ἀλλήλους; πρός + αὐτόν/αὐτούς	18,11; 20,5.14*; 22,23; 23,12*; 24,12		0	7/8
τὰ περὶ ἑαυτοῦ (VKa)	24,27		1	0/1
Reciprocal	20,5.14*; 22,23		1	6/7

→ ἀπαρνέομαι ἑαυτόν; ἀρνέομαι ἑαυτόν; ἕτερος + ἑαυτοῦ; ἔχω ἐν ἑαυτῷ/ἑαυτοῖς; λαμβάνω ἑαυτῷ; μένω καθ' ἑαυτόν

Characteristic of Luke
GOULDER 1989; MORGENTHALER 1958L

	Lk	Acts	Mt	Mk
ἑαυτοῦ, sandwiched (between article and noun) DENAUX 2009 L***; GOULDER 1989*	2,3; 9,60; 11,21; 13,34; 14,33		1	0
ἔρχομαι εἰς ἑαυτόν VOGEL 1899C	15,17		0	0
προσέχετε ἑαυτοῖς BOISMARD 1984 Ab61; GOULDER 1989; HAWKINS 1909add, NEIRYNCK 1985; PLUMMER 1922 lii ; VOGEL 1899C	12,1; 17,3; 21,34	5,35; 20,28	0	0

Literature
COLLISON 1977 125 [ἀφ' ἑαυτοῦ: noteworthy phenomena]; 198-199 [for possessive: linguistic usage of Luke: probable]; 200 [ἐν ἑαυτῷ/ἑαυτοῖς: linguistic usage of Luke's "other source-material": certain]; 200-201 [for σεαυτοῦ: linguistic usage of Luke: likely]; 201 [ποιήσατε ἑαυτοῖς/προσέχετε ἑαυτοῖς: noteworthy phenomena]; DENAUX 2009 Laⁿ [προσέχετε ἑαυτοῖς]; JEREMIAS 19 80 211: "Das eigentlich für ihn Charakteristische beim Gebrauch von προσέχειν ist jedoch die Verbindung des pluralischen Imperativs mit dem Dativ des Reflexivpronomens"; REHKOPF 1959 95 [λέγειν/εἰπεῖν ἐν ἑαυτῷ: vorlukanisch]; SCHÜRMANN 1953 32-33; 1957 11 [Luk scheint keine Vorliebe für die Verbindung von ἑαυτοῦ mit Präpositionen zu haben]; 1961 276 [λέγειν/εἰπεῖν ἐν ἑαυτῷ].

NEIRYNCK, Frans, Ἀπῆλθεν πρὸς ἑαυτόν: Lc 24,12 et Jn 20,10. — ETL 54 (1978) 104-118; = ID., Evangelica, 1982, 441-455 (455: note additionnelle; Appendix, Evangelica II, 1991, 799).

SCHWARZ, Günther, ἄφες τοὺς νεκροὺς θάψαι τοὺς ἑαυτῶν νεκρούς. — ZNW 72 (1981) 272-276.

STEINHAUSER, M.G., Noah in His Generation: An Allusion in Luke 16 8b, "εἰς τὴν γενεὰν τὴν ἑαυτῶν" — ZNW 79 (1988) 152-157.

TILLER, Patrick A., Reflexive Pronouns in the New Testament. — FilolNT 15 (29-30, 2002) 43-63.

ἐάω 2 + 7/8 (Mt 1)	allow			
Word groups	Lk	Acts	Mt	Mk
ἐάω + direct object, without infinitive (VKa)		5,38*	0	0
ἐάω ἕως (LN: stop)	22,51		0	0
ἐάω absolutely used (VKb)	22,51		0	0
ἐάω nautical term (VKc)		27,40	0	0

Characteristic of Luke
BOISMARD 1984 Bb86; DENAUX 2009 lA*; GOULDER 1989; HARNACK 1906 40.53; HAWKINS 1909B. 187; PLUMMER 1922 lx

Literature
HAUCK 1934 [Vorzugswort]; JEREMIAS 1980 295: "ἐάω ist lk Vorzugswort"; REHKOPF 1959 62-63 [ἐᾶτε ἕως τούτου].

ἑβδομήκοντα 2 + 3	seventy			
Word groups	Lk	Acts	Mt	Mk
ἑβδομήκοντα δύο (VKa)	10,1.17		0	0
ἑβδομήκοντα ἕξ (VKc)		27,37	0	0
ἑβδομήκοντα πέντε (VKb)		7,14	0	0

Literature
DENAUX 2009 La^n.

Ἔβερ 1	Eber (Lk 3,35)

ἐγγίζω 18 + 6 (Mt 7/8, Mk 3)				
1. come near (movement) (Lk 18,40); 2. come near (time) (Lk 21,8)				
Word groups	Lk	Acts	Mt	Mk
ἐγγίζω (+) εἰς (VKd)	18,35; 19,29; 24,28		1	1
ἐγγίσας DENAUX 2009 La^n	18,40; 24,15	21,33	0	0
ἤγγικεν (+) ἡ βασιλεία (VKa) → **ἔγγυς** ἐστιν ἡ βασιλεία	10,9.11		3	1

Characteristic of Luke
BOISMARD 1984 Eb60; CADBURY 1920 172; GASTON 1973 65 [Lked?]; GOULDER 1989; HAWKINS 1909add; HENDRIKS 1986 434; MORGENTHALER 1958L; NEIRYNCK 1985; PLUMMER 1922 lx

	Lk	Acts	Mt	Mk
ἐγγίζω absolutely used (place) (VKc) DENAUX 2009 L***	12,33; 18,40; 19,41; 24,15	21,33; 23,15	1	1
ἐγγίζω absolutely used (time) (VKb) DENAUX 2009 L***	21,8.20.28; 22,1	7,17	2	0

ἐγγίζω/ἐγγύς + dative → **ἐγγύς** + dat.; cf. Heb 7,19; Jam 4,8[1.2] BOISMARD 1984 cb25; DENAUX 2009 LA*; NEIRYNCK 1985	7,12; 15,1.25; 19,11; 22,47	9,3.38; 10,9; 22,6; 27,8	0/1	0
ἐγγίζω+ dative→ **ἐγγύς** + dat. DENAUX 2009 La*	7,12; 15,1.25; 22,47	9,3;10,9; 22,6	0	0
ὡς ἤγγισεν DENAUX 2009 L***; PLUMMER 1922 lii	7,12; 15,25; 19,29.41		0	0

Literature

VON BENDEMANN 2001 428: "ἐγγίζειν ist ein von Lukas bevorzugtes verbum"; COLLISON 1977 46 [linguistic usage of Luke: certain]; DENAUX 2009 Lan; EASTON 1910 147 [especially characteristic of L]; HAUCK 1934 [Vorzugswort]; JEREMIAS 1980 157: "lk Vorzugswort"; RADL 1975 406 [ἐγγίζω; ἐγγίσας]; REHKOPF 1959 93 [ἐγγίζειν = προσέρχεσθαι: vorlukanisch].

BERKEY, Robert F., Ἐγγίζειν, φθάνειν, and Realized Eschatology. — *JBL* 82 (1963) 177-187.
CAMPBELL, J.Y., "The Kingdom of God Has Come". — *ExpT* 48 (1936-37) 91-94.
CLARK, Kenneth W., "Realized Eschatology". — *JBL* 59 (1940) 367-383. Esp. 367-374.
DODD, Charles H., "The Kingdom of God Has Come". — *ExpT* 48 (1936-37) 138-142.
HUTTON, W.R., The Kingdom of God Has Come. — *ExpT* 64 (1952-53) 89-91.
PORTER, Stanley E., *Studies in the Greek New Testament*. Esp. 125-138: "'In the Vicinity of Jericho': Luke 18:35 in the Light of Its Synoptic Parallels" (129-136: "A solution based upon the verb ἐγγίζειν; 137-138 : "Luke 18:35 and the spatial-locational sense of ἐγγίζειν").

ἐγγράφω 1
record (Lk 10,20)

Literature
HAUCK 1934 [seltenes Alleinwort].

ἐγγύς 3 + 3 (Mt 3, Mk 2)

1. near (place) (Lk 19,11); 2. near (time) (Lk 21,30.31)

Word groups	Lk	Acts	Mt	Mk
ἐγγύς ἐστιν ἡ βασιλεία → **ἤγγικεν** ἡ βασιλεία	21,31		2	0
ἐγγύς + dative DENAUX 2009 lA[n]	19,11	9,38; 27,8	0	0
ἐγγύς ... Ἰερουσαλήμ; cfr. Jn 11,18 DENAUX 2009 LA[n]	19,11	1,12		
ἐγγύς concerning time (*VK*b) DENAUX 2009 L[n]	21,30.31		0	0

Characteristic of Luke	Lk	Acts	Mt	Mk
ἐγγύς/ἐγγίζω + dative → **ἐγγίζω** + dat. BOISMARD 1984 Cb25; DENAUX 2009 LA*; NEIRYNCK 1985;	7,12; 15,1.25; 19,11; 22,47	9,3.38; 10,9; 22,6; 27,8	0	0

Literature
JEREMIAS 1980 278 [ἐγγὺς ... Ἰερουσαλήμ: red.].

ἐγείρω 18/19 + 13/14 (Mt 36, Mk 18[19])

1. cause to stand up (Acts 3,7); 2. stand up (Lk 5,23); 3. cause to wake up (Acts 12,7); 4. cause to exist (Lk 3,8); 5. raise to life (Lk 20,37); 6. restore; 7. heal
ἐγείρομαι: 1. stand up (Acts 9,8); 2. wake up; 3. make war against (Lk 21,10)

Word groups	Lk	Acts	Mt	Mk
ἐγείρομαι + ἐπί with accusative (VKe)	21,10		1	1
ἐγείρω (+) ἐκ (τῶν) νεκρῶν (SCa; VKa) → (ἡ) ἀνάστασις (ἡ) (ἐκ) (τῶν) νεκρῶν; ἀνίστημι ἐκ νεκρῶν; cf. ἐγείρω ἀπὸ τῶν νεκρῶν (SCb; VKb) Mt 14,2; 27,64; 28,7	9,7	3,15; 4,10; 13,30	1	1/2[3]
ἐγείρω νεκρούς (VKd)		26,8	1	0
ἐγείρω (+) τῇ τρίτῃ ἡμέρᾳ → ἀνίστημι τῇ τρίτῃ ἡμέρᾳ; cf. ἐγείρω μετὰ τρεῖς ἡμέρας Mt 27,63	9,22	10,40	3	0
νεκροὶ ἐγείρονται (SCc; VKc)	7,22; 20,37		1	1
νεκρός + ἐγείρω → (ἡ) ἀνάστασις (ἡ) (ἐκ) (τῶν) νεκρῶν	7,22; 9,7; 20,37	3,15; 4,10; 13,30; 26,8	6	2/3[4]
ἐγείρω resurrection of Jesus (SCd) → ἀνίστημι	9,22; 24,6.34	3,15; 4,10; 5,30; 10,40; 13,30.37	9	2[3]

Characteristic of Luke	Lk	Acts	Mt	Mk
ἐγερθείς → διεγερθείς CREDNER 1836 139	8,24*; 11,8		9	0

Literature

COLLISON 1977 37.82 [noteworthy phenomena]; EASTON 1910 160 [ἐγείρω in the sense of "make effective": cited by Weiss as characteristic of L, and possibly corroborative]; 176 [ἐγερθείς: possible Hebraisms in the Lucan Writings, as classed by Dalman]; JEREMIAS 1980 197 [ἐγερθείς: red.].

KENDALL, Daniel – O'COLLINS, Gerald, Christ's Resurrection and the Aorist Passive of ἐγείρω. — Greg 74 (1993) 725-735.
LACY, John A., Ἠγέρθη – He Has Risen. — BiTod 36 (1968) 2532-2535.
RODRÍGUEZ CARMONA, Antonio, Origen de las fórmulas neotestamentarias de resurrección con anistánai y egeírein. — EstE 55 (1980) 27-58.
SABUGAL, Santos, Anástasis. Resucitó y resucitaremos (BAC), Madrid, 1993. 712 pp.

ἐγκάθετος 1　　spy (Lk 20,20)

Literature
HAUCK 1934 [seltenes Alleinwort].

BORMANN, Lukas, Recht, Gerechtigkeit und Religion, 2001. Esp. 178-179.

ἐγκακέω 1　　become discouraged (Lk 18,1)

Literature
HAUCK 1934 [seltenes Alleinwort].

ἐγκρύπτω 1 (Mt 1)　　put into (Lk 13,21)

ἔγκυος 1　　pregnant (Lk 2,5)

Literature
HAUCK 1934 [seltenes Alleinwort].

ἐγώ 213/229 + 186/201 (Mt 212/232, Mk 106[107]/114) → κἀγώ			I, me	

Word groups

ἐγώ	Lk	Acts	Mt	Mk
αὐτὸς ἐγώ	24,39[3] v.l.	10,26	0	0
ἐγώ (+) εἰμί / εἰμί (+) ἐγώ with predicate (SCc; VKc) DENAUX 2009 Lan	1,18[1].19; 7,8[1]; 19,22; 22,27; 24,39[3]	9,5; 10,21.26; 13,25[2]; 18,10[1]; 21,39[1]; 22,3.8[3]; 23,6[1]; 26,15[2].29[2]; 27,23[2]	5	0
ἐγώ εἰμί without predicate (SCb; VKb) → σὺ εἶ	21,8[2]; 22,70		3	3
ἐγὼ (δὲ) λέγω ὑμῖν / ἐγὼ ὑμῖν λέγω (SCg; VKe)	16,9; 20,8		7	1
ἐγὼ μέν (SCd; VKd) → ἡμεῖς/ὑμεῖς μέν	3,16[1]	22,3 v.l.; 26,9	1	0/1
ἐγώ + σύ	22,32	9,5; 22,8[3]; 26,15[2]	2	1
ἰδοὺ ἐγώ (SCa; VKa) → ἰδοὺ ἡμεῖς	7,27*; 10,3*; 23,14[2]; 24,49[1]	9,10; 10,21; 20,25[1]	4	0/1
καὶ ἐγώ (SCf; VKf) → κἀγώ; καὶ ἐμοί; καὶ ἡμεῖς/σύ/ὑμεῖς; cf. καὶ γὰρ ἐγώ Lk 7,8	2,48*; 16,9; 19,23*; 24,49[1] v.l.	10,26; 26,29[2]	0/2	0
οὐδὲ ἐγώ (VKg)	20,8		1	1

ἐμοῦ		Lk	Acts	Mt	Mk
ἐμοῦ dependent on verb (VKa)		10,16[1]		0	0
ἕνεκεν ἐμοῦ (SCa); cf. ἕνεκεν τοῦ ὀνόματός μου Lk 21,12; Mt 19,29		9,24		4	3
τὸ/τὰ περὶ ἐμοῦ and similar (VKb) → τὰ περὶ ἡμῶν DENAUX 2009 LA[n]		22,37[2]	23,11	0	0

μου	Lk	Acts	Mt	Mk
μου before the noun (SCa; VKc)	6,47[2]; 7,44*.44[2].45[2].46[2] v.l.; 10,29; 12,18[1]; 14,23.24.26[2].27[2].33; 19,8.23	1,8; 2,26[1] v.l.; 21,13[1]	7	2/3
μου + preposition (VKa)	4,7 v.l.8*; 9,23[1]; 14,27[1]; 19,27[3]	2,25[1]; 10,30[2]	5	4
μου dependent on adjective (VKb)	3,16		4	1
μου dependent on verb (VKe)	6,47[2]; 8.45.45*.46[1]; 23,42	1,4; 15,13; 22,1; 24,13; 25,11[1]; 26,3.29[1]	2	3
πατήρ μου (SCb) → πατήρ σου; πατήρ/πατέρες ἡμῶν/ὑμῶν	2,49[2]; 9,59[3]; 10,22[2]; 15,17[1].18; 16,27; 22,29[2]; 24,49[2]		17/20	0
μου in an absolute genitive (VKd) DENAUX 2009 lA[n]	22,53[1]	22,17[2]; 24,20; 25,15	0	

→ ἔθνος μου; λαός μου; θάπτω τὸν πατέρα μου

ἐμοί		Lk	Acts	Mt	Mk
καὶ ἐμοί → καὶ ἐγώ; καὶ ἡμῖν/σοί/ὑμῖν		15,29[1]	10,28*	0	0
τί ἐμοὶ καὶ σοί (VKa) → τί ἡμῖν καὶ σοί		8,28[1]		0	1

μοι	Lk	Acts	Mt	Mk
ἀκολούθει/ἀκολουθείτω μοι	5,27; 9,23[2].59[1]; 18,22	12,8	4	3

με	Lk	Acts	Mt	Mk
ἐγώ/με with τό + infinitive (VKa)	10,35; 22,15	11,15; 19,21[1]	2	1

Characteristic of Luke	Lk	Acts	Mt	Mk
ἐγὼ γάρ GOULDER 1989	1,18; 8,46; 21,15	9,16[1]; 21,13[2]	0	0
ἐγὼ δέ without λέγω ὑμῖν (SCe; VKe) → ἡμεῖς/σὺ/ὑμεῖς δέ DENAUX 2009 lA*	15,17[2]; 22,27.32	22,8[1].28[2]; 25,25; 26,15[1]	0	0

| μοι (ἔστιν/γίνεται) (VKa) → ἡμῖν (ἐστιν) DENAUX 2009 lA* | 1,38.43[1]; 9,38[2] | 1,8*; 7,49[1]; 9,15[1]; 18,10[2]; 22,6[1].17[1]; 24,11 | 0 | 1 |

Literature

COLLISON 1977 140 [μετ’ ἐμοῦ: linguistic usage of Luke’s “other source-material”: likely]; 198 [ἐγὼ δέ: noteworthy phenomena]; DENAUX 2009 La[n] [ἐγὼ γάρ]; JEREMIAS 1980 39 [ἐγὼ γάρ: red.]; RADL 1975 406 [ἐγώ nom.; ἐγὼ γάρ; ἐγὼ δέ]; SCHÜRMANN 1955 61 [das enklitische μου]; 1957 86-87.105 [ἐγὼ δέ: Vermutung luk R]; 129 [τὸ περὶ ἐμοῦ].

ELLIOTT, James K., New Testament Linguistic Usage, 1992. Esp. 47-48: “πρός με or πρὸς ἐμέ in the New Testament”.

FUCHS, Albert, Sprachliche Untersuchungen zu Mattäus und Lukas, 1971. Esp. 180-181 [ἐγὼ γάρ …].

HINNEBUSCH, Paul, “In My Father’s House … About My Father’s Business” (Luke 2:49). — BiTod 27 (1966) 1893-1899.

SYLVA, Dennis D., The Cryptic Clause en tois tou patros mou dei einai me in Luke 2,49b. — ZNW 78 (1987) 132-140.

ἐδαφίζω 1

1. raze (Lk 19,44); 2. kill (Lk 19,44)

Literature

HAUCK 1934 [seltenes Alleinwort].

ἐθίζω 1   be in the habit of

Characteristic of Luke	Lk	Acts	Mt	Mk
κατὰ τὸ εἰθισμένον → τὸ εἰωθός; κατὰ τὸ ἔθος CREDNER 1836 134-135; HARNACK 1906 70; PLUMMER 1922 lxiii	2,27		0	0

Literature

HAUCK 1934 [seltenes Alleinwort]; SCHÜRMANN 1957 5 [κατὰ τὸ εἰθισμένον].

ἔθνος 13 + 43/44 (Mt 15, Mk 6)   nation

Word groups	Lk	Acts	Mt	Mk
ἔθνος + proper name (geographical) (VKc)		8,9; 10,22; 13,19	0	0
ἔθνος ἐπὶ ἔθνος (VKd)	21,10[1.2]		2	2
ἔθνος + λαός (VKf)	2,32	4.25.27; 15,14; 26,17.23	1	0
ἔθνος μου (VKe)		24,17; 26,4; 28,19	0	0
πᾶν ἔθνος singular → πάντα τὰ ἔθνη; cf. Rev 7,9; 14,6		2,5; 10,35; 17,26	0	0
πάντα τὰ ἔθνη (SCb; VKb) → πᾶν ἔθνος singular; ἅπας/ὅλος/πᾶς ὁ λαός; πᾶς ὁ ὄχλος; ἅπαν/πᾶν τὸ πλῆθος	12,30; 21,24[1]; 24,47	14,16; 15,17	5	2

Characteristic of Luke

HENDRIKS 1986 468; MORGENTHALER 1958A

	Lk	Acts	Mt	Mk
ἔθνος + determinative; cf. Jn 11,48 BOISMARD 1984 Bb15; DENAUX 2009 lA*; NEIRYNCK 1985	7,5; 12,30; 23,2	2,5; 8,9; 10,22; 17,26; 24,17; 26,4; 28,19	0	0
ἔθνος = Jewish nation; cf. Jn 11,48.50.51.52; 18,35 BOISMARD 1984 cb153; DENAUX 2009 lA*; NEIRYNCK 1985	7,5; 23,2	10,22; 24,2.10.17; 26,4; 28,19	0	0
(τὰ) ἔθνη (LN: heathen; SCa; VKa); see also πάντα τὰ ἔθνη DENAUX 2009 lA**	2,32; 18,32; 21,24²·³.25; 22,25	4,25.27; 7,45; 9,15; 10,45; 11,1.18; 13,19.42*.46.47.48; 14,2.5.27; 15,3.7.12.14.19. 23; 18,6; 21,11.19.21.25; 22,21; 26,17.20.23; 28,28	7	2

Literature

GERSDORF 1816 256 [φῶς εἰς ἀποκάλυψιν ἐθνῶν]; RADL 1975 406 [ἔθνος; ἔθνος "im Singular, bezogen auf die Juden"].

DAHL, Nils A., "A People for His Name" (Acts XV. 14). — NTS 4 (1957-58) 319-327.
DUPONT, Jacques, Λαὸς ἐξ ἐθνῶν (Act. XV. 14). — NTS 3 (1956-57) 47-50.
MUTHURAJ, J.G., The Meaning of ἔθνος and ἔθνη and its Significance to the Study of the New Testament. — Bangalore Theological Forum 29 (1997) 3-36.

ἔθος 3 + 7	custom

Word groups	Lk	Acts	Mt	Mk
(τὰ) ἔθη (VKa) Jewish customs BOISMARD 1984 Aa26; HARNACK 1906 53		6,14; 16,21; 21,21; 26,3; 28,17	0	0

Characteristic of Luke

DENAUX 2009 lA*; HARNACK 1906 70; HAWKINS 1909B; PLUMMER 1922 lx

	Lk	Acts	Mt	Mk
τὸ ἔθος singular; cf. Jn 19,40; Heb 10,25 BOISMARD 1984 cb75; HARNACK 1906 53; NEIRYNCK 1985	1,9; 2,42; 22,39	15,1	0	0
κατὰ τὸ ἔθος (VKb) → κατὰ τὸ εἰθισμένον GOULDER 1989; HARNACK 1906 70.148; PLUMMER 1922 lii	1,9; 2,42; 22,39		0	0

Literature

COLLISON 1977 138 [κατὰ τὸ ἔθος: noteworthy phenomena]; DENAUX 2009 Laⁿ [τὸ ἔθος singular]; Lⁿ [κατὰ τὸ ἔθος]; EASTON 1910 149 [κατὰ τὸ ἔθος; especially characteristic of L]; GERSDORF 1816 173-174 [κατὰ τὸ ἔθος]; HAUCK 1934 [Vorzugswort]; JEREMIAS 1980 29: "κατὰ τὸ ἔθος findet sich im NT ausschließlich im LkEv"; RADL 1975 406 [ἔθος; κατὰ τὸ ἔθος; ἔθη]; REHKOPF 1959 95 [κατὰ τὸ ἔθος]; SCHÜRMANN 1957 5 [κατὰ τὸ ἔθος].

BORMANN, Lukas, Recht, Gerechtigkeit und Religion, 2001. Esp. 202.
WILSON, Stephen G., Luke and the Law (SNTS MS, 50). Cambridge: University Press, 1963, VII-142 p. Esp. 1-11: "Legal terminology in Luke-Acts" [ἔθος; ἐντολή; νόμος].

εἰ 53 + 35 (Mt 55, Mk 35)	
1. if (Lk 4,3); 2. because; 3. that, whether (Acts 26,23)	

Word groups	Lk	Acts	Mt	Mk
εἰ + optative (VKr); cf. 1 Cor 14,10; 15,37; 1 Pet 3,14.17 BOISMARD 1984 Ca67		17,11.27; 20,16; 24,19; 25,20; 27,12.39	0	0
εἰ ἄρα (VKa) BOISMARD 1984 Ca39; PLUMMER 1922 lxiii		7,1 v.l.; 8,22; 17,27	0	1
εἰ δέ (VKd)	11,18.19.20; 12,28	5,39; 18,15; 23,9; 25,11²	6	0/1
εἰ δέ τις/τι (VKg)		19,39	0	0
εἰ ἤδη	12,49		0	1/2
εἰ (δὲ) καὶ → ἂν/ἐάν/ὅταν (δὲ) καί	11,8.11*.18; 18,4		0/1	1
εἰ μέν (VKh) → ἐὰν/κἂν μέν		18,14	0	0
εἰ μὲν ... εἰ δέ; cf. 2 Cor 11,4 BOISMARD 1984 Aa87		18,14(-15); 19,38 (-39); 25,11^{1.2}	0	0
εἰ μὲν οὖν (VKj) → εἰ οὖν		18,14 v.l.; 19,38; 25,11¹	0	0
εἰ μή (LN: except that; SCa; VKk) → ἐάν (δὲ/γὰρ) μή; εἰ μὴ (...) μόνον/μόνος	4,26.27; 5,21; 6,4; 8,51; 10,22^{1.2}; 11,29; 17,18; 18,19	11,19; 21,25*; 26,32	14/17	13/14
εἰ μήτι (VKl)	9,13		0	0
εἰ ... οὐ/οὐδέ → ἂν/ἐὰν ... οὐ	5,36; 12,39; 14,26; 16,31	5,39; 25,11¹	7	3/4
εἰ οὖν (SCc; VKm) → εἰ μὲν οὖν; cf. ἐὰν οὖν Mt 5,19.25; 6,22; 24,26	11,13.36; 12,26; 16,11	11,17	3	0
εἴ πως/εἴπως (VKn)		27,12	0	0
εἴ τις / εἴτις (VKp)	9,23; 14,26; 19,8	13,15; 24,19.20*; 25,5	2	6/7
καὶ εἰ → καὶ ἐάν; κἂν	6,32; 16,12; 19,8		6	4

→ εἰ βούλει; δέομαι εἰ; ἐπερωτάω εἰ; κρίνω εἰ; οὐ ... εἰ μή(τι); οὐδεὶς ... εἰ μή; εἰ ... οὐδείς; πυνϑάνομαι εἰ

Characteristic of Luke	Lk	Acts	Mt	Mk
εἰ + direct question BOISMARD 1984 cb5; DENAUX 2009 lA*; NEIRYNCK 1985	6,9; 11,11*; 13,23; 14,3*; 22,49	1,6; 7,1; 19,2¹; 21,37; 22,25.27*	2	0
εἰ interrogative (SCd) PLUMMER 1922 lxiii	6,7.9; 11,11*; 13,23; 14,3*.28.31; 22,49; 23,6	1,6; 4,19; 5,8; 7,1; 8,22; 10,18; 17,11.27; 19,2^{1.2}; 21,37; 22,25.27*; 23,9; 25,20; 27,12.39	4	7
εἰ δὲ μή γε (SCb; VKf); cf. εἰ δὲ μή Mk 2,21.22 CREDNER 1836 137; DENAUX 2009 L***; GOULDER 1989*; HAWKINS 1909L; PLUMMER 1922 lx	5,36.37; 10,6; 13,9; 14,32		2	0
εἰ οὐ DENAUX 2009 L***; GOULDER 1989*	11,8; 12,26; 14,26; 16,11.12.31		2	1

Literature

COLLISON 1977 102 [εἰ δὲ μή γε: linguistic usage of Luke: probable]; 104 [direct/indirect questions: likely]; 105 [+ particle + interrogative word: certain]; 105 [εἰ οὐ: linguistic usage of Luke's "other source-material": certain]; HARNACK 1906 34 [unassuming εἰ very nearly = ἐπεί (Acts 4,9; 11,17; 16,15)]; HAUCK 1934 [Vorzugsverbindung: εἰ δὲ μή γε]; JEREMIAS 1980 231: "εἰ als Fragepartikel vor direkter Rede ... wird also von Lukas nicht ungern geschrieben"; RADL 1975 407 ["zur Einleitung eines direkten Fragesatzes"]; REHKOPF 1959 93 [εἰ καί: vorlukanisch]; SCHÜRMANN 1961 280 [εἰ καί: protoluk R weniger wahrscheinlich].

BOYER, James L., First Class Conditions: What Do They Mean?.— *Grace Theological Journal* 2 (1981) 76-114.
—, Second Class Conditions in New Testament Greek. — *Grace Theological Journal* 3 (1982) 81-88.
—, Third (and Fourth) Class Conditions. — *Grace Theological Journal* 3 (1982) 163-175.
GREENLEE, J. Harold, "If" in the New Testament. — *BTrans* 13 (1962) 39-43.
ROBERTS, J.W., Some Aspects of Conditional Sentences in the Greek New Testament. — *BTrans* 15 (1964) 70-76.
THRALL, Margaret E., *Greek Particles in the New Testament*, 1962. Esp. 9-10 [εἰ δὲ μή γε].
WILSON, W.A.A., "But me no Buts". — *BTrans* 15 (1964) 173-180. [εἰ μή]

εἶδος 2

1. form (Lk 3,22; 9,29); 2. sight

Literature

HAUCK 1934 [seltenes Alleinwort].

εἴκοσι 1 + 2   twenty

Word groups	Lk	Acts	Mt	Mk
εἴκοσι χιλιάδες	14,31		0	0
ἑκατὸν εἴκοσι (*VK*d)		1,15	0	0

εἰκών 1 (Mt 1, Mk 1)

1. image; 2. likeness; 3. representation (Lk 20,24)

Literature

ELTESTER, Friedrich-Wilhelm, *Eikon im Neuen Testament* (BZNW, 23). Berlin: Töpelmann, 1958, XVI-166 p. Esp. 1-25: "Das Wort Eikon".

εἰμί 361/378 + 279/286 (Mt 289/300, Mk 192/210)

1. be (Lk 12,38); 2. be identical; 3. exist (Acts 17,28[1]); 4. happen (Lk 22,49); 5. be in a place (L k 2,49; 17,31); 6. be possible (Acts 2,29); 7. belong (Lk 19,2); 8. represent

Word groups	Lk	Acts	Mt	Mk
ἀνάστασιν μὴ εἶναι	20,27	23,8	1	1
ἀρεστόν ἐστίν BOISMARD 1984 Ab118; NEIRYNCK 1985		6,2; 12,3[1]	0	0
γνωστόν (+) ἐστίν → γνωστὸν **ἐγένετο** BOISMARD 1984 Aa6		2,14; 4,10; 13,38; 28,22.28	0	0
διὰ τὸ (+) εἶναι (*SC*c; *VK*d) DENAUX 2009 La[n]	2,4; 11,8; 19,11	18,3[1]; 27,4	0	0
δυνατόν ἐστίν		2,24; 20,16	1	1
δυνατός ἐστίν + infinitive DENAUX 2009 LA[n]	14,31	11,17	0	0
ἐγώ εἰμί / εἰμὶ ἐγώ with predicate DENAUX 2009 lAn	1.18.19; 7,8; 19,22; 22,27; 24,39	9,5[2]; 10,21.26; 13,25[2]; 18,10[1]; 21,39; 22,3[1].8[2]; 23,6[2]; 26,15[2].29; 27,23	5	0

ἐγώ εἰμί without predicate → σὺ εἶ	21,8; 22,70²		3	3
εἰμί + dative	1,7¹.14.36.45; 2,7.10; 6,32.33.34; 7,41; 8,30.42; 9,13.38; 10,12.14.39; 11,30.41; 12,20.24; 14,10	2,14.39; 4,10.32³; 7,5.44; 8,21¹; 9,15; 10,6; 13,38; 18,10²; 19,25; 20,16; 21,9.23; 22,15; 24,10.11; 25,16; 28,28	8	2/4
εἰμί + genitive	4,7; 5,3; 9,55*; 18,16; 20,38	1,7; 9,2; 21,11; 23,6¹; 27,23	6/7	5
εἰμί + perfect participle	1,7³; 2,26; 4,16.17; 5,1.17³.18; 6,40²; 8,2; 9,32.45; 12,2.6.35.52; 14,8; 15,24².32*; 18,34; 19,17; 20,6¹; 23,15.38 v.l.51.55; 24,38	1,17; 2,13; 4,31; 5,25; 8,16; 9,33; 12,6.12; 13,48; 14,26; 16,9; 18,25; 19,32; 20,8².13; 21,29.33²; 22,20.29²; 25,10.14; 26,26	9	6
εἰμί + present participle	1,10.20.21.22; 2,8.33.51; 3,23¹; 4,20.31.33.38.44; 5,10².16.17¹·².29²; 6,12.43; 8,32.40; 9, 18¹.53; 11,1.14¹; 13,10. 11*.11; 14,1; 15,1; 17,35; 19,47; 21,17.24. 37; 22,69; 23,8.51 v.l.53; 24,13.32.53	1,10.13.14; 2,2.5.42; 4,36; 8,1.13.28; 9,9.28; 10,24.30; 11,5; 12,5.6.12.20; 14,7; 16,9.12²; 18,7; 19,14; 21,3; 22,19.20	13/15	25/26
εἰμί + ὁ + aorist participle	8,12.14; 20,2; 22,64	7,38; 9,21	3	2
εἰμί + ὁ + present participle	7,19.20; 8,21; 16,15; 24,21	1,20	7	4
εἰμί ἀντιπέρα	8,26		0	0
εἰμί (+) ἀπό DENAUX 2009 Lⁿ	8,43; 21,11²		0	0/1
εἰμί + ἀσύμφωνος + πρὸς ἀλλήλους		28,25	0	0
εἰμί + ἄχρι		2,29	0	0
εἰμί (+) εἰς	3,5; 5,17⁴; 11,7; 23,19 v.l.11,7	7,12; 8,20.23; 13,47	1	1/3
εἰμί (+) εἰς replacing the predicate nominative (LN: become) → γίνομαι + εἰς replacing the predicate nom.; cf. ἔχω εἰς Mt 21,46	3,5	8,20.23; 13,47	1	1
εἰμί (+) ἐκ	12,15; 20,4; 22,3 .58¹; 23,7¹	2,25; 4,6; 5,38.39; 19,25; 21,8; 23,34; 24,10; 27,22	4	3
εἰμί + ἔμπροσθεν	14,2		0	0
εἰμί (+) ἐν	1,80; 2,7.8.25¹.44.49; 4,25.27.32.33; 5,12; 7,25.37; 8,43; 9,12; 10,12.14; 11,1.21; 12,15; 15,7.25; 17,24.26; 18,2.3; 21,23 v.l.25.37; 22,27.53¹; 23,7².12.19.40; 24,6.53	1,8; 2,17.29; 4,12¹.34; 5,12.25; 7,2.12 v.l.44; 9,10.36¹.38²; 10,1*; 11,5.11.22; 12,18; 13,1¹.15; 16,3.12²; 17,28¹; 18,10².24; 19,1.16; 20,8¹.10; 21,20; 25,5; 26,21	19/21	14/17
εἰμί + ἐντός	17,21		0	0
εἰμί + ἐνώπιον DENAUX 2009 Lⁿ	1,15; 14,10; 16,15*		0	0
εἰμί + ἕως	1,80; 9,41	1,8	1	1
εἰμί (+) κατά + accusative/genitive	9,50*.50¹; 11,23²; 17,30; 21,11¹; 22,53¹	11,1; 13,1¹; 25,23*	2	3

εἰμί (+) μετά + genitive	1,66²; 5,29².34; 6,3; 11,7.23¹; 15,31¹; 22,53¹.59¹; 23,43	7,9; 9,28.39; 10,38; 11,21; 18,10¹; 20,34	8	8
εἰμί + παρά + dative	18,27	10,6	1	1
εἰμί + πρό		14,13	0	0
εἰμί (+) πρός + accusative/dative	9,41; 23,12; 24,29	28,25	1	5
εἰμί τις (LN: be important)		5,36; 8,9	0	0
εἰμί + ὑπέρ + accusative/genitive	6,40¹; 9,50²		1	1
εἰμί + ὑπό + accusative		4,12²	0	0
εἶναι (accusative + infinitive) (SCb)	2,44.49; 4,41²; 9,20.33²; 20,6².20.27.41; 23,2	4,32²; 5,36; 8,9.37*; 13,25¹. 47; 16,13.15; 17,7.29; 18,5.28; 23,8; 28,6	4	4/6
εἶναι + nominative (SCa; VKa)	14,26.27.33; 22,24	2,12; 16,13 v.l.; 17,18.20; 18,15²	2	2
τοῦ εἶναι (VKf)		13,47		
εἰς χολὴν πικρίας + εἰμί (LN: be terribly envious)		8,23	0	0
ἐστίν + neuter plural subject (SCc; VKd)	11,21.41; 14,17; 15,31²; 18,27	15,18*; 18,15¹	2/3	2/3
ἐστίν μοι → γίνεταί μοι DENAUX 2009 lAⁿ	9,38	1,8 v.l.; 9,15; 18,10²; 24,11	0	0
ἤμην/ἦς + adverb of place		2,1	3	6/7
θέλει + εἶναι (LN: it means)		2,12; 17,20	0	0
λιμὸς + ἔσται / λιμοὶ ἔσονται → ἐγένετο λιμός	21,11¹	11,28	1	1
μέλλει ἔσεσθαι		11,28; 24,15; 27,10	0	0
ὅ ἐστίν (LN: that means)		4,36	2	9
οὐδείς ἐστίν	1,61; 7,28¹; 18,29		0	2
οὐδέν (+) ἐστίν	12,2	21,24; 25,11	3	1
οὐκ εἰμί without predicate nominative (VKd) DENAUX 2009 LAⁿ	22,58²	13,25²	0	0
οὕτως (+) ἔσται	11,30; 15,7; 17,24.26	27,25	8	0
συ (+) εἶ → ἐγώ εἰμί	3,22; 4,41; 7,19.20; 22,67.70; 23,3.37.39	13,33; 21,38; 22,27	6	5
τοῦτ' ἔστίν (LN: that means)		1,19; 19,4	1	1
φιλός εἰμί → φίλος γίνομαι	11,8		0	0
ὄν/οὖσα/ὄν in an absolute genitive	14,32; 22,53¹	7,5; 9,38¹; 18,12; 19,36¹; 27,2.9	0	4
ὄν/οὖσα/ὄν with the article: nominalized participle	6,3; 11,23¹	20,34; 22,9; 28,17	1	1/2
ἔσεσθαι BOISMARD 1984 Aa42		11,28; 23,30; 24,15; 27,10	0	0
ἐσόμενος	22,49		0	0
ἐστίν impersonal (VKe)	8,17; 9,33¹; 10,42; 16,17; 17,1; 18,25; 22,38; 24,29	4,19; 6,2; 10,28; 12,3¹; 19,36²; 20,35; 28,22	12/14	12
ἦσθα/ἤμεθα		27,37	3	1

→ ἐγγύς ἐστιν ἡ βασιλεία; ἡμῖν ἐστίν; καλόν ἐστίν + inf.; μακάριόν ἐστίν; ὁμοία ἐστίν ἡ βασιλεία; σιωπᾶν εἰμί; σοῦ/ὑμῶν ἐστίν; ἔστιν τί σοι; τί οὖν ἐστίν; τόπος ἐστίν; χρεία ἐστίν

Characteristic of Luke

HENDRIKS 1986 434

	Lk	Acts	Mt	Mk
verb + noun/pronoun + εἶναι + τι/τινά BOISMARD 1984 Eb13; DENAUX 2009 lA*; NEIRYNCK 1985	4,41²; 20,41; 23,2	5,36; 8,9.37*; 16,15; 17,7.29; 28,6	0	1

δοκεῖ εἶναι BOISMARD 1984 Db40; NEIRYNCK 1985	22,24	17,18	0	0
εἴη optative BOISMARD 1984 Ab6; DENAUX 2009 L***; GOULDER 1989*; HAWKINS 1909L; NEIRYNCK 1985	1,29; 3,15; 8,9; 9,46; 15,26; 18,36; 22,23	8,20; 10,17; 20,16; 21,33[1]	0	0
εἰμί + dative (= to have); cf. Jn 18,10.39; 19,40; Rom 9,2; 1 Cor 9,16; 11,14.15; Eph 6,12; Jam 4,17 BOISMARD 1984 cb26; DENAUX 2009 L***; GOULDER 1989*; HAWKINS 1909L; NEIRYNCK 1985	1,14; 2,7.10; 6,32.33.34; 7,41; 8,30.42; 9,13.38; 10,39; 12,20.24; 14,10	4,32[3]; 7,5.44; 8,21[1]; 10,6; 18,10[2]; 21,9; 24,10.11; 25,16	3	2
εἰμι ἐν τῷ ἱερῷ BOISMARD 1984 Bb110; DENAUX 2009 La*; NEIRYNCK 1985	21,37; 22,53[1]; 24,53	5,25	0	1
εἰμί (+) ἐπί + accusative/dative/genitive DENAUX 2009 L***	2,25[2].40; 4,27; 15,7; 17,31.34.35; 21,23	1,15; 2,1.44*.44; 4,33; 8,27	0	2/3
εἰμι ἐπί + genitive of time → γίνομαι ἐπί + genitive of time BOISMARD 1984 cb22; NEIRYNCK 1985	4,27		0	0
εἰμι ἐπὶ τὸ αὐτό; cf. 1 Col 7,5; 11,20 BOISMARD 1984 cb16 ; NEIRYNCK 1985	17,35	1,15; 2,1.44	0	0
εἰμί + ὁ + perfect participle DENAUX 2009 LA*	20,17; 22,28	2,16; 10,42	0	1
εἰμί (+) σύν DENAUX 2009 lA*	7,12[2]; 22,56; 24,44	4,13[2]; 8,20; 13,7; 14,4; 22,9; 27,2	0	1
εἶναι after preposition and article DENAUX 2009 L***; GOULDER 1989*; HAWKINS 1909L	2,4.6; 5,12; 9,18[1]; 11,1.8; 19,11	18,3[1]; 19,1; 27,4	0	0
ἐν τῷ (+) εἶναι (SCd; VKe) DENAUX 2009 L***	2,6; 5,12; 9,18[1]; 11,1	19,1	0	0
ἐστὶν αὐτῷ/αὐτοῖς → ὑπάρχω αὐτῷ/αὐταῖς DENAUX 2009 L***	1,7[1]; 2,7.26; 7,2; 8,42	7,5; 19,31	2	0
ἐστίν μέγας, said of someone BOISMARD 1984 Ab87; NEIRYNCK 1985	1,15.32; 9,48	8,9	0	0
ἐστὶν (+) σοι → γίνεταί σοι DENAUX 2009 La*	1,14; 8,30; 14,10	8,21[1]	1	0
ἦν/ἦσαν + participle → εἰμί (ὁ) + participle aorist/perfect/present; ἦν διδάσκων CREDNER 1936 139; HARNACK 1906 31.70; HAWKINS 1909add	1,7[3].10.21.22; 2,8.26.33. 51; 3,23[1]; 4,16.17.20.31. 33.38.44; 5,1.16.17[1.2.3]. 18.29[2]; 6,12; 8,2.32.40; 9,32.45.53; 11,14[1]; 13,10.11*.11; 14,1; 15,1. 24[2].32*; 18,34; 19,47; 21,37; 23,8.19.38 v.l.51.53.55; 24,13.32.53	1,10.13.14.17; 2,2.5.42; 4,31; 8,1.13.16.28; 9,9.28.33; 10,24. 30; 11,5; 12,5.6. 12.20; 13,48; 14,7.26; 16,9.12[2]; 18,7.25; 19,14.32; 20,8[2].13; 21,3.29; 22,19.20. 29[2]	8/10	25/26
οὗ ἦν/ἦσαν + participle BOISMARD 1984 Ab27; DENAUX 2009 lA*; NEIRYNCK 1985	4,16.17; 23,53	1,13; 2,2; 12,12; 20,8[2]	0	0
καὶ αὐτὸς ἦν; cf. καὶ αὐτὸς ἤμην Acts 22,20[1] DENAUX 2009 L***; GOULDER 1989*	1,22; 3,23[1]; 5,1.17[1]; 17,16; 19,2.2*		0	2

τίς ἐστίν οὗτος	5,21; 7,49; 8,25; 9,9		1	1
DENAUX 2009 L***; PLUMMER 1922 lxiii				
ὤν/οὖσα/ὄν	2,5;3,23²; 6,3; 8,43;	5,17;7,2.5.12;	5	7/9
GOULDER 1989	11,23¹; 12,28; 13,16;	8,23;9,2.38.39¹³;		
	14,32; 20,36³;	11,1.22; 13,1;		
	22,3.53¹; 23,7².12;	14,13; 15,32;		
	24,6².44	16,3.21; 17,16;		
		18,12.24; 19,31.		
		35².36¹; 20,34;		
		21,8; 22,5.9;		
		24,10.24; 25,23*;		
		26,3.21; 27,2.9;		
		28,.25		

→ εἰμί/γίνομαι ἐτῶν; μάρτυς (εἰμί/γίνομαι) + genitive; εἰμί/γίνομαι ἐν τῇ πόλει; ἦν
προσευχόμενον; πυνθάνομαι τίς/τί εἴη; εἰμὶ σύν + dative

Literature

BDR 353,1: "εἶναι mit Partizip Präsens: die meisten ntl Beispiele entfallen auf Lk und den ersten
Teil der Apg (1–13)"; COLLISON 1977 47 [εἴη: linguistic usage of Luke: certain; articular inf. after
prepositions: certain]; 103 [εἶναι δέ: probable]; DENAUX 2009 LAⁿ [δοκεῖ εἶναι]; LAⁿ [εἰμι ἐπί +
genitive of time; ἐστίν μέγας, said of someone]; lAⁿ [εἰμι ἐπὶ τὸ αὐτό]; lAn [ὤν/οὖσα/ὄν];
EASTON 1910 177 [εἶναι with the participle: possible Hebraisms in the Lucan Writings, as classed
by Dalman]; HAUCK 1934 [Vorzugsverbindung: διὰ τὸ εἶναι; εἰμι + dative; Stileigentümlichkeit:
εἴη optat.]; JEREMIAS 1980 24: "προβεβηκότες … ἦσαν: Die periphrastische Konjugation beim
Perfektsystem (bestehend aus einer Form von εἶναι + artikellosem Part.perf. …) ist gut griechisch:
damit hängt es zusammen, daß diese Konstruktion im lk Doppelwerk so häufig, bei den anderen
beiden Synoptikern dagegen vergleichsweise selten ist"; 43 [εἶναι + Part.praes.: red.]; 48
εἴη "unsere Stelle ist der erste Beleg für die vielseitige Verwendung, die der Optativ in den beiden
Lukasschriften gefunden hat"; 270 [εἰμὶ ἐπὶ τὸ αὐτό: red.]; RADL 1975 407 [εἰμί + dat.; ὄν; ὢν
ἐκ]; SCHÜRMANN 1955 36-39 [omission of copula ἐστιν in Luke]; 1957 89 [εἶναι ὡς: luk R
weniger wahrscheinlich]; 1961 277 [ὡς εἶναι].

BARR, James, *The Semantics of Biblical Language*, 1961. Esp. 58-72: "The verb 'to be'".

BEYER, Klaus, *Semitische Syntax im Neuen Testament*. I/1, 1962. Esp. 63-65:
"Satzeinleitendes καὶ ἔσται mit Zeitbestimmung".

BJÖRCK, Gudmund, *ἦν διδάσκων: Die periphrastischen Konstruktionen im Griechischen*
(Skrifter utgivna av K. Humanistika Vetenskops- Samfundet i Uppsala, 32.2.). Uppsala:
Almqvist and Wiksell, 1940. Esp. 74-85.

DE JONGE, Henk J., Sonship, Wisdom, Infancy: Luke II.41-51a. — *NTS* 24 (1977-78) 317-
354. Esp. "I must be about the affairs of my Father".

FANNING, Buist M., *Verbal Aspect*, 1990. Esp. 309-323 [periphrastic constructions].

NEBE, Gottfried, Das ἔσται in Lk 11,36 – ein neuer Deutungsvorschlag. — *ZNW* 83
(1992) 108-114. Esp. 108-110 [discussion of three important publications on the topic: Bultmann,
Hahn, Allison]; 110: "Doch lässt sich für dieses ἔσται nicht nur ein futurisch-zeitlicher Sinn
vertreten, sondern als andere Möglichkeit auch ein voluntativ-imperativischer".

SYLVA, Dennis D., The Cryptic Clause *en tois tou patros mou dei einai me* in Luke 2,49b.
— *ZNW* 78 (1987) 132-140.

VERBOOMEN, Alain, *L'imparfait périphrastique dans l'Évangile de Luc et dans la
Septante: Contribution à l'étude du système verbal du grec néotestamentaire* (Académie
royale de Belgique. Classe des Lettres. Fonds René Draguet, 10). Leuven, Peeters, 1993,
XIV-92 p.

εἵνεκεν 1

ἕνεκεν: 1. on account of; 2. in order that; 3. because of (Lk 4,18)

Word groups	Lk	Acts	Mt	Mk
οὗ εἴνεκεν → οὗ ἕνεκεν/χάριν; τίνος ἕνεκα/ἕνεκεν	4,18		0	0

εἰρήνη 14 + 7 (Mt 4, Mk 1)

1. peace (Lk 19,42); 2. freedom from worry

Word groups	Lk	Acts	Mt	Mk
εἰρήνη ἐν ἀνθρώποις εὐδοκίας	2,14		0	0
εἰρήνη ὑμῖν (VKc)	24,36		0	0
εἰς εἰρήνην (VKf)	7,50; 8,48	7,26	0	1
ἐν εἰρήνῃ (SCb; VKe)	2,29; 11,21	16,36	0	0
DENAUX 2009 La[n]				
ἐν οὐρανῷ εἰρήνη	19,38		0	0
εὐαγγελίζομαι εἰρήνην		10,36	0	0
μετ᾽ εἰρήνης (VKg)		15,33	0	0
τὰ πρὸς εἰρήνην (VKd)	14,32; 19,42		0	0
DENAUX 2009 L[n]				

Characteristic of Luke

DENAUX 2009 L***; GOULDER 1989*; HAWKINS 1909L; HENDRIKS 1986 433;
MORGENTHALER 1958L

	Lk	Acts	Mt	Mk
πορεύου εἰς εἰρήνην (SCa) / πορεύεσθε ἐν εἰρήνῃ; cf. ὕπαγε εἰς εἰρήνην Mk 5,34 BOISMARD 1984 Ab115; NEIRYNCK 1985; PLUMMER 1922 liii; VOGEL 1899C	7,50; 8,48	16,36	0	0

Literature

VON BENDEMANN 2001 420; COLLISON 1977 172-173 [linguistic usage of Luke's "other source-material": probable; but a linguistic usage of Luke cannot be ruled out]; DENAUX 2009 La[n] [πορεύου εἰς εἰρήνην (SCa) / πορεύεσθε ἐν εἰρήνῃ]; EASTON 1910 160 [εἰρήνη of literal (military) peace: cited by Weiss as characteristic of L, and possibly corroborative]; GERSDORF 1816 232 [δόξα ἐν ὑψίστοις θεῷ καὶ ἐπὶ γῆς εἰρήνη]; 254 [νῦν ἀπολύεις τὸν δοῦλόν σου, δέσποτα, κατὰ τὸ ῥῆμά σου ἐν εἰρήνῃ]; HAUCK 1934 [Vorzugswort]; SCHÜRMANN 1955 25-26 [τὰ πρὸς εἰρήνην ... als luk verdächtigt].

ARICHEA, Daniel C., Jr., Peace in the New Testament. — BTrans 38 (1987) 201-206.
BAARLING, Heinrich, Friede im Himmel: Die lukanische Redaktion von Lk 19,38 und ihre Deutung. — ZNW 76 (1985) 170-186. [ἐν οὐρανῷ εἰρήνη καὶ δόξα ἐν ὑψίστοις]
BOHUYTRON SOLANO, José Antonio, ¿En qué modo es significativo el término "paz" para el retrato lucano de Jesús? Diss. Roma, Pont. Univ. Greg., 1996, 410 p. (dir. R. F. O'Toole).
DELEBECQUE, Édouard, Études grecques, 1976. Esp. 25-38: "Le 'gloria' des anges (2,14)".
GILLETT, D., Shalom : content for a slogan. — Themelios 1 (1976) 80-84. [NTA 21, 20]
GUERRA GÓMEZ, Manuel, Análisis filológico-teológico y traducción del himno de los ángeles en Belén, 1989. Esp. 49-53: "εἰρήνη – 'paz, salvación'".
KLASSEN, William, "A Child of Peace" (Luke 19,6) in First Century Context. — NTS 27 (1981) 488-506.
KARIAMADAM, Paul, "Peace in Heaven..." (Lk. 19:38b) – An Explanation. — Bible Bhashyam 23 (1997) 256-268.
KLEMM, Matthys, Εἰρήνη im neutestamentlichen Sprachsystem: Eine Bestimmung von lexikalischen Bedeutungen durch Wortfeld-Funktionen und deren Darstellung mittels

EDV (Forum Theologiae Linguisticae, 8). Bonn: Linguistica Biblica, 1977, 294 p.
LOOKWOOD, G., *Eirēnē* Reaffirmed. — *Lutheran Theological Journal* 21 (1987) 123-132.
PRETE, Benedetto, Il senso della formula "en eirênêi" in Luca 2,29. — *Chiesa per il mondo*. 1: *Saggi storico-biblici: Miscellanea teologico-pastorale nel LXX del card. Michele Pellegrino*. Bologna: Dehoniane, 1974, 39-60; = ID., *L'opera di Luca*, 1986, 167-184.
SWARTLEY, Willard M., Politics or Peace (*eirēnē*) in Luke's Gospel. — CASSIDY, Richard J. – SHARPER, Philip J. (eds.), *Political Issues in Luke-Acts*. Maryknoll, NY: Orbis, 1983, 18-37.
VAN LEEUWEN, Willem Silvester, *Eirene in het Nieuwe Testament: Een semasiologische, exegetische bijdrage op grond van de Septuaginta en de joodsche literatuur*. Wageningen: H. Veenman & Zonen, 1940, 232 p. — Diss. Leiden, 1940 (dir. J. De Zwaan).

εἰς 226/242 + 302/312 (Mt 218/227, Mk 165[168]/180)

1. to (extension); 2. into (extension) (Lk 2,15; Acts 17,10); 3. on (location) (Lk 15,22); 4. inside (location) (Lk 9,61; 11,7); 5. among (location) (Acts 4,17); 6. in order to (purpose) (Lk 2,32); 7. so that (result); 8. by (means) (Acts 7,53); 9. with reference to (content) (Acts 2,25); 10. to the point of (degree) (Lk 13,11); 11. to (change of state) (Lk 13,19); 12. to (experiencer); 13. on behalf of (benefaction); 14. by (guarantor); 15. for (time) (Lk 12,19); 16. at (time) (Acts 13,42); 17. until (time)

Word groups	Lk	Acts	Mt	Mk
γίνομαι/εἰμί + εἰς replacing the predicate nominative (*LN*: become; *SC*h; *VK*h); cf. ἔχω + εἰς Mt 21,46	3,5^{1.2}; 13,19^2; 20,17	4,11; 5,36; 8,20.23; 13,47^2	2	2
εἰς with composite verb ἀνα-/ἐπανα-/συνανα- (*SC*c; *VK*c)	2,4^{1.2}.22.42*; 4,5*; 5,4^1; 9,16.28; 13,11; 14,10; 18,10.31; 19,28; 22,66 *v.l.*; 24,51	1,11^2.13; 2,34; 3,1; 7,21; 9,39; 10,4.16; 11,2.10; 13,31; 15,2; 16,34; 20,3.13*; 21,4 *v.l.*6^1.12.15; 22,13; 24,11; 25,1.9	16	9[10]13
εἰς with composite verb εἰσ-/παρεισ-/συνεισ- (*SC*b; *VK*b)	1,9.40; 4,16^2.38; 6,4.6; 7,1^2.36.44; 8,30.32.33^1.41.51 *v.l.*; 9,4.34.52; 10,5.8.10^1.38; 11,4; 17,12.27; 18,17.24.25; 19,45; 21,21^2; 22,3.10^{1.3}.40.46.54; 24,26	3,2.3.8; 5,21^1; 9,6.8.17.28; 10,24; 11,8.12.20; 13,14^2; 14,1.14 *v.l.*20.22; 16,15.40*; 17,20; 18,7.19^2; 19,8.30; 20,29; 21,8^2.26.28.29.37; 22,24; 23,16.33; 25,23; 28,16	27/29	34/35
εἰς with composite verb ἐν- (*SC*d; *VK*d)	5,3; 6,39; 8,22^1.37; 10,36; 12,5; 13,21; 14,5 *v.l.*	1,11^1; 2,27.31; 9,1; 21,6^1 *v.l.*; 27,6^2	10/11	5/6
εἰς with reference to time (*SC*a; *VK*a)	1,20.33.50.55; 12,19; 13,9; 18,5	4,3^2; 13,42	5/6	3
εἰς + ἀνά (*VK*u)	10,1		0	1
εἰς + ἀπό (*VK*j)	1,26; 2,4^1.15; 4,38; 8,29 *v.l.*33^1; 9,5; 10,30; 24,51	1,11^2.12.25; 2,22; 8,26; 11,27; 12,19; 13,13^{1.2}.14^1.29.31; 16,11^1.40*; 18,6.22^1; 20,6.17; 21,1^1.7; 25,1; 26,18^1	5	3
εἰς αὐτό/οὐδέν/τοῦτο/τί (*SC*g; *VK*g)	4,43*	5,36; 9,21^2; 19,3^1; 26,16; 27,6^2	3	3

εἰς + ἄχρι/ἕως (VKs)	24,50*	13,47²; 20,6; 26,11; 28,15	1	2
εἰς + διά + accusative/genitive (VKl)	23,19*.25	14,22; 17,10¹; 23,31; 24,17	1	3
εἰς + ἐκ/ἔξω (LN: completely; VKk)	2,4¹; 4,38 v.l.; 10,7.11; 16,4; 17,24; 21,4; 24,50*	1,25 v.l.; 7,3; 13,34; 15,22; 16,40* v.l.; 18,1; 23,10; 28,17	8	6
εἰς + ἐν (VKm)	1,26; 2,27; 4,1*.14.16²; 6,6.12; 7,11; 8,22; 17,31; 21,21^{1.2}; 24,13	2,38 v.l.; 7,39; 11,27; 26,12.20*	6	4/5
εἰς + ἐπί +accusative/dative (VKp)	1,33; 9,5; 11,33; 24,47²	2,38; 3,1; 4,5*.17; 16,19; 20,13*; 26,18¹	2	3/4
εἰς + κατά + accusative/genitive (VKn)	2,41.42*; 4,16²; 8,33²; 22,39	16,7	4	4
εἰς + μετά + accusative/genitive (VKr)	1,39¹; 11,7; 15,13; 22,33¹; 24,52	9,28; 20,29; 25,1; 26,12	2	4/5
εἰς (τό) + adjective neuter singular (SCf; VKf)	4,35; 5,19; 6,8; 8,17; 13,11	17,21	0	4
εἰς τό (μή) + infinitive (SCe; VKe)	4,29*; 5,17; 20,20*	3,19; 7,19	3	1
εἰς τὸ οὖς / τὰ ὦτα (LN: privately)	1,44; 9,44	11,22	1	1
εἰς + παρά + accusative (VKz)	18,14		0	0
εἰς + περί + genitive (VKv)	4,37; 5,14	11,22; 15,2	1	2
εἰς + πρός + accusative (VKq)	1,26-27; 4,26; 19,29	9,2¹; 15,2; 20,6; 28,23	2	4
εἰς + σύν (VKw) DENAUX 2009 Laⁿ	5,19	3,4¹.8; 8,20; 14,20²; 15,22; 18,18; 25,23	0	0
εἰς τέλος (LN: completely)	18,5		2	1
εἰς + ὑπέρ + accusative/genitive (VKy) DENAUX 2009 LAⁿ	16,8	21,13	0	0
εἰς + ὑπό (VKt) DENAUX 2009 Lan	1,26 v.l.; 8,29; 11,33; 14,8¹; 16,22	5,21¹; 23,30 v.l.; 26,6	1	1
εἰς + χολὴν πικρίας εἰμί (LN: be terribly envious)		8,23	0	0
κατέχω εἰς (LN: head for)		27,40	0	0
τίθεμαι + εἰς τὰ ὦτα (LN: ᵃlisten carefully to; ᵇremember well)	9,ᵇ44		0	0

→ εἰς τὸν/τοὺς **αἰῶνα/αἰῶνας**; **ἀναβαίνω** εἰς (τὸ ἱερόν/Ἱεροσόλυμα/τὴν Ἰουδαίαν/τὸ ὄρος/τὸ πλοῖον); **ἀναβλέπω** εἰς τὸν οὐρανόν; **ἀνάγω** εἰς; **ἀναφέρω** εἰς; **ἀπαγγέλλω** εἰς; **ἀπάγω** εἰς; **ἀπέρχομαι** εἰς (τὸν οἶκον); **ἀποβαίνω** εἰς; **ἀποστέλλω** εἰς; **ἀποφέρω** εἰς; **αὐλίζομαι** εἰς; εἰς **ἄφεσιν** (τῶν) ἁμαρτιῶν; **ἀφορίζω** εἰς; **βάλλω** εἰς (τὸ) πῦρ / (τὴν) φυλακήν; **βαπτίζω** εἰς; **βασιλεύω** εἰς τοὺς αἰῶνας; **βλασφημέω** εἰς τὸ πνεῦμα; **βλέπω** εἰς; **διαβαίνω** εἰς; **διέρχομαι** εἰς τὸ πέραν; εἰς **ἑαυτόν/ούς**; **ἐγγίζω** εἰς; **εἰμι** εἰς; εἰς **εἰρήνην**; **εἰσάγω** εἰς (τὸ ἱερόν); **εἰσέρχομαι** εἰς τὴν βασιλείαν/τὸ ἱερόν/τὴν οἰκίαν/τὸν οἶκον; **εἰσπορεύομαι** εἰς τὴν βασιλείαν/τὸ ἱερόν/οἰκίαν; **εἰσφέρω** εἰς (τὰς ἀκοάς/πειρασμόν); **ἐκβάλλω** εἰς; **ἐκφέρω** εἰς; **ἐμβαίνω** εἰς (τὸ πλοῖον); **ἐμβλέπω** εἰς; **ἐξάγω** εἰς; **ἐξαποστέλλω** εἰς; **ἐξέρχομαι** εἰς (τὸ ὄρος); **ἐπανάγω** εἰς; **ἐπιβάλλω** τὴν χεῖρα ἐπ' ἄροτρον καὶ βλέπω εἰς τὰ ὀπίσω; **ἐπιστρέφω** εἰς (τὰ ὀπίσω); **ἔρχομαι** + εἰς; **ἔρχομαι** εἰς τὴν βασιλείαν/τὸ ἱερόν/Ἱερουσαλήμ/τὴν οἰκίαν/τὸν οἶκον; **ἥκω** εἰς; εἰς **θάνατον**; εἰς τὸν **θερισμόν**; εἰς τὸ **ἰᾶσθαι**; εἰς τὰ **ἴδια**; **καλέω** εἰς γάμον; **καταβαίνω** ἀπὸ … εἰς; **κατάγω** εἰς; **κατέρχομαι** (ἀπὸ …) εἰς; **κατοικέω** εἰς; **κεῖμαι** εἰς; εἰς **κεφαλὴν** γωνίας; **κλίνω** τὸ πρόσωπον εἰς τὴν γῆν; οἱ εἰς **μακράν**; εἰς **μαρτύριον**; εἰς τὸ **μέσον**; **μεταβαίνω** εἰς; **μετανοέω** εἰς; εἰς **μνημεῖον** τίθημι; εἰς (τὴν/τὰς) **ὁδόν/ὁδούς**; εἰς τὰ **ὀπίσω**; **ἀκούω** εἰς τὸ **οὖς** / τὰ ὦτα; εἰς τὸ παντελές; παραδίδωμι εἰς (τὰς χεῖρας); εἰς τὸ πέραν; πίπτω εἰς; πιστεύω εἰς; πίστις εἰς; ἀνα/ἐμ/ἐπιβαίνω εἰς (τὸ) πλοῖον; πλουτέω εἰς θεόν; ποιέω τι εἰς; πορείαν ποιέω εἰς Ἱεροσόλυμα; πορεύομαι εἰς Ἱεροσόλυμα / κώμην / οἶκον/ τὸ ὄρος; προάγω εἰς; συνάγω εἰς; συνέρχομαι εἰς; εἰς σωτηρίαν; τίθημι εἰς φυλακήν; τύπτω εἰς; ὑπάγω εἰς; εἰς φάνερον ἐλθεῖν; φέρω εἰς; φεύγω εἰς; εἰς (τὰς) χεῖρας; εἰς Χριστόν

Characteristic of Luke

HENDRIKS 1986 468; MORGENTHALER 1958A

	Lk	Acts	Mt	Mk
εἰς + ἔμπροσθεν/ἐνώπιον/ πρό (VKx) DENAUX 2009 L***	5,19; 10,1; 15,18.21; 19,28	10,4	0	0

→ ἄγω εἰς; ἁμαρτάνω εἰς; ἀναβαίνω εἰς Ἱερουσαλήμ; ἀτενίζω εἰς; γίνομαι εἰς; γίνομαι εἰς + place; ἔρχομαι εἰς ἑαυτόν; εἰσέρχομαι εἰς τὴν συναγωγήν; καταβαίνω εἰς; κατέρχομαι εἰς; μετάνοια εἰς; εἰς τὸν οἶκον + gen.; βαπτίζω εἰς τὸ ὄνομα; ἀναλαμβάνω εἰς τὸν οὐρανόν; παραγίνομαι εἰς; παραδίδωμι + (εἰς τό +) inf.; παραδίδωμι εἰς φυλακήν; πέμπω εἰς; πίστις εἰς (κύριον/Χριστὸν) Ἰησοῦν; πορεύομαι εἰς + place; πορεύομαι εἰς Ἱερουσαλήμ; πορεύου εἰς εἰρήνην; προσκυνέω εἰς + place; τίθημι εἰς; τίθημι εἰς τὴν καρδίαν; ὑποστρέφω εἰς (Ἱερουσαλήμ/τὸν οἶκον); εἰς χώραν μακράν

Literature

VON BENDEMANN 2001 416: "εἰς für klassisch zu erwartendes ἐν entspricht lukanischem Sprachgebrauch"; BDR §402: "Der substantivierter Inf. mit Präp. im Akkusativ: 1. διὰ τό zur Bezeichnung des Grundes, häufig Lk/Apg, bei Paulus nur Phil 1,7. 2. εἰς τό zur Bezeichnung des Zwecks oder der Folge, vorwiegend bei Paulus und Hb und wohl ohne Unterschied von τοῦ mit Inf. bei Luk."; COLLISON 1977 126-128 [εἰς for ἐν; for ἐπί; for πρός; for κατά + genitive; for purpose; semitisms; ἐπιστρέφω εἰς: noteworthy phenomena]; 128 [ὑποστρέφω + εἰς: linguistic usage of Luke: certain]; 129-130 [adverbial expressions: noteworthy phenomena]; 147 [εἰς τὰ ὀπίσω]; EASTON 1910 157 [εἰς τὰ ὦτα: probably characteristic of L]; 166 [εἰς χώραν μακράν: cited by Weiss as characteristic of L, and possibly corroborative]; GERSDORF 1816 217 [ἀνέβη δὲ καὶ Ἰωσὴφ - εἰς πόλιν Δαυίδ - ἀπογράψασθαι]; JEREMIAS 1980 58 [εἰς τὰ ὦτα: red.]; 59 [εἰς instead of ἐν: red.]; 151 [εἰς τὰς ἀκοάς: red.]; RADL 1975 408 [εἰς instead of ἐν; εἰς "bezogen auf Jerusalem"; 408 [εἰσέρχομαι εἰς]; REHKOPF 1959 93 [vorlukanisch]; SCHÜRMANN 1961 280 [protoluk R weniger wahrscheinlich].

BAUMERT, Norbert, Εἰς τό mit Infinitif. — FilolNT 11 (21-22, 1998) 7-24.

DELLING, Gerhard, Die Bezugnahme von neutestamentlichem εἰς auf Vorgegebenes. — BÖCHER, O. – HAACKER, K. (eds.), Verborum Veritas. FS G. Stählin, 1970, 211-223.

GARCÍA PÉREZ, José Miguel, El relato del Buen Ladrón (Lc 23,39-43), 1986. Esp. 276-280: "La preposición ἐν/εἰς".

GREENLEE, J. Harold, The Preposition εἰς in the New Testament. — BTrans 3 (1952) 12-14.

MANTEY, Julius Robert, The Causal Use of eis in the New Testament. — JBL 70 (1951) 45-48

—, On Causal eis again, — JBL 70 (1951) 309-311.

MARCUS, Ralph, On Causal eis. — JBL 70 (1951) 129-130.

READ-HEIMERDINGER, Jenny, The Bezan Text of Acts, 2002. Esp. 192-197: "εἰς-ἐν".

εἷς 43/48 + 21 (Mt 66, Mk 44/47)

1. one (number) (Lk 17,15); 2. one (indefinite) (Lk 22,50); 3. one (unit)

Word groups	Lk	Acts	Mt	Mk
ἀπὸ μιᾶς (LN: one by one; VKr)	14,18		0	0

εἷς + genitive	5,12.17; 8,22; 9,8*; 11,46; 12,27; 13,10; 15,15.19.21*.26; 17,2.22; 20,1; 22,47; 23,39; 24,1	1,22; 20,7; 23,17	17	12
εἷς + three (VKl)	9,33[1.2.3]		3	3
εἷς + two (VKk)	5,3; 7,41; 12,6; 16,13[1.2]; 17,34[1.2]. 35; 18,10; 23,39; 24,18	1,24	16	6
εἷς (ἐκ) τῶν δώδεκα (SCc; VKc) → τις τῶν μαθητῶν; cf. εἷς τῶν μαθητῶν Mk 13,1	22,47		2	3
εἷς … εἷς (SCa)	9,33[1.2.3]		11	15
εἷς (+) ἐκ (VKa)	12,6; 15,4; 17,15; 22,50	11,28	5	2
εἷς ὁ θεός (VKd) → μόνος ὁ θεός	18,19		0/1	2/3
εἷς (+) οὐ (VKe); cf. εἷς + μή Mt 18,10	11,46; 12,6; 15,4	20,31	6	1
εἷς + πᾶς/πάντες/πολλοί (VKj)	10,(41-)42; 18,22	17,26; 19,34	2	3
εἷς τις (VKg) → δύο τινές	22,50		0	1/2
(τὸ) ἕν / καθ' ἕν (VKn)	10,42; 18,22	21,19	0	1
καθ' ἕν ἕκαστον		21,19	0	0
(ἐν +) τῇ μιᾷ (VKq)	24,1	20,7	0	1
(η) μία τῶν σαββάτων	24,1	20,7	1	1
μία ὥρα	22,59		2	1
τῶν μικρῶν τούτων εἷς	17,2		4	1
οὐδὲ εἷς (VKf)		4,32	1	1

Characteristic of Luke

	Lk	Acts	Mt	Mk
δύο + noun + ὁ εἷς … ὁ ἕτερος DENAUX 2009 L***	7,41; 16,13[1.2]; 17,34[2].35; 18,10		2	0
εἷς ἕκαστος (SCd; VKb) BOISMARD 1984 Eb16; DENAUX 2009 lA*; NEIRYNCK 1985; PLUMMER 1922 lx	4,40; 16,5	2,3.6; 17,27; 20,31; 21,19.26	1	0
εἷς … ἕτερος (SCb; VKh); cf. 1 Cor 4,6 BOISMARD 1984 cb109; DENAUX 2009 L*** [ὁ εἷς … ὁ ἕτερος]; GOULDER 1989 [ὁ εἷς … ὁ ἕτερος]; NEIRYNCK 1985	7,41; 16,13[1.2]; 17,34[2].35; 18,10; 23,39(-40)	23,6	2	0
ἐν μιᾷ τῶν DENAUX 2009 L***; GOULDER 1989*; HAWKINS 1909L; PLUMMER 1922 lii	5,12.17; 8,22; 13,10; 20,1		0	0
ἐν μιᾷ τῶν ἡμερῶν PLUMMER 1922 lii	5,17; 8,22; 20,1		0	0
μία τῶν ἡμερῶν DENAUX 2009 L***	5,17; 8,22; 17,22; 20,1		0	0

Literature

COLLISON 1977 185 [εἷς … ἕτερος: noteworthy phenomena]; 213 [indefinite pronoun: linguistic usage of Luke's "other source-material": certain]; DENAUX 2009 L[n] [ἐν μιᾷ τῶν ἡμερῶν]; HAUCK 1934 [Vorzugsverbindung: μία τῶν ἡμερῶν]; JEREMIAS 1980 256 [εἷς ἕκαστος + Gen.part.: red.]; PLUMMER 1922 lxi [εἷς in the sense of τις (5,12.17; 8,22; 13,10; 20,1) or of πρῶτος (24,1)]; RADL 1975 408 [εἷς … ἕτερος]; 425 [πορεύομαι εἷς + place]; SCHÜRMANN 1957 8-9 [εἷς für τις: ein korrelatives zweites εἷς von Luk vermieden]; 9, n. 29 [ἐν μιᾷ τῶν ἡμερῶν … πόλεων … συναγωγῶν in den von Luk gebildeten Perikopenanfängen, in der er von einer geformten Redeweise abhängig zu sein scheint].

BLACK, Matthew, The Aramaic Dimension in Q with Notes on Luke 17.22 Matthew 24.26 (Luke 17.23). — JSNT 40 (1990) 33-41. Esp.38: "The day of the son of man (Lk. 17.22)".

BURCHARD, Christoph, Fußnoten zum neutestamentlichen Griechisch II, 1978. Esp. 146-149: "Lk 5,12.17; 8,22; 13,10; 20,1 ἐν μιᾷ τῶν…".

DODD, Charles H., New Testament Translation Problems. — BTrans 27 (1976) 301-311.

Esp. 305-307: "τῇ μιᾷ τῶν σαββάτων"; 28 (1977) 101-116.
FEE, Gordon D., "One Thing is Needful"?, Luke 10:42. — EPP, E.J. – FEE, G.D. (eds.),
New Testament Textual Criticism. FS B.M. Metzger, 1981, 71-75.
GILLIESON, T., A Plea for Proportion: St. Luke x.38-42. — *ExpT* 59 (1947-48) 111-112.
[πολλά ... ἑνός].
NORTH, J. Lionel, ὀλίγων δέ ἐστιν χρεία ἢ ἑνός (Luke 10.42): Text, Subtext and
Context. — *JSNT* 66 (1997) 3-13. [NTA 42, 266]
WILCOX, Max, Semitisms in the New Testament, 1984. Esp. 1009: "ἀπὸ μιᾶς (Luke 14:18)";
"ἐν μιᾷ τῶν ἡμερῶν = 'one day'".

εἰσάγω 3 + 6

1. lead into (Lk 2,27; 14,21; 22,54); 2. carry in (Acts 7,45)

Word groups	Lk	Acts	Mt	Mk
εἰσάγω (+) εἰς + place → (ἀν/ἀπ/ἐξ/ἐπαν/κατ/προ/ συν/ὑπ)ἄγω εἰς + place DENAUX 2009 1Aⁿ	22,54	9,8; 21,28.29.37; 22,24	0	0
εἰσάγω εἰς τὸ ἱερόν → ἀναβαίνω/ εἰσπορεύομαι/(εἰσ)ἔρχομαι εἰς τὸ ἱερόν; cf. εἴσειμι εἰς τὸ ἱερόν Acts 3,3; 21,26		21,28.29		
κελεύω + εἰσάγειν → κελεύω + (ἀπ)ἄγειν BOISMARD 1984 Ab26; NEIRYNCK 1985		22,24	0	0
εἰσάγομαι passive → (ἀν/ἀπ/ἐπισυν/κατ/συν)ἄγομαι passive		21,37; 22,24	0	0
εἰσήγαγον → (ἀν/ἀπ/κατ)ἤγαγον; cf. συνήγαγον Mt 22,10; 27,27 DENAUX 2009 1Aⁿ	22,54	7,45; 9,8	0	0

Characteristic of Luke

BOISMARD 1984 Bb87; DENAUX 2009 1A*; GOULDER 1989; HAWKINS 1909B; NEIRYNCK
1985; PLUMMER 1922 lx

	Lk	Acts	Mt	Mk
εἰσάγω transitive → (ἀν/ἀπ/ἐξ/ἐπισυν/κατ/προ/ προσ/συν)ἄγω transitive DENAUX 2009 1A*	2,27; 14,21; 22,54	7,45; 9,8; 21,28.29.37; 22,24	0	

Literature

GERSDORF 1816 252; HAUCK 1934 [Vorzugswort]; JEREMIAS 1980 95: "lk Vorzugswort";
RADL 1975 408 [εἰσάγω; εἰσάγω "bezogen auf den Tempel"]; SCHNEIDER 1969 74-75.163
[Vorzugswörter und -ausdrücke des Luk].

εἰσακούω 1 + 1 (Mt 1)

1. listen to (Lk 1,13; Acts 10,31); 2. obey

Literature

HARNACK 1906 71 (ET 100) [εἰσηκούσθη, of prayers, occurs besides (1,13) only in Acts 10,31;
cf. Mt 6,7].

DANOVE, Paul, Verbs of Experience, 1999. Esp. 155.172.

εἰσέρχομαι 50/52 + 34/35 (Mt 36/40, Mk 30/33)

1. move into (Lk 7,1; Acts 1,13); 2. happen; 3. begin (Lk 9,46); 4. begin to experience (Lk 22,40)

Word groups	Lk	Acts	Mt	Mk
εἰσέρχομαι + infinitive → (ἀπ/ἐξ/προ/προσ/ συν)ἔρχομαι + inf.	19,7; 24,29		1	1
εἰσέρχομαι (+) ἄγγελος → ἀπέρχομαι + ἄγγελος; cf. ἐξέρχομαι ἄγγελος Mt 13,49; προσέρχομαι (+) ἄγγελος Mt 4,11; 28,2 DENAUX 2009 LA[n]	9,52	10,3	0	0
εἰσέρχομαι + ἀπαγγέλλω → ἀποστέλλω/(ἀπ/ δι/κατ/προσ)ἔρχομαι/(εἰσ)πορεύομαι/ ὑποστρέφω/φεύγω + ἀπαγγέλλω/ διαγγέλλω/διηγέομαι/κηρύσσω		11,12(-13); 23,16	0	0
εἰσέρχομαι (+) διά + genitive (VKg)	13,24[1]; 18,25[1]	14,22	2/3	0/1
εἰσέρχομαι εἰς (+) τὴν βασιλείαν (SCb; VKb) → εἰσπορεύομαι/ ἔρχομαι εἰς τὴν βασιλείαν	18,17.24*.25[2]	14,22	5/6	5
εἰσέρχομαι (+) εἰς τὸ ἱερόν → εἰσέρχομαι εἰς τὸν ναόν; ἀναβαίνω/εἰσάγω/ εἰσπορεύομαι/ἔρχομαι εἰς τὸ ἱερόν; cf. εἴσειμι εἰς τὸ ἱερόν Acts 3,3; 21,26	19,45	3,8; 5,21	1	2
εἰσέρχομαι (+) εἰς (+) κώμην / πολίν or name of city	7,1; 9,52;10,38;17,12; 22,10	9,6; 10,24;11,20; 14,20; 23,33; 28,16	5	4
εἰσέρχομαι εἰς τὸν ναόν → εἰσέρχομαι εἰς τὸ ἱερόν	1,9		0	0
εἰσέρχομαι (+) εἰς (+) τὴν οἰκίαν / τὸν οἶκον (SCa; VKa) → (ἀπ)ἔρχομαι εἰς τὴν οἰκίαν / τὸν οἶκον	1,40; 4,38; 6,4; 7,36.44; 8,41.51*; 9,4; 10,5	9,17; 11,12; 16,15; 18,7; 21,8	3/4	6
εἰσέρχομαι (+) εἰς τὴν συναγωγήν (SCf)	4,16; 6,6	13,14; 14,1; 18,19; 19,8	0	2
εἰσέρχομαι ἐκ (VKm)	17,7		0	0
εἰσέρχομαι + ἐν (VKl)	9,46		0	0
εἰσέρχομαι + ἐξέρχομαι (SCe; VKf)	8,33; 9,4; 10,10; 11,(24-)26; 14,23; 15,28	1,21; 10,(23-) 24; 14,20; 16,40; 21,8	3	6
εἰσέρχομαι καὶ ἐξέρχομαι (LN: live with) → εἰσπορεύομαι καὶ ἐκπορεύομαι		1,21	0	0
εἰσέρχομαι + ἐπί + accusative (VKj) → (ἀπ/ἐξ/ἐπ) ἔρχομαι ἐπί + acc.		1,21	0	0
εἰσέρχομαι + εὑρίσκω → (ἀπ/δι/ἐξ/κατ) ἔρχομαι/(εἰσ)πορεύομαι + εὑρίσκω DENAUX 2009 lA[n]	24,3	5,10; 10,27	0	0
εἰσέρχομαι + τοῦ + infinitive (SCd; VKe)	24,29		0	0
εἰσέρχομαι + ὑπό + accusative (VKk)	7,6		1	0

Characteristic of Luke	Lk	Acts	Mt	Mk
εἰσελθὼν absolute ... εὑρίσκω BOISMARD 1984 Ab180; NEIRYNCK 1985	24,3	5,10	0	0
εἰσέρχομαι + ἀναγκάζω/παραβιάζομαι /παρακαλέω DENAUX 2009 La**	8,32.41; 14,23; 15,28; 24,29	14,22; 16,15.40	1	1

εἰσέρχομαι πρός (+ accusative) (*VK*h) → (ἀπ/κατ)ἔρχομαι πρός + acc.; cf. Rev 3,20 BOISMARD 1984 cb107; HARNACK 1906 42; NEIRYNCK 1985	1,28	10,3; 11,3; 16,40; 17,2; 28,8	0	2

Literature

DENAUX 2009 LAⁿ [εἰσελθών absolute ... εὑρίσκω]; HARNACK 1906 34; RADL 1975 408 [εἰσέρχομαι εἰς]; SCHÜRMANN 1953 94 [εἰσέρχεσθαι; εἰσέρχεσθαι εἰς].

JEREMIAS, Joachim, Lukas 7,45: εἰσῆλθον. — *ZNW* 51 (1960) 131.

KREUZER, Siegfried, Der Zwang des Boten – Beobachtungen zu Lk 14,23 und 1 Kor 9,16. — *ZNW* 76 (1985) 123-128.

WINDISCH, Hans, Die Sprüche vom Eingehen in das Reich Gottes. — *ZNW* 27 (1928) 163-192.

εἰσπορεύομαι 5 + 4 (Mt 1, Mk 8) move into

Word groups	Lk	Acts	Mt	Mk
εἰσπορεύομαι + εἰς τὴν βασιλείαν → (εἰσ)ἔρχομαι εἰς τὴν βασιλείαν	18,24		0	0
εἰσπορεύομαι εἰς τὸ ἱερόν → ἀναβαίνω/εἰσάγω/(εἰσ) ἔρχομαι εἰς τὸ ἱερόν; cf. εἴσειμι εἰς τὸ ἱερόν Acts 3,3; 21,26		3,2	0	0
εἰσπορεύομαι + εἰς οἰκίαν → πορεύμαι εἰς οἶκον	22,10		0	0
εἰσπορεύομαι + εὑρίσκω → (ἀπ/δι/εἰσ/ἐξ/κατ)ἔρχομαι/ πορεύομαι + εὑρίσκω	19,30		0	1
εἰσπορεύομαι καὶ ἐκπορεύομαι (*LN*: live with) → εἰσέρχομαι καὶ ἐξέρχομαι		9,28	0	0
εἰσπορεύομαι + κηρύσσω → ἀποστέλλω/(ἀπ/δι/εἰσ/ κατ/προσ)ἔρχομαι/πορεύομαι/ὑποστρέφω/φεύγω + ἀπαγγέλλω/διαγγέλλω/διηγέομαι/κηρύσσω		28,30(-31)	0	0

Characteristic of Luke	Lk	Acts	Mt	Mk
(οἱ) εἰσπορευόμενοι (*VK*a) BOISMARD 1984 Ab77; NEIRYNCK 1985	8,16; 11,33; 19,30	3,2; 28,30	0	0

Literature

COLLISON 1977 49 [linguistic usage of Luke: certain]; DENAUX 2009 Laⁿ [(οἱ) εἰσπορευόμενοι]; JEREMIAS 1980 205: "Das substantivierte pluralische Partizip οἱ εἰσπορευόμενοι begegnet im NT nur im Doppelwerk"; SCHÜRMANN 1953 96 [Vorliebe des Luk für πορεύεσθαι und seine Komposita].

εἰσφέρω 4 + 1 (Mt 1)

1. bring in (Lk 5,18.19; 12,11); 2. cause to (Lk 11,4; Acts 17,20?)

Word groups	Lk	Acts	Mt	Mk
εἰσφέρω εἰς τὰς ἀκοάς (*LN*: ᵃcause to hear; ᵇspeak about)		17,ᵃ20	0	0
εἰσφέρω εἰς πειρασμόν	11,4		1	0
εἰσφέρω metaphorically (*VK*a)	11,4	17,20	1	0

Characteristic of Luke

BOISMARD 1984 Eb47; DENAUX 2009 L***; GOULDER 1989*; HAWKINS 1909 18; NEIRYNCK 1985; PLUMMER 1922 lx

Literature

COLLISON 1977 93 [noteworthy phenomena]; HAUCK 1934 [Vorzugswort].

εἶτα 1 (Mk 4)

1. afterwards (Lk 8,12); 2. furthermore

εἴωθα 1 + 1 (Mt 1, Mk 1)   be in the habit of

Characteristic of Luke	Lk	Acts	Mt	Mk
τὸ εἰωθός → τὸ εἰθισμένον BOISMARD 1984 Ab175; CREDNER 1836 134-135; HARNACK 1906 70 (κατὰ τὸ εἰωθός); NEIRYNCK 1985; PLUMMER 1922 lxiii [κατὰ τὸ εἰωθός].	4,16	17,2	0	0

Literature

DENAUX 2009 LA[n] [τὸ εἰωθός]; JEREMIAS 1980 29: "Der Apg-Beleg zeigt, daß das substantivierte Part.perf. τὸ εἰωθός lukanisch ist"; SCHÜRMANN 1957 5 [κατὰ τὸ εἰωθός: luk Wendung].

CHILTON, Bruce, Announcement in Nazara, 1981. Esp. 153-154.

ἐκ 87/94 + 84/94 (Mt 82/86, Mk 65[66]/71[73])

1. out of (extension) (Lk 23,55); 2. because of (reason) (Lk 12,15); 3. by (means) (Lk 8,3; 16,9); 4. with (instrument); 5. with (manner) (Lk 10,27); 6. from (source) (Acts 22,14); 7. from (dissociation) (Acts 28,4[2]); 8. from (derivation) (Lk 2,36; Acts 4,6); 9. one of (part-whole) (Lk 24,13); 10. from (cessation); 11. when (time); 12. since (time) (Lk 18,21); 13. with (price); 14. of (substance)

Word groups	Lk	Acts	Mt	Mk
εἷς (+) ἐκ (SCf) → τις/τίς ἐκ	12,6; 15,4[1.2]; 17,15; 22,50	11,28	5	2
ἐκ + composite verb ἀνα- (SCe; VKe) → ἀπό + composite verb ἀνα-	2,4[1]; 4,38*; 12,36; 16,31; 24,46	2,30 v.l.; 3,22; 6,9; 7,37; 8,39; 10,41; 13,34; 17,3.31; 20,30	0/1	4
ἐκ + composite verb ἀπο- (SCe; VKe) → ἀπό + composite verb ἀπο-	2,35	24,7*	1	1/2
ἐκ + composite verb ἐκ- (SCb; VKb) → ἀπό + composite verb ἐκ-	4,22.35*; 6,42; 11,49 v.l.	3,23; 7,3[1.2].4.10.40; 12,7.11.17; 13,17.42*; 15,22.24; 16,40*; 17,33; 19,16; 22,18; 26,17[1.2]; 27,30[2]; 28,3*	13/15	15/16
ἐκ + composite verb κατα- (SCd; VKd) → ἀπό + composite verb κατα-		11,5	4	1
ἐκ + composite verb συν- (SCc; VKc) → ἀπό + composite verb συν-; cf. ἐκ + composite verb ἐπισυν- Mk 13,27	6,44[2]; 23,55	19,33	4	0
ἐκ + ἀπό (VKl)	2,4[1]	26,4	2	1

ἐκ + εἰς (*LN*: completely; *VK*j)	2,4[1]; 4,38*; 10,7.11; 16,4; 17,24; 21,4[1]	1,25*; 7,3[1,2]; 13,34; 15,22; 16,40* *v.l.*; 18,1; 23,10; 28,17	7	5
ἐκ + ἐν (*VK*k)	12,15	7,4; 15,21; 22,18	4/5	2
ἐξ (+) ἐτῶν → ἀπ᾽ ἐτῶν BOISMARD 1984 cb29; NEIRYNCK 1985		9,33; 24,10	0	0
ἐκ ... ἕως (*VK*m) → ἀπὸ ... ἕως	20,42(-43); 22,16*	2,34(-35)	3	3
ἐκ + κατά + accusative (*VK*u)		15,21	0	0
ἐκ + μετά + accusative/ genitive (*VK*n)		24,7*	2	1
ἐκ τοῦ ὄχλου → ἀπὸ τοῦ ὄχλου; διὰ τὸν ὄχλον	11,27; 12,13	19,33	0	1
ἐκ + περί + accusative (*VK*s)		22,6	0	0
ἐκ + πρός + accusative (*VK*r) DENAUX 2009 LA[n]	11,6	10,15; 16,40*; 23,30*	0	0
ἐκ + σύν (*VK*v)		15,22	0	0
ὁ/ἡ/τὸ ἐκ (*SC*f; *VK*f)		6,9; 11,2; 15,23	3	0
τίς (+) ἐκ (*SC*f) → εἷς/τις ἐκ; τίς/τις/τινες numeral ἐξ αὐτῶν	11,5.11; 12,25; 14,28; 15,4[1]; 17,7[1]; 22,23	6,9	4	0
ἐκ adverb of place (*SC*g; *VK*g)	23,8	10,15; 11,9[1]	3	2/3
ἐκ time (*SC*a; *VK*a) → ἀπό time	1,15; 8,27*; 18,21; 23,8	3,2; 9,33; 14,8; 15,21; 24,10; 26,4	0/1	2/3

→ ἀναβαίνω ἐκ; → (ἡ) ἀνάστασις (ἡ) (ἐκ) (τῶν) νεκρῶν; ἀνατολὴ ἐξ ὕψους; ἀνίστημι ἐκ νεκρῶν; ἐξ ἀριστερῶν; γυνὴ ἐκ τοῦ ὄχλου; ἐκ δεξιῶν (κάθημαι); ἐκ δευτέρου; δύναμις ἐξ ὕψους; ἐγείρω ἐκ (τῶν) νεκρῶν; εἰμι ἐκ; εἷς (ἐκ) τῶν δώδεκα; εἰσέρχομαι ἐκ; ἐκβάλλω ἐκ; ἐξάγω ἐκ; ἐξέρχομαι ἐκ (ἐξ Ἰερουσαλήμ); ἔρχομαι + ἐκ; θρὶξ ἐκ τῆς κεφαλῆς; ἐξ ὅλης τῆς ἰσχύος; ἐκ καρποῦ τῆς ὀσφύος; καταβαίνω ἐκ; (χωλὸς) ἐκ κοιλίας μητρός; λαμβάνω ἐκ; ἐκ μέσου; μεταβαίνω ἐκ; ἐκ νεκρῶν; ἐκ οὐρανοῦ; πάλιν ἐκ δευτέρου; πᾶς ἐκ; πατὴρ ἐξ οὐρανοῦ; πίπτω (ἐκ); ποιέω τι ἐκ; πολλοί ... ἐκ; ἐκ τοῦ στόματός τινος; συλλέγω ἐκ; τις + ἐκ; τις ἐκ τοῦ ὄχλου; τίς ἐξ ὑμῶν; ἐξ ὑμῶν; ὑποστρέφω ἐκ; φεύγω ἐκ; ἐκ τῆς χειρός (proper sense); ἐκ (τῆς) χειρός / τῶν χειρῶν others; χορτάζομαι ἐκ

Characteristic of Luke	Lk	Acts	Mt	Mk
τις (+) ἐκ (*SC*f) → εἷς/τίς ἐκ; τίς/τις/τινες numeral ἐξ αὐτῶν DENAUX 2009 lA*	11,15.54; 12,13	11,20; 15,2.24; 17,4	0	1

Literature

COLLISON 1977 130 [partitive: linguistic usage of Luke's "other source-material": certain, but Luke can also introduce it into his source; τις ἐκ: noteworthy phenomena]; 132 [τίς ἐξ ὑμῶν: likely]; HAUCK 1934 [Vorzugsverbindung: τίς (γὰρ/δὲ) ἐξ (ὑμῶν); RADL 1975 399 [ἀνάστασις ἐκ νεκρῶν]; 407 [ὧν ἐκ]; SCHÜRMANN 1953 102 [ἀπό instead of ἐκ]; 1957 12-13 [τίς ἐξ (ἡμῶν/αὐτῶν)].

READ-HEIMERDINGER, Jenny, *The Bezan Text of Acts*, 2002. Esp. 187-192: "ἀπό-ἐκ".

ἕκαστος 5 + 11 (Mt 4, Mk 1)   each

Word groups	Lk	Acts	Mt	Mk
ἕκαστος ἡμῶν/ὑμῶν DENAUX 2009 lA[n]	13,15	2,38; 17,27	0	0

ἕκαστος (+) ἴδιος (*VK*b)	2,3 *v.l.*; 6,44	2,6.8	1	0
καθ' ἓν ἕκαστον (*VK*e)		21,19	0	0
ἕκαστος adjective (*VK*a)	6,44		0	0

Characteristic of Luke

CADBURY 1920 115; MORGENTHALER 1958A

	Lk	Acts	Mt	Mk
εἷς ἕκαστος (*SC*a; *VK*c) BOISMARD 1984 Eb16; DENAUX 2009 IA*; NEIRYNCK 1985; PLUMMER 1922 lx	4,40; 16,5	2,3.6; 17,27; 20,31; 21,19.26	1	0
ἕκαστος + genitive plural BOISMARD 1984 Db5; DENAUX 2009 IA*; GOULDER 1989 (part.gen.); NEIRYNCK 1985	4,40; 13,15; 16,5	2,3.38; 11,29; 17,27; 21,19(?).26	0	0

Literature

JEREMIAS 1980 256 [εἷς ἕκαστος + Gen.part.: red.].

ἑκατόν 3/4 (Mt 4, Mk 3) — one hundred

Word groups	Lk	Acts	Mt	Mk
ἑκατὸν εἴκοσι (*VK*c)		1,15	0	0
ἑκατὸν ἑξήκοντα (*VK*f)	24,13*		0	0

ἑκατονταπλασίων 1 (Mt 1, Mk 1) — hundred times as much (Lk 8,8)

ἑκατοντάρχης 2/4 + 12 (Mt 1/4) — Roman officer

Word groups	Lk	Acts	Mt	Mk
ἑκατοντάρχης + στρατιώτης		21,32; 27,31	0	0
ἑκατοντάρχαι plural (*VK*a)		21,32; 23,17.23	0	0

Characteristic of Luke

BOISMARD 1984 cb6; DENAUX 2009 IA*; MORGENTHALER 1958A; NEIRYNCK 1985;
PLUMMER 1922 lx

Literature

HAUCK 1934 [Vorzugsverbindung: ἑκατοντάρχου δέ τινος]; JEREMIAS 1980 151
[ἑκατοντάρχης/ος: red.].

BORMANN, Lukas, *Recht, Gerechtigkeit und Religion*, 2001. Esp. 212.

ἑκατόνταρχος 1 + 1/9 (Mt 3/4) — Roman officer (Lk 7,2)

Word groups	Lk	Acts	Mt	Mk
ἑκατόνταρχος + στρατιώτης		21,32 *v.l.*	0	0

Literature

BORMANN, Lukas, *Recht, Gerechtigkeit und Religion*, 2001. Esp. 212.

ἐκβάλλω 20/21 + 5 (Mt 28, Mk 16[18])

1. throw out (Lk 20,12); 2. drive out (Acts 16,37); 3. send out (Lk 10,2); 4. lead out; 5. exorcise (Lk 9,49); 6. cause to be

Word groups	Lk	Acts	Mt	Mk
ἐκβάλλω + ἀπό (VKb)		13,50	0/1	0[1]
ἐκβάλλω (+) δαιμόνιον (SCa); cf. ἐκβάλλω σατανᾶν Mt 12,26; Mk 3,23	9,49; 11,14.15.18.19[1]. 20; 13,32		7	7[9]
ἐκβάλλω (+) εἰς (VKc)	10,2	27,38	6	1
ἐκβάλλω + ἐκ (VKa)	6,42[2]		6	1
ἐκβάλλω (+) ἔξω (VKd) → βάλλω ἔξω	4,29; 8,54*; 13,28; 20,15	7,58; 9,40	1	1
ἐκβάλλω τὸ ὄνομα (LN: slander; VKf)	6,22		0	0
ἐκβάλλω of human beings	4,29; 10,2; 13,28; 19,45; 20,12.15	7,58; 9,40; 13,50; 16,37	8	4

Characteristic of Luke	Lk	Acts	Mt	Mk
ἐκβάλλω ἔξω τῆς πόλεως BOISMARD 1984 Ab176; NEIRYNCK 1985	4,29	7,58	0	0

Literature

DENAUX 2009 LA[n] [ἐκβάλλω ἔξω τῆς πόλεως]; RADL 1975 409 [ἐκβάλλω; ἐκβάλλω "bezogen auf (menschliche) Personen"].

FERRARO, Giuseppe, "Oggi e domani e il terzo giorno" (osservazioni su *Luca* 13,32.33). — *RivBib* 16 (1968) 397-407. Esp. 401-407: "Considerazioni sul vocabolario di Luca 13,32.33" [ἐκβάλλειν δαιμόνια; ἰάσεις ἀποτελῶ; τελειοῦσθαι e πορεύεσθαι; ἀπολέσθαι].

ἐκδίδομαι 1 (Mt 2, Mk 1)   rent out (Lk 20,9)

ἐκδικέω 2

1. give justice (Lk 18,3.5); 2. revenge; 3. punish

Literature

BORMANN, Lukas, *Recht, Gerechtigkeit und Religion*, 2001. Esp. 180.

ἐκδίκησις 3 + 1

1. give justice (Lk 18,7.8); 2. revenge; 3. punishment (Lk 21,22)

Characteristic of Luke	Lk	Acts	Mt	Mk
ἐκδίκησιν ποιέω (VKa) BOISMARD 1984 Ab116; NEIRYNCK 1985	18,7.8	7,24	0	0

Literature

COLLISON 1977 181 [noteworthy phenomena]; DENAUX 2009 La[n]; La[n] [ἐκδίκησιν ποιέω]; EASTON 1910 160 [ἐκδίκησις punishment: cited by Weiss as characteristic of L, and possibly corroborative]; JEREMIAS 1980 271: "ποιέω τὴν ἐκδίκησιν ... findet sich im NT nur Lk 18,7f.; Apg 7,24. ... Lk 18,7f. wird die Person, der Recht verschafft wird, im Genitiv eingeführt, Apg 7,24 im Dativ. Da Lukas selbst in der Apg mit Dativ konstruiert, ist die Konstruktion mit Genitiv (Lk 18,7f.) der Tradition zuzuschreiben".

BORMANN, Lukas, *Recht, Gerechtigkeit und Religion*, 2001. Esp. 180-181.

ἐκδύω 1 (Mt 2, Mk 1)	take off clothes (Lk 10,30)

ἐκεῖ 16 + 6/7 (Mt 28/29, Mk 11/13)   there

Word groups	Lk	Acts	Mt	Mk
ἐκεῖ + ἐκεῖθεν	9,4		0	1
ἰδοὺ ἐκεῖ → ἰδοὺ ὧδε	17,21 v.l.23		0	0/1
ὅπου + ἐκεῖ (VKa); cf. οὗ + ἐκεῖ Mt 18,20	12,34; 17,37		2	1/2
ὧδε + ἐκεῖ (VKb)	17,21.23		0	1

Literature
COLLISON 1977 151 [linguistic usage of Luke: likely; it may also be a linguistic usage of Luke's "other source material"]; RADL 1975 409 ["im Gefolge einer Zielangabe"]; SCHÜRMANN 1953 101 [καὶ ἐκεῖ von Luk vermieden; κἀκεῖ relativ häufig].

ἐκεῖθεν 3 + 4/5 (Mt 12, Mk 5/7)   from there

Word groups	Lk	Acts	Mt	Mk
οἱ ἐκεῖθεν (VKd)	16,26 v.l.		0	0
ἐκεῖθεν + ἀποπλέω → κἀκεῖθεν ἀποπλέω BOISMARD 1984 Aa137		13,4	0	0
ἐκεῖθεν + ἐκεῖ (VKc)	9,4		0	1
ἐξέρχομαι ἐκεῖθεν (VKa) → κἀκεῖθεν + (ἐξ)έρχομαι	9,4; 12,59		1	2/3

ἐκεῖνος 33/38 + 22/23 (Mt 54/57, Mk 20[23]/25)   that

Word groups	Lk	Acts	Mt	Mk
ὁ ἄνθρωπος ἐκεῖνος → ὁ ἀνὴρ ἐκεῖνος; ἀνὴρ/ἄνθρωπος οὗτος; γυνὴ αὕτη	11,26; 22,22	16,35	3/4	2
ὁ ἀνὴρ ἐκεῖνος → ὁ ἄνθρωπος ἐκεῖνος; ἀνὴρ/ἄνθρωπος οὗτος; γυνὴ αὕτη	14,24		0	0
ἐκεῖνος after noun (VKa)	2,1; 4,2; 6,48.49; 9,5; 10,12[1.2].31; 11,26; 12,37.38.43.45.46; 14,21*.24; 15,14.15; 17,9*; 18,3; 19,27*; 20,1*.35; 21,34; 22,22	1,19; 2,18.41; 3,23; 7,41; 8,8; 9,37; 12,6; 14,21; 16,3.35; 19,16.23; 20,2; 28,7	39/42	9/10
ἐκεῖνος before noun (VKb)	5,35; 6,23; 7,21; 9,36; 12,47; 13,4; 17,31; 20,18; 21,23	8,1; 12,1; 16,33	11	8
ἐκεῖνος with reference to time (SCb) → ὁ αἰὼν ἐκεῖνος; ἡ ἡμέρα ἐκείνη; ὁ ἐκεῖνος καίρος; νὺξ ἐκείνη; ἐν ἐκείνῃ τῇ ὥρᾳ / τῇ ὥρᾳ ἐκείνῃ	2,1; 4,2; 5,35; 6,23; 7,21; 9,36; 10,12[1]; 17,31; 20,1*.35; 21,23.34	2,18.41; 7,41; 8,1; 9,37; 12,1.6; 16,33; 19,23	22	10/11
ἐκεῖνος + ἀλλήλων(VKe)		21,6	0	0
ἐκεῖνος … ὅς	12,37.43; 13,4; 22,22		2/3	1
ἐκεῖνος + οὗτος (VKc) → ἄλλος/ ἕτερος/κἀκεῖνος + οὗτος DENAUX 2009 L[n]	18,14; 20,(34-)35		0	0

Characteristic of Luke

→ κατὰ τὸ **καιρὸν** ἐκεῖνον

Literature

JEREMIAS 1980 275: "Lokaler Genitiv mit Ellipse von ὁδός findet sich im NT nur im LkEv: 5,19 ποίας und 19,4 ἐκείνης"; SCHÜRMANN 1953 38 [unbetonte ἐκεῖνος].

CIGNELLI, Lino – PIERRI, Rosario, *Sintassi di Greco biblico*. I.a, 2003. Esp. 68-74: "Concordanza dei pronomi dimostrativi" [ὅδε, οὗτος, ἐκεῖνος].

CRAGHAN, John F., A Redactional Study of Lk 7,21 in the Light of Dt 19,15. — *CBQ* 29 (1967) 353-367. Esp. 52-56: "The redactor's hand" [ἐν αὐτῇ/ἐκείνῃ τῇ ὥρᾳ].

ELLIOTT, James K., New Testament Linguistic Usage, 1992. Esp. 42-44: "ἐκεῖνος in the Gospels and Acts".

JEREMIAS, Joachim, Ἐν ἐκείνῃ τῇ ὥρᾳ, (ἐν) αὐτῇ τῇ ὥρᾳ. — *ZNW* 42 (1949) 214-217.

ἐκζητέω 2 + 1

1. seek diligently (Acts 15,17); 2. bring charges against (Lk 11,50.51)

Word groups	Lk	Acts	Mt	Mk
ἐκζητέω ἀπό → αἰτέω/ζητέω παρά + gen.; (ἀπ)αἰτέω/κωλύω ἀπό	11,51		0	0

Literature

DENAUX 2009 La[n] ; HAUCK 1934 [seltenes Alleinwort].

BORMANN, Lukas, *Recht, Gerechtigkeit und Religion*, 2001. Esp. 180.

ἐκκομίζω* 1   carry out (Lk 7,12)

Literature

HAUCK 1934 [seltenes Alleinwort].

ἐκκόπτω 3 (Mt 4)

1. cut down/off (Lk 3,9; 13,7.9); 2. do away with

ἐκκρεμάννυμι 1

ἐκκρέμαμαι: 1. consider seriously (Lk 19,48); 2. persist in (Lk 19,48)

Literature

HAUCK 1934 [seltenes Alleinwort].

ἐκλέγομαι 4 + 7 (Mk 1)

1. select (Lk 6,13; Acts 1,2); 2. choose (Lk 9,35; 10,42; 14,7; Acts 13,17)

Word groups	Lk	Acts	Mt	Mk
ἐκλέγομαι + infinitive (VKa)		1,24; 15,7	0	0
(υἱὸς ὁ) + ἐκλελεγμένος (VKc) → υἱὸς (ὁ) **ἀγαπητός**	9,35		0	0

Characteristic of Luke
DENAUX 2009 L***; GOULDER 1989*

Literature
COLLISON 1977 93 [noteworthy phenomena]; HAUCK 1934 [Vorzugswort].

ἐκλείπω 3

1. fail (Lk 16,9); 2. depart; 3. cease (event) (Lk 22,32; 23,45); 4. cease (state)

Characteristic of Luke
GOULDER 1989

Literature
VON BENDEMANN 2001 430; COLLISON 1977 94 [noteworthy phenomena]; DENAUX 2009 Lⁿ; EASTON 1910 153 [probably characteristic of L]; REHKOPF 1959 93 [vorlukanisch]; SCHÜRMANN 1957 106 [Sprache der LXX]. SAWYER, John F.A., Why Is a Solar Eclipse Mentioned in the Passion Narrative (Luke XXIII.44-5)? — JTS 23 (1972) 124-128.

ἐκλεκτός 2 (Mt 4/5, Mk 3)   chosen (Lk 18,7; 23,35)

ἐκμάσσω 2   wipe dry (Lk 7,38.44)

ἐκμυκτηρίζω*** 2   ridicule (Lk 16,14; 23,35)

Word groups	Lk	Acts	Mt	Mk
ἐκμυκτηρίζω + λέγων	23,35		0	0

Characteristic of Luke
PLUMMER 1922 liii

Literature
DENAUX 2009 Lⁿ; EASTON 1910 160 [cited by Weiss as characteristic of L, and possibly corroborative]; HAUCK 1934 [seltenes Alleinwort]; JEREMIAS 1980 69 [ἐκμυκτηρίζω + λέγων: red.].

ἐκπειράζω 2 (Mt 1)

1. test (Lk 4,12; 10,25); 2. try to trap (Lk 10,25); 3. tempt (Lk 10,25)

Word groups	Lk	Acts	Mt	Mk
ἐκπειράζω + λέγων	10,25		0	0

Literature
JEREMIAS 1980 69 [ἐκπειράζω + λέγων: red.].

ἐκπλήσσομαι 3 + 1 (Mt 4, Mk 5) | be greatly astounded

Word groups	Lk	Acts	Mt	Mk
ἐκπλήσσομαι (+) ἐπί + dative (VKa) → θαυμάζω ἐπί + dat.	4,32; 9,43	13,12	2	2
ἐκπλήσσομαι ἐπὶ τῇ διδαχῇ	4,32	13,12	2	2
πάντες ἐξεπλήσσοντο; cf. Mk 11,18 πᾶς ὁ ὄχλος	9,43		0	0
ἐξεπλήσσετο → πάντες ἐθαύμαζον/ἐθαύμασαν				

Literature

HARNACK 1906 149

DANOVE, Paul, Verbs of Experience, 1999. Esp. 166-167.177.

ἐκπνέω 1 (Mk 2) | die (Lk 23,46)

ἐκπορεύομαι 3 + 3 (Mt 5/6, Mk 11) | depart out of

Word groups	Lk	Acts	Mt	Mk
εἰσπορεύομαι καὶ ἐκπορεύομαι (LN: live with) → εἰσέρχομαι καὶ ἐξέρχομαι		9,28	0	0
ἐκπορεύομαι absolute (VKa)		19,12; 25,4	0/1	0
BOISMARD 1984 Aa129				

Characteristic of Luke

CREDNER 1836 139

ἐκριζόω 1 (Mt 2) | uproot (Lk 17,6)

ἔκστασις 1 + 4 (Mk 2)

1. amazement (Lk 5,26); 2. ecstatic vision (Acts 10,10; 11,5)

Word groups	Lk	Acts	Mt	Mk
ἔκστασις = vision		10,10; 11,5; 22,17	0	0
BOISMARD 1984 Aa89				

Characteristic of Luke

PLUMMER 1922 lx

Literature

HAUCK 1934 [Vorzugswort].

ἐκτείνω 3 + 3 (Mt 6, Mk 3) | stretch out

Word groups	Lk	Acts	Mt	Mk
ἀγκύρας + ἐκτείνω (VKa)		27,30	0	0
ἐκτείνω τὴν χεῖρα	5,13; 6,10	4,30; 26,1	5	2
ἐκτείνω τὰς χεῖρας ἐπί + accusative (LN: arrest)	22,53		0	0

ἐκτελέω 2 | complete (Lk 14,29.30)

Characteristic of Luke
PLUMMER 1922 liii

Literature
DENAUX 2009 Lⁿ; HAUCK 1934 [seltenes Alleinwort].

ἐκτενῶς 1 + 1
1. continuously (Lk 22,14; Acts 12,5); 2. eagerly (Lk 22,44; Acts 12,5)

Word groups	Lk	Acts	Mt	Mk
ἐκτενέστερον comparative (*VKa*)	[22,44]		0	0

Characteristic of Luke
VOGEL 1899B

Literature
DENAUX 2009 LAⁿ; JEREMIAS 1980 294 [red.].

SCHNEIDER, Gerhard, Engel und Blutschweiß (Lk 22,43-44): "Redaktionsgeschichte" im Dienste der Textkritik. — *BZ* NF 20 (1976) 112-116. Esp. 113-115: "Vokabular und Stil von Lk 22,43.44"; = ID., *Lukas, Theologe der Heilsgeschichte*, 1985, 153-157. Esp. 154-156.
TUCKETT, Christopher M., Luke 22,43-44: The "Agony" in the Garden and Luke's Gospel. — DENAUX, Adelbert (ed.), *New Testament Textual Criticism and Exegesis*. FS J. Delobel, 2002, 131-144. Esp. 133-135: "Vocabulary and style"

ἕκτος 3 + 1 (Mt 2, Mk 1) | sixth

Word groups	Lk	Acts	Mt	Mk
ὥρα ἕκτη (*VKa*) → ὥρα ἐνάτη/τρίτη	23,44	10,9	2	1

ἐκφέρω 1 + 4 (Mk 1)
1. carry out (Lk 15,22); 2. lead out; 3. grow

Word groups	Lk	Acts	Mt	Mk
ἐκφέρω + εἰς → (ἀνα/ἀπο)φέρω εἰς		5,15	0	0

Characteristic of Luke
BOISMARD 1984 Eb34; NEIRYNCK 1985

ἐκφεύγω 1 + 2
1. flee from (Acts 16,27; 19,16); 2. escape (Lk 21,36)

ἐκχέω/ἐκχύννω 3 + 6 (Mt 2, Mk 1/2)
1. cause to flow out (Lk 5,37; 11,50; 22,20); 2. scatter; 3. give in abundance (Acts 2,33); 4. cause to fully experience (Acts 2,33)

Word groups	Lk	Acts	Mt	Mk
αἷμα (+) ἐκχέω/ἐκχύννω (*LN*: murder; *VK*b)	11,50; 22,20	22,20	1	1
ἐκχέω/ἐκχύννω + (ἅγιον) πνεῦμα (*VK*a)		2,17.18.33; 10,45	0	0

Literature

SCHÜRMANN 1955 23-24.65-69.73-81 [(τὸ ὑπὲρ ὑμῶν) ἐκχυννόμενον]; 77, n. 279 [αἷμα ἐκχεῖν].

DELEBECQUE, Édouard, *Études grecques*, 1976. Esp. 109-121: "Le pain et la coupe de la dernière cène (22,17-20)".

PETZER, Kobus H., Style and Text in the Lucan Narrative of the Institution of the Lord's Supper, 1991. Esp. 120.

ἐκχωρέω 1

depart (Lk 21,21)

ἐλαία 4 (Mt 3, Mk 3)

1. olive (tree) (Lk 19,29.37; 21,37; 22,39); 2. olive (fruit)

Word groups	Lk	Acts	Mt	Mk
ὄρος τῶν ἐλαιῶν	19,37; 22,39		3	3
ὄρος τὸ καλούμενον Ἐλαιῶν; cf. ὄρος τὸ καλούμενον Ἐλαιών Lk 19,29*; 21,37*; Acts 1,12 DENAUX 2009 La[n]	19,29; 21,37	1,12	0	0

Characteristic of Luke

BOISMARD Ab117; HAWKINS 1909LA(?); NEIRYNCK 1985 [ἐλαιών].

Literature

HAUCK 1934 [häufiges Alleinwort]; JEREMIAS 1980 284: "Der Ölberg wird von Lukas in zweifacher Weise benannt: 1. τὸ ὄρος τῶν ἐλαιῶν 'Olivenberg' (Lk 19,37; 22,39) ist die traditionelle Bezeichnung wie wir sie bei Mk und Mt je dreimal lesen; 2. nur im Doppelwerk kommt im NT vor: τὸ ὄρος τὸ καλούμενον Ἐλαιών der 'Olivenhain' genannte Berg (Lk 19,29; 21,37/Apg 1,12)".

ἔλαιον 3 (Mt 3, Mk 1)

olive oil

Word groups	Lk	Acts	Mt	Mk
ἔλαιον + ἀλείφω (*VK*a); cf. ἔλαιον + χρίω Heb 1,9	7,46		0	1

Literature

PAFFENROTH 1997 75.

ἐλαύνω 1 (Mk 1)

drive along (Lk 8,29)

ἐλάχιστος 4 (Mt 5)

1. very small (Lk 19,17); 2. least important (value) (Lk 16,10[1.2]); 3. least important (status)

Word groups	Lk	Acts	Mt	Mk
ἐλάχιστος + πολύς → ὀλιγός + πολύς	16,10[1.2]		0	0

Characteristic of Luke	Lk		Acts	Mt	Mk
ἐλάχιστον neuter without noun; cf. 1 Cor 4,3 DENAUX 2009 L***; GOULDER 1989; HAWKINS 1909L	12,26; 16,10[1.2]; 19,17			0	0

Literature

HAUCK 1934 [häufiges Alleinwort].

ANDERSON, Fred C., Luke xvi.10. — ExpT 59 (1947-48) 278-279.

ἐλέγχω 1 (Mt 1) rebuke

Word groups	Lk	Acts	Mt	Mk
ἐλέγχομαι passive (VKa)	3,19		0	0

ἐλεέω 4 (Mt 8, Mk 3) show mercy

Word groups	Lk	Acts	Mt	Mk
ἐλέησον (VKb)	16,24; 17,13; 18,38.39		5	2

Literature

EASTON 1910 153 [probably characteristic of L; not noted by Weiss]; PAFFENROTH 1997 81.

ἐλεημοσύνη 2 + 8 (Mt 3/4)

1. acts of charity (Acts 10,4); 2. donation (Lk 11,41; 12,33; Acts 3,2)

Word groups	Lk	Acts	Mt	Mk
ἐλεημοσύνην αἰτέω		3,2	0	0
ἐλεημοσύνην δίδωμι (VKb) DENAUX 2009 L[n]	11,41; 12,33		0	0
ἐλεημοσύνην ποιέω (VKa) → ἔλεον ποιέω VOGEL 1899C		9,36; 10,2; 24,17	2/3	0
ἐλεημοσύναι plural (VKc) BOISMARD 1984 Aa27		9,36; 10,2.4.31; 24,17	0	0

Characteristic of Luke				
PLUMMER 1922 lx				
	Lk	Acts	Mt	Mk
ἐλεημοσύνη singular BOISMARD 1984 cb145; NEIRYNCK 1985	11,41; 12,33	3,2.3.10	3/4	0

Literature

DENAUX 2009 1An; EASTON 1910 153 [ἐλεημοσύνην δίδωμι: probably characteristic of L];
JEREMIAS 1980 206 [δίδωμι ἐλεημοσύνην: trad.].

BLACK, Matthew, An Aramaic Approach to the Gospels and Acts. [3]1967. Esp. 2 [Lk 11,41:
δότε ἐλεημοσύνην].

HEILIGENTHAL, Roman, Werke der Barmherzigkeit oder Almosen? Zur Bedeutung von *eleēmosunē*. — *NT* 25 (1983) 289-301. [NTA 28,442]
SCHWARZ, Günther, "Gebt ... den Inhalt als Almosen"? (Lukas 11,40.41). — *BibNot* 75 (1994) 26-30.

ἔλεος 6 (Mt 3)   mercy

Word groups

Word groups	Lk	Acts	Mt	Mk
ἔλεον ποιέω (VKb) → ἐλεημοσύνην ποιέω; cf. ἔλεον δίδωμι 2 Tim 1,16 DENAUX 2009 L^n	1,72; 10,37		0	0
ἔλεος (+) μετά + genitive DENAUX 2009 L^n	1,58.72; 10,37		0	0

Characteristic of Luke

DENAUX 2009 L***; GOULDER 1989; HARNACK 1906 141; HAWKINS 1909 18

	Lk	Acts	Mt	Mk
ἔλεος neuter CREDNER 1836 137; DENAUX 2009 L***	1,50.54.58.72.78; 10,37		0	0

Literature

EASTON 1910 149 [ποιέω ἔλεος μετ' αὐτοῦ: especially characteristic of L]; GERSDORF 1816 202 [τὸ ἔλεος αὐτοῦ μετ' αὐτῆς]; HAUCK 1934 [Vorzugswort]; PLUMMER 1922 lxi [ποιεῖν/μεγαλύνειν ἔλεος μετά: Hebrew influence].

GERBER, Daniel, Les employs d'ἔλεος en Luc-Actes. — BONS, Eberhard (ed.), *"Car c'est l'amour qui me plait, non le sacrifice…": Recherches sur Osée 6:6 et son interpretation juive et chrétienne* (Supplements to tthe Journal for the Study of Judaism, 88). Leiden – Boston: Brill, 2004, 81-95.

Ἐλιακίμ 1 (Mt 2)   Eliakim (Lk 3,30)

Ἐλιέζερ 1   Eliezer (Lk 3,29)

Ἐλισάβετ 9   Elisabeth

Literature

LAURENTIN, René, Traces d'allusions étymologiques en Luc 1–2 (II). — *Bib* 38 (1957) 1-23. Esp. 1-4: "Zacharie et Élisabeth".

Ἐλισαῖος 1   Elisha (Lk 4,27)

ἑλκόομαι* 1   have sores (Lk 16,20)

Literature

HAUCK 1934 [seltenes Alleinwort].

ἕλκος 1	sore (Lk 16,21)

Ἐλμαδάμ 1	Elmadam (Lk 3,28)

ἐλπίζω 3 + 2 (Mt 1)
1. hope (for) (Lk 23,8; 24,21); 2. expect (Lk 6,34)

Word groups	Lk	Acts	Mt	Mk
ἐλπίζω ὅτι (VKb)	24,21	24,26	0	0
DENAUX 2009 LA[n]				
ἐλπίζω + infinitive (VKa); cf. ἐλπίς + inf. Acts 24,15; 27,20	6,34; 23,8	26,7	0	0
DENAUX 2009 La[n]				

Characteristic of Luke
BOISMARD 1984 Eb35; DENAUX 2009 La*; GOULDER 1989; NEIRYNCK 1985

Literature
JEREMIAS 1980 145: "Von den Evangelien konstruiert nur das dritte ἐλπίζω mit dem Infinitiv…; das ist lukanischer Sprachgebrauch … ist das Subjekt des Infinitivs mit dem des regierendem Verbums ἐλπίζω identisch. Unterschieden sich beide, so läßt Lukas auf ἐλπίζω einen ὅτι-Satz folgen".

ἐμαυτοῦ 2 + 4 (Mt 1) | myself (Lk 7,7.8)

Characteristic of Luke
DENAUX 2009 IA*

Literature
RADL 1975 409.

ἐμβαίνω 3 + 0/1 (Mt 5/6, Mk 5)
1. embark (Lk 5,3; 8,22.37); 2. step into

Word groups	Lk	Acts	Mt	Mk
ἐμβαίνω (+) εἰς → ἀνα/ἀπο/δια/κατα/μεταβαίνω εἰς; cf. ἐπιβαίνω εἰς Acts 21,6*	5,3; 8,22.37	21,6*	5/6	4/5
ἐμβαίνω εἰς (τὸ) πλοῖον → ἀναβαίνω εἰς τὸ πλοῖον; cf. ἐμβαίνω εἰς ἓν τῶν πλοίων Lk 5,3; ἐπιβαίνω εἰς τὸ πλοῖον Acts 21,6*	8,22.37	21,6*	5/6	4/5

ἐμβάλλω 1 | throw in (Lk 12,5)

Literature
HAUCK 1934 [seltenes Alleinwort].

ἐμβλέπω 2 + 2 (Mt 2, Mk 4)
1. look straight at (Lk 20,17; 22,61); 2. think about

Word groups	Lk	Acts	Mt	Mk
ἐμβλέπω εἰς (VKa)		1,11	1	0

Ἐμμαοῦς 1

Emmaus (Lk 24,13)

ἐμός 3 (Mt 4/5, Mk 2)

mine

Word groups	Lk	Acts	Mt	Mk
τὰ ἐμά (VKc); cf. τὸ ἐμόν Mt 20,23; 25,27; Mk 10,40	15,31		1	0

Literature

KILPATRICK, George D., The Possessive Pronouns in the New Testament. — *JTS* 42 (1941) 184-186; = ID., *Principles and Practice*, 1990, 161-162.
PETZER, Kobus H., Style and Text in the Lucan Narrative of the Institution of the Lord's Supper, 1991. Esp. 116.

ἐμπαίζω 5 (Mt 5, Mk 3)

1. mock (Lk 14,29; 18,32; 22,63; 23,11.36); 2. trick

Word groups	Lk	Acts	Mt	Mk
ἐμπαίζω λέγων	14,29(-30)		0	0
ἐμπαίζομαι passive (VKa)	18,32		1	0

Literature

EASTON 1910 153 [probably characteristic of L]; JEREMIAS 1980 69 [ἐμπαίζω + λέγων: red.].

ἐμπίμπλημι 2 + 1

1. satisfy with food (Lk 1,53; 6,25); 2. enjoy

Word groups	Lk	Acts	Mt	Mk
ἐμπίμπλημι + πεινάω DENAUX 2009 L[n]	1,53; 6,25		0	0

Characteristic of Luke

BOISMARD 1984 cb165; CREDNER 1836 142; HARNACK 1906 142; NEIRYNCK 1985; PLUMMER 1922 lx

Literature

DENAUX 2009 La[n]; EASTON 1910 160 [cited by Weiss as characteristic of L, and possibly corroborative]; HAUCK 1934 [seltenes Alleinwort].

DUPONT, Jacques, *Les Béatitudes*, III, 1973. Esp. 46-47.

ἐμπίπτω 2/3 (Mt 1)

1. fall into (Lk 6,39); 2. experience (Lk 10,36)

Word groups	Lk	Acts	Mt	Mk
ἐμπεσών → (ἐπι/κατα/περι/προσ)πεσών; cf. Jn 12,24; Rom 11,22; 1 Cor 14,25; ἀναπεσών Jn 13,25; παραπεσών Heb 6,6	10,36		0	0
ἐμπίπτω aorist → (ἀνα/ἐπι/κατα/περι/προσ/συμ)πίπτω aorist; cf. ἀποπίπτω Acts 9,18; ἐκπίπτω Acts 12,7; 27,17.26.29.32	10,36		1	0

ἔμπροσθεν 10 + 2 (Mt 18, Mk 2/3)

1. in front of (Lk 5,19); 2. on the front; 3. in the judgement of

Word groups	Lk	Acts	Mt	Mk
ἔμπροσθεν τῶν ἀγγέλων τοῦ θεοῦ → ἐνώπιον τῶν ἀγγέλων τοῦ θεοῦ	$12,8^2$		0	0
ἔμπροσθεν τῶν ἀνθρώπων (VKa) → ἐνώπιον τῶν ἀνθρώπων	$12,8^1$		5	0
ἔμπροσθεν τοῦ θεοῦ → ἐναντίον/ἐνώπιον (τοῦ) θεοῦ		10,4	0	0
ἔμπροσθεν adverb (VKb) DENAUX 2009 L^n	19,4.28		0	0

→ εἰμι ἔμπροσθεν; εἰς + ἔμπροσθεν; ἐν + ἔμπροσθεν; πορεύομαι ἔμπροσθεν

Literature

COLLISON 1977 146 [noteworthy phenomena]; EASTON 1910 153 [probably characteristic of L; not noted by Weiss].

ἐμπτύω 1 (Mt 2, Mk 3)   spit (Lk 18,32)

ἔμφοβος 2 + 2/3   terrified

Characteristic of Luke

PLUMMER 1922 lix; VOGEL 1899B

	Lk	Acts	Mt	Mk
ἔμφοβος γενόμενος; cf. ἔμφοβοι ἐγένοντο Acts 22,9* BOISMARD 1984 Ab78; NEIRYNCK 1985	24,5.37	10,4; 24,25	0	0

Literature

DENAUX 2009 LA^n; LA^n [ἔμφοβος γενόμενος]; EASTON 1910 167 [ἔμφοβος γενόμενος: classed by Weiss as characteristic of L on insufficient (?) evidence]; JEREMIAS 1980 311 [ἔμφοβος γενόμενος: red.]; RADL 1975 409.

ἐν 361/381 + 279/296 (Mt 293/307, Mk 132[135]/153)

1. in (location) (Lk 7,37); 2. among (location) (Lk 7,16); 3. on (location); 4. at (location); 5. in (state) (Lk 16,23); 6. into (extension) (Lk 7,17); 7. in union with (association) (Lk 2,27^1); 8. with (attendant circumstances) (Lk 9,26); 9. with (instrument) (Lk 14,31; 22,49); 10. with (manner) (Lk 18,8); 11. with regard to (specification); 12. of (substance) (Acts 7,14); 13. to (experiencer); 14. by (agent) (Acts 17,31^3); 15. by (guarantor); 16. by (means) (Lk 24,35); 17. because (reason) (Acts 7,29); 18. so that (result) (Lk 1,17); 19. when (time) (Lk 9,36); 20. during (time) (Lk 1,5); 21. in (content) (Acts 10,48)

Word groups	Lk	Acts	Mt	Mk
ἐν with composite verb ἐν- (SCd; VKf)	10,20[2]	3,25; 25,24; 28,30	4	1
ἐν with reference to scripture (SCb; VKd)	2,23.24; 3,4[1]; 10,26; 20,42; 24,27.44	1,20[1]; 7,42[1]; 13,33.35.38.40; 18,24; 24,14	3	2
ἐν with reference to time (SCa;VKa) → ἐν ᾧ/οἷς time; ἐν τάχει	1,5.7.18.25[1].26.36.39.59; 2,1.36; 3,1; 4,2.5.16.25[1].31; 5,17.35; 6,1.2*.6.7.12[1].23[1]; 7,11.21; 8,1.13.22; 9,36[2].37*; 10,12.21[1]; 12,12.38[1,2].42.46[1,2]; 13,1.10[2]. 14[1,2].31; 14,5; 17,24.26[1,2].28.31[1]; 18,30[1,2]; 19,42; 20,1[1].10*.19; 21,6.23[2].36; 22,7; 23,7[2].12[1].29; 24,13.18[2]	1,6.15[1].21[1].21*; 2,17.18.41; 5,37; 6,1[1]; 7,13.20[1].41[1]; 8,1[1]; 9,37[1]; 10,40; 11,27; 13,41; 16,33; 17,31[1]; 18,9; 20,7.26; 27,7	32/34	11/16
ἐν + ἄχρι(ς) (VKx)		2,29; 7,17(-18)	0	0
ἐν + διά (VKu)	1,77(-78); 6,1; 24,53	2,22.43*; 5,12; 9,25; 15,7.12; 18,9; 21,19	4	3
ἐν + εἰς (VKk)	1,26; 2,27[1]; 4,1[1] v.l.14.16; 6,6.12[1]; 7,11; 8,22; 17,31[3]; 21,21[1,3]; 24,13	2,38*; 7,39; 11,27; 26,12.20 v.l.	6	4/5
ἐν + ἐκ (VKm)	12,15	7,4; 15,21; 22,18	4/5	2
ἐν + ἔμπροσϑεν/πρός + accusative (VKq)	1,26(-27); 12,8[1,2]; 20,10*; 21,38; 23,12[2]	6,1[1]; 9,10[2]; 17,17[2]	4/5	2/3
ἐν τῷ Ἰησοῦ/κυρίῳ (VKc)		4,2; 11,23*	0	0
ἐν + κατά + accusative (VKh)	2,29; 4,16; 8,1; 10,31; 22,53	2,46[1]; 5,42; 13,1; 14,1; 15,21; 17,17[2]; 18,4; 19,9; 24,12[2].14	3	2
ἐν μεγάλῳ (LN: in a long time)		26,29[2]	0	0
ἐν + μετά + accusative/ genitive (VKl)	2,46[1]; 11,31.32; 18,4; 21,27; 22,28.53; 23,12[1].43	1,3.5; 5,37; 7,7.38[1]. 45; 9,28*; 24,18[2]; 26,12; 28,11[1]	9	6[7]
ἐν + μεταξύ (VKw)	16,26		0	0
ἐν ὀλίγῳ (LN: [a]in a short time; [b]easily); cf. Eph 3,3 CREDNER 1836 138		26,[a]28.[a]29	0	0
ἐν + παρά + accusative/ dative/genitive (VKs)	2,52	7,16[2]; 9,43; 10,32	1	0
ἐν + παρεκτός/σύν (VKy)		4,27; 21,29; 26,29[2]	0	0
ἐν τῷ (καϑ)έξῆς (LN: later) DENAUX 2009 L[n]	7,11; 8,1		0	0
ἐν + ὑπό + genitive (VKj)	1,26 v.l.	17,13	1	1
ἐν ᾧ/οἷς time (LN: as long as; SCa; VKb) → ἐν ᾧ/οἷς others	5,34; 12,1; 19,13		0	1
ὁ/ἡ/τὸ ἐν (SCg; VKe)	5,7 v.l.; 6,41[1,2].42[1,3]; 11,2[1]*.35	7,34; 8,1[2].14; 13,26; 16,4	17/19	2/5
προβαίνω ἐν ἡμέραις (LN: be old) DENAUX 2009 L[n]	1,7.18; 2,36		0	0
ἐν instrumental (SCf)	1,51; 11,15.18.19[1,2].20; 14,31.34; 20,2.8; 22,49	4,7[2,3].9.12[3]; 7,35*	12/13	9

212   ἐν

| ὁ/ἡ/τὸ (+) ἐν used as a noun (SCc; VKe) | 8,15¹; 17,31³; 21,21¹·²·³; 24,35¹ | 4,24; 14,15; 16,32; 17,11.24¹; 26,20 | 4 | 1 |

→ ἐν ἀγαλλιάσει; ἐν ἀγρῷ; ἄγω ἐν; ἀναβαίνω ἐν καρδίᾳ; ἐν τῇ ἀναστάσει; ἐν ἀνθρώποις; ἀπόκειμαι ἐν; ἐν ἀρχῇ; (καὶ) ἐν (δὲ) τῷ + inf. ... καὶ αὐτός; ἐν ἀφέσει (τῶν) ἁμαρτιῶν; βάλλω ἐν (τῇ) φυλακῇ; βαπτίζω ἐν (πνεύματι ἁγίῳ / πυρί / ὕδατι); ἐν γαστρὶ ἔχω/συλλαμβάνω; ἐν γῇ; ἐν τῇ γῇ; (καὶ) ἐγένετο (δὲ) (ἐν τῷ + inf.) ... καὶ αὐτός/αὐτοί; ἐν τῷ δευτέρῳ; διατηρέω ἐν τῇ καρδίᾳ; ἐν δικαιοσύνῃ; ἐν (τῇ) δόξῃ; ἐν δυνάμει; ἐν ἑαυτῷ/ἑαυτοῖς; εἰμὶ ἐν; ἐν τῷ εἶναι; (ἐν) τῇ μιᾷ; ἐν ποίᾳ ἐξουσίᾳ; εἰρήνη ἐν ἀνθρώποις εὐδοκίας; ἐν εἰρήνῃ; εἰσέρχομαι ἐν; ἐξέρχομαι ἐν; ἔρχομαι + ἐν; ἐν ἑτέρῳ; ἐν ἔτει; ἔχω ἐν ἑαυτῷ/ἑαυτοῖς; ζῶ ἐν; θαυμάζω ἐν τῷ + inf.; θησαυρὸς ἐν οὐρανῷ; κάθημαι ἐν (μέσῳ); καθίζω ἐν; ἐν καιρῷ; καταβαίνω ἐν; κατάκειμαι ἐν; κεῖμαι ἐν; ἐν τῇ κρίσει; λέγω/εἶπον ἐν ἑαυτῷ/ἐν τῇ καρδίᾳ; ἐν λόγῳ; ἐν τῷ μέσῳ; ἐν μνήματι τίθημι; ἐν τῇ ὁδῷ; ὁμολογέω ἐν; ἐν οὐρανῷ εἰρήνη; ἐν παραβολαῖς; πατάσσω ἐν; πατὴρ ὁ ἐν (τοῖς) οὐρανοῖς; περιπατέω ἐν στολαῖς; ἐν τῷ περισσεύειν; πίπτω ἐν μέσῳ; ποιέω τι ἐν; πορεύομαι ἐν; ἐν (τῷ/ἑτέρῳ) σαββάτῳ; (ἐν) τοῖς σάββασιν; σκανδαλίζομαι ἐν; ἐν τῇ σκοτίᾳ, ἐν πάσῃ σοφίᾳ; ἐν στιγμῇ χρόνου; συμβάλλω ἐν τῇ καρδίᾳ; τίθημι ἐν (μνημείῳ/φυλακῇ); ἐν ὑπομονῇ; (δόξα) ἐν (τοῖς) ὑψίστοις; χαίρω ἐν; ἐν χειρί

Characteristic of Luke

HENDRIKS 1986 428.434.448

	Lk	Acts	Mt	Mk
ἐν + ἀπό (VKr) DENAUX 2009 L***	1,26; 7,21; 8,43; 9,37*; 12.52.58; 13,7; 16,23³	2,17.18; 10,30¹; 11,27; 15,7; 26,4¹	1/2	1
ἐν + ἔναντι/ἐναντίον/ ἐνώπιον (VKt) DENAUX 2009 L***	1,6.8².17¹.75; 16,15; 24,19	4,10²; 10,30²	0	0
ἐν + ἕνεκα/περί + accusative/genitive (VKn) DENAUX 2009 L***	3,15; 7,17; 13,1; 24,44	10,3; 26,21	1	1/2
ἐν + ἐπί + accusative/dative/genitive (VKp) DENAUX 2009 L***	1,17²; 2,14¹; 3,1.2; 4,27; 11,2²*; 12,52; 13,4; 15,7; 19,44²; 20,19; 21,6.23*.25²; 22,30	1,21*; 2,17.18.19; 4,5.27; 8,1¹; 11,15²	3/4	1
ἐν + ἕως/μέχρι (VKv); cf. ἐν + πρό Mt 24,38 DENAUX 2009 LA*	1,80; 24,49	1,8²; 10,30¹(?)	1	0
ἐν τῷ + infinitive (SCe; VKg) → ἐν τῷ εἶναι; cf. Rom 3,4; 15,13; 1 Cor 11,21; Gal 4,18; Heb 2,8; 8,13; ἐγένετο ἐν τῷ + inf. BOISMARD 1984 cb1; CREDNER 1836 135; DENAUX 2009 L***; GOULDER 1989*; HAWKINS 1909L; NEIRYNCK 1985; PLUMMER 1922 lxii	1,8¹.21¹; 2,6.27².43¹; 3,21; 5,1.12¹; 8,5.40. 42; 9,18.29.33.34.36¹. 51; 10,35.38; 11,1¹.27. 37; 12,15; 14,1; 17,11.14; 18,35; 19,15; 24,4¹.15.30.51	2,1; 3,26; 4,30; 8,6; 9,3; 11,15¹; 19,1¹	3	2/3
ἐν τάχει (LN: [very] soon) BOISMARD 1984 db28; CREDNER 1836 138; NEIRYNCK 1985	18,8	12,7; 22,18; 25,4	0	0
ὁ ἐν + name of a city/region BOISMARD 1984 Ea6	21,21	8,1; 16,4; 17,11; 26,20	1	1

→ γίνομαι ἐν ἑαυτῷ; (καὶ) ἐγένετο (δὲ) ἐν τῷ + inf.; γέγραπται ἐν βίβλῳ; δυνατὸς ἐν; ἐν μιᾷ τῶν (ἡμερῶν); ἐν ἐξουσίᾳ; (ἐν) αὐτῇ τῇ ἡμέρᾳ; ἐν ταῖς ἡμέραις + gen.; ἐν ταῖς ἡμέραις + proper name; ἐν ταῖς ἡμέραις ταύταις; εἰμι ἐν τῷ ἱερῷ; ἵστημι ἐν μέσῳ (τινῶν); ἐν αὐτῷ τῷ καιρῷ; κατακλείω ἐν φυλακῇ; κατοικέω ἐν; μένω ἐν; ἐν μέσῳ; ἐν αὐτῇ τῇ οἰκίᾳ; ἐν τούτῳ; πιστὸς ἐν; ἐν τῷ πνεύματι without determinative; (εἰμι/γίνομαι) ἐν (τῇ) πόλει; ἐν πολλῷ; προβαίνω ἐν ἡμέραις; (ἐν) (τῇ) ἡμέρᾳ τοῦ σαββάτου / τῶν σαββάτων; ποιέω σημεῖα καὶ τέρατα ἐν; συνάγω ἐν + place; διαλέγομαι ἐν τῇ συναγωγῇ; σῴζω ἐν; τίθεμαι/τίθημι ἐν τῇ καρδίᾳ / ἐν τῷ πνεύματι; ὑπάρχω ἐν; (ἐν) αὐτῇ τῇ ὥρᾳ

Literature

BDR § 404: "Der substantivierte Inf. mit Präp. im Dativ: Nur ἐν τῷ (hauptsächlich Lk). 1. Vorwiegend in temporalem Sinn; …mit dem Inf. Präs. 'während' (durativ), mit dem Inf. Aor. (nur Lk) 'als', 'nachdem' (momentan) … Aramäisch ist diese Konstruktion nicht"; COLLISON 1977 131 [ἐν + articular infinitive: linguistic usage of Luke: certain]; 132 [ἐν preceded by καὶ ἐγένετο/ἐγένετο δέ; ἐν prefactory: lintuistic usages of Luke: certain]; 133 [ἐν + ἡμέρα; ἐν preceded by ἐγένετο; ἐν prefactory: linguistic usage of Luke: certain]; 134 [ἐν + demonstrative: linguistic usage of Luke: probable, but the possibility of a linguistic usage of Luke's "other source-material" cannot be exluded; ἐν + ἡμέρα + genitive: linguistic usage of Luke's "other source-material": probable]; 135 [ἐν + relative pronoun: linguistic usage of Luke: probable; ἐν μέσῳ: noteworthy phenomena]; DENAUX 2009 1Aⁿ [ἐν τάχει (*LN*: [very] soon)]; EASTON 1910 177 [ἐν τῷ with infinitive: possible Hebraisms in the Lucan Writings, as classed by Dalman]; GERSDORF 1816 193 [ἐν ἀνθρώποις]; 220-222 [ἀνέκλινεν αὐτὸν ἐν φάτνῃ]; HAUCK 1934 [Vorzugsverbindung: τὰ ἐν; (ἐγένετο) (δὲ) ἐν τῷ + inf.; ἐν ταῖς ἡμέραις ταύταις; ἐν αὐτῇ τῇ ἡμέρᾳ/ὥρᾳ; ἐν μιᾷ τῶν (ἡμέρῶν/πόλεων); ἐν οἷς; ἐν τοῖς τοῦ πατρός; καὶ ἐγένετο ἐν]; JEREMIAS 1980 15-16: "Die starke Bevorzugung des ἐν temp. im Markusstoff geht auf die Redaktion zurück. Was die 71 Belege für das temporale ἐν im Nicht-Markusstoff des LkEv anlangt, so können wir dank des Umstandes, daß es sich weithin um geprägtes Gut handelt, 21 mit einiger Wahrscheinlichkeit als vorlukanisch und 39 als lukanisch bestimmen (lediglich an 11 Stellen muß die Zuweisung an die Tradition oder Redaktion offen bleiben)"; 26 [ἐγένετο δέ + ἐν τῷ + acc. + inf.: red.]; 28-29: "Stilistisch ist für die lukanische Verwendung von ἐν τῷ c.inf. zweierlei kennzeichnend: 1) Während Lukas im allgemeinen, dem Üblichen folgend, ἐν τῷ mit Inf.praes. verbindet, wählt er als einziger neutestamentlicher Autor zur Bezeichnung der Vorzeitigkeit nach ἐν τῷ den Inf.aor. (9mal). 2) Außerdem läßt er ἐν τῷ c.inf. nicht weniger als 18mal auf das spezifisch lukanische periphrastische ἐγένετο folgen"; 195: "ἐν τῷ εἶναι: im NT nur im Doppelwerk"; 228: "Die fünf Perikopeneinleitungen des NT mit ἐν μιᾷ τῶν (…) sind eine Eigentümlichkeit des Lukasevangeliums"; REHKOPF 1959 95 [λέγειν/εἰπεῖν ἐν ἑαυτῷ: vorlukanisch]; SCHNEIDER 1969 76-77.163: "ἐν μέσῳ mit Genitiv des Ortes ist bei Luk beliebt" [Vorzugswörter und -ausdrücke des Luk]; SCHÜRMANN 1953 13 [ἐν τῷ + infinitive]; 1957 25 [Luk schreibt gern ein temporales ἐν]; 125 [τελεσθῆναι ἐν ἐμοί: sehr wahrscheinlich luk R].

DELEBECQUE, Édouard, *Études grecques*, 1976. Esp. 40: "ἐν τοῖς τοῦ Πατρός μου".

GRANT, Lawrence Otto, *The History of ἐν τῷ with the Infinitive and Its Bearing on Luke's Writings*. Diss. Southern Baptist Theol. Sem., 1945.

GREENLEE, J. Harold, The Preposition εἰς in the New Testament. — *BTrans* 3 (1952) 12-14. Esp. 13-14: "The relationship of εἰς and ἐν".

GUERRA GÓMEZ, Manuel, Análisis filológico-teológico y traducción del himno de los ángeles en Belén, 1989. Esp. 53-55: "ἐν ἀνθρώποις (in) hominibus, entre-en (para) los hombres".

HARLÉ, Paul, Un "private-joke" de Paul dans le livre des Actes (XXVI.28-29). — *NTS* 24 (1977-78) 527-533. Esp. 529-532 [ἐν ὀλίγῳ].

HUTTON, W.R., The Salt Sections. — *ExpT* 58 (1946-47) 166-168. Esp. 166-167 [ἐν τίνι].

—, Considerations for the Translation of Greek en. — *BTrans* 9 (1958) 163-170.

MARTIN, Raymond A., Syntactical Evidence of Aramaic Sources in Acts I–XV, 1964. Esp. 41-42: "The relative frequency of certain prepositions in relation to the frequency of ἐν".

NEIRYNCK, Frans, La matière marcienne dans l'évangile de Luc, 1973. Esp. 184.186-187 [ἐν τῷ + inf.]; ²1989. Esp. 94.96-97; = ID., *Evangelica*, 1982. Esp. 64.66-67.

READ-HEIMERDINGER, Jenny, *The Bezan Text of Acts*, 2002. Esp. 192-197: "εἰς-ἐν".

SOISALON-SOININEN, Imari, *Die Infinitive in der Septuaginta*, 1965. Esp. 80-95 [ἐν τῷ + inf.].

SYLVA, Dennis D., The Cryptic Clause *en tois tou patros mou dei einai me* in Luke 2,49b. — *ZNW* 78 (1987) 132-140.

TURNER, Nigel, The Preposition *en* in the New Testament. — *BTrans* 10 (1959) 113-120.

URBÁN, Angel, El doble aspecto estatico-dinamico de la preposicion ἐν en el NT. —

URBÁN, A. – MATEOS, J. – ALEPUZ, M., *Estudios de Nuevo Testamento*. II, 1977, 15-62.

ἔναντι 1 + 1/2

1. in front of (Lk 1,8); 2. in the judgment of (Acts 8,21)

Word groups	Lk	Acts	Mt	Mk
ἔναντι + ἐν → ἐναντίον/ἐνώπιον + ἐν	1,8		0	0

Characteristic of Luke

HARNACK 1906 70.74; HAWKINS 1909LA; MORGENTHALER 1958*; PLUMMER 1922 lii; VOGEL 1899A

	Lk	Acts	Mt	Mk
ἔναντι/ἐναντίον BOISMARD 1984 Ab50; DENAUX 2009 L***; NEIRYNCK 1985	1,6.8; 20.26; 24,19	8,21	0	0

Literature

DENAUX 2009 LA[n]; HAUCK 1934 [seltenes Alleinwort]; JEREMIAS 1980 22 [red.].

SOLLAMO, Raija, Some ‚improper' prepositions such as *enōpion, enantion, enanti*, etc. in the Septuagint and early Koine Greek. — *VT* 25 (1975) 773-782. [NTA 20, 724]

ἐναντίον 3 + 2 (Mk 0/1)

1. in front of (Lk 20,26; Acts 8,32); 2. in the judgment of (Lk 1,6; 24,19)

Word groups	Lk	Acts	Mt	Mk
ἐναντίον τοῦ θεοῦ → ἐνώπιον (τοῦ) θεοῦ DENAUX 2009 L[n]	1,6; 24,19		0	0
ἐναντίον + ἐν → ἔναντι/ἐνώπιον + ἐν DENAUX 2009 L[n]	1,6; 24,19		0	0

Characteristic of Luke

GOULDER 1989; HARNACK 1906 70; HAWKINS 1909LA; MORGENTHALER 1958*; PLUMMER 1922 lii

	Lk	Acts	Mt	Mk
ἐναντίον/ἔναντι BOISMARD 1984 Ab50; DENAUX 2009 L***; NEIRYNCK 1985	1,6.8; 20.26; 24,19	8,21	0	0

Literature

VON BENDEMANN 2001 437; COLLISON 1977 146 [noteworthy phenomena]; DENAUX 2009 La[n]; EASTON 1910 154 [probably characteristic of L]; HAUCK 1934 [seltenes Alleinwort]; JEREMIAS 1980 22 [ἐναντίον τοῦ θεοῦ: red.].

SOLLAMO, Raija, Some ‚improper' prepositions such as *enōpion, enantion, enanti*, etc. in the Septuagint and early Koine Greek. — *VT* 25 (1975) 773-782. [NTA 20, 724]

ἔνατος 1 + 3 (Mt 3, Mk 2)   ninth

Word groups	Lk	Acts	Mt	Mk
ὥρα (+) ἐνάτη → ὥρα ἕκτη/τρίτη	23,44	3,1; 10,3.30	3	2

ἕνδεκα 2 + 2 (Mt 1, Mk [1])   eleven

Word groups	Lk	Acts	Mt	Mk
οἱ ἕνδεκα → οἱ **δώδεκα**	24,9.	2,14	0	0[1]
DENAUX 2009 La[n]	33			
ἕνδεκα ἀπόστολοι → **δώδεκα** ἀπόστολοι; cf. ἕνδεκα μαθηταί Mt 28,16		1,26	0	0

Characteristic of Luke

BOISMARD 1984 Bb101; DENAUX 2009 LA*; NEIRYNCK 1985

Literature

JEREMIAS 1980 311: "τοῖς ἕνδεκα: Die Zahl elf kommt im NT nur Mt 28,16; Lk 24,9.33/Apg 1,26; 2,14 vor, an allen fünf Stellen vom Zwölferkreis ohne Judas gesagt. Es handelt sich um einen von Lukas bevorzugten Sprachgebrauch".

PLEVNIK, Joseph, "The Eleven and Those with Them" according to Luke. [Lk 24,9] — *CBQ* 40 (1978) 205-211.

ἐνδέχεται 1 — be possible (Lk 13,33)

Literature

HAUCK 1934 [seltenes Alleinwort].

ἐνδιδύσκω 1/2 (Mk 1) — clothe (Lk 8,27*; 16,19)

ἔνδοξος 2

1. splendid (Lk 7,25; 13,17); 2. honored

Literature

DENAUX 2009 L[n].

ἔνδυμα 1 (Mt 7) — clothing

Word groups	Lk	Acts	Mt	Mk
ἔνδυμα + σῶμα → **ἐνδύω** + σῶμα	12,23		1	0

ἐνδύω 4 + 1 (Mt 3, Mk 3/4) — clothe

Word groups	Lk	Acts	Mt	Mk
ἐνδύω ἱμάτιον; cf. ἐνδύω ἔνδυμα Mt 22,11; ἐνδύω + χιτών Mk 6,9	8,27		1	1
ἐνδύω + σῶμα → **ἔνδυμα** + σῶμα	12,22		1	0
ἐνδύω proper use (*VK*a)	8,27; 12,22; 15,22	12,21	3	3/4

ἐνεδρεύω 1 + 1

1. be in ambush (Acts 23,21); 2. make plans against (Lk 11,54)

Characteristic of Luke; cf. ἐνέδρα Acts 23,16; 25,3; ἐνέδρον Acts 23,16*

BOISMARD 1984 ab79; HAWKINS 1909LA; MORGENTHALER 1958*; NEIRYNCK 1985; PLUMMER 1922 liii; VOGEL 1899A

Literature
DENAUX 2009 LAⁿ; HAUCK 1934 [seltenes Alleinwort]; JEREMIAS 1980 210 [red.].

ἔνειμι 1 | be inside (Lk 11,41)

Literature
HAUCK 1934 [seltenes Alleinwort].

ἕνεκα 1 + 2 (Mt 1)

ἕνεκεν: 1. on account of; 2. in order that; 3. because of (Lk 6,22)

Word groups	Lk	Acts	Mt	Mk
ἕνεκα τούτων (VKa)		26,21	0	0
τίνος ἕνεκα (VKb) → οὗ εἵνεκεν/ἕνεκεν; τίνος ἕνεκεν		19,32	0	0

Characteristic of Luke
→ ἕνεκα + ἐν

Literature
JEREMIAS 1980 138: "Während das NT sonst durchgängig ἕνεκεν/εἵνεκεν (also mit
Schlußkonsonant) schreibt, begegnet an vier Stellen die attische Form mit Schlußvokal (ἕνεκα),
davon dreimal im Doppelwerk".

ἕνεκεν 3 + 1 (Mt 6, Mk 5)

1. for the sake of (Lk 9,24; 18,29; 21,12); 2. in order that; 3. because of (Lk 4,18; Acts
28,20)

Word groups	Lk	Acts	Mt	Mk
ἕνεκεν ἐμοῦ	9,24		4	3
ἕνεκεν τοῦ ὀνόματός μου	21,12		1	0
οὗ ἕνεκεν (VKb) → οὗ εἵνεκεν/χάριν; τίνος ἕνεκα/ἕνεκεν	4,18*		0	0
τίνος ἕνεκεν (VKb) → οὗ εἵνεκεν/ἕνεκεν; τίνος ἕνεκα		19,32*	0	0

ἐνενήκοντα 2 (Mt 2) | ninety

Word groups	Lk	Acts	Mt	Mk
ἐνενήκοντα ἐννέα (VKa)	15,4.7		2	0

Literature
PAFFENROTH 1997 76 [ἐνενήκοντα ἐννέα].

ἐνέχω 1 (Mk 1)

1. have grudge against; 2. be hostile toward (Lk 11,53)

ἐνθάδε 1 + 5 | here (Lk 24,41)

Characteristic of Luke

BOISMARD 1984 cb27; NEIRYNCK 1985; PLUMMER 1922 lx

Literature

DENAUX 2009 lAⁿ; JEREMIAS 1980 125: "das von den Attizisten empfohlene ἐνθάδε"; RADL 1975 409.

ἔνθεν 1 (Mt 1) | from there (Lk 16,26)

Literature

LEE, John A.L. – HORSLEY, G.H.R., A Lexicon of the New Testament, 2, 1998. Esp. 74.82.

ἐνιαυτός 1 + 2

1. one year (Acts 11,26; 18,11); 2. era (Lk 4,19)

Word groups	Lk	Acts	Mt	Mk
ἐνιαυτός + μήν (VKa) → **ἔτος** + μήν		18,11	0	0

ἐνισχύω 1 + 1

1. strengthen (Lk 22,43); 2. regain strength (Acts 9,19)

Characteristic of Luke

HAWKINS 1909LA; MORGENTHALER 1958*(?); VOGEL 1899A

Literature

DENAUX 2009 LAⁿ; HAUCK 1934 [seltenes Alleinwort]; JEREMIAS 1980 294 [red.].

BRUN, Lyder, Engel und Blutschweiß Lc 22,43-44. — ZNW 32 (1933) 265-276.
SCHNEIDER, Gerhard, Engel und Blutschweiß (Lk 22,43-44): "Redaktionsgeschichte" im Dienste der Textkritik. — BZ NF 20 (1976) 112-116. Esp. 113-115: "Vokabular und Stil von Lk 22,43.44"; = ID., Lukas, Theologe der Heilsgeschichte, 1985, 153-157. Esp. 154-156.
TUCKETT, Christopher M., Luke 22,43-44: The "Agony" in the Garden and Luke's Gospel. — DENAUX, Adelbert (ed.), New Testament Textual Criticism and Exegesis. FS J. Delobel, 2002, 131-144. Esp. 133-135: "Vocabulary and style"

ἐννέα 3 (Mt 2) | nine

Word groups	Lk	Acts	Mt	Mk
ἐνενήκοντα ἐννέα (VKa)	15,4.7		2	0

Literature

PAFFENROTH 1997 76 [ἐνενήκοντα ἐννέα].

ἐννεύω 1 | gesture (Lk 1,62)

Literature

HAUCK 1934 [seltenes Alleinwort].

ἐνοχλέω 1	afflict

Literature
HAUCK 1934 [seltenes Alleinwort].

ἐντέλλομαι 1 + 2 (Mt 4/5, Mk 2/2)		command		
Word groups	Lk	Acts	Mt	Mk
ἐντέλλομαι + τοῦ + infinitive (VKa)	4,10		1	0

Literature
MAKUJINA, John, Verbs Meaning "Command" in the New Testament: Determining the Factors Involved in the Choice of Command-Verbs. — EstBíb 56 (1998) 357-369. Esp. 358-359: "Παραγγέλλω"; 359-361: "Κελεύω"; 361-362: "Ἐντέλλω"; 362-364: "Διαστέλλω"; 364-366: "-τάσσω complex"; 366-367: "Λέγω". [NTA 43, 57]

ἐντεῦθεν 2/3 (Mt 0/1)				
1. from here (Lk 4,9; 13,31); 2. from this				
Word groups	Lk	Acts	Mt	Mk
ἐντεῦθεν κάτω	4,9		0	0

Literature
DENAUX 2009 L^n.

ἔντιμος 2				
1. valuable (Lk 7,2); 2. honoured (Lk 14,18)				
Word groups	Lk	Acts	Mt	Mk
ἐντιμότερος comparative (VKa)	14,8		0	0

Literature
DENAUX 2009 L^n; EASTON 1910 160 [cited by Weiss as characteristic of L, and possibly corroborative]; HAUCK 1934 [seltenes Alleinwort];.

ἐντολή 4 + 1 (Mt 6/7, Mk 6/8)		commandment		
Word groups	Lk	Acts	Mt	Mk
ἐντολή + ἵνα (VKg)		17,15	0	0
ἐντολή + τοῦ κυρίου; cf. ἐντολὴ τοῦ θεοῦ Mt 15,3; Mk 7,8.9	1,6		0	0
ἐντολὴν λαμβάνω (VKc)		17,15	0	0

Literature
REHKOPF 1959 93 [vorlukanisch].

WILSON, Stephen H., Luke and the Law (SNTS MS, 50). Cambridge: University Press, 1963, VII-142 p. Esp. 1-11: "Legal terminology in Luke-Acts" [ἔθος; ἐντολή; νόμος].

ἐντός 1 (Mt 1)				
1. among (Lk 17,21); 2. what is inside				

Word groups

→ εἰμι ἐντός

Literature

ALLEN, P.M.S., Luke xvii.21: ἰδοὺ γάρ, ἡ βασιλεία τοῦ θεοῦ ἐντὸς ὑμῶν ἐστίν. — *ExpT* 49 (1937-38) 476-477; 50 (1938-39) 233-235.

BALLARD, Frank, Luke xvii.21. — *ExpT* 38 (1926-27) 331.

GRIFFITHS, J. Gwyn, ἐντὸς ὑμῶν (Luke xvii.21). — *ExpT* 63 (1951-52) 30-31.

—, "Within You" (Luke XVII.21). — *BTrans* 4 (1953) 7-8.

LEBOURLIER, Jean, *Entos hymōn*. Le sens "au milieu de vous" est-il possible? — *Bib* 73 (1992) 259-262.

LEWIS, F. Warburton, Luke xvii.21. — *ExpT* 38 (1926-27) 187-188.

RAKOCY, W., *Entos hymōn* (Lk 17,21): królestwo Boże 'w was' czy 'pośród was'. — *ColcT* 71 (2001) 31-40.

RIESENFELD, Harald, Gudsriket – här eller där, mitt ibland människor eller inom dem? Till Luk 17:20-21. — *SEÅ* 47 (1982) 93-101.

—, Le règne de Dieu, parmi vous ou en vous? (*Luc 17,20-21*). — *RB* 98 (1991) 190-198.

RÜSTOW, Alexander, Ἐντὸς ὑμῶν ἐστιν: Zur Deutung von Lukas 17,20-21. — *ZNW* 51 (1960) 197-224. Esp. 197-203 [παρατηρέω/παρατήρησις]; 203-204 [ἀστραπή]; 208-218 [ἐντός].

SCHWARZ, Günther, Οὐκ ... μετὰ παρατηρήσεως? — *BibNot* 59 (1991) 45-48. [παρατήρησις and ἐντὸς ὑμῶν ἐστιν].

SLEDD, Andrew, The Interpretation of Luke xvii.21. — *ExpT* 50 (1938-39) 235-237.

SNEED, Richard, "The Kingdom of God is within You" (Lk 17,21). — *CBQ* 24 (1962) 363-382.

STROBEL, August, Die Passa-Erwartung als urchristliches Problem in Lc 17,20f. — *ZNW* 49 (1958) 157-196.

ἐντρέπω 3 (Mt 1, Mk 1)

1. make ashamed; ἐντρέπομαι: 2. respect (Lk 18,2.4; 20,13)

ἐντυλίσσω 1 (Mt 1)

1. wrap (Lk 23,53); 2. roll up

ἐνώπιον 22/23 + 13/15

1. in front of (Lk 1,19; Acts 10,30); 2. in the opinion of (Lk 12,6; 15,18)

Word groups	Lk	Acts	Mt	Mk
ἐνώπιον τῶν ἀγγέλων τοῦ θεοῦ → **ἔμπροσθεν** τῶν ἀγγέλων τοῦ θεοῦ DENAUX 2009 Lⁿ	12,9²; 15,10		0	0
ἐνώπιον τῶν ἀνθρώπων (*VK*c) → **ἔμπροσθεν** τῶν ἀνθρώπων DENAUX 2009 Lⁿ	12,9¹; 16,15¹		0	0
ἐνώπιον + ἐν → **ἔναντι/ἐναντίον** + ἐν DENAUX 2009 Laⁿ	1,17.75; 16,15²	4,10; 10,30	0	0
→ **ἁμαρτάνω** ἐνώπιον; **εἰμι** ἐνώπιον; **εἰς** + ἐνώπιον; **προσκυνέω** ἐνώπιον; **τίθημι** ἐνώπιον				

Characteristic of Luke

BOISMARD 1984 Eb1; DENAUX 2009 L***; GOULDER 1989*; HARNACK 1906 51.72.145;
HAWKINS 1909 L; HENDRIKS 1986 428.433.448; MORGENTHALER 1958LA; NEIRYNCK 1985;
PLUMMER 1922 lx

	Lk	Acts	Mt	Mk
ἐνώπιον (τοῦ) θεοῦ (SCa; VKa) → **ἔμπροσθεν/ἐναντίον**	1,6*.19;	4,19; 7,46;	0	0
τοῦ θεοῦ	12,6;	8,21*;		
PLUMMER 1922 lx	16,15^2	10,4*.31.33		
ἐνώπιον (τοῦ) κυρίου (SCa; VKb); cf. ἐνώπιον αὐτοῦ Lk	1,15.76		0	0
1,17.75				
PLUMMER 1922 lx				
παρίστημι ἐνώπιον	1,19	4,10	0	0
BOISMARD 1984 Ab192; NEIRYNCK 1985				

→ **χάρις** ἐνώπιον τοῦ θεοῦ

Literature

VON BENDEMANN 2001 425; COLLISON 1977 147 [linguistic usage of Luke: certain; it is also
probable that this is a linguistic usage of Luke's "other source-material"]; DENAUX 2009 L^n
[ἐνώπιον (τοῦ) κυρίου]; LA^n [ἐνώπιον (τοῦ) θεοῦ; παρίστημι ἐνώπιον]; EASTON 1910 177
[possible Hebraisms in the Lucan Writings, as classed by Dalman]; GERSDORF 1816 171 [ἐνώπιον
τοῦ θεοῦ]; HAUCK 1934 [seltenes Alleinwort]; JEREMIAS 1980 36 [ἐνώπιον κυρίου: trad.]; 38:
"hat er eine ausgesprochene Vorliebe für ἐνώπιον"; RADL 1975 409.

SOLLAMO, Raija, Some ‚improper' prepositions such as *enōpion, enantion, enanti*, etc. in
	the Septuagint and early Koine Greek. — *VT* 25 (1975) 773-782. [NTA 20, 724]
WALLS, A.F., "In the Presence of the Angels" (Luke xv 10). — *NT* 3 (1959) 314-316.
WIKENHAUSER, Alfred, Ἐνώπιος-ἐνώπιον-κατενώπιον. — *BZ* 8 (1910) 263-270.
WILCOX, Max, Semitisms in the New Testament, 1984. Esp. 1012-1013: "ἐνώπιον in
	Luke 15:18,21".

Ἐνώς 1

Enos (Lk 3,38)

Ἐνώχ 1

Enoch (Lk 3,37)

ἕξ 2 + 3 (Mt 1, Mk 1)

six (Lk 4,25; 13,14)

Word groups	Lk	Acts	Mt	Mk
ἑβδομήκοντα ἕξ (VKb)		27,37	0	0
διακόσιοι ἑβδομήκοντα ἕξ (VKc)		27,37	0	0

ἐξάγω 1 + 8 (Mk 1/2)

lead out

Word groups	Lk	Acts	Mt	Mk
ἐξάγω εἰς + place (VKc) → (ἀν/ἀπ/εἰσ/ἐπαν/κατ/ προ/συν/ὑπ)ἄγω εἰς + place	24,50 v.l.	21,38	0	0

ἐξάγω (+) ἐκ (VKa) → **ἐξάγω** ἔξω		7,40; 12,17; 13,17	0	0
ἐξάγω ἔξω (VKb) → **ἐξάγω** ἐκ	24,50		0	0/1
ἐξάγω ἕως location (VKd) → **ἄγω/διώκω/**	24,50		0	0
(δι/ἐξ)ἔρχομαι/καταβαίνω/πορεύομαι ἕως				
ἐξάγω πρός + accusative (place) → **(ἀπ)ἄγω** πρός + acc.	24,50		0	0
ἐξάγω transitive → **(ἀν/ἀπ/εἰσ/ἐπισυν/κατ/προ/ προσ/συν)ἄγω** transitive DENAUX 2009 lAn	24,50	5,19; 7,36.40; 12,17; 13,17; 16,37.39; 21,38	0	1

Characteristic of Luke
BOISMARD 1984 Bb102; NEIRYNCK 1985; PLUMMER 1922 lx

Literature
DENAUX 2009 lAn; JEREMIAS 1980 84 [ἐξάγω ἕως: red.]; 323: "ἐξάγω ist lk Vorzugswort".

ἐξαιτέομαι* 1   ask with success (Lk 22,31)

Literature
HAUCK 1934 [seltenes Alleinwort]; SCHÜRMANN 1957 103 [möglicherweise luk R].

ἐξαίφνης 2 + 2 (Mk 1)   immediately (Lk 2,13; 9,39; Acts 8,3; 22,6)

Characteristic of Luke
BOISMARD 1984 Bb103; CREDNER 1936 142; DENAUX 2009 LA*; NEIRYNCK 1985; PLUMMER 1922 lx

Literature
GERSDORF 1816 230 [καὶ ἐξαίφνης ἐγένετο σὺν τῷ ἀγγέλῳ πλῆθος στρατιᾶς οὐρανίου αἰνούντων τὸν θεόν].

DAUBE, David, *The Sudden in the Scriptures.* Leiden: Brill, 1964, VII-86 p. Esp. 30-32.

ἐξανίστημι 1 + 1 (Mk 1)   stand up

Word groups	Lk	Acts	Mt	Mk
ἐξανίστημι σπέρμα (LN: beget)	20,28		0	1

Characteristic of Luke	Lk	Acts	Mt	Mk
ἐξανέστη and cognate ἀνέστη + participle → **ἀνέστη** + part. BOISMARD 1984 Ab68; NEIRYNCK 1985	10,25	5,36; 6,9; 15,5	0	0

Literature
DENAUX 2009 lA[n] [ἐξανέστη and cognate ἀνέστη + participle].

ἐξαποστέλλω 3/4 + 7 (Mk 0[1])
1. send out (Lk 1,53; 20,10.11; Acts 17,14); 2. send a message (Acts 13,26)

Word groups	Lk	Acts	Mt	Mk
ἐξαποστέλλω + infinitive (VKc)		11,22; 17,14	0	0
ἐξαποστέλλω + ἄγγελος → **ἀποστέλλω** + ἄγγελος		12,11	0	0
ἐξαποστέλλω + εἰς (VKa) → **ἀποστέλλω/πέμπω** εἰς		7,12; 9,30; 22,21	0	0
ἐξαποστέλλω + εἰς + person → **ἀποστέλλω** εἰς + person		22,21	0	0

Characteristic of Luke

BOISMARD 1984 вb66; CREDNER 1836 139; DENAUX 2009 IA*; GOULDER 1989; HARNACK 1906 142; HAWKINS 1909 L; NEIRYNCK 1985; PLUMMER 1922 lix; VOGEL 1899в

	Lk	Acts	Mt	Mk
ἐξαποστέλλω τινὰ κενόν (VKb); cf. ἀποστέλλω τινὰ κενόν Mk 12,3 CREDNER 1836 141; HARNACK 1906 142.151	1,53; 20,10.11		0	0

Literature

COLLISON 1977 94 [noteworthy phenomena]; DENAUX 2009 Lⁿ [ἐξαποστέλλω τινὰ κενόν]; GERSDORF 1816 200 [ἐξαπέστειλεν κενούς]; HAUCK 1934 [häufiges Alleinwort]; JEREMIAS 1980 84 [ἐξαποστέλλω ἕως: red.]; 209 [ἐξαποστέλλω εἰς + person: red.]; 322: "ἐξαποστέλλω ist lk Vorzugswort".

ἐξαστράπτω*** 1	glisten (Lk 9,29)

Literature

HAUCK 1934 [seltenes Alleinwort].

ἐξέρχομαι 44/45 + 30/33 (Mt 43/46, Mk 38[39]/40)

1. go out (Lk 2,1; Acts 17,15); 2. pass away (Acts 16,19)

Word groups	Lk	Acts	Mt	Mk
διηγέομαι + ἐξέρχομαι → παραγγέλλω + **ἐξελθεῖν**; διηγέομαι + ἀπέρχομαι		12,17	0	0
εἰσέρχομαι καὶ ἐξέρχομαι (LN: live with) → εἰσπορεύομαι καὶ **ἐκπορεύομαι**		1,21	0	0
ἐξέρχομαι + genitive (VKk)		8,7; 16,39*	2	0
ἐξέρχομαι + infinitive → (ἀπ/εἰσ/προ/ προσ/συν)**έρχομαι** + inf.	2,1; 6,12; 7,24.25.26; 8,5.35; 14,18	11,25	6	3/4
ἐξέρχομαι participle without place of destination (VKl)	1,22; 4,42; 9,6; 10,35*; 14,18; 15,28; 21,37; 22,39	12,9.10.17; 16,36; 21,5.8; 28,3	9	7[8]
ἐξέρχομαι ἀπό + person → **ἐξέρχομαι** ἀπό + person (exorcism) DENAUX 2009 Lⁿ	5,8; 8,46		0	0
ἐξέρχομαι + ἀπό + place → **ἐξέρχομαι** ἀπό + person (exorcism); ἀποβαίνω/(ἐπ/ κατ)**έρχομαι/πορεύομαι/ὑποστρέφω** ἀπό	9,5; 17,29	16,40; 28,3	3/5	1
ἐξέρχομαι + ἕως (VKj) → (δι/παρ)**έρχομαι** ἄχρι/ἕως	12,59	21,5; 28,15*	1	0

ἐξέρχομαι (+) εἰς (VKb)	6,12; 7,24; 10,10; 14,21.23	11,25; 14,20; 16,10; 28,15*	9/10	7/8
ἐξέρχομαι + εἰς τὸ ὄρος → **ἀναβαίνω/ πορεύομαι** εἰς τὸ ὄρος; **κατέρχομαι** ἀπὸ τοῦ ὄρους	6,12		1	1
ἐξέρχομαι + εἰσέρχομαι	8,33; 9,4; 10,10; 11,24[1](-26); 14,23; 15,28	1,21; 10,23(-24); 14,20; 16,40; 21,8	3	6
ἐξέρχομαι (+) ἐκ (VKc)	4,35[1] v.l.	7,3.4; 15,24; 16,40[1] v.l.; 17,33; 22,18; 28,3 v.l.	5/6	10
ἐξέρχομαι (+) ἐκεῖθεν/κἀκεῖθεν	9,4; 11,53; 12,59	7,4; 16,(12-)13	1	4
ἐξέρχομαι + ἐν + place (VKd)	7,17		0	0
ἐξέρχομαι + ἐξ Ἰερουσαλήμ → **ἔρχομαι** εἰς Ἰερουσαλήμ; **κατέρχομαι** ἀπὸ Ἰεροσολύμων		22,18	0	0
ἐξέρχομαι ἔξω (VKe) → **ἀπέρχομαι** ἔξω	22,62	16,13	3	1
ἐξέρχομαι + ἐπί + accusative (place) (VKf) → **(ἀπ/εἰσ/ἐπ)ἔρχομαι** ἐπί + acc.	8,27; 22,52	1,21	1	1
ἐξέρχομαι + εὑρίσκω → **(ἀπ/δι/εἰσ/κατ) ἔρχομαι/(εἰσ)πορεύομαι** + εὑρίσκω	8,35	11,(25-).26	4	1
ἐξέρχομαι κατά + genitive (VKg) → **ἔρχομαι** κατά + acc.	4,14		0	0
ἐξέρχομαι + παρά + accusative/genitive (VKh) → **ἔρχομαι** παρά + acc./gen.; cf. ἐξέρχομαι ἔμπροσθεν Mk 2,12	2,1; 6,19	16,13	0	1
ἐξέρχομαι σύν; cf. Jn 18,1 BOISMARD 1984 CA11		10,23; 14,20; 16,3	0	0

Characteristic of Luke

GASTON 1973 64 [Lked]

	Lk	Acts	Mt	Mk
δαιμόνιον ἐξέρχεται (SCa); cf. in a similar meaning of ἐξέρχεται Mt 8,32; 12,43.44; Mk 1,25.26; 5,8.13; 9,25.26.29; Lk 4,35[1].36; 8,29; 11,24[1.2]; Acts 8,7; 16,18[1.2]; cf. δαιμόνιον εἰσέρχεται Lk 8,30.33 DENAUX 2009 L***	4,35[2].41; 8,2.33.35[2].38; 11,14		1	2
ἐξελθὼν absolute ... πορεύομαι BOISMARD 1984 Ab60; NEIRYNCK 1985	4,42; 22,39	12,17; 16,36; 21,5	0	0
ἐξέρχομαι + ἀπό DENAUX 2009 L***; GOULDER 1989*; HARNACK 1906 40	4,35[1.2].41; 5,8; 8,2.29.33.35[2].38. 46; 9,5; 11,24[1]; 17,29	16,18[1].40[1]; 19,12*; 28,3	5	1
ἐξέρχομαι ἀπό + person (exorcism) → **ἐξέρχομαι** ἀπό + person/place; **ἀποχωρέω** ἀπό BOISMARD 1984 Bb88; DENAUX 2009 L***; HAWKINS 1909L; NEIRYNCK 1985; PLUMMER 1922 lxii	4,35[1.2].41; 8,2.29.33.35[2].38; 11,24[1]	16,18[1]; 19,12*	2	0
παραγγέλλω ... ἐξελθεῖν → **διηγέομαι** + **ἐξέρχομαι** BOISMARD 1984 Ab191; NEIRYNCK 1985	8,29	16,18[1]	0	0

Literature

VON BENDEMANN 2001 413 [ἐξέρχεσθαι ἀπό]; 426 [ἐξέρχεσθαι + πορεύεσθαι]; COLLISON 1977 123 [ἐξέρχομαι + ἀπό: linguistic usage of Luke: certain]; DENAUX 2009 LA[n] [παραγγέλλω + ἐξελθεῖν], IA[n] [ἐξελθὼν absolute ... πορεύομαι]; HAUCK 1934

[Vorzugsverbindung: ἐξέρχομαι ἀπό]; JEREMIAS 1980 177: "Bei der Analyse der zehn Belege für exorzistisches ἐξέρχεσθαι ἀπό im Doppelwerk ... ganz sicher lukanisch"; 234: "Lukanisch ist insbesondere die semitisierende Kombination von ἐξέρχομαι und πορεύομαι"; RADL 1975 400 [ἐξέρχομαι + ἀπό]; 409 [ἐξέρχομαι; ἐξέρχομαι + πορεύομαι]; SCHÜRMANN 1953 102 [ἐξέρχεσθαι ἀπό].

DENAUX, Adelbert, L'hypocrisie des pharisiens et le dessein de Dieu, 1973. Esp. 259; [2]1989. Esp. 169.

GARCÍA PÉREZ, José Miguel, El Endemoniado de Gerasa (Lc 8,26-39), 1986. Esp. 127-137.

ἔξεστιν 5 + 4/5 (Mt 9/10, Mk 6)

1. be possible (Acts 2,29); 2. ought to (Lk 6,2.4.9; 14,3; 20,22)

Word groups	Lk	Acts	Mt	Mk
ἔξεστιν + accusative + infinitive (VKa)	6,4; 20,22		0	1
ἔξεστιν + inf. + ἤ + inf.	6,9		0	0
ἔξεστιν + inf. + ἤ οὐ	14,3; 20,22		1	1
ἐξόν (VKb)		2,29	1	0
ἔξεστιν question	6,9; 14,3; 20,22	21,37; 22,25	4	3

ἐξηγέομαι 1 + 4

1. tell fully (Lk 24,35; Acts 10,8); 2. make fully known

Characteristic of Luke
BOISMARD 1984 bb67; NEIRYNCK 1985; PLUMMER 1922 lx; VOGEL 1899B

Literature
DENAUX 2009 IA[n]; JEREMIAS 1980 319 [red.].

ἑξήκοντα 1 (Mt 2, Mk 2)   sixty

Word groups	Lk	Acts	Mt	Mk
ἑκατὸν ἑξήκοντα (VKc)	24,13 v.l.		0	0

ἑξῆς 2 + 3   next, soon afterward

Word groups	Lk	Acts	Mt	Mk
τῇ (+) ἑξῆς (LN: the next day) DENAUX 2009 IA[n]	9,37	21,1; 25,17; 27,18	0	0
ἐν τῷ ἑξῆς (LN: later) → ἐν τῷ καθεξῆς	7,11		0	0

Characteristic of Luke
BOISMARD 1984 Ab51; CREDNER 1836 142; HARNACK 1906 51; HAWKINS 1909LA.add; MORGENTHALER 1958*; NEIRYNCK 1985; PLUMMER 1922 lii; VOGEL 1899A

Literature
COLLISON 1977 152 [noteworthy phenomena]; DENAUX 2009 IA[n]; HAUCK 1934 [häufiges Alleinwort]; JEREMIAS 1980 156 [red.]; RADL 1975 403 [ἐγένετο + ἡμέρα/σάββατον/(καθ) ἑξῆς/καιρός]; 409.

KÜRZINGER, Joseph, Lk 1,3: ... ἀκριβῶς καθεξῆς σοι γράψαι. — *BZ* NF 18 (1974)
249-255. [NTA 19, 575]
VÖLKEL, Martin, Exegetische Erwägungen zum Verständnis des Begriffs καθεξῆς im
lukanischen Prolog. — *NTS* 20 (1973-74) 289-299. Esp. 295. [NTA 19, 127]

ἐξίστημι 3 + 8 (Mt 1, Mk 4)

1. astonish greatly (Lk 8,56; 24,22; Acts 8,9.11); ἐξίσταμαι: 2. be greatly astonished
(Lk 2,47); 3. be insane

Word groups	Lk	Acts	Mt	Mk
ἐξίστημι + ἐπί + dative (*VK*d)	2,47		0	0
ἐξίσταντο δὲ πάντες οἱ ἀκούοντες DENAUX 2009 LA[n]	2,47	9,21	0	0

Characteristic of Luke

BOISMARD 1984 cb129; CREDNER 1836 141; HARNACK 1906 149; NEIRYNCK 1985;
PLUMMER 1922 lx

	Lk	Acts	Mt	Mk
ἐξίσταντο δὲ πάντες; cf. καὶ ἐξίσταντο πάντες Mt 12,23; ἐξίστασθαι πάντας Mk 2,12 BOISMARD 1984 Ab118; HARNACK 1906 149; NEIRYNCK 1985	2,47	2,12; 9,21	0	0
ἐξίστημι τι/τινά (*VK*a) BOISMARD 1984 Ab119; NEIRYNCK 1985	24,22	8,9.11	0	0

Literature

DENAUX 2009 lA[n] [ἐξίσταντο δὲ πάντες, ἐξίστημι τι/τινά]; GERSDORF 1816 267 [ἐξίσταντο
δὲ πάντες οἱ ἀκούοντες αὐτοῦ]; JEREMIAS 1980 101 [ἐξίσταντο δὲ πάντες οἱ ἀκούοντες:
red.]; 316: "Transitives ἐξίστημι ('verwirren') im NT nur Lk 24,22/Apg 8,9.11".

DANOVE, Paul, Verbs of Experience, 1999. Esp. 167-168.177.

ἔξοδος 1

1. departure; 2. death (Lk 9,31)

Literature

HAUCK 1934 [seltenes Alleinwort].

ἐξομολογέω 2 + 1 (Mt 2, Mk 1)

1. profess; 2. admit (Lk 22,6; Acts 19,18); 3. give thanks; 4. praise (Lk 10,21)

Word groups	Lk	Acts	Mt	Mk
ἐξομολογέω + dative (*VK*c)	10,21		1	0
ἐξομολογέω active (*VK*a)	10,21; 22,6		1	0

Literature

BORMANN, Lukas, *Recht, Gerechtigkeit und Religion*, 2001. Esp. 190.
GEORGE, Augustin, La prière. — ID., *Études*, 1978, 395-427. Esp. 402-405: "Le vocabulaire
lucanien de la prière".

ἐξουθενέω 2 + 1 (Mk 0/1) | despise (Lk 18,9; 23,11; Acts 4,11)

Literature

DENAUX 2009 La[n]; EASTON 1910 160 [cited by Weiss as characteristic of L, and possibly corroborative]; JEREMIAS 1980 273 [red.].

ἐξουσία 16 + 7 (Mt 10, Mk 10)

1. authority to rule (Lk 19,17); 2. jurisdiction (Lk 4,6; 23,7); 3. symbol of authority; 4. ruler (Lk 12,11); 5. control (Acts 5,4); 6. power (Lk12,5); 7. supernatural power; 8. right to judge

Word groups	Lk	Acts	Mt	Mk
ἐν ποίᾳ ἐξουσίᾳ	20,2[1].8		3	3
ἐν ἐξουσίᾳ absolute (VKd); cf. κατ᾽ ἐξουσίαν Mk 1,27 DENAUX 2009 L[n]	4,32.36		0	0
ἐξουσία + ἀρχή DENAUX 2009 L[n]	12,11; 20,20		0	0
ἐξουσία + δόξα	4,6		0	0
ἐξουσία + δύναμις DENAUX 2009 L[n]	4,36; 9,1; 10,19		0	0
αἱ ἐξουσίαι (VKc)	12,11		0	0
ἐξουσίαν δίδωμι (VKb)	4,6; 9,1; 10,19; 20,2[2]	8,19	4	3
ἐξουσίαν ἔχω (VKa)	5,24; 12,5; 19,17	9,14	2	3
ἐξουσίαν λαμβάνω		26,10	0	0
τασσόμενος ὑπὸ ἐξουσίαν	7,8		0/1	0

Literature

COLLISON 1977 173 [linguistic usage of Luke: certain]; EASTON 1910 154 [ἐξουσία with subjective genitive: probably characteristic of L].

BORMANN, Lukas, *Recht, Gerechtigkeit und Religion*, 2001. Esp. 116.
WINK, Walter, *Naming the Powers*, 1984. Esp. 15-17.157.

ἐξουσιάζω 1 | reign (Lk 22,25)

Literature

SCHÜRMANN 1957 71 [vermutlich luk R].

BORMANN, Lukas, *Recht, Gerechtigkeit und Religion*, 2001. Esp. 116.

ἔξω 10/11 + 10/11 (Mt 9, Mk 10)

1. outside (Lk 8,20; Acts 16,13); 2. away

Word groups	Lk	Acts	Mt	Mk
(ἐκ)βάλλω (+) ἔξω	4,29; 8,54*; 13,28; 14,35; 20,15	7,58; 9,40	3	1
ἔξω + genitive (VKa)	4,29; 13,33; 20,15	4,15; 7,58; 14,19; 16,13; 21,5.30	3	4
ἔξω + preposition (VKb)	24,50	5,23*	1	3
ἔξω + εἰς	24,50 v.l.	26,11	1	1

→ ἀπέρχομαι ἔξω; ἐξάγω ἔξω; ἐξέρχομαι ἔξω; ἵσταμαι ἔξω

Characteristic of Luke	Lk	Acts	Mt	Mk
ἐκβάλλω ἔξω τῆς πόλεως BOISMARD 1984 Ab176; NEIRYNCK 1985	4,29	7,58	0	0

Literature
COLLISON 1977 152 [noteworthy phenomena]; DENAUX 2009 LAⁿ [ἐκβάλλω ἔξω τῆς πόλεως];
RADL 1975 409-410 [ἔξω; ἔξω τῆς πόλεως].

ἔξωθεν 2 (Mt 3, Mk 2)

1. from outside; 2. outside (Lk 11,39.40); 3. the outside of

Word groups	Lk	Acts	Mt	Mk
ἔξωθεν + ἔσωθεν; cf. ἐκτός + ἐντός Mt 23,26	11,39.40		3	0
τὸ ἔξωθεν used as a noun (VKb)	11,39.40		1	0

ἑορτή 3/4 + 0/1 (Mt 2, Mk 2)   festival

Word groups	Lk	Acts	Mt	Mk
κατὰ ἑορτήν (VKc); cf. κατὰ τὸ ἔθος τῆς ἑορτῆς Lk 2,42	23,17*		1	1
ἑορτὴ τῶν ἀζύμων → ἡμέρα τῶν ἀζύμων; πάσχα + ἄζυμος	22,1		0	0
ἑορτή (+) πάσχα DENAUX 2009 Lⁿ	2,41; 22,1		0	0

ἐπαγγελία 1 + 8

1. promise (Lk 2,39); 2. agreement (Acts 23,21)

Word groups	Lk	Acts	Mt	Mk
κατ' ἐπαγγελίαν (VKb)		13,23	0	0
λαμβάνω + ἐπαγγελίαν; cf. λαμβάνω + παραγγελίαν Acts 16,24		2,33	0	0

Characteristic of Luke
BOISMARD 1984 Db6; NEIRYNCK 1985

	Lk	Acts	Mt	Mk
ἐπαγγελία τοῦ πατρός BOISMARD 1984 Ab177; NEIRYNCK 1985	24,49	1,4	0	0

Literature
DENAUX 2009 IAⁿ, LAⁿ [ἐπαγγελία τοῦ πατρός]; JEREMIAS 1980 322 [ἐπαγγελία τοῦ
πατρός: red.].

ἐπαθροίζω* 1   ἐπαθροίζομαι: gather together more (Lk 11,29)

Literature
HAUCK 1934 [seltenes Alleinwort].

ἐπαινέω 1   praise (Lk 16,8)

Literature
COLLISON 1977 90 [noteworthy phenomena].
SCHWARZ, Günther, "…lobte den betrügerischen Verwalter"? (Lukas 16,8a). — *BZ* NF 18 (1974) 94-95. Esp. 94: "…, wer in V. 8a (…) mit dem κύριος gemeint ist … erledigt sich von selbst, wenn die Fehlübersetzung der entscheidenden Vokabeln (ἐπῄνεσεν und φρονίμως) korrigiert sein wird". [NTA 19, 588]

ἐπαίρω 6 + 5 (Mt 1)

1. raise (Lk 11,27; Acts 2,14); ἐπαίρομαι: 2. rise up against; 3. be arrogant

Word groups	Lk	Acts	Mt	Mk
ἐπαίρω τὴν κεφαλήν (*LN*: have courage)	21,28		0	0
ἐπαίρω χεῖρας	24,50		0	0
ἐπαίρω τὴν φωνήν + λέγων		14,11; 22,22	0	0

Characteristic of Luke

BOISMARD 1984 cb158; DENAUX 2009 L***; GOULDER 1989*; HAWKINS 1909 L; NEIRYNCK 1985

	Lk	Acts	Mt	Mk
ἐπαίρω τοὺς ὀφθαλμούς (*LN*: look; *SC*a; *VK*a) → (δι)ἀνοίγω τοὺς ὀφθαλμούς; (ἐπ)αἴρω τὴν φωνήν GOULDER 1989	6,20; 16,23; 18,13		1	0
ἐπαίρω (and cognate αἴρω) τὴν φωνήν (*LN*: speak loudly; *VK*b) → αἴρω φωνήν; ἐπαίρω τοὺς ὀφθαλμούς BOISMARD 1984 Ab45; NEIRYNCK 1985	11,27; 17,13	2,14; 4,24; 14,11; 22,22	0	0
ἐπαίρω τὴν φωνήν PLUMMER 1922 lii; VOGEL 1899C	11,27	2,14; 14,11; 22,22	0	0

Literature
VON BENDEMANN 2001 420: "ἐπαίρειν ist lukanisches Vorzugsverb"; COLLISON 1977 49 [linguistic usage of Luke's "other source-material": likely]; DENAUX 2009 lAⁿ [ἐπαίρω τὴν φωνήν; ἐπαίρω (and cognate αἴρω) τὴν φωνήν]; EASTON 1910 154 [probably characteristic of L]; HAUCK 1934 [Vorzugswort]; JEREMIAS 1980 69 [ἐπαίρω τὴν φωνήν + λέγων: red.]; 203 ["übertragener Gebrauch von ἐπαίρω in der Bedeutung 'aufheben, erheben'": red.]; RADL 1975 410 [ἐπαίρω; ἐπαίρω τὴν φωνήν]; REHKOPF 1959 96 [ὀφθαλμοὺς ἐπαίρειν]; SCHÜRMANN 1961 284 [ὀφθαλμοὺς ἐπαίρειν: protoluk R nicht beweisbar].
VALLAURI, Emiliano, … Alzati gli occhi … (Lc. 6,20; Giov. 6,5). — *BibOr* 27 (1985) 163-169.

ἐπαισχύνομαι 2 (Mk 2)   be ashamed of (Lk 9,26[1.2])

Characteristic of Luke

CREDNER 1836 138

Literature
DUPONT, Jacques, *Le discours de Milet*, 1962. Esp. 64-65.75.
VORSTER, Willem S., *Aischunomai en stamverwante woorde in die Nuwe Testament*. Pretoria: Universiteit van Suid-Africa, 1979, XVIII-299 p. Esp. 67-87: "Αἰσχύνομαι"; 87-100: "ἐπαισχύνομαι"; 100-121: "καταισχύνω".

ἐπαιτέω 2	beg (Lk 16,3; 18,35)

Characteristic of Luke
PLUMMER 1922 liii

Literature
DENAUX 2009 Lⁿ; HAUCK 1934 [seltenes Alleinwort].

ἐπάν 2 (Mt 1)	whenever (Lk 11,22.34)

ἐπανάγω 2 (Mt 1)	
1. return to; 2. put out to sea (Lk 5,3.4)	

Word groups	Lk	Acts	Mt	Mk
ἐπανάγω ἀπό + genitive → ἀνάγομαι ἀπό; cf. ἐκπλέω ἀπό Acts 20,6	5,3		0	0
ἐπανάγω εἰς + place → (ἀν/ἀπ/εἰσ/ἐξ/κατ/προ/συν/ὑπ)άγω εἰς + place	5,4		1	0

Characteristic of Luke
CREDNER 1836 139

Literature
HAUCK 1934 [Vorzugswort].

ἐπαναπαύομαι 1	
1. remain (Lk 10,6); 2. trust in	

Characteristic of Luke
CREDNER 1836 139

Literature
HAUCK 1934 [seltenes Alleinwort].

ἐπανέρχομαι 2	return to (Lk 10,35; 19,15)

Characteristic of Luke
CREDNER 1836 139; PLUMMER 1922 liii

Literature
DENAUX 2009 Lⁿ; EASTON 1910 160 [cited by Weiss as characteristic of L, and possibly corroborative]; HAUCK 1934 [seltenes Alleinwort].

ἐπάνω 5 (Mt 8/9, Mk 1)	
1. on, above, over (Lk 4,39; 10,19; 11,44); 2. more than; 3. superior (Lk 19,17.19)	

Word groups	Lk	Acts	Mt	Mk
ἐπάνω adverb (VKa)	11,44		0	1
→ ἐφίστημι ἐπάνω; περιπατέω ἐπάνω				

Literature

COLLISON 1977 153 [avoids literal sense: linguistic usage of Luke: likely; used metaphorically: likely].

ἐπεί 1/2 (Mt 3, Mk 1) — because (Lk 1,34; Acts 13,46*)

Word groups	Lk	Acts	Mt	Mk
ἐπεί expression of time (VKa)	7,1*		0	0

ἐπειδή 2 + 3 (Mt 0/1)

1. because (Lk 11,6); 2. when (Lk 7,1)

Word groups	Lk	Acts	Mt	Mk
ἐπειδή δέ (VKc)		13,46 v.l.	0	0
ἐπειδή expression of time (VKa)	7,1		0	0

Characteristic of Luke

BOISMARD 1984 db16; NEIRYNCK 1985

Literature

COLLISON 1977 113 [noteworthy phenomena]; DENAUX 2009 1A[n]; HAUCK 1934 [seltenes Alleinwort]; JEREMIAS 1980 151 [red.].

ἐπειδήπερ* 1 — because (Lk 1,1)

Literature

BDR § 456,3: "Kausale Konjunktionen: ἐπειδήπερ nur Lk 1,1 'da (nun) einmal', nimmt auf eine bereits bekannte Tatsache Bezug"; GERSDORF 1816 160; HAUCK 1934 [seltenes Alleinwort].

ALEXANDER, Loveday, The Preface to Luke's Gospel, 1993. Esp. 108-109.
CADBURY, Henry J., Commentary on the Preface of Luke, 1922. Esp. 492.

ἐπεισέρχομαι 1 — happen

Literature

HAUCK 1934 [seltenes Alleinwort].

DAUBE, David, The Sudden in the Scriptures. Leiden: Brill, 1964, VII-86 p. Esp. 34-38: "To come upon".

ἔπειτα 1 (Mk 0/1) — later

Word groups	Lk	Acts	Mt	Mk
ἔπειτα enumeration (VKa)	16,7		0	0

ἐπέρχομαι 3/4 + 4

1. arrive (Lk 1,35; Acts 14,19); 2. assault (Lk 11,22); 3. happen (Lk 21,26; Acts 13,40)

Word groups	Lk	Acts	Mt	Mk
τὰ ἐπερχόμενα (VKb)	21,26		0	0
ἐπέρχομαι ἀπό → ἀποβαίνω/ἀποχωρέω/(ἀπ/ἐξ)ἔρχομαι/ πορεύομαι/ὑποστρέφω ἀπό		14,19	0	0

Characteristic of Luke

BOISMARD 1984 cb7; DENAUX 2009 1A*; GOULDER 1989; HAWKINS 1909B; NEIRYNCK 1985; PLUMMER 1922 lix

	Lk	Acts	Mt	Mk
ἐπέρχομαι ἐπί τινα (VKa) → (ἀπ/εἰσ/ἐξ)ἔρχομαι ἐπί + acc. BOISMARD 1984 Ab120; NEIRYNCK 1985	1,35; 21,35*	1,8; 8,24; 13,40 v.l.	0	0

Literature

VON BENDEMANN 2001 420: "typisch lukanisch"; DENAUX 2009 1A^n, 1A^n [ἐπέρχομαι ἐπί τινα]; HAUCK 1934 [Vorzugswort]; JEREMIAS 1980 51: "ἐπέρχεσθαι ist lukanisches Vorzugswort"; RADL 1975 410.

DAUBE, David, The Sudden in the Scriptures. Leiden: Brill, 1964, VII-86 p. Esp. 34-38: "To come upon".

SCHNEIDER, Gerhard, Lk 1,34. 35 als redaktionelle Einheit. — BZ NF 15 (1971) 255-259. Esp. 256-257: "Lk 1,35 ist nach Wortschatz, Stil und Theologie 'lukanisch'".

—, Jesu geistgewirkte Empfängnis (Lk 1,34f): Zur Interpretation einer christologischen Aussage. — TPQ 119 (1971) 105-116. Esp. 110; = ID., Lukas, Theologe der Heilsgeschichte, 1985, 86-97. Esp. 91.

ἐπερωτάω 17/18 + 2/3 (Mt 8, Mk 25/26)

1. ask (Lk 3,10); 2. ask for; 3. interrogate (Acts 5,27)

Word groups	Lk	Acts	Mt	Mk
ἐπερωτάω + 2 accusatives (to ask someone something) (VKb) → ἐρωτάω + 2 acc.	20,40		0	2
ἐπερωτάω + ἀποκρίνομαι → αἰτέω/ἐρωτάω + ἀποκρίνομαι	3,10(-11); 9,18(-19); 17,20; 20,(39-)40; 23,3*.9	5,27(-29)	4	10/18
ἐπερωτάω εἰ (VKa)	6,9; 23,6	1,6*	1	3
ἐπερωτάω (+) λέγω/εἶπον → ἐρωτάω + λέγω/εἶπον	3,10.14; 8,9 v.l.30 v.l.; 9,18; 17,20; 18,18.40 v.l.; 20,21.27(-28); 21,7; 22,64; 23,3*	1,6*; 5,27(-28)	6	5/6

Characteristic of Luke

CADBURY 1920 160 [aorist]; GASTON 1973 65 [Lked?]

Literature

COLLISON 1977 72 [imperfect: noteworthy phenomena]; JEREMIAS 1980 69 [ἐπερωτάω + λέγων: red.].

ELLIOTT, James K., Ἐρωτᾶν and ἐπερωτᾶν in the New Testament. — FilolNT 2 (1989) 205-206.

ἐπέχω 1 + 2

1. be alert for; 2. hold firmly to; 3. watch (Lk 14,7; Acts 3,5); 4. stay on (Acts 19,22)

Characteristic of Luke
BOISMARD 1984 cb166; NEIRYNCK 1985

Literature
DENAUX 2009 IA[n]; JEREMIAS 1980 237: "Intransitiv gebrauchtes ἐπέχω findet sich im NT nur Lk 14,7/Apg 3,5; 19,22; 1 Tim 4,16".

ἐπηρεάζω 1 (Mt 0/1)   mistreat (Lk 6,28)

Literature
HAUCK 1934 [seltenes Alleinwort].

ἐπί 161/169 + 170/175 (Mt 122/132, Mk 71[72]/80)

1. upon (location) (Acts 5,30); 2. at (location) (Lk 22,30); 3. among (location) (Acts 1,21); 4. before (location) (Acts 25,12); 5. toward (extension) (Acts 20,13); 6. onto (extension); 7. upon (responsibility); 8. to (experiencer) (Acts 5,35; 7,11; 19,13); 9. by (instrument); 10. against (opposition) (Lk 12,52); 11. for (benefaction) (Acts 21,24); 12. and (addition); 13. over (authority) (Lk 1,33; Acts 8,27); 14. because of (reason) (Lk 1,29); 15. in order to (purpose); 16. concerning (content) (Acts 2,38); 17. in view of (basis) (Lk 4,25; Acts 4,27); 18. up to (degree) (Acts 4,17); 19. at, when (time) (Acts 3,1); 20. during (time) (Acts 13,31); 21. by (agent)

Word groups

ἐπί + genitive	Lk	Acts	Mt	Mk
ἐπί concerning time (SCad; VKa)	3,2[1]; 4,27	11,28[2]	1	1
ἐπί with composite verb ἀνα- (SCaa; VKc)	12,54		1	2
ἐπί with composite verb ἐπι- (SCab; VKb)	8,16 v.l.		2	0
ἐπί with composite verb κατα- (SCac; VKd)	12,42; 22,30[2]	2,30 v.l.; 6,3; 7,27; 8,28; 9,33; 10,11.34; 12,21; 17,26; 20,9[1]; 25,6.17	9	0
ὁ/ἡ/τὸ + ἐπί used as a noun (VKe)	8,13	12,20	1	2
other instances with genitive	2,14; 4,11.25[1].29; 5,18.24; 6,17; 8,16; 11,2*; 12,3; 17,31.34; 18,8; 20,37; 21,23. 25; 22,21.30[1].40.	2,19; 5,15.23.30; 8,27; 10,39; 12,20; 21,23.40; 23,30; 24,19.20.21; 25,9.10.26[1.2]; 26,2; 27,44[2]	22	14

→ ἀνατέλλω ἐπὶ δυσμῶν; ἐπὶ γῆς; ἐπὶ τῆς γῆς; ἐπὶ τῶν δωμάτων; ἐφ᾽ ἑαυτοῦ/ἑαυτῶν; εἰμι ἐπί; κάθημαι ἐπί; καθίζω ἐπί; καθίστημι ἐπί; κατάκειμαι ἐπί; κατοικέω ἐπί; ἐπὶ κλίνης; κρεμάννυμι ἐπὶ ξύλου; προάγω ἐπί; φέρω ἐπί; ἐπὶ χειρῶν

ἐπί + dative	Lk	Acts	Mt	Mk
ἐπί giving the basis for a state of being, an action or a result (SCbe)	1,14.29.47; 2,20.33.47; 4,4.4*.22.32; 5,5.9; 7,13; 9,43[1.2].48.49*; 11,22; 13,17; 15,7[1.2].10; 18,9; 20,26; 21,8; 24,47	3,10[2].12.16; 4,9.21; 5,35; 8,2; 11,19; 13,12; 14,3[1]; 15,31; 20,38; 26,6	10	10
ἐπί with composite verb ἀνα- (SCba)		4,9	0/1	1

ἐπί 233

	Lk	Acts	Mt	Mk
ἐπί with composite verb ἐπι- (SCbb; VKg)		8,16; 28,14*	1	0/1
ἐπί with composite verb κατα- (SCbc; VKh)	5,25 v.l.; 12,44	2,26; 3,10¹; 9,33 v.l.	1	0/2
ἐπί τούτῳ → ἐπὶ τοῦτο		3,12	0	0

→ ζῶ ἐπ᾿ ἄρτῳ; βαπτίζω ἐπὶ (τῷ) ὀνόματι; διαμερίζομαι ἐπί; ἐφ᾿ ἑαυτοῖς; εἰμι ἐπί; εἰς + ἐπί; ἐκπλήσσομαι ἐπί (τῇ διδαχῇ); ἐξίστημι ἐπί; ἐπιπίπτω ἐπί; ἔρχομαι + ἐπί; ζῶ ἐπί; κάθημαι ἐπί; καθίστημι ἐπί; κατάκειμαι ἐπί; μακροθυμέω ἐπί; πείθω ἐπί; πιστεύω ἐπί; προσέχω ἐπί; προστίθημι ἐπί; σπλαγχνίζομαι ἐπί

ἐπί + accusative	Lk	Acts	Mt	Mk
ἀναβαίνω ἐπὶ + καρδίαν (LN: begin to think)		7,23	0	0
ἐκτείνω τὰς χεῖρας ἐπί (LN: arrest)	22,53		0	0
ἐπί + adverb (VKt) BOISMARD 1984 Aa17		4,17; 10,16; 11,10; 20,9²; 24,4; 28,6	0	0
ἐπί with composite verb ἀνα- (SCca; VKm)	5,19; 10,6²; 19,4	7.18.23; 10,9; 14,10; 20,13²	3/4	1
ἐπί with composite verb ἐπανα- (VKp)	10,6¹		1	1
ἐπί with composite verb ἐπι- (SCcb; VKl)	1,12.16.17.35.48; 5,36; 9,38.62; 10,34; 15,5.20; 17,4*; 19,35; 20,19; 21,12¹.34.35¹	1,8; 4,29; 5,18.28²; 8,17.24; 9,17.35; 10,10 v.l.17.44; 11,11.15¹·².21; 13,11² v.l. 40*.50; 14,15; 15,10.17¹·².19; 19,12 v.l.16.17; 20,37; 21,27; 26,18.20; 27,20; 28,3	5/8	2[3]/5
ἐπί with composite verb κατα- (SCcc; VKn)	3,22; 5,11.25.27; 8,6; 12,14; 19,30; 21,35²; 22,44	2,3.30; 7,10¹·².27 v.l.; 10,11*; 17,26 v.l.; 21,32	2/3	4/5
ἐπὶ πλεῖον → ἐπὶ πολύ; cf. 2 Tit 2,16; 3,9; ἐπὶ πλείονας ἡμέρας Acts 27,20; ἐπὶ πλείονα χρόνον Acts 18,20		4,17¹; 20,9²; 24,4	0	0
ἐπὶ πολύ (LN: a long time) → ἐπὶ πλεῖον; cf. ἐπὶ πολλὰς ἡμέρας Acts 16,18		28,6	0	0
ἐπὶ τὴν κεφαλήν (LN: responsibility)		18,6	0	0
ἐπὶ τοῦτο → ἐπὶ τούτῳ; εἰς τοῦτο	4,43		0	0
ἐπὶ τρίς		10,16; 11,10	0	0
ἐπιστρέφω καρδίας + ἐπί (LN: make friendly toward)	1,17		0	0
ἐφ᾿ ἱκανόν (LN: for a long time)		20,11	0	0
πίπτω (+) ἐπί (LN: cause to suffer); cf. πίπτω ἐπί + gen. Mk 9,20; 14,35	8,6 v.l.8*; 11,17²; 13,4; 20,18¹·²; 23,30	1,26; 9,4; 10,25; 13,11²	6	1
ὁ/ἡ/τὸ ἐπί used as a noun (VKs)	8,13 v.l.		0	0
other instances with accusative	1,33.65; 2,8.25.40; 3,2²; 4,9.18.25³.36; 5,12; 6,29.35. 48.48*.49; 7,13 v.l. 44; 8,27; 9,1.5; 10,9.11*.19;	1,21; 2,17.18¹·²; 4,22.27².33; 5,5.11¹·²; 7,11.54.57; 8,1.26.32.36; 9,11.21.42; 10,10.45; 11,17.28¹; 12,10.12; 13,11¹·².51; 14,13; 16,19.31; 17,6.14.19; 18,12;	55	28

11,17[1].18.33; 12,11.49.53[3.4.5.6].58; 14,31; 15,4; 17,16; 19,5.14.23. 27.41.43.44; 21,10[1.2]. 12[2]; 22,52[1.2]; 23,1.28[1.2.3].33.44.48; 24,1.12.22.24	19, 6.12.13; 20,13[1]; 21,5.35; 22,19; 24,8*; 25,12; 26,16; 27,43.44[3]	

→ ἀναβαίνω ἐπί; ἀνάγω ἐπί; ἀπέρχομαι ἐπί; βασιλεύω ἐπί; ἐπὶ (...) τὴν γῆν; ἐγένετο
θάμβος/φόβος ἐπί; ἐφ᾽ ἑαυτόν/ούς; διαμερίζομαι ἐφ᾽ ἑαυτόν; ἐγείρομαι ἐπί; ἔθνος ἐπὶ
ἔθνος; εἰμι ἐπί; εἰς + ἐπί; εἰσέρχομαι ἐπί; ἐξέρχομαι ἐπί; ἐπιβάλλω τὴν χεῖρα ἐπ᾽ ἄροτρον
καὶ βλέπω εἰς τὰ ὀπίσω; ἐπιβιβάζω ἐπί; ἐπιπίπτω ἐπὶ τὸν τράχηλον; ἐπιστρέφω ἐπί;
ἐπιτίθημι ζυγὸν ἐπὶ τὸν τράχηλον; ἔρχομαι + ἐπί; ἐφίστημι ἐπί; ἥκω ἐπί; κάθημαι ἐπί;
καθίζω ἐπί; καθίστημι ἐπί; καταβαίνω ἐπί; κατάγω ἐπί; κατάκειμαι ἐπί; κατοικέω ἐπί; ὁ
κλῆρος πίπτει ἐπί; ἐπικαλέομαι τὸ ὄνομά τινος ἐπί τινα; πίπτω ἐπὶ πρόσωπον; πιστεύω
ἐπί; προέρχομαι ἐπὶ τὸ πλοῖον; ἐπὶ (τὸ) πρόσωπον (πάσης τῆς γῆς); ἐπὶ σάββατα τρία;
σπλαγχνίζομαι ἐπί; συνάγω ἐπὶ (τὸ αὐτό); τίθημι ἐπί; τρέχω ἐπί; τύπτω ἐπί; ὑπάγω ἐπί;
ἐπί + ὑπό + acc.; φέρω ἐπί; ἐπὶ χρόνον

Characteristic of Luke
HENDRIKS 1986 468

	Lk	Acts	Mt	Mk
εἰμὶ ἐπὶ τὸ αὐτό; cf. 1 Cor 7,5 BOISMARD 1984 cb16; NEIRYNCK 1985	17,35	1,15; 2,1.44	0	0
ἐπ᾽ ἀληθείας (LN: really; SCae) BOISMARD 1984 cb73; NEIRYNCK 1985; PLUMMER 1922 lix	4,25[1]; 20,21; 22,59	4,27[1]; 10,34	0	2
ἐπί + accusative of time (SCcd; VKk); cf. Rom 7,1; 1 Cor 7,39; Gal 4,1; Heb 11,30; 2 Pet 1,13 BOISMARD 1984 cb58; DENAUX 2009 L***; GOULDER 1989; HARNACK 1906 41.51; HAWKINS 1909 187; NEIRYNCK 1985	4,25[2]; 10,35; 12,25; 18,4	3,1; 4,5; 13,31; 16,18; 17,2; 18,20; 19,8.10.34; 20,11; 27,20	0	0/1
ἐπί + dative GOULDER 1989	1,14.29.47.59;2,20.3 3.47; 3,20; 4,4[1.2]*.22.32; 5,5.9; 7,13; 9,43[1.2].48; 11,22; 12,44.52[1.2].53[1.2] 53[3] v.l. 53[4] v.l.;13,17; 15,7[1.2].10; 16,26*; 18,7.9; 19,41 v.l.44 v.l.; 20,26; 21,6.8; 23,38; 24,25.47	2,26.38;3,10[1.2].11.12.16; 4,9.17[2].18.21; 5,9.28[1].35.40; 7,33; 8,2.16; 11,19; 13,12; 14,3[1.2]; 15,14*.31;20,38; 21,24; 26,6; 27,44[1]; 28,14*	18/21	16/22
ἐπὶ τὸ αὐτό (VKr) → συνάγω ἐπὶ τὸ αὐτό BOISMARD 1984 Eb33; GOULDER 1989*; NEIRYNCK 1985	17,35	1,15; 2,1.44.47; 4,26	1	0
ἐφ᾽ ὑμᾶς DENAUX 2009 L***; GOULDER 1989	10,6[2].9; 11,20; 12,14; 19,14; 21,12[1].34; 24,49	1,8.21	3	0

→ ἄγω ἐπί + acc.; ἀπάγω ἐπί + acc.; ἐπὶ τὴν αὔριον; γενόμενος ἐπὶ τοῦ τόπου; γίνομαι ἐπί
+ acc.; γίνομαι ἐπί + gen. of time; ἐγένετο θάμβος/φόβος ἐπί; εἰμι ἐπί + gen. of time; ἐν + ἐπί
+ acc./dat./gen.; ἐπέρχομαι ἐπί + acc.; ἐπιβάλλω τὰς χεῖρας ἐπί + acc.; ἐπέπεσεν φόβος ἐπί +
acc.; ἐπιπίπτω ἐπί + acc./dat./gen.; ἐπιστρέφω ἐπὶ τὸν θεόν/κύριον; ἐπιτίθημι τὰς χεῖρας ἐπί

+ acc.; ἐπὶ ἔτη; θαυμάζω ἐπί + dat.; ἵστημι ἐπί + gen.; κλαίω ἐπί; κρίνομαι ἐπί + gen.; ἐπὶ τῷ ὀνόματι; πιστεύω ἐπὶ τὸν κύριον; πνεῦμα + verb of movement + ἐπί + acc.; πορεύομαι ἐπί + acc.; πίπτω ἐπὶ τοὺς πόδας; τίθημι ἐπί; ἐπὶ τὸν τράχηλον; χαίρω ἐπί + dat.

Literature

COLLISON 1977 136 [ἐπί + accusative = against/before: noteworthy phenomena; ἐπ' ἀληθείας: linguistic usage of Luke: probable]; 137 [θαυμάζω ἐπί: linguistic usage of Luke: certain]; DENAUX 2009 1Aⁿ [εἰμὶ ἐπὶ τὸ αὐτό] [lAn: ἐπὶ τὸ αὐτό]; EASTON 1910 155 [θαυμάζω ἐπί: probably characteristic of L; not in Weiss]; 156 [κλαίω ἐπί: probably characteristic of L]; 158 [τόπος after ἐπί: probably characteristic of L]; 166 [ἔρχομαι ἐπί: cited by Weiss as characteristic of L, and possibly corroborative]; 167 [ἐπιπίπτω ἐπί: classed by Weiss as characteristic of L on insufficient (?) evidence]; GERSDORF 1816 256 [θαυμάζοντες ἐπὶ τοῖς λαλουμένοις]; JEREMIAS 1980 126: "ἐπί c.acc. de tempore findet sich im NT – abgesehen von der Wendung ἐφ' ὅσον (χρόνον) – ausschließlich im lk Doppelwerk"; 126 [ἐπ' ἀληθείας: trad.]; 192 [ἐπὶ τὴν αὔριον]: "ἐπί c. acc. de tempore ist lukanisch"; RADL 1975 410 ["in forensischem Zusammenhang"]; 425 [πορεύομαι ἐπί]; SCHÜRMANN 1957 52-53 [ἐπί + gen. auf die Frage "wo" ... gut als luk R möglich, aber geradesogut vorluk].

FERGUSON, E., "When You Come together": *Epi To Auto* in Early Christian Literature. — *Restoration Quarterly* 16 (1973) 202-208.

GUERRA GÓMEZ, Manuel, Análisis filológico-teológico y traducción del himno de los ángeles en Belén, 1989. Esp. 46-47: "Ἐπὶ γῆς = 'sobre (en) la tierra'".

READ-HEIMERDINGER, Jenny, *The Bezan Text of Acts*, 2002. Esp. 197-201: "ἐπί".

WILCOX, Max, Semitisms in the New Testament, 1984. Esp. 1010-1011: "ἐπὶ τὸ αὐτό (Acts 2:47; cf. also 1:15; 2:44, 46 [D])".

ἐπιβάλλω 5 + 4 (Mt 2, Mk 4)

1. throw on; 2. put on, lay on (Lk 5,36; 9,62; 20,19; 21,12); 3. splash into; 4. belong to (Lk 15,12); 5. think about seriously; 6. begin

Word groups	Lk	Acts	Mt	Mk
ἐπιβάλλω + ἐπίβλημα (*VK*a); cf. ἐπιράπτω ἐπίβλημα Mk 2,21	5,36		1	0
ἐπιβάλλω τὴν χεῖρα ἐπ' ἄροτρον καὶ βλέπω εἰς τὰ ὀπίσω (*LN*: start to do and then hesitate)	9,62		0	0
ἐπιβάλλω intransitive (*VK*b)	15,12		0	2

Characteristic of Luke	Lk	Acts	Mt	Mk
ἐπιβάλλω τὴν χεῖρα/τὰς χεῖρας (*LN*: arrest; *SC*a); cf. Jn 7,30.44 BOISMARD 1984 cb108; NEIRYNCK 1985	9,62; 20,19; 21,12	4,3; 5,18; 12,1; 21,27	1	1

Literature

VON BENDEMANN 2001 416: "ἐπιβάλλειν findet sich zwar bei Lukas relativ häufig, aber in anderer Bedeutung, insbesondere mit singularischem Objekt χεῖρα immer in malam partem"; DENAUX 2009 lAn [ἐπιβάλλω τὴν χεῖρα/τὰς χεῖρας + dative or + ἐπί + accusative]; RADL 1975 410 [ἐπιβάλλω; ἐπιβάλλω τὰς χεῖρας (τὴν χεῖρα) (ἐπί)].

DERRETT, J. Duncan M., *Law in the New Testament*. London: Darton, XLVI-503 p. Esp. 104.106 [Lk 15,12].

ἐπιβιβάζω 2 + 1 | cause to mount

Word groups	Lk	Acts	Mt	Mk
ἐπιβιβάζω + ἐπί + accusative DENAUX 2009 L[n]	10,34; 19,35		0	0

Characteristic of Luke

BOISMARD 1984 Ab121; CREDNER 1836 138; HARNACK 1906 29; HAWKINS 1909LA; MORGENTHALER 1958*; NEIRYNCK 1985; PLUMMER 1922 lii; VOGEL 1899A

Literature

DENAUX 2009 La[n]; HAUCK 1934 [seltenes Alleinwort]; JEREMIAS 1980 192 [red.].

FERNÁNDEZ MARCOS, Natalio, La unción de Salomón y la entrada de Jesús en Jerusalén: 1 Re 1,33-40/Lc 19,35-40. — *Bib* 68 (1987) 89-97. Esp. 90-92: "Ἐπεβίβασαν τὸν Ἰησοῦν".

ἐπιβλέπω 2

1. notice; 2. pay attention to (Lk 1,48; 9,38); 3. help (Lk 9,38); 4. pay respect to

Literature

DENAUX 2009 L[n]; GERSDORF 1816 200 [ὅτι ἐπέβλεψεν ἐπὶ τὴν ταπείνωσιν]; HARNACK 1906 141.151 [ἐπίβλεπειν ἐπί].

ἐπίβλημα 2 (Mt 1, Mk 1)   patch

Word groups	Lk	Acts	Mt	Mk
ἐπιβάλλω + ἐπίβλημα; cf. ἐπιράπτω ἐπίβλημα Mk 2,21	5,36		1	0

ἐπιγινώσκω 7 + 13 (Mt 6, Mk 4)

1. know about (Lk 1,4); 2. understand (Acts 25,10); 3. learn about (Lk 7,37; Acts 22,24; 23,28; 28,1); 4. recognize (Lk 24,16; Acts 12,14); 5. acknowledge

Word groups	Lk	Acts	Mt	Mk
βούλομαι + ἐπιγνῶναι → βούλομαι **γνῶναι**		23,28	0	0
δύναμαι + ἐπιγνῶναι→ δύναμαι + **γνῶναι** (Acts 17,19; 21,34)		24,8.11	0	0
ἐπιγινώσκω περί + genitive (*VK*b)	1,4	24,8	0	0

Characteristic of Luke

MORGENTHALER 1958A

	Lk	Acts	Mt	Mk
ἐπιγινώσκω + ὅτι (*VK*a) → **γινώσκω** + ὅτι; cf. Rom 1,32; 2 Cor 1,14; 13,5 BOISMARD 1984 cb89; DENAUX 2009 lA*; GOULDER 1989; HARNACK 1906 38; NEIRYNCK 1985	1,22; 7,37; 23,7	3,10; 4,13; 19,34; 22,29; 24,11; 28,1	1	1

Literature

COLLISON 1977 94 [noteworthy phenomena]; EASTON 1910 167 [ἐπιγινώσκω (ὅτι): classed by Weiss as characteristic of L on insufficient (?) evidence]; GERSDORF 1816 162 [ἵνα ἐπιγνῷς περὶ ὧν κατηχήθης λόγων τὴν ἀσφάλειαν]; JEREMIAS 1980 314: "Das Kompositum ἐπιγινώσκω schreibt Lukas gern (…). In der Bedeutung 'Wiedererkennen' kommt es nur bei ihm vor"; RADL 1975 402 [βούλομαι (ἐπι)γνῶναι]; 406 [δύναμαι + (ἐπι)γνῶναι]; 410 [ἐπιγινώσκω].

DANOVE, Paul, Verbs of Experience, 1999. Esp. 159.174.

ἐπιγραφή 2 (Mt 1, Mk 2)	inscription (Lk 20,24; 23,38)

ἐπιδείκνυμι 1/3 + 2 (Mt 3)

1. cause to be seen (Lk 17,14; Lk 24,40*); 2. show to be true (Acts 18,28)

Word groups	Lk	Acts	Mt	Mk
ἐπιδείκνυμι to make clear (VKa) → δείκνυμι		18,28	0	0
ἐπιδείκνυμι imperative → (ἀνα)δείκνυμι imperative	17,14		0	0

ἐπιδίδωμι 5/6 + 2 (Mt 2)

1. give to (Lk 4,17; 11,11.12; 24,30.42); 2. yield (Acts 27,15)

Word groups	Lk	Acts	Mt	Mk
ἐπιδίδωμι (+) αἰτέω → δίδωμι + αἰτέω/ζητέω; λαμβάνω/ παρατίθημι + αἰτέω; εὑρίσκω + (ἀνα/ἐπι)ζητέω; cf. ἀποδίδωμι + αἰτέω Mt 27,58	11,11.12		2	0
ἐπιδίδωμι + ἄρτον → δίδωμι ἄρτον	24,30		0	0
ἐπιδίδωμι + ἐσθίω	24,42(-43v.l.)		0	0
ἐπιδίδωμι nautical term (VKa)		27,15	0	0

Characteristic of Luke

BOISMARD 1984 cb76; DENAUX 2009 L***; GOULDER 1989; HAWKINS 1909 L; NEIRYNCK 1985

Literature

HAUCK 1934 [Vorzugswort].

CHILTON, Bruce, Announcement in Nazara, 1981. Esp. 155.

ἐπιζητέω 2/3 + 3 (Mt 3, Mk 0/1)

1. try to find out (Lk 4,42; Acts 12,19); 2. desire (Lk 12,30; Acts 13,7)

Word groups	Lk	Acts	Mt	Mk
ἐπιζητέω + εὑρίσκω → (ἀνα)ζητέω + εὑρίσκω; ζητέω + δίδωμι; αἰτέω + (ἐπι)δίδωμι/λαμβάνω		12,19	0	0
ἐπιζητέω σημεῖον (VKa) → ζητέω σημεῖον	11,29*		2	0/1
ἐπιζητέω + infinitive (VKb)		13,7	0	0

ἐπιθυμέω 4 + 1 (Mt 2)

1. desire greatly (Lk 15,16; 16,21; 17,22; 22,15); 2. lust (Acts 20,33)

Word groups	Lk	Acts	Mt	Mk
ἐπιθυμέω + genitive (VKc)		20,33	0/1	0

Characteristic of Luke

DENAUX 2009 L***†; GOULDER 1989*; HAWKINS 1909 †18

	Lk	Acts	Mt	Mk
ἐπιθυμία ἐπιθυμέω (VKb) HARNACK 1906 43; PLUMMER 1922 lxiii	22,15		0	0

Literature

COLLISON 1977 94 [noteworthy phenomena]; HAUCK 1934 [Vorzugswort]; REHKOPF 1959 93 [vorlukanisch]; SCHÜRMANN 1953 5-7 [ἐπιθυμία ἐπιθύμησα Lk 22,15: vermutlich luk R einer vorluk T]; 1961 280 [protoluk R weniger wahrscheinlich].

ἐπιθυμία 1 (Mk 1)

1. deep desire (Lk 22,15); 2. lust

Characteristic of Luke	Lk	Acts	Mt	Mk
ἐπιθυμία ἐπιθυμέω (VKc) HARNACK 1906 43; PLUMMER 1922 lxiii	22,15		0	0

ἐπίκειμαι 2 + 1

1. lie on; 2. press against (Lk 5,1); 3. be in force; 4. keep on (Lk 23,23); 5. exist

Literature

DENAUX 2009 La^n; JEREMIAS 1980 129: "ἐπίκειμαι: kommt in der Bedeutung 'be-, herandrängen, zusetzen' im NT nur im lk Doppelwerk vor".

ἐπικρίνω 1

decide (Lk 23,24)

Literature

HAUCK 1934 [seltenes Alleinwort].

KILPATRICK, George D., Ἐπιθύειν and ἐπικρίνειν in the Greek Bible. — ZNW 74 (1983) 151-153; = ID., Principles and Practice, 1990, 191-194.

ἐπιλαμβάνομαι 5 + 7 (Mt 1, Mk 1)

1. take hold of (Lk 9,47; 14,4; 23,26); 2. arrest (Acts 21,33); 3. trap (Lk 20,20.26); 4. help; 5. be concerned for; 6. experience

Word groups	Lk	Acts	Mt	Mk
ἐπιλαμβάνομαι metaphorically (VKa) DENAUX 2009 L^n	20,20.26		0	0

Characteristic of Luke

CADBURY 1920 172.175; CREDNER 1836 138; DENAUX 2009 L***; GASTON 1973 64 [Lked]; GOULDER 1989*; HAWKINS 1909 L; PLUMMER 1922 lx

	Lk	Acts	Mt	Mk
ἐπιλαβόμενος + finite verb BOISMARD 1984 Bb18; DENAUX 2009 IA*; NEIRYNCK 1985	9,47; 14,4; 23,26	9,27; 16,19; 17,19; 18,17; 21,30; 23,19	0	0

ἐπιλαμβάνομαι τινα	9,47; 23,26	9,27; 16,19; 18,17	0	0
BOISMARD 1984 Ab52; NEIRYNCK 1985				

Literature

COLLISON 1977 49 [linguistic usage of Luke: probable]; DENAUX 2009 IAⁿ [ἐπιλαμβάνομαι
τινα]; HAUCK 1934 [Vorzugswort]; JEREMIAS 1980 236: "lk Vorzugswort"; "Abgesehen von drei
Ausnahmen (Lk 20,20.26; Apg 21,33) erscheint das Verbum im Doppelwerk stets als Partizipium
aor.med. (ἐπιλαβόμενος), das den begleitenden Umstand nennt"; RADL 1975 410
[ἐπιλαμβάνομαι; ἐπιλαβόμενος].

BORMANN, Lukas, *Recht, Gerechtigkeit und Religion*, 2001. Esp. 181.
BURCHARD, Christoph, Fußnoten zum neutestamentlichen Griechisch, 1970. Esp. 165: "Act
9,27 ἐπιλαβόμενος".

ἐπιλανθάνομαι 1 (Mt 1, Mk 1)

1. forget; 2. neglect (Lk 12,6)

ἐπιλείχω** 1   lick (Lk 16,21)

Literature

HAUCK 1934 [seltenes Alleinwort].

ἐπιμελέομαι 2

1. take care of (Lk 10,34.35); 2. think about

Literature

DENAUX 2009 Lⁿ; HARNACK 1906 54; HAUCK 1934 [seltenes Alleinwort]; JEREMIAS 1980 192
[red.]; PAFFENROTH 1997 83-84 [pre-Lukan].

ἐπιμελῶς 1   carefully (Lk 15,8)

Literature

HARNACK 1906 54; HAUCK 1934 [seltenes Alleinwort]; JEREMIAS 1980 192 [red.];
PAFFENROTH 1997 83-84 [pre-Lukan].

ἐπιούσιος 1 (Mt 1)

1. daily (Lk 11,3); 2. today

Literature

BDAG 2000 376-377 [literature].

BAKER, Aelred, What Sort of Bread Did Jesus Want Us to Pray for? — *New Blackfriars*
54 (1973) 125-129.
BISCHOFF, A., Ἐπιούσιος. — *ZNW* 7 (1906) 266-271.
BLACK, Matthew, The Aramaic of τὸν ἄρτον ἡμῶν τὸν ἐπιούσιον (Matt. vi.11 = Luke
xi.3). — *JTS* 42 (1941) 186-189.
BOISMARD, Marie-Émile, « Notre Pain Quotidien » (Mt 6,11) . — *RB* 102 (1995) 371-378.

BOURGOIN, H., Le pain quotidien. — *Cahiers du Cercle Ernest Renan* (Paris) 25 (1977) 1-17.

—, Ἐπιούσιος expliqué par la notion de préfixe vide. — *Bib* 60 (1979) 91-96.

BRAUN, François-Marie, Le pain dont nous avons besoin. *Mt 6*,11; *Lc 11*,3. — *NRT* 100 (1978) 559-568.

DELEBECQUE, Édouard, *Études grecques*, 1976. Esp. 167-181: "Le pain du *Pater* (11,3)".

DEWAILLY, Louis-Marie, "Donne-nous notre pain": Quel pain? Note sur la quatrième demande du Pater. — *RSPT* 64 (1980) 561-588.

FALCONE, Sebastian A., The Kind of Bread We Pray for in the Lord's Prayer. — McNAMARA, Robert F. (ed.), *Essays in Honor of Joseph P. Brennan*. Rochester, NY: Saint Bernard's Seminary, 1976, 36-59.

HEMER, Colin, Ἐπιούσιος. — *JSNT* 22 (1984) 81-94.

HULTGREN, Arland J., The Bread of Petition of the Lord's Prayer. — *ATR* 11 (1990) 41-54.

KORTING, Georg, *Das Vaterunser und die Unheilabwehr: Ein Beitrag zur ἐπιούσιον-Debatte (Mt 6,11/Lk 11,3)* (NTAbh, NF 48), Münster: Aschendorff, 2004, XXVI-791 p. Esp. 1-199: "ἐπιούσιον in der Brotbitte des Vaterunsers (Mt 6,11/Lk 11,3) als ein philologisches Problem. Zum Forschungsstand".

METZGER, Bruce M., How Many Times Does "Epiousios" Occur Outside the Lord's Prayer? — *ExpT* 69 (1957-58) 52-54.

NIJMAN, M. & K.A. WORP, "ΕΠΙΟΥΣΙΟΣ" in a Documentary Paper?. — *NT* 41 (1999) 231-234.

NOBER, Petrus, Num bis relata sit, extra orationem Dominicam, vox epiousios? — *VD* 34 (1956) 349-351.

ORCHARD, Bernard, The Meaning of ton epiousion (Mt 6:11 = Lk 11:3). — *BTB* 3 (1973) 274-282.

SHEARMAN, Thomas G., "Our Daily Bread". — *JBL* 53 (1934) 110-117.

V[OGT], Ernst, Ὁ ἄρτος ὁ ἐπιούσιος = ὁ ἄρτος ὁ τῆς ἐπιούσης. — *Bib* 35 (1954) 136-137.

ἐπιπίπτω 2 + 6/8 (Mk 1)

1. press against (Lk 15,20); 2. happen (Lk 1,12; Acts 19,17)

Word groups	Lk	Acts	Mt	Mk
ἐπιπίπτω + dative (*VK*a)		20,10	0	1
ἐπιπίπτω + ἐπί + dative (*VK*b) → ἐπέπεσεν φόβος ἐπί + acc.; **πίπτω** ἐπί + acc.		8,16	0	0
ἐπιπίπτω ἐπὶ τὸν τράχηλον (*LN*: embrace; *SC*b) DENAUX 2009 LAⁿ	15,20	20,37	0	0
ἐπιπίπτει (+) τὸ πνεῦμα τὸ ἅγιον (*SC*c)		8,(15-)16; 10,44; 11,15	0	0
ἐπιπεσών → (ἐμ/κατα/περι/προσ)πεσών; cf. Jn 12,24; Rom 11,22; 1 Cor 14,25; ἀναπεσών Jn 13,25; παραπεσών Heb 6,6		20,37	0	0

Characteristic of Luke

BOISMARD 1984 Bb89; CREDNER 1836 138.141 [as a description for extraordinary being]; DENAUX 2009 IA*; HAWKINS 1909 187; NEIRYNCK 1985; PLUMMER 1922 lx

	Lk	Acts	Mt	Mk
φόβος + ἐπιπίπτειν (and cognate πίπτειν) ἐπί τινα (*SC*a) → ἐγένετο θάμβος/φόβος ἐπί + acc.; ἐπλήσθην θάμβους/φόβου; φόβος λαμβάνει + acc. BOISMARD 1984 cb126; HARNACK 1906 71.74; NEIRYNCK 1985; VOGEL 1899c	1,12	19,17	0	0

| ἐπιπίπτω aorist → (ἀνα/ἐμ/κατα/περι/προσ/συμ) πίπτω aorist; cf. ἀποπίπτω Acts 9,18; ἐκπίπτω Acts 12,7; 27,17.26.29.32 DENAUX 2009 lA* | 1,12; 15,20 | 10,44; 11,15; 19,17; 20,10.37 | 0 | 0 |
| ἐπιπίπτω ἐπί + acc./dat./gen. DENAUX 2009 lA*; HARNACK 1906 71 | 1,12; 15,20 | 8,16; 10,44; 11,15; 19,17; 20,37 | 0 | 0 |

Literature

DENAUX 2009 LAⁿ [φόβος + ἐπιπίπτειν (and cognate πίπτειν) ἐπί τινα]; EASTON 1910 167 [ἐπιπίπτω ἐπί: classed by Weiss as characteristic of L on insufficient (?) evidence]; JEREMIAS 1980 32: "φόβος ἐπέπεσεν ἐπ᾽ αὐτὸν: Diese Wendung ist ein Septuagintismus"; RADL 1975 410 [ἐπιπίπτω; ἐπιπίπτω ἐπί].

WILCOX, Max, *The Semitisms in Acts*, 1965. Esp. 67 [Lk 15,20; Acts 20,37].

ἐπιπορεύομαι 1   arrive (Lk 8,4)

Literature
HAUCK 1934 [seltenes Alleinwort].

ἐπιρίπτω 1   throw on (Lk 19,35)

Literature
HAUCK 1934 [seltenes Alleinwort].

ἐπισιτισμός 1   food (Lk 9,12)

Literature
HAUCK 1934 [seltenes Alleinwort].

ἐπισκέπτομαι 3 + 4 (Mt 2)

1. select carefully (Acts 6,3); 2. visit (Lk 1,68.78; 7,16; Acts 7,23); 3. take care of (Acts 15,14); 4. be present

Word groups

	Lk	Acts	Mt	Mk
ἐπισκέπτομαι + infinitive (VKa)		15,14	0	0

Characteristic of Luke
BOISMARD 1984 cb86; HARNACK 1906 143; NEIRYNCK 1985; PLUMMER 1922 lx

Literature
COLLISON 1977 95 [noteworthy phenomena]; DENAUX 2009 lAn; EASTON 1910 154 [probably characteristic of L]; GERSDORF 1816 206 [ὅτι ἐπεσκέψατο]; 212 [ἐπισκέψεται ἡμᾶς ἀνατολὴ ἐξ ὕψους]; JEREMIAS 1980 73 [trad.].

DENAUX, Adelbert, The Theme of Divine Visits and Human (In)Hospitality in Luke-Acts: Its Old Testament and Graeco-Roman Antecedents. — VERHEYDEN, J. (ed.), *The Unity of Luke-Acts*, 1999, 255-279. Esp. 271-272.275-276.

GEHMAN, Henry S., ἐπισκέπτομαι, ἐπισκέψις, ἐπίσκοπος, and ἐπισκοπή in the Septuagint in Relation to פקד and other Hebrew Roots - a Case of Semantic Development Similar to that of Hebrew. — *VT* 22 (1972) 197-207. [NTA17, 38]

ἐπισκιάζω 2 + 1 (Mt 1, Mk 1) | cast a shadow upon (Lk 1,35; 9,34; Acts 5,15)

Literature
BDAG 2000 379 [literature].

ALLGEIER, Arthur, Ἐπισκιάζειν Lk 1,35. — *BZ* 14 (1917) 338-343.
HEHN, Johannes, Ἐπισκιάζειν Lk 1,35. — *BZ* 14 (1917) 147-152.
LEE, John A.L. – HORSLEY, G.H.R., A Lexicon of the New Testament, 2, 1998. Esp. 76.
SCHNEIDER, Gerhard, Lk 1,34. 35 als redaktionelle Einheit. — *BZ* NF 15 (1971) 255-259.
  Esp. 256-257: "Lk 1,35 ist nach Wortschatz, Stil und Theologie 'lukanisch'".
—, Jesu geistgewirkte Empfängnis (Lk 1,34f): Zur Interpretation einer christologischen Aussage. — *TPQ* 119 (1971) 105-116. Esp. 110; = ID., *Lukas, Theologe der Heilsgeschichte*, 1985, 86-97. Esp. 91.

ἐπισκοπή 1 + 1
1. visitation (Lk 19,44); 2. office as a church leader (Acts 1,20); 3. position of responsibility (Acts 1,20)

Literature
EASTON 1910 154 [probably characteristic of L].
See also ἐπισκέπτομαι.

GEHMAN, Henry S., ἐπισκέπτομαι, ἐπισκέψις, ἐπίσκοπος, and ἐπισκοπή in the Septuagint in Relation to פקד and other Hebrew Roots - a Case of Semantic Development Similar to that of Hebrew. — *VT* 22 (1972) 197-207. [NTA17, 38]

ἐπιστάτης 7 | master

Word groups

Word groups	Lk	Acts	Mt	Mk
Ἰησοῦ ἐπιστάτα	17,13		0	0

Characteristic of Luke
CREDNER 1836 134; DENAUX 2009 L***; GASTON 1973 64 [Lked]; GOULDER 1989*; HAWKINS 1909 L

	Lk	Acts	Mt	Mk
ἐπιστάτα DENAUX 2009 L***; PLUMMER 1922 lii	5,5; 8,24[1.2].45; 9,33.49; 17,13		0	0

Literature
HAUCK 1934 [häufiges Alleinwort]; JEREMIAS 1980 132: "ἐπιστάτης begegnet im NT ausschließlich im dritten Evangelium (7mal), und zwar stets als am Satzanfang stehende Anrede an Jesus"; SCHÜRMANN 1957 28 [ἐπιστάτα luk Sprachgebrauch].

BORMANN, Lukas, *Recht, Gerechtigkeit und Religion*, 2001. Esp. 136.
BRANDT, Pierre-Yves & Alessandra LUKINOVICH, L'adresse à Jésus dans les évangiles synoptiques. — *Bib* 82 (2001) 17-50. Esp. 33-34.
GLOMBITZA, Otto, Die Titel διδάσκαλος und ἐπιστάτης für Jesus bei Lukas. — *ZNW* 49 (1958) 275-278.

ἐπιστρέφω 7/8 + 11 (Mt 4/5, Mk 4)

1. return (Lk 2,39); 2. change one's beliefs; 3. cause to change beliefs (Lk 1,16); 4. change one's ways; ἐπιστρέφομαι: 5. turn around

Word groups

Word groups	Lk	Acts	Mt	Mk
ἐπιστρέφω (+) εἰς (VKc)	2,39	3,19; 26,18	1	0
ἐπιστρέφω (+) ἐπί + accusative (VKa)	1,16.17; 17,4 v.l.	9,35; 11,21; 14,15; 15,19; 26,18.20	0/1	0
ἐπιστρέφω καρδίας + ἐπί + accusative (LN: make friendly toward)	1,17		0	0
ἐπιστρέφω εἰς τὰ ὀπίσω (VKd)	17,31		1	1
ἐπιστρέφω πρός (VKb)	17,4	3,19 v.l.; 9,40	1	0
ἐπιστρέφω transitive (VKe) DENAUX 2009 Lⁿ	1,16.17		0	0

Characteristic of Luke

CREDNER 1836 138; GOULDER 1989; MORGENTHALER 1958A

	Lk	Acts	Mt	Mk
ἐπιστρέφω ἐπὶ (τὸν) θεόν/κύριον (SCa) BOISMARD 1984 Ab25; NEIRYNCK 1985	1,16	9,35; 11,21; 14,15; 15,19; 26,18.20	0	0
ἐπιστρέφω + μετανοέω BOISMARD 1984 Ab136; NEIRYNCK 1985	17,4	3,19; 26,20	0	0
ἐπιστρέψας → ὑποστρέψας; cf. Jam 5,20; 2 Pet 2,22; Rev 1,12; cf. ἀναστρέψας Acts 5,22; συστρέψας Acts 28,3 CREDNER 1936 139	22,32	9,40; 15,36; 16,18	0	0

Literature

COLLISON 1977 128 [ἐπιστρέφω εἰς: noteworthy phenomena]; DENAUX 2009 lAⁿ [ἐπιστρέφω ἐπὶ (τὸν) θεόν/κύριον; ἐπιστρέφω + μετανοέω; ἐπιστρέψας]; EASTON 1910 160-161 [cited by Weiss as characteristic of L, and possibly corroborative]; GERSDORF 1816 185 [ἐπιστρέφειν ἐπὶ τὸν θεόν/κύριον]; HAUCK 1934 [Vorzugswort]; SCHÜRMANN 1957 108-109 [ἐπιστρέψας: wahrscheinlich luk R].

GEORGE, Augustin, La conversion. — ID., Études, 1978, 351-368.

HEZEL, Francis X., "Conversion" and "Repentance" in Lucan Theology. — BiTod 37 (1968) 2596-2602.

JUNG, Chang-Wook., Infancy Narrative, 2004. Esp. 111-112 [ἐπιστρέψαι - ἐπί].

LEE, R.E., Luke xxii.32. — ExpT 38 (1926-27) 233-234.

MÉNDEZ-MORATALLA, Fernando, The Paradigm of Conversion in Luke. London – New York: T&T Clark, 2004, XII-255 p. Esp. 15-18: "Linguistic Analysis".

MICHIELS, Robrecht, La conception lucanienne de la conversion. — ETL 41 (1965) 42-78.

PICKAR, Charles H., The Prayer of Christ for Saint Peter. — CBQ 4 (1942) 133-140. Esp. 137-140 [Lk 22,31-32].

PRETE, Benedetto, Il testo di Luca 24,47: "Sarà predicata a tutte le genti la conversione per il perdono dei peccati". — ID., L'opera di Luca, 1986, 328-351. Esp. 342-344: "Il vocabolario degli Atti sulla conversione".

RIESENFELD, Harald, Omvändelse i Lukasevangeliet. — SEÅ 35 (1971) 44-60.

TAEGER, Jens-Wilhelm, Der Mensch und sein Heil, 1982. Esp. 127-130: "ἐπιστροφή/ἐπιστρέφειν ἐπὶ τὸν κύριον ([τὸν θεόν])"; 139-147: "μετανοεῖν καὶ ἐπιστρέφειν".

THOMSON, P., ἐπιστρέφω (Luke xxii.32). — ExpT 38 (1926-27) 468.

ἐπισυνάγω 3 (Mt 3, Mk 2)

1. cause to come together (Lk 13,34); ἐπισυνάγομαι: 2. come together (Lk 12,1; 17,37)

Word groups	Lk	Acts	Mt	Mk
ἐπισυνάγομαι passive → (ἀν/ἀπ/εἰσ/κατ/συν)άγομαι passive	12,1; 17,37		0	1
ἐπισυνάγω transitive → (ἀν/ἀπ/εἰσ/ἐξ/κατ/προ/προσ/ συν)άγω transitive	12,1; 13,37; 17,37		2	2

Literature

HAUCK 1934 [Vorzugswort].

ἐπισχύω 1   persist in

Word groups	Lk	Acts	Mt	Mk
ἐπισχύω λέγων	23,5		0	0

Literature

HAUCK 1934 [seltenes Alleinwort]; JEREMIAS 1980 69 [ἐπισχύω + λέγων: red.].

ἐπιτάσσω 4 + 1 (Mk 4)   command

Word groups	Lk	Acts	Mt	Mk
ἐπιτάσσω τοῖς + πνεύμασιν (VKa)	4,36		0	1

Characteristic of Luke

PLUMMER 1922 1x

Literature

MAKUJINA, John, Verbs Meaning "Command" in the New Testament: Determining the Factors Involved in the Choice of Command-Verbs. — EstBíb 56 (1998) 357-369. Esp. 358-359: "Παραγγέλλω"; 359-361: "Κελεύω"; 361-362: "Ἐντέλλω"; 362-364: "Διαστέλλω"; 364-366: "-τάσσω complex"; 366-367: "Λέγω". [NTA 43, 57]

ἐπιτίθημι 5/6 + 14 (Mt 7, Mk 7[8]/9)

1. place on (Lk 4,40; 13,13; 15,5; 23,26); 2. add; 3. subject to (Lk 10,30; Acts 16,23) ἐπιτίθεμαι: 4. give (Acts 28,10); 5. attack (Acts 18,10)

Word groups	Lk	Acts	Mt	Mk
ἐπιτίθημι ζυγὸν ἐπὶ τὸν τράχηλον (LN: load down with obligations)		15,10	0	0
ἐπιτίθημι (+) (τὰς)χεῖρας + dative (SCa; VKa) → ἐπιτίθημι τὰς χεῖρας ἐπί + acc.; ἐπιβάλλω τὴν χεῖρα/τὰς χεῖρας + dative or + ἐπί + acc.; cf. ἐπιτίθημι τὴν χεῖρα + dative Mk 7,32; ἐπίθεσις τῶν χειρῶν Acts 8,18	4,40; 13,13	6,6; 8,19; 9,12; 13,3; 19,6; 28,8	2	3
ἐπιτίθημι τὰς χεῖρας ἐπί + acc. (SCa; VKb) → ἐπιτίθημι τὰς χεῖρας + dat.; ἐπιβάλλω τὴν χεῖρα/τὰς χεῖρας + dative or + ἐπί + acc.; cf. ἐπιτίθημι τὴν χεῖρα ἐπί + acc. Mt 9,18; τίθημι τὰς χεῖρας ἐπί + acc. Mk 10,16; ἐπίθεσις τῶν χειρῶν Acts 8,18 BOISMARD 1984 ca46; HARNACK 1906 42		8,17; 9,17	0	1[2]

Characteristic of Luke
MORGENTHALER 1958A

Literature
WELLS, Louise, *The Greek Language of Healing*, 1998. Esp. 202.

ἐπιτιμάω 12 (Mt 6/7, Mk 9/10)

1. rebuke (Lk 4,35.39); 2. command (Lk 8,24)

Word groups	Lk	Acts	Mt	Mk
ἐπιτιμάω + ἵνα (*VK*a)	18,39		2/3	3
ἐπιτιμάω + λέγω → **ἀπαγγέλλω/παραγγέλλω** + λέγω/εἶπον; cf. διαστέλλομαι + λέγω Mk 8,15; ἐντέλλομαι + λέγω Mt 17,9	4,35		1	4

Literature
JEREMIAS 1980 69 [ἐπιτιμάω + λέγων: red.].

ἐπιτρέπω 4 + 5 (Mt 2/3, Mk 2)   allow

Word groups	Lk	Acts	Mt	Mk
ἐπιτρέπομαι passive (*VK*a)		26,1; 28,16	0	0

Characteristic of Luke
GOULDER 1989; HAWKINS 1909 187

ἐπίτροπος 1 (Mt 1)

1. foreman (Lk 8,3); 2. guide

Literature
BORMANN, Lukas, *Recht, Gerechtigkeit und Religion*, 2001. Esp. 151.

ἐπιφαίνω 1 + 1

1. illuminate (Lk 1,79); ἐπιφαίνομαι: 2. appear (Acts 27,20)

Word groups	Lk	Acts	Mt	Mk
ἐπιφαίνω + σκότος	1,79		0	0

Characteristic of Luke
HARNACK 1906 54.73.146; VOGEL 1899B

Literature
DENAUX 2009 LAⁿ.

ἐπιφωνέω 1 + 3   cry out (Acts 12,22; 21,34; 22,24)

Word groups	Lk	Acts	Mt	Mk
ἐπιφωνέω + λέγω → **(ἀνα/προσ)φωνέω** + λέγω/εἶπον	23,21		0	0

Characteristic of Luke

BOISMARD 1984 Ab80; CADBURY 1920 177; CREDNER 1836 138; HAWKINS 1909LA; MORGENTHALER 1958*; NEIRYNCK 1985; PLUMMER 1922 lii; VOGEL 1899A

Literature

DENAUX 2009 IA[n]; HAUCK 1934 [seltenes Alleinwort]; JEREMIAS 1980 57: "Lukas hat eine Vorliebe für Worte der Stammsilbe -φων"; 69 [ἐπιφωνέω + λέγων: red.]; 304 "im NT nur im Doppelwerk"; RADL 1975 411.

ἐπιφώσκω 1 (Mt 1)	dawn (Lk 23,54)

Literature

BLACK, Matthew, *An Aramaic Approach to the Gospels and Acts*, 1967. Esp. 136-138.
GARDNER-SMITH, Percival, Ἐπιφωσκεῖν. — *JTS* 27 (1925-26) 179-181.
VAN WIELE, Inge, *De inleiding op het lege-grafverhaal (Lc 23,54-56a): Een filologisch-retorische analyse*. Diss. lic. Leuven, 1996, XXVII-130 p. (dir. A. Denaux). Esp. 71-91.

ἐπιχειρέω 1 + 2	try (Lk 1,1; Acts 9,29; 19,13)

Characteristic of Luke

BOISMARD 1984 Ab122; CREDNER 1836 142; HAWKINS 1909LA; MORGENTHALER 1958*; NEIRYNCK 1985; PLUMMER 1922 lii; VOGEL 1899A

Literature

DENAUX 2009 IA[n]; GERSDORF 1816 160; HAUCK 1934 [seltenes Alleinwort].

ALEXANDER, Loveday, *The Preface to Luke's Gospel*, 1993. Esp. 109-110 [Lk 1,1].
CADBURY, Henri J., Commentary on the Preface of Luke, 1922. Esp. 493-494 [Lk 1,1].
GLÖCKNER, Richard, *Die Verkündigung des Heils beim Evangelisten Lukas*, 1975. Esp. 11-12: "Zum Begriff ἐπιχειρεῖν".
HEAD, Peter M., Papyrological Perspectives on Luke's Predecessors (Luke 1,1). — P.J. WILLIAMS – A.D. CLARKE – P.M. HEAD – D. INSTONE-BREWER (eds.), *The New Testament in Its First Century Setting: Essays on Context and Background in Honour of B.W. Winter on His 65th Birthday*, Grand Rapids, MI – Cambridge, Eerdmans, 2004, 30-45. Esp. 35-38.

ἐπιχέω 1	pour on (Lk 10,34)

Literature

HAUCK 1934 [seltenes Alleinwort].

ἑπτά 6 + 8 (Mt 9, Mk 8[9])	seven

Word groups	Lk	Acts	Mt	Mk
ἑπτὰ ἡμέραι (VKa)		20,6; 21,4.27; 28,14	0	0

ἑπτάκις 2 (Mt 2)	seven times (Lk 17,4[1.2])

Literature

EASTON 1910 161 [ἑπτάκις τῆς ἡμέρας: cited by Weiss as characteristic of L, and possibly corroborative].

ἐργάζομαι 1 + 3 (Mt 4, Mk 1)

1. work (Lk 13,14); 2. do business; 3. perform (Acts 10,35); 4. bring about

Word groups	Lk	Acts	Mt	Mk
ἐργάζομαι δικαιοσύνην; cf. ποιέω δικαιοσύνην Mt 6,1		10,35	0	0
ἔργον ἐργάζομαι (VKc)		13,41	1	1
ἐργάζομαι intransitive (VKa)	13,14	18,3	2	0

ἐργασία 1 + 4

1. behavior; 2. business (Acts 19,25); 3. profit (Acts 16,19)

Word groups	Lk	Acts	Mt	Mk
δίδωμι ἐργασίαν (LN: do one's best)	12,58		0	0

Characteristic of Luke

BOISMARD 1984 Bb68; HARNACK 1906 35.51; NEIRYNCK 1985; PLUMMER 1922 lix

Literature

DENAUX 2009 IA[n]; HARNACK 1907 43; HAUCK 1934 [häufiges Alleinwort]; JEREMIAS 1980 225 [red.].

ἐργάτης 4 + 1 (Mt 6)

1. worker (Lk 10,2[1.2].7); 2. doer (Lk 13,27)

Word groups	Lk	Acts	Mt	Mk
ἐργάτης + attributive genitive (VKb)	13,27		0	0
πάντες ἐργάται ἀδικίας	13,27		0	0

Literature

JEREMIAS 1980 232 [πάντες ἐργάται ἀδικίας: red.].

HARAGUCHI, Takaaki, Das Unterhaltsrecht des frühchristlichen Verkündigers: Eine Untersuchung zur Bezeichnung ἐργάτης im Neuen Testament. — ZNW 84 (1993) 178-195. Esp. 186-194: "Ἐργάτης in der synoptischen Tradition".

ἔργον 2 + 10/11 (Mt 6, Mk 2)

1. act (Lk 11,48; Acts 26,20); 2. work (Lk 24,39; Acts 13,2); 3. workmanship

Word groups	Lk	Acts	Mt	Mk
ἔργα ἀγαθά (VKb); cf. ἔργα καλά Mt 5,16		9,36	0	0
ἔργα τῶν χειρῶν		7,41	0	0
ἔργον ἐργάζομαι (VKd)		13,41[1]	1	1
ἔργον + λόγος (VKh)	24,19	7,22	0	0
DENAUX 2009 LA[n]				

Literature
KLEIST, James A., *Ergon* in the Gospels. — *CBQ* 6 (1944) 61-68.

ἔρημος 10/12 + 9 (Mt 8, Mk 9)
1. uninhabited (Acts 1,20); 2. lonely place (Lk 5,16); 3. forsaken

Word groups	Lk	Acts	Mt	Mk
ἔρημος + ἔπαυλις (*VK*d)		1,20	0	0
ἔρημος + ὁδός (*VK*b)		8,26	0	0
ἔρημος + οἶκος (*VK*c)	13,35*		1	0
τόπος ἔρημος (*LN*: lonely place; *VK*a)	4,42; 9,10*.12		2	5
ἔρημος as adjective (*SC*a)	4,42; 9,10*.12; 13,35*	1,20; 8,26	3	5

Characteristic of Luke
GASTON 1973 64 [Lked]

	Lk	Acts	Mt	Mk
αἱ ἔρημοι GOULDER 1989; HAWKINS 1909add	1,80; 5,16; 8,29		0	0

Literature
DENAUX 2009 Lⁿ [αἱ ἔρημοι]; GERSDORF 1816 212 [ἦν ἐν ταῖς ἐρήμοις]; JEREMIAS 1980 77: "Der generalisierende Plural αἱ ἔρημοι (subst.) findet sich im NT nur im dritten Evangelium (3mal)".

FUNK, Robert, The Wilderness. — *JBL* 78 (1959) 205-214.
MAHFOUZ, Hady, *La fonction littéraire et théologique de Lc 3,1-20*, 2003. Esp. 59-62 [ἐν τῇ ἐρήμῳ].

ἐρημόω 1 (Mt 1)   ἐρημόομαι: be destroyed (Lk 11,17)

ἐρήμωσις 1 (Mt 1, Mk 1)   be destroyed (Lk 21,20)

ἔριφος 1 (Mt 1)   he-goat (Lk 15,29)

ἔρχομαι 101/103 + 50/56 (Mt 114/121, Mk 85/87)
1. go, come (Lk 3,3); 2. come (Lk 7,33); 3. become; 4. happen to

Word groups	Lk	Acts	Mt	Mk
ὁ αἰὼν ὁ ἐρχόμενος → ὁ **αἰὼν** ἐκεῖνος	18,30		0	1
διελθὼν ... ἔρχομαι BOISMARD 1984 Aa41		12,10[1]; 14,24; 19,1; 20,2	0	0
ἔρχομαι + dative or genitive (*VK*h)	12,39.40; 13,14; 14,1; 24,1	9,17; 13,13	5	1
ἔρχομαι + infinitive → **ἀπ/εἰσ/ἐξ/ προ/προσ/συνέρχομαι** + inf.	1,59; 3,12; 4,34; 5,7[1].32; 6,18; 9,56*; 11,31; 12,49; 19,10	18,21*	11/12	5

ἔρχομαι + ἀπαγγέλλω/κηρύσσω → ἀπ/δι/εἰσ/κατ/προσέρχομαι / ἀποστέλλω / (εἰσ)πορεύομαι / ὑποστρέφω / φεύγω + ἀπαγγέλλω / διαγγέλλω / διηγέομαι / κηρύσσω	3,3	4,23	1	3
ἔρχομαι + ἀπό (SCa; VKf) → ἀνα/καταβαίνω / ἀπ/ἐξ/ἐπ/ κατέρχομαι / ἥκω / πορεύομαι / ὑποστρέφω ἀπό	13,7; 23,26	3,20; 18,2	0	4
ἔρχομαι + ἄχρι/ἕως (VKu) → (ἐξ)ἄγω / διώκω / δι/ἐξέρχομαι / καταβαίνω / πορεύομαι ἕως; cf. ἀπέρχομαι + ἕως Mt 26,36; προάγω + ἕως Mt 14,22 DENAUX 2009 lA^n	4,42; 19,13 v.l.	11,5; 20,6; 28,15	0	0
ἔρχομαι + διά + genitive (VKm)	17,1^2		1	1/2
ἔρχομαι (+) εἰς (LN: result in; SCb; VKa) → ἀπέρχομαι/ἥκω εἰς	2,27.51; 3,3; 4,16; 8,17.51; 14,1; 15,6.17; 16,28; 18,5; 23,42	8,40; 9,21; 11,20; 13,13.14*.51; 14,24; 15,30*; 17,1; 18,1.7*; 19,1*.27; 20,2.6.14. 15; 21,1.8; 22,11; 27,8; 28,13.14.15.16*. 23	21/23	21
ἔρχομαι εἰς τὴν βασιλείαν → εἰσέρχομαι/εἰσπορεύομαι εἰς τὴν βασιλείαν	23,42		0	0
ἔρχομαι + εἰς τὸ ἱερόν → ἀναβαίνω/εἰσάγω/εἰσέρχομαι/ εἰσπορεύομαι εἰς τὸ ἱερόν; cf. εἴσειμι εἰς τὸ ἱερόν Acts 3,3; 21,26	2,27		1	0
ἔρχομαι + εἰς Ἰερουσαλήμ → ἐξέρχομαι ἐξ Ἰερουσαλήμ; κατέρχομαι ἀπὸ Ἰεροσολύμων; cf. ἀπ/εἰσέρχομαι (+) εἰς Ἰεροσόλυμα Mt 16,21; 21,10; Mk 11,11; ἔρχομαι ἀπὸ Ἰεροσολύμων Mk 7,1		8,27	0	2
ἔρχομαι (+) εἰς τὴν οἰκίαν / τὸν οἶκον → ἀπ/εἰσέρχομαι εἰς τὴν οἰκίαν / τὸν οἶκον	8,51; 14,1; 15,6	18,7*	6	3
ἔρχομαι + ἐκ (VKk)	5,17; 11,31		1	0/1
ἔρχομαι (+) ἐν (SCc; VKg)	2,27; 9,26; 12,38*. 38; 13,14.35; 19,13. 38; 21,27; 23,42 v.l.		7/8	6
ἔρχομαι (+) ἐπί + accusative (SCd; VKc) → ἀπέρχομαι/ἥκω ἐπί + acc.	14,31; 19,5; 23,33; 24,1	7,11; 8,36; 12,10.12; 19,6; 24,8*	7	2
ἔρχομαι + ἐπί + dative (SCd; VKe)	21,8		1	1
ἔρχομαι (+) (ἀν)εὑρίσκω→ ἀπ/δι/εἰσ/ἐξ/κατέρχομαι / (εἰσ)πορεύομαι + εὑρίσκω	2,16.44(-45); 8,35; 11,25; 12,37.38.43; 13,6.7; 18,8; 22,45; 24,23	18,2; 19,1*; 28,14	5/6	6
ἔρχομαι μετά + accusative (VKp)		13,25; 19,4	1	0
ἔρχομαι + μετά + genitive (VKn)	14,31; 17,20^2; 21,27	25,23	3	5
ἔρχομαι (+) ὀπίσω (SCe; VKj)	9,23; 14,27		2	1/2

ἔρχομαι + παρά + accusative/ genitive (VKl) → ἐξέρχομαι παρά + acc./gen.	8,49		1	1
ἔρχομαι + πρός + accusative (SCf; VKb) → ἀπ/εἰσ/κατέρχομαι / ἥκω πρός + acc.	1,43; 6,47; 7,7; 8,35; 14,26; 15,20; 18,3.16; 22,45	4,23; 17,15; 20,6; 21,11; 22,13; 28,23	12/13	12/13
ἔρχομαι + σύν (VKx)		11,12	0	0
ἡμέραι ἐλεύσονται → ἡμέραι ἥξουσιν	5,35; 17,22; 21,6		1	1
κἀκεῖθεν ἔρχομαι → ἐκεῖθεν / κἀκεῖθεν + ἐξέρχομαι		20,15; 21,1; 28,15	0	0
ὁ υἱὸς τοῦ ἀνθρώπου (+) ἔρχομαι	7,34; 9,56*; 12,40; 18,8; 19,10; 21,27		7/9	3

→ τῷ ἐρχομένῳ **σαββάτῳ**; εἰς **φάνερον** ἐλθεῖν

Characteristic of Luke	Lk	Acts	Mt	Mk
ἔρχομαι + βασιλεία τοῦ θεοῦ → ἀναφαίνω/φθάνω + βασιλεία τοῦ θεοῦ DENAUX 2009 L***	11,2; 17,20[1.2]; 22,18		1	1
ἔρχομαι εἰς ἑαυτόν VOGEL 1899C	15,17		0	0
ἔρχομαι κατά + accusative (VKv) → ἐξέρχομαι κατά + gen. BOISMARD 1984 Ab123; NEIRYNCK 1985	10,32. 33	16,7	0	0
ἡμέραι ἔρχονται/ἐλεύσονται/ἥξουσιν DENAUX 2009 L***; GOULDER 1989*	5,35; 17,12; 19,43; 21,6; 23,29			

Literature

CADBURY 1920 177 ["Forms of ἔρχομαι or its compounds frequently disappear in Luke's reproduction of his sources"]; COLLISON 1977 50 [ἐρχόμενος: linguistic usage of Luke's "other source-material": certain]; DENAUX 2009 La[n] [ἔρχομαι κατά + accusative]; EASTON 1910 161 [ἔρχεσθαι πρός με, metaphorical, of Christ: cited by Weiss as characteristic of L, and possibly corroborative]; 166 [ἔρχομαι ἐπί: cited by Weiss as characteristic of L, and possibly corroborative]; 175 [ἐλθών, ἐρχόμενος: possible Hebraisms in the Lucan Writings, as classed by Dalman]; GERSDORF 1816 202-203 [καὶ ἐγένετο ἐν τῇ ἡμέρα τῇ ὀγδόῃ ἦλθον]; 203 [ἦλθον περιτεμνεῖν]; 239 [καὶ ἦλθαν σπεύσαντες]; 252 [καὶ ἦλθεν ἐν τῷ πνεύματι]; 265 [ἦλθον ἡμέρας ὁδὸν καὶ ἀνεζήτουν αὐτόν]; JEREMIAS 1980 84 [ἔρχομαι ἕως: red.]; 241 [ἔρχεται ὀπίσω μου: red.]; RADL 1975 411; SCHÜRMANN 1953 77-78 [ἦλθεν ἡ ἡμέρα Lk 22,7 vermutlich luk R].

GARCÍA PÉREZ, José Miguel, El relato del Buen Ladrón (Lc 23,39-43), 1986. Esp. 272-276: "El verbo ἔρχομαι".

LEVINSOHN, Stephen H., Ἔρχομαι and πορεύομαι in Luke-Acts: Two Orientation Strategies. — Notes on Translation 15 (2001) 13-30.

ἐρωτάω 15/16 + 7 (Mt 4, Mk 3/4)

1. ask (Lk 9,45); 2. ask for (Acts 3,3)

Word groups	Lk	Acts	Mt	Mk
ἐρωτάω + 2 accusatives (to ask someone something) (VKd) → ἐπερωτάω + 2 acc.	20,3		1/2	1
ἐρωτάω + ἀποκρίνομαι → αἰτέω/ἐπερωτάω + ἀποκρίνομαι	20,3; 22,68; 23,3		2	1
ἐρωτάω + ἵνα (VKb)	7,36; 16,27		0	1

ἐρωτάω + λέγω/εἶπον → **ἐπερωτάω** + λέγω/εἶπον	7,4*; 20,3; 23,3	1,6	2	0/1
ἐρωτάω + λόγος	20,3		1	1
ἐρωτάω + περί + genitive (VKe)	4,38; 9,45		1	0

Characteristic of Luke

DENAUX 2009 L***; GASTON 1973 65 [Lked?]; GOULDER 1989*; HAWKINS 1909 L; MORGENTHALER 1958L

	Lk	Acts	Mt	Mk
ἐρωτάω + infinitive (VKa); cf. Jn 4,40; 1 Thess 5,12	5,3;	3,3; 10,48; 16,39;	0	0
BOISMARD 1984 cb8; DENAUX 2009 1A*; NEIRYNCK 1985	8,37	18,20; 23,18		
ἐρωτάω ὅπως (VKc)	7,3;	23,20	0	0
BOISMARD 1984 Ab124; NEIRYNCK 1985	11,37			

Literature

DENAUX 2009 La[n] [ἐρωτάω ὅπως]; EASTON 1910 161 [ἐρωτάω "make request": cited by Weiss as characteristic of L, and possibly corroborative]; HAUCK 1934 [Vorzugswort]; JEREMIAS 1980 69 [ἐρωτάω + λέγων: red.]; 130: "lukanisches und johanneisches Vorzugswort"; "Da wir ὅπως als lukanisch erkannten (…), bestätigt sich die Regel, daß bei den Verben des Bittens die Ergänzung mit dem Infinitiv und mit ὅπως lukanisch ist, die Ergänzung mit ἵνα dagegen auf die Tradition zurückgeht".

ELLIOTT, James K., Ἐρωτᾶν and ἐπερωτᾶν in the New Testament. — *FilolNT* 2 (1989) 205-206.

ἐσθής 2 + 3   clothing (Lk 23,11; 24,4)

Word groups	Lk	Acts	Mt	Mk
ἐσθὴς λαμπρά (VKa) / λευκή	23,11	1,10; 10,30	0	0
DENAUX 2009 1A[n]				

Characteristic of Luke

PLUMMER 1922 lix; BOISMARD 1984 Db20; NEIRYNCK 1985

Literature

DENAUX 2009 1A[n]; EASTON 1910 167 [classed by Weiss as characteristic of L on insufficient (?) evidence]; JEREMIAS 1980 302 [red.].

MARCONI, Gilberto, La veste (esthēs) come categoria ermeneutica del "vedere" e semantica del divino negli scritti lucani, ovvero l'estetica non-umana di Luca. — *RivBib* 39 (1991) 3-23.

ἐσθίω/ἔσθω 33 + 7 (Mt 24, Mk 27/29)
1. eat (Lk 5,30); 2. destroy

Word groups	Lk	Acts	Mt	Mk
δίδωμι (+) φαγεῖν; cf. δίδωμι + πιεῖν Mt 27,34	8,55; 9,13		3	3
ἐπιδίδωμι + ἐσθίω	24,(42-)43		0	0
ἐσθίω (+) (τὸν) ἄρτον / (τοὺς) ἄρτους (SCb; VKb)	6,4[1.2]; 7,33; 9,(16-)17; 14,1.15	27,35	3	7
ἐσθίω (+) μετά + genitive	5,30; 7,36; 22,11.15		2	4
ἐσθίω (+) τὸ πάσχα (VKd)	22.8.11.15.16		1	2
ἐσθίω + χορτάζω	9,17; 15,16		3	3
λαμβάνω (+) ἐσθίω	6,4[1]; 9,(16-)17; 24,43	27,35	5	3/4

Characteristic of Luke	Lk	Acts	Mt	Mk
ἐσθίω καὶ πίνω (SCa; VKa) → συνεσθίω + συμπίνω; cf. τρώγω + πίνω Mt 24,38 DENAUX 2009 L*** (?); GOULDER 1989	5,30.33; 7,33.34; 10,7; 12,19.29.45; 13,26; 17,8$^{1.2}$.27.28; 22,30	9,9; 23,12. 21	6	0/1

Literature

COLLISON 1977 50 [ἐσθίειν + πίνειν: linguistic usage of Luke: probable; it may also have been a linguistic usage of Luke's "other source-material"]; SCHÜRMANN 1955 90-91 n. 312 [ἄρτον ἐσθίειν]; 1957 48-49 [φαγεῖν (καὶ) πιεῖν].

AMELING, W., Φάγωμεν καὶ πίωμεν. Griechische Parallellen zu zwei Stellen aus dem Neuen Testament. — Zeitschrift für Papyrologie und Epigraphik 60 (1985) 35-43. [Lk 12,19]

Ἐσλί 1
Esli (Lk 3,25)

ἑσπέρα 1 + 2
evening (Lk 24,29; Acts 4,3; 28,23)

Characteristic of Luke

BOISMARD 1984 Ab81; HAWKINS 1909LA; MORGENTHALER 1958*; NEIRYNCK 1985; PLUMMER 1922 lii; VOGEL 1899A

Literature

DENAUX 2009 lA^n; HAUCK 1934 [seltenes Alleinwort]; JEREMIAS 1980 318 [red.].

DENAUX, Adelbert & Inge VAN WIELE, The Meaning of the Double Expression of Time in Luke 24,29. — J. VERHEYDEN – G. VAN BELLE – J.G. VAN DER WATT (eds.), Miracles and Imagery in Luke and John. FS Ulrich Busse (BETL, 218), Leuven, 2008, 67-88. Esp. 70-77 [πρὸς ἑσπέραν].

Ἐσρώμ 1 (Mt 2)
Hezron (Lk 3,33)

ἔσχατος 6 + 3 (Mt 10/11, Mk 5)
1. final(ly) (Lk 11,26); 2. least important (Lk 14,10)

Word groups	Lk	Acts	Mt	Mk
τὰ ἔσχατα (VKe)	11,26		1	0
ἐσχάτη ἡμέρα (VKa)		2,17	0	0
ἔσχατος + πρῶτος (VKf)	11,26; 13,30$^{1.2}$		8	3
ἕως ἐσχάτου (VKc); cf. ἐπ᾽ ἐσχάτου Heb 1,2; 1 Pet 1,20; Jud 18		1,8; 13,47	0	0

Literature

BURCHARD, Christoph, Fußnoten zum neutestamentlichen Griechisch, 1970. Esp. 161-163: "Act 1,8 ἕως ἐσχάτου τῆς γῆς".

VAN UNNIK, Willem C., Der Ausdruck ἕως ἐσχάτου τῆς γῆς (Apostelgeschichte 1:8) und sein alttestamentlicher Hintergrund. — Studia Biblica et Semitica: Theodoro Christiano Vriezen qui munere professoris theologiae per XXV annos functus est, ab amicis, collegis, discipulis dedicata. Wageningen: Veenman & Zonen, 1966, 335-349; = ID., Sparsa Collecta, I, 1973, 386-401.

ἔσωθεν 3 (Mt 4, Mk 2)

1. from inside (Lk 11,7); 2. within (Lk 11,39.40); 3. the inner being

Word groups	Lk	Acts	Mt	Mk
τὸ (+) ἔσωθεν (VKb)	11,39.40		0	0
DENAUX 2009 L[n]				
ἔσωθεν + genitive (VKa)	11,39		0	0
ἔσωθεν + ἔξωθεν; cf. ἐντός + ἐκτός Mt 23,26	11,39.40		3	0

Literature

SCHWARZ, Günther, "Gebt ... den Inhalt als Almosen"? (Lukas 11,40.41). — BibNot 75 (1994) 26-30.

ἕτερος 32/33 + 17/18 (Mt 10/11, Mk 0[1])

1. different (Lk 9,29); 2. another (Lk 6,6)

Word groups	Lk	Acts	Mt	Mk
ἄλλος ... ἕτερος		4,12	1	0
ἐν ἑτέρῳ scripture (VKf)		13,35	0	0
ἐν ἑτέρῳ σαββάτῳ	6,6		0	0
ἕτερός τις (VKd) → **ἄλλος** τις		8,34; 27,1	0	0
ἕτερος + ἑαυτοῦ (VKe)		8,34	0	0
ἕτερος + οὗτος → **ἄλλος/ἐκεῖνος/**	20,11(-12)		1	0
κἀκεῖνος + οὗτος				
ἕτερος + πρῶτος	14,(18-)19; 16,(5-)7		1	0
ἕτερος + τρίτος	20,11(-12)		0	0
τῇ + ἑτέρᾳ (LN: the next day; VKg) → τῇ		20,15; 27,3	0	0
ἐχομένῃ ἡμέρᾳ				
οὐδεὶς ἕτερος → οὐδεὶς **ἄλλος**		17,21	0	0

Characteristic of Luke

BOISMARD 1984 Eb45; DENAUX 2009 L***; GASTON 1973 65 [Lked?]; GOULDER 1989*; HAWKINS 1909 L; HENDRIKS 1986 428.433.434.448.466; MORGENTHALER 1958LA; NEIRYNCK 1985

	Lk	Acts	Mt	Mk
δύο + noun + ὁ εἷς ... ὁ ἕτερος	7,41; 16,13[1.2]; 17,34.35;		2	0
DENAUX 2009 L***	18,10			
εἷς ... ἕτερος (VKa); cf. 1 Cor 4,6	7,41; 16,13[1.2]; 17,34.35;	23,6	2	0
BOISMARD 1984 cb109; DENAUX 2009 L***;	18,10; 23,(39-)40			
GOULDER 1989; NEIRYNCK 1985				
ἕτερος enumeration (VKc)	8,6.7.8; 14,19.20; 16,7;		2	0
DENAUX 2009 L***	19,20; 20,11			
ἕτεροι πολλοί (VKb) (SCh; VKl); cf. ἄλλοι	3,18; 8,3; 22,65	15,35	1	0
πολλοί Mk 7,4; 15,41; πολλοὶ ἄλλοι Mk 12,5				
BOISMARD 1984 Bb104; DENAUX 2009 La*;				
NEIRYNCK 1985				

Literature

VON BENDEMANN 2001 413: "nicht-duales ἕτερος entspricht lukanischem Stil"; BDR § 306,1: "Pronominaladjektiva: ἕτερος ist neben ἀμφότεροι im NT das einzige dualische Pronomen, aber nicht mehr bei allen Verfassern zu belegen (hauptsächlich Lk und Apg)"; COLLISON 1977 184 [linguistic usage of Luke: certain]; 185 [εἷς ... ἕτερος: noteworthy phenomenon]; HAUCK 1934

[Vorzugswort]; JEREMIAS 1980 110-111: "Kennzeichnend für den lukanischen Sprachgebrauch von ἕτερος ist, daß a) ἕτερος bei Lukas seine klassische dualische Bedeutung praktisch aufgegeben hat ... b) Abgesehen von ... (ὁ) εἷς/ὁ ἕτερος begegnet dualisches ἕτερος im NT nur an zwei Stellen im dritten Evangelium: Lk 5,7; 14,31; hier folgt Lukas seiner Vorlage. c) Die Gegenüberstellung (ὁ) εἷς/ὁ ἕτερος ... schreibt Lukas teils von sich aus (Apg 23,6, hier jedoch adjektivisch), teils übernimmt er sie aus der Tradition (Lk 16,13^{bis} par. Mt 6,24^{bis})"; RADL 1975 408 [εἷς ... ἕτερος]; SCHNEIDER 1969 84.103.163 [Vorzugswörter und -ausdrücke des Luk].

ELLIOTT, James K., The Use of ἕτερος in the New Testament. — ZNW 60 (1969) 140-141. [NTA 14, 414]

SANDIYAGU, Virginia R., Ἕτερός and ἄλλος in Luke. — NT 48 (2006) 105-131.

ἔτι 16/17 + 5 (Mt 8, Mk 5/6)

1. still (Lk 8,49); 2. in addition (Lk 14,26); 3. nevertheless

Word groups	Lk	Acts	Mt	Mk
ἔτι + absolute genitive (VKc)	8,49; 9,42; 14,32; 15,20; 22,47.60; 24,41	10,44	3	2
ἔτι δέ (VKd)	9,42; 14,26 v.l.; 15,20; 22,47 v.l.; 24,41	2,26	0/1	0
DENAUX 2009 Laⁿ				
ἔτι (αὐτοῦ) λαλοῦντος (SCa)	8,49; 22,47.60		3	2
ἔτι τε καί	14,26	21,28	0	0
DENAUX 2009 LAⁿ				
οὐκ/οὐδέ/οὔτε ... ἔτι (SCb; VKa)	16,2; 20,36.40*		0	0
→ μηκέτι; οὐκέτι; cf. οὐδὲν ...				
ἔτι Mt 5,13				
DENAUX 2009 Lⁿ				
τί ἔτι (VKb)	22,71		2	2

Characteristic of Luke
GOULDER 1989; MORGENTHALER 1958L

Literature
COLLISON 1977 153 [linguistic usage of Luke: likely; it may also be a linguistic use of Luke's "other source-material"; ἔτι ὤν:noteworthy phenomenon]; JEREMIAS 1980 241 [ἔτι δέ καί; ἔτι τε καί: red.]; RADL 1975 411 [ἔτι; ἔτι τε καί]; SCHNEIDER 1969 90.164: [ἔτι mit genitivus absolutus; ἔτι + Partizip + Nomen: Bei Luk beliebte Konstruktionen].

ἑτοιμάζω 14 + 1 (Mt 7, Mk 5/6)   make ready

Word groups	Lk	Acts	Mt	Mk
ἑτοιμάζω + accusative (person) (VKb)		23,23	0	0
ἑτοιμάζω + ἵνα (VKf)	22,8		0	1
ἑτοιμάζω interrogative (VKd)	17,8		0	0

Characteristic of Luke
GOULDER 1989; MORGENTHALER 1958L

Literature
VON BENDEMANN 2001 416; EASTON 1910 147 [especially characteristic of L].

ἕτοιμος 3 + 2 (Mt 4, Mk 1)   ready

Word groups	Lk	Acts	Mt	Mk
ἕτοιμος of human beings (VKa)	12,40; 22,33	23,15.21	2	0

Characteristic of Luke	Lk	Acts	Mt	Mk
ἕτοιμος + infinitive BOISMARD 1984 Db41; NEIRYNCK 1985	22,33	23,15	0	0

Literature

DENAUX 2009 LAⁿ [ἕτοιμος + infinitive]; SCHÜRMANN 1957 31 [ἕτοιμος(ἑτοίμως)].

ἔτος 15 + 11 (Mt 1, Mk 2) | year

Word groups	Lk	Acts	Mt	Mk
δι' ἐτῶν (LN: after years) → δι' ἡμερῶν		24,17	0	0
δώδεκα ἔτη	2,42; 8,42.43		1	2
ἐν ἔτει (VKb)	3,1		0	0
ἔτος + μήν → ἐνιαυτός + μήν	4,25		0	0
κατ' ἔτος (VKd)	2,41		0	0
ἕως ἐτῶν ὀγδοήκοντα τεσσάρων	2,37		0	0
τεσσεράκοντα ἔτη (LN: very long time); cf. Heb 3,10.17; cf. τεσσερακονταετής Acts 7,23; 13,18 BOISMARD 1984 Ba14		4,22; 7,30.36.42; 13,21	0	0

Characteristic of Luke

BOISMARD 1984 Eb42; DENAUX 2009 L***; GOULDER 1989*; HARNACK 1906 148; HAWKINS 1909 L; MORGENTHALER 1958LA; NEIRYNCK 1985; PLUMMER 1922 lx

	Lk	Acts	Mt	Mk
ἀπὸ/ἐξ ἐτῶν; cf. Rom 15,23 BOISMARD 1984 cb29; NEIRYNCK 1985	8,43	9,33; 24,10	0	0
εἰμι/γίνομαι ἐτῶν (VKa); cf. 1 Tim 5,9 BOISMARD 1984 cb77; CREDNER 1836 137; DENAUX 2009 L***; NEIRYNCK 1985	2,37.42; 3,23; 8,42	4,22	0	1
ἐπὶ ἔτη (VKc) BOISMARD 1984 Ab179; NEIRYNCK 1985	4,25	19,10	0	0

Literature

DENAUX 2009 lAⁿ [ἀπὸ/ἐξ ἐτῶν], LAⁿ [ἐπὶ ἔτη]; GERSDORF 1816 260 [ὡς ἐτῶν ὀγδοήκοντα τεσσάρων]; 264 [κατ' ἔτος]; HAUCK 1934 [Vorzugswort]; JEREMIAS 1980 126 [ἐπὶ ἔτη τρία: red.]; 228 [ἔτη δεκαοκτώ: red.].

CADBURY, Henry J., Some Lukan Expressions of Time (Lexical Notes on Luke-Acts VII). — JBL 82 (1963) 272-278.

DE JONGE, Henk J., Sonship, Wisdom, Infancy: Luke II.41-51a. — NTS 24 (1977-78) 317-354. Esp. 317-324: "When he was twelve".

εὐαγγελίζω 10 + 15 (Mt 1) | tell the good news

Word groups	Lk	Acts	Mt	Mk
εὐαγγελίζομαι + ἄγγελος DENAUX 2009 Lⁿ	1,19; 2,10		0	0

εὐαγγελίζομαι + ἀποστέλλω DENAUX 2009 La[n]	1,19; 4,18.43	10,36	0	0
εὐαγγελίζομαι εἰρήνην (VKf)		10,36	0	0
εὐαγγελίζομαι + κηρύσσω (VKg) → **εὐαγγελίζομαι** + διδάσκω (Acts 5,42; 15,35); cf. κηρύσσω (+) τὸ εὐαγγέλιον Mt 4,23; 9,35; 24,14; 26,13; Mk 1,14; 13,10; 14,9; [16,15] DENAUX 2009 L[n]	4,18; 8,1		0	0
εὐαγγελίζομαι (+) λαός DENAUX 2009 L[n]	2,10; 3,18; 20,1		0	0
εὐαγγελίζομαι (+) τὸν Ἰησοῦν/Χριστόν (SCb; VKc) BOISMARD 1984 Aa48		5,42; 8,35; 11,20; 17,18	0	0
εὐαγγελίζομαι (+) τὸν λόγον (SCc)		8,4; 15,35	0	0
εὐαγγελίζομαι passive (VKb)	7,22; 16,16		1	0

Characteristic of Luke

BOISMARD 1984 Eb2; CADBURY 1920 114; CREDNER 1836 140; DENAUX 2009 L***; GASTON 1973 66 [Lked?]; GOULDER 1989*; HAWKINS 1909 19; MORGENTHALER 1958LA; NEIRYNCK 1985; PLUMMER 1922 lix; VOGEL 1899D

	Lk	Acts	Mt	Mk
εὐαγγελίζομαι τινα; cf. Gal 1,16; 1 Pet 1,12 BOISMARD 1984 Bb105; CREDNER 1836 140; DENAUX 2009 lA*; HARNACK 1906 29.51; NEIRYNCK 1985	3,18; 20,1	8,25.40; 13,32; 14,15.21; 16,10	0	0
εὐαγγελίζομαι τι; see also **εὐαγγελίζομαι** τὸν Ἰησοῦν/Χριστόν; cf. εὐαγγελίζομαι + inf. Acts 14,15 BOISMARD 1984 Db2; DENAUX 2009 L***; NEIRYNCK 1985	1,19; 2,10; 4,43; 8,1	8,4; 10,36; 13,32; 15,35; 17,18	0	0
εὐαγγελίζομαι τὴν βασιλείαν / περὶ τῆς βασιλείας (SCa; VKe); cf. τὸ εὐαγγέλιον τῆς βασιλείας Mt 4,23; 9,35; 24,14; Mk 1,14 v.l. GOULDER 1989	4,43; 8,1; 16,16	8,12	0	0
εὐαγγελίζομαι καὶ διδάσκω (VKg) → **εὐαγγελίζομαι** + κηρύσσω BOISMARD 1984 Ab110; NEIRYNCK 1985	20,1	5,42; 15,35	0	0

Literature

VON BENDEMANN 2001 413: "εὐαγγελίζεσθαι τὴν βασιλείαν τοῦ θεοῦ ... typisch lukanisch"; 431: "mediales εὐαγγελίζεσθαι findet sich in den Synoptikern nur bei Lukas"; COLLISON 1977 51 [linguistic usage of Luke: certain]; DENAUX 2009 La[n] [εὐαγγελίζομαι τὴν βασιλείαν / περὶ τῆς βασιλείας]; lA[n] [εὐαγγελίζομαι καὶ διδάσκω]; GERSDORF 1816 187 [εὐαγγελίζεσθαι σοι ταῦτα]; HAUCK 1934 [Vorzugswort]; JEREMIAS 1980 39: "Mediales εὐαγγελίζεσθαι findet sich in den Geschichtswerken des NT nur bei Lukas".

BURCHARD, Christoph, Formen der Vermittlung christlichen Glaubens im Neuen Testament: Beobachtungen anhand von κήρυγμα, μαρτυρία und verwandten Wörtern. — EvT 38 (1978) 313-340. Esp. 321-325: "Lukas".

DE VIRGILIO, Giuseppe, L'impiego di "evangelizzare" (εὐαγγελίζεσθαι) nell'opera di Luca. — LEONARDI, G. – TROLESE, F.G.B. (eds.), San Luca Evangelista, 2000, 283-297.

DUPONT, Jacques, Le discours de Milet, 1962. Esp. 115.117.

KÜMMEL, Werner Georg, "Das Gesetz und die Propheten gehen bis Johannes" – Lukas 16,16 im Zusammenhang der heilsgeschichtlichen Theologie der Lukasschriften. — BÖCHER, O. – HAACKER, K. (eds.), Verborum Veritas. FS G. Stählin, 1970, 89-102. Esp. 95.

MAHFOUZ, Hady, *La fonction littéraire et théologique de Lc 3,1-20*, 2003. Esp. 313-317.
PARKER, J.F., *Εὐαγγέλιον – εὐαγγελίζω: A Contextual Analysis of Their Meaning in the New Testament and the Apostolic Fathers*. Diss. New Orleans, 1990 (dir. J.W. Dukes).
VIRGILIO, G. de, Εὐαγγελίζειν nel terzo vangelo. — *CS* 16 (1995) 587-598.

εὖγε 1	good (value) (Lk 19,17)

Literature
HAUCK 1934 [seltenes Alleinwort].

εὐγενής 1 + 1
1. important (Lk 19,12); 2. open-minded (Acts 17,11)

Word groups	Lk	Acts	Mt	Mk
ἄνθρωπός τις εὐγενής → ἄνθρωπός τις πλούσιος	19,12		0	0
εὐγενέστερος comparative (*VK*a)		17,11	0	0

Literature
DENAUX 2009 LA[n].

εὐδοκέω 2 (Mt 3, Mk 1)
1. be pleased with, to (Lk 3,22; 12,32); 2. enjoy; 3. prefer

Word groups	Lk	Acts	Mt	Mk
εὐδοκέω + infinitive (*VK*a)	12,32		0	0

εὐδοκία 2 (Mt 1)
1. what pleases (Lk 2,14; 10,21); 2. desire

Word groups	Lk	Acts	Mt	Mk
ἄνθρωποι εὐδοκίας	2,14		0	0
εἰρήνη ἐν ἀνθρώποις εὐδοκίας	2,14		0	0

Literature
BERGER, Paul-Richard, Lk 2,14: ἄνθρωποι εὐδοκίας: Die auf Gottes Weisung mit Wohlgefallen beschenkten Menschen. — *ZNW* 74 (1983) 129-144.
—, Menschen ohne "Gottes Wohlgefallen" Lk 2,14? — *ZNW* 76 (1985) 119-122.
DEICHGRÄBER, Reinhard, Lk 2,14: ἄνθρωποι εὐδοκίας. — *ZNW* 51 (1960) 132.
DELEBECQUE, Édouard, *Études grecques*, 1976. Esp. 25-38: "Le 'gloria' des anges (2,14)".
DERRETT, J. Duncan M., Ἄνθρωποι εὐδοκίας (Lk 2:14b). — *FilolNT* 11 (1998) 101-106. Esp. 101-102: "The problem"; 102-103: "A Greek word with a Hebrew meaning"; 103-105: "The angelic host". [NTA 44, 971]
DODD, Charles H., New Testament Translation Problems. — *BTrans* 27 (1976) 301-311; 28 (1977) 101-116. Esp. 104-110: "εὐδοκεῖν, εὐδοκία".
EULENSTEIN, Rolf, Und den Menschen ein Wohlgefallen (Lk 2,14). Ein Beispiel für Sinn und Umfang philologischer Arbeit an Neuen Testament. — *Wort und Dienst* 18 (1985) 93-103.
FITZMYER, Joseph A., "Peace Upon Earth Among Men of His Good Will" (Lk 2:14). — *TS* 19 (1958) 225-227; = ID., *Essays on the Semitic Background of the New Testament*, London: Chapman, 1971, 101-104.

GUERRA GÓMEZ, Manuel, Análisis filológico-teológico y traducción del himno de los ángeles en Belén, 1989. Esp. 55-76: "Εὐδοκία(ς). Su etimología, origen y significados".

—, "… Eudokia (bondad, benevolencia) en medio de los hombres", nombre o designación de Jesucristo en el himno de los ángeles (Lc 2,14 y comienzo del "Gloria…" de la Misa). — *RevistCatTeol* 14 (1989) 203-222.

HANSACK, Ernst, Luk 2,14: "Friede den Menschen auf Erden, die guten Willens sind"? Ein Beitrag zur Übersetzungskritik der Vulgata. — *BZ* NF 21 (1977) 117-118. Esp. 118: "die beiden geschilderten Übersetzungsmöglichkeiten …, nämlich die synthetische Methode ('*benevolentiae*') und die analytische Methode ('*bona voluntas*'). … "Guter Wille" für '*bona voluntas*' ist also ein Übersetzungsfehler der Neuzeit" … die lateinische Version denkt *nicht* 'an den menschlichen guten Willen', sondern an das göttliche 'Wohlwollen'".

HUNZINGER, Claus-Hunno, Neues Licht auf Lc 2,14 ἄνϑρωποι εὐδοκίας. — *ZNW* 44 (1952-53) 85-90.

—, Ein weiterer Beleg zu Lc 2,14 ἄνϑρωποι εὐδοκίας. — *ZNW* 49 (1958) 129-130.

JEREMIAS, Joachim, ῎Ανϑρωποι εὐδοκίας (Lk 2,14). — *ZNW* 28 (1929) 13-20.

KILPATRICK, Ross S., The Greek Syntax of Luke 2.14. — *NTS* 34 (1988) 472-475.

MOODY, Robert A., "Men of Good-will". — *ExpT* 50 (1938-39) 563.

MÜLLER, Theodore, Observations on Some New Testament Texts Based on Generative-Transformational Grammar. — *BTrans* 29 (1978) 117-120. Esp. 117: "Luke 2.14b καὶ ἐπὶ γῆς εἰρήνη ἐν ἀνθρώποις εὐδοκίας". [NTA 22, 712]

RAD, Gerhard VON, Noch einmal Lc 4,14 ἄνϑρωποι εὐδοκίας. — *ZNW* 29 (1930) 111-115.

ROPES, James H., "Good Will Toward Men" (Luke 2,14). — *HTR* 10 (1917) 52-56.

SCHWARZ, Günther, Der Lobgesang der Engel (Lukas 2,14): Emendation und Rückübersetzung. — *BZ* NF 15 (1971) 260-264.

—, …ἄνϑρωποι εὐδοκίας"? (Lk 2,14). — *ZNW* 75 (1984) 136-137. [NTA 26, 143]

SMOTHERS, Edgar R., ἐν ἀνθρώποις εὐδοκίας. — *RechSR* 24 (1934) 86-93.

WILLIAMS, A. Lukyn, "Glory to God in the Highest, and on Earth Peace among Men of Good-will" (Luke ii.14). — *ExpT* 50 (1938-39) 283-284.

WOBBE, Joseph, Das Gloria (Lk 2,14). — *BZ* 22 (1934) 118-152.224-245; 23 (1936) 358-364.

εὐεργέτης 1   benefactor (Lk 22,25)

Literature

HAUCK 1934 [seltenes Alleinwort]; SCHÜRMANN 1957 72-73 [schwacher Verdacht auf luk R].

DANKER, Frederick W., The Endangered Benefactor in Luke-Acts. — *SBL 1981 Seminar Papers*, 39-48.

LULL, David J., The Servant-Benefactor as a Model of Greatness (Luke 22:24-30). — *NT* 28 (1986) 289-305.

NOCK, Arthur D., Soter and Euergetes. — JOHNSON, Sherman Elbridge (ed.), *The Joy of Study: Papers on New Testament and Related Subjects Presented to Honor Frederick Clifton Grant*. New York: MacMillan Company, 1951, 127-148.

εὔθετος 2

1. suitable (Lk 9,62); 2. useful (Lk 14,35)

Word groups	Lk	Acts	Mt	Mk
εὔθετος + dative	9,62		0	0
εὔθετος + εἰς	14,35		0	0

Literature
DENAUX 2009 L[n]; HARNACK 1906 54; HAUCK 1934 [seltenes Alleinwort].

εὐθέως 6/8 + 9 (Mt 13/15, Mk 1/40) immediately, then

Word groups	Lk	Acts	Mt	Mk
εὐθέως + ἀνίστημι → παραχρῆμα + ἀνίστημι; cf.		9,34	0	0/1
εὐθύς ἀνίστημι Mk 5,42; εὐθύς ἐγείρω Mk 2,12				
εὐθέως δέ (VKb) → παραχρῆμα δέ		17,14	2/4	0
εὐθέως δὲ τότε		17,14	0	0
εὐθέως οὖν (VKc)		22,29	0	0
καὶ εὐθέως (SCb) → καὶ εὐθύς/παραχρῆμα	5,13; 6,49*	9.18.20.34; 12,10; 21,30	8	1/23
ὅταν ... εὐθέως; cf. ὅταν ... εὐθύς Mk 4,15.16.29 DENAUX 2009 L[n]	12,54; 21,9		0	0/3
οὐκ εὐθέως (VKd) DENAUX 2009 L[n]	14,5; 21,9		0	0
ὡς + εὐθέως		16,10	0	0

Characteristic of Luke
VOGEL 1899D

Literature
COLLISON 1977 155 [linguistic usage of Luke's "other source-material": probable]; JEREMIAS 1980 219 [red.]; RADL 1975 411.

DAUBE, David, *The Sudden in the Scriptures*. Leiden: Brill, 1964, VII-86 p. Esp. 63-65: "At Once: Luke"; 69-71: "Acts".

MATEOS, Juan, Εὐθύς y sinonimos en el evangelio de Marcos y demas escritos del Nuevo Testamento. — URBÁN, A. – MATEOS, J. – ALEPUZ, M., *Estudios de Nuevo Testamento*. II: Cuestiones de gramatica y lexico, 1977, 103-139.

PERNOT, Hubert, *Études sur la langue des Évangiles*, 1927. Esp. 181-187.

RYDBECK, Lars, *Fachprosa*, 1967. Esp. 167-176.

εὐθύς adv. 1 + 1 (Mt 5, Mk 41/43) immediately, then

Word groups	Lk	Acts	Mt	Mk
καὶ εὐθύς (SCb) → καὶ εὐθέως/παραχρῆμα	6,49	10,16	1/3	25

Literature
EASTON 1910 176 [possible Hebraisms in the Lucan Writings, as classed by Dalman].

DAUBE, David, *The Sudden in the Scriptures*. Leiden: Brill, 1964, VII-86 p. Esp. 63-65: "At Once: Luke"; 69-71: "Acts".

MATEOS, Juan, Εὐθύς y sinonimos en el evangelio de Marcos y demas escritos del Nuevo Testamento. — URBÁN, A. – MATEOS, J. – ALEPUZ, M., *Estudios de Nuevo Testamento*. II: Cuestiones de gramatica y lexico, 1977, 103-139.

PERNOT, Hubert, *Études sur la langue des Évangiles*, 1927. Esp. 181-187.

RYDBECK, Lars, *Fachprosa*, 1967. Esp. 167-176.

εὐθύς adj. 2 + 3 (Mt 1, Mk 1)
1. straight (Lk 3,4.5; Acts 9,11); 2. upright (Acts 8,21; 13,10)

Word groups	Lk	Acts	Mt	Mk
εὐθύς name of a street (VKa)		9,11	0	0

εὐκαιρία 1 (Mt 1)   opportunity (Lk 22,6)

εὔκοπος 3 (Mt 2, Mk 2)   easy

Word groups	Lk	Acts	Mt	Mk
εὐκοπώτερος comparative (VKa)	5,23; 16,17; 18,25		2	2

εὐλαβής 1 + 3   pious

Word groups	Lk	Acts	Mt	Mk
ἀνὴρ εὐλαβής → ἄνθρωπος **εὐλαβής**; ἀνήρ + **ἀγαθός/ δίκαιος**; cf. ἀνὴρ + εὐσεβής Acts 10,(1-)2; 22,12*		2,5; 8,2; 22,12	0	0
ἄνθρωπος + εὐλαβής → ἀνὴρ **εὐλαβής**; ἄνθρωπος + **ἀγαθός/δίκαιος**	2,25		0	0

Characteristic of Luke
BOISMARD 1984 Ab82; CREDNER 1836 142; HARNACK 1906 74; HAWKINS 1909LA; MORGENTHALER 1958*; NEIRYNCK 1985; PLUMMER 1922 lii; VOGEL 1899A

Literature
DENAUX 2009 IA[n]; GERSDORF 1816 246 [δίκαιος καὶ εὐλαβής]; HAUCK 1934 [seltenes Alleinwort].

εὐλογέω 13/14 + 1/2 (Mt 5/6, Mk 5/6)
1. praise (Lk 2,28); 2. bless (Lk 1,42); 3. act kindly toward

Word groups	Lk	Acts	Mt	Mk
εὐλογέω τὸν θεόν (SCc; VKb) → **αἰνέω/δοξάζω** τὸν θεόν; **εὐλογητός** + θεός DENAUX 2009 L[n]	1,64; 2,28; 24,53		0	0
εὐλογέω τὸν θεόν + verb of saying → **αἰνέω/δοξάζω** τὸν θεόν + verb of saying	2,28		0	0
εὐλογέω (+) ἄρτον + (κατα)κλάω (SCb; VKd) → **εὐχαριστέω** ἄρτον	9,16; 24,30		2	2
εὐλογέω + χαρά → **αἰνέω** + χαίρω	24,(52-)53		0	0
εὐλογημένος (SCa; VKa)	1,28*.42[1.2]; 13,35; 19,38		3	2

Characteristic of Luke
GOULDER 1989; HAWKINS 1909add; MORGENTHALER 1958L

Literature
COLLISON 1977 51 [linguistic usage of Luke's "other source-material": probable]; EASTON 1910 147 [especially characteristic of L]; GERSDORF 1816 204 [εὐλογῶν τὸν θεόν]; 257 [καὶ εὐλόγησεν αὐτούς]; JEREMIAS 1980 70 [εὐλογῶν τὸν θεόν: red.]; 141(-142) [6,27-28: trad.]; "ἀγαπᾶτε ... ποιεῖτε ... εὐλογεῖτε ... προσεύχεσθε: Die asyndetische Aufreihung von Imperativen wird von Lukas in dem von ihm übernommenen Markusstoff konsequent beseitigt"; SCHÜRMANN 1953 28; 1955 46-47.

GEORGE, Augustin, La prière. — ID., *Études*, 1978, 395-427. Esp. 402-405: "Le vocabulaire lucanien de la prière".
LÉGASSE, Simon, Εὐλογεῖν et εὐχαριστεῖν. — *Mens concordat voci. Mélanges A.G. Martimort*, Paris, 1983, 431-435.
MULLINS, TERENCE Y., Ascription as a Literary Form. — *NTS* 19 (1973) 194-205. [NTA 17, 842: The most comon types are woes (*ouai*), eulogies (*eulogētos* or *eulogēmenos*) and beatitudes (*makarios*)]
OBERMANN, Andreas, *An Gottes Segen ist alles gelegen: Eine Untersuchung zum Segen im Neuen Testament* (BThSt, 37), Neukirchen, 1998. 142 pp.

εὐλογητός 1 (Mk 1)   to be praised

Word groups	Lk	Acts	Mt	Mk
εὐλογητός + θεός → **αἶνος/δόξα** θεῷ; **εὐλογέω** τὸν θεόν	1,68		0	0

Literature
GEORGE, Augustin, La prière. — ID., *Études*, 1978, 395-427. Esp. 402-405: "Le vocabulaire lucanien de la prière".
LEE, John A.L. – HORSLEY, G.H.R., A Lexicon of the New Testament, 2, 1998. Esp. 77.82.
MULLINS, Tenrence Y., Ascription as a Literary Form. — *NTS* 19 (1973) 194-205. [NTA 17, 842: The most comon types are woes (*ouai*), eulogies (*eulogētos* or *eulogēmenos*) and beatitudes (*makarios*)]

εὑρίσκω 45 + 35 (Mt 27, Mk 11)
1. discover (Lk 11,24); 2. learn (Lk 19,48; Acts 17,27; 19,19); 3. attain (Lk 1,30); 4. begin to experience (Acts 7,46); εὑρίσκομαι: 5. be found to be

Word groups	Lk	Acts	Mt	Mk
εὑρίσκω + accusative and participle	2,12; 7,10; 8,35; 11,25; 12,37.43; 19,30	5,23; 9,2; 10,27; 27,6	5	4
εὑρίσκω + infinitive (*VKf*) DENAUX 2009 Lⁿ	6,7; 17,18		0	0
εὑρίσκω + ἀπ/δι/εἰσ/ἐξ/ κατέρχομαι (*VKd*)	8,35; 9,12 *v.l.*; 11,24; 19,32; 22,13; 24,3.24	5,10; 9,(32-)33; 10,27; 11,26; 13,6; 17,23; 19,1	6	2
εὑρίσκω + ἀπόλλυμι lose	15,4.6.8.9².24.32		2	0
εὑρίσκω (+) ἔρχομαι (*VKc*) → **ἀνευρίσκω** + ἔρχομαι	2,(44-)45; 8,35; 11,25; 12,37.38.43; 13,6.7; 18,8; 22,45; 24,23	18,2; 19,1 *v.l.*; 28,14	5/6	6
εὑρίσκω + (ἀνα/ἐπι)ζητέω (*VKb*) → **αἰτέω** + (ἐπι)δίδωμι/ λαμβάνω; **δίδωμι** + ζητέω	2,45; 5,(18-)19; 11,9.10.24; 13,6.7; 15,8; 19,(47-)48; 24,3(-5)	11,(25-)26; 12,19; 17,(5-)6.27	6	2
εὑρίσκω (+) (εἰσ)πορεύομαι (*VKe*)	9,12; 15,4; 19,30		3	1
εὑρήσετε	2,12; 11,9; 19,30		3	1

Characteristic of Luke
GOULDER 1989; MORGENTHALER 1958LA

	Lk	Acts	Mt	Mk
εὑρίσκομαι passive (*VKa*) DENAUX 2009 La**	9,36; 15,24.32; 17,18	5,39; 8,40	1	0

εὑρίσκω + acc. part. immediately following DENAUX 2009 L***; GOULDER 1989	8,35; 11,25; 12,37.43; 22,45; 23,2; 24,33	5,23; 10,27; 23,29	1	0
εὑρίσκω τινά + participle with accusative; cf. Jn 11,17 VOGEL 1899C	2,46; 23,2	24,5.12	0	0
εἰσελθὼν absolute … εὑρίσκω BOISMARD 1984 Ab180; NEIRYNCK 1985	24,3	5,10	0	0
χάριν εὑρίσκω/ἔχω → χάριν ἔχω; cf. Heb 4,16 BOISMARD 1984 Db30; NEIRYNCK 1985	1,30; 17,9	2,47; 7,46[1]	0	0

Literature

COLLISON 1977 109 [μή + participle: noteworthy phenomena]; DENAUX 2009 LAⁿ [εὑρίσκω τινά + participle with accusative; εἰσελθὼν absolute … εὑρίσκω; χάριν εὑρίσκω]; GERSDORF 1816 266 [καὶ μὴ εὑρόντες ὑπέστρεψαν]; HAUCK 1934 [Vorzugswort]; RADL 1975 411 [εὑρίσκω; εὑρίσκω "mit Akkusativ und Partizip und dessen Akkusativobjekt"].

BROX, Norbert, Suchen und Finden: Zur Nachgeschichte von Mt 7,7b/Lk 11,9b. — HOFFMANN, P. – BROX, N. – PESCH, W. (eds.), *Orientierung an Christus. FS J. Schmid*, 1973, 17-36.

CHILTON, Bruce, Announcement in Nazara, 1981. Esp. 157.

LEE, John A.L., A Non-Aramaism in Luke 6:7. — *NT* 33 (1991) 28-34. Esp. 28: "In Luke 6:7 εὑρίσκω is found in a context requiring the sense of 'find a way (to)', 'be able(to)': … This use, also found in the text of D at 11:54 and 13:24, has been the subject of remark since the time of Wellhausen, who suggested that an Aramaism was involved"; 29-32 [parallels in Greek literature and papyri]; 34: "We may reasonably conclude, then, that our use of εὑρίσκω is not only amply established for Koine Greek, but also has its roots in the earlier language. There is no reason to regard it as in any way unGreek or as unavailable to a writer such as Luke".

WILCOX, Max, Semitisms in the New Testament, 1984. Esp. 1011-1012: "εὑρίσκειν = 'to be able'"; 1012: "εὑρεθῆναι εἰς (Acts 8:40)".

εὐτόνως 1 + 1   vigorously (Lk 23,10; Acts 18,28)

Characteristic of Luke

BOISMARD 1984 Ab181; HAWKINS 1909LA; MORGENTHALER 1958*; NEIRYNCK 1985; PLUMMER 1922 liii; VOGEL 1899A

Literature

DENAUX 2009 LAⁿ; HAUCK 1934 [seltenes Alleinwort]; JEREMIAS 1980 302 [red.].

εὐφορέω* 1   produce much fruit (Lk 12,16)

Literature

HAUCK 1934 [seltenes Alleinwort].

εὐφραίνω 6 + 2

1. make glad; εὐφραίνομαι: 2. rejoice (Acts 2,26); 3. celebrate (Lk 15,23.29.32; Acts 7,41)

Characteristic of Luke

BOISMARD 1984 cb135; DENAUX 2009 L***; GOULDER 1989*; HAWKINS 1909 L; NEIRYNCK 1985

Literature

COLLISON 1977 52 [linguistic usage of Luke's "other source-material": certain]; EASTON 1910 154-155 [probably characteristic of L; not noted by Weiss]; HAUCK 1934 [häufiges Alleinwort]; PAFFENROTH 1997 81; REHKOPF 1959 94 [vorlukanisch]; SCHÜRMANN 1961 271.

εὐχαριστέω 4 + 2 (Mt 2, Mk 2)

1. thank (Lk 17,16; 18,11; 22,17.19); 2. be thankful

Word groups	Lk	Acts	Mt	Mk
εὐχαριστέω ἄρτον (VKa) → **εὐλογέω** ἄρτον + (κατα)κλάω	22,19	27,35	1	1
εὐχαριστέω + ὅτι (VKb)	18,11		0	0

Characteristic of Luke

GOULDER 1989

Literature

BDAG 2000 416 [literature]; COLLISON 1977 51-52 [noteworthy phenomena]; SCHÜRMANN 1953 53-60; 1955 45-47.92-93.

GEORGE, Augustin, La prière. — ID., *Études*, 1978, 395-427. Esp. 402-405: "Le vocabulaire lucanien de la prière".

LÉGASSE, Simon, Εὐλογεῖν et εὐχαριστεῖν. — *Mens concordat voci. Mélanges A.G. Martimort*, Paris, 1983, 431-435.

PETZER, Kobus H., Style and Text in the Lucan Narrative of the Institution of the Lord's Supper, 1991. Esp. 121.

SCHWANK, Benedict, « Dankend brach er ». Eucharistie – was bedeutet mir das? — *Erbe und Auftrag* 77 (2001) 497-505.

ἐφημερία 2

work group (Lk 1,5.8)

Characteristic of Luke

PLUMMER 1922 liii

Literature

DENAUX 2009 L[n]; HAUCK 1934 [seltenes Alleinwort].

SCHWARZ, Günther, ΕΞ ΕΦΗΜΕΡΙΑΣ ΑΒΙΑ? (Lukas 1,5). — *BibNot* 53 (1990) 30-31.

ἐφίστημι 7 + 11

ἐφίσταμαι: 1. stand at (Lk 4,39; 24,4); 2. be near (Lk 24,4; Acts 22,20); 3. happen; 4. attack (Acts 17,5); 5. be imminent; 6. begin (Acts 28,2); 7. continue

Word groups	Lk	Acts	Mt	Mk
ἐφεστώς (VKa) → **(παρ/συν)εστώς** CREDNER 1836 140		22,20; 28,2	0	0
ἐφίστημι ἐπί + accusative (VKb) DENAUX 2009 IA[n]	21,34	10,17; 11,11	0	0
ἐφίστημι ἐπάνω (VKc)	4,39		0	0

ἐφίστημι + ἄγγελος → **(παρ)ἵστημι** + ἄγγελος; ἀπέστη/ἀπῆλθεν ὁ ἄγγελος/διάβολος DENAUX 2009 LAⁿ	2,9	12,7	0	0

Characteristic of Luke

BOISMARD 1984 Bb45; DENAUX 2009 L***; GOULDER 1989*; HARNACK 1906 39.51; HAWKINS 1909 L; MORGENTHALER 1958A; NEIRYNCK 1985; PLUMMER 1922 lix; VOGEL 1899D

	Lk	Acts	Mt	Mk
ἐπιστάς CREDNER 1836 139; DENAUX 2009 lA*	2,38; 4,39; 10,40	6,12; 17,5; 22,13; 23,11.27	0	0

Literature

EASTON 1910 167 [classed by Weiss as characteristic of L on insufficient (?) evidence]; GERSDORF 1816 261 [ἐπιστᾶσα ἀνθωμολογεῖτο τῷ κυρίῳ]; HAUCK 1934 [häufiges Alleinwort]; JEREMIAS 1980 80: "lukanisch"; RADL 1975 411 [ἐφίστημι; ἐπιστάς].

ἐφοράω 1 + 1	pay attention to

Characteristic of Luke

ἐπεῖδον BOISMARD 1984 Ab178; HARNACK 1906 73; HAWKINS 1909LA; NEIRYNCK 1985	1,25	4,29	0	0

Literature

DENAUX 2009 LAⁿ, LAⁿ [ἐπεῖδον]; HAUCK 1934 [seltenes Alleinwort]; JEREMIAS 1980 46 [red.].

ἔχθρα 1	enmity (Lk 23,12)

ἐχθρός 8 + 2 (Mt 7, Mk 1)	be enemy of

Word groups	Lk	Acts	Mt	Mk
ἐχθρός + genitive (thing) (VKa)		13,10	0	0
ἐχθρός + ἀγαπάω → **ἐχθρός** + μισέω; **πλησίον** + ἀγαπάω	6,27.35		1	0
ἐχθρός + μισέω → **ἐχθρός** + ἀγαπάω	1,71; 6,27		1	0

Literature

BDAG 2000 419 [literature]; EASTON 1910 155 [ἐχθροί in the plural: probably characteristic of L].

SCHWARZ, Günther, αγαπατε τους εχθρους υμων Mt 5,44a / Lk 6,27a(35a): Jesu Forderung *kat' exochen*. — *BibNot* 12 (1980) 32-34.

ἔχιδνα 1 + 1 (Mt 3)	
1. snake (Acts 28,3); 2. evil person (Lk 3,7)	

Word groups	Lk	Acts	Mt	Mk
γεννήματα ἐχιδνῶν	3,7		3	0

Literature

REHKOPF 1959 98 [γεννήματα ἐχιδνῶν: "Substantiva in Anrede bei den Synoptikern"].

MAHFOUZ, Hady, *La fonction littéraire et théologique de Lc 3,1-20*, 2003. Esp. 179-180 [γεννήματα ἐχιδνῶν].

ἔχω 77/78 + 44/46 (Mt 74/75, Mk 69[70]/72)

1. possess (Lk 15,8); 2. hold on to; 3. hold a view (Lk 14,19); 4. wear; 5. be able to (Lk 7,42); 6. experience (Lk 7,33; Acts 28, 9); 7. be (Acts 7,1); 8. cause; 9. content marker (Acts 23,25)
ἐχόμενος: 10. neighboring

Word groups	Lk	Acts	Mt	Mk
ἀνάγκην ἔχω (VKc)	14,18[1]; 23,17*		0	0
ἔχω with two accusative objects (SCc; VKm)	3,8; 6,8; 14,18[2]. 19; 19,20; 20,33	13,5; 20,24*	2	4
ἔχω βαπτισθῆναι	12,50		1	0
ἔχω (+) γυναῖκα	20,28.33		0	2
ἔχω δαιμόνιον; cf. ἔχω πνεῦμα δαιμονίου ἀκαθάρτου Lk 4,33; ἔχω λεγιῶνα Mk 5,15	7,33; 8,27		1	0
ἔχω ἐλπίδα		24,15	0	0
ἔχω ἐν γαστρί (LN: be pregnant; VKf)	21,23		3	1
ἔχω ἐν ἑαυτῷ/ἑαυτοῖς (SCb; VKk); cf. ἔχω μεθ' ἑαυτῶν Mt 15,30; 26,11[1]; Mk 2,19 v.l.; 8,14; 14,7[1]		28,29*	1	2
ἔχω ἐξουσίαν (SCd; VKa)	5,24; 12,5; 19,17	9,14	2	3
ἔχω ὅ/ποῦ/τί (VKe)	9,58; 11,6; 12,17	25,26[2]	2	2/3
ἔχω πρός + accusative (VKl) (against someone); cf. 1 Cor 6,1; Col 3,13; cf. ἔχω κατά + gen. Mt 5,23; Mk 11,25 BOISMARD 1984 Ca69		19,38; 24,19; 25,19	0	0
ἔχω πίστιν	17,6	14,9	2	2
ἔχω πνεῦμα		8,7; 16,16	0	0
ἔχω πνεῦμα πύθωνα (LN: be a fortuneteller)		16,16	0	0
ἔχω (+) χρείαν (SCe; VKb)	5,31[1]; 9,11; 15,7; 19,31.34; 22,71	2,45; 4,35	6	4
ἔχω ὦτα (LN: be able to hear)	8,8; 14,35		3	3
κακῶς ἔχων (LN: be sick; SCf; VKg)	5,31[2]; 7,2		4/5	4
οὕτως ἔχω (VKh); cf. Rev 2,15 BOISMARD 1984 Aa60		7,1; 12,15; 17,11; 24,9	0	0
τὸ νῦν ἔχον (VKq)		24,25	0	0
πωλέω ὅσα ἔχεις + ἀκολουθέω	18,22		1	1
τέλος ἔχω	22,37		0	1
ἔχω intransitive (VKj) (exc. VKg/h/q)		1,12; 15,36; 21,13	0	1[2]

Characteristic of Luke	Lk	Acts	Mt	Mk
τῇ ἐχομένῃ (ἡμέρᾳ) (LN: the next day) / ἐχόμενος (LN: neighboring; VKp) → τῇ **ἑτέρᾳ** BOISMARD 1984 Ab125; HAWKINS 1909 186; NEIRYNCK 1985; PLUMMER 1922 liii; VOGEL 1899C	13,33	20,15; 21,26	0	0
ἔχω + infinitive (SCa; VKd); cf. Jn 8,26; 16,12 BOISMARD 1984 Eb53; DENAUX 2009 L***; GOULDER 1989*; HAWKINS 1909L; NEIRYNCK 1985	7,40.42; 12,4.50; 14,14	4,14; 23,17.18.19; 25,26[1].26[2] v.l.; 28,19	1	0
ἔχω, opening parable DENAUX 2009 L***; GOULDER 1989*	11,5; 15,4.8.11;1 6,1;17,7		1	0

			0	0
ἔχω, first word in clause, pres. ind. act. DENAUX 2009 L***; GOULDER 1989*	7,40; 16,28.29; 19,25; 24,41			
χάριν ἔχω/εὑρίσκω → χάριν εὑρίσκω BOISMARD 1984 Db30; NEIRYNCK 1985	1,30;17,9	2,47; 7,46[1]	0	0

Literature

VON BENDEMANN 2001 424 [ἔχω + inf.]; 426: "Die elliptische Wendung τῇ ἐχομένῃ ist lukanisch"; COLLISON 1977 53 [in introduction to parable: linguistic usage of Luke's "other source-material": certain]; 109 [μὴ ἔχων: linguistic usage of Luke's "other source-material": probable]; DENAUX 2009 lA[n] [τῇ ἐχομένῃ (ἡμέρᾳ)/ ἐχόμενος], LA[n] [χάριν ἔχω/εὑρίσκω]; HAUCK 1934 [Vorzugswort; Vorzugsverbindung: ἔχω βαπτισθῆναι; ἔχω σοί τι εἰπεῖν]; JEREMIAS 1980 169: "ἔχω mit folgendem Infinitiv = 'können', 'müssen' findet sich … im Doppelwerk elfmal"; 234: "Das Medium von ἔχω, von der Zeit gesagt ('darauffolgend'), begegnet im NT nur Lk 13,33 / Apg 20,15; 21,26"; PLUMMER 1922 lxii [The quite classical ἔχειν τι is common (vii.42, ix.58, xi.6, xii.17,50, xiv.14)]; RADL 1975 411 [ἔχω + inf.; ἔχω τι; οὕτως ἔχω]; SCHÜRMANN 1957 121 [ἔχων c. acc. verwendet Luk gern]; 129 [τέλος ἔχει Lk 22,37 luk R weniger wahrscheinlich].

ANDERSEN, T. David, The Meaning of ἔχοντες χάριν πρός in Acts 2.47. — NTS 34 (1988) 604-610.

ἕως 28/31 + 22 (Mt 49, Mk 15)

1. until (Lk 12,50); 2. while (Lk 17,8); 3. as far as (Lk 2,15); 4. to the point of (Lk 22,51); 5. as much as

Word groups	Lk	Acts	Mt	Mk
ἀπὸ … ἕως (SCj; VKk) → ἐκ … ἕως; ἀπὸ… ἄχρι/μέχρι	11,51; 22,18; 23,5	1,22; 8,10; 28,23	14	4
ἐάω ἕως (LN: stop)	22,51		0	0
ἐκ … ἕως → ἀπὸ… ἕως	20,(42-)43; 22,16 v.l.	2,(34-)35	2	1
ἕως conjunction followed by indicative (SCb; VKb)	13,35; 19,13*		2/3	1
ἕως preposition with reference to number (SCh)	22,51	8,10	6	2
ἕως preposition with reference to time (SCf)	1,55*.80; 2,37; 9,41; 11,51; 16,16*; 23,44	1,22; 7,45; 8,40; 13,20; 28,23	13	5
ἕως ἄν + subjunctive (SCc; VKc)	9,27; 13,35 v.l.; 20,43; 21,32	2,35	11	3
ἕως + ἐν → μέχρι + ἐν DENAUX 2009 Lan	1,80; 24,49	1,8	1	0
ἕως ἐσχάτου; cf. ἐπ᾽ ἐσχάτου Heb 1,2; 1 Pet 1,20; Jud 18		1,8; 13,47	0	0
ἕως ἐτῶν ὀγδοήκοντα τεσσάρων	2,37		0	0
ἕως καί → ὥστε καί; cf. ἵνα καί Mk 1,38; 11,25	12,59		0	0
ἕως τοῦ + infinitive (VKf)		8,40		
ἕως οὗ + indicative (LN: a. until; b. while; SCe; VKd) → ἄχρι οὗ; cf. ἕως ὅτου + indicative Mt 5,25; μέχρις οὗ Mk 13,30	13,21; 24,49 v.l.	21,26	2	0
ἕως πότε (VKh)	9,41		2	2
ἕως ὧδε	23,5		0	0
οὐ (+) ἕως; cf. οὐ + μέχρις Mk 13,30	9,27; 12,59; 13,35; 21,32; 22,16.18.34		11	3

→ ἄγω ἕως; διώκω ἕως; εἰμὶ ἕως; εἰς + ἕως; ἐξάγω ἕως; ἐξέρχομαι ἕως; ἔρχομαι ἕως;
καταβαίνω ἕως; λέγω ὑμῖν/σοι … οὐ μὴ … ἕως (ἄν); οὐκέτι … ἕως; ἕως (τοῦ) οὐρανοῦ;
ἕως τούτου; παρέρχομαι ἕως; πορεύομαι ἕως

Characteristic of Luke	Lk	Acts	Mt	Mk
διέρχομαι ἕως → **διέρχομαι** + ἄχρι; (ἐξ/παρ)**έρχομαι** + ἄχρι/ἕως BOISMARD 1984 Ab112; HARNACK 1906 146; NEIRYNCK 1985; PLUMMER 1922 lii	2,15	9,38; 11,19.22	0	0
ἕως conjunction followed by subjunctive (*SC*a; *VK*a) DENAUX 2009 L***	12,59; 15,4; 17,8; 21,32 *v.l.*; 22,34		1/6	1/2
ἕως + other preposition (*VK*j) BOISMARD 1984 Bb106; NEIRYNCK 1985	24,50	17,14; 21,5; 26,11	0	1
ἕως preposition with reference to location (*SC*g) CREDNER 1836 137	2,15; 4,29.42; 10,15[1.2]; 19,13*; 23,5; 24,50	1,8; 9,38; 11,19.22; 13,47; 17,14.15; 21,5; 23,23; 26,11	6	3
ἕως ὅτου + subjunctive (*LN*: [a]until; [b]while; *SC*d; *VK*e) → **ἕως** οὗ + subjunctive; cf. ἕως ὅτου + indic. (*SC*e) Mt 5,25 CREDNER 1836 136; GOULDER 1989	12,50; 13,8; 15,8 *v.l.*; 22,16.18 *v.l.*		0	0
ἕως οὗ + subjunctive (*LN*: a. until; b. while; *SC*d; *VK*d) → **ἕως** ὅτου + subjunctive; ἄχρι οὗ; cf. μέχρις οὗ Mk 13,30 GOULDER 1989	12,50 *v.l.*59 *v.l.*; 15,4 *v.l.*8; 22,18; 24,49	23,12.14.21; 25,21	4/5	0

Literature

VON BENDEMANN 20001 424: "ἕως ὅτου c. conj. aor. findet sich im Neuen Testament nur bei Lukas"; COLLISON 1977 114 [ἕως + subjunctive, but without ἄν: linguistic usage of Luke: likely; ἕως ὅτου: linguistic usage of Luke's "other source-material": likely; ἕως οὗ: noteworthy phenomena]; DENAUX 2009 L[n] [ἕως ὅτου + subjunctive]; lA[n] [διέρχομαι ἕως]; lAn [ἕως + other preposition]; GERSDORF 1816 212 [ἕως ἡμέρας ἀναδείξεως]; 236 [διέλθωμεν δὴ ἕως Βηθλέεμ]; JEREMIAS 1980 84 [διέρχομαι / ἄγω / διώκω / ἐξάγω / ἐξαποστέλλω / ἔρχομαι / πορεύομαι / προπέμπω ἕως: red.]; 247 [ἕως οὗ: red.]; 323: "ἕως als uneigentliche Präposition findet sich mit einer weiteren Präposition verbunden im NT nur im Doppelwerk"; RADL 1975 412 [ἕως "als Präposition mit Ortsbestimmung"]; REHKOPF 1959 62-63 [ἐᾶτε ἕως τούτου]; 94 [ἕως (temp. Konjunktion ohne ἄν); ἕως ὅτου: vorlukanisch]; SCHÜRMANN 1953 19 [ἕως ὅτου]; 37 [ἕως οὗ Vorzugswendung des Luk; cf. III,24]; 1961 271 [ἕως ὅτου]; 281 [ἕως (temp. Konjunktion ohne ἄν): protoluk R weniger wahrscheinlich].

BURCHARD, Christoph, Fußnoten zum neutestamentlichen Griechisch, 1970. Esp. 161-163: "Act 1,8 ἕως ἐσχάτου τῆς γῆς".
—, Fußnoten zum neutestamentlichen Griechisch II, 1978. Esp. 145-146: "Lk 2,15 διέλθωμεν δὴ ἕως Βηθλέεμ".
VAN UNNIK, Willem C., Der Ausdruck ἕως ἐσχάτου τῆς γῆς (Apostelgeschichte 1:8) und sein alttestamentlicher Hintergrund. — *Studia Biblica et Semitica: Theodoro Christiano Vriezen qui munere professoris theologiae per XXV annos functus est, ab amicis, collegis, discipulis dedicata*. Wageningen: Veenman & Zonen, 1966, 335-349; = ID., *Sparsa Collecta*, I, 1973, 386-401.

Z

Ζακχαῖος 3	Zacchaeus (Lk 19,2.5.8)

Ζαχαρίας 10 (Mt 1) | Zechariah

Word groups	Lk	Acts	Mt	Mk
αἷμα Ζαχαρίου	11,51		1	0
Ζαχαρίας father of John the Baptist (VKa) DENAUX 2009 (L***)	1,5.12.13.18.21.40.59.67; 3,2		0	0
Ζαχαρίας son of Barachias (VKb)	11,51		1	0

Literature

JEREMIAS 1980 210 [αἷμα Ζαχαρίου: trad.; "Artikellosen Genitivverbindungen übernahm Lukas aus der Überlieferung"].

LAURENTIN, René, Traces d'allusions étymologiques en Luc 1–2 (II). — *Bib* 38 (1957) 1-23. Esp. 1-4: "Zacharie et Élisabeth".

Ζεβεδαῖος 1 (Mt 6, Mk 4) | Zebedee (Lk 5,10)

ζεῦγος 2 | pair (Lk 2,24; 14,19)

Characteristic of Luke

PLUMMER 1922 liii

Literature

DENAUX 2009 Lⁿ; HAUCK 1934 [seltenes Alleinwort].

ζηλωτής 1 + 3

1. enthusiast (Acts 21,20; 22,3); 2 nationalist (Lk 6,15; Acts 1,13?)

Word groups	Lk	Acts	Mt	Mk
Σίμων + ὁ ζηλωτής (VKa); cf. Σίμων ὁ Καναναῖος Mt 10,4; Mk 3,18 DENAUX 2009 LAⁿ	6,15	1,13	0	0

Characteristic of Luke

BOISMARD 1984 Db21; NEIRYNCK 1985

Literature

BDAG 2000 427; DENAUX 2009 lAⁿ.

ζημιόω 1 (Mt 1, Mk 1)

1. suffer loss (Lk 9,25); 2. undergo punishment

Word groups	Lk	Acts	Mt	Mk
ζημιόω + κερδαίνω (VKa)	9,25		1	1

ζητέω 25/28 + 10 (Mt 14, Mk 10)

1. try to find (Lk 2,48.49); 2. seek information (Lk 12,29); 3. desire; 4. demand (Lk 12,48); 5. try (Lk 5,18); 6. try to obtain (Lk 12,31); 7. attempt to find

Word groups	Lk	Acts	Mt	Mk
ζητέω + direct object → ἀναζητέω + direct object	2,45*.48.49; 4,42*; 5,18	9,11; 10,19.21; 17,27	2	3
ζητέω + indirect question (VKb)	12,29; 22,2		0	3
ζητέω + ἀπόλλυμι lose → εὑρίσκω + ἀπόλλυμι lose DENAUX 2009 Lⁿ	15,8; 17,33; 19,10		0	0
ζητέω + δίδωμι → αἰτέω + (ἐπι) δίδωμι/λαμβάνω/παρατίθημι; ἀνα/ἐπιζητέω + εὑρίσκω; cf. ἐπιζητέω + δίδωμι Mt 12,39; 16,4	11,29; 12,48		0	1
ζητέω (+) εὑρίσκω (VKc) → ζητέω + δίδωμι; ἀνα/ἐπιζητέω + εὑρίσκω; αἰτέω + (ἐπι)δίδωμι/λαμβάνω	2,45*; 5,18(-19); 11,9. 10.24; 13,6.7; 15,8; 19,47(-48); 24,(3-)5	17,5(-6).27	6	2
ζητέω παρά → (ἀπ)αἰτέω ἀπό/παρά; ἐκζητέω/κωλύω ἀπό	11,16; 12,48		0	1
ζητέω (+) σημεῖον (VKe) → ἐπιζητέω σημεῖον	11,16.29		0	2
ζητέω τὴν ψυχήν (LN: want to kill; VKd) → ἀπόλλυμι/ζῳογονέω/ σῴζω τὴν ψυχήν; cf. εὑρίσκω τὴν ψυχήν Mt 10,39; 16,25	17,33		1	0

Characteristic of Luke

GOULDER 1989; MORGENTHALER 1958L

	Lk	Acts	Mt	Mk
ζητέω + infinitive (VKa) DENAUX 2009 L***	5,18; 6,19; 9,9; 11,54*; 13,24; 17,33; 19,3.47; 20,19	13,8; 16,10; 17,5; 21,31; 27,30	3	1

Literature

VON BENDEMANN 2001 414: "ζητεῖν bei Lukas häufig mit Inifinitiv"; GERSDORF 1816 270 [τί ὅτι ἐζητεῖτέ με]; RADL 1975 412.

BORMANN, Lukas, Recht, Gerechtigkeit und Religion, 2001. Esp. 181-182.
BROX, Norbert, Suchen und Finden: Zur Nachgeschichte von Mt 7,7b/Lk 11,9b. — HOFFMANN, P. – BROX, N. – PESCH, W. (eds.), Orientierung an Christus. FS J. Schmid, 1973, 17-36.
DELEBECQUE, Édouard, Études grecques, 1976. Esp. 48-50 [2,41-52].

Ζοροβαβέλ 1 (Mt 2) | Zerubbabel (Lk 3,27)

ζύμη 2 (Mt 4, Mk 2)

1. yeast (Lk 13,21); 2. pretense (Lk 12,1)

Word groups	Lk	Acts	Mt	Mk
ζύμη + τῶν Φαρισαίων (VKa)	12,1		3	1

Literature

MITTON, C. Leslie, New Wine in Old Wineskins. IV: Leaven. — ExpT 84 (1972-73) 339-343.

ζυμόω 1 (Mt 1)	use yeast (Lk 13,21)

ζῶ 9 + 12 (Mt 6, Mk 2[3])
1. live (Lk 2,36); 2. live again (Lk 15,32); 3. behave (Lk 15,13)

Word groups	Lk	Acts	Mt	Mk
(ὁ) θεὸς (ὁ) ζῶν (VKa)		14,15	2	0
ζῶ + dative (VKf)	20,38²		0	0
ζῶ + ἐν (VKg)		17,28	0	0
ζῶ + ἐπί + dative (VKh) → ζῶ ἐπ᾽ ἄρτῳ	4,4		1	0
ζῶ + (ἀπο)θνήσκω (VKb); cf. ζῶ + τελευτάω Mt 9,18		9,(37-)41; 25,19	0	0
ζῶ + κατά + accusative (VKk)		26,5	0	0
ζῶ + νεκρός (VKc) → ἀναζάω + νεκρός	15,32; 20,38¹; 24,5	10,42	1	1
θεὸς + τῶν ζώντων	20,38¹·²		1/2	1/2

Characteristic of Luke
GOULDER 1989

	Lk	Acts	Mt	Mk
ζῆν infinitive HARNACK 1906 40	24,23	22,22; 25,19.24; 28,4	0	0

Literature
DENAUX 2009 IAⁿ [ζῆν infinitive]; EASTON 1910 161 [ζάω "become alive": cited by Weiss as characteristic of L, and possibly corroborative]; RADL 1975 412 [ζῶ; ζῆν].

LEE, John A.L., The Future of ζῆν in Late Greek. — NT 22 (1980) 289-298.
SABUGAL, Santos, Anástasis. Resucitó y resucitaremos (BAC), Madrid, 1993. 712 pp.

ζωγρέω 1	control (Lk 5,10)

ζωή 5/6 + 8 (Mt 7, Mk 4)   life

Word groups	Lk	Acts	Mt	Mk
ζωὴ αἰώνιος (SCa; VKa)	10,25; 18,18.30	13,46.48	3	2
ζωὴν ... δίδωμι		17,25	0	0
ζωὴν αἰώνιον κληρονομέω; cf. βασιλείαν κληρονομέω Mt 25,34 DENAUX 2009 Lⁿ	10,25; 18,18		0	0

Literature
HILL, David, Greek Words and Hebrew Meanings, 1967. Esp. 191-192: "The use of ζωή αἰώνιος in the New Testament: The Synoptic Gospels".

ζῳογονέω 1 + 1
1. keep alive (Lk 17,33; Acts 7,19); 2. make live

Word groups	Lk	Acts	Mt	Mk
ζῳογονέω + ἀπόλλυμι	17,33		0	0

| ζῳογονέω τὴν ψυχήν → ἀπόλλυμι/ζητέω/σῴζω τὴν ψυχήν | 17,33 | | 0 | 0 |

Literature
DENAUX 2009 LAⁿ; HAUCK 1934 [seltenes Alleinwort]; JEREMIAS 1980 269-270 [red.].

H

ἤ 45/52 + 35/39 (Mt 68/73, Mk 33/40)
1. or (Lk 5,23); 2. than (Lk 9,13)

Word groups	Lk	Acts	Mt	Mk
ἀλλ' ἤ (VKj)	12,51		0	0
ἤ after a comparative (SCd; VKf)	5,23; 9,13; 10,12.14; 16,17; 18,25	24,11*; 25,6	5/6	2/3
ἤ in a comparison (SCd; VK1)	15,7; 17,2; 18,14*	17,21¹	2	3
ἤ interrogative except ἤ πῶς / τίς / τί / ἐν τίνι (SCc; VKc)	7,19.20; 13,4		5	0
ἤ ... ἤ (LN: either ... or; SCg)	16,13¹·²	17,21¹·²	4	0
ἤ ἰδού → ἀλλ'/πλὴν ἰδού	17,21 v.l.23v.l.?		0	0/1
ἤ ἵνα	17,2		0	0
ἤ καί (VKe)	11,11* v.l.12; 12,41; 18,11		1	0
ἤ πῶς (SCb; VKb)	6,42*		2	0
ἤ (+) τίς / τί / ἐν τίνι interrogative (SCa; VKa)	12,11¹·².29*; 14,31; 15,8; 20,2	3,12¹; 7,49	4	2/3
μᾶλλον (+) ἤ (SCe; VKg)		4,19; 5,29; 20,35; 27,11	1	0
πρὶν ἤ (SCf; VKh)	2,26; 22,34*	2,20*; 7,2; 25,16	1	1

→ ἀργύριον ἤ χρυσίον; ἔξεστιν + inf. + ἤ + inf.; ἔξεστιν + inf. + ἤ οὐ

Characteristic of Luke	Lk	Acts	Mt	Mk
ἤ γάρ (VKk) CREDNER 1836 137	16,13¹; 18,14*		0	0

→ πλείων ἤ

Literature
COLLISON 1977 103 [ἤ disjunctive particle between sayings: linguistic usage of Luke's "other source-material": certain]; 105 [ἤ disjunctive particle between questions: linguistic usage of Luke: probable]; SCHÜRMANN 1957 33 [Luk liebt ... Doppelgliederungen mit καί oder ἤ]; 84 [mit ἤ gegliederte Fragen ... eher vorluk Ursprung].

THRALL, Margaret E., Greek Particles in the New Testament, 1962. Esp. 16-20 [ἀλλ' ἤ for ἀλλά].

ἡγεμονεύω* 2
be governor (Lk 2,2; 3,1)

Characteristic of Luke
PLUMMER 1922 liii

Literature
DENAUX 2009 Lⁿ; GERSDORF 1816 216 [ἡγεμονεύοντος τῆς Συρίας κυρηνίου]; HAUCK 1934 [seltenes Alleinwort]; SCHÜRMANN 1957 77-78 [ἡγεμονεύω, ἡγεμονία, ἡγεμών].

BORMANN, Lukas, Recht, Gerechtigkeit und Religion, 2001. Esp. 116.

ἡγεμονία 1 — government (Lk 3,1)

Literature
HAUCK 1934 [seltenes Alleinwort].

BORMANN, Lukas, *Recht, Gerechtigkeit und Religion*, 2001. Esp. 116.

ἡγεμών 2 + 6/7 (Mt 10/11, Mk 1)
1. ruler; 2. governor (Lk 20,20; 21,12)

Word groups	Lk	Acts	Mt	Mk
ἡγεμὼν καὶ βασιλεύς	21,12	26,30	1	1
ἡγεμόνες plural (VKa)	21,12		2	1

Literature
BORMANN, Lukas, *Recht, Gerechtigkeit und Religion*, 2001. Esp. 116-117.

ἡγέομαι 1 + 4 (Mt 1)
1. be of opinion; 2. guide (Lk 22,26); 3. govern (Acts 7,10)

Characteristic of Luke	Lk	Acts	Mt	Mk
ἡγούμενος (VKa) BOISMARD 1984 Db22; NEIRYNCK 1985; VOGEL 1899B	22,26	7,10; 14,12; 15,22	1	0

Literature
DENAUX 2009 lAn, lAn [ἡγούμενος].

ἤδη 10 + 3 (Mt 7, Mk 8/9) — already

Word groups	Lk	Acts	Mt	Mk
ἤδη in absolute genitive (VKa)	7,6; 19,37	27,9[1]	0	3
εἰ ἤδη (VKc)	12,49		0	1/2
ἤδη δέ (VKb)	3,9; 7,6		1	0

Literature
REHKOPF 1959 94 [vorlukanisch]; SCHÜRMANN 1961 276.

ἡδονή 1
1. pleasure (Lk 8,14); 2. passion

Literature
HAUCK 1934 [seltenes Alleinwort].

ἡδύοσμον 1 (Mt 1) — mint (Lk 11,42)

ἥκω 5 + 0/1 (Mt 4, Mk 1)
1. arrive (Lk 12,46; 13,29.35; 15,27; 19,43); 2. be here; 3. happen

Word groups	Lk	Acts	Mt	Mk
ἥκω ἀπό (VKa) → ἔρχομαι + ἀπό	13,29		1	1
ἥκω εἰς (VKb) → ἔρχομαι + εἰς		28,23*	0	0
ἥκω + ἐπί + accusative (VKd) → ἔρχομαι + ἐπί + acc.	19,43		1	0
ἥκω πρός + accusative (VKe) → ἔρχομαι πρός + acc.		28,23*	1	0

Characteristic of Luke	Lk	Acts	Mt	Mk
ἡμέραι ἥξουσιν/ἔρχονται/ἐλεύσονται→ ἡμέραι **ἐλεύσονται** DENAUX 2009 L***; GOULDER 1989*	5,35[1]; 17,22[1]; 19,43; 21,6; 23,29		1	1

Literature

COLLISON 1977 95 [noteworthy phenomena]; REHKOPF 1959 94 [vorlukanisch]; SCHÜRMANN 1961 276.

Ἡλί 1 Heli (Lk 3,23)

Ἡλίας 7/8 (Mt 9, Mk 9) Elijah

Word groups	Lk	Acts	Mt	Mk
Ἡλίας + Μωϋσῆς (VKa)	9,30.33		2	2

ἡλικία 3 (Mt 1)

1. lifetime (Lk 12,25); 2. mature; 3. stature (Lk 2,52; 19,3)

Literature

EASTON 1910 161 [ἡλικία: "stature": cited by Weiss as characteristic of L, and possibly corroborative]; REHKOPF 1959 94 [vorlukanisch]; SCHÜRMANN 1961 273.

SCHWARZ, Günther, οτι τη ηλικια μικρος ην. [Lk 19,3] — *BibNot* 8 (1979) 23-24.
—, Προσθεῖναι ἐπὶ τὴν ἡλικίαν αὐτοῦ πῆχυν ἕνα. — *ZNW* 71 (1980) 244-247.

ἥλιος 3 + 4 (Mt 5, Mk 4) sun

Word groups	Lk	Acts	Mt	Mk
ἥλιος + ἄστρον DENAUX 2009 LA[n]	21,25	27,20	0	0
ἥλιος + σελήνη	21,25	2,20	1	1
ἥλιος + σκότος; cf. ἥλιος + σκοτίζω Mt 24,29; Mk 13,24 DENAUX 2009 lA[n]	23,44(-45)	2,20; 13,11	0	0

Literature

GRÁNDEZ, Rufino María, Crítica textual de Lc 23,45a: καὶ ἐσκοτίσθη ὁ ἥλιος. — *Scriptorium Victoriense* (Vitoria) 44 (1997) 5-20.

ἡμεῖς 69/76 + 125/138 (Mt 49/51, Mk 23/24) we, us

Word groups

ἡμεῖς	Lk	Acts	Mt	Mk
ἡμεῖς δέ (VKb) → ἐγὼ/σὺ/ὑμεῖς δέ DENAUX 2009 1Aⁿ	24,21	6,4; 20,6.13; 21,7; 23,15	0	0
ἡμεῖς μέν → ἐγὼ/ὑμεῖς μέν	23,41		0	0
ἰδοὺ ἡμεῖς (VKf) → ἰδοὺ ἐγώ	18,28		1	1
πάντες ἡμεῖς (VKe) → πάντων ἡμῶν; πάντας ἡμᾶς; πάντες ὑμεῖς		2,32; 10,33	0	0

ἡμῶν	Lk	Acts	Mt	Mk
ἕκαστος ἡμῶν (VKf) → τίς/ἕκαστος/οὐδεὶς ὑμῶν		17,27	0	0
ἡμῶν in absolute genitive (VKd)		16,16[1]; 20,7; 21,10*.17[1]; 26,14; 27,18.27	1	0
ἡμῶν after preposition + genitive (VKa)	9,49.50*[1.*2]; 16,26[1]; 24,22[1].29	1,22[1]; 7,27; 9,38; 15,9.24	2	2
ἡμῶν in the prepositive position (SCa; VKc)		16,20	1	0
ἡμῶν with verb + genitive (VKb) DENAUX 2009 1An	20,14	7,40[2]; 24,4	0	1
θεὸς ἡμῶν; cf. θεέ μου Mt 27,46; θεός μου Mk 15,34	1,78[1]	2,39; 3,22*	0	1
πάντων + ἡμῶν (VKe) → παντές ἡμεῖς; πάντας ἡμᾶς; παντῶν ὑμῶν		26,14	0	0
τὰ περὶ ἡμῶν (VKg) → τὸ/τὰ περὶ ἐμοῦ		28,15[1]	0	0

ἡμῖν	Lk	Acts	Mt	Mk
ἡμῖν dependent on adjective (VKb)		28,22	1	0
ἡμῖν (ἐστιν) (VKc) → μοι (ἔστιν/γίνεται)	4,34[1]; 9,13	19,25; 21,23	4	1
καὶ ἡμῖν → καὶ ἡμεῖς/ἡμᾶς; καὶ ἐμοί/σοί/ὑμῖν		11,17; 15,8.28; 16,17	0	0
τί ἡμῖν καὶ σοί → τί ἐμοὶ καὶ σοί	4,34[1]		1	1

ἡμᾶς	Lk	Acts	Mt	Mk
ἡμᾶς after preposition + accusative (VKa)	12,41; 16,26[2]; 19,14; 23,15.30[1]	1,21[2]; 3,4; 5,28; 7,27 v.l.; 11,15; 14,11; 21,11	3	2
καὶ ἡμᾶς → καὶ ἡμεῖς/ἡμῖν DENAUX 2009 Lⁿ	11,45; 23,39		0	0
πάντας ἡμᾶς (VKb) → πάντες ἡμεῖς; πάντων ἡμῶν		28,2[2]	0	0

Characteristic of Luke

HENDRIKS 1986 468; MORGENTHALER 1958LA

	Lk	Acts	Mt	Mk
ἡμῖν after preposition + dative (VKa) DENAUX 2009 1A**	1,1; 7,16; 24,24.32[2]	1,17.22; 2,29; 15,7*; 21,16.18; 27,2	1	0
καὶ ἡμεῖς (VKa) → καὶ ἡμῖν/ἡμᾶς; καὶ ἐγώ/σύ/ὑμεῖς DENAUX 2009 1A*	3,14; 23,41	5,32; 10,39.47; 13,32; 14,15	1	0
πατήρ/πατέρες ἡμῶν (SCb) → πατήρ μου/σου / πατέρες ὑμῶν DENAUX 2009 1A*	1,55.72.73[1]; 11,2*	3,13.25*; 4,25; 5,30; 7,2.11.12.15.19[2].38[1].39. 44.45[1.2]; 13,17; 15,10[1]; 22,14; 26,6; 28,25*	2	1
→ θεὸς τῶν πατέρων σου/ἡμῶν				

Literature

SCHÜRMANN 1957 73-74.86-87 [ἡμεῖς δέ].

PICKETT, Velma B., Those Problem Pronouns: *We, Us* and *Our* in the New Testament. — *BTrans* 15 (1964) 88-92.

ἡμέρα 83/85 + 94 (Mt 45, Mk 27)				
1. day (Lk 13,14); 2. daylight period; 3. period (Lk 1,23); 4. daylight (Lk 4,42); 5. court of justice				

Word groups	Lk	Acts	Mt	Mk
ἄγει ἡμέραν DENAUX 2009 L[n]	4,(1-)2; 24,21		0/1	0
ἀνίστημι/ἐγείρω (+) τῇ τρίτῃ ἡμέρᾳ; cf. ἀνίστημι/ἐγείρω μετὰ τρεῖς ἡμέρας Mt 27,63; Mk 8,31; 9,31; 10,34	9,22; 18,33; 24,7.46	10,40	3	0/1
ἀφ' ἡμερῶν ἀρχαίων (LN: long ago)		15,7	0	0
ἄχρι τῆς ἡμέρας ταύτης → ἄχρι ἧς ἡμέρας BOISMARD 1984 Aa76		2,29; 23,1; 26,22	0	0
ἄχρι ἧς ἡμέρας → ἄχρι τῆς ἡμέρας ταύτης	1,20; 17,27	1,2	1	0
δι' ἡμερῶν (LN: few days later) → δι' ἐτῶν		1,3	0	1
διατρίβω (+) ἡμέρας		16,12; 20,6[3]; 25,6.14	0	0
ἐσχάτη ἡμέρα (VKg)		2,17	0	0
ἡμέρα with cardinal number, except μία τῶν ἡμερῶν (SCc; VKc)	2,21.46; 4,2[1]; 9,28; 13,14[1]	1,3; 9,9; 20,6[2.3]; 21,4. 7.27; 24,1.11; 25,1.6; 28,7.12.13.14.17	9	9
ἡμέρα with ordinal number, except τρίτη ἡμέρα (SCc; VKe)	1,59	7,8; 10,30; 20,18; 27,33[2]	0	1
ἡμέρα τῶν ἀζύμων → ἑορτὴ τῶν ἀζύμων; πάσχα + ἄζυμος; cf. ἡ πρώτη τῶν ἀζύμων Mt 26,17	22,7	12,3; 20,6[1]	0	1
ἡ ἡμέρα αὕτη (SCa) → ἡ ἡμέρα ἐκείνη; αἱ ἡμέραι αὗται; ὁ αἰὼν οὗτος; οὗτος καιρός; αὕτη ἡ νύξ DENAUX 2009 lA[n]	19,42; 24,21	2,29; 23,1; 26,22	0	0
ἡ ἡμέρα ἐκείνη (SCa; VKa) → ἡ ἡμέρα αὕτη; αἱ ἡμέραι ἐκείναι; ὁ αἰὼν ἐκεῖνος; ὁ ἐκεῖνος καιρός; νὺξ ἐκείνη; ἐν ἐκείνη τῇ ὥρᾳ / τῇ ὥρᾳ ἐκείνη	6,23; 10,12; 17,31; 21,34	2,41; 8,1	6	4
ἡμέρα (+) ἱκανή → χρόνος ἱκανός		9,23.43; 18,18; 27,7	0	0
ἡμέρα κυρίου		2,20	0	0
ἡμέρα + μεγάλη		2,20	0	0
ἡμέρα + ὁ υἱὸς τοῦ ἀνθρώπου → ὥρα + ὁ υἱὸς τοῦ ἀνθρώπου DENAUX 2009 L[n]	17,22[2].24.26[2].30		0	0
ἡμέρα + νύξ (VKk)	2,37; 18,7; 21,37	9,24; 20,31; 26,7	3	2
ἡμέραι τινές BOISMARD 1984 Aa18		9,19; 10,48; 15,36; 16,12; 24,24; 25,13	0	0
ἡμέρα + ὥρα (VKl)	12,46	2,15; 10,3.30	3	1
αἱ ἡμέραι ἐκείναι (SCb; VKb) → ἡ ἡμέρα ἐκείνη; αἱ ἡμέραι αὗται	2,1; 4,2[2]; 5,35[2]; 9,36; 20,1 v.l.; 21,23	2,18; 7,41; 9,37	6	5/6
ἡμέρας (+) καὶ νυκτός	18,7	9,24	0	0
πλείους (+) ἡμέραι		13,31; 21,10; 24,11; 25,6.14; 27,20	0	0
προβαίνω ἐν ἡμέραις (LN: be old) DENAUX 2009 L[n]	1,7.18; 2,36		0	0

πρώτη ἡμέρα		20,18	0	1
συμπληροῦται ἡ ἡμέρα → ἐπλήσθησαν αἱ **ἡμέραι**; τελειόω τὰς **ἡμέρας** DENAUX 2009 LA[n]	9,51	2,1	0	0
τελειόω τὰς ἡμέρας → ἐπλήσθησαν αἱ **ἡμέραι**; συμπληροῦται ἡ **ἡμέρα**	2,43		0	0
τρίτη (+) ἡμέρα (SCe; VKf) → **ὥρα** τρίτη	9,22; 18,33; 24,7.21.46	10,40	4	0/2
→ ἡ **σήμερον** (ἡμέρα)				

Characteristic of Luke

GOULDER 1989; HENDRIKS 1986 428.434.448.468; MORGENTHALER 1958LA

	Lk	Acts	Mt	Mk
αἱ ἡμέραι αὗται (SCb) → ἡ **ἡμέρα** αὕτη; αἱ **ἡμέραι** ἐκεῖναι DENAUX 2009 L***	1,24.39; 6,12; 23,7; 24,18	1,5.15; 3,24; 5,36; 6,1; 11,27; 21,15.38	0	0
(ἐν) αὐτῇ τῇ ἡμέρᾳ → ἐν αὐτῷ τῷ **καιρῷ**; (ἐν) αὐτῇ τῇ **ὥρᾳ** GOULDER 1989*; NEIRYNCK 1985; PLUMMER 1922 lii	13,31*; 23,12; 24,13			
(ἐν) αὐτῇ τῇ ἡμέρᾳ/καιρῷ/ ὥρᾳ BOISMARD 1984 Ab4; DENAUX 2009 L***	2,38; 10,21; 12,12; 13,1.31*; 20,19; 23,12; 24,13.33	16,18; 22,13	0	0
ἐν μιᾷ τῶν ἡμερῶν PLUMMER 1922 lii	5,17; 8,22; 20,1			
ἐν ταῖς ἡμέραις + genitive DENAUX 2009 L***; GOULDER 1989*	1,5.7.18; 4,25;17,26.28	5,37; 13,41	0	0
ἐν ταῖς ἡμέραις + proper name; cf. Acts 7,45 ἕως τῶν ἡμερῶν Δαυίδ DENAUX 2009 L***; HARNACK 1906 69	1,5; 4,25; 17,26.28		0	0
ἐν ταῖς ἡμέραις ταύταις BOISMARD 1984 Ab34; DENAUX 2009 L***; GOULDER 1989*; HARNACK 1906 138; HAWKINS 1909L; NEIRYNCK 1985; PLUMMER 1922 lii.	1,39; 6,12; 23,7; 24,18	1,15; 6,1; 11,27	0	0
ἡμέρα + liturgical determinative; cf. Jn 12,1; 19,31 BOISMARD 1984 Bb107; DENAUX 2009 L***; NEIRYNCK 1985	4,16; 13,14.16; 14,5; 22,7; 23,54	2,1; 12,3; 13,14; 16,13; 20,6[1].16	0	1
(ἡ) ἡμέρα / (αἱ) ἡμέραι + genitive of person(s) (SCg; VKj) DENAUX 2009 L***	1,5.7.18.75; 4,25; 17,22[2].24.26[1.2].28	2,20; 7,45; 13,41	3	0
ἡμέρα + αὕτη; cf. Heb 1,2 BOISMARD 1984 Bb6; DENAUX 2009 L***; HARNACK 1906 52; NEIRYNCK 1985	1,24.39; 6,12; 19,42; 23,7; 24,18.21	1,5.15; 2,29; 3,24; 5,36; 6,1; 11,27; 21,15.38; 23,1; 26,22	0	0
ἡμέρα γίνεται BOISMARD 1984 Bb19; DENAUX 2009 lA*; HARNACK 1906 52; HAWKINS 1909L.B; NEIRYNCK 1985; PLUMMER 1922 lii	4,42; 6,13; 22,66	12,18; 16,35; 23,12; 27,29.33[1].39	0	1
(ἐν) (τῇ) ἡμέρᾳ τοῦ σαββάτου / τῶν σαββάτων (SCj) DENAUX 2009 L***; GOULDER 1989; HARNACK 1906 31; HAWKINS 1909 187; PLUMMER 1922 lii; VOGEL 1899C	4,16; 13,14[2].16; 14,5	13,14; 16,13		

ἡμέραι ἥξουσιν/ἐλεύσονται/ἔρχονται DENAUX 2009 L***; GOULDER1989*	5,35[1]; 17,22[1]; 19,43; 21,6; 23,29		1	1
ἡμέρας γενομένης; cf. ὀψίας γενομένης Mt 8,16; 14,15.23; 16,2; 20,8; 26,20; 27,57; Mk 1,32; 4,35; 6,47; 14,17; 15,42 VOGEL 1899C	4,42	12,18; 16,35; 23,12	0	1
ἡμέρας ὁδός → σαββάτου ὁδός BOISMARD 1984 Ab187; NEIRYNCK 1985	2,44		0	0
καθ' ἡμέραν (SCh; VKn); cf. καθημερινός Acts 6,1 CADBURY 1920 117; CREDNER 1836 138; DENAUX 2009 L***; HAWKINS 1909L; PLUMMER 1922 lx	9,23; 11,3; 16,19; 19,47; 22,53	2,46.47; 3,2; 16,5; 17,11; 19,9	1	1
τὸ καθ' ἡμέραν BOISMARD 1984 Ab126; NEIRYNCK 1985	11,3; 19,47	17,11 v.l.	0	0
κλίνει ἡ ἡμέρα PLUMMER 1922 liii	9,12; 24,29		0	0
μετὰ δὲ ἡμέρας; cf. Jn 4,43 BOISMARD 1984 Bb69; NEIRYNCK 1985	1,24	15,36; 21,15; 24,1	0	0
μία τῶν ἡμερῶν (SCd; VKd) DENAUX 2009 L***	5,17; 8,22; 17,22[2]; 20,1		0	0
νύκτα καὶ ἡμέραν BOISMARD 1984 cb38; NEIRYNCK 1985	2,37	20,31; 26,7	0	1
ἐπλήσθησαν αἱ ἡμέραι → συμπληροῦται ἡ ἡμέρα; τελειόω τὰς ἡμέρας; ἐπλήσθη ὁ χρόνος DENAUX 2009 L***	1,23; 2,6.21.22		0	0

→ μετ' οὐ πολλὰς ἡμέρας

Literature

COLLISON 1977 133 [ἐν + ἡμέρα: linguistic usage of Luke: certain]; 134 [ἐν + ἡμέρα + genitive: linguistic usage of Luke's "other source-material": probable]; 137 [καθ' ἡμέραν: linguistic usage of Luke: certain]; DENAUX 2009 L[n] [(ἐν) αὐτῇ τῇ ἡμέρᾳ; ἐν μιᾷ τῶν ἡμερῶν; τὸ καθ' ἡμέραν; κλίνει ἡ ἡμέρα], lA[n] [μετὰ δὲ ἡμέρας; ἡμέρας γενομένης]; EASTON 1910 155 [ἡμέρα τοῦ σαββάτου: probably characteristic of L]; 161 [ἐπτάκις τῆς ἡμέρας: cited by Weiss as characteristic of L, and possibly corroborative]; GERSDORF 1816 162 [ἐγένετο ἐν ταῖς ἡμέραις]; 164 [ἐν ταῖς ἡμέραις Ἡρῴδου]; 188 [ἄχρι ἧς ἡμέρας γένηται ταῦτα]; 192 [μετὰ δὲ ταύτας τὰς ἡμέρας]; 198 [ἀναστᾶσα δὲ Μαριὰμ ἐν ταῖς ἡμέραις ταύταις]; 202-203 [καὶ ἐγένετο ἐν τῇ ἡμέρᾳ τῇ ὀγδόῃ ἦλθον]; 211-212 [πάσαις ταῖς ἡμέραις ἡμῶν]; 212 [ἕως ἡμέρας ἀναδείξεως]; 212 [ἐγένετο δὲ ἐν ταῖς ἡμέραις ἐκείναις]; 265 [ἦλθον ἡμέρας ὁδὸν καὶ ἀνεζήτουν αὐτόν]; HARNACK 1907 48; HAUCK 1934 [Vorzugsverbindung: (τὸ) καθ' ἡμέραν; ἐγένετο ἡμέρα; ἐν αὐτῇ τῇ ἡμέρᾳ; ἐν ταῖς ἡμέραις ταύταις]; JEREMIAS 1980 46 [μετὰ δὲ ταύτας τὰς ἡμέρας; ἐν ἡμέραις αἷς: red.]; 55 [ἐν ταῖς ἡμέραις ταύταις: red.]; 77 [ἡμέρας ἀναδείξεως: "Artikellose Genitivverbindung": trad.]; 99: "er verbindet Fest- und Sabbathbezeichnungen mit ἡμέρα bzw. ἡμέραι"; 120: "Die Wendung (ἐν) τῇ ἡμέρᾳ τῶν σαββάτων / τοῦ σαββάτου ist ein Septuagintismus, der im NT nur im lukanischen Doppelwerk vorkommt: trad."; 249 [μετ' οὐ πολλὰς ἡμέρας: litotes: red.]; 266 [ἐλεύσονται ἡμέραι: red.]; 267 [μίαν τῶν ἡμερῶν: red.]; 299: "Die Verbindung von ἡμέρα mit γίνομαι zur Umschreibung des Tagesanbruchs findet sich im NT nur im lk Doppelwerk"; PAFFENROTH 1997 81 [ἡμέρα τοῦ σαββάτου (singular)]; PLUMMER 1922 lxi [ἐν ταῖς ἡμέραις; τῇ ἡμέρᾳ τοῦ σαββάτου: Hebrew influence]; RADL 1975 403 [ἐγένετο + ἡμέρα]; 405 [διατρίβω ἡμέρας]; 412 [ἡμέρα; "Lukas liebt Umschreibungen mit ἡμέρα: z.B. καθ' ἡμέραν; ἄχρι τῆς ἡμέρας ταύτης; ἡμέρα τῶν σαββάτων/τοῦ σαββάτου]; 413 [ἡμέραι ἱκαναί]; 424 [πλείους + ἡμέραι].

CADBURY, Henry J., Some Lukan Expressions of Time (Lexical Notes on Luke-Acts VII).
— JBL 82 (1963) 272-278.

CLARK, D.J., After Three days. — *BTrans* 30 (1979) 340-343. [NTA 24, 30]

DE JONGE, Henk J., Sonship, Wisdom, Infancy: Luke II.41-51a. — *NTS* 24 (1977-78) 317-354. Esp. 324-327: "After three days".

MEALAND, David, "After Not Many Days" in Acts 1.5 and Its Hellenistic Context. — *JSNT* 42 (1991) 69-77. [μετὰ ἡμέρας πολλάς]

PERRY, John M., The Three Days in the Synoptic Passion Predictions. — *CBQ* 48 (1986) 637-654. [τῇ τρίτῃ ἡμέρᾳ]

PRETE, Benedetto, Valore dell'espressione ἀφ' ἡμερῶν ἀρχαίων in *Atti* 15,7: Nesso cronologico, oppure istanza teologica della Chiesa delle origini? — *BibOr* 13 (1971) 119-133; = ID., *L'opera di Luca*, 1986, 494-508. Esp. 500-503: "L'uso dell'espressione ἀπ' αἰῶνος negli scritti di Luca"; 503-504: "Le espressioni ἀπ' ἀρχῆς e ἐν ἀρχῇ negli scritti di Luca"; 504-506: "La formula ἀφ' ἡμερῶν ἀρχαίων nel contesto di Atti 15,1-35"; 506-508: "La formula ἀφ' ἡμερῶν ἀρχαίων: espressione di un'istanza della Chiesa primitiva".

WILCOX, Max, Semitisms in the New Testament, 1984. Esp. 1009: "ἐν μιᾷ τῶν ἡμερῶν = 'one day'".

ἡμιθανής 1 | half dead (Lk 10,30)

Literature

HAUCK 1934 [seltenes Alleinwort].

BURCHARD, Christoph, Fußnoten zum neutestamentlichen Griechisch, 1970. Esp. 158-159.

ἥμισυς 1 (Mk 1) | one half (Lk 19,8)

Ἤρ 1 | Er (Lk 3,28)

Ἡρῴδης 14 + 8/9 (Mt 13, Mk 8) | Herod

Word groups	Lk	Acts	Mt	Mk
Ἡρῴδης (ὁ) βασιλεύς	1,5	12,1	2	1
Ἡρῴδης (+) Ἰωάννης	9,7.9		1	5
Ἡρῴδης (+) Πιλᾶτος DENAUX 2009 La^n	3,1; 23,(6-)7$^{1.2}$.11.12. (13-)15	4,27	0	0
Ἡρῴδης Herod Agrippa (SCc; VKc)		12,1.6.11.19.20*.21	0	0
Ἡρῴδης Herod Antipas tetrarch (SCb; VKb)	3,1.19$^{1.2}$; 8,3; 9,7.9; 13,31; 23,7$^{1.2}$.8. 11.12.15	4,27; 13,1	4	8
Ἡρῴδης Herod the Great (SCa; VKa)	1,5	23,35	9	0

Literature

GERSDORF 1816 167 [Ἡρῴδου τοῦ βασιλέως].

Ἡρῳδιάς 1 (Mt 2, Mk 3) | Herodias (Lk 3,19)

Ἠσαΐας 2 + 3 (Mt 6/7, Mk 2) | Isaiah (Lk 3,4; 4,17)

Word groups	Lk	Acts	Mt	Mk
διὰ Ἠσαΐου τοῦ προφήτου (SCa; VKa)		28,25	4/5	0

ἡσυχάζω 2 + 2

1. rest (Lk23,56); 2. live quiet life; 3. remain quiet (Lk 14,4)

Characteristic of Luke
BOISMARD 1984 Bb108; HARNACK 1906 52; NEIRYNCK 1985; PLUMMER 1922 lix; VOGEL 1899B

Literature
DENAUX 2009 LA[n]; JEREMIAS 1980 236 [red.]; RADL 1975 412.

ἦχος 2 + 1

1. sound (Lk 21,25; Acts 2,2); 2. information (Lk 4,37)

Word groups	Lk	Acts	Mt	Mk
τὸ ἦχος (VKa)	21,25		0	0

Characteristic of Luke
BOISMARD 1984 cb30; NEIRYNCK 1985; VOGEL 1899B

Literature
COLLISON 1977 181 [noteworthy phenomena]; DENAUX 2009 La[n]; HAUCK 1934 [seltenes Alleinwort].

θάλασσα 3 + 10 (Mt 16/17, Mk 19)

1. sea (Lk 17,2.6; 21,25; Acts 14,15); 2. lake (Acts 7,36; 10,6)

Word groups	Lk	Acts	Mt	Mk
γῆ + θάλασσα (VKd)	21,25	4,24; 7,36; 14,15	1	1
ἡ ἐρυθρὰ θάλασσα (VKc)		7,36	0	0

Literature
THEIßEN, Gerd, "Meer" und "See" in den Evangelien: Ein Beitrag zur Lokalkoloritforschung. — SNTU 10 (1985) 5-25. Esp. 9-13: "Der 'See Gennesaret' und das lukanische Doppelwerk".

θάμβος 2 + 1   astonishment (Lk 4,36; 5,9; Acts 3,10)

Word groups	Lk	Acts	Mt	Mk
τὸ θάμβος (VKa)		3,10	0	0
θάμβος + περιέχει + accusative → ἐγένετο θάμβος ἐπί + acc.; φόβος λαμβάνει + acc.	5,9		0	0
ἐπλήσθην θάμβους → ἐγένετο θάμβος ἐπί + acc.; ἐπλήσθην φόβου		3,10	0	0

Characteristic of Luke

BOISMARD 1984 Ab127; HAWKINS 1909LA; MORGENTHALER 1958*; NEIRYNCK 1985; PLUMMER 1922 lii; VOGEL 1899A

	Lk	Acts	Mt	Mk
ἐγένετο ϑάμβος/φόβος ἐπί + accusative → **ϑάμβος** περιέχει + acc.; ἐπλήσϑην **ϑάμβους**; ἐγένετο **φόβος** ἐπί + acc. BOISMARD 1984 Ab72; NEIRYNCK 1985	1,65; 4,36	5,5.11	0	0

Literature

COLLISON 1977 181 [noteworthy phenomena]; DENAUX 2009 La[n]; LA[n] [ἐγένετο ϑάμβος/ φόβος ἐπί + accusative]; JEREMIAS 1980 32 [ἐγένετο ϑάμβος ἐπί τινα; ϑάμβος περιέσχεν τινά; ἐπλήσϑησαν ϑάμβους καὶ ἐκστάσεως: red.]; 136 [red.]; HAUCK 1934 [Vorzugswort].

ϑάνατος 7 + 8 (Mt 7, Mk 6)
1. death (Lk 23,15); 2. plague

Word groups	Lk	Acts	Mt	Mk
αἰτία ϑανάτου (SCc) → αἴτιος/ἄξιος **ϑανάτου** BOISMARD 1984 Aa113		13,28; 28,18	0	0
εἰς ϑάνατον (SCa; VKa)	22,33		1/2	1
ϑάνατον ὁράω/εἶδον (VKh); cf. ϑάνατον ϑεωρέω Jn 8,51	2,26			
ϑανάτου γεύομαι (VKf)	9,27		1	1
κρίμα ϑανάτου	24,20		0	0
σκία ϑανάτου (SCb)	1,79		1	0

Characteristic of Luke	Lk	Acts	Mt	Mk
αἴτιος/ἄξιος ϑανάτου → αἰτία **ϑανάτου** DENAUX 2009 IA*; VOGEL 1899C	23,15.22	23,29; 25,11.25; 26,31	0	0
πράσσω τι/οὐδὲν ἄξιον ϑανάτου; cf. Rom 1,32 BOISMARD 1984 Ab100; NEIRYNCK 1985	23,15	25,11.25; 26,31	0	0

Literature

DENAUX 2009 IA[n] [πράσσω τι/οὐδὲν ἄξιον ϑανάτου]; JEREMIAS 1980 303 [οὐδὲν ἄξιον ϑανάτου: red.]; RADL 1975 400 [ἄξιον ϑανάτου πράσσω]; 412 [αἰτία/αἴτιον/ἄξιον ϑανάτου]; SCHÜRMANN 1957 31 [Lk 22,33: εἰς ϑάνατον πορεύεσϑαι: wahrscheinlich luk Mk-R].

ϑανατόω 1 (Mt 3, Mk 2)
1. execute (Lk 21,16); 2. stop completely

ϑάπτω 3 + 4 (Mt 3)   bury

Word groups	Lk	Acts	Mt	Mk
ἄφες τοὺς νεκροὺς ϑάψαι τοὺς ἑαυτῶν νεκρούς (LN: that is not the issue)	9,60		1	0
ϑάπτω τὸν πατέρα μου (LN: take care of one's father until death)	9,59		1	0
ϑάπτομαι passive (VKa) DENAUX 2009 LA[n]	16,22	2,29	0	0

Literature

SCHWARZ, Günther, ἄφες τοὺς νεκροὺς ϑάψαι τοὺς ἑαυτῶν νεκρούς. — ZNW 72 (1981) 272-276.

Θάρα 1	Terah (Lk 3,34)

ϑαυμάζω 13 + 5 (Mt 7/8, Mk 4/6)   be amazed

Word groups

Word groups	Lk	Acts	Mt	Mk
ϑαυμάζω (+) ἀκούω → ϑαυμάζω + (ὁράω/)εἶδον	2,18; 7,9		2	0
ϑαυμάζω + ἀπιστέω	24,(11-)12.41		0	0
DENAUX 2009 Lⁿ				
ϑαυμάζω ἐν τῷ + infinitive (VKh)	1,21		0	0
ϑαυμάζω (+) (ὁράω/)εἶδον → ϑαυμάζω + ἀκούω	11,38	3,12; 7,31; 13,41	1	0
ϑαυμάζω ὅτι (VKf)	11,38		0	0
ϑαυμάζω περί + genitive (VKb)	2,18		0	0

Characteristic of Luke

GOULDER 1989; MORGENTHALER 1958L

	Lk	Acts	Mt	Mk
ϑαυμάζω ἐπί	2,33; 4,22; 9,43;	3,12	0	0
BOISMARD 1984 Ab53; DENAUX 2009 L***;	20,26			
GOULDER 1989*; HAWKINS 1909L; NEIRYNCK				
1985; PLUMMER 1922 lx				
ϑαυμάζω τινα/τι (VKd); cf. Jn 5,28; Jude 16	7,9; 24,12	7,31		
BOISMARD 1984 cb167; NEIRYNCK 1985				
ὁ δὲ ... ἰδὼν ἐϑαύμασεν	11,38	7,31		
BOISMARD 1984 Ab174; NEIRYNCK 1985				
πάντες ἐϑαύμαζον/ἐϑαύμασαν → πάντες	1,63; 2,18; 4,22; 9,43		1	
ἐξεπλήσσοντο				
DENAUX 2009 L***				

Literature

VON BENDEMANN 2001 421: "ϑαυμάζειν begegnet im dritten Evangelium häufig"; COLLISON 1977 137 [ϑαυμάζω ἐπί: linguistic usage of Luke: certain]; DENAUX 2009 Laⁿ [ϑαυμάζω τινα/τι], LAⁿ [ὁ δὲ ... ἰδὼν ἐϑαύμασεν]; EASTON 1910 155 [ϑαυμάζω ἐπί: probably characteristic of L; not in Weiss]; GERSDORF 1816 189-190 [καὶ ἐϑαύμαζον ἐν τῷ χρονίζειν ἐν τῷ ναῷ]; 240 [καὶ πάντες οἱ ἀκούσαντες ἐϑαύμασεν περὶ τῶν λαληϑέντων]; 256 [ϑαυμάζοντες ἐπὶ τοῖς λαλουμένοις]; HAUCK 1934 [Vorzugswort; Vorzugsverbindung: ϑαυμάζω ἐπί]; JEREMIAS 1980 44 [ἐϑαύμαζον ἐν τῷ χρονίζειν: red.]; 69 [ϑαυμάζω + λέγων: red.]; 96 [ϑαυμάζω ἐπί + dat.: red.]; 155: "Transitives ϑαυμάζω ('sich wundern über') kommt im NT nur im Doppelwerk ... vor".

DANOVE, Paul, Verbs of Experience, 1999. Esp. 169-170.178.

DAUER, Anton, Lk 24,12 – Ein Produkt lukanischer Redaktion? — F. VAN SEGBROECK, et al. (eds.), The Four Gospels 1992. FS F. Neirynck, 1992, II, 1697-1716.

—, Zur Authentizität von Lk 24,12. — ETL 70 (1994) 294-318.

MUDDIMAN, John, A Note on Reading Luke XXIV.12. — ETL 48 (1972) 542-548.

NEIRYNCK, Frans, The Uncorrected Historic Present in Lk XXIV.12. — ETL 48 (1972) 548-553; = ID., Evangelica, 1982, 329-334 (334: additional note; Appendix, Evangelica II, 1991, 798).

—, Once More Lk 24,12. — *ETL* 70 (1994) 319-340.
—, A Supplementary Note on Lk 24,12. — *ETL* 72 (1996) 425-430; = ID., *Evangelica III*, 2001, 572-578.
—, Luke 24,12: An Anti-Docetic Interpolation? — DENAUX, A. (ed.), *New Testament Textual Criticism and Exegesis*. FS J. Delobel, 2002, 145-158. Esp. 148.
Ó FEARGHAIL, Fearghus, Rejection in Nazareth: Lk 4,22. — *ZNW* 75 (1984) 60-72. Esp. 65-67 [μαρτυρέω]; 67 [ϑαυμάζω]; 67-69 [οἱ λόγοι τῆς χάριτος].
ROBERTS, J.H., Θαυμάζω: An Expression of Pereplexity in Some Examples of Papyri Letters. — *Neotestamentica* 26 (1991) 109-122.

ϑεάομαι 3 + 3/4 (Mt 4, Mk 0[2])

1. look at (Lk 5,27. 7,24; 23,55); 2. visit

Word groups	Lk	Acts	Mt	Mk
ϑεάομαι + (ὁράω/)εἶδον→ ἀτενίζω/(ἀνα)βλέπω/ϑεωρέω + (ὁράω/)εἶδον; cf. βλέπω + ὁράω Mk 8,15.24; ἐμβλέπω + εἶδον Mk 14,67; περιβλέπω + εἶδον Mk 5,32; 9,8	7,24(-25)		2	0

Literature
HAUCK 1934 [Vorzugswort].

ϑεῖον 1

1. sulphur (Lk 17,29); 2. divine being

Word groups	Lk	Acts	Mt	Mk
ϑεῖον + πῦρ	17,29		0	0

ϑέλημα 4/5 + 3 (Mt 6, Mk 1)

BDAG 2000: 1. (objective sense) what is willed (Lk 11,2; 12,47; 22,42); 2. (subjective sense) will (Lk 23,35)

Word groups	Lk	Acts	Mt	Mk
ϑέλημα τοῦ ϑεοῦ/αὐτοῦ		22,14	0	1
ϑέλημα τοῦ κυρίου	12,47[1]	21,14	0	0
ϑέλημα + ποιέω (SCa; VKa)	12,47[2]	13,22	3	1
ϑελήματα (VKg)		13,22	0	0

Literature
DUPONT, Jacques, *Le discours de Milet*, 1962. Esp. 121-123.
LÓPEZ-PEGO, Alvaro, Evolución del significado de ϑέλημα, 'voluntad', del Antiguo al Nuevo Testamento. — *EstBib* 58 (2000) 309-346.

ϑέλω 28 + 14/16 (Mt 42/43, Mk 25)

1. purpose (Lk 13,31); 2. be of an opinion; 3. desire (Lk 13,34[1]); 4. enjoy (Lk 20,46)

Word groups	Lk	Acts	Mt	Mk
ἐὰν ϑέλῃς absolute → εἰ βούλει	5,12		1	1
ϑέλει + εἶναι (LN: it means)		2,12; 17,20	0	0
ϑέλω with finite verb (SCa; VKa)	9,54; 18,41; 22,9		5	5

θέλω + acc.	5,39; 12,49		5	2
θέλω + inf.	1,62; 8,20; 9,23.24; 10,24.29; 13,31.34[1]; 14,28; 15,28; 16,26; 18,13; 19,14.27; 20,46; 23,8.20	2,12; 7,28.39; 10,10; 14,13; 16,3; 17,18.20; 19,33; 24,27; 25,9[1.2]; 26,5	23	10
θέλω (+) δύναμαι → βούλομαι + δύναμαι	5,12; 16,26		1	4
θέλω ἵνα (SCb; VKb)	6,31		1	3
θέλω τι/τινά (SCc; VKc)	5,39; 12,49		4	2
θέλων ὁ θεός (VKh)		18,21	0	0
ποσάκις θέλω (SCd; VKd); cf. ὅσα θέλω Mt 17,12; Mk 9,13; ὡς θέλω Mt 15,28; 26,39	13,34[1]		1	0

Literature
VON BENDEMANN 2001 418 [θέλω + inf.]; GERSDORF 1816 204 [τὸ τί ἂν θέλοι].

RIESENFELD, Harald, *Zum Gebrauch von telô im Neuen Testament* (Arbeiten und Mitteilungen aus dem Neutestamentischen Seminar zu Uppsala). Uppsala: Ruthbert, 1936, 16 p.
SEPER, F.H., Καὶ τί θέλω εἰ ἤδη ἀνήφθη (Lc 12,49b). — *VD* 36 (1958) 147-153.

θεμέλιον 3 + 1
1. foundation (Acts 16,26); 2. basis
θεμέλιος: 3. foundation (Lk 6,48.49; 14,29); 4. foundation stone

Word groups	Lk	Acts	Mt	Mk
τὰ θεμέλια (VKa)		16,26	0	0
θεμέλιον τίθημι (VKc) DENAUX 2009 L[n]	6,48; 14,29		0	0

Literature
DENAUX 2009 La[n]; EASTON 1910 161 [θεμέλιον τίθημι: cited by Weiss as characteristic of L, and possibly corroborative].

θεός 122/125 + 166/179 (Mt 51/56, Mk 48[49]/52)
1. God (Acts 17,24); 2. god (Acts 28,6); 3. goddess (Acts 19,37)

Word groups	Lk	Acts	Mt	Mk
ὁ ἅγιος τοῦ θεοῦ	4,34		0	1
αἶνος/δόξα τῷ θεῷ/εὐλογητός (+) θεός → αἰνέω/δοξάζω/εὐλογέω τὸν θεόν; cf. αἰνέω τῷ θεῷ Rev 19,5 DENAUX 2009 La[n]	1,68; 2,14; 17,18; 18,43[1]	12,23	0	0
ἄνθρωπος singular + θεός → ἄνθρωποι plural + θεός; ἄνθρωπος singular + κύριος	4,4*; 18,2.4; 22,69; 23,47	7,56; 10,28; 12,22; 17,29	2	2
βασιλεία (τοῦ) θεοῦ (SCg) → βασιλεία τοῦ θεοῦ + ἀναφαίνω/ἔρχομαι/φθάνω	4,43; 6,20; 7,28; 8,1.10; 9,2. 11.27.60.62; 10,9.11; 11,20[2]; 12,31*; 13,18. 20.28.29; 14,15; 16,16; 17,20[1.2].21; 18,16.17.24. 25.29; 19,11; 21,31; 22,16.18; 23,51	1,3; 8,12; 14,22; 19,8; 20,25*; 28,23.31	5	14/15

δάκτυλος θεοῦ	11,20		0	0
δίδωμι δόξαν τῷ θεῷ (*LN*: promise to tell truth) → δοξάζω τὸν **θεόν**; **δίδωμι** δόξαν DENAUX 2009 LA[n]	17,18	12,23	0	0
δόξα θεοῦ → δόξα **κυρίου**		7,55[1]	0	0
δουλεύω θεῷ → δουλεύω τῷ **κυρίῳ**	16,13		1	0
δοῦλος θεοῦ		16,17	0	0
δύναμις τοῦ θεοῦ → δύναμις **κυρίου**	22,69	8,10	1	1
δύναται ὁ θεός → ὁ **δυνατός** DENAUX 2009 L[n]	3,8; 5,21		0	0
εἷς/μόνος (ὁ) θεός (*SC*c; *VK*h)	5,21; 18,19		0/1	2/3
ἐκκλησία θεοῦ		20,28	0	0
ἔμπροσθεν/ἐναντίον (τοῦ) θεοῦ → ἔμπροσθεν/ ἐνώπιον τῶν **ἀγγέλων** τοῦ θεοῦ / τῶν **ἀνθρώπων** / τοῦ **κυρίου** DENAUX 2009 La[n]	1,6; 24,19	8,21 *v.l.*; 10,4	0	0
εὐαγγέλιον + τοῦ θεοῦ		20,24	0	1
εὐλογέω τὸν θεόν → εὐλογέω τὸν **θεόν** + verb of saying; αἶνος/ δόξα τῷ θεῷ / εὐλογητός + **θεός**; αἰνέω/δοξάζω τὸν **θεόν** DENAUX 2009 L[n]	1,64; 2,28; 24,53		0	0
θεός + attributive adjective (*VK*p)	8,28	16,17; 17,23; 24,14	0	1
θεὸς Ἀβραάμ/Ἰσαάκ/Ἰακώβ (*SC*b; *VK*f)	20,37[1.2.3]	3,13[1.2.3]; 7,32[2].32[1*.2*].46*	3	3
θεός + ἀγαπάω/ἀγάπη → **κύριος** + ἀγαπάω/ἀγάπη	10,27; 11,42		1	1
θεός + ἄνθρωπος (*SC*e; *VK*t)	2,14.52; 4,4*; 12,8.9; 16,15[1.2]; 18,2.4.11.27; 22,69; 23,47	5,4.29.(38-)39; 7,56; 10,28; 12,22; 14,11.15; 16,17; 17,30; 18,13; 24,16	5	5
θεός + δεσπότης/σωτήρ (*VK*d)	1,47	4,24*; 5,31; 13,23		
θεὸς ἡμῶν (*VK*l); cf. θεέ μου (*VK*j) Mt 27,46[1.2]; θεός μου (*VK*k) Mk 15,34[1.2]	1,78	2,39; 3,22 *v.l.*	0	1
θεὸς (ὁ) ζῶν (*VK*m)		14,15	2	0
θεός + τῶν ζώντων (*VK*n)	20,38		1/2	1/2
θεὸς τῶν πατέρων σου/ἡμῶν BOISMARD 1984 Aa49		3,13[4]; 5,30; 7,32[1]; 22,14	0	0
θεὸς (τοῦ) Ισραήλ (*VK*g)	1,68	13,17	1	0
θεός + κόσμος (*VK*v)		17,24	0	0
θεός + πατέρες (*VK*e)		3,13[4].25; 5,30; 7,32[1].45; 13,17.33; 22,14; 26,6	0	0
θεός + πατήρ (*VK*c) → **κύριος** + πατήρ		2,33	0	0/1
ὁ θεὸς (+) ἐποίει/ἐποίησεν + διά + genitive BOISMARD 1984 Ba16		2,22[2]; 15,12; 19,11; 21,19		
ὁ θεὸς ὁ σωτήρ	1,47		0	0
τὰ τοῦ θεοῦ (*VK*q)	20,25[1]		2	2
μεγαλειότης τοῦ θεοῦ → μεγαλύνω + **θεός/κύριος**; **δυνατός** + μεγάλα; cf. μεγαλεῖος τοῦ θεοῦ Acts 2,11 DENAUX 2009 La[n]	1,46.58	19,17		

μεγαλύνω (+) θεός → μεγαλειότης τοῦ θεοῦ; δυνατός + μεγάλα; μεγαλύνω + κύριος		10,46	0	0
ὁδὸς τοῦ θεοῦ → ὁδὸς τοῦ κυρίου	20,21	18,26	1	1
οἶκος τοῦ θεοῦ	6,4		1	1
πειράζω τὸν θεόν → πειράζω τὸ πνεῦμα		15,10	0	0
προσευχὴ τοῦ θεοῦ	6,12		0	0
ῥῆμα θεοῦ → λόγος τοῦ θεοῦ; ῥῆμα Ἰησοῦ/τοῦ κυρίου; cf. ῥῆμά σου Lk 1,38; 2,29	3,2; 4,4*		0	0
σοφία τοῦ θεοῦ	11,49		0	0
υἱοὶ (τοῦ) θεοῦ	20,36		1	0
υἱός (+) θεός (SCd; VKs)	1,16.32.35; 3,(23-)38; 4,3.9.41; 8,28; 12,8; 20,36; 22,69.70	3,25; 7,56; 8,37*; 9,20	10	4
υἱός (τοῦ) θεοῦ (LN: Son of God) → Ἰησοῦς (ὁ) υἱὸς (τοῦ) θεοῦ	1,35; 4,3.9.41; 8,28; 22,70	8,37*; 9,20	10	4
χάρις ἐνώπιον τοῦ θεοῦ		7,46	0	0
χάρις παρὰ θεῷ DENAUX 2009 L[n]	1,30; 2,52		0	0
θεοί plural (SCf; VKx)		7,40; 14,11; 19,26	0	0

→ ἡ δεξιὰ (τῆς δυνάμεως) τοῦ θεοῦ; δοῦλος (τοῦ) θεοῦ; δυνατὸς παρὰ τῷ θεῷ; δῶρον τοῦ θεοῦ; θέλημα τοῦ θεοῦ/αὐτοῦ; θέλων ὁ θεός; πλουτέω εἰς θεόν

Characteristic of Luke

GOULDER 1989; HAWKINS 1909add; HENDRIKS 1986 428.434.448.468; MORGENTHALER 1958LA

	Lk	Acts	Mt	Mk
ἄγγελος/ἄγγελοι τοῦ θεοῦ → θεός + ἄγγελος; ἄγγελος κυρίου; cf. Jn 1,51; Gal 4,14 BOISMARD 1984 Cb72; NEIRYNCK 1985	12,8.9; 15,10	10,3; 27,23	0/1	0
αἰνέω τὸν θεόν → δοξάζω/εὐλογέω τὸν θεόν; αἶνος/δόξα τῷ θεῷ / εὐλογητός + θεός; αἰνέω τὸν θεόν + verb of saying; cf. αἰνέω τῷ θεῷ Rev 19,5 BOISMARD 1984 Ab30; DENAUX 2009 LA*; GOULDER 1989; NEIRYNCK 1985	2,13.20; 19,37; 24,53 v.l.	2,47; 3,8.9	0	0
ἄνθρωποι plural + θεός → ἄνθρωπος singular + θεός; ἄνθρωποι plural + κύριος GOULDER 1989	2,14.52; 12,8.9; 16,15[1.2]; 18,11.27	5,4.29.(38-)39; 14,11.15; 16,17; 17,30; 18,13; 24,16	3	3
βουλὴ τοῦ θεοῦ PLUMMER 1922 lii	7,30	2,23; 13,36; 20,27	0	0
δοξάζω τὸν θεόν → αἰνέω/εὐλογέω τὸν θεόν; αἶνος/δόξα τῷ θεῷ / εὐλογητός + θεός; δοξάζω τὸν θεόν + verb of saying; cf. δοξάζω τὸν λόγον τοῦ κυρίου Acts 13,48 DENAUX 2009 L***; GOULDER 1989*; HAWKINS 1909L; PLUMMER 1922 lxi	2,20; 5,25.26; 7,16[1]; 13,13; 17,15; 18,43[1]; 23,47	4,21; 11,18[1]; 21,20	2	1
ἐνώπιον (τοῦ) θεοῦ → ἔμπροσθεν/ἐναντίον (τοῦ) θεοῦ; ἐνώπιον τῶν ἀγγέλων τοῦ θεοῦ DENAUX 2009 lA*; PLUMMER 1922 lx	1,6 v.l.19; 12,6; 16,15[2]	4,19[1]; 7,46; 10,4 v.l..31.33	0	0

ἐπιστρέφω ἐπὶ (τὸν) θεόν/κύριον → ἐπιστρέφω ἐπὶ (τὸν) **κύριον** BOISMARD 1984 Ab25; NEIRYNCK 1985	1,16	9,35; 11,21; 14,15; 15,19; 26,18.20	0	0
θεός anarthrous GOULDER 1989	1,35.78; 2,14.40.52; 3,2;4,4; 11,20; 12,21; 16,13; 18,19 v.l.; 20,36.37²·³.38	5,29.39; 7,55; 12,22; 14,15; 17,23; 20,21	12/15	5/9
θεός + preposition (VKr) DENAUX 2009 L***	1,6.8.19.26.30.37.47 ; 2,52; 12,6.21; 16,15²; 18,27; 24,19	2,22¹; 4,19¹.24; 5,39; 6,11; 7,46; 8,21; 10,4.31.33.33*. 41. 42; 12,5; 14,15; 15,19; 20,21; 24,15.16; 26,6.18.20.22	4	2
θεός + ἄγγελος (VKu) → ἄγγελος/ἄγγελοι τοῦ **θεοῦ** DENAUX 2009 L*** (?)	1,26; 2,13; 12,8.9; 15,10	7,35; 10,3; 12,23; 27,23	0/1	0
θεός + κύριος (SCa; VKa) [DENAUX 2009 L*** (?)]	1,6.8(-9).(46-)47; 16,13	2,36; 10,33; 17,24; 20,21.24; 28,31	0	0[1]
θεός + λαός (VKw) DENAUX 2009 L*** (?)	1,68; 7,16².29; 18,43²; 24,19	2,47; 3,9; 10,41; 13,17; 15,14	0	0
ὁ θεὸς ὁ ὕψιστος; cf. Hebr 7,1 HARNACK 1906 36	8,28	16,17	0	1
κύριος ὁ θεός BOISMARD 1984 Db17; GOULDER 1989; NEIRYNCK 1985	1,16.32.68; 4,8.12; 10,27; 20,37¹	2,39; 3,22; 7,37 v.l.	3	2
λόγος τοῦ θεοῦ → ῥῆμα **θεοῦ**; **ἀκούω** τὸν λόγον τοῦ θεοῦ/κυρίου; λόγος τοῦ **κυρίου** BOISMARD 1984 Eb55; DENAUX 2009 L***; GOULDER 1989*; HAWKINS 1909L; NEIRYNCK 1985; PLUMMER 1922 lx	5,1; 8,11.21; 11,28	4,31; 6,2.7; 8,14; 11,1; 12,24; 13,5. 7.44*.46.48*; 16,32*; 17,13; 18,11	1	1
παῖς τοῦ θεοῦ (of Jesus); cf. παῖς σου Acts 4,27.30; παῖς μου Mt 12,18; cf. παῖς τοῦ θεοῦ (of Israel) Lk 1,54 (αὐτοῦ); Acts 4,25 (σου); cf. παῖς τοῦ θεοῦ (of David) Lk 1,69 (αὐτοῦ) BOISMARD 1984 Ab39; CREDNER 1836 140; NEIRYNCK 1985		3,13⁴.26	0	0
περὶ τῆς βασιλείας τοῦ θεοῦ BOISMARD 1984 Ab71; NEIRYNCK 1985	9,11	1,3; 8,12; 19,8	0	0
φοβέομαι τὸν θεόν BOISMARD 1984 Cb67; DENAUX 2009 lA*; NEIRYNCK 1985	18,2.4; 23,40	10,2¹.22.34(-35); 13,16.26		
χάρις (τοῦ) θεοῦ/κυρίου → χάρις τοῦ **κυρίου**; cf. χάρις αὐτοῦ Acts 20,32 BOISMARD 1984 Db9; NEIRYNCK 1985	2,40	11,23; 13,43; 14,26; 15,11.40*; 20,24		

→ **βασιλεία** τοῦ θεοῦ + ἔρχομαι; **ἐνώπιον** τῶν ἀγγέλων τοῦ θεοῦ; **λαλέω** with God as speaker; **λαλέω** τὸν λόγον τοῦ θεοῦ/κυρίου; **πιστεύω** τῷ θεῷ; **ὑψόομαι** τῇ δεξιᾷ (τοῦ θεοῦ); ὁ **χριστὸς** (τοῦ) θεοῦ/κυρίου

Literature

VON BENDEMANN 2001 413: "κηρύσσειν τὴν βασιλείαν τοῦ θεοῦ ... und εὐαγγελίζεσθαι τὴν βασιλείαν τοῦ θεοῦ ... sind typisch lukanisch"; 436: "αἰνέω τὸν θεόν findet sich im Neuen

Testament nur beim auctor ad Theophilum"; COLLISON 1977 46 [δοξάζω τὸν ϑεόν: linguistic usage of Luke: likely]; 170 [ἡ βασιλεία τοῦ ϑεοῦ: certain]; DENAUX 2009 Laⁿ [ἄγγελος/ ἄγγελοι τοῦ ϑεοῦ], [IAⁿ: βουλὴ τοῦ ϑεοῦ; ἐπιστρέφω ἐπὶ (τὸν) ϑεόν/κύριον; περὶ τῆς βασιλείας τοῦ ϑεοῦ; χάρις (τοῦ) ϑεοῦ]; GERSDORF 1816 171 [ἐνώπιον τοῦ ϑεοῦ]; 204 [εὐλογῶν τὸν ϑεόν]; 240 [δοξάζοντες καὶ αἰνοῦντες τὸν ϑεόν]; HAUCK 1934 [Vorzugsverbindung: λόγος τοῦ ϑεοῦ]; JEREMIAS 1980 22 [ἐναντίοντοῦ ϑεοῦ: red.]; 54 [1,37 red.: οὐκ ἀδυνατήσει παρὰ τοῦ ϑεοῦ πᾶν ῥῆμα: ist ein freies Zitat von Gen 18,14 LXX: μὴ ἀδυνατεῖ παρὰ τῷ ϑεῷ ῥῆμα; Lukas hat ein πᾶν zugefügt und παρά mit dem Genitiv (LXX: Dativ) konstruiert. Sowohl das stilistische Feilen am LXX-Text wie die Verstärkung durch πᾶς ist typisch lukanisch"; 83 [αἰνέω τὸν ϑεόν: red.]; 208-209 [τοῦ ϑεοῦ: red.]; RADL 1975 430 [χάρις ϑεοῦ]; SCHNEIDER 1969 93.163 [λόγος/λόγον τοῦ ϑεοῦ].

BAUGH, Steven M., Phraseology and the Reliability of Acts. — NTS 36 (1990) 290-294. [ἡ ϑεά Acts 19,27 / ἡ ϑεός Acts 19,37]

BOVER, José M., "Quod nascetur (ex te) sanctum vocabitur filius Dei" (Lc. 1,35). — Bib 1 (1920) 92-94.

—, "Quod nascetur (ex te) sanctum vocabitur filius Dei" (Lc., 1,35). — EstE 8 (1929) 381-392.

DAWSEY, James M., What's in a Name? Characterization in Luke. — BTB 16 (1986) 143-147. Esp. 146-147: "Luke's use of 'son of God'".

DELEBECQUE, Édouard, Études grecques, 1976. Esp. 25-38: "Le 'gloria' des anges (2,14)".

DOBLE, Peter, The Paradox of Salvation, 1996. Esp. 25-69: "Luke's use of δοξάζειν τὸν ϑεόν".

GEORGE, Augustin, Jésus Fils de Dieu dans l'Évangile selon saint Luc. — RB 72 (1965) 185-209; = ID., Études, 1978, 215-236.

—, Note sur quelques traits lucaniens de l'expression "Par le doigt de Dieu" (Luc XI,20). — Sciences Ecclésiastiques 18 (1966) 461-466; = "Par le doigt de Dieu" (Luc 11,20). — ID., Études, 1978, 127-132.

—, Le règne de Dieu. —ID., Études, 1978, 285-306.

GLOVER, Warren W., "The Kingdom of God" in Luke. — BTrans 29 (1978) 231-237.

GUERRA GÓMEZ, M., Análisis filológico-teológico y traducción del himno de los ángeles en Belén, 1989. Esp. 42-46: "ἐν ὑψίστοις ϑεῷ" = 'en las alturas a Dios' o 'al Dios Altísimo'".

HAHN, Ferdinand, Christologische Hoheitstitel, 1963. Esp. 280-346: "Gottessohn".

LOEWEN, Jacob, The Names of God in the New Testament. — BTrans 35 (1984) 208-211. Esp. 208-209: "Ho theos, 'God, god'".

MAHFOUZ, Hady, La fonction littéraire et théologique de Lc 3,1-20, 2003. Esp. 55-57 [ῥῆμα ϑεοῦ].

MUÑOZ IGLESIAS, Salvador, Lucas 1,35b. — La idea de Dios en la Biblia. XXVIII Semana Biblica Española (Madrid 23-27 sept. 1968). Madrid: Consejo Superior de Investigaciones Cientificas, 1971, 303-324.

PRIEUR, Alexander, Die Verkündigung der Gottesherrschaft: Exegetische Studien zum lukanischen Verständnis von βασιλεία τοῦ ϑεοῦ (WUNT, II/89). Tübingen: Mohr, 1996, VIII-336 p.

READ-HEIMERDINGER, Jenny, The Bezan Text of Acts, 2002. Esp. 275-310: "Ὁ Κύριος and ὁ ϑεός".

RESE, Martin, Alttestamentliche Motive in der Christologie des Lukas, 1969. Esp. 131-133: "Προφήτης, ἅγιος, δίκαιος, ἀρχηγός, σωτήρ und υἱὸς ϑεοῦ in der Apostelgeschichte"; 203-204: "υἱὸς ὑψίστου bzw. ϑεοῦ im Lukasevangelium".

SCHLOSSER, Jacques, Les logia du Règne: Étude sur le vocable "Basileia tou theou" dans la prédication de Jésus. Thèse présentée devant l'Université de Strasbourg II, le 16 décembre 1978. Lille: Atelier national de reproduction des thèses, 1982, x-714 p.

WILCOX, Max, The "God-Fearers" in Acts – A Reconsideration. — JSNT 13 (1981) 102-122. [φοβούμενοι τὸν ϑεόν]

Θεόφιλος 1 + 1

Theophilus (Lk 1,3; Acts 1,1)

Literature

CADBURY, Henri J., Commentary on the Preface of Luke, 1922. Esp. 507-508.

θεραπεία 2 (Mt 0/1)

1. healing (Lk 9,11); 2. household servants (Lk 12,42)

Literature

VON BENDEMANN 2001 414: "θεραπεία im Neuen Testament nur Lk 9,11: 12,42 diff Mt 24,45 (aber differente Bedeutung); Apk 22,2"; DENAUX 2009 L[n]; HAUCK 1934 [seltenes Alleinwort]

θεραπεύω 14 + 5 (Mt 16, Mk 5/6)

1. heal (Lk 4,23); 2. serve (Acts 17,25)

Word groups	Lk	Acts	Mt	Mk
θεραπεύω (+) νόσος (VKd)	4,40; 7,21; 9,1		4	1/2

Characteristic of Luke	Lk	Acts	Mt	Mk
θεραπεύομαι passive (VKa); cf. Jn 5,10; Rev 13,3.12 BOISMARD 1984 cb90; DENAUX 2009 L***; HARNACK 1906 43; NEIRYNCK 1985	5,15; 6,18; 8,2.43;13,14[2]	4,14; 5,16; 8,7; 17,25; 28,9	1	0
θεραπεύω absolute (VKb) DENAUX 2009 L***	6,7; 9,6; 13,14[1.2]; 14,3		1	1
θεραπεύω ἀπό (VKc) → ἰάομαι ἀπό DENAUX 2009 L***; GOULDER 1989*; HAWKINS 1909L; PLUMMER 1922 lii	5,15; 6,18; 7,21; 8,2		0	0

Literature

VON BENDEMANN 2001 413 "θεραπεύειν ἀπό im Neuen Testament nur bei Lukas"; COLLISON 1977 124 [θεραπεύω ἀπό: linguistic usage of Luke: certain]; HAUCK 1934 [Vorzugsverbindung: θεραπεύω ἀπό]; JEREMIAS 1980 154 [θεραπεύω ἀπό: red.].

AUNE, David E., Lexical Glosses and Definitions of θεραπεύω. — DONALDSON, A. – SAILORS, T.B. (eds.), New Testament Greek and Exegesis. FS G.F. Hawthorne, 2003, 11-22.

NOLLAND, John, Classical and Rabbinic Parallels to "Physician, Heal Yourself" (Lk. iv 23). — NT 21 (1979) 193-209.

WELLS, Louise, The Greek Language of Healing, 1998. Esp. 120-155.

θερίζω 3 (Mt 3)

reap

Word groups	Lk	Acts	Mt	Mk
θερίζω + σπείρω (VKa)	12,24; 19,21.22		3	0

θερισμός 3 (Mt 6, Mk 1)

1. reaping; 2. harvest (Lk 10,2[1.2.3])

Word groups	Lk	Acts	Mt	Mk
εἰς τὸν θερισμόν (VKa)	10,2[3]		1	0

θέρος 1 (Mt 1, Mk 1) | summer (Lk 21,30)

θεωρέω 7 + 14 (Mt 2, Mk 7)
1. look at (Lk 10,18; Acts 7,56); 2. understand (Acts 17,22); 3. experience

Word groups	Lk	Acts	Mt	Mk
θεωρέω + indirect question (VKb)		21,20	0	2
θεωρέω + ἀκούω → βλέπω / ὁράω/εἶδον / συνίημι + ἀκούω		19,26	0	0
θεωρέω + (ὁράω/)εἶδον→ (ἀνα)βλέπω/ἀτενίζω/θεάομαι + (ὁράω/)εἶδον; cf. βλέπω + ὁράω Mk 8,15.24; ἐμβλέπω + εἶδον Mk 14,67; περιβλέπω + εἶδον Mk 5,32; 9,8	24,39		0	0
θεωρέω (+) ὅτι (VKa) → (ὁράω/)εἶδον ὅτι		19,26; 27,10	0	1
θεωρέω absolute (VKc)	14,29; 23,35		1	1

Literature
HILLS, Julian V., Luke 10.18 – Who Saw Satan Fall? — JSNT 46 (1992) 25-40.
[ἐθεώρουν]

θεωρία 1 | spectacle (Lk 23,48)

Literature
HAUCK 1934 [seltenes Alleinwort].

θηλάζω 2/3 (Mt 2, Mk 1)
1. nurse (of a baby) (Lk 11,27; 21,23); 2. nurse a baby

θηρεύω 1 | catch in mistake (Lk 11,54)

θησαυρίζω 1 (Mt 2)
1. treasure up (Lk 12,21); 2. cause to happen

θησαυρός 4/5 (Mt 9, Mk 1)
1. storeroom (Lk 6,45); 2. treasure box; 3. treasure (Lk 12,33.34; 18,22)

Word groups	Lk	Acts	Mt	Mk
θησαυρός + ἐν οὐρανῷ / ἐν τοῖς οὐρανοῖς (SCa)	12,33; 18,22		2	1

θνήσκω 2 + 2 (Mt 1, Mk 1) | die (Lk 7,12; 8,49; Acts 14,19; 25,19)

Word groups	Lk	Acts	Mt	Mk
ϑνῄσκω + ζῶ → **ἀποϑνῄσκω** + ζῶ; cf. τελευτάω + ζῶ Mt 9,18		25,19	0	0

ϑορυβάζω** 1   ϑορυβάζομαι: be upset (Lk 10,41)

Literature
HAUCK 1934 [seltenes Alleinwort].

ϑραύω 1   oppress (Lk 4,18)

Literature
HAUCK 1934 [seltenes Alleinwort].

ϑρηνέω 2 (Mt 1)
1. wail (Lk 23,27); 2. sing funeral songs (Lk 7,32); 3. lament (Lk 23,27)

Word groups	Lk	Acts	Mt	Mk
ϑρηνέω + κλαίω	7,32		0	0
ϑρηνέω + κόπτομαι → **κλαίω** + κόπτομαι	23,27		0	0

ϑρίξ 4 + 1 (Mt 3, Mk 1)   hair

Word groups	Lk	Acts	Mt	Mk
τρίχες τῆς κεφαλῆς (*VK*b)	7,38.44 *v.l.*; 12,7		1	0
ϑρίξ singular (*VK*a)	21,18	27,34	1	0

Characteristic of Luke	Lk	Acts	Mt	Mk
ϑρίξ ἀπὸ/ἐκ τῆς κεφαλῆς HARNACK 1906 54	21,18	27,34	0	0

Literature
DENAUX 2009 LA[a] [ϑρὶξ ἀπὸ/ἐκ τῆς κεφαλῆς].

ϑρόμβος* 1   clot of blood (Lk 22,44)

Literature
HAUCK 1934 [seltenes Alleinwort].

BRUN, Lyder, Engel und Blutschweiß Lc 22,43-44. — *ZNW* 32 (1933) 265-276.
SCHNEIDER, Gerhard, Engel und Blutschweiß (Lk 22,43-44): "Redaktionsgeschichte" im
  Dienste der Textkritik. — *BZ* NF 20 (1976) 112-116. Esp. 113-115: "Vokabular und Stil von
  Lk 22,43.44"; = ID., *Lukas, Theologe der Heilsgeschichte*, 1985, 153-157. Esp. 154-156.
TUCKETT, Christopher M., Luke 22,43-44: The "Agony" in the Garden and Luke's Gospel.
  — DENAUX, Adelbert (ed.), *New Testament Textual Criticism and Exegesis*. FS J.
  Delobel, 2002, 131-144. Esp. 133-135: "Vocabulary and style".

ϑρόνος 3 + 2 (Mt 5)

1. throne (Lk 1,52; 22,30); 2. ruler; 3. supernatural power; 4. authority to rule (Lk 1,32); 5. place of ruling

Literature
BORMANN, Lukas, *Recht, Gerechtigkeit und Religion*, 2001. Esp. 117.
WINK, Walter, *Naming the Powers*, 1984. Esp. 18-20.

ϑυγάτηρ 9 + 3 (Mt 8, Mk 5/6)

1. daughter (own) (Lk 8,42); 2. daughter (address) (Lk 8,48); 3. female descendant (Lk 13,16); 4. female inhabitant (Lk 23,28)

Word groups	Lk	Acts	Mt	Mk
ϑυγάτηρ ᾿Ααρών/᾿Αβραάμ (*VK*d) → σπέρμα/τέκνον/υἱός + ᾿Αβραάμ DENAUX 2009 L[n]	1,5; 13,16		0	0
ϑυγάτηρ ᾿Ιερουσάλημ (*LN*: people of Jerusalem; *VK*c)	23,28		0	0
ϑυγάτηρ + μήτηρ (*VK*a) → υἱός + μήτηρ	12,53[1.2]		1	0
ϑυγάτηρ + υἱός (*VK*b)		2,17; 7,21	1	0

Literature
GERSDORF 1816 171 [ἐκ τῶν ϑυγατέρων ᾿Ααρών]; HARNACK 1906 70 (ET 97) [ϑυγατέρων ᾿Ααρών, without the article, like ϑυγατέρα ᾿Αβραάμ XIII,16]; JEREMIAS 1980 230 [ϑυγάτηρ ᾿Αβραάμ: trad.]; REHKOPF 1959 94 [vorlukanisch]; 99 [ϑύγατηρ: "Substantiva in Anrede bei den Synoptikern"]; SCHÜRMANN 1961 273.

ϑυμίαμα 2

1. incense (Lk 1,11); 2. incense offering (Lk 1,10)

Literature
DENAUX 2009 L[n].

ϑυμιάω 1 — offer incense (Lk 1,9)

Literature
HAUCK 1934 [seltenes Alleinwort].

ϑυμός 1 + 1

1. fury (Lk 4,28, Acts 19,28); 2. intense desire

Literature
DENAUX 2009 LA[n].

ϑύρα 4 + 10 (Mt 4/5, Mk 6)

1.door (Lk 11,7; 13,24.[25].[1.2]; Acts 12,13); 2. entrance

Word groups	Lk	Acts	Mt	Mk
ϑύρα (+) ἀνοίγω (*LN*: make possible; *VK*b) → ϑύρα +	13,25[2]	5,19.23;	0	0

(ἀπο)κλείω/κρούω; ἀνοίγω τὴν **πύλην** / τὸν **πυλῶνα** DENAUX 2009 lA[n]	13,25[2]	5,19.23; 14,27; 16,26.27	0	0
θύρα + (ἀπο)κλείω (*VK*a) → **θύρα** + ἀνοίγω/κρούω	11,7; 13,25[1]	21,30	2	0
ἡ θύρα τοῦ πυλῶνος		12,13	0	0
θύρα + κρούω → **θύρα** + ἀνοίγω/(ἀπο)κλείω DENAUX 2009 LA[n]	13,25[2]	12,13	0	0
στενὴ θυρά; cf. στενὴ πύλη Mt 7,13.14	13,24		0	0

θυσία 2 + 2 (Mt 2, Mk 1/2)　　sacrifice (Lk 2,24; 13,1; Acts 7,41.42)

Word groups	Lk	Acts	Mt	Mk
προσφέρω θυσίαν; cf. προσφορά + θυσία (*VK*b) Eph 5,2; Heb 10,5.8		7,42	0	0
θυσίαι plural (*VK*a)	13,1	7,42	0	1

Literature
MARROW, Stanley B., Principles for Interpreting the New Testament Soteriological Terms.
— *NTS* 36 (1990) 268-280. *Esp.* 275-276: "Expiation and sacrifice".

θυσιαστήριον 2 (Mt 6)　　altar (Lk 1,11; 11,51)

Literature
KLAUCK, Hans-Josef, *Thysiastērion – eine Berichtigung*. — *ZNW* 71 (1980) 274-277.

θύω 4 + 4 (Mt 1, Mk 1)
　　1. sacrifice (Lk 22,7; Acts 14,13); 2. slaughter (Lk 15,23.27.30)

Word groups	Lk	Acts		Mt	Mk
τὸ πάσχα θύω (*VK*b)	22,7			0	1

Characteristic of Luke
GOULDER 1989

	Lk	Acts		Mt	Mk
θύω/ἐπιθύειν; cfr. Jn 10,10; 1 Cor 5,7; 10,20 BOISMARD 1984 cb154; DENAUX 2009 LA**; NEIRYNCK 1985	15,23.27. 30; 22,7	10,13; 11,7; 14,13.18		1	1

Literature
COLLISON 1977 95 [noteworthy phenomena]; DENAUX 2009 L(***) ; HAWKINS 1909 19.

KILPATRICK, George D., The Meaning of *thuein* in the New Testament. — *BTrans* 12
(1961) 130-132.

Θωμᾶς 1 + 1 (Mt 1, Mk 1)　　Thomas (Lk 6,15; Acts 1,13)

I

Ἰάϊρος 1 (Mk 1)　　Jairus (Lk 8,41)

Ἰακώβ 4 + 8 (Mt 6, Mk 1) — Jacob

Word groups	Lk	Acts	Mt	Mk
Ἀβραάμ + Ἰσαάκ + Ἰακώβ (VKb)	3,34; 13,28; 20,37	3,13; 7,32	2	1
(ὁ) θεὸς Ἰακώβ (SCb) → θεὸς Ἀβραάμ/Ἰσαάκ	20,37	3,13; 7,32.46 v.l.	1	1
Ἰακώβ + Ἰωσήφ (VKc)		7,14	0	0
οἶκος Ἰακώβ (VKd) DENAUX 2009 LAⁿ	1,33	7,46	0	0
Ἰακώβ son of Isaac (SCa; VKa)	1,33; 3,34; 13,28; 20,37	3,13; 7,8^{1.2}.12.14.15.32.46	4	1

Ἰάκωβος 8 + 7 (Mt 6, Mk 15) — James

Word groups	Lk	Acts	Mt	Mk
Ἰάκωβος + Ἰωάννης + Πέτρος	6,14; 8,51; 9,28	1,13^{1}	1	3
Ἰάκωβος brother of Jesus (SCd; VKd)		12,17; 15,13; 21,18	1	1
Ἰάκωβος father of Judas (SCe; VKe) DENAUX 2009 LAⁿ	6,16	1,13^{3}	0	0
Ἰάκωβος son of Alphaeus (SCb; VKb)	6,15	1,13^{2}	1	1
Ἰάκωβος son of Mary (SCc; VKc)	24,10		1	2
Ἰάκωβος son of Zebedee (SCa; VKa)	5,10; 6,14; 8,51; 9,28.54	1,13^{1}; 12,2	3	11

Ἰανναί 1 — Jannai (Lk 3,24)

ἰάομαι 11/12 + 4/5 (Mt 4, Mk 1)

1. heal (Lk 6,18); 2. renew

Word groups	Lk	Acts	Mt	Mk
εἰς τὸ ἰᾶσθαι (VKc)	5,17		0	0
ἰάομαι ἀπό (VKb) → θεραπεύω ἀπό	6,18		0	1

Characteristic of Luke

DENAUX 2009 L***; GASTON 1973 64 [Lked]; GOULDER 1989*; HAWKINS 1909 L; MORGENTHALER 1958L; PLUMMER 1922 lx

	Lk	Acts	Mt	Mk
ἰάομαι middle transitive (VKa) DENAUX 2009 L***	4,18*; 5,17; 6,19; 9,2.11.42; 14,4; 22,51	9,34; 10,38; 28,8.27	1	0
ἰάομαι proper sense; cf. Jn 4,47; 5,13 BOISMARD 1984 cb95; DENAUX 2009 L***; HARNACK 1906 42; NEIRYNCK 1985	5,17; 6,18.19; 7,7; 8,47; 9,2.11.42; 14,4; 17,15; 22,51	3,11*; 9,34; 10,38; 28,8	3	1

Literature

VON BENDEMANN 2001 414: "Die Statistik für ἰᾶσθαι ist eindeutig: Mk1x/Mt 4x/Lk11x/Apg4x"; HAUCK 1934 [Vorzugswort]; JEREMIAS 1980 154-155: "lk Vorzugswort"; "Lk hat für ἰάομαι/ἴασις einen für ihn kennzeichnenden Sprachgebrauch bevorzugt. a. ... im eigentlichen Sinn ... b. ... mit ἀπό ... c. ... in aktiver Bedeutung...".

HORSLEY, G.H.R. – LEE, John A.L., A Lexicon of the New Testament, 1, 1997. Esp. 75-76.
WELLS, Louise, The Greek Language of Healing, 1998. Esp. 155-179.

Ἰάρετ 1	Jared (Lk 3,37)

ἴασις 1 + 2	healing (Lk 13,32; Acts 4,22.30)

Characteristic of Luke

BOISMARD 1984 Ab128; HAWKINS 1909LA; MORGENTHALER 1958*; NEIRYNCK 1985; PLUMMER 1922 lii; VOGEL 1899A

Literature

DENAUX 2009 lA[n]; HAUCK 1934 [seltenes Alleinwort]; JEREMIAS 1980 154 [red.].

FERRARO, Giuseppe, "Oggi e domani e il terzo giorno" (osservazioni su *Luca* 13,32,33).
— *RivBib* 16 (1968) 397-407. Esp. 401-407: "Considerazioni sul vocabolario di Luca 13,32.33" [ἐκβάλλειν δαιμόνια; ἰάσεις ἀποτελῶ; τελειοῦσθαι e πορεύεσθαι; ἀπολέσθαι].
HORSLEY, G.H.R. – LEE, John A.L., A Lexicon of the New Testament, 1, 1997. Esp. 76.82.

ἰατρός 3 (Mt 1, Mk 2)	physician (Lk 4,23; 5,31; 8,43)

Word groups	Lk	Acts	Mt	Mk
ἰατροί plural (*VK*a)	8,43		0	0

Literature

HORSLEY, G.H.R. – LEE, John A.L., A Lexicon of the New Testament, 1, 1997. Esp. 76-78.
NOLLAND, John, Classical and Rabbinic Parallels to "Physician, Heal Yourself" (Lk. iv 23). — *NT* 21 (1979) 193-209.

ἴδιος 6/7 + 16 (Mt 10/11, Mk 8/9)	
1. one's own (Acts 4,32); 2. peculiar (Lk 6,44; Acts 1,25); 3. individually	

Word groups	Lk	Acts	Mt	Mk
εἰς τὰ ἴδια (*VK*d)		21,6	0	0
τὰ ἴδια (*VK*c)	18,28	21,6	0	0
DENAUX 2009 LA[n]				
οἱ ἴδιοι (*LN*: his own people; *VK*e)		4,23; 24,23	0	0
ἴδιος + ἕκαστος (*VK*f)	2,3*; 6,44	2,6.8	1	0
κατ᾿ ἰδίαν (*LN*: privately; *SC*a; *VK*a); cf. κατὰ μόνας Mk 4,10	9,10; 10,23	23,19	6	7

Characteristic of Luke

CADBURY 1920 194

Literature

RADL 1975 412.

TILLER, Patrick A., Reflexive Pronouns in the New Testament. — *FilolNT* 15 (29-30, 2002) 43-63.

ἰδού 57/59 + 23 (Mt 62, Mk 7/12)	
1. look! (Lk 13,35); 2. indeed (Lk 13,16)	

Word groups	Lk	Acts	Mt	Mk
ἀλλ'/ἤ/πλὴν ἰδού (VKd)	17,21*.23²; 22,21	13,25	0	0/1
ἰδοὺ ἐγώ (SCd; VKj)	7,27 v.l.; 10,3 v.l.; 23,14; 24,49	9,10; 10,21; 20,25	4	0/1
ἰδοὺ ἡμεῖς (VKk)	18,28		1	1
ἰδοὺ ὧδε/ἐκεῖ (VKf)	17,21¹.21*.23¹·²		1	0/2
καὶ νῦν ἰδού (SCc; VKe) BOISMARD 1984 Aa94		13,11; 20,22.25	0	0
ὅτι ἰδού (VKg)	23,29	5,25	0	1
οὐχ ἰδού (VKh)		2,7	0	0
→ (καὶ) ἰδοὺ ἄνθρωπος/γυνή				

Characteristic of Luke	Lk	Acts	Mt	Mk
ἰδού without verb instead of ἔρχομαι CADBURY 1920 178	5,13.18; 23,50		0	0
ἰδοὺ γάρ (SCb; VKc); cf. 2 Cor 7,11 BOISMARD 1984 Bb46; CREDNER 1836 137; DENAUX 2009 L***; GOULDER 1989*; HARNACK 1906 139; HAWKINS 1909L; NEIRYNCK 1985; PLUMMER 1922 lx	1,44.48; 2,10; 6,23; 17,21²	9,11	0	0
καὶ ἰδού (SCa; VKa) → (καὶ) (ἰδού) ἄνδρες δύο; καὶ ἰδοὺ ἀνήρ/ ἄνθρωπος + ὄνομα PLUMMER 1922 lxi	1,20.31.36; 2,9*.25; 5,12.18; 7,12.37; 8,41; 9,30.38.39; 10,25; 11,31.32.41; 13,11.30; 14,2; 19,2; 23,14.15.50; 24,4.13.49	1,10; 5,28; 8,27; 10,17 v.l.30; 11,11; 12,7; 16,1; 27,24	28	0/1
καὶ ἰδού in apodosis BOISMARD 1984 Bb109; DENAUX 2009 La*; NEIRYNCK 1985	5,12; 7,12; 24,4	1,10	1	0
(καὶ) ἰδοὺ ... καί + verb (same subject) BOISMARD 1984 Ab35; DENAUX 2009 L***; NEIRYNCK 1985	1,36; 5,18; 7,37; 13,11; 19,2	5,9	0	0
→ (καὶ) ἰδοὺ + (ὁ) ἀνήρ; καὶ ἰδοὺ ἀνήρ/ἄνθρωπος + ὄνομα				

Literature

BDAG 2000 468 [literature]; COLLISON 1977 106-107 [linguistic usage of Luke's "other source-material": certain]; 107-108 [καὶ ἰδού: certain]; 108 [ἰδοὺ γάρ: certain; temporal ἰδού: probable]; DENAUX 2009 Lⁿ [ἰδού without verb instead of ἔρχομαι]; GERSDORF 1816 187 [καὶ ἰδού]; 199 [ἰδοὺ γάρ]; 245 [καὶ ἰδοὺ ἄνθρωπος ἦν]; HAUCK 1934 [Vorzugsverbindung: ἰδοὺ γάρ]; JEREMIAS 1980 41-42 [καὶ ἰδού]: "hebraisierende Partikelverbindung"; "Für die Beantwortung der Frage, ob die 26 Belege für καὶ ἰδού im LkEv traditionell oder redaktionell sind oder ob sie sich auf beide Größen verteilen, haben wir eine ganze Reihe von Anhaltspunkten. 1. Beginnen wir mit der Redaktion, so ist festzustellen a) καὶ ἰδοὺ ἀνήρ ... ist ein markanter Lukanismus ... b) καὶ ἰδού, nach periphrastischen καὶ ἐγένετο den Anschlußsatz einleitend ..., ist ebenfalls lukanisch... c) Weiter ist zu nennen: καὶ ἰδού zur Einleitung des Nachsatzes nach Kunjunktionalsatz mit ὡς temp. (Biblizismus) ... d) Ellipse des Verbum finitum nach (καὶ) ἰδού + Nominativ bei gleichem Subjekt im Vorder- und im Anschlußsatz schreibt Lukas als einziger neutestamentlicher Autor ... e) καὶ ἰδού in Verbindung mit Futurum instans ('ab sofort') findet man im Doppelwerk auch sonst: Lk 1,20 ... / Apg 13,11 ... 2. Viel geringer ist dagegen der Raum, den das καὶ ἰδού in der vorlukanischen Tradition einnimmt. Es handelt sich um a) καὶ ἰδού als Perikopenanfang ..., b) καὶ ἰδοὺ ἄνθρωπος..., nicht lukanisch ... und c) die Ellipse von ἐστίν nach καὶ ἰδού Lk 11,31f., die aus dem Logiengut stammt, wie die Parallele Mt 12,41f. zeigt"; [52-53 καὶ ἰδού red.] ; 60 [ἰδοὺ γάρ findet sich im NT (außer 2Kor 7,11) nur im lk Doppelwerk]; PLUMMER 1922 lxi [the frequent use of ἰδού and καὶ ἰδού: Hebrew influence]; RADL 1975 413 [ἰδού; καὶ ἰδού; καὶ νῦν ἰδού]; REHKOPF 1959 94 [ἰδοὺ γάρ: vorlukanisch]; SCHÜRMANN 1953 93; 1957 16 [ἰδού eine Vorzugswendung des Matth und Luk]; 1961 273 [ἰδοὺ γάρ].

DICKERSON, Patrick L., The New Character Narrative in Luke-Acts, 1997. Esp. 293-298: "The elements of the Lukan new character narrative" [τις/ἰδοὺ ἀνὴρ/γυνὴ ὀνόματι]; 301: "The use of the word ἰδού in Matthew and Luke".
FIEDLER, Peter, *Die Formel "Und siehe" im Neuen Testament* (SANT, 20). München: Kösel, 1969, 96 p. Esp. 13-48: "Das sprachliche Problem".
KILPATRICK, George D., Ἰδού and ἴδε in the Gospels. — *JTS* NS 18 (1967) 425-426. [NTA 12, 561]; = ID., *Principles and Practice*, 1990, 205-206.
VAN OTTERLOO, Roger, Towards an Understanding of 'Lo' and 'Behold'. Functions of ἰδοὺ and ἴδε in the Greek New Testament. — *OPTAT* (Dallas, TX) 2 (1988) 34-64.

ἰδρώς 1	sweat (Lk 22,44)

Literature

BRUN, Lyder, Engel und Blutschweiß Lc 22,43-44. — *ZNW* 32 (1933) 265-276.
SCHNEIDER, Gerhard, Engel und Blutschweiß (Lk 22,43-44): "Redaktionsgeschichte" im Dienste der Textkritik. — *BZ* NF 20 (1976) 112-116. Esp. 113-115: "Vokabular und Stil von Lk 22,43.44"; = ID., *Lukas, Theologe der Heilsgeschichte*, 1985, 153-157. Esp. 154-156.
TUCKETT, Christopher M., Luke 22,43-44: The "Agony" in the Garden and Luke's Gospel. — DENAUX, Adelbert (ed.), *New Testament Textual Criticism and Exegesis*. FS J. Delobel, 2002, 131-144. Esp. 133-135: "Vocabulary and style".

ἱερατεία 1	priesthood (Lk 1,9)

ἱερατεύω 1	be a priest (Lk 1,8)

ἱερεύς 5/6 + 3/4 (Mt 3, Mk 2)	priest

Word groups	Lk	Acts	Mt	Mk
ἱερεῖς + γραμματεῖς (*VK*c)	20,1*		0	0
ἱερεύς + ἀρχιερεῖς (*VK*d)		5,24*	0	0
ἱερεύς τις DENAUX 2009 L[n]	1,5; 10,31		0	0
ἱερεὺς τοῦ Διός (*VK*f)		14,13	0	0
ἱερεῖς plural (*VK*b)	6,4; 17,14; 20,1*	4,1; 6,7	2	1

Literature

GERSDORF 1816 169 [ἱερεύς τις ὀνόματι Ζαχαρίας]; HARNACK 1906 70 (ET 97) [ἱερεύς τις ὀνόματι]; HAUCK 1934 [Vorzugsverbindung: ἱερεύς τις]; JEREMIAS 1980 15 [ἱερεύς τις: red.].

BACHMANN, Michael, *Jerusalem und der Tempel*, 1980. Esp. 172-186: "Kultusbeamte".

Ἰεριχώ 3 (Mt 1, Mk 2)	Jericho (Lk 18,35)

ἱερόν 14 + 25 (Mt 11, Mk 9)	temple

Word groups	Lk	Acts	Mt	Mk
ἀναβαίνω/εἰσάγω/εἰσπορεύομαι/ (εἰσ)ἔρχομαι (+) εἰς τὸ ἱερόν →	2,27; 18,10; 19,45	3,1.2[2].8; 5,21; 21,28.29	2	2

ἐίσέρχομαι εἰς τὴν **συναγωγήν**; εἰσέρχομαι εἰς τὸν **ναόν**; cf. εἴσειμι εἰς τὸ ἱερόν Acts 3,3; 21,26				
Ἀρτέμιδος ἱερόν (*VK*c)		19,27	0	0
ἱερόν (+) διδάσκω (*SC*a; *VK*a)	19,47; 20,1; 21,37	5,21.25.42; 21,28	2	3
ἱερόν + προσεύχομαι →**ὄρος** + προσεύχομαι DENAUX 2009 LAⁿ (?)	18,10	22,17	0	0
ἱερόν + συναγωγή (*VK*e)		24,12	0	0

Characteristic of Luke
GASTON 1973 66 [Lked?]; MORGENTHALER 1958A

	Lk	Acts	Mt	Mk
εἰμι ἐν τῷ ἱερῷ BOISMARD 1984 Bb110; DENAUX 2009 La*; NEIRYNCK 1985	21,37; 22,53; 24,53	5,25	0	1
στρατηγὸς τοῦ ἱεροῦ (*LN*: commander of the Temple guard; *VK*d) PLUMMER 1922 lii	22,52	4,1; 5,24	0	0

Literature
BDAG 2000 470; DENAUX 2009 IAⁿ [στρατηγὸς τοῦ ἱεροῦ].

DE JONGE, Henk J., Sonship, Wisdom, Infancy: Luke II.41-51a. — *NTS* 24 (1977-78) 317-354. Esp. 327-330: "In the temple".

Ἰεροσόλυμα 4/6 + 22/26 (Mt 11, Mk 10) — Jerusalem

Word groups	Lk	Acts	Mt	Mk
ἀναβαίνω εἰς Ἰεροσόλυμα → καταβαίνω ἀπὸ Ἰεροσολύμων; ἀναβαίνω εἰς **Ἰερουσαλήμ**; cf. ἐπιβαίνω εἰς Ἰεροσόλυμα Acts 21,4; συναναβαίνω + εἰς Ἰεροσόλυμα Mk 15,41; συναναβαίνω + εἰς Ἰερουσαλήμ Acts 13,31	2,42*; 18,31*	11,2*; 21,15; 25,1.9	2	2
Ἰεροσόλυμα + Ἰουδαία (*SC*b; *VK*e)		26,20	2	1
καταβαίνω ἀπὸ Ἰεροσολύμων → ἀναβαίνω εἰς Ἰεροσόλυμα; καταβαίνω ἀπὸ **Ἰερουσαλήμ**		25,7	0	1
κατέρχομαι ἀπὸ Ἰεροσολύμων → ἔρχομαι εἰς/ἐξέρχομαι ἐξ **Ἰερουσαλήμ**; cf. ἀπ/εἰσέρχομαι (+) εἰς Ἰεροσόλυμα Mt 16,21; 21,10; Mk 11,11; ἔρχομαι ἀπὸ Ἰεροσολύμων Mk 7,1		11,27	0	0
πορεύομαι εἰς Ἰεροσόλυμα → πορεύομαι εἰς **Ἰερουσαλήμ**		19,21; 25,20	0	0
πορείαν ποιέω εἰς Ἰεροσόλυμα	13,22		0	0

Characteristic of Luke
MORGENTHALER 1958A

Literature
See Ἰερουσαλήμ.

Ἰερουσαλήμ 27/29 + 37/45 (Mt 2) — Jerusalem

Word groups	Lk	Acts	Mt	Mk
ἔρχομαι εἰς/ἐξέρχομαι ἐξ + Ἰερουσαλήμ → κατέρχομαι ἀπὸ **Ἰεροσολύμων**		8,27; 22,18	0	2

θυγάτηρ Ἰερουσαλήμ	23,28		0	0
ἡ (πόλις) Ἰερουσαλήμ (VKc)	21,20 v.l.; 24,49*	5,28	0	0
Ἰερουσαλήμ Ἰερουσαλήμ (VKf)	13,34		2	0
Ἰερουσαλήμ + Ἰουδαία (SCb; VKe) DENAUX 2009 La[n]	5,17; 6,17	1,8	0	0
Ἰερουσαλήμ + οἶκος	$13,34^{1.2}$(-35)		1	0
Ἰερουσαλήμ + τὰ τέκνα → πόλις + τὰ τέκνα	$13,34^{1.2}$; $23,28^1$		1	0
καταβαίνω ἀπὸ Ἰερουσαλήμ → ἀναβαίνω εἰς Ἰερουσαλήμ; καταβαίνω ἀπὸ Ἰεροσολύμων DENAUX 2009 LA[n]	10,30	8,26	0	0
ὅλη + Ἰερουσαλήμ (VKd); cf. πᾶσα Ἰεροσόλυμα Mt 2,3		21,31	0	0

Characteristic of Luke

BOISMARD 1984 Bb84; CREDNER 1836 136; DENAUX 2009 L***; GOULDER 1989*; HAWKINS 1909 L; HENDRIKS 1986 428.433.434. 441.448.468; MORGENTHALER 1958LA; NEIRYNCK 1985

	Lk	Acts	Mt	Mk
ἀναβαίνω (+) εἰς Ἰερουσαλήμ → καταβαίνω ἀπὸ Ἰερουσαλήμ; ἀναβαίνω εἰς Ἰεροσόλυμα; cf. ἐπιβαίνω εἰς Ἰεροσόλυμα Acts 21,4; συναναβαίνω + εἰς Ἰεροσόλυμα Mk 15,41; συναναβαίνω + εἰς Ἰερουσαλήμ Acts 13,31 DENAUX 2009 lA*	18,31; 19,28	11,2; 15,2; 21,4 v.l.12. 15*; 24,11	0	0
πορεύομαι (+) εἰς Ἰερουσαλήμ → πορεύομαι εἰς Ἰεροσόλυμα; cf. εἰσπορεύομαι καὶ ἐκπορεύομαι εἰς Ἰερουσαλήμ Acts 9,28 DENAUX 2009 L***	2,41; 9,51.53; 17,11	19,21*; 20,22; 25,20*	0	0
ὑποστρέφω εἰς Ἰερουσαλήμ DENAUX 2009 lA*	2,45; 24,33.52	$1,12^1$; 8,25; 12,25; 13,13; 22,17	0	0

Literature

COLLISON 1977 181 [noteworthy phenomena]; EASTON 1910 155 [probably characteristic of L]; HAUCK 1934 [Vorzugswort]; JEREMIAS 1980 91-92 [red.]; SCHÜRMANN 1957 110, n. 386 [luk Spracheigentümlichkeit].

BACHMANN, Michael, *Jerusalem und der Tempel*, 1980. Esp. 13-66: "Die beiden Formen des Namens Jerusalem".

BARTLET, J. Vernon, The Twofold Use of "Jerusalem" in the Lucan Writings. — *ExpT* 13 (1901-02) 157-158. [Hebraic and Hellenistic form of Jerusalem]

DE LA POTTERIE, Ignace, Les deux noms de Jérusalem dans l'évangile de Luc. — *RSR* 69 (1981) 57-70.

JEREMIAS, Joachim, Ἰερουσαλήμ/Ἰεροσόλυμα. — *ZNW* 65 (1974) 273-276. Esp. 275-276: "Das lukanische Doppelwerk".

MORALES GOMEZ, G., *Jerusalén en la doble obra Lucana*. Barcelona: Facultad de teologia. Seccion San Paciano, 1981, 735 p.

—, Jerusalén-Jerosolima en el vocabulario y la geografia de Lucas. — *RevistCatTeol* 7 (1982) 131-186.

NEIRYNCK, Frans, La matière marcienne dans l'évangile de Luc, 1973. Esp. 183; [2]1989. Esp. 93; = ID., *Evangelica*, 1982. Esp. 63.

READ-HEIMERDINGER, Jenny, *The Bezan Text of Acts*, 2002. Esp. 311-344: "The spelling of Jerusalem".
ROSS, J.M., The Spelling of Jerusalem in Acts. — *NTS* 38 (1992) 474-476.
SCHÜTZ, Roland, Ἰερουσαλήμ und Ἰεροσόλυμα im Neuen Testament. — *ZNW* 11 (1910) 169-187.
SYLVA, Dennis D., Ierousalēm and Hierosoluma in Luke-Acts. — *ZNW* 74 (1983) 207-221. Esp. 208-211: "Former studies of the problem"; 211-212: "The Lukan use of Jerusalem terms"; 212-220: "A complementary-clarificatory use of Jerusalem terms in Luke-Acts". [NTA 28, 524]
WINTER, Paul, "Nazareth" and "Jerusalem" in Luke Chs. 1 and 2. — *NTS* 3 (1957) 136-142. Esp. 136-139 [Ναζαρέθ]; 139-142 [Ἰερουσαλήμ/Ἰεροσόλυμα].

Ἰεσσαί 1 + 1 (Mt 2)   Jesse (Lk 3,32)

Ἰησοῦς 88/100 + 69/73 (Mt 152/176, Mk 80[82]/92)   Jesus

Word groups	Lk	Acts	Mt	Mk
διὰ Ἰησοῦ Χριστοῦ		10,36	0	0
ἐν τῷ Ἰησοῦ → ἐν τῷ **κυρίῳ**		4,2	0	0
Ἰησοῦ ἐπιστάτα (*VK*s)	17,13		0	0
Ἰησοῦς (ὁ) κύριος / κύριος (+) Ἰησοῦς (*SC*f; *VK*j); cf. Ἰησοῦς Χριστός, οὗτός ἐστιν πάντων κύριος Acts 10,36	24,3	1,21; 4,33; 7,59; 8,16; 9,17.28*; 11,17.20; 15,11; 16,31; 19,5. 10*.13^1.17; 20,24.35; 21,13; 28,31	0	0[1]
Ἰησοῦς (ὁ) κύριος ἡμῶν (*VK*k)		15,26; 20,21	0	0
Ἰησοῦς (ὁ) Ναζωραῖος / (ὁ) Ναζαρηνός / (ὁ) ἀπὸ Ναζαρέθ (*SC*m; *VK*v)	4,34; 18,37; 24,19	2,22; 3,6; 4,10; 6,14; 10,38; 22,8; 26,9	2	4
Ἰησοῦς σωτήρ (*VK*l)		13,23	0	0
Ἰησοῦς υἱὸς Δαυίδ (*SC*h; *VK*n)	18,38		1	1
Ἰησοῦς + (ὁ) υἱὸς (τοῦ) θεοῦ (*SC*g; *VK*m)	8,28^2	8,37*; 9,20	0/1	2
Ἰησοῦς + (ὁ) υἱὸς + (τοῦ) Ἰωσήφ (*SC*j; *VK*p)	3,23		0	0
Ἰησοῦς (+) Χριστός (*SC*d; *VK*e)		2,38; 3,6; 4,10.33 *v.l.*; 8,12.37*; 9,34; 10,36.48; 11,17; 15,11 *v.l.*26; 16,18.31 *v.l.*; 20,21 *v.l.*; 28,31	2/3	1
Ἰησοῦς ὁ παῖς / τὸ παιδίον (*SC*l; *VK*t) DENAUX 2009 1A^n	2,27.43	3,13.26*; 4,27.30	0	0
Ἰησοῦς ὁ χριστός (*VK*g)		5,42 *v.l.*; 9,34 *v.l.*	0/1	0
λόγος + Ἰησοῦ		20,35	0	0
(τὰ)(περὶ) (τοῦ) Ἰησοῦ (*VK*z)	24,19	18,25; 28,23.31	1	0
ὄνομα (τοῦ) Ἰησοῦ (*SC*p; *VK*y) → ὄνομα (τοῦ) **κυρίου**; see also **ὄνομα** (τοῦ) Ἰησοῦ (Χριστοῦ) BOISMARD 1984 ca28		2,38; 3,6; 4,10.18.30; 5,40; 8,12.16; 9,27.28*; 10,48; 15,26; 16,18; 19,5.13^1.17; 21,13; 26,9	0	0
οὗτος ὁ Ἰησοῦς BOISMARD 1984 Aa95; NEIRYNCK 1985		1,11; 2,32.36	0	0

πίστις εἰς (κύριον/Χριστὸν) Ἰησοῦν; cf. Col 2,5; πίστις εἰς ἐμέ Acts 26,18 BOISMARD 1984 ca19		20,21; 24,24	0	0
πνεῦμα Ἰησοῦ		16,7	0	0
σῶμα (τοῦ) (+) Ἰησοῦ	23,52; 24,3		2	2
Χριστὸς (ὁ) Ἰησοῦς (SCd; VKf)		3,20; 5,42; 17,3; 18,5.28; 19,4 v.l.; 24,24	0	0
Ἰησοῦς Jesus Nave (SCa; VKa)		7,45	0	0
Ἰησοῦς Jesus son of Eliezer (SCb; VKb)	3,29		0	0
→ ἀδελφοί brothers of Jesus				

Characteristic of Luke

GASTON 1973 66 [Lked?]

	Lk	Acts	Mt	Mk
ὁ κύριος Ἰησοῦς BOISMARD 1984 Db1; NEIRYNCK 1985	24,3	1,21; 4,33; 7,59; 8,16; 11,17.20; 15,11.26; 16,31; 19,5.13^l.17; 20,21.24.35; 21,13; 28,31	0	0
→ βαπτίζω in the name of Jesus; εὐαγγελίζομαι τὸν Ἰησοῦν; κηρύσσω τὸν Ἰησοῦν				

Literature

COLLISON 1977 95 [Ἰησοῦς vocative: noteworthy phenomena]; DENAUX 2009 IAⁿ [ὁ κύριος Ἰησοῦς]; RADL 1975 420 [ὄνομα τοῦ κυρίου Ἰησοῦ]; SCHÜRMANN 1955 54-55 [κύριος Ἰησοῦς].

LAURENTIN, René, Traces d'allusions étymologiques en Luc 1–2 (I). — Bib 37 (1956) 435-456. Esp. 444-447: "Jésus".

READ-HEIMERDINGER, Jenny, The Bezan Text of Acts, 2002. Esp. 254-274: "Titles of Jesus" [(ὁ) Ἰησοῦς; Ἰησοῦς ὁ Ναζωραῖος; ὁ παῖς; ὁ ἅγιος παῖς σου Ἰησοῦς; (ὁ) Χριστός; Χριστὸς Ἰησοῦς; Ἰησοῦς Χριστός; Ἰησοῦς Χριστὸς ὁ Ναζωραῖος; (ὁ) κύριος; (ὁ) κύριος Ἰησοῦς; ὁ κύριος Ἰησοῦς Χριστός].

ἱκανός 9/10 + 18/19 (Mt 3, Lk 3)

1. enough (degree); 2. intense (Acts 22,16); 3. adequate; 4. enough (quantity) (Lk 22,38); 5. many (Acts 12,12); 6. large (Lk 7,12; 8,27)

Word groups	Lk	Acts	Mt	Mk
ἐφ᾽ ἱκανόν (LN: for a long time)		20,11	0	0
(τὸ) ἱκανόν (SCd; VKd)	22,38; 23,8 v.l.	17,9; 20,11	0	1
ἱκανός + infinitive (SCa; VKa)	3,16		1	1
ἱκανός + ἵνα (SCb; VKb)	7,6		1	0

Characteristic of Luke

DENAUX 2009 IA**; GASTON 1973 66 [Lked?]; GOULDER 1989; HAWKINS 1909A.187; MORGENTHALER 1958A; PLUMMER 1922 lx; VOGEL 1899D

	Lk	Acts	Mt	Mk
ἱκανός concerning time (SCc; VKc) → ἐφ᾽ ἱκανόν; ἱκανὴ ἡμέρα; ἱκανὸς χρόνος BOISMARD 1984 Ab8; CADBURY 1920 196; DENAUX 2009 IA*; NEIRYNCK 1985	8,27; 20,9; 23,8	8,11; 9,23.43; 14,3; 18,18; 20,11; 27,7.9	0	0

ἱκανός = numerous, many; cf. 1 Cor 11,30	7,11*.12;	8,11; 9,23.43; 11,24.26;	1	1
BOISMARD 1984 Bb33; CREDNER 1836 141;	8,27.32;	12,12; 14,3.21; 18,18; 19,26;		
DENAUX 2009 L***; NEIRYNCK 1985	20,9; 23,8.9	20,8.37; 22,6; 27,7.9		
ὄχλος ἱκανός	7,12	11,24.26; 19,26	0	1
BOISMARD 1984 Bb116; NEIRYNCK 1985				

Literature

COLLISON 1977 186 [quantitative: linguistic usage of Luke: likely; it seems "likely" also that this is a linguistic usage of Luke's "other source-material"]; DENAUX 2009 lAn [ὄχλος ἱκανός]; EASTON 1910 161 [ἱκανός "much", "great": cited by Weiss as characteristic of L, and possibly corroborative]; HAUCK 1934 [Vorzugswort]; JEREMIAS 1980 157-158: "Vorzugswort des Lukas"; 301 [ὄχλος ἱκανός; χρόνος ἱκανός: red.]; RADL 1975 413 [ἱκανός; ἱκανός "bei Zeitbestimmungen"; ἡμέραι ἱκαναί]; REHKOPF 1959 94 [vorlukanisch]; SCHÜRMANN 1957 132-134 [ἱκανόν ἐστιν Bedeutung "genügend" auch luk möglich]; 1961 281 [protoluk R weniger wahrscheinlich].

FINLAYSON, S.K., "The Enigma of the Swords". — *ExpT* 50 (1938-39) 563.
WESTERN, W., "The Enigma of the Swords". — *ExpT* 50 (1938-39) 377.
—, The Enigma of the Swords, St. Luke xxii.38. — *ExpT* 52 (1940-41) 357.

| ἱκμάς 1 | moisture (Lk 8,6) |

Literature
HAUCK 1934 [seltenes Alleinwort].

| ἱλάσκομαι 1 | 1. forgive; 2. show mercy (Lk 18,13) |

Literature
BDAG 2000 474 [literature].

HILL, David, *Greek Words and Hebrew Meanings*, 1967. Esp. 23-48: "The interpretation of ἱλάσκεσθαι and related words in the Septuagint and in the New Testament".

| ἱμάς 1 + 1 (Mk 1) | 1. strap (Lk 3,16); 2. whipping (Acts 22,25) |

Word groups	Lk	Acts	Mt	Mk
λύω τὸν ἱμάντα → λύω τὸ ὑπόδημα	3,16		0	1

| ἱματίζω 1 (Mk 1) | clothe (Lk 8,35) |

| ἱμάτιον 10 + 8 (Mt 13/16, Mk 12) | 1. clothing (Acts 18,6); 2. coat (Lk 6,29) |

Word groups	Lk	Acts	Mt	Mk
ἱμάτιον ἐνδύω; cf. ἔνδυμα/χιτών (+) ἐνδύω	8,27		1	1
Mt 22,11; Mk 6,9				

| ἱμάτιον + ἱματισμός/χιτών (VKb); cf.
ἱμάτιον + χλαμύς Mt 27,31
κράσπεδον τοῦ ἱματίου | 6,29; 7,25

8,44 | 9,39 | 1/2

2 | 0

1 |
| ἱμάτιον singular (SCa; VKa) | 5,36[1.2]; 6,29; 8,27.44; 22,36 | 12,8 | 7 | 5 |

ἱματισμός 2 + 1 (Mt 0/1)   clothing (Lk 7,25; 8,29; Acts 20,33)

Word groups	Lk	Acts	Mt	Mk
ἱματισμός + ἱμάτιον → χιτών + ἱμάτιον	7,25		0/1	0

Characteristic of Luke
BOISMARD 1984 cb31; NEIRYNCK 1985; PLUMMER 1922 lx; VOGEL 1899B

Literature
DENAUX 2009 La[n]; HAUCK 1934 [seltenes Alleinwort]; JEREMIAS 1980 163: "lukanisch".

ἵνα 46/47 + 15/16 (Mt 39/40, Mk 64)
1. in order to (Acts 22,24); 2. as a result (Lk 9,45); 3. that (Lk 21,36); 4. namely

Word groups	Lk	Acts	Mt	Mk
ἀλλ᾽ ἵνα (VKr)		4,17	0	2
ἢ ἵνα (VKv)	17,2		0	0
ἵνα + future indicative (SCa; VKb)	14,10; 20,10	5,15 v.l.; 21,24	0	0/1
ἵνα δέ (VKh)	5,24	24,4	2	1
ἵνα κἄν (VKl); cf. ἵνα εἰ Mk 14,35		5,15	0	1
ἵνα (…) μή (SCb; VKe)	8,10.12.31; 9,45; 14,29 v.l.; 16,28; 18,5; 22,32.46	2,25; 4,17; 5,26*; 24,4	8	6
ἵνα μήποτε (SCc; VKf); cf. ἵνα μηδείς Mt 16,20; Mk 5,43; 6,8; 7,36; 8,30; 9,9	14,29		0	0
ἵνα ὅ (VKp)		8,19	0	1
ἵνα ὅταν (SCd; VKm) DENAUX 2009 L[n]	14,10; 16,4.9		0	0
τοῦτο ἵνα (VKx)	1,43	9,21	0	0

→ ἀναβαίνω + ἵνα; γίνομαι ἵνα; δέομαι ἵνα; ἐντολή + ἵνα; ἐπιτιμάω + ἵνα; ἐρωτάω + ἵνα; ἑτοιμάζω + ἵνα; θέλω ἵνα; ἱκανός + ἵνα; λέγω/εἶπον ἵνα; παρακαλέω ἵνα; ποιέω … ἵνα; προσεύχομαι ἵνα

Literature
BDAG 2000 476-477 [literature]; COLLISON 1977 110 [ἵνα ὅταν: linguistic usage of Luke's "other source-material": certain]; 115 [non telic: linguistic usage of Luke: likely]; PAFFENROTH 1997 87-88; SCHÜRMANN 1957 48.106 [(nicht) finales ἵνα].

CADOUX, C.J., The Imperatival Use of ἵνα in the New Testament. — *JTS* 42 (1941) 165-173.
CARAGOUNIS, Chrys C., *The Development of Greek and the New Testament*, 2004. Esp. 218-226.
DEER, Donald S., More about the Imperatival *hina*. — *BTrans* 24 (1973) 328-329.
GREENLEE, J. Harold, Ἵνα Clauses and Related Expressions. — *BTrans* 6 (1955) 12-16.
GREENLEE, J. Harold, Ὅτι and ἵνα Content Clauses. — *Notes on Translation* 14 (2000)

49-53. [NTA 46, 74]
LARSEN, I., The Use of *Hina* in the New Testament, with Special Reference in the Gospel of John. — *Notes on Translation* (Dallas, TX) 2 (1988) 28-34.
MEECHAM, H.G., The Imperatival Use of ἵνα in the New Testament. — *JTS* 43 (1942) 179-180.
MORRICE, W.G., The Imperatival ἵνα. — *BTrans* 23 (1972) 326-330.
SALOM, A.P., The Imperatival Use of ἵνα in the New Testament. – *AusBibRev* 6 (1958) 123-141.

ἵνατί 1 + 2 (Mt 2) | why? (Lk 13,7; Acts 4,25; 7,26)

Ἰορδάνης 2 (Mt 6, Mk 4) | Jordan River (Lk 3,3; 4,1)

Ἰουδαία 10 + 12 (Mt 8, Mk 3)
1. Judea (Lk 1,5); 2. Jewess

Word groups	Lk	Acts	Mt	Mk
ἀναβαίνω + εἰς τὴν Ἰουδαίαν → κατέρχομαι ἀπὸ τῆς **Ἰουδαίας**	2,4		0	0
Ἰουδαία + Ἰερουσαλήμ/Ἱεροσόλυμα	5,17; 6,17	1,8; 26,20	2	1
κατέρχομαι (+) ἀπὸ τῆς Ἰουδαίας → ἀναβαίνω εἰς τὴν **Ἰουδαίαν**		12,19; 15,1; 21,10	0	0
πᾶσα ἡ Ἰουδαία (*SC*a; *VK*a) → ὅλη ἡ **Ἰουδαία**	6,17	1,8	1	0
συναγωγὴ τῆς Ἰουδαίας → συναγωγὴ τῶν **Ἰουδαίων**	4,44		0	0
ἡ χώρα τῆς Ἰουδαίας (*VK*b) → χώρα τῶν **Ἰουδαίων**		8,1; 26,20	0	0

Characteristic of Luke
GASTON 1973 66 [Lked?]

	Lk	Acts	Mt	Mk
καθ' ὅλης τῆς Ἰουδαίας VOGEL 1899C	23,5	9,31; 10,37	0	0
ὅλη ἡ Ἰουδαία → πᾶσα ἡ **Ἰουδαία** BOISMARD 1984 Ab83; NEIRYNCK 1985	7,17; 23,5	9,31; 10,37	0	0

Literature
BDAG 2000 [Acts 2,9: literature]; DENAUX 2009 IAⁿ [καθ' ὅλης τῆς Ἰουδαίας], LAⁿ [ὅλη ἡ Ἰουδαία]; EASTON 1910 161 [cited by Weiss as characteristic of L, and possibly corroborative]; JEREMIAS 1980 17-18 [trad.]; 70 [ὅλη ἡ Ἰουδαία: red.].

BACHMANN, Michael, *Jerusalem und der Tempel*, 1980. Esp. 67-131: "Der Gebrauch von Ἰουδαία".
KÖHLER, Ludwig, Ἰουδαίαν in Acts 2,9. — *ExpT* 22 (1910-11) 230-231.

Ἰουδαῖος 5 + 79/82 (Mt 5, Mk 7)
1. Jew (Lk 7,3; 23,3.37.38); 2. Judean (Lk 23,51)

Word groups	Lk	Acts	Mt	Mk
ἀνήρ/ἄνθρωπος (+) Ἰουδαῖος (*SC*b; *VK*e)		10,28; 13,6; 21,39; 22,3	0	0
βασιλεὺς τῶν Ἰουδαίων ΣΞα; ηΚγ˚	23,3.37.38		4	5

	Lk	Acts	Mt	Mk
γυνὴ Ἰουδαία (VKf)		16,1	0	0
(ὧ) (ἄνδρες) Ἰουδαῖοι (VKd)		2,14; 18,14²	0	0
Ἰουδαῖος + Ἕλλην (SCd; VKk)		14,1²; 16,1; 18,4; 19,10.17; 20,21	0	0
Ἰουδαῖοί τε καὶ Ἕλλήναι; cf. Rom 3,9; 1 Cor 1,24 BOISMARD 1984 ca47		14,1; 19,10.17; 20,21	0	0
λαὸς τῶν Ἰουδαίων		12,11	0	0
νόμος τῶν Ἰουδαίων		25,8	0	0
οἵτινες ἀπό + place + Ἰουδαῖοι BOISMARD 1984 Aa96		17,13; 21,27; 24,19	0	0
πάντες (οἱ) Ἰουδαῖοι; cf. Jn 18,20 BOISMARD 1984 ca29		18,2²; 21,21; 22,12; 24,5; 26,4	0	1
πόλις τῶν Ἰουδαίων (VKc)	23,51		0	0
πρεσβύτεροι τῶν Ἰουδαίων → πρεσβύτεροι τοῦ Ἰσραήλ DENAUX 2009 LAⁿ	7,3	25,15		
συναγωγὴ τῶν Ἰουδαίων (SCc; VKj) → συναγωγὴ τῆς Ἰουδαίας BOISMARD 1984 Aa66		13,5.42*; 14,1¹; 17,1.10	0	0
χώρα τῶν Ἰουδαίων (VKb) → ἡ χώρα τῆς Ἰουδαίας		10,39	0	0

Characteristic of Luke

DENAUX 2009 IA**; HENDRIKS 1986 468; MORGENTHALER 1958A

Literature

KRAEMER, R.S., On the Meaning of the Term "Jew" in Greco-Roman Inscriptions. — HTR 82 (1989) 25-53.

LOWE, Malcolm, Who Were the Ἰουδαῖοι? — NT 18 (1976) 101-130. Esp. 102-110: "Semantics and history"; 126-128: "Ἰουδαῖοι in the synoptics". [NTA 21, 328]

TOMSON, Peter J., The Names Israel and Jew in Ancient Judaism and in the New Testament II. — Bijdragen 47 (1986) 266-289. [NTA 31, 527]

Ἰούδας 8/9 + 8 (Mt 10, Mk 4)

1. Judah or Judas (person) (Lk 3,30; 6,16; Acts 5,37; 9,11; 15,22); 2. Judah (tribe); 3. Judah (land) (Lk 1,39).

Word groups	Lk	Acts	Mt	Mk
Ἰούδας ὁ Γαλιλαῖος (SCc; VKc)		5,37	0	0
Ἰούδας (+) Ἰσκαριώτης/Ἰσκαριώθ (SCf; VKf)	6,16²; 22,3.		5	3
Ἰούδας ὁ καλούμενος Βαρσαββᾶς (SCg; VKg)		15,22	0	0
Ἰούδας + παραδίδωμι	22,3(-4); 22,48		5	3
Ἰούδας + προδότης	6,16		0	0
Judas of Damascus (SCd; VKd)		9,11	0	0
Ἰούδας son of Jacob (SCa; VKa)	3,33		4	0
Ἰούδας son of Joanna (VKj)	3,26*		0	0
Ἰούδας son of Joseph (SCb; VKb)	3,30		0	0
Ἰούδας Ἰακώβου, the apostle (SCe; VKe) DENAUX LAⁿ	6,16¹	1,13	0	0

Literature

BDAG 2000 479 [literature].

GÄRTNER, Bertil, Die rätselhaften Termini Nazoräer und Iskariot (Horae Soederblomianae, 4). Lund: Gleerup, 1957, 68 p. Esp. 5-36: "Nazareth, Nazoräer und das Mandäertum"; 37-68: "Judas Iskariot".

Ἰσαάκ 3 + 4 (Mt 4, Mk 1) | Isaac

Word groups	Lk	Acts	Mt	Mk
Ἀβραάμ + Ἰσαάκ + Ἰακώβ (VKa)	3,34; 13,28; 20,37	3,13; 7,32	2	1
(ὁ) θεὸς (+) Ἰσαάκ → θεὸς Ἀβραάμ/Ἰακώβ	20,37	3,13v.l.?; 7,32	1	1

ἰσάγγελος** 1 | like an angel (Lk 20,36)

Literature
HAUCK 1934 [seltenes Alleinwort].

Ἰσκαριώθ 1 (Mk 2) | Iscariot

Word groups	Lk	Acts	Mt	Mk
Ἰούδας Ἰσκαριώθ	6,16		0	2

Literature
ARBEITMAN, Yoël, The Suffix of Iskariot. — JBL 99 (1980) 122-124.
CANE, Anthony, Contested Meanings of the Name 'Judas Iscariot'. — ExpT 112 (2000) 44-45.
EHRMAN, Albert, Judas Iscariot and Abba Saqqara. — JBL 97 (1978) 572-573.
GÄRTNER, Bertil, Die rätselhaften Termini Nazoräer und Iskariot (Horae Soederblomianae, 4). Lund: Gleerup, 1957, 68 p. Esp. 5-36: "Nazareth, Nazoräer und das Mandäertum"; 37-68: "Judas Iscariot".

Ἰσκαριώτης 1/2 (Mt 2, Mk 0/2) | Iscariot

Word groups	Lk	Acts	Mt	Mk
Ἰούδας Ἰσκαριώτης	6,16*; 22,3		2	0/3

Literature
VOGT, E., Ἰσκαριώτης = hypocrita, proditor. — Bib 35 (1954) 404-405.

ἴσος 1 + 1 (Mt 1, Mk 2) | equal (Lk 6,34; Acts 11,7)

Word groups	Lk	Acts	Mt	Mk
τὰ ἴσα (VKa)	6,34		0	0

Ἰσραήλ 12 + 15/16 (Mt 12, Mk 2) | Israel

Word groups	Lk	Acts	Mt	Mk
θεὸς (+) (τοῦ) Ἰσραήλ (SCe; VKe)	1,68	13,17	1	0
οἶκος Ἰσραήλ (LN: people of Israel; SCb; VKb)		2,36; 7,42	2	0
πρεσβύτεροι τοῦ Ἰσραήλ → πρεσβύτεροι τῶν Ἰουδαίων		4,8*	0	0
φυλή + τοῦ Ἰσραήλ (SCc; VKc) → λαὸς Ἰσραήλ	22,30		1	0

Characteristic of Luke	Lk	Acts	Mt	Mk
λαὸς Ἰσραήλ (SCd; VKd) → φυλή + τοῦ Ἰσραήλ BOISMARD 1984 Ab56; NEIRYNCK 1985	2,32	4,10.27; 13,17.24	1	0
υἱοὶ Ἰσραήλ (LN: people of Israel; SCa; VKa) BOISMARD 1984 Db18; NEIRYNCK 1985	1,16	5,21; 7,23.37; 9,15; 10,36	1	0

Literature

DENAUX 2009 lAn [λαὸς Ἰσραήλ; υἱοὶ Ἰσραήλ]; GERSDORF 1816 200 [ἀντελάβετο Ἰσραήλ παιδὸς αὐτοῦ]; 256 [δόξαν λαοῦ σου Ἰσραήλ]; RADL 1975 413 [Ἰσραήλ; οἶκος/λαὸς/υἱοὶ Ἰσραήλ].

TOMSON, Peter J., The Names Israel and Jew in Ancient Judaism and in the New Testament II. — *Bijdragen* 47 (1986) 266-289. [NTA 31, 527]
VOORWINDE, S., How Jewish Is *Israel* in the New Testament. — *Reformed Theological Review* 67 (2008) 61-90. [NTA 53, 101]

ἵστημι 26 + 35 (Mt 21, Mk 10)

1. put; 2. maintain; 3. establish; 4. pay; 5. select; 6. propose
ἵσταμαι: 7. stand (Acts 5,25); 8. stand up; 9. be in a place; 10. cease (Lk 8,44; Acts 8,38); 11. continue to be; 12. remain firmly (Lk 11,18)

Word groups	Lk	Acts	Mt	Mk
ἔστηκα/ἑστήκειν, perfect and pluperfect (SCc)	1,11; 5,1.2; 8,20; 9,27; 13,25; 18,13; 23,10.35.49	1,11; 4,14; 5,23.25; 7,33.55.56; 9,7; 12,14; 16,9; 21,40; 22,25; 24,21; 25,10; 26,6.22	11	3/4
ἵσταμαι ἔξω; cf. κάθημαι ἔξω Mt 26,69	8,20; 13,25		2	0
ἵστημι followed by participle	7,38; 8,20; 13,25; 23,10.35.49	1,11; 3,8; 26,6.22	3	0
ἵστημι (ἀπὸ) μακρόθεν/πόρρωθεν DENAUX 2009 Lⁿ	17,12; 18,13; 23,49		0	0
ἵστημι + ἄγγελος → ἐφ/παρίστημι + ἄγγελος; ἀπέστη/ἀπῆλθεν ὁ ἄγγελος/διάβολος DENAUX 2009 LAⁿ	1,11	11,13	0	0
ἵστημι + παρὰ τοὺς πόδας → παρακαθέζομαι πρὸς τοὺς πόδας	7,38		0	0
ὁ υἱὸς τοῦ ἀνθρώπου ἑστὼς ἐκ δεξιῶν τοῦ θεοῦ → ὁ υἱὸς τοῦ ἀνθρώπου καθήμενος ἐκ δεξιῶν (τοῦ θεοῦ)		7,56	0	0
ἵσταμαι passive (SCb; VKb)	11,18; 18,11.40; 19,8; 21,36; 24,17	2,14; 5,20; 11,13; 17,22; 25,18; 27,21	5	3/4
ἵστημι transitive (SCa; VKa)	4,9; 9,47	1,23; 4,7; 5,27; 6,6.13; 7,60; 17,31; 22,30	4	2

Characteristic of Luke	Lk	Acts	Mt	Mk
ἀναστὰς ἔστη HARNACK 1906 43	6,8		0	0
ἔστην DENAUX 2009 L***; GOULDER 1989*	6,8.17; 8,44; 24,36	1,23; 4,7; 5,27; 6,6; 10,30	1	1

ἑστώς (VKd) → ἐφεστώς/παρεστώς/ συνεστώς; cf. ἑστηκώς Mt 16,28 v.l.; 27,47; Mk 3,31* v.l.; 9,1; 11,5; 13,14 CREDNER 1836 139.140	1,11; 5,1.2; 9,27; 18,13	4,14; 5,23.25; 7,55.56; 16,9; 21,40; 22,25; 24,21; 25,10	5/7	0/1
ἵστημι ἐν μέσῳ (τινῶν) BOISMARD 1984 Ab129; NEIRYNCK 1985	24,36	17,22; 27,21	0	0
ἵστημι ἐπί + genitive BOISMARD 1984 Eb36; NEIRYNCK 1985	6,17	5,23; 21,40; 24,20; 25,10	0	1
σταθείς/σταθέντες BOISMARD 1984 Ab14; CREDNER 1836 139; DENAUX 2009 IA*; GOULDER 1989; HARNACK 1906 52; HAWKINS 1909L.B; NEIRYNCK 1985; PLUMMER 1922 lxii; VOGEL 1899D	18,11.40; 19,8	2,14; 5,20; 11,13; 17,22; 25,18; 27,21	0	0

Literature

VON BENDEMANN 2001 434: "Das Partizip σταθείς/σταθέντες für den begleitenden Umstand findet sich nur im lukanischen Doppelwerk"; DENAUX 2009 IAⁿ [ἵστημι ἐν μέσῳ (τινῶν)], IAn [ἵστημι ἐπί + genitive]; EASTON 1910 162 [ἵστημι in the aorist passive: cited by Weiss as characteristic of L, and possibly corroborative]; 176 [ἑστώς/σταθείς: possible Hebraisms in the Lucan Writings, as classed by Dalman]; GERSDORF 1816 180 [ἑστὼς ἐκ δεξιῶν]; JEREMIAS 1980 273: "σταθείς/σταθέντες (begleiten der Umstand) im NT ausschließlich im lk Doppelwerk … Wir haben es mit einem markanten Lukanismus zu tun"; 302: "Finite Formen von ἕστηκα/εἱστήκειν + Part.coniunct. finden sich im Doppelwerk häufiger als im übrigen NT"; RADL 1975 413 [ἵστημι; ἵστημι transitive; σταθείς; ἑστώς].

BERGSON, L., στας, ἑστώς, κτλ. Entbehrliches und ergänzendes Partizip. — Eranos (Oslo) 93 (1995) 65-68. [NTA 42, 95]

ἰσχυρός 4 (Mt 4, Mk 3)

1. powerful (Lk 3,16); 2. strong (Lk 11,21.22); 3. intense (Lk 15,14); 4. great

Word groups	Lk	Acts	Mt	Mk
λιμὸς ἰσχυρά → λιμὸς μέγας/μεγάλη	15,14		0	0
ἰσχυρότερος comparative (SCa; VKa)	3,16; 11,22		1	1

Literature

LÉGASSE, Simon, L'"homme fort" de Luc xi 21-22. — NT 5 (1962) 5-9.

ἰσχύς 1 (Mk 2)

1. capability; 2. strenght (Lk 10,27)

Word groups	Lk	Acts	Mt	Mk
ἐξ ὅλης τῆς ἰσχύος (VKa)	10,27 v.l.		1	1

ἰσχύω 8 + 6 (Mt 4, Mk 4)

1. be capable of (Lk 13,24); 2. be strong (Lk 16,3); 3. be healthy

Word groups	Lk	Acts	Mt	Mk
ἰσχύω κατά + genitive (VKc)		19,16	0	0
ἰσχύω + κράτος; cf. ἰσχύς κράτος Eph 1,19; 6,10		19,20	0	0

Characteristic of Luke				
Goulder 1989; Vogel 1899d				
	Lk	Acts	Mt	Mk
ἰσχύω + infinitive; cf. Jn 21,6	6,48; 8,43; 14,6.29.30; 16,3;	6,10; 15,10;	2	2
Boismard 1984 Cb 2; Neirynck 1985	20,26	25,7; 27,16		
οὐκ/μὴ ἰσχύω	6,48; 8,43; 13,24;	6,10; 25,7	2	2
Denaux 2009 L***	14,6.29.30; 16,3; 20,26			

Literature

von Bendemann 2001 427: "charakteristisch lukanisch ist die Negation mit folgendem Infinitiv"; Collison 1977 53 [with negative particle: linguistic usage of Luke: certain]; Denaux 2009 Lan [ἰσχύω + infinitive]; Easton 1910 162 [cited by Weiss as characteristic of L, and possibly corroborative]; Hauck 1934 [Vorzugswort]; Jeremias 1980 150 [red.]; Radl 1975 413-414 [ἰσχύω; οὐκ/μὴ ἰσχύω].

ἴσως 1	probably (Lk 20,13)

Literature

Hauck 1934 [seltenes Alleinwort].

Ἰτουραῖος 1	Ituraean (Lk 3,1)

ἰχθύς 7 (Mt 5, Mk 4)	fish

Word groups	Lk	Acts	Mt	Mk
δύο ἰχθύες (VKa)	9,13.16		2	3
ἰχθύς + ἄρτος; cf. ἰχθύδιον + ἄρτος Mt 15,34; Mk 8,(6-)7	9,13.16		4	3

Ἰωανάν 1	Joanan (Lk 3,27)

Ἰωάννα 2	Joanna (Lk 8,3; 24,10)

Ἰωάννης 31 + 24 (Mt 26, Mk 26)	John

Word groups	Lk	Acts	Mt	Mk
Ἡρῴδης (+) Ἰωάννης	9,7.9		1	5
Ἰάκωβος + Ἰωάννης + Πέτρος	6,14; 8,51; 9,28	1,13	1	3
Ἰωάννης (+) βαπτίζω/βάπτισμα	3,16; 7,29; 20,4	1,5.22; 10,37; 11,16; 13,24; 18,25; 19,3.4	3	5
Ἰωάννης ὁ βαπτιστής (VKb) → John the Baptist; cf. Ἰωάννης ὁ βαπτίζων (VKc) Mk 1,4; 6,14.24	7,20.28 v.l..33; 9,19		7	2/3
Ἰωάννης ὁ ἐπικαλούμενος Μᾶρκος (SCe; VKk); see also Acts 13,5.13		12,12.25 v.l.; 15,37	0	0
οἱ μαθηταὶ Ἰωάννου (SCb; VKd)	5,33		1	2

Πέτρος + Ἰωάννης (VKf)	6,14; 8,51; 9,28; 22,8	1,13; 3,1.3.4.11; 4,13.19; 8,14	1	4
John the Baptist (SCa; VKa) → Ἰωάννης ὁ βαπτιστής	1,13.60.63; 3,2.15.16.20; 7,18¹·².22.24¹·².28.29; 9,7.9; 11,1; 16,16; 20,4.6	1,5.22; 10,37; 11,16; 13,24.25; 18,25; 19,3.4	15	9
Ἰωάννης father of Simon Peter (VKh); cf. Ἰωνᾶς Jn 1,42*; 21,15*.16*.17*		13,5.13	0	0
Ἰωάννης Jewish priest (SCd; VKj)		4,6	0	0
Ἰωάννης son of Zebedee (SCc; VKe)	5,10; 6,14; 8,51; 9,28.49.54; 22,8	12,2	3	0

Characteristic of Luke

GASTON 1973 66 [Lked?]

Literature

BDAG 2000 485-486 [literature].

LAURENTIN, René, Traces d'allusions étymologiques en Luc 1–2 (I). — *Bib* 37 (1956) 435-456. Esp. 441-444: "Jean".

Ἰωβήδ 1 (Mt 2) | Obed (Lk 3,32)

Ἰωδά 1 | Joda (Lk 3,26)

Ἰωνάμ 1 | Jonam (Lk 3,30)

Ἰωνᾶς 4 (Mt 5) | Jonah

Word groups	Lk	Acts	Mt	Mk
κήρυγμα Ἰωνᾶ	11,32¹		1	0
σημεῖον Ἰωνᾶ; cf. σημεῖον + Ἰωνᾶς Lk 11,30	11,29		2	0
Ἰωνᾶς the prophet (VKa)	11,29.30.32¹·²		5	0

Literature

BDAG 2000 486 [literature].

SCHMITT, Götz, Das Zeichen des Jona. — *ZNW* 69 (1978) 123-129.

Ἰωρίμ 1 | Jorim (Lk 3,29)

Ἰωσήφ 8/11 + 7 (Mt 11/12, Mk 2) | Joseph

Word groups	Lk	Acts	Mt	Mk
Ἰησοῦς + (ὁ) υἱὸς + (τοῦ) Ἰωσήφ	3,23		0	0
Ἰωσήφ + ἀπὸ Ἁριμαθαίας (SCf; VKf)	23,50(-51)		2	2

		1,23	0	0
Ἰωσὴφ καλούμενος Βαρσαββᾶς (SCh; VKh)		1,23	0	0
Ἰωσὴφ + ὁ ἐπικληθεὶς Βαρναβᾶς (SCg; VKg)		4,36	0	0
Ἰωσὴφ + Ἰακώβ		7,14	0	0
Ἰωσὴφ husband of Mary (SCd; VKd)	1,27; 2,4.16. 33*.43*; 3,23; 4,22		7/8	0
Ἰωσὴφ son of Jacob (SCa; VKa)		7,9.13[1.2].14.18	0	0
Ἰωσὴφ son of Joda (VKk)	3,26*		0	0
Ἰωσὴφ son of Jonam (SCb; VKb)	3,30		0	0
Ἰωσὴφ son of Mattathias (SCc; VKc)	3,24		0	0

Literature
GERSDORF 1816 217 [ἀνέβη δὲ καὶ Ἰωσὴφ - εἰς πόλιν Δαυίδ - ἀπογράψασθαι].

Ἰωσήχ 1

Josech (Lk 3,26)

K

κἀγώ 6/8 + 4/6 (Mt 9, Mk 0/1)   and I, but I → καὶ ἐγώ

Word groups	Lk	Acts	Mt	Mk
κἀμοί (VKg) DENAUX 2009 1A[n]	1,3	8,19; 10,28	0	0

Literature
SCHÜRMANN 1957 41-42 [relative Häufigkeit der Krasis bei Luk].

καθαιρέω 3 + 3 (Mk 2)

1. lower (Lk 1,52); 2. take down (Lk 23,53); 3. tear down (Lk 12,18); 4. destroy (Acts 13,19); 5. do away with (Acts 19,27)

Word groups	Lk	Acts	Mt	Mk
καθαιρέω (+) ἀπό (VKa) → ἀφαιρέω ἀπό DENAUX 2009 LA[n]	1,52	13,29	0	0

Characteristic of Luke
BOISMARD 1984 cb110; HARNACK 1906 142; NEIRYNCK 1985; PLUMMER 1922 lx

Literature
DENAUX 2009 LAn.

καθαρίζω 7 + 3 (Mt 7, Mk 4)

1. make clean (Lk 11,39); 2. purify (Acts 10,15); 3. heal (Lk 4,27)

Word groups	Lk	Acts	Mt	Mk
καθαρίζω + λεπρός/λεπροί/λέπρα (SCa)	4,27; 5,12.13; 7,22; 17,(12-)14.(12-)17		4	2
καθαρίσθητι (VKb)	5,13		1	1

Literature

WELLS, Luise, *The Greek Language of Healing*, 1998. Esp. 191-195.

καθαρισμός 2 (Mk 1)   purification (Lk 2,22; 5,14)

καθαρός 1 + 2 (Mt 3)

1. clean; 2. pure (Lk 11,41; Acts 20,26)

Word groups	Lk	Acts	Mt	Mk
καθαρός + ἀπό (VKc)		20,26	0	0

Literature

DUPONT, Jacques, *Le discours de Milet*, 1962. Esp. 125-134.

καθέζομαι 1 + 2 (Mt 1)   sit (down) (Lk 2,46; Acts 6,15; 20,9)

καθεξῆς 2 + 3   one after another

Wordgroups

	Lk	Acts	Mt	Mk
ἐν τῷ καθεξῆς → ἐν τῷ ἑξῆς	8,1		0	0

Characteristic of Luke

BOISMARD 1984 Ab54; CREDNER 1836 137; HAWKINS 1909LA.add; MORGENTHALER 1958*; NEIRYNCK 1985; PLUMMER 1922 lii; VOGEL 1899A

Literature

VON BENDEMANN 2001 413: "καθεξῆς (im Neuen Testament nur: Lk 1,3; 8,1; Apg 3,24; 11,4; 18,23)"; DENAUX 2009 IAⁿ; GERSDORF 1816 162; HAUCK 1934 [häufiges Alleinwort]; JEREMIAS 1980 156 [red.]; RADL 1975 403 [ἐγένετο + (καθ)ἑξῆς].

ALEXANDER, Loveday, *The Preface to Luke's Gospel*, 1993. Esp. 131-132.
CADBURY, Henri J., Commentary on the Preface of Luke, 1922. Esp. 504-505.
KÜRZINGER, Joseph, Lk 1,3: ... ἀκριβῶς καθεξῆς σοι γράψαι. — *BZ* NF 18 (1974) 249-255. [NTA 19, 575]
LOOKWOOD, G.J., The Reference to Order in Luke's Preface. — *Concord Theological Quaterly* 59 (1995) 101-104,
MOESSNER, David P., The Meaning of καθεξῆς in the Lukan Prologue as a Key to the Distinctive Contribution of Luke's Narrative Among the "Many". — Frans VAN SEGBROECK, et al. (eds.), *The Four Gospels 1992*. FS F. Neirynck, 1992, II, 1513-1528.
MUSSNER, Franz, Καθεξῆς im Lukasprolog. — ELLIS, E.E. – GRÄBER, E. (eds.), *Jesus und Paulus*. FS W.G. Kümmel, 1975, 253-255. [Lk 1,3]

PRETE, Benedetto, Struttura del Vangelo di Luca. — ID., *L'opera di Luca*, 1986, 34-79. Esp. 67-71: "L'avverbio καθεξῆς".

SCHNEIDER, Gerhard, Zur Bedeutung von καθεξῆς im lukanischen Doppelwerk. — *ZNW* 68 (1977) 128-131. [NTA 22, 116]; = ID., *Lukas, Theologe der Heilsgeschichte*, 1985, 31-34.

VÖLKEL, Martin, Exegetische Erwägungen zum Verständnis des Begriffs καθεξῆς im lukanischen Prolog. — *NTS* 20 (1973-74) 289-299. [NTA 19, 127]

καθεύδω 2 (Mt 7, Mk 8)
1. sleep (Lk 8,52; 22,46); 2. be dead

Word groups	Lk	Acts	Mt	Mk
καθεύδω ἀνίστημι (*VK*d); cf. Eph 5,14; καθεύδω + ἐγείρω Mt 8,24(-25); 9,(24-)25; 25,5(-7); 26,45(-46); Mk 4,27.38; 14,41(-42)	22,46		0	0
καθεύδω + ἀποθνῄσκω (*VK*c)	8,52		1	1

κάθημαι 13 + 6/7 (Mt 19, Mk 11)
1. sit (down) (Acts 3,10); 2. reside (Lk 21,35; Acts 14,8)

Word groups	Lk	Acts	Mt	Mk
κάθημαι ἐκ δεξιῶν (*SC*b; *VK*c); cf. καθίζω ἐκ δεξιῶν Mt 20,21.23; Mk 10,37.40; [16,19]	20,42; 22,69	2,34	2	2
κάθημαι + ἐν (*SC*d; *VK*e)	1,79; 7,32; 10,13		4	1
κάθημαι ἐπί + accusative (*SC*g; *VK*k)	5,27; 21,35		2	1
κάθημαι ἐπί + dative (*SC*g; *VK*j)		3,10	0	0
κάθημαι ἐπί + genitive (*SC*f; *VK*h)	22,30	8,28; 20,9*	2	0
κάθημαι + μέσος / ἐν μέσῳ (*SC*h; *VK*l); cf. κάθημαι μετά + gen. Mt 26,58	22,55		0	0
κάθημαι (+) παρά + accusative (*SC*j; *VK*m)	8,35; 18,35		2	1
κάθημαι (+) πρός + accusative (*VK*p) DENAUX 2009 LA[n]	22,56	3,10	0	0
ὁ υἱὸς τοῦ ἀνθρώπου καθήμενος ἐκ δεξιῶν (τοῦ θεοῦ) → ὁ υἱὸς τοῦ ἀνθρώπου **ἑστὼς** ἐκ δεξιῶν τοῦ θεοῦ	22,69		1	1

Literature
COLLISON 1977 54 [linguistic usage of Luke: likely]; EASTON 1910 175-176 [καθίσας, καθήμενος: possible Hebraisms in the Lucan Writings, as classed by Dalman].

καθίζω 7/8 + 9 (Mt 8/9, Mk 7[8])
1. sit (down) (Lk 4,20); 2. cause to sit (down); 3. remain (Lk 24,49; Acts 18,11); 4. appoint

Word groups	Lk	Acts	Mt	Mk
καθίζω ἐν (*SC*b; *VK*e)	5,3 *v.l.*; 24,49		1	1
καθίζω (+) ἐπί + accusative (*SC*d; *VK*h)	19,30	2,3.30	0/1	2
καθίζω ἐπί + genitive (*SC*c; *VK*f)	20,30*	2,30 *v.l.*; 12,21; 25,6.17	3	0
καθίζω σύν (*VK*k)		8,31	0	0
καθίζω transitive (*VK*a)		2,30	0	0

Characteristic of Luke				
CREDNER 1836 139				
	Lk	Acts	Mt	Mk
καϑίζω = remain VOGEL 1899A	24,49	18,11	0	0
καϑίσας → συγκαϑίσας; cf. Jn 8,2; Eph 1,20 CREDNER 1836 139; GOULDER 1989; PLUMMER 1922 lxii	5,3; 14,28.31; 16,6	12,21; 16,13; 25,6.17	2	2

Literature
COLLISON 1977 54 [linguistic usage of Luke's "other source-material": probable]; DENAUX 2009 LAn [καϑίσας, καϑίζω = remain]; EASTON 1910 175-176 [καϑίσας, καϑήμενος: possible Hebraisms in the Lucan Writings, as classed by Dalman]; HARNACK 1906 149 [καϑεζόμενος/ν ptc. Lk 1,46; Acts 20,9]; JEREMIAS 1980 242: "Das abundante Partizipium καϑίσας ist ein Semitismus, der sich im NT (außer Mt 13,48) nur bei Lukas findet"; 322: "καϑίσατε in der Bedeutung 'sich aufhalten' kommt im NT nur Lk 24,49 / Apg 18,11 vor".

καϑίημι 1 + 3 — let down (Lk 5,19; Acts 9,25; 10,11; 11,5)

Characteristic of Luke
BOISMARD 1984 Ab84; HAWKINS 1909LA; MORGENTHALER 1958*; NEIRYNCK 1985; PLUMMER 1922 lii

Literature
DENAUX 2009 lA[n]; HAUCK 1934 [seltenes Alleinwort].

καϑίστημι 3 + 5 (Mt 4)
1. appoint (Lk 12,14.42.44); 2. cause to be

Word groups	Lk	Acts	Mt	Mk
καϑίστημι (+) ἐπί + accusative (SCc; VKd) DENAUX 2009 lA[n]	12,14	7,10.27	0	0
καϑίστημι + ἐπί + dative (SCb; VKc)	12,44		1	0
καϑίστημι + ἐπί (+) genitive (SCa; VKb)	12,42	6,3; 7,27	3	0
καϑιστάνω (SCd; VKa)		17,15	0	0

Literature
TALBERT, Charles H., *Reading Luke-Acts in Its Mediterranean Milieu* (SupplNT, 107). Leiden-Boston: Brill, 2003, XII-255 p. Esp. 21-27: "The semantic field of succession thinking"; 43-50: "The concept of succession and Luke-Acts".

καϑοπλίζω 1 — arm fully (Lk 11,21)

Literature
HAUCK 1934 [seltenes Alleinwort].

καϑότι 2 + 4
1. because (Lk 1,7; 19,9; Acts 2,24); 2. to the degree that (Acts 2,45)

Word groups	Lk	Acts	Mt	Mk
καθότι ἄν (VKa)		2,45; 4,35	0	0
καθότι ἄν + τις → ἐάν + τις		2,45; 4,35	0	0
καθότι καί → διό(τι)/ὅτι καί	19,9		0	0

Characteristic of Luke
BOISMARD 1984 Ab36; CREDNER 1836 137; DENAUX 2009 IA*; HARNACK 1906 70; HAWKINS 1909LA; MORGENTHALER 1958*; NEIRYNCK 1985; PLUMMER 1922 lii; VOGEL 1899A

Literature
BDR § 456,4: "καθότι (nur Lk und Apg)"; GERSDORF 1816 172 [καθότι ἦν ἡ Ἐλισάβετ στεῖρα]; HAUCK 1934 [seltenes Alleinwort]; JEREMIAS 1980 24 [red.].

καθώς 17 + 11/12 (Mt 3, Mk 8)
1. to the degree that (Acts 11,29); 2. inasmuch as; 3. just as (Lk 11,30); 4. when (Acts 7,17); 5. how (Acts 15,14)

Word groups	Lk	Acts	Mt	Mk
καθώς + verb of saying (SCd) DENAUX 2009 Lan	1,2.55.70; 2,20; 5,14; 11,1; 19,32; 22,13; 24,24	2,4; 7,44.48; 15,14	2	3
καθὼς γάρ (VKj) → ὡς/ὥσπερ γάρ	11,30		0	0
καθὼς γέγραπται (SCa; VKb) → ὡς γέγραπται	2,23	7,42; 15,15	1	3
καθὼς δέ time (VKa) → ὡς δέ		7,17	0	0
καθὼς ἐγένετο DENAUX 2009 L[n]	11,30; 17,26.28		0	0
καθὼς καί (SCb; VKg) → ὁμοίως/οὕτως/ ὡς/ὥσπερ καί DENAUX 2009 La[n]	6,31v.l.36; 11,1; 24,24	2,22 v.l.; 10,47*; 15,8	0	0
καὶ καθώς (VKf) → καὶ οὕτως/ὡς DENAUX 2009 L[n]	6,31; 17,26		0	0
οὕτως καθώς (VKh) → καθώς ὁμοίως	24,24		0	0
ποιέω καθώς → ποιέω ὡς		2,22	1	0

Characteristic of Luke
GOULDER 1989; HAWKINS 1909add; MORGENTHALER 1958LA

	Lk	Acts	Mt	Mk
καθώς + ὁμοίως/οὕτως (SCc; VKd) → ὡς + οὕτως DENAUX 2009 L***	6,31; 11,30; 17,26.28; 24,24		0	0

Literature
CADBURY 1919/20 142; COLLISON 1977 155-156 [linguistic usage of Luke: certain]; CREDNER 1836 137; DENAUX 2009 Lan; GERSDORF 1816 242 [καθὼς ἐλαλήθη πρὸς αὐτούς]; 245 [καθὼς γέγραπται]; HAUCK 1934 [Vorzugswort]; SCHÜRMANN 1957 44 [καθώς kann nicht als Vorzugswort des Luk gelten (vgl. A12)].

CADBURY, Henri J., Commentary on the Preface of Luke, 1922. Esp. 496-497.
ELLIOTT, James K., Καθώς and ὥσπερ in the New Testament. — FilolNT 4 (1991) 55-58. Esp. 55: "In Luke the καθώς clause usually follows the main clause: 1:2,55,70, 2:20,23, 5:14, 6:36, 11:1, 19:32, 22:13,29, 24:24,39. There are four exceptions (6:31, 11:30, 17:26,28) where καθώς clause precedes. In each of these, the main clause is introduced by an expression which

refers back to the καθώς"; 56: "In Acts 2:4,22, 7:42,44,48, 15:8,14,15, 22:3 the καθώς-clause follows the main clause. At 7:17, 11:29 it precedes but with no resumptive word following"; 58: "It [ὥσπερ] appears at Luke 17:24 also, but at Luke 18:11 we should read ὡς. At Acts 2:2, 3:17, 11:15 ὥσπερ follows. At 2:2 a noun has to be supplied from the main clause and ὥσπερ is equivalent to 'like,' but at 3:17, 11:15 a verb is wanted. ... Καθώς predominates in Luke (seventeen against one)".

ZEMEK, G.J., Awesome Analogies: *Kathôs* Constructs in the NT. — *JEvTS* 38 (1995) 337-348.

καί 1469/1564 +1110/1154 (Mt 1178/1240, Mk 1078[1091]/1156)

1. and (Lk 3,10); 2. and then (Acts 5,21); 3. also (Lk 2,36); 4. yet (Lk 4,26); 5. then (Lk 4,5)

Word groups	Lk	Acts	Mt	Mk
ἄμα/γε καί (*VK*p) → γε	24,21	24,26[1]	1	0
ἂν/ἐὰν/εἰ/ὅταν (δὲ) καί (*VK*z)	11,8.11* *v.l.*18; 12,39*; 14,34; 18,4[2]; 22,68*	23,35	2/3	1
ἄρα καί (*VK*y)		11,18[2]	0	0
γὰρ/οὖν καί (*VK*r)	3,18	3,19; 17,23[1].28[4]	2	0
διότι / (καθ)ότι καί (*VK*v) → διὸ καί	4,43; 8,25[1]; 19,9	2,29[1].36[1]; 10,45[2]; 11,1[2]; 13,35; 17,13[1]	1	2/3
ἕως/ὥστε καί (*VK*x); cf. ἵνα καί Mk 1,38[2]; 11,25[2] DENAUX 2009 1A[n]	12,59	5,15[1]; 19,12[1]	0	0
ἢ καί (*VK*s)	11,11*.12; 12,41; 18,11		1	0
καθὼς καί → ὁμοίως/οὕτως/ ὡς καί; ὥσπερ καί DENAUX 2009 La[n]	[6,36]; 11,1[2]; 24,24[3]	2,22*; 10,47 *v.l.*; 15,8[2]	0	0
καί γε/καίγε/καίτοιγε (*VK*e)	19,42*	2,18[1]; 14,17*; 17,27[2]	0	0
καὶ ἐάν/εἰ/ὅταν/ὅτε (*VK*j)	2,21[1].22.42; 5,35; 6,13[1].22[1]. 32[1].33[1] *v.l.*34[1]; 10,6; 11,12 *v.l.*; 12,38[1]*.55[1]; 16,12; 17,3.4[1]; 19,8.31; 22,14[1]; 23,33	1,13[1]; 11,2*; 22,20[1]	16/18	23/24
καὶ ἐγώ/σύ (*VK*f) → κἀγώ	1,76; 2,35.48*; 4,34; 8,28[2]; 10,15.37; 15,29[2]; 16,9; 19,19[2].23*.42[1]; 22,32.58[2]; 24,49 *v.l.*	10,26.28*; 23,3[1]; 25,10; 26,29[4]	8/10	3
καὶ ἡμεῖς/ὑμεῖς (*VK*g)	3,14[2]; 6,31*; 11,45.46[1]; 12,29[1].36[1].40; 16,26[2]; 17,10; 21,31; 23,39.41	5,32[1]; 7,51[3]; 10,39[1]. 47; 11,17; 13,32; 14,15[2]; 15,8[2].28; 16,17	14	3
καὶ ἰδών/ἰδόντες → ἰδὼν/ἰδόντες δέ	2,48[1]; 5,20; 7,13[1]; 10,31.32[2].33[2]; 17,14[1]; 19,7	7,24[1]; 9,40[3]; 11,23[1]; 14,9; 16,27.40[1]	9	9
καὶ καθώς (*VK*k) → καὶ οὕτως/ὡς DENAUX 2009 L[n]	6,31; 17,26[1]		0	0
καὶ μή/μηδείς (*VK*b); cf. καὶ μηκέτι Mk 9,25[2]	1,20[2]; 2,45; 3,8; 5,19; 6,37[1.3]. 49[1]; 10,4.10; 11,4[3].24; 12,21. 29[3].47; 13,11[3].14; 14,29; 18,1.16; 24,23[1]	1,20[1]; 12,19[1]; 13,28; 15,38; 18,9; 19,36; 24,23; 27,15	12	9/10
καὶ νῦν ἰδού BOISMARD 1984 Aa94		13,11[1]; 20,22.25	0	0
καὶ πόθεν/πῶς (*VK*m) → καὶ ὅτι	1,43; 12,50; 20,44	2,8; 9,27[3]	0	3

καὶ οὐ/οὐκέτι/οὔτε (VKa)	1,7^1; 2,43^2; 4,2^1; 6,46.48^3; 7,32$^{2.3}$; 8,14^4.19^2; 9,40^2.53; 10,24$^{2.4}$; 11,6.8; 12,39*; 13,6^2. 7^1.24.34^2; 14,5^2.6.26^1.30; 15,19*.21*.28; 17,22; 18,4^1.34^3; 19,3^2.44^3.48; 20,21^3.26^1.31*; 24,18	4,12.16; 6,10^1; 7,5^1.11^3.53; 8,39; 9,9^2; 12,9^2.22; 13,46^2; 16,7; 24,12	32/33	21/24
καὶ οὐ μή/οὐδέ/οὐδείς/ οὐδέποτε (VKc)	4,27^2; 5,37^1.39; 6,37$^{2.4}$; 9,36^3; 10,19^3.22^1; 15,16^2.29^1	4,32^2; 15,9^1 v.l.; 18,10.17; 28,26$^{2.4}$	6/7	9/10
καὶ τὰ νῦν CREDNER 1836 134		4,29^1; 5,38^1; 20,32^1; 27,22^1	0	0
μὴ καί (VKt); cf. οὐχὶ καί Mt 5,46.47^2 DENAUX 2009 LA^n	16,28	25,27	0	0
ὁμοίως/οὕτως/ὡς καί (VKu) → καθὼς καί; cf. ὥσπερ καί; cf. ὡσαύτως καί Mt 25,17^1*; Mk 14,31 v.l.	5,33^2; 9,54*; 17,10.28*; 21,31; 22,36^1	11,17; 13,33; 17,28^3; 22,5^1; 25,10	10	3
ὡς + καί	2,15*; 7,12^1; 11,2*	1,10^2; 7,51^2; 10,17*	1/2	0
ὥσπερ καί (VKc) → καθὼς/ὁμοίως/ οὕτως/ὡς καί BOISMARD 1984 Aa167		3,17^2; 11,15	0	0

→ (καὶ) (ἰδού) **ἄνδρες** δύο; (καὶ) ἰδού + **ἄνθρωπος/γυνή**; **ἀπεκρίθη** καὶ εἶπεν; καὶ **ἀποκριθεὶς** λέγει/εἶπεν/ἔρεῖ; **ἀπόστολοι** καὶ πρεσβύτεροι; **ἀργύριον** καὶ χρυσίον; καὶ ἐν τῷ + inf. ... καὶ **αὐτός**; **ἡγεμὼν** καὶ **βασιλεύς**; καὶ **ἐγένετο** (ἐν τῷ + inf.) ... καὶ αὐτός/αὐτοί; **καί** + **γίνομαι**; **γραμματεῖς** καὶ Φαρισαῖοι ὑποκριταί; **δέκα** καὶ ὀκτώ; **διαπορεύομαι/διέρχομαι/διοδεύω** κατὰ + place + participle καί participle; **εἰσέρχομαι** καὶ ἐξέρχομαι; **εἰσπορεύομαι** καὶ ἐκπορεύομαι; **ἐπιβάλλω** τὴν χεῖρα ἐπ' ἄροτρον καὶ βλέπω εἰς τὰ ὀπίσω; καὶ **εὐθέως**; καὶ **εὐθύς**; **ἡμέρας** καὶ νυκτός; **καθώς** + **καί**; **καλὸς** καὶ ἀγαθός; ἀπερίτμητος **καρδίαις** καὶ τοῖς ὠσίν; **λιμοὶ** καὶ λοιμοί; ὑπηρέτης καὶ **μάρτυς**; **οἶνος** καὶ σίκερα; ὁ **οὐρανὸς** καὶ ἡ γῆ; κυριὸς (τοῦ) **οὐρανοῦ** καὶ (τῆς) γῆς; καὶ **παραχρῆμα**; ἄνδρες ἀδελφοὶ καὶ **πατέρες**; κατὰ **πόλιν** καὶ κώμην / πόλεις καὶ κώμας; **προφῆται** καὶ ἀπόστολοι; **πρῶτον** τε καί; **σήμερον** καὶ αὔριον; ἀχλὺς καὶ **σκότος** πίπτει; στόμα καὶ **σοφία**; **τί** ἐμοὶ/ἡμῖν καὶ σοί; **Φαρισαῖοι** καὶ νομικοί/νομοδιδάσκαλοι; **ὡσαύτως** (δὲ) καί

Characteristic of Luke

HENDRIKS 1986 435

	Lk	Acts	Mt	Mk
ἀλλὰ καί (VKw); cf. ἀλλὰ γε καί Lk 24,21; ἀλλὰ κἄν Mt 21,21 DENAUX 2009 IA*; GOULDER 1989	12,7; 16,21^2; 24,22	19,27^1; 21,13^2; 26,29^1; 27,10^3	0	0
δὲ καί (VKq); cf. Jn 2,2; 3,23; 15,24; 18,2.5.18^2; 19,19^1.39; 21,25; δὲ κἀκεῖνος Lk 20,11 BOISMARD 1984 Eb61; CREDNER 1836 135; DENAUX 2009 L***; GOULDER 1989*; HAWKINS 1909L; NEIRYNCK 1985; PLUMMER 1922 lxiii; SCHÜRMANN 1957 65-66	2,4^1; 3,9^1.12^1; 4,41^1; 5,10^1.36^1; 6,6*.39; 9,61; 10,32^1; 11,18; 12,54^1.57; 14,12^1.26^7 v.l.34; 15,28. 32^1; 16,1^1.22^2; 18,1*.9^1; 19,19^1; 20,12^2.31^2; 21,2*.16^1; 22,24.68*; 23,32.35^2.38.55*; 24,37	2,7.26^2; 3,1; 5,16^1; 9,24^1; 11,7^1; 12,25; 13,5^2; 14,27^1; 15,32^1 v.l..35^1; 16,1^1; 17,18^1; 19,27^2 v.l.28.31; 20,11^1; 21,16; 22,28; 23,34^1; 24,9.26^1 v.l.	6/8	2/3
διὸ καί → διότι/(καθ)ότι καί BOISMARD 1984 Db19; NEIRYNCK 1985	1,35^3	10,29; 13,35 v.l.; 24,26^2	0	0
καί in apodosis → καὶ ἰδού in apodosis DENAUX 2009 L***; GOULDER 1989*; HAWKINS 1909L	2,21^2; 7,12^1; 11,34$^{1.2}$; 13,25^2(?); 24,4^2	1,10^2	1	0

καὶ αὐτός/αὐτή/αὐτοί/αὐταί nominative BOISMARD 1984 Eb58; CADBURY 1920 150; CREDNER 1836 135; DENAUX 2009 L***; GOULDER 1989*; HAWKINS 1909L; NEIRYNCK 1985; PLUMMER 1922 lix	$1,17^1.22^2.36^2$; $2,28^1.37^1$. 50; 3,23; 4,15; $5,1^2.14^1$. $17^2.37^2$; 6,20; $7,12^2$; $8,1^2$. $22^1.41^2$ $v.l.42$; $9,36^2.51$; 10,38*; $11,4^2.46^2$; $14,1^2$. 12^2; 15,14; $16,24^1.28$; $17,11^2.13.16^2$; $18,34^1$; $19,2^{2.3}.9$; 20,42*; 22,23. 41^1; 23,51*; $24,14.15^3$. $25^1.28^2.31^2.35^1.52$	2,22*; $8,13^1$; $15,32^2$; $21,24^3$; $22,20^2$; $24,15^1.16^1$; 25,22; 27,36	4/6	5[6]/7
καὶ αὐτός (VKh) (all cases) → καὶ οὗτος DENAUX 2009 L***	$1,17^1.22^2.36^2$; $2,28^1.37^1.38^1.50$; 3,23; $4,8^2.15$; $5,1^2.14^1.17^2.37^2$; 6,20; $7,12^2$; $8,1^2.22^1.41^2$ $v.l.42$; $9,36^2.51$; 10,38*; $11,[14^2].46^2$; $14,1^2.9^2.12^2$; 15,14; $16,24^1.28$; $17,11^2.13.16^2$; $18,34^1$; $19,2^{2.3}.9$; 20,42*; $22,23.41^1$; $23,7^2.51$*; $24,14.15^3.25^1.28^2.31^2.35^1.5$ 2	2,22*; $8,13^1$; $15,9^2$. $27^2.32^2$; $21,24^3$; $22,20^2$; $24,15^1.16^1$; 25,22.25*; 27,36	6/8	6/9
καὶ γάρ (VKd) CADBURY 1920 145; CREDNER 1836 137; GOULDER 1989; HAWKINS 1909add	$1,66^2$; $6,32^2.33^{1.2}$ $v.l.34^2$ $v.l.$; $7,8^1$; $11,4^2$; $22,37^2.59^3$	$19,40^1$	3	2/3
καὶ ἰδού (VKn) PLUMMER 1922 lxi	$1,20^1.31^1.36^1$; $2,9^1$ $v.l.25^1$; $5,12^2.18^1$; $7,12^1.37^1$; $8,41^1$; $9,30^1.38.39^1$; 10,25; $11,31^2.$ $32^2.41$; $13,11^1.30^1$; 14,2; $19,2^1$; $23,14.15.50^1$; $24,4^2.13.49$	$1,10^2$; $5,28^1$; $8,27^2$; $10,17$*$.30^2$; 11,11; $12,7^1$; $16,1^3$; 27,24	28	0/1
καὶ ἰδού in apodosis; see also ἐγένετο … καί → καί in apodosis BOISMARD 1984 Bb109; DENAUX 2009 La*; NEIRYNCK 1985	$5,12^2$; $7,12^1$; $24,4^2$	$1,10^2$	1	0
καὶ ὅτι (VKm) → καὶ πόθεν/πῶς DENAUX 2009 lA*	4,11; $7,16^2$	$9,27^2$; $14,22.27^2$; $17,3^3$; $22,29^2$	0	1
καὶ οὗτος/αὕτη nominative; cf. Jn 17,25 BOISMARD 1984 Eb44; DENAUX 2009 L***; GOULDER 1989; HAWKINS 1909L; NEIRYNCK 1985; PLUMMER 1922 lii	$1,36^3$; $2,12^1.38^1$ $v.l.$; $7,12^2$ $v.l.$; $8,13^1.41^2.42$ $v.l.$; $16,1^2$; $20,28^1.30$*; $22,56^2.59^2$	17,7	0	1
καὶ οὗτος (VKh) → καὶ αὐτός; cf. καὶ ἐκεῖνος Mt 20,4¹; Mk 4,20¹ DENAUX 2009 L***	$1,36^3$; $2,12^1.38^1$ $v.l.$; $3,20^1$; 5,6; $7,12^2$ $v.l.$; $8,13^1.41^2.42$ $v.l.$; 12,31; $13,17^1$; $16,1^2$; $19,19^1$; $20,12^2.28^1.30$*; $22,56^2.59^2$; 23,46*; $24,40^1$	$1,9^1$; 7,60; 14,18; 15,15; 17,7; $19,40^2$; 20,36; 26,30*; 28,29*	1/2	2[3]
καὶ οὕτως (VKk) → καὶ καθώς/ὡς BOISMARD 1984 Da12	24,46*	$7,8^2$; 17,32 $v.l.$; $27,44^2$; 28,14	0	0
καὶ ὡς (VKk) → καὶ καθώς/οὕτως; cf. Heb 7,9 BOISMARD 1984 Bb17; DENAUX 2009 L***; NEIRYNCK 1985; PLUMMER 1922 lii	2,39; $8,47^2$; $15,25^1$; 17,28*; 18,11; 19,5.41; $22,66^1$; 23,26.55; 24,32*$.35^2$	$1,10^1$; 8,32; 13,18	0	1

μήποτε καί → μὴ καί BOISMARD 1984 Ab186; NEIRYNCK 1985	14,12²	5,39	0	0
ὅς καί BOISMARD 1984 Eb38; DENAUX 2009 lA**; HARNACK 1906 43; NEIRYNCK 1985	6,13³.14¹.16*; 7,49²; 10,30².39²; 12,59 v.l.; 23,27*.51²*	1,3¹.11.19 v.l.; 7,45; 10,39³; 11,30¹; 12,4; 13,22²; 17,34¹; 22,5³; 24,6¹·².15¹; 26,10¹.12*.26; 27,23; 28,10¹	1	4/5
ὅ τε + noun + καὶ ὁ + noun; cf. Heb 2,11 BOISMARD 1984 Bb21; DENAUX 2009 lA*; NEIRYNCK 1985	15,2²; 23,12	5,24; 8,38³; 17,10.14; 18,5; 26,23.30¹	0	0
τε καί DENAUX 2009 L***	12,45³; 14,26⁷; 21,11³; 22,66²	1,1; 2,9⁴.10¹.11¹; 4,27¹; 5,14; 8,12²; 9,2.6¹*.15.18².24². 29; 14,1².5¹; 15,9².32¹; 19,10.17¹.27²; 20,21¹; 21,12.28³; 22,4²; 24,3.15².26¹; 26,3.20¹.22¹	1	0
τε ... καὶ ... καί; cf. Phil 1,7; Heb 9,2 BOISMARD 1984 Bb81; DENAUX 2009 lA*; NEIRYNCK 1985	2,16³·⁴; 21,11¹·²	1,8²·³.13²·³·⁴; 6,12¹·²·³; 9,18²-19; 13,1²·³; 21,25¹·²·³.30¹·²·³; 22,23¹·²	0	0

→ ἄνδρες (τε) καὶ γυναῖκες; (καὶ) ἰδού + (ὁ) ἀνήρ; καὶ ἰδοὺ ἀνήρ + ὄνομα; καὶ ἰδοὺ ἄνθρωπος + ὄνομα; καὶ ἐγένετο; (καὶ) ἐγένετο (δὲ) + expression of time; (καὶ) ἐγένετο (δὲ) ἐν τῷ + inf.; ἐγένετο ..., καί; (καὶ) ἰδού ... καί + verb; Ἰουδαῖοί τε καὶ Ἑλλήναι; Μωϋσῆς καὶ προφῆται; νύκτα καὶ ἡμέραν; καὶ οἶκος; καὶ μετὰ ταῦτα; (καὶ) παραγενόμενος (δέ); ποιέω σημεῖα καὶ τέρατα ἐν; imperative of movement + καί + πορεύου; τε (...) καί

Literature

COLLISON 1977 48 [καὶ εἶπεν beginning sentences: linguistic usage of Luke's "other source material": certain]; 100 [ἀλλὰ καί: noteworthy phenomena]; 103 [δὲ καί: linguistic usage of Luke: certain]; 107-108 [καὶ ἰδού: linguistic usage of "other source-material": certain]; 110 [καὶ ὅτε (ἐγένετο): linguistic usage of Luke: likely]; 112 [τε ... καί: linguistic usage of Luke: certain]; 116 [καί and δέ; καὶ γάρ: noteworthy phenomena]; 117-118 [καί + nominative personal pronoun]; 117 [καί + nominative demonstrative pronoun: linguistic usage of Luke: certain; καὶ ὡς temporal: likely; καὶ ὡς attendant circumstances: likely]; DENAUX 2009 lAⁿ [διὸ καί], LAⁿ [μήποτε καί]; EASTON 1910 148 [καὶ αὐτός: especially characteristic of L]; 159 [Φαρισαῖοι καὶ γραμματεῖς: cited by Weiss as characteristic of L, and possibly corroborative]; 177 [καὶ ἐγένετο: possible Hebraisms in the Lucan Writings, as classed by Dalman]; GERSDORF 1816 187 [καὶ ἰδού]; 239 [καὶ ἀνεῦραν τήν τε Μαριάμ]; 242-244 [καὶ ὅτε]; 245 [καὶ ἰδοὺ ἄνθρωπος ἦν]; GOULDER 1989 805 [καί = also: Lk 124; Acts 91; Mt 60; Mk 36]; HAUCK 1934 [Vorzugswort; Vorzugsverbindung: ἔλεγεν (δὲ) καί (παραβολήν) (πρός); καὶ αὐτός/αὐτή/αὐτοί; δὲ καί; καὶ γάρ; καὶ ἐγένετο; καὶ οὗτος/τοῦτο]; JEREMIAS 1980 20 [καί relativum: trad.]; 25-26 [καὶ ἐγένετο: red.]; 41-42 [καὶ ἰδού]: "hebraisierende Partikelverbindung"; "Für die Beantwortung der Frage, ob die 26 Belege für καὶ ἰδού im LkEv traditionell oder redaktionell sind oder ob sie sich auf beide Größen verteilen, haben wir eine ganze Reihe von Anhaltspunkten. 1. Beginnen wir mit der Redaktion, so ist festzustellen a) καὶ ἰδοὺ ἀνήρ ... ist ein markanter Lukanismus ... b) καὶ ἰδού, nach periphrastischen καὶ ἐγένετο den Anschlußsatz einleitend ..., ist ebenfalls lukanisch... c) Weiter ist zu nennen: καὶ ἰδού zur Einleitung des Nachsatzes nach Kunjunktionalsatz mit ὡς temp. (Biblizismus) ... d) Ellipse des Verbum finitum nach (καὶ) ἰδού + Nominativ bei gleichem Subjekt im Vorder- und im Anschlußsatz schreibt Lukas als einziger neutestamentlicher Autor ... e) καὶ ἰδού in Verbindung mit Futurum instans ('ab sofort') findet man im Doppelwerk auch sonst: Lk 1,20 .... / Apg 13,11 ... 2. Viel geringer ist dagegen der Raum, den das καὶ ἰδού in der vorlukanischen *Tradition* einnimmt. Es handelt sich um a) καὶ ἰδού als Perikopenanfang ..., b) καὶ ἰδοὺ ἄνθρωπος..., nicht lukanisch ... und c) die Ellipse von ἐστίν nach καὶ ἰδού Lk 11,31f., die aus dem Logiengut stammt, wie die Parallele Mt 12,41f. zeigt"; 78-79 [δὲ καί: red.]; 174: " ὅς καί nach Relativ-Pronomen ... im lk Doppelwerk ... 20mal. Von den vier auf das LkEv entfallenden Belegen (6,13.14; 7,49; 10,30) sind die beiden ersten (Lk 6,13.14) lukanische Markusbearbeitung; zusammen mit den sechzehn Apg-Belegen zeigen sie, daß Lukas die Wendung bevorzugt"; PAFFENROTH 1997 86-87; RADL 1975 398 [ἀλλὰ καί]; 401 [καὶ αὐτός]; 402 [καὶ ἐγένετο]; 403 [ἐγένετο καί + finite verb; ἐγένετο + καὶ αὐτός + finite verb]; 404 [δὲ καί]; 411 [ἔτι; ἔτι τε καί]; 413 [καὶ ἰδού; καὶ νῦν ἰδού]; 414 [καί after relative pronoun]; 418 [καὶ νῦν]; 421 [οὐ μόνον ... ἀλλὰ καί]; 428 [τε ... καί]; 430 [ὡς καί]; REHKOPF 1959 93 [εἰ καί]; 94 [καὶ αὐτός (αὐτοί) unbetont; καὶ γάρ]; 95 [καὶ ὡς (temporal): vorlukanisch]; SCHNEIDER 1969 91-92.163 [καὶ στραφείς von Jesus: Vorzugswörter und -ausdrücke des Luk]; 106.164: "καὶ ὡς (temporal) scheint luk Eigentümlichkeit zu sein" [Vorzugswörter und -ausdrücke des Luk]; SCHÜRMANN 1955 34-36 [καί... ὡσαύτως: die luk vermutlich Ergebnis einer vorluk R]; 44 [Luk vermeidet das anreihende καί]; 1957 32-33 [luk eine ausgesprochene Vorliebe für τὲ ... καί, begegnet καί...καί]; 33 [Luk liebt Doppelgliederungen mit καί oder η]; 128 [καὶ γάρ: luk R nicht nachweisbar]; 1961 271 [καὶ ὡς]; 276 [καὶ γάρ]; 280 [εἰ καί: protoluk R weniger wahrscheinlich]; 281 [καὶ αὐτός (αὐτοί) unbetont: protoluk R weniger wahrscheinlich].

BEYER, Klaus, *Semitische Syntax im Neuen Testament*. I/1, 1962. Esp. 29-62: "Satzeinleitendes καὶ ἐγένετο mit Zeitbestimmung"; 63-65: "Satzeinleitendes καὶ ἔσται mit Zeitbestimmung"; 66-72: "Καί zur Einleitung des Nachsatzes".

DELEBECQUE, Édouard, *Études grecques*, 1976. Esp. 123-165: "La vivante formule καὶ ἐγένετο".

DENAUX, Adelbert, The Delineation of the Lukan Travel Narrative within the Overall Structure of the Gospel of Luke. — FOCANT, Camille (ed.), *The Synoptic Gospels: Source Criticism and the New Literary Criticism* (BETL, 110). Leuven: Leuven University Press – Peeters, 1993, 357-392. Esp. 377-382: "The structural function of the καὶ ἐγένετο-Formula".

FIEDLER, Peter, *Die Formel "Und siehe" im Neuen Testament* (SANT, 20). München: Kösel, 1969, 96 p. Esp. 13-48: "Das sprachliche Problem".

GUERRA GÓMEZ, M., Análisis filológico-teológico y traducción del himno de los ángeles en Belén, 1989. Esp. 47-49: "La partícula καί y sus significados".

HOOPERT, D.A., The Greek Conjunction καί Used with a Personal Pronoun. Exemplification or Appliucations intriduced by the Conjunction καί. — OPTAT (Dallas, TX) 3 (1989) 83-89.

JOHANNESSOHN, Martin, Das biblische καὶ ἐγένετο und seine Geschichte. — *Zeitschrift für vergleichende Sprachforschung* 53 (1926) 161-212.

KILPATRICK, George D., Three Problems of New Testament Text. — NT 21 (1979) 289-292. Esp. 290: "Luke v. 1 καὶ ἐγένετο"; = ID., *Principles and Practice*, 1990, 241-244. Esp. 242.

LARSEN, I., Notes on the Function of γάρ, οὖν, μέν, δέ, καί, and τέ in the Greek New Testament. — *Notes on Translation* (Dallas) 5 (1991) 35-47.

LEVISOHN, Stephen H., *Textual Connections in Acts*, 1987. Esp. 86-120: "de and kaí".

MARSHALL, Alfred, A Note on τε ... καί. — BTrans 5 (1954) 182-183.

MARTIN, Raymond A., Syntactical Evidence of Aramaic Sources in Acts I–XV, 1964. Esp. 40-41: "Proportions of δέ to καί".

MICHAELIS, Wilhelm, Das unbetonte καὶ αὐτός bei Lukas. — *StudTheol* 4 (1951) 86-93.

MOST, William G., Did St. Luke Imitate the Septuagint? — JSNT 15 (1982) 30-41. Esp. 33-38 [καί; καὶ ἐγένετο]. [NTA 27, 128]

NEIRYNCK, Frans, La matière marcienne dans l'évangile de Luc, 1973. Esp. 183-193 [καὶ ἐγένετο]; [2]1989. Esp. 93-103; = ID., *Evangelica*, 1982. Esp. 63-67.

READ-HEIMERDINGER, Jenny, *The Bezan Text of Acts*, 2002. Esp. 204-211: "δέ, καί and τε".

REILING, Jannes, The Use and Translation of *kai egeneto*, "and it happened", in the New Testament. — *BTrans* 16 (1965) 153-163.

RIUS-CAMPS, Josep, El καὶ αὐτός en los encabezamientos lucanos, ¿una fórmula anafórica? — *FilolNT* 2 (1989) 187-192.

ROBSON, Edward Alfred, *Kai-Configurations in the Greek New Testament*. Diss. Graduate School of Syracuse University, 1980, X-354, 97 and 458 p.

SCHNEIDER, Gerhard, Lk 1,34. 35 als redaktionelle Einheit. — *BZ* NF 15 (1971) 255-259. Esp. 256-257: "Lk 1,35 ist nach Wortschatz, Stil und Theologie 'lukanisch'" [διὸ καί].

—, Jesu geistgewirkte Empfängnis (Lk 1,34f): Zur Interpretation einer christologischen Aussage. — *TPQ* 119 (1971) 105-116. Esp. 110; = ID., *Lukas, Theologe der Heilsgeschichte*, 1985, 86-97. Esp. 91.

THRALL, Margaret E., *Greek Particles in the New Testament*, 1962. Esp. 11-16 [ἀλλὰ γε καί, ἀλλὰ μενοῦν γε καί].

URBÁN, Angel, La coordinada modal en el Nuevo Testamento. — *FilolNT* 1 (1988) 193-208. Esp. 200-201 [Lk 12,46; 18,1; 20,1.31; Acts 8,25; 9,9; 10,42; 16,20-21; 20,2]; 207: "Summary: The article makes a detailed study of ... 'the modal coordinate sentence', found when of two verbal clauses, joined by the conjunction καί/τε or τε καί (also in the negative form), one indicates the *mode* of doing or taking place of the action/state expressed by the other".

VICENT, Antonio, El valor atenuado de *dio kai* = ('por eso en cierto modo') dentro y fuera del N.T. — *EstBib* 32 (1973) 57-76. [NTA 18, 405]

Καϊάφας 1 + 1 (Mt 2) | Caiaphas (Lk 3,2; Acts 4,6)

Καϊνάμ 2 | Cainan

Word groups	Lk	Acts	Mt	Mk
Καϊνάμ son of Arphaxad (VKa)	3,36		0	0
Καϊνάμ son of Enos (VKb)	3,37		0	0

καινός 5 + 2 (Mt 4/5, Mk 4[5]/6)

1. new (time) (Lk 5,38; 22,20); 2. new (class) (Lk 5,36[1.2.3]); 3. previously unknown (Acts 17,19.21)

Word groups	Lk	Acts	Mt	Mk
καινὴ διαθήκη (VKb)	22,20		0/1	0/1
καινὴ διδαχή (VKd)		17,19	0	1
καινός + νεός (VKf)	5,38		1	1
καινός + παλαιός (SCa; VKg)	5,36[1.3].38(-39)		2	2
καινότερος comparative (VKa)		17,21	0	0

Literature

DELEBECQUE, Édouard, *Études grecques*, 1976. Esp. 109-121: "Le pain et la coupe de la dernière cène (22,17-20)".

HAGENE, Sylvia, *Zeiten der Wiederherstellung*, 2003. Esp. 276-299: "Bund und 'neuer Bund' im lkDW".

PETZER, Kobus H., *Style and Text in the Lucan Narrative of the Institution of the Lord's Supper*, 1991. Esp. 118-119.

καιρός 13/14 + 9 (Mt 10, Mk 5)

1. occasion; 2. period of time (Lk 8,13[1]); 3. era; 4. opportunity (Acts 24,25)

Word groups	Lk	Acts	Mt	Mk
ἐκεῖνος ὁ καιρός (SCb; VKb) → οὗτος καιρός; ὁ αἰὼν ἐκεῖνος; ἡ ἡμέρα ἐκείνη; αἱ ἡμέραι ἐκεῖναι; νὺξ ἐκείνη; ἐν ἐκείνῃ τῇ ὥρᾳ / τῇ ὥρᾳ ἐκείνῃ		12,1; 19,23	3	0
ἐν καιρῷ / τῷ καιρῷ absolute (VKd)	12,42; 20,10		1	1
καιρὸς πειρασμοῦ	8,13[2]		0	0
κατὰ (+) καιρόν (VKh)		12,1; 19,23	0	0
κατὰ τὸ καιρὸν ἐκεῖνον BOISMARD 1984 Aa136		12,1; 19,23	0	0
οὗτος καιρός (VKc) → ἐκεῖνος ὁ καιρός; ὁ αἰὼν οὗτος; ἡ ἡμέρα αὕτη; αἱ ἡμέραι αὗται; αὕτη ἡ νύξ DENAUX 2009 L[n]	12,56; 18,30		0	0
πρὸς καιρὸν (LN: for a while; VKg); cf. 1 Cor 7,5; πρὸς καιρὸν ὥρας 2 Thess 2,17	8,13[1]		0	0
χρόνοι + καιροί; cf. 1 Thess 5,1		1,7	0	0
καιροί plural (SCa; VKa)	21.24.24*	1,7; 3,20; 14,17; 17,26	2	0

Characteristic of Luke	Lk	Acts	Mt	Mk
ἄχρι καιροῦ (VKf) PLUMMER 1922 liii	4,13	13,11	0	0
αὐτὸς ὁ καιρός/ἡμέρα/ὥρα BOISMARD 1984 Ab4; DENAUX 2009 L***; NEIRYNCK 1985	2,38; 10,21;13,1.31; 20,19; 23,12; 24,13.33		0	0

Literature

DENAUX 2009 LA[n] [ἄχρι καιροῦ]; RADL 1975 403 [ἐγένετο + καιρός] .

BURNS, A.L., Two Words for "Time" in the New Testament. — AusBibRev 3 (1953) 7-22.

FERRARO, Giuseppe, Καιροὶ ἀναψύξεως: annotazioni su Atti 3,20. — RivBib 23 (1975) 67-78.

GALLET, B., Kairos et 'le' kairos chez les historiens grecs de l'époque classique. — Revue des Études Anciennes 109 (2007) 491-516. [NTA 53,96]

SCHWARZ, Günther, την τροφην ([το] σιτομετριον] εν καιρω? Mt 24,45 / Lk 12,42. — BibNot 59 (1991) 44.

Καῖσαρ 7 + 10/11 (Mt 4, Mk 4)

1. Caesar (Lk 20,22); 2. Emperor (Lk 2,1)

Word groups	Lk	Acts	Mt	Mk
Καῖσαρ Αὐγοῦστος (VKb)	2,1		0	0
τὰ Καίσαρος (VKa)	20,25[1]		1	1
Κλαύδιος Καῖσαρ (VKd)		11,28*	0	0
Τιβέριος Καῖσαρ (VKc)	3,1		0	0

Characteristic of Luke

BOISMARD 1984 cb152; MORGENTHALER 1958A; NEIRYNCK 1985

Literature
BORMANN, Lukas, *Recht, Gerechtigkeit und Religion*, 2001. Esp. 117-118.
MARYKS, Robert, A. Il latinismi del Nuovo testamento, 2000. Esp. 25.

καίω 2 (Mt 1/2)

1. burn (Lk 12,35; 24,32); 2. ignite

Word groups	Lk	Acts	Mt	Mk
καίω metaphorically (*VK*b)	24,32		0	0

κἀκεῖθεν 1 + 8/9 (Mk 1/2)

1. (and) from there (Lk 11,53; Acts 14,26); 2. then (Acts 13,21)

Word groups	Lk	Acts	Mt	Mk
κἀκεῖθεν with reference to time (*VK*a)		13,21	0	0
κακεῖθεν ἀποπλέω → ἐκεῖθεν ἀποπλέω BOISMARD 1984 Aa137		14,26; 20,15	0	0
κἀκεῖθεν (+) (ἐξ)ἔρχομαι→ ἔρχομαι ἐκεῖθεν	11,53	7,4; 16,12(-13); 20,15; 21,1; 28,15	0	2

Characteristic of Luke
BOISMARD 1984 Bb20; HAWKINS 1909 187; NEIRYNCK 1985

Literature
DENAUX 2009 lAn; JEREMIAS 1980 210 [red.]; SCHÜRMANN 1953 100 [κἀκεῖνος, κακεῖθεν, κακεῖ].

κἀκεῖνος 4 + 3 (Mt 2, Mk 2)   and that

Word groups	Lk	Acts	Mt	Mk
κἀκεῖνος + οὗτος → ἄλλος/ἐκεῖνος/ἕτερος + οὗτος	11,42	5,37	1	0

Characteristic of Luke
GOULDER 1989

Literature
SCHÜRMANN 1953 100 [κἀκεῖνος, κακεῖθεν, κακεῖ].

κακοποιέω 1 (Mk 1)

1. do evil (Lk 6,9); 2. injure

Literature
COLLISON 1977 88 [noteworthy phenomena].

κακός 2 + 4 (Mt 3, Mk 2)

1. bad (moral) (Lk 23,22; 2. bad (value) (Lk 16,25); 3. harmed (Acts 28,5); 4. incorrect

Word groups	Lk	Acts	Mt	Mk
τὰ κακά (VKb) → τὰ ἀγαθά	16,25		0	0
κακὸν πάσχω (VKf)		28,5	0	0
κακὸν ποιέω (SCa; VKc) → καλῶς ποιέω	23,22	9,13	1	1
κακὸν πράσσω (VKd)		16,28	0	0
κακός + ἀγαθός	16,25		0	0

Literature

TAEGER, Jens-Wilhelm, *Der Mensch und sein Heil*, 1982. Esp. 43-44: "Verwandte Begriffe (πονηρός, κακός, ἄτοπος)".

κακοῦργος 3 — evildoer (Lk 23,32.33.39)

Literature

COLLISON 1977 181 [noteworthy phenomena]; DENAUX 2009 L[n].

BORMANN, Lukas, *Recht, Gerechtigkeit und Religion*, 2001. Esp. 203.

κακῶς 2 + 0/1 (Mt 7, Mk 4)

1. evil (Acts 23,5); 2. harm; 3. incorrect; 4. severely

Word groups	Lk	Acts	Mt	Mk
κακῶς ἔχων (LN: be ill; SCa; VKa)	5,31; 7,2		4/5	4

κάλαμος 1 (Mt 5, Mk 2)

1. reed (plant) (Lk 7,24); 2. reed (stalk); 3. pen; 4. measuring rod

Literature

SCHWARZ, Günther, "Ein Rohr, vom Wind bewegt"? (Matthäus 11,7 par. Lukas 7,24). — *BibNot* 83 (1996) 19-21.

καλέω 43 + 18 (Mt 26/27, Mk 4)

1. name (Lk 2,4); 2. call (Lk 1,32); 3. summon (Lk 19,13; Acts 4,18); 4. call to a task; 5. invite (Lk 14,9) [6.consider (Lk 15,19.21; 1,32?)]

Word groups	Lk	Acts	Mt	Mk
καλέω + εἰς γάμον	14,8[1]		2	0
καλέω τὸ ὄνομα (SCa; VKa); cf. ἐπικαλέω τὸ ὄνομα (SCa) Acts 2,21; 9,14.21; 15,17; 22,16	1,13.31; 2,21[1]		3	0
καλέω + ὄνομα + proper name	1,13.31.59; 2,21[1]; 19,2		3	0
καλέω (ἐπὶ) (τῷ) ὀνόματι (SCb; VKb) DENAUX 2009 L[n]	1,59.61; 19,2		0	0
κεκλημένος (SCd; VKe)	14,7.8[2].17.24		3	0
κληθείς (VKf); cf. ἐπικληθείς Mt 10,3*; Acts 4,36; 12,25 DENAUX 2009 LA[n]	2,21[2]	24,2	0	0

→ Ἰούδας ὁ καλούμενος Βαρσαββᾶς; Μαρία ἡ καλουμένη **Μαγδαληνή**

Characteristic of Luke; cf. μετακαλέομαι Acts 7,14; 10,32; 20,17; 24,25
CREDNER 1836 140; GOULDER 1989; HENDRIKS 1986 434.466; MORGENTHALER 1958L

	Lk	Acts	Mt	Mk
καλέω + ὄνομα DENAUX 2009 L***	1,13.31.59.61; 2,21[1]; 19,2		3	0
καλέω + λέγω/εἶπον/ἐρῶ → παρα/προσ/συγκαλέω + λέγω/εἶπον; cf. ἐπικαλέω + λέγω Acts 7,59 DENAUX 2009 L***	7,39; 14,9.10; 19,13		1	0
καλούμενος (SCc; VKd) → ὄρος τὸ καλούμενον Ἐλαιῶν/Ἐλαιών; cf. Heb 5,4; 11,8; Rev 1,9; 12,9; 16,16; 19,11; ἐπικαλούμενος pass. Lk 22,3*; Acts 10,18; 11,13; 12,12.25 v.l.; 15,22* BOISMARD 1984 Bb111; CREDNER 1836 140; DENAUX 2009 L***; GOULDER 1989*; HAWKINS 1909L; NEIRYNCK 1985	1,36; 6,15; 7,11; 8,2; 9,10; 10,39; 19,2.29; 21,37; 22,3; 23,33	1,12.23; 3,11; 7,58; 8,10; 9,11; 10,1; 13,1; 15,22.37; 27,8.14.16	0	0
υἱός (singular) τινος καλεῖται; cf. υἱοὶ θεοῦ κληθήσονται Mt 5,9 DENAUX 2009 L***	1,32.35; 15,19.21		0	0

Literature

COLLISON 1977 179 [articular participle as appositive: linguistic usage of Luke: certain]; EASTON 1910 162 [καλούμενος of persons: cited by Weiss as characteristic of L, and possibly corroborative]; GERSDORF 1816 196: "Nur dem Lucas ist ὁ καλούμενος, ἡ καλ., τὸ καλ. üblich"; HAUCK 1934 [häufiges Alleinwort]; JEREMIAS 1980 53: "Das Partizip καλούμενος zur Einführung des Namens oder Beinamens einer Person oder Sache findet sich im NT außer in der Offb (3mal) nur im Doppelwerk"; 284: "Der Ölberg wird von Lukas in zweifacher Weise benannt: 1. τὸ ὄρος τῶν ἐλαιῶν 'Olivenberg' (Lk 19,37; 22,39) ist die traditionelle Bezeichnung wie wir sie bei Mk und Mt je dreimal lesen; 2. nur im Doppelwerk kommt im NT vor: τὸ ὄρος τὸ καλούμενον Ἐλαιών der 'Olivenhain' genannte Berg (Lk 19,29; 21,37/Apg 1,12); καλούμενος zur Einführung des Namens einer Örtlichkeit ist redaktionell"; SCHÜRMANN 1957 72 [καλεῖν "bei Namen rufen", "mit Nehmen nennen" bei Luk relative häufig].

BOVER, José M., "Quod nascetur (ex te) sanctum vocabitur filius Dei" (Lc. 1,35). — *Bib* 1 (1920) 92-94.

—, "Quod nascetur (ex te) sanctum vocabitur filius Dei" (Lc., 1,35). — *EstE* 8 (1929) 381-392.

JUNG, Chang-Wook, *Infancy Narrative*, 2004. Esp. 80 [κληθήσεται with ἅγιον, Lk 2,23]; 196-199 [καλέσεις τὸ ὄνομα αὐτοῦ + name, Lk 1,13b].

MUÑOZ IGLESIAS, Salvador, Lucas 1,35b. — *La idea de Dios en la Biblia. XXVIII Semana Biblica Española (Madrid 23-27 sept. 1968)*. Madrid: Consejo Superior de Investigaciones Cientificas, 1971, 303-324.

NEIRYNCK, Frans, La matière marcienne dans l'évangile de Luc, 1973. Esp. 183 [καλούμενος]; [2]1989. Esp. 93; = ID., *Evangelica*, 1982. Esp. 63.

SCHNEIDER, Gerhard, Lk 1,34. 35 als redaktionelle Einheit. — *BZ* NF 15 (1971) 255-259. Esp. 256-257: "Lk 1,35 ist nach Wortschatz, Stil und Theologie 'lukanisch'".

—, Jesu geistgewirkte Empfängnis (Lk 1,34f): Zur Interpretation einer christologischen Aussage. — *TPQ* 119 (1971) 105-116. Esp. 110; = ID., *Lukas, Theologe der Heilsgeschichte*, 1985, 86-97. Esp. 91.

VICENT CERNUDA, Antonio, 'Considerar' acepción axiológica de καλέω y su presencia en la Biblia. — *Augustinianum* 15 (1975) 445-445. [NTA 21, 22] [Lk 1,25b ; 15,19.21 : 'to be considered' and not 'to be named']

καλός 9 +1 (Mt 21, Mk 11)

1. good (moral) (Lk 8,15²); 2. good (value) (Lk 6,43); 3. advantageous; 4. fitting (Lk 9,33); 5. beautiful (Lk 21,5); 6. important

Word groups	Lk	Acts	Mt	Mk
Καλοὶ λιμένες (VKh)		27,8	0	0
καλόν ἐστιν + infinitive (SCa; VKa); cf. καλόν ἐστιν + εἰ Mt 26,24; Mk 9,42; 14,21	9,33		4	5
καλὸς καὶ ἀγαθός (VKg)	8,15²		0	0
καλὸς καρπός	3,9; 6,43²		5	0
λίθος καλός (LN: gem)	21,5		0	0

Literature
SCHÜRMANN 1957 7 [(οὐ) καλόν ἐστι (μᾶλλον): vermutlich luk Mk-R].

καλύπτω 2 (Mt 2)

1. cover (Lk 8,16; 23,30); 2. keep secret

καλῶς 4 + 3 (Mt 2/3, Mk 5[6])

1. good (moral) (Lk 6,26; 20,39); 2. good (value) (Lk 6,27.48); 3. accurate; 4. important; 5. please; 6. certainly (Acts 25,10)

Word groups	Lk	Acts	Mt	Mk
κάλλιον (VKc)		25,10	0	0
καλῶς ποιέω (SCa; VKa) → κακὸν ποιέω/πράσσω	6,27	10,33	1/2	1

κάμηλος 1 (Mt 3, Mk 2)   camel (Lk 18,25)

κἄν 3 + 1 (Mt 2/3, Mk 2[3])   even if (Lk 12,38¹·²; 13,9)

Word groups	Lk	Acts	Mt	Mk
ἵνα κἄν; cf. ἵνα εἰ Mk 14,35		5,15	0	1
κἄν μέν (VKc) → ἐὰν/εἰ μέν (οὖν)	13,9		0	0
κἄν at least (VKd)		5,15	0	2

καρδία 22/24 + 20/21 (Mt 16/17, Mk 11/12)

1. inner self (Lk 10,27); 2. inside

Word groups	Lk	Acts	Mt	Mk
ἀναβαίνω ἐν καρδίᾳ → ἀναβαίνω ἐπὶ καρδίαν	24,38		0	0
ἀναβαίνω ἐπὶ καρδίαν (LN: begin to think) → ἀναβαίνω ἐν καρδίᾳ		7,23	0	0
ἀπερίτμητος καρδίαις καὶ τοῖς ὠσίν (LN: obstinate)		7,51	0	0
διανοίγω τὴν καρδίαν (LN: cause to be open minded) → διανοίγω τοὺς ὀφθαλμούς / τὸν νοῦν		16,14	0	0

ἐπιστρέφω καρδίας + ἐπί (*LN*: make friendly toward)	1,17		0	0
καρδία + διαλογίζομαι → **καρδία** + διαλογισμός	3,15; 5,22		0	2
καρδία + στόμα (*SC*b; *VK*c)	6,45²		2/3	0
καρδία + ψυχή → **πνεῦμα/σῶμα** + ψυχή	10,27	4,32	1	1/2
κατανύσσομαι τὴν καρδίαν (*LN*: be greatly troubled)		2,37	0	0
(λέγω/)εἶπον ἐν τῇ καρδίᾳ	12,45		1	0
πληρόω + τὴν καρδίαν (*LN*: cause to think)		5,3	0	0
οἱ συντετριμμένοι τὴν καρδίαν	4,18*		0	0
συνθρύπτω + τὴν καρδίαν (*LN*: cause great sorrow)		21,13	0	0
τίθεμαι ἐν τῇ καρδίᾳ (*LN*: treasure up in mind)	1,66		0	0
τίθημι εἰς τὴν καρδίαν	21,14 *v.l.*		0	0
καρδίαι plural (*SC*a; *VK*a) DENAUX 2009 Lan	1,17; 2,35; 3,15; 5,22; 16,15; 21,14.34; 24,38 *v.l.*	7,39.51.54; 14,17; 15,9	2	2/3

Characteristic of Luke	Lk	Acts	Mt	Mk
καρδία + verbal expression (ἀναβαίνω ἐν καρδίᾳ/ἐπὶ καρδίαν / βαρέω τὰς καρδίας / διαλογίζομαι/ διατηρέω/συμβάλλω ἐν τῇ καρδίᾳ / διαλογισμὸς καρδίας / διαπρίομαι ταῖς καρδίαις / ἐπίνοια τῆς καρδίας / κατανύσσομαι τὴν καρδίαν / πρόθεσις τῆς καρδίας / συνθρύπτω / συντετριμμένος τὴν καρδίαν / τίθημι ἐν ταῖς καρδίαις CREDNER 1836 134; DENAUX 2009 L***	1,66; 2,19.35.51; 3,15; 4,18*; 5,22; 9,47; 21,14.34; 24,38	2,37; 5,4; 7,23.54; 8,22; 11,23; 21,13	0	2
καρδία + διαλογισμός → **καρδία** + διαλογίζομαι GOULDER 1989	2,35; 9,47; 24,38		1	1
τίθημι ἐν τῇ καρδίᾳ (*LN*: make up mind) BOISMARD 1984 Ab130; NEIRYNCK 1985; VOGEL 1899C	21,14	5,4	0	0

Literature

COLLISON 1977 66 [τίθημι + ἐν καρδίᾳ: noteworthy phenomena]; DENAUX 2009 Laⁿ [τίθημι ἐν τῇ καρδίᾳ]; EASTON 1910 158 [τίθεσθαι ἐν ταῖς καρδίαις: probably characteristic of L]; JEREMIAS 1980 71: "Wendungen mit übertragenem τίθημι + folgendem ἐν ('zu Herzen nehmen', 'sich vornehmen') schreibt im NT nur Lukas"; PLUMMER 1922 lxi [combination with ἐν τῇ καρδίᾳ or ἐν ταῖς καρδίαις, such as διαλογίζεσθαι, διατηρεῖν, θέσθαι, συμβάλλειν: Hebrew influence]; RADL 1975 414: "in hebraisierenden Wendungen bei Lukas"; 428 [τίθεμαι ἐν καρδίᾳ].

DELEBECQUE, Édouard, *Études grecques*, 1976. Esp. 17-23.

FUCHS, Albert, *Sprachliche Untersuchungen zu Mattäus und Lukas*, 1971. Esp. 175-178 [θέτε οὖν ἐν ταῖς καρδίαις ὑμῶν].

JUNG, Chang-Wook, *Infancy Narrative*, 2004. Esp. 106-111 [καρδίας πατέρων: Lk 1,17].

LERLE, Ernst, Καρδία als Bezeichnung für den Mageneingang. — *ZNW* 76 (1985) 292-294. [Acts 14,17]

SCHWARZ, Günther, μηποτε βαρηθωσιν υμων αι καρδιαι. [Lk 21,34] — *BibNot* 10 (1979) 40.

WILCOX, Max, *The Semitisms in Acts*, 1965. Esp. 62-63 [Lk 1,66; Acts 5,4].

καρπός 12 + 1 (Mt 19, Mk 5)	
1. fruit (Lk 3,8); 2. harvest; 3. deed	

Word groups	Lk	Acts	Mt	Mk
ἀπὸ τοῦ καρποῦ δίδωμι; cf. καρπὸν δίδωμι (SCb; VKc) Mt 13,8; Mk 4,7.8; καρπὸν ἀποδίδωμι (LN: bear fruit; VKd) Mt 21,41	20,10		0	0
ἐκ καρποῦ τῆς ὀσφύος (LN: offspring)		2,30	0	0
καλὸς καρπός	3,9; 6,43²		5	0
καρπὸν ποιέω (LN: ᵃproduce fruit, ᵇcause results; SCa; VKa); cf. καρπὸν (ἀνα)φέρω (VKb) Mt 7,18 v.l.; Jn 12,24; 15,2¹·².4.5.8.16¹	3,ᵃ8.ᵃ9; 6,43ᵃ¹·ᵃ²; 8,ᵃ8; 13,ᵃ9		11	0
καρπός + δένδρον	3,9; 6,43¹·².44		9	0
καρπὸς τῆς κοιλίας (LN: child)	1,42		0	0

Literature

HARNACK 1906 139 (ET: 201: "There is nothing to compare in the Gospel with ὁ καρπὸς τῆς κοιλίας, but in Acts ii:30 we find ὁ καρπὸς τῆς ὀσφύος αὐτοῦ"); JEREMIAS 1980 57: "(ὁ) καρπὸς τῆς κοιλίας Lk 1,42/τῆς ὀσφύος Apg 2,30 (cit.) sind hebraisierende gewählte Bezeichnungen für Nachkommenschaft (der Frau bzw. des Mannes), die sich im NT nur im lk Doppelwerk an den genannten beiden Stellen finden".

καρποφορέω 1 (Mt 1, Mk 2)

1. bear fruit (Lk 8,15); 2. cause results

κάρφος 3 (Mt 3)

splinter, speck (Lk 6,41.42¹·²)

κατά 43/46 + 90/97 (Mt 37/38, Mk 23/24)

1. down, toward (extension) (Lk 10,32); 2. along (extension) (Lk 10,4; Acts 25,3; 26,13); 3. throughout (extension) (Lk 8,39; Acts 9,42); 4. facing toward (location) (Acts 8,26; 27,12); 5. among (location) (Lk 9,6; Acts 9,31; 21,21); 6. opposite (location) (Acts 27,5.7); 7. when (time); 8. about (time) (Acts 16,25); 9. in name of (guarantor); 10. against (opposition) (Lk 11,23); 11. in accordance with (isomorphic) (Lk 2,22); 12. from … to (distributive) (Lk 2,41; Acts 8,3); 13. with regard to (specification) (Acts 25,14); 14. with (association) (Acts 17,28; 26,3)

Word groups	Lk	Acts		
ὁ + noun + ὁ κατά + geographical name BOISMARD 1984 Aa58		2,10; 11,1; 24,5; 27,5	0	0
κατά + πᾶς (accusative) in a temporal expression BOISMARD 1984 Aa50		13,27; 15,21²; 17,17; 18,4	0	0
κατά + genitive	**Lk**	**Acts**	**Mt**	**Mk**
κακόω τὴν ψυχὴν + κατά (LN: cause to dislike)		14,2	0	0
κατὰ τοῦ νόμου/τοῦ τόπου → κατὰ (τὸν) νόμον BOISMARD 1984 Aa145		6,13; 21,28		
μετά + κατά + gen.	11,23		1	0
κατά hostile against (SCa)	6,7*; 9,50.50*; 11,23; 23,14	4,26¹·²; 6,13; 14,2; 16,22; 19,16; 21,28; 24,1; 25,2.3¹.7*.15.27; 27,14	14/15	6

κατά with reference to location (SCb; VKb)	4,14; 8,33; 23,5	9,31.42; 10,37; 13,49*	1	1/2

→ εἰμι κατά; εἰς + κατά; ἐξέρχομαι κατά; ἰσχύω κατά; κατηγορέω κατά; συνάγω κατά ; κατά + ὑπέρ + gen.; φέρω κατά; κατὰ τοῦ Χριστοῦ

κατά + accusative	Lk	Acts	Mt	Mk
καθ᾽ ἓν ἕκαστον; cf. κατά + numeral (VKt) Mk 6,40[1.2]		21,19	0	0
κατ᾽ ἰδίαν (LN: privately; SCf; VKd)	9,10; 10,23	23,19	6	7
κατὰ λόγον + ἀνέχομαι (LN: accept a complaint)		18,14	0	0
κατὰ μόνας (LN: alone; SCg; VKe)	9,18		0	1
κατὰ πάντα (VKr)		3,22; 17,22.25*	0	0
κατὰ σάρκα (VKh)		2,30*	0	0
κατὰ τί (VKq)	1,18		0	0
κατὰ (τὸν) νόμον (SCh; VKj) → κατὰ τοῦ νόμου; κρίνω κατὰ τὸν νόμον; cf. κατὰ τὸ εἰρημένον ἐν τῷ νόμῳ κυρίου Lk 2,24; κατὰ τὸ εἰθισμένον τοῦ νόμου Lk 2,27; κατὰ ἀκρίβειαν τοῦ πατρῴου νόμου Acts 22,3 DENAUX 2009 IA[n]	2,22.39	22,12; 23,3; 24,6*.14[2]	0	0

→ διαπορεύομαι κατὰ πόλεις καὶ κώμας; διέρχομαι κατὰ τὰς κώμας; διοδεύω κατὰ πόλιν καὶ κώμην; καθ᾽ ἑαυτόν; εἰμι κατά; εἰς + κατά; ἐκ + κατά; ἐν + κατά; κατὰ ἑορτήν; κατ᾽ ἐπαγγελίαν; κατ᾽ ἔτος; ζῶ κατά; μένω καθ᾽ ἑαυτόν; κατὰ μέσον (τῆς νυκτός); κατ᾽ οἶκον/οἶκους; κατὰ τὸ ὡρισμένον; ποιέω (τι) κατά; κατὰ πόλιν καὶ κώμην / πόλεις καὶ κώμας; πορεύομαι κατά; κατὰ τὸ ῥῆμα; κατὰ πᾶν σάββατον; σῴζω κατά; κατὰ τόπους

Characteristic of Luke

HENDRIKS 1986 468; MORGENTHALER 1958A

	Lk	Acts	Mt	Mk
τὸ/τὰ κατά BOISMARD 1984 Db11; DENAUX 2009 LA*; NEIRYNCK 1985	2,39; 11,3; 19,47	17,11; 24,22; 25,14	0	0
κατά + accusative GOULDER 1989	1,9.18.38; 2,22.24.27.29.31.39.41.42; 4,16; 6,23.26; 8,1.2.39; 9,6.10.18.23; 10,4.23.31.32.33; 11,3; 13,22; 15,14; 16,19; 17,30; 19,47; 21,11, 22,22.39.53; 23,17*.56	2,10.30*.46.47; 3,2.13.17.22; 5,15*.42; 7,44; 8,1.3.26.36; 11,1; 12,1; 13,1.22.23.27; 14,1.23; 15,11.21[1.2].23.36; 16,5.7[1.2]*.25; 17,2.11.17.22.25*.28; 18,4.14.15; 19,9.20.23; 20,20.23; 21,19.21.28; 22,3.12.19; 23,3.19.31; 24,5.6*.12.14[1.2].22; 25,3[2].14.16.23; 26,3.5.11.13; 27,2.5.7[1.2].25.27.29; 28,16	21	17
κατά + accusative of time (SCd) BOISMARD 1984 Eb9; CADBURY 1920 117; DENAUX 2009 L***; NEIRYNCK 1985	2,41; 9,23; 11,3; 16,19; 19,47; 22,53; 23,17*	2,46[1].47; 3,2; 8,26; 12,1; 13,27; 15,21[2]; 16,5.25; 17,11.17; 18,4; 19,9.23; 27,27	2	1
κατά in a distributive sense; cf. Tit 1,5; Heb 9,25; 10,1.3 BOISMARD 1984 Cb59; DENAUX 2009 L***; GOULDER 1989; NEIRYNCK 1985	8,1.4; 9,6; 13,22; 21,11	2,46[1]; 5,15*.42; 8,1.3; 14,23; 15,21[1].36; 20,20.23; 22,19	1	1

κατὰ τό + part. perf. DENAUX 2009 L***; GOULDER 1989*	2,24.27; 4,16; 22,22	17,2; 23,31	0	0
κατὰ τὸ (αὐτό) / τὰ (αὐτά) (SCk; VKn) BOISMARD 1984 Ab70; GOULDER 1989; NEIRYNCK 1985	6,23.26; 17,30	14,1	0	0
καθ᾽ (πᾶσαν) ἡμέραν (SCe; VKf); cf. καθημερινός Acts 6,1 CADBURY 1920 117; CREDNER 1836 138; DENAUX 2009 L***; HAWKINS 1909L; PLUMMER 1922 lx	9,23; 11,3; 16,19; 19,47; 22,53	2,46[1].47; 3,2; 16,5; 17,11.17; 19,9	1	1
τὸ καθ᾽ ἡμέραν BOISMARD 1984 Ab126; NEIRYNCK 1985	11,3; 19,47	17,11 v.l.	0	0
καθ᾽ ὅλης BOISMARD 1984 Ab55; NEIRYNCK 1985; PLUMMER 1922 lii	4,14; 23,5	9,31.42; 10,37; 13,49*	0	0
κατὰ πρόσωπον (LN: [a]in front of; [b]in person; SCj; VKm); cf. 2 Cor 10,1.7; Gal 2,11 PLUMMER 1922 lxi	2,[a]31	3,[a]13; 25,[a]16	0	0

→ γενόμενος κατὰ τὸν τόπον; γίνομαι κατά + acc. of place; κατὰ τὸ εἰθισμένον; κατὰ τὸ εἰρημένον; κατὰ τὸ εἰωθός; κατὰ τὸ ἔθος; ἔρχομαι κατά + acc.; καθ᾽ ὅλης τῆς Ἰουδαίας; κατὰ τὸ καιρὸν ἐκεῖνον; κατὰ τὴν ὁδόν; κατὰ πόλιν/πόλεις; καθ᾽ ὃν τρόπον; κατὰ τὸ ὡρισμένον;

Literature

COLLISON 1977 137 [κατά + genitive = against, avoided: linguistic usage of Luke: likely; καθ᾽ ἡμέραν: probable]; 138 [κατὰ τὰ αὐτά: probable; καθ᾽ ὅλης: likely; κατά + accusative = according: linguistic usage of Luke: likely; linguistic usage of Luke's "other source-material": also probable; κατὰ τὸ ἔθος: noteworthy phenomena]; DENAUX 2009 La[n] [κατὰ τὸ αὐτό / τὰ αὐτά]; L[n] [τὸ καθ᾽ ἡμέραν]; lA[n] [καθ᾽ ὅλης; κατὰ πρόσωπον]; EASTON 1910 149 [κατὰ τὸ ἔθος: especially characteristic of L]; GERSDORF 1816 173-174 [κατὰ τὸ ἔθος]; 244 [κατὰ τὸν νόμον Μωϋσέως]; 245 [κατὰ τὸ εἰρημένον]; 256 [κατὰ πρόσωπον]; 264 [κατ᾽ ἔτος]; HAUCK 1934 [Vorzugsverbindung: κατὰ τὰ αὐτὰ (γάρ); κατὰ πόλιν; (τὸ) καθ᾽ ἡμέραν]; JEREMIAS 1980 29: "κατὰ τὸ ἔθος findet sich im NT ausschließlich im LkEv ... Auffallend sind die Alternativwendungen: κατὰ τὸ εἰωθός (...) und κατὰ τὸ εἰθισμένον (...)";118: "καθ᾽ ὅλου/ὅλης + Subst. des Ortes im Gen. begegnet im NT nur im lk Doppelwerk"; 175-176: "Lukas hat eine Vorliebe für räumliches κατά c.acc."; 184 [κατὰ τὴν ὁδόν: red.]; 231 [κατὰ πόλεις καὶ κώμας: red.]; RADL 1975 414 [κατά + acc.; κατὰ τὸν νόμον]; 419 [κατὰ τὴν ὁδόν]; 424 [κατὰ πόλιν(πόλεις)]; 426 [κατὰ πρόσωπον]; REHKOPF 1959 95 [κατά (gemäss); κατὰ τὸ ἔθος: vorlukanisch]; SCHÜRMANN 1961 282 [κατά (= gemäss): protoluk R weniger wahrscheinlich].

BACHMANN, Michael, Jerusalem und der Tempel, 1980. Esp. 78-84.97-103 [καθ᾽ ὅλης].

GARCÍA PÉREZ, José Miguel, El Endemoniado de Gerasa (Lc 8,26-39), 1986. Esp. 119-123 [καθ᾽ ὅλην τὴν πόλιν].

καταβαίνω 13 + 19 (Mt 11, Mk 6)	move down

Word groups	Lk	Acts	Mt	Mk
καταβαίνω (+) ἀπό (SCa; VKa) → ἀποβαίνω/κατέρχομαι ἀπό	9,54; 10,30	8,26; 25,7	4/5	3/4
καταβαίνω ἀπὸ ... εἰς → κατέρχομαι ἀπὸ ... εἰς	10,30		0	0
καταβαίνω ἀπὸ Ἰερουσαλήμ → → καταβαίνω ἀπὸ Ἰεροσολύμων (Acts 25,7); ἀναβαίνω εἰς Ἰεροσόλυμα/Ἰερουσαλήμ; κατέρχομαι ἀπὸ Ἰεροσολύμων DENAUX 2009 LAⁿ	10,30	8,26	0	0
καταβαίνω + ἐκ (SCc; VKc) → ἀνα/μεταβαίνω ἐκ		11,5	2	1
καταβαίνω ἐν + place(VKd)	10,31		0	0
καταβαίνω + ἐπί + accusative (SCd; VKe) → ἀναβαίνω ἐπί + acc.	3,22; [22,44]	10,11 v.l.	1	0/1
καταβαίνω ἕως (SCe; VKf)	10,15		1	0
καταβαίνω πρός + accusative (VKg) → διαβαίνω/κατέρχομαι πρός + acc. BOISMARD 1984 ca48		10,21; 14,11	0	0
καταβάς absolute + verb BOISMARD 1984 Aa139		8,15; 20,10	0	0

Characteristic of Luke	Lk	Acts	Mt	Mk
καταβαίνω εἰς (SCb; VKb) → ἀνα/ἀπο/δια/ἐμ/ μεταβαίνω/κατέρχομαι εἰς; cf. Jn 2,12; Eph 4,9; Rev 13,13; ἐπιβαίνω εἰς Acts 21,6* BOISMARD 1984 cb91; DENAUX 2009 lA*; NEIRYNCK 1985	8,23; 10,30; 18,14	7,15; 8,26.38; 14,25; 16,8; 18,22; 25,6	0	1/2
καταβαίνω μετά + genitive BOISMARD 1984 Ab131; NEIRYNCK 1985	2,51; 6,17	24,1	0	0

Literature

DENAUX 2009 Laⁿ [καταβαίνω μετά + genitive]; GERSDORF 1816 271: "Lucas allein schreibt καταβαίνειν μετά τινος"; RADL 1975 414 [καταβαίνων μετά + gen.].

SCHNEIDER, Gerhard, Engel und Blutschweiß (Lk 22,43-44): "Redaktionsgeschichte" im Dienste der Textkritik. — BZ NF 20 (1976) 112-116. Esp. 113-115: "Vokabular und Stil von Lk 22,43.44"; = ID., Lukas, Theologe der Heilsgeschichte, 1985, 153-157. Esp. 154-156.

κατάβασις 1   slope (Lk 19,37)

Literature
HAUCK 1934 [seltenes Alleinwort].

καταβολή 1 (Mt 1/2)   creation

Word groups	Lk	Acts	Mt	Mk
ἀπὸ καταβολῆς κόσμου	11,50		2	0

καταγελάω 1 (Mt 1, Mk 1)   laugh at (Lk 8,53)

κατάγω 1 + 7/8

1. lead down (Acts 9,30); 2. bring to shore (Lk 5,11); κατάγομαι: 3. arrive at land (Acts 27,3)

Word groups	Lk	Acts	Mt	Mk
κατάγω + εἰς + person		23,15	0	0
κατάγω (+) εἰς + place →		9,30; 21,3*;	0	0
(ἀν/ἀπ/εἰσ/ἐξ/ἐπαν/προ/συν/ὑπ) ἄγω εἰς + place; cf.		23,20.28; 27,3;		
καταντάω εἰς + place Acts 16,1; 18,19.24; 21,7; 25,13;		28,12		
27,12; 28,13				
κατάγω + ἐπί + accusative (place) → (ἀν)ἄγω ἐπί + acc.	5,11		0	0
(place); (ἀπ/συν/ὑπ)ἄγω ἐπί + acc. (person); προάγω ἐπί				
+ gen. (person)				
κατάγομαι passive → (ἀν/ἀπ/εἰσ/ἐπισυν/συν)ἄγομαι		21,3*; 27,3; 28,12	0	0
passive				
κατάγω nautical term (VKa)	5,11	21,3*; 27,3; 28,12	0	0
DENAUX 2009 lA[n]				
κατάγω transitive → (ἀν/ἀπ/εἰσ/ἐξ/ἐπισυν/προ/προσ/	5,11	9,30; 21,3*;	0	0
συν)ἄγω transitive		22,30; 23,15.		
DENAUX 2009 lA[n]		20.28; 27,3; 28,12		
κατήγαγον → (ἀν/ἀπ/εἰσ)ἤγαγον; cf. συνήγαγον Mt		9,30	0	0
22,10; 27,27				

Characteristic of Luke
BOISMARD 1984 Bb28; HARNACK 1906 44.52; NEIRYNCK 1985; PLUMMER 1922 lix

Literature
DENAUX 2009 lA[n]; RADL 1975 414.

καταδέω 1 | wrap (Lk 10,34)

Literature
HAUCK 1934 [seltenes Alleinwort].

καταδικάζω 2 (Mt 2) | condemn (Lk 6,37[1.2])

Literature
BORMANN, Lukas, *Recht, Gerechtigkeit und Religion*, 2001. Esp. 179.

καταισχύνω 1 | put to shame (Lk 13,17)

Literature
PAFFENROTH 1997 79 [αἰσχύνη/αἰσχύνομαι/καταισχύνω: prelukan].

VORSTER, Willem S., Aischunomai *en stamverwante woorde in die Nuwe Testament*.
Pretoria: Universiteit van Suid-Africa, 1979, XVIII-299 p. Esp. 67-87: "Αἰσχύνομαι"; 87-
100: "ἐπαισχύνομαι"; 100-121: "καταισχύνω".

κατακαίω 1 + 1 (Mt 3) | burn down (Lk 3,17; Acts 19,19)

Word groups	Lk	Acts	Mt	Mk
κατακαίω + πῦρ (VKa); cf. καίω + πῦρ Mt 13,40*	3,17		2	0

Literature

SCHWARZ, Günther, Τὸ δὲ ἄχυρον κατακαύσει. — *ZNW* 72 (1981) 264-271. [NTA 26, 464]

κατάκειμαι 3 + 2 (Mk 4)

1. lie down (Lk 5,25; Acts 28,8); 2. recline to eat (Lk 5,29); 3. eat a meal (Lk 7,37)

Word groups	Lk	Acts	Mt	Mk
κατάκειμαι ἐν → ἀπόκειμαι/κεῖμαι ἐν; cf. ἀνάκειμαι ἐν Mt 9,10	7,37		0	1
κατάκειμαι ἐπί + accusative (*VK*a)	5,25		0	0
κατάκειμαι ἐπί + dative (*VK*c)	5,25 *v.l.*	9,33 *v.l.*	0	0/1
κατάκειμαι ἐπί + genitive (*VK*b)		9,33	0	0

Literature

COLLISON 1977 95 [noteworthy phenomena].

κατακλάω 1 (Mk 1)   break into pieces

Word groups	Lk	Acts	Mt	Mk
κατακλάω ἄρτον → κλάσις τοῦ ἄρτου; κλάω ἄρτον	9,16		0	1
κατακλάω + εὐλογέω → κλάω + εὐλογέω	9,16		0	1

Literature

TAYLOR, Justin, La fraction du pain en Luc-Actes. — VERHEYDEN, J. (ed.), *The Unity of Luke-Acts*, 1999, 281-295.

κατακλείω 1 + 1   put into prison

Word groups	Lk	Acts	Mt	Mk
κατακλείω ἐν φυλακῇ → βάλλω/παραδίδωμι/τίθημι εἰς (τὴν) φυλακήν / ἐν (τῇ) φυλακῇ DENAUX 2009 LAⁿ	3,20	26,10	0	0

Characteristic of Luke

BOISMARD 1984 Ab182; HAWKINS 1909LA; MORGENTHALER 1958*; NEIRYNCK 1985; PLUMMER 1922 liii; VOGEL 1899A

Literature

DENAUX 2009 LAⁿ; HAUCK 1934 [seltenes Alleinwort]; JEREMIAS 1980 112 [κατέκλεισεν ἐν φυλακῇ: red.].

MAHFOUZ, Hady, *La fonction littéraire et théologique de Lc 3,1-20*, 2003. Esp. 92-93 [κατακλείω ἐν φυλακῇ].

κατακλίνω 5

1. cause to recline to eat (Lk 9,14.15); κατακλίνομαι: 2. recline to eat (Lk 7,36; 14,8; 24,30)

Characteristic of Luke

DENAUX 2009 L***; GOULDER 1989*; HAWKINS 1909 19; PLUMMER 1922 lii

Literature

COLLISON 1977 90 [noteworthy phenomena]; HAUCK 1934 [häufiges Alleinwort]; JEREMIAS 1980 237: "Lukas bevorzugt die κατα-Komposita der Verben des Zu-Tische-Liegens, während die Tradition die ἀνα-Komposita vorzieht".

κατακλυσμός 1 (Mt 2) | flood (Lk 17,27)

κατακολουθέω 1 + 1 | follow along behind (Lk 23,55; Acts 16,17)

Characteristic of Luke

BOISMARD 1984 Ab183; HARNACK 1906 36.54; HAWKINS 1909LA; MORGENTHALER 1958*; NEIRYNCK 1985; PLUMMER 1922 liii; VOGEL 1899A

Literature

DENAUX 2009 LA[n]; HAUCK 1934 [seltenes Alleinwort]; JEREMIAS 1980 310 [red.].

κατακρημνίζω 1 | throw down a cliff (Lk 4,29)

Literature

HAUCK 1934 [seltenes Alleinwort].

BORMANN, Lukas, *Recht, Gerechtigkeit und Religion*, 2001. Esp. 182.

κατακρίνω 2 (Mt 4, Mk 2[3]) | condemn (Lk 11,31.32)

Literature

BORMANN, Lukas, *Recht, Gerechtigkeit und Religion*, 2001. Esp. 184-185.

καταλείπω 4 + 5/6 (Mt 4, Mk 4)

1. leave (Lk 20,31); 2. leave behind (Lk 5,28; 15,4); 3. leave to exist; 4. neglect (Acts 6,2); 5. no longer relate to; 6. leave off helping (Lk 10,40)

Word groups	Lk	Acts	Mt	Mk
καταλείπω + ἀκολουθέω → ἀφίημι/πωλέω + ἀκολουθέω	5,28		0	0
καταλείπομαι passive (VKb)		2,31*; 25,14	0	0
καταλείπω transitive (person) (VKa)	10,40; 20,31	18,19; 24,27	3	2

καταλιθάζω * 1 | stone to death (Lk 20,6)

Literature

HAUCK 1934 [seltenes Alleinwort].

BORMANN, Lukas, *Recht, Gerechtigkeit und Religion*, 2001. Esp. 182-183.

κατάλυμα 2 (Mk 1)

1. inn (Lk 2,7); 2. room (Lk 22,11)

Characteristic of Luke
PLUMMER 1922 lx

Literature
BENOIT, Pierre, "Non erat eis locus in diversorio" (Lc 2,7). — DESCAMPS, A. – DE HAL-
LEUX, A. (eds.), *Mélanges bibliques en hommage au R.P. Béda Rigaux*, 1970, 173-186.
DERRETT, J.D.M., Luke 2.7 Again. — *NTS* 45 (1999) 263. [NTA 43, 1735]
KERR, A.J., "No Room in the Kataluma". — *ExpT* 103 (1991-92) 15-16.
KIPGEN, Kaikhohen, Translating *kataluma* in Luke 2.7. — *BTrans* 34 (1983) 442-443.
LAVERDIÈRE, E., No Room for Them in the Inn. — *Emmanuel* 91 (1985) 552-557.
OLLEY, John W., God on the Move – A Further Look at *Kataluma* in Luke. — *ExpT* 103
(1991-92) 300-301.
PAX, Elpidius, "Denn sie fanden keinen Platz in der Herberge": Jüdisches und
frühchristliches Herbergswesen. — *BibLeb* 6 (1965) 285-288.
TRUDINGER, L. Paul, "No Room in the Inn": A Note on Luke 2:7. — *ExpT* 102 (1990-91)
172-173.
WINANDY, J., Du *kataluma* à la crèche. — *NTS* 44 (1998) 618-622.

καταλύω 3 + 3 (Mt 5, Mk 3)

1. tear down (Lk 21,6); 2. destroy (Acts 6,14); 3. put an end to (Acts 5,38); 4. make
invalid; 5. be a guest (Lk 9,12; 19,7)

Word groups	Lk	Acts	Mt	Mk
καταλύω active intransitive (*VK*a) DENAUX 2009 L[n]	9,12; 19,7		0	0

Literature
JEREMIAS 1980 277: "Intransitives καταλύω ('übernachten', 'einkehren') ist im NT nur zweimal,
beide Stellen im dritten Evangelium belegt".

κατανεύω* 1   gesture (Lk 5,7)

Literature
HAUCK 1934 [seltenes Alleinwort].

κατανοέω 4 + 4 (Mt 1)

1. consider closely (Lk 12,24.27); 2. be concerned about (Lk 6,41; Acts 27,39); 3.
understand completely (Lk 20,30); 4. notice (Acts 27,39)

Characteristic of Luke
BOISMARD 1984 Eb22; DENAUX 2009 L***; GOULDER 1989*; HAWKINS 1909 19; NEIRYNCK
1985; PLUMMER 1922 lx

Literature
COLLISON 1977 54 [linguistic usage of Luke: probable]; HAUCK 1934 [Vorzugswort]; JEREMIAS

1980 217 [red.].

DANOVE, Paul, Verbs of Experience, 1999. Esp. 162.175.

καταξιόω 1/2 + 1   regard as worthy

Word groups	Lk	Acts	Mt	Mk
καταξιόω + infinitive → ἄξιος/ἀξιόω + inf. DENAUX 2009 LAn	20,35; 21,36*	5,41	0	0

Characteristic of Luke
BOISMARD 1984 cb111; NEIRYNCK 1985

Literature
VON BENDEMANN 2001 437; DENAUX 2009 LAn; HAUCK 1934 [seltenes Alleinwort]; JEREMIAS 1980 154 [καταξιόω + inf.: red.].

καταπατέω 2 (Mt 2)
1. trample on (Lk 8,5; 12,1); 2. despise

Literature
JEREMIAS 1980 211 [red.].

καταπέτασμα 1 (Mt 1, Mk 1)   curtain (Lk 23,45)

καταπίπτω 1 + 2
1. fall (Lk 8,6); 2. fall down (Acts 26,14; 28,6)

Word groups	Lk	Acts	Mt	Mk
καταπεσών → (ἐμ/ἐπι/περι/προσ)πεσών; cf. Jn 12,24; Rom 11,22; 1 Cor 14,25; ἀναπεσών Jn 13,25; παραπεσών Heb 6,6		26,14	0	0
καταπίπτω aorist → (ἀνα/ἐμ/ἐπι/περι/προσ/συμ)πίπτω aorist; cf. ἀποπίπτω Acts 9,18; ἐκπίπτω Acts 12,7; 27,17.26.29.32 DENAUX 2009 LAn	8,6	26,14	0	0

Characteristic of Luke
BOISMARD 1984 Ab132; HARNACK 1906 41; HAWKINS 1909LA; MORGENTHALER 1958*; NEIRYNCK 1985

Literature
DENAUX 2009 lAn; HAUCK 1934 [seltenes Alleinwort].

καταπλέω* 1   sail toward shore (Lk 8,26)

Literature
HAUCK 1934 [seltenes Alleinwort].

καταράομαι 1 (Mt 1/2, Mk 1) curse (Lk 6,28)

καταργέω 1
1. put an end to; 2. put a stop to; 3. invalidate (Lk 13,7); καταργέομαι: 4. be freed; 5. cease

Literature
DODD, Charles H., Some Problems of New Testament Translation. — *BTrans* 13 (1962) 145-157. Esp. 151-152: "*katargein*".

καταρτίζω 1 (Mt 2, Mk 1)
1. make adequate (Lk 6,40); 2. produce; 3. create

Word groups	Lk	Acts	Mt	Mk
κατηρτισμένος (*VK*a)	6,40		0	0

κατασκευάζω 2 (Mt 1, Mk 1)
1. make ready (Lk 1,17; 7,27); 2. build

Word groups	Lk	Acts	Mt	Mk
κατασκευάζω τὴν ὁδόν (*LN*: make ready)	7,27		1	1

κατασκηνόω 1 + 1 (Mt 1, Mk 1) make a nest (Lk 13,19; Acts 2,26)

κατασκήνωσις 1 (Mt 1) nest (Lk 9,58)

κατασύρω 1 drag off forcefully (Lk 12,58)

Literature
HAUCK 1934 [seltenes Alleinwort].

BORMANN, Lukas, *Recht, Gerechtigkeit und Religion*, 2001. Esp. 183.

κατασφάζω 1 slaughter (Lk 19,27)

καταφιλέω 3 + 1 (Mt 1, Mk 1) kiss (Lk 7,38.45; 15,20; Acts 20,37)

Word groups	Lk	Acts	Mt	Mk
καταφιλέω τοὺς πόδας (*VK*a) DENAUX 2009 L[n]	7,38.45		0	0

Characteristic of Luke
BOISMARD 1984 Bb112; NEIRYNCK 1985; PLUMMER 1922 lx; VOGEL 1899B

Literature
COLLISON 1977 89 [noteworthy phenomena]; DENAUX 2009 Lan; EASTON 1910 156 [probably characteristic of L]; JEREMIAS 1980 168: "lukanisch"; PAFFENROTH 1997 81.

LOSS, Nicolò Maria, Amore d'amicizia nel Nuovo Testamento, 1977. Esp. 22.

καταφρονέω 1 (Mt 2) | despise (Lk 16,13)

καταψύχω 1 | make cool (Lk 16,24)

Literature
HAUCK 1934 [seltenes Alleinwort].

κατέναντι 1 (Mt 1/2, Mk 3)
1. opposite (Lk 19,30); 2. in the judgement of

Word groups	Lk	Acts	Mt	Mk
κατέναντι adverb (VKa)	19,30		0	0

κατέρχομαι 2 + 13
1. move down (Lk 4,31; 9,37); 2. arrive at land (Acts 18,22)

Word groups	Lk	Acts	Mt	Mk
κατέρχομαι ἀπὸ … εἰς (SCc) → καταβαίνω ἀπὸ … εἰς		11,27; 12,19	0	0
κατέρχομαι ἀπὸ Ἱεροσολύμων → ἔρχομαι εἰς / ἐξέρχομαι ἐξ Ἱερουσαλήμ; καταβαίνω ἀπὸ Ἱεροσολύμων/Ἱερουσαλήμ		11,27	0	0
κατέρχομαι ἀπὸ τῆς Ἰουδαίας → ἀναβαίνω εἰς τὴν Ἰουδαίαν		12,19; 15,1; 21,10	0	0
κατέρχομαι ἀπὸ τοῦ ὄρους → ἀναβαίνω/ ἐξέρχομαι/πορεύομαι εἰς τὸ ὄρος	9,37		0	0
κατέρχομαι εἰς (SCb) → καταβαίνω εἰς DENAUX 2009 IA[n]	4,31	8,5; 13,4; 15,30; 18,22; 19,1; 21,3; 27,5	0	0
κατέρχομαι + εὑρίσκω → (ἀπ/δι/εἰσ/ἐξ)ἔρχομαι + εὑρίσκω; εἰσπορεύομαι + εὑρίσκω		9,32(-33); 19,1	0	0
κατέρχομαι + κηρύσσω → ἀποστέλλω / (ἀπ/δι/εἰσ/προσ)ἔρχομαι / (εἰσ)πορεύομαι / ὑποστρέφω / φεύγω + ἀπαγγέλλω / διαγγέλλω / διηγέομαι / κηρύσσω		8,5	0	0
κατέρχομαι πρός + accusative (VKb) → (ἀπ/εἰσ)ἔρχομαι/καταβαίνω πρός + acc.		9,32	0	0

Characteristic of Luke
BOISMARD 1984 Bb8; DENAUX 2009 IA*; HARNACK 1906 52; HAWKINS 1909B.187; MORGENTHALER 1958A; NEIRYNCK 1985; PLUMMER 1922 lix

	Lk	Acts	Mt	Mk
κατέρχομαι ἀπό (SCa; VKa) → ἀνα/καταβαίνω / (ἀπ/ἐξ/ἐπ)ἔρχομαι / πορεύομαι / ὑποστρέφω ἀπό BOISMARD 1984 Ab37; NEIRYNCK 1985	9,37	11,27; 12,19; 15,1; 18,5; 21,10	0	0

Literature

COLLISON 1977 95 [noteworthy phenomena]; DENAUX 2009 IAⁿ [κατέρχομαι ἀπό]; HAUCK 1934 [Vorzugswort]; RADL 1975 415 [κατέρχομαι; κατέρχομαι "mit Beziehung auf Jerusalem bzw. Judäa"].

κατεσθίω 3 (Mt 1/2, Mk 2)

1. eat up (Lk 8,5); 2. destroy utterly; 3. rob (Lk 20,47); 4. waste (Lk 15,30); 5. exploit completely

Word groups	Lk	Acts	Mt	Mk
κατεσθίω metaphorically (VKb)	15,30; 20,47		0/1	1

Literature

SCHWARZ, Günther, "Die Häuser der Witwen verzehren"? (Markus 12,40 / Lk 20,47). — BibNot 88 (1997) 45-46.

κατευθύνω 1   guide

Word groups	Lk	Acts	Mt	Mk
κατευθύνω τοὺς πόδας (LN: guide behavior)	1,79		0	0

κατέχω 3 + 1 (Mt 0/1)

1. prevent; 2. continue belief (Lk 8,15); 3. possess; 4. control (Lk 4,42); 5. occupy (Lk 14,9)

Word groups	Lk	Acts	Mt	Mk
κατέχω εἰς (LN: head for)		27,40	0	0
κατέχω nautical term (VKc)		27,40	0	0

Characteristic of Luke

BOISMARD 1984 Db23; HARNACK 1906 54; HAWKINS 1909add; NEIRYNCK 1985

Literature

COLLISON 1977 96 [noteworthy phenomena]; DENAUX 2009 Laⁿ; HAUCK 1934 [häufiges Alleinwort]; JEREMIAS 1980 237 [red.].

κατηγορέω 4/5 + 9 (Mt 2, Mk 3)   accuse

Word groups	Lk	Acts	Mt	Mk
κατηγορέω κατά + genitive (VKd)	23,14		0	0
κατηγορέω + λέγων	23,2	24,2	0	0
κατηγορέω accuse of something (accusative) (VKc)		22,30	0	0
κατηγορέω accuse someone (genitive) of something (accusative) (VKa)		25,11; 28,19	0	2

Characteristic of Luke; cf. κατήγορος Acts 23,30.35; 24,8*; 25,16.18

BOISMARD 1984 cb159; NEIRYNCK 1985

Literature

DENAUX 2009 lAn; JEREMIAS 1980 69 [κατηγορέω + λέγων: red.].

BORMANN, Lukas, *Recht, Gerechtigkeit und Religion*, 2001. Esp. 183.

κατηχέω 1 + 3

1. teach (Lk 1,4; Acts 18,25); 2. inform (Lk 1,4; Acts 21,14)

Characteristic of Luke

BOISMARD 1984 Db24; NEIRYNCK 1985

Literature

DENAUX 2009 lA[n]; GERSDORF 1816 162 [ἵνα ἐπιγνῷς περὶ ὧν κατηχήθης λόγων τὴν ἀσφάλειαν]; HAUCK 1934 [seltenes Alleinwort].

ALEXANDER, Loveday, *The Preface to Luke's Gospel*, 1993. Esp. 139.

CADBURY, Henri J., Commentary on the Preface of Luke, 1922. Esp. 508-509.

MOURLON BEERNAERT, Pierre, Le verbe grec *katêchein* dans le N.T. — *Lumen Vitae* 44 (1989) 377-387.

κατισχύω 2 (Mt 1)

1. be fully able (Lk 21,36); 2. be strong enough (Lk 21,36); 3. defeat

κατοικέω 2 + 20 (Mt 4)   dwell (Lk 11,26; 13,4)

Word groups	Lk	Acts	Mt	Mk
κατοικέω + εἰς (VKb)		2,5; 7,4	2	0
κατοικέω ἐν + name of place		2,5; 7,2.4; 9,22; 11,29;	0	0
BOISMARD 1984 Aa19		13,27		
κατοικέω ἐπί + accusative/genitive (VKc)		17,26	0	0

Characteristic of Luke

BOISMARD 1984 Eb32; DENAUX 2009 lA*; MORGENTHALER 1958A; NEIRYNCK 1985

	Lk	Acts	Mt	Mk
κατοικέω transitive (VKa) (+ accusative of place); cf. Rev 17,2 BOISMARD 1984 Bb90; NEIRYNCK 1985	13,4	1,19; 2,9.14; 4,16; 9,32.35; 19,10.17	1	0
πάντες οἱ κατοικοῦντες BOISMARD 1984 Bb29; NEIRYNCK 1985	13,4	1,19; 2,14; 4,16; 9,35; 19,10.17; 22,12	0	0

Literature

DENAUX 2009 lAn [κατοικέω transitive (VKa) (+ accusative of place)]; lA[n] [πάντες οἱ κατοικοῦντες]; JEREMIAS 1980 226: "Kennzeichnend für seinen Sprachgebrauch ist der transitive Gebrauch des Verbums, wie er im NT (außer Mt 23,21; Offb 17,2) nur an unserer Stelle [Lk 13,4] und im zweiten Teil des lk Doppelwerkes (8mal) vorliegt, sowie die Häufigkeit des Partizips (Lk 1/Apg 14), insbesondere in der als Ersatz für Ἱεροσολυμίτης dienenden Wendung οἱ κατοικοῦντες Ἱερουσαλήμ".

κάτω 1 + 2 (Mt 2, Mk 2)

1. low (location) (Acts 2,19); 2. down to (direction) (Lk 4,9; Acts 20,9)

Word groups	Lk	Acts	Mt	Mk
ἐντεῦθεν κάτω	4,9		0	0

καύσων 1 (Mt 1)	scorching heat (Lk 12,55)

Καφαρναούμ 4 (Mt 4, Mk 3)	Capernaum

Word groups	Lk	Acts	Mt	Mk
ἡ Καφαρναούμ (VKa)	4,23		0	0
Καφαρναοὺμ πόλις (VKb)	4,31		0	0
πόλις + Γαλιλαία + Καφαρναούμ → πόλις + Γαλιλαία + **Ναζαρέθ**	4,31		0	0

κεῖμαι 6/7 (Mt 3)				
1. recline (Lk 2,12); 2. be in a place; 3. exist (Lk 2,34)				

Word groups	Lk	Acts	Mt	Mk
κεῖμαι εἰς (SCa; VKa) DENAUX 2009 L[n]	2,34; 12,19		0	0
κεῖμαι ἐν (SCb; VKb) → ἀπό/κατάκειμαι ἐν; cf. ἀνάκειμαι ἐν Mt 9,10 DENAUX 2009 L[n]	2,12.16		0	0
κεῖμαι + πρός + accusative (SCc; VKe)	3,9		1	0

Characteristic of Luke

DENAUX 2009 L***†; GOULDER 1989*; HAWKINS 1909 †L

	Lk	Acts	Mt	Mk
κείμενος DENAUX 2009 L***; GOULDER 1989*	2,12.16; 12,19; 23,53; 24,12*		1	0

Literature

REHKOPF 1959 95 [vorlukanisch]; SCHÜRMANN 1961 276.

SILVA, Moisés, New Lexical Semitisms? — ZNW 69 (1978) 253-257. Esp. 255: "κεῖσθαι".

κελεύω 1 + 17/18 (Mt 7/8)	command

Word groups	Lk	Acts	Mt	Mk
κελεύω + present infinitive (VKb)		16,22; 21,34; 22,24; 23,3.35; 24,8*; 25,21; 27,43	0	0

Characteristic of Luke

BOISMARD 1984 cb71; MORGENTHALER 1958A; NEIRYNCK 1985

	Lk	Acts	Mt	Mk
κελεύω + (ἀπ/εἰσ)ἄγειν BOISMARD 1984 Ab26; NEIRYNCK 1985	18,40	12,19; 21,34; 22,24; 23,10; 25,6.17	0	0

Literature

DENAUX 2009 lAn; lA[n] [κελεύω + (ἀπ/εἰσ)ἄγειν]; HAUCK 1934 [Vorzugswort]; RADL 1975

415 [κελεύω + ἄγω/εἰσάγω].

MAKUJINA, John, Verbs Meaning "Command" in the New Testament: Determining the Factors Involved in the Choice of Command-Verbs. — *EstBíb* 56 (1998) 357-369. Esp. 358-359: "Παραγγέλλω"; 359-361: "Κελεύω"; 361-362: "'Εντέλλω"; 362-364: "Διαστέλλω"; 364-366: "-τάσσω complex"; 366-367: "Λέγω". [NTA 43, 57]

κενός 3 + 1 (Mk 1)

1. without anything (Lk 1,53; 20,10.11); 2. foolish; 3. without result; 4. without purpose; 5. untrue

Word groups	Lk		Acts	Mt	Mk
κενά noun (*VK*b)			4,25	0	0

Characteristic of Luke	Lk	Acts	Mt	Mk
ἐξαποστέλλω τινὰ κενόν; cf. ἀποστέλλω τινὰ κενόν Mk 12,3 CREDNER 1836 141; HARNACK 1906 151	1,53; 20,10.11		0	0

Literature
DENAUX 2009 Lⁿ [ἐξαποστέλλω τινὰ κενόν]; GERSDORF 1816 200 [ἐξαπέστειλεν κενούς].

κεραία 1 (Mt 1)   part of letter (Lk 16,17)

κεράμιον 1 (Mk 1)   jar (Lk 22,10)

κέραμος 1   tile (Lk 5,19)

Literature
HAUCK 1934 [seltenes Alleinwort].

κέρας 1

1. horn; 2. corner; 3. power (Lk 1,69)

Word groups	Lk	Acts	Mt	Mk
κέρας σωτηρίας (*VK*a)	1,69		0	0

Literature
GERSDORF 1816 206 [κέρας σωτηρίας].

κεράτιον* 1   carob pod (Lk 15,16)

Literature
HAUCK 1934 [seltenes Alleinwort].

κερδαίνω 1 + 1 (Mt 6, Mk 1)

1. make profit (Lk 9,25); 2. avoid (Acts 27,21)

Word groups	Lk	Acts	Mt	Mk
κερδαίνω + ζημιόω	9,25		1	1

κεφαλή 7/8 + 5 (Mt 12, Mk 8)
1. head (Lk 7,46); 2. superior

Word groups	Lk	Acts	Mt	Mk
εἰς κεφαλὴν γωνίας (LN: cornerstone; SCb; VKb); cf. 1 Pet 2,7	20,17	4,11	1	1
ἐπαίρω τὴν κεφαλήν (LN: have courage)	21,28		0	0
ἐπὶ τὴν κεφαλήν (LN: responsibility)		18,6	0	0
τὴν κεφαλὴν κλίνω (LN: lie down to rest; VKd)	9,58		1	0

Characteristic of Luke	Lk	Acts	Mt	Mk
θρίξ (ἐκ/ἀπὸ) τῆς κεφαλῆς (SCa; VKa) DENAUX 2009 La*	7,38.44*; 12,7; 21,18	27,34	1	0

κῆπος 1
garden (Lk 13,19)

Literature
HAUCK 1934 [seltenes Alleinwort].

κήρυγμα 1 (Mt 1, Mk 0[1])
preaching

Word groups	Lk	Acts	Mt	Mk
κήρυγμα Ἰωνᾶ (VKb)	11,32		1	0

Literature
HERMANN, Ingo, Kerygma und Kirche. — BLINZLER, J. – KUSS, O. – MUßNER, F. (eds.), *Neutestamentliche Aufsätze.* FS J. Schmid, 1963, 110-114.

κηρύσσω 9 + 8 (Mt 9, Mk 12[14])
1. announce; 2. tell (Lk 8,39); 3. preach (Lk 3,3)

Word groups	Lk	Acts	Mt	Mk
ἀποστέλλω / εἰσπορεύομαι / (ἀπ/δι/κατ) ἔρχομαι + κηρύσσω; cf. ἐξέρχομαι / μεταβαίνω/περιάγω/πορεύομαι + κηρύσσω Mt 4,23; 9,35; 10,7; 11,1; Mk [16,15.20]	3,3; 4,18.19.(43-)44; 8,39; 9,2	8,5; 20,25; 28,(30-)31	0	4
κηρύσσω + dative (VKe) DENAUX 2009 IAⁿ	4,18	8,5; 10,42	0	0[1]
κηρύσσω τὸ βάπτισμα (VKd)	3,3	10,37	0	1
κηρύσσω + διδάσκω (SCa; VKa) → **κηρύσσω** + εὐαγγελίζομαι		28,31	3	0
κηρύσσω + εὐαγγελίζομαι → **κηρύσσω** + διδάσκω; cf. κηρύσσω τὸ εὐαγγέλιον (SCb; VKb) Mt 4,23; 9,35; 24,14; 26,13; Mk 1,14; 13,10; 14,9; [16,15] DENAUX 2009 Lⁿ	4,18; 8,1		0	0

		Lk	Acts	Mt	Mk
κηρύσσω + ὅτι (VKf); cf. κηρύσσω ἵνα Mk 6,12		9,20; 10,42	0		0
κηρύσσω (+) συναγωγή → διδάσκω + συναγωγή	4,19(-20).44	9,20; 15,21	2		1
κηρύσσω τὸν Ἰησοῦν (SCd) → κηρύσσω τὸν Χριστόν; εὐαγγελίζομαι τὸν Ἰησοῦν/Χριστόν; cf. 2 Cor 11,4 BOISMARD 1984 ca49		9,20; 19,13	0		0
κηρύσσω τὸν Χριστόν (SCd) → κυρύσσω τὸν Ἰησοῦν; εὐαγγελίζομαι τὸν Ἰησοῦν/Χριστόν		8,5	0		0

Characteristic of Luke	Lk	Acts	Mt	Mk
κηρύσσω τὴν βασιλείαν (SCc; VKc); cf. κηρύσσω τὸ εὐαγγέλιον τῆς βασιλείας Mt 4,23; 9,35; 24,14; Mk 1,14 v.l.; κηρύσσω + βασιλεία Mt 3,1; 4,17; 10,7 BOISMARD 1984 Ab85; NEIRYNCK 1985	8,1; 9,2	20,25; 28,31	0	0

Literature

VON BENDEMANN 2001 413: "κηρύσσειν τὴν βασιλείαν τοῦ θεοῦ ... typisch lukanisch"; DENAUX 2009 LA[n] [κηρύσσω τὴν βασιλείαν]; JEREMIAS 1980 176 [κηρύσσω τὴν βασιλείαν τοῦ θεοῦ: red.]; RADL 1975 415 [κηρύσσω; κηρύσσω τὴν βασιλείαν (τοῦ θεοῦ)].

BURCHARD, Christoph, Formen der Vermittlung christlichen Glaubens im Neuen Testament: Beobachtungen anhand von κήρυγμα, μαρτυρία und verwandten Wörtern. — EvT 38 (1978) 313-340. Esp. 321-325: "Lukas".

DUPONT, Jacques, Le discours de Milet, 1962. Esp. 115-117.

GRUMM, Meinert H., Translating kērussō and Related Verbs. — BTrans 21 (1970) 176-179.

MAHFOUZ, Hady, La fonction littéraire et théologique de Lc 3,1-20, 2003. Esp. 115-117.

κιβωτός 1 (Mt 1)

1. boat (Lk 17,27); 2. box

κινδυνεύω 1 + 2

1. be in danger (Lk 8,23); 2. run a risk (Acts 19,27.40)

Characteristic of Luke

BOISMARD 1984 cb32; NEIRYNCK 1985

Literature

DENAUX 2009 lA[n]; HAUCK 1934 [seltenes Alleinwort].

κίχρημι 1   lend (Lk 11,5)

Literature

HAUCK 1934 [seltenes Alleinwort].

BORMANN, Lukas, Recht, Gerechtigkeit und Religion, 2001. Esp. 164.

κλάδος 1 (Mt 3, Mk 2)   branch (Lk 13,19)

κλαίω 11 + 2 (Mt 2, Mk 3[4]) | weep

Word groups	Lk	Acts	Mt	Mk
κλαίω ἐπί + acc. (VKc) DENAUX 2009 L[n]	19,41; 23,28[1.2]		0	0
κλαίω + θρηνέω (VKb)	7,32		0	0
κλαίω + κόπτομαι → θρηνέω + κόπτομαι	8,52[1]		1	0
κλαίω + πενθέω (VKa)	6,25		0	0[1]
μὴ κλαῖε/κλαίετε DENAUX 2009 L[n]	7,13; 8,52[2]; 23,28[1]		0	0
οἱ κλαίοντες (VKd)	6,21		0	0

Characteristic of Luke
DENAUX 2009 L***; GOULDER 1989*; HAWKINS 1909 19; MORGENTHALER 1958L

Literature
COLLISON 1977 55 [linguistic usage of Luke's "other source-material": probable; linguistic usage of Luke: also likely]; 109 [μὴ κλαῖε: noteworthy phenomena]; EASTON 1910 156 [κλαίω ἐπί: probably characteristic of L]; HAUCK 1934 [Vorzugswort; Vorzugsverbindung: κλαίω ἐπί]; REHKOPF 1959 95 [vorlukanisch]; SCHÜRMANN 1961 282 [protoluk R weniger wahrscheinlich].

DUPONT, Jacques, Les Béatitudes, III, 1973. Esp. 69-78: "Ceux qui pleurent".

κλάσις 1 + 1 | breaking

Word groups	Lk	Acts	Mt	Mk
κλάσις τοῦ ἄρτου → (κατα)κλάω ἄρτον DENAUX 2009 LA[n]	24,35	2,42	0	0

Characteristic of Luke
BOISMARD 1984 Ab184; HAWKINS 1909LA; MORGENTHALER 1958*; NEIRYNCK 1985; PLUMMER 1922 liii; VOGEL 1899A

Literature
DENAUX 2009 LA[n]; HAUCK 1934 [seltenes Alleinwort]; JEREMIAS 1980 320: "Die Genitivverbindung ἡ κλάσις τοῦ ἄρτου kommt in der urchristlichen Literatur nur im lukanischen Doppelwerk vor".

TAYLOR, Justin, La fraction du pain en Luc-Actes. — VERHEYDEN, J. (ed.), The Unity of Luke-Acts, 1999, 281-295.

κλάσμα 1 (Mt 2, Mk 4) | piece (Lk 9,17)

Literature
TAYLOR, Justin, La fraction du pain en Luc-Actes. — VERHEYDEN, J. (ed.), The Unity of Luke-Acts, 1999, 281-295.

κλαυθμός 1 + 1 (Mt 7) | weeping (Lk 13,28; Acts 20,37)

Word groups	Lk	Acts	Mt	Mk
κλαυθμός +βρυγμός (SCa; VKa); cf. κλαυθμὸς καὶ ὀδυρμός Mt 2,18	13,28		6	0

κλάω 2 + 4 (Mt 3, Mk 3) — break

Word groups	Lk	Acts	Mt	Mk
κλάω + εὐλογέω (VKb) → κατακλάω + εὐλογέω	24,30		2	1
κλάω + εὐχαριστέω (VKa)	22,19	27,35	1	1

Characteristic of Luke	Lk	Acts	Mt	Mk
κλάω ἄρτον singular (LN: have a meal; SCa; VKb) → κατακλάω ἄρτον; κλάσις τοῦ ἄρτου; cf. 1 Cor 10,16; 11,24 BOISMARD 1984 cb146; NEIRYNCK 1985	22,19; 24,30	2,46; 20,7.11; 27,35	1	1

Literature

DENAUX 2009 lAn [κλάω ἄρτον singular]; SCHÜRMANN 1955 57 [κλᾶν ἄρτον ist dem klassischen Griechisch fremd].

DELEBECQUE, Édouard, Études grecques, 1976. Esp. 109-121: "Le pain et la coupe de la dernière cène (22,17-20)".

SCHWANK, B., « Dankend brach er ». Eucharistie – was bedeutet mir das? — Erbe und Auftrag 77 (2001) 497-505.

TAYLOR, Justin, La fraction du pain en Luc-Actes. — VERHEYDEN, J. (ed.), The Unity of Luke-Acts, 1999, 281-295.

κλείς 1 (Mt 1)

1. key; 2. means of (Lk 11,52)

κλείω 2 + 2 (Mt 3) — close

Word groups	Lk	Acts	Mt	Mk
κλείω + ἀνοίγω → ἀποκλείω/κρούω + ἀνοίγω		5,23	0	0
κλείω + θύρα	11,7	21,30	2	0
κλείω τὸν οὐρανόν (VKa) → (δι)ἀνοίγω τὸν οὐρανόν	4,25		0	0

Κλεοπᾶς 1 — Cleopas (Lk 24,18)

κλέπτης 2 (Mt 3) — thief (Lk 12,33.39)

Word groups	Lk	Acts	Mt	Mk
κλέπτης + διορύσσω	12,39		3	0

κλέπτω 1 (Mt 5, Mk 1) — steal (Lk 18,20)

κληρονομέω 2 (Mt 3, Mk 1)

1. receive; 2. inherit (Lk 10,25; 18,18)

Word groups	Lk	Acts	Mt	Mk
κληρονομέω ζωὴν αἰώνιον (VKb); cf. κληρονομέω βασιλείαν Mt 25,34	10,25; 18,18		1	1

κληρονομία 2 + 2 (Mt 1, Mk 1)

1. possession (Acts 7,5); 2. inheritance (Lk 12,13; 20,14)

Word groups	Lk	Acts	Mt	Mk
κληρονομίαν δίδωμι BOISMARD 1984 Aa140		7,5; 20,32	0	0
κληρονομία + ἐπαγγέλλομαι		7,5	0	0

Literature
BORMANN, Lukas, *Recht, Gerechtigkeit und Religion*, 2001. Esp. 151.
DUPONT, Jacques, *Le discours de Milet*, 1962. Esp. 181.249.251.261-284.

κληρονόμος 1 (Mt 1, Mk 1)

1. receiver; 2. heir (Lk 20,14)

κλῆρος 1 + 5/6 (Mt 1/2, Mk 1)

1. lot (Lk 23,34); 2. possession; 3. ministry (Acts 1,17); 4. responsibility; 5. part (Acts 1,17; 26,18)

Word groups	Lk	Acts	Mt	Mk
βάλλω κλῆρον	23,34		1	1
δίδωμι κλήρους		1,26[1]	0	0
ὁ κλῆρος πίπτει ἐπί + accusative (LN: choose by lot)		1,26[2]	0	0
κλήροι plural (VKa)	23,34	1,26[1]	0	0

Characteristic of Luke
BOISMARD 1984 Ca30

Literature
BEARDSLEE, William A., The Casting of Lots at Qumran and in the Book of Acts. — *NT* 4 (1960) 245-252. [1,26]
DUPONT, Jacques, *Le discours de Milet*, 1962. Esp. 262.266-269.275.
LOHFINK, Gerhard, Der Losvorgang in Apg 1,26. — *BZ* NF 19 (1975) 247-249. [ἔδωκαν κλήρους αὐτοῖς]
THORNTON, L.S., The Choice of Matthias. — *JTS* 46 (1945) 51-59.

κλίβανος 1 (Mt 1)   oven (Lk 12,28)

κλίνη 3 + 0/1 (Mt 2, Mk 3)   bed (Lk 5,18; 8,16; 17,34)

Word groups	Lk	Acts	Mt	Mk
ἐπὶ κλίνης; cf. ἐπὶ τὴν κλίνην Mk 7,30	5,18; 17,34		1	0

| κλίναι plural (*VK*a) | | 5,15* | 0 | 1 |

Literature

HAUCK 1934 [Vorzugsverbindung: ἐπὶ κλίνης].

κλινίδιον* 2 | cot (Lk 5,19.24)

Characteristic of Luke

PLUMMER 1922 liii

Literature

DENAUX 2009 L[n]; HAUCK 1934 [seltenes Alleinwort].

κλίνω 4 (Mt 1)

1. bow (Lk 9,58; 24,5); 2. put to fight; 3. decline (Lk 9,12; 24,29); 4. begin to end (Lk 9,12)

Word groups	Lk	Acts	Mt	Mk
τὴν κεφαλὴν κλίνω (*LN*: lie down to rest)	9,58		1	0
κλίνω τὸ πρόσωπον εἰς τὴν γῆν (*LN*: prostrate oneself)	24,5		0	0
κλίνω intransitive (*VK*a) DENAUX 2009 L[n]	9,12; 24,29		0	0

Characteristic of Luke

DENAUX 2009 L***; GOULDER 1989*; HAWKINS 1909 19

	Lk	Acts	Mt	Mk
κλίνει ἡ ἡμέρα PLUMMER 1922 liii	9,12; 24,29		0	0

Literature

DENAUX 2009 L[n] [κλίνει ἡ ἡμέρα]; HAUCK 1934 [Vorzugswort]; JEREMIAS 1980 318 [κέκλικεν ἤδη ἡ ἡμέρα: red.].

DENAUX, Adelbert & Inge VAN WIELE, The Meaning of the Double Expression of Time in Luke 24,29. – J. VERHEYDEN - G. VAN BELLE - J.G. VAN DER WATT (eds.), *Miracles and Imagery in Luke and John. FS Ulrich Busse* (BETL, 218), Leuven, 2008, 67-88. Esp. 78-86 [κλίνει ἡ ἡμέρα]

κλισία 1 | eating group (Lk 9,14)

Literature

HAUCK 1934 [seltenes Alleinwort].

κλύδων 1 | wave (Lk 8,24)

Literature

HAUCK 1934 [seltenes Alleinwort].

κοιλία 7/8 + 2 (Mt 3, Mk 1)

1. belly (L 15,16; 2. womb (Lk 1,15.41.42.44; 2,21; 11,27; 23,29); 3. feelings; 4. desires

Word groups	Lk	Acts	Mt	Mk
ἐκ κοιλίας μητρός (SCa; VKa) → **χωλὸς** ἐκ κοιλίας μητρός	1,15	3,2; 14,8	1	0
ἐν τῇ κοιλίᾳ + συλλαμβάνω → ἐν **γάστρι/γήρει** συλλαμβάνω	2,21		0	0
καρπὸς τῆς κοιλίας (LN: child)	1,42		0	0
κοιλία + μαστός DENAUX 2009 L[n] (?)	11,27; 23,29		0	0
ἡ κοιλία βαστάζει (LN: be pregnant with)	11,27		0	0
κοιλίαι plural (VKc)	23,29		0	0

Characteristic of Luke	Lk	Acts	Mt	Mk
κοιλία = womb; cf. Jn 3,4; Gal 1,15 BOISMARD 1984 cb33; DENAUX 2009 L***; GOULDER 1989*; HAWKINS 1909 19; NEIRYNCK 1985	1,15.41.42.44; 2,21; 11,27; 23,29	3,2; 14,8	1	0

Literature

VON BENDEMANN 2001 420: "sprachlich lukanisch"; EASTON 1910 162 [κοιλία "womb": cited by Weiss as characteristic of L, and possibly corroborative]; HARNACK 1906 72 [ἐκ κοιλίας μητρός]; JEREMIAS 1980 36 [ἐκ κοιλίας μητρός: "Artikellose Genitivverbindung": trad.]; 57 [καρπὸς τῆς κοιλίας: red.]; PLUMMER 1922 lxi [ἐκ κοιλίας μητρός: Hebrew influence].

κοιμάομαι 1 + 3 (Mt 2)

1. sleep (Lk 22,45; Acts 12,6); 2. be dead (Acts 7,60; 13,36)

κοινωνός 1 (Mt 1)   partner

Word groups	Lk	Acts	Mt	Mk
κοινωνός + dative (VKa)	5,10		0	0

Literature

BAUMERT, Norbert, *Koinonein und metechein – Synonym? Eine umfassende semantische Untersuchung* (SBB, 51). Stuttgart: Verlag Katholisches Bibelwerk, 2003, 564 p.
BORMANN, Lukas, *Recht, Gerechtigkeit und Religion*, 2001. Esp. 151-152.
CAMPBELL, J.Y., Κοινωνία and Its Cognates in the New Testament. — *JBL* 51 (1932) 352-380.

κοιτή 1

1. bed (Lk 11,7); 2. sexual life; 3. sexual immorality

κόκκος 2 (Mt 2, Mk 1)   Seed (Lk 13,19; 17,6)

κολλάω 2 + 5 (Mt 1)

κολλάομαι: 1. join (Lk 15,15; Acts 8,29); 2. cling to (Lk 10,11)

Characteristic of Luke

BOISMARD 1984 cb136; DENAUX 2009 lA*; NEIRYNCK 1985; PLUMMER 1922 lx

Literature

JEREMIAS 1980 186 [red.].

BURCHARD, Christoph, Fußnoten zum neutestamentlichen Griechisch, 1970. Esp. 159-160: "Lc 15,15; Act 5,13; 8,29; 9,26; 10,28; 17,34 κολλᾶσθαι".

HARRILL, J. Albert, The Indentured Labor of the Prodigal Son (Luke 15:15). — *JBL* 115 (1996) 714-717.

SCHWARZ, Günther, "Er hängte sich an einen Bürger"? (Lukas 15,15a). — *BibNot* 85 (1996) 24-25. [NTA 42, 269]

TAEGER, Jens-Wilhelm, *Der Mensch und sein Heil*, 1982. Esp. 149-150.

κόλπος 3 + 1

1. lap (Lk 16,22.23); 2. fold (Lk 6,38); 3. bay (Acts 27,39)

Word groups	Lk	Acts	Mt	Mk
κόλπος (+) Ἀβραάμ (*LN*: heaven) DENAUX 2009 L[n]	16,22.23		0	0
κόλποι plural (*VK*a)	16,23		0	0
κόλπος bay (*VK*b)		27,39	0	0

Characteristic of Luke

BOISMARD 1984 cb112; NEIRYNCK 1985

Literature

DENAUX 2009 La[n]; EASTON 1910 162 [κόλπος "bosom": cited by Weiss as characteristic of L, and possibly corroborative].

κομίζω 1 (Mt 1)

1. carry to (Lk 7,37); 2. cause to experience; κομίζομαι: 3. receive; 4. receive back

Word groups	Lk	Acts	Mt	Mk
κομίζω active (*VK*a)	7,37		0	0

κονιορτός 2 + 2 (Mt 1) dust (Lk 9,5; 10,11; Acts 13,51; 22,23)

Characteristic of Luke

BOISMARD 1984 cb34; DENAUX 2009 LA*; NEIRYNCK 1985; PLUMMER 1922 lx

Literature

HAUCK 1934 [Vorzugswort].

κοπιάω 2 + 1 (Mt 2)

1. labor (Lk 5,5; 12,27; Acts 20,35); 2. be tired; 3. lose heart

Literature

HARNACK, Adolf VON, Κόπος (κοπιᾶν, οἱ κοπιῶντες) im frühchristlichen Sprachgebrauch. — *ZNW* 27 (1928) 1-10.

κόπος 2 (Mt 1, Mk 1)

1. labor; 2. trouble (Lk 11,7; 18,5)

Word groups	Lk	Acts	Mt	Mk
παρέχω + κόπον/κόπους	11,7; 18,5		1	1
κόποι plural (*VK*a)	11,7		1	1

Literature

PAFFENROTH 1997 76.

HARNACK, Adolf VON, Κόπος (κοπιᾶν, οἱ κοπιῶντες) im frühchristlichen Sprachgebrauch. — *ZNW* 27 (1928) 1-10.

κοπρία 1/2

dung heap (Lk 14,35; 13,8*)

Literature

HAUCK 1934 [seltenes Alleinwort].

κόπριον 1

dung (Lk 13,8)

κόπτω 2 (Mt 3, Mk 1)

1. cut; κόπτομαι: 2. mourn (Lk 8,52; 23,27)

Word groups	Lk	Acts	Mt	Mk
κόπτομαι + θρηνέω/κλαίω	8,52; 23,27		1	0
κόπτομαι (*SC*a)	8,52; 23,27		2	0

κόραξ 1

crow, raven (Lk 12,24)

Literature

HAUCK 1934 [seltenes Alleinwort].

κόρος 1

cor (Lk 16,7)

Literature

HAUCK 1934 [seltenes Alleinwort].

κοσμέω 2 (Mt 3)

beautify (Lk 11,25; 21,5)

κόσμος 3 + 1 (Mt 8/9, Mk 2[3])

1. universe (Acts 17,24); 2. earth (Lk 12,30); 3. world system; 4. people; 5. adorning; 6. adornment; 7. tremendous amount

Word groups	Lk	Acts	Mt	Mk
ἀπὸ καταβολῆς κόσμου (SCa; VKh)	11,50		2	0
κόσμος + θεός		17,24	0	0
κόσμος ὅλος (VKb) → ὅλη/πᾶσα ἡ **γῆ**	9,25		2	2

Literature

BDAG 2000 563 [literature].

JOHNSTON, George, Οἰκουμένη and κόσμος in the New Testament. — NTS 10 (1963-64) 352-360.

κόφινος 1 (Mt 2, Mk 2) | large basket (Lk 9,17)

Literature

MURRAY, J.O.F., A Note by the Late Dr Hort on the Words κόφινος, σπυρίς, σαργάνη. — JTS 10 (1908-09) 567-571.

κράζω 3 + 11 (Mt 12, Mk 10/12) | shout

Word groups	Lk	Acts	Mt	Mk
κράζω + λέγω/εἶπον (VKb) → **ἀνακράζω/** **κραυγάζω** + λέγω/εἶπον	4,41*	14,14(-15); 16,17; 19,28	9	4/5
κράζω + σιωπάω	19,40		1	1
κράζω (+) φωνή		7,57.60; 19,34; 24,21	1	1/2
κράζω (+) φωνῇ μεγάλη (VKa) → **ἀνακράζω/βοάω/** **(ἀνα)φωνέω** + φωνῇ μεγάλη		7,57.60	1	1/2

Literature

COLLISON 1977 96 [Luke avoids κράζω: linguistic usage of Luke: likely]; HARNACK 1906 36 [κράζω + λέγων]; JEREMIAS 1980 69 [κράζω + λέγων: red.].

KINMAN, Brent Rogers, "The Stones Will Cry Out" (Luke 19,40) – Joy on Judgment. — Bib 75 (1994) 232-235.

κραιπάλη* 1 | drunken dissipation (Lk 21,34)

Literature

HAUCK 1934 [seltenes Alleinwort].

Κρανίον 1 (Mt 1, Mk 1) | skull (Lk 23,33)

κράσπεδον 1 (Mt 3, Mk 1)
1. fringe (Lk 8,44); 2. tassel

Word groups	Lk	Acts	Mt	Mk
κράσπεδον τοῦ ἱματίου	8,44		2	1

κραταιόω 2

κραταιόομαι: 1. become strong (Lk 2,40); 2. become powerful (Lk 1,80)

κρατέω 2 + 4 (Mt 12, Mk 15)

1. hold on (Lk 8,54; Acts 3,11); 2. control (Lk 24,16; Acts 2,24); 3. arrest (Acts 24,6); 4. keep; 5. accomplish (Acts 27,13)

Word groups	Lk	Acts	Mt	Mk
κρατέω + genitive (thing) (VKa) → κρατέω τῆς χειρός	8,54	27,13	1	3
κρατέω τοῦ + infinitive (VKb)	24,16		0	0

Literature

SCHWARZ, Günther, οι δε οφθαλμοι αυτων εκρατουντο? (Lukas 24,16a). — BibNot 55 (1990) 16-17.
WELLS, Luise, The Greek Language of Healing, 1998. Esp. 200-201.

κράτιστος 1 + 3   most excellent (Lk 1,3)

Characteristic of Luke

BOISMARD 1984 Ab86; HAWKINS 1909LA; MORGENTHALER 1958*; NEIRYNCK 1985; VOGEL 1899A

Literature

DENAUX 2009 IA[n]; GERSDORF 1816 162 [κράτιστε Θεόφιλε]; HAUCK 1934 [seltenes Alleinwort].

ALEXANDER, Loveday, The Preface to Luke's Gospel, 1993. Esp. 132-133 [Lk 1,3].
CADBURY, Henri J., Commentary on the Preface of Luke, 1922. Esp. 505-507 [Lk 1,3].

κράτος 1 + 1

1. power (Acts 19,20); 2. mighty deed (Lk 1,51)

Word groups	Lk	Acts	Mt	Mk
κράτος + ἰσχύω; cf. κράτος + ἰσχύς (VKa) Eph 1,19; 6,10		19,20	0	0

Characteristic of Luke

HARNACK 1906 74.151

Literature

DENAUX 2009 LA[n]; PLUMMER 1922 lxi [ποιεῖν κράτος: Hebrew influence].

LEE, John A.L., A History of New Testament Lexicography, 2003. Esp. 297-304.

κραυγάζω 1 + 1 (Mt 1/2)   shout (Lk 4,41; Acts 22,23)

Word groups	Lk	Acts	Mt	Mk
κραυγάζω + λέγω (VKa) → (ἀνα)κράζω + λέγω/εἶπον	4,41		0/1	0

κραυγή 1 + 1 (Mt 1)

1. shout (Lk 1,42; Acts 23,9); 2. weeping

Word groups	Lk	Acts	Mt	Mk
ἀναφωνέω κραυγῇ μεγάλῃ → **φωνῇ** μεγαλῇ + βοάω/(ἀνα)κράζω/ (ἀνα)φωνέω	1,42		0	0
(λέγω/)εῖπον + κραυγή → λέγω/εῖπον + **φωνή**	1,42		0	0

Characteristic of Luke	Lk	Acts	Mt	Mk
κραυγὴ μεγάλη (VKa) → **φωνὴ** μεγάλη CREDNER 1836 141; HARNACK 1906 139	1,42	23,9	0	0

Literature

DENAUX 2009 LAⁿ [κραυγὴ μεγάλη]; GERSDORF 1816 198 [ἀνεφώνησεν κραυγῇ μεγάλῃ]; HARNACK 1906 131 [ἀναφωνέω κραυγῇ μεγάλῃ]; JEREMIAS 1980 57 [κραυγῇ μεγάλῃ: red.]; RADL 1975 417 [μέγας + κραυγή].

κρεμάννυμι 1 + 3 (Mt 2)

1. cause to hang (Lk 23,39; Acts 5,30; 10,39); κρέμαμαι: 2. hang from (Acts 28,4); 3. depend upon

Word groups	Lk	Acts	Mt	Mk
κρεμάννυμι ἐπὶ ξύλου (LN: crucify); cf. Gal 3,13		5,30; 10,39	0	0
κρεμάννυμι intransitive (VKa)		28,4	1	0

Characteristic of Luke

BOISMARD 1984 Ab133; NEIRYNCK 1985; PLUMMER 1922 lx

Literature

JEREMIAS 1980 306: "Von der Kreuzigung gebrauchtes κρεμάννυμι findet sich im NT außer Gal 3,13 cit. nur im Doppelwerk".

BORMANN, Lukas, Recht, Gerechtigkeit und Religion, 2001. Esp. 183.

κρημνός 1 (Mt 1, Mk 1)   steep slope (Lk 8,33)

κρίμα 3 + 1 (Mt 1/2, Mk 1)

1. legal decision (Acts 24,25); 2. authority to judge; 3. verdict (Lk 23,40; 24,20); 4. condemnation (Lk 20,47); 5. lawsuit; 6. judgment (Acts 24,25)

Word groups	Lk	Acts	Mt	Mk
κρίμα θανάτου (VKc)	24,20		0	0
κρίμα + λαμβάνω (VKb)	20,47		0/1	1
τὸ κρίμα τὸ μέλλον (VKe)		24,25	0	0

Literature

EASTON 1910 162 [cited by Weiss as characteristic of L, and possibly corroborative].

BORMANN, Lukas, Recht, Gerechtigkeit und Religion, 2001. Esp. 183-184.

GARCÍA PÉREZ, José Miguel, El relato del Buen Ladrón (Lc 23,39-43), 1986. Esp. 291-293: "El término κρίμα".

κρίνον 1 (Mt 1)	wild flower (Lk 12,27)

Literature

SUESS, G.E.M., Lilies in the Field. — *Jerusalem Perspective* 46-47 (1994) 18-23.

κρίνω 6 + 21/22 (Mt 6)

1. decide (Acts 3,13); 2. prefer; 3. evaluate (Acts 4,19); 4. hold a view (Lk 7,43; Acts 15,19); 5. make legal decision (Acts 23,3); 6. condemn (Acts 13,27); 7. rule (Lk 22,30)

Word groups	Lk	Acts	Mt	Mk
κρίνω + (τοῦ) infinitive (*VK*j); cf. 1 Cor 2,2; 5,3; Tit 3,12		3,13; 16,15; 20,16; 21,25; 25,25; 27,1	0	0
κρίνω εἰ (*VK*k)		4,19	0	0
κρίνομαι ἐπί + genitive; cf. 1 Cor 6,1 BOISMARD 1984 ca50		24,21; 25,9	0	0
κρίνω κατὰ τὸν νόμον (*VK*d)		23,3; 24,6*	0	0
κρίνω μή + infinitive (*VK*l)		15,19	0	0
κρίνομαι περί + genitive (*VK*e) BOISMARD 1984 Aa54		23,6; 24,21; 25,9.20	0	0
κρίνω τὴν οἰκουμένην (*VK*c)		17,31	0	0

Characteristic of Luke

DENAUX 2009 1A**; MORGENTHALER 1958A

	Lk	Acts	Mt	Mk
κρίνω in the wider sense DENAUX 2009 1A*; HARNACK 1906 34.52	7,43; 12,57	4,19; 13,46; 15,19; 16,4.15; 20,16; 21,25; 25,25; 26,8; 27,1	0	0

Literature

JEREMIAS 1980 171: "κρίνω in der abgeschwächten Bedeutung 'urteilen, meinen, erklären, halten' im NT außer bei Paulus (dreimal) nur bei Lukas" (Lk 7,43; Acts 4,19; 13,46; 15,19; 16,15; 26,8); 224: "In der Bedeutung 'sich entscheiden für, beschließen, sich vornehmen, wollen' ... kommt κρίνω im NT außer 6mal bei Paulus nur im lk Doppelwerk (Ev 1/Apg 6mal) vor"; RADL 1975 415 [κρίνω; κρίνω + inf.; κρίνω περί].

BORMANN, Lukas, *Recht, Gerechtigkeit und Religion*, 2001. Esp. 184.

κρίσις 4 + 1 (Mt 12, Mk 0/2)

1. legal decision; 2. authority to judge; 3. court of justice; 4. verdict; 5. condemnation; 6. justice (Lk 11,42; Acts 8,33); 7. judgment (Lk 10,14; 11,31.32); 8. basis for judgment; 9. punishment

Word groups	Lk	Acts	Mt	Mk
ἐν τῇ κρίσει (*SC*b; *VK*d)	10,14; 11,31.32		2	0

Literature

BORMANN, Lukas, *Recht, Gerechtigkeit und Religion*, 2001. Esp. 185.

κριτής 6 + 4 (Mt 3)	judge

Word groups	Lk	Acts	Mt	Mk
κριτής τις	18,2		0	0
κριταί plural (VKa)	11,19	13,20	1	0

Characteristic of Luke

DENAUX 2009 L***†; GOULDER 1989*; HAWKINS 1909 †L

Literature

HAUCK 1934 [Vorzugsverbindung: κριτής τις].

BORMANN, Lukas, *Recht, Gerechtigkeit und Religion*, 2001. Esp. 185.

κρούω 4 + 2 (Mt 2)   knock

Word groups	Lk	Acts	Mt	Mk
κρούω + θύρα (VKa) → ἀνοίγω/(ἀπο)κλείω + θύρα DENAUX 2009 LA^n	13,25	12,13	0	0

Characteristic of Luke

DENAUX 2009 L***†; GOULDER 1989*; HAWKINS 1909 †L

	Lk	Acts	Mt	Mk
κρούω + ἀνοίγω → (ἀπο)κλείω + ἀνοίγω DENAUX 2009 L*** (?)	11,9.10; 12,36; 13,25	12,16	2	0

κρύπτη* 1   secret place (Lk 11,33)

Literature

HAUCK 1934 [seltenes Alleinwort].

κρυπτός 2/3 (Mt 5/7, Mk 1)   secret (Lk 8,17; 12,2)

κρύπτω 2/3 (Mt 7)

1. keep safe; 2. made invisible; 3. hide; 4. keep secret (Lk 18,34; 19,42)

Word groups	Lk	Acts	Mt	Mk
κρύπτω ἀπό → ἀποκρύπτω/παρακαλύπτω ἀπό	18,34; 19,42		2	0

Literature

EASTON 1910 163 [cited by Weiss as characteristic of L, and possibly corroborative].

κτάομαι 2 + 3 (Mt 1)   acquire (Lk 18,12; 21,19; Acts 1,18; 8,20; 22,28)

Word groups	Lk	Acts	Mt	Mk
κτάομαι τὴν ψυχήν (LN: protect oneself)	21,19		0	0

Characteristic of Luke

BOISMARD 1984 cb78; DENAUX 2009 IA*; NEIRYNCK 1985; PLUMMER 1922 lx

Literature
RADL 1975 415.

κτῆνος 1 + 1 | beast of burden (Lk 10,34; Acts 23,24)

Literature
DENAUX 2009 LA[n]; HAUCK 1934 [seltenes Alleinwort]; JEREMIAS 1980 192 [red.].

κυκλόω 1 + 1
1. go around; 2. surround (Lk 21,20; Acts 14,20)

Literature
DENAUX 2009 LA[n]; HAUCK 1934 [seltenes Alleinwort].

κύκλῳ 1 (Mk 3) | around

Word groups	Lk	Acts	Mt	Mk
κύκλῳ κῶμαι	9,12		0	1

Κυρηναῖος 1 + 3 (Mt 1, Mk 1) | a Cyrenian (Lk 23,26; Acts 6,9; 11,20; 13,1)

Κυρήνιος 1 | Quirinius (Lk 2,2)

κυριεύω 1 | rule (Lk 22,25)

Literature
BORMANN, Lukas, *Recht, Gerechtigkeit und Religion*, 2001. Esp. 152.
CLARK, Kenneth W., The Meaning of [κατα]κυριεύειν. – ELLIOTT, J.K. (ed.), *Studies in New Testament Language and Text*. FS George D. Kilpatrick, 1976, 100-105.

κύριος 104/109 + 107/122 (Mt 80/84, Mk 16[18]/20)
1. Lord (Lk 1,6); 2. owner (Lk 19,33); 3. ruler; 4. sir (Lk 19,16)

Word groups	Lk	Acts	Mt	Mk
ἄνθρωποι plural + κύριος → ἄνθρωπος singular + **κύριος**; ἄνθρωποι plural + **θεός** DENAUX 2009 LA[n]	1,25; 12,36	15,17[1].26	0	0
ἄνθρωπος singular + κύριος → ἄνθρωποι plural + **κύριος**; ἄνθρωπος singular + **θεός**	6,5		2	1
δικαιώματα τοῦ κυρίου (*SC*ag) → νόμος **κυρίου**	1,6		0	0
δόξα κυρίου → δόξα **θεοῦ**	2,9[2]		0	0

δουλεύω κυρίῳ → δουλεύω **θεῷ**		20,19	0	0
δύναμις κυρίου (*SC*ae) → δύναμις τοῦ **θεοῦ**	5,17		0	0
ἐν τῷ κυρίῳ → ἐν τῷ Ἰησοῦ		11,23 *v.l.*	0	0
ἐντολή + τοῦ κυρίου; cf. ἐντολὴ τοῦ **θεοῦ** Mt 15,3; Mk 7,8.9	1,6		0	0
ἡμέρα κυρίου (*VK*w)		2,20	0	0
κύριε κύριε (*SC*bf; *VK*r)	6,46[1.2]; 13,25[1.2]		6	0
κύριος ἀγαπάω → **θεός** + ἀγαπάω/ἀγαπή	10,27		1	1
κύριος + βασιλεύς (*VK*d)	19,38		0	0
κύριος + δοῦλος (*VK*m); see also **κύριος** as master (of a slave); **κύριος** + οἰκέτης	12,37.43.45.46. 47; 14,21.22.23; 19,16.18.20	4,29	22/23	0
κύριος (ἡμῶν) Ἰησοῦς (*SC*ba; *VK*h)	24,3	1,21; 4,33; 7,59; 8,16; 9,17.28 *v.l.*; 11,20; 15,11; 16,31; 19,5.10 *v.l.*13.17; 20,21.24.35; 21,13	0	0[1]
κύριος (ἡμῶν) Ἰησοῦς Χριστός (*SC*bb; *VK*j); see also **κύριος** + χριστός		4,33 *v.l.*; 11,17; 15,11 *v.l.*26; 16,31 *v.l.*; 20,21 *v.l.*; 28,31	0	0
κύριος + οἰκέτης → **κύριος** as master (of a slave); **κύριος** + δοῦλος	16,13		0	0
κύριος (τοῦ) οὐρανοῦ καὶ (τῆς) γῆς (*VK*n)	10,21	17,24	1	0
κύριος πάντων (*VK*p)		10,36	0	0
κύριος + πατήρ (*VK*c) → **θεός** + πατήρ/πατέρες	10,21		1	0/1
κύριος + σωτήρ (*VK*e)	2,11		0	0
κύριος + υἱός (*VK*l)	6,5; 20,44		5	2
κύριος + υἱὸς τοῦ ἀνθρώπου (*SC*bd)	6,5		1	1
κύριος (+) χριστός (*SC*aj.bj; *VK*k); see also **κύριος** (ἡμῶν) Ἰησοῦς Χριστός DENAUX 2009 IA[n]	2,11.26	2,36; 3,20; 4,26		
λέγει κύριος of scripture (*VK*y)		7,49; 15,17[2]	0	0
μεγαλύνω (+) κύριος → **δυνατός** + μεγάλα; μεγαλύνω + **θεός**; μεγαλειότης τοῦ **θεοῦ** DENAUX 2009 La[n]	1,46.58	19,17	0	0
ναὸς τοῦ κυρίου	1,9		0	0
νόμος κυρίου (*SC*ag) → δικαίωματα τοῦ **κυρίου**; cf. νόμος τοῦ **θεοῦ** Mt 15,6* DENAUX 2009 L[n]	2,23[1].24.39		0	0
ὄνομα κυρίου (*SC*ah; *VK*s) → ὄνομα (τοῦ) Ἰησοῦ	13,35; 19,38	2,21	2	1/2
ὄνομα τοῦ κυρίου (*SC*bh)		9,28; 10,48*	0	0
ὄνομα τοῦ κυρίου (…) Ἰησοῦ (Χριστοῦ) (*SC*bg)		8,16; 10,48* *v.l.*; 15,26; 19,5.13.17; 21,13; 22,16*	0	0
ὀνομάζω τὸ ὄνομα κυρίου (*LN*: say that one belongs to the Lord); cf. 2 Tit 2,19		19,13	0	0
τὰ περὶ τοῦ κυρίου (*VK*x)		18,25*; 28,31	0	0
προστίθημι τῷ κυρίῳ		5,14; 11,24	0	0
ῥῆμα τοῦ κυρίου (*SC*bc; *VK*u) → λόγος τοῦ **κυρίου**; ῥῆμα (τοῦ) **θεοῦ** DENAUX 2009 LA[n]	22,61[2]	11,16	0	0

σῶμα (τοῦ) κυρίου	24,3		0	0
φόβος τοῦ κυρίου		9,31	0	0
κύριε (1x) (SCbf)	5,8.12; 7,6; 9,54.57*.[59].61; 10,17.40; 11,1; 12,41; 13,23.25; 17,37; 18,41; 19,8²; 22,33.38.49; 23,42*	1,6; 7,59.60; 9,5.6¹*.10².13; 22,8.10¹.19; 26,15¹	21/24	1
κύριοι plural (VKz)	16,13; 19,33	16,16.19.30	2	0
κύριος The Lord (God) (SCa); see also ἄγγελος κυρίου; δικαιώματα τοῦ κυρίου; δύναμις κυρίου; κύριος ὁ θεός; κύριος (τοῦ) οὐρανοῦ καὶ (τῆς) γῆς; κύριος + χριστός; νόμος κυρίου; ὄνομα κυρίου; πνεῦμα κυρίου; χεὶρ κυρίου	1,9.15.17.25.28.38. 45.46.58; 2,9².15. 22.23².38*; 4,19; 20,42¹	1,24; 2,25.34¹.47; 3,20; 4,29; 7,31.33.49; 8,22.24; 9,31; 10,14.33; 11,8; 12,11. 17; 13,2.10; 15,17¹·²; 16,10*.14; 17,27*; 20,28*; 21,14.20*	6	5
κύριος as master (of a slave) (SCc); see also κύριος + δοῦλος/οἰκέτης	9,57*; 12,36.37.42². 43.45.46.47; 13,8; 14,21.22.23; 16,3. 5¹·².13; 19,16.18. 20.25; 23,42*	16,16.19	23	0
κύριος as 'sir' (SCd)		10,4; 16,30; 25,26	2	0
→ θέλημα τοῦ κυρίου				

Characteristic of Luke

HARNACK 1906 33; HENDRIKS 1986 428.434.448; MORGENTHALER 1958LA

	Lk	Acts	Mt	Mk
ἄγγελος κυρίου (SCab; VKt) → ἄγγελος τοῦ θεοῦ; cf. ἄγγελος αὐτοῦ Mt 4,6; Mk 13,27 v.l.; Lk 4,10; Acts 12,11; ἄγγελος μου Mt 11,10; Mk 1,2; Lk 7,27 HARNACK 1906 71	1,11; 2,9¹	5,19; 7,30*; 8,26; 12,7.23	5	0
ἐνώπιον (τοῦ) κυρίου → ἔμπροσθεν/ἐναντίον/ἐνώπιον τῶν ἀγγέλων τοῦ θεοῦ / τῶν ἀνθρώπων / (τοῦ) θεοῦ PLUMMER 1922 lx	1,15.76		0	0
ἐπιστρέφω ἐπὶ (τὸν) κύριον/θεόν → ἐπιστρέφω ἐπὶ (τὸν) θεόν BOISMARD 1984 Ab25; NEIRYNCK 1985	1,16	9,35; 11,21²; 14,15; 15,19; 26,20	0	0
κύριος for Jesus (Christ) (SCb); see also κύριε (κύριε); κύριος (ἡμῶν) Ἰησοῦς (Χριστός); κύριος + υἱὸς τοῦ ἀνθρώπου; κύριος + χριστός; λόγος/ῥῆμα τοῦ κυρίου; (τὸ) ὄνομα τοῦ κυρίου DENAUX 2009 lA**	1,43.76; 3,4; 7,13. 19.31*; 10,1.39.41; 11,39; 12,42¹; 13,15; 16,8; 17,5.6; 18,6; 19,8¹.31.34; 20,42².44; 22,31*. 61¹; 24,34	2,20.34²; 5,14; 9,1.5*. 6²*.10¹.11.15.27. 35. 42; 10,36; 11,21².23. 24; 13,12.47; 14,3.23; 15,40; 16,15; 18,8.9. 25; 20,19; 22,10²; 23,11; 26,15²	6/7	5[6]
ὁ κύριος in narrative; cf. Jn 4,11; 6,23; 11,2; 20,20; 21,12 DENAUX 2009 L***; GOULDER 1989*; HAWKINS 1909L	7,13.19; 10,1.39.41; 12,42¹; 13,15; 17,5.6; 18,6; 19,8¹; 22,61¹		0	0[2]
κύριος ὁ θεός (SCaa; VKa) BOISMARD 1984 db17; GOULDER 1989; NEIRYNCK 1985	1,16.32.68; 4,8.12; 10,27; 20,37	2,39; 3,22; 7,37*	3	2

κύριος + θεός (*VK*b) DENAUX 2009 lA*	1,6.(8-)9.46(-47); 16,13	2,36; 10,33; 17,24; 20,21.24; 28,31	0	0[1]
ὁ κύριος Ἰησοῦς BOISMARD 1984 Db1; NEIRYNCK 1985	24,3	1,21; 4,33; 7,59; 8,16; 11,17.20; 15,11.26; 16,31; 19,5.13.17; 20,21. 24.35; 21,13; 28,31	0	0
ὁ λόγος τοῦ κυρίου (*SC*bc; *VK*u) → ῥῆμα τοῦ **κυρίου**; **ἀκούω** τὸν λόγον θεοῦ/κυρίου; λόγος τοῦ **θεοῦ** BOISMARD 1984 Da1; PLUMMER 1922 lix	22,61[2] *v.l.*	8,25; 12,24*; 13,44.48.49; 14,25*; 15,35.36; 16,32; 19,10.20; 20,35	0	0
ὁδὸς (τοῦ) κυρίου/αὐτοῦ → ὁδὸς τοῦ **θεοῦ** BOISMARD 1984 Aa146	1,76; 3,4	13,10; 18,25	1	1
πνεῦμα κυρίου (*SC*ad) BOISMARD 1984-Da19	4,18	5,9; 8,39	0	0
χάρις (τοῦ) κυρίου/θεοῦ (*VK*v) → χάρις (τοῦ) **θεοῦ**; cf. κύριος + χάρις αὐτοῦ Acts 14,3 BOISMARD 1984 Db9; NEIRYNCK 1985	2,40	11,23; 13,43;14,26; 15,11.40; 20,24	0	0
χεὶρ κυρίου (*SC*af) BOISMARD 1984 Ab153; NEIRYNCK 1985; PLUMMER 1922 lii	1,66	11,21[1]; 13,11	0	0

→ **λαλέω** τὸν λόγον τοῦ θεοῦ/κυρίου; **πίστις** εἰς (κύριον/Χριστὸν) Ἰησοῦν; **πιστεύω** τῷ κυρίῳ / ἐπὶ τὸν κύριον; ὁ **χριστὸς** (τοῦ) θεοῦ/κυρίου

Literature

BDAG 2000 576-579 [literature]; DENAUX 2009 L[n] [ἐνώπιον (τοῦ) κυρίου]; lA[n] [ἐπιστρέφω ἐπὶ (τὸν) κύριον; ὁ κύριος Ἰησοῦς; πνεῦμα κυρίου; χάρις (τοῦ) κυρίου/θεοῦ; χεὶρ κυρίου]; EASTON 1910 149 [κύριος, of Christ: especially characteristic of L]; GERSDORF 1816 193 [κύριος - ἐπεῖδεν]; 238 [ὁ κύριος ἐγνώρισεν ἡμῖν]; 245 [ἐν νόμῳ κυρίου]; 252 [τὸν χριστὸν κυρίου]; HARNACK 1906 139 (ET: 201: "It is well known that St. Luke constantly uses ὁ κύριος for Christ"); HAUCK 1934 [ὁ κύριος in narrative: häufiges Alleinwort]; JEREMIAS 1980 23-24: "In der lukanischen Kindheitsgeschichte liest man den Titel (ὁ) κύριος im ganzen 27mal; nicht weniger als 24mal davon ... ist er auf Gott bezogen, nur 3mal (1,43.76; 2,11) auf Jesus. Diese Anwendung des Titels κύριος auf Gott ist nicht-lukanischer Sprachgebrauch"; 31 [ἄγγελος κυρίου: trad.]; 36 [κύριος ὁ θεός: trad.]; 57: "110 Belege für den christologischen Bezug des Kyriostitels, die sich im lk Doppelwerk finden. Lukas läßt den theologischen Bezug des Titels zurücktreten, weil ihm der christologische der geläufige war... Bei diesem muß unterschieden werden zwischen der Anwendung des Titels auf den irdischen und auf den erhöhten Herrn. Die 14 Stellen des LkEv, an denen der irdische Herr in der Erzählung ὁ κύριος genannt wird, und die 19 Belege im LkEv für die Anrede des Irdischen mit κύριε sind ... vorlukanisch. Das Gros der Stellen jedoch, die den Kyriostitel christologisch verwenden, ist im Doppelwerk auf den Erhöhten bezogen und findet sich in der Apg. Diese Stellen stammen aus der Feder des Lukas, wie schon die vielen Belege in der Apg zeigen, aber auch die zahlreichen mit ihnen zusammenhängenden missionstheologischen Termini, für die Lukas eine Vorliebe hat"; RADL 1975 415 [εἶπεν δὲ ... ὁ κύριος]; 419-420 [ὄνομα τοῦ κυρίου Ἰησοῦ]; REHKOPF 1959 95 [vorlukanisch]; 99 [κύριε (von Menschen): "Substantiva in Anrede bei den Synoptikern"]; SCHNEIDER 1969 93.163 [ὁ λόγος τοῦ κυρίου: Vorzugswörter und -ausdrücke des Luk]; SCHÜRMANN 1955 54-55 [(ὁ) κύριος (ἡμῶν) Ἰησοῦς (ohne Χριστός)]; 1957 28-29 [κύριε als Anrede "mögliche luk Sprechweise" (130)]; 1961 282-283 [protoluk R weniger wahrscheinlich].

BORMANN, Lukas, *Recht, Gerechtigkeit und Religion*, 2001. Esp. 152-153.

BOUSSET, Wilhelm, *Jesus der Herr: Nachträge und Auseinandersetzungen zu Kurios Christos.* Göttingen: Vandenhoeck & Ruprecht, 1916, 95 p.

BRANDT, Pierre-Yves & Alessandra LUKINOVICH, L'adresse à Jésus dans les évangiles synoptiques. — *Bib* 82 (2001) 17-50.

BUTH, Randall, Luke 19:31-34, Mishnaic Hebrew, and Bible Translation: Is κύριοι τοῦ πώλου singular? — *JBL* 104 (1985) 680-685.

DAWSEY, James M., What's in a Name? Characterization in Luke. — *BTB* 16 (1986) 143-147. Esp. 145-146: "Luke's use of 'Lord'".

DE LA POTTERIE, Ignace, Le titre *kurios* appliqué à Jésus dans l'évangile de Luc. — DESCAMPS, A. – DE HALLEUX, A. (eds.), *Mélanges bibliques en hommage au R.P. Béda Rigaux*, 1970, 117-146.

DICKEY, E., Κύριε, δέσποτα, *domine*. Greek Politeness in the Roman Empire. — *JHS* 121 (2001) 1-11.

DUNN, James D.G., Κύριος in Acts. — LANDMESSER, Christof – ECKSTEIN, Hans-Joachim – LICHTENBERGER, Hermann (eds.), *Jesus Christus als die Mitte der Schrift: Studien zur Hermeneutik des Evangeliums* (BZNW, 86). Berlin – New York: de Gruyter, 1997, 363-378.

GEORGE, Augustin, Jésus "Seigneur". — ID., *Études*, 1978, 237-255.

GREENLEE, J. Harold, Kurios "Lord". — *BTrans* 1 (1950) 106-108.

HAGENE, Sylvia, *Zeiten der Wiederherstellung*, 2003. Esp. 189-193: "Besonderheiten der Verwendung von κύριος bei Lukas".

HAHN, Ferdinand, *Christologische Hoheitstitel*, 1963. Esp. 67-125: "Kyrios".

KILPATRICK, George D., "Kurios" in the Gospels. — *L'évangile hier et aujoud'hui: Mélanges offerts au Professeur Franz-J. Leenhardt*. Genève: Labor et Fides, 1968, 65-70; = ID., *Principles and Practice*, 1990, 207-212.

—, Kyrios in the Gospels. — *Δελτίον τοῦ ΕΦΣΑ, 1969*, Famagusta, 1970; = ID., *Principles and Practice*, 1990, 213-215.

—, The Gentiles and the Strata of Luke. — BÖCHER, O. – HAACKER, K. (eds.), *Verborum Veritas*. FS G. Stählin, 1970, 83-88. Esp. 84-85; = ID., *Principles and Practice*, 1990, 313-318. Esp. 317.

—, Κύριος Again. — HOFFMANN, P. – BROX, N. – PESCH, W. (eds.), *Orientierung an Christus*. FS J. Schmid, 1973, 214-219; = ID., *Principles and Practice*, 1990, 216-222.

LOEWEN, Jacob, The Names of God in the New Testament. — *BTrans* 35 (1984) 208-211. Esp. 209-210: "Kurios".

O'NEILL, John C., The Use of "κύριος" in the Book of Acts. — *AusBibRev* 4 (1954-55) 17-47; = *ScotJT* 8 (1955) 155-174.

PHILIPOSE, John, Kurios in Luke: A Diagnosis. — *BTrans* 43 (1992) 325-333.

PRETE, Benedetto, "Oggi vi è nato … il Salvatore che è il Cristo Signore" (*Lc* 2,11). — *RivBib* 34 (1986) 289-325. Esp. 317-320: "Signore (κύριος)".

READ-HEIMERDINGER, Jenny, *The Bezan Text of Acts*, 2002. Esp. 254-274: "Titles of Jesus" [(ὁ) Ἰησοῦς; Ἰησοῦς ὁ Ναζωραῖος; ὁ παῖς; ὁ ἅγιος παῖς σου Ἰησοῦς; (ὁ) Χριστός; Χριστὸς Ἰησοῦς; Ἰησοῦς Χριστός; Ἰησοῦς Χριστὸς ὁ Ναζωραῖος; (ὁ) κύριος; (ὁ) κύριος Ἰησοῦς; ὁ κύριος Ἰησοῦς Χριστός]; 275-310: "Ὁ Κύριος and ὁ θεός".

REID, John, "Lord" and "the Lord" in Acts. — *ExpT* 15 (1903-04) 296-300.

RESE, Martin, *Alttestamentliche Motive in der Christologie des Lukas*, 1969. Esp. 126-131: "Κύριος in der Apostelgeschichte"; 205-206: "Κύριος im Lukasevangelium".

SCHNEIDER, Gerhard, Gott und Christus als κύριος nach der Apostelgeschichte. — ZMIJEWSKI, Josef – NELLESSEN, Ernst (eds.), *Begegnung mit dem Wort. Festschrift für Heinrich Zimmermann* (BBB, 53). Bonn: Hanstein, 1980, 161-174; = ID., *Lukas, Theologe der Heilsgeschichte*, 1985, 213-226.

SCHWARZ, Günther, "…lobte den betrügerischen Verwalter"? (Lukas 16,8a). — *BZ* NF 18 (1974) 94-95. Esp. 94: "…, wer in V. 8a (…) mit dem κύριος gemeint ist … erledigt sich von selbst, wenn die Fehlübersetzung der entscheidenden Vokabeln (ἐπήνεσεν und φρονίμως)

korrigiert sein wird". [NTA 19, 588]
STEINHAUSER, Michael G., Noah in His Generation: An Allusion in Luke 16 8b, "εἰς τὴν γενεὰν τὴν ἑαυτῶν" — ZNW 79 (1988) 152-157.
VOSS, Gerhard, Die Christologie der lukanischen Schriften in Grundzügen, 1965. Esp. 45-60: "Σωτήρ und κύριος als herrscherliche Jesusprädikate".
WINTER, Paul, Lukanische Miszellen. — ZNW 49 (1958) 65-77. Esp. 67-75: "Lc 2,11: χριστὸς κύριος oder χριστὸς κυρίου"?

κύων 1 (Mt 1)

1. dog (Lk 16,21); 2. bad person; 3. pervert

κωλύω 6 + 6 (Mt 1, Mk 3)   prevent

Word groups	Lk	Acts	Mt	Mk
κωλύω + (τοῦ) infinitive (VKc)	23,2	8,36; 10,47; 16,6; 24,23	1	0
κωλύω + ἀπό → (ἀπ)αἰτέω/(ἐκ)ζητέω ἀπό/παρά	6,29		0	0
κωλύω τινά τινός (VKb)		27,43	0	0
τί κωλύει; (VKa)		8,36	0	0

Characteristic of Luke
BOISMARD 1984 Eb54; GOULDER 1989; NEIRYNCK 1985; PLUMMER 1922 lx

Literature
COLLISON 1977 96 [noteworthy phenomena]; DENAUX 2009 LAn; HAUCK 1934 [Vorzugswort]; JEREMIAS 1980 143: "Lukas hat eine gewisse Vorliebe für κωλύειν... Die Person, die an etwas gehindert bzw. von etwas abgehalten wird, führt er regelmäßig im Akkusativ ein (9,49; 11,52; 18,16/Apg 8,36; 11,17; 24,23; 27,43), einzig an unserer Stelle [Lk 6,29] mit semitisierendem ἀπό; sie gibt sich damit als vorlukanisch zu erkennen"; RADL 1975 415.

ARGYLE, A.W., O. Cullmann's Theory concerning κωλύειν. — ExpT 67 (1955-56) 17.

κώμη 12 + 1 (Mk 4, Mk 7/8)

1. village (Lk 5,17); 2. people of a village (Acts 8,25)

Word groups	Lk	Acts	Mt	Mk
διαπορεύομαι κατὰ πόλεις καὶ κώμας / **διέρχομαι** κατὰ τὰς κώμας / διοδεύω κατὰ πόλιν καὶ κώμην + participle καί participle	8,1; 9,6; 13,22		0	0
εἰσέρχομαι εἰς κώμην → εἰσέρχομαι εἰς **πολίν** DENAUX 2009 Ln	9,52; 10,38; 17,12		0	1
κατὰ πόλιν καὶ κώμην / πόλεις καὶ κώμας	8,1; 13,22		0	0
κύκλῳ κώμαι	9,12		0	1
κώμη + ἀγρός (SCb; VKb) → **πόλις** + ἀγρός	9,12		0	2
κώμη + πόλις (SCa; VKa)	8,1; 13,22		2	1
κώμη τις	10,38; 17,12		0	0
πορεύομαι (+ εἰσέρχομαι) εἰς κώμην/κώμας	9,12.52.56; 10,38; 24,13.28		1	0

Characteristic of Luke	Lk	Acts	Mt	Mk
κώμη/πόλις/χώρα + determinative of region → **πόλις/χώρα** + determ. of region	1,26; 4,31; 5,17	8,1.5; 26,20	0	0

BOISMARD 1984 Bb34; DENAUX 2009 LA*; NEIRYNCK 1985

κώμη + proper name (VKc) → **πόλις/χώρα** + proper name; κώμη (τῶν) **Σαμαριτῶν** BOISMARD 1984 cb35; DENAUX 2009 La*; NEIRYNCK 1985	5,17; 9,52; 24,13	8,25	0	1

Literature
HAUCK 1934 [Vorzugsverbindung: κώμη τις].

Κωσάμ 1   Cosam (Lk 3,28)

κωφός 4 (Mt 7, Mk 3)
1. mute (Lk 1,22; 11,14[1.2]); 2. deaf (Lk 7,22)

Word groups	Lk	Acts	Mt	Mk
κωφός ἀκούω	7,22		1	1
κωφός + λαλέω	11,14[2]		3	0
κωφός + τυφλός (VKa)	7,22		4/5	0
κωφός + χωλός	7,22		1	0

Literature
WEISSENRIEDER, A., *Images of Illness in the Gospel of Luke*, 2003. Esp. 119-123: "Κωφός in the New Testament".

Λ

λαγχάνω 1 + 1
1. receive (Acts 1,17); 2. choose by lot; 3. be chosen by lot (Lk 1,9)

Literature
DENAUX 2009 LA[n]; GERSDORF 1816 174 [ἔλαχε τοῦ θυμιᾶσαι].

Λάζαρος 4   Lazarus

Word groups	Lk	Acts	Mt	Mk
Λάζαρος mendicant (VKb) DENAUX 2009 (L[n])	16,20.23.24.25		0	0

λαῖλαψ 1 (Mk 1)   windstorm

Word groups	Lk	Acts	Mt	Mk
λαῖλαψ ἀνέμου	8,23		0	1

λαλέω 31 + 59/63 (Mt 26, Mk 19[21]/22)   speak

Word groups	Lk	Acts	Mt	Mk
ἀκούω τινὸς λαλοῦντος; cf. Jn 1,37 BOISMARD 1984 Ba10		2,6.11; 6,11; 10,46; 14,9	0	0
ἄρχομαι (+) λαλεῖν DENAUX 2009 1Aⁿ	7,15	2,4; 11,15	0	0
γλώσσαις (+) λαλέω (SCe; VKf)		2,4.11; 10,46; 19,6	0	0[1]
ἔτι αὐτοῦ λαλοῦντος	8,49; 22,47.60		3	2
κωφός + λαλέω	11,14		3	0
λαλέω (+) λέγω/εἶπον (VKg) → ὀνομάζω/συλλαλέω + λέγω	5,4; 12,3; 24,6(-7)	8,26; 26,14*.22.31; 28,25(-26)	4	1
λαλέω (+) τὸν λόγον (SCb; VKb) → λαλέω (τὸ) ῥῆμα	24,44	4,29.31; 8,25; 11,19; 13,46; 14,25; 16,6.32	0	4
λαλέω τὸν λόγον τοῦ θεοῦ/κυρίου; cf. Heb 13,7 BOISMARD 1984 Ca31		4,29.31; 8,25; 13,46; 16,32	0	0
λαλέω + μετὰ παρρησίας (VKe); cf. λαλέω παρρησίᾳ Mk 8,32		4,29.31	0	0
λαλέω πρὸς ἀλλήλους → δια/συλλαλέω + πρὸς ἀλλήλους DENAUX 2009 LAⁿ	2,15	26,31	0	0
λαλέω + φωνή (VKj)		22,9; 26,14*	0	0
τὰ λαληθέντα/λαληθησόμενα (VKl)	2,18		0	0
τὰ λαλούμενα (VKk) → τὸ λαλούμενον DENAUX 2009 1Aⁿ	2,33	13,45; 16,14	0	0
τὰ λελαλημένα (VKm)	1,45		0	0
πρὸς τὸ οὖς λαλέω (LN: whisper)	12,3		0	0

Characteristic of Luke	Lk	Acts	Mt	Mk
λαλέομαι passive GOULDER 1989; DENAUX 2009 L***; HARNACK 1906 140	1,45; 2,17. 18.20.33	9,6; 13,42.45.46; 16,14; 17,19; 22,10; 27,25	1	1
λαλέομαι/λέγεσθαι ὑπό + genitive → λέγομαι ὑπό + gen.; cf. Heb 9,19 BOISMARD 1984 Cb12; DENAUX 2009 1A*; HARNACK 1906 33; NEIRYNCK 1985	2,18; 9,7	8,6; 13,45; 16,14; 17,19; 27,11	0	0
λαλέω with an angel as speaker → λέγω/εἶπον + ἄγγελος as subject; cf. Jn 12,29 BOISMARD 1984 Eb37; NEIRYNCK 1985	1,19	7,38; 8,26; 10,7; 23,9	0	0
λαλέω with God as subject; cf. other references with God as speaker (SCg) Lk 1,45; Acts 7,44; 27,25 BOISMARD 1984 Db25; NEIRYNCK 1985	1,55.70	3,21; 7,6	0	0
λαλέω of the prophets DENAUX 2009 1A*; VOGEL 1899C	1,70; 24,25	3,21.22.24; 26,22; 28,25	0	0
λαλέω περί + gen. DENAUX 2009 La*; GOULDER 1989*	2,33.38; 9,11	2,31	0	0
λαλέω πρός + accusative (person) (SCa; VKa) → verb of saying πρός + acc.; cf. 1 Thess 2,2; Heb 5,5; 11,18 BOISMARD 1984 Bb70; CREDNER 1836 138; DENAUX 2009 L***; HARNACK 1906 143.146.151; NEIRYNCK 1985; PLUMMER 1922 lxii	1,19.55; 2,15.18.20; 24,44	3,22; 4,1; 8,26; 9,29; 11,14.20; 21,39; 26,14*.26. 31; 28,25	0	0
λαλέω (τὸ) ῥῆμα / (τὰ) ῥήματα (SCc; VKc) → λαλέω τὸν λόγον; διαλαλέω τὸ ῥῆμα; cf. Jn 3,34; 6,63; 8,20; 14,10 BOISMARD 1984 Cb156; DENAUX 2009 1A*; NEIRYNCK 1985	2,17.50	5,20; 6,11.13; 10,44; 11,14; 13,42	1	0

λαλέω + στόμα (SCf; VKh)	1,64.70;	3,21	1	0
DENAUX 2009 La* (?)	6,45			
τὸ λαλούμενον → τὰ λαλούμενα; cf. 1 Cor 14,9	2,33	13,45; 16,14	0	0
BOISMARD 1984 cb36; HARNACK 1906 52;				
NEIRYNCK 1985				

Literature

DENAUX 2009 lAⁿ [λαλέω with an angel as speaker, τὸ λαλούμενον], [LAⁿ: λαλέω with God as subject]; GERSDORF 1816 186 [λαλῆσαι πρὸς σέ]; 207 [ἐλάλησεν διὰ στόματος τῶν ἁγίων ἀπ᾽ αἰῶνος προφητῶν αὐτοῦ]; HARNACK 1906 73-74; HAUCK 1934 [Vorzugsverbindung: λαλέω πρός]; JEREMIAS 1980 33 [λαλέω πρός + acc.: red.]; 69 [λαλέω + λέγων: red.]; 84 [λαλέω πρὸς ἀλλήλους: red.]; RADL 1975 415 [λαλέω; λαλέομαι; τὰ λαλούμενα(λελαλημένα) (ὑπό)].

JASCHKE, Helmut, "λαλεῖν" bei Lukas: Ein Beitrag zur lukanischen Theologie. — BZ NF 15 (1971) 109-114. Esp. 110-111: "Das 'Reden' der Propheten"; 112-113: "Das 'Reden' Jesu"; 113-114: "Das 'Reden' der 'Apostel'".

λαμβάνω 21/23 + 29/30 (Mt 53/58, Mk 20/21)

1. take (hold of) (Lk 13,19.21; Acts 27,35); 2. acquire (Lk 19,12); 3. receive (Lk 11,10); 4. collect; 5. select; 6. come to believe; 7. exploit by deception; 8. experience; 9. cause to experience; 10. put on (clothes); 11. do

Word groups	Lk	Acts	Mt	Mk
λαμβάνω + accusative (person) (VKa)	5,26; 7,16; 9,39	2,23*; 9,25; 16,3; 24,27	2	4
λαμβάνω αἰτέω (SCh; VKs) → αἰτέω + (ἐπι)δίδωμι/παρατίθημι; δίδωμι + ζητέω; εὑρίσκω + (ἀνα/ἐπι)ζητέω	11,10		3	1
λαμβάνω ἄφεσιν ἁμαρτιῶν (SCj; VKp) BOISMARD 1984 Aa141		10,43; 26,18	0	0
λαμβάνω (+) ἄρτον (SCa)	6,4; 9,16; 22,19; 24,30	27,35	6/7	5
λαμβάνω (+) βασιλείαν (LN: become a king) DENAUX 2009 Lⁿ	19,12.15		0	0
λαμβάνω (+) γυναῖκα/αὐτήν (SCb; VKb); cf. παραλαμβάνω γυναῖκα Mt 1,20.24	20,28.29.30*.31		0	3/4
λαμβάνω διά + genitive (VKg)		10,43	0	0
λαμβάνω δύναμιν (VKm)		1,8	0	0
λαμβάνω ἑαυτῷ (VKc); cf. λαμβάνω μεθ᾽ ἑαυτῶν Mt 25,32	19,12		0	0
λαμβάνω ἐκ (VKd)		15,14	0	0
λαμβάνω ἐντολήν		17,15	0	0
λαμβάνω ἐξουσίαν (VKn)		26,10	0	0
λαμβάνω (+) ἐσθίω	6,4; 9,16(-17); 24,43	27,35	5	3/4
λαμβάνω + ἐπαγγελίαν/παραγγελίαν (VKq)		2,33; 16,24	0	0
λαμβάνω θάρσος (LN: take courage)		28,15	0	0
λαμβάνω + κρίμα (SCg; VKk)	20,47		0/1	1
λαμβάνω (+) παρά + genitive (SCe; VKf) → ἀπολαμβάνω παρά; cf. (ἀπο)λαμβάνω ἀπό Mt 17,25; Mk 7,33; 12,2; ἀναλαμβάνω ἀπό Acts 1,11 DENAUX 2009 lAn	6,34	2,33; 3,5; 17,9; 20,24; 26,10	0	1

	Lk	Acts	Mt	Mk
λαμβάνω πνεῦμα (ἅγιον) → **λαμβάνω +** πνεῦμα; cf. Jn 20,22 BOISMARD 1984 Ba13		8,15.17.19; 10,47; 19,2	0	0
λαμβάνω (+) πνεῦμα (SCc) → **λαμβάνω** πνεῦμα (ἅγιον) DENAUX 2009 lAⁿ (?)	9,39	1,8; 2,33.38; 8,15. 17.19; 10,47; 19,2	0	0
λαμβάνω πρόσωπον (LN: show favoritism; VKj)	20,21		0	0
λαμβάνω τροφήν; cf. μεταλαμβάνω τροφῆς Acts 2,46; 27,33.34; προσλαμβάνομαι τροφῆς Acts 27,36 BOISMARD 1984 Aa35		9,19	0	0
φόβος + λαμβάνει + accusative → **ἐγένετο** θάμβος/φόβος ἐπί + acc.; **ἐπέπεσεν** φόβος ἐπί + acc.; θάμβος **περιέχει** + acc.; **ἐπλήσθην** θάμβους/φόβου	7,16		0	0

Literature

COLLISON 1977 82 [redundant participle: noteworthy phenomena]; RADL 1975 416.

DELEBECQUE, Édouard, *Études grecques*, 1976. Esp. 109-121: "Le pain et la coupe de la dernière cène (22,17-20)".

Λάμεχ 1   Lamech (Lk 3,36)

λαμπρός 1 + 1

1. shining (Lk 23,11; Acts 10,30); 2. sparkling; 3. glamorous

Word groups	Lk	Acts	Mt	Mk
ἐσθὴς λαμπρά → ἐσθὴς **λευκή** DENAUX 2009 LAⁿ	23,11	10,30	0	0

Literature
DENAUX 2009 LAⁿ.

JOÜON, Paul, Luc 23,11: ἐσθῆτα λαμπράν. — *RechSR* 26 (1936) 80-85.

λαμπρῶς* 1   luxuriously (Lk 16,19)

Literature
HAUCK 1934 [seltenes Alleinwort].

λάμπω 1 + 1 (Mt 3)   shine (Lk 17,24; Acts 12,7)

Word groups	Lk	Acts	Mt	Mk
λάμπω + φῶς → **περιλάμπω** + φῶς; cf. φῶς + περιαστράπτω Acts 9,3; 22,6		12,7	1	0

Literature
JEREMIAS 1980 267 [red.].

λανθάνω 1 + 1 (Mk 1)

1. escape notice (Lk 8,47; Acts 26,26); 2. forget; 3. not know

λαξευτός*** 1   hewn out of rock (Lk 23,53)

Literature
HAUCK 1934 [seltenes Alleinwort].

λαός 36 + 48 (Mt 14/15, Mk 2/3)

1. nation (Lk 2,31); 2. people of God (Acts 3,23); 3. crowd (Acts 21,36); 4. common
people

Word groups	Lk	Acts	Mt	Mk
οἱ ἄρχων/πρῶτοι τοῦ λαοῦ (SCd; VKf); cf. ἀρχιερεῖς τοῦ λαοῦ Mt 2,4; 21,23; 26,3.47; 27,1; γραμματεῖς τοῦ λαοῦ Mt 2,4; πρεσβύτεροι τοῦ λαοῦ Mt 21,23; 26,3.47; 27,1 DENAUX 2009 1Aⁿ	19,47	4,8; 23,5	0	0
εὐαγγελίζομαι (+) λαός DENAUX 2009 Lⁿ	2,10; 3,18; 20,1		0	0
λαὸς αὐτοῦ (= θεοῦ/κυρίου) (SCe) DENAUX 2009 Lⁿ	1,68.77; 7,16		0	0
λαός + ἔθνος (SCg; VKk) DENAUX 2009 1An (?)	2,32	4,25.27; 15,14; 26,17.23	1	0
λαὸς τῶν Ἰουδαίων (SCf; VKj)		12,11	0	0
λαός μου/σου (SCe; VKg)	2,32	7,34; 23,5	1	0
ὁ λαὸς οὗτος (SCb; VKc)	9,13; 21,23	13,17¹; 28,26.27	2	1
ὅλος ὁ λαός (SCa; VKb) → ἅπας/πᾶς ὁ **λαός** BOISMARD 1984 Bb36; NEIRYNCK 1985		2,47	0	0
πρεσβυτέριον τοῦ λαοῦ; cf. πρεσβύτεροι τοῦ λαοῦ Mt 21,23; 26,3.47; 27,1	22,66		0	0
λαοί plural (SCj; VKl) DENAUX 2009 1Aⁿ	2,31	4,25.27	0	0

Characteristic of Luke
DENAUX 2009 L***; GASTON 1973 64 [Lked]; GOULDER 1989; HAWKINS 1909 20; HENDRIKS
1986 428.434.448.468; MORGENTHALER 1958LA

	Lk	Acts	Mt	Mk
ἅπας/πᾶς ὁ λαός (SCa; VKa) → ὅλος ὁ **λαός**; πάντα τὰ **ἔθνη**; πᾶς ὁ **ὄχλος**; ἅπαν/πᾶν τὸ **πλῆθος**; cf. Heb 9,19¹·² BOISMARD 1984 Bb36; DENAUX 2009 L***; GOULDER 1989; HAWKINS 1909L; NEIRYNCK 1985; PLUMMER 1922 lx	2,10.31; 3,21; 7,29; 8,47; 9,13; 18,43; 19,48; 20,6.45; 21,38; 24,19	3,9.11; 4,10; 5,34; 10,41; 13,24	1	0
διδάσκω τὸν λαόν BOISMARD 1984 Ab111; NEIRYNCK 1985	20,1	4,2; 5,25	0	0

λαός singular BOISMARD 1984 cb85; DENAUX 2009 L***; NEIRYNCK 1985	1,10.17.21.68.77; 2,10.32; 3,15.18.21; 6,17; 7,1.16.29; 8,47; 9,13; 18,43; 19,47.48; 20,1.6.9. 19.26.45; 21,23.38; 22,2.66; 23,5.13.14. 27.35; 24,19	2,47; 3,9.11.12.23; 4,1.2.8. 10.17.21; 5,12.13.20.25. 26.34.37; 6,8.12; 7,17.34; 10,2.41.42; 12,4.11; 13,15. 17$^{1.2}$.24.31; 15,14; 18,10; 19,4; 21,28.30.36.39.40; 23,5; 24,17.23; 28,17.26.27	14/15	2/3
λαός + θεός DENAUX 2009 L*** (?)	1,68; 7,16.29; 18,43; 24,19	2,47; 3,9; 10,41; 13,17^1; 15,14	0	0
λαὸς Ἰσραήλ (SCf; VKh) → φυλὴ τοῦ Ἰσραήλ BOISMARD 1984 Ab56; NEIRYNCK 1985	2,32	4,10.27; 13,17^1.24	1	0
πλῆθος (πολὺ) τοῦ λαοῦ (SCh) BOISMARD 1984 Ab97; NEIRYNCK 1985	1,10; 6,17; 23,27	21,36	0	0
φοβέομαι τὸν λαόν BOISMARD 1984 Ab151; NEIRYNCK 1985	20,19; 22,2	5,26	0	0

Literature

COLLISON 1977 173-174 [linguistic usage of Luke: certain]; 174 [ἅπας/πᾶς ὁ λαός: certain];
DENAUX 2009 lA^n [διδάσκω τὸν λαόν], La^n [πλῆθος (πολὺ) τοῦ λαοῦ; φοβέομαι τὸν λαόν];
lAn [λαὸς Ἰσραήλ]; EASTON 1910 156 [πᾶς ὁ λαός: probably characteristic of L]; 165
[πρεσβυτέριον τοῦ λαοῦ: cited by Weiss as characteristic of L, and possibly corroborative];
GERSDORF 1816 188 [καὶ ἦν ὁ λαὸς προσδοκῶν – καὶ ἐθαύμαζον]; 231 [πάντων τῶν
λαῶν]; 256 [δόξαν λαοῦ σου Ἰσραήλ]; HAUCK 1934 [Vorzugswort; Vorzugsverbindung: πρὸς
τὸν λαὸν λέγειν; πᾶς/ἅπας ὁ λαός]; JEREMIAS 1980 30: "lukanisches Vorzugswort"; 81:
"Insbesondere die Kombination πᾶς (ἅπας) + ὁ λαός findet sich gehäuft im lk Doppelwerk";
RADL 1975 416 [λαός]; 424 [πλῆθος τοῦ λαοῦ]; SCHNEIDER 1969 163 [Vorzugswörter und -
ausdrücke des Luk].

CITRON, Bernhard, The Multitude in the Synoptic Gospels. — ScotJT 7 (1954) 408-418.
   Esp. 409-411: "Terminology" [πλῆθος, λαός, ὄχλος].
DAHL, Nils A., "A People for His Name" (Acts XV. 14). — NTS 4 (1957-58) 319-327.
DUPONT, Jacques, Λαὸς ἐξ ἐθνῶν (Act. XV. 14). — NTS 3 (1956-57) 47-50.
KILPATRICK, George D., Λαοί at Lk II. 31 and Acts IV. 25, 27. — JTS NS 16 (1965) 127;
   = ID., Principles and Practice, 1990, 312.
—, The Gentiles and the Strata of Luke. — BÖCHER, O. – HAACKER, K. (eds.), Verborum
   Veritas. FS G. Stählin, 1970, 83-88. Esp. 83; = ID., Principles and Practice, 1990, 313-
   318. Esp. 313-314.
KODELL, Jerome, Luke's Use of Laos, "People," Especially in the Jerusalem Narrative (Lk
   19,28–24,53). — CBQ 31 (1969) 327-343.
MAHFOUZ, Hady, La fonction littéraire et théologique de Lc 3,1-20, 2003. Esp. 256-263.
PRETE, Benedetto, "Il popolo che Dio si è scelto" negli scritti di Luca. — Sacra Doctrina
   26 (1981) 173-204; = ID., L'opera di Luca, 1986, 355-375.

λατρεύω 3 + 5 (Mt 1)	worship			
Word groups	**Lk**	**Acts**	**Mt**	**Mk**
λατρεύω + προσκυνέω (VKb)	4,8		1	0

Characteristic of Luke

BOISMARD 1984 Db12; DENAUX 2009 lA*; GOULDER 1989; HARNACK 1906 52.145; HAWKINS
1909B; NEIRYNCK 1985

Literature

GERSDORF 1816 261 [λατρεύουσα νύκτα καὶ ἡμέραν]; HAUCK 1934 [Vorzugswort].

BACHMANN, Michael, *Jerusalem und der Tempel*, 1980. Esp. 332-369: "Gebet".
GEORGE, Augustin, La prière. — ID., *Études*, 1978, 395-427. Esp. 402-405: "Le vocabulaire lucanien de la prière".
REICKE, Bo, Some Reflections on Worship in the New Testament. — HIGGINS, A.J.B. (ed.), *New Testament Essays: Studies in Memory of Thomas Walter Manson 1893-1958*. Manchester: University Press, 1959, 194-209.

λάχανον 1 (Mt 1, Mk 1) | garden plant (Lk 11,42)

λεγιών 1 (Mt 1, Mk 2)
1. Legion (Lk 8,30); 2. army unit

Literature

MATEOS, Juan, Terminos relacionados con "Legion" en Mc 5,2-20. — *FilolNT* 1 (1988) 211-215.
MARYKS, Robert, A. Il latinismi del Nuovo testamento, 2000. Esp. 27.

λέγω 533/554 + 234/247 (Mt 505/510, Mk 289[290]/311)
1. speak (Lk 7,24); 2. name (Lk 22,47); 3. call (Lk 22,1); 4. mean (Acts 9,36); 5. imply

Word groups

λέγω	Lk	Acts	Mt	Mk
verb of saying + pleonastic participle λέγων	1,63.67; 3,10.14[1].16; 4,35.36; 5,12. 21.30; 7,4.6.16. 19.20[2].39[2]; 8,54; 9,18[1].35.38; 10,25; 12,16[2].17; 14,3[2].7[2].(29-) 30; 15,2.3[2].6.9; 17,13; 18,(1-)2.16.18.38; 19,7. 14.(29-)30. (37-)38; 20,2[2].5[1]. 14.21[1].(27-)28; 21,7; 22,(41-)42.57.59. 64; 23,2[1]. 3[1].5.18.21.35. 39.47; 24,(6-)7.29	1,6; 2,7.40; 3,25; 4,(15-)16; 5,(22-)23. (27-)28; 6,11; 8,26; 11,18; 13,15[1]; 14,11; 15,13; 16,9.15.17.28. 35; 19,28; 20,23; 21,40; 22,22.26; 23,9; 24,2; 26,31; 27,(9-)10. 33; 28,(25-)26[1]	47/48	30/32
ἀκούων/ἀκούσας + λέγω → ἀκούων/ἀκούσας + εἶπον; ἀκούσας + ἀποκρίνομαι	1,66	8,50*; 9,21; 11,18; 19,28; 22,26	3	6
ἀμὴν λέγω ὑμῖν → ἀληθῶς/ναὶ **λέγω** ὑμῖν; cf. ἀμὴν γὰρ λέγω ὑμῖν Mt 5,18; 10,23; 13,17; 17,20[2]; ἀμὴν λέγω δὲ ὑμῖν Lk 13,35[1] *v.l.*; ἀμὴν δὲ λέγω ὑμῖν Mk 14,9; ἀμήν σοι λέγω Lk 23,43[2]; ἀμὴν λέγω σοι Mt 5,26; 26,34; Mk 14,30[2]	4,24[2]; 12,37; 18,17.29[2]; 21,32		25	11/12

ἀμὴν λέγω ὑμῖν ὅτι	4,24[2]; 12,37; 13,35[1] v.l.; 18,29[2]; 21,32		10	8
ἀμὴν λέγω (δὲ) ὑμῖν / σοι λέγω without ὅτι	13,35[1] v.l.; 18,17; 23,43[2]		15	3/4
ἀποστέλλω/πέμπω + λέγων → ἀποστέλλω εἰπών	7,6.19.20[2]; 19,14.(29-)30	13,15[1]; 16,35	6	2
δοκεῖτε ὅτι …; οὐχί, λέγω ὑμῖν, ἀλλ'… DENAUX 2009 L[n]	12,51; 13,(2-)3.(4-)5		0	0
τὸ λέγειν/λέγεσθαι (VKh) DENAUX 2009 L[n]	9,7; 11,27[1]		0	0
λέγει κύριος of Scripture		7,49; 15,17	0	0
λέγω + double accusative (SCd; VKd) → λέγω + infinitive	9,18[2].20[2]; 18,19[2]; 20,37.41[2]; 23,2[2]	4,32; 5,36; 8,9; 10,28; 17,7; 24,14; 28,6	1/3	5
λέγω + infinitive (SCv) → λέγω + double accusative	9,18[2].20[2]; 11,18; 20,27*.41[2]; 23,2[2]; 24,23[1.2]	4,32; 5,36; 8,9; 15,24*; 17,7; 21,4.21; 23,8.12; 28,6	5	3
λέγω with reference to scripture (SCx)	3,4*; 20,37.42[1]	2,17.25.34[1]; 3,25; 7,48; 13,35; 28,26[1]	15	2
λέγω + ἄγγελος as subject → εἶπον + ἄγγελος as subject; λαλέω with an angel as speaker	24,23[2]	8,26; 12,7.8[2]; 27,(23-)24	2	0
λέγω + ἀπαγγέλλω/παραγγέλλω (VKj) → λέγω + ἐπιτιμάω; εἶπον + ἀπαγγέλλω/παραγγέλλω	8,20*; 9,21	5,(22-)23.25*; 22,26	1	0
λέγω (+) ἀποκρίνομαι (SCf; VKk) → εἶπον/ἐρῶ + ἀποκρίνομαι; ἀποκρίνομαι λέγων; καὶ ἀποκριθεὶς λέγει; ὁ δὲ ἀποκριθεὶς λέγει; ἀποκιθεὶς δὲ λέγει/ἔλεγεν; cf. λόγον ἀποκρίνομαι Mt 22,46	3,11.16; 4,4*; 8,50*; 11,45[1]; 13,8.14; 14,3[2]; 17,37[1]; 23,40*	15,13; 24,10	6	12/18
λέγω (ἀνα)βοάω (VKl)	9,38; 18,38		1	0/1
λέγω + διαλογίζομαι/ συλλογίζομαι (SCg; VKm)	5,21; 12,17; 20,5.14		2	1/2
λέγω + διδάσκω (SCh; VKn); cf. λέγω ἐν τῇ διδαχῇ Mk 4,2; 12,38	20,21[2]	21,21	1	4
λέγω ἐν ἑαυτῷ (LN: think to oneself; SCb; VKb) → εἶπον ἐν ἑαυτῷ	3,8[1]; 7,49		2	0
λέγω + ἐπιτιμάω (SCs) → λέγω + ἀπαγγέλλω/παραγγέλλω; cf. λέγω + διαστέλλομαι Mk 8,15; λέγω + ἐντέλλομαι Mt 17,9	4,35; 23,40*		1	4
λέγω + (ἐπ)ἐρωτάω (SCj; VKp) → εἶπον + (ἐπ)ἐρωτάω	3,10.14[1]; 7,4 v.l.; 8,9*.30*; 9,18[1]; 18,18. 40*; 20,21[1].(27-)28; 21,7; 22,64; 23,3[1]	1,6; 5,(27-)28	7/8	6/7
λέγω ἵνα (VKe) → εἶπον ἵνα; cf. ἐκλέγω ἵνα 1 Cor 1,27[1.2].28		19,4[2]	0	0
λέγω (+) (ἐπι/παρα/προσ/συγ)καλέω (SCk.l; VKq) → εἶπον/ἐρῶ + (προσ/συγ)καλέω; λόγος + παράκλησις	7,4; 15,6.9; 16,5; 18,16	2,40; 7,59; 16,9.15; 27,33	5	7/8
λέγω (+) (ἀνα)κράζω/κραυγάζω (SCn; VKs) → εἶπον + (ἀνα)κράζω	4,33*.41; 23,18	14,(14-)15; 16,17; 19,28	9	5/6
λέγω + (συλ)λαλέω/ὀνομάζω (SCp; VKt) → εἶπον + λαλέω	4,36; 24,(6-)7	8,26; 19,13; 26,14 v.l.22.31; 28,(25-)26[1]	4	1

λέγω + λόγος (*VK*w) → εἶπον/ἐρῶ + λόγος	3,4*	13,15²; 15,24*	0	0
λέγω μηδενί → εἶπον μηδενί	9,21		0	2
λέγω (+) ὅτι (*SC*u) → εἶπον/ἐρῶ ὅτι	1,24; 3,8¹ *v.l.*8²; 4,21.24².25 *v.l.*41; 5,26.36; 6,5 *v.l.*; 7,4.16; 8,49; 9,7; 10,12.24; 12,27 *v.l.*37.44. 54².55; 13,14.35¹ *v.l.*; 14,24.30; 15,2.7; 17,10; 18,8.29²; 19,7.26.40² *v.l.*42; 20,5¹; 21,3².5¹.8² *v.l.*32; 22,16.18. 37.70²; 23,5; 24,7. 34	2,13; 5,23; 6,11.14; 11,3; 15,5; 18,13; 19,26; 20,23; 26,31	33/39	38/40
λέγω οὖν → εἶπον οὖν DENAUX 2009 Lⁿ	3,7; 13,18		0	0
λέγω πρὸς ἀλλήλους; cf. διαλέγομαι + πρὸς ἀλλήλους Mk 9,34	8,25²	28,4	0	1
λέγω + προσέρχομαι → εἶπον + προσέρχομαι	13,31	22,26	2	0
λέγω (+) προφήτης/προφητεύω (*SC*t; *VK*x) → εἶπον + προφήτης; cf. λέγω + προφητεία Mt 13,14	1,67; 3,4*	7,48; 8,34²; 26,22; 28,(25-)26¹	11	0
λέγω (+) ῥῆμα/διάλεκτος (*VK*y) → εἶπον + ῥῆμα DENAUX 2009 IAⁿ	18,34	11,16; 21,40; 26,14	0	0
λέγω (+) ὑμῖν / ὑμῖν λέγω / σοὶ λέγω / λέγω σοί (introducing a speech) (*SC*w)	3,8²; 4,24².25; 5,24²; 6,27; 7,9². 14².26.28.47; 9,27; 10,12.24; 11,8.9.51; 12,4.5. 8.22².27.37.44.51. 59; 13,3.5.24.35¹; 14,24; 15,7.10; 16,9; 17,34; 18,8. 14.17.29²; 19,26. 40²; 20,8²; 21,3². 32; 22,16.18.34². 37; 23,43²	5,38	59	18/19
λέγω ὑμῖν / σοι … οὐ μὴ … ἕως (ἄν); cf. λέγω ὑμῖν … οὐ μὴ … μέχρις οὗ Mk 13,30	9,27; 12,59; 13,35¹; 21,32; 22,16.18		6	2
λέγω + (ἐπι/προσ)φωνέω (*SC*q; *VK*u) → εἶπον + (ἀνα/προσ)φωνέω	7,32; 8,8.54; 23,21	16,28; 21,40	1	2
λέγω (+) φωνή (*SC*r; *VK*z)	3,22*; 4,33*; 9,35; 17,13; 19,(37-)38	9,4; 11,7; 14,11; 16,28; 22,7.22; 26,14	3	1/3
ναὶ λέγω ὑμῖν → ἀληθῶς/ἀμὴν λέγω ὑμῖν	7,26; 11,51; 12,5		1	0
πείθομαι τοῖς λεγομένοις BOISMARD 1984 Aa150		27,11; 28,24	0	0
σὺ λέγεις; cf. σὺ εἶπας Mt 26,25.64	23,3		1	2
ὑμεῖς (+) λέγετε	9,20; 22,70		2	2
λέγεται (*SC*e; *VK*f)		9,36	1	0

λεγόμενος (SCe; VKg)	18,34; 22,1.47	3,2; 6,9; 8,6; 13,45*; 27,11; 28,24	13	1
εἶπον	Lk	Acts	Mt	Mk
ἀκούων/ἀκούσας + εἶπον → ἀκούων/ἀκούσας + **λέγω**; ἀκούσας + **ἀποκρίνομαι**	7,9[1]; 14,(14-)15; 18,22.26; 20,16	2,37; 4,24; 17,32; 21,20	4	0
ἀναστάς + εἶπεν BOISMARD 1984 ca5		1,15; 13,16; 15,7	1	0
ἀποκρίνομαι + εἶπον πρός + accusative (SCd)	5,22.31; 6,3; 7,40[1]; 8,21; 14,3[1]; 20,3[1]; 24,18	4,19	1	0
ἀποστέλλω εἰπών → ἀποστέλλω/πέμπω **λέγων**	22,8		0	0
εἶπον + infinitive (SCk)	9,54[2]; 12,13[2]; 19,15	11,12; 22,24	1	2
εἶπον with reference to scripture (SCm)	10,27; 20,42[2]	3,22; 4,25; 7,3.7.27. 33.35.37.40; 13,22	2	3
εἶπον + ἄγγελος as subject (+ μὴ φοβοῦ/φοβεῖσθε) → **λέγω** + ἄγγελος as subject; **λαλέω** with an angel as speaker	1,13.19.28 v.l.30.35; 2,10	5,19; 10,3; 11,13	1	0
εἶπον + ἀπαγγέλλω/ παραγγέλλω (VKe) → **λέγω** + ἀπαγγέλλω/παραγγέλλω DENAUX 2009 La[n]	5,14; 8,56; 9,21 v.l.	4,23	0	0
εἶπον (+) ἀποκρίνομαι (SCb; VKf) → **λέγω/ἐρῶ** + ἀποκρίνομαι; **ἀποκριθεὶς** (δὲ) εἶπεν; **ἀπεκρίθη** καὶ εἶπεν; καὶ **ἀποκριθεὶς** εἶπεν; ὁ δὲ **ἀποκριθεὶς** εἶπεν	1,19.35.60; 4,8.12[1]; 5,5.22.31; 6,3; 7,22. 40[1].43[1]; 8,21; 9,19.20[3]. 41.49; 10,27.41; 11,7; 13,2.15; 14,3[1].5 v.l.; 15,29; 17,17.20; 19,40[1]; 20,3[1].24 v.l.34 v.l.39[1]; 22,51; 24,18	4,19; 5,29; 8,24[1].34[1].37*[2]; 19,15; 21,13*; 25,9	43/44	6/19
εἶπον (+) ἐν ἑαυτῷ (SCa; VKa) → **λέγω** ἐν ἑαυτῷ	7,39[1]; 16,3; 18,4		2	0
εἶπον (+) ἐν τῇ καρδίᾳ (SCa)	12,45		1	0
εἶπον + (ἐπ)ἐρωτάω (VKh) → **λέγω** + (ἐπ)ἐρωτάω DENAUX 2009 L[n]	17,20; 20,3[2]		0	0
εἶπον (+) ἵνα (SCe; VKd) → **λέγω** ἵνα	4,3[2]; 10,40[2]		2	2
εἶπον + (προσ/συγ)καλέω (SCf; VKj) → **λέγω/ἐρῶ** + (ἐπι/παρα/προσ/συγ)καλέω	7,39[1]; 14,10 v.l.; 18,16 v.l.; 19,13; 23,(13-)14	6,2; 23,23	4	2
εἶπον + (ἀνα)κράζω (VKk) → **λέγω** + (ἀνα)κράζω/ κραυγάζω	8,28		0	0/1
εἶπον + κραυγή (SCj) → **εἶπον** + φωνή	1,42		0	0
εἶπον (+) λαλέω (VKl) → **λέγω** + (συλ)λαλέω/ὀνομάζω DENAUX 2009 L[n]	5,4; 12,3		0	0
εἶπον (+) λέγω (SCg; VKm)	7,39[1]; 12,16[1]; 14,3[1]; 15,3[1]; 20,2[1].5[2]; 21,5[2]		3	3
εἶπον (+) λόγος (VKq) → **λέγω/ἐρῶ** + λόγος	7,7; 20,3[2]; 22,61 v.l.	20,35	4	0
εἶπον μηδενί → **λέγω** μηδενί	5,14; 8,56		3	1
εἶπον (+) ὅτι (SCl) → **λέγω/ἐρῶ** ὅτι	1,61; 4,12[1].43; 9,22; 15,27; 19,9; 22,61; 24,46	3,22; 19,21; 23,20	4	5/8

εἶπον οὖν → **λέγω** οὖν	10,40[2]; 19,12		1	0
εἶπον + προσέρχομαι → **λέγω** + προσέρχομαι	9,12	23,14	15/16	0
εἶπον + προφήτης (VKt) → **λέγω** + προφήτης/ προφητεύω		21,(10-)11[1]	0	0
εἶπον + ῥῆμα (VKr) → **λέγω** + ῥῆμα/διάλεκτος	22,61	28,25	0/1	1
εἶπόν τε / εἶπέν τε → **ἀπεκρίθη** τε; cf. ἔφη τε Acts 10,28; 23,5 BOISMARD 1984 Aa12		2,37; 5,35; 12,8 v.l.17; 19,2.3[1]; 21,20; 22,8	0	0
εἶπον + (ἀνα/προσ)φωνέω (SCh; VKn) → **λέγω** + (ἐπι/προσ)φωνέω	1,42; 13,12; 16,2.24; 23,46[1]		1	1
εἶπον + φωνή (SCj; VKs) → **λέγω** + φωνή; **εἶπον** + κραυγή DENAUX 2009 La[n]	1,42 v.l.; 8,28; 11,27[2]; 23,46[1]	4,24; 14,10	0	0/1
στραφεὶς (+) εἶπεν	7,9[1]; 10,23; 14,25; 22,61; 23,28		2	0
εἶπας participle BOISMARD 1984 Aa43		7,37; 22,24; 24,22; 27,35	0	0

ἐρῶ	Lk	Acts	Mt	Mk
ἐρῶ with reference to scripture (SCh)	2,24; 4,12[2]	2,16; 13,34.40	19/20	0/1
ἐρῶ ἀποκρίνομαι (SCe; VKe) → **λέγω/εἶπον** + ἀποκρίνομαι; καὶ **ἀποκριθεὶς** ἐρεῖ	13,25[2]		1	1
ἐρῶ (+) καλέω (SCf; VKf) → **λέγω/εἶπον** + (ἐπι/παρα/προσ/συγ)καλέω DENAUX 2009 L[n]	14,9.10		0	0
ἐρῶ + λέγω (SCd; VKg); cf. τὸ ῥῆθεν + λέγω Mt 1,22; 2,15.17; 4,14; 8,17; 12,17; 13,35; 21,4; 22,31; 27,9; ὁ ῥηθείς + λέγω Mt 3,3	13,27[1]		0	0
ἐρῶ (+) λόγος (VKh) → **λέγω/εἶπον** + λόγος DENAUX 2009 LA[n]	12,10	20,38	0	0
ἐρῶ + νόμος	2,24		0	0
ἐρῶ ὅτι (SCg)	19,31	13,34; 20,38	3	0

Characteristic of Luke

GASTON 1973 64 [Lked: εἰπεῖν]; GOULDER 1989 [εἰπεῖν]; HENDRIKS 1986 428.441 [εἶπεν].434 [εἶπον].448.466 [εἶπον]; MORGENTHALER 1958L

	Lk	Acts	Mt	Mk
ἀληθῶς λέγω ὑμῖν → ἀμὴν/ναὶ **λέγω** ὑμῖν GOULDER 1989; HAWKINS 1909add	9,27; 12,44; 21,3[2]		0	0
ἄρχομαι λέγειν (SCa; VKa) GOULDER 1989	3,8[1]; 4,21; 7,24.49; 11,29; 12,1; 13,26; 20,9; 23,30		3	7/8
εἶπεν δέ / εἶπαν δέ; cf. Jn 8,11; 12,6; 21,23; cf. εἶπον δέ Acts 11,8; 22,10[1] BOISMARD 1984 Bb1; CADBURY 1920 169; DENAUX 2009 L***; GOULDER 1989*; HARNACK 1906 71; HAWKINS 1909 L; NEIRYNCK 1985; PLUMMER 1922 lxiii; SCHÜRMANN 1957 120	1,13.34.38; 4,3[1].24[1]; 6,8.9.39; 7,48.50; 8,25[1]; 9,9.13[1].14.20[1].50.59[1].60.61.62; 10,18.28.37[2]; 11,2[1].39; 12,13[1].15. 16[1].20.22[1].41[1]; 13,7.23[1]; 15,3[1].11. 21.22; 16,3.25.27.31; 17,1.6[1].22; 18,6[1].9.19[1]. 26.28; 19,9.19; 20,13.41[1]; 22,36.52. 60[1].67[3].70[1]; 24,17.44	1,6; 3,6; 5,3; 7,1.33; 8,29; 9,5.15; 10,4[2]; 11,12; 12,8[1].17 v.l.; 18,9; 19,4[1]; 21,39; 23,20; 25,10	0	0

εἶπεν παραβολήν → **λέγω** παραβολήν; cf. εἶπεν διὰ παραβολῆς Lk 8,4 DENAUX 2009 L***; GOULDER 1989*; HAWKINS 1909L; PLUMMER 1922 lx	6,39; 12,16[1]; 15,3[1]; 18,9; 19,11; 20,19; 21,29		0	1
εἶπον/εἶπεν πρός + accusative (SCc; VKb) → **λέγω** πρός + acc.; verb of saying **πρός** + acc. BOISMARD 1984 Bb7; CREDNER 1836 138; DENAUX 2009 L***; HARNACK 1906 71; NEIRYNCK 1985; PLUMMER 1922 lxii; SCHÜRMANN 1953 4-5	1,13.18.34.61; 2,15*. 34.48.49; 3,12.13. 14 v.l.; 4,23[1].43; 5,4.10.22.31. 33.34; 6,3.9; 7,40[1]. 50; 8,21.22; 9,3.13[1].14.33. 43.50.57.59[1].62; 10,26.29; 11,1.5[1].39; 12,15.16[1].22[1]; 13,7.23[2]; 14,3[1].5.23.25; 15,3[1].22; 17,1.22; 18,9.31; 19,5.8.9.13. 33.39; 20,2[1] v.l.3[1].19.23.25.41[1]; 22,15. 52; 23,4.14.22; 24,5.17.18.25.32.44	1,7; 2,29.37; 3,22 v.l.; 4,8.19.23; 5,9*. 35; 7,3; 8,20; 9,10[1]. 15; 10,21; 12,8[1].15[1]; 15,7.36; 18,6.14; 19,2.2*.3[1] v.l.; 21,37[2]; 22,8.10[2].21. 25; 23,3; 28,21	2	2
εἰπών participle DENAUX 2009 L*** GOULDER 1989*	5,13*; 9,22; 19,28.30*; 22,8; 23,46; 24,4	1,9; 4,25; 7,26.27.35.37 v.l.40.60; 10,3; 11,13; 18,21; 19,21; 20,36; 22,24 v.l.; 23,7; 24,22 v.l.; 26,30*; 27,35 v.l.; 28,25.29*	0	1
εἴρηκεν/-ται GOULDER 1989	4,12; 22,13 v.l.	8,24; 13,34; 17,28; 20,38 v.l.	1	0
τὸ εἰρημένον (SCa; VKa); cf. Rom 4,18 BOISMARD 1984 cb28; NEIRYNCK 1985; PLUMMER 1922 lxiii (κατὰ τὸ εἰρημένον)	2,24	2,16; 13,40	0	0
ἔλεγεν δέ / ἔλεγον δέ; cf. Jn 6,71; 10,20 DENAUX 2009 L***; HAWKINS 1909L; PLUMMER 1922 lxiii	5,36; 9,23; 10,2; 12,54[1]; 13,6; 14,7[1].12; 16,1; 18,1		1	1
ἔλεγεν δὲ καί DENAUX 2009 L***	5,36; 12,54[1]; 14,12; 16,1		0	0
ἔλεγεν δὲ παραβολήν GOULDER 1989 DENAUX 2009 L***;	5,36; 13,6; 14,7[1]; 18,1		0	0
λαλέομαι/λέγομαι ὑπό + genitive → **λαλέομαι** ὑπό + gen.; cf. Eph 2,11[1] BOISMARD 1984 cb12; DENAUX 2009 IA*; NEIRYNCK 1985	2,18; 9,7	8,6; 13,45; 16,14; 17,19; 27,11	0	0
τὸ λεγόμενον; cf. Heb 8,1 BOISMARD 1984 Bb113; NEIRYNCK 1985	18,34	8,6; 28,24; 27,11	0	0
λέγω παραβολήν → **εἶπεν** παραβολήν DENAUX 2009 L***; GOULDER 1989; HAWKINS 1909L	5,36; 12,41[2]; 13,6; 14,7[1]; 18,1; 20,9		0	0

| λέγω πρός + accusative (person) (*SCc*; *VKc*) → εἶπον πρός + acc. BOISMARD 1984 cb141; DENAUX 2009 L***; NEIRYNCK 1985; PLUMMER 1922 lxii | 4,21; 5,36; 7,24; $8,25^2$; 9,23; 10,2; 11,53*; $12,1.41^2$; $14,7^{1.2}$; 16,1; $20,2^2.9$; 24,10 | 2,7 *v.l.*12; 3,25; 23,30; 26,14; 28,4.17 | 0 | 4 |

→ τὸ πνεῦμα (τὸ ἅγιον) εἶπεν + dat.; εἶπον φωνῇ μεγαλῇ

Literature

VON BENDEMANN 2001 414: "ἔλεγεν δὲ c. πρός ist typisch lukanisch"; 415 [ἀποκριθεὶς + εἶπεν]: "Kennzeichnend lukanisch ist dabei die Verbindung mit δέ"; 418-419: "ὁ δὲ εἶπεν ist lukanisch"; 419 [λέγω ὑμῖν]; 427 [λέγειν παραβολήν]; COLLISON 1977 47 [εἶπεν δέ beginning sentences: linguistic usage of Luke: certain; but the possibility that it was also a linguistic usage of Luke cannot be excluded]; 48 [καὶ εἶπεν beginning sentences: linguistic usage of Luke's "other source-material": certain]; 55 [ἔλεγεν/ἔλεγον: linguistic usage of Luke: certain]; 56 [ἔλεγεν δέ: nearly certain; ἔλεγεν δὲ καί: likely; λέγω γὰρ ὑμῖν ὅτι: noteworthy phenomena]; 57 [λέγω δὲ ὑμῖν: linguistic usage of Luke: probable; σοί/ὑμῖν λέγω: likely]; 83 [pleonastic λέγων: noteworthy phenomena]; 119 [λέγων ὅτι: linguistic usage of Luke: certain]; 179 [λεγόμενος: noteworthy phenomena]; DENAUX 2009 Lⁿ [ἀληθῶς λέγω ὑμῖν], IAⁿ [τὸ εἰρημένον,τὸ λεγομένον]; EASTON 1910 163 [λεγόμενος "called": cited by Weiss as characteristic of L, and possibly corroborative]; 176 [λέγων after a verb of speaking; ἀποκριθεὶς εἶπεν: possible Hebraisms in the Lucan Writings, as classed by Dalman]; GERSDORF 1816 180 [εἶπεν δὲ πρὸς αὐτόν]; 186 [καὶ εἶπεν Ζαχαρίας πρὸς τὸν ἄγγελον]; 196 [εἶπεν δὲ Μαριὰμ πρὸς τὸν ἄγγελον]; 236 [εἶπον πρὸς ἀλλήλους]; 245 [κατὰ τὸ εἰρημένον]; HAUCK 1934 [Vorzugsverbindung: λέγω/εἶπον πρός; λέγω/εἶπον παραβολὴν πρός; διὰ τὸ λέγεσθαι; ἀληθῶς λέγω ὑμῖν; ἔλεγεν/εἶπον δέ]; JEREMIAS 1980 33: "1. εἶπεν (-ον, -αν) δέ ... am Satzbeginn ... profilierten Lukanismus... 2. Auch πρός c.acc. nach Verba dicendi zur Bezeichnung des (der) Angeredeten ... ist ausgesprochen lukanisch"; 68(-70): "das pleonastische λέγων ist eine lukanische Vorzugswendung"; 91 [τὸ εἰρημένον: red.]; 124: "λέγειν/εἰπεῖν παραβολήν ist eine lk Vorzugswendung"; 171 [ὁ δὲ εἶπεν αὐτῷ: trad.]; 223: "Vorlukanisch ist auch das parenthetische λέγω ὑμῖν"; 224: "ἔλεγεν δέ am Satzbeginn ist lukanisch"; RADL 1975 400-401 [ἀποκριθεὶς εἶπεν: "Septuagintismus"]; 407 [εἶπον; εἰπών; εἰπών "im Gefolge eines Verbums"; εἴπας; "zu ἐρῶ gehörige Perfekt- und Plusquamperfektformen"; εἰρήκει]; 408 [εἶπεν/εἶπαν δέ; εἶπεν πρός; εἶπεν δέ "mit unmittelbar folgendem Subjekt"; εἶπεν δὲ ... ὁ κύριος; εἶπεν δέ, "gefolgt von πρός und dem Subjekt (oder umgekehrt)"]; 416: "Luke frequently adds the participle λέγων to various expressions of saying"; 421 [καὶ ταῦτα εἰπών]; 425 [πρός "bei Verben des Sagens"]; REHKOPF 1959 61-62 [ἀποκριθεὶς ... εἶπεν: vorlukanisch]; 93 [εἶπεν(ον, αν) αὐτῷ (αὐτῇ/αὐτοῖς); λέγειν/εἰπεῖν/ἐρεῖν: vorlukanisch]; 95 [λέγω γὰρ ὑμῖν; ναὶ λέγω ὑμῖν; λέγειν/εἰπεῖν ἐν ἑαυτῷ: vorlukanisch]; 97 [ὑμῖν λέγω: vorlukanisch]; SCHNEIDER 1969 87.164 [Verbum finitum mit folgendem λέγων: Bei Luk beliebte Konstruktionen]; 89.164 [εἶπεν δέ mit folgendem Subjekt: Bei Luk beliebte Konstruktionen]; 112.163: "Das Partizip λέγοντες ist für Luk außerordentlich gut bezeugt" [Vorzugswörter und -ausdrücke des Luk]; 163 [εἶπαν "am Anfang eines Satzes oder einer Wendung"]; SCHÜRMANN 1953 14-16 [λέγω γὰρ ἡμῖν ὅτι luk R weniger wahrscheinlich]; 83.86 [Lk εἶπεν (-ον, -αν) instead of hist. pres. λέγει (-οντων) in Mk]; 89 [Den Aorist εἶπα schreibt Luk relative häufig]; 97 [Lk ἐρεῖν instead of εἰπεῖν in Mk/Mt]; 103 [Plqpf. εἰρήκα vermutlich luk R]; 1957 30 [λέγων (λέγοντες) eine Rede oder Frage einführend: luk sprachgebrauch]; 121 [εἶπεν δὲ αὐτοῖς: wahrscheinlich luk R einer vorluk T]; 1961 276 [λέγω γὰρ ὑμῖν; λέγειν/εἰπεῖν ἐν ἑαυτῷ; ναὶ λέγω ὑμῖν; εἶπεν(ον, αν) αὐτῷ (αὐτῇ/αὐτοῖς)]; 280 [λέγειν/εἰπεῖν: protoluk R weniger wahrscheinlich]; 280-281 [ἐρεῖ: protoluk R nicht beweisbar]; 285 [ὑμῖν λέγω: protoluk R nicht beweisbar].

DANOVE, Paul., Λέγω Melding in the Septuagint and New Testament. — *FilolNT* 16 (31-32, 2003) 19-31.

λέγω – λέπρα 375

DENAUX, Adelbert, L'hypocrisie des pharisiens et le dessein de Dieu, 1973. Esp. 259 [verb + λέγων]; ²1989. Esp. 169.
JOÜON, Paul, "Respondit et dixit". — *Bib* 13 (1932) 309-314.
MAKUJINA, John, Verbs Meaning "Command" in the New Testament: Determining the Factors Involved in the Choice of Command-Verbs. — *EstBíb* 56 (1998) 357-369. Esp. 358-359: "Παραγγέλλω"; 359-361: "Κελεύω"; 361-362: "Ἐντέλλω"; 362-364: "Διαστέλλω"; 364-366: "-τάσσω complex"; 366-367: "Λέγω". [NTA 43, 57]
NEIRYNCK, Frans, Recent Developments in the Study of Q. — DELOBEL, J. (ed.), *Logia: Les paroles de Jésus – The Sayings of Jesus* (BETL, 59). Leuven: Peeters – University Press, 1982, 29-75. Esp. 56-69 [λέγω ὑμῖν].
POYTRESS, Vern Sheridan, Translating λέγω in Acts. — *WestTJ* 64 (2002) 273-278.
SAMAIN, É., L'évangile de Luc. Un témoignage ecclésial et missionaire. Lc 1,1-4; 4,14-15. — *AssSeign* 34 (1973) 60-73. Esp. 226-246.
SCHNEIDER, Gerhard, Lk 1,34. 35 als redaktionelle Einheit. — *BZ* NF 15 (1971) 255-259. Esp. 256-257: "Lk 1,35 ist nach Wortschatz, Stil und Theologie 'lukanisch'".
—, Jesu geistgewirkte Empfängnis (Lk 1,34f): Zur Interpretation einer christologischen Aussage. — *TPQ* 119 (1971) 105-116. Esp. 109; = ID., *Lukas, Theologe der Heilsgeschichte*, 1985, 86-97. Esp. 90.

λεῖος 1
smooth (Lk 3,5)

Literature
HAUCK 1934 [seltenes Alleinwort].

λείπω 1
1. be in need; 2. not possessed (Lk 18,22); 3. ought to (Lk 18,22)

Word groups	Lk	Acts	Mt	Mk
λείπω intransitive (*VK*a)	18,22		0	0

λειτουργία 1
1. service (Lk 1,23); 2. ministry; 3. performance of religious duties (Lk 1,23)

Literature
GEORGE, Augustin, La prière. — ID., *Études*, 1978, 395-427. Esp. 402-405: "Le vocabulaire lucanien de la prière".
HILHORST, Anton, Termes chrétiens issus du vocabulaire de la démocratie athénienne. — *FilolNT* 1 (1988) 27-32. Esp. 29-30.

λέπρα 2 (Mt 1, Mk 1)
leprosy

Word groups	Lk	Acts	Mt	Mk
λέπρα + καθαρίζω → **λεπρός** + καθαρίζω	5,12.13		1	1
πλήρης λέπρας	5,12		0	0

Literature
BDAG 2000 592 [literature]; HAUCK 1934 [Vorzugsverbindung: πλήρης λέπρας].

HULSE, E.V., The Nature of Biblical 'Leprosy' and the Use of Alternative Medical Terms in Modern Translations of the Bible. — *Palestine Exploration Quarterly* 107 (1975) 87-105. [NTA 20, 374]

WEISSENRIEDER, Annette, *Images of Illness in the Gospel of Luke*, 2003. Esp. 168-187: "The image of λέπρα in the Gospel of Luke and the expanded frame of reference in Luke 17:11-19",

λεπρός 3 (Mt 4, Mk 2)   leper

Word groups	Lk	Acts	Mt	Mk
λεπρός (+) καθαρίζω → λέπρα + καθαρίζω	4,27; 7,22; 17,12(-14.17)		3	1

Literature
EASTON 1910 163 [cited by Weiss as characteristic of L, and possibly corroborative]; PAFFENROTH 1997 82.

λεπτόν 2 (Mk 1)   small coin (Lk 12,59; 21,2)

Literature
JEREMIAS 1980 225 [red.].

Λευΐς 4 (Mk 1)   Levi

Word groups	Lk	Acts	Mt	Mk
Λευΐς son of Alphaeus, disciple of Jesus (*SC*c; *VK*d)	5,27.29		0	1
Λευΐς son of Melchi (*SC*a; *VK*b)	3,24		0	0
Λευΐς son of Simeon (*SC*b; *VK*c)	3,29		0	0

Λευΐτης 1 + 1   Levite (Lk 10,32; Acts 4,36)

Literature
DENAUX 2009 LA[n].

λευκός 1 + 1 (Mt 3, Mk 2)
1. white (Acts 1,10); 2. radiant (Lk 9,29)

Word groups	Lk	Acts	Mt	Mk
ἐσθὴς λευκή → ἐσθὴς λαμπρά		1,10	0	0

λῆρος 1   pure nonsense (Lk 24,11)

Literature
HAUCK 1934 [seltenes Alleinwort].

ληστής 4 (Mt 4, Mk 3)
1. robber (Lk 10,30.36; 19,46); 2. rebel (Lk 22,52)

Word groups	Lk	Acts	Mt	Mk
σπήλαιον λῃστῶν (VKa)	19,46		1	1

Literature

BDAG 2000 594 [literature].

BORMANN, Lukas, *Recht, Gerechtigkeit und Religion*, 2001. Esp. 203.

DODD, Charles H., Some Problems of New Testament Translation. — *BTrans* 13 (1962) 145-157. Esp. 146-147: *"lêstês"*.

λίαν 1 (Mt 4, Mk 4)	very

Word groups	Lk	Acts	Mt	Mk
λίαν with a verb (SCa; VKa)	23,8		2	1

λιθοβολέω 1 + 3 (Mt 2, Mk 0/1)	stone to death (Lk 13,34; Acts 7,58.59; 14,5)

Characteristic of Luke

BOISMARD 1984 ca70

λίθος 14/15 + 2 (Mt 11, Mk 8/9)	

1. stone (substance) (Acts 17,29); 2. stone (piece) (Lk 11,11)

Word groups	Lk	Acts	Mt	Mk
λίθος + ἄρτος	4,3		2	0
λίθος καλός (LN: gem; VKa)	21,5		0	0
λίθος μυλικός (VKb)	17,2		0	0/1

Literature

KINMAN, Brent Rogers, "The Stones Will Cry Out" (Luke 19,40) – Joy on Judgment. — *Bib* 75 (1994) 232-235.

λικμάω 1 (Mt 1)	crush (Lk 20,18)

λίμνη 5	lake

Word groups	Lk	Acts	Mt	Mk
λίμνη lake Gennesareth (VKa) DENAUX 2009 L[n]	5,1.2; 8,22.23.33		0	0

Characteristic of Luke

CADBURY 1920 186; CREDNER 1836 134; GOULDER 1989*; HAWKINS 1909 L

Literature

COLLISON 1977 182 [noteworthy phenomena]; HAUCK 1934 [häufiges Alleinwort]; JEREMIAS 1980 129 [red.].

THEIßEN, Gerd, "Meer" und "See" in den Evangelien: Ein Beitrag zur Lokalkoloritforschung. — *SNTU* 10 (1985) 5-25. Esp. 9-13: "Der 'See Gennesaret' und das lukanische Doppelwerk".

λιμός 4 + 2 (Mt 1, Mk 1)

1. famine (Lk 4,25; 15,14; 21,11); 2. hunger (Lk 15,17)

Word groups	Lk	Acts	Mt	Mk
λιμοί plural (VKb)	21,11		1	1
λιμοὶ καὶ λοιμοί	21,11		0/1	0
λιμὸς ἰσχυρά	15,14		0	0
λιμὸς μέγας/μεγάλη	4,25	11,28	0	0

Characteristic of Luke	Lk	Acts	Mt	Mk
ἡ λιμός (VKa)	15,14	11,28	0	0
BOISMARD 1984 Ab185; NEIRYNCK 1985				

Literature

DENAUX 2009 L(***); LAⁿ [ἡ λιμός]; EASTON 1910 163 [λιμὸς ἐγένετο: cited by Weiss as characteristic of L, and possibly corroborative]; HAWKINS 1909 20; JEREMIAS 1980 127.249 [ἡ λιμός: red.]; PAFFENROTH 1997 82 [λιμὸς ἐγένετο].

PAFFENROTH, Kim, Famines in Luke-Acts. — ExpT 112 (2000-01) 405-407.
THIERING, B.E., The Three and a Half Years of Elijah (Lk IV 25; Jas V 17). — NT 23 (1981) 41-55.

λογίζομαι 1 + 1 (Mk 0/2)

1. reason about; 2. keep mental record; 3. hold a view (Lk 22,37); 4. charge to account

Word groups	Lk	Acts	Mt	Mk
λογίζομαι passive (VKc)	22,37	19,27	0	0/1

λόγος 32/33 + 65 (Mt 33, Mk 23[24])

1. statement; 2. speech (Acts 14,12); 3. gospel (Acts 19,20); 4. treatise (Acts 1,1); 5. Word; 6. account (Lk 16,2); 7. reason (Acts 10,29); 8. event (Acts 8,21); 9. appearance; 10. accusation (Acts 19,38)

Word groups	Lk	Acts	Mt	Mk
αἴρω τὸν λόγον → ἀκούω/(ἀπο) δέχομαι τὸν **λόγον**; cf. συναίρω λόγον Mt 18,23; 25,19	8,12		0	1
ἀκούω (+) τὸν λόγον / τοὺς λόγους / τῶν λόγων → ἀκούω τὸν **λόγον** / τὸν **λόγον** τοῦ θεοῦ/κυρίου / **ῥήματα**; αἴρω/(ἀπο)δέχομαι (τὸν) **λόγον**; cf. ἠκούσθη ὁ λόγος Acts 11,22	5,1; 6,47; 8,15.21; 10,39; 11,28	2,22; 4,4; 5,5.24; 10,44; 13,7.44; 15,7; 19,10	9	3
ἀπαγγέλλω + τοὺς λόγους τούτους → ἀπαγγέλλω τὰ **ῥήματα** ταῦτα		16,36	0	0
διὰ λόγου (VKj)		15,27.32	0	0
διακονία τοῦ λόγου		6,4	0	0
εὐαγγελίζομαι (+) τὸν λόγον		8,4; 15,35	0	0

καταγγέλλω τὸν λόγον BOISMARD 1984 Aa97		13,5; 15,36; 17,13	0	0
κατὰ λόγον + ἀνέχομαι (LN: accept a complaint)		18,14	0	0
λαλέω τὸν λόγον τοῦ θεοῦ/κυρίου; cf. Heb 13,7 BOISMARD 1984 Ca31		4,29.31; 8,25; 13,46; 16,32	0	0
λόγοι plural (SCa; VKa)	1,4.20; 3,4; 4,22; 6,47; 9,26.28.44; 21,33; 23,9; 24,17.44	2,22.40; 5,5.24; 7,22; 15,15.24; 16,36; 20,35	9	3
λόγον (+) ἀποδίδωμι (SCe; VKd) → μαρτύριον ἀποδίδωμι	16,2	19,40	1	0
λόγον (+) λαλέω (SCb; VKb) → ῥῆμα (δια)λαλέω	24,44	4,29.31; 8,25; 11,19; 13,46; 14,25; 16,6.32	0	4
λόγον λέγω/εἶπον/ἐρῶ / λόγῳ λέγω (SCc; VKc); λέγω + λόγος	3,4 v.l.; 7,7; 12,10; 20,3; 22,61*	13,15; 15,24 v.l.; 20,35.38	4	1
λόγος with reference to Jesus' teaching (SCm)	4,22.32.36; 6,47; 8,12.13.15; 9,26.44; 10,39; 21,33; 24,44	1,1	16	16
λόγος with reference to scripture (SCn)	3,4	15,15	0	0
ὁ λόγος ηὔξανεν BOISMARD 1984 Aa98		6,7; 12,24; 19,20	0	0
λόγος + ἔργον (VKl) DENAUX 2009 LAⁿ (?)	24,19	7,22		
λόγος + ἐρωτάω (VKf)	20,3		1	1
λόγος Ἰησοῦ		20,35	0	0
λόγος οὗτος →ῥῆμα τοῦτο; τὰ ῥήματα ταῦτα	4,36; 7,17; 9,28.44; 24,17.44	2,22; 5,5.24; 7,29; 8,21; 15,6; 16,36; 22,22	7	1
λόγος + παράκλησις → λέγω + παρακαλέω		13,15	0	0
λόγος + πληρόω → γεγραμμένα/ γραφή/ῥῆμα + πληρόω	1,20		0	0
λόγος (+) ποιέω (SCd; VKe)	6,47; 8,21	1,1; 20,24	2	0
λόγος πολύς/πλείων; cf. Heb 5,11 BOISMARD 1984 Ca13		2,40; 15,32; 20,2	0	0
λόγους + ἀντιβάλλω πρὸς ἀλλήλους	24,17		0	0
λόγῳ / ἐν λόγῳ (SCh; VKk)	7,7; 23,9; 24,19	2,40; 7,22; 10,29; 15,24; 20,2	3	1
ποιέομαι λόγου (LN: be of opinion)		20,24	0	0
ὑπηρέτης τοῦ λόγου	1,2		0	0

Characteristic of Luke

GASTON 1973 64 [Lked]; MORGENTHALER 1958A

	Lk	Acts	Mt	Mk
ἀκούω τὸν λόγον → ἀκούω τὸν λόγον/ῥήματα; ἀκούω τὸν λόγον τοῦ θεοῦ/κυρίου; αἴρω /(ἀπο)δέχομαι (τὸν) λόγον; cf. ἠκούσθη ὁ λόγος Acts 11,22; παρακούω τὸν λόγον Mk 5,36 HAWKINS 1909add	5,1; 8,15.21; 10,39; 11,28	4,4; 10,44; 13,7.44; 15,7; 19,10	6	3
ἀκούω τὸν λόγον τοῦ θεοῦ/κυρίου → ἀκούω τὸν λόγον/ῥήματα BOISMARD 1984 Ab31; DENAUX 2009 L***; GOULDER 1989; NEIRYNCK 1985	5,1; 8,21; 10,39 (αὐτοῦ); 11,28	13,7.44; 19,10	0	0

(ἀπο)δέχομαι (τὸν) λόγον → ἀκούω/αἴρω τὸν **λόγον/ῥήματα**; cf. 1 Thess 1,6; 2,13; Jam 1,21; δέχομαι λόγια Acts 7,38 BOISMARD 1984 cb144; NEIRYNCK 1985	8,13	2,41; 8,14; 11,1; 17,11	0	0
λόγος with reference to the gospel message (*SC*l); see also **λόγος** τοῦ θεοῦ/κυρίου DENAUX 2009 1A*	1,2.4	2,41; 4,4.29; 6,4; 8,4; 10,36.44; 11,19; 13,26; 14,3.25; 15,7; 16,6; 17,11; 18,5; 20,7.32	0	0
λόγος τοῦ θεοῦ (*SC*j) → **ῥῆμα** θεοῦ; cf. Jn 8,55; 10,35; 17,14.17 BOISMARD 1984 Eb55; CADBURY 1920 114 DENAUX 2009 L***; GOULDER 1989*; HAWKINS 1909L; NEIRYNCK 1985; PLUMMER 1922 lx	5,1; 8,11.21; 11,28	4,31; 6,2.7; 8,14; 11,1; 12,24; 13,5.7.44 *v.l.*46. 48 *v.l.*; 16,32 *v.l.*; 17,13; 18,11	1	1
λόγος τοῦ κυρίου (*SC*k) → **ῥῆμα** τοῦ κυρίου BOISMARD 1984 Da1; PLUMMER 1922 lix	22,61*	8,25; 12,24 *v.l.*; 13,44.48.49; 14,25 *v.l.*; 15,35.36; 16,32; 19,10.20; 20,35	0	0
λόγος τῆς χάριτος BOISMARD 1984 Ab134; NEIRYNCK 1985	4,22	14,3; 20,32	0	0

Literature

VON BENDEMANN 2001 413: "Λόγος τοῦ θεοῦ ist typisch lukanisches Syntagma ... Zur Verbindung von Hören und λόγος vgl. die Belege in Apg 4,4; 10,44; 11,22; 13,7; 15,7; 19,10; 28,28"; DENAUX 2009 1A[n] [(ἀπο)δέχομαι (τὸν) λόγον; λόγος τῆς χάριτος]; HAUCK 1934 [Vorzugsverbindung: λόγος τοῦ θεοῦ]; JEREMIAS 1980 50: "LkEv 4,22 hat den Plural τοῖς λόγοις τῆς χάριτος αὐτοῦ, dagegen Apg 14,3; 20,32 (τῷ λόγῳ τῆς χάριτος αὐτοῦ) den Singular mit Personalpronomen"; 129 [λόγος τοῦ θεοῦ: von Lukas bevorzugter Terminus]; 193 [τὸν λόγον αὐτοῦ: "Seine (Jesu) Verkündigung": red.]; RADL 1975 416 [λόγος; ἀκούω τὸν λόγον]; SCHNEIDER 1969 93.163 [ὁ λόγος τοῦ κυρίου: Vorzugswörter und -ausdrücke des Luk].

CADBURY, Henry J., Commentary on the Preface of Luke, 1922. Esp. 500 [Lk 1,2].

KODELL, Jerome, "The Word of God Grew": The Ecclesial Tendency of λόγος in Acts 1,7; 12,24; 19,20. — *Bib* 55 (1974) 505-519.

ORSATTI, Mauro, La parola: Appunti su un'originale espressione degli Atti degli Apostoli. — *La Parola e le parole* (Quaderni teologici del Seminario di Brescia). Brescia: Morcelliana, 2003, 73-90. Esp. 74-84: "Rilievi statistici e filologici sul termine 'parola'".

TAEGER, Jens-Wilhelm, *Der Mensch und sein Heil*, 1982. Esp. 123-125: "δέχεσθαι τὸν λόγον (τοῦ θεοῦ)"; 125-127: "ἀποδέχεσθαι τὸν λόγον αὐτοῦ (= des Petrus)"; 163-177: "ὁ λόγος τοῦ θεοῦ / τοῦ κυρίου) ηὔξανεν"; 177-178: "διεφέρετο ὁ λόγος τοῦ κυρίου".

λοιμός 1 + 1 (Mt 0/1)

1. plague (Lk 21,11); 2. troublemaker (Acts 24,5)

Word groups	Lk	Acts	Mt	Mk
λιμοὶ καὶ λοιμοί	21,11		0/1	0

Characteristic of Luke

HAWKINS 1909LA; MORGENTHALER 1958*

Literature

DENAUX 2009 LA[n]; HAUCK 1934 [seltenes Alleinwort].

λοιπός 6 + 6 (Mt 4, Mk 2) | remaining

Word groups	Lk	Acts	Mt	Mk
τὰ λοιπά (VKc)	12,26		0	1
τὸ λοιπόν (VKa)		27,20	1	1
λοιπός + genitive (VKd)	18,11		0	0

Characteristic of Luke	Lk	Acts	Mt	Mk
οἱ λοιποι plural	8,10; 12,26; 18,9.11;	2,37; 5,13; 17,9; 27,44;	4	3
GOULDER 1989; HARNACK 1906 43	24,9.10	28,9		

Literature

JEREMIAS 1980 111-112: "καὶ αἱ λοιπαί: Lukas fügt wiederholt einen generalisierenden Ausdruck zu bereits spezifierten Wendungen hinzu".

λύκος 1 + 1 (Mt 2)

1. wolf (Lk 10,3; Acts 20,29); 2. fierce person (Acts 20,29)

Word groups	Lk	Acts	Mt	Mk
λύκος + ἀρήν; cf. λύκος + πρόβατον Mt 7,15; 10,16	10,3		0	0
λύκος βαρεῖς (VKa)		20,29	1	0

λύπη 1

1. regret; 2. sadness (Lk 22,45)

Λυσανίας 1 | Lysanias (Lk 3,1)

λυσιτελέω 1 | λυσιτελεῖ: be advantageous (Lk 17,2)

Literature

HAUCK 1934 [seltenes Alleinwort].

λυτρόομαι 1 | liberate (Lk 24,21)

Literature

EASTON 1910 149 [especially characteristic of L]; SCHÜRMANN 1957 91-92.

BOURASSA, François, Rédemption. — Science et Esprit 21 (1969) 19-33. [NTA 14, 67]
DE LORENZI, Lorenzo, Gesù λυτρωτής: Atti 7,35. — RivBib 8 (1960) 31-41. Esp. 35-36.
HILL, David, Greek Words and Hebrew Meanings, 1967. Esp. 66-81: "The λύτρον-words in the New Testament".
WILCOX, Max, Semitisms in the New Testament, 1984. Esp. 1013-1014: "λυτροῦσθαι τὸν Ἰσραηλ (Luke 24:21), and λύτρωσις Ιερουσαλημ (Luke 2:38; cf. 1:68)".

λύτρωσις 2 | liberation (Lk 1,68; 2,38)

Literature

DENAUX 2009 L[n]; EASTON 1910 149 [especially characteristic of L] ; SCHÜRMANN 1957 91-92.

BORMANN, Lukas, *Recht, Gerechtigkeit und Religion*, 2001. Esp. 148.

DE LORENZI, Lorenzo, Gesù λυτρωτής: Atti 7,35. — *RivBib* 8 (1960) 31-41. Esp. 36.

HILL, David, *Greek Words and Hebrew Meanings*, 1967. Esp. 66-81: "The λύτρον-words in the New Testament".

MARROW, Stanley B., Principles for Interpreting the New Testament Soteriological Terms. — *NTS* 36 (1990) 268-280. Esp. 272-274: "Redemption and ransom".

WILCOX, Max, Semitisms in the New Testament, 1984. Esp. 1013-1014: "λυτροῦσθαι τὸν Ἰσραηλ (Luke 24:21), and λύτρωσις Ἰερουσαλημ (Luke 2:38; cf. 1:68)".

λυχνία 2 (Mt 1, Mk 1)	lampstand (Lk 8,16; 11,33)

λύχνος 6 (Mt 2, Mk 1)	lamp

Word groups	Lk	Acts	Mt	Mk
λύχνοι plural (*VK*b)	12,35		0	0

Characteristic of Luke

DENAUX 2009 L***†; GOULDER 1989*; HAWKINS 1909 †L ; PLUMMER 1922 lx

	Lk	Acts	Mt	Mk
ἅπτω λύχνον → (ἀν/περι)ἅπτω + πῦρ/πυρά BOISMARD 1984 Ab69; GOULDER 1989*; HARNACK 1906 54; HAWKINS 1909 186; NEIRYNCK 1985	8,16; 11,33; 15,8		0	0

Literature

BDAG 2000 606 [Lk 11,34: literature]; DENAUX 2009 La[n] [ἅπτω λύχνον]; HAUCK 1934 [Vorzugswort].

HAHN, Ferdinand, Die Worte vom Licht Lk 11,33-36. — HOFFMANN, P. – BROX, N. – PESCH, W. (eds.), *Orientierung an Christus*. FS J. Schmid, 1973, 107-138.

λύω 7 + 6 (Mt 6/7, Mk 5)	

1. untie (Lk 3,16); 2. set free (Lk 13,16); 3. destroy (Acts 27,41); 4. dismiss (Acts 13,43); 5. transgress; 6. permit; 7. do away with (Acts 2,24); 8. put an end to

Word groups	Lk	Acts	Mt	Mk
λύω (+) ἀπό → **ἀπολύω/ῥύομαι** ἀπό	13,15.16	22,30 *v.l.*	0	0
λύω βοῦν/πῶλον or human being (*VK*a)	13,15.16; 19,30.33[1.2]	22,30; 24,26*	1	3
λύω (+) δέω/δεσμός (*VK*c)	13,16; 19,30	22,(29-)30	5	3
λύω τὸν ἱμάντα / τὸ ὑπόδημα (*VK*b)	3,16	7,33; 13,25	0	1

Λώτ 3	Lot (Lk 17,28.29.32)

M

Μάαθ 1	Maath (Lk 3,26)

Μαγδαληνή 2 (Mt 3, Mk 3[4]) Magdalene

Word groups	Lk	Acts	Mt	Mk
ἡ Μαγδαληνή Μαρία (VKb)	24,10		0	0
Μαρία ἡ καλουμένη Μαγδαληνή (VKa)	8,2		0	0

μαθητής 37/39 + 28/30 (Mt 72/75, Mk 46)
1. follower (Acts 6,1); 2. pupil (Lk 6,40)

Word groups	Lk	Acts	Mt	Mk
δύο μαθηταί / δύο τῶν μαθητῶν (VKf)	7,18²; 19,29		1/2	2
οἱ δώδεκα μαθηταί (SCc; VKd) → δώδεκα ἀπόστολοι; cf. ἕνδεκα μαθηταί Mt 28,16	9,1*		3/4	0
μαθηταί disciples of John (SCa; VKa)	5,33; 7,18¹·²; 11,1²		3	3
μαθηταί + προσκαλέομαι → δώδεκα + προσκαλέομαι	7,18²		1	3
μαθητής + διδάσκαλος (SCe; VKj)	6,40; 19,39; 22,11		5	2
μαθητής + ὄχλος (SCf; VKl)	6,17; 7,11; 9,16. 18; 12,1; 19,39	6,7; 11,26	9	9
ὄχλος + μαθητῶν → πλῆθος τῶν μαθητῶν	6,17		0	0
τις τῶν μαθητῶν (SCd; VKg) → εἷς (ἐκ) τῶν δώδεκα; cf. εἷς τῶν μαθητῶν Mk 13,1	11,1¹	11,29	0	1

Characteristic of Luke
GASTON 1973 66 [Lked?]

	Lk	Acts	Mt	Mk
μαθητής singular (VKk); see also μαθητής + διδάσκαλος DENAUX 2009 1A*	14.26.27.33	9,10.26; 16,1; 21,16	1	0
πλῆθος τῶν μαθητῶν → ὄχλος μαθητῶν BOISMARD 1984 Ab195; NEIRYNCK 1985	19,37	6,2	0	0

Literature
DENAUX 2009 LAⁿ [πλῆθος τῶν μαθητῶν].

Μαθθαῖος 1 + 1 (Mt 2, Mk 1) Matthew (Lk 6,15; Acts 1,13)

Μαθθάτ 2 Matthat

Word groups	Lk	Acts	Mt	Mk
Μαθθάτ father of Heli (VKa)	3,24		0	0
Μαθθάτ father of Jorim (VKb)	3,29		0	0

Μαθουσαλά 1 Methuselah (Lk 3,37)

μακαρίζω 1 regard as happy (Lk 1,48)

μακάριος 15 + 2 (Mt 13) happy

Word groups	Lk	Acts	Mt	Mk
μακάριόν ἐστιν (VKb)		20,35	0	0
μακάριον + μᾶλλον (VKc)		20,35	0	0
μακάριος + ὅτι	1,45; 6,20.21[1.2]; 14,14		10	0

Literature

HARNACK 1906 140 (ET: 202: "μακάριος, wanting in St. Mark, and occurring in St. Matthew, apart from the Beatitudes, only four times; in Luke's Gospel, however, eleven times").

DUPONT, Jacques, *Les Béatitudes*, II, 1969. Esp. 324-338.

MULLINS, Tenrence Y., Ascription as a Literary Form. — *NTS* 19 (1973) 194-205. [NTA 17, 842: The most comon types are woes (*ouai*), eulogies (*eulogētos* or *eulogēmenos*) and beatitudes (*makarios*)]

TOPEL, L. John, *Children of a Compassionate God: A Theological Exegesis of Luke 6:20-49*. Collegeville, MN: The Liturgical Press, 2001, XVII-340. Esp. 62-67.

μακράν 2 + 3 (Mt 1, Mk 1)   far (away)

Word groups	Lk	Acts	Mt	Mk
οἱ εἰς μακράν (VKa)		2,39	0	0
οὐ μακράν	7,6	17,27	0	0
DENAUX 2009 LA[n]				
ὑπάρχω οὐ + μακρὰν ἀπό; cf. ἀπέχω μακράν Lk 15,20		17,27	0	0
ἀπέχω + οὐ μακρὰν ἀπό; cf. ἀπέχω μακράν Lk 15,20	7,6		0	0

Literature

HAUCK 1934 [seltenes Alleinwort; Vorzugsverbindung: μακρὰν ἀπέχω].

CADBURY, Henry J., Litotes in Acts. — BARTH, E.H. – COCROFT, R.E. (eds.), *Festschrift to Honor F. Wilbur Gingrich*, 1972, 70-84. Esp. 62-63 [οὐ μακράν].

μακρόθεν 4 (Mt 2, Mk 5)   far (away)

Word groups	Lk	Acts	Mt	Mk
ἀπὸ μακρόθεν (SCa; VKa)	16,23; 23,49		0	0
DENAUX 2009 L[n]				
ἵστημι + (ἀπὸ) μακρόθεν → ἵστημι πόρρωθεν	18,13; 23,49		0	0
DENAUX 2009 L[n]				

Literature

PAFFENROTH 1997 82; REHKOPF 1959 95 [vorlukanisch]; SCHNEIDER 1969 75-76.164: "Lk läßt ἀπό vor μακρόθεν weg" [Vorzugswörter und -ausdrücke des Luk].

μακροθυμέω 1 (Mt 2)

1. be patient; 2. delay in (Lk 18,7)

Word groups	Lk	Acts	Mt	Mk
μακροθυμέω ἐπί + dative (VKa)	18,7		2	0

Literature

BEYER, Klaus, *Semitische Syntax im Neuen Testament*. I/1, 1962. Esp. 268, n. 1.

LJUNGVIK, H.L., Zur Erklärung einer Lk-Stelle (Luk. XVIII. 7). — *NTS* 10 (1963-64) 289-294. Esp. 293-294: "In den Worten καὶ μακροθυμεῖ ἐπ᾽ αὐτοῖς, so aufgefasst, liegt, so scheint es mir, *die eigentliche Pointe* der Darstellung. Sie dienen auch durch ihre Anknüpfung an die Parabel v.2-5 dazu, diese und die darauf folgende Belehrung zu einer natürlichen Einheit zusammenzufügen. Und endlich wird so der ganze Vers 7 logisch im besten Einklag mit der Schlußfolgerung V. 8a stehen: 'Ich sage euch, er wird ihnen Recht verschaffen und zwar in Kürze'".

RIESENFELD, Harald, Zu μακροθυμεῖν (Lk 18,7). — BLINZLER, J. – KUSS, O. – MUßNER, F. (eds.), *Neutestamentliche Aufsätze*. FS J. Schmid, 1963, 214-217.

SAHLIN, Harald, *Zwei Lukasstellen* (Symbolae Biblicae Upsalienses, 4). Uppsala, 1945. Esp. 9-20.

WIFSTAND, Albert, Lk XVIII. 7. — *NTS* 11 (1964) 72-74.

μακρός 3 (Mt 0/1, Mk 1)

1. long (time) (Lk 20,47); 2. far (away) (Lk 15,13; 19,12)

Word groups	Lk	Acts	Mt	Mk
μακρά adverb (*VK*a)	20,47		0/1	1
εἰς χώραν μακράν DENAUX 2009 Lⁿ	15,13; 19,12		0	0

Literature

EASTON 1910 166 [εἰς χώραν μακράν: cited by Weiss as characteristic of L, and possibly corroborative]

μαλακός 1 (Mt 2)

1. soft (Lk 7,25); 2. homosexual

Μαλελεήλ 1   Maleleel (Lk 3,37)

μᾶλλον 5/6 + 7 (Mt 9, Mk 5/6)

1. more (than) (Lk 5,15; 7,36; 9,42; 10,48; 15,11; Acts 20,35); 2. instead (Acts 27,11)

Word groups	Lk	Acts	Mt	Mk
μακάριον + μᾶλλον		20,35	0	0
μᾶλλον (+) ἤ(περ) (*VK*e)		4,19; 5,29; 20,35; 27,11	1	0
πολλῷ μᾶλλον (*SC*a; *VK*a)	18,39		1	1
πόσῳ μᾶλλον (*SC*b; *VK*b)	11,13; 12.24.28		2	0
πόσῳ μᾶλλον ... οὕτως; cf. πολλῷ μᾶλλον οὕτως Mt 6,30	12,28		1	0

Literature

COLLISON 1977 156 [as comparative adverb: linguistic usage of Luke: likely].

DUPONT, Jacques, *Le discours de Milet*, 1962. Esp. 333-335 [μᾶλλον ἤ].

μαμωνᾶς 3 (Mt 1)   wordly wealth (Lk 16,9.11.13)

Literature

COLELLA, Pasquale, Zu Lk 16,7. — *ZNW* 64 (1973) 124-126.
DELEBECQUE, Édouard, *Études grecques*, 1976. Esp. 89-97: "Le régisseur infidèle (16,1-13)".
RÜGER, Hans Peter, Μαμωνας. — *ZNW* 64 (1973) 127-131.

Μάρϑα 4	Martha (Lk 10,38.40.41[1.2])			
Word groups	Lk	Acts	Mt	Mk
Μάρϑα Μάρϑα (*VK*a)	10,41[1.2]		0	0

Μαρία 4 + 1 (Mt 8, Mk 7[8])	Mary

Literature

BADG 2000 616-617 [literature]; JEREMIAS 1980 46-47: "Im LkEv kommt der Name der Mutter Jesu nur in der Kindheitsgeschichte vor. Auffälligerweise alternieren die semitische Form Μαριάμ ... und die hellenisierte Form Μαρία ... Außerdem fällt auf, daß Μαριάμ außer 2,16 (wo der Artikel anaphorisch ist) stets artikellos gebraucht wird, Μαρία dagegen an beiden Stellen den Artikel hat. ... so legt sich der schluß nahe, daß die semitische Form Μαριάμ der Tradition, die hellenisierte Form Μαρία der Redaktion zugehört".

Μαριάμ 13 + 1 (Mt 3)	Mary

Word groups	Lk	Acts	Mt	Mk
Μαριάμ Mary Magdalene (*SC*b; *VK*b)	8,2; 24,10[1]		3	3[4]
Μαριάμ mother of James (*SC*c; *VK*c)	24,10[2]		3	3
Μαριάμ mother of Jesus (*SC*a; *VK*a)	1,27.30.34.38.39.41.46.56; 2,5.16.19.34	1,14	5	1
Μαριάμ mother of John Mark (*SC*e; *VK*f)		12,12	0	0
Μαριάμ sister of Martha (*SC*d; *VK*e) DENAUX 2009 L[n]	10,39.42		0	0

Characteristic of Luke

HENDRIKS 1986 434

Literature

BADG 2000 616-617 [literature]; DENAUX 2009 Lan; GERSDORF 1816 194 [Μαριάμ]; 196 [εἶπεν δὲ Μαριάμ πρὸς τὸν ἄγγελον]; 239 [καὶ ἀνεῦραν τήν τε Μαριάμ]; JEREMIAS 1980 46-47: "Im LkEv kommt der Name der Mutter Jesu nur in der Kindheitsgeschichte vor. Auffälliger-weise alternieren die semitische Form Μαριάμ ... und die hellenisierte Form Μαρία ... Außerdem fällt auf, daß Μαριάμ außer 2,16 (wo der Artikel anaphorisch ist) stets artikellos gebraucht wird, Μαρία dagegen an beiden Stellen den Artikel hat. ... so legt sich der schluß nahe, daß die semitische Form Μαριάμ der Tradition, die hellenisierte Form Μαρία der Redaktion zugehört".

GEORGE, Augustin, La mère de Jésus. — ID., *Études*, 1978, 429-464.
LAURENTIN, René, Traces d'allusions étymologiques en Luc 1–2 (II). — *Bib* 38 (1957) 1-23. Esp. 5-12: "Marie".

μαρτυρέω 1/2 + 11/12 (Mt 1)	

1. witness (Acts 22,5); 2. speak well of (Lk 4,22)

Word groups	Lk	Acts	Mt	Mk
μαρτυρέομαι passive (VKa)		6,3; 10,22; 16,2; 22,12; 26,22*	0	0
μαρτυρέομαι ὑπό + genitive; cf. Rom 3,21; 3 Jn 12 BOISMARD 1984 ca72		10,22; 16,2; 22,12	0	0
μαρτυρέω + dative (VKc)	4,22	10,43; 13,22; 14,3; 15,8; 22,5; 26,22*	1	0
μαρτυρέω + infinitive (VKe)		10,43	0	0

Characteristic of Luke
MORGENTHALER 1958A

Literature
DENAUX 2009 1An; RADL 1975 416.

BROX, Norbert, *Zeugen und Märtyrer: Untersuchungen zur frühchristlichen Zeugnis-Terminologie* (SANT, 5). München: Kösel, 1961, 250 p. Esp. 43-69: "Der technische Wortgebrauch bei Lukas".

Ó FEARGHAIL, Fearghus, Rejection in Nazareth: Lk 4,22. — *ZNW* 75 (1984) 60-72. Esp. 65-67 [μαρτυρέω]; 67 [θαυμάζω]; 67-69 [οἱ λόγοι τῆς χάριτος].

TRITES, Allison A., *The New Testament Concept of Witness*, 1977. Esp. 72-74.

μαρτυρία 1 + 1 (Mk 3)
1. witness; 2. testimony (Lk 22,71); 3. reputation

Word groups	Lk	Acts	Mt	Mk
μαρτυρία περί + genitive (VKe)		22,18	0	0

Literature
BORMANN, Lukas, *Recht, Gerechtigkeit und Religion*, 2001. Esp. 185-186.

BROX, Norbert, *Zeugen und Märtyrer: Untersuchungen zur frühchristlichen Zeugnis-Terminologie* (SANT, 5). München: Kösel, 1961, 250 p. Esp. 43-69: "Der technische Wortgebrauch bei Lukas".

TRITES, Allison A., *The New Testament Concept of Witness*, 1977. Esp. 67-68.

μαρτύριον 3 + 2 (Mt 3, Mk 3)
1. witness (Lk 21,23); 2. testimony (Lk 5,14; 9,5)

Word groups	Lk	Acts	Mt	Mk
εἰς μαρτύριον (SCa; VKa)	5,14; 9,5; 21,13		3	3
μαρτύριον ἀποδίδωμι → λόγον ἀποδίδωμι; cf. ὅρκους ἀποδίδωμι Mt 5,33		4,33	0	0
σκηνὴ τοῦ μαρτυρίου (SCb; VKb)		7,44	0	0

Literature
BORMANN, Lukas, *Recht, Gerechtigkeit und Religion*, 2001. Esp. 186.

BROX, Norbert, *Zeugen und Märtyrer: Untersuchungen zur frühchristlichen Zeugnis-Terminologie* (SANT, 5). München: Kösel, 1961, 250 p. Esp. 43-69: "Der technische Wortgebrauch bei Lukas".

HARTMAN, Lars, *Testimonium linguae*, 1963. Esp. 57-75: "'Ἀποβήσεται ὑμῖν εἰς μαρτύριον".

TRITES, Allison A., *The New Testament Concept of Witness*, 1977. Esp. 68-71.

μάρτυς 2 + 13 (Mt 2, Mk 1)

1. witness (Lk 11,48; 24,48); 2. martyr (Acts 22,20)

Word groups	Lk	Acts	Mt	Mk
μάρτυς + θεός (VKa)		22,15 (αὐτός)	0	0
ὑπηρέτης καὶ μάρτυς		26,16	0	0

Characteristic of Luke
DENAUX 2009 lA*; MORGENTHALER 1958A

	Lk	Acts	Mt	Mk
μάρτυς (εἰμι/γίνομαι) + genitive; cf. Rom 1,9 BOISMARD 1984 Ab9; NEIRYNCK 1985	24,48	1,8.22; 2,32; 3,15; 5,32; 10,39; 13,31; 22,15; 26,16	0	0

Literature
DENAUX 2009 lA[n] [μάρτυς (εἰμι/γίνομαι) + genitive]; JEREMIAS 1980 322: "μάρτυς als Bezeichnung des urchristlichen Zeugen im NT findet sich ganz überwiegend im Doppelwerk".

BORMANN, Lukas, *Recht, Gerechtigkeit und Religion*, 2001. Esp. 186-188.

BROX, Norbert, *Zeugen und Märtyrer: Untersuchungen zur frühchristlichen Zeugnis-Terminologie* (SANT, 5). München: Kösel, 1961, 250 p. Esp. 43-69: "Der technische Wortgebrauch bei Lukas".

GÜNTHER, Ernst, Zeuge und Märtyrer. — *ZNW* 47 (1956) 145-161.

HAGENE, Sylvia, *Zeiten der Wiederherstellung*, 2003. Esp. 160: "Beobachtungen zur Wortfamilie μαρτύς κτλ. im lkDW".

SCHNEIDER, Gerhard, Die zwölf Apostel als "Zeugen": Wesen, Ursprung und Funktion einer lukanischen Konzeption. — SCHEELE, Paul-Werner – SCHNEIDER, Gerhard (eds.), *Christuszeugnis der Kirche: Theologische Studien*. Essen: Verlag Fredebeul & Koenen, 1970, 39-65; = ID., *Lukas, Theologe der Heilsgeschichte*, 1985, 61-85.

TRITES, Allison A., *The New Testament Concept of Witness*, 1977. Esp. 66-67.

μαστιγόω 1 (Mt 3, Mk 1)

1. beat with a whip (Lk 18,32); 2. punish

Word groups	Lk	Acts	Mt	Mk
μαστιγόω ἀποκτείνω; cf. μαστιγόω + σταυρόω Mt 20,19; 23,34; φραγελλόω + σταυρόω Mt 27,26; Mk 15,15	18,33		1	1

μάστιξ 1 + 1 (Mk 3)

1. flogging (Acts 22,24); 2. disease (Lk 7,21)

Word groups	Lk	Acts	Mt	Mk
μάστιξ (beating with a) whip (VKa)		22,24	0	0

μαστός 2 | breast

Word groups	Lk	Acts	Mt	Mk
κοιλία + μαστός DENAUX 2009 L[n]	11,27; 23,29		0	0

Literature
VON BENDEMANN 2001 420; DENAUX 2009 L[n].

Ματταθά 1	Mattatha (Lk 3,31)

Ματταθίας 2	Mattathias

Word groups	Lk	Acts	Mt	Mk
Ματταθίας son of Amos (VKa)	3,25		0	0
Ματταθίας son of Semei (VKb)	3,26		0	0

μάχαιρα 5 + 2 (Mt 7, Mk 3)
1. sword (Lk 21,24; 22,36.38.49.52); 2. war; 3. death; 4. discord

Word groups	Lk	Acts	Mt	Mk
μάχαιραι plural (VKa)	22,38.52		2	2
στόμα μαχαίρης (VKb)	21,24		0	0

Literature
SCHÜRMANN 1957 124 [Lk 22,36 μάχαιρα luk R weniger wahrscheinlich].

FINLAYSON, S.K., "The Enigma of the Swords". — ExpT 50 (1938-39) 563.

HEILIGENTHAL, Roman, Wehrlosigkeit oder Selbstschutz? Aspekte zum Verständnis des lukanischen Schwertwortes. — NTS 41 (1995) 39-58.

NAPIER, T.M., The Enigma of the Swords. — ExpT 49 (1937-38) 467-470.

SCHWARZ, Günther, κυριε, ιδου μαχαιραι ωδε δυο. [Lk 22,38] — BibNot 8 (1979) 23.

WESTERN, W., "The Enigma of the Swords". — ExpT 50 (1938-39) 377.

—, The Enigma of the Swords, St. Luke xxii.38. — ExpT 52 (1940-41) 357.

μεγαλειότης 1 + 1
1. prominence (Acts 19,27); 2. mighty power (Lk 9,43)

Word groups	Lk	Acts	Mt	Mk
μεγαλειότης τοῦ θεοῦ →μεγαλύνω + θεός/κύριος; δυνατός + μεγάλα; cf. μεγαλεῖος τοῦ θεοῦ Acts 2,11	9,43		0	0

Characteristic of Luke → μεγαλύνω; cf. μεγαλεῖος Lk 1,49*; Acts 2,11

VOGEL 1899B

	Lk	Acts	Mt	Mk
μεγαλειότης (and cognates μεγαλύνω/ μεγαλεῖος) BOISMARD 1984 cb113; DENAUX 2009 1A*; NEIRYNCK 1985	1,46.49*; 9,43	2,11; 5,13; 10,46; 19,17.27	1	0

Literature
DENAUX 2009 LA[n]; HAUCK 1934 [Vorzugswort].

μεγαλύνω 2 + 3 (Mt 1)
1. make large (Lk 1,58); 2. praise greatness of (Lk 1,46; Acts 10,46); 3. honor highly (Acts 5,13)

Word groups	Lk	Acts	Mt	Mk
μεγαλύνω + θεός →μεγαλύνω + κύριος; μεγαλειότης τοῦ θεοῦ; δυνατός +μεγάλα		10,46	0	0
μεγαλύνω (+) κύριος →μεγαλύνω + θεός DENAUX 2009 La[n]	1,46.58	19,17	0	0

Characteristic of Luke →μεγαλειότης; cf. μεγαλεῖος Lk 1,49*; Acts 2,11

DENAUX 2009 lA*; HARNACK 1906 140.151; PLUMMER 1922 lx

	Lk	Acts	Mt	Mk
μεγαλύνω (and cognates μεγαλειότης/μεγαλεῖος) BOISMARD 1984 Cb113; DENAUX 2009 lA*; NEIRYNCK 1985	1,46.49 *; 9,43	2,11; 5,13; 10,46; 19,17.27	1	0

Literature

GERSDORF 1816 200 [μεγαλύνει ἡ ψυχὴ τὸν κύριον].

GEORGE, Augustin, La prière. — ID., *Études*, 1978, 395-427. Esp. 402-405: "Le vocabulaire lucanien de la prière".

μέγας 26/27 + 30/33 (Mt 20, Mk 15)

1. great (quantity) (Lk 5,29); 2. great (degree) (Acts 4,33); 3. large (Acts 10,11); 4. important (Lk 7,16; Acts 8,10); 5. surprising

Word groups	Lk	Acts	Mt	Mk
ἀναφωνέω κραυγῇ μεγάλῃ →φωνῇ μεγαλῇ + βοάω/(ἀνα)κράζω/(ἀνα)φωνέω	1,42		0	0
δύναμις (+) μεγάλη (VKf)		4,33[1]; 8,10[2].13	0	0
ἐν μεγάλῳ (LN: in a long time; VKc)		26,29	0	0
ἡμέρα + μεγάλη (VKg)		2,20	0	0
θλῖψις μεγάλη (VKk)		7,11	1	0
λιμὸς μέγας/μεγάλη →λιμὸς ἰσχυρά DENAUX 2009 LA[n]	4,25	11,28		
μεγάλα noun (VKb)	1,49		0	0
μεγάλα δυνατός →μεγαλύνω + θεός/κύριος; μεγαλειότης τοῦ θεοῦ; cf. δυνατός + μεγαλεῖος Lk 1,49 v.l.	1,49		0	0
μέγας + μικρός/μικρότερος (VKn) → μείζων + μικρότερος DENAUX 2009 lA[n]	9,48	8,10[1]; 26,22	0	0
μέγας + ὀλίγος/ἐλάχιστος (VKp)		26,29	1	0
σημεῖον μέγα (VKh)	21,11[2]	6,8	1	0
φωνῇ μεγαλῇ + βοάω/(ἀνα)κράζω/(ἀνα)φωνέω → ἀναφωνέω κραυγῇ μεγάλη; cf. φωνῇ μεγαλῇ + ἀναβοάω Mt 27,46	1,42 v.l.; 4,33; 8,28; 23,46	7,57.60; 8,7; 16,28	1/2	3

Characteristic of Luke	Lk	Acts	Mt	Mk
ἐστιν μέγας, said of someone BOISMARD 1984 Ab87; HARNACK 1906 72; NEIRYNCK 1985	1,15.32; 9,48	8,9	0	0
φόβος μέγας (SCa; VKj); cf. Rev 11,11 BOISMARD 1984 cb125; CREDNER 1836 141; NEIRYNCK 1985; PLUMMER 1922 lx	2,9; 8,37	2,44*; 5,5.11	0	1
φωνή/κραυγή μεγάλη (SCb; VKl) → φωνῇ μεγάλη + βοάω/(ἀνα)κράζω/(ἀνα)φωνέω; εἶπον φωνῇ μεγαλῇ CREDNER 1836 141; PLUMMER 1922 lx	1,42; 4,33; 8,28; 17,15; 19,37; 23,23.46	7,57.60; 8,7; 14,10; 16,28; 23,9; 26,24	2/3	4

χαρὰ μεγάλη (SCc; VKm) → **πολλὴ** χαρά CREDNER 1836 141; PLUMMER 1922 lx	2,10; 24,52	8,8*; 15,3	2	0

Literature

COLLISON 1977 186 [attributive use: linguistic usage of Luke: certain. It may also have been a linguistic usage of Luke's "other source-material"]; 187 [φωνὴ μεγάλη: probable]; DENAUX 2009 Laⁿ [ἔστιν μέγας, said of someone], LAn [φόβος μέγας]; GERSDORF 1816 195 [οὗτος ἔσται μέγας]; 198 [ἀναφωνέω κραυγῇ μεγάλη / φωνέω φωνῇ μεγαλῇ]; 227 [χαρὰν μεγάλην]; JEREMIAS 1980 57: "κραυγῇ μεγαλῇ: Selten. In LXX nur Ex 11,6; 12,30. Im NT nur im Doppelwerk (Lk 1,42; Apg 23,9)"; RADL 1975 416-417 [μέγας + φόβος; χαρά; φωνή; κραυγή]; SCHÜRMANN 1957 67.75 [μέγας superlative; μείζων].

CADBURY, Henri J., Lexical Notes on Luke-Acts, II, 1926. Esp. 194-195: "ἦν συνεχομένη πυρετῷ μεγάλῳ".

STRELAN, Rick, Recognizing the Gods (Acts 14.8-10). — NTS 46 (2000) 488-503. Esp. 490-493: "The stare"; 493-501: "The loud voice".

μέθη 1   drunkenness (Lk 21,34)

μεθίστημι 1 + 2

1. cause to move (Acts 13,22); 2. cause to change (Lk 16,4); 3. mislead (Acts 19,26) μεθίσταμαι: 1. cease

Word groups	Lk	Acts	Mt	Mk
μεθίσταμαι passive → (ἀποκαθ)ίσταμαι passive	16,4		0	0

Characteristic of Luke
BOISMARD 1984 cb168; NEIRYNCK 1985; PLUMMER 1922 lix

Literature
DENAUX 2009 lAⁿ.

μεθύσκομαι 1   get drunk (Lk 12,45)

Literature
HAUCK 1934 [seltenes Alleinwort].

μείγνυμι 1 (Mt 1)   mix (Lk 13,1)

μείζων 7 (Mt 9, Mk 3)

1. more; 2. superior to (Lk 7,28); 3. older

Word groups	Lk	Acts	Mt	Mk
μείζων + μικρότερος (VKa) → **μέγας** + μικρός/μικρότερος	7,28²		2	1
μείζων + νεώτερος (VKb)	22,26		0	0

Μελεά 1   Melea (Lk 7,31)

μέλει 1 + 1 (Mt 1, Mk 2)
1. think about; 2. be anxious about (Lk 10,40; Acts 18,17)

Word groups	Lk	Acts	Mt	Mk
οὐ μέλει (SCa)	10,40		1	2

μέλλω 12 + 34/35 (Mt 9/10, Mk 2)
1. be about to (Lk 21,7); 2. must be (Lk 9,44); 3. wait (Acts 22,16)

Word groups	Lk	Acts	Mt	Mk
τὸ κρίμα τὸ μέλλον		24,25	0	0
μέλλει + aorist infinitive (VKa)		12,6	0	0
μέλλει + future infinitive (VKb) → μέλλει ἔσεσθαι		11,28; 23,30*; 24,15.25 v.l.; 27,10	0	0
(τὸ) μέλλον / (τὰ) μέλλοντα noun (LN: future; SCa; VKc) → ὁ μέλλων	13,9; 21,36	26,22	0	1
μέλλω of divine destiny (SCb)	9,31.44; 21,7. 36; 24,21	13,34; 17,31; 20,38; 24,15.25; 26,22.23	4	2
μέλλων without the article + infinitive; cf. Heb 8,5; 10,27; Jam 2,12; 2 Pet 2,6 BOISMARD 1984 ca14		3,3; 13,34; 18,14; 20,3.7.13[1.2]; 21,37; 23,15.20.27; 26,2.22; 27,2.30	1	0
ὁ μέλλων (SCa) → (τὸ) μέλλον / (τὰ) μέλλοντα	3,7; 22,23; 24,21	22,29; 24,25	2	0
ὀργὴ ἡ μέλλουσα	3,7		1	0

Characteristic of Luke
DENAUX 2009 IA**; GASTON 1973 66 [Lked?]; HARNACK 1906 41 [Acts]; HENDRIKS 1986 468; MORGENTHALER 1958A

	Lk	Acts	Mt	Mk
ἤμελλεν,-ον DENAUX 2009 L***; GOULDER 1989	7,2; 9,31; 10,1; 19,4	12,6; 16,27; 27,33	0	0
μέλλει γίνεσθαι; cf. Rev 1,19 BOISMARD 1984 Bb114; NEIRYNCK 1985	21,7.36	26,22; 27,33	0	0
μέλλω πράσσειν BOISMARD 1984 Ab197; NEIRYNCK 1985	22,23	5,35	0	0

Literature
VON BENDEMANN 2001 414 "Imperfekt von μέλλειν c. inf. findet sich in den Synoptikern nur bei Lukas"; COLLISON 1977 58 [present/imperfect: linguistic usage of Luke: probable]; DENAUX 2009 LA[n] [μέλλει γίνεσθαι; μέλλω πράσσειν]; EASTON 1910 163 [ἤμελλον: cited by Weiss as characteristic of L, and possibly corroborative]; JEREMIAS 1980 152; 289 [red.]; RADL 1975 417 [μέλλω; μέλλω + inf.]; SCHÜRMANN 1957 13 [Luk braucht μέλλειν auffallend häufig].

ELLIOTT, James K., Textual Variation Involving the Augment in the Greek New Testament. — ZNW 69 (1978) 247-252.

MAHFOUZ, Hady, La fonction littéraire et théologique de Lc 3,1-20, 2003. Esp. 180-181 [μέλλουση ὀργή].

Μελχί 2
Melchi

Word groups	Lk	Acts	Mt	Mk
Μελχί son of Addi (VKb)	3,28		0	0

Μελχί son of Janna (VKa)	3,24		0	0

μέν 10/12 + 48/51 (Mt 20, Mk 5/7[8])
1. and; 2. indeed (Lk 22,22)

Word groups	Lk	Acts	Mt	Mk
ἐγὼ μέν	3,16	22,3*; 26,9	1	0
εἰ/ἐὰν/κἂν μέν (VKc)	10,6*; 13,9	18,14; 19,38; 25,11	1	0
εἰ μέν … εἰ δέ; cf. 2 Cor 11,4 BOISMARD 1984 Aa87		18,14(-15); 19,38(-39); 25,11	0	0
ἡμεῖς μέν	23,41		0	0
ὁ μέν used as pronoun (VKg)		1,6; 2,41; 5,41; 8,4.25; 14,4; 15,3.30; 17,32; 23,18; 28,5.24	1/3	0/1
μέν + ἀλλά (LN: on the one hand … on the other hand; VKd)		4,16(-17)	0	1
μέν γάρ (VKb); cf. Rom 7,14*; 1 Cor 5,3; 11,7.18; 12,8; 14,17; 2 Cor 9,1; 11,4; Heb 6,16*; 7,18.20; 8,4 v.l. 7*; 12,10 BOISMARD 1984 Da11; CREDNER 1836 137		3,22 v.l.; 4,16; 13,36; 23,8; 25,11 v.l.; 28,22	0	0
μέν … δέ (LN: [a]some … others; [b]on the one hand … on the other hand)	3,16.17*.18 (-19); 10,2. 6*; 11,48; 13,9; 23,33. 41	1,5; 2,41(-42); 3,13(-14); 5,23*; 8,4 (-5).25(-26); 9,7.31(-32); 11,16.19 (-20); 12,5; 13,36(-37); 14,3.4.12*; 15,3(-4).30(-31); 16,5(-6); 17,12(-13). 17(-18).32; 18,14(-15); 19,15.38(-39); 21,39; 22,3*.9; 23,8.18(-19). 31(-32); 25,4.11; 27,41.44; 28,5(-6).24	20	4/7[8]
μέν + πλήν (LN: on the one hand … on the other hand; VKe)	22,22		0	0
μέν without ἀλλά/δέ/ πλήν (SCb; VKf)	8,5	1,1; 3,21.22; 4,16; 27,21; 28,22	0	1
μὲν οὖν without ἀλλά/δέ/ πλήν (SCc; VKf)		1,6 v.l.18; 5,41; 13,4; 17,30; 19,32; 23,22; 26,4.9	0	0
ὁ μὲν οὖν + participle + verb BOISMARD 1984 Aa3		1,6; 2,41; 8,4.25; 11,19; 15,3.30; 23,18.31; 28,5	0	0
ὁ μὲν οὖν + noun; cf. Jn 19,24 BOISMARD 1984 Ba5		9,31; 12,5; 16,5; 17,30; 23,22.31; 25,4; 26,4	0	0
ὅς + μέν (VKh) → ὅς δέ	8,5; 23,33	3,13; 27,44	6	2
ὑμεῖς μέν		3,13	0	0

Characteristic of Luke
CADBURY 1920 145-146; HENDRIKS 1986 468; MORGENTHALER 1958A

	Lk	Acts	Mt	Mk
μέν on itself; cf. Jn 7,12; 11,6 BOISMARD 1984 Eb4; HENDRIKS 1986 468; NEIRYNCK 1985	3,18	1,1.6.18; 2,41; 3,13.21; 5,41; 8,25; 9,31; 11,19; 13,4; 14,3; 15,3.30; 16,5; 17,12.17. 30; 19,32; 21,39; 23,18.22.31; 25,4; 26,4. 9; 27,21; 28,5.22	0	0
μὲν οὖν (γε) (SCa; VKa) → εἰ μὲν οὖν CREDNER 1836 137; HARNACK 1906 40.52	3,18	1,6.18; 2,41; 5,41; 8,4.25; 9,31; 11,19; 12,5; 13,4; 14,3; 15,3.30; 16,5; 17,12.17.30; 18,14 v.l.; 19,32. 38; 23,18.22.31; 25,4.11; 26,4.9; 28,5	0	[1]

Literature
DENAUX 2009 IA[n] [μέν on itself; μὲν οὖν (γε)];JEREMIAS 1980 110: "*Fortleitendes μὲν οὖν ist*

lukanische Vorzugswendung"; RADL 1975 417 [μέν; μὲν οὖν]; SCHÜRMANN 1957 5-6 [bei Luk weniger Vorliebe für μέν-δέ als für μέν; häufig ist μέν durch οὖν verstärkt].

LARSEN, I., Notes on the Function of γάρ, οὖν, μέν, δέ, καί, and τέ in the Greek New Testament. — Notes on Translation (Dallas) 5 (1991) 35-47.
LEVISOHN, Stephen H., Textual Connections in Acts, 1987. Esp. 137-150: "oun and men oun".
READ-HEIMERDINGER, Jenny, The Bezan Text of Acts, 2002. Esp. 225-240: "οὖν, μέν and μὲν οὖν".

Μεννά 1	Menna (Lk 3,31)

μενοῦν 1

1. on the contrary (Lk 11,28); 2. therefore; 3. surely

Literature

HAUCK 1934 [seltenes Alleinwort].

THRALL, Margaret E., Greek Particles in the New Testament, 1962. Esp. 11-16 [ἀλλά γε καί, ἀλλὰ μενοῦν γε καί]; 34-36 [μενοῦν].

μένω 7 + 13/14 (Mt 3, Mk 2)

1. stay (Lk 10,7; Acts 27,31); 2. wait for (Acts 20,5); 3. continue to exist; 4. keep on

Word groups

Word groups	Lk	Acts	Mt	Mk
μένω + dative (VKg) ; cf. ἐπιμένω + dat. Acts 13,43*		$5,4^2$	0	0
μένω καθ' ἑαυτόν (VKc)		28,16	0	0
μένω μετά + genitive (VKd)	$24,29^1$		0	0
μένω (+) παρά + dative (VKe); cf. ἐπιμεῖναι παρά + dat. Acts 28,14; ξενίζω παρά + dat. Acts 10,6; 21,16		9,43; 18,3.20 v.l.; 21,7.8	0	0
μένω transitive (VKa) BOISMARD 1984 Aa142		20,5.23	0	0

Characteristic of Luke; cf. ἐμμένω Acts 14,22; 28,30; ἐπιμένω Acts 10,48; 12,16; 13,43*; 15,34*; 21,4.10; 28,12.14

CREDNER 1836 140; DENAUX 2009 IA**; GOULDER 1989; HARNACK 1906 35

	Lk	Acts	Mt	Mk
μένω ἐν + place; cf. Jn 7,9; 8,35; 11,6; 2 Tim 4,20; ἐπιμένω + acc. of time Acts 10,48; 21,4.10; 28,14 BOISMARD 1984 cb169; DENAUX 2009 LA*; NEIRYNCK 1985	8,27; 10,7; 19,5	9,43; 20,5.15* ; 27,31	0	0
μένω σύν + person (VKf) BOISMARD 1984 Ab135; HARNACK 1906 143; NEIRYNCK 1985	1,56; $24,29^2$	28,16	0	0

Literature

DENAUX 2009 La^n [μένω σύν + person]; GERSDORF 1816 201 [ἔμεινεν δὲ Μαριὰμ σὺν αὐτῇ]; HARNACK 1906 43 [Acts 5,4 μένον ἔμενεν]; 44 [ἐπιμένειν: Acts 7x; combined with ἡμέραι: 10,48; 21,4.10; 28,14]; JEREMIAS 1980 63-64: "Bei dem Verbum μένειν ... führt Lukas den Gastgeber mit παρά c.dat. ein (...); wenn dafür Lk 1,56; 24,29b σύν, 24,29a μετά c.gen. gesagt wird, so wird das die Stimme der Tradition sein"; 100: "Lukas schreibt gern Verbkomposita mit μένω"; RADL 1975 417 [μένω; μένω "mit einer Person im Akkusativ"; μένω παρά + dat.]; SCHÜRMANN 1957 38 [μένειν: luk Wortwahl?].

μερίζω 1 (Mt 3, Mk 4)

1. divide (Lk 12,13); 2. distribute; 3. give part; 4. assign responsibility

Word groups	Lk	Acts	Mt	Mk
μερίζομαι middle (VKb)	12,13		0	0

μέριμνα 2 (Mt 1, Mk 1)   anxiety (Lk 8,14; 21,34)

μεριμνάω 5 (Mt 7)   be anxious about

Word groups	Lk	Acts	Mt	Mk
μεριμνάω + dative (VKd)	12,22		1	0
μεριμνάω περί + accusative/genitive (VKa)	10,41; 12,26		1	0

Literature

FUCHS, Albert, Sprachliche Untersuchungen zu Mattäus und Lukas, 1971. Esp. 173-174 [μὴ μεριμνήσητε πῶς ἢ (τί)].

μερίς 1 + 2   (Lk 10,42; Acts 8,21; 16,12)

1. portion (Acts 8,21); 2. district (Acts 16,12)

Characteristic of Luke

BOISMARD 1984 cb170; HARNACK 1906 52; NEIRYNCK 1985; PLUMMER 1922 lix

Literature

DENAUX 2009 lA[n]; HAUCK 1934 [seltenes Alleinwort].

μεριστής** 1   divider (Lk 12,14)

Literature

BORMANN, Lukas, Recht, Gerechtigkeit und Religion, 2001. Esp. 153.

μέρος 4 + 7 (Mt 4, Mk 1)

1. part (Lk 11,36; 12,46; 15,12; 24,42); 2. side; 3. region; 4. group (Acts 23,9); 5. business (Acts 19,27); 6. to some degree

Word groups	Lk	Acts	Mt	Mk
διέρχομαι τὰ μέρη BOISMARD 1984 Aa125		19,1; 20,2	0	0
τὰ μέρη of a place (SCa; VKa)		2,10; 19,1; 20,2	3	1

Literature

VON BENDEMANN 2001 421: "lukanisch ist dagegen mit einiger Sicherheit μέρος"; RADL 1975 417.

μέσον 12/13 + 8 (Mt 6/7, Mk 5)   the middle

Word groups	Lk	Acts	Mt	Mk
διὰ μέσον/μέσου (VKb) → **διέρχομαι** διὰ μέσου/μέσον DENAUX 2009 Lⁿ	4,30; 17,11		0	0
εἰς τὸ μέσον (SCb; VKc); cf. εἰς μέσον Mk 14,60	4,35; 5,19; 6,8		0	1/2
ἐκ μέσου (VKd)		17,33; 23,10	1	0
ἐν τῷ μέσῳ (SCd; VKe)		4,7	1	0
κάθημαι μέσος / ἐν μέσῳ; cf. κάθημαι μετά + gen. Mt 26,58	22,55 v.l.		0	0
κατὰ μέσον (VKf)		27,27	0	0
κατὰ μέσον τῆς νυκτός		27,27	0	0

Characteristic of Luke
GOULDER 1989; MORGENTHALER 1958LA

	Lk	Acts	Mt	Mk
ἐν μέσῳ (SCc) → **πίπτω** ἐν μέσῳ GOULDER 1989; PLUMMER 1922 lxii	2,46; 8,7; 10,3; 21,21; 22,27.55; 24,36	1,15; 2,22; 17,22; 27,21	3	2
ἵστημι ἐν μέσῳ (τινῶν) BOISMARD 1984 Ab129; NEIRYNCK 1985	24,36	17,22; 27,21	0	0

Literature

COLLISON 1977 135 [ἐν μέσῳ: noteworthy phenomena]; DENAUX 2009 lAⁿ [ἵστημι ἐν μέσῳ (τινῶν)]; GERSDORF 1816 267 [ἐν μέσῳ τῶν διδασκάλων]; RADL 1975 417 [ἐκ μέσου]; SCHNEIDER 1969 76-77.163: "ἐν μέσῳ mit Genitiv des Ortes ist bei Luk beliebt" [Vorzugswörter und -ausdrücke des Luk].

μεσονύκτιον 1 + 2 (Mk 1)   midnight (Lk 11,5; Acts 16,25; 20,7)

Characteristic of Luke
BOISMARD 1984 Cb37; NEIRYNCK 1985; PLUMMER 1922 lx

μέσος 2 + 2 (Mt 1)

1. among; 2. in the middle (Lk 22,55; 23,45; Acts 1,18; 26,13)

Word groups	Lk	Acts	Mt	Mk
κάθημαι μέσος / ἐν μέσῳ; cf. κάθημαι μετά + gen. Mt 26,58	22,55		0	0

Characteristic of Luke
DENAUX 2009 LA*; GASTON 1973 66 [Lked?]; GOULDER 1989; MORGENTHALER 1958LA

Literature

RADL 1975 417 [μέσος]; SCHNEIDER 1969 78.164 [Vorzugswörter und -ausdrücke des Luk]; SCHÜRMANN 1957 88 [Luk verwendet μέσος relativ häufig: ἐν μέσῳ + gen.].

μετά 63/64 + 65/67 (Mt 71, Mk 52/54[58])

1. with (association) (Acts 24,1); 2. with (accompanying object) (Lk 22,52); 3. with (combinative) (Lk 13,1); 4. with (attendant circumstances) (Lk 14,9); 5. with (experiencer) (Acts 7,9); 6. against (opposition); 7. after (time) (Lk 1,24); 8. among (location) (Lk 24,5); 9. beyond (location); 10. with (benefaction) (Lk 11,23[1]); 11. with (means) (Acts 2,28)

Word groups

→ εἰς + μετά; ἐκ + μετά; ἐν + μετά; ἔρχομαι μετά

μετά + genitive	Lk	Acts	Mt	Mk
εἰμὶ μετά + genitive (be with someone) (SCe) → μετά + the person assured of God's or Jesus' helpful presence	1,66; 5,29.34; 6,3; 11,7.23[1]; 15,31; 22,53.59; 23,43	7,9; 9,28.39; 10,38; 11,21; 18,10; 20,34	8	6
μετά + the person assured of God's or Jesus' helpful presence (SCf) → εἰμὶ μετά + genitive	1,28.58.66.72	7,9; 10,38; 11,21; 14,27; 15,4; 18,10	4	0
μετ' ἀλλήλων (SCc; VKc)	23,12		0	0
οἱ μετ' αὐτοῦ (SCa; VKa) → οἱ σὺν αὐτῷ/αὐτοῖς	6,3.4; 8,45*		3	3[4]
μετὰ δυναμέως	21,17		1	1
μετά + κατά + gen. (SCd; VKd)	11,23[1]		1	0

→ ἀκολουθέω μετά; μετ' εἰρήνης; εἰς + μετά; ἐκ + μετά; ἔλεος μετά; ἐν + μετά; ἔρχομαι μετά; ἐσθίω μετά; λαλέω μετὰ παρρησίας; μένω μετά; μετὰ ὄχλου; μετὰ σπουδῆς; συνάγω μετά; τίθημι μετά; ὑπάγω μετά; μετὰ χαρᾶς

μετά + accusative	Lk	Acts	Mt	Mk
μετά + accusative with reference to time (SCj; VKf)	1,24; 2,46; 15,13; 22,58	1,5; 15,36; 20,6; 21,15; 24,1[1].24; 25,1; 27,14; 28,11.13.17	5	6
other instances with accusative (SCj; VKj)	9,28; 12,5; 22,20	1,3; 5,37; 7,4.5; 10,37.41; 12,4; 13,15.25; 15,13; 19,4.21; 20,1.29	5	3[4]
μετὰ παρρησίας BOISMARD 1984 Aa62		2,29; 4,29.31; 28,31	0	0

Characteristic of Luke	Lk	Acts	Mt	Mk
καὶ μετὰ ταῦτα; cf. Rev 15,5 BOISMARD 1984 Bb71; NEIRYNCK 1985	5,27; 12,4; 17,8	7,7; 13,20	0	0
καταβαίνω μετά + genitive BOISMARD 1984 Ab131; NEIRYNCK 1985	2,51; 6,17	24,1[2]	0	0
μετά + genitive expressing a state of mind BOISMARD 1984 Eb64; NEIRYNCK 1985	1,39; 8,13; 10,17; 14,9; 24,52	2,29; 4,29.31; 15,33; 17,11; 20,19; 24,3; 28,31	2	3
μετὰ ταῦτα (SCh; VKh) DENAUX 2009 L***; GOULDER 1989; HAWKINS 1909L	5,27; 10,1; 12,4; 17,8; 18,4	7,7; 13,20; 15,16; 18,1	0	0[2]
μετὰ τό + infinitive (SCg; VKg) BOISMARD 1984 Eb56; NEIRYNCK 1985; PLUMMER 1922 lxii	12,5; 22,20	1,3; 7,4; 10,41; 15,13; 19,21; 20,1	1	2[3]
οὐ μετά / μετ' οὐ; cf. οὐδὲ μετά Acts 24,18[2] BOISMARD 1984 Ab38; NEIRYNCK 1985	15,13	1,5; 5,26; 24,18[1]; 27,14	0	0

→ γίνομαι μετά + gen.; μετὰ δὲ ἡμέρας; ποιέω μετά + gen.; μετ' οὐ πολύ / μετ' οὐ πολλὰς ἡμέρας

Literature

VON BENDEMANN 2001 416: "μετὰ ... ταῦτα ist eine lukanische Vorzugsverbindung"; COLLISON

1977 139 [μετὰ ταῦτα: linguistic usage of Luke: probable]; 140 [μετ᾽ ἐμοῦ: linguistic usage of Luke's "other source-material": likely]; DENAUX 2009 Laⁿ [καὶ μετὰ ταῦτα; καταβαίνω μετά + genitive], lAⁿ [οὐ μετά / μετ᾽ οὐ]; EASTON 1910 149 [ποιέω ἔλεος μετ᾽ αὐτοῦ: especially characteristic of L]; GERSDORF 1816 192 [μετὰ δὲ ταύτας τὰς ἡμέρας]; HAUCK 1934 [Vorzugsverbindung: μετὰ (δὲ) ταῦτα]; JEREMIAS 1980 29 [μετὰ τό + inf.: red.]; 183 [μετὰ ταῦτα: red.]; RADL 1975 414 [καταβαίνων μετά + gen.]; SCHÜRMANN 1957 32 [μέτα für σύν].

PETZER, Kobus H., Style and Text in the Lucan Narrative of the Institution of the Lord's Supper, 1991. Esp. 118: "μετὰ τὸ δειπνῆσαι".

μεταβαίνω 1 + 1 (Mt 6)
1. depart (Lk 10,7; Acts 18,7); 2. become

Word groups	Lk	Acts	Mt	Mk
μεταβαίνω εἰς → ἀνα/ἀπο/δια/ἐμ/καταβαίνω εἰς; cf. ἐπιβαίνω εἰς Acts 21,6*	10,7		0	0
μεταβαίνω ἐκ (VKb) → ἀνα/καταβαίνω ἐκ	10,7		0	0

μεταδίδωμι 1 — share (Lk 3,11)

μετανοέω 9 + 5 (Mt 5, Mk 2) — repent

Word groups	Lk	Acts	Mt	Mk
μετανοέω ἀπό (VKa); cf. μετάνοια ἀπό Heb 6,1		8,22	0	0
μετανοέω εἰς (VKb) → μετάνοια εἰς	11,32		1	0

Characteristic of Luke
GOULDER 1989

	Lk	Acts	Mt	Mk
μετανοέω + ἐπιστρέφω (VKe) BOISMARD 1984 Ab136; NEIRYNCK 1985	17,4	3,19; 26,20	0	0

Literature

VON BENDEMANN 2001 431: "lukanisches Stichwort"; COLLISON 1977 58 [linguistic usage of Luke's "other source-material": probable]; DENAUX 2009 lAⁿ [μετανοέω + ἐπιστρέφω].

GEORGE, Augustin, La conversion. — ID., Études, 1978, 351-368.

MÉNDEZ-MORATALLA, Fernando, The Paradigm of Conversion in Luke. London – New York: T&T Clark, 2004, XII-255 p. Esp. 15-18: "Linguistic Analysis".

MICHIELS, Robrecht, La conception lucanienne de la conversion. — ETL 41 (1965) 42-78.

PINTO LEÓN, A., μετάνοια εἰς. — QOL (Tlalpan, Mexico) 11 (1996) 19-34. [NTA 42, 105]

PRETE, Benedetto, Il testo di Luca 24,47: "Sarà predicata a tutte le genti la conversione per il perdono dei peccati". — ID., L'opera di Luca, 1986, 328-351. Esp. 340-341: "L'importanza della conversione negli scritti lucani".

RIESENFELD, Harald, Omvändelse i Lukasevangeliet. — SEÅ 35 (1971) 44-60.

TAEGER, Jens-Wilhelm, Der Mensch und sein Heil, 1982. Esp. 130-147: "μετάνοια/μετανοεῖν".

TOSATO, Angelo, Per una revisione degli studi sulla metanoia neotestamentaria. — RivBib 23 (1975) 3-45. Esp. 3-9: "Il problema circa la semantica di μετανοεῖν/μετάνοια nel NT".

μετάνοια 5 + 6 (Mt 2/3, Mk 1/2) — repentance

Word groups	Lk	Acts	Mt	Mk
δίδωμι μετάνοιαν; cf. 2 Tim 2,25 BOISMARD 1984 ca52		5,31; 11,18	0	0
μετάνοια + ἄφεσις ἁμαρτιῶν (VKc)	3,3; 24,47	5,31	0	1

Characteristic of Luke
BOISMARD 1984 Eb59; GOULDER 1989; HAWKINS 1909add; NEIRYNCK 1985

	Lk	Acts	Mt	Mk
βάπτισμα μετανοίας (VKd) BOISMARD 1984 cb18; NEIRYNCK 1985	3,3	13,24; 19,4	0	1
μετάνοια εἰς (VKa) → μετανοέω εἰς DENAUX 2009 LA*	3,3; 24,47	11,18; 20,21	0	1

Literature
DENAUX 2009 lAn; JEREMIAS 1980 246 [red.]; 322 [μετάνοιαν εἰς ἄφεσιν ἁμαρτιῶν: red.].

DIRKSEN, Aloys H., *The New Testament Concept of Metanoia* (Universitas Catholica Americae Washingtonii. S. facultas theologica, 34). Diss. Washington, DC, The Catholic University of America, 1932, XI-257 p.

GEORGE, Augustin, La conversion. — ID., *Études*, 1978, 351-368.

HAUDEBERT, Pierre, La *métanoia*, des Septante à Saint Luc. – CAZELLES, H. (ed.), *La vie de la Parole*. FS P. Grelot, 1987, 355-366.

HEZEL, Francis X., "Conversion" and "Repentance" in Lucan Theology. — *BiTod* 37 (1968) 2596-2602.

MAHFOUZ, Hady, *La fonction littéraire et théologique de Lc 3,1-20*, 2003. Esp. 122-133.

MÉNDEZ-MORATALLA, Fernando, *The Paradigm of Conversion in Luke*. London – New York: T&T Clark, 2004, XII-255 p. Esp. 15-18: "Linguistic Analysis".

MICHIELS, Robrecht, La conception lucanienne de la conversion. — *ETL* 41 (1965) 42-78.

PINTO LEÓN, A., μετάνοια εἰς. — *QOL* (Tlalpan, Mexico) 11 (1996) 19-34. [NTA 42, 105]

PRETE, Benedetto, Il testo di Luca 24,47: "Sarà predicata a tutte le genti la conversione per il perdono dei peccati". — ID., *L'opera di Luca*, 1986, 328-351. Esp. 340-341: "L'importanza della conversione negli scritti lucani".

TAEGER, Jens-Wilhelm, *Der Mensch und sein Heil*, 1982. Esp. 130-147: "μετάνοια/μετανοεῖν".

TOSATO, Angelo, Per una revisione degli studi sulla metanoia neotestamentaria. — *RivBib* 23 (1975) 3-45. Esp. 3-9: "Il problema circa la semantica di μετανοεῖν/μετάνοια nel NT".

UDICK, William S., Metanoia as Found in the Acts of the Apostles. – Some Inferences and Reflections. — *BiTod* 28 (1967) 1943-1946.

μεταξύ 2 + 3 (Mt 2)

1. between (location) (Lk 11,51; Acts 12,6); 2. between (association) (Lk 16,26; Acts 15,9); 3. next (Acts 13,42)

Word groups	Lk	Acts	Mt	Mk
μεταξύ adverb (VKa)		13,42	0	0
μεταξύ + ἐν	16,26		0	0

μετεωρίζομαι 1 — be anxious about (Lk 12,29)

Literature

HARNACK 1907 10; HAUCK 1934 [seltenes Alleinwort].

μέτοχος 1	companion (Lk 5,7)

μετρέω 1 (Mt 2, Mk 2)
1. measure; 2. give a measure (Lk 6,38)

Word groups	Lk	Acts	Mt	Mk
μέτρῳ μετρέω (VKb)	6,38		1	1

μέτρον 2 (Mt 2, Mk 1)	measure

Word groups	Lk	Acts	Mt	Mk
μέτρῳ μετρέω (VKa)	6,38²		1	1

μέχρι 1 + 2 (Mt 2/3, Mk 1)
1. until (Lk 16,16; Acts 20,7); 2. as far as; 3. to the degree that

Word groups	Lk	Acts	Mt	Mk
ἀπό ... μέχρι → ἀπό ... ἄχρι/ἕως		10,30	0	0
μέχρι + ἐν → ἕως + ἐν		10,30	0	0

Literature

KÜMMEL, Werner Georg, "Das Gesetz und die Propheten gehen bis Johannes" – Lukas 16,16 im Zusammenhang der heilsgeschichtlichen Theologie der Lukasschriften. — BÖCHER, O. – HAACKER, K. (eds.), *Verborum Veritas*. FS G. Stählin, 1970, 89-102. Esp. 94.

μή 140/153 + 64/68 (Mt 128/139, Mk 76[77]83)
1. not (Lk 8,18); 2. marker of a question (Lk 22,35); 3. so that not (Acts 27,42)

Word groups	Lk	Acts	Mt	Mk
βλέπω/σκοπέω/φοβέομαι + μή (SCp; VKs); cf. ὁράω μή Mt 18,10; 24,6	11,35; 21,8[1]	5,26; 13,40; 23,10; 27,17.29	1	1
ἐάν (δὲ/γὰρ) μή (SCa; VKa)	13,3.5	3,23; 8,31; 15,1; 27,31	8	5
εἰ (...) μή + finite verb (SCc; VKc)		26,32	1	2
εἰ μή without predicate (LN: except that; SCd: only; VKd) → εἰ μή (...) μόνον/μόνος	4,26.27; 5,21; 6,4; 8,51; 10,22^{1.2}; 11,29; 17,18; 18,19	11,19; 21,25*	13/16	11/12
ἵνα (...) μή (SCf; VKf)	8,10^{1.2}.12.31; 9,45; 14,29*; 16,28; 18,5; 22,32.46	2,25; 4,17; 5,26 v.l.; 24,4	8	7
μή + indicative (VKq); see also εἰ (...) μή + finite verb; μή as interrogative; οὐ μή + future indicative		8,31	0/1	0/1

(τὸ) μή + infinitive (SCl; VKn)	2,26; 4,42; 8,6; 11,42; 17,1; 18,1; 20,7.27; 21,14; 22,34*.40; 24,16	1,4; 4,18.20; 5,28. 40; 7,19; 9,38 v.l.; 10,47; 14,18; 15,19.38[2]; 19,31; 20,20.27; 21,4. 12.21; 23,8; 25,24.27; 27,21	9	4/5
μή as interrogative (SCq; VKt)	5,34; 10,15; 11,11[1*.2*]. 12*; 17,9; 22,35	7,28.42	4	1/3
μή + optative (SCn; VKr) DENAUX 2009 LA[n]	3,15*; 20,16	27,42	0	0
μή γένοιτο	20,16		0	0
μή καί → μήποτε καί	16,28	25,27	0	0
μή κλαῖε/κλαίετε DENAUX 2009 L[n]	7,13; 8,52; 23,28		0	0
μή οὖν	12,7 v.l.; 21,8[2] v.l.		5	0
μή ποτε (VKj)	3,15*; 4,11*; 12,58*; 14,8*.12*.29*; 21,34*	5,39*; 28,27*	0/8	0/2
μή που (LN: so that not; SCh; VKh); cf. μή τι Mk 14,19[1*.2*]		27,29	0	0
μή (+) τις; cf. μήτι + τις Acts 10,47	11,36; 12,4; 22,35	8,31; 27,42	2/3	1/3
ὅπως (...) μή (SCg; VKg) → ὅπως μηδέν/μηδέ	16,26	20,16	1	0
ὅς/ὅσος/ὅστις ἄν/ἐὰν (...) μή (SCb; VKb)	7,23; 8,18; 9,5; 10,10; 18,17[1]	3,23	3	3/4
οὐ/οὐχὶ μή + aorist subjunctive (SCj; VKk)	1,15; 6,37[2.4]; 8,17; 9,27; 10,19; 12,59; 13,35; 18,7.17[2]. 30; 21,18.32.33 v.l.; 22,16.18.67. 68	13,41; 28,26[1.2]	16/17	8[9]/10
οὐ μή + future indicative (SCk; VKl)	9,27 v.l.; 10,19 v.l.; 18,7 v.l.; 21,33; 22,34*		3/4	2/[3]
φοβέομαι μή BOISMARD 1984 Da8		5,26; 23,10; 27,17.29	0	0

→ ἀνάστασιν + μὴ εἶναι; μὴ δυνάμενος; μὴ ἰσχύω; καὶ μή; καὶ οὐ μή; κρίνω μή + inf.; λέγω ὑμῖν / σοι ... οὐ μή ... ἕως (ἄν); οὐ ... εἰ μή(τι); μὴ φοβοῦ / μὴ φοβεῖσθε

Characteristic of Luke	Lk	Acts	Mt	Mk
εἰ δὲ μή γε (SCe; VKe); cf. εἰ δὲ μή Mk 2,21.22 CREDNER 1836 137; DENAUX 2009 L***; HAWKINS 1909L; PLUMMER 1922 lx	5,36.37; 10,6; 13,9; 14,32		2	0
μή + participle (SCm; VKp) GOULDER 1989	1,20; 2,45; 3,9.11; 5,19; 6,49; 7,30.33.42; 9,33; 11,231.2.24.36; 12,42.21. 33.47.48; 13,11; 14,29; 18,21.2; 19,26.27; 22,36; 24,23	5,7; 9,9.26; 12,19; 13,11; 15,381; 17,6; 20,22.29; 21,14.34; 27,7.15	16	6

→ μὴ φοβοῦ singular; μὴ φοβοῦ + vocative

Literature

VON BENDEMANN 2001 437 [μὴ γένοιτο]; COLLISON 1977 102 [εἰ δὲ μή γε: linguistic usage of Luke: probable]; 108 [pleonastic; + articular infinitive: likely]; 109 [μὴ φοβοῦ; μὴ ἔχων: linguistic usage of Luke's "other source-material": probable; μὴ κλαῖε; μή + participle of εὑρίσκω: noteworthy phenomena]; GOULDER 1989 806 [A.(?)- καί μή - non A. (?): 2/0/6 Lk 12,21]; HARNACK 1906 149 (ET: 213: "μή causal: Lk 2,45; 3,9: a delicate Lukan touch"); HAUCK 1934

[Vorzugswort: μήγε; Vorzugsverbindung: εἰ δὲ μή γε]; RADL 1975 406 [μὴ δυνάμενος]; 417-418 [μή; "οὐ negiert den Indikativ, μή die übrigen Modi einschließlich Infinitiv und Partizipium"; μή + inf; μή "mit dem Infinitiv als Verbot"; τοῦ μή + inf.]; 419 [οἶδα with μή]; 430 [φοβέομαι + μή]; SCHÜRMANN 1957 26 [μὴ εἰδέναι; pleonastisches μή + Inf.].

JUNG, Chang-Wook, *Infancy Narrative*, 2004. Esp. 97-99 [οὐ μή].
MARSHALL, Alfred, Οὐ and μή Questions. — *BTrans* 4 (1953) 41-42.
MITIKU, A., The Use of Οὐ Μή in the New Testament: Emphatic or Mild Negation?. — *Faith & Mission* [Wake Forest, NC] 22 (2005) 85-104.
MOULTON, James Hope, *A Grammar of New Testament Greek*. Vol. I: *Prolegomena*. EdinburgH: T. &T. Clark, ³1908 (repr. 1988). Esp. 187-192.
THRALL, Margaret E., *Greek Particles in the New Testament*, 1962. Esp. 9-10 [εἰ δὲ μή γε].
WILSON, W.André A., "But me no Buts". — *BTrans* 15 (1964) 173-180. [εἰ μή]

μηδέ 7/10 + 2/3 (Mt 11, Mk 6/8)

1. and not (Acts 4,18); 2. not even

Word groups	Lk	Acts	Mt	Mk
μηδέ + aorist subjunctive (*SC*a)	3,14; 17,23		8	2
μηδέ + infinitive (*SC*b; *VK*d)		4,18; 21,21; 23,8*	0	2
μηδέ + participle (*VK*e)	7,33*; 12,47*		0	1/2
ὅπως … μηδέ (*VK*c) → ὅπως (…) **μή/μηδέν**	16,26		0	0

μηδείς 9/10 + 21/23 (Mt 5, Mk 9)   no one, nothing

Word groups	Lk	Acts	Mt	Mk
καὶ μηδείς → καὶ **οὐδείς**	10,4	13,28; 19,36; 24,23	0	1
λέγω/εἶπον μηδενί	5,14; 8,56; 9,21		3	3
μηδείς + double negative (*VK*g)		4,17	0	3
ὅπως μηδέν (*VK*b) → ὅπως (…) **μή/μηδέ**		8,24	0	0

Characteristic of Luke

MORGENTHALER 1958A

	Lk	Acts	Mt	Mk
μηδέν/οὐδέν + epithet → **οὐδέν** + epithet; cf. 1 Cor 13,7 BOISMARD 1984 cb69; DENAUX 2009 IA*; NEIRYNCK 1985	3,13; 23, 15.41	15,28; 16,28; 17,21; 19,36; 23,9.29; 25,25; 28,5.6; 26,31	0	0
μηδέν + infinitive (*VK*c); cf. 1 Cor 1,7; 2 Cor 11,5; 13,7; 1 Thess 3,3; 1 Tim 5,14; Tit 3,2; Heb 10,2 BOISMARD 1984 cb138; DENAUX 2009 IA*; NEIRYNCK 1985	5,14; 8,56; 9,21	4,17; 10,28; 15,28; 19,36; 21,25*; 23,14.22; 24,23; 25,25; 28,18	0	0
μηδέν + participle BOISMARD 1984 Eb5; DENAUX 2009 IA*; NEIRYNCK 1985	4,35; 6,35	4,21; 9,7; 10,20; 11,12.19; 13,28; 19,40; 23,29; 25,17; 27,33*; 28,6	0	1
μηδὲν αἴτιον (no guilt) → **οὐδὲν/οὐϑὲν** αἴτιον GOULDER 1989; VOGEL 1899A		19,40	0	0
μηδὲν/οὐδέν πλέον BOISMARD 1984 Ab194; NEIRYNCK 1985	3,13	15,28	0	0
παραγγέλλω μηδενί + verb of saying BOISMARD 1984 Ab93; NEIRYNCK 1985	5,14; 8,56; 9,21	23,22	0	0
→ μηδὲν **ἄξιον** θανάτου πράσσω				

Literature

DENAUX 2009 LA[n] [μηδὲν/οὐδέν πλέον], La[n] [παραγγέλλω μηδενί + verb of saying]

SCHWARZ, Günther, Μηδὲν ἀπελπίζοντες. — ZNW 71 (1980) 133-135. [NTA 26, 521]

μηκέτι 1 + 3 (Mt 1, Mk 4)	no longer (Lk 8,49)			
Word groups	**Lk**	**Acts**	**Mt**	**Mk**
μηκέτι + double negative (VKe)		4,17; 25,24	0	2
μηκέτι + infinitive (VKb)		4,17; 25,24	0	2
μηκέτι + participle (VKc)		13,34	0	0

μήν 5 + 5	month			
Word groups	**Lk**	**Acts**	**Mt**	**Mk**
μήν + ἐνιαυτός/ἔτος (VKa) DENAUX 2009 LA[n]	4,25	18,11	0	0

Characteristic of Luke

BOISMARD 1984 db7; GOULDER 1989*; HARNACK 1906 52; NEIRYNCK 1985; PLUMMER 1922 lix

Literature

DENAUX 2009 L(***); HAWKINS 1909 20.

CADBURY, Henry J., Some Lukan Expressions of Time (Lexical Notes on Luke-Acts VII). — JBL 82 (1963) 272-278.

μηνύω 1 + 1	inform (Lk 20,37; Acts 23,30)

Literature

DENAUX 2009 LA[n]; HAUCK 1934 [seltenes Alleinwort].

μήποτε 7 + 2 (Mt 8, Mk 2)				
1. never; 2. can be (Lk 3,15); 3. so that not (Acts 5,39)				

Word groups	**Lk**	**Acts**	**Mt**	**Mk**
ἵνα μήποτε (VKa); cf. ἵνα μηδείς Mt 16,20; Mk 5,43; 6,8; 7,36; 8,30; 9,9	14,29		0	0
μήποτε interrogative (VKd)	3,15		0	0
προσέχω μήποτε	21,43		0	0

Characteristic of Luke	**Lk**	**Acts**	**Mt**	**Mk**
μήποτε καί BOISMARD 1984 Ab186; NEIRYNCK 1985	14,12	5,39	0	0

Literature

DENAUX 2009 LA[n] [μήποτε καί].

μήτε 6/7 + 8 (Mt 6, Mk 0/1)　nor

Word groups	Lk	Acts	Mt	Mk
μήτε + infinitive (*VK*b)	9,3[5]	23,8[1.2].12[1.2].21[1.2]	3	0/1
μήτε + participle (*VK*c)	7,33*.33	27,20[1.2]	2	0

Characteristic of Luke
GASTON 1973 64 [Lked]

Literature
RADL 1975 418.

μήτηρ 17/18 + 4 (Mt 26/27, Mk 17)
1. mother (Lk 1,60); 2. archetype (Lk 8,21)

Word groups	Lk	Acts	Mt	Mk
ἐκ κοιλίας μητρός (*SC*a; *VK*a) → χωλὸς ἐκ κοιλίας μητρός	1,15	3,2; 14,8	1	0
μήτηρ + ἀδελφή/ἀδελφός (*SC*c; *VK*d); cf. μήτηρ + κοράσιον Mt 14,11; Mk 6,28	8,19.20.21; 14,26	1,14	7	7
μήτηρ + θυγάτηρ (*SC*d; *VK*e)	12,53[1.2]		3	2
μήτηρ (τοῦ Ἰησοῦ) (the mother of Jesus) (*SC*g)	1,43; 2,33.34.48.51; 8,19.20.21	1,14	12	5
μήτηρ + παιδίον/παῖς/τέκνον (*SC*f; *VK*g) → πατήρ + παιδίον/παῖς/τέκνον	1,(59-)60; 2,43*.48; 8,51; 14,26		6	3
μήτηρ + πατήρ (*SC*b; *VK*b)	2,33.48; 8,51; 12,53[1.2]; 14,26; 18,20		8/9	8
μήτηρ + πενθερά	12,53[1.2]		1	0
μήτηρ + υἱός (*SC*e; *VK*f) → πατήρ + υἱός	7,12		3	0

μήτι 2 + 1 (Mt 4, Mk 2/3)　marker of a question

Word groups	Lk	Acts	Mt	Mk
εἰ μήτι (*VK*a)	9,13		0	0

Characteristic of Luke	Lk	Acts	Mt	Mk
μήτι δύναται + infinitive BOISMARD 1984 Ab173; NEIRYNCK 1985	6,39	10,47	0	0

Literature
DENAUX 2009 LA[n] [μήτι δύναται + infinitive].

μήτρα 1　womb

Word groups	Lk	Acts	Mt	Mk
ἄρσεν διανοῖγον μήτραν (*LN*: firstborn son)	2,23		0	0

Literature
JUNG, Chang-Wook, *Infancy Narrative*, 2004. Esp. 81-83.

μικρός 5 + 2 (Mt 8, Mk 5)

1. little (quantity) (Lk 12,32); 2. little (size) (Lk 19,3); 3. little (degree); 4. short (time); 5. short (measurement) (Lk 19,3); 6. young; 7. unimportant (Lk 7,28; 9,48; 17,2; Acts 8,10)

Word groups	Lk	Acts	Mt	Mk
μικρός/μικρότερος + μέγας/μείζων (VKf)	7,28; 9,48	8,10; 26,22	2	1
μικρότερος comparative (SCa; VKa)	7,28; 9,48		2	1
τῶν μικρῶν τούτων εἷς	17,2		4	1

Literature

REHKOPF 1959 99 [τὸ μικρὸν ποίμνιον: "Substantiva in Anrede bei den Synoptikern"].

SCHWARZ, Günther, οτι τη ηλικια μικρος ην. [Lk 19,3] — BibNot 8 (1979) 23-24.

μιμνῄσκομαι 6 + 2 (Mt 3)

1. remember (Lk 1,54); 2. remember and respond

Word groups	Lk	Acts	Mt	Mk
μιμνῄσκομαι passive (VKc)		10,31	0	0
μιμνῄσκομαι ὅτι (VKa) → μνημονεύω ὅτι	16,25		2	0
μιμνῄσκομαι ὡς (VKb)	24,6		0	0

Characteristic of Luke

DENAUX 2009 L***†; GOULDER 1989*; HAWKINS 1909 †L

	Lk	Acts	Mt	Mk
μιμνῄσκομαι + genitive	23,42; 24,8	11,16	1	
BOISMARD 1984 Eb65; NEIRYNCK 1985				

Literature

COLLISON 1977 59 [linguistic usage of Luke's "other source-material": certain]; EASTON 1910 156 [μιμνῄσκομαι aorist passive with active sense: probably characteristic of L]; HAUCK 1934 [Vorzugswort]; REHKOPF 1959 95 [μνησθῆναι].

μισέω 7 (Mt 5/6, Mk 1)   hate

Word groups	Lk	Acts	Mt	Mk
μισέομαι passive (VKc)	21,17		2	1
μισέω + ἀγαπάω	6,27; 16,13		2	0
μισέω + δουλεύω → ἀγαπάω + δουλεύω	16,13		1	0
μισέω + ἐχθρός → ἀγαπάω + ἐχθρός	1,71; 6,27		1	0

Literature

EASTON 1910 163 [οἱ μισοῦντες: cited by Weiss as characteristic of L, and possibly corroborative].

DERRETT, J. Duncan M., Hating Father and Mother (Luke 14:26; Matthew 10:37) . — Downside Review 117 (1999) 251-272.

DUPONT, Jacques, Les Béatitudes, I, 1958. Esp. 309.

—, Les Béatitudes, II, 1969. Esp. 286-287: "La haine".

LACHS, Samuel T., Hebrew Elements in the Gospels and Acts . — The Jewish Querterly Review 71 (1980) 31-43. Esp. 40-41: Lk 14,26-27..

μίσϑιος 2/3	hired worker (Lk 15,17.19.21*)

Literature

DENAUX 2009 L[n]; HAUCK 1934 [seltenes Alleinwort].

μισϑός 3 + 1 (Mt 10, Mk 1)	
1. wages (Lk 10,7); 2. reward (Lk 6,32.35; Acts 1,10)	

Literature

BDAG 2000 653 [literature].

SCHWARZ, Günther, "Seiner Nahrung" oder "seines Lohnes"? (Mt 10,10e / Lc 10,7c). — *BibNot* 65 (1992) 40-41.

μνᾶ 9	monetary unit, mina

Literature

DENAUX 2009 L(***); HAUCK 1934 [seltenes Alleinwort]; HAWKINS 1909 20

μνῆμα 3 + 2 (Mk 2/4)	grave			

Word groups	Lk	Acts	Mt	Mk
ἐν μνήματι + τίϑημι (VKa) → εἰς μνημεῖον τίϑημι; cf. ἐν μνημείῳ τίϑημι Mt 27,60; Mk 6,29; 15,46	23,53	7,16	0/1	0
μνήματα plural (VKb) → μνημεῖα plural	8,27		2	0

Characteristic of Luke

PLUMMER 1922 lx

Literature

KILPATRICK, George D., Style and Text, 1967. Esp. 156-157; = ID., *Principles and Practice*, 1990. Esp. 57-59.

μνημεῖον 7/9 + 1 (Mt 7, Mk 8/9)	
1. grave (Lk 11,44); 2. monument (Lk 11,47)	

Word groups	Lk	Acts	Mt	Mk
εἰς μνημεῖον τίϑημι (VKa) → ἐν μνήματι τίϑημι; cf. ἐν μνημείῳ τίϑημι Mt 27,60; Mk 6,29; 15,46		13,29	0	0
μνημεῖα plural (VKb) → μνήματα plural	11,44.47.48*		4	1/2

Literature

JEREMIAS 1980 207 [red.].

KILPATRICK, George D., Style and Text, 1967. Esp. 156-157; = ID., *Principles and Practice*, 1990. Esp. 57-59.

μνημονεύω 1 + 2 (Mt 1, Mk 1)

1. remember (Lk 17,32; Acts 20,31.35); 2. keep thinking about; 3. remember and respond; 4. remember and mention

Word groups	Lk	Acts	Mt	Mk
μνημονεύω ὅτι (VKc) → μιμνῄσκομαι ὅτι		20,31	0	0

μνηστεύομαι 2 (Mt 1/2)

promise in marriage (Lk 1,27; 2,5)

μόγις 1

1. μόγις/μόλις: scarcely (Lk 9,39); 2. with difficulty (Lk 9,39)

Characteristic of Luke

HARNACK 1906 52;

	Lk	Acts	Mt	Mk
μόγις/μόλις	9,39	14,18;	0	0
BOISMARD 1984 Bb[72]; DENAUX 2009 lA*; NEIRYNCK 1985		27,7.8.16		

μόδιος 1 (Mt 1, Mk 1)

container (Lk 11,33)

Literature

MARYKS, Robert A., Il latinismi del Nuovo testamento, 2000. Esp. 29.

μοιχεύω 3 (Mt 4, Mk 1)

commit adultery (Lk 16,18[1.2]; 18,20)

μοιχός 1

adulterer (Lk 18,11)

Literature

BORMANN, Lukas, Recht, Gerechtigkeit und Religion, 2001. Esp. 153.

μονογενής 3

unique (Lk 7,12; 8,42; 9,38)

Word groups	Lk	Acts	Mt	Mk
μονογενής υἱός DENAUX 2009 L[n]	7,12; 9,38		0	0

Characteristic of Luke

GOULDER 1989; HAWKINS 1909add

Literature

COLLISON 1977 187 [noteworthy phenomena]; DENAUX 2009 L[n]; JEREMIAS 1980 157: "μονογενής hat im NT nur im LkEv, und zwar hier an allen drei Stellen, profane Bedeutung".

μόνον 1 + 8 (Mt 8, Mk 3)

1. only (Lk 8,50); 2. alone

Word groups	Lk	Acts	Mt	Mk
εἰ μὴ μόνον (SCb; VKg) → εἰ μὴ (...) μόνος		11,19	2	1/2
οὐ μόνον (δὲ) ... ἀλλά (SCa; VKa) → οὐ ... μόνος		19,26.27; 21,13; 26,29;	1	0
... ἀλλά		27,10		

Literature
RADL 1975 421 [οὐ μόνον ... ἀλλὰ καί].

DEER, Donald, Supplying "Only" in Translation. — BTrans 38 (1987) 227-234.

μόνος 9 (Mt 6, Mk 3)
1. only one; 2. alone (Lk 9,36)

Word groups	Lk	Acts	Mt	Mk
αὐτὸς μόνος (SCc; VKc)	4,8		2	1
εἰ μὴ μόνος (SCb; VKb) → εἰ μὴ (...) μόνον	5,21; 6,4		2	0
κατὰ μόνας (LN: alone; SCd; VKd)	9,18		0	1
μόνος ὁ θεός → εἷς ὁ θεός	5,21		0	0
οὐ ... μόνος ... ἀλλά (SCa; VKa) → οὐ μόνον (δὲ) ... ἀλλά	4,4 v.l.		1	0

μόσχος 3   calf

Word groups	Lk	Acts	Mt	Mk
μόσχος σιτευτός DENAUX 2009 Lⁿ	15,23.27.30		0	0

Literature
VON BENDEMANN 2001 429: "μόσχος σιτευτός findet sich im Neuen Testament nur in Lk 15,23.27.30".

μυλικός 1** (Mk 0/1)   of a mill

Word groups	Lk	Acts	Mt	Mk
λίθος μυλικός	17,2		0	0/1

Literature
HAUCK 1934 [seltenes Alleinwort].

μυριάς 1 + 2
1. ten thousand (Acts 19,19); 2. countless (Lk 12,1; Acts 21,20)

Word groups	Lk	Acts	Mt	Mk
μυριάδες τοῦ ὄχλου	12,1		0	0
μυριάδες πέντε		19,19	0	0

Characteristic of Luke
BOISMARD 1984 Db33; NEIRYNCK 1985; VOGEL 1899C

Literature
DENAUX 2009 lAⁿ; HAUCK 1934 [seltenes Alleinwort].

μύρον 4 (Mt 2/3, Mk 3)	perfume			
Word groups	Lk	Acts	Mt	Mk
ἀλείφω (τῷ) μύρῳ (VKa) DENAUX 2009 Lⁿ	7,38.46		0	0
μύρα plural (VKb)	23,56		0	0

μυστήριον 1 (Mt 1, Mk 1)	secret			
Word groups	Lk	Acts	Mt	Mk
μυστήρια plural (VKa)	8,10		1	0
μυστήριον τῆς βασιλείας (VKb)	8,10		1	1

μωραίνω 1 (Mt 1)	cause to become nonsense (Lk 14,34)

Μωϋσῆς 10 + 19 (Mt 7, Mk 8)
1. Moses (Lk 9,30); 2. the Law (of Moses)

Word groups	Lk	Acts	Mt	Mk
Μωϋσῆς ἔγραψεν; cf. Μωϋσῆς + γράφω Lk 24,44; Mk 10,4	20,28		0	1
Μωϋσῆς + Ἠλίας (VKc)	9,30.33		2	2
νόμος Μωϋσέως + προφῆται (SCc) → **Μωϋσῆς** καὶ προφῆται DENAUX 2009 LAⁿ (?)	24,44	28,23	0	0

Characteristic of Luke	Lk	Acts	Mt	Mk
Μωϋσῆς καὶ προφῆται (SCb; VKe) → νόμος **Μωϋσέως** + προφῆται; cf. Jn 1,45 BOISMARD 1984 Bb115; GOULDER 1989; NEIRYNCK 1985	16,29. 31; 24,27	26,22	0	0
Μωϋσῆς + νόμος (SCa; VKd); cf. Jn 7,23; 1 Cor 9,9; Heb 10,28 BOISMARD 1984 cb147; NEIRYNCK 1985	2,22; 24,44	13,38; 15,5; 28,23	0	0

Literature
DENAUX 2009 lAⁿ [Μωϋσῆς + νόμος], Laⁿ [Μωϋσῆς καὶ προφῆται].

N

Ναασσών 1 (Mt 2)	Nahshon (Lk 3,32)

Ναγγαί 1	Naggai (Lk 3,25)

Ναζαρά 1 (Mt 1)	Nazareth (Lk 4,16)

Literature
BDAG 2000 664 [literature]; EASTON 1910 163 [cited by Weiss as characteristic of L, and possibly corroborative].

OESTERLEY, W.O.E., Nazarene and Nazareth. — *ExpT* 52 (1940-41) 410-412.
RÜGER, Hans Peter, Ναζαρέθ/Ναζαρά Ναζαρηνός/Ναζωραῖος. — *ZNW* 72 (1981) 257-263. [NTA 26, 419]

Ναζαρέθ 4 + 1 (Mt 1)   Nazareth

Word groups	Lk	Acts	Mt	Mk
Ἰησοῦς (ὁ) ἀπὸ Ναζαρέθ → Ἰησοῦς (ὁ) **Ναζαρηνός**; Ἰησοῦς (ὁ) **Ναζωραῖος**		10,38	1	1
πόλις + Γαλιλαία + Ναζαρέθ → πόλις + Γαλιλαία + **Καφαρναούμ**	1,26; 2,4.39		0	0

Literature
BDAG 2000 664 [literature].

OESTERLEY, W.O.E., Nazarene and Nazareth. — *ExpT* 52 (1940-41) 410-412.
RÜGER, Hans Peter, Ναζαρέθ/Ναζαρά Ναζαρηνός/Ναζωραῖος. — *ZNW* 72 (1981) 257-263. [NTA 26, 419]
WINTER, Paul, "Nazareth" and "Jerusalem" in Luke Chs. 1 and 2. — *NTS* 3 (1957) 136-142. Esp. 136-139 [Ναζαρέθ]; 139-142 [Ἰερουσαλήμ/Ἰεροσόλυμα].

Ναζαρηνός 2 (Mk 4)   Nazarene

Word groups	Lk	Acts	Mt	Mk
Ἰησοῦς ὁ Ναζαρηνός → Ἰησοῦς (ὁ) ἀπὸ **Ναζαρέθ**; Ἰησοῦς (ὁ) **Ναζωραῖος**	4,34; 24,19		0	4

Literature
JEREMIAS 1980 315 [trad.].

CHACÓN GALLARDO, Luis, Santo de Dios, Nazareno, Nazareo. —*EstBib* 64 (2006) 31-49.
OESTERLEY, W.O.E., Nazarene and Nazareth. — *ExpT* 52 (1940-41) 410-412.
PARENTE, Fausto, Ναζαρηνός – Ναζωραῖος: An Unsolved Riddle in the Synoptic Tradition. — *Scripta Classica Israelica* 15 (1996) 185-201. [NTA 42, 187]
RÜGER, Hans Peter, Ναζαρέθ/Ναζαρά Ναζαρηνός/Ναζωραῖος. — *ZNW* 72 (1981) 257-263. [NTA 26, 419]
TREVES, M., Nazōraioi, zēlōtai, nazarēnos. — *Cahiers du Cercle Ernest-Renan* 19 (1971) 51-54. [NTA 16, 67]

Ναζωραῖος 1/2 + 7 (Mt 2; Mk 0/1)   Nazarene

Word groups	Lk	Acts	Mt	Mk
ἡ τῶν Ναζωραίων αἵρεσις (VKa)		24,5	0	0
Ἰησοῦς (ὁ) Ναζωραῖος → Ἰησοῦς (ὁ) ἀπὸ **Ναζαρέθ**; Ἰησοῦς (ὁ) **Ναζαρηνός**	18,37; 24,19*	2,22; 3,6; 4,10; 6,14; 22,8; 26,9	1	0/1

Characteristic of Luke
BOISMARD 1984 cb155; NEIRYNCK 1985

Literature
BDAG 2000 664-665 [literature]; DENAUX 2009 1An; JEREMIAS 1980 315 [red.]; RADL 1975 418.

CHACÓN GALLARDO, Luis, Santo de Dios, Nazareno, Nazareo. —*EstBib* 64 (2006) 31-49.

GÄRTNER, Bertil, *Die rätselhaften Termini Nazoräer und Iskariot* (Horae Soederblomianae, 4). Lund: Gleerup, 1957, 68 p. Esp. 5-36: "Nazareth, Nazoräer und das Mandäertum"; 37-68: "Judas Iskariot".

OESTERLEY, W.O.E., Nazarene and Nazareth. — *ExpT* 52 (1940-41) 410-412.

O'NEILL, John C., Jesus of Nazareth. — *JTS* 50 (1999) 135-142.

PARENTE, F., Ναζαρηνός - Ναζωραῖος. An Unsolved Riddle in the Synoptic Tradition. — *Scripta Classica Israelica* 15 (1996) 185-201. [NTA 42, 187]

READ-HEIMERDINGER, Jenny, *The Bezan Text of Acts*, 2002. Esp. 254-274: "Titles of Jesus" [(ὁ) Ἰησοῦς; Ἰησοῦς ὁ Ναζωραῖος; ὁ παῖς; ὁ ἅγιος παῖς σου Ἰησοῦς; (ὁ) Χριστός; Χριστὸς Ἰησοῦς; Ἰησοῦς Χριστός; Ἰησοῦς Χριστὸς ὁ Ναζωραῖος; (ὁ) κύριος; (ὁ) κύριος Ἰησοῦς; ὁ κύριος Ἰησοῦς Χριστός].

RÜGER, Hans Peter, Ναζαρέθ/Ναζαρά Ναζαρηνός/Ναζωραῖος. — *ZNW* 72 (1981) 257-263. [NTA 26, 419]

TREVES, M., Nazōraioi, zēlōtai, nazarēnos. — *Cahiers du Cercle Ernest-Renan* 19 (1971) 51-54. [NTA 16, 67]

Ναθάμ 1	Nathan (Lk 3,31)

ναί 4 + 2 (Mt 9, Mk 0/1)	yes (Acts 5,8; 22,27)

Word groups	Lk	Acts	Mt	Mk
ναὶ λέγω ὑμῖν (*VK*c) → ἀληθῶς/ἀμὴν λέγω ὑμῖν	7,26; 11,51; 12,5		1	0

Literature

COLLISON 1977 150 [noteworthy phenomena]; REHKOPF 1959 95 [ναὶ λέγω ὑμῖν: vorlukanisch]; SCHÜRMANN 1961 276 [ναὶ λέγω ὑμῖν].

Ναιμάν 1	Naaman (Lk 4,27)

Ναΐν 1	Nain (Lk 7,11)

ναός 4 + 2/3 (Mt 9, Mk 3)	
1. temple (Lk 1,9.21.22; 23,45); 2. model of a shrine (Acts 19,24)	

Word groups	Lk	Acts	Mt	Mk
εἰσέρχομαι εἰς τὸν ναόν → ἀναβαίνω/εἰσάγω/ εἰσπορεύομαι/ (εἰσ)ἔρχομαι εἰς τὸ ἱερόν	1,9		0	0
ναοί plural (*VK*e) BOISMARD 1984 Aa144		7,48*; 17,24; 19,24	0	0
ναὸς τοῦ κυρίου (*VK*b)	1,9		0	0

Literature

GERSDORF 1816 174 [εἰς τὸν ναὸν τοῦ κυρίου].

BALTZER, Klaus, The Meaning of the Temple in the Lukan Writings. — *HTR* 58 (1965) 263-277.

Ναούμ 1	Nahum (Lk 3,25)

Ναχώρ 1	Nahor (Lk 3,34)

νεανίσκος 1 + 4 (Mt 2, Mk 2)   young man

Word groups	Lk	Acts	Mt	Mk
νεανίσκοι plural (VKa)		2,17; 5,10	0	0/1

Literature

REHKOPF 1959 99 [Lk 7,14 νεανίσκε: "Substantiva in Anrede bei den Synoptikern"].

νεκρός 14 + 17/18 (Mt 12, Mk 7/8[9])
1. dead (Lk 7,15); 2. useless; 3. ineffective

Word groups	Lk	Acts	Mt	Mk
ἀνάστασις νεκρῶν without article BOISMARD 1984 Da6		17,32; 23,6; 24,15*.21; 26,23	0	0
ἀπὸ νεκρῶν (SCf)	16,30		3	0
ἄφες τοὺς νεκροὺς θάψαι τοὺς ἑαυτῶν νεκρούς (LN: that is not the issue)	9,60$^{1.2}$		1	0
ἐκ νεκρῶν (SCg)	9,7; 16,31; 20,35; 24,46	3,15; 4,2.10; 10,41; 13,30.34; 17,3.31	1	4[5]/6
νεκρός + ἀνίστημι intransitive (SCd; VKd) → (ἡ) ἀνάστασις (ἡ) (ἐκ) (τῶν) **νεκρῶν**	16,31; 24,46	10,41; 17,3	0/1	3
νεκρός + ἀνίστημι transitive (SCe; VKd) → (ἡ) ἀνάστασις (ἡ) (ἐκ) (τῶν) **νεκρῶν**		13,34; 17,31	0	0
νεκρός + (ἀνα)ζῶ (SCb; VKb)	15,24.32; 20,38; 24,5	10,42	1	1
νεκρός + ἐγείρω (SCc; VKc) → (ἡ) ἀνάστασις (ἡ) (ἐκ) (τῶν) **νεκρῶν**	7,22; 9,7; 20,37	3,15; 4,10; 13,30; 26,8	6	2/3[4]

Characteristic of Luke	Lk	Acts	Mt	Mk
ἡ ἀνάστασις ἡ ἐκ (τῶν) νεκρῶν (SCa; VKa) → **νεκρός** + ἀνίστημι/ἐγείρω BOISMARD 1984 Ab158; NEIRYNCK 1985	20,35	4,2	1	0

Literature

RADL 1975 399 [ἀνάστασις (ἡ) (ἐκ) (τῶν) νεκρῶν].

EHRHARDT, Arnold A.T., Lass die Toten ihre Toten begraben. — StudTheol 6 (1953) 128-164. [Lk 9,60]

PERLES, Felix, Zwei Übersetzungsfehler im Text der Evangelien. — ZNW 19 (1919-20) 96. [Lk 9,60; 14,35]

—, Noch einmal Mt 8,22 Lk 9,60, sowie Joh 20,17. — ZNW 25 (1926) 286-287.

SCHWARZ, Günther, ἄφες τοὺς νεκροὺς θάψαι τοὺς ἑαυτῶν νεκρούς. — ZNW 72 (1981) 272-276. [Lk 9,60]

νέος 7 + 2 (Mt 2, Mk 2/3)
1. new (time) (Lk 5,38); 2. new (class)

Word groups	Lk	Acts	Mt	Mk
Νέα πόλις (VKb)		16,11	0	0
νεός + καινός	5,38		1	1
νεός + παλαίος	5,37[1].39		1	1
νεώτερος comparative (VKa) DENAUX 2009 La[n]	15,12.13; 22,26	5,6	0	0
νεώτερος + μείζων	22,26		0	0
ὁ νεώτερος υἱός → ὁ υἱὸς ὁ πρεσβύτερος	15,13		0	0
οἶνος νέος (LN: new wine)	5,37[1.2].38		2	2/3

Literature
SCHÜRMANN 1957 76-77 [Nicht nur νέος schreibt Luk relative häufig, sondern speziell auch den Komparativ νεώτερος].

DUPONT, Jacques, Vin vieux, vin nouveaux (Luc 5,39). — CBQ 25 (1963) 286-304. Esp. 286 n. 1.

νεότης 1 + 1 (Mt 0/1, Mk 1) youth (Lk 18,21; Acts 26,4)

νεφέλη 5 + 1 (Mt 4, Mk 4) cloud

Characteristic of Luke	Lk	Acts	Mt	Mk
νεφέλη in context of apparitions CREDNER 1836 138	9,34[1.2].35; 21,27	1,9	4	4

Literature
SABOURIN, Leopold, The Biblical Cloud – Terminology and Traditions. — BTB 4 (1974) 290-311.

νήθω 1 (Mt 1) spin (Lk 12,27)

νήπιος 1 (Mt 2) small child (Lk 10,21)

Literature
BDAG 2000 671 [literature 1,b,β].

DUPONT, Jacques, Les "simples" (petâyim) dans la Bible et à Qumrân. À propos des νήπιοι de Mt. 11,25; Lc. 10,21. — Studi sull'Oriente e la Bibbia offerti al P. Giovanni Rinaldi nel 60° compleanno da allievi, colleghi, amici. Genova: Studio e Vita, 1967, 329-336; = ID., Études, II, 1985, 583-591.

Νηρί 1 Neri (Lk 3,27)

νηστεία 1 + 2 (Mt 0/1, Mk 0/1)
1. fasting (Lk 2,37); 2. hunger; 3. festival of atonement (Acts 27,9)

Word groups	Lk	Acts	Mt	Mk
νηστεία + προσεύχομαι → **νηστεύω** + προσεύχομαι; cf. νηστεία + προσευχή (*VK*a) Mt 17,21*; Mk 9,29*		14,23	0	0

Characteristic of Luke	Lk	Acts	Mt	Mk
νηστεία/εύω + praying → **νηστεύω** + praying BOISMARD 1984 Ab88; NEIRYNCK 1985	2,37; 5,33	10,30*; 13,3; 14,23	0	0

Literature
DENAUX 2009 lA[n]; LA[n] [νηστεία/εύω + praying]; GERSDORF 1816 261 [νηστείαις καὶ δεήσεσιν].

νηστεύω 4 + 2/3 (Mt 8, Mk 6)   fast

Word groups	Lk	Acts	Mt	Mk
νηστεύω + προσεύχομαι (*VK*b) → **νηστεία** + προσεύχομαι νηστεύω πυκνά (*VK*a); cf. νηστεύω πολλά Mt 9,14[1]	5,33	10,30*; 13,3	0 0	0 0

Characteristic of Luke	Lk	Acts	Mt	Mk
νηστεύω/εία + praying → **νηστεία** + praying BOISMARD 1984 Ab88; NEIRYNCK 1985	2,37; 5,33	10,30*; 13,3; 14,23	0	0

Literature
DENAUX 2009 LA[n] [νηστεία/εύω + praying]

νικάω 1   conquer

Word groups	Lk	Acts	Mt	Mk
νικάω transitive (*VK*a)	11,22		0	0

Νινευίτης 2 (Mt 1)   a Ninevite (Lk 11,30.32)

νομίζω 2 + 7 (Mt 3)

1. suppose (Lk 2,44; 3,23); νομίζομαι: 2. do customarily.

Word groups	Lk	Acts	Mt	Mk
νομίζομαι passive (*VK*b)	3,23	16,13 *v.l.*	0	0
νομίζω with following (acc. +) infinitive DENAUX 2009 lA[n]	2,44	7,25; 8,20; 14,19; 16,13.27; 17,29		
νομίζω ὅτι (*VK*a)		21,29	3	0

Characteristic of Luke
BOISMARD 1984 cb171; HARNACK 1906 31-32.148-149; NEIRYNCK 1985; PLUMMER 1922 lx

Literature
DENAUX 2009 lAn; GERSDORF 1816 265 [νομίσαντες δὲ αὐτὸν εἶναι]; JEREMIAS 1980 100: "νομίζω mit folgendem (acc.c.) inf. findet sich im NT außer 2mal bei Paulus nur im lk Doppelwerk (7mal)"; 114: "νομίζω ist lk Vorzugswort"; RADL 1975 418 [νομίζω; νομίζω participle; "bei Matth. folgt stets ὅτι, bei Lukas der Acc. c. Infinit.". DANOVE, Paul, Verbs of Experience, 1999. Esp. 163.175-176.

νομικός 6 (Mt 1)

1. about the law (adj.); 2. interpreter of the law (subst.) (Lk 10,25); 3. lawyer (subst.)

Word groups	Lk	Acts	Mt	Mk
Φαρισαῖοι καὶ νομικοί (SCa; VKa) → Φαρισαῖοι καὶ νομοδιδάσκαλοι	7,30; 14,3		1	0

Characteristic of Luke
CREDNER 1836 134 [νομικός instead of γραμματεῖς]; DENAUX 2009 L***; GOULDER 1989; HAWKINS 1909 L; PLUMMER 1922 lx

Literature
COLLISON 1977 174-175 [linguistic usage of Luke: probable]; HAUCK 1934 [Vorzugswort]; REHKOPF 1959 95 [vorlukanisch]; SCHÜRMANN 1961 276.

BORMANN, Lukas, *Recht, Gerechtigkeit und Religion*, 2001. Esp. 153-155.
DICKERSON, Patrick L., The New Character Narrative in Luke-Acts, 1997, 291-312. Esp. 305-308: "The use of νομικός in Luke 10:25".
KILPATRICK, George D., Scribes, Lawyers and Lucan Origins. — *JTS* NS 1 (1950) 56-60; = ID., *Principles and Practice*, 1990, 245-249.
—, The Gentiles and the Strata of Luke. — BÖCHER, O. – HAACKER, K. (eds.), *Verborum Veritas*. FS G. Stählin, 1970, 83-88. Esp. 85-86; = ID., *Principles and Practice*, 1990, 313-318. Esp. 315-316.
KLIJN, A.F.J., Νομικός in St. Luke's Gospel. — *JTS* NS 2 (1951) 166-170.
NEIRYNCK, Frans, Luke 10:25-28: A Foreign Body in Luke? — PORTER, Stanley E. – JOYCE, Paul – ORTON, David E. (eds.), *Crossing the Boundaries: Essays in Biblical Interpretation in Honour of Michael D. Goulder*. Leiden – New York: Brill, 1994, 149-165; = ID., *Evangelica III*, 2001, 267-282.
—, The Minor Agreements and Lk 10,25-28. — *ETL* 71 (1995) 151-160. Esp. 154-156: "Νομικός in Luke"; = ID., *Evangelica III*, 2001, 283-294. Esp. 287-290.
—, Luke 9,22 and 10,25-28: The Case for Independent Redaction. — *ETL* 75 (1999) 123-132. Esp. 130-132: "Νομικός in Lk"; = ID., *Evangelica III*, 2001, 295-306. Esp. 303-306.

νομοδιδάσκαλος 1 + 1   teacher of the Law (Lk 5,17; Acts 5,34)

Word groups	Lk	Acts	Mt	Mk
Φαρισαῖοι καὶ νομοδιδάσκαλοι → Φαρισαῖοι καὶ νομικοί	5,17		0	0

Characteristic of Luke
BOISMARD 1984 cb114; NEIRYNCK 1985; VOGEL 1899B

Literature
DENAUX 2009 LA[n]; JEREMIAS 1980 166 [red.].

BORMANN, Lukas, *Recht, Gerechtigkeit und Religion*, 2001. Esp. 156-157.
HORSLEY, G.H.R. – LEE, John A.L., A Lexicon of the New Testament, 1, 1997. Esp. 79.82-84.

νόμος 9 + 17/19 (Mt 8/9)

1. law (Acts 18,15); 2. the Law (Lk 2,23); 3. the Scriptures

Word groups	Lk	Acts	Mt	Mk
τὰ κατὰ τὸν νόμον (VKh) DENAUX 2009 LAⁿ	2,39	24,14	0	0
κατὰ (τὸν) νόμον → κατὰ τοῦ **νόμου**; **κρίνω** κατὰ τὸν νόμον; cf. κατὰ τὸ εἰρημένον ἐν τῷ νόμῳ κυρίου Lk 2,24; κατὰ τὸ εἰθισμένον τοῦ νόμου Lk 2,27; κατὰ ἀκρίβειαν τοῦ πατρῴου νόμου Acts 22,3 DENAUX 2009 lAⁿ	2,22.39	22,12; 23,3; 24,6*.14	0	0
κατὰ τοῦ νόμου → κατὰ (τὸν) **νόμον**; κατὰ τοῦ **τόπου** BOISMARD 1984 Aa145		6,13; 21,28	0	0
νόμον + τηρέω (VKx) → φυλάσσω τὸν **νόμον**		15,5.24*	0	0
νόμος + ἀναγινώσκω/ἀνάγνωσις (SCd; VKt)	10,26	13,15	1	0
νόμος + γράφω (SCe; VKr) DENAUX 2009 Laⁿ (?)	2,23; 10,26; 24,44	24,14	0	0
νόμος τῶν Ἰουδαίων (VKd)		25,8	0	0
νόμος + κρίνω (VKu)		23,3; 24,6*	0	0
νόμος κυρίου (SCa; VKa) → **δικαιώματα** τοῦ κυρίου; cf. νόμος τοῦ θεοῦ Mt 15,6* DENAUX 2009 Lⁿ	2,23.24.39		0	0
νόμος + (λέγω/)ἐρῶ (VKs)	2,24		0	0
νόμος + προφῆται (LN: the sacred writings; SCc; VKk)	16,16; 24,44	13,15; 24,14; 28,23	4	0
παρὰ τὸν νόμον		18,13	0	0
φυλάσσω τὸν νόμον → **νόμον** τηρέω; cf. Gal 6,13 BOISMARD 1984 ca59		7,53; 21,24	0	0

Characteristic of Luke	Lk	Acts	Mt	Mk
νόμος Μωϋσέως (SCb; VKl); cf. Jn 7,23; 1 Cor 9,9; Heb 10,28 BOISMARD 1984 cb147; NEIRYNCK 1985	2,22; 24,44	13,38; 15,5; 28,23	0	0

Literature

COLLISON 1977 182 [ἐν νόμῳ κυρίου: noteworthy phenomena]; DENAUX 2009 lAⁿ [νόμος Μωϋσέως]; GERSDORF 1816 244 [κατὰ τὸν νόμον Μωϋσέως]; 245 [ἐν τῷ νόμῳ κυρίου]; 262 [ἅπαντα τὰ κατὰ τὸν νόμον]; JEREMIAS 1980 90 [κατὰ τὸν νόμον Μωϋσέως: red.]; RADL 1975 414 [κατὰ τὸν νόμον]; 418 [νόμος].

BORMANN, Lukas, *Recht, Gerechtigkeit und Religion*, 2001. Esp. 118-121.
JERVELL, Jacob, The Law in Luke-Acts. — *HTR* 64 (1971) 21-36.
JUNG, Chang-Wook, *Infancy Narrative*, 2004. Esp. 69-72.74-78.
WILSON, Stephen G., *Luke and the Law* (SNTS MS, 50). Cambridge: University Press, 1963, VII-142 p. Esp. 1-11: "Legal terminology in Luke-Acts" [ἔθος; ἐντολή; νόμος].

νόσος 4 + 1 (Mt 5, Mk 1/2) — sickness

Word groups	Lk	Acts	Mt	Mk
νόσος (+) θεραπεύω	4,40; 7,21; 9,1		4	1/2

Literature

JEREMIAS 1980 162 [red.].

νοσσία 1 — brood (Lk 13,34)

Literature

HAUCK 1934 [seltenes Alleinwort].

νοσσός 1   young bird (Lk 2,24)

Literature

HAUCK 1934 [seltenes Alleinwort].

JUNG, Chang-Wook, *Infancy Narrative*, 2004. Esp. 87.

νότος 3 + 2 (Mt 1)

1. south (Lk 11,31; 13,29); 2. south wind (Lk 12,55; Acts 27,13; 28,13)

Word groups	Lk	Acts	Mt	Mk
ἀπό + νότου → ἀπὸ ἀνατολῶν/βορρᾶ/δυσμῶν	13,29		0	0
βασίλισσα νότου (*VK*a)	11,31		1	0

Characteristic of Luke

BOISMARD 1984 cb115; DENAUX 2009 La*; HARNACK 1906 54; NEIRYNCK 1985

νοῦς 1

1. mind (Lk 24,45); 2. way of thinking

Word groups	Lk	Acts	Mt	Mk
διανοίγω + τὸν νοῦν (*LN*: cause to be open minded) → διανοίγω τὴν καρδίαν / τοὺς ὀφθαλμούς	24,45		0	0

νύμφη 2 (Mt 1)

1. bride; 2. daughter-in-law (Lk 12,53$^{1.2}$)

Word groups	Lk	Acts	Mt	Mk
νύμφη + πενθερά	12,53$^{1.2}$		1	0

νυμφίος 2 (Mt 6, Mk 3)   bridegroom (Lk 5,34.35)

νυμφών 1 (Mt 1/2, Mk 1)   wedding hall

Word groups	Lk	Acts	Mt	Mk
υἱοὶ τοῦ νυμφῶνος (*LN*: wedding guests)	5,34		1	1

νῦν 14 + 25/29 (Mt 4, Mk 3)

1. now (Lk 2,29); 2. just now

Word groups	Lk	Acts	Mt	Mk
ἀλλὰ νῦν → **νῦν** δέ	22,36		0	0
καὶ τὰ νῦν CREDNER 1836 134		4,29; 5,38; 20,32; 27,22	0	0
καὶ νῦν ἰδού BOISMARD 1984 Aa94		13,11; 20,22.25	0	0
νῦν attributive (*VK*f)		22,1*	0	0
νῦν δέ → ἀλλὰ **νῦν**	16,25; 19,42; 22,69		0	0
νῦν οὖν BOISMARD 1984 Aa57		10,33; 15,10; 16,36; 23,15	0	0
τό/τὰ νῦν BOISMARD 1984 Aa32		4,29; 5,38; 17,30; 20,32; 24,25; 27,22	0	0
τὸ νῦν ἔχον / τὰ νῦν (*SC*c; *VK*c)		4,29; 5,38; 17,30; 20,32; 24,25; 27,22	0	0

Characteristic of Luke

DENAUX 2009 L***; GOULDER 1989; HAWKINS 1909 L; MORGENTHALER 1958LA

	Lk	Acts	Mt	Mk
ἀπὸ τοῦ νῦν (*SC*a; *VK*b); cf. Jn 8,11; 2 Cor 5,16 BOISMARD 1984 Bb47; CREDNER 1836 134; DENAUX 2009 L***; GOULDER 1989*; HARNACK 1906 141; HAWKINS 1909L; NEIRYNCK 1985; PLUMMER 1922 lix; SCHÜRMANN 1953 36	1,48; 5,10; 12,52; 22,18.69	18,6	0	0

Literature

COLLISON 1977 158 [νῦν in eschatological context: linguistic usage of Luke's "other source-material": certain]; 158-159 [ἀπὸ τοῦ νῦν: linguistic usage of Luke: likely]; EASTON 1910 145 [ἀπὸ τοῦ νῦν: especially characteristic of L]; HAUCK 1934 [Vorzugswort; Vorzugsverbindung: ἀπὸ τοῦ νῦν]; JEREMIAS 1980 60 [ἀπὸ τοῦ νῦν: red.]; RADL 1975 400 [ἀπὸ τοῦ νῦν]; 413 [καὶ ἰδού; καὶ νῦν ἰδού]; 418 [νῦν; καὶ νῦν]; SCHNEIDER 1969 119.163 [ἀπὸ τοῦ νῦν: Vorzugswörter und -ausdrücke des Luk]; SCHÜRMANN 1953 36 ["Luk scheint keine Vorliebe für ein einfaches νῦν zu haben"; rather preference for composite expressions with νῦν: νῦν δέ, καὶ νῦν, νῦν οὖν, νυνί, τὸ νῦν ἔχον, τὰ νῦν, and ἀπὸ τοῦ νῦν]; 1961 279 [ἀπὸ τοῦ νῦν: protoluk R weniger wahrscheinlich].

DECKER, Rodney J., The Semantic Range of νῦν in the Gospels as Related to Temporal Deixis. — *Trinity Journal* 16 (1995) 187-217.

DUPONT, Jacques, *Les Béatitudes*, III, 1973. Esp. 100-109.

MINEAR, Paul S., A Note on Luke XXII,36. — *NT* 7 (1964-65) 128-134. Esp. 133-134 [ἀλλὰ νῦν]: "To Luke it was on the very night (and at the very *table* where) Jesus took bread *that he was betrayed*. It is this betrayal, set over against Jesus' intercession, that marks for Luke the extent and the limit of 'the power of darkness' (vs. 53), and the boundary between the two kingdoms (vs.24-30)".

THRALL, Margaret E., *Greek Particles in the New Testament*, 1962. Esp. 30-34.

νύξ 7 + 16 (Mt 9/10, Mk 4/5)

1. night (time) (Lk 2,8); 2. night (darkness)

Word groups	Lk	Acts	Mt	Mk
αὕτη ἡ νύξ → **νὺξ** ἐκείνη; ὁ **αἰὼν** οὗτος; ἡ **ἡμέρα** αὕτη; οὗτος **καιρός**	12,20; 17,34	27,23	2	1/2

			0	0
δι' ὅλης νυκτός (*SCd*); cf. διὰ παντὸς νυκτός Mk 5,5	5,5		0	0
ἡμέρας (+) καὶ νυκτός (*SCa*; *VK*a) DENAUX 2009 LA[n]	18,7	9,24	0	0
κατὰ μέσον τῆς νυκτός		27,27[2]	0	0
νὺξ ἐκείνη → αὕτη ἡ **νύξ**; ὁ **αἰὼν** ἐκεῖνος; ἡ **ἡμέρα** ἐκείνη; αἱ **ἡμέραι** ἐκεῖναι; ὁ ἐκεῖνος **καιρός**; ἐν ἐκείνῃ τῇ **ὥρᾳ** / τῇ **ὥρᾳ** ἐκείνῃ		12,6	0	0
νὺξ + ἡμέρα (*SCb*; *VK*c)	2,37; 18,7; 21,37	9,24; 20,31; 26,7	3	2
νὺξ + ὅραμα		16,9; 18,9	0	0
φυλακὴ τῆς νυκτός (*SCc*; *VK*d)	2,8		1	1
ὥρα τῆς νυκτός (*VK*e)		16,33; 23,23	0	0

Characteristic of Luke
MORGENTHALER 1958A

	Lk	Acts	Mt	Mk
διὰ νυκτός (*SCd*; *VK*f) → δι' ὅλης **νυκτός** BOISMARD 1984 Ab57; NEIRYNCK 1985	5,5	5,19; 16,9; 17,10; 23,31	0	0
νύκτα καὶ ἡμέραν BOISMARD 1984 cb38; NEIRYNCK 1985	2,37	20,31; 26,7	0	1
τῇ νυκτί BOISMARD 1984 Bb73; NEIRYNCK 1985	12,20; 17,34	12,6; 23,11; 27,23	0	1

Literature
VON BENDEMANN 2001 423: "ταύτῃ τῇ νυκτί ist lukanisches Syntagma"; DENAUX 2009 lA[n] [διὰ νυκτός], lAn [τῇ νυκτί]; RADL 1975 421 [ταύτῃ τῇ νυκτί]; SCHÜRMANN 1955 55 [temporal dative ταύτῃ τῇ νυκτί].

STROBEL, August, A. Merx über Lc 17,20f. — *ZNW* 51 (1960) 133-134.

[νὺξ παρατηρήσεως]

Νῶε 3 (Mt 2)	Noah (Lk 3,36; 17,26.27)

ξηραίνω 1 (Mt 3, Mk 6/7)	
1. cause to wither; ξηραίνομαι: 2. become dry (Lk 8,6); 3. become ripe; 4. become stiff	

ξηρός 3 (Mt 2, Mk 1)	
1. dry (Lk 23,31); 2. paralyzed (Lk 6,6.8)	

ξύλον 2 + 4 (Mt 2, Mk 2)	
1. wood; 2. firewood (Lk 23,31); 3. tree (Lk 23,31); 4. club (Lk 22,52); 5. stocks (Acts 16,24); 6. cross (Acts 5,30)	

Word groups	Lk	Acts	Mt	Mk
κρεμάννυμι ἐπὶ ξύλου (*LN*: crucify; *VK*b); cf. Gal 3,13		5,30; 10,39	0	0
ξύλον = the cross; cf. 1 Pet 2,24 BOISMARD 1984 ca15		5,30; 10,39; 13,29	0	0

O

ὁ, ἡ, τό 2629 + 2668 (2777+1504)		the		

Word groups	Lk	Acts	Mt	Mk
article as implicit, implied participle (MGM 734)		13,9	2	0
article followed by an adjective (MGM 729-30)	1,36¹·².39².49¹.58¹·².65¹; 2,44³·⁴; 3,5¹·².16²; 4,35³; 5,7¹.19⁵; 6,8⁵.24¹.32².33². 34.35³; 7,15¹.28¹.43¹; 8,10⁴; 9.8.19³.60¹·²; 10,9¹; 11,21¹.26¹; 12,26.46⁴.57; 13,11.17³;14,14².21⁷; 15,12¹; 16,10¹·².11².12¹. 15⁵.21³.22¹·⁴.25¹·³; 17,2³. 18²; 18,7³.9².11³.13⁶.27²; 19,8²·⁴; 20,37¹; 22,1².7². 26¹·²; 23,29¹.35⁵.49¹; 24,5⁴. 9³.10³	2,33¹; 3,14; 4,23¹·³; 5,6. 13¹; 7,48¹.52⁵; 9,13².32¹. 41¹; 13,34¹·².35; 14,15¹; 17,5².9¹·³.21; 19,32²; 20,15²; 21,6².12¹.34²; 22,14⁴.30²; 23,8; 24,23²; 25,5¹; 27,12².44¹; 28,9¹.16¹*	91/ 96	35 [36]
article followed by a demonstrative pronoun (MGM 730)	9,48⁴; 19,26²v.l.	15,38¹; 17,6².24¹	6	3
article followed by a pronoun (MGM 729-30)	5,33⁴; 6,30²; 15,31²; 16,12¹; 17,34³.35².36²*; 18,10³.16³; 19,20¹; 22,42³; 23,40¹	27,3¹	7	1
article followed by a proper noun in the genitive (MGM 727)	5,33²; 20,4*.25²; 24,10²	13,22¹; 15,1¹; 23,35³	7	9
article followed by a (pro)noun in the genitive (other cases) (MGM 727)	2,49¹; 16,8⁸	11,23²; 16,33⁴; 26,12²	5	3/4
article followed by οὖ or μή (MGM 732-33)	3,11²; 11,23¹·²; 12,48¹; 19,26².27²; 22,36²		4	0
article in stead of a demonstrative pronoun (MGM 731)		17,28²	0	0
article with adverb (other than temporal) (MGM 735)	8,22²; 9,62²; 10,27⁷; 11,39³·⁶.40²; 16,26*; 17,31⁶; 19,4	7,27²	11	9
article with temporal adverb (MGM 735)	1,48³; 5,10⁴; 7,11¹; 8,1¹; 10,35¹; 12,52¹; 22,18¹.69¹	3,24²; 4,3².5¹.29¹; 5,38¹; 10,9¹.23¹.24¹; 14,20³; 17,30⁴; 18,6⁴; 19,40¹; 20,7⁴.32¹; 21,1².8¹; 22,30¹; 23,32¹; 25,6¹.17¹.23¹; 27,18.22¹	8	3

article with two nouns, the governing noun being anarthrous (MGM 727-28)	1,2¹.26³.70; 2,25¹; 4,9³.17¹. 26.29².38²; 7,3².12³; 8,28². 41¹; 10,21⁴; 14,5; 15,17; 20,36.43²; 21,26¹; 23,51³	1,18¹.22¹; 2,30².35²; 3,18².20¹.21²; 4,4³.8.25¹. 32²; 5,41²; 6,1³; 7,42³. 45⁵.49³.55²; 10,12²·³; 13,13³. 24¹; 14,5¹; 16,12¹.7²; 17,1³.26¹.29¹; 18,12¹; 19,35³; 21,20⁵. 30².39¹; 22,3¹; 23,5². 7¹.29; 24,5¹; 27,5⁴.12³. 23².42¹	18	5
article with two nouns, the governed noun being anarthrous (MGM 727-28)	1,5¹.16¹.32².33¹.40¹; 2,22³. 24³; 3,4³; 4,25¹; 5,1⁵; 7,29⁴; 8,41v.l.; 11,29³.31⁶. 32³; 16,22³; 17,26¹.28¹.32; 20,4. 37³; 23,7¹	1,22¹; 2,38¹; 3,6¹.13¹; 4,10¹; 5,9².12⁴; 7,13⁴*. 16².21.23³.32³.37³. 45⁶. 46².58⁴; 8,12⁴; 10,36². 48¹; 12,2.12³; 15,5⁴.16¹; 16,7³; 17,5⁴; 18,25⁶; 19,3²; 21,8²; 23,16²; 25,10²; 26,9¹; 28,23⁵	21	17/18
article with two nouns (other cases) (MGM 727-28)	1,8².9¹·⁴.10³.11¹.23¹.27¹. 41¹.42¹.43¹.44¹.48¹.59⁴.68¹;2, 22¹.27⁷.41².42¹; 3,6¹.9². 16².27-38 (*passim*); 4,9¹. 14².16².22¹.43².44; 5,1².9¹. 24¹.34²; 6,4¹.5².12³.20⁴.22³. 49³; 7,1².12¹.28².30².34¹. 36².37².38⁴; 8,10¹·²;11³.24³. 26¹.35⁵.37¹·².44¹·³.51²; 9,2¹. 11².20¹.22¹.26²·⁵.27³.43¹. 44³.51².56¹*.60³.62⁴; 10,2³. 9².11⁵.39²; 11,15¹.20².30². 31²·⁴.34¹.42⁵.47¹.48¹.49¹.50¹; 12,1¹.7¹.8².9³.10¹.31¹*. 40¹.47³.56¹; 13,14⁵.16³.18¹. 19¹.20¹.28².29¹; 14,1².14¹. 15².17².21⁵; 15,10¹.12³.15¹; 16,2¹.8²·⁴·⁶.9¹.16³.21².24¹. 27¹; 17,20²·⁴.21¹.22²·³.24⁴. 26²·³.30³; 18,6².7².8².16³. 17¹.25¹.29².31⁴; 19,10¹.11². 37¹·²·³.44². 47³; 20,10².15². 20².21¹.47²; 21,27¹.31¹.36²; 22,1¹.3².7¹.16¹.18¹·³.22¹. 25².39².48¹.54¹.61⁴.69²·⁴.70¹; 23,3².35³.37¹.38¹.45². 51⁴.52²; 24,3¹.7¹.35³.49¹	1,3³.4¹.14².25¹; 2,1².10¹. 11².31¹.33¹·³.38³.42¹·⁴; 3,1².2¹.13⁴.15¹.16¹.25¹; 4,1³.13¹.18².26¹.30³.31³. 32¹.33¹.35¹.37²; 5,2³.3⁶.12¹.16¹.19¹.24². 30¹.37².40²; 6,2²·⁴.4². 7¹·³; 7,2².17¹.20².30¹.32¹. 33².34¹.41².42².43¹·³.44¹. 45². 52⁴.56²; 8,1⁵.5¹.9². 10¹.12².14³.16¹. 18²·³. 20².22³. 25².32¹.37²*; 9,1².20³.27⁴.28¹.31³·⁵; 10,45³; 11,1⁴.6¹.12³.16¹. 22².23³; 12,3².7².11⁴.12¹. 13¹.14¹.20¹.24¹; 13,5¹·³. 7².10¹.12³.14³.15¹.25². 27³.36¹.44³.46³.48².50⁴. 51²; 14,1¹.2².2³.4¹.6¹.13². 22¹·⁴.26¹; 15,3⁴.5².7³.10². 11¹.15¹.17¹.20².26².35¹. 36².40¹; 16,13¹.19².26¹. 27².32¹.33¹; 17,10⁴.13⁵. 26².30¹; 18,25¹; 19,5¹.8¹. 10³.13⁵.17³.20¹27²; 20,6¹.16⁴.17².19³.24⁵·⁶. 28⁴·⁶.32³.35².37¹; 21,11¹.13³.14¹.26⁵·⁶.35³. 36¹; 22,9³.11¹.14²; 23,4². 9¹·².16¹; 24,4⁴.5⁶; 25,8². 15².21²; 26,13².18²; 27,19².32².40³; 28,7².8¹. 17¹.20²23².31¹	220	92
article with cardinal number (MGM 731)	7,41¹; 8,1⁴; 9,12²; 10,17¹.36¹; 13,4¹; 15,4¹; 16,13¹; 17,17²·³.34².35²; 18,10²; 20,31².33³; 22,3³.47²; 24,1¹.9².33²	1,24; 2,14²; 6,2¹; 20,7¹; 21,8⁴	16	18 [19]
article with ordinal number (MGM 731)	1,26²; 11,26³; 12,38¹·²; 13,32²; 14,18; 18,33²; 19,16¹.18¹.47⁵; 20,29.30.31¹	3,1⁴; 7,8³.13¹; 10,30²; 13,33⁴.50⁴; 25,2²; 27,19¹; 28,7³.	12	5

article with aorist participle (MGM 732-33)	1,45¹.66¹; 2,17².18¹·².21³; 6,49¹; 7,10².39²; 8,12³. 14¹·³.36¹·².45²; 9,17.48³; 10,11².13².16⁴.36².37²; 11,27⁴.40¹.51¹; 12,9¹.10³. 47².48¹; 14,9¹; 15,30²; 17,9².10; 18,26¹; 19,27²; 20,2¹.18¹.35¹; 22,64; 23,47².48¹·³; 24,18¹	1,11⁴.16⁴·⁵; 4,4¹.11²·⁴.21¹. 24¹.25¹.32².36¹; 5,9⁴; 7,35³.37².38¹.52³; 8,4¹. 32³; 9,17⁴.21²; 11,19¹. 21¹; 12,25²; 13,31¹; 15,33².38¹; 17,6².24²; 19,19¹; 20,19²; 21,38²; 23,13¹; 26,4³	47/ 48	10/ [15]
article with future participle (MGM 732-33) DENAUX 2009 LAⁿ	22,49²	20,22²	0	0
article with perfect participle (MGM 732-33)	1,19².45².79¹; 2,15⁵.24². 27⁷; 3,13²; 4,16¹; 5,24⁴; 7,32.49; 8,34².56³; 9,27¹. 32²; 11,50³; 13,17.34³. 14,7¹.10².12¹.15¹.24²; 15,6⁵; 18,9¹.31²; 19,10³. 24¹.32; 20,17²; 21,15.22². 35¹; 22,22³.27¹·³.28¹.37¹; 24,12⁴.14.44²	2,16¹; 3,10¹·⁵; 4,12³.14²; 5,7²; 10,17⁴.33².41².42²; 13,12².29¹.40¹; 15,16²·³; 16,4³; 17,2¹; 18,27⁴; 19,18¹; 20,32⁷; 21,20⁴; 23,2².4¹.31²; 24,14³; 26,18⁶.30³; 28,2⁴	21/ 22	15/ 16
article with participle (other cases) (MGM 733)	1,35².36².50².65¹.71; 2,38².47²; 3,11¹·³; 5,31²·³; 6,3².18³.27¹·³.28¹·².29¹·⁴.30¹ .32¹·³.47; 7,14².19².20².25¹; 8,3.4.5¹.8³.16¹.21².34¹; 9,7¹.11⁴.48⁴; 10.8.16¹·²·³; 11,10¹·²·³.28¹.33¹.41; 12,4². 5¹.21; 13,9.17¹.23.33; 14,11¹·².29.31.35; 16,15¹. 18¹·².21¹.26; 18,14²·³.24². 34²; 19,24¹.26¹.45²; 20,17³. 27; 21,4⁴.23¹·².26¹·²; 22,21¹. 23².25⁴.26¹·³.27²·⁴.36¹; 24,21¹	1,19¹.20²; 2,7.9¹.14⁴.47⁴; 3,2³; 4,16.32².34²; 5,5². 11².32⁵; 6,15¹; 7,24¹. 44⁵; 8,6².7; 9,14².21¹·³. 35¹; 10,7².35.38³.43³. 44⁵; 12,9¹; 13,16¹.26¹. 27¹.39.45³; 14,12³; 15,19¹.21¹ 16,11.14⁴; 17,15¹.17³·⁵; 19,4².12¹. 13².22²; 20,15¹·³.20¹. 34².35¹; 21,18¹; 22,5⁴. 9¹·⁴.11³.19².20⁴29¹; 24,25²; 25,16¹; 26,13⁴; 27,11⁴. 24².40⁵.43⁴; 28,17¹.24². 30	92/ 93	39/ 41
article + participle preceded by a noun (MGM 732-33)	2,15⁵.17².21³; 4,22³; 6,8²; 7,39²; 9,32⁵; 10,11².13². 23³; 11,27⁴.44⁴.50³; 12,47²; 13,4⁵.17⁴; 14,24²; 15,6⁵. 30²; 18,7⁴.30³; 19,27².29²; 20,46²; 21,37⁵; 22,1³.19². 20⁶.63²; 23,33²	3,2³; 4,11²·⁴.14²; 6,9³; 7,38⁵; 8,26²; 9,7².11³. 17⁴.32²; 10,7².17⁴; 11,1¹. 19³.22⁴; 12,10³; 13,27⁵; 14,3²; 15,16²; 16,3³.4³; 17,24²; 18,21¹; 20,32⁵; 21,28².38²; 24,25³; 26,4³; 28,2⁴.9²	26	9/ 10
article + participle preceded by a proper noun (MGM 732-33)	1,19²; 6,15; 8,2; 11,51¹; 13,34¹; 22,3¹	1,11⁴.16⁴.23; 4,36¹; 7,37²; 9,22²; 10,18; 11,13³; 12,12⁴.25²; 13,1³; 15,22⁵.37²	9/10	3
article + preposition preceded by a noun (MGM 734-35)	5,36⁴; 6,41²·⁶.42³·⁹; 11,13³. 35²; 20,35⁴	2,10³; 3,16⁵; 4,2⁵; 7,34³; 8,1⁴; 10,23³; 15,23⁴; 24,5³; 26,4²·³; 27,5²; 28,9²	22	6
article + preposition preceded by an anarthrous noun (MGM 734-35)	11,2*	10,38¹; 12,20¹; 16,4⁵; 18,15; 25,23⁵; 26,18⁷.22¹	1	2
article + preposition (other cases) (MGM 734-35)	2,39¹; 5,9¹; 6,3².4⁵; 8,12¹. 13¹.15¹.45⁵*; 9,32².61¹;	1,3²; 2,5¹.39³; 4,24⁷; 5,17².21⁴; 6,9¹·⁴; 11,2;	14	11/ 12

	Lk	Acts	Mt	Mk
	10,7²; 14,32; 17,24²·³.31⁵; 19,42²; 21,21¹·⁴·⁵; 22,37³. 49¹; 24,19².24¹.27².33³.35¹	12,1⁴; 13,13²; 14,15⁵; 15,5¹; 16,32³; 17,11¹·³*. 24⁴; 18,25⁴; 19,8²; 23,11³.15³; 24,10⁴. 14³·⁴.22²·⁵; 25,14³; 26,20¹; 27,44²; 28,7¹.10².15².31²		
article + μή + infinitive (MGM 731)	4,42²; 8,6²; 17,1²	7,19⁵; 10,47²; 14,18²; 20,20².27¹; 21,12²	2	1
nom. art. for vocative (MGM 728-29)	6,20.21¹·².25¹·²; 8,54²; 10,21⁶; 11,2v.l.39²; 12,32¹; 18,11².13⁵	4,24³.25; 13,41¹	6	5
εἰς τό (μή) + infinitive (SCe; VKe)	4,29*; 5,17⁴; 20,20*	3,19¹; 7,19⁵	3	1
ἡ δέ, αἱ δέ (MGM 726-27)	1,29¹	5,8²; 9,40⁴; 12,15²	4/5	2
ὁ + noun + ὁ κατά + geographical name BOISMARD 1984 Aa58		2,10; 11,1; 24,5; 27,5	0	0
ὁ/ἡ/τὸ (+) ἐν used as a noun (SCc; VKe)	8,15¹; 17,31³; 21,21¹·²·³; 24,35¹	4,24; 14,15; 16,32; 17,11.24¹; 26,20	4	1
οἱ δέ as pronoun (VKe)	5,33¹; 7,4; 8,12.13.25² v.l.; 9,13².19¹.45; 14,4; 19,34; 20,5.11.12.24; 22,9.35.38¹. 71; 23,5.11.21.23; 24,19.42	4,21.24; 5,33; 7,25²; 9,29; 10,22; 12,15¹·³; 13,51; 14,4; 16,31; 17,18.32²; 19,2.3; 21,20.32; 28,6¹.21.24	26/ 27	17/ 21
ὁ δέ as pronoun (VKc)	3,13; 4,40².43; 5,34 v.l.; 6,8*.10; 7,40.43; 8,10¹.21. 24².30².48.52².56; 9,21.59²; 10,26.27.29.37¹; 11,46; 12,14; 13,8.23²; 14,16; 15,12.27.29.31; 16,6¹·².7².30; 17,37; 18,21.23.27.29.41; 20,17.25; 21,8; 22,10.25.33. 34.36.38².57.70²; 23,3².22	3,5; 7,2; 8,31; 9,5².10²; 10,4¹; 19,3*; 21,37; 22,14.27²; 25,22*; 26,15² v.l.	41/4 5	27/ 31
ὁ μέν ... ὁ δέ, ἄλλος δέ (MGM 726)		14,4³·⁵; 17,32¹·²; 28,24¹·³	1	0
ο(ἱ) μέν (MGM 726-27)		1,6¹; 2,41¹; 5,41¹; 8,4¹.25¹; 15,3¹.30¹; 23,18¹	0	0
πρὸς τό + infinitive (SCcc; VKe)	18,1	3,19*	5	1
τὰ πρὸς εἰρήνην (VKd) DENAUX 2009 Lⁿ	14,32; 19,42		0	0
τό + infinitive	5,17³; 8,6²; 12,5²; 18,1; 22,20²	1,3¹; 3,19¹; 7,4².19⁵; 10,41⁴; 15,13¹; 19,21⁴; 20,1¹; 25,11	12	10 [11]
τὸ/τὰ περὶ ἐμοῦ and similar (VKb) → τὰ περὶ ἡμῶν DENAUX 2009 LAⁿ	22,37²	23,11	0	0

Characteristic of Luke	Lk	Acts	Mt	Mk
article + sentence (MGM 735) DENAUX 2009 L***; PLUMMER 1922 lxii	1,62²; 9,46; 19,48¹; 22,2³.4².23¹.24¹.37²	4,21²; 22,30²	1	1
article + participle preceded by an anarthrous noun (MGM 732-33) DENAUX 2009 lA*	7,32; 23,49²	1,12¹; 4,12³; 7,35³; 10,1. 41²; 11,21¹; 19,11¹.17¹. 26³; 20,19²; 27,14	2	0

article + preposition followed by a noun (MGM 734) DENAUX 2009 lA*	$6,42^3$; $16,10^2.15^5$	$8,14^1$; $10,45^1$; $15,23^4$; $16,2$; $17,13^1.28^1(?)$; $18,27^{3*}$; $19,25^2.38$; $20,21^1$; $21,21^1.27^2$; $22,1$; $23,21$; $25,27$; $26,3$; $27,2^1$	1	1
διὰ τό + infinitive BOISMARD 1984 cb163; CREDNER 1836 135; GOULDER 1989; HAWKINS 1909add; NEIRYNCK 1985; PLUMMER 1922 lxii	$2,4^3$; $6,48^4$; $8,6^2$; $9,7^3$; $11,8^1$; $18,5^1$; $19,11^1$; $23,8^3$	$4,2^1$; $8,11^1$; $12,20^4$; $18,2^3.3^1$; $27,4^2.9^2$; $28,18$	3	3
εἰμί + ὁ + perfect participle DENAUX 2009 LA*	$20,17$; $22,28$	$2,16$; $10,42$	0	1
ἐν τῷ + infinitive BOISMARD 1984 cb1; CREDNER 1836 135; DENAUX 2009 L***; GOULDER 1989*; HAWKINS 1909L; NEIRYNCK 1985; PLUMMER 1922 lxii	$1,8^1.21^3$; $2,6^1.27^1.43^2$; $3,21^1$; $5,1^1.12^1$; $8,5^4.40^1$. 42^1; $9,18^1.29^1.33^1.34^1.36^1$. 51^1; $10,35^3.38$; $11,1^1.27^1$. 37; $12,15^1$; $14,1^1$; $17,11.14$; $18,35^1$; $19,15^1$; $24,4.15.30.51^1$	$2,1^1$; $3,26^3$; $4,30^1$; $8,6^4$; $9,3^1$; $11,15^1$; $19,1^1$	3	2/3
ἐν τῷ (+) εἶναι (SCd; VKe) DENAUX 2009 L***	$2,6$; $5,12$; $9,18^1$; $11,1$	$19,1$	0	0
κατὰ τό + part. perf. DENAUX 2009 L***; GOULDER 1989*	$2,24.27$; $4,16$; $22,22$	$17,2$; $23,31$	0	0
κατὰ τὸ (αὐτό) / τὰ (αὐτά) (SCk; VKn) BOISMARD 1984 Ab70; GOULDER 1989; NEIRYNCK 1985	$6,23.26$; $17,30$	$14,1$	0	0
μετὰ τό + infinitive (SCg; VKg) BOISMARD 1984 Eb56; NEIRYNCK 1985; PLUMMER 1922 lxii	$12,5^2$; $22,20^2$	$1,3^1$; $7,4^2$; $10,41^4$; $15,13^1$; $19,21^4$; $20,1^1$	1	2[3]
ὁ + phrase + noun DENAUX 2009 lA**; HAWKINS 1909A; GOULDER 1989	$1,70$; $6,42^4$; $9,12^4.37^1$; $16,10^2.15^4$; $19,30$	$5,16^2$; $8,14^1$; $10,45^1$; $13,42^1$; $15,23^1$; $16,2$; $17,13^1.28^1$; $19,25^1.38^1$; $20,21^1.26$; $21,21^1.27^2$; $22,1$; $23,21$; $25,27$; $26,3.11^2$; $27,2^2$	2	3
ὅ τε + noun + καὶ ὁ + noun BOISMARD 1984 Bb21; DENAUX 2009 lA*; NEIRYNCK 1985	$15,2$; $23,12^{1.2}$	$5,24^{2.3}$; $8,38^{3.4}$; $17,10^{2.3}.14^{4.5}$; $18,5^{2.3}$; $26,23^{2.3}.30^{1.2}$	0	0
τά + genitive HARNACK 1906 149	$2,49^2$; $20,25^{1.2}$		5/6	4
οἱ σὺν αὐτῷ/αὐτοῖς → οἱ μετ᾽ αὐτοῦ DENAUX 2009 LA*; GOULDER 1989*	$5,9^2$; $8,45*$; $9,32^1$; $24,33^2$	$5,17.21^1$; $19,38$	0	1
τά + participle GOULDER 1989	$9,7^2$; $11,21^3.41$; $12,33^1$; $16,1^2$; $17,9^2.10$; $18,31^2.34^2$; $21,22^2.36^1$; $23,48^3$; $24,18^1.44^2$	$10,33^2$; $13,29^1$; $15,16^3$; $16,4^3$; $20,22^2$	10	3/[4]
τὰ περί + genitive (SCac; VKd) DENAUX 2009 lA*; HARNACK 1906 45	$22,37$ v.l.; $24,19^2.27^3$	$1,3^2$; $8,12$ v.l.; $18,25^4$; $19,8^2$; $23,11^2.15^3$; $24,10^4.22^2$; $28,15^2.23$ v.l.31^3	0	0/1

τό + indirect question cf. 1 Tess 4,1; Rom 8,26 DENAUX 2009 L***; GOULDER 1989;	1,62²; 9,46; 19,48¹; 22,2³.4².23¹.24	4,21²; 22,30²	0	0
τό + perfect participle DENAUX 2009 L***; GOULDER 1989*	1,35²; 2,15³.24².27⁷; 3,13²; 8,34².35¹.56⁴; 20,17²; 22,37²; 24,12⁴	2,16¹; 5,7²; 13,12².40¹; 23,31²	2	1
τὸ καθ' ἡμέραν BOISMARD 1984 Ab126; NEIRYNCK 1985	11,3; 19,47	17,11 v.l.	0	0
τὸ/τὰ κατά BOISMARD 1984 Db11; DENAUX 2009 LA*; NEIRYNCK 1985	2,39; 11,3; 19,47	17,11; 24,22; 25,14	0	0
τὸ τίς/τί (nominalized indirect question) (SCk) → τὸ πῶς; cf. Rom 8,26 BOISMARD 1984 Bb53; DENAUX 2009 L***; GOULDER 1989*; HAWKINS 1909L; NEIRYNCK 1985	1,62²; 9,46; 19,48¹; 22,23¹.24	22,30³	0	0
τό, τά before preposition DENAUX 2009 L***; GOULDER 1989*; HAWKINS 1909 L	2,39¹; 8,15¹; 10,7²; 14,32; 19,42²; 22,37³; 24,19².27³.35¹	1,3²; 4,24⁷; 14,15³; 17,24⁴; 18,25⁴; 19,8; 23,11³.15³; 24,10⁴.14³.22²·⁴; 25,14³; 28,7¹.10².15².31	1	1
τοῦ + infinitive DENAUX 2009 L***; GOULDER 1989*; HAWKINS 1909 L; PLUMMER 1922 lxiii	1,9³.57³.73².77¹.79²; 2,6³. 21¹·⁵.24¹.27⁶; 4,10².42²; 5,7³; 8,5²; 9,51⁵; 10,19²; 12, 42⁶; 17,1²; 21,22¹; 22,6.15².31²; 24,16². 25². 29².45²	3,2⁴.12³; 5,31³ᵛ·¹·; 7,19³; 8,40²; 9,15²; 10,25¹.47²; 13,47²; 14,9².18²; 15,20¹; 18,10¹; 20,3³.20².27¹. 30¹; 21,12²; 23,15⁴·⁵.20²; 26,18¹·⁵; 27,1¹.20	7	1
τοῦ + infinitive after noun DENAUX 2009 L***;	1,57³; 2,6².21¹; 10,19²; 22,6	14,9²; 27,20	0	0
τοῦ + infinitive after preposition DENAUX 2009 LA*;	2,21¹; 22,15²	8,40²; 23,15⁴	1	0
τοῦ μή + infinitive DENAUX 2009 lA*;	4,42²; 17,1²; 24,16²	10,47²; 14,18²; 20,20².27¹; 21,12²	0	0
πρὸ τοῦ + infinitive (SCa; VKa) PLUMMER 1922 lxii	2,21⁵; 22,15²	23,15⁴	1	0

Literature

COLLISON 1977 190 [τό + indirect question: linguistic usage of Luke: certain], τοῦ + infinitive [linguistic usage of Luke: certain; it may also be a linguistic usage of Luke's 'other source-material']; DENAUX 2009 Lan [διὰ τό + infinitive]; Laⁿ [κατὰ τὸ (αὐτό) / τὰ (αὐτά)]; Lⁿ [τὸ καθ' ἡμέραν]; SCHÜRMANN 1953 12 [τοῦ + infinitive: vermutlich luk R], 13 [διὰ τό + infinitive: vermutlich luk R]; 1957 11 [τό + indirect question], 12 [τὸ τίς/τί (nominalized indirect question)], 129 [τὰ περί + genitive: wahrscheinlich luk R; τό, τά before preposition: wahrscheinlich luk R]; 1963 12 [πρὸ τοῦ + infinitive]

BAUMERT, Norbert, Εἰς τό mit Infinitif. — FilolNT 11 (21-22, 1998) 7-24.

CARAGOUNIS, Chrys C., The Development of Greek and the New Testament, 2004. Esp. 203-205 [The Use of τό in Indirect Questions: Lk 1,62]

COLLWELL, Ernest C., A Definite Rule for the Use of the Article in the Greek NT. — JBL 52 (1933) 12-21.

FUNK, Robert W., The Syntax of the Greek Article: Its Importance for Critical Pauline Problems (PhD dissertation), Vanderbilt University, 1953.

KLUIT, Adrianus, Vindiciae Articuli ὁ, ἡ, τό in Novo Testamento, Traiecti ad Rhenum: Paddenburg, 1768.

426 ὁ, ἡ, τό – ὁδός

MIDDLETON, Thomas Fanshaw, *The Doctrine of the Greek Article Applied to the Criticism and Illustration of the New Testament*, new [3d] ed., rev. by H.J. Rose, London: J.G.F. & J. Rivington, 1841.
ROBERTS, J.W., Exegetical Helps, The Greek Noun with and without the Article. — *Restoration Quaterly* 14 (1971) 28-44.
TEEPLE, Howard, The Greek Article with Personal Names in the Synoptic Gospels. — *NTS* 19 (1973) 302-317.
WALLACE, Daniel B., The Semantic Range of the Article-Noun-Kai-Noun Plural Construction in the NT. — *Grace Theological Journal* 4 (1983) 59-84.

ὀγδοήκοντα 2

eighty (Lk 2,37; 16,7)

Word groups	Lk	Acts	Mt	Mk
ὀγδοήκοντα τέσσαρες (*VKa*)	2,37		0	0

ὄγδοος 1 + 1

eight (Lk 1,59; Acts 7,8)

ὅδε 1/2 + 1/2

(Lk 16,25*; Acts 15,23*)

1. this (Lk 10,39; Acts 21,11); 2. such and such

Characteristic of Luke
BOISMARD 1984 Db42; NEIRYNCK 1985

Literature
DENAUX 2009 LA[n]; JEREMIAS 1980 193: "Das Demonstrativpronomen ὅδε ... findet sich in den Geschichtsbüchern des NT nur im lk Doppelwerk".

CIGNELLI, Lino – PIERRI, Rosario, *Sintassi di Greco biblico*. I.a, 2003. Esp. 68-74: "Concordanza dei pronomi dimostrativi" [ὅδε, οὗτος, ἐκεῖνος].

ὁδεύω 1

travel (Lk 10,33)

Literature
HAUCK 1934 [seltenes Alleinwort]; JEREMIAS 1980 191: "Das Simplex ... ist wahrscheinlich nicht lukanisch, da Lukas selbst das Kompositum διοδεύω schreibt".

ὁδηγέω 1 + 1 (Mt 1)

1. guide (Lk 6,39); 2. guide in learning (Acts 8,31)

ὁδός 20 + 20 (Mt 22, Mk 16/17)

1. road (Lk 9,57); 2. journey (Lk 2,44); 3. way of life; 4. Christian way of life (Acts 9,2)

Word groups	Lk	Acts	Mt	Mk
εἰς ὁδόν (*SCc; VKc*)	1,79		1	2

	Lk	Acts	Mt	Mk
εἰς τὴν ὁδόν (SCc; VKd)	9,3		0	1/2
εἰς ὁδούς	3,5		0	0
εἰς τὰς ὁδούς (SCc; VKd)	14,23		1	0
ἐν τῇ ὁδῷ (SCb; VKb)	9,57; 10,31; 12,58; 19,36; 24,32.35	9,17.27	5	6
κατασκευάζω τὴν ὁδόν (LN: make ready)	7,27		1	1
ὁδός metaphorically, as term for the Christian belief (SCh) BOISMARD 1984 Aa8		9,2; 18,25.26; 19,9.23; 22,4; 24,14.22	0	0
ὁδός + genitive (thing) (VKf)	1,79	2,28; 16,17	1	0
ὁδός + ἔρημος		8,26	0	0
ὁδὸς σωτηρίας; cf. Lk 1,79 ὁδὸς εἰρήνης; Acts 2,28 ὁδοὺς ζωῆς HARNACK 1906 37		16,17	0	0
ὁδὸς τοῦ θεοῦ (SCe; VKg)	20,21	18,26v.l.?	1	1
ὁδὸς (τοῦ) κυρίου/αὐτοῦ (SCf; VKh)	1,76; 3,4	13,10; 18,25	1	1
ὁδοί plural (SCg; VKj) DENAUX 2009 LAn	1,76; 3,5; 14,23	2,28; 13,10; 14,16	2	0
παρὰ τὴν ὁδόν (SCa)	8,5.12; 18,35		3	3
πορεύομαι + ὁδόν		8,39	0	0

Characteristic of Luke	Lk	Acts	Mt	Mk
κατὰ τὴν ὁδόν (SCd; VKe) BOISMARD 1984 Ab89; NEIRYNCK 1985	10,4	8,36; 24,14; 25,3; 26,13	0	0
ἡμέρας/σαββάτου ὁδός (LN: Sabbath journey) BOISMARD 1984 Ab187 NEIRYNCK 1985	2,44	1,12	0	0
ὁδὸς (τοῦ) κυρίου BOISMARD 1984 Aa146	1,76; 3,4	13,10; 18,25	1	1

Literature

BDAG 2000 691-692 [literature]; DENAUX 2009 IAⁿ [κατὰ τὴν ὁδόν], LAⁿ [ἡμέρας/σαββάτου ὁδός]; JEREMIAS 1980 184 [red.: κατὰ τὴν ὁδόν]; RADL 1975 419 [ὁδός "im übertragenen Sinn"; κατὰ τὴν ὁδόν].

LYONNET, Stanislas, "La voie" dans les Actes des Apôtres. — RechSR 69 (1981) 149-164.
MAHFOUZ, Hady, La fonction littéraire et théologique de Lc 3,1-20, 2003. Esp. 145-146.

ὀδούς 1 + 1 (Mt 8, Mk 1) tooth

Word groups	Lk	Acts	Mt	Mk
βρυγμὸς τῶν ὀδόντων (LN: gnashing of teeth; SCa; VKa)	13,28		6	0
βρύχω τοὺς ὀδόντας (LN: ᵃgnash the teeth; ᵇbe furious); cf. τρίζω τοὺς ὀδόντας Mk 9,18		7,ᵃ54	0	0

ὀδυνάομαι 3 + 1

1. be in great pain (Lk 16,24.25); 2. be terribly worried (Lk 2,48; Acts 20,38)

Characteristic of Luke

BOISMARD 1984 Ab90; CREDNER 1836 142; HARNACK 1906 149; HAWKINS 1909LA.add; MORGENTHALER 1958*; NEIRYNCK 1985; PLUMMER 1922 lii; VOGEL 1899A

Literature

DENAUX 2009 Laⁿ; GERSDORF 1816 269 [ὀδυνώμενοι ἐζητοῦμέν σέ]; HAUCK 1934 [seltenes Alleinwort]; JEREMIAS 1980 101 [red.]; RADL 1975 419.

ὅθεν 1 + 3 (Mt 4)

1. from where (Lk 11,24; Acts 28,13); 2. because of (Acts 26,19)

Word groups	Lk	Acts	Mt	Mk
ὅθεν location (VKa)	11,24	14,26; 28,13	3	0

ὀθόνιον 1

linen cloth

Literature

BDAG 2000 69 [literature].

DAUER, Anton, Zur Authentizität von Lk 24,12. — ETL 70 (1994) 294-318.
MUDDIMAN, John, A Note on Reading Luke XXIV.12. — ETL 48 (1972) 542-548.
NEIRYNCK, Frank, The Uncorrected Historic Present in Lk XXIV.12. — ETL 48 (1972)
    548-553; = ID., Evangelica, 1982, 329-334 (334: additional note; Appendix, Evangelica
    II, 1991, 798).
—, Once More Lk 24,12. — ETL 70 (1994) 319-340.

οἶδα 25/26 + 19 (Mt 24/25, Mk 21/22)

1. know (Lk 2,49); 2. know how to (Lk 11,13); 3. understand; 4. remember; 5. honor

Word groups	Lk	Acts	Mt	Mk
οἶδα + infinitive (SCd; VKd)	4,41; 11,13; 12,56[1.2]		1	0/1
οἶδα + interrogative pronoun (SCb; VKb)	4,34; 12,39; 13,25. 27; 20,7; 23,34	7,40; 19,32	4	7
οἶδα + relative pronoun (SCc; VKc)	9,33.55*; 22,60	2,30; 3,17; 12,9.11; 16,3;	1	1
οἶδα (+) ὅτι (SCa; VKa)	2,49; 5,24; 8,53; 12,30; 19,22; 20,21	2,30; 3,17; 12,9.11; 16,3; 20,22(-23).25.29; 23,5; 26,27	9	3/4

Characteristic of Luke

GASTON 1973 66 [Lked?]

Literature

RADL 1975 419 [οἶδα with μή].

DANOVE, Paul, Verbs of Experience, 1999. Esp. 163-164.176.
DUPONT, Jacques, Le discours de Milet, 1962. Esp. 31-33.88.
McKAY, K.L., On the Perfect and Other Aspects in New Testament Greek, 1981. Esp. 297-
    309: "Knowing".

οἰκέτης 1 + 1

house servant (Lk 16,13; Acts 10,7)

Word groups	Lk	Acts	Mt	Mk
οἰκέτης + κύριος → δοῦλος + κύριος	16,13		0	0

Characteristic of Luke

BOISMARD 1984 Db43; NEIRYNCK 1985

Literature

DENAUX 2009 LA[n]; HAUCK 1934 [seltenes Alleinwort]; JEREMIAS 1980 258 [red.].

οἰκία 24/26 + 12 (Mt 25/26, Mk 18/19)
1. house (Lk 5,29); 2. family; 3. lineage 4. property

Word groups	Lk	Acts	Mt	Mk
(εἰσ)ἔρχομαι εἰς (τὴν) (+) οἰκίαν (SCf) → (ἀπ/εἰσ)ἔρχομαι εἰς τὸν **οἶκον**	4,38; 7,36*.44; 8,51; 9,4; 10,5	9,17; 18,7[1]	8	4
εἰσπορεύομαι + εἰς οἰκίαν → πορεύμαι εἰς **οἶκον**	22,10		0	0
οἰκία + genitive referring to the owner of the house (SCc; VKd) → **οἶκος** + gen. referring to the owner of the house	4,38; 5,29; 7,37.44; 8,51; 20,47; 22,54	9,11; 10,17.32; 12,12; 16,32; 17,5; 18,7[1]	8/9	9
οἰκία + ἀγρός/χωρίον (SCd; VKe)	17,31	4,34	2	3
οἰκία + πόλις (SCe; VKg)	10,7[3](-8)		3	0
οἰκίαι plur. (VKh)	20,47	4,34	1/2	2
αἱ οἰκίαι τῶν χηρῶν	20,47		0/1	1
οἰκίαν οἰκοδομέω (SCa; VKa) → **οἶκον** οἰκοδομέω	6,48[1].49[1]		2	0
οἰκοδεσπότης + οἰκία (SCb; VKb); cf. οἰκία + κύριος Mk 13,35	22,11		1	0
σαρόω + οἰκία → σαρόω + **οἶκος**	15,8		0	0

Characteristic of Luke	Lk	Acts	Mt	Mk
ἐν αὐτῇ τῇ οἰκίᾳ PLUMMER 1922 lii	10,7[1]		0	0

Literature
BDAG 2000 693 [literature Lk 10,38 v.l.); SCHÜRMANN 1953 97-98 [Lk 22,11: τῆς οἰκίας vermutlich luk R].

BORMANN, Lukas, *Recht, Gerechtigkeit und Religion*, 2001. Esp. 157.
BRANDT, Pierre-Yves – LUKINOVICH, Alessandra, Οἶκος et οἰκία chez Marc comparé à Matthieu et Luc. — *Bib* 78 (1997) 525-533.
NICKLIN, T., "House" and "Home" in New Testament Greek. — *ExpT* 49 (1937-38) 566-568.
SCHWARZ, Günther, "Die Häuser der Witwen verzehren"? (Markus 12,40 / Lk 20,47). — *BibNot* 88 (1997) 45-46.

οἰκοδεσπότης 4 (Mt 7, Mk 1)   master of household

Word groups	Lk	Acts	Mt	Mk
οἰκοδεσπότης + δοῦλος → **δεσπότης** + δοῦλος	14,21		2	0
οἰκοδεσπότης τῆς οἰκίας (VKb); cf. οἰκοδεσπότης + οἰκία αὐτοῦ Mt 24,43; οἰκία + κύριος Mk 13,35	22,11		0	0

Literature
REHKOPF 1959 96 [vorlukanisch]; SCHÜRMANN 1961 276.

οἰκοδομέω 12 + 4/5 (Mt 8, Mk 4)
1. build (Lk 6,48); 2. make more able (Acts 20,32)

Word groups	Lk	Acts	Mt	Mk
οἰκοδομέομαι middle and passive (VKe) DENAUX 2009 La[n]	4,29; 6,48[2]	9,31	0	0

οἰκοδομέω (+) οἰκίαν/οἶκον (VKb)	6,48¹.49	7,47.49	2	0
οἰκοδομέω τινί τι (VKc)	7,5	7,47.49	0	0
DENAUX 2009 1Aⁿ				
οἱ οἰκοδομοῦντες (VKa)	20,17	4,11*	1	1

Characteristic of Luke
GOULDER 1989

Literature
DUPONT, Jacques, *Le discours de Milet*, 1962. Esp. 250-260.
TAEGER, Jens-Wilhelm, *Der Mensch und sein Heil*, 1982. Esp. 156-160.

οἰκονομέω 1   manage a household (Lk 16,2)

Literature
HAUCK 1934 [seltenes Alleinwort].

οἰκονομία 3
1. task; 2. plan; 3. manage a household (Lk 16,2.3.4)

Literature
LEE, John A.L., *A History of New Testament Lexicography*, 2003. Esp. 305-310.
REUMANN, John, The Use of *Oikonomia* and Related Terms in Greek Sources to about
    A.D. 100. — *Ekklesiastikos Pharos* [AddisAbeba] 60 (1978) //482-579; 61 (1979) 563-
    603; *Ekklēsia kai Theologia/ Church and Theology* [London] 1 (1980) 368-430; 2
    (1981) 591-617; 3 (1982) 115-140. [NTA 23,771; 24,31; 26, 418; 28, 445]
RICHTER, Gerhard, *Oikonomia: Der Gebrauch des Wortes Oikonomia im Neuen
    Testament, bei den Kirchenvätern und in der theologischen Literatur bis ins 20.
    Jahrhundert* (Arbeiten zur Kirchengeschichte, 90). Berlin – New York: de Gruyter,
    2005, IX-753 p. Esp. 33-92: "Oikonomia im Neuen Testament".

οἰκονόμος 4
1. manager of a household (Lk 12,42; 6,1.3.8); 2. administrator

Word groups	Lk	Acts	Mt	Mk
οἰκονόμος τῆς ἀδικίας (VKb)	16,8		0	0
οἰκονόμος + φρόνιμος	12,42; 16,8		0	0
DENAUX 2009 Lⁿ				

Literature
BDAG 2000 698 [literature]; DENAUX 2009 L(***); HAWKINS 1909 20

BORMANN, Lukas, *Recht, Gerechtigkeit und Religion*, 2001. Esp. 157-158.
CORLEY, Bruce, The Intertestamental Perspective of Stewardship. — *Southwestern
    Journal of Theology* 13 (1971) 15-24. [NTA 16, 57]
DELEBECQUE, Édouard, *Études grecques*, 1976. Esp. 89-97: "Le régisseur infidèle (16,1-13)".
HATCH, Edwin, *Essays*, 1889. Esp. 62-63.
HENDRICKS, W.L., Stewardship in the New Testament. — *Southwestern Journal of
    Theology* 13 (1971) 25-33. [NTA 16, 61]

οἶκος 33/35 + 25 (Mt 10, Mk 13)

1. house, temple (Lk 11,51); 2. family (Acts 10,2); 3. lineage (Lk 1,27); 4. property (Acts 7,10)

Word groups	Lk	Acts	Mt	Mk
(ἀπ/εἰσ)ἔρχομαι (+) εἰς τὸν οἶκον → (εἰσ)ἔρχομαι εἰς (τὴν) **οἰκίαν**	1,23.40; 5,25; 6,4; 7,36; 8,41; 14,1; 15,6	11,12; 16,15[2]; 21,8	2	6
καὶ οἶκος / σὺν οἴκῳ metaphorically after καί/σύν BOISMARD 1984 Aa20		7,10; 10,2; 11,14; 16,15[1].31; 18,8	0	0
κατ' οἶκον/οἴκους / κατὰ τοὺς οἴκους (SCe; VKe)		2,46; 5,42; 8,3; 20,20	0	0
οἶκοι plural (VKg)	16,4	8,3; 20,20	1	0
οἶκον (+) οἰκοδομέω (VKf) → **οἰκίαν** οἰκοδομέω		7,47.49	0	0
οἶκος + genitive referring to the owner of the house (SCd; VKd) → **οἰκία** + gen. referring to the owner of the house	1,23.40.56; 5,24.25; 7,36; 8,41; 9,61; 10,38*; 11,24; 12,39; 13,35; 14,1.23; 16,4.27; 18,14; 19,5.46[1]; 22,54*	7,10.20; 10,2.22.30; 11,12.13.14; 16,15[1].31.34 v.l.; 18,8; 21,8	6	6
οἶκος (+) Δαυίδ (SCc; VKc) DENAUX 2009 L[n]	1,27.69; 2,4		0	0
οἶκος + ἔρημος	13,35 v.l.		1	0
οἶκος Ἰακώβ (SCb; VKc) DENAUX 2009 LA[n]	1,33	7,46	0	0
οἶκος τοῦ θεοῦ (SCa; VKa)	6,4		1	1
οἶκος + Ἰερουσαλήμ	13,(34-)35		1	0
οἶκος Ἰσραήλ (LN: people of Israel; SCb; VKb)		2,36; 7,42	2	0
οἶκος + πατριά (VKh)	2,4		0	0
οἶκος + πατρός DENAUX 2009 LA[n]	16,27	7,20	0	0
οἶκος προσευχῆς	19,46[2]		1	1
πορεύομαι + εἰς οἶκον → εἰσπορεύομαι εἰς **οἰκίαν**	5,24		0	0
σαρόω + οἶκος → σαρόω + **οἰκία**	11,24(-25)		1	0

Characteristic of Luke

GOULDER 1989; HAWKINS 1909add; MORGENTHALER 1958LA

	Lk	Acts	Mt	Mk
εἰς τὸν οἶκον + gen. GOULDER 1989	1,23.40.56; 5,24.25; 6,4; 7,36; 8,39.41; 9,61; 10,38*; 11,24; 14,1; 16,4.27; 18,14; 22,54*	10,22; 11,12; 16,15.34 v.l.; 21,8	4	6/7
οἶκος family CREDNER 1836 134; GOULDER 1989*; HARNACK 1906 34.138; HAWKINS 1909L; PLUMMER 1922 lxi	1,27.33.69; 2,4; 10,5; 11,17[1.2]; 16,27; 19,9	2,36; 7,10.42.46; 10,2; 11,14; 16,15[1].31; 18,8	3	3
ὑποστρέφω εἰς τὸν οἶκον DENAUX 2009 L***; GOULDER 1989*	1,56; 7,10; 8,39; 11,24		0	0

Literature

DENAUX 2009 Lan [εἰς τὸν οἶκον + gen.; οἶκος family]; GERSDORF 1816 206-207 [ἐν οἴκῳ Δαυίδ]; 217 [διὰ τὸ εἶναι αὐτὸν ἐξ οἴκου].

BORMANN, Lukas, *Recht, Gerechtigkeit und Religion*, 2001. Esp. 158-160.
BRANDT, Pierre-Yves – LUKINOVICH, Alessandra, **Οἶκος** et οἰκία chez Marc comparé à Matthieu et Luc. — *Bib* 78 (1997) 525-533.
BRYANT, H.E., Note on Luke xi.7. — *ExpT* 50 (1938-39) 525-526. [οἶκος ἐπὶ οἶκον].
DELLING, Gerhard, Zur Taufe von "Häusern" im Urchristentum. — *NT* 7 (1964-65) 285-311. [οἶκος in Acts]
NICKLIN, T., "House" and "Home" in New Testament Greek. — *ExpT* 49 (1937-38) 566-568.
WEIGANDT, Peter, Zur sogenannten "Oikosformel". — *NT* 6 (1963) 49-74.

οἰκουμένη 3 + 5 (Mt 1)

1. earth (Lk 4,5; 21,26); 2. empire (Lk 2,1); 3. people (Acts 17,31)

Word groups	Lk	Acts	Mt	Mk
κρίνω τὴν οἰκουμένην		17,31	0	0
ὅλη/πᾶσα (+) ἡ οἰκουμένη (*SC*a; *VK*a)	2,1	11,28; 19,27	1	0

Characteristic of Luke

BOISMARD 1984 Eb17; DENAUX 2009 1A*; GOULDER 1989; HAWKINS 1909B; NEIRYNCK 1985; PLUMMER 1922 lx

Literature

HAUCK 1934 [Vorzugswort]; JEREMIAS 1980 78: "οἰκουμένη ist lk Vorzugswort"; RADL 1975 419.

BORMANN, Lukas, *Recht, Gerechtigkeit und Religion*, 2001. Esp. 121-122.
JOHNSTON, George, **Οἰκουμένη** and κόσμος in the New Testament. — *NTS* 10 (1963-64) 352-360.

οἰκτίρμων 2   merciful (Lk 6,36[1.2])

Literature

HAUCK 1934 [seltenes Alleinwort].

DUPONT, Jacques, L'appel à imiter Dieu en Mt 5,48 et Lc 6,36. — *RivBib* 14 (1966) 137-158; = ID., *Études*, II, 1985, 529-550. Esp. 536-538: "'Parfait' et 'miséricordieux'".
NAVONE, John, Divine Mercy and Human Mercy. — *BiTod* 29 (1967) 2024-2026.

οἰνοπότης 1 (Mt 1)   drunkard (Lk 7,34)

οἶνος 6 (Mt 4, Mk 5)   wine

Word groups	Lk	Acts	Mt	Mk
βάλλω (+) οἶνον	5,37.38		2	1
οἶνος καὶ σίκερα (*VK*c)	1,15		0	0
οἶνος νέος (*LN*: new wine; *VK*a)	5,37[1.2].38		2	2/3

ὀκτώ 3/5 + 2   eight

Word groups	Lk	Acts	Mt	Mk
δέκα καὶ ὀκτώ (VKa) → δεκαοκτώ	13,4*.11*.16		0	0

ὀλιγόπιστος 1 (Mt 4) | little faith

Word groups	Lk	Acts	Mt	Mk
ὀλιγόπιστοι vocative; cf. ὀλιγόπιστε Mt 14,31	12,28		3	0

ὀλίγος 6/7 + 10 (Mt 6/7, Mk 4)
1. few (Lk 12,23); 2. slight (Lk 7,47[1.2]; Acts 12,18); 3. little (Lk 5,3)

Word groups	Lk	Acts	Mt	Mk
ἐν ὀλίγῳ (LN: [a]in a short time; [b]easily; SCd; VKc); cf. Eph 3,3 CREDNER 1836 138		26,[a]28.[a]29	0	0
ὀλίγον adverb (SCa; VKa)	5,3; 7,47[2]		0	2
ὀλίγος + μέγας; cf. ἐλάχιστος + μέγας Mt 5,19		26,29	0	0
ὀλίγος + πολύς → ἐλάχιστος + πολύς	7,47[1.2]; 10,2. 42*; 12,(47-)48, 13,23(-24)	17,4.12; 26,29 v.l.	5/6	0
οὐκ ὀλίγος (SCc; VKg) BOISMARD 1984 Aa9; HARNACK 1906 39		12,18; 14,28; 15,2; 17,4.12; 19,23.24; 27,20	0	0
χρόνος οὐκ ὀλίγος → πλείων/πολὺς χρόνος		14,28	0	0

Characteristic of Luke

MORGENTHALER 1958A

Literature

RADL 1975 419.

CADBURY, Henry J., Litotes in Acts. — BARTH, E.H. – COCROFT, R.E. (eds.), *Festschrift to Honor F. Wilbur Gingrich*, 1972, 70-84. Esp. 62-63 [οὐκ ὀλίγος].

FEE, Gordon D., "One Thing is Needful"?, Luke 10:42. — EPP, E.J. – FEE, G.D. (eds.), *New Testament Textual Criticism*. FS B.M. Metzger, 1981, 71-75.

HARLÉ, Paul, Un "private-joke" de Paul dans le livre des Actes (XXVI.28-29). — *NTS* 24 (1977-78) 527-533. Esp. 529-532 [ἐν ὀλίγῳ].

ὅλος 17 + 19/22 (Mt 22/23, Mk 18/19)
1. whole (Lk 5,5); 2. complete (quantity); 3. complete (degree)

Word groups	Lk	Acts	Mt	Mk
noun + ὅλος without article (VKc) → ὅλος + noun without article		11,26; 28,30	0	0
δι' ὅλης νυκτός; cf. διὰ παντὸς νυκτός Mk 5,5	5,5		0	0
ἐξ ὅλης τῆς ἰσχύος	10,27[3] v.l.		0	0
καθ' ὅλου/ὅλης + noun of place DENAUX 2009 1A[n]	4,14; [8,39]; 23,5	9,31.42; 10,37	0	0
κόσμος ὅλος	9,25		2	2

ὅλη ἡ γῆ → **πᾶσα** ἡ γῆ	23,44		2	1
ὅλη + Ἰερουσαλήμ; cf. πᾶσα Ἰεροσόλυμα Mt 2,3		21,31	0	0
ὅλη καρδία	10,27		1	2
ὅλη (+) ἡ οἰκουμένη → **πᾶσα** ἡ οἰκουμένη		11,28; 19,27	1	0
ὅλη ἡ ψυχή → **ὅλον** τὸ σῶμα; **πᾶσα** ψυχή	10,27[2]		1	1/2
ὅλον τὸ σῶμα → **ὅλη** ἡ ψυχή	11,34.36[1]		4	0
ὅλος + noun without article (VKb) → noun + **ὅλος** without article DENAUX 2009 LA[n]	5,5; 10,27[1] v.l.	9,42 v.l.; 19,27 v.l.; 21,31	0/1	0/2
ὅλος with expressions of place (SCa) → **ὅλη** ἡ γῆ / Ἰερουσαλήμ / ἡ Ἰουδαία / ἡ οἰκουμένη / ἡ πόλις; κόσμος **ὅλος**	1,65; 4,14; 7,17; 8,39; 9,25; 23,5.44	2,2; 7,11; 9,31.42; 10,37; 11,28; 13,6.49; 19,27.29*; 21,30.31	8	7
ὅλος with expressions of time (SCb) → δι' **ὅλης** νυκτός	5,5	11,26; 28,30	1	0
ὁ ... ὅλος (VKa)	9,25; 11,36[1]	19,29*; 21,30	2	2

Characteristic of Luke	Lk	Acts	Mt	Mk
καθ' ὅλης BOISMARD 1984 Ab55; NEIRYNCK 1985; PLUMMER 1922 lii	4,14; 23,5	9,31.42; 10,37; 13,49 v.l.	0	0
καθ' ὅλης τῆς Ἰουδαίας VOGEL 1899c	23,5	9,31; 10,37	0	0
ὅλη ἡ Ἰουδαία → **πᾶσα** ἡ Ἰουδαία BOISMARD 1984 Ab83; NEIRYNCK 1985	7,17; 23,5	9,31; 10,37	0	0
ὅλη ἡ πόλις → **πᾶσα** ἡ πόλις BOISMARD 1984 cb121; NEIRYNCK 1985	8,39	19,29*; 21,30	0	1
ὅλος ὁ λαός → **ἅπας/πᾶς** ὁ λαός; **ἅπαν/πᾶν** τὸ πλῆθος; **πάντα** τὰ ἔθνη; **πᾶς** ὁ ὄχλος BOISMARD 1984 Bb36; NEIRYNCK 1985		2,47	0	0

Literature

COLLISON 1977 138 [καθ' ὅλης: linguistic usage of Luke: likely]; DENAUX 2009 LA[n] [καθ' ὅλης; ὅλη ἡ Ἰουδαία]; IA[n] [καθ' ὅλης τῆς Ἰουδαίας]; JEREMIAS 1980 70 [ὅλη ἡ Ἰουδαία: red.]; 118: "καθ' ὅλου/ὅλης + Subst. des Ortes im Gen. begegnet im NT nur im lk Doppelwerk".

BACHMANN, Michael, Jerusalem und der Tempel, 1980. Esp. 78-84.97-103 [καθ' ὅλης].
GARCÍA PÉREZ, José Miguel, El Endemoniado de Gerasa (Lc 8,26-39), 1986. Esp. 119-123 [καθ' ὅλην τὴν πόλιν].

ὄμβρος 1	rainstorm (Lk 12,54)

Literature
HAUCK 1934 [seltenes Alleinwort].

ὁμιλέω 2 + 2	talk (with) (Lk 24,14.15; Acts 20,11; 24,26)

Word groups	Lk	Acts	Mt	Mk
ὁμιλέω πρὸς ἀλλήλους → verb of saying **πρός** + acc.	24,14		0	0

Characteristic of Luke
BOISMARD 1984 Ab91; CREDNER 1836 142; HARNACK 1906 52; HAWKINS 1909LA; MORGENTHALER 1958*; NEIRYNCK 1985; PLUMMER 1922 lii; VOGEL 1899A

Literature

DENAUX 2009 LAⁿ; HAUCK 1934 [seltenes Alleinwort; Vorzugsverbindung: ὁμιλέω πρός];
JEREMIAS 1980 313 [red.]; SCHÜRMANN 1957 10, n. 40 [luk R].

| ὀμνύω 1 + 1/2 (Mt 13, Mk 2) | | make an oath | | |

Word groups	Lk	Acts	Mt	Mk
ὀμνύω + accusative (VKa)	1,73	7,17*	0	0
ὀμνύω + infinitive (VKd)		2,30 v.l.	0	0

Characteristic of Luke	Lk	Acts	Mt	Mk
ὀμνύω ὅρκον/ὅρκῳ (SCb; VKe)	1,73	2,30	0	0
BOISMARD 1984 Ab188; NEIRYNCK 1985				

Literature

DENAUX 2009 LAⁿ [ὀμνύω ὅρκον/ὅρκῳ]; GERSDORF 1816 207 [ὅρκον ὃν ὤμοσεν]; JEREMIAS
1980 74-75: "ὅρκον ὃν ὤμοσεν: Die klassische Figura etymologica (= Verstärkung des Verbs
durch einen *Akkusativ* des inneren Objekts, der ein dem Verb stammgleiches bzw. sinnverwandtes
Substantiv benutzt) liebt Lukas nicht. ... Vielmehr bevorzugt Lukas die Verstärkung des Verbums
durch ein stammgleiches Substantiv im *Dativ*".

| ὅμοιος 9 + 1 (Mt 9, Mk 0/1) | | similar | | |

Word groups	Lk	Acts	Mt	Mk
ὁμοία ἐστὶν (+) ἡ βασιλεία	13,18.19-20.21		6	0
(SCa) → ὁμοιόω + βασιλεία				
ὅμοιος (ἐστιν) + dative	6,47.48.49; 7,31.32; 12,36; 13,18.19.21	17,29	9	0/1
ὅμοιος ἐστιν after direct question	7,32; 13,19.21		1	0

Literature

COLLISON 1977 187 [ὅμοιος ἐστιν: linguistic usage of Luke: likely].

| ὁμοιόω 3 + 1 (Mt 8, Mk 1) | | | | |

1. be similar to (Acts 14,11); 2. compare (Lk 7,31; 13,18.20)

Word groups	Lk	Acts	Mt	Mk
ὁμοιόω active (SCa; VKa)	7,31; 13,18.20		1/2	1
ὁμοιόω + βασιλεία (SCb) → ὁμοία ἐστὶν ἡ βασιλεία	13,18.20		4	1

| ὁμοίως 11/12 (Mt 3, Mk 1/2) | | similarly | | |

Word groups	Lk	Acts	Mt	Mk
ὁμοίως + καθώς (VKd) → οὕτως + καθώς	6,31; 17,28		0	0
DENAUX 2009 Lⁿ				
ὁμοίως (δὲ) καί (VKa) →	5,10.33; 10,32; 17,28 v.l.; 22,36		3	1
καθώς/οὕτως/ὡς/ὥσπερ καί				

| Characteristic of Luke | | | | |

DENAUX 2009 L***; GOULDER 1989*; HAWKINS 1909 L; HENDRIKS 1986 433;
MORGENTHALER 1958L

Literature

COLLISON 1977 159 [linguistic usage of Luke's "other source-material": probable; linguistic usage of Luke: also likely;]; EASTON 1910 156 [probably characteristic of L]; HAUCK 1934 [Vorzugswort]; REHKOPF 1959 96 [vorlukanisch]; SCHÜRMANN 1957 122-123; 1961 283 [protoluk R nicht beweisbar].

ὁμολογέω 2 + 3 (Mt 4)

1. profess (Lk 12,8[1.2]); 2. admit (Acts 24,14); 3. declare (Acts 7,17)

Word groups	Lk	Acts	Mt	Mk
ὁμολογέω ἐν + person (VKa)	12,8[1.2]		2	0
ὁμολογέω + ὅτι (VKb)		24,14	1	0

Literature

BDR 220,3: "Semitismus ist ὁμολογεῖν ἔν τινι".

BORMANN, Lukas, Recht, Gerechtigkeit und Religion, 2001. Esp. 188-190.
NESTLE, Eberhard, Zum neutestamentlichen Griechisch. — ZNW 7 (1906) 279-280.
[ὁμολογεῖν ἔν in Lk 12,8 is a "Syrismus"; ὁμολογεῖν + dative is a Hebraism].

ὀνειδίζω 1 (Mt 3, Mk 1[2])

1. insult (Lk 6,22); 2. reprimand

Literature

DUPONT, Jacques, Les Béatitudes, II, 1969. Esp. 290-292: "Les outrages".

ὄνειδος 1 | disgrace (Lk 1,25)

Literature

HAUCK 1934 [seltenes Alleinwort].

ὄνομα 34 + 60 (Mt 22, Mk 14/15[16])

1. name (Lk 1,61); 2. person (Acts 1,15); 3. reputation; 4. category (Lk 9,48)

Word groups	Lk	Acts	Mt	Mk
noun + τις adjective + ὀνόματι + proper name; cf. ἀνὴρ δέ τις Ἀνανίας ὀνόματι Acts 5,1; Ἰουδαῖος δέ τις Ἀπολλῶς ὀνόματι Acts 18,24 DENAUX 2009 IA[n]	1,5; 10,38; 16,20	8,9; 9,33; 10,1; 16,1	0	0
ἁγιάζω τὸ ὄνομα / τὸ ὄνομα ἅγιον	1,49; 11,2		1	0
ἀνὴρ δέ τις ὀνόματι + proper name BOISMARD 1984 Aa71		5,1; 8,9; 10,1	0	0
ἄνθρωπος + ὀνόματι / ᾧ ὄνομα + proper name → ἀνὴρ/γυνὴ ὀνόματι	2,25	9,33	1	0

βαπτίζω εἰς (τὸ) ὄνομα / ἐν/ἐπὶ (τῷ) ὀνόματι (in the name of Jesus); cf. εἰς τὸ ὄνομα τοῦ πατρός Mt 28,19; εἰς τὸ ὄνομα Παύλου 1 Cor 1,13 BOISMARD 1984 Aa39		2,38; 8,16; 10,48; 19,5	0	0
βαστάζω τὸ ὄνομα (LN: inform)		9,15	0	0
διὰ τοῦ ὀνόματος BOISMARD 1984 Aa147		4,30; 10,43	0	0
ἐκβάλλω τὸ ὄνομα (LN: slander)	6,22		0	0
ἕνεκεν τοῦ ὀνόματός μου	21,12		1	0
ἐπικαλέω τὸ ὄνομα; cf. Rom 10,13; 1 Cor 1,2; Jam 2,7 BOISMARD 1984 Ca68		2,21; 9,14.21; 15,17; 22,16	0	0
ἐπικαλέομαι τὸ ὄνομά τινος ἐπί τινα (LN: be people of); cf. Jam 2,7		15,17	0	0
ὄνομα + proper name (SCb; VKj); cf. τοὔνομα + proper name Mt 27,57	1,5[1.2].13.26.27[1.2].31.59.63; 2,21.25; 5,27; 8,41; 10,38; 16,20; 19,2; 23,50; 24,13.18	5,1.34; 8,9; 9,10.11.12. 33.36; 10,1; 11,28; 12,13; 13,6.8; 16,1.14; 17,34; 18,2.7.24; 19,24; 20,9; 21,10; 27,1; 28,7	5	5
ὄνομα αὐτοῦ/μου/σου and similar, of Jesus' name (SCn)	9,48.49; 10,17; 21,8.12.17; 24,47	3,16[1.2]; 4,17; 5,28.41; 9,14. 15.16.21; 10,43; 22,16	11	6
ὄνομα (τοῦ) Ἰησοῦ (SCj; VKh) → ὄνομα (τοῦ) Ἰησοῦ Χριστοῦ; ὄνομα τοῦ κυρίου / τοῦ κυρίου Ἰησοῦ / τοῦ κυρίου ἡμῶν Ἰησοῦ Χριστοῦ BOISMARD 1984 Ca28		2,38; 3,6; 4,10.18.30; 5,40; 8,12.16; 9,27.28 v.l.; 10,48; 15,26; 16,18; 19,5.13[1].17; 21,13; 26,9	0	0
ὄνομα (τοῦ) Ἰησοῦ Χριστοῦ (SCh; VKh) → ὄνομα (τοῦ) Ἰησοῦ; ὄνομα κυρίου / τοῦ κυρίου / τοῦ κυρίου Ἰησοῦ / τοῦ κυρίου ἡμῶν Ἰησοῦ Χριστοῦ		2,38; 3,6; 4,10; 8,12; 10,48; 16,18	0	0
ὄνομα (+) καλέω + proper name (SCc)	1,13.31.59; 2,21; 19,2		3	0
ὄνομα + καλέω (SCa; VKa) → ἐπικαλέω τὸ ὄνομα DENAUX 2009 L*** (?)	1,13.31.59.61; 2,21; 19,2		3	0
ὄνομα κυρίου (SCf: name of the Lord God; VKg) → ὄνομα (τοῦ) Ἰησοῦ; ὄνομα (τοῦ) Ἰησοῦ Χριστοῦ; ὄνομα τοῦ κυρίου / τοῦ κυρίου Ἰησοῦ / τοῦ κυρίου ἡμῶν Ἰησοῦ Χριστοῦ	13,35; 19,38	2,21	2	1/2
ὄνομα τοῦ κυρίου (SCl) → ὄνομα (τοῦ) Ἰησοῦ; ὄνομα (τοῦ) Ἰησοῦ Χριστοῦ; ὄνομα κυρίου / τοῦ κυρίου Ἰησοῦ / τοῦ κυρίου ἡμῶν Ἰησοῦ Χριστοῦ		9,28; 10,48 v.l.	0	0
ὄνομα τοῦ κυρίου ἡμῶν Ἰησοῦ Χριστοῦ (SCm) → ὄνομα (τοῦ) Ἰησοῦ; ὄνομα (τοῦ) Ἰησοῦ Χριστοῦ; ὄνομα κυρίου / τοῦ κυρίου / τοῦ κυρίου Ἰησοῦ		15,26; 18,8*; 22,16 v.l.	0	0
ὄνομα τοῦ κυρίου Ἰησοῦ (SCk) → ὄνομα (τοῦ) Ἰησοῦ; ὄνομα (τοῦ) Ἰησοῦ Χριστοῦ; ὄνομα κυρίου / τοῦ κυρίου / τοῦ κυρίου ἡμῶν Ἰησοῦ Χριστοῦ		8,16; 9,28 v.l.; 18,4*; 19,5.13.17; 21,13	0	0

ὄνομα + ὀνομάζω (VKb)		19,13	0	0
ὀνομάζω + τὸ ὄνομα κυρίου (LN: say that one belongs to the Lord); cf. 2 Tit 2,19		19,13	0	0
ὀνόματα plural (VKk)	10,20	1,15; 18,15	1	1
τις adjective + noun + ὀνόματι + proper name		5,34; 9,10.36; 16,14; 18,2; 20,9; 21,10	0	0
ὑπὲρ τοῦ ὀνόματος suffer, die BOISMARD 1984 Aa59		5,41; 9,16; 15,26; 21,13	0	0

Characteristic of Luke

GOULDER 1989; HENDRIKS 1986 468; MORGENTHALER 1958LA

	Lk	Acts	Mt	Mk
ἀνὴρ ὀνόματι / ᾧ ὄνομα + proper name → ἄνθρωπος/γυνὴ **ὀνόματι** + proper name BOISMARD 1984 Bb14; DENAUX 2009 L***; HARNACK 1906 32; NEIRYNCK 1985	1,27[1]; 8,41; 19,2; 23,50	5,1; 8,9; 9,12; 10,1; 13,6; 18,24	0	0
γυνὴ ὀνόματι + proper name → ἀνὴρ/ἄνθρωπος **ὀνόματι** DENAUX 2009 lA*	1,13; 10,38	5,1; 16,14; 17,34; 18,2	0	0
ἐπὶ τῷ ὀνόματι BOISMARD 1984 cb116; NEIRYNCK 1985	1,59; 9,48; 21,8; 24,47	2,38; 4,17.18; 5,28.40	2	3
καὶ ἰδοὺ ἀνήρ/ἄνθρωπος + ὄνομα DENAUX 2009 L***	2,25; 8,41; 19,2; 23,50		0	0
ὄνομα nominative, in "whose name was" DENAUX 2009 L***; HAWKINS 1909L	1,5[2].26.27[1.2]; 2,25; 8,41; 24,13	13,6	0	1
ὄνομα + proper name BOISMARD 1984 Bb9; DENAUX 2009 L***; NEIRYNCK 1985	1,5[1.2].26.27[1.2]; 2,25; 5,27; 8,41; 10,38; 16,20; 19,2; 23,50; 24,13.18	5,1.34; 8,9; 9,10.11.12.33.36; 10,1; 11,28; 12,13; 13,6; 16,1.14; 17,34; 18,2.7.24; 19,24; 20,9; 21,10; 27,1; 28,7	1	2
ὄνομα αὐτοῦ/μου/σου and similar, of God's name (SCg) DENAUX 2009 LA*	1,49; 11,2	15,14.17		
ὀνόματι meaning 'by name', 'named'or 'called' CADBURY 1920 154-155; CREDNER 1836 139; DENAUX 2009 L***; GOULDER 1989*; HARNACK 1906 32; HAWKINS 1909L; PLUMMER 1922 lx	1,5[1]; 5,27; 10,38; 16,20; 19,2; 23,50; 24,18	5,1.34; 8,9; 9,10.11.12.33.36; 10,1; 11,28; 12,13; 16,1.14; 17,34; 18,2.7.24; 19,24; 20,9; 21,10; 27,1; 28,7	1	1
ᾧ/ᾗ ὄνομα DENAUX 2009 L***; GOULDER 1989*	1,26.27; 2,25; 8,41; 23,50; 24,13.18 v.l.	13,6	0	0

→ **βαπτίζω** in the name of Jesus

Literature

DENAUX 2009 lAn; GERSDORF 1816 169 [ἱερεύς τις ὀνόματι Ζαχαρίας]; 194 [ᾧ ὄνομα Ἰωσήφ]; 203 [ἐπὶ τῷ ὀνόματι τοῦ πατρὸς αὐτοῦ]; HAUCK 1934 [Vorzugswort: ὀνόματι; Vorzugsverbindung: ᾗ/ᾧ ὄνομα; τὸ ὄνομα + gen.]; JEREMIAS 1980 15: "ὀνόματι: lukanische Vorzugswendung; insbesondere die Wortfolge Nachgestelltes adjektivisches τις + ὀνόματι + Eigenname"; 46: "ᾗ ὄνομα … ᾧ ὄνομα: Die elliptische Wendung: Relativpronomen im Dativ + artikelloses ὄνομα + Eigenname begegnet im NT nur im Doppelwerk"; 65 [trad.] ; RADL 1975 419 [ὄνομα; ὀνόματι "('mit Namen' mit Eigenname (ohne Verbum)"; ὑπὲρ τοῦ ὀνόματος; ὄνομα τοῦ κυρίου Ἰησοῦ]; 429 [τις ὀνόματι].

BRATCHER, Robert G., "The Name" in Prepositional Phrases in the New Testament. — *BTrans* 14 (1963) 72-80.

DICKERSON, Patrick L., The New Character Narrative in Luke-Acts, 1997. Esp. 293-298: "The elements of the Lukan new character narrative" [τις/ἰδοὺ ἀνὴρ/γυνὴ ὀνόματι].

DUPONT, Jacques, *Les Béatitudes*, II, 1969. Esp. 292-293: "Un nom mauvais" [ὄνομα ὡς πονηρόν].

FOULKES, Irene W., Two Semantic Problems in the Translation of Acts 4.5-20. — *BTrans* 29 (1978) 121-125. Esp. 122-123: "ὄνομα 'name'"; 124-125: "σῴζειν 'save, heal', and σωτηρία 'salvation, healing'".

HEIMERDINGER, Jenny, Word Order in Koine Greek, 1996. Esp. 152-155: "ὀνόματι"; = READ-HEIMERDINGER, Jenny, *The Bezan Text of Acts*, 2002. Esp. 85-88.

HEITMÜLLER, Wilhelm, *"Im Namen Jesu"*, 1903.

JUNG, Chang-Wook, *Infancy Narrative*, 2004. Esp. 149-159 [Lk 1,5]; 196-197 [καλέσεις τὸ ὄνομα + gen. + name].

TOLMIE, D. François, Die vertaling van ὄνομα-uitdrukkings in die Nuwe Testament. — *HTS* 901-918.

WINK, Walter, *Naming the Powers*, 1984. Esp. 21-22.

ὀνομάζω 2 + 1 (Mk 1)

1. give a name to (Lk 6,13.14); 2. pronounce a name (Acts 19,13); 3. speak about ὀνομάζομαι: 4. be known

Word groups	Lk	Acts	Mt	Mk
ὄνομα + ὀνομάζω (VKa)		19,13	0	0
ὀνομάζω + λέγω → (συλ)λαλέω + λέγω/εἶπον		19,13	0	0
ὀνομάζω + τὸ ὄνομα κυρίου (LN: say that one belongs to the Lord)		19,13	0	0

ὄνος 1/2 (Mt 3)   donkey (Lk 13,15; 14,5*)

Word groups	Lk	Acts	Mt	Mk
ὄνος + βοῦς	13,15		0	0

Literature
PAFFENROTH 1997 77.

ὄντως 2 (Mk 1)   really (Lk 23,47; 24,34)

Literature
COLLISON 1977 150 [noteworthy phenomena]; JEREMIAS 1980 308 [red.].

ὄξος 1 (Mt 1/2, Mk 1)   sour wine (Lk 23,36)

ὄπισθεν 2 (Mt 2, Mk 1)

1. from behind (Lk 8,44; 23,26); 2. on the back of; 3. on the outside

Word groups	Lk	Acts	Mt	Mk
ὄπισθεν adverb	8,44		1	1
ὄπισθεν preposition + genitive	23,26		1	0

ὀπίσω 7/8 + 2 (Mt 6, Mk 6)
1. behind (Lk 7,38); 2. after (Acts 5,37; 20,30)

Word groups	Lk	Acts	Mt	Mk
εἰς τὰ ὀπίσω (SCa; VKb)	9,62; 17,31		0	1
ἐπιβάλλω τὴν χεῖρα ἐπ' ἄροτρον καὶ βλέπω εἰς τὰ ὀπίσω (LN: start to do and then hesitate)	9,62		0	0
ὀπίσω absolute (VKa)	7,38		1	1
→ ὀπίσω ἑαυτῶν; ἐπιστρέφω (εἰς τὰ) ὀπίσω; ἔρχομαι + ὀπίσω; πορεύομαι ὀπίσω; ὑπάγω ὀπίσω				

Literature
COLLISON 1977 147 [εἰς τὰ ὀπίσω: noteworthy phenomena]; EASTON 1910 166 [cited by Weiss as characteristic of L, and possibly corroborative].

ὅπου 5 + 2 (Mt 13, Mk 15/17)
1. where (place) (Lk 9,57; 12,33.34; 17,37; 22,11; Acts 17,1; 20,6); 2. where (circumstance); 3. since; 4. in the case of

Word groups	Lk	Acts	Mt	Mk
ὅπου ἄν/ἐάν (SCa; VKa)	9,57		3	5
ὅπου γάρ (VKb)	12,34		1/2	0
ὅπου + ἐκεῖ (SCb; VKe); cf. οὗ + ἐκεῖ Mt 18,20	12,34; 17,37		2	1/2
ποῦ + ὅπου (VKf)	22,11		0	1

Literature
KILPATRICK, George D., Style and Text, 1967. Esp. 159-160; = ID., Principles and Practice, 1990. Esp. 61-62.

ὀπτασία 2 + 1   vision (Lk 1,22; 24,23; Acts 26,19)

Word groups	Lk	Acts	Mt	Mk
ὀπτασία of apparitions of angels → ὤφθη of apparitions of angels	1,(19-)22; 24,23		0	0
ὁράω ὀπτασίαν; cf. εἶδον/ὄψομαι + ὅραμα Acts 7,31; 9,12; 10,3.17; 11,5; 16,9.10	1,22; 24,23		0	0
DENAUX 2009 Lⁿ				

Characteristic of Luke
BOISMARD 1984 cb39; CREDNER 1836 138; NEIRYNCK 1985; PLUMMER 1922 lix; VOGEL 1899B

Literature
DENAUX 2009 Laⁿ; EASTON 1910 163 [cited by Weiss as characteristic of L, and possibly corroborative]; GERSDORF 1816 191 [ὅτι ὀπτασίαν ἑώρακεν].

ὀπτός 1	broiled, baked (Lk 24,42)

ὅπως 7 + 14/15 (Mt 17/18, Mk 1/2)

1. how (Lk 24,20); 2. so that (Acts 8,24; 9,17); 3. somehow (Lk 24,20)

Word groups	Lk	Acts	Mt	Mk
ὅπως adverb of mood (*VK*a)	24,20		0	0
ὅπως + indicative (*VK*d)	24,20		0/1	0/1
ὅπως + present subjunctive (*VK*e)	10,2 *v.l.*; 16,26		1	0
ὅπως ἐάν → **ὅπως** ἄν		9,2	0	0
ὅπως (…) μή/μηδέ/μηδέν (*VK*c)	16,26	8,24; 20,16	1	0

Characteristic of Luke	Lk	Acts	Mt	Mk
ὅπως after verbs of asking (*SC*b; *VK*f) → **αἰτέομαι** ὅπως;	7,3; 10,2;	8,15.24; 9,2;	2	0
δέομαι ὅπως; **ἐρωτάω** ὅπως; **παρακαλέω** ὅπως;	11,37	23,20; 25,3		
προσεύχομαι ὅπως				
BOISMARD 1984 cb40; DENAUX 2009 1A*; NEIRYNCK 1985				
ὅπως ἄν (*SC*a; *VK*b) → **ὅπως** ἐάν; ἀφ᾽ **οὗ/πρὶν** ἄν	2,35	3,20; 9,2 *v.l.*;	0/1	0
BOISMARD 1984 Ab189; NEIRYNCK 1985		15,17		

Literature

BDR § 436,2: "Das unbestimmte Relativum ὅπως in indirekter Frage für πῶς nur Lk 24,20";
DENAUX 2009 1A[n] [ὅπως ἄν]; JEREMIAS 1980 94: "Eine besondere Bemerkung erfordern die
Verben des 'Bittens' und 'Forderns'. Für diese Wortgruppe gilt zwar auch, daß ihre (klassische)
Ergänzung durch den Infinitiv lukanisch ist, dagegen die (hellenistische) Ergänzung durch ἵνα-Sätze
nicht-lukanisch, doch liegt zwischen diesen beiden Polen bei den Verben des Bittens ein
Zwischenstadium: Die Ergänzung durch ὅπως. Dieser Übergangscharakter der Konstruktion mit
ὅπως kommt u.a. darin zum Ausdruck, daß Lukas diese Konstruktion teils aus der
Logienüberlieferung übernimmt…, teils von sich aus schreibt"; 97: "ὅπως ἄν mit Konjunktiv des
Aorists, eine der LXX geläufige Konstruktion, begegnet im NT, abgesehen von einem paulinischen
Bibelzitat, nur in den beiden Teilen des Doppelwerks"; RADL 1975 420.

ὁράω 81/85 + 66/67 (Mt 72, Mk 52/53)

1. see (Lk 1,12); 2. pay attention to (Lk 12,15); 3. understand; 4. visit (Acts 19,21); 5.
experience (Lk 2,26); 6. learn about; 7. cause to happen

Word groups

ὁράω	Lk	Acts	Mt	Mk
ὁράω + accusative with participle (*SC*c; *VK*e) → **εἶδον/ὄψομαι** +		8,23	0	1
accusative with participle				
ὁράω + indirect interrogative (*VK*b) → **εἶδον** + indirect interrogative		22,26*	0	0
ὁράω + ἀκούω (*VK*n) → **εἶδον** + ἀκούω; **βλέπω/θεωρέω/συνίημι**		22,15	0	0
+ ἀκούω				
ὁράω ὀπτασίαν (*SC*b; *VK*h) → **εἶδον/ὄψομαι** + ὅραμα/ὅρασιν	1,22;		0	0
DENAUX 2009 L[n]	24,23			
ὁράω + ὀφθαλμός (*SC*f; *VK*j) → **εἶδον** + ὀφθαλμός;	16,23		0	0
ἀτενίζω/(ἀνα/δια)βλέπω + ὀφθαλμός				

εἶδον	Lk	Acts	Mt	Mk
εἶδον + accusative with participle	5,2; 7,25; 9,32.49; 12,54;	3,3.9; 7,24.55; 9,12;	18	16/18
(*SC*c; *VK*e) → **ὁράω/ὄψομαι** +	18,24; 21,1.2.20.31;	10,3; 11,5.13; 16,27;		
accusative with participle	22,56; 23,8[3]	22,18; 26,13; 28,4		

	Lk	Acts	Mt	Mk
εἶδον + indirect interrogative (*SC*k; *VK*b) → ὁράω + indirect interrogative	19,3		1	4
εἶδον + ἀκούω (*SC*j; *VK*n) → ὁράω + ἀκούω; **βλέπω/θεωρέω/ συνίημι** + ἀκούω	2,20; 7,22; 10,24[1.2]; 23,8[2]	4,20; 7,34[2]; 22,14; 28,26.27	3	0
εἶδον + ἀτενίζω/(ἀνα)βλέπω/ θεάομαι/θεωρέω/ (*SC*e; *VK*m); cf. ὁράω + βλέπω Mk 8,15.24; εἶδον + ἐμβλέπω Mk 14,67; εἶδον + περιβλέπω Mk 5,32; 9,8	7,25; 10,24[1]; 19,5*; 21,1; 22,56; 24,39[2]	6,15; 7,55; 11,6; 14,9; 28,26	4	1
εἶδον (+) θαυμάζω → ἀκούω + θαυμάζω	11,38	3,12; 7,31; 13,41	1	0
εἶδον (+) ὅραμα (*SC*b; *VK*h) → ὁράω ὀπτασίαν; **ὄψομαι** ὅραμα/ὅρασιν; **βλέπω** ὅραμα		7,31; 9,12; 10,3.17; 11,5; 16,10	0	0
εἶδον (+) ὅτι (*SC*a; *VK*a) → **θεωρέω** ὅτι	8,47; 17,15; 24,39[2]	8,18; 12,3; 14,9; 16,19	3	6
εἶδον + ὀφθαλμός (*SC*f; *VK*j) → ὁράω + ὀφθαλμός; **ἀτενίζω/ (ἀνα/δια)βλέπω** + ὀφθαλμός	2,30	9,40; 28,27	2	0
εἶδον + **ὄψομαι** (*SC*d; *VK*l) DENAUX 2009 IA[n]	17,22[1]	7,34[1.2](-35); 26,16[2]	0	0
εἶδον περί + genitive (*VK*c)		15,6	0	0
εἶδον σημεῖον (*SC*h; *VK*k)	23,8[3]		1	0
εἶδον (+) σπλαγχνίζομαι	7,13; 10,33; 15,20		2	1
ἴδετε (*SC*g; *VK*g)	21,29; 24,39[1.2]	13,41	1	1
καὶ ἰδών/ἰδόντες → **ἰδών/ἰδόντες** δέ	2,48; 5,20; 7,13; 10,31. 32.33; 17,14; 19,7	7,24; 9,40; 11,23; 14,9; 16,27.40	9	9

ὄψομαι	Lk	Acts	Mt	Mk
ὄψομαι + accusative with participle (*SC*c; *VK*e) → ὁράω/εἶδον + accusative with participle	13,28; 21,27		2	2
ὄψομαι + εἶδον (*SC*d; *VK*l)	17,22[2]	7,(34-)35; 26,16[2]	0	0
ὄψομαι ὅραμα/ὅρασιν (*SC*b; *VK*h) → ὁράω ὀπτασίαν; **εἶδον** + ὅραμα; **βλέπω** ὅραμα		2,17; 16,9	0	0
ὤφθη of apparitions of angels → **ὀπτασία** of apparitions of angels; **ἄγγελος** object of ὁράω DENAUX 2009 LA[n]	1,11; [[22,43]]	7,30.35	0	0
→ ὁράω/εἶδον **θανάτον**				

Characteristic of Luke	Lk	Acts	Mt	Mk
εἶδον + ἀπαγγέλλω; cf. ἑώρακα + ἀπαγγέλλω Lk 9,36; ὄψομαι + ἀπαγγέλλω Mt 28,10 DENAUX 2009 La*	7,22; 8,34.36.47	11,13	0	1
ἰδών/ἰδόντες absolute BOISMARD 1984 cb97; NEIRYNCK 1985	1,12.29*; 2,17; 5,8; 7,39; 9,54; 10,32.33; 11,38; 17,14; 18,15.43; 19,7	3,12; 7,31; 16,40	6	0
ἰδών/ἰδόντες δέ → καὶ **ἰδών/ἰδόντες** BOISMARD 1984 cb164; GOULDER 1989; NEIRYNCK 1985	2,17; 5,8.12; 7,39; 8,28.34.47; 9,54; 13,12; 18,15.24; 20,14; 22,49.56; 23,47	3,12; 8,18; 12,3; 13,45	9	3
ὁ δὲ ... ἰδὼν ἐθαύμασεν BOISMARD 1984 Ab174; NEIRYNCK 1985	11,38	7,31	0	0

ὤφϑη aorist passive (SCa) DENAUX 2009 L***; GOULDER 1989	1,11; 9,31; [[22,43]]; 24,34	2,3; 7,2.26.30.35; 9,17; 13,31; 16,9; 26,16[1]	1	1
ὤφϑη + dative BOISMARD 1984 Eb10; DENAUX 2009 1A*; HARNACK 1906 71; NEIRYNCK 1985	1,11; 24,34	2,3; 7,2.26; 9,17; 13,31; 16,9; 26,16[1]	1	1

Literature

VON BENDEMANN 2001 421: "Partizipiales ἰδών entspricht lukanischen Sprachgebrauch";
DENAUX 2009 Lan [ἰδών/ἰδόντες absolute], LA[n] [ὁ δὲ ... ἰδὼν ἐθαύμασεν]; GERSDORF 1816
180 [ὤφϑη δὲ αὐτῷ ἄγγελος κυρίου]; 238 [καὶ ἴδωμεν τὸ ῥῆμα τοῦτο τὸ γεγονός]; JERE-
MIAS 1980 31 [ὤφϑη: red.]; 86 [ἰδών/ἰδόντες δέ: red.]; RADL 1975 407 [εἶδον; ἰδών; ἰδὼν δέ].

BRUN, Lyder, Engel und Blutschweiß Lc 22,43-44. — ZNW 32 (1933) 265-276. [ὤφϑη]
FIEDLER, Peter, Die Formel "Und siehe" im Neuen Testament (SANT, 20). München:
    Kösel, 1969, 96 p. Esp. 13-48: "Das sprachliche Problem".
KILPATRICK, George D., Ἰδού and ἴδε in the Gospels. — JTS NS 18 (1967) 425-426.
    [NTA 12, 561]; = ID., Principles and Practice, 1990, 205-206.
SCHNEIDER, Gerhard, Engel und Blutschweiß (Lk 22,43-44): "Redaktionsgeschichte" im
    Dienste der Textkritik. — BZ NF 20 (1976) 112-116. Esp. 113-115: "Vokabular und Stil von
    Lk 22,43.44"; = ID., Lukas, Theologe der Heilsgeschichte, 1985, 153-157. Esp. 154-156.
TUCKETT, Christopher M., Luke 22,43-44: The "Agony" in the Garden and Luke's Gospel.
    — DENAUX, A. (ed.), New Testament Textual Criticism and Exegesis. FS J. Delobel,
    2002, 131-144. Esp. 133-135: "Vocabulary and style".

ὀργή 2/3 (Mt 1, Mk 1)
1. anger; 2. punishment (Lk 3,7)

Word groups	Lk	Acts	Mt	Mk
ὀργή + dative; cf. ὀργίζομαι + dat. Mt 5,22	21,23		0	0
ὀργὴ ἡ μέλλουσα (VKa)	3,7		1	0

Literature
MAHFOUZ, Hady, La fonction littéraire et théologique de Lc 3,1-20, 2003. Esp. 180-181
    [μέλλουση ὀργή].

ὀργίζομαι 2 (Mt 3)
be very angry (Lk 14,21; 15,28)

ὀρεινός 2
mountainous region (Lk 1,39.65)

Literature
DENAUX 2009 L[n]; HARNACK 1906 138; HAUCK 1934 [seltenes Alleinwort].

ὀρϑρίζω*** 1
get up early (Lk 21,38)

Characteristic of Luke	Lk	Acts	Mt	Mk
ὀρϑρίζω and cognates ὀρϑρινός, ὄρϑρος BOISMARD 1984 Ab92; GOULDER 1989; NEIRYNCK 1985	21,38; 24,1.22	5,21	0	0

Literature

DENAUX 2009 Lⁿ [ὀρθρίζω and cognates ὀρθρινός, ὄρθρος]; EASTON 1910 163 [cited by Weiss as characteristic of L, and possibly corroborative]; HAUCK 1934 [seltenes Alleinwort]; JEREMIAS 1980 284-285 [red.].

ὀρθρινός 1	early in the morning (Lk 24,22)

Characteristic of Luke	Lk	Acts	Mt	Mk
ὀρθρινός and cognates ὀρθρίζω, ὄρθρος	21,38;	5,21	0	0
BOISMARD 1984 Ab92; GOULDER 1989; NEIRYNCK 1985	24,1.22			

Literature

DENAUX 2009 Lⁿ [ὀρθρίζω and cognates ὀρθρινός, ὄρθρος]; EASTON 1910 163 [cited by Weiss as characteristic of L, and possibly corroborative]; HAUCK 1934 [seltenes Alleinwort]; JEREMIAS 1980 284-285 [red.].

ὄρθρος 1 + 1	
1. early morning; 2. daybreak (Lk 24,1; Acts 5,21)	

Characteristic of Luke	Lk	Acts	Mt	Mk
ὄρθρος and cognates ὀρθρίζω, ὀρθρινός	21,38; 24,1.22	5,21	0	0
BOISMARD 1984 Ab92; GOULDER 1989; NEIRYNCK 1985				

Literature

DENAUX 2009 LAⁿ, Laⁿ [ὀρθρίζω and cognates ὀρθρινός, ὄρθρος]; EASTON 1910 163 [cited by Weiss as characteristic of L, and possibly corroborative]; JEREMIAS 1980 284-285 [red.].

WALLACE, R.W., ὄρθρος. —Transactions of the American Philological Association 119 (1989) 201-207.

ὀρθῶς 3 (Mk 1)	correct(ly) (Lk 7,43; 10,28; 20,21)

Characteristic of Luke

GOULDER 1989; PLUMMER 1922 lx

Literature

JEREMIAS 1980 171 [red.].

BORMANN, Lukas, Recht, Gerechtigkeit und Religion, 2001. Esp. 203-204.

ὀρίζω 1 + 5	
1. decide (Lk 22,22; Acts 11,29); 2. appoint (Acts 10,42; 17,31)	

Characteristic of Luke

BOISMARD 1984 cb41; NEIRYNCK 1985; PLUMMER 1922 lix; VOGEL 1899B

	Lk	Acts	Mt	Mk
(κατὰ) τὸ ὡρισμένον (VKa)	22,22		0	0
CREDNER 1836 134-135; PLUMMER 1922 lxiii				

Literature

DENAUX 2009 IAⁿ; HAUCK 1934 [Vorzugswort]; JEREMIAS 1980 288 [red.]; SCHÜRMANN 1957 4-5 [sehr wahrscheinlich luk Mk-R].

ALLEN, Leslie C., The Old Testament Background of (ΠΡΟ)‘ΟΡΙΖΕΙΝ in the New Testament. — *NTS* 17 (1970-71) 104-108.

ὅρκος 1 + 1 (Mt 4, Mk 1) — oath

Characteristic of Luke	Lk	Acts	Mt	Mk
ὀμνύω ὅρκον/ὅρκῳ (SCa; VKa) BOISMARD 1984 Ab188; NEIRYNCK 1985	1,73	2,30	0	0

Literature

DENAUX 2009 LAⁿ [ὀμνύω ὅρκον/ὅρκῳ]; GERSDORF 1816 207 [ὅρκον ὃν ὤμοσεν]; JEREMIAS 1980 74: "ὅρκον ὃν ὤμοσεν: Die klassische Figura etymologica (= Verstärkung des Verbs durch einen *Akkusativ* des inneren Objekts, der ein dem Verb stammgleiches bzw. sinnverwandtes Substantiv benutzt) liebt Lukas nicht. … Vielmehr bevorzugt Lukas die Verstärkung des Verbums durch ein stammgleiches Substantiv im *Dativ*".

ὁρμάω 1 + 2 (Mt 1, Mk 1) — rush (Lk 8,33; Acts 7,57; 19,29)

Word groups	Lk	Acts	Mt	Mk
ὁρμᾶν BOISMARD 1984 Ca54		7,57; 19,29	1	1

ὄρνις 1 (Mt 1) — bird (Lk 13,34)

ὄρος 12/13 + 3 (Mt 16, Mk 11) — mountain

Word groups	Lk	Acts	Mt	Mk
ἀναβαίνω εἰς τὸ ὄρος; cf. καταβαίνω ἀπὸ τοῦ ὄρους Mt 8,1; καταβαίνω ἐκ τοῦ ὄρους Mt 17,9; Mk 9,9	9,28		3	1
ἐξέρχομαι + εἰς τὸ ὄρος	6,12		0	0
κατέρχομαι + ἀπὸ τοῦ ὄρους	9,37		0	0
τὰ ὄρη (SCc; VKf)	21,21; 23,30		2	2/3
τὸ ὄρος τῶν ἐλαιῶν (SCa; VKa)	19,37; 22,39		3	3
(τὸ) ὄρος τὸ καλούμενον Ἐλαιῶν/Ἐλαιών (SCb; VKb) DENAUX 2009 Laⁿ	19,29; 21,37	1,12	0	0
ὄρος + προσεύχομαι → ἱερόν + προσεύχομαι	6,12; 9,28; 22,39(-40)		1	1
ὄρος Σινᾶ (VKd)		7,30.38	0	0
πορεύομαι + εἰς τὸ ὄρος	22,39		1	0
ὑψηλὸς ὄρος	4,5*		2	1

Literature

EASTON 1910 163 [τὸ ὄρος τῶν ἐλαιῶν: cited by Weiss as characteristic of L, and possibly corroborative]; JEREMIAS 1980 284: "Der Ölberg wird von Lukas in zweifacher Weise benannt: 1. τὸ ὄρος τῶν ἐλαιῶν 'Olivenberg' (Lk 19,37; 22,39) ist die traditionelle Bezeichnung wie wir sie bei Mk und Mt je dreimal lesen; 2. nur im Doppelwerk kommt im NT vor: τὸ ὄρος τὸ καλούμενον Ἐλαιών der 'Olivenhain' genannte Berg (Lk 19,29; 21,37/Apg 1,12); καλούμενος zur Einführung des Namens einer Örtlichkeit ist redaktionell".

ὀρχέομαι 1 (Mt 2, Mk 1)   dance (Lk 7,32)

ὅς 189/197 + 224/227 (Mt 125/135, Mk 86[87]/95)   who; which

Word groups	Lk	Acts	Mt	Mk
ὅς in a construction according to sense (VKp) DENAUX 2009 1Aⁿ	6,18	15,17.36; 26,17	0	0
ἀφ' οὗ ἄν → ὅπως/πρὶν ἄν	13,25		0	0
ἄχρι ἧς ἡμέρας (SCr) → ἄχρι τῆς ἡμέρας **ταύτης**	1,20[1]; 17,27	1,2[1]	1	0
ἐκεῖνος ... ὅς (SCj; VKj)	12,37.43; 13,4; 22,22		2/3	1
ἐν ᾧ/οἷς time (LN: as long as; SCq; VKu)	5,34; 12,1; 19,13		0	1
ἐν ᾧ/οἷς others (SCq)	1,78; 19,30[1]; 21,6[2]; 22,7; 23,29[1]	1,21 v.l.; 2,8; 4,12.31; 7,20[1]; 10,12; 11,11.14[2]; 17,23[1].31[1].34; 19,16; 20,25.28[1]; 24,18; 26,12	6	2
ἵνα ὅ		8,19	0	1
ὅ ἐστιν (LN: that means; SCn; VKq)		4,36	2	9
ὅς after cardinal number (VKm)	5,3; 6,13; 13,4.14; 17,12; 24,18*	1,11[1].24 v.l.; 6,3; 24,21	3	2
ὅς with pleonastic pronoun (SCm; VKn)	3,16.17	3,13 v.l.; 15,17	1	2
ὅς (δ'/γάρ) (+) ἄν/ἐάν (SCg; VKg) → **ὅσος/ὅστις** ἄν/ἐάν	4,6; 7,23; 8,18[1.2]; 9,4. 24[1.2].26.48[1.2]; 10,5.8.10. 22; 12,8; 13,25; 17,33[1.2]; 18,17; 20,18	2,21; 7,3.7; 8,19	35/37	20/24
ὅς ἄν/ἐάν ... μή → **ὅσος/ὅστις** ἄν/ἐάν ... μή	7,23; 8,18[2]; 10,10; 18,17		3	3/4
ὅς γάρ (SCd; VKd)	6,38; 8,18[1]; 9,24[1].26.50		2	6
ὅς δέ (SCc; VKc) → **ὅς** μέν	7,47[2]; 9,24[2]; 10,5.8 v.l.10; 12,20; 17,29.33[2]; 20,18; 23,33[2]	3,6; 13,37; 27,44[2]	8	5
ὅς (+) μέν (SCb; VKb) → **ὅς** δέ	8,5; 23,33[1]	3,13; 27,44[1]	6	2
ὅς ὅταν	8,13[1]		0	2
ὅς οὖν (SCf; VKf); cf. ὅς δή Mt 13,23		17,23[2]	2	1
ὅς ... οὗτος (SCh; VKh) → οὗτος ..., **ὅς**; cf. ὅστις ... οὗτος Mt 18,4	9,24[2].26; 20,17.47	3,6; 4,10[1.2]; 8,32; 17,23[2]	2	4/5
ὅς τε (SCe; VKe) → **ὅς** καί		26,16[1.2].22	0	0
οὗ εἵνεκεν/ἕνεκεν → **τίνος** ἕνεκα/ἕνεκεν	4,18		0	0
οὗ χάριν (VKz)	7,47[1]		0	0
πᾶς adjective or with determinative + ὅς → πᾶς adjective + **ὅστις**	14,33; 21,4	1,21; 15,17.36; 20,25.28[1]; 24,8[2]	3	
τίς ... ὅς (SCk; VKk)	5,21; 7,49; 9,9; 12,42; 17,7; 24,17	10,17.21[2]; 19,35; 23,19	3	2
→ δι' ἣν **αἰτίαν**; **ἔχω** ὅ; **οὐαί** (τῷ ἀνθρώπῳ) δι' οὗ; **οὕτως** ... ὃν τρόπον				

Characteristic of Luke

HENDRIKS 1986 433.468; MORGENTHALER 1958LA

	Lk	Acts	Mt	Mk
ἀνθ' ὧν (*SC*p; *VK*r); cf. 2 Thess 2,10 BOISMARD 1984 Bb95; GOULDER 1989; HAWKINS 1909add; NEIRYNCK 1985; PLUMMER 1922 lix	1,20[2]; 12,3[1]; 19,44	12,23	0	0
ἀφ' ἧς / ἀφ' οὗ since (*SC*t; *VK*s); cf. 2 Pet 3,4; Rev 16,18 BOISMARD 1984 Cb42; DENAUX 2009 L***; GOULDER 1989; NEIRYNCK 1985	7,45; 13,7.25; 24,21	20,18; 24,11	0	0
ἄχρι (δὲ) οὗ (*LN*: [a]before, [b]until; *SC*r; *VK*w) → ἕως οὗ; cf. μέχρις οὗ Mk 13,30 HARNACK 1906 51	21,[b]24	7,[b]18[1]; 27,[a]33	0	0
ἕως οὗ/ ὅτου (*SC*s; *VK*x) → ἄχρι (δὲ) οὗ; ἕως ὅτου GOULDER 1989	12,50*.59*; 13,8.21[2]; 15,4*.8; 22,16.18; 24,49	21,26; 23,12.14.21; 25,21	6/7	0
ὅς in attraction (of the relative pronoun to a noun, expressed or understood) DENAUX 2009 L***; GOULDER 1989*; HAWKINS 1909L	1,4; 2,20; 3,19; 5,9; 9,36.43; 12,46[1.2]; 15,16; 19,37; 23,41; 24,25	1,1.22; 2,22; 3,21[2].25; 7,16.17.45[2]; 8,24; 9,36[1.2]; 10,39[1]; 13,38; 17,31[2]; 20,38; 21,19.24; 22,10.15; 24,8[2].21; 25,18[2]; 26,2.16[1.2].22	2	1
ὅς in attraction (of the relative pronoun after πάντων/πᾶσιν) BOISMARD 1984 Ab7; DENAUX 2009 L***; HARNACK 1906 148; NEIRYNCK 1985	2,20; 3,19; 9,43; 24,25	1,1; 3,21[2]; 10,39[1]; 13,38; 22,10; 24,8[2]; 26,2	0	0
ὅς καί (*SC*e; *VK*e) → ὅς τε; cf. Jn 21,20 BOISMARD 1984 Eb38; DENAUX 2009 1A**; HARNACK 1906 43; NEIRYNCK 1985	6,13.14.16 *v.l.*; 7,49; 10,30.39; 12,59*; 23,27 *v.l.*51 *v.l.*	1,3.11[1].19*; 7,45[1]; 10,39[2]; 11,30; 12,4; 13,22[1]; 17,34; 22,5; 24,6[1.2].15; 26,10.12 *v.l.*26; 27,23[2]; 28,10	1	4/5
οὗτος …, ὅς (*SC*h; *VK*h) → ὅς … οὗτος; οὗτος … ὅστις DENAUX 2009 L***	2,15.37 *v.l.*; 5,21; 6,3; 7,27[1].49; 8,13[2]; 9,9; 13,16; 19,15; 21,6[1]; 24,17.44	1,16 *v.l.*25; 2,24.33.36; 3,16; 7,4.35.38.39.40[2]; 17,3; 21,23; 24,6[1.2].8[2].21; 25,24; 28,4	4	2
πᾶς ὅς (*SC*a; *VK*a); cf. πᾶς ὅστις Mt 7,24; 10,32; 19,29 DENAUX 2009 L***	2,20; 3,19; 9,43; 12,8.10.48[1]; 19,37; 24,25	1,1; 2,21; 3,21[2]; 10,39[1]; 13,38; 22,10; 26,2	1/2	0
περὶ οὗ/ἧς/ὧν DENAUX 2009 1A*	1,4; 7,27[1]; 9,9	19,40; 24,13; 25,15.18[1].24.26; 26,7	1	0
τις … ὅς/ὅστις (*SC*l; *VK*l) → τις … ὅστις BOISMARD 1984 Cb81; DENAUX 2009 1A*; NEIRYNCK 1985	8,2[1].27*; 9,27; 16,1.20*	3,2; 8,9; 9,33; 10,5.6.11; 11,20; 13,6; 14,8; 15,24; 16,1.14.16; 17,34; 18,7; 21,16; 24,1.19; 25,14 .19; 27,8.39	0	0/2
→ ᾧ/ἧ ὄνομα, ὅς παραγενόμενος + verb; καθ' ὃν τρόπον				

Literature

COLLISON 1977 114 [ἕως οὗ: noteworthy phenomena]; 123 [ἀνθ᾽ ὧν: noteworthy phenomena]; 124-125 [ἀφ᾽ οὗ/ἀφ᾽ ἧς]; 205 [attraction to antecedent: linguistic usage of Luke: certain; linguistic usage of Luke's "other source-material": also possible]; 206 [implied demonstrative: certain; linguistic usage of Luke's "other source-material": also possible; ὅς + pleonastic καί / ὅς + ἐγένετο: noteworthy phenomena]; 207 [ὅς + participle: linguistic usage of Luke's "other source-material": likely; ὅς ἄν: noteworthy phenomena]; DENAUX 2009 Lᵃⁿ [ἀνθ᾽ ὧν], IAⁿ [ἄχρι (δὲ) οὗ]; EASTON 1910 158-159 [ἀνθ᾽ ὧν: cited by Weiss as characteristic of L, and possibly corroborative]; GERSDORF 1816 188 [ἀνθ᾽ ὧν]; HARNACK 1906 33.42.43: "die Erzählung wird in einem Relativsatz fortgeführt" [Acts 2,24; 3,3; 11,6; 16,14; 23,29; 25,16; 28,8.10]; HAUCK 1934 [Vorzugsverbindung: οἷς οὐκ ἐστιν; ἧ/ᾧ ὄνομα; Stileigentümlichkeit: ὅς in attraction]; JEREMIAS 1980 43 [ἀνθ᾽ ὧν: red.]; 88: "Die Attractio relativi findet sich in Lk/Apg ganz erheblich häufiger als in den übrigen Evangelien ... sie ist also lukanische Vorzugswendung. Insbesondere liebt Lukas die Attractio relativi nach πάντα"; 172: "Im LkEv begegnen nebeneinander elliptisches ἀφ᾽ οὗ ... und ἀφ᾽ ἧς ... beides erstarrte Formeln mit der Bedeutung 'seitdem'. Im Blick auf den Beleg in der Apg (24,11) wird man erwägen, ἀφ᾽ ἧς dem Evangelisten und ἀφ᾽ οὗ der Tradition zuzuschreiben"; 174: "ὅς καί: καί nach Relativ-Pronomen ... im lk Doppelwerk ... 20mal. Von den vier auf das LkEv entfallenden Belegen (6,13.14; 7,49; 10,30) sind die beiden ersten (Lk 6,13.14) lukanische Markusbearbeitung; zusammen mit den sechzehn Apg-Belegen zeigen sie, daß Lukas die Wendung bevorzugt"; RADL 1975 420 [ὅς; ὅς "zur Einleitung eines Hauptsatzes"; "Attraktion des Relativpronomens"]; REHKOPF 1959 91 [ἀνθ᾽ ὧν: vorlukanisch]; SCHÜRMANN 1957 74 [ὅς ἄν (ἐάν)]; 1961 273 [ἀνθ᾽ ὧν].

CADBURY, Henri J., The Relative Pronouns in Acts and Elsewhere. — *JBL* 42 (1923) 150-157. [ὅς, ὅστις].

CIGNELLI, L. – PIERRI, R., *Sintassi di Greco biblico*. I.a, 2003. Esp. 75-95: "Concordanza dei pronomi relativi" [ὅς, ὅστις, ὅσος, οἷος].

DELEBECQUE, Édouard, L'hellénisme de la "relative complexe" dans le Nouveau Testament et principalement chez saint Luc. — *Bib* 62 (1981) 229-238.

FUCHS, Albert, *Sprachliche Untersuchungen zu Mattäus und Lukas*, 1971. Esp. 181-183 [ἧ Relativpronomen].

SPOTTORNO, Victoria, The Relative Pronoun in the New Testament. Some Critical Remarks — *NTS* 28 (1982) 132-141. [ὅς, ὅστις; ὅσος, ὅσπερ].

ὁσιότης 1

1. holiness (Lk 1,75); 2. dedication (Lk 1,75)

ὅσος 10 + 17 (Mt 15/16, Mk 14/15)

1. as many as (Acts 3,24); 2. as much as (Lk 11,8); 3. to the degree that; 4. as long as

Word groups	Lk	Acts	Mt	Mk
ὅσος ἄν/ἐάν (*SC*b; *VK*h) → ὅς/ὅστις ἄν/ἐάν	9,5	2,39; 3,22	6	2/4
ὅσος ἄν/ἐάν ... μή → ὅς/ὅστις ἄν/ἐάν ... μή	9,5		0	0/1
ὅσος γάρ (*VK*f)		4,34	0	0
πάντα ὅσα ἔχω/κτάομαι	4,40; 18,12.22		3	1
πᾶς/ἅπας (...) ὅσος (*SC*a; *VK*a)	4,40; 18,12.22	2,39; 3,22.24; 5,36.37	7/8	4
πᾶς (...) ὅσος ἄν (*SC*c); cf. πᾶς (...) ὅσος ἐάν Mt 7,12; 23,3; Mk 3,28		2,39; 3,22	1/3	0/2
→ **πωλέω** ὅσα ἔχεις + ἀκολουθέω				

Literature

CADBURY, Henri, The Relative Pronouns in Acts and Elsewhere. — JBL 42 (1923) 150-157. [ὅς, ὅστις].
CIGNELLI, L. – PIERRI, R., Sintassi di Greco biblico. I.a, 2003. Esp. 75-95: "Concordanza dei pronomi relativi" [ὅς, ὅστις, ὅσος, οἷος].
DELEBECQUE, Édouard, L'hellénisme de la "relative complexe" dans le Nouveau Testament et principalement chez saint Luc. — Bib 62 (1981) 229-238.
SPOTTORNO, Victoria, The Relative Pronoun in the New Testament. Some Critical Remarks — NTS 28 (1982) 132-141. [ὅς, ὅστις; ὅσος, ὅσπερ].

ὀστέον 1 (Mt 1)	bone (Lk 24,39)

ὅστις 18 + 24 (Mt 29/31, Mk 5/6)	whoever; whatever

Word groups	Lk	Acts	Mt	Mk
ὅστις after a cardinal number (SCh; VKj)	9,30; 15,7	23,(13-)14.21	1	0
ὅστις (δ') ἄν/ἐάν (SCe; VKe) → ὅς/ὅσος ἄν/ἐάν	10,35	3,23	2	1
ὅστις ἄν/ἐάν … μή → ὅς/ὅσος ἄν/ἐάν … μή		3,23	0	0
οὗτος … ὅστις (SCf; VKf); cf. ὅστις … οὗτος Mt 18,4	8,15	10,47; 16,17; 17,11	1	0/1
πᾶς (adjective) ὅστις (SCa; VKa) → πᾶς ὅς; πᾶς (adjective) + ὅς; cf. πᾶς ὅστις Mt 7,24; 10,32; 19,29		3,23		

Characteristic of Luke	Lk	Acts	Mt	Mk
ἥτις DENAUX 2009 L***; GOULDER 1989*	2,4.10; 7,37.39; 8,3.26.43; 10,42; 12,1; 23,55	3,23; 11,28; 12,10; 16,12.16	3/4	0
οἵτινες + participle + principal verb; cf. Eph 4,19; Heb 2,3 BOISMARD 1984 cb64; NEIRYNCK 1985	8,15	8,15; 11,20; 13,43; 17,10; 23,14.33; 28,18	1	0
ὅστις instead of the relative pronoun DENAUX 2009 lA**; HARNACK 1906 30	1,20; 2,4.10; 7,37.39; 8,3.26. 43; 9,30;10,42; 12,1; 23,19.55	5,16; 8,15; 11,20.28; 12,10; 13,31.43; 16,12. 16.17; 17,10.11; 21,4; 23,14.21.33; 24,1; 28,18	5	2
τις … ὅστις (SCg; VKg) → τις … ὅς BOISMARD 1984 cb81; NEIRYNCK 1985		11,20; 16,16; 24,1	1/2	1
→ ὅστις παραγενόμενος + verb				

Literature

VON BENDEMANN 2001 414: "ὅστις/ἥτις/ὅτι für einfaches Relativum ist lukanisch"; COLLISON 1977 208 [avoided as indefinite pronoun: linguistic usage of Luke: probable; implied demonstrative: probable; ὅστις = ὅς: linguistic usage of Luke's other source-material: nearly certain]; DENAUX 2009 lAn [οἵτινες + participle + principal verb]; JEREMIAS 1980 43: "Der im klassischen Sprachgebrauch seltene Ersatz des einfachen Relativpronomens durch ὅστις, ἥτις, ὅτι wird im NT besonders von Lukas angewendet"; RADL 1975 420 [ὅστις; οἵτινες]: "Lukas benutzt in der Apg 'die Pronomina ἥτις, οἵτινες, αἵτινες als bestimmte Relativa".

CADBURY, Henry, The Relative Pronouns in Acts and Elsewhere. — JBL 42 (1923) 150-157. [ὅς, ὅστις].

CIGNELLI, L. – PIERRI, R., *Sintassi di Greco biblico*. I.a, 2003. Esp. 75-95: "Concordanza dei pronomi relativi" [ὅς, ὅστις, ὅσος, οἷος].
SPOTTORNO, Victoria, The Relative Pronoun in the New Testament. Some Critical Remarks — *NTS* 28 (1982) 132-141. [ὅς, ὅστις; ὅσος, ὅσπερ].

ὀσφύς 1 + 1 (Mt 1, Mk 1)
1. waist (Lk 12,35); 2. genitals (Acts 2,30)

Word groups	Lk	Acts	Mt	Mk
ἐκ καρποῦ τῆς ὀσφύος (*LN*: offspring; *VK*a)		2,30	0	0
περιζώννυμαι τὴν ὀσφύν (*LN*: get ready); cf. Eph 6,14	12,35		0	0

ὅταν 29 + 2 (Mt 19, Mk 21)
1. whenever (Lk 12,11); 2. when (Lk 5,35); 3. as often, as; 4. as long as

Word groups	Lk	Acts	Mt	Mk
ἀλλ᾽ ὅταν DENAUX 2009 Lⁿ	14,10[1].13		0	0
ἵνα ὅταν (*SC*d; *VK*d) DENAUX 2009 Lⁿ	14,10[2]; 16,4.9		0	0
καὶ ὅταν → καὶ ὅτε	5,35; 6,22[2]; 12,55		2	6
ὃς ὅταν (*SC*f; *VK*f)	8,13		0	2
ὅταν + future indicative (*SC*l; *VK*m)	13,28		0	0
ὅταν δέ (*SC*b; *VK*b) → ὅτε δέ	12,11; 21,9.20		6	3/4
ὅταν … εὐθέως (*SC*h; *VK*j); cf. ὅταν … εὐθύς Mk 4,15.16.29 DENAUX 2009 Lⁿ	12,54; 21,9		0	0/3
ὅταν καί → ἂν/εἰ/ἐὰν (δὲ) καί		23,35	0	0
ὅταν οὖν (*SC*c; *VK*c)	11,34 *v.l.*		3	0
ὅταν … τότε (*SC*g; *VK*h)	5,35; 11,24; 21,20		3	2
οὐαὶ ὅταν	6,26		0	0
ὡς ὅταν (*VK*g); cf. ὡς ἐάν Mk 4,26 *v.l.*	11,36		0	0

Literature
COLLISON 1977 110 [ἵνα ὅταν: linguistic usage of Luke's "other source-material": certain].

ὅτε 12 + 10 (Mt 12/13, Mk 12/13)
1. when (Lk 2,21); 2. as long as

Word groups	Lk	Acts	Mt	Mk
καὶ ὅτε → καὶ ὅταν	2,21.22.42; 6,13; 22,14; 23,33	1,13; 11,2 *v.l.*; 22,20	2/3	5/6
ὅτε + aorist subjunctive (*SC*c; *VK*k)	13,35		0	0
ὅτε + future indicative after a substantive (*VK*h)	17,22		0	0

Characteristic of Luke	Lk	Acts	Mt	Mk
ὅτε δέ (*SC*a; *VK*b) → ὅταν δέ BOISMARD 1984 Eb66	15,30	8,12.39; 11,2; 12,6; 21,5.35; 27,39; 28,16	3	0/2

Literature
COLLISON 1977 110 [καὶ ὅτε (ἐγένετο): linguistic usage of Luke: likely; καὶ ὅτε: linguistic usage

of Luke's "other source-material": also likely]; DENAUX 2009 lAn [ὅτε δέ]; GERSDORF 1816 242-244 [καὶ ὅτε]; RADL 1975 403 [ὅτε δὲ ἐγένετο]; 420-421 [ὅτε]; SCHÜRMANN 1953 78 [von sich aus schreibt Luk ὅτε immer nur in Verbindung mit καί oder δέ]; 105-106 [von sich aus scheint Luk die Wendung ὅτε δὲ ἐγένετο zu schreiben … Luk (schreibt) ein καί bei ὅτε meist in Abhängigkeit von einer V]; 1957 117 [ein einfaches ὅτε vermeidet Luk].

ὅτι 174/184 + 123 (Mt 140/150, Mk 100[102]/110)

1. that (Lk 24,21); 2. because (Lk 4,41[2]); 3. namely (Lk 2,49; Acts 5,4)

Word groups	Lk	Acts	Mt	Mk
διὰ τί; ὅτι (SCb; VKk)	19,31		1	0
δοκεῖτε ὅτι …; οὐχί, λέγω ὑμῖν, ἀλλ'… DENAUX 2009 L[n]	12,51; 13,2(-3).4-(5)		0	0
ὅτι + accusative with infinitive (VKe)		27,10	0	0
ὅτι after interrogative (SCa; VKb)	2,49[1]; 4,36; 8,25; 12,17; 16,3	5.4.9	4	3/6
ὅτι as a causal conjunction (SCd)	1,37.48.49.68; 2,11.30; 4,6. 32.41[2].43[2]; 5,8; 6,19.20.21[1.2]. 24.25[1.2].35; 7,47; 8,30.37.42; 9,12.38.49.53; 10,13.21[1.2]; 11,18.31.32.42.43.44.46.47. 48.52; 12,15.17.32.40; 13,2[2]. 24.31.33; 14,11.14.17; 15,6. 9.24.27[2].32; 16,3.8[1.2].15.24; 17,9; 18,14; 19,3.4.17.21.43; 21,22; 22,22; 23,29.31.40; 24,29.39[2]	1,5.17; 2,6.25.27; 4,16.21; 5,38.41; 6,1; 8,20.33; 9,15; 10,14.20.38; 11,8.24; 13,41; 17,18; 20,35[2]; 22,15.21	51/52	15
ὅτι in prolepsis (VKc)	12,24; 24,7	3,10; 4,13[2]; 9,20; 13,33; 16,3; 21,29	1	4
ὅτι recitative (VKd)	1,25.61; 2,23; 3,8*; 4,4.10.11.21.41[1].43[1]; 5,26.36; 7,4.16[1].22*; 8,20*.49	3,22; 5,23.25; 6,11; 7,6; 11,3; 13,34[2]; 15,1; 16,36; 17,6; 18,13; 19,21; 23,5[2].22; 25,8; 28,25	13/16	25/29
ὅτι with reference to scripture (SCc)	2,23; 4,4.10.11	2,30.31; 3,22; 7,6; 13,34[2]; 23,5[2]	4	5
ὅτι δέ (VKl)		13,34[1]	0	0
ὅτι ἰδού	23,29	5,25	0	1
ὅτι καί → διό(τι)/καθότι καί	4,43[1]; 8,25	2,29.36; 10,45; 11,1; 17,13	1	2/3
οὐαὶ … ὅτι	6,24.25[1.2]; 10,13; 11,43.44.46.47.52		7	0
οὕτως … ὅτι (VKm)		7,6; 13,34[2]	0	0
πλὴν ὅτι (VKj)		20,23[1]	0	0
τίς + ὅτι → τί ὅτι	2,49[1]; 4,36; 8,25; 12,17; 16,3	5.4.9	4	3/6

→ γινώσκω ὅτι; ἐλπίζω ὅτι; εὐχαριστέω + ὅτι; θαυμάζω ὅτι; θεωρέω ὅτι; κηρύσσω ὅτι; λέγω /εἶπον/ἐρῶ ὅτι; μακάριος + ὅτι; μιμνήσκομαι ὅτι; μνημονεύω ὅτι; νομίζω ὅτι; οἶδα ὅτι; ὁμολογέω ὅτι; (ὁράω)/εἶδον ὅτι; πείθω ὅτι; πιστεύω ὅτι; πυνθάνομαι ὅτι; ὑποδείκνυμι ὅτι

Characteristic of Luke	Lk	Acts	Mt	Mk
καὶ ὅτι → καὶ πόθεν/πῶς DENAUX 2009 lA*	4,11; 7,16[2]	9,27; 14,22.27; 17,3[2]; 22,29[2]	0	1
ὅτι after demonstrative (VKa) DENAUX 2009 L***	4,36; 10,11.20[1]; 12,39; 24,44	16,36; 20,29; 24,14.21	1	0

τί ὅτι → τίς + ὅτι	2,49[1]	5,4.9	0	0/1
BOISMARD 1984 Ab148; HARNACK 1906 149; NEIRYNCK 1985; VOGEL 1899C				
→ ἐπιγινώσκω + ὅτι				

Literature

COLLISON 1977 118 [ὅτι recitative: linguistic usage of Luke: likely; it may also be a linguistic usage of Luke's "other source-material"]; 119 [λέγων ὅτι: certain; it may also be a linguistic usage of Luke's "other source-material"; causal ὅτι: certain; linguistic usage of Luke's "other source-material": certain]; DENAUX 2009 lAⁿ [τί ὅτι]; GERSDORF 1816 192 [ὅτι οὕτω μοι πεποίηκεν κύριος]: "Das ὅτι recitativum od. pleonasticum kommt bei'm Lucas zum öftern vor"; 206 [ὅτι ἐπεσκέψατο]; 270 [τί ὅτι ἐζητεῖτέ με]; PLUMMER 1922 lxiii [after τοῦτο he has ὅτι in Gospel and Acts (x.11, xii.39, etc.); Mt. and Mk. never; Jn. only after διὰ τοῦτο]; RADL 1975 421 [ὅτι; ὅτι recitativum]; SCHÜRMANN 1953 35 [ὅτι nach (ἀμὴν) λέγω (γὰρ) ὑμῖν]; 98 [ὅτι recitativum].

BAUMERT, Norbert, Konsekutives ὅτι in biblischen Griechisch? — *BibNot* 107-108 (2001) 5-11.
CADBURY, Henri J., Lexical Notes on Luke-Acts, IV, 1929.
DELEBECQUE, Édouard, *Études grecques*, 1976. Esp. 41-42 [τί ὅτι].
ELLIOTT, James K., The Position of Causal "ὅτι" Clauses in the New Testament. — *FilolNT* 3 (1990) 155-157.
GARCÍA PÉREZ, José Miguel, El relato del Buen Ladrón (Lc 23,39-43), 1986. Esp. 293-297: "El extraño ὅτι".
GREENLEE, J. Harold, Ὅτι and ἵνα Content Clauses. — *Notes on Translation* 14 (2000) 49-53. [NTA 46, 74]
JUNG, Chang-Wook, *Infancy Narrative*, 2004. Esp. 72-74 [ὅτι Lk 2,23].
WINTER, Paul, Ὅτι Recitativum in Luke I 25, 61, II 23. — *HTR* 48 (1955) 213-216.
—, Ὅτι "recitativum" in Lc 1,25. 61; 2,23. — *ZNW* 46 (1955) 261-263.
ZEDDA, Silverio, L'ὅτι di Lc 1,45: "che" o "perché"? — *RivBib* 39 (1991) 193-199.

ὅτου 3/5 (Mt 1)

Characteristic of Luke	Lk	Acts	Mt	Mk
ἕως ὅτου + subjunctive (*LN*: ᵃuntil) → ἕως οὗ + subjunctive; cf. ἕως ὅτου + indic. Mt 5,25 CREDNER 1836 136; GOULDER 1989	12,50; 13,8; 15,8*; 22,16.18*		0	0

Literature

DENAUX 2009 Ln; REHKOPF 1959 94 [ἕως ὅτου]; SCHÜRMANN 1961 271 [ἕως ὅτου].

οὗ 5 + 8 (Mt 3)

1. where (place) (Lk 4,16.17; 10,1; 23,53; 24,28); 2. where (circumstance)

Word groups	Lk	Acts	Mt	Mk
τόπος οὗ (*VK*d) DENAUX 2009 Lⁿ	4,17; 10,1		0	0
πορεύομαι οὗ	24,28		0	0

Characteristic of Luke

BOISMARD 1984 cb160; DENAUX 2009 lA**; GOULDER 1989; HARNACK 1906 31; HAWKINS 1909A; NEIRYNCK 1985

οὖ – οὐ   453

	Lk	Acts	Mt	Mk
οὗ ἦν/ἦσαν + participle BOISMARD 1984 Ab27; DENAUX 2009 IA*; NEIRYNCK 1985	4,16.17; 23,53	1,13; 2,2; 12,12; 20,8	0	0

Literature

COLLISON 1977 159-160 [linguistic usage of Luke: likely]; HAUCK 1934 [Vorzugswort];
JEREMIAS 1980 120 [red.]; RADL 1975 421.

KILPATRICK, George D., Style and Text, 1967. Esp. 159-160; = ID., *Principles and Practice*,
1990. Esp. 61-62.

οὐ 172/182 + 111/112 (Mt 198/203, Mk 115[117]/127)

1. not (Lk 4,2); 2. marker of question (Lk 2,49)

Word groups	Lk	Acts	Mt	Mk
ἀλλ᾽ οὐ → ἀλλ᾽ οὐδέ/οὐχί	21,9	7,48	0	4
ἄν/ἐάν ... οὐ (SCs; VKt); cf. κἄν ... οὐ Mt 26,35; Mk [16,18]	18,17; 22,67.68	13,41; 15,1; 27,31	3	5
εἰ ... οὐ (SCr; VKs) → εἰ ... οὐδέ	5,36; 12,39; 14,26²	5,39; 25,11	7	3
οὐ in a double negative (SCc; VKc)	4,2; 8,43.51 v.l.; 10,19; 18,13; 20,40*; 22,16 v.l.; 23,53	4,12; 8,39; 19,40; 20,27; 26,26¹	4	8
οὐ + future indicative as prohibitive (SCa; VKa)	4,12; 10,42	23,5²	9	0
οὐ interrogative (SCb; VKb)	2,49; 4,22*; 9,55*; 10,40; 11,40; 12,56; 13,15.16; 14,5; 15,4; 17,17*.18; 18,7; 24,18	2,7; 5,28; 9,21; 13,10; 21,38	17	15
οὐ + participle (SCg)	6,42	7,5²; 19,11; 28,2	2	0
οὐ (μόνον) ... ἀλλά (καί) (SCh; VKh) → οὐδέ/οὐδείς ... ἀλλά	4,4 v.l.; 5,31.32; 7,6²(-7); 8,27².52; 9,56*; 18,13; 20,21.38; 22,26.53; 24,6	1,7(-8); 2,15(-16); 4,16(-17); 5,4; 7,39; 10,34(-35).41; 13,25¹; 16,37; 18,20(-21); 19,26¹.27; 21,13; 26,19(-20).25.29; 27,10	24	21
οὐ + ἄλλος (SCn; VKn); cf. οὐ + ἑαυτοῦ Mt 27,42; Mk 15,31		4,12	0	2
οὐκ ἄν (SCe; VKe)	12,39		4	1
οὐ + ἅπας/πᾶς (VKq); cf. οὐχί + πᾶς Mt 13,56	1,37; 14,33²; 21,15	10,41	4	2
οὐ γάρ (SCf; VKf) → οὐδὲ/ οὐδείς/οὐκέτι/οὔτε γάρ	6,43.44; 7,6²; 8,17¹.52; 9,50*; 16,2; 23,34	2,15.34; 16,37; 20,27; 22,22; 26,26²	5	6/7
οὐ ... δέ (SCj; VKj) → οὐδείς ... ἀλλά/δέ	6,40; 7,44.45¹.46; 15,28	2,34; 3,6; 12,14; 27,39	4	4
οὐ ... εἰ μή(τι) (SCk; VKk); cf. οὐ ... ἐὰν μή Mt 26,42; Mk 3,27; 4,22	6,4; 8,51; 9,13; 11,29; 17,18		7/8	5
οὐ + εἷς (SCp; VKp) → οὐδὲ εἷς; cf. μή + εἷς Mt 18,10	11,46; 12,6; 15,4	20,31	6	1
οὐκ ἔτι (VKg) → μηκέτι; οὐδὲ ἔτι; οὐκέτι	16,2; 20,40*		0	0

	Lk	Acts	Mt	Mk
οὐ + ἕως (SCl; VKl); cf. οὐ + μέχρις Mk 13,30	9,27; 12,59; 13,35; 21,32; 22,16.18.34		11	3
οὐχ ἰδού		2,7	0	0
οὐ μή (SCd; VKd) → οὐχὶ μή	1,15; 6,37$^{1.2}$; 8,17^3; 9,27; 10,19; 12,59; 13,35; 18,7.17.30*; 21,18.32.33; 22,16.18.34 v.l.67.68	13,41; 28,26$^{1.2}$	19/20	10[11]
οὐκ ὀλίγος BOISMARD 1984 Aa9; HARNACK 1906 39		12,18; 14,28; 15,2; 17,4.12; 19,23.24; 27,20	0	0
οὐ ... οὐδέ (SCu)	6,43.44; 7,6^2(-7); 8,17^2; 12,24$^{1.2}$.27.33; 16,31; 17,20(-21); 18,4^2	2,27; 4,12; 7,5^1; 8,21^1; 9,9; 16,21; 17,24(-25); 24,18	13	1
οὐ + τις (VKr) → οὐδὲ/ οὐδεὶς/οὔτε ... τις DENAUX 2009 1A^n	8,51; 12,15	25,16.26; 26,26^1	0	0/1
οὐχ ὡς (SCq)		28,19	2	1

→ οὐκ εἰμί; ἔξεστιν + inf. + ἢ οὐ; οὐκ εὐθέως; οὐκ ἰσχύω; καὶ οὐ; καὶ οὐ μή; λέγω ὑμῖν / σοι ... οὐ μή ... ἕως (ἄν); (ἀπέχω/ὑπάρχω) οὐ μακρὰν (ἀπό); οὐ μέλει; οὐ μόνον (δὲ) ... ἀλλά; οὐ ... μόνος ... ἀλλά; οὐχ ... οὕτως; οὐ ... πολύς; οὐχ ὁ τυχών; χρόνος οὐκ ὀλίγος

Characteristic of Luke

	Lk	Acts	Mt	Mk
οὐ μετά / μετ᾽ οὐ → μετ᾽ οὐ πολύ / μετ᾽ οὐ πολλὰς ἡμέρας; cf. οὐδὲ μετά Acts 24,18 BOISMARD 1984 Ab38; NEIRYNCK 1985	15,13	1,5; 5,26; 24,18^1; 27,14	0	0

→ εἰ οὐ; οὐ πρῶτον

Literature

BDR § 430: "Die Negation beim Partizip: ... Im NT ist μή die Regel, ... 2. Dagegen in Lk und Apg einige Beispiele von klass. οὐ"; COLLISON 1977 105 [linguistic usage of Luke's "other source-material": certain]; DENAUX 2009 1A^n [οὐ μετά / μετ᾽ οὐ]; GERSDORF 1816 270 [οὐκ ᾔδειτε]; HARNACK 1906 39 [This litotes (οὐκ ὀλίγος and similar negative expressions) occurs in Lk-Acts at least 17 times, and is as good as absent elsewhere in the NT]; 72 (ET: 101: "οὐ μή in Acts exclusively in quotations"); JEREMIAS 1980 147: "οὐ beim Partizip ist eines der vielen Beispiele des Lukas für das Bemühen um ein sorgfältiges Griechisch"; RADL 1975 421 [οὐ μόνον (... ἀλλὰ καί)]; SCHÜRMANN 1953 17-18 [οὐ,οὐ μή].

CADBURY, Henry J., Litotes in Acts. — BARTH, E.H. – COCROFT, R.E. (eds.), Festschrift to Honor F. Wilbur Gingrich, 1972, 70-84. Esp. 59-61 [οὐκ ἄσημος]; 61-62 [οὐ μετρίως]; 62-63 [οὐκ ὀλίγος]; 63-64 [οὐχ ὁ τύχων]; 64 [οὐ πολύς]; 64-65 [οὐ ἀμάρτυρον]; 65-66 [οὐ μακράν].
JUNG, Chang-Wook, Infancy Narrative, 2004. Esp. 115-116 [οὐ - πᾶς].
MITIKU, A., The Use of Οὐ Μή in the New Testament: Emphatic or Mild Negation? . — Faith & Mission [Wake Forest, NC] 22 (2005) 85-104.

οὐ 2 (Mt 3, Mk 1) | no (Lk 4,3; 20,22)

οὐαί 15 (Mt 13/14, Mk 2/3) | horror, woe

Word groups	Lk	Acts	Mt	Mk
ἀλλὰ οὐαί (VKf) → πλὴν οὐαί	11,42		0	0
οὐαί + nominative (VKa)	6,25^2		0	0/1
οὐαί placed after a substantive (VKh)	11,46		0	0

οὐαὶ (τῷ ἀνθρώπῳ) δι᾽ οὗ	17,1; 22,22	2	1
οὐαὶ ... γάρ	6,26; 21,23	0	0
οὐαὶ δέ (SCa; VKc)	17,1 v.l.; 21,23 v.l.	3/4	2
οὐαὶ ὅταν (VKe)	6,26	0	0
οὐαὶ ... ὅτι	6,24.25[1.2]; 10,13[1.2]; 11,43.44.46.47.52	8	0
οὐαί σοι → οὐαὶ ὑμῖν	10,13[1.2]	2	0
οὐαὶ ὑμῖν → οὐαί σοι	6,24.25[1]; 11,42.43.44.47.52	6	0
πλὴν οὐαί (SCb; VKg) → ἀλλὰ οὐαί	6,24; 17,1; 22,22	1	0

Characteristic of Luke	Lk	Acts	Mt	Mk
οὐαὶ ὑμῖν τοῖς GOULDER 1989	6,24; 11,42.43.46.52		0	0

Literature

COLLISON 1977 121 [πλὴν οὐαί: noteworthy phenomena]; 160 [noteworthy phenomena]; DENAUX 2009 Ln [οὐαὶ ὑμῖν τοῖς]; SCHÜRMANN 1957 5-6 [πλὴν οὐαί].

DUPONT, Jacques, *Les Béatitudes*, III, 1973. Esp. 28-30.
MARGOT, Jean-Claude, The Translation of οὐαί. — *BTrans* 19 (1968) 26-27.
MULLINS, T.Y., Ascription as a Literary Form. — *NTS* 19 (1973) 194-205. [NTA 17, 842: The most comon types are woes (*ouai*), eulogies (*eulogētos* or *eulogēmenos*) and beatitudes (*makarios*)]

οὐδέ 21/22 + 12/14 (Mt 27/28, Mk 9[10]/13)

1. and not (Lk 6,43; Acts 17,25); 2. not even (Lk 18,13; Acts 7,5)

Word groups	Lk	Acts	Mt	Mk
ἀλλ᾽ οὐδέ → ἀλλ᾽ οὐ/οὐχί DENAUX 2009 LA[n]	23,15	19,2	0	0
διὸ οὐδέ	7,7		0	0
εἰ ... οὐδέ (VKm) → εἰ ... οὐ; cf. ἐὰν ... οὐδέ (VKn) Mt 6,15	16,31		0	0/1
καὶ οὐδέ		4,32	0	3
οὐ ... οὐδέ (... οὐδέ) (SCg); cf. οὔπω ... οὐδέ Mt 16,9.10; Mk 8,17	6,43.44; 7,(6-)7; 8,17; 12,24[1.2]. 27[1].33; 16,31; 17,(20-)21; 18,4	2,27; 4,12; 7,5; 8,21; 9,9; 16,21; 17,(24-)25; 24,18	15	1
οὐδέ in a double negative (SCb; VKb); cf. οὐδ᾽ οὐ μή Mt 24,21	18,13		2	1
οὐδέ interrogative (SCa; VKa)	6,3; 23,40		2	2
οὐδέ ... ἀλλά (SCd; VKg)	7,7; 11,33; 18,13	4,32	2	1
οὐδέ + ἄπας (VKk) → οὐ ἄπας/πᾶς	21,15*		0	0
οὐδὲ γάρ (SCc; VKe) → οὐ/οὐδεὶς/ οὐκέτι/οὔτε γάρ; cf. οὐδέπω γάρ Acts 8,16 DENAUX 2009 lA[n]	20,36	4,12.34	0	0
οὐδὲ ἐγώ	20,8		1	1
οὐδὲ εἷς (VKj) → οὐ + εἷς		4,32	1	0
οὐδὲ ... ἔτι (VKf) → μηκέτι; οὐκ ἔτι; οὐκέτι	20,36		0	0
οὐδὲ ... τις (SCf; VKl) → οὐ/οὐδεὶς/ οὔτε... τις		4,32.34; 17,25	3	0

οὐδείς 33/36+ 25/28 (Mt 19/20, Mk 26)　　　no one, nothing

Word groups	Lk	Acts	Mt	Mk
εἰ ... οὐδείς (SCe; VKf)		25,11[2]	0	0

		5,36	0	0
εἰς οὐδέν → εἰς **αὐτό/τοῦτο/τί**				
καὶ οὐδείς → καὶ **μηδείς**	4,27; 5,37.39; 9,36[1]; 10,19.22; 15,16	15,9*; 18,10.17	4	4/5
οὐδείς in a double negative (SCa; VKa) → **οὐθείς** in a double negative	4,2; 8,43.51*; 9,36[1.2]; 10,19; 20,40; 23,53	4,12; 8,16; 26,26*	1	15
οὐδείς ..., ἀλλά/δέ (SCb; VKc) → **οὐ/οὐδὲ ... ἀλλά; οὐ ... δέ**	5,5.36.37(-38); 8,16; 11,33	5,13; 19,27*; 21,24	1	4
οὐδεὶς ἄλλος/ἕτερος (VKl)		4,12; 17,21	0	0
οὐδεὶς αὐτῶν DENAUX 2009 La[n]	4,26.27	8,16	0	0
οὐδεὶς γάρ (SCh; VKj) → **οὐ/οὐδὲ/ οὐκέτι/οὔτε** γάρ;		27,34	1	1
οὐδεὶς δέ (SCg; VKh)	8,16; 11,33 v.l.; 12,2		1	0
οὐδεὶς ... εἰ μή (SCc; VKd); cf. οὐδεὶς ... ἐὰν μή Mk 3,27; 10,29	4,26.27; 8,51*; 10,22; 18,19		5/6	6/7
οὐδεὶς (+) ἐκτός/πλήν (SCd; VKe); cf. οὐδείς + χωρίς Mt 13,34		26,22; 27,22	0	0
οὐδείς ἐστιν	1,61; 7,28; 18,29		0	2
οὐδεὶς (οὐκ) ἔτι / οὐκέτι (VKb)	20,40		1	5
οὐδεὶς ... τις → οὐ/οὐδὲ/οὔτε ... τις		26,31	1	0
οὐδεὶς (+) ὑμῶν		27,34	0	0
οὐδέν neuter noun (SCf; VKg)	4,2; 5,5; 9,36[2]; 10,19; 12,2; 18,34; 20,40; 22,35*; 23,9	4,14; 5,36; 9,8; 15,9*; 18,17; 19,27*; 20,20; 21,24; 25,10.11[1]; 26,22.26*	10	9
οὐδέν (+) ἐστιν	12,2	21,24; 25,11[1]	3	1

Characteristic of Luke	Lk	Acts	Mt	Mk
gnomic οὐδείς DENAUX 2009 L***; GOULDER 1989	4,24; 5,36.37.39; 8,16; 9,62; 10,22; 11,33; 12,2; 16,13; 18,19		3/4	5
οὐδείς adjective DENAUX 2009 IA*	4,24; 16,13	20,24.33; 25,18; 27,22	0	1
οὐδείς/**οὐθείς** + determinative → **οὐθείς** + determinative; cf. Jn 13,28; 21,12 BOISMARD 1984 Eb41; DENAUX 2009 L***; NEIRYNCK 1985	4,26.27; 9,36[2]; 14,24; 18,34; 19,30	5,13; 8,16; 18,17; 20,20; 21,24; 25,11[1]; 26,26; 27,34	0	1
οὐδέν/ μηδέν + epithet → **μηδέν** + epithet; cf. Rom 14,14; Gal 5,10; 2 Tim 2,14; Heb 2,8 BOISMARD 1984 cb69; DENAUX 2009 IA*; NEIRYNCK 1985	3,13; 23,15.41	15,28; 16,28; 17,21; 19,36; 23,9; 26,31; 28,5	0	0
οὐδὲν αἴτιον (no guilt) → **μηδὲν/οὐθὲν** αἴτιον GOULDER 1989	23,4.14*.22		0	0
→ οὐδὲν **ἄξιον** θανάτου πράσσω				

Literature

DENAUX 2009 L[n] [οὐδὲν αἴτιον]; JEREMIAS 1980 300 [οὐδὲν ... αἴτιον: red.]; RADL 1975 421 [οὐδὲν κακόν].

οὐδέποτε 2 + 3 (Mt 5, Mk 2)   never (Lk 15,29[1.2]; Acts 10,14; 11,8; 14,8)

Word groups	Lk	Acts	Mt	Mk
καὶ οὐδέποτε	15,29		0	0

οὐθείς 2 + 3/4 — no one, nothing (Lk 22,35; 23,14)

Word groups	Lk	Acts	Mt	Mk
οὐθείς in a double negative (*VK*a) → οὐδείς in a double negative		26,26	0	0
οὐθέν + αἴτιον → μηδὲνοὐδὲν αἴτιον	23,14		0	0

Characteristic of Luke
BOISMARD 1984 cb9; NEIRYNCK 1985

	Lk	Acts	Mt	Mk
οὐθείς/οὐδείς + determinative → οὐδείς + determinative BOISMARD 1984 Eb41; DENAUX 2009 L***; NEIRYNCK 1985	4,26.27; 9,36[2]; 14,24; 18,34; 19,30	5,13; 8,16; 18,17; 20,20; 21,24; 25,11[1]; 26,26; 27,34	0	0

Literature
DENAUX 2009 lA[n]; JEREMIAS 1980 292: "Die in hellenistischer Zeit zurückgedrängten Formen οὐθείς/μηθείς finden sich im NT außer 2mal bei Pls nur im Doppelwerk"; SCHÜRMANN 1957 120 [wahrscheinlich LukR].

οὐκέτι 3/4 + 3 (Mt 2, Mk 7) — no longer

Word groups	Lk	Acts	Mt	Mk
οὐκέτι in a double negative (*SC*a; *VK*a)	20,40; 22,16*	8,39	1	6
οὐκέτι γάρ → οὐ/οὐδὲ/οὐδείς/οὔτε γάρ	20,40		0	0
οὐκέτι ... ἕως (*VK*c)	22,16*		0	1

οὖν 33/48 + 61/68 (Mt 56/58, Mk 5[6]/11)
1. therefore (Lk 8,18); 2. indeed (Acts 26,9); 3. but (Acts 2,30)

Word groups	Lk	Acts	Mt	Mk
εἰ (μὲν) οὖν (*SC*a; *VK*a); cf. ἐὰν οὖν Mt 5,19.25; 6,22; 24,26	11,13.36; 12,26; 16,11	11,17; 18,14*; 19,38; 25,11	3	0
εὐθέως οὖν		22,29	0	0
λέγω/εἶπον οὖν	3,7; 10,40; 13,18; 19,12		1	0
μὴ οὖν (*SC*d; *VK*f)	12,7*; 21,8*		5	0
νῦν οὖν BOISMARD 1984 Aa57		10,33[2]; 15,10; 16,36; 23,15	0	0
ὃς οὖν; cf. ὃς δή Mt 13,23		17,23	2	1
ὅταν οὖν (*SC*c; *VK*d)	11,34*		3	0
οὖν after imperative	3,8; 8,18; 10,2.40; 11,35; 13,7; 21,14	3,19; 8,22; 10,32; 13,40	10	1
οὖν in an interrogative phrase (*SC*f; *VK*m)	3,10; 7,31.42; 10,36*; 20,5*.15.17.33; 21,7; 22,70	15,10; 19,3; 21,22	11	3/4
οὖν καί → γὰρ καί DENAUX 2009 LA[n]	3,18	3,19	0	0
οὕτως οὖν; cf. οὕτως δέ Mt 20,26 *v.l.*; Mk 10,43	14,33		0	0
πάλιν οὖν → πάλιν δέ	23,20*		0	0
πᾶς οὖν → πᾶς τε	3,9		6	0
σὺ/ὑμεῖς οὖν	4,7; 12,40*; 22,70	23,21	1	0/1

τί οὖν ἐστιν;		21,22	0	0
τίς οὖν	3,10; 7,31.42; 10,36*; 20,5*.15.17	19,3; 21,22	4	3
οὖν in third place (*VK*n); see also μὲν/μὴ **οὖν**	12,40*; 13,14; 16,27; 20,5*.33	2,33; 19,3; 28,20	3/4	1/2

Characteristic of Luke
GASTON 1973 66 [Lked?]

	Lk	Acts	Mt	Mk
μὲν οὖν (γε) (*SC*e; *VK*k) →εἰ μὲν οὖν CREDNER 1836 137; HARNACK 1906 52	3,18	1,6.18; 2,41; 5,41; 8,4.25; 9,31; 11,19; 12,5; 13,4; 14,3; 15,3.30; 16,5; 17,12.17.30; 18,14*; 19,32.38; 23,18.22.31; 25,4.11; 26,4.9; 28,5	0	0[1]
→ὁ **μὲν** οὖν + part. + verb; ὁ **μὲν** οὖν + noun				

Literature
COLLISON 1977 111 [τίς οὖν: linguistic usage of Luke: likely]; DENAUX 2009 1Aⁿ [μὲν οὖν (γε)]; RADL 1975 417 [μὲν οὖν]; 421 [οὖν].

LARSEN, I., Notes on the Function of γάρ, οὖν, μέν, δέ, καί, and τέ in the Greek New Testament. — *Notes on Translation* (Dallas) 5 (1991) 35-47.
LEVISOHN, Stephen H., *Textual Connections in Acts*, 1987. Esp. 137-150: "*oun* and *men oun*".
PARKER, David C., The Translation of οὖν in the Old Latin Gospels. — *NTS* 31 (1985) 252-276.
READ-HEIMERDINGER, Jenny, *The Bezan Text of Acts*, 2002. Esp. 225-240: "οὖν, μέν and μὲν οὖν".
THRALL, Margaret E., *Greek Particles in the New Testament*, 1962. Esp. 10-11 [ἄρα/οὖν].

οὔπω 1 + 0/1 (Mt 2/3, Mk 5) — not yet

Word groups	Lk	Acts	Mt	Mk
οὔπω in a double negative (*SC*b; *VK*b)	23,53	8,16*	0	1
οὔπω γάρ (*VK*c)		8,16*	0	0

οὐράνιος 1 + 1 (Mt 7) — heavenly (Lk 2,13; Acts 26,19)

Characteristic of Luke	Lk	Acts	Mt	Mk
στρατιὰ οὐράνιος (*LN*: ranks of angels) → στρατιὰ τοῦ **οὐρανοῦ** VOGEL 1899C	2,13		0	0

οὐρανός 35/37 + 26 (Mt 82/86, Mk 17[18]/20)
1. sky (Acts 2,5); 2. heaven (Lk 11,13); 3. God (Lk 15,18.21)

Word groups	Lk	Acts	Mt	Mk
ἀναβλέπω εἰς τὸν οὐρανόν	9,16		1	2
ἀναλαμβάνω εἰς τὸν οὐρανόν VOGEL 1899B		1,11²; 10,16	0	0[1]
(δι)ἀνοίγω τὸν οὐρανόν	3,21	7,56; 10,11	1	0
ἀπὸ (τοῦ) οὐρανοῦ	9,54; 17,29; 21,11; 22,43	9,3 *v.l.*	2	1

	Lk	Acts	Mt	Mk
δυνάμεις τῶν οὐρανῶν; cf. αἱ δυνάμεις αἱ ἐν τοῖς οὐρανοῖς Mt 13,25	21,26		1	0
ἐκ (+) οὐρανοῦ	3,22; 10,18; 11.13.16; 17,24[1]; 20,4.5	2,2; 9,3; 11,5.9; 22,6	5	4
ἐν οὐρανῷ εἰρήνη	19,38		0	0
ἕως (τοῦ) οὐρανοῦ (VKh)	10,15		1	0
θησαυρὸς (+) ἐν οὐρανῷ / ἐν τοῖς οὐρανοῖς	12,33; 18,22		2	1
κλείω τὸν οὐρανόν	4,25		0	0
κύριος (+) (τοῦ) οὐρανοῦ καὶ (τῆς) γῆς (VKd)	10,21	17,24	1	0
οὐρανοί plural (SCa; VKa)	10,20; 11,2*; 12,33; 18,22; 21,26	2,34; 7,56	55/59	5/6
οὐρανός + γῆ (SCd; VKc)	4,25; 10,21; 11,2*; 12,56; 16,17; 21,33; 22,43(-44)	2,19; 4,24; 7,49; 10,12; 11,6; 14,15; 17,24	12/13	2
ὁ οὐρανὸς καὶ ἡ γῆ (LN: universe)	10,21; 12,56; 16,17; 21,33	4,24; 17,24	4	1
ὁ πατὴρ ὁ ἐν (τοῖς) οὐρανοῖς / ἐξ οὐρανοῦ (SCc); cf. πατὴρ ὁ οὐράνιος Mt 5,48; 6,14.26.32; 15,13; 18,35; 23,9	11,2*.13		13/15	1/2
πετεινὰ τοῦ οὐρανοῦ (LN: wild birds)	8,5; 9,58; 13,19	10,12; 11,6	3	1/2
πρόσωπον (+) τοῦ οὐρανοῦ (VKe) → πρόσωπον τῆς γῆς	12,56		1	0
στρατιὰ τοῦ οὐρανοῦ (LN: supernatural powers) → στρατιὰ οὐράνιος VOGEL 1899C		7,42	0	0
ἡ ὑπὸ τὸν οὐρανόν (LN: on earth; VKg)	17,24[1.2]		0	0

Characteristic of Luke	Lk	Acts	Mt	Mk
ὑπὸ τὸν οὐρανόν; cf. Col 1,23 VOGEL 1899C	17,24[1.2]	2,5; 4,12	0	0

Literature

COLLISON 1977 96-97 [noteworthy phenomena]; DENAUX 2009 LAⁿ [ὑπὸ τὸν οὐρανόν]; GERSDORF 1816 232-235 [καὶ ἐγένετο ὡς ἀπῆλθον ἀπ᾽ αὐτῶν εἰς τὸν οὐρανὸν οἱ ἄγγελοι]; JEREMIAS 1980 113-114 [οὐρανός sing.].

BAARDA, Heinrich, Friede im Himmel: Die lukanische Redaktion von Lk 19,38 und ihre Deutung. — ZNW 76 (1985) 170-186. [ἐν οὐρανῷ εἰρήνη καὶ δόξα ἐν ὑψίστοις]
SCHNEIDER, Gerhard, Engel und Blutschweiß (Lk 22,43-44): "Redaktionsgeschichte" im Dienste der Textkritik. — BZ NF 20 (1976) 112-116. Esp. 113-115: "Vokabular und Stil von Lk 22,43.44"; = ID., Lukas, Theologe der Heilsgeschichte, 1985, 153-157. Esp. 154-156.
TUCKETT, Christopher M., Luke 22,43-44: The "Agony" in the Garden and Luke's Gospel. — DENAUX, Adelbert (ed.), New Testament Textual Criticism and Exegesis. FS J. Delobel, 2002, 131-144. Esp. 133-135: "Vocabulary and style".

οὖς 7 + 5 (Mt 7, Mk 4/5)

1. ear (Lk 1,44); 2. hearing (Lk 4,21)

Word groups	Lk	Acts	Mt	Mk
ἀκούω + εἰς τὰ ὦτα (LN: hear in secret)		11,22	1	0

ἀπερίτμητος καρδίαις καὶ τοῖς ὠσίν (*LN*: obstinate)		7,51	0	0
ἔχω ὦτα (*LN*: be able to hear)	8,8; 14,35		3	3
οὖς (+) ἀκούω (*SC*a; *VK*a)	8,8; 12,3; 14,35	11,22; 28,27[1.2]	7	3/4
οὖς + ὀφθαλμός (*SC*b; *VK*c)		28,27[1.2]	3	1
πρὸς τὸ οὖς (*LN*: privately)	12,3		0	0
πρὸς τὸ οὖς λαλέω (*LN*: whisper)	12,3		0	0
συνέχω τὰ ὦτα (*LN*: refuse to listen)		7,57	0	0
τίθεμαι + εἰς τὰ ὦτα (*LN*: [a]listen carefully to; [b]remember well)	9,[b]44		0	0
τοῖς ὠσὶν βαρέως ἀκούω (*LN*: be mentally dull)		28,27	1	0
ὦτα ἀκούειν ἀκουέτω	8,8; 14,35		0/3	2/3

Characteristic of Luke	Lk	Acts	Mt	Mk
εἰς τὰ ὦτα (*LN*: privately); cf. ἐν τοῖς ὠσίν Lk 4,21; εἰς τὸ οὖς Mt 10,27 HARNACK 1906 139; PLUMMER 1922 lxii	1,44; 9,44	11,22	0	1

Literature

COLLISON 1977 66 [τίθημι + οὖς: noteworthy phenomena]; EASTON 1910 157 [οὖς / εἰς τὰ ὦτα: probably characteristic of L]; GERSDORF 1816 199 [ἐγένετο ἡ φωνή - εἰς τὰ ὦτά μου].

ULRICHS, Karl Friedrich, Some Notes on Ears in Luke-Acts especially in Lk. 4.21. — *BibNot* 98 (1999) 28-31. [NTA 44, 975]

οὐσία 2   property (Lk 15,12.13)

Characteristic of Luke

PLUMMER 1922 liii

Literature

DENAUX 2009 L[n]; HAUCK 1934 [seltenes Alleinwort].

BORMANN, Lukas, *Recht, Gerechtigkeit und Religion*, 2001. Esp. 160.

οὔτε 4/10 + 14/16 (Mt 6, Mk 4/5)   nor

Word groups	Lk	Acts	Mt	Mk
οὔτε γάρ (*VK*d)	20,36*	4,12*	0	0
οὔτε … ἔτι (*VK*h) → οὐκ/οὐδὲ … ἔτι	20,36*		0	0
οὔτε … τις → οὐ/οὐδὲ/οὐδείς … τις		24,12[1]; 25,8[3]; 28,21[2]	0	0
→ καὶ οὔτε				

Literature

RADL 1975 421.

οὗτος 229/243 + 237/246 (Mt 147/154, Mk 75[78]/89)   this

Word groups	Lk	Acts	Mt	Mk
ὁ αἰὼν οὗτος → αὕτη ἡ νύξ; ἡ ἡμέρα αὕτη; οὗτος καιρός; ὁ αἰὼν ἐκεῖνος; υἱοὶ τοῦ αἰῶνος τούτου	16,8; 20,34		1/3	0/1

ὁ ἀνὴρ οὗτος → ὁ ἄνθρωπος οὗτος; γυνὴ αὕτη; ὁ ἀνὴρ/ἄνθρωπος ἐκεῖνος BOISMARD 1984 Aa37		9,13; 19,37; 23,27; 24,5; 25,5*	0	0
αὕτη ἡ νύξ → ὁ αἰὼν οὗτος; ἡ ἡμέρα αὕτη; οὗτος καιρός; νὺξ ἐκείνη	12,20; 17,34	27,23	2	1/2
αὐτὸς (+) οὗτος/οὗτοι (VKg)		24,15.20; 25,25	0	0
ἄχρι τῆς ἡμέρας ταύτης → ἄχρι ἧς ἡμέρας BOISMARD 1984 Aa76		2,29; 23,1; 26,22	0	0
γενεὰ αὕτη	7,31; 11,29.30.31.32.50. 51; 17,25; 21,32		6	4
γυνὴ αὕτη → ὁ ἀνὴρ/ἄνθρωπος οὗτος; ἀνὴρ/ἄνθρωπος ἐκεῖνος	7,44[1]		0	0
ἡ πόλις αὕτη / αὕτη ἡ πόλις BOISMARD 1984 Ba17		4,27; 16,12; 18,10; 22,3	1	0
διὰ τοῦτο (SCg; VKk)	11,19.49; 12,22; 14,20	2,26	10/11	3
εἰς/ἐπὶ τοῦτο (VKl) → εἰς αὐτό/οὐδέν/τί	4,43	9,21[3]; 26,16	0	1
ἐν τούτῳ (SCk; VKp) DENAUX 2009 lA[n]	10,20	13,39; 24,16	0	0
ἕνεκα τούτων (SCh; VKm); cf. ἕνεκα /ἕνεκεν τούτου Mt 19,5; Mk 10,7		26,21	0	0
ἐπὶ τούτῳ (VKr)		3,12	0	0
ἕως τούτου (VKq)	22,51		0	0
καὶ οὗτος → καὶ αὐτός; cf. Jn 17,25; cf. καὶ ἐκεῖνος Mt 20,4; Mk 4,20	1,36; 2,12.38*; 3,20; 5,6; 7,12*; 8,13.41.42*; 12,31; 13,17; 16,1; 19,19; 20,12.28.30*; 22,56.59 24,40	1,9; 7,60[2]; 14,18; 15,15; 17,7; 19,40[2]; 20,36; 26,30*; 28,29*	1/2	2[3]
λόγος οὗτος → ῥῆμα τοῦτο; τὰ ῥήματα ταῦτα	4,36; 7,17; 9,28.44; 24,17.	2,22; 5,5.24[1]; 7,29; 8,21; 15,6; 16,36; 22,22	7	1
τῶν μικρῶν τούτων εἷς	17,2		4	1
ὁ + participle (+) οὗτος (SCd; VKe)	8,14; 9,48[2]; 12,5	15,38; 17,6.24	7/8	2
ὃς (+) οὗτος (SCc; VKc) → οὗτος ...,ὅς	9,24.26; 20,17[2].47	3,6; 4,10[1]; 8,32; 17,23	2	4/5
οὗτος as adjective coming before a noun (SCa; VKa)	1,24; 2,2; 7,44[1]; 9,48[1]; 12,20.31 v.l.; 13,6.8; 14,30; 15,24; 17,34; 18,11[2]; 22,15.20.37.42; 23,7; 24,21[2]	1,11; 2,32.36; 5,36; 7,35[1].60[1]; 10,30; 11,27; 14,15[2]; 15,17 v.l.. 28; 16,12.17[2].20; 17,19; 19,25.27; 21,38; 22,4.22; 23,1.13.18; 24,21; 27,23; 28,20[1].28	23/27	10
οὗτος before a number (VKb)	10,36	1,24	3	0
οὗτος + ἄλλος/ἐκεῖνος/ἕτερος/ κἀκεῖνος (SCe; VKf); cf. οὗτος + ὁ μέλλων Mt 12,32	7,8[1]; 11,42; 18,14; 20,(11-)12.16.34(-35)	5,37	3	3
οὗτος γάρ	6,23*.26*; 12,30[1]	26,16; 27, 34	3/4	1
οὗτος ὁ Ἰησοῦς BOISMARD 1984 Aa95		1,11; 2,32.36	0	0
οὗτος (+) καιρός → ὁ αἰὼν οὗτος; αὕτη ἡ νύξ; ἡ ἡμέρα αὕτη; ἐκεῖνος ὁ καιρός DENAUX 2009 L[n]	12,56; 18,30		0	

οὗτος ... ὅστις → **οὗτος** ... ὅς; cf. ὅστις ... οὗτος Mt 18,4	8,15	10,47; 16,17²; 17,11¹	1	0/1
ταῦτα in stead of τὰ αὐτά (VKh)	6,23*.26*; 17,30*		0	0
τοῦτ' + ἔστιν (LN: that means; SCf; VKj)		1,19; 19,14	1	1
τοῦτο subject of γίνεσθαι BOISMARD 1984 ca66		5,24²; 10,16; 11,10; 19,10.17; 28,9	3	1
τοῦτο (+) ἵνα	1,43	9,21³	0	0

→ ἀνταποκρίνομαι πρὸς ταῦτα; ἀπαγγέλλω τοὺς λόγους τούτους / τὰ ῥήματα ταῦτα / περὶ πάντων τούτων; ἄνδρες/ἄνθρωποι τῆς γενεᾶς ταύτης; ὁ λαὸς οὗτος

Characteristic of Luke

GASTON 1973 66 [Lked?]; HENDRIKS 1986 428.434.448; MORGENTHALER 1958LA; PLUMMER 1922 lxiii

	Lk	Acts	Mt	Mk
ὁ ἄνθρωπος οὗτος →ὁ ἀνὴρ **οὗτος**; γυνὴ **αὕτη**; ὁ ἀνὴρ/ἄνθρωπος ἐκεῖνος; cf. Jn 18,17.29 BOISMARD 1984 Bb61; DENAUX 2009 L***; GOULDER 1989*; HARNACK 1906 36; NEIRYNCK 1985	2,25; 14,30; 23,4.14¹·².47	4,16; 5,28².35.38¹; 6,13¹; 16,17².20; 22,26; 23,9; 26,31.32; 28,4	0	2
ἡ γραφὴ αὕτη BOISMARD 1984 cb104; NEIRYNCK 1985	4,21	8,35		1
ἐν ταῖς ἡμέραις ταύταις BOISMARD 1984 Ab34; DENAUX 2009 L***; GOULDER 1989; HARNACK 1906 138; HAWKINS 1909L; NEIRYNCK 1985; PLUMMER 1922 lii.lx	1,39; 6,12; 23,7; 24,18	1,15; 6,1; 11,27	0	0
ἡ ἡμέρα αὕτη / αἱ ἡμέραι αὗται → αὕτη ἡ νύξ; ἡ **ἡμέρα** ἐκείνη; αἱ ἡμέραι ἐκείναι; cf. Heb 1,2 BOISMARD 1984 Bb6; DENAUX 2009 L***; HARNACK 1906 52; NEIRYNCK 1985	1,24.39; 6,12; 19,42; 23,7; 24,18.21²	1,5.15; 2,29; 3,24; 5,36; 6,1; 11,27; 21,15.38; 23,1; 26,22	0	0
καὶ μετὰ ταῦτα; cf. Rev 15,5 BOISMARD 1984 Bb71; NEIRYNCK 1985	5,27; 12,4; 17,8	7,7¹; 13,20	0	0
καὶ οὗτος nominative → καὶ **αὐτός**; cf. Jn 17,25; cf. καὶ ἐκεῖνος Mt 20,4; Mk 4,20 BOISMARD 1984 Eb44; DENAUX 2009 L***; GOULDER 1989*; HAWKINS 1909L; NEIRYNCK 1985; PLUMMER 1922 lii	1,36; 2,12.38*; 7,12*; 8,13.41.42*; 16,1; 20,28.30*; 22,56.59	17,7	0	1
μετὰ ταῦτα (SCj; VKn) DENAUX 2009 L***; GOULDER 1989; HAWKINS 1909L	5,27; 10,1; 12,4; 17,8; 18,4	7,7¹; 13,20; 15,16; 18,1	0	0[2]
οὗτος contemptuous GOULDER 1989	4,22; 5,21; 7,31.39; 11,29.32.50.51; 13,2¹.4*.32; 15,2.30; 17,25; 18,11².27; 21,4¹; 23,2	1,18; 2,40; 6,13¹; 9,21¹; 16,20; 17,7; 18,13; 19,26; 21,28¹; 28,4	4	4
οὗτος ..., ὅς (SCc; VKc) → ὅς ... **οὗτος** **οὗτος** ... ὅστις DENAUX 2009 IA*	2,15.37*; 5,21; 6,3; 7,27.49; 8,13; 9,9; 13,16¹; 19,15; 21,6; 24,17.44	1,16*.25; 2,23.33.36; 3,16¹; 7,4.35¹.38.40; 17,3; 21,23; 24,5.8.21; 25,24; 28,4	4	2

ἡ παραβολὴ αὕτη DENAUX 2009 L***; GOULDER 1989*	4,23; 8,9.11; 12,41; 13,6; 15,3; 18,9; 20,9.19		2	1
ταῦτα in narrative texts DENAUX 2009 L***; HENDRIKS 1986 441.448	1,65; 2,19; 4,28; 5,27; 7,9; 8,8; 9,34; 10,1; 11,27.53*; 13,17; 14,6.15; 16,14; 18,23; 19,11.28; 23,49; 24,9.10.11.36	1,9; 5,5*.11; 7,54; 10,44; 11,18; 13,42; 14,18; 16,38; 17,8.11; 18,1; 19,21; 20,36; 21,12; 24,9.22*; 26,24.30*; 27,35; 28,29*	4	2
τοῦτον = him; cf. ταύτην Lk 13,15; τούτου Acts 13,23.38 DENAUX 2009 L***; HAWKINS 1909L	9,26; 12,5; 19,14; 20,12.13; 23,2.18	2,23; 3,16; 5,31.37; 7,35; 10,40; 13,27; 15,38; 16,3; 25,24	1	0
τὸ ῥῆμα τοῦτο → τὰ ῥήματα ταῦτα; λόγος οὗτος DENAUX 2009 L***; GOULDER 1989*	2,15; 9,451.2; 18,342		0	0
τὰ ῥήματα ταῦτα →ῥῆμα τοῦτο BOISMARD 1984 Ab29; DENAUX 2009 lA*; GOULDER 1989*; NEIRYNCK 1985	1,65; 2,19; 24,11	5,32; 10,44; 13,42; 16,38	0	0
ταῦτα/τοῦτο + verb of saying DENAUX 2009 L***	8,8; 9,34; 11,45; 13,17; 19,28; 23,46; 24,36.40 v.l.	1,8; 7,60; 14,18; 19,41; 20,36; 23,7; 27,35	2	1
τίς ἐστιν οὗτος ὅς DENAUX 2009 L***; PLUMMER 1922 lxiii	5,21; 7,49; 8,25; 9,9		1	1

→ ἀκούω ταῦτα; ἀπαγγέλλω ταῦτα

Literature

COLLISON 1977 139 [μετὰ ταῦτα: linguistic usage of Luke: probable]; 202 [anaphoric: certain]; 203 [αὐτός for οὗτος: probable; it may also have been a linguistic usage of Luke's "other source-material"]; 203-204 [contemptuous: linguistic usage of Luke's "other source-material": probable]; 204 [ἡ γενεὰ αὕτη: linguistic usage of Luke: certain; οὗτος + ῥῆμα: certain; τὴν παραβολὴν ταύτην: certain]; DENAUX 2009 Lan [οὗτος contemptuous], La[n] [καὶ μετὰ ταῦτα]; EASTON 1910 163-164 [τὴν παραβολὴν ταύτην: cited by Weiss as characteristic of L, and possibly corroborative]; GERSDORF 1816 195 [οὗτος ἔσται μέγας]; 196 [καὶ οὗτος μὴν ἕκτος]; 198 [ἀναστᾶσα δὲ Μαριὰμ ἐν ταῖς ἡμέραις ταύταις]; 213 [αὕτη ἀπογραφὴ πρώτη ἐγένετο]; 258 [καὶ ἦν Ἄννα προφῆτις - αὕτη προβεβηκυῖα - ζήσασα]; HARNACK 1906 36 [οὗτος to repeat the subject very common in Acts (8,26; 9,36; 10,6.32.36; 13,7; 14,9; 16,17; 18,25.26 etc.)]; HAUCK 1934 [Vorzugsverbindung: καὶ οὗτος/τοῦτο; μετὰ (δὲ) ταῦτα; ἐν ταῖς ἡμέραις ταύταις]; JEREMIAS 1980 53 [καὶ οὗτος: red.]; 183: "Stellt man die Belege für das Vorkommen von μετὰ ταῦτα in den Synoptikern zusammen, so erhält man ein eindeutiges Bild: einer Fehlanzeige bei Matthäus und Markus steht ein neunmaliges Vorkommen im Doppelwerk gegenüber"; 71 [τὸ ῥῆμα τοῦτο/ τὰ ῥήματα ταῦτα: ein Septuagintismus, der sich im NT nur in lk Doppelwerk findet]; 212: "Emphatisches τοῦτον/ταύτην ist kennzeichnend für das Doppelwerk"; RADL 1975 421 [οὗτος; ταῦτα; καὶ ταῦτα εἰπών; ὁ ἄνθρωπος οὗτος; ταύτῃ τῇ νυκτί]; 423 [περὶ τούτων]; REHKOPF 1959 62-63 [ἐᾶτε ἕως τούτου]; SCHÜRMANN 1953 10-11 [οὗτος, αὕτη, τοῦτο gewöhnlich nach dem Substantiv].

CIGNELLI, L. – PIERRI, R., *Sintassi di Greco biblico*. I.a, 2003. Esp. 68-74: "Concordanza dei pronomi dimostrativi" [ὅδε, οὗτος, ἐκεῖνος].

MEINERTZ, Max, "Dieses Geschlecht" im Neuen Testament. — *BZ* NF 1 (1957) 283-289.

SCHÜRMANN, Heinz, Lk 22,42a das älteste Zeugnis für Lk 22,20? — *MüTZ* 3 (1952) 185-188.

οὕτω(ς) 21/23 + 27 (Mt 32/33, Mk 10/11)

1. thus (Lk 1,25; Acts 23,11); 2. as follows (Acts 7,6); 3. so (degree) (Lk 9,15)

Word groups	Lk	Acts	Mt	Mk
ἐὰν … οὕτως (VKe)	19,31		0	0
καθώς + οὕτως (SCb; VKb) → καθώς + ὁμοίως DENAUX 2009 Lⁿ	11,30; 17,26; 24,24		0	0
καὶ οὕτως → καὶ **καθώς/ώς** BOISMARD 1984 Da12	24,46*	7,8; 17,33 v.l.; 27,44; 28,14	0	0
οὕτω (SCj)		23,11	0	0
οὕτως γάρ (SCe; VKk)		13,8.47; 20,13	3	0
οὕτως ἔσται	11,30; 15,7; 17,24.26	27,25	8	0
οὕτως ἔχω (SCh; VKn); cf. Rev 2,15 BOISMARD 1984 Aa60		7,1; 12,15; 17,11; 24,9	0	0
οὕτως (…) καί (SCd; VKj) → **καθώς/ὁμοίως/ώς/ὥσπερ** καί	11,30; 17,10.26; 21,31	23,11	5	2
οὕτως … ὃν τρόπον (VKd) BOISMARD 1984 Aa149		1,11; 27,25	0	0
οὕτως … ὅτι		7,6; 13,34	0	0
οὕτως οὖν (SCf; VKl); cf. οὕτως δέ Mt 20,26 v.l.; Mk 10,43	14,33		1	
οὕτως + ὥστε (VKh)		14,1	0	0
οὐχ (…) οὕτως (SCg; VKm); cf. οὐχί … οὕτως Mt 5,47*; οὐδέποτε … οὕτως Mt 9,33; Mk 2,12; οὐδὲ … οὕτως 14,59	22,26	8,32	2	1
πόσῳ μᾶλλον … οὕτως (SCc; VKf); cf. πολλῷ μᾶλλον οὕτως Mt 6,30	12,28		1	0
ὥσ(περ) + οὕτως (SCa; VKa)	17,24	8,32; 23,11	5	1

Literature

COLLISON 1977 161 [linguistic usage of Luke's "other source-material", but in 2 instances it is from the hand of Luke: nearly certain]; RADL 1975 411 [οὕτως ἔχω]; SCHÜRMANN 1955 35 [οὕτω(ς) καί]; 1957 73 [οὕτω(ς); οὕτως + εἶναι].

οὐχί 18 + 2/3 (Mt 9/10)

1. not (Lk 6,39); 2. marker of a question (Lk 4,22)

Word groups	Lk	Acts	Mt	Mk
ἀλλ' οὐχί (VKa) → ἀλλ' **οὐ/οὐδέ**	17,8		0	0
δοκεῖτε ὅτι …; οὐχί, λέγω ὑμῖν, ἀλλ'… DENAUX 2009 Lⁿ	12,51; 13,(2-)3.(4-)5		0	0
ἐὰν … οὐχί (SCc; VKk)	15,8		2	0
οὐχί in an interrogative phrase (SCd)	4,22; 6,39; 12,6; 14,28.31; 15,8; 17,8.17; 22,27; 23,39; 24,26.32	5,4; 7,50	9	0
οὐχὶ ἰδού (VKh)		2,7*	0	0
οὐχὶ μή (VKd) → **οὐ** μή	18,30		0	0

Characteristic of Luke

DENAUX 2009 L***; GOULDER 1989; MORGENTHALER 1958L

	Lk	Acts	Mt	Mk
οὐχὶ … ἀλλά (SCb; VKj) DENAUX 2009 L***; GOULDER 1989*; HAWKINS 1909L	1,60; 12,51; 13,3.5; 16,30		0	0
→ οὐχὶ **πρῶτον**				

Literature

COLLISON 1977 120 [linguistic usage of Luke's "other source-material": probable; οὐχὶ ἀλλά: certain]; EASTON 1910 149 [οὐχί, ἀλλά: especially characteristic of L]; GERSDORF 1816 204 [οὐχὶ ... ἀλλά: "so schreibt nur Lucas und Paulus"]; HAUCK 1934 [Vorzugswort]; REHKOPF 1959 96 [οὐχὶ ... ἀλλά (ἀλλ᾽ οὐχί): vorlukanisch]; SCHÜRMANN 1957 84 [luk R weniger wahrscheinlich]; 1961 283-284 [οὐχὶ ... ἀλλά (ἀλλ᾽ οὐχί)/οὐχί: protoluk R nicht beweisbar].

ὀφειλέτης 1 (Mt 2)

1. debtor; 2. one who must; 3. sinner (Lk 13,4)

Literature

PAFFENROTH 1997 82.

ὀφείλω 5 + 1 (Mt 6)

1. be in debt (Lk 7,41; 16,5.7); 2. must (Lk 17,10); 3. ought; 4. sin against (Lk 11,4)

Word groups	Lk	Acts	Mt	Mk
ὀφείλω + infinitive (*VK*a)	17,10	17,29	0	0

Literature

COLLISON 1977 59 [linguistic usage of Luke's "other source-material": probable]; PAFFENROTH 1997 82.

BORMANN, Lukas, *Recht, Gerechtigkeit und Religion*, 2001. Esp. 160-161.

ὀφθαλμός 17 + 7 (Mt 24/26, Mk 7)

1. eye (Lk 4,20); 2. sight (Acts 1,9); 3. understanding (Lk 19,42)

Word groups	Lk	Acts	Mt	Mk
(δι)ἀνοίγω (+) τοὺς ὀφθαλμούς (*LN*: cause to be able to see; *SC*d; *VK*e) → ἐπαίρω τοὺς ὀφθαλμούς; διανοίγω τὴν **καρδίαν** / τὸν **νοῦν**	24,31	9,8.40; 26,18	2	0
καμμύω τοὺς ὀφθαλμούς (*LN*: refuse to learn)		28,27	1	0
ὀφθαλμός + ἀτενίζω (*SC*c; *VK*c)	4,20		0	0
ὀφθαλμός + (ἀνα/δια)βλέπω (*SC*b; *VK*b)	6,41[1].42[2.4]; 10,23	1,9; 9,8.18	2/3	2
ὀφθαλμός + ὁράω/εἶδον (*SC*a; *VK*a)	2,30; 16,23	9,40; 28,27[2]	2	0
ὀφθαλμός + οὖς		28,27[1.2]	3	1
ὀφθαλμὸς πονηρός (*LN*: [a]jealous; [b]stingy; *SC*e; *VK*f)	11,34[2]		2	1

Characteristic of Luke	Lk	Acts	Mt	Mk
ἐπαίρω τοὺς ὀφθαλμούς (*LN*: look; *SC*f) → (δι) ἀνοίγω τοὺς ὀφθαλμούς; (ἐπ)αίρω τὴν **φωνήν** GOULDER 1989	6,20; 16,23; 18,13		1	0

Literature

REHKOPF 1959 96 [ὀφθαλμοὺς ἐπαίρειν: vorlukanisch]; SCHÜRMANN 1961 284 [ὀφθαλμοὺς ἐπαίρειν: protoluk R nicht beweisbar].

CHILTON, Bruce, Announcement in Nazara, 1981. Esp. 159.

VALLAURI, Emiliano, ... Alzati gli occhi ... (Lc. 6,20; Giov. 6,5). — *BibOr* 27 (1985) 163-169.

ὄφις 2 (Mt 3, Mk 0[1])

1. snake (Lk 10,19; 11,11); 2. evil person

Word groups	Lk	Acts	Mt	Mk
ὄφις + σκορπίος	10,19; 11,11(-12)		0	0

Literature

GRELOT, Pierre, Étude critique de Luc 10,19. — *RechSR* 69 (1981) 87-100. Esp. 92-96: "Pourquoi des serpents et des scorpions?".

ὀφρύς 1

cliff (Lk 4,29)

Literature

HAUCK 1934 [seltenes Alleinwort].

ὄχλος 41 + 22 (Mt 50, Mk 38/39)

1. crowd (Lk 5,29); 2. common people

Word groups	Lk	Acts	Mt	Mk
ἀνὴρ ἀπὸ τοῦ ὄχλου / γυνὴ/τις ἐκ τοῦ ὄχλου DENAUX 2009 Lⁿ	9,38; 11,27; 12,13		0	0
ἀπολύω τὸν ὄχλον; cf. ἀπολύω τοὺς ὄχλους Mt 14,15.22.23; 15,39	9,12		0	1
ἄτερ ὄχλου (*VK*j)	22,6		0	0
διὰ τὸν ὄχλον → ἀπὸ/ἐκ τοῦ **ὄχλου**	5,19; 8,19		0	2
ἐκ τοῦ ὄχλου → ἀπὸ τοῦ **ὄχλου**; διὰ τὸν **ὄχλον**	11,27; 12,13	19,33	0	1
μετὰ ὄχλου (*VK*k)		24,18	0	0
μυριάδες τοῦ ὄχλου (*VK*h)	12,1		0	0
ὄχλοι πολλοί (*SC*b; *VK*b) → **ὄχλος** πολύς; πάντες οἱ **ὄχλοι**	5,15; 14,25		6/7	0
ὄχλος in a constructio ad sensum (*VK*l)	6,19	6,7	1	1
ὄχλος + ἀκολουθέω/συμπαραγίνομαι/συμπνίγω/ συμπορεύομαι/συναντάω/σύνειμι/συνέρχομαι/ συνεφίστημι/συνέχω → **πλῆθος** + ἀκολουθέω/συνάγω/συνέρχομαι	5,15; 7,9.11; 8,4.42.45; 9,11.37; 14,25; 23,48	16,22	7	3
ὄχλος + μαθητής	6,17; 7,11; 9,16.18; 12,1; 19,39	6,7; 11,26	9	9
ὄχλος + μαθητῶν	6,17		0	0
ὄχλος (+) πολύς (*SC*a; *VK*a) → **ὄχλοι** πολλοί; πᾶς ὁ **ὄχλος**; **πλῆθος** πολύ; cf. ὄχλος πλεῖστος Mt 21,8; Mk 4,1	5,29; 6,17; 7,11; 8,4; 9,37	6,7	3	6/8
πάντες οἱ + ὄχλοι (*SC*d; *VK*d) → **ὄχλοι** πολλοί	23,48		1	0
πᾶς ὁ ὄχλος (*SC*c; *VK*c) → **ὄχλος** πολύς; πάντα τὰ **ἔθνη**; ἄπας/ὅλος/πᾶς ὁ **λαός**; ἅπαν/πᾶν τὸ **πλῆθος**	6,19; 13,17	21,27	1	4/5

Characteristic of Luke

GASTON 1973 64 [Lked]

	Lk	Acts	Mt	Mk
ἀπὸ τοῦ ὄχλου → διὰ τὸν **ὄχλον**; ἐκ τοῦ **ὄχλου** GOULDER 1989	9,38; 19,3.39		0	2
ὄχλοι plural VOGEL 1899D	3,7.10; 4,42; 5,3.15; 7,24; 8,42.45; 9,11.18; 11,14.29; 12,54; 14,25; 23,4.48	8,6; 13,45; 14,11.13.18.19; 17,13	29	1

ὄχλος + genitive BOISMARD 1984 Ab58; NEIRYNCK 1985	5,29; 6,17; 7,12	1,15; 6,7	0	0
ὄχλος ἱκανός (SCe; VKe) BOISMARD 1984 Bb116; NEIRYNCK 1985	7,12	11,24.26; 19,26	0	1

Literature

VON BENDEMANN 2001 420: "Der Plural ὄχλοι ist typisch lukanisch"; DENAUX 2009 lAn [ὄχλος ἱκανός], Laⁿ [ὄχλος + genitive]; JEREMIAS 1980 104: "οἱ ὄχλοι plural: red.]; 157: "ὄχλος mit folgendem Genitiv findet sich im NT nur im Doppelwerk"; 158 [ὄχλος ἱκανός: red.]; RADL 1975 422 [ὄχλος; ὄχλοι].

CITRON, Bernhard, The Multitude in the Synoptic Gospels. — ScotJT 7 (1954) 408-418.
Esp. 409-411: "Terminology" [πλῆθος, λαός, ὄχλος].
DAUBE, David, ὄχλος in Mark ii.4 (Luke v.19). — ExpT 50 (1938-39) 138-139.
MAHFOUZ, Hady, La fonction littéraire et théologique de Lc 3,1-20, 2003. Esp. 177-178.
PARK, Tae-Sik, ῎Οχλος im Neuen Testament. Diss. Göttingen, 1994, 362 p.

ὀψώνιον 1

1. pay (Lk 3,14); 2. money for support; 3. result

Literature

HAUCK 1934 [seltenes Alleinwort].

BORMANN, Lukas, Recht, Gerechtigkeit und Religion, 2001. Esp. 161.
CARAGOUNIS, Chrys, Opsōnion: A Reconsideration of Its Meaning. — NT 16 (1974) 35-57. [NTA 19, 31]

Π

παγίς 1

1. snare (Lk 21,35); 2. danger; 3. control

Literature

HAUCK 1934 [seltenes Alleinwort].

παιδεύω 2 + 2

1. teach (Acts 7,22); 2. discipline; 3. punish (Lk 23,16.22)

Word groups	Lk	Acts	Mt	Mk
παιδεύομαι passive (VKa)		7,22; 22,3	0	0

Characteristic of Luke

BOISMARD 1984 Db26; DENAUX 2009 LA*; NEIRYNCK 1985

παιδίον 13/14 (Mt 18, Mk 12)

1. child (generic) (Lk 2,27); 2. child (own) (Lk 11,7); 3. child (endearment)

Word groups	Lk	Acts	Mt	Mk
John the Baptist as παιδίον → Ἰησοῦς ὁ παῖς	1,59.66.76.80		0	0
DENAUX Ln				
Jesus as παιδίον → Ἰησοῦς ὁ παῖς	2,17.22*.27.40		9	0
παιδίον + γονεῖς (VKe) → τέκνον + γονεῖς	2,27		0	0
παιδίον + μήτηρ (SCb; VKb)	1,59(-60)		5	1
παιδίον + πατήρ (SCd; VKd)	1,59		0	2

Literature

GERSDORF 1816 263 [τὸ δὲ παιδίον - ἐκραταιοῦτο - πληρούμενον σοφία]; REHKOPF 1959 96 [vorlukanisch]; 99 [παιδίον: "Substantiva in Anrede bei den Synoptikern"]; SCHÜRMANN 1961 273.

KILPATRICK, George D., Style and Text, 1967. Esp. 157-159; = ID., Principles and Practice, 1990. Esp. 59-61.

παιδίσκη 2 + 2 (Mt 1, Mk 2)   slave girl (Lk 12,45; 22,56; Acts 12,13; 16,16)

Word groups	Lk	Acts	Mt	Mk
παιδίσκη + παῖς (VKb)	12,45		0	0
παιδίσκη τις	22,56	16,16	0	0
DENAUX 2009 LA[n]				

Literature

HAUCK 1934 [Vorzugsverbindung: παιδίσκη τις].

παῖς 9 + 6 (Mt 8)

1. child (generic) (Lk 8,51); 2. child (own); 3. slave (Lk 7,7)

Word groups	Lk	Acts	Mt	Mk
ἅγιος παῖς		4,27.30	0	0
Ἰησοῦς ὁ παῖς → Ἰησοῦς τὸ παιδίον	2,43		0	0
παῖς Δαυίδ	1,69	4,25	0	0
DENAUX 2009 LA[n]				
παῖς + μήτηρ/πατήρ (SCb; VKb)	2,43 v.l.; 8,51; 9,42	4,25	0	0
DENAUX 2009 La[n]				
παῖς + παιδίσκη (VKc)	12,45		0	0
David as παῖς τοῦ θεοῦ (SCe; VKe)	1,69		0	0
Israel as παῖς τοῦ θεοῦ (SCd; VKe)	1,54	4,25	0	0
DENAUX 2009 LA[n]				

Characteristic of Luke	Lk	Acts	Mt	Mk
Jesus as παῖς τοῦ θεοῦ (SCc; VKd)		3,13.26; 4,27.30	1	0
BOISMARD 1984 Ab39; CREDNER 1836 140; NEIRYNCK 1985; PLUMMER 1922 lx				
ἡ παῖς (SCa; VKa)	8,51.54		0	0
PLUMMER 1922 liii				

Literature

BDAG 2000 750-751 [literature: Jesus as παῖς τοῦ θεοῦ]; DENAUX 2009 L[n] [ἡ παῖς]; GERSDORF 1816 200 [ἀντελάβετο Ἰσραὴλ παιδὸς αὐτοῦ]; 206-207 [Δαυὶδ (τοῦ) παιδὸς αὐτοῦ]; JEREMIAS 1980 62: "Παῖς θεοῦ als archaisierende theokratische Prädikation für Israel, David, Jesus findet sich im NT außer in einem LXX-Zitat (Mt 12,18 cit. Jes 42,1) nur im traditionellen Formelgut des Doppelwerkes".

DIMONT, C.T., Children or Servants? (Luke xi.7). — *ExpT* 9 (1897-98) 382.

KILPATRICK, George D., Style and Text, 1967. Esp. 157-159; = ID., *Principles and Practice*, 1990. Esp. 59-61.

READ-HEIMERDINGER, Jenny, *The Bezan Text of Acts*, 2002. Esp. 254-274: "Titles of Jesus" [(ὁ) Ἰησοῦς; Ἰησοῦς ὁ Ναζωραῖος; ὁ παῖς; ὁ ἅγιος παῖς σου Ἰησοῦς; (ὁ) Χριστός; Χριστὸς Ἰησοῦς; Ἰησοῦς Χριστός; Ἰησοῦς Χριστὸς ὁ Ναζωραῖος; (ὁ) κύριος; (ὁ) κύριος Ἰησοῦς; ὁ κύριος Ἰησοῦς Χριστός].

SOUTER, A., The Translation of παῖς, etc., in the English Bible. — *ExpT* 9 (1897-98) 240, 382.

SPARKS, Hedley Frederik Davis, The Centurion's παῖς. — *JTS* 42 (1941) 179-181.

παίω 1 (Mt 1, Mk 1)

1. hit (Lk 22,64); 2. sting

Literature

NEIRYNCK, Frans, Τίς ἐστιν ὁ παίσας σε: Mt 26,68/Lk 22,64 (diff. Mc 14,65). — *ETL* 63 (1987) 5-47; = ID., *Evangelica II*, 1991, 95-138.

—, Goulder and the Minor Agreements. — *ETL* 73 (1997) 84-93. Esp. 85 [Lk 6,19 πάντας; Lk 4,15 αὐτῶν]; 91-92 [τίς ἐστιν ὁ παίσας σε;]. [NTA 42, 185]; = ID., *Evangelica III*, 2001, 307-318. Esp. 308-309; 315-317.

πάλαι 1 (Mt 1, Mk 1/2)

1. long ago (Lk 10,13); 2. all the time; 3. already

παλαιός 5 (Mt 3, Mk 3)

1. old (time) (Lk 5,36$^{1.2}$.37.39$^{1.2}$); 2. old (class); 3. long ago

Word groups	Lk	Acts	Mt	Mk
παλαιός + καινός/νέος (*VKc*)	5,36$^{1.2}$.37.39^{1}		2	2

Literature

DUPONT, Jacques, Vin vieux, vin nouveaux (Luc 5,39). — *CBQ* 25 (1963) 286-304. Esp. 286 n. 1.

παλαιόω 1   (Lk 12,33)

1. make old; παλαιόομαι: 1. become old

Literature

HAUCK 1934 [seltenes Alleinwort].

πάλιν 3 + 5/6 (Mt 17/18, Mk 28/29)

1. again (Lk 6,43; 13,20; 23,20); 2. also; 3. on the other hand

Word groups	Lk	Acts	Mt	Mk
πάλιν δέ (SCa; VKb)	23,20	18,21 v.l.	2	0
πάλιν ἐκ δευτέρου (SCb; VKf)		10,15	1	0
πάλιν οὖν (VKc)	23,20 v.l.		0	0

Literature

COLLISON 1977 163 [noteworthy phenomena].

MATEOS, Juan, Contribuciones al DGENT (Diccionario Griego-Español del Nuevo Testamento): Πάλιν en el Nuevo Testamento. — FilolNT 7 (1994) 65-80. Esp. 65-68: "Datos de los Diccionarios" [Zorell, Bauer-Aland, Louw-Nida]; 68-78: "Analisis del lexema".

παμπληθεί 1   all together (Lk 23,18)

Literature

HAUCK 1934 [seltenes Alleinwort].

πανδοχεῖον* 1   inn (Lk 10,34)

Literature

HAUCK 1934 [seltenes Alleinwort].

ROYSE, James R., A Philonic Use of πανδοχεῖον (Lk x 34). — NT 23 (1981) 193-194.

πανδοχεύς* 1   innkeeper (Lk 10,35)

Literature

HAUCK 1934 [seltenes Alleinwort].

πανοπλία 1   weapens and armor (Lk 11,22)

πανουργία 1   treachery (Lk 20,23)

Literature

HAUCK 1934 [seltenes Alleinwort].

BORMANN, Lukas, Recht, Gerechtigkeit und Religion, 2001. Esp. 204.

πανταχοῦ 1 + 3/4 (Mk 1[2])   everywhere (Lk 9,6)

Word groups	Lk	Acts	Mt	Mk
πανταχοῦ + πᾶς/πάντη (VKa)		17,30; 21,28*; 24,3	0	0

Characteristic of Luke; cf. πανταχῇ Acts 21,28	Lk	Acts	Mt	Mk
πανταχοῦ/πανταχῇ BOISMARD 1984 cb79; NEIRYNCK 1985	9,6	17,30;21,28; 24,3; 28,22	0	0
πανταχοῦ PLUMMER 1922 lx; VOGEL 1899B	9,6	17,30; 24,3; 28,22		

Literature

DENAUX 2009 1An; JEREMIAS 1980 276 [red.].

παντελής 1

1. forever; 2. completely (Lk 13,11)

Word groups	Lk	Acts	Mt	Mk
εἰς τὸ παντελές (*LN*: [a]forever; [b]completely); cf. Heb 7,25	13,[b]11		0	0

πάντοθεν 1 (Mk 1)

1. from all directions (Lk 19,43); 2. all over

πάντοτε 2 (Mt 2, Mk 2/3) — always

Word groups	Lk	Acts	Mt	Mk
πάντοτε + πᾶς (*VK*g)	15,31		0	0
πάντοτε προσεύχομαι (*VK*f)	18,1		0	0

πάντως 1 + 2/3

1. certainly (Lk 4,23; Acts 21,22; 28,4); 2. indeed

Characteristic of Luke

BOISMARD 1984 Db34; HARNACK 1906 40.52; NEIRYNCK 1985

Literature

DENAUX 2009 1A[n]; JEREMIAS 1980 124: "Da Lukas eine Vorliebe für Wendungen mit πᾶς hat, entspricht das Adverb πάντως seinem Sprachgefühl".

LEE, G.M., Πάντως "Perhaps"? — *ZNW* 64 (1973) 152.
LEE, G.M., Further on Πάντως "Perhaps"? — *NT* 19 (1977) 240. [NTA 22, 347] [Lk 4,23]

παρά 29/30 + 29/35 (Mt 18/20, Mk 16[17])

1. at (location) (Lk 9,47; Acts 16,13); 2. among (location); 3. from (extension) (Lk 2,1; 6,19); 4. from (source) (Acts 3,2); 5. for (agent) (Lk 1,37); 6. in opinion of (viewpoint participation) (Lk 1,30); 7. contrary to (opposition) (Acts 18,13); 8. instead of (contrast); 9. with (association) (Lk 11,37); 10. because of (reason); 11. beyond (degree) (Lk 13,2); 12. less (quantity)

Word groups	Lk	Acts	Mt	Mk
ὁ παρά (*VK*a)	10,7		0	3
παρά + genitive	**Lk**	**Acts**	**Mt**	**Mk**
ὁ παρά + genitive (*SC*aa)	10,7		0	2
others with genitive (*SC*a)	1,37.45; 2,1; 6,19.34; 8,49; 11,16; 12,48	2,33; 3,2.5; 7,16; 9,2.14; 10,22; 17,9; 20,24; 22,5.30*; 24,8; 26,10.12*.22*; 28,22	5/6	5[6]

→ ἀκούω παρά; ἀπολαμβάνω παρά; ἐν + παρά; ἐξέρχομαι παρά; ἔρχομαι παρά

παρά + dative	Lk	Acts	Mt	Mk
παρά concerning persons (SCb; VKc)	1,30.37 v.l.; 2,52; 9,47; 11,37; 18,27[1.2]; 19,7	9,43; 10,6[1]; 18,3.20*; 21,7.8.16; 26,8; 28,14	6/7	3
παρ' ἑαυτῷ (VKd)	9,47		0/1	0
→ εἰμι παρά; ἐν + παρά; μένω παρά				

παρά + accusative	Lk	Acts	Mt	Mk
παρά adversative (SCcc; VKj)		18,13	0	0
παρά with reference to location (SCca; VKg)	5,1.2; 7,38; 8,5.12.35.41; 10,39*; 17,16; 18,35	4,35.37*; 5,2.10*; 7,58; 10,6[2].32; 16,13; 22,3	7	7
τίθημι παρὰ τοὺς πόδας (LN: turn over to) → τίθημι πρὸς τοὺς πόδας; cf. ἀποτίθεμαι παρὰ τοὺς πόδας Acts 7,58		4,35.37*; 5,2	0	0
→ εἰς + παρά; ἐν + παρά; ἐξέρχομαι παρά; ἔρχομαι παρά; ἵστημι παρὰ τοὺς πόδας; κάθημαι παρά; παρὰ τὸν νόμον; παρὰ τὴν ὁδόν; πίπτω παρά; πλείων παρά; ἀνατρέφομαι παρὰ τοὺς πόδας; τίθημι παρά				

Characteristic of Luke	Lk	Acts	Mt	Mk
παρά in a comparison (SCcb; VKh) DENAUX 2009 L***; GOULDER 1989; HAWKINS 1909L	3,13; 13,2.4; 18,14		0	0
παρὰ τοὺς πόδας BOISMARD 1984 Bb22; DENAUX 2009 L***; GOULDER 1989*; HAWKINS 1909L; NEIRYNCK 1985; PLUMMER 1922 lxiii	7,38; 8,35.41; 10,39*; 17,16	4,35.37*; 5,2.10*; 7,58; 22,3	1	0
→ λαμβάνω παρά; πίπτω παρὰ τοὺς πόδας; χάρις παρὰ θεῷ				

Literature

BDR § 245: "Umschreibung der Steigerungsform durch den Positiv. 3. "Positiv statt Komparativ. a) wenn die Vergleichung mit παρά oder ὑπέρ geschieht"; COLLISON 1977 140 [παρά + accusative = comparative particle: linguistic usage of Luke's "other source-material": likely]; EASTON 1910 149 [παρά + acc. in the sense of 'beyond': especially characteristic of L]; 167 [παρὰ τοὺς πόδας: classed by Weiss as characteristic of L on insufficient (?) evidence]; HAUCK 1934 [Vorzugsverbindung: παρὰ τοὺς πόδας]; JEREMIAS 1980 54 [1,37 red.: οὐκ ἀδυνατήσει παρὰ τοῦ θεοῦ πᾶν ῥῆμα: ist ein freies Zitat von Gen 18,14 LXX: μὴ ἀδυνατεῖ παρὰ τῷ θεῷ ῥῆμα; Lukas hat ein πᾶν zugefügt und παρά mit dem Genitiv (LXX: Dativ) konstruiert. Sowohl das stilistische Feilen am LXX-Text wie die Verstärkung durch πᾶς ist typisch lukanisch"; 168: "παρὰ τοὺς πόδας ist eine lk Vorzugswendung"; PAFFENROTH 1997 88 [παρά (with acc., comparative), dative (instead of πρός + acc.); RADL 1975 417 [μένω παρά + dat.]; 422 [παρά + gen.]; REHKOPF 1959 96 [παρά c. Akk.: vorlukanisch]; SCHÜRMANN 1961 271 [παρά c. acc.].

JUNG, Chang-Wook, Infancy Narrative, 2004. Esp. 116-119 [παρά + gen.: Lk 1,37].

παραβιάζομαι 1 + 1 | urge

Word groups	Lk	Acts	Mt	Mk
παραβιάζομαι + εἰσέρχομαι → ἀναγκάζω/παρακαλέω + εἰσέρχομαι	24,29	16,15	0	0
παραβιάζομαι + λέγων	24,29		0	0

Characteristic of Luke

BOISMARD 1984 Ab190; HARNACK 1906 35.54; HAWKINS 1909LA; MORGENTHALER 1958*; NEIRYNCK 1985; PLUMMER 1922 liii; VOGEL 1899A

Literature

DENAUX 2009 LAⁿ; HAUCK 1934 [seltenes Alleinwort]; JEREMIAS 1980 69 [παραβιάζομαι + λέγων: red.]; 318 [red.].

παραβολή 18 (Mt 17, Mk 13)

1. parable (Lk 8,10); 2. archetype

Word groups	Lk	Acts	Mt	Mk
διὰ παραβολῆς (VKb)	8,4		0	0
ἐν παραβολαῖς (SCa; VKa)	8,10		6	4
λέγω παραβολήν + λέγων	14,7; 18,1(-2)		0	0

Characteristic of Luke

GASTON 1973 64 [Lked]

	Lk	Acts	Mt	Mk
λέγω (+) παραβολήν DENAUX 2009 L***; HAWKINS 1909L; PLUMMER 1922 lx	5,36; 12,41; 13,6; 14,7; 18,1; 20,9		0	0
εἶπεν (+) παραβολήν; cf. εἶπεν διὰ παραβολῆς Lk 8,4 DENAUX 2009 L***; GOULDER 1989*; HAWKINS 1909L; PLUMMER 1922 lii.lx	6,39; 12,16; 15,3; 18,9; 19,11; 20,19; 21,29		0	1
παραβολὴ (+) αὕτη DENAUX 2009 L***; GOULDER 1989*	4,23; 8.9.11; 12,41; 13,6; 15,3; 18,9; 20,9.19		2	1
τὴν παραβολὴν ταύτην DENAUX 2009 L***	4,23; 12,41; 13,6; 15,3; 18,9; 20,9.19	0	1	1

Literature

COLLISON 1977 204 [τὴν παραβολὴν ταύτην: linguistic usage of Luke: certain]; EASTON 1910 163-164 [τὴν παραβολὴν ταύτην: cited by Weiss as characteristic of L, and possibly corroborative]; HAUCK 1934 [Vorzugsverbindung: λέγω/εἶπον παραβολήν (πρός)]; JEREMIAS 1980 69 [λέγω παραβολήν + λέγων: red.]; 124: "λέγειν/εἰπεῖν παραβολήν ist eine lk Vorzugswendung".

HATCH, Edwin, *Essays*, 1889. Esp. 64-71.
SIDER, John W., The Meaning of *Parabole* in the Usage of the Synoptic Evangelists. — *Bib* 62 (1981) 453-470.

παραγγέλλω 4 + 11 (Mt 2, Mk 2[3])   command

Word groups	Lk	Acts	Mt	Mk
παραγγέλλω + λέγω/εἶπον → **ἀπαγγέλλω/ἐπιτιμάω** + λέγω/ εἶπον; cf. διαστέλλομαι + λέγω Mk 8,15; ἐντέλλομαι + λέγω Mt 17,9	5,14; 8,56; 9,21		1	0
παραγγελίᾳ παραγγέλλω (VKa) HARNACK 1906 43		5,28	0	0
παραγγέλλω + aorist infinitive (VKc); cf. 1 Cor 7,10 DENAUX 2009 Lan	5,14; 8,29. 56; 9,21 v.l.	10,42; 16,18; 23,22	1	1

Characteristic of Luke

GASTON 1973 64 [Lked]; MORGENTHALER 1958A; PLUMMER 1922 lx

	Lk	Acts	Mt	Mk
παραγγέλλω + present infinitive (*VK*b); cf. 2 Thess 3,6; 1 Tim 1,3; 6,17 BOISMARD 1984 cb60; NEIRYNCK 1985	9,21	1,4; 4,18; 5,28.40; 15,5; 16,23; 17,30; 23,30	0	0
παραγγέλλω + ἐξελθεῖν BOISMARD 1984 Ab191; NEIRYNCK 1985	8,29	16,18	0	0
παραγγέλλω μηδενί + verb of saying BOISMARD 1984 Ab93; NEIRYNCK 1985	5,14; 8,56; 9,21	23,22	0	0

Literature

COLLISON 1977 59 [linguistic usage of Luke: probable]; DENAUX 2009 lAn; lA[n] [παραγγέλλω + present infinitive], LA[n] [παραγγέλλω + ἐξελθεῖν], La[n] [παραγγέλλω μηδενί + verb of saying]; HAUCK 1934 [Vorzugswort]; RADL 1975 422.

BORMANN, Lukas, *Recht, Gerechtigkeit und Religion*, 2001. Esp. 136.
MAKUJINA, John, Verbs Meaning "Command" in the New Testament: Determining the Factors Involved in the Choice of Command-Verbs. — *EstBíb* 56 (1998) 357-369. Esp. 358-359: "Παραγγέλλω"; 359-361: "Κελεύω"; 361-362: "Ἐντέλλω"; 362-364: "Διαστέλλω"; 364-366: "-τάσσω complex"; 366-367: "Λέγω". [NTA 43, 57]

παραγίνομαι 8 + 20/21 (Mt 3, Mk 1)

1. come (Lk 7,4); 2. come to help; 3. appear in a place (Acts 25,7)

Word groups

	Lk	Acts	Mt	Mk
ὅς/ὅστις παραγενόμενος + verb BOISMARD 1984 Aa61		9,39; 10,32*; 11,23; 17,10; 18,27	0	0
παραγενόμενος δέ + subject → γενομένης δέ + subject DENAUX 2009 lA[n]	7,20	5,21.25; 25,7	0	0
παραγίνομαι εἰς; cf. Jn 8,2 BOISMARD 1984 ca16		9,26; 13,14; 15,4; 17,10	1	0
παραγίνομαι + (τοῦ +) infinitive (*VK*b)	12,51		1	0
παρεγένετο δέ → ἐγένετο δέ DENAUX 2009 L[n]	8,19; 19,16		0	0

Characteristic of Luke

BOISMARD 1984 cb10; DENAUX 2009 L***; GOULDER 1989*; HAWKINS 1909L; MORGENTHALER 1958A; NEIRYNCK 1985; PLUMMER 1922 lx

	Lk	Acts	Mt	Mk
(καὶ) παραγενόμενος (δέ), in the beginning of a sentence BOISMARD 1984 Ab19; DENAUX 2009 lA*; NEIRYNCK 1985	7,20; 14,21	5,21.25; 9,26; 14,27; 15,4; 25,7	0	0
παραγενόμενος + ἀπαγγέλλω; cf. παραγίνομαι + ἀπαγγέλλω Lk 8,19(-20); Acts 5,22; παραγίνομαι + ἀναγγέλλω Acts 14,27; 15,4 BOISMARD 1984 Ab94; NEIRYNCK 1985	14,21	5,25; 23,16; 28,21	0	0
παραγίνομαι absolute use (*VK*a) DENAUX 2009 lA*	14,21; 19,16	5,21.22.25; 9,39; 10,32*.33; 11,23; 14,27; 18,27; 21,18; 23,16.35; 24,17.24; 25,7; 28,21	1	1
παραγίνομαι πρός BOISMARD 1984 Bb74; CREDNER 1836 138; DENAUX 2009 La*; NEIRYNCK 1985; VOGEL 1899B	7,4.20; 8,19; 11,6	20,18	0	0

Literature

VON BENDEMANN 2001 413: "Παραγίνεσθαι ... mit πρός konstruiert findet sich das Verb mit Ausnahme von Mt 3,13 nur im lukanischen Doppelwerk"; COLLISON 1977 96-97 [noteworthy phenomena]; DENAUX 2009 [IAⁿ : παραγενόμενος + ἀπαγγέλλω]; EASTON 1910 164 [cited by Weiss as characteristic of L, and possibly corroborative]; HAUCK 1934 [Vorzugswort]; JEREMIAS 1980 152: "Die Statistik weist παραγίνομαι als markantes lukanisches Vorzugswort aus"; 153: "Vorzugsweise benutzt er das Partizip von παραγίνομαι als Übergangswendung... Die Konstruktion παραγίνομαι πρός τινα findet sich außer Mt 3,13 nur im Doppelwerk"; RADL 1975 422 [παραγίνομαι; παραγενόμενος].

παράδεισος 1 | paradise (Lk 23,43)

παραδίδωμι 17 + 13/14 (Mt 31/32, Mk 20)

1. give over (Lk 4,6); 2. betray, hand over (Lk 9,44); 3. instruct (Lk 1,2); 4. grant

Word groups	Lk	Acts	Mt	Mk
Ἰούδας + παραδίδωμι → Ἰούδας + προδότης	22,(3-)4; 22,48		5	3
παραδίδωμι (+) εἰς (SCc; VKc)	21,12; 24,20	8,3; 14,26; 22,4	3	2
παραδίδωμι + (εἰς τό +) infinitive (SCd; VKd); cf. Rom 1,24.28; παραδίδωμι ἵνα Mt 27,26; Mk 15,15 BOISMARD 1984 ca74		7,42; 12,4; 16,4	2	0
παραδίδωμι εἰς (τὰς) χεῖρας (LN: deliver to control of; SCb; VKb)	9,44; 24,7	21,11; 28,17	2	2
παραδίδωμι τὴν ψυχήν (LN: risk) → δίδωμι (τὸ) πνεῦμα; cf. δίδωμι τὴν ψυχήν Mt 20,28; Mk 10,45		15,26	0	0
ὁ υἱὸς τοῦ ἀνθρώπου + παραδίδωμι	9,44; 18,(31-)32; 22,22.48; 24,7		5	4

Characteristic of Luke	Lk	Acts	Mt	Mk
παραδίδωμι εἰς φυλακήν/τήρησιν → βάλλω/κατακλείω/τίθημι εἰς (τὴν) φυλακήν / ἐν (τῇ) φυλακῇ BOISMARD 1984 Ab137; NEIRYNCK 1985	21,12	8,3; 22,4	0	0

Literature

DENAUX 2009 [IAⁿ : παραδίδωμι εἰς φυλακήν/τήρησιν]; SCHÜRMANN 1957 18-19 [Partizip von παραδιδόναι].

ALEXANDER, Loveday, *The Preface to Luke's Gospel*, 1993. Esp. 118-119.

BORMANN, Lukas, *Recht, Gerechtigkeit und Religion*, 2001. Esp. 190.

CADBURY, Henry J., Commentary on the Preface of Luke, 1922. Esp. 497.

TALBERT, Charles H., Succession in Mediterranean Antiquity. Part I: The Lukan Milieu; Part 2: Luke Acts. — *SBL SP* 37 (1998) 148-168.169-179.

—, *Reading Luke-Acts in Its Mediterranean Milieu* (SupplNT, 107). Leiden-Boston: Brill, 2003, XII-255 p. Esp. 21-27: "The semantic field of succession thinking"; 43-50: "The concept of succession and Luke-Acts".

παράδοξος 1

1. incredible (Lk 5,26); 2. unusual (Lk 5,26)

Literature

HAUCK 1934 [Vorzugswort].

παραιτέομαι 3 + 1 (Mk 1)

1. ask for (Lk 14,18[1.2].19: excuse); 2. not pay attention; 3. reject; 4. not associate with; 5. refuse to obey (Acts 25,11)

παρακαθέζομαι 1   sit down by

Word groups	Lk	Acts	Mt	Mk
παρακαθέζομαι πρὸς τοὺς πόδας → (καθ)ἵστημι παρὰ/πρὸς τοὺς πόδας	10,39		0	0

Literature

HAUCK 1934 [seltenes Alleinwort].

παρακαλέω 7 + 22 (Mt 9, Mk 9)

1. ask for earnestly (Acts 28,20); 2. invite (Lk 8,41); 3. call together to (Acts 28,20); 4. encourage (Acts 14,22)

Word groups	Lk	Acts	Mt	Mk
παρακαλέω + εἰσέρχομαι → ἀναγκάζω/παραβιάζομαι + εἰσέρχομαι	8,32.41; 15,28	14,22; 16,15.40	1	1
παρακαλέω ἵνα (SCb; VKc)	8,31.32		1	5
παρακαλέω (+) λέγω → παράκλησις + λόγος; (προσ/συγ)καλέω + λέγω/εἶπον/ἐρῶ; cf. ἐπικαλέω + λέγω Acts 7,59	7,4	2,40; 16,9.15; 27,33	3	3
παρακαλέω ὅπως (SCc; VKd)		25,2(-3)	1	0

Characteristic of Luke

MORGENTHALER 1958A

	Lk	Acts	Mt	Mk
παρακαλέω + infinitive (SCa; VKb) BOISMARD 1984 Eb7; NEIRYNCK 1985	8,41	8,31; 9,38 v.l.; 11,23; 13,42; 14,22; 19,31; 21,12; 24,4; 27,33.34; 28,14.20	0	1

Literature

VON BENDEMANN 2001 429 [παρακαλέω + inf.]; DENAUX 2009 lAn; HARNACK 1906 29 [" παρακαλέω Von Gott nur in den Act. gebraucht" (2,39; 13,2; 16,10)]; 34 [παρακαλέω + λέγων]; JEREMIAS 1980 69 [παρακαλέω + λέγων: red.]; 111: "παρακαλέω wird von Lukas gern in der Bedeutung 'ermahnen' gebraucht"; 153: "Lukas ergänzt παρακαλέω gern durch pleonastisches λέγων + direkte Rede, öfter auch durch Infinitiv (Lk 8,41/Apg elfmal), vereinzelt durch ὅπως (Apg 25,2f.)"; 253: "Wie die übrigen Verben des Bittens wird παρακαλέω von Lukas meist mit einem Infinitiv konstruiert"; RADL 1975 422 [παρακαλέω; παρακαλέω + inf.; παρακαλέω "ohne persönliches Akkusativobjekt".

GRAYSTON, Kenneth, A Problem of Translation. The meaning of *parakeleō, paraklēsis* in the New Testament. — *Scripture Bulletin* 11 (1980) 27-31. [NTA 27, 461]
MAHFOUZ, Hady, *La fonction littéraire et théologique de Lc 3,1-20*, 2003. Esp. 311-313.

παρακαλύπτω 1	make secret			
Word groups		Lk	Acts	Mt	Mk
παρακαλύπτω ἀπό → (ἀπο)κρύπτω ἀπό		9,45		0	0

Literature

HAUCK 1934 [seltenes Alleinwort].

παράκλησις 2 + 4

1. encouragement, consolation (Lk 2,25; 6,24; Acts 13,15); 2. earnest request

Word groups	Lk	Acts	Mt	Mk
παράκλησις λόγος (VKc) → παρακαλέω + λέγω		13,15	0	0

Characteristic of Luke

BOISMARD 1984 Db13; DENAUX 2009 IA*; HAWKINS 1909B; NEIRYNCK 1985

Literature

HAUCK 1934 [Vorzugswort]; JEREMIAS 1980 93: "Lukas selbst ... verwendet das Wort nur im nichteschatologischen Sinn".

GRAYSTON, Kenneth, A Problem of Translation. The meaning of *parakelēo, paraklēsis* in the New Testament. — *Scripture Bulletin* 11 (1980) 27-31. [NTA 27, 461]

παρακολουθέω 1 (Mk 0[1])

1. be follower of; 2. investigate carefully (Lk 1,3); 3. happen along

Literature

GERSDORF 1816 162 [παρηκολουθηκότι - ἀκριβῶς].

ALEXANDER, Loveday, *The Preface to Luke's Gospel*, 1993. Esp. 128-130.
CADBURY, Henry J., Commentary on the Preface of Luke, 1922. Esp. 501-502.
MOESSNER, David P., "Eyewitnesses", "Informed Contemporaries", and "Unknown Inquirers": Josephus' Criteria for Authentic Historiography and the Meaning of παρακολουθέω. — *NT* 38 (1996) 105-122.
—, The Lukan Prologues in the Light of Ancient Narrative Hermeneutics: *παρηκολουθηκότι* and the Credentialed Author. — VERHEYDEN, J. (ed.), *The Unity of Luke-Acts*, 1999, 399-417.
ROPES, James Hardy, St. Luke's Preface; ἀσφάλεια and παρακολουθεῖν. — *JTS* 25 (1923-24) 67-71.

παρακύπτω 1

1. bend over (Lk 24,12); 2. look into; 3. desire to learn

Literature

DAUER, Anton, Lk 24,12 – Ein Produkt lukanischer Redaktion? — F. VAN SEGBROECK, et al. (eds.), *The Four Gospels 1992*. FS F. Neirynck, 1992, II, 1697-1716.

—, Zur Authentizität von Lk 24,12. — *ETL* 70 (1994) 294-318.

MUDDIMAN, John, A Note on Reading Luke XXIV.12. — *ETL* 48 (1972) 542-548.

NEIRYNCK, Frans, The Uncorrected Historic Present in Lk XXIV.12. — *ETL* 48 (1972) 548-553; = ID., *Evangelica*, 1982, 329-334 (334: additional note; Appendix, *Evangelica II*, 1991, 798).

—, Παρακύψας βλέπει: Lc 24,12 et Jn 20,5. — *ETL* 53 (1977) 113-152. [NTA 22, 130]; = ID., *Evangelica*, 1982, 401-440 (Appendix, *Evangelica II*, 1991, 799).

—, Once More Lk 24,12. — *ETL* 70 (1994) 319-340.

—, Luke 24,12: An Anti-Docetic Interpolation? — DENAUX, A. (ed.), *New Testament Textual Criticism and Exegesis*. FS J. Delobel, 2002, 145-158. Esp. 148.

παραλαμβάνω 6 + 6 (Mt 16, Mk 6)

1. bring along with (Lk 9,28); 2. lead aside; 3. learn from someone; 4. welcome; 5. receive appointment; 6. be taught by

Word groups	Lk	Acts	Mt	Mk
παραλαβών DENAUX 2009 1An	9,10.28; 18,31	15,39; 16,33; 21,24.26.32; 23,18	2	1

Literature

RADL 1975 422 [παραλαμβάνω; παραλαβών].

BURCHARD, Christoph, Fußnoten zum neutestamentlichen Griechisch II, 1978. Esp. 156-157: "Lk 9,10; Act 16,33; 21,24.26 u.ö. παραλαβών".

παράλιος 1   coastal region (Lk 6,17)

Literature

HAUCK 1934 [seltenes Alleinwort].

παραλύω 2 + 2   παραλύομαι: be paralyzed

Characteristic of Luke

BOISMARD 1984 Ab95; NEIRYNCK 1985

	Lk	Acts	Mt	Mk
παραλελυμένος; cf. Heb 12,12 PLUMMER 1922 lii; VOGEL 1899B	5,18.24	8,7; 9,33	0	0

Literature

DENAUX 2009 LAⁿ; LAⁿ [παραλελυμένος] ; HAUCK 1934 [Vorzugswort].

CADBURY, Henri J., Lexical Notes on Luke-Acts, II, 1926. Esp. 204-205: "παραλελυμένος".

παρασκευή 1 (Mt 1, Mk 1)   day of preparation (Lk 23,54)

Literature

BDAG 2000 771 [literature].

MATEOS, Juan, Σάββατα, σάββατον, προσάββατον, παρασκευή. — *FilolNT* 3 (1990) 19-38. Esp. 26-28: "En el evangelio de Lucas"; 29-30: "En Hechos y en las cartas paulinas".

παρατηρέω 3 + 1 (Mk 1)

1. watch closely (Lk 6,7; 14,1; 20,20; Acts 9,24); 2. observe custom

Characteristic of Luke

BOISMARD 1984 cb117; NEIRYNCK 1985; PLUMMER 1922 lx

	Lk	Acts	Mt	Mk
παρατηρεῖν/-ησις DENAUX 2009 L***; GOULDER 1989	6,7; 14,1; 17,20; 20,20	9,24	0	0

Literature

COLLISON 1977 97 [noteworthy phenomena]; EASTON 1910 164 [παρατηρέω active: cited by Weiss as characteristic of L, and possibly corroborative]; JEREMIAS 1980 236 [red.]; RADL 1975 422.

RÜSTOW, Alexander, Ἐντὸς ὑμῶν ἐστιν: Zur Deutung von Lukas 17,20-21. — *ZNW* 51 (1960) 197-224. Esp. 197-203 [παρατηρέω/παρατήρησις]; 203-204 [ἀστραπή]; 208-218 [ἐντός].

παρατήρησις* 1 | close watch (Lk 17,20)

Characteristic of Luke	Lk	Acts	Mt	Mk
παρατηρησις/-εῖν DENAUX 2009 L***; GOULDER 1989	6,7; 14,1; 17,20; 20,20	9,24	0	0

Literature

HAUCK 1934 [seltenes Alleinwort]; JEREMIAS 1980 236 [red.].

CHRUPCAŁA, Lesław D., "Il regno di Dio non verrà μετὰ παρατηρήσεως (Lc 17,20b). — *Antonianum* 72 (1997) 39-52.
RÜSTOW, Alexander, Ἐντὸς ὑμῶν ἐστιν: Zur Deutung von Lukas 17,20-21. — *ZNW* 51 (1960) 197-224. Esp. 197-203 [παρατηρέω/παρατήρησις]; 203-204 [ἀστραπή]; 208-218 [ἐντός].
SCHWARZ, Günther, Οὐκ ... μετὰ παρατηρήσεως? — *BibNot* 59 (1991) 45-48.
SNEED, Richard, "The Kingdom of God is within You" (Lk 17,21). — *CBQ* 24 (1962) 363-382.
STROBEL, August, Die Passa-Erwartung als urchristliches Problem in Lc 17,20f. — *ZNW* 49 (1958) 157-196.
—, A. Merx über Lc 17,20f. — *ZNW* 51 (1960) 133-134. [νὺξ παρατηρήσεως]

παρατίθημι 5 + 4 (Mt 2, Mk 4)

1. give food to (Lk 9,16; 10,8; 11,6; Acts 16,34)
παρατίθεμαι: 1. entrust to (Lk 12,48; 23,46; Acts 14,23); 2. show to be true (Acts 17,3)

Word groups	Lk	Acts	Mt	Mk
παρατίθημι + αἰτέω → (ἐπι)δίδωμι/λαμβάνω + αἰτέω; ζητέω + δίδωμι	12,48		0	0
παρατίθημι + ἄρτους	9,16; 11,(5-)6		0	2
παρατίθεμαι middle (VKa) DENAUX 2009 1A[n]	12,48; 23,46	14,23; 17,3; 20,32	0	0
παρατίθεμαι passive (VKb)	10,8		0	0

Literature

DUPONT, Jacques, Le discours de Milet, 1962. Esp. 236-242.
GEORGE, Augustin, La prière. — ID., Études, 1978, 395-427. Esp. 402-405: "Le vocabulaire lucanien de la prière".

παραφέρω 1 (Mk 1)

1. drive along; 2. mislead

Word groups	Lk	Acts	Mt	Mk
παραφέρω τὸ ποτήριον ἀπό (LN: cause not to experience)	22,42		0	1

Literature

BLAISING, Craig A., Gethsemane: A Prayer of Faith. — JEvTS 22 (1979) 333-343.

παραχρῆμα 10 + 6/7 (Mt 2)   suddenly

Word groups	Lk	Acts	Mt	Mk
παραχρῆμα + present indicative (VKb)	19,11		0	0
παραχρῆμα (+) ἀνίστημι → εὐθέως + ἀνίστημι; cf. εὐθύς + ἀνίστημι Mk 5,42; εὐθύς + ἐγείρω Mk 2,12 DENAUX 2009 L[n]	4,39; 5,25; 8,55		0	0
παραχρῆμα δέ (VKa) → εὐθέως δέ	4,39	3,7; 12,23; 13,11 v.l.		

Characteristic of Luke

BOISMARD 1984 Bb31; CADBURY 1920 199; CREDNER 1836 142; DENAUX 2009 L***; GASTON 1973 64 [Lked]; GOULDER 1989*; HAWKINS 1909L; HENDRIKS 1986 434; MORGENTHALER 1958L; NEIRYNCK 1985; PLUMMER 1922 lx; VOGEL 1899D

	Lk	Acts	Mt	Mk
καὶ παραχρῆμα DENAUX 2009 L***	5,25; 8,44; 13,13; 18,43; 22,60		0	0
παραχρῆμα a sudden effect in the context of miracles DENAUX 2009 L***	1,64; 4,39; 5,25; 8,44.47.55; 13,13; 18,43	3,7; 5,10; 12,23; 13,11; 16,26	0	0
παραχρῆμα at the beginning of a sentence BOISMARD 1984 Ab15; DENAUX 2009 L***; NEIRYNCK 1985	4,39; 5,25; 8,44; 13,13; 18,43; 22,60	3,7; 12,23; 13,11	0	0

Literature

VON BENDEMANN 2001 435: "im lukanischen Doppelwerk beschreibt es nahezu ausschließlich den 'auf der Stelle' eintretenden Effekt von Heilungs- oder Straf-'Wundern'"; COLLISON 1977 154 [linguistic usage of Luke: certain; in a context of miracle: certain]; GERSDORF 1816 204:

"παραχρῆμα, ein Wort das sich im Ev. u. der Apostg. zum öftern findet"; HAUCK 1934 [Vorzugswort]; JEREMIAS 1980 70: "παραχρῆμα ist ein ausgesprochenes Vorzugswort der lukanischen Redaktion".

DAUBE, David, *The Sudden in the Scriptures*. Leiden: Brill, 1964, VII-86 p. Esp. 40-43: "Straightway: Luke"; 43-45: "Acts"; 45-46: "Luke and Acts".
FABRICIUS, C., Zu παραχρῆμα bei Lukas. — *Eranos* (Stockholm) 83 (1985) 62-66.
NEIRYNCK, Frans, La matière marcienne dans l'évangile de Luc, 1973. Esp. 183; [2]1989.
Esp. 93; = ID., *Evangelica*, 1982. Esp. 63.
PERNOT, Hubert, *Études sur la langue des Évangiles*, 1927. Esp. 181-187.
RYDBECK, Lars, *Fachprosa*, 1967. Esp. 167-176.

πάρειμι 1 + 5 (Mt 1)

1. be present (Lk 13,1); 2. arrive (Acts 17,6; 12,20)

Word groups	Lk	Acts	Mt	Mk
παρῆσαν (= 'they had arrived') DENAUX 2009 LA[n]	13,1	12,20	0	0
πάρεισιν (= 'they have arrived')		10,21; 17,6	0	0

Literature
VON BENDEMANN 2001 424; DENAUX 2009 lAn; JEREMIAS 1980 226: "Kennzeichnend für den lukanischen Sprachgebrauch von πάρειμι ist die Verwendung des Präsens πάρεισιν im perfektischen Sinn 'sie sind gekommen' Apg 17,6; 10,21 sowie des Imperfekts παρῆσαν im Sinne von 'sie waren gekommen', 'sie kamen' Lk 13,1/Apg 12,20".

παρεμβάλλω 1   surround (Lk 19,43)

Literature
HAUCK 1934 [seltenes Alleinwort].

παρέρχομαι 9 + 2/3 (Mt 9, Mk 5)

1. pass by (Lk 18,37); 2. arrive (Lk 12,37); 3. disobey (Lk 11,42); 4. pass away (Lk 21,32); 5. pass (of time) (Acts 27,9)

Word groups	Lk	Acts	Mt	Mk
παρέρχομαι + ἄχρι/ἕως → (δι/ἐξ)ἔρχομαι + ἄχρι/ἕως; cf. παρέρχομαι + μέχρι Mk 13,30	21,32		2	0

Characteristic of Luke	Lk	Acts	Mt	Mk
παρέρχομαι transitive (VKb) BOISMARD 1984 cb43; NEIRYNCK 1985	11,42; 15,29	16,8	0	1
παρελθών BOISMARD 1984 Ab138; NEIRYNCK 1985	12,37; 17,7	16,8	0	0

Literature
COLLISON 1977 97 [noteworthy phenomena]; DENAUX 2009 La[n] [παρελθών]; EASTON 1910 164 [παρέρχομαι "come": cited by Weiss as characteristic of L, and possibly corroborative]; JEREMIAS 1980 133-134 [παρελθών: trad.]; 207: "In der Bedeutung 'übertreten' (ein Gebot), 'mißachten' findet sich παρέρχομαι im NT nur im Nicht-Markusstoff (Lk 11,42; 15,29); gleiches

gilt für abundantes παρελθών (12,37; 17,7)"; 220: "Abundantes παρελθών findet sich im NT nur im Nicht-Markusstoff des LkEv (12,37; 17,7), an beiden Stellen bezogen auf die Bedienung bei Tisch, nicht lukanisch".

παρέχω 4 + 5 (Mt 1, Mk 1)

1. continue to offer (Lk 6,29) or to be (Acts 22,2); 2. cause to happen (Lk 7,4; 11,7; 18,5); 3. cause to experience (Acts 28,2)

Word groups	Lk	Acts	Mt	Mk
παρέχω πίστιν → προστίθημι πίστιν		17,31	0	0
παρέχομαι middle (VKa) DENAUX 2009 LAⁿ	7,4	19,24	0	0

Characteristic of Luke

BOISMARD 1984 Eb14; DENAUX 2009 L***†; GOULDER 1989*; HARNACK 1906 36; HAWKINS 1909L†; NEIRYNCK 1985

	Lk	Acts	Mt	Mk
παρέχω (+) κόπον/κόπους †HAWKINS 1909L	11,7; 18,5		1	1

Literature

DENAUX 2009 Lⁿ [παρέχω (+) κόπον/κόπους]; HAUCK 1934 [Vorzugswort]; RADL 1975 422-423.

παρθενία 1   virginity (Lk 2,36)

Literature

HAUCK 1934 [seltenes Alleinwort].

παρθένος 2 + 1 (Mt 4/5)

1. virgin (female) (Lk 1,27$^{1.2}$); 2. virgin (male); 3. unmarried person (Acts 21,9)

Word groups	Lk	Acts	Mt	Mk
παρθένος concerning Mary (VKa)	1,27$^{1.2}$		0/1	0

Literature

BDAG 2000 777 [literature].

CARMIGNAC, Jean, The Meaning of παρθένος in Luke 1.27: A Reply to C.H. Dodd. — BTrans 28 (1977) 327-330.

DODD, Charles H., New Testament Translation Problems. — BTrans 27 (1976) 301-311. Esp. 301-305 [παρθένος Lk 1,27]; 28 (1977) 101-116.

MASSINGBERD FORD, J., The Meaning of "Virgin". — NTS 12 (1965-66) 293-299.

RODRÍGUEZ, Isidoro, Consideración filologica sobre el mensaje de la anunciación, 1958. Esp. 228: "παρθένος".

παρίημι 1

1. avoid (Lk 11,42); παρίεμαι: 1. be weak

παρίστημι 3 + 13 (Mt 1, Mk 6)

1. cause to be in a place (Lk 2,22; Acts 1,3); 2. cause to be; 3. cause to exist; 4. provide (Acts 23,24); 5. hand over (Acts 23,33); 6. show to be true (Acts 24,13)
παρίσταμαι: 1. stand near (Lk 19,24; Acts 4,26); 2. be at; 3. be in front of (Lk 1,19; Acts 27,24); 4. be now; 5. come (Acts 27,23); 6. help

Word groups	Lk	Acts	Mt	Mk
παρίστημι + ἄγγελος → (ἐφ)ἵστημι + ἄγγελος; ἀπέστη/ἀπῆλθεν ὁ ἄγγελος/διάβολος DENAUX 2009 LA[n]	1,19	27,23	0	0

Characteristic of Luke
MORGENTHALER 1958A; VOGEL 1899B

	Lk	Acts	Mt	Mk
παρεστώς → (ἐφ/συν)εστώς CREDNER 1836 140	19,24	23,2.4	0	2
παρίστημι transitive (SCa; VKa) BOISMARD 1984 Eb28; NEIRYNCK 1985	2,22	1,3; 9,41; 23,24.33; 24,13	1	0
παρίστημι ἐνώπιον BOISMARD 1984 Ab192; NEIRYNCK 1985	1,19	4,10	0	0

Literature
DENAUX 2009 lAn [παρίστημι transitive], LA[n] [παρίστημι ἐνώπιον]; GERSDORF 1816 244 [παραστῆσαι τῷ κυρίῳ]; RADL 1975 423 [παρίστημι; παρέστην; παρίσταμαι als "terminus technicus in Epiphanien"].

παροικέω 1

1. dwell temporarily (Lk 24,18); 2. live as a foreigner

Literature
ELLIOTT, John H., *A Home for the Homeless: A Sociological Exegesis of 1 Peter, Its Situation and Strategy.* London: SCM, 1982, XIV-306 p. Esp. 23-58 [πάροικος, παροικέω].

πᾶς 158/169 + 172/181 (Mt 129/131, Mk 66[68]/73)

1. all (Lk 4,6); 2. any (Lk 3,9; Acts 22,3); 3. total (Acts 4,29); 4. whole (Lk 1,10; Acts 6,5); 5. every kind of (Acts 2,5)

Word groups	Lk	Acts	Mt	Mk
ἀπαγγέλλω (+) πάντα / περὶ πάντων; cf. ἀπαγγέλλω ἅπαντα Mt 28,11	7,18; 24,9		1	0
κατὰ πάντα (SCn)		3,22; 17,22.25 v.l.	0	0
κατὰ + πᾶς (accusative) in a temporal expression BOISMARD 1984 Aa50		13,27; 15,21; 17,17; 18,4	0	0
κατὰ πᾶσαν ἡμέραν		17,17	0	0
οὐ πᾶς (SCl; VKs); cf. οὐχὶ πᾶς Mt 13,56[1]		10,41	2	0
οὐ + πᾶς → οὐ(δέ) + ἅπας; cf. οὐχί + πᾶς Mt 13,56[1]	1,37; 14,33[1]	10,41	4	2

πᾶν ἔθνος singular → **πάντα** τὰ ἔθνη; cf. Rev 7,9; 14,6 BOISMARD 1984 Da9		2,5; 10,35; 17,26	0	0
πᾶν ῥῆμα → **πάντα** τὰ ῥήματα	1,37; 4,4*		3/4	0
πᾶν τὸ συνέδριον		22,30	0	0
πάντα (SCg; VKh)	1,3; 2,39; 3,20; 4,7 v.l.; 5,11.28; 9,43³; 10,22; 11,41; 14,17*; 15,13.14; 18,28*; 21,32	1,24; 4,32*; 9,32; 10,36; 17,22.25² v.l.; 20,35	8/10	13
τὰ πάντα (SCg; VKj)		17,25²	0	1
πάντα τὰ ἔθνη → **πᾶν** ἔθνος singular; **ἅπας/ὅλος/πᾶς** ὁ λαός; **ἅπαν/πᾶν** τὸ πλῆθος; **πᾶς** ὁ ὄχλος	12,30; 21,24; 24,47	14,16; 15,17	5	2
πάντες DENAUX 2009 lAn	1,63.66; 2,3.18; 2,47; 4,22.28; 6,26; 8,40.52; 9,17.43¹; 13,3.5.27; 14,18.29; 15,1; 19,7; 20,38; 21,4¹; 22,70; 23,48.49	1,14; 2,1.4.12.14.32. 44; 3,24; 4,21; 5,17.36.37; 6,15; 8,1.10; 9,21.26.35; 10,33¹.43¹; 16,33; 17,7.21; 18,17; 19,7; 20,25; 21,18.20; 21,24; 22,3; 25,24; 26,4; 27,36	18	14
οἱ πάντες (VKe)		19,7	0	0
πάντες οἱ / πάντα τά (SCe; VKf) DENAUX 2009 lAn	2,39; 5,9	2,39; 4,24; 5,17; 14,15; 16,32; 17,24; 24,14	2	1
πάντες ἄνδρες → **πάντες** (οἱ) ἄνθρωποι		19,7	0	0
πάντες (οἱ) ἄνθρωποι → **πάντες** ἄνδρες DENAUX 2009 Laⁿ	6,26; 13,4	22,15	0	0
πάντες ἐργάται ἀδικίας	13,27		0	0
πάντες ἡμεῖς/ὑμεῖς DENAUX 2009 lAn	9,48	2,32; 3,16; 4,10¹; 10,33¹; 20,25.32 v.l.; 22,3; 26,14; 28,2	2	0
πάντες (οἱ) Ἰουδαῖοι; cf. Jn 18,20 BOISMARD 1984 ca29		18,2; 21,21; 22,12; 24,5; 26,4	0	1
πάντες (…) ὅσοι (SCk; VKm) → **ἅπαντες** (…) ὅσοι	4,40*; 18,12.22	2,39; 3,22.24; 5,36.37	7/8	4
πᾶς adjective or with determinative + ὅς/ὅστις	14,33¹; 21,4²	1,21; 3,23; 15,17.36; 20,25.28; 24,8	3	0
πᾶς followed by a demonstrative or personal pronoun (SCb; VKb) → **ἅπας** followed by a pronoun	6,10; 7,18; 16,26; 24,21	2,32; 3,16; 4,10¹.33; 10,33¹; 20,36; 22,3; 24,8; 28,2	3/5	0/2
πᾶς following a demonstrative or personal pronoun (SCb; VKb) → **ἅπας** following a pronoun	12,30.31*; 16,14; 18,21; 21,12.36²; 24,9¹	1,14; 7,50; 15,17*; 16,33; 17,7; 20,25	8/10	4
πᾶς following a noun (SCa; VKa) → **ἅπας** following a noun	7,35 v.l.; 12,7; 21,24	4,29; 8,40; 15,36; 16,26¹; 17,21.30 v.l.; 27,20	4	1
πᾶς + proper name (SCd; VKd) DENAUX 2009 lAn	6,17; 13,2	1,8; 2,36; 4,10²; 13,24; 17,21; 18,2; 19,17¹.26; 21,21; 22,12; 24,5; 26,4	2	2
πᾶς γάρ (VKq) → **ἅπας** γάρ	11,10; 20,38; 21,4¹		6	5
πᾶς δέ (VKp)	6,30 v.l.; 9,43²; 12,48	2,44; 3,24; 8,1; 26,14 v.l.	2	[1]
πᾶς (+) εἷς → **πολύς** + εἷς	18,22	17,26¹; 19,34	2	3
πᾶς ἐκ (VKt)	14,33¹		0	0

πᾶς (...) ὅσος ἄν; cf. πᾶς (...) ὅσος ἐάν Mt 7,12; 23,3; Mk 3,28		2,39; 3,22	1/3	0/2
πᾶς οὖν/τε (VKr)	3,9	5,42; 8,1 v.l.; 21,18; 26,14.20	6	0
πᾶς (+) ὁ ὄχλος / πάντες (+) οἱ ὄχλοι → ἅπας/ὅλος/πᾶς ὁ λαός; ἅπαν/πᾶν τὸ πλῆθος; πάντα τὰ ἔθνη	6,19; 13,17[2]; 23,48	21,27	2	4/5
(ὁ) πᾶς χρόνος BOISMARD 1984 Aa166		1,21; 20,18	0	0
πᾶς + πανταχοῦ/πάντοτε; cf. πάντῃ + πανταχοῦ Acts 24,3 DENAUX 2009 LA[n]	15,31	17,30; 21,28 v.l.	0	0
πᾶσα ἡ γῆ → ὅλη ἡ γῆ	4,25; 21,35[2]		1	0
πᾶσα ἡ Ἰουδαία → ὅλη ἡ Ἰουδαία	6,17	1,8	1	0
πᾶσα ἡ οἰκουμένη → ὅλη ἡ οἰκουμένη	2,1		0	0
πᾶσα ἡ πόλις → ὅλη ἡ πόλις		13,44	2	0
πᾶσα ψυχή → ὅλη ἡ ψυχή		2,43; 3,23; 27,37	0	0
πᾶσαι αἱ γραφαί → πάντα τὰ γεγραμμένα	24,27[1]		0	0
ὕστερον δὲ πάντων	20,32*		1	0

→ κύριος πάντων; ἐπὶ πρόσωπον πάσης τῆς γῆς; κατὰ πᾶν σάββατον; πᾶσα σάρξ; ἐν πάσῃ σοφίᾳ; πᾶς τόπος

Characteristic of Luke

CADBURY 1920 115; GASTON 1973 66 [Lked?]; HENDRIKS 1986 434.468; PLUMMER 1922 lxii

	Lk	Acts	Mt	Mk
attraction of relative pronoun after πάντων/πᾶσιν BOISMARD 1984 Ab7; DENAUX 2009 L***	2,20; 3,19; 9,43; 24,25	1,1; 3,21; 10,39; 13,38; 22,10; 24,8; 26,2	0	0
διὰ παντός (LN: [a]regularly; [b]always; SCm; VKu) CREDNER 1836 142	[b]24,53	2,[b]25; 10,[b]2; 24,[b]16	1	1
δὲ πάντες DENAUX 2009 L***	2,47; 8,52; 9,43[1]; 22,70; 23,49	2,12; 9,21; 18,17; 17,21	0	1
ἐξίσταντο δὲ πάντες; cf. καὶ ἐξίσταντο πάντες Mt 12,23; ἐξίστασθαι πάντας Mk 2,12[2] BOISMARD 1984 Ab118; HARNACK 1906 149; NEIRYNCK 1985	2,47	2,12; 9,21	0	0
ἐπλήσθησαν πάντες; cf. πλησθῆναι πάντα Lk 21,22; ἐπλήσθησαν ἅπαντες Acts 4,31 BOISMARD 1984 Ab96; NEIRYNCK 1985	4,28	2,4	0	0
ὅς in attraction (of the relative pronoun after πάντων/πᾶσιν) BOISMARD 1984 Ab7; DENAUX 2009 L***; HARNACK 1906 148; HAWKINS 1909L; NEIRYNCK 1985	2,20; 3,19; 9,43[3]; 24,25	1,1; 3,21; 10,39; 13,38; 22,10; 24,8; 26,2	0	0
πᾶν/ἅπαν τὸ πλῆθος → ἅπας/ὅλος/πᾶς ὁ λαός; πάντα τὰ ἔθνη; πᾶς ὁ ὄχλος; ἅπαν τὸ πλῆθος; πλῆθος πολύ BOISMARD 1984 Ab28; HARNACK 1906 71; NEIRYNCK 1985	1,10	6,5; 15,12; 25,24*	0	0
πάντα τὰ γεγραμμένα → πᾶς ὁ + part.; πᾶσαι αἱ γραφαί; cf. Gal 3,10 BOISMARD 1984 Bb98; NEIRYNCK 1985; SCHÜRMANN 1953 11; VOGEL 1899C	18,31; 21,22; 24,44	13,29; 24,14	0	0

πάντα τὰ ῥήματα → **πᾶν** ῥῆμα; τὰ ῥήματα **ἅπαντα** BOISMARD 1984 Ab62; DENAUX 2009 L***; NEIRYNCK 1985	1,65; 2,19.51; 7,1	5,20	0	0
πάντες αὐτοί; cf. 1 Cor 15,10 BOISMARD 1984 cb118; NEIRYNCK 1985	6,10	4,33; 19,17; 20,36	1	0
πάντες οἱ ἀκούοντες/ἀκούσαντες → **πᾶς** ὁ + part. BOISMARD 1984 Ab16; DENAUX 2009 lA*; HARNACK 1906 147; NEIRYNCK 1985; VOGEL 1899C	1,66; 2,18.47	5,5.11; 9,21; 10,44; 26,29	0	0
πάντες ἐξεπλήσσοντο / ἐθαύμαζον/ἐθαύμασαν; cf. Mk 11,18 πᾶς ὁ ὄχλος ἐξεπλήσσετο DENAUX 2009 L***	1,63; 2,18; 4,22; 9,43$^{1.2}$		1	0
πάντες οἱ κατοικοῦντες → **πᾶς** ὁ + part.; cf. Rev 13,8 BOISMARD 1984 Bb29; NEIRYNCK 1985; VOGEL 1899C	13,4	1,19; 2,14; 4,16; 9,35; 19,10.17; 22,12	0	0
πάντες οἱ προφῆται (of the OT) BOISMARD 1984 Bb50; DENAUX 2009 lA*; GOULDER 1989; NEIRYNCK 1985	11,50; 13,28; 24,27^1	3,18.24; 10,43^1	1	0
πᾶς + article → **ἅπας** + article DENAUX 2009 lA*	2,39.51; 21,4^2	2,14; 6,15; 13,29; 16,33	0	0
πᾶς following a participle (SCc; VKc) → **ἅπας** following a part. DENAUX 2009 lA*	6,40; 9,7	2,14; 20,32	1	0
πᾶς ὁ + participle → **πάντες** οἱ ἀκούοντες/ἀκούσαντες / κατοικοῦντες / πάντα τὰ γεγραμμένα; **ἅπας** ὁ + part. DENAUX 2009 L***	1,66.71; 2,18.38.47; 6,47; 12,44; 13,17^1; 14,10. 11.29; 16,18. 18*; 17,10; 18,14.31; 19,26; 20,18; 21,22.35.36^2; 23,48; 24,14. 44	1,19; 4,16; 5,5.11; 6,15; 9,14.21.35; 10,33^2.38.43^2.4 4; 13,39; 19,10; 22,12; 25,24; 26,29; 27,24; 28,30	11	0
πᾶς/ἅπας/ὅλος ὁ λαός → **ἅπαν/πᾶν** τὸ πλῆθος; **πάντα** τὰ ἔθνη; **πᾶς** ὁ ὄχλος; **ἅπας/ὅλος** ὁ λαός BOISMARD 1984 Bb36; DENAUX 2009 L***; NEIRYNCK 1985	2,10.31; 7,29; 8,47; 9,13; 18,43; 19,48; 20,6*.45; 21,38; 24,19	2,47; 3,9.11; 4,10; 5,34; 10,41; 13,24	1	0
πᾶς ὁ λαός PLUMMER 1922 lx; DENAUX 2009 L***	2,10.31; 7,29; 8,47; 9,13; 18,43; 20,6*.45; 21,38; 24,19	3,9.11; 4,10; 5,34; 10,41; 13,24	1	0
πᾶς/ἅπας ὁ λαός DENAUX 2009 L***; GOULDER 1989; HAWKINS 1909L	2,10.31; 7,29; 8,47; 9,13; 18,43; 19,48 20,6.45; 21,38; 24,19	3,9.11; 4,10; 5,34; 10,41; 13,24	1	0
πᾶς ὅς (SCh; VKk); cf. πᾶς ὅστις Mt 7,24; 10,32; 19,29 DENAUX 2009 L***	2,20; 3,19; 9,43^3; 12,8. 10.48; 19,37; 24,25	1,1; 2,21; 3,21; 10,39; 13,38; 22,10; 26,2	1/2	0
περὶ πάντων DENAUX 2009 lA*	3,19; 7,18; 24,14	1,1; 22,10; 24,8; 26,2		
ὡς (δὲ) ἐτέλεσαν πάντα → ὡς δὲ ἐτέλεσαν **ἅπαντα** VOGEL 1899C	2,39	13,29	0	0
→ πᾶσιν **ὑμῖν**				

Literature

VON BENDEMANN 2001 428 [πᾶς ὁ]; 430 [διὰ παντός] 436 [περὶ πασῶν; περὶ πάντων]; COLLISON 1977 174 [ἅπας/πᾶς ὁ λαός: linguistic usage of Luke: certain]; 176 [ἅπας/πᾶς τὸ πλῆθος: noteworthy phenomena]; DENAUX 2009 lAn; lA[n] [διὰ παντός, ἐξίσταντο δὲ πάντες, ἅπαν/πᾶν τὸ πλῆθος, πάντες οἱ κατοικοῦντες]; lAn [πάντες αὐτοί]; LA[n] [ἐπλήσθησαν πάντες]; La[n] [πάντα τὰ γεγραμμένα]; LA[n] [ὡς (δὲ) ἐτέλεσαν πάντα]; EASTON 1910 156 [πᾶς ὁ λαός: probably characteristic of L], GERSDORF 1816 174 [πᾶν τὸ πλῆθος ἦν τοῦ λαοῦ προσευχόμενον]; 179 [πᾶν τὸ πλῆθος τοῦ λαοῦ]; 205 [πάντα τὰ ῥήματα ταῦτα]; 231 [πάντων τῶν λαῶν]; 240 [πάντα συνετήρει τὰ ῥήματα ταῦτα συμβάλλουσα ἐν τῇ καρδίᾳ αὐτῆς]; 241 [ἐπὶ πᾶσιν οἷς ἤκουσαν καὶ εἶδον]; 272 [διετήρει πάντα τὰ ῥήματα ταῦτα]; HAUCK 1934 [Vorzugswort; Vorzugsverbindung: πᾶς ὁ λαός]; JEREMIAS 1980 30: "Lukas hat, verglichen mit den anderen Evangelisten, eine Vorliebe für Wendungen mit πᾶς ὁ ...; insbesondere bevorzugt er πᾶς ὁ + Partizip"; 31 [πᾶς/πᾶς ὁ/Attractio relativi mit πᾶς: red.]; 54 [1,37 red.]: "οὐκ ἀδυνατήσει παρὰ τοῦ θεοῦ πᾶν ῥῆμα: ist ein freies Zitat von Gen 18,14 LXX: μὴ ἀδυνατεῖ παρὰ τῷ θεῷ ῥῆμα; Lukas hat ein πᾶν zugefügt und παρά mit dem Genitiv (LXX: Dativ) konstruiert. Sowohl das stilistische Feilen am LXX-Text wie die Verstärkung durch πᾶς ist typisch lukanisch"; 72 [πάντες οἱ ἀκούοντες/ἀκούσαντες: red.]; 101 [ἐξίσταντο δὲ πάντες οἱ ἀκούοντες: red.]; 112 [3,20 red.]: "ἐπὶ πᾶσιν: Lukas hat eine Vorliebe für rhetorische Verstärkung durch πᾶς"; 144: "Substantiviertes Partizip nach πᾶς ('jeder') schreibt Lukas mit Vorliebe ... Ganz anders liegt es bei der Wendung πᾶς + Partizip ohne Artikel. Sie findet zich bei Lukas nur ganz vereinzelt, nämlich an unserer Stelle [Lk 6,30] παντὶ αἰτοῦντί σε δίδου und 11,4 ἀφίομεν παντὶ ὀφείλοντι ἡμῖν. Die Seltenheit der Belege zeigt, daß wir es mit nicht-lukanischem Sprachgebrauch zu tun haben"; 232 [πάντες ἐργάται ἀδικίας: red.]; 323: "διὰ παντός: lukanisch"; RADL 1975 423 [πᾶς; πάντες αὐτοί]; 424 [ἅπαν(πᾶν) τὸ πλῆθος]; SCHNEIDER 1969 122.163 [δὲ πάντες: Vorzugswörter und -ausdrücke des Luk]; 123.164 [πάντες: Vorzugswörter und -ausdrücke des Luk].

CADBURY, Henri J., Commentary on the Preface of Luke, 1922. Esp. 503-504 [Lk 1,3].
HEIMERDINGER, Jenny, Word Order in Koine Greek, 1996. Esp. 163-164: "πᾶς"; = READ-HEIMERDINGER, Jenny, The Bezan Text of Acts, 2002. Esp. 97-99.
NEIRYNCK, Frans, Goulder and the Minor Agreements. — ETL 73 (1997) 84-93. Esp. 85 [Lk 6,19 πάντας; Lk 4,15 αὐτῶν]; 91-92 [τίς ἐστιν ὁ παίσας σε;]. [NTA 42, 185]; = ID., Evangelica III, 2001, 307-318. Esp. 308-309; 315-317.
NESTLE, Eberhard, Luke i. 3. — ExpT 13 (1901-02) 139-140.

πάσχα 7 + 1 (Mt 4, Mk 5)

1. Passover festival (Lk 22,1); 2. Passover meal (Lk 22,13); 3. Passover lamb (Lk 22,7)

Word groups	Lk	Acts	Mt	Mk
ἐσθίω (+) τὸ πάσχα	22,8.11.15		1	2
πάσχα + ἄζυμος	22,1.7		1	2
πάσχα (+) ἑορτή (VKa) → ἑορτή/ἡμέρα τῶν ἀζύμων DENAUX 2009 L[n]	2,41; 22,1		0	0
τὸ πάσχα θύω	22,7		0	1

Literature

BDAG 2000 784-785 [literature]; SCHÜRMANN 1953 7-9 [τὸ πάσχα φαφεῖν].

BUSSBY, F., A Note on πάσχα in the Synoptic Gospels. — ExpT 59 (1947-48) 194-195.

πάσχω 6 + 5 (Mt 4, Mk 3)

1. suffer (Lk 22,15); 2. experience

Word groups	Lk	Acts	Mt	Mk
δεῖ (+) παθεῖν	9,22; 17,25; 24,26	9,16; 17,3	1	1
κακόν + πάσχω		28,5	0	0
παθεῖν absolute meaning 'suffer death'	22,15; 24,46	1,3; 3,18; 17,3	0	0
DENAUX 2009 1A[n]				
πάσχω + ὑπέρ + genitive (VKf)		9,16	0	0
πολλὰ παθεῖν	9,22; 17,25		1	1

Characteristic of Luke	Lk	Acts	Mt	Mk
παθεῖν infinitive	9,22; 17,25; 22,15;	1,3; 3,18; 9,16;	1	1
DENAUX 2009 L***; GOULDER 1989*	24,26.46	17,3		

Literature

JEREMIAS 1980 286 "παθεῖν: absolut gebraucht, in der Bedeutung 'den Tod erleiden' findet sich im NT nur Lk 22,15; 24,46/Apg 1,3; 3,18; 17,3; Hebr 9,26, ist also eine von Lukas bevorzugte Wendung"; RADL 1975 423 [πάσχω; παθεῖν]; SCHÜRMANN 1953 13-14 [παθεῖν].

πατάσσω 2 + 3 (Mt 2, Mk 1)

1. strike a blow (Lk 22,49.50); 2. strike down (Acts 7,24; 12,23)

Word groups	Lk	Acts	Mt	Mk
πατάσσω ἐν (VKa)	22,49		0	0

Characteristic of Luke

BOISMARD 1984 Eb48; NEIRYNCK 1985

Literature

SCHÜRMANN 1957 130-131

πατέω 2

1. step on (Lk 10,19); 2. trample; 3. trample on (Lk 21,24); 4. conquer (Lk 21,24)

Literature

HAUCK 1934 [seltenes Alleinwort].

πατήρ 56 + 35/36 (Mt 63/64, Mk 18/19)

1. father (Lk 2,48); 2. parents; 3. ancestor (Lk 1,73; Acts 3,13); 4. Father (title for God) (Lk 6,36); 5. father (title for person) (Acts 7,2); 6. elder (Acts 22,1); 7. archetype; 8. leader

Word groups	Lk	Acts	Mt	Mk
ἄνδρες ἀδελφοὶ καὶ πατέρες		7,2; 22,1	0	0
δόξα + τοῦ πατρός	9,26		1	1
θάπτω τὸν πατέρα μου (LN: take	9,59		1	0
care of one's father until death)				
θεὸς τῶν πατέρων σου/ἡμῶν		3,13; 5,30; 7,32;	0	0
BOISMARD 1984 Aa49		22,14		
οἶκος πατρός	16,27[2]	7,20	0	0
DENAUX 2009 LA[n]				

	Lk	Acts	Mt	Mk
πατὴρ ἐξ οὐρανοῦ → πατὴρ ὁ ἐν (τοῖς) οὐρανοῖς	11,13		0	0
πατὴρ ὁ ἐν (τοῖς) οὐρανοῖς (SCa; VKa) → πατὴρ ἐξ οὐρανοῦ; cf. πατὴρ ὁ οὐράνιος Mt 5,48; 6,14.26.32; 15,13; 18,35; 23,9²	11,2 v.l.		13/15	1/2
πατὴρ κυριός → πατήρ/πατέρες + θεός	10,21		1	0/1
πατήρ + μήτηρ (SCe; VKe)	2,33.48; 8,51; 12,53^{1.2}; 14,26; 18,20		8/9	8
πατήρ μου → πατήρ σου/ἡμῶν/ὑμῶν	2,49; 9,59; 10,22¹; 15,17.18¹; 16,27²; 22,29; 24,49		17/20	0
πατήρ + παιδίον/παῖς (SCh; VKh) → πατήρ + τέκνον; μήτηρ + παιδίον/παῖς/τέκνον	1,59; 8,51; 9,42	4,25	0	2
πατήρ/πατέρες ὑμῶν → πατήρ μου/σου/ἡμῶν	6,36; 11,47.48; 12,30(?).32	3,25; 7,51.52; 28,25	15	1/2
πατήρ σου → πατήρ μου/ἡμῶν/ὑμῶν	2,48; 15,27; 18,20	7,32	5/7	2
πατήρ + τέκνον (SCg; VKg) → πατήρ + παιδίον/παῖς; μήτηρ + παιδίον/παῖς/τέκνον	1,17; 2,48; 11,13; 14,26	13,32(-33)	3	2
πατήρ + υἱός (SCf; VKf) → μήτηρ + υἱός	9,26; 10,22^{2.3}; 11,11; 12,53^{1.2}; 15,(11-)12¹. 18²(-19).21	3,25; 16,1	7	
πατήρ/πατέρες + θεός → πατήρ + κυριός		2,33; 3,13.25; 5,30; 7,32.45; 13,17.(32-).33; 22,14; 26,6	0	0/1
προστίθημι πρὸς τοὺς πατέρας αὐτοῦ (LN: bury)		13,36	0	0
πατήρ human father(s)	1,17.32.55.59.62.67.7 2. 73; 2,33.48; 3,8; 6,23. 26; 8,51; 9,42.59; 11,11.47.48; 12,53^{1.2}; 14,26; 15,12^{1.2}.17.18^{1.2}. 20^{1.2}.21.22.27.28.29; 16,24.27^{1.2}.30; 18,20	3,13.25; 4,25; 5,30; 7,2^{1.2}.4.11. 12.14..15.19.20. 32.38.39. 44.45^{1.2}. 51.52; 13,17.32. 36; 15,10; 16,1.3; 22,1.14; 26,6; 28,8.25	18	14
πατήρ referring to David (SCl; VKl)	1,32	4,25	0	1
πατήρ referring to God (SCd)	2,49; 6,36; 9,26; 10,21^{1.2}. 22^{1.2.3}; 11,2.13; 12,30.32; 22,29.42; 23,34.46.49	1,4.7; 2,33	30	3
πατήρ referring to Jacob (SCk; VKk)		7,14	0	0

Characteristic of Luke	Lk	Acts	Mt	Mk
ἐπαγγελία τοῦ πατρός BOISMARD 1984 Ab177; NEIRYNCK 1985	24,49	1,4	0	0
πάτερ absolute DENAUX 2009 L***; GOULDER 1989*	10,21; 11,2; 15,12².18².21; 22,42; 23,34*.46		0	0
πατέρες plural (SCm; VKm) DENAUX 2009 L***	1,17.55. 72; 6,23.26; 11,47.48	3,13.22*.25; 5,30; 7,2¹.11.12.15.19.32. 38.39.44.45^{1.2}.51. 52; 13,17.32.36; 15,10; 22,1.14; 26,6; 28,25	2	0

οἱ πατέρες ἡμῶν/ὑμῶν/αὐτῶν DENAUX 2009 L***; GOULDER 1989	1,55.72; 6,23.26; 11,47.48	3,13.22 v.l.25; 5,30; 7,11.12.15.19.38.39.44.4 $5^{1.2}$.51.52; 13,17; 22,14; 26,6; 28,25	2	0
οἱ πατέρες fathers of Israel; cf. Jn 4,20; 6,31.49.58; 7,22; Rom 9,5; 11,28; 15,8; 1 Cor 10,1; Heb 1,1 BOISMARD 1984 cb96; DENAUX 2009 L***; NEIRYNCK 1985	1,55.72; 6,23.26; 11,47.48	3,13.25; 5,30; 7,11.12.15.19.38. $39.44.45^{1.2}.51.52;$ 13,17.32; 15,10; 22,14; 26,6; 28,25	2	0
πατήρ referring to Abraham (SCj; VKj) DENAUX 2009 L***	1,55.73; 3,8; 16,24.27^1.30	$7,2^2$	1	0
πατήρ/πατέρες ἡμῶν → πατήρ μου/σου/ὑμῶν DENAUX 2009 lA*	1,55.72.73; 11,2 v.l.	3,13.25 v.l.; 4,25; 5,30; 7,2.11.12.15.19.38.39. $44.45^{1.2}$; 13,17; 15,10; 22,14; 26,6; 28,25 v.l.	2	1

Literature

BDAG 2000 787 [literature]; DENAUX 2009 LA^n [ἐπαγγελία τοῦ πατρός]; GERSDORF 1816 270 [ἐν τοῖς τοῦ πατρός]; HAUCK 1934 [Vorzugswendung: ἐν τοῖς τοῦ πατρός]; JEREMIAS 1980 322 [ἐπαγγελία τοῦ πατρός: red.]; REHKOPF 1959 99 [πάτερ: "Substantiva in Anrede bei den Synoptikern"].

DE JONGE, Henk J., Sonship, Wisdom, Infancy: Luke II.41-51a. — NTS 24 (1977-78) 317-354. Esp. 330-331: "Your father and I"; 331-337: "I must be about the affairs of my Father"; 351-353: "My Father".

HINNEBUSCH, Paul, "In My Father's House … About My Father's Business" (Luke 2:49). — BiTod 27 (1966) 1893-1899.

LE ROUX, L.V., Style and Text of Acts 4:25(a). — Neotestamentica 25 (1991) 29-32.

SCHLOSSER, Jacques, Le Dieu de Jésus. Étude exégétique (LD, 129), Paris, Cerf, 1987 140-150.157-175.

SYLVA, Dennis D., The Cryptic Clause en tois tou patros mou dei einai me in Luke 2,49b. — ZNW 78 (1987) 132-140.

πατριά 1 + 1

1. lineage (Lk 2,4); 2. nation (Acts 3,25)

Word groups	Lk	Acts	Mt	Mk
πατρία Δαυίδ	2,4		0	0
πατρία + οἶκος	2,4		0	0

Literature
DENAUX 2009 LA^n; HARNACK 1906 74.

BORMANN, Lukas, Recht, Gerechtigkeit und Religion, 2001. Esp. 161.

πατρίς 2 (Mt 2, Mk 2)   homeland (Lk 4,23.24)

παύω 3 + 6

1. cause to cease; παύομαι: 2. cease (Lk 5,4; 8,24; 11,1)

Characteristic of Luke
DENAUX 2009 lA*; GOULDER 1989; HAWKINS 1909B; PLUMMER 1922 lix

	Lk	Acts	Mt	Mk
παύω + participle; cf. Eph 1,16; Col 1,9; Heb 10,2 BOISMARD 1984 cb119; NEIRYNCK 1985	5,4	5,42; 6,13; 13,10; 20,31; 21,32	0	0

Literature

VON BENDEMANN 2001 419; DENAUX 2009 IA[n] [παύω + participle]; HAUCK 1934
[Vorzugswort]; JEREMIAS 1980 131 [παύομαι + part.: red.]; RADL 1975 423.

πέδη 1 (Mk 2)	fetter (Lk 8,29)

πεδινός 1	level (Lk 6,17)

Literature

HAUCK 1934 [seltenes Alleinwort].

πείθω 4 + 17 (Mt 3, Mk 0/1)

1. persuade (Acts 12,20); 2. trust (perfect only) (Lk 11,22; 18,9)
πείθομαι: 3. obey; 4. be a follower (Acts 5,36); 5. be certain (Lk 16,31; 20,6)

Word groups	Lk	Acts	Mt	Mk
πείθομαι τοῖς λεγομένοις BOISMARD 1984 Aa150		27,11; 28,24	0	0
πείθω ἐπί + dative (VKd) DENAUX 2009 L[n]	11,22; 18,9		0	0/1
πείθω + ὅτι (VKa)	18,9		0	0
πείθω τινὰ περί τινος; cf. Heb 6,9 BOISMARD 1984 Aa151		19,8; 28,23	0	0

Characteristic of Luke

CREDNER 1836 142; DENAUX 2009 IA*; MORGENTHALER 1958A

	Lk	Acts	Mt	Mk
πείθομαι BOISMARD 1984 Db3; DENAUX 2009 IA*; HARNACK 1906 52; NEIRYNCK 1985	16,31; 20,6	5,36.37.39; 17,4; 21,14; 23,21; 26,26; 27,11; 28,24	0	0
πείθω + (accusative +) infinitive (VKb); cf. Rom 2,19; 2 Cor 10,7 BOISMARD 1984 cb120; NEIRYNCK 1985	20,6	13,43; 26,26.28	0	0

Literature

DENAUX 2009 IA[n] [πείθω + (accusative +) infinitive]; JEREMIAS 1980 272 [πεποιθότας: red.];
RADL 1975 423 [πείθω; πείθομαι; πείσας].

HARLÉ, Paul, Un "private-joke" de Paul dans le livre des Actes (XXVI.28-29). — *NTS* 24
(1977-78) 527-533. Esp. 527-529.

TAEGER, Jens-Wilhelm, *Der Mensch und sein Heil*, 1982. Esp. 147-149.

πεινάω 5 (Mt 9, Mk 2)

1. be hungry (Lk 1,53; 4,2; 6,3.21.25); 2. desire strongly

Word groups	Lk	Acts	Mt	Mk
ἐμπίμπλημι (+) πεινάω DENAUX 2009 Lⁿ	1,53; 6,25		0	0

Literature

DUPONT, Jacques, *Les Béatitudes*, II, 1969. Esp. 37-39: "Les affamés".
—, *Les Béatitudes*, III, 1973. Esp. 45-46.

πειράζω 2/3 + 5 (Mt 6, Mk 4)

1. examine; 2. try to trap (Lk 11,16); 3. tempt (Lk 4,2); 4. attempt (Acts 9,26; 16,7; 24,6)

Word groups	Lk	Acts	Mt	Mk
πειράζω + διάβολος → πειρασμός + διάβολος	4,2		1	0
πειράζω + infinitive (*VK*d) BOISMARD 1984 Aa100		9,26; 15,10; 16,7; 24,6		
πειράζω τὸ πνεῦμα/τὸν θεόν (*VK*b)		5,9; 15,10	0	0

Literature

BDAG 2000 793 [literature]; RADL 1975 423 [πειράζω; πειράζω + inf.]; SCHÜRMANN 1957 39-40 [luk R].

GIBSON, Jeffrey B., *The Temptation of Jesus in Early Christianity* (JSNT SS, 112), Sheffffield, 1995. Esp. 325-326 [Instances of the Verb πειράζω in Classical and Hellenistic Greek]
HATCH, Edwin, *Essays*, 1889. Esp. 71-73.

πειρασμός 6 + 1 (Mt 2, Mk 1)

1. testing (Lk 8,13); 2. temptation (Lk 4,13)

Word groups	Lk	Acts	Mt	Mk
εἰσφέρω + εἰς πειρασμόν	11,4		1	0
καιρὸς πειρασμοῦ (*VK*a)	8,13		0	0
πειρασμὸς διάβολος → πειράζω + διάβολος	4,13		0	0
πειρασμοί plural (*VK*b) DENAUX 2009 LAⁿ	22,28	20,19	0	0

Characteristic of Luke

DENAUX 2009 L***†; GOULDER 1989*; HAWKINS 1909 L†

Literature

HAUCK 1934 [Vorzugswort] ; SCHÜRMANN 1957 39-40 [luk R].

DUPONT, Jacques, *Le discours de Milet*, 1962. Esp. 36-39.
HATCH, Edwin, *Essays*, 1889. Esp. 71-73.
KNOWLES, Michael P., Once More "Lead Us Not *Eis peirasmon*". — *ExpT* 115 (2003-04) 191-194.
PORTER, Stanley E., Mt 6:13 and Lk 11:4: "Lead us not into temptation". — *ExpT* 101 (1990) 359-362.

πέμπω 10 + 11/12 (Mt 4, Mk 1)

1. send (someone) (Lk 20,11; Acts 15,22); 2. send (by someone) (Acts 11,29); 3. send word (Lk 7,6.19; Acts 19,31); 4. cause to experience

Word groups	Lk	Acts	Mt	Mk
πέμπω + infinitive (VKe) → ἀποστέλλω + inf.	15,15		0	0
πέμπω δοῦλον → ἀποστέλλω δοῦλον	20,11		0	0
πέμπω (+) λέγων → ἀποστέλλω λέγων/εἶπον	7,6.19		0	0
DENAUX 2009 Lⁿ				

Characteristic of Luke; cf. ἐκπέμπω Acts 13,4; 17,10; προπέμπω Acts 15,3; 20,38; 21,5
DENAUX 2009 L***†; GOULDER 1989*; HAWKINS 1909L†; MORGENTHALER 1958LA

	Lk	Acts	Mt	Mk
πέμπω εἰς (VKb) → (ἐξ)ἀποστέλλω εἰς; cf. Eph 6,22; Phil 4,16; Col 4,8; 1 Pet 2,14; Rev 1,11; μεταπέμπομαι εἰς Acts 10,22; 25,3; προπέμπω εἰς Acts 20,38 BOISMARD 1984 Eb57; DENAUX 2009 1A*; NEIRYNCK 1985	4,26; 15,15; 16,27	10,5.32; 11,29; 15,22; 20,17	1	1
πέμπω πρός + accusative (VKc) → ἀναπέμπω/ἀποστέλλω πρός + acc.; cf. Jn 16,7; Eph 6,22; Phil 2,25; Col 4,8; Tit 3,12 BOISMARD 1984 Eb29; DENAUX 2009 1A*; NEIRYNCK 1985	4,26; 7,6 v.l.19	10,33; 15,25; 19,31; 23,30; 25,21*	0	0

Literature

EASTON 1910 164 [cited by Weiss as characteristic of L, and possibly corroborative]; HAUCK 1934 [Vorzugswort]; JEREMIAS 1980 69 [πέμπω + λέγων: red.].

DI MARCO, Angelico Salvatore, Πέμπω: per una ricerca del "campo semantico" nel NT. — RivBib 40 (1992) 385-419.

LOHMEYER, Monika, Der Apostelbegriff im Neuen Testament: Eine Untersuchung auf dem Hintergrund der synoptischen Aussendungsrede (SBB, 29). Stuttgart: Katholisches Bibelwerk, 1995, XI-472 p. Esp. 141-154: "ἀποστέλλειν und πέμπειν".

πενθερά 3 (Mt 2, Mk 1) mother-in-law (Lk 4,38; 12,53[1.2])

Word groups	Lk	Acts	Mt	Mk
μήτηρ + πενθερά	12,53[1.2]		1	0
νύμφη + πενθερά	12,53[1.2]		1	0

πενθέω 1 (Mt 2, Mk 0[1]) be sad

Word groups	Lk	Acts	Mt	Mk
πενθέω + κλαίω (VKa)	6,25		0	0[1]

Literature

DUPONT, Jacques, Les Béatitudes, II, 1969. Esp. 35-37: "Les affligés".

πενιχρός 1 poor (Lk 21,2)

Literature

HAUCK 1934 [seltenes Alleinwort].

πεντακισχίλιοι 1 (Mt 2, Mk 2) | five thousand (Lk 9,14)

πεντακόσιοι 1 | five hundred (Lk 7,41)

πέντε 9 + 5 (Mt 12, Mk 3) | five

Word groups	Lk	Acts	Mt	Mk
ἑβδομήκοντα πέντε (VKb)		7,14	0	0
μυριάδες πέντε (VKd)		19,19	0	0
χιλιάδες πέντε (VKc)		4,4	0	0

Literature

JEREMIAS 1980 107.261 [Lk 16,28: πέντε ἀδελφοί: trad.: "Lukas bevorzugt die Nachstellung der Kardinalzahl"].

πεντεκαιδέκατος 1 | fifteenth (Lk 3,1)

πεντήκοντα 3 + 1 (Mk 1) | fifty (Lk 7,41; 9,14; 16,6; Acts 13,20)

πέραν 1 (Mt 7, Mk 7) | across

Word groups	Lk	Acts	Mt	Mk
εἰς τὸ πέραν (SCa; VKa) → **διέρχομαι** εἰς τὸ πέραν	8,22		4	5

Literature

ELLINGTON, John, Where Is the Other Side? — BTrans 38 (1987) 221-226.

πέρας 1 (Mt 1)

1. limit (Lk 11,31); 2. conclusion

περί 45 + 72/74 (Mt 28, Mk 22[23]/25)

1. around (location) (Lk 13,8); 2. about (content) (Lk 2,38); 3. about (time) (Acts 22,6); 4. because (reason) (Lk 19,37); 5. on behalf of (benefaction); 6. with (association) (Acts 13,13); 7. with regard to (specification) (Acts 15,2)

Word groups	Lk	Acts	Mt	Mk
περὶ δέ (VKa)		21,25	4	2
περὶ μὲν γάρ (VKb)		28,22	0	0
περί + genitive	Lk	Acts	Mt	Mk
περί + genitive DENAUX 2009 Lan	1,1.4; 2,17[1.2].18; 2,27.33.38; 3,15.19[1.2]; 4,10.14.37.38; 5,14.15; 6,28; 7,3.17.18.24.27; 9,9.11.45; 11,53; 12,26; 13,1; 16,2; 19,37; 21,5; 22,32.37; 23,8; 24,4.14.19.27.44	1,1.3.16; 2,29.31; 5,24; 7,52; 8,12.15.34[1.2.3]; 9,13; 10,19; 11,22; 12,5; 13,29; 15,2.6; 17,32; 18,25; 19,8.23.40[1.2.3]; 21,21.24.25; 22,10.18; 23,6.11.15.20.29; 24,8.10.13.21[1.2].22.24.25; 25,9.15.16.18.19[1.2].20[1.2].24.26; 26,1.2.7.26; 28,15.21[1.2].22.23.31	20	13

περί + proper name (SCab; VKf) DENAUX 2009 LAn	3,15.19[1]; 7,3.24; 13,1; 24,19	1,16; 2,29; 18,25; 25,19[2]; 28,23.31	2	2
περὶ αὐτοῦ of Jesus DENAUX 2009 Lan	2,27.33; 4,17.37; 5,15; 7,17; 23,8	13,29	1	3
other instances with genitive (SCa)	1,1; 2,17[1.2].18.27.33.38; 3,19[2]; 4,10.14.37.38; 5,14.15; 6,28; 7,17.18; 9,11.45; 11,53; 12,26; 16,2; 19,37; 21,5; 22,32; 23,8; 24,4.14.44	1,1; 2,31; 5,24; 7,52; 8,12.15.34[1.2.3]; 9,13; 10,19; 11,22; 12,5; 13,29; 15,2.6; 17,32; 18,15; 19,23.40[1.3]; 21,21.24.25; 22,10.18; 23,6.20.29; 24,8.21[1.2].24.25; 25,9.16. 19[1].20[1.2]; 26,1.2.26; 28,21[1.2].22	17	12/14

→ ἀπαγγέλλω περί; γράφω περί; (τὰ) περὶ ἑαυτοῦ; τὸ/τὰ περὶ ἐμοῦ; εἰς + περί; ἐπιγινώσκω περί; ἐρωτάω περί; τὰ περὶ ἡμῶν; θαυμάζω περί; τὰ (περὶ) τοῦ Ἰησοῦ; τὰ (περὶ) τοῦ κυρίου; μαρτυρία περί; μεριμνάω περί; ὁράω/εῖδον περί

περί + accusative	Lk	Acts	Mt	Mk
περί with reference to location (SCba; VKg)	13,8; 17,2; 22,49	13,13; 21,8*; 22,6[2]; 28,7	3	7[8]
περί with reference to time (SCbb; VKh)		10,3.9; 22,6[1]	5	1
other instances with accusative (VKj)	10,40.41	19,25	0	1

→ ἐκ + περί; μεριμνάω περί

Characteristic of Luke

GASTON 1973 64 [Lked]; HENDRIKS 1986 434; MORGENTHALER 1958LA

	Lk	Acts	Mt	Mk
τὰ περί + genitive (SCac; VKd) DENAUX 2009 1A*	22,37 v.l.; 24,19.27	1,3; 8,12 v.l.; 18,25; 19,8 (v.l.?); 23,11.15; 24,10.22; 28,15.23 v.l.31	0	0/1
ἀκούω περί + genitive BOISMARD 1984 Bb25; DENAUX 2009 L***; GOULDER 1989; NEIRYNCK 1985	7,3; 9,9; 16,2; 23,8	9,13; 11,22; 17,32; 24,24	0	2
οἱ περί + accusative (SCbc; VKc) HARNACK 1906 41	22,49	13,13; 21,8*	1	1/2[3]
τὸ/τὰ περί + accusative/genitive; cf. Eph 6,22; Phil 1,27; 2,19.20.23; Col 4,8 BOISMARD 1984 cb139; DENAUX 2009 1A*; HARNACK 1906 45.52 [+ gen.]; NEIRYNCK 1985; PLUMMER 1922 lix	22,37; 24,19.27	1,3; 8,12 v.l.; 18,25; 19,8; 23,11.15; 24,10.22; 28,7.15.28 v.l.31	0	0
περὶ οὗ/ἧς/ὧν (SCaa; VKe) DENAUX 2009 1A*	1,4; 7,27; 9,9	19,40[2]; 24,13; 25,15.18.24.26; 26,7	1	0

→ περὶ τῆς βασιλείας τοῦ θεοῦ; διδάσκω τὰ περί; ἐν + περί + acc./gen.; εὐαγγελίζομαι περὶ τῆς βασιλείας; κρίνομαι περί + gen.; λαλέω περί + gen.; πείθω τινὰ περί τινος; ποιέω περί + gen.; προσεύχομαι περί + gen.

Literature

COLLISON 1977 140 [περὶ αὐτοῦ of Jesus: linguistic usage of Luke: certain]; HAUCK 1934 [Vorzugsverbindung: τὰ περί; Vorzugsverbindung/Stileigentümlichkeit:τὸ περὶ ἐμου]; JEREMIAS 1980 255 [ἀκούω τι περί τινος: red.]; 293: "Der substantivierte präpositionale Ausdruck τὸ περί τινος begegnet singularisch im NT nur an unserer Stelle [Lk 22,37]. Da Lk/Apg (wie Paulus) die Wendung sonst pluralisch (τὰ περί τινος) gebrauchen, wird unsere Stelle der Tradition zuzuschreiben sein"; 315 [τὰ περί + gen.: red.]; RADL 1975 419 [τὰ περί]; 423 [περί + gen.; περὶ τούτων]; SCHÜRMANN 1957 106 [περί = "im Interesse von" möglicherweise luk R]; 129 [τὸ περὶ ἐμου].

BARTSCH, Hans-Werner, Jesu Schwertwort, Lukas XXII. 35-38: Überlieferungsgeschichtliche Studie. — NTS 20 (1973-74) 190-203. Esp. 196-198: "Die Handschrift des Lukas".

περιάπτω 1	start a fire

Word groups	Lk	Acts	Mt	Mk
περιάπτω active → ἅπτω active; cf. ἀν/καθάπτω Acts 28,2*.3	22,55		0	0
περιάπτω πῦρ → (ἀν)ἅπτω λύχνον/πῦρ/πυράν	22,55		0	0

περιβάλλω 2/3 + 1 (Mt 5, Mk 2)	
1. clothe (Lk 12,27; 19,43*; 23,11; Acts 12,8); 2. adorn	

περιβλέπομαι 1 (Mk 6)	look around (Lk 6,10)

περιέχω 1 + 0/1	
1. contain (Acts 15,23*); 2. experience (Lk 5,9)	

Word groups	Lk	Acts	Mt	Mk
θάμβος περιέχει + accusative → ἐγένετο θάμβος/φόβος ἐπί + acc.; ἐπέπεσεν φόβος ἐπί + acc.; φόβος λαμβάνει + acc.; ἐπλήσθην θάμβους/φόβου	5,9		0	0

Characteristic of Luke
VOGEL 1899B

περιζώννυμι 3 + 0/1	περιζώννυμαι: be girded (Lk 12,35.37; 17,8; Acts 12,8*)

Word groups	Lk	Acts	Mt	Mk
περιζώννυμαι τὴν ὀσφύν (LN: get ready); cf. Eph 6,14	12,35		0	0

Literature
COLLISON 1977 60 [linguistic usage of Luke's "other source-material": likely]; EASTON 1910 157 [probably characteristic of L]; HAUCK 1934 [seltenes Alleinwort]; PAFFENROTH 1997 77.

περικαλύπτω 1 (Mk 1)	cover (Lk 22,64)

περίκειμαι 1 + 1 (Mk 1)	
1. be around; 2. be put around (Lk 17,2); 3. wear (Acts 28,20); 4. be in many ways	

περικρύβω** 1	conceal (Lk 1,24)

Literature
HAUCK 1934 [seltenes Alleinwort].

περικυκλόω 1	surround (Lk 19,43)

Literature
HAUCK 1934 [seltenes Alleinwort].

περιλάμπω 1 + 1 | shine around (Lk 2,9; Acts 26,13)

Word groups	Lk	Acts	Mt	Mk
περιλάμπω + φῶς → λάμπω + φῶς; cf. περιαστράπτω + φῶς Acts 9,3; 22,6		26,13	0	0

Characteristic of Luke
BOISMARD 1984 Ab193; HARNACK 1906 73; HAWKINS 1909LA; MORGENTHALER 1958*; NEIRYNCK 1985; PLUMMER 1922 liii; VOGEL 1899A

Literature
DENAUX 2009 LAⁿ; HAUCK 1934 [seltenes Alleinwort]; JEREMIAS 1980 80: "Lukas hat eine Vorliebe für die Derivate des Stammes λαμπ-".

περίλυπος 2 (Mt 1, Mk 2) | very sad (Lk 18,23.24)

περιοικέω* 1 | live nearby (Lk 1,65)

Literature
HAUCK 1934 [seltenes Alleinwort].

περίοικος 1 | neighbor (Lk 1,58)

Literature
HAUCK 1934 [seltenes Alleinwort].

περιπατέω 5 + 8 (Mt 7, Mk 8[9]/10)
1. walk (Lk 5,23; 7,22; 11,44; 20,26; 24,17); 2. behave (Acts 21,21)

Word groups	Lk	Acts	Mt	Mk
περιπατέω + dative (VKa)		21,21	0	0
περιπατέω ἐν στολαῖς	20,46		0	1
περιπατέω ἐπάνω (VKg)	11,44		0	0

περιπίπτω 1 + 1
1. run into (Acts 27,41); 2. fall into hands of (Lk 10,30); 3. experience

Word groups	Lk	Acts	Mt	Mk
περιπεσών → (ἐμ/ἐπι/κατα/προσ)πεσών; cf. Jn 12,24; Rom 11,22; 1 Cor 14,25; ἀναπεσών Jn 13,25; παραπεσών Heb 6,6		27,41	0	0

Characteristic of Luke	Lk	Acts	Mt	Mk
περιπίπτω aorist → (ἀνα/ἐμ/ἐπι/κατα/προσ/συμ)πίπτω aorist cf. ἀποπίπτω Acts 9,18; ἐκπίπτω Acts 12,7; 27,17.26.29.32 HARNACK 1906 54	10,30	27,41	0	0

Literature

DENAUX 2009 LAⁿ; LAⁿ [περιπίπτω aorist]; HAUCK 1934 [seltenes Alleinwort]; JEREMIAS 1980 191: "Eigentlich gebraucht findet sich περιπίπτω nur im Doppelwerk".

περιποιέομαι 1 + 1   acquire (Lk 17,33; Acts 20,28)

Word groups	Lk	Acts	Mt	Mk
τὴν ψυχὴν αὐτοῦ περιποιέομαι (*LN*: save oneself)	17,33		0	0

Literature

DENAUX 2009 LAⁿ; HAUCK 1934 [seltenes Alleinwort]; JEREMIAS 1980 269 [red.].

περισπάομαι 1   be distracted and anxious (Lk 10,40)

Literature

HAUCK 1934 [seltenes Alleinwort].

περίσσευμα 1 (Mt 1, Mk 1)   abundance (Lk 6,45)

Literature

SWELLENGREBEL, J.L., Puzzles in Luke. — *BTrans* 17 (1966) 118-122. Esp. 120-121 [Lk 6,45 ἐκ γὰρ περισσεύματος καρδίας].

περισσεύω 4 + 1 (Mt 5, Mk 1)

1. be in abundance (Lk 9,17; 21,4; Acts 16,5); 2. provide in abundance; 3. have more than enough (Lk 12,15; 15,17); 4. excessive; 5. cause to be intense; 6. have greater advantage

Word groups	Lk	Acts	Mt	Mk
ἐν τῷ περισσεύειν (*VK*c)	12,15		0	0
τὸ περισσεῦον (*VK*a)	21,4		2	1
τὸ περισσεῦσαν (*VK*b)	9,17		0	0
περισσεύω + ὑστέρημα (*VK*f); cf. 1 Cor 9,12; περισσεύω + ὑστερέω 1 Cor 8,8; Phil 4,12; περισσεύω + ὑστέρησις Mk 12,44; περίσσευμα + ὑστέρημα 1 Cor 8,14[1.2]	21,4		0	0
περισσεύομαι middle (*VK*h)	15,17		0	0

Literature

TAEGER, Jens-Wilhelm, *Der Mensch und sein Heil*, 1982. Esp. 181-183: "περισσεύειν τῷ ἀριθμῷ / ἐγενήθη ἀριθμός".

περισσός 4 (Mt 3/4, Mk 4/5)   1. advantage; 2. exceptional; 3. superfluous; 4. unnecessary; 5. *comparative*: excessive

Word groups	Lk	Acts	Mt	Mk
περισσότερον comparative (*SC*a; *VK*a)	7,26; 12,4.48; 20,47		1/2	3

περιστερά 2 (Mt 3, Mk 2) | dove, pigeon (Lk 2,24; 3,22)

Word groups	Lk	Acts	Mt	Mk
περιστερά singular (VKa)	3,22		1	1
πνεῦμα + περιστερά	3,22		1	1

Literature

KECK, Leander E., The Spirit and the Dove. — *NTS* 17 (1970-71) 41-67.
TELFER, W., The form of the Dove. — *JTS* 29 (1928) 238-242.

περιτέμνω 2 + 5/6 | circumcise

Word groups	Lk	Acts	Mt	Mk
περιτέμνω active (VKa)	1,59; 2,21	7,8; 15,5; 16,3; 21,21	0	0

Characteristic of Luke

BOISMARD 1984 Bb57; DENAUX 2009 lA*†; HAWKINS 1909B; NEIRYNCK 1985

Literature

BDAG 2000 807 [literature]; GERSDORF 1816 203 [ἦλθον περιτεμνεῖν].

περίχωρος 5 + 1 (Mt 2, Mk 1/2) | surrounding region

Word groups	Lk	Acts	Mt	Mk
περίχωρος + proper name (VKa)	3,3; 8,37		1	1

Characteristic of Luke

BOISMARD 1984 cb148; GASTON 1973 64 [Lked]; GOULDER 1989; NEIRYNCK 1985;
PLUMMER 1922 lx.

Literature

COLLISON 1977 175 [linguistic usage of Luke: certain]; DENAUX 2009 Lan; JEREMIAS 1980 118
[red.]; RADL 1975 424.

πετεινόν 4 + 2 (Mt 4, Mk 2) | bird

Word groups	Lk	Acts	Mt	Mk
(τὰ) πετεινὰ τοῦ οὐρανοῦ (LN: wild birds; SCa; VKa)	8,5; 9,58; 13,19	10,12; 11,6	3	1/2

πέτρα 3/4 (Mt 5, Mk 1) | bedrock (Lk 6,48; 8,6.13)

Πέτρος 19/20 + 56/58 (Mt 23/24, Mk 19[20]) | Peter

Word groups	Lk	Acts	Mt	Mk
Πέτρε vocative DENAUX 2009 lA[n]	22,34	10,13; 11,7	0	0

Πέτρος + Ἀνδρέας (SCb; VKd)	6,14	1,13	2	1
Πέτρος + Ἰάκωβος + Ἰωάννης (SCc; VKe)	6,14; 8,51; 9,28	1,13	1	3
Πέτρος + Ἰωάννης (SCd; VKe)	6,14; 8,51; 9,28; 22,8	1,13; 3,1.3.4.11; 4,13.19; 8,14	1	4
Πέτρος καὶ οἱ ἀπόστολοι and similar phrases (SCf; VKf) DENAUX 2009 1A[n]	8,45 v.l.; 9,32	2,14.37; 5,29	0	0
Σίμων (ὁ καλούμενος/ λεγόμενος and similar) Πέτρος (SCa; VKa)	5,8; 6,14	10,5.18.32; 11,13	3	2

Characteristic of Luke

CREDNER 1836 136; GASTON 1973 65 [Lked]; HENDRIKS 1986 468; MORGENTHALER 1958A

	Lk	Acts	Mt	Mk
Πέτρος without the article (SCe; VKg) DENAUX 2009 1A*	5,8; 6,14; 8,51; 9,20.28; 18,28 v.l.; 22,8.34	1,15; 2,14 v.l.38; 3,1.3.4.6.12 v.l.; 4,8; 5,3 v.l.8.15.29; 8,14.20; 9,32.38.39; 10,5.9.13.21.32.34.46; 11,2. 4.7; 12,3; 15,7	2/3	2/3

Literature

BDAG 2000 139 [literature]; JEREMIAS 1980 292: "Πέτρε: Dieser Vokativ findet sich im NT nur Lk 22,34/Apg 10,13; 11,7 und könnte lukanisch sein".

CARAGOUNIS, Chrys C., *Peter and the Rock* (BZNW, 58). Berlin – New York: de Gruyter, 1990, IX-157 p. Esp. 7-57: "The philological evidence".

CLAVIER, Henri, Πέτρος καὶ πέτρα. — ELTESTER, W. (ed.), *Neutestamentliche Studien für Rudolf Bultmann zu seinem siebstigsten Geburtstag am 20. August 1954* (BZNW, 21). Berlin: Töpelmann, 1954, [2]1957, 94-109. Esp. 101-109: "Le problème linguistique".

ELLIOTT, James K., Κῆφας: Σίμων Πέτρος: ὁ Πέτρος: An Examination of New Testament Usage. — NT 14 (1972) 241-256. Esp. 250-252: "The addition of Πέτρος"; 252-254: "Arthrous/anarthrous Πέτρος". [NTA 17, 836]

FITZMYER, Joseph A., Aramaic Kepha' and Peter's Name in the New Testament. — BEST, E. – WILSON, R.McL. (eds.), *Text and Interpretation*. FS M. Black, 1979, 121-132; = ID., *To Advance the Gospel*, 1981, 112-124.

MIGUENS, Manuel, Kephâs, ho pétros y el primado de Pedro. — SBF/LA 17 (1967) 348-364.

πήγανον* 1 | rue (Lk 11,42)

Literature

HAUCK 1934 [seltenes Alleinwort].

BISCHOP, Eric F.F., Rue – πήγανον. — ExpT 59 (1947-48) 81.

CORRENS, Dietrich, Die Verzehntung der Raute: Luk xi 42 und M Schebi ix 1. — NT 6 (1963) 110-112.

NESTLE, Eberhard, "Anise" and "Rue". — ExpT 15 (1903-04) 528.

—, Eine semitische schriftliche Quelle fur Matthäus und Lukas. — ZNW 7 (1906) 260-261.

πήρα 4 (Mt 1, Mk 1) | traveler's bag (Lk 9,3; 10,4; 22,35.36)

Characteristic of Luke

PLUMMER 1922 lx

| **πῆχυς** 1 (Mt 1) | cubit (Lk 12,25) |

Literature

SCHWARZ, Günther, Προσθεῖναι ἐπὶ τὴν ἡλικίαν αὐτοῦ πῆχυν ἕνα. — *ZNW* 71 (1980) 244-247.

| **πιέζω** 1 | press down (Lk 6,38) |

Literature

HAUCK 1934 [seltenes Alleinwort].

| **πικρῶς** 1 (Mt 1) | with agony (Lk 22,62) |

| **Πιλᾶτος** 12 + 3 (Mt 9, Mk 10) | Pilate |

Word groups	Lk	Acts	Mt	Mk
Πιλᾶτος + Ἡρῴδης	3,1; 23,6($-7^{1.2}$).11.12.13(-15)	4,27	0	0
Πόντιος Πιλᾶτος (*SC*a; *VK*a)	3,1	4,27	0/1	0
Πιλᾶτος without the article (*SC*b; *VK*b)	3,1; 13,1; 23,6.13.24	3,13; 4,27; 13,28	2	1/2

| **πίμπλημι** 13 + 9 (Mt 2) | |

1. fill completely (Lk 5,7); 2. make happen (Lk 21,22)
πίμπλαμαι: 3. come to an end (Lk 1,33); 4. completely (Lk 5,26; Acts 3,10)

Word groups	Lk	Acts	Mt	Mk
γεγραμμένα + πίμπλημι → γεγραμμένα/γραφή/λόγος/ῥῆμα + **πληρόω/τελέω**	21,22		0	0
ἐπλήσθη/ἐπλήσθησαν with reference to time (*SC*b; *VK*c) → ἐπλήσθησαν αἱ **ἡμέραι**; ἐπλήσθη ὁ **χρόνος**; **τελειόω** with reference to time; **συμπληροῦται** ἡ ἡμέρα DENAUX 2009 Lⁿ	1,23.57; 2,6.21.22		0	0
ἐπλήσθην θάμβους/φόβου → **ἐγένετο** θάμβος/φόβος ἐπί + acc.; **ἐπέσεν** φόβος ἐπί + acc.; φόβος **λαμβάνει** + acc.; θάμβος **περιέχει** + acc. DENAUX 2009 LAⁿ	5,26	3,10	0	0
ζήλου πίμπλημι BOISMARD 1984 Aa152		5,17; 13,45	0	0
πίμπλημι active (*VK*b)	5,7		1	0

Characteristic of Luke

BOISMARD 1984 Bb11; CREDNER 1936 141; DENAUX 2009 L***; GOULDER 1989*; HARNACK 1906 72; HAWKINS 1909 L; HENDRIKS 1986 434; MORGENTHALER 1958L; NEIRYNCK 1985; PLUMMER 1922 lx?

	Lk	Acts	Mt	Mk
Passive form of πίμπλημι with gen. abstr. DENAUX 2009 L***	1,15.41.67; 4,28; 5,26; 6,11	2,4; 3,10; 4,8.31; 5,17; 9,17; 13,9.45; 19,29	0	0

ἐπλήσθην πνεύματος ἁγίου (SCa; VKa) BOISMARD 1984 Ab20; DENAUX 2009 lA*; HARNACK 1906 72; NEIRYNCK 1985	1,15.41.67	2,4; 4,8.31; 9,17; 13,9	0	0
ἐπλήσθησαν πάντες; cf. πλησθῆναι πάντα Lk 21,22; ἐπλήσθησαν ἅπαντες Acts 4,31 BOISMARD 1984 Ab96; NEIRYNCK 1985	4,28; 21,22	2,4	0	0
→ ἐπλήσθησαν αἱ ἡμέραι				

Literature

COLLISON 1977 60 [linguistic usage of Luke's "other source-material": highly probable, but, the possibility that Luke has introduced it a few times cannot be excluded]; DENAUX 2009 La^n [ἐπλήσθησαν πάντες]; EASTON 1910 157 [πίμπλημι in temporal sense: probably characteristic of L, not in Weiss]; 167 [πίμπλημι, in general use: classed by Weiss as characteristic of L on insufficient (?) evidence]; GERSDORF 1816 184 [πλησθήσεται ἔτι ἐκ κοιλίας μητρὸς αὐτοῦ]; 191-192 [καὶ ἐγένετο ὡς ἐπλήσθησαν]; 198.206 [ἐπλήσθη πνεύματος ἁγίου]; 202 [τῇ δὲ Ἐλισάβετ ἐπλήσθη ὁ χρόνος]; 219-220 [ἐγένετο δὲ ἐν τῷ εἶναι αὐτοὺς ἐκεῖ ἐπλήσθησαν]; 242.244 [καὶ ὅτε ἐπλήσθησαν]; 243 [ἐπλήσθησαν ἡμέραι ὀκτώ]; HAUCK 1934 [Vorzugswort/Vorzugsverbindung: πνεύματος ἁγίου πλησθήσεται]; JEREMIAS 1980 35: "lukanisches Vorzugswort"; 36: "Kennzeichnend für Lukas ist vor allem die Verbindung des Passivs von πίμπλημι mit Gen. abstr. (im NT nur Lk 6/Apg 9), insbesondere mit πνεύματος ἁγίου (…). Dagegen ist die Verwendung des Passivs von πίμπλημι zur Bezeichnung des Ablaufs einer Zeitspanne der Tradition zuzuweisen"; RADL 1975 424.

JUNG, Chang-Wook, *Infancy Narrative*, 2004. Esp. 170-179 [πίμπλημι pass. with ἡμέρα or χρόνος].

πινακίδιον* 1	tablet (Lk 1,63)

Literature

HAUCK 1934 [seltenes Alleinwort].

πίναξ 1 (Mt 2, Mk 2)	plate (Lk 11,39)

πίνω 17 + 3 (Mt 15, Mk 7[8]/10)	
1. drink (Lk 22,18); 2. soak up	

Characteristic of Luke	Lk	Acts	Mt	Mk
πίνω + ἐσθίω/ἔσθω (SCa; VKa); cf. πίνω + τρώγω Mt 24,38; συμπίνω καὶ συνεσθίω Acts 10,41 DENAUX 2009 L*** (?); GOULDER 1989	5,30.33; 7,33.34; 10,7; 12,19.29.45; 13,26; 17,8$^{1.2}$.27.28; 22,30	9,9; 23,12.21	6	0/1

Literature

COLLISON 1977 50 [ἐσθίειν + πίνειν: linguistic usage of Luke: probable]; SCHÜRMANN 1957 49 [ἐσθίειν (καὶ) πίνειν; φαγεῖν (καὶ) πεῖν].

AMELING, W., Φάγωμεν καὶ πίωμεν. Griechische Parallellen zu zwei Stellen aus dem Neuen Testament. — *Zeitschrift für Papyrologie und Epigraphik* 60 (1985) 35-43. [Lk 12,19]

πίπτω 17/20 + 9/10 (Mt 19, Mk 8)

1. fall (Lk 8,7; Acts 20,9); 2. fall down (Lk 10,18; Acts 5,5); 3. prostrate oneself before (Lk 5,12); 4. be destroyed; 5. die; 6. cease; 7. happen (Acts 13,11); 7. worsen; 8. come to an end; 9. become inadequate; 10. experience

Word groups	Lk	Acts	Mt	Mk
ἀχλὺς καὶ σκότος πίπτει (*LN*: become blind)		13,11	0	0
ὁ κλῆρος πίπτει ἐπί + accusative (*LN*: choose by lot)		1,26	0	0
πίπτω aorist → (ἀνα/ἐμ/ἐπι/κατα/ περι/προσ/συμ)πίπτω aorist; cf. ἀποπίπτω Acts 9,18; ἐκπίπτω Acts 12,7; 27,17.26.29.32	5,12; 8,5.7.8.14.41; 10,18; 13,4; 16,17; 17,16; 20,18[1.2]; 23,30	1,26; 5,5.10; 9,4; 10,25; 13,11; 20,9; 22,7	13	5
πίπτω fall down as a sign of devotion (*SCf*)	5,12; 8,41; 17,16	10,25	6	2
πίπτω ἀπό (*SCa*; *VKa*); cf. ἀποπίπτω ἀπό Acts 9,18	16,21	20,9; 27,34*	2	0
πίπτω εἰς (*SCb*; *VKb*)	6,39*; 8,8.14; 14,5	22,7	2/3	2
πίπτω (ἐκ) + gen. (*SCc*; *VKc*)	10,18; 16,17	27,34* v.l.	0/1	1
πίπτω ἐν μέσῳ (*VKd*)	8,7		0	0
πίπτω ἐπὶ/παρά/πρὸς τοὺς πόδας → προσπίπτω τοῖς γόνασιν; cf. πίπτω εἰς τοὺς πόδας Mt 18,29 v.l.; προσ-πίπτω πρὸς τοὺς πόδας Mk 7,25 DENAUX 2009 LAn	8,41; 17,16	5,10; 10,25	0	1
πίπτω ἐπὶ πρόσωπον (*VKh*)	5,12; 17,16		2	0
πίπτω παρά + accusative (*SCg*; *VKj*)	8,5.41; 17,16	5,10 v.l.	1	1
πίπτω πρός + accusative (*VKk*)		5,10	0	1

Characteristic of Luke	Lk	Acts	Mt	Mk
πεσών → ἐμ/ἐπι/κατα/περι/προσπεσών; cf. Jn 12,24; Rom 11,22; 1 Cor 14,25; ἀναπεσών Jn 13,25; παραπεσών Heb 6,6 CREDNER 1836 139	5,12; 8,14.41; 10,18; 20,18	5,5; 9,4; 10,25	5	1
πίπτω ἐπί + accusative (*LN*: cause to suffer; *SCe*; *VKg*) → πίπτω ἐπὶ πρόσωπον; προσπίπτω τοῖς γόνασιν; cf. πίπτω ἐπί + gen. Mk 9,20; 14,35 GOULDER 1989	8,6*.8 v.l.; 11,17; 13,4; 20,18[1.2]; 23,30	1,26; 9,4; 10,25; 13,11	6	1

Literature

HAUCK 1934 [Vorzugsverbindung: πεσὼν παρὰ τοὺς πόδας].

SPITTA, Friedrich, Der Satan als Blitz. — *ZNW* 9 (1908) 160-163. [Lk 10,18]
WEBSTER, Charles A., St. Luke x.18. Ἐθεώρουν τὸν σατανᾶν ὡς ἀστραπὴν ἐκ τοῦ οὐρανοῦ πεσόντα. — *ExpT* 57 (1945-46) 52-53.

πιστεύω 9 + 37/39 (Mt 11, Mk 10[14]/15)

1. think to be true (Lk 1,20); 2. trust (Lk 16,11); 3. have Christian faith (Acts 4,32); 4. entrust (Lk 16,11)

Word groups	Lk	Acts	Mt	Mk
οἱ πεπιστευκότες BOISMARD 1984 Aa33		15,5; 18,27; 19,18; 21,20.25	0	0

	Lk	Acts	Mt	Mk
πιστεύω + dative (SCa; VKa) → **πιστεύω** transitive; **πιστός** + dat.	1,20; 20,5	5,14; 8,12; 13,41 v.l.; 16,34; 18,8[1]; 24,14; 26,27[1]; 27,25	4/5	1[3]
πιστεύω + infinitive (VKj)		8,37*; 15,11	0	0
πιστεύω transitive (VKf) → **πιστεύω** + dat. DENAUX 2009 LA[n]	16,11	13,41	0	0
πιστεύω + ἀπειθέω (SCd; VKh); cf. πιστεύω + ἀπιστία Mk 9,24; [16,14]; πιστεύω + ἀπιστέω Mk [16,16]; πίστις + ὀλιγοπιστία Mt 17,20		14,1(-2)	0	0
πιστεύω (+) εἰς (SCb; VKb) → **πίστις** εἰς		10,43; 14,23; 19,4	1	1
πιστεύω (+) ἐπί + accusative (SCc; VKe); cf. πιστὸς ἐπί + accusative Mt 25,21[2].23[2]		9,42; 11,17; 16,31; 22,19	1	0
πιστεύω ἐπί + dative (SCc; VKd)	24,25		0	0
πιστεύω τῷ θεῷ; cf. Tit 3,8 BOISMARD 1984 ca56		16,34; 27,25		
πιστεύω τῷ κυρίῳ / ἐπὶ τὸν κύριον; cf. πιστεύω ἐπί σε Acts 22,19 BOISMARD 1984 Aa22		5,4; 9,42; 11,17; 16,31; 18,8[1]	0	0
πιστεύω (+) ὅτι (SCe)	1,45	9,26; 27,25	1	2
πιστεύω + σῴζω → **πίστις** + σῴζω; cf. πιστεύω + σωτήρ Tit 1,3 DENAUX 2009 LA[n]	8,12.50	15,11; 16,31	0	[1]

Literature

BOTHA, J.Eugene, *The Meanings of pisteúō in the Greek New Testament: A Semantic-Lexicographical Study.* — *Neotestamentica* 21 (1987) 225-240.

HAGER, Jens, *Das Verbum πιστεύω in den vier Evangelien.* Diss. Graz, 1959.

LINDSAY, Dennis Ray, *Josephus and Faith: Πίστις and πιστεύειν as Faith Terminology in the Writings of Flavius Josephus and in the New Testament* (Arbeiten zur Geschichte des antiken Judentums und des Urchristentums, 19). Leiden: Brill, 1993, XIV-212 p. — Diss. Tübingen, 1991 (dir. O. Betz). Esp. 113-155: "Πιστεύειν in the writings of Flavius Josephus and the NT".

—, The Roots and Development of the πιστ- Word Group as Faith Terminology. — *JSNT* 49 (1993) 103-118.

TAEGER, Jens-Wilhelm, *Der Mensch und sein Heil*, 1982. Esp. 106-123: "πίστις / πιστεύειν".

WERNINK, J.R., *Exegetische studiën over πίστις en πιστεύειν in het Nieuwe Testament.* Rotterdam: Van der Meer & Verbruggen, 1858, VIII-166 p.

WILCOX, Max, *The Semitisms in Acts*, 1965. Esp. 85-86 [πιστεύω ἐπί].

πίστις 11 + 15/16 (Mt 8, Mk 5)

1. what can be believed (Acts 17,31); 2. trust (Acts 24,24); 3. trustworthiness; 4. Christian faith; 5. doctrine; 6. promise

Word groups	Lk	Acts	Mt	Mk
πίστιν ἔχω (SCa; VKa)	17,6	14,9	2	2
πίστιν παρέχω/προστίθημι (SCb; VKb) DENAUX 2009 LA[n]	17,5	17,31	0	0
πίστις ἡ διά + genitive (VKg)		3,16[2]	0	0
πίστις (ἡ) εἰς (SCc; VKh) → **πιστεύω** εἰς		20,21; 24,24; 26,18	0	0
πίστις εἰς (κύριον/Χριστὸν) Ἰησοῦν; cf. Col 2,5 BOISMARD 1984 ca19		20,21; 24,24; 26,18 (ἐμέ)	0	0
πίστις + σῴζω (SCd) → **πιστεύω** + σῴζω; cf. πίστις + σωτηρία 2 Tim 3,15; 1 Pet 1,5.9	7,50; 8,48; 17,19; 18,42	14,9	1	2

Literature

VON BENDEMANN 2001 432: "πίστις ist lukanische Vorzugsvokabel"; SCHÜRMANN 1957 107 [πίστις Lk 18,8; 22,32 späterer Gemeindesprachgebrauch].

BORMANN, Lukas, *Recht, Gerechtigkeit und Religion*, 2001. Esp. 204-205.

DELEBECQUE, Édouard, *Études grecques*, 1976. Esp. 99-107: "'Foi', moutarde et sycomore (17,5-6)".

LINDSAY, Dennis Ray, *Josephus and Faith: Πίστις and πιστεύειν as Faith Terminology in the Writings of Flavius Josephus and in the New Testament* (Arbeiten zur Geschichte des antiken Judentums und des Urchristentums, 19). Leiden: Brill, 1993, XIV-212 p. — Diss. Tübingen, 1991 (dir. O. Betz). Esp. 77-111: "Πίστις in the writings of Flavius Josephus and the NT".

LINDSAY, Dennis Ray, The Roots and Development of the πιστ- Word Group as Faith Terminology. — *JSNT* 49 (1993) 103-118.

LÜHRMAN, Dieter, Pistis im Judentum. — *ZNW* 64 (1973) 19-38. [NTA 18, 403]

MOULE, Charles F.D., The Biblical Conception of "Faith". — *ExpT* 68 (1956-57) 157, 222.

PATHRAPANKAL, J., You Shal Be My Witnesses. — *Clergy Monthly* (Ranchi) 37 (1973) 184-197. [NTA 18, 404]

PRETE, Benedetto, Il senso della formula "coloro che sono stati santificati per la fede in me" (*At* 26,18c). — *RivBib* 35 (1987) 313-320. Esp. 314-316: "Motivi di carattere filologico".

SHEARER, Thomas, The Concept of "Faith" in the Synoptic Gospels. — *ExpT* 69 (1957-58) 3-6.

TAEGER, Jens-Wilhelm, *Der Mensch und sein Heil*, 1982. Esp. 106-123: "πίστις / πιστεύειν".

TORRANCE, Thomas F., One Aspect of the Biblical Conception of Faith. — *ExpT* 68 (1956-57) 111-114.

—, The Biblical Conception of "Faith". — *ExpT* 68 (1956-57) 221-222.

WERNINK, J.R., *Exegetische studiën over πίστις en πιστεύειν in het Nieuwe Testament*. Rotterdam: Van der Meer & Verbruggen, 1858, VIII-166 p.

πιστός 6 + 4 (Mt 5)

1. trusting (Acts 16,15); 2. trustworthy (Lk 16,11); 3. sure (Acts 13,34)

Word groups	Lk	Acts	Mt	Mk
πιστός + dative (VKd) → πιστεύω + dat.		16,15	0	0
πιστὸς ἐν (SCa; VKf); cf. πιστὸς ἐπί + acc. Mt 25,21^2.23^2; πιστεύω ἐν Mk 1,15 DENAUX 2009 L^n	16,10$^{1.2}$.11.12; 19,17		0	0
οἱ πιστοί noun (VKb)		10,45	0	0

Literature

HARNACK 1906 34 [πιστός = believer, only in Acts 10,45; 16,1.15]; REHKOPF 1959 96 [πιστός (in profanem Sinn): vorlukanisch]; SCHÜRMANN 1961 276.

BORMANN, Lukas, *Recht, Gerechtigkeit und Religion*, 2001. Esp. 205.

LINDSAY, Dennis Ray, *Josephus and Faith: Πίστις and πιστεύειν as Faith Terminology in the Writings of Flavius Josephus and in the New Testament* (Arbeiten zur Geschichte des antiken Judentums und des Urchristentums, 19). Leiden: Brill, 1993, XIV-212 p. — Diss. Tübingen, 1991 (dir. O. Betz). Esp. 157-164: "Πιστός in the writings of Flavius Josephus and the NT".

—, The Roots and Development of the πιστ- Word Group as Faith Terminology. — *JSNT* 49 (1993) 103-118.

πλανάω 1 (Mt 8, Mk 4)

1. deceive (Lk 21,8); πλανάομαι: 2. wander about; 3. stray from the truth

πλατεῖα 3 + 1 (Mt 2) | wide street (Lk 10,10; 13,26; 14,21; Acts 5,15)

Word groups	Lk	Acts	Mt	Mk
εἰς τὰς πλατείας DENAUX 2009 Laⁿ	10,10; 14,21	5,15	0	0

Characteristic of Luke
BOISMARD 1984 Eb49; NEIRYNCK 1985

Literature
VON BENDEMANN 2001 428 [εἰς τὰς πλατείας]; REHKOPF 1959 96 [vorlukanisch]; SCHÜRMANN 1961 284 [protoluk R nicht beweisbar].

πλείων 9 + 19 (Mt 7, Mk 1/2)

1. more (quantity) (Acts 2,40); 2. more (degree) (Lk 7,42); 3. more appropriate

Word groups	Lk	Acts	Mt	Mk
ἐπὶ πλεῖον (*VK*h) → ἐπὶ **πολύ**; cf. 2 Tit 2,16; 3,9; ἐπὶ πλείονας ἡμέρας Acts 27,20; ἐπὶ πλείονα χρόνον Acts 18,20		4,17; 20,9; 24,4	0	0
λόγος πλείων → λόγος **πολύς** BOISMARD 1984 Ca13		2,40		
τὸ πλεῖον (*SC*d; *VK*g)	7,43		0	0
οἱ πλείονες/πλείους (*VK*b) HARNACK 1906 52		19,32; 27,12	0	0
πλείων παρά + accusative (*VK*e)	3,13		0	0
πλείων + πλήν + genitive (*VK*d)		15,28	0	0
πλείων χρόνος → **πολὺς** χρόνος; χρόνος οὐκ **ὀλίγος**		18,20	0	0
πλείους (+) ἡμέραι		13,31; 21,10; 24,11; 25,6.14; 27,20	0	0
πλείων ἤ (*SC*b; *VK*c) DENAUX 2009 LAⁿ	9,13	24,11 *v.l.*; 25,6	0/1	0
πλείων temporal BOISMARD 1984 Aa5		4,22; 13,31; 18,20; 21,10; 24,11.17; 25,6.14; 27,20	0	0
πλέον (*VK*a) DENAUX 2009 LAⁿ	3,13	15,28	0	0

Characteristic of Luke
MORGENTHALER 1958A

	Lk	Acts	Mt	Mk
μηδὲν πλέον (*SC*a) BOISMARD 1984 Ab194; NEIRYNCK 1985	3,13	15,28	0	0
πλείων without comparative value (absolute use) (*SC*d; *VK*j) DENAUX 2009 IA*	7,42.43; 11,53	2,40; 13,31; 18,20; 19,32; 21,10; 24,17; 25,14; 27,12.20; 28,23	1	0

Literature

DENAUX 2009 lAn; LAⁿ [μηδὲν πλέον]; JEREMIAS 1980 108 [πλέον: red.]; RADL 1975 424 [πλείων; πλείους + ἡμέραι].

ELLIOTT, James K., The Two Forms of the Third Declension Comparative Adjectives in the New Testament. — *NT* 19 (1977) 234-239.

MUSSIES, Gerard, The Declension of the -(ί)ων Comparatives in New Testament Greek. — *NT* 6 (1963) 233-238.

πλεονεξία 1 (Mk 1)

1. greed (Lk 12,15); 2. exploitation

Literature

BDAG 2000 824 [literature].

MALHERBE, Abraham J., The Christianization of a *Topos* (Luke 12:13-34). — *NT* 38 (1996) 123-135.

πλέω 1 + 4 — sail (Lk 8,23; Acts 21,3; 27,2.6.24)

Characteristic of Luke; cf. ἐκπλέω Acts 15,39; 18,18; 20,6

BOISMARD 1984 Bb75; HARNACK 1906 54; HAWKINS 1909 187; NEIRYNCK 1985

Literature

DENAUX 2009 lAⁿ.

πληγή 2 + 2

1. hit (Lk 10,30; 12,48; Acts 16,23); 2. wound (Acts 16,33); 3. plague; 4. distress

Characteristic of Luke

BOISMARD 1984 Db27; NEIRYNCK 1985

Literature

VON BENDEMANN 2001 424: "πληγή in den Synoptikern nur bei Lukas"; DENAUX 2009 LAⁿ; EASTON 1910 164 [cited by Weiss as characteristic of L, and possibly corroborative].

πλῆθος 8 + 16/17 (Mk 2)

1. large number; 2. crowd (Acts 2,6)

Word groups	Lk	Acts	Mt	Mk
ἐσχίσθη τὸ πλῆθος BOISMARD 1984 Aa160		14,4; 23,7	0	0
ἅπαν τὸ πλῆθος DENAUX 2009 Laⁿ	8,37; 19,37; 23,1	25,24	0	0
πᾶν τὸ πλῆθος DENAUX 2009 lAⁿ	1,10	6,5; 15,12	0	0

πλῆθος + ἀκολουθέω/συνάγω/συνέρχομαι→ ὄχλος + ἀκολουθέω/συμπαραγίνομαι/συμπνίγω/συμπορεύομαι/ συναντάω/σύνειμι/συνέρχομαι/συνεφίστημι/συνέχω	23,27	2,6; 5,16; 15,30; 21,36	0	1
(τὸ) πλῆθος συνέρχεται BOISMARD 1984 Aa158		2,6; 5,16	0	0
πληθή plural (VKc)		5,14	0	0

Characteristic of Luke

BOISMARD 1984 Bb117; DENAUX 2009 L***; GOULDER 1989*; HARNACK 1906 71; HAWKINS 1909 L; MORGENTHALER 1958A; NEIRYNCK 1985; PLUMMER 1922 lx

	Lk	Acts	Mt	Mk
ἅπαν/πᾶν τὸ πλῆθος (SCa; VKa) → πάντα τὰ ἔθνη; ἅπας/ὅλος/πᾶς ὁ λαός; πᾶς ὁ ὄχλος BOISMARD 1984 Ab28; DENAUX 2009 L***; GOULDER 1989*; HAWKINS 1909 L; HARNACK 1906 71; NEIRYNCK 1985	1,10; 8,37; 19,37; 23,1	6,5; 15,12; 25,24	0	0
ἅπαν/πᾶν/πολύ πλῆθος (SCb; VKb) → ὄχλος πολύς CREDNER 1936 141; DENAUX 2009 L***	1,10; 2,13; 5,6; 6,17; 8,37; 19,37; 23,1.27	2,6; 4,32; 5,14.16; 6,2.5; 14,1.4; 15,12.30; 17,4; 19,9; 21,22.36; 23,7; 25,24; 28,3	0	2
πλῆθος of things HARNACK 1906 39.54 ["elsewhere used only of men"]	5,6	28,3	0	0
πλῆθος (πολὺ) τοῦ λαοῦ BOISMARD 1984 Ab97; HARNACK 1906 71; NEIRYNCK 1985	1,10; 6,17; 23,27	21,36	0	0
πλῆθος τῶν μαθητῶν BOISMARD 1984 Ab195; NEIRYNCK 1985	19,37	6,2	0	0

Literature

COLLISON 1977 175 [linguistic usage of Luke: probable]; 176 [ἅπαν/πᾶν τὸ πλῆθος; πολὺ πλῆθος: noteworthy phenomena]; DENAUX 2009 LAⁿ [πλῆθος of things, πλῆθος τῶν μαθητῶν]; Laⁿ [πλῆθος (πολὺ) τοῦ λαοῦ]; EASTON 1910 164 [cited by Weiss as characteristic of L, and possibly corroborative]; GERSDORF 1816 174 [πᾶν τὸ πλῆθος ἦν τοῦ λαοῦ προσευχόμενον]; 179-180 [πᾶν τὸ πλῆθος τοῦ λαοῦ]; 230-231 [καὶ ἐξαίφνης ἐγένετο σὺν τῷ ἀγγέλῳ πλῆθος στρατιᾶς οὐρανίου αἰνούντων τὸν θεόν]; HAUCK 1934 [Vorzugswort]; JEREMIAS 1980 30: "πλῆθος ist lukanisches Vorzugswort"; 132 [πλῆθος πολύ: red.]; 305: "πλῆθος τοῦ λαοῦ: Diese Genitivverbindung findet sich im NT ausschließlich im lk Doppelwerk"; RADL 1975 424 [πλῆθος; ἅπαν(πᾶν) τὸ πλῆθος; πλῆθος τοῦ λαοῦ; πλῆθος πολύ].

CITRON, Bernhard, The Multitude in the Synoptic Gospels. — ScotJT 7 (1954) 408-418.
Esp. 409-411: "Terminology" [πλῆθος, λαός, ὄχλος].
TAYLOR, Justin, The Community of Jesus' Disciples. — Proceedings of the Irish Biblical Association 21 (1998) 25-32.

πλήμμυρα 1	flood (Lk 6,48)

Literature
HAUCK 1934 [seltenes Alleinwort].

πλήν 15 + 4 (Mt 5, Mk 1) | but, except

Word groups	Lk	Acts	Mt	Mk
μέν + πλήν	22,22		0	0
οὐδεὶς …, πλήν; cf. οὐδεὶς …, ἐκτός Acts 26,33; οὐδεὶς …, χωρὶς Mt 13,34		27,22	0	0
πλείων + πλήν + genitive		15,28	0	0
πλήν + genitive (SCa; VKa) BOISMARD 1984 ca20		8,1; 15,28; 27,22	0	1
πλὴν ἰδού → ἀλλ'/ ἢ ἰδού	22,21		0	0
πλὴν ὅτι		20,23	0	0
πλὴν οὐαί → ἀλλὰ οὐαί	6,24; 17,1; 22,22		1	0

Characteristic of Luke
DENAUX 2009 L***; GOULDER 1989*; HAWKINS 1909 L; HENDRIKS 1986 433; MORGENTHALER 1958L; PLUMMER 1922 lx

Literature
VON BENDEMANN 2001 417; COLLISON 1977 121 [linguistic usage of Luke: certain; πλὴν οὐαί: noteworthy phenomena]; HAUCK 1934 [Vorzugswort]; RADL 1975 424; REHKOPF 1959 96 [πλήν als Adv.; πλὴν ὅτι: vorlukanisch]; SCHÜRMANN 1957 5-6 [πλὴν (οὐαί); πλήν "ausser" (attisch), "jedoch", "indessen" (vulgär)]; 1961 276 [πλήν als Adverb].

DUPONT, Jacques, Les Béatitudes, I, 1958. Esp. 312.
—, Les Béatitudes, III, 1973. Esp. 30-34.
FRID, Bo, A Brief Note in plēn in Roman times. — SEÅ 51-52 (1986-87) 65-71.
LEE, John A.L., A History of New Testament Lexicography, 2003. Esp. 311-315.
THRALL, Margaret E., Greek Particles in the New Testament, 1962. Esp. 20-24: "Πλήν as an adversative and progressive conjunction"; 67-70 [πλήν in Lk 22,42].
WILSON, W.A.A., "But me no Buts". — BTrans 15 (1964) 173-180.

πλήρης 2 + 8 (Mt 2, Mk 2/3)
1. full (Lk 4,1; 5,12); 2. complete (Acts 6,5); 3. very many (Acts 9,36)

Word groups	Lk	Acts	Mt	Mk
πλήρης λέπρας	5,12		0	0
πλήρης + two genitives; cf. Jn 1,14 BOISMARD 1984 ba9		6,3.5.8; 9,36; 11,24; 13,10	0	0
πλήρης indeclinable (VKa)		6,5	0	1

Characteristic of Luke
CREDNER 1836 141; PLUMMER 1922 lx

	Lk	Acts	Mt	Mk
πλήρης for persons + genitive; cf. Jn 1,14 BOISMARD 1984 bb76; DENAUX 2009 lA*; NEIRYNCK 1985; VOGEL 1899D	4,1; 5,12	6,3.5.8; 7,55; 9,36; 11,24; 13,10; 19,28	0	0
πλήρης πνεύματος ἁγίου; cf. πλήρης πνεύματος καὶ σοφίας Acts 6,3 BOISMARD 1984 Ab98; NEIRYNCK 1985	4,1	6,5; 7,55; 11,24	0	0
πλήρης πνεύματος χάριτος (without ὤν) → πλήρης πνεύματος VOGEL 1899C		6,8	0	0

Literature

DENAUX 2009 IAⁿ [πλήρης πνεύματος ἁγίου]; HAUCK 1934 [Vorzugsverbindung: πλήρης λέπρας; πλήρης πνεύματος ἁγίου]; JEREMIAS 1980 114-115: "πλήρης mit Genitiv ist lk Vorzugswendung".

LEE,G.M., Indeclinable *plērēs* (Moulton *Proleg.* 50) . — *NT* 17 (1975) 304.

πληροφορέω 1

1. make happen (Lk 1,1); 2. proclaim; 3. accomplish
πληροφορέομαι: 4. be completely certain

Characteristic of Luke

CREDNER 1836 142

Literature

BDAG 2000 827 [literature].

ALEXANDER, Loveday, *The Preface to Luke's Gospel*, 1993. Esp. 111-112.
CADBURY, Henri J., Commentary on the Preface of Luke, 1922. Esp. 495-496.

πληρόω 9/10 + 16 (Mt 16/17, Mk 2/3)

1. fill (Lk 3,5; Acts 2,2); 2. make complete (Acts 9,23); 3. finish (Acts 12,25); 4. provide fully; 5. proclaim completely; 6. give true meaning; 6. cause to happen
πληρόομαι: 7. come to an end (Acts 7,30); 8. be completely (Acts 13,52)

Word groups	Lk	Acts	Mt	Mk
πληρόω + γεγραμμένα/γραφή → **πίμπλημι/τελέω** + γεγραμμένα/γραφή	4,21; 21,22*; 24,44	1,16	2	1/2
πληρόω + τὴν καρδίαν (*LN*: cause to think)		5,3	0	0
πληρόω + λόγος/ῥῆμα; cf. πληρόω + ῥηθέν Mt 1,22; 2,15.17.23; 4,14; 8,17; 12,17; 13,35; 21,4; 27,9.35* DENAUX 2009 Lⁿ	1,20; 7,1		0	0
πληρόω active (*SC*a; *VK*a)	7,1; 9,31	2,2.28; 3,18; 5,3.28; 12,25; 13,25.27; 14,26	3	0
πληρόω = to end (profane sense) DENAUX 2009 IAn	7,1	7,23.30; 9,23; 12,25; 13,25; 14,26; 19,21; 24,27	0	1
πληρόω with reference to scripture (*SC*b; *VK*b)	4,21; 21,22*; 24,44	1,16; 13,27	2	1/2
πληρόω with reference to a sermon (*SC*c; *VK*b)	1,20; 7,1		10/11	0

Characteristic of Luke; cf. ἐκπληρόω Acts 13,33

CREDNER 1836 141

	Lk	Acts	Mt	Mk
πληρόω with reference to time (*SC*d; *VK*c); cf. Jn 7,8 BOISMARD 1984 cb80; NEIRYNCK 1985	21,24	7,23.30; 9,23; 24,27	0	1

Literature
DENAUX 2009 lAn [πληρόω with reference to time]; EASTON 1910 167 [πληρόω in temporal
sense: classed by Weiss as characteristic of L on insufficient (?) evidence]; GERSDORF 1816 264
[πληρούμενον σοφίᾳ]; JEREMIAS 1980 151: "Der Gebrauch von πληρόω im rein profanen Sinne
von 'beendigen' ist kennzeichnend für das lk Doppelwerk"; 179: "Das Simplex πληροῦμαι, de
tempore gebraucht, ist lukanisch"; RADL 1975 424 [πληρόω "Zum Vorkommen sinnverwandter
Wörter und zur Unterscheidung zwischen Erfüllung der Schrift und Erfüllung zeitlicher
Gegebenheiten – die letztere begegnet bei Lukas häufig"; πληρόω after ὡς δέ].

BLACK, Matthew, The "Fulfilment" in the Kingdom of God. — *ExpT* 57 (1945-46) 25-26.
—, *An Aramaic Approach*, [3]1967. Esp. 228-236.
MOULE, Charles F.D., Fulfilment-Words in the New Testament: Use and Abuse. — *NTS*
    14 (1968) 293-320.

πλησίον 3 + 1 (Mt 3, Mk 2)
1. nearby; 2. neighbor (Lk 10,27.29.36; Acts 7,27)

Word groups	Lk	Acts	Mt	Mk
πλησίον + ἀγαπάω → **ἐχθρός** + ἀγαπάω	10,27		3	2

Literature
BDAG 2000 830 [literature]; HAUCK 1934 147: "Exk 10: Der Nächste".

πλοῖον 8 + 19 (Mt 13, Mk 17/18)   boat

Word groups	Lk	Acts	Mt	Mk
ἀναβαίνω εἰς τὸ πλοῖον (*SC*a; *VK*a)		21,6	1	1
ἐμβαίνω εἰς (τὸ) πλοῖον (*SC*b; *VK*b); cf. ἐμβαίνω εἰς ἓν τῶν πλοίων Lk 5,3[1]	8,22.37	21,6 *v.l.*	5/6	4/5
ἐπιβαίνω εἰς τὸ πλοῖον (*VK*c)		21,6 *v.l.*	0	0
ἐπιβαίνω + πλοίῳ (*VK*d); cf. πλοῖον + ἐπιβαίνω Acts 21,2		27,2	0	0
πλοῖον + ἀνάγομαι DENAUX 2009 lA[n]	8,22	20,13; 21,2; 27,2; 28,11	0	0
πλοῖον + φορτίον / ἀποφορτίζομαι γόμον		21,3; 27,10	0	0
προέρχομαι ἐπὶ τὸ πλοῖον		20,13	0	0

Characteristic of Luke
MORGENTHALER 1958A

Literature
HILGERT, Earle, *The Ship and Related Symbols in the New Testament*. Assen: Royal Van
    Gorcum, 1962. — Diss. Basel.

πλούσιος 11 (Mt 3, Mk 2)
1. rich (Lk 16,1); 2. in abundance

Word groups	Lk	Acts	Mt	Mk
ἄνθρωπός (+) τις (+) πλούσιος → ἄνθρωπός τις **εὐγενής** DENAUX 2009 L[n]	12,16; 16,1.19		0	0

| (οἱ) πλούσιοι (*VK*a) → (οἱ) **πτωχοί** | 6,24; 21,1 | | 0 | 1 |

Characteristic of Luke
DENAUX 2009 L***; GOULDER 1989*; HAWKINS 1909 L; MORGENTHALER 1958L

	Lk	Acts	Mt	Mk
πλούσιος + πτωχός DENAUX 2009 L*** (?)	6,(20-)24; 14,12(-13); 16,19(-20).22		0	1

Literature
VON BENDEMANN 2001 427; HAUCK 1934 [Vorzugswort].

DUPONT, Jacques, *Les Béatitudes*, III, 1973. Esp. 43-45.
FURFEY, Paul H., Πλούσιος and Cognates in the New Testament. — *CBQ* 5 (1943) 243-263.

πλουτέω 2
1. be rich (Lk 1,53; 12,21); 2. become rich; 3. be generous; 4. have a great deal of

Word groups	Lk	Acts	Mt	Mk
πλουτέω εἰς θεόν (*VK*b)	12,21		0	0

Literature
VON BENDEMANN 2001 423; DENAUX 2009 L[n]

πλοῦτος 1 (Mt 1, Mk 1)
1. riches (Lk 8,14); 2. extreme

πλύνω 1
wash (Lk 5,2)

πνεῦμα 36/38 + 70/71 (Mt 19, Mk 23)
1. Holy Spirit (Lk 1,15); 2. spirit (Lk 1,17; Acts 23,8); 3. evil spirit (Lk 9,39); 4. ghost (Lk 24,37); 5. inner being (Lk 1,47; Acts 17,16); 6. way of thinking; 7. wind; 8. breath

Word groups	Lk	Acts	Mt	Mk
βαπτίζω ἐν πνεύματι ἁγίῳ → βαπτίζω ἐν **ὕδατι**	3,16	1,5; 11,16	1	1
βλασφημέω + εἰς τὸ πνεῦμα	12,10		0	1
διὰ (+) πνεύματος (ἁγίου)		1,2; 4,25; 11,28; 21,4	0	0
δύναμις τοῦ πνεύματος	4,14		0	0
ἐκχέω/ἐκχύννω + (ἅγιον) πνεῦμα		2,17.18.33; 10,45	0	0
ἐπιπίπτει (+) τὸ πνεῦμα τὸ ἅγιον		8,15(-16); 10,44; 11,15	0	0
ἐπιτάσσω τοῖς πνεύμασιν	4,36		0	1
ἔχω πνεῦμα πύθωνα (*LN*: be a fortuneteller)		16,16	0	0
ζέω τῷ πνεύματι (*LN*: show enthusiasm)		18,25	0	0

λαμβάνω + πνεῦμα → λαμβάνω **πνεῦμα** (ἅγιον) DENAUX 2009 IA[n] (?)	9,39	1,8; 2,33.38; 8,15.17.19; 10,47; 19,2[1]	0	0
λαμβάνω πνεῦμα (ἅγιον) → λαμβάνω + **πνεῦμα**; cf. Jn 20,22 BOISMARD 1984 Ba13		8,15.17.19; 10,47; 19,2	0	0
πειράζω τὸ πνεῦμα → πειράζω τὸν **θεόν**		5,9	0	0
πνεῦμα (τὸ) ἀκάθαρτον (LN: unclean spirit; SCe; VKf) → (τὸ) **πνεῦμα** (τὸ) πονηρόν	4,36; 6,18; 8,29; 9,42; 11,24	5,16; 8,7	2	11
πνεῦμα ἀσθενείας / πνεῦμα + ' ἀσθένεια DENAUX 2009 LA[n]	8,2; 13,11	5,16; 19,12	0	0
πνεῦμα (+) δαιμόνιον (+) ἀκάθαρτος; cf. Rev. 18,2 DENAUX 2009 L[n]	4,33; 8,29; 9,42		0	0
πνεῦμα (τὸ ἅγιον) εἶπεν + dative BOISMARD 1984 Aa63		8,29; 10,19; 11,12; 13,2	0	0
πνεῦμά μου (SCc; VKb)		2,17.18	3	0
πνεῦμα Ἰησοῦ (VKd)		16,7	0	0
πνεῦμα + περιστερά	3,22		1	1
πνεῦμα (+) σάρξ	24,39	2,17	1	1
πνεῦμα + σοφία DENAUX 2009 IA[n](?)	2,40*	6,3.10	0	0
πνεῦμα + ὕδωρ	3,16	1,5; 10,47; 11,16	1	1
πνεῦμα + ψυχή → **καρδία/σῶμα** + ψυχή	1,(46-)47		1	0
πνεῦμα evil spirit, demon (SCe)	4,33.36; 6,18; 7,21; 8,2.29; 9,39.42; 10,20; 11,24.26; 13,11	5,16; 8,7; 19,15.16	2	11
πνεῦμα = τὸ πνεῦμα τὸ ἅγιον (SCb)	2,27; 4,1[2].14	2,4[2]; 6,3.10; 8,18.29; 10,19; 11,12.28; 16,16.18; 20,22; 21,4	3	2

Characteristic of Luke
HENDRIKS 1986 468; MORGENTHALER 1958A

	Lk	Acts	Mt	Mk
δίδωμι (τὸ) πνεῦμα → **παραδίδωμι** τὴν ψυχήν; cf. Jn 3,34 BOISMARD 1984 Eb46; NEIRYNCK 1985	11,13	5,32; 8,18; 15,8	0	0
δύναμις + πνεῦμα DENAUX 2009 L***	1,17.35; 4,14.36	1,8; 10,38	0	0
ἐν τῷ πνεύματι without determinative BOISMARD 1984 Eb67; NEIRYNCK 1985	2,27; 4,1[2]	19,21	0	0
ἔχω πνεῦμα HARNACK 1906 35	4,33; 13,11	8,7; 16,16; 19,13	0	3
ἐπλήσθην πνεύματος (ἁγίου) BOISMARD 1984 Ab20; DENAUX 2009 IA*; NEIRYNCK 1985	1,15.41.67	2,4[1]; 4,8.31; 9,17; 13,9	0	0
πλήρης πνεύματος ἁγίου; cf. πλήρης πνεύματος καὶ σοφίας Acts 6,3 BOISMARD 1984 Ab98; NEIRYNCK 1985	4,1[1]	6,5; 7,55; 11,24	0	0
πνεῦμα + verb of movement + ἐπί + accusative (person) BOISMARD 1984 Ab59; NEIRYNCK 1985	1,35	1,8; 10,44; 11,15; 19,6	0	0

πνεῦμα (τὸ) ἅγιον (*SC*a; *VK*a) BOISMARD 1984 cb162; DENAUX 2009 IA**; GOULDER 1989; HARNACK 1906 72; NEIRYNCK 1985	1,15.35.41.67; 2,25.26; 3,16.22; 4,1¹; 10,21; 11,13; 12,10.12	1,2.5.8.16; 2,4¹.33.38; 4,8.25.31; 5,3.32; 6,3 *v.l.*5; 7,51.55; 8,15.17. 18 *v.l.*19; 9,17.31; 10,38.44.45.47; 11,15. 16.24; 13,2.4.9.52; 15,8.28; 16,6; 19,2¹·². 6; 20,23.28; 21,11; 28,25	5	4
πνεῦμα κυρίου (*SC*d; *VK*c) BOISMARD 1984 Da19	4,18	5,9; 8,39	0	0
(τὸ) πνεῦμα (τὸ) πονηρόν (*LN*: evil spirit) → **πνεῦμα** (τὸ) ἀκάθαρτον BOISMARD 1984 Bb48; DENAUX 2009 IA*; NEIRYNCK 1985; PLUMMER 1922 lii	7,21; 8,2; 11,26	19,12.13.15.16	1	0
πνεύματα plural (*SC*f; *VK*h) DENAUX 2009 L***	4,36; 6,18; 7,21; 8,2; 10,20; 11,26	5,16; 8,7; 19,12.13	0	0
πνεύματα plural of evil spirits (*SC*e; *VK*g); see also **πνεῦμα** (τὸ) ἀκάθαρτον DENAUX 2009 L***	7,21; 8,2; 10,20; 11,26	19,12.13	2	0
τίθεμαι ἐν τῷ πνεύματι (*LN*: make up mind) → τίθεμαι/τίθημι ἐν τῇ **καρδίᾳ** VOGEL 1899C		19,21	0	0

Literature

BDAG 2000 836 [literature]; COLLISON 1977 171 [πνεῦμα ἀκάθαρτον: linguistic usage of Luke: likely]; 176 [πνεῦμα ἅγιον: nearly certain]; DENAUX 2009 IAⁿ [δίδωμι (τὸ) πνεῦμα,πλήρης πνεύματος ἁγίου, πνεῦμα + verb of movement + ἐπί + accusative (person), πνεῦμα κυρίου], Laⁿ [ἐν τῷ πνεύματι without determinative]; GERSDORF 1816 182: "Sehr üblich ist dem Lucas auch der Ausdruck πνεῦμα ἅγιον"; 186 [ἐν πνεύματι καὶ δυνάμει Ἠλίου]; 196 [πνεῦμα ἅγιον ἐπελεύσεται ἐπὶ σέ]; 198.206 [ἐπλήσθη πνεύματος ἁγίου]; 246-247 [πνεῦμα ἦν ἅγιον] 252 [καὶ ἦλθεν ἐν τῷ πνεύματι]; HAUCK 1934 [Vorzugswort; Vorzugsverbindung: πλήρης πνεύματος ἁγίου / πνεῦμα (τὸ) ἅγιον / πνεύματος ἁγίου πλησθήσεται; (τὸ) πνεῦμα (τὸ) πονηρόν]; 55-56: "Exk 6: Der heilige Geist bei Lk"; JEREMIAS 1980 115 [πλήρης πνεύματος ἁγίου: charakteristisch für Lukas]; 115 [4,1: τῷ πνεύματι: trad.]; 162 [πνεῦμα πονηρόν: red.]; 202 [ἀκάθαρτον πνεῦμα: trad.].

BAER, Heinrich VON, *Der Heilige Geist in den Lukasschriften* (BWANT, 39). Stuttgart: Kohlhammer, 1926, VII-220 p. Esp. 20-38: "Die Abgrenzung des Heiligen Geistes, in seinem speziellen Sinne, vom Pneuma im allgemeinen (kosmischen, psychologischen usw.) Gebrauch dieses Wortes im N.T."; 38-43: "Das Pneuma Hagion und andere Korrelatbegriffe an den Lukasschriften".

BÖCHER, Otto, Wasser und Geist. — BÖCHER, O. – HAACKER, K. (eds.), *Verborum Veritas*. FS G. Stählin, 1970, 197-209.

BRATCHER, Robert G., Biblical Words Describing Man: Breath, Life, Spirit. — *BTrans* 34 (1983) 201-209. Esp. 205-209: "Pneuma, 'wind, breath, spirit'".

BÜCHSEL, Friedrich, *Der Geist Gottes im Neuen Testament*. Gütersloh: Bertelsmann, 1926, X-516 p. Esp. 37-54: "Πνεῦμα im griechischen Sprachgebrauch".

DODD, Charles H., Some Problems of New Testament Translation. — *BTrans* 13 (1962) 145-157. Esp. 152-153: "*pneuma*".

FITZMYER, Joseph A., The Role of the Spirit in Luke-Acts. — VERHEYDEN, J. (ed.), *The Unity of Luke-Acts*, 1999, 165-183.

HILL, David, *Greek Words and Hebrew Meanings*, 1967. Esp. 241-256: "The background and biblical usage of the term πνεῦμα: The Synoptic Gospels"; 257-265: "The Acts of the Apostles".

HUR, Jo, *A Dynamic Reading of the Holy Spirit in Luke-Acts* (JSNT SS, 211). Sheffield:

Academic Press, 2001, 372 p. Esp. 37-86: "The usage of *rûah/pneuma* in the extratext of Luke-Acts as literary repertoire".

KILPATRICK, George D., The Gentiles and the Strata of Luke. — BÖCHER, O. – HAACKER, K. (eds.), *Verborum Veritas*. FS G. Stählin, 1970, 83-88. Esp. 86 [πνεῦμα ἀκάθαρτον/ πονηρόν]; = ID., *Principles and Practice*, 1990, 313-318. Esp. 315-316.

MOWERY, Robert L., The Articular References to the Holy Spirit in the Synoptic Gospels. — *Biblical Research* (Chicago) 31 (1986) 26-45.

PAIGE, Terence, Who Believes in "Spirit"? Πνεῦμα in Pagan Usage and Implications for the Gentile Christian Mission. — *HTR* 65 (2002) 417-436.

PITT FRANCIS, D., The Holy Spirit: A Statistical Inquiry. — *ExpT* 96 (1985) 136-137. [NTA 29, 870] "The NT 'power' references to the Holy Spirit do not contain the definite article, wheres the 'person' references invariably do".

PRETE, Benedetto, Lo Spirito Santo nell'opera di Lucas. — *Divus Thomas* 102 (1999) 3-172.

READ-HEIMERDINGER, Jenny, *The Bezan Text of Acts*, 2002. Esp. 145-172: "The Holy Spirit".

SCHNEIDER, Gerhard, Lk 1,34. 35 als redaktionelle Einheit. — *BZ* NF 15 (1971) 255-259. Esp. 256-257: "Lk 1,35 ist nach Wortschatz, Stil und Theologie 'lukanisch'".

—, Jesu geistgewirkte Empfängnis (Lk 1,34f): Zur Interpretation einer christologischen Aussage. — *TPQ* 119 (1971) 105-116. Esp. 109; = ID., *Lukas, Theologe der Heilsgeschichte*, 1985, 86-97. Esp. 90.

SCHOEMAKER, William Ross, The Use of רוח in the Old Testament, and of πνεῦμα in the New Testament: A Lexicographical Study. — *JBL* 23 (1904) 13-67.

SWELLENGREBEL, J.L., Puzzles in Luke. — *BTrans* 17 (1966) 118-122. Esp. 122 [Lk 8,55 καὶ ἐπέστρεψεν τὸ πνεῦμα αὐτῆς].

πνέω 1 + 1 (Mt 2)   blow (Lk 12,55; Acts 27,15*.40)

Word groups	Lk	Acts	Mt	Mk
ἡ πνέουσα as a noun (*VK*a)		27,40	0	0

πόθεν 4 (Mt 5, Mk 3)
1. whence (Lk 13,25.27; 20,7); 2. how; 3. why (Lk 1,43)

Word groups	Lk	Acts	Mt	Mk
καὶ πόθεν → καὶ ὅτι/πῶς	1,43		0	1

ποιέω 88/91 + 68/71 (Mt 86/89, Mk 47/52)
1. do (Lk 5,33; 13,2); 2. perform (Lk 1,51); 3. cause to be; 4. work; 5. make (Lk 3,4); 6. behave toward; 7. assign to a task; 8. make profit (Lk 19,18)

Word groups	Lk	Acts	Mt	Mk
διηγέομαι + ὅσα + ἐποίησαν DENAUX 2009 L[n]	8,39; 9,10		0	0
ἔλεον (+) ποιέω → ἐλεημοσύνην ποιέω DENAUX 2009 L[n]	1,72; 10,37[1]		0	0
ὁ θεὸς ἐποίει/ἐποίησεν + διά + genitive BOISMARD 1984 Ba16		2,22; 15,12; 19,11; 21,19	0	0

	Lk	Acts	Mt	Mk
ποιέομαι λόγου (LN: be of opinion)		20,24	0	0
ποιέω + accusative + infinitive (SCe; VKf)	5,34		1	2/3
ποιέω + double accusative (SCd; VKe)	3,4; 15,19.21*; 19,46	2,36; 7,19; 15,17 v.l.; 20,24	14	4
ποιέω + infinitive DENAUX 2009 1A[n]	1,25; 5,34	7,43; 17,26; 25,3	0	0
ποιέω (εἰς τό, πρὸς τό / τοῦ, ὡς) + infinitive (SCf; VKj); cf. ποιέω ..., ὅπως Mt 6,2[2]		3,12; 7,19; 20,24	3	0/1
ποιέω + participle (VKk)		10,33; 21,13	0	1/2
ποιέω + temporal expression (SCb; VKc); cf. Rev 13,5 BOISMARD 1984 ca76		15,33; 18,23; 20,3	1	0
ποιέω ἵνα (SCg; VKh)	16,4	16,30	1	2
ποιέω (+) καρπόν (LN: [a]produce fruit; [b]cause results)	3,[a]8.[a]9; 6,43[a1.a2]; 8,[a]8; 13,[a]9		11	0
ποιέω + καθώς → **ποιέω ὡς**		2,22	1	0
ποιέω (+) λόγος	6,47; 8,21	1,1; 20,24	2	0
ποιέω σημεῖα καὶ τέρατα ἐν BOISMARD 1984 Aa64		2,22; 6,8; 7,36; 15,12	0	0
ποιέω τι εἰς (SCl; VKq) DENAUX 2009 LA[n]	22,19	24,17	0	0
ποιέω τι ἐκ (VKr) DENAUX 2009 LA[n]	16,9	17,26		
ποιέω τι ἐν (SCm; VKs)	23,31		1	0
ποιέω (τι) κατά + accusative (SCn; VKu)	2,27; 6,23.26	7,44	1	0
ποιέω + ὡς (SCh; VKl) → **ποιέω καθώς**	15,19.21*		3	0
ποιήσατε ἑαυτοῖς DENAUX 2009 L[n]	12,33; 16,9		0	0
τὸ ποιῆσαι/τὸ ποιεῖν (VKa) DENAUX 2009 LA[n]	2,27	7,19	0	0
πορείαν ποιέω εἰς Ἱεροσόλυμα → **πορεύομαι εἰς Ἱεροσόλυμα/ Ἱερουσαλήμ**	13,22			
τί ποιήσωμεν DENAUX 2009 LA[n]	3,12.14	2,37; 4,16		

→ **ποιέω ἄριστον**; ποιέομαι **δεήσεις**; ποιέω **δεῖπνον**; ποιέω **δοχήν**; ποιέω τὸ **θέλημα**; **κακὸν** ποιέω; **καλῶς** ποιέω

Characteristic of Luke	Lk	Acts	Mt	Mk
δεῖ ... ποιεῖν/ποιῆσαι BOISMARD 1984 ca40	11,42	9,6; 16,30	1	0
ἐκδίκησιν ποιέω BOISMARD 1984 Ab116; NEIRYNCK 1985	18,7.8	7,24	0	0
ἐλεημοσύνην ποιέω → **ἐλεημοσύνην αἰτέω/δίδωμι**; **ἔλεον ποιέω** VOGEL 1899C		9,36; 10,2; 24,17	2	0
ποιέομαι middle (SCa; VKb) DENAUX 2009 1A*; HARNACK 1906 52	5,33; 13,22	1,1[1]; 8,2 v.l.; 20,24; 23,13; 25,17; 27,18	0	0
ποιέω with adverb of mood (SCc; VKd) GOULDER 1989	1,25; 2,48; 3,11; 6,10 v.l.27. 31[2]; 9,15; 10,37[2]; 12,43; 16,8	5,34; 10,33; 12,8	7/8	4
ποιέω (τί/τινα) + dative (SCj; VKm); cf. ποιέω τί τινα Mt 27,22; Mk 15,12 CREDNER 1836 134	1,25.49.68; 2,48; 5,29; 6,11.23.26.27.31[1.2]; 8,39[1.2]; 9,33; 12,33; 16,9; 18,41; 20,15	4,16; 7,24.40; 9,13; 10,2; 15,3; 28,17	13	12
ποιέω μετά + genitive (SCp; VKv) BOISMARD 1984 Ab99; CREDNER 1836 134; HARNACK 1906 144; NEIRYNCK 1985	1,72; 10,37[1]	14,27; 15,4	0	0

ποιέω περί + genitive BOISMARD 1984 Ab196; NEIRYNCK 1985	2,27	1,1	0	0
ποιέω (τι) πρός + accusative (VKw) CREDNER 1836 138	12,47		0	0
ποιούμενος/ποιησάμενος BOISMARD 1984 Db35; NEIRYNCK 1985	13,22	23,13; 25,17	0	0
τί ποιήσω DENAUX 2009 L***	12,17; 16,3.4; 20,13	22,10[1]	0	1
τί ποιήσω/-μεν/-σιν; DENAUX 2009 L***; GOULDER 1989	3,12.14; 12,17; 16,3.4; 19,48; 20,13; [23,34]	22,10[1]	0	2

Literature

COLLISON 1977 201 [ποιήσατε ἑαυτοῖς: noteworthy phenomena]; DENAUX 2009 La[n] [ἐκδίκησιν ποιέω], LA[n] [ποιέω μετά + genitive, ποιέω περί + genitive], lA[n] [ποιούμενος/ ποιησάμενος]; EASTON 1910 149 [ποιέω ἔλεος μετ' αὐτοῦ: especially characteristic of L]; [ποίει(=εἴτω) ὁμοίως: cited by Weiss as characteristic of L, and possibly corroborative]; GERSDORF 1816 200 [ὅτι ἐποίησέν μοι μεγάλα ὁ δυνατός]; 206 [καὶ ἐποίησεν λύτρωσιν]; 207 [ποιῆσαι ἔλεος μετὰ τῶν πατέρων ἡμῶν]; 269 [τί ἐποίησας ἡμῖν οὕτως]; JEREMIAS 1980 141(-142) [6,27-28: trad.]: "ἀγαπᾶτε ... ποιεῖτε ... εὐλογεῖτε ... προσεύχεσθε: Die asyndetische Aufreihung von Imperativen wird von Lukas in dem von ihm übernommenen Markusstoff konsequent beseitigt"; 216 [τί ποιήσω: red.]; 231 [ποιοῦμαι: red.]; RADL 1975 424 [ποιέομαι Medium].

MAHFOUZ, Hady, La fonction littéraire et théologique de Lc 3,1-20, 2003. Esp. 88 [ποιέω ... πονηρόν].
SCHWARZ, Günther, "Gebt ... den Inhalt als Almosen"? (Lukas 11,40.41). — BibNot 75 (1994) 26-30.
WILCOX, Max, The Semitisms of Acts, 1965. Esp. 84-85 [ποιέω μετά].

ποικίλος 1 (Mt 1, Mk 1)
of various kinds (Lk 4,40)

ποιμαίνω 1 + 1 (Mt 1)
1. shepherd (Lk 17,7; Acts 20,28); 2. guide and help; 3. rule

ποιμήν 4 (Mt 3, Mk 2)
1. shepherd (Lk 2,8.15.18.20); 2. minister

Word groups	Lk	Acts	Mt	Mk
ποιμένες plural (VKb)	2,8.15.18.20		0	0

ποίμνη 1 (Mt 1)
1. flock (Lk 2,8); 2. follower of Christ

ποίμνιον 1 + 2
follower of Christ (Lk 12,32; Acts 20,28.29)

Characteristic of Luke
BOISMARD 1984 cb172; NEIRYNCK 1985

Literature

DENAUX 2009 IAⁿ; REHKOPF 1959 99 [τὸ μικρὸν ποίμνιον: "Substantiva in Anrede bei den Synoptikern"].

ποῖος 8 + 4 (Mt 7, Mk 4/5)

1. which (Lk 20,2); 2. what kind of (Acts 7,49)

Word groups	Lk	Acts	Mt	Mk
ἐν ποίᾳ ἐξουσίᾳ (VKa)	20,2.8		3	3
ποῖος in an ellipse (VKc)	24,19		1	0

Literature

JEREMIAS 1980 275: "Lokaler Genitiv mit Ellipse von ὁδός findet sich im NT nur im LkEv: 5,19 ποίας und 19,4 ἐκείνης".

πόλεμος 2 (Mt 2, Mk 2)

1. war (Lk 14,31; 21,9); 2. fight

Word groups	Lk	Acts	Mt	Mk
πολέμοι plural (VKb)	21,9		2	2

πόλις 39/40 + 43/44 (Mt 27, Mk 8/9)

1. town (Lk 4,29); 2. city (Lk 19,41); 3. inhabitants of city (Acts 13,44)

Word groups	Lk	Acts	Mt	Mk
αἱ + preposition + πόλεις BOISMARD 1984 Aa153		5,16; 26,11	0	0
διαπορεύομαι κατὰ πόλεις καὶ κώμας / διοδεύω κατὰ πόλιν καὶ κώμην + participle καί participle → **διέρχομαι** κατὰ τὰς κώμας DENAUX 2009 Lⁿ	8,1; 13,22		0	0
ἡ πόλις αὕτη / αὕτη ἡ πόλις BOISMARD 1984 Ba17		4,27; 16,12²; 18,10; 22,3	1	0
κατὰ πόλιν καὶ κώμην / πόλεις καὶ κώμας DENAUX 2009 Lⁿ	8,1; 13,22		0	0
Νέα πόλις		16,11	0	0
πᾶσα ἡ πόλις (SCg; VKh) → **ὅλη ἡ πόλις**		13,44	2	0
πόλις + proper name (SCa; VKa) → **κώμη/χώρα** + proper name; πόλις τῶν Ἰουδαίων; ἡ (πόλις) Ἰερουσαλήμ; πόλις τῆς **Σαμαρείας**; πόλις (τῶν) **Σαμαριτῶν**	1,26.39; 2,4¹·².11.39; 4,31; 7,11; 9,10.52*; 23,51; 24,49 v.l.	5,16; 8,5; 11,5; 14,6; 16,11.12¹. 14; 19,35; 21,39; 27,8	3	0
πόλις + ἀγρός (SCe; VKf) → **κώμη** + ἀγρός	8,34		0	2
πόλις + Γαλιλαία + Ναζαρέθ/Καφαρναούμ DENAUX 2009 Lⁿ	1,26; 2,4¹.39; 4,31		0	0
πόλις Δαυίδ	2,4².11		0	0
πόλις + κώμη (SCd; VKd)	8,1; 13,22		2	1
πόλις + οἰκία (VKe)	10,(7-)8		3	0
πόλις + τὰ τέκνα → Ἰερουσαλήμ + τὰ τέκνα	19,41(-44)	21,5	3	0
πόλεις plural (SCb; VKb)	4,43; 5,12; 13,22; 19,17.19	5,16; 8,40; 14,6; 16,4; 26,11	5	2

Characteristic of Luke

GASTON 1973 66 [Lked?]; GOULDER 1989; MORGENTHALER 1958LA

	Lk	Acts	Mt	Mk
εἰμι/γίνομαι ἐν τῇ πόλει (SCh; VKj) BOISMARD 1984 Ab21; DENAUX 2009 L***; NEIRYNCK 1985	5,12; 7,37; 18,2.3; 23,19	8,8; 11,5; 18,10	0	0
εἰσέρχομαι εἰς πολίν → εἰσέρχομαι εἰς **κώμην** HARNACK 1906 45	9,52; 10,8.10; 22,10	9,6; 14,20	3	1
ἐκβάλλω ἔξω τῆς πόλεως BOISMARD 1984 Ab176; NEIRYNCK 1985	4,29	7,58	0	0
ἐν (τῇ) πόλει singular; cf. 2 Cor 11,26 BOISMARD 1984 Bb32; DENAUX 2009 L***; GOULDER 1989; NEIRYNCK 1985	2,11; 5,12; 7,37; 18,2.3; 23,19; 24,49	4,27; 8,8.9; 11,5; 16,12; 18,10; 21,29; 22,3	1	0
κατὰ πόλιν/πόλεις (SCf; VKg); cf. Tit 1,5; καθ᾿ ὅλην τὴν πόλιν Lk 8,39; κατὰ τὴν πόλιν Acts 24,12; κατ᾿ ἐκκλησίαν Acts 14,23; κατ᾿ οἶκον Acts 2,46; 5,42 BOISMARD 1984 Bb30; DENAUX 2009 LA*; HAWKINS 1909B; NEIRYNCK 1985	8,1.4; 13,22	15,21.36; 20,23	0	0
ὅλη ἡ πόλις (SCh; VKj) → πᾶσα ἡ **πόλις** BOISMARD 1984 cb121; NEIRYNCK 1985	8,39	19,29 v.l.; 21,30	0	1
πόλις/κώμη/χώρα + determinative of region → **κώμη/χώρα** + determinative of region; cf. Jn 4,5 BOISMARD 1984 Bb34; DENAUX 2009 1A*; NEIRYNCK 1985	1,26; 4,31; 5,17	8,1.5; 14,6; 26,20		
πόλις + name of the city; cf. Rev 21,2.10 BOISMARD 1984 cb122; HARNACK 1906 32.52; NEIRYNCK 1985	2,4[1].39	11,5; 16,14; 27,8	0	0

Literature

DENAUX 2009 Lan; LA[n] [ἐκβάλλω ἔξω τῆς πόλεως]; IA[n] [πόλις + name of the city]; GERSDORF 1816 193 [εἰς πόλιν τῆς Γαλιλαίας]; 216 [εἰς τὴν ἰδίαν πόλιν]; 217 [ἀνέβη δὲ καὶ Ἰωσὴφ - εἰς πόλιν Δαυίδ - ἀπογράψασθαι]; 263 [εἰς πόλιν ἑαυτῶν]; HARNACK 1906 138 [ET 200] [ad Lk 1,39: πόλιν Ἰούδα, like πόλις Δαβείδ, St. Luke ii.4,11 is copied from the style of the LXX (γῆ, οἶκος φυλὴ Ἰούδα). Or is Ἰούδα the corrupted form of the name of the town, as in St. Luke πόλις Ναζαρέτ, πόλις Ἰόππη, πόλις Θυάτειρα, πόλις Λαταία?]; HAUCK 1934 [Vorzugsverbindung: κατὰ πόλιν]; JEREMIAS 1980 176 [Lk 8,1 luk.]; RADL 1975 409-410 [ἔξω τῆς πόλεως]; 424-425 [πόλις; κατὰ πόλιν(πόλεις); ἐν τῇ πόλει ταύτῃ; πόλις "mit folgendem Eigennamen"; πόλις "mit Landschaftsnamen im Genitiv"].

BORMANN, Lukas, Recht, Gerechtigkeit und Religion, 2001. Esp. 122-123.

CONN, H., Lucan Perspective and the City. — Missiology 13 (1985) 409-428.

GARCÍA PÉREZ, José Miguel, El Endemoniado de Gerasa (Lc 8,26-39), 1986. Esp. 119-123 [καθ᾿ ὅλην τὴν πόλιν]; 123-127 [ἐκ τῆς πόλεως].

SCHWARZ, Günter, "Auch den anderen Städten"? (Lukas IV.43a). — NTS 23 (1976-77) 344.

WILCOX, Max, Semitisms in the New Testament, 1984. Esp. 1014: "πόλις מדינה in Luke 1:39b".

πολίτης 2 + 1	citizen (Lk 15,15; 19,14; Acts 21,39)

Characteristic of Luke

BOISMARD 1984 Ab139; NEIRYNCK 1985; PLUMMER 1922 lii; VOGEL 1899B

Literature

DENAUX 2009 La[n]; EASTON 1910 164 [πολῖται: cited by Weiss as characteristic of L, and possibly corroborative]; JEREMIAS 1980 250 [red.].

BORMANN, Lukas, *Recht, Gerechtigkeit und Religion*, 2001. Esp. 123.

πολλαπλασίων 1 (Mt 0/1)	many times as much (Lk 18,30)

πολύς 51/52 + 46/50 (Mt 61/63, Mk 59/62)

1. many (Lk 4,25; Acts 2,40); 2. much (Acts 11,21); 3. great (Lk 7,47; Acts 21,40)

Word groups	Lk	Acts	Mt	Mk
ἐν πολλῷ (*SC*e; *VK*h) DENAUX 2009 L[n]	$16,10^{1.2}$	26,29*	0	0
ἐπὶ πολύ (*LN*: a long time) → ἐπὶ πλεῖον; cf. ἐπὶ πολλὰς ἡμέρας Acts 16,18		28,6	0	0
λόγος πολύς → λόγος πλείων BOISMARD 1984 ca13		15,32; 20,2	0	0
οὗ (+) πολύς (*SC*l; *VK*q)	15,13	1,5; 27,14	2	1
ὄχλος πολύς / πλῆθος πολύ (*SC*n)	$5,6.15.29; 6,17^{1.2};$ 7,11; 8,4; 9,37; 14,25; 23,27	6,7; 14,1; 17,4	9/10	8/10
πλῆθος πολὺ τοῦ λαοῦ	6,17		0	0
πολλοὶ + ἐκ (*SC*b; *VK*c)		17,12	0	0
πολλοὶ τῶν (*SC*b; *VK*d) DENAUX 2009 lAn	1,16	$4,4; 8,7^{1}; 13,43;$ 18,8; 19,18; 26,10	1	0
πολύς + demonstrative pronoun (*SC*j; *VK*m)		1,5	0	1/3
πολὺς δέ; cf. Jn 11,19; 2 Cor 6,10; Heb 12,9 BOISMARD 1984 Ca21		$2,43$ *v.l.*$; 4,4; 8,7^{2};$ 15,7; 16,23 *v.l.*; 21,40; 23,10; 27,14.21 *v.l.*; 28,6	1	1/2
πολὺς δέ + noun + γινόμενος BOISMARD 1984 Aa79		15,7; 21,40; 23,10	0	0
πολύς τε BOISMARD 1984 Aa23		2,43; 6,7; 8,25; 11,21; 16,23; 19,18; 26,10; 27,21	0	0
πολύς + εἷς (*VK*n) → πᾶς + εἷς; cf. πολύς + ἄλλος Mk 11,8	10,41(-42)		0	0
πολύς + ἐλάχιστος/ὀλίγος (*SC*k; *VK*p)	$7,47^{1.2}; 10,2.41$ *v.l.*; 12,47(-48); $13,(23-)24; 16,10^{1.2}$	17,4.12; 26,29*	5/6	1
πολλὴ χαρά → χαρὰ μεγάλη; cf. πᾶσα χαρά Rom 15,13; Phil 2,29; Jam 1,2 PLUMMER 1922 lx		8,8	0	0
πολύς + χρόνος → πλείων χρόνος; χρόνος οὐκ ὀλίγος	8,29		1	0
πολλῷ μᾶλλον (*SC*f; *VK*j) → ποσῷ μᾶλλον	18,39		1	1
πολλά (*SC*c; *VK*e)	9,22; 17,25; 23,8*		4	16
(οἱ) πολλοί used as a noun (*SC*a; *VK*a)	1,1.14.16; 2,34; 4,41; $7,21^{1}; 13,24;$ 14,16; 21,8	$4,4; 8,7^{1.2}; 9,13.42;$ 10,27; 13,43; 17,12; 18,8; 19,18; 26,10	15	15

Characteristic of Luke	Lk	Acts	Mt	Mk
ἕτεροι πολλοί / ἕτερα πολλά (SCh; VKl); cf. ἄλλοι πολλοί Mk 7,4; 15,41; πολλοὶ ἄλλοι Mk 12,5 BOISMARD 1984 Bb104; DENAUX 2009 La*; NEIRYNCK 1985	3,18; 8,3; 22,65	15,35	1	0
μετ' οὐ πολύ / μετ' οὐ πολλὰς ἡμέρας HARNACK 1906 52	15,13	1,5; 27,14	0	0
πολύ (SCd; VKf) DENAUX 2009 L**; GOULDER 1989	$7,47^2$; $12,48^{1.2.3}$	18,27; 27,14; 28,6	0	1
πολύς with reference to time (SCm); cf. Jn 2,12; 5,6; Rom 15,23 BOISMARD 1984 cb173; NEIRYNCK 1985	2,36; 8,29; $12,19^2$; 15,13	1,5; 16,18; 24,10; 27,14; 28,6	1	2

Literature

DENAUX 2009 IA[n] [μετ' οὐ πολύ / μετ' οὐ πολλὰς ἡμέρας], IAn [πολύς with reference to time]; JEREMIAS 1980 110-111 [πολλὰ ... καί; πολλὰ ... ἕτερα: red.]; 249 [μετ' οὐ πολλὰς ἡμέρας: litotes: red.]; RADL 1975 424 [πλῆθος πολύ].

ALEXANDER, Loveday, *The Preface to Luke's Gospel*, 1993. Esp. 109 [Lk 1,1].
BAUER, Johannes B., Πολλοί Lk I,1. — *NT* 4 (1960) 263-266; = ID., *Scholia Biblica et Patristica*, 1972, 73-78.
CADBURY, Henry J., Commentary on the Preface of Luke, 1922. Esp. 492-493 [Lk 1,1].
—, Litotes in Acts. — BARTH, E.H. – COCROFT, R.E. (eds.), *Festschrift to Honor F. Wilbur Gingrich*, 1972, 70-84. Esp. 64 [οὐ πολύς].
GILLIESON, T., A Plea for Proportion: St. Luke x.38-42. — *ExpT* 59 (1947-48) 111-112. [πολλὰ ... ἑνός].
MEALAND, David L., The Phrase "Many Proofs" in Acts 1,3 and in Hellenistic Writers. — *ZNW* 80 (1989) 134-135. [ἐν πολλοῖς τεκμηρίοις]

πονηρία 1 + 1 (Mt 1, Mk 1)   wickedness (Lk 11,39; Acts 3,26)

Word groups	Lk	Acts	Mt	Mk
πονηρίαι plural (VKa)		3,26	0	1

Literature

HATCH, Edwin, *Essays*, 1889. Esp. 77-82.
TAEGER, Jens-Wilhelm, *Der Mensch und sein Heil*, 1982. Esp. 33-34: "Verwandte Begriffe (πονηρία, ἀδικία, κακία)".

πονηρός 13/14 + 8 (Mt 26, Mk 2)

1. wicked (Lk 6,35); 2. worthless; 3. guilty; 4. be sick (Lk 11,34)

Word groups	Lk	Acts	Mt	Mk
γενεὰ πονηρά	11,29		2	0
δοῦλος πονηρός → δοῦλος ἀγαθός; cf. δοῦλος κακός Mt 24,48	19,22		1	0
ὀφθαλμός + πονηρός (LN: [a]jealous; [b]stingy)	11,34			1
(τὰ) πονηρά (SCd; VKd)	3,19	25,18	2	0
(ὁ) πονηρός (LN: the Evil one) / (τὸ) πονηρόν (SCb; VKb)	$6,45^{1.2.3}$; 11,4*	28,21	6	0
(οἱ) πονηροί used as a noun (SCc; VKc)	6,35		3	0
πονηρότερα comparative (SCa; VKa)	11,26		1	0

Characteristic of Luke
PLUMMER 1922 1x?

	Lk	Acts	Mt	Mk
(τὸ) πνεῦμα (τὸ) πονηρόν (*LN*: evil spirit; *SC*e) → πνεῦμα (τὸ) ἀκάθαρτον BOISMARD 1984 Bb48; DENAUX 2009 1A*; NEIRYNCK 1985; PLUMMER 1922 1ii	7,21; 8,2; 11,26	19,12.13. 15.16	1	0

Literature
BDAG 2000 852 [literature, 3a]; HAUCK 1934 [Vorzugsverbindung: (τὸ) πνεῦμα (τὸ) πονηρόν]; JEREMIAS 1980 112 [περὶ πάντων ὧν ἐποίησεν πονηρῶν: Attractio relativi: red.]; 162: "πνεῦμα πονηρόν begegnet im NT außer Mt 12,45 nur im lk Doppelwerk"; RADL 1975 425; REHKOPF 1959 98 [ἀγαθὲ/πονηρὲ δοῦλε: "Substantiva in Anrede bei den Synoptikern"].

DUPONT, Jacques, *Les Béatitudes*, II, 1969. Esp. 292-293: "Un nom mauvais" [ὄνομα ὡς πονηρόν].

HATCH, Edwin, *Essays*, 1889. Esp. 77-82.

MAHFOUZ, Hady, *La fonction littéraire et théologique de Lc 3,1-20*, 2003. Esp. 88 [ποιέω … πονηρόν].

TAEGER, Jens-Wilhelm, *Der Mensch und sein Heil*, 1982. Esp. 43-44: "Verwandte Begriffe (πονηρός, κακός, ἄτοπος)".

Πόντιος 1 + 1 (Mt 0/1)   Pontius

Word groups	Lk	Acts	Mt	Mk
Πόντιος Πιλᾶτος	3,1	4,27	0/1	0

πορεία 1

1. journey (Lk 13,22); 2. business activity

Word groups	Lk	Acts	Mt	Mk
πορείαν ποιέω εἰς Ἱεροσόλυμα → **πορεύομαι** εἰς Ἱεροσόλυμα/ Ἱερουσαλήμ	13,22		0	0

Literature
HAUCK 1934 [seltenes Alleinwort]; JEREMIAS 1980 175 [πορείαν ποιοῦμαι: red.].

πορεύομαι 51 + 37/38 (Mt 29/30, Mk 0[3]/4)

1. go (Lk 7,9); 2. travel (Lk 10,38); 3. go away; 4. behave (Lk 1,6); 5. die (Lk 22,22)

Word groups	Lk	Acts	Mt	Mk
πορευθείς + imperative	7,22; 13,32; 14,10; 17,14; 22,8		6	1
πορεύομαι + dative of mood (*SC*1 *VK*n) BOISMARD 1984 ca57		9,31; 14,16	0	0
πορεύομαι ἀπαγγέλλω → **ἀποστέλλω/ εἰσπορεύομαι/(ἀπ/δι/εἰσ/κατ/προσ)ἔρχομαι/ ὑποστρέφω/φεύγω** + ἀπαγγέλλω/διαγγέλλω/ διηγέομαι/κηρύσσω	7,22		1/2	1

πορεύομαι + διέρχομαι DENAUX 2009 La[n]	4,30; 17,11	19,21	0	0
πορεύομαι (+ εἰσέρχομαι) εἰς κώμην/κώμας	9,12.52.56; 10,38; 24,13.28[1]		1	0
πορεύομαι εἰς οἶκον → **εἰσπορεύμαι** εἰς οἰκίαν	5,24		0	0
πορεύομαι + εἰς τὸ ὄρος → **ἀναβαίνω/ἐξέρχομαι** εἰς τὸ ὄρος; **κατέρχομαι** ἀπὸ ὄρους	22,39		1	0
πορεύομαι ἔμπροσθεν (SCd; VKe)	19,28		0	0
πορεύομαι (+) ἐν except for phrases referring to time (SCe; VKf)	1,6; 9,57	16,36	0	0
πορεύομαι + εὑρίσκω → **εἰσπορεύομαι** / **(ἀπ/δι/εἰσ/ἐκ/ κατ)ἔρχομαι** + εὑρίσκω	9,12; 15,4		3	0
πορεύομαι ἕως referring to location (SCg; VKh) → **(ἐξ)ἄγω/διώκω/(δι/ἐξ)ἔρχομαι/καταβαίνω** ἕως		17,14; 23,23	0	0
πορεύομαι (+) κατά + accusative, except for phrases referring to time (SCh; VKj)	22,22.39	8,36; 16,7 v.l.	0	0
πορεύομαι + ὁδόν (SCa; VKa)		8,39	0	0
πορεύομαι ὀπίσω (VKk)	21,8		0	0
πορεύομαι + οὗ or adverb of place (SCj; VKl)	13,31; 24,28[1.2]		1	0
πορεύομαι (+) πρός + accusative (SCk; VKm)	11,5; 15,18; 16,30	27,3; 28,26	3	0

Characteristic of Luke

CREDNER 1836 139; GASTON 1973 66 [Lked?]; GOULDER 1989; HARNACK 1906 35.70.148; HENDRIKS 1986 434; MORGENTHALER 1958LA; SCHÜRMANN 1957 5.31; VOGEL 1899D

	Lk	Acts	Mt	Mk
imperative of movement + καί + πορεύου BOISMARD 1984 Ab141; NEIRYNCK 1985	13,31	8,26; 10,20	0	0
ἀναστάς + πορεύομαι; cf. ἀνάστηθι + πορεύου Acts 8,26 BOISMARD 1984 Ab40; DENAUX 2009 lA*; NEIRYNCK 1985	1,39; 15,18; 17,19	8,27; 9,11; 10,20; 22,10	0	0
ἐξελθὼν absolute ... πορεύομαι BOISMARD 1984 Ab60; DENAUX 2009 lA*; NEIRYNCK 1985	4,42[1]; 22,39	12,17; 16,36; 21,5	1	0
πορεύομαι + infinitive (SCm; VKp) DENAUX 2009 L***	2,3; 14,19.31; 19,12		0/1	0
πορεύομαι + participle; cf. Rom 15,25 BOISMARD 1984 Bb49; NEIRYNCK 1985	19,28	5,41; 8,39; 10,20; 20,22; 22,5	0	0
πορεύομαι ἀπό (SCb; VKb) → **ἀπο/καταβαίνω/ἀποχωρέω/(ἀπ/ἐξ/ἐπ/ κατ) ἔρχομαι/ὑποστρέφω** ἀπό BOISMARD 1984 cb45; NEIRYNCK 1985	4,42[2]; 16,30	5,41	2	0
πορεύομαι εἰς + place (SCc; VKd); cf. Jn 7,35; Rom 15,24.25; 1 Tim 1,3; 2 Tim 4,10; Jam 4,13; 1 Pet 3,22 BOISMARD 1984 cb123; DENAUX 2009 L***; NEIRYNCK 1985	1,39; 2,3.41; 4,42[1]; 5,24; 7,11.50; 8,48; 9,12.51.53.56; 17,11; 19,12; 22,33.39; 24,13	1,11.25; 12,17; 16,7.16; 18,6; 19,21; 20,1.22; 22,5.10; 25,20; 26,12	5	0[2]
πορεύομαι εἰς Ἱεροσόλυμα/ Ἰερουσαλήμ → **πορείαν** ποιέω εἰς Ἱεροσόλυμα; cf. εἰσπορεύομαι καὶ ἐκπορεύομαι εἰς Ἰερουσαλήμ Acts 9,28 DENAUX 2009 L***	2,41; 9,51.53; 17,11	19,21; 20,22; 25,20	0	0
πορεύομαι εἰς (τὸν) τόπον BOISMARD 1984 Ab140; NEIRYNCK 1985	4,42[1]; 14,10	1,25; 12,17	0	0
πορεύομαι ἐπί + accusative (SCf; VKg) BOISMARD 1984 Bb77; NEIRYNCK 1985	15,4	8,26; 9,11; 17,14; 25,12	1	0

πορεύομαι σύν; cf. 1 Cor 16,4[2] BOISMARD 1984 cb46; NEIRYNCK 1985	7,6	10,20; 26,13	0	0
πορεύου εἰς εἰρήνην / πορεύεσθε ἐν εἰρήνῃ (SCn); cf. ὕπαγε εἰς εἰρήνην Mk 5,34 BOISMARD 1984 Ab115; NEIRYNCK 1985; VOGEL 1899C	7,50; 8,48	16,36	0	0
πορεύου εἰς εἰρήνην PLUMMER 1922 liii;	7,50; 8,48		0	0
πορεύου/πορεύθητι absolute; cf. Jn 4,50 BOISMARD 1984 cb44; DENAUX 2009 lA*; NEIRYNCK 1985	10,37; 17,19	5,20; 9,15; 22,21; 24,25	1	0

Literature

VON BENDEMANN 2001 415: "Πορεύεσθαι ist lukanisches Vorzugsverb"; COLLISON 1977 60-61 [linguistic usage of Luke: certain; linguistic usage of Luke's "other Source-material": also highly probable]; 61 [πορεύομαι + εἰς: linguistic usage of Luke: certain]; DENAUX 2009 Lan; lA[n] [imperative of movement + καί + πορεύου; πορεύομαι + participle; πορεύομαι σύν]; LA[n] [πορεύομαι εἰς (τὸν) τόπον], lAn [πορεύομαι ἐπί + accusative], La[n] [πορεύου εἰς εἰρήνην / πορεύεσθε ἐν εἰρήνῃ], L[n] [πορεύου εἰς εἰρήνην]; EASTON 1910 175 [πορεύομενος, πορευθείς: possible Hebraisms in the Lucan Writings, as classed by Dalman]; GERSDORF 1816 198 [ἀναστᾶσα - ἐπορεύθη]; 216 [καὶ ἐπορεύοντο πάντες ἀπογράφεσθαι]; HAUCK 1934 [Vorzugswort]; JEREMIAS 1980 23: "πορεύομαι ist zwar unzweifelhaft lukanisches Vorzugswort, läßt sich jedoch für einige Verwendungsarten der Tradition zuweisen. Dazu gehört: a] πορεύομαι ἐν in übertragenem Sinn..., da Lukas selbst übertragenes πορεύομαι mit Dativ konstruiert ...; b] pleonastisches πορεύομενος/πορευθείς ... c] πορεύεσθαι ἐν τῇ ὁδῷ (= 'seines Weges ziehen' Lk 9,57), da Lukas selbst πορεύεσθαι κατὰ τὴν ὁδόν (Apg 8,36) bzw. πορεύεσθαι τὴν ὁδὸν αὐτοῦ (8,39) schreibt; d] πορεύομαι mit finalem Infinitiv ...; e) die Stellen, an denen die Matthäusparallele das Verb als vorlukanisch erweist ... und f) der Friedensgruß πορεύου εἰς εἰρήνην"; 56: "πορεύεσθαι ... ist ein Verb, das Lukas ... gern gebraucht"; 84 [πορεύομαι ἕως: red.]; 234: "Lukanisch ist insbesondere die semitisierende Kombination von ἐξέρχομαι und πορεύομαι"; 245 [πορεύομαι ἐπί: red.]; 251 [πορεύομαι + ἀναστάς: red.]; RADL 1975 405 [διέρχομαι + πορεύομαι]; 409 [ἐξέρχομαι + πορεύομαι]; 425 [πορεύομαι; πορεύου; πορεύομαι εἰς + place; πορεύομαι "mit Jerusalem als Ziel"; πορεύομαι ἐπί]; SCHÜRMANN 1953 86.90 [luk. Vorliebe für πορεύεσθαι und einige seiner Komposita].

DENAUX, Adelbert, L'hypocrisie des pharisiens et le dessein de Dieu, 1973. Esp. 260-261; [2]1989. Esp. 170-171.

FERRARO, Giuseppe, "Oggi e domani e il terzo giorno" (osservazioni su Luca 13,32,33). — RivBib 16 (1968) 397-407. Esp. 401-407: "Considerazioni sul vocabolario di Luca 13,32.33" [ἐκβάλλειν δαιμόνια; ἰάσεις ἀποτελῶ; τελειοῦσθαι e πορεύεσθαι; ἀπολέσθαι].

LEVINSOHN, S. H., Ἔρχομαι and πορεύομαι in Luke-Acts: Two Orientation Strategies. — Notes on Translation 15 (2001) 13-30.

PRETE, Benedetto, Il testo di Luca 13,31-33: Unità letteraria e insegnamento cristologico. — BibOr 24 (1982) 59-79; = ID., L'opera di Luca, 1986, 80-103. Esp. 233.236-239.

πόρνη 1 (Mt 2)   prostitute

Word groups	Lk	Acts	Mt	Mk
πόρναι plural (VKb)	15,30		2	0

πόρρω 2 (Mt 1, Mk 1)   far away (Lk 14,32; 24,28)

Word groups	Lk	Acts	Mt	Mk
πορρώτερον comparative (SCa; VKa)	24,28		0	0

Literature

EASTON 1910 157 [probably characteristic of L]; PAFFENROTH 1997 82.

πόρρωϑεν 1

1. long before; 2. far away (Lk 17,12)

Word groups	Lk	Acts	Mt	Mk
ἵστημι πόρρωϑεν →ἵστημι (ἀπὸ) μακρόϑεν	17,12		0	0

Literature

EASTON 1910 157 [probably characteristic of L]; PAFFENROTH 1997 82.

πορφύρα 1 (Mk 2) | purple cloth (Lk 16,19)

ποσάκις 1 (Mt 2) | how often

Word groups	Lk	Acts	Mt	Mk
ποσάκις θέλω; cf. ὅσα θέλω Mt 17,12; Mk 9,13; ὡς θέλω Mt 15,28; 26,39	13,34		1	0

πόσος 6 + 1 (Mt 8, Mk 6)

1. how many (Lk 15,17; Acts 21,20); 2. how much (Lk 16,5); 3. how great

Word groups	Lk	Acts	Mt	Mk
πόσῳ μᾶλλον (SCa; VKa) → πολλῷ μᾶλλον	11,13; 12,24.28		2	0
πόσῳ μᾶλλον ... οὕτως; cf. πολλῷ μᾶλλον οὕτως Mt 6,30	12,28		1	0

ποταμός 2 + 1 (Mt 3, Mk 1) | river (Lk 6,48.49; Acts 16,13)

ποταπός 2 (Mt 1, Mk 2) | what sort of (Lk 1,29; 7,39)

Literature

GERSDORF 1816 195 [ποταπὸς εἴη ὁ ἀσπασμὸς οὗτος].

ποτέ 1/8 + 0/2 (Mt 0/8, Mk 0/2)

1. ever; 2. when (Lk 22,32)

Word groups	Lk	Acts	Mt	Mk
μή ποτε (VKa)	3,15*; 4,11*; 12,58*; 14,8*.12*.29*; 21,34*	5,39*; 28,27*	0/8	0/2

Literature

SCHÜRMANN 1957 108 [möglicherweise luk R].

πότε 4 (Mt 7, Mk 5) | when (Lk 9,41; 12,36; 17,20; 21,7)

Word groups	Lk	Acts	Mt	Mk
ἕως πότε (SCa; VKa)	9,41		2	2

ποτήριον 5 (Mt 7/8, Mk 6/7) — cup (Lk 11,39; 22,17.20$^{1.2}$.42)

Word groups	Lk	Acts	Mt	Mk
παραφέρω τὸ ποτήριον ἀπό (LN: cause not to experience)	22,42		0	1

Literature
BLAISING, Craig A., Gethsemane: A Prayer of Faith. — *JEvTS* 22 (1979) 333-343.
DELEBECQUE, Édouard, *Études grecques*, 1976. Esp. 109-121: "Le pain et la coupe de la dernière cène (22,17-20)".
PETZER, Kobus H., Style and Text in the Lucan Narrative of the Institution of the Lord's Supper, 1991. Esp. 117-121.

ποτίζω 1 (Mt 5, Mk 2)
1. give to drink (Lk 13,15); 2. irrigate

ποῦ 7 (Mt 4, Mk 3)
1. where (place) (Lk 22,11); 2. where (circumstance) (Lk 8,25)

Word groups	Lk	Acts	Mt	Mk
ἔχω ποῦ	9,58; 12,17		1	0
ποῦ in an indirect question with the subjunctive (SCb; VKb); cf. ποῦ in an indirect question with the indicative Mt 2,4; Mk 15,47	9,58; 12,17		1	0
ποῦ + ὅπου	22,11		0	1

Characteristic of Luke
GOULDER 1989

Literature
COLLISON 1977 111 [linguistic usage of Luke: likely]; JEREMIAS 1980 275 [ποῦ (= 'wo?' in direkten Fragen: red.).

πούς 19 + 19 (Mt 10, Mk 6) — foot

Word groups	Lk	Acts	Mt	Mk
ἀνατρέφομαι + παρὰ τοὺς πόδας (LN: be taught by)		22,3	0	0
βῆμα ποδός (LN: square yard = meter)		7,5	0	0
ἵστημι + παρὰ / παρακαθέζομαι πρὸς τοὺς πόδας DENAUX 2009 L^n	7,38^1; 10,39		0	0
καταφιλέω (+) τοὺς πόδας DENAUX 2009 L^n	7,38^2.45		0	0
κατευθύνω τοὺς πόδας (LN: guide behavior)	1,79		0	0
πίπτω + ἐπὶ τοὺς πόδας (VKe); cf. πίπτω εἰς τοὺς πόδας Mt 18,29*		10,25	0	0
πίπτω παρὰ/πρὸς τοὺς πόδας → προσπίπτω τοῖς **γόνασιν**; cf. προσπίπτω πρὸς τοὺς πόδας Mk 7,25 DENAUX 2009 LAn	8,41; 17,16	5,10	0	1

	15,22; 24,39.40	21,11	3	2
πούς + χείρ (*SCc*; *VK*f)	15,22; 24,39.40	21,11	3	2
πρὸς τοὺς πόδας (*SCb*; *VK*b)	10,39	4,37; 5,10	0	2
τίθημι (+) παρὰ/πρὸς τοὺς πόδας (*LN*: turn over to); cf. ἀποτίθεμαι παρὰ τοὺς πόδας Acts 7,58		4,35.37; 5,2	0	0
ὑποπόδιον τῶν ποδῶν (*LN*: be under someone's control); cf. Heb 1,13; 10,13 DENAUX 2009 lA[n]	20,43	2,35; 7,49	0/2	0/1

Characteristic of Luke
GOULDER 1989; MORGENTHALER 1958LA

	Lk	Acts	Mt	Mk
παρὰ τοὺς πόδας (*SCa*; *VK*a) BOISMARD 1984 Bb22; DENAUX 2009 L***; GOULDER 1989*; HAWKINS 1909L; NEIRYNCK 1985; PLUMMER 1922 lxiii	7,38[1]; 8,35.41; 10,39 *v.l.*; 17,16	4,35.37 *v.l.*; 5,2.10 *v.l.*; 7,58; 22,3	1	0

Literature
EASTON 1910 167 [παρὰ τοὺς πόδας: classed by Weiss as characteristic of L on insufficient (?) evidence]; HAUCK 1934 [Vorzugsverbindung: παρὰ τοὺς πόδας]; JEREMIAS 1980 168: "παρὰ τοὺς πόδας ist eine lk Vorzugswendung".

HOFIUS, Otfried, Fußwaschung als Erweis der Liebe: Sprachliche und sachliche Anmerkungen zu Lk 7,44b. — *ZNW* 81 (1990) 171-177.
WILCOX, Max, Semitisms in the New Testament, 1984. Esp. 1008-1009: "ἀνάστηθι ἐπὶ τοὺς πόδας σου (Acts 14:10)".

πρᾶγμα 1 + 1 (Mt 1)
1. event (Lk 1,1); 2. undertaking; 3. lawsuit

Literature
ALEXANDER, Loveday, *The Preface to Luke's Gospel*, 1993. Esp. 112.
CADBURY, Henri J., Commentary on the Preface of Luke, 1922. Esp. 496.
GLÖCKNER, Richard, *Die Verkündigung des Heils beim Evangelisten Lukas*, 1975. Esp. 15-21: "Zum Begriff πρᾶγμα".

πραγματεύομαι 1
do business (Lk 19,13)

Literature
BORMANN, Lukas, *Recht, Gerechtigkeit und Religion*, 2001. Esp. 161.

πράκτωρ 2
officer (Lk 12,58[1.2])

Characteristic of Luke
PLUMMER 1922 liii

Literature
DENAUX 2009 L[n]; HAUCK 1934 [seltenes Alleinwort].

BORMANN, Lukas, *Recht, Gerechtigkeit und Religion*, 2001. Esp. 162.

πρᾶξις 1 + 1 (Mt 1)
1. deed (Lk 23,51; Acts 19,18); 2. function

Literature
BORMANN, Lukas, *Recht, Gerechtigkeit und Religion*, 2001. Esp. 205.

πράσσω 6 + 13
1. do (Lk 22,23; Acts 3,17; 26,26); 2. receive (Lk 3,13; 19,23); 3. experience

Word groups	Lk	Acts	Mt	Mk
κακὸν + πράσσω → **κακὸν/καλῶς** ποιέω		16,28	0	0
πράσσομαι passive (*VK*d)	23,15	26,26	0	0
πράσσω intransitive (*SC*b; *VK*e)		3,17; 15,29; 17,7	0	0
πράσσω as technical term referring to certain economical	3,13;		0	0
activities: collect taxes, duties, interest,... (*SC*a; *VK*b)	19,23			
πράττω (*VK*a)		17,7 *v.l.*; 19,36 *v.l.*	0	0

Characteristic of Luke
BOISMARD 1984 Eb11; DENAUX 2009 L***; HAWKINS 1909 21; MORGENTHALER 1958A; NEIRYNCK 1985

	Lk	Acts	Mt	Mk
μέλλω πράσσειν	22,23	5,35	0	0
BOISMARD 1984 Ab197; NEIRYNCK 1985				
οὐδὲν/τι ἄξιον θανάτου πράσσω; cf. Rom 1,32	23,15	25,11.25; 26,31	0	0
BOISMARD 1984 Ab100; NEIRYNCK 1985				

Literature
COLLISON 1977 98 [noteworthy phenomena]; DENAUX 2009 LA[n] [μέλλω πράσσειν], lA[n] [οὐδὲν/τι ἄξιον θανάτου πράσσω]; HAUCK 1934 [häufiges Alleinwort]; JEREMIAS 1980 289 [ὁ τοῦτο μέλλων πράσσειν: red.]; RADL 1975 425 [πράσσω; πράσσω ἄξιον θανάτου].

BORMANN, Lukas, *Recht, Gerechtigkeit und Religion*, 2001. Esp. 205-206.

πρεσβεία 2   representative

Word groups	Lk	Acts	Mt	Mk
ἀποστέλλω πρεσβείαν	14,32; 19,14		0	0

Characteristic of Luke
PLUMMER 1922 liii

Literature
DENAUX 2009 L[n]; EASTON 1910 165 [πρεσβείαν ἀποστέλλω: cited by Weiss as characteristic of L, and possibly corroborative]; HAUCK 1934 [seltenes Alleinwort].

BORMANN, Lukas, *Recht, Gerechtigkeit und Religion*, 2001. Esp. 123-124.

πρεσβυτέριον 1 + 1
1. high council of Jews (Lk 22,66; Acts 22,5); 2. group of elders

Word groups	Lk	Acts	Mt	Mk
πρεσβυτέριον + ἀρχιερεῖς + γραμματεῖς → **πρεσβύτεροι** + ἀρχιερεύς/εῖς + γραμματεῖς	22,66		0	0
πρεσβυτέριον τοῦ λαοῦ	22,66		0	0

Characteristic of Luke
BOISMARD 1984 Ab198; NEIRYNCK 1985; PLUMMER 1922 lix; VOGEL 1899B

Literature
DENAUX 2009 LAⁿ; EASTON 1910 165 [πρεσβυτέριον τοῦ λαοῦ: cited by Weiss as characteristic of L, and possibly corroborative]; JEREMIAS 1980 299: "Während die oberste jüdische Behörde im NT allgemein τὸ συνέδριον (bei Josephus auch ἡ βουλή) genannt wird, finden sich daneben im lk Doppelwerk noch die hellenistischen Bezeichnungen τὸ πρεσβυτέριον (Lk 22,66/Apg 22,5) und ἡ γερουσία".

πρεσβύτερος 5 + 18 (Mt 12/13, Mk 7)
1. older (Lk 7,3; 9,22; 15,25; 20,1: 22,52); 2. of ancient times

Word groups	Lk	Acts	Mt	Mk
ἀπόστολοι καὶ πρεσβύτεροι (*VKf*) BOISMARD 1984 Aa15		15,2.4.6.22.23; 16,4	0	0
πρεσβύτεροι + ἀρχιερεῖς (*SCc*; *VKc*)	9,22; 20,1; 22,52	4,23; 23,14; 24,1; 25,15	9	5
πρεσβύτεροι + ἀρχιερεύς/εῖς + γραμματεῖς → **πρεσβυτέριον** + ἀρχιερεῖς + γραμματεῖς; **πρεσβύτεροι** + ἄρχοντες + γραμματεῖς	9,22; 20,1		3	5
πρεσβύτεροι + ἀρχιερεῖς + στρατηγοί	22,52		0	0
πρεσβύτεροι + ἄρχοντες + γραμματεῖς → **πρεσβύτεροι** + ἀρχιερεύς/εῖς + γραμματεῖς		4,5	0	0
πρεσβύτεροι + γραμματεῖς (*SCc*; *VKc*)	9,22; 20,1	4,5; 6,12	3	5
(οἱ) πρεσβύτεροι + ἐκκλησία (*VKg*)		14,23; 15,4.22; 20,17	0	0
πρεσβύτεροι τῶν Ἰουδαίων / τοῦ Ἰσραήλ (*SCe*; *VKe*) DENAUX 2009 LAⁿ	7,3	4,8 *v.l.*; 25,15	0	0
ὁ υἱὸς ὁ πρεσβύτερος → ὁ **νεώτερος** υἱός	15,25		0	0
(οἱ) πρεσβύτεροι among the Christians (*SCf*)		11,30; 14,23; 15,2.4.6.22.23; 16,4; 20,17; 21,18		
πρεσβύτερος adjective: comparative (*SCa*; *VKa*) DENAUX 2009 LAⁿ	15,25	2,17	0	0

Characteristic of Luke
MORGENTHALER 1958A

Literature
JEREMIAS 1980 152 [πρεσβύτεροι τῶν Ἰουδαίων: red.].

BORMANN, Lukas, *Recht, Gerechtigkeit und Religion*, 2001. Esp. 212-213.

CLAUSSEN, Carsten, *Versammlung, Gemeinde, Synagoge*, 2002. Esp. 264-273: "Πρεσβύτερος".

DUPONT, Jacques, *Le discours de Milet*, 1962. Esp. 141-143.

KLIJN, A.F.J., Scribes, Pharisees, Highpriests and Elders in the New Testament. — *NT* 3 (1959) 259-267.

πρεσβύτης 1	old man (Lk 1,18)

πρίν 2 + 3 (Mt 3, Mk 2)	before

Word groups	Lk	Acts	Mt	Mk
πρὶν ἄν → ἀφ᾽ οὗ/ὅπως ἄν	2,26		0	0
πρὶν ἤ (SCa; VKa)	2,26v.l.?; 22,34*	2,20 v.l.; 7,2; 25,16	1	1

πρό 7/8 + 7/8 (Mt 5, Mk 1)

1. in front of (location) (Acts 12,14); 2. before (time) (Acts 13,24); 3. above (value)

Word groups	Lk	Acts	Mt	Mk
πρό with reference to location (SCb; VKb); cf. Jam 5,9		5,23*; 12,6.14;	0	0
BOISMARD 1984 ca22		14,13		
→ εἰμι + πρό; εἰς + πρό; πρὸ **προσώπου** αὐτοῦ				

Characteristic of Luke	Lk	Acts	Mt	Mk
πρὸ τοῦ + infinitive (SCa; VKa)	2,21; 22,15	23,15	1	0
PLUMMER 1922 lxii				
πρὸ προσώπου (LN: previous; SCc; VKc) →	1,76*; 7,27;	13,24	1	1
ἀποστέλλω πρὸ προσώπου	9,52; 10,1			
BOISMARD 1984 Ab101; NEIRYNCK 1985; PLUMMER				
1922 lxi				

Literature

DENAUX 2009 Ln [πρὸ προσώπου]; EASTON 1910 157 [πρὸ προσώπου αὐτοῦ: probably characteristic of L]; HAUCK 1934 [Vorzugsverbindung: πρὸ τοῦ + inf.]; JEREMIAS 1980 89: "πρὸ τοῦ: Lukas hat eine Vorliebe für den präpositionalen substantivierten Infinitiv"; RADL 1975 426 [πρὸ προσώπου]; REHKOPF 1959 96 [πρὸ προσώπου: vorlukanisch]; SCHÜRMANN 1953 12-13 [πρὸ τοῦ c. inf. vermutlich luk R]; 1961 273 [πρὸ προσώπου].

προάγω 1 + 4 (Mt 6, Mk 5)

1. go prior to; 2. go in front of (Lk 18,39); 3. bring forward (Acts 17,5; 25,26); 4. happen previously; 5. fail to obey

Word groups	Lk	Acts	Mt	Mk
προάγω εἰς + place → (ἀν/ἀπ/εἰσ/ἐξ/ἐπαν/κατ/		17,5	4	3
συν/ὑπ)ἄγω εἰς + place				
προάγω + ἐπί + genitive (person) → (ἀν/κατ)ἄγω ἐπί +		25,26	0	0
acc. (place); (ἀπ/συν/ὑπ)ἄγω ἐπί + acc. (person)				
προάγω bring forward (VKa)		12,6; 16,30; 17,5; 25,26	0	0
προάγω transitive → (ἀν/ἀπ/εἰσ/ἐξ/ἐπισυν/κατ/		12,6; 16,30; 17,5; 25,26	6	3
προσ/συν)ἄγω transitive				

Literature

RADL 1975 425.

προβαίνω 3 (Mt 1, Mk 1)	move on

Word groups	Lk	Acts	Mt	Mk
προβαίνω ἐν ἡμέραις (*LN*: be old) DENAUX 2009 Lⁿ	1,7.18; 2,36		0	0

Literature

GERSDORF 1816 258 [αὕτη προβεβηκυῖα - ζήσασα]; JEREMIAS 1980 24 [προβεβηκότες ... ἦσαν: red. "die periphrastische Konjugation beim Perfektsystem"]; 25 [προβεβηκότες ἐν ταῖς ἡμέραις: trad.].

JUNG, Chang-Wook, *Infancy Narrative*, 2004. Esp. 179-193 [προβαίνω + ἐν (ταῖς) ἡμέραις (εἰμι)].

προβάλλω 1 + 1

1. sprout leaves (Lk 21,30); 2. BDAG 2000: put forward (Acts 19,33)

Characteristic of Luke

BOISMARD 1984 Ab199; HAWKINS 1909LA; MORGENTHALER 1958*; NEIRYNCK 1985; PLUMMER 1922 liii; VOGEL 1899A

Literature

DENAUX 2009 LAⁿ; HAUCK 1934 [seltenes Alleinwort].

πρόβατον 2 + 1 (Mt 11, Mk 2)

1. sheep (Lk 15,4.6); 2. follower of Christ

Word groups	Lk	Acts	Mt	Mk
πρόβατον + σφαγή (*VK*a)		8,32	0	0

προδότης 1 + 1   betrayer

Word groups	Lk	Acts	Mt	Mk
Ἰούδας + προδότης → Ἰούδας + παραδίδωμι	6,16		0	0

Characteristic of Luke

VOGEL 1899A

	Lk	Acts	Mt	Mk
προδότης γίνομαι BOISMARD 1984 Ab200; NEIRYNCK 1985	6,16	7,52	0	0

Literature

DENAUX 2009 LAⁿ; Laⁿ [προδότης γίνομαι]; HAUCK 1934 [Vorzugswort].

BORMANN, Lukas, *Recht, Gerechtigkeit und Religion*, 2001. Esp. 190.

προέρχομαι 2 + 3 (Mt 1, Mk 2)

1. go on (Lk 1,17); 2. go along (Acts 12,10); 3. go prior to (Acts 20,5); 4. lead (Lk 22,47)

Word groups	Lk	Acts	Mt	Mk
προέρχομαι + infinitive → (ἀπ/εἰσ/ἐξ/προσ/συν)έρχομαι + inf.	1,17		0	0
προέρχομαι ἐπὶ τὸ πλοῖον		20,13	0	0
προέρχομαι τινα (VKa)	22,47		0	1

Characteristic of Luke
PLUMMER 1922 lix

Literature
EASTON 1910 165 [cited by Weiss as characteristic of L, and possibly corroborative]; GERSDORF 1816 185 [καὶ αὐτὸς προελεύσεται].

πρόθεσις 1 + 2 (Mt 1, Mk 1)   plan (Lk 6,4; Acts 11,23; 27,13)

Word groups	Lk	Acts	Mt	Mk
ἄρτος τῆς προθέσεως (LN: consecrated bread; VKb)	6,4		1	1
πρόθεσις τῆς καρδίας		11,23	0	0

προκόπτω 1
1. progress (Lk 2,52); 2. accomplish; 3. increase; 4. draw to a close

Literature
GERSDORF 1816 272 [προέκοπτεν σοφίᾳ καὶ ἡλικίᾳ].

προμελετάω* 1   plan ahead (Lk 21,14)

Literature
HAUCK 1934 [seltenes Alleinwort].

BORMANN, Lukas, Recht, Gerechtigkeit und Religion, 2001. Esp. 191.
FUCHS, Albert, Sprachliche Untersuchungen zu Mattäus und Lukas, 1971. Esp. 178.

προπορεύομαι 1 + 1
1. precede (Lk 1,76); 2. lead (Acts 7,40)

Characteristic of Luke
HARNACK 1906 73.145; HAWKINS 1909LA; MORGENTHALER 1958*; PLUMMER 1922 liii

Literature
DENAUX 2009 LA[n]; GERSDORF 1816 212 [προπορεύσῃ γὰρ πρὸ προσώπου]; HAUCK 1934 [seltenes Alleinwort].

πρός 166/173 + 133/144 (Mt 42/44, Mk 65/68)
1. to (extension) (Lk 23,7); 2. against (extension) (Acts 26,14); 3. at (location) (Acts 5,10); 4. among (location); 5. to (experiencer) (Acts 3,25); 6. about (content); 7. with (association) (Acts 3,25); 8. for (purpose) (Acts 3,10); 9. end in (result); 10. according

to (correspondence) (Lk 12,47); 11. toward (time) (Lk 24,29); 12. at (time); 13. to the point of (degree); 14. with regard to (specification) (Lk 14,6; 20,19); 15. in opinion of (view-point participant) (Acts 24,16); 16. against (opposition) (Acts 19,38); 17. compared to (comparison)

Word groups	Lk	Acts	Mt	Mk
πρός + genitive (SCa; VKa)		27,34	0	0
→ ὑπάρχω πρός				
πρός + dative (SCb; VKb)	19,37		0	1
→ εἰμι πρός				
πρός + accusative				
πρός + accusative, verb of saying not explicitly mentioned BOISMARD 1984 Aa24		2,38; 5,9; 9,11; 19,2^2; 25,22; 26,28	0	0
πρός with composite verb προσ- (SCcb; VKd)	4,11	13,36	1	2
πρός in an elliptical construction (SCcf; VKh)		5,9; 9,6*.11; 19,2^2; 25,22; 26,28	1	0
πρὸς τό + infinitive (SCcc; VKe)	18,1	3,19*	5	1
πρός with reference to time (SCcg; VKj) DENAUX 2009 L^n	8,13; 24,29		0	0
πρὸς καιρόν (LN: for a while); cf. 1 Cor 7,5; πρὸς καιρὸν ὥρας 1 Thess 2,17	8,13		0	0
πρὸς κέντρα λακτίζω (LN: hurt by resistance)		26,14^2	0	0
τίθημι πρὸς τοὺς πόδας (LN: turn over to) → τίθημι παρὰ τοὺς πόδας		4,37	0	0
other instances with accusative (SCc)	1,27.28.43; 3,9; 4,26$^{1.2}$.40; 6,47; 7,3.4. 6*.7.19.20$^{1.2}$.44; 8,4. 19.35; 9,41; 10,22*. 23.39; 11,5^2.6; 12,3. 47.58; 13,34; 14,6.26; 15,18.20; 16,20.26$^{1.2}$. 30; 17,4; 18,3.16.29; 19,35; 20,10; 21,38; 22,45.52*.56; 23,7.15. 28; 24,12.50	3,2.10.11.25^1; 4,23^1; 5,10$^{1.2}$; 8,14; 9,27.32.38. 40; 10,3.21*.33; 11,3.11. 30; 12,20; 13,15^1; 14,11; 15,2^2.25.33; 16,40; 17,2. 15^2; 18,21; 19,31; 20,6.18; 21,11.18; 22,13; 23,17. 18$^{1.2}$.24.30^1; 24,15*.19; 25,21; 26,6*.9; 27,3; 28,8.23.26.30	35/37	44/46

→ ἄγω πρός; ἀναπέμπω πρός; ἀνταποκρίνομαι πρὸς ταῦτα; ἀπάγω πρός; ἀπέρχομαι πρός (ἑαυτόν); ἀποστέλλω πρός; πρὸς αὐτόν/αὐτήν/αὐτούς/αὐτάς; γογγύζω πρός; πρὸς ἑαυτόν/ἑαυτούς; εἰμι πρός; τὰ πρὸς εἰρήνην; πρός + εἰς; πρός + ἐκ; πρός + ἐν; ἐξάγω πρός; ἐπιστρέφω πρός; ἔρχομαι + πρός; ἥκω πρός; κάθημαι πρός + acc.; κατέρχομαι πρός; κεῖμαι πρός; πρὸς τὸ οὖς (λαλέω); παρακαθέζομαι πρὸς τοὺς πόδας; πίπτω πρός; πρὸς τοὺς πόδας; ποιέω (τι) πρός; πορεύομαι πρός; προστίθημι πρὸς τοὺς πατέρας αὐτοῦ; στραφεὶς πρός; τίθημι πρός; ὑπάρχω πρός; πρός + ὑπέρ + gen.

Characteristic of Luke
CADBURY 1920 202-203; CREDNER 1836 138; GASTON 1973 65 [Lked]; HARNACK 1906 144; HENDRIKS 1986 428.434.448.466; MORGENTHALER 1958LA

	Lk	Acts	Mt	Mk
noun or adjective with πρός + accusative (SCcd; VKf)	1,80; 23,12	2,47; 6,1; 7,31*; 9,2; 10,13.15; 12,5;	0	0

		13,15².31. 32; 15,2¹; 17,15¹; 19,38; 22,1.5.15; 24,16; 25,19; 27,12; 28,25¹		
DENAUX lA*				
verb of saying πρός + accusative (SCca; VKc) → ἀντιβάλλω, ἀπαγγέλλω, ἀποκρίνομαι, διαλαλέω, διαλογίζομαι, λαλέω, λέγω/εἶπον, ὁμιλέω, συζητέω, συλλαλέω, συλλογίζομαι, συμβάλλω, φημὶ πρός; cf. φωνὴ πρὸς αὐτόν Acts 7,31*; 10,13.15 CREDNER 1836 138; DENAUX 2009 L***; GOULDER 1989*; HAWKINS 1909L; SCHÜRMANN 1953 4-5	1,13.18.19.34.55.61.73; 2,15. 18.20.34.48.49; 3,12.13.14*; 4,4.21.23. 36.43; 5,4.10.22. 30.31. 33.34.36; 6,3.9.11; 7,24.40.50; 8,21.22.25; 9,3. 13.14.23.33.43.50.57.59.62; 10,2.26.29; 11,1.5¹.39.53*; 12,1.3.15.16.22.41¹·²; 13,7.23; 14,3.5.7¹·².23.25; 15,3.22; 16,1; 17,1.22; 18,7*.9.11.31; 19,5.8.9.13.33.39; 20,2.3.5.9. 14.19.23.25.41; 22,15.23.52. 70; 23,4.14.22; 24,5.10.14. 17¹·².18.25.32.44¹·²	1,7; 2,7*.12.29.37.38 v.l.; 3,12.22*.22.25²; 4,1.8.15.19.23².24; 5,8.9 v.l.35; 7,3; 8,20. 24.26; 9,10.15.29; 10,21.28; 11,2.14.20; 12,8.15.21; 15,7.36; 16,36.37; 17,17; 18,6.14; 19,2¹·² v.l.3*; 21,37.39; 22,8.10.21. 25; 23,3.22.30²; 24,12; 25,16.22 v.l.; 26,1.14¹.26.28 v.l.31; 28,4.17.21.25²	1	14/15
τὰ πρός + accusative (SCce; VKg) HARNACK 1906 43	14,28*.32; 19,42	23,30²; 28,10	0	1

→ πρὸς ἀλλήλους; εἰσέρχομαι πρός; ἔχω πρός; καταβαίνω πρός; παραγίνομαι πρός; πέμπω πρός; πίπτω πρός τοὺς πόδας; ποιέω (τι) πρός; φημὶ πρός

Literature

VON BENDEMANN 2001 414 [Verbum dicendi c. πρός c. acc.]; COLLISON 1977 145 [πρός following verbs of saying: noteworthy phenomena]; 202 [πρὸς ἀλλήλους: linguistic usage of Luke: certain]; DENAUX 2009 Lan; EASTON 1910 161 [ἔρχεσθαι πρός με, metaphorical, of Christ: cited by Weiss as characteristic of L, and possibly corroborative]; GERSDORF 1816 267 [καὶ πρὸς αὐτὸν ἡ μήτηρ αὐτοῦ εἶπεν]; HAUCK 1934 [Vorzugsverbindung: πρὸς αὐτούς (ἔφη/λέγω/εἶπον); λέγω/εἶπον (δὲ) πρός; (δια/συλ)λαλέω πρός; ἀποκρίνομαι πρός; ὁμιλέω πρός]; JEREMIAS 1980 33: "πρός c.acc. nach Verba dicendi zur Bezeichnung des (der) Angeredeten … ist ausgesprochen lukanisch"; 84 [πρὸς ἀλλήλους; (δια/συλ)λαλέω + πρὸς ἀλλήλους: red.]; RADL 1975 398 [πρὸς ἀλλήλους]; 408 [εἶπεν πρός; εἶπεν δέ, "gefolgt von πρός und dem Subjekt (oder umgekehrt)"]; 425-426 [πρός + acc.; πρός bei Verben des Sagens"]; SCHNEIDER 1969 125.164: "Πρός in Verbindung mit ἔφη bei Erwähnung der Adressaten eines Wortes erscheint im NT nur in den lk Schriften" [Bei Luk beliebte Konstruktionen]; 125.164 [πρός + acc.: Vorzugs-wörter und -ausdrücke des Luk]; SCHÜRMANN 1955 25-26 [τὰ πρὸς εἰρήνην als luk verdächtigt].

ANDERSEN, T. David, The Meaning of ἔχοντες χάριν πρός in Acts 2.47. — NTS 34 (1988) 604-610.

CHEETHAM, F.P., Acts ii.47: ἔχοντες χάριν πρὸς ὅλον τὸν λαόν. — ExpT 74 (1962-63) 214-215.

ELLIOTT, James K., New Testament Linguistic Usage, 1992. Esp. 47-48: "πρός με or πρὸς ἐμέ in the New Testament".

NEIRYNCK, Frans, La matière marcienne dans l'évangile de Luc, 1973. Esp. 183 [verb of saying + πρός]; ²1989. Esp. 93; = ID., Evangelica, 1982. Esp. 63.

—, Ἀπῆλθεν πρὸς ἑαυτόν: Lc 24,12 et Jn 20,10. — ETL 54 (1978) 104-118; = ID., Evangelica, 1982, 441-455 (455: note additionnelle; Appendix, Evangelica II, 1991, 799).

προσάγω 1 + 2/3 (Mt 0/1)

1. bring into presence (Lk 9,41; Acts 16,20); 2. approach (Acts 27,27)

Word groups	Lk	Acts	Mt	Mk
προσάγω + dative → (ἀπ)ἄγω πρός + acc. (person); ἄγω ἐπί + acc.		16,20; 27,27	0	0
προσάγω transitive → (ἀν/ἀπ/εἰσ/ἐξ/ἐπισυν/κατ/προ/ συν)ἄγω transitive DENAUX 2009 LAⁿ	9,41	12,6*; 16,20	0	0

Characteristic of Luke
HARNACK 1906 52; PLUMMER 1922 lix

προσαναβαίνω 1   move up to (Lk 14,10)

Literature
HAUCK 1934 [seltenes Alleinwort].

προσαναλόω 1   spend much (Lk 8,43)

προσδαπανάω ** **1**   spend in addition (Lk 10,35)

Literature
HAUCK 1934 [seltenes Alleinwort].

BORMANN, Lukas, *Recht, Gerechtigkeit und Religion*, 2001. Esp. 150.

προσδέχομαι 5 + 2 (Mk 1)

1. accept (Acts 24,15); 2. welcome (Lk 15,2); 3. wait for (Lk 2,25.38; 12,36; 23,51)

Word groups	Lk	Acts	Mt	Mk
προσδέχομαι τινα (*VK*a)	12,36; 15,2		0	0

Characteristic of Luke
BOISMARD 1984 Eb23; DENAUX 2009 L***; GOULDER 1989*; HAWKINS 1909L; NEIRYNCK 1985; PLUMMER 1922 lx

Literature
VON BENDEMANN 2001 428; COLLISON 1977 62 [linguistic usage of Luke's "other source-material": likely]; EASTON 1910 157 [probably characteristic of L]; GERSDORF 1816 246 [προσδεχόμενος παράκλησιν τοῦ Ἰσραήλ]; HAUCK 1934 [Vorzugswort]; JEREMIAS 1980 193 [red.].

BARTOLOMÉ, Juan J., Comer en común: Una costumbre tipica de Jesús y su proprio comentario (Lc 15). — *Sal* 44 (1982) 669-712. Esp. 687-689: "Estudio del lenguaje y del estilo"; 701 [προσδέχομαι].

προσδοκάω 6 + 5 (Mt 2)

1. wait with anxiety (Acts 27,33); 2. expect (Lk 7,20)

Word groups	Lk	Acts	Mt	Mk
προσδοκάω + (accusative with) infinitive (VKa)		3,5; 28,6[1]	0	0

Characteristic of Luke

BOISMARD 1984 cb132; DENAUX 2009 L***; GOULDER 1989*; HARNACK 1906 41; HAWKINS 1909 L; NEIRYNCK 1985; PLUMMER 1922 lx; VOGEL 1899D

Literature

COLLISON 1977 62 [linguistic usage of Luke: probable]; HAUCK 1934 [Vorzugswort; Stileigentümlichkeit]; JEREMIAS 1980 44 [red.].

MAHFOUZ, Hady, *La fonction littéraire et théologique de Lc 3,1-20*, 2003. Esp. 255-256.

προσδοκία 1 + 1	expectation (Lk 21,26; Acts 12,11)

Characteristic of Luke

BOISMARD 1984 Ab201; HAWKINS 1909LA; MORGENTHALER 1958*; NEIRYNCK 1985; PLUMMER 1922 liii; VOGEL 1899A

Literature

DENAUX 2009 LA[n]; HAUCK 1934 [seltenes Alleinwort]; JEREMIAS 1980 44 [red.].

προσεργάζομαι* 1	earn in addition (Lk 19,16)

Literature

HAUCK 1934 [seltenes Alleinwort].

προσέρχομαι 10 + 10/13 (Mt 51/53, Mk 5)

1. approach (Lk 23,52); 2. seek association with (Acts 10,28); 3. agree with

Word groups	Lk	Acts	Mt	Mk
προσέρχομαι + infinitive (SCb; VKb) → (ἀπ/εἰσ/ἐξ/προ/συν)ἔρχομαι + inf.		7,31; 12,13	1	0
προσέρχομαι + ἀπαγγέλλω → ἀποστέλλω/ (ἀπ/δι/εἰσ/κατ)έρχομαι/(εἰσ)πορεύομαι/ ὑποστρέφω/φεύγω + ἀπαγγέλλω/ διαγγέλλω/διηγέομαι/κηρύσσω		22,26	0	0
προσέρχομαι + λέγω/εἶπον or other verb of saying (SCa; VKa)	8,24; 9,12.42; 13,31; 20,27; 23,52	7,31; 9,1; 10,28; 22,26.27; 23,14; 24,23*	29	2

Characteristic of Luke

GASTON 1973 65 [Lked]

Literature

DENAUX, Adelbert, L'hypocrisie des pharisiens et le dessein de Dieu, 1973. Esp. 259; [2]1989. Esp. 169.

προσευχή 3 + 9 (Mt 2/3, Mk 2)

1. prayer (Lk 6,12; 19,46; 22,45); 2. place for prayer (Acts 16,13)

Word groups	Lk	Acts	Mt	Mk
οἶκος προσευχῆς (VKe)	19,46		1	1
προσευχή + ἀναβαίνω → ἀναβαίνω + **προσεύξασθαι**		3,1; 10,4	0	0
προσευχή + δέησις (VKc)		1,14 v.l.	0	0
προσευχὴ τοῦ θεοῦ (VKb)	6,12		0	0
προσευχαί plural (VKf)		2,42; 10,4	0	0
προσευχή place of prayer (SCa)		16,13.16	0	0

Characteristic of Luke
BOISMARD 1984 Eb31; NEIRYNCK 1985

Literature
DENAUX 2009 lAn.

CLAUSSEN, C., *Versammlung, Gemeinde, Synagoge*, 2002. Esp. 114-120: "Προσευχή".
DUPONT, Jacques, La prière et son efficacité dans l'Évangile de Luc. — *RechSR* 69 (1981)
45-56; = ID., *Études*, II, 1985, 1055-1065.
GEORGE, Augustin, La prière. — ID., *Études*, 1978, 395-427. Esp. 402-405: "Le vocabulaire
lucanien de la prière".
HENGEL, Martin, Proseuche und Synagoge. Jüdische Gemeinde, Gotteshaus und
Gottesdienst in der Diaspora und in Palästina. — JEREMIAS, G. – KUHN, H.-W. –
STEGEMANN, H. (eds.), *Tradition und Glaube. Das frühe Christentum in seiner Umwelt.
Festgabe für Karl Georg Kuhn zum 65. Geburtstag*, Göttingen: Vandenhoeck &
Ruprecht, 1971, 157-184.
PRETE, Benedetto, Motivazioni e contenuti della preghiera di Gesù nel Vangelo di Luca.
— DE GENNARO, G. (ed.), *La preghiera nella Bibbia: Storia, struttura e pratica
dell'esperienza religiosa*. Napoli: Dehoniane, 1983, 293-327; = ID., *L'opera di Luca*,
1986, 80-103. Esp. 85-86: "Il vocabolario lucano della preghiera".
ZARB, Seraphinus M., De Judaeorum προσευχή in Act XVI,13,16. — *Angelicum* 5 (1928) 91-
108.

προσεύχομαι 19 + 16 (Mt 15/16, Mk 10/11) | pray

Word groups	Lk	Acts	Mt	Mk
προσευξάμενος + "to lay the hands on"		6,6; 13,3;	0	0
BOISMARD 1984 Aa103		28,8		
προσεύχομαι + infinitive (SCc; VKf)	22,40		0	0
προσεύχομαι with Jesus as subject (SCa)	3,21; 5,16; 6,12; 9,18.28. 29; 11,1[1]; 22,40.41.44		5	5
προσεύχομαι (+) ἱερόν	18,10	22,17	0	0
DENAUX 2009 LA[n]				
προσεύχομαι ἵνα (SCc; VKg)	22,46		2	3
προσεύχομαι + λέγων	22,41(-42)		0	0
προσεύχομαι + νηστεία/νηστεύω (VKk) → **δέησις** + νηστεία/νηστεύω; cf. προσευχή + νηστεία Mt 17,21*; Mk 9,29 v.l.		10,30 v.l.; 13,3; 14,23	0	0
προσεύχομαι + ὅπως (SCc; VKh)		8,15	0	0
προσεύχομαι (+) ὄρος	6,12; 9,28; 22,(39-)40		1	1
προσεύχομαι πάντοτε	18,1		0	0
προσεύχομαι τι (SCb; VKd)	18,11		0	1
προσεύχομαι ὑπέρ + genitive (VKb)	6,28 v.l.		1	0

Characteristic of Luke

GASTON 1973 66 [Lked?]

	Lk	Acts	Mt	Mk
ἀναβαίνω + προσεύξασθαι → **προσευχή** + ἀναβαίνω BOISMARD 1984 cb14; NEIRYNCK 1985	9,28; 18,10	10,9	1	0
ἦν προσευχόμενον HARNACK 1906 70-71	1,10; 5,16	12,12	0	0
προσεύχομαι περί + genitive (VKa) BOISMARD 1984 db44; NEIRYNCK 1985	6,28	8,15	0	0

Literature

BDAG 2000 879 [literature]; COLLISON 1977 63 [linguistic usage of Luke: certain; of Jesus: certain]; DENAUX 2009 La[n] [ἦν προσευχόμενον], LA[n] [προσεύχομαι περί + genitive]; GERSDORF 1816 174 [πᾶν τὸ πλῆθος ἦν τοῦ λαοῦ προσευχόμενον]; 180 [ἦν προσευχόμενον]; JEREMIAS 1980 69 [προσεύχομαι + λέγων: red.]; 31 [ἦν ... προσευχόμενον: red.]; 141(-142) [6,27-28: trad.]: "ἀγαπᾶτε ... ποιεῖτε ... εὐλογεῖτε ... προσεύχεσθε: Die asyndetische Aufreihung von Imperativen wird von Lukas in dem von ihm übernommenen Markusstoff konsequent beseitigt"; RADL 1975 404 [θεὶς τὰ γόνατα + προσεύχομαι]; 426 [προσεύχομαι].

DUPONT, Jacques, La prière et son efficacité dans l'Évangile de Luc. — RechSR 69 (1981) 45-56; = ID., Études, II, 1985, 1055-1065.
GEORGE, Augustin, La prière. — ID., Études, 1978, 395-427. Esp. 402-405: "Le vocabulaire lucanien de la prière".
PRETE, Benedetto, Motivazioni e contenuti della preghiera di Gesù nel Vangelo di Luca. — DE GENNARO, G. (ed.), La preghiera nella Bibbia: Storia, struttura e pratica dell'esperienza religiosa. Napoli: Dehoniane, 1983, 293-327; = ID., L'opera di Luca, 1986, 80-103. Esp. 85-86: "Il vocabolario lucano della preghiera".
SCHNEIDER, Gerhard, Engel und Blutschweiß (Lk 22,43-44): "Redaktionsgeschichte" im Dienste der Textkritik. — BZ NF 20 (1976) 112-116. Esp. 113-115: "Vokabular und Stil von Lk 22,43.44"; = ID., Lukas, Theologe der Heilsgeschichte, 1985, 153-157. Esp. 154-156.
TUCKETT, Christopher M., Luke 22,43-44: The "Agony" in the Garden and Luke's Gospel. — DENAUX, Adelbert (ed.), New Testament Textual Criticism and Exegesis. FS J. Delobel, 2002, 131-144. Esp. 133-135: "Vocabulary and style".

προσέχω 4 + 6 (Mt 6)

1. be alert for (Lk 12,1; 17,3; 20,46; 21,34); 2. consider carefully (Acts 8,6); 3. continue to believe; 4. continue to give oneself to

Word groups	Lk	Acts	Mt	Mk
προσέχω (+) ἀπό (SCa; VKa) → **φυλάσσω** ἀπό	12,1; 20,46		5	0
προσέχω + ἐπί + dative (SCa; VKb)		5,35	0	0
προσέχω + μήποτε (VKc)	21,43		0	0

Characteristic of Luke	Lk	Acts	Mt	Mk
προσέχετε ἑαυτοῖς (VKe) BOISMARD 1984 Ab61; GOULDER 1989; HAWKINS 1909add; NEIRYNCK 1985; PLUMMER 1922 lii; VOGEL 1899c	12,1; 17,3; 21,43	5,35; 20,28	0	0
προσέχω with the meaning "give heed" HARNACK 1906 33		8,6.10.11; 16,14	0	0

Literature

COLLISON 1977 201 [ποιήσατε ἑαυτοῖς/προσέχετε ἑαυτοῖς: noteworthy phenomena];
DENAUX 2009 Lⁿ [προσέχετε ἑαυτοῖς]; EASTON 1910 165 [προσέχετε (ἑαυτοῖς) without
ἀπό: cited by Weiss as characteristic of L, and possibly corroborative]; HAUCK 1934
[Vorzugsverbindung: προσέχω δέ]; JEREMIAS 1980 211: "Das eigentlich für ihn Charakteristische
beim Gebrauch von προσέχειν ist jedoch die Verbindung des pluralischen Imperativs mit dem Dativ
des Reflexivpronomens".

DOBBELER, Axel VON, Mission und Konflikt: Beobachtungen zu προσέχειν in Act 8,4-
13. — *BibNot* 84 (1996) 16-22.

DUPONT, Jacques, *Le discours de Milet*, 1962. Esp. 136-141.

TAEGER, Jens-Wilhelm, *Der Mensch und sein Heil*, 1982. Esp. 152-153.

προσκαλέομαι 4 + 9/10 (Mt 6, Mk 9)

1. call to oneself (Lk 7,18; 15,26; 16,5; 18,16); 2. call to a task (Acts 16,10)

Word groups	Lk	Acts	Mt	Mk
προσκαλέομαι + λέγω/εἶπον → **(παρα/συγ)καλέω** + λέγω/εἶπον/ἐρῶ; cf. ἐπικαλέω + λέγω Acts 7,59	16,5; 18,16	6,2; 23,23	5	5/6
προσκαλέομαι + μαθηταί/δώδεκα (*SC*a)	7,18	6,2	2	5
προσκαλέομαι of a divine call (*SC*b)		2,39; 13,2; 16,10	0	0
προσκαλέομαι finite verbe (*VK*a)	18,16	2,39; 13,2; 16,10	0	2

Characteristic of Luke	Lk	Acts	Mt	Mk
προσκαλεσάμενος ἕνα/δύο + genitive GOULDER 1989	7,18; 15,26; 16,5	23,17.23*	0	0

Literature

JEREMIAS 1980 69 [προσκαλέω + λέγων: red.].

προσκόπτω 1 (Mt 2)

1. strike against (Lk 4,11); 2. stumble; 3. take offense

Word groups	Lk	Acts	Mt	Mk
προσκόπτω transitive (*VK*a)	4,11		1	0

προσκυνέω 3 + 4 (Mt 13, Mk 2)

1. worship (Lk 4,7.8; 24,52); 2. prostrate oneself before (Acts 10,25)

Word groups	Lk	Acts	Mt	Mk
προσκυνέω εἰς + place BOISMARD 1984 Aa155		8,27; 24,11	0	0
προσκυνέω ἐνώπιόν (*VK*c)	4,7		0	0
προσκυνέω + λατρεύω	4,8		1	0
προσκυνέω τινά (*VK*a)	4,8; 24,52		1	1
προσκυνέω to the devil (*SC*c)	4,7		1	0
προσκυνέω to God (*SC*a)	4,8	8,27; 24,11	1	0
προσκυνέω to human beings (*SC*d)		10,25	1	0
προσκυνέω to Jesus (*SC*b)	24,52		10	2

Literature

BDAG 2000 883 [literature].

BACHMANN, Michael, *Jerusalem und der Tempel*, 1980. Esp. 332-369: "Gebet".
GEORGE, Augustin, La prière. — ID., *Études*, 1978, 395-427. Esp. 402-405: "Le vocabulaire lucanien de la prière".
KILPATRICK, George D., Style and Text, 1967. Esp. 154-156; = ID., *Principles and Practice*, 1990. Esp. 55-57.

προσπίπτω 3 + 1 (Mt 1, Mk 3)

1. prostrate oneself before (Lk 5,8; 8,28.47; Acts 16,29); 2. strike against

Word groups	Lk	Acts	Mt	Mk
προσπίπτω τοῖς γόνασιν → πίπτω ἐπὶ/παρὰ/πρὸς τοὺς πόδας	5,8		0	0
προσπεσών → (ἐμ/ἐπι/κατα/περι)πεσών; cf. Jn 12,24; Rom 11,22; 1 Cor 14,25; ἀναπεσών Jn 13,25; παραπεσών Heb 6,6	8,47		0	0
προσπίπτω aorist → (ἀνα/ἐμ/ἐπι/κατα/περι/συμ)πίπτω aorist; cf. ἀποπίπτω Acts 9,18; ἐκπίπτω Acts 12,7; 27,17.26.29.32	5,8; 8,28.47	16,29	1	2

Characteristic of Luke

PLUMMER 1922 lx

προσποιέομαι 1   act as though (Lk 24,28)

Literature

HAUCK 1934 [seltenes Alleinwort].

προσρήγνυμι** 2   strike against (Lk 6,48.49)

Literature

HAUCK 1934 [seltenes Alleinwort].

προστάσσω 1 + 3 (Mt 2/3, Mk 1)

1. command (Lk 5,14); 2. arrange for (Acts 17,26)

Word groups	Lk	Acts	Mt	Mk
προστάσσω with accusative + infinitive (VKa)		10,48	0	0
προστάσσομαι passive (VKb)		10,33; 17,26	0	0

Literature

MAKUJINA, John, Verbs Meaning "Command" in the New Testament: Determining the Factors Involved in the Choice of Command-Verbs. — *EstBíb* 56 (1998) 357-369. Esp. 358-359: "Παραγγέλλω"; 359-361: "Κελεύω"; 361-362: "Ἐντέλλω"; 362-364: "Διαστέλλω"; 364-366: "-τάσσω complex"; 366-367: "Λέγω". [NTA 43, 57]

προστίθημι 7 + 6 (Mt 2, Mk 1)

1. add (Lk 3,20); 2. give (Lk 12,31)
προστίθεμαι: 3. continue (Lk 19,11); 4. proceed (Acts 12,3)

Word groups	Lk	Acts	Mt	Mk
προστίθημι + ἐπί + dative	3,20		0	0
προστίθημι + τῷ κυρίῳ		5,14; 11,24	0	0
προστίθημι (τί) τινι (VKa)	12,31; 17,5	5,14; 11,24	1	1
προστίθημι + πίστιν → **παρέχω** πίστιν	17,5		0	0
προστίθημι πρὸς τοὺς πατέρας αὐτοῦ (LN: bury; VKc)		13,36	0	0

Characteristic of Luke

BOISMARD 1984 cb93; DENAUX 2009 L***; GASTON 1973 65 [Lked]; GOULDER 1989*;
HAWKINS 1909 L; NEIRYNCK 1985; PLUMMER 1922 lx

	Lk	Acts	Mt	Mk
προστίθημι + infinitive (VKb)	20,11.12	12,3	0	0
BOISMARD 1984 Ab142; NEIRYNCK 1985				

Literature

COLLISON 1977 64 [linguistic usage of Luke: certain; προστίθημι = again: noteworthy
phenomena]; DENAUX 2009 Laⁿ [προστίθημι + infinitive]; HAUCK 1934 [Vorzugswort];
JEREMIAS 1980 112: "προστίθημι ist eine von Lukas bevorzugte Vokabel … Es fällt auf, daß sich
im dritten Evangelium die Konstruktion von προστίθημι mit τι ἐπί τι (Lk 12,25 par. Mt 6,27)
neben der mit τι ἐπί τινι (Lk 3,20) findet. Da die Konstruktion von ἐπί mit dem Akkusativ (Lk
12,25) nach Ausweis der Mt-Parallele der Tradition zugehört, wird unsere Stelle [Lk 3,20], die ἐπί
mit dem Dativ konstruiert, der Redaktion zuzuweisen sein. Ferner findet sich im NT *nur* in Lk/Apg
die semitisierende Verwendung von προστίθημι zur Umschreibung der Adverbien 'wiederum,
weiterhin' (Lk 3/Apg 1). Lukas schreibt in diesen Fällen mit LXX προσέθετο (Med.) c.inf.".

TAEGER, Jens-Wilhelm, *Der Mensch und sein Heil*, 1982. Esp. 155:
"προστιθέναι/προστίθεσθαι (τῷ κυρίῳ".

προσφέρω 4/5 + 3 (Mt 15, Mk 3/4)

1. bring to (Lk 5,14; 18,15; 23,36; Acts 7,42); 2. bring into presence (Lk 23,14); 3.
present to
προφέρομαι: 4. behave toward

Word groups	Lk	Acts	Mt	Mk
προσφέρω θυσίαν (VKc); cf. προσφορά + θυσία Eph 5,2; Heb 10,5.8		7,42	0	0
προσφέρω προσφοράν (VKa)		21,26	0	0
προσφέρω τι (VKd)	23,36	8,18	2	1
προσφέρω (sacrificial) gifts (SCa)	5,14	7,42; 21,26	4	1

προσφωνέω 4 + 2 (Mt 1)

1. address (Acts 21,40); 2. call out to (Lk 7,32; 23,30); 3. call to oneself (Lk 6,13; 13,12)

Word groups	Lk	Acts	Mt	Mk
προσφωνέω + λέγω/εἶπον → (**ἀνα/ἐπι)φωνέω** + λέγω/εἶπον	7,32; 13,12	21,40	1	0
προσφωνέω τινά (VKa)	6,13		0	0

Characteristic of Luke

BOISMARD 1984 Bb78; CADBURY 1920 177; DENAUX 2009 L***; GOULDER 1989*; HAWKINS 1909 L; NEIRYNCK 1985; PLUMMER 1922 lx; VOGEL 1899B

Literature

HAUCK 1934 [Vorzugswort]; JEREMIAS 1980 69 [προσφωνέω + λέγων: red.]; 229 [red.].

προσψαύω* 1

1. touch (Lk 11,46); 2. touch to help (Lk 11,46)

Literature

HAUCK 1934 [seltenes Alleinwort].

πρόσωπον 13/15 + 12 (Mt 10, Mk 3)

1. face (Lk 9,29); 2. person; 3. surface (Lk 21,35); 4. appearance (Lk 12,56); 5. presence (Acts 2,28); 6. in front of (Lk 10,1; Acts 7,45)

Word groups	Lk	Acts	Mt	Mk
ἀπὸ προσώπου (SCd; VKa) ; cf. 2 Thess 1,9; Rev 6,16; 12,14 BOISMARD 1984 Da14		3,20; 5,41; 7,45	0	0
ἀποστέλλω + πρὸ προσώπου; cf. προκηρύσσω πρὸ προσώπου Acts 13,24	7,27; 9,52; 10,1		1	1
ἐπὶ (τὸ) πρόσωπον (SCa; VKd)	5,12; 17,16; 21,35	17,26 v.l.	2	0
ἐπὶ πρόσωπον πάσης τῆς γῆς; cf. ἐπὶ παντὸς προσώπου τῆς γῆς Acts 17,26	21,35		0	0
κλίνω τὸ πρόσωπον εἰς τὴν γῆν (LN: prostrate oneself)	24,5		0	0
πίπτω ἐπὶ πρόσωπον	5,12; 17,16		2	0
πρὸ προσώπου αὐτοῦ	9,52; 10,1		0	0
πρόσωπον λαμβάνω (LN: show favoritism; VKh)	20,21		0	0
πρόσωπον + τοῦ οὐρανοῦ → πρόσωπον τῆς γῆς	12,56		1	0
στηρίζω τὸ πρόσωπον (LN: decide firmly)	9,51		0	0
πρόσωπα plural (VKj)	24,5		1	0

Characteristic of Luke	Lk	Acts	Mt	Mk
κατὰ πρόσωπον (LN: ᵃin front of; ᵇin person; SCb; VKe); cf. 2 Cor 10,1.7; Gal 2,11 PLUMMER 1922 lxi	2,ᵃ31	3,ᵃ13; 25,ᵃ16	0	0
πρὸ προσώπου (LN: previous; SCc; VKf) BOISMARD 1984 Ab101; NEIRYNCK 1985; PLUMMER 1922 lxi	1,76*; 7,27; 9,52; 10,1	13,24	1	1
πρόσωπον τῆς γῆς → πρόσωπον τοῦ οὐρανοῦ BOISMARD 1984 Ab143; NEIRYNCK 1985; VOGEL 1899C	12,56; 21,35	17,26	0	0

Literature

VON BENDEMANN 2001 415 [πρὸ προσώπου αὐτοῦ]; DENAUX 2009 lAⁿ [κατὰ πρόσωπον], Laⁿ [πρόσωπον τῆς γῆς]; EASTON 1910 157 [πρὸ προσώπου αὐτοῦ: probably characteristic of L]; 176 [possible Hebraisms in the Lucan Writings, as classed by Dalman]; GERSDORF 1816 212 [προπορεύσῃ γὰρ πρὸ προσώπου]; 256 [κατὰ πρόσωπον]; JEREMIAS 1980 179: "Die artikellose präpositionale Wendung πρὸ προσώπου τινός ist ein Septuagintismus, der bei allen drei Synoptikern in dem LXX-Zitat Mal 3,1 vorkommt (Mt 11,10 par. Mk 1,2 par. Lk 7,27), sonst nur im lukanischen Doppelwerk"; 283: "ἐπὶ πρόσωπον πάσης τῆς γῆς: = die 'Erdoberfläche' (Septuagintismus), im NT nur im Doppelwerk"; PLUMMER 1922 lxi [πρὸ προσώπου, κατὰ πρόσωπον: Hebrew influence]; RADL 1975 426 [πρόσωπον; κατὰ πρόσωπον; πρὸ προσώπου]; REHKOPF 1959 96 [πρὸ προσώπου]; SCHÜRMANN 1961 273 [πρὸ προσώπου].

προτρέχω 1	run in front of			
Word groups	**Lk**	**Acts**	**Mt**	**Mk**
- δραμ - (VKa)	19,4		0	0

προϋπάρχω 1 + 1   exist formerly (Lk 23,12; Acts 8,9)

Characteristic of Luke
BOISMARD 1984 Ab202; HAWKINS 1909LA; MORGENTHALER 1958*NEIRYNCK 1985; PLUMMER 1922 liii; VOGEL 1899A

Literature
DENAUX 2009 LA[n]; HAUCK 1934 [seltenes Alleinwort]; JEREMIAS 1980 303 [red.].

πρόφασις 1 + 1 (Mt 0/1, Mk 1)

1. pretense (Acts 27,30); 2. excuse (Lk 20,47)

προφέρω 2   produce (Lk 6,45$^{1.2}$)

Characteristic of Luke
PLUMMER 1922 liii

Literature
DENAUX 2009 L[n]; HAUCK 1934 [seltenes Alleinwort].

προφητεύω 2 + 4 (Mt 4, Mk 2)   speak inspired utterances (Lk 1,67; 22,64)

Word groups	**Lk**	**Acts**	**Mt**	**Mk**
ὁ προφητεύων (VKd)		21,9	0	0
προφητεύω λέγω → **προφήτης** + λέγω/εἶπον; cf. προφητεία + λέγω Mt 13,14	1,67		1	0

Literature
JEREMIAS 1980 69 [προφητεύω + λέγων: red.].

προφήτης 29/31 + 30 (Mt 37/39, Mk 6/7)   prophet

Word groups	**Lk**	**Acts**	**Mt**	**Mk**
ἅγιος + προφήτης DENAUX 2009 LA[n]	1,70	3,21	0	0

ἀνὴρ προφήτης	24,19		0	0
διὰ (+) τοῦ προφήτου/τῶν προφητῶν → διὰ Ἠσαίου τοῦ προφήτου	1,70; 18,31	2,16; 3,21; 28,25	13	0
προφῆται καὶ ἀπόστολοι (VKf)	11,49		0	0
προφῆται + νόμος/Μωϋσῆς (LN: the sacred writings; SCb; VKb)	16,16.29.31; 24,27.44	13,15; 24,14; 26,22; 28,23	4	0
προφῆται + νόμος Μωϋσέως DENAUX 2009 LAⁿ (?)	24,44	28,23	0	0
προφήτης + proper name (except VKa) (VKd)	7,28*	13,1; 15,32; 21,10	0	0
προφήτης + proper name referring to the OT (VKa)	3,4; 4,17.27; 11,29*	2,16; 3,24; 8,28.30; 13,20; 28,25	8/9	1/2
προφήτης referring to Jesus (SCd; VKc)	7,16.39; 9,8.19; 24,19	3,22.23; 7,37	2	1
προφήτης referring to John the Baptist (SCc)	1,76; 7,28*; 20,6		3	1
προφήτης + λέγω/εἶπον → προφητεύω + λέγω; cf. προφητεία + λέγω Mt 13,14	3,4 v.l.	7,48; 8,34; 21,10(-11); 26,22; 28,25(-26)	10	0
προφήτης τις DENAUX 2009 Lⁿ	9,8.19		0	0
προφήτης Hebrew Bible (SCa, except SCb)	1,70; 3,4; 4,17.27; 6,23; 9,8.19; 10,24; 11,29*.47.50; 13,28; 18,31; 24,25	2,16.30; 3,18.21.24.25; 7,42.48.52; 8,28.30.34; 10,43; 13,20.27.40; 15,15; 26,27; 28,25	21	4
προφήτης Christian prophets (SCe)	11,49	11,27; 13,1; 15,32; 21,10	4	0

Characteristic of Luke	Lk	Acts	Mt	Mk
λαλέω of the prophets DENAUX 2009 IA*; VOGEL 1899C	1,70; 24,25	3,21.22.24; 26,22; 28,25	0	0
πάντες οἱ προφῆται (of the OT) BOISMARD 1984 Bb50; DENAUX 2009 IA*; GOULDER 1989; NEIRYNCK 1985	11,50; 13,28; 24,27	3,18.24; 10,43	1	0
Μωϋσῆς καὶ προφῆται; cf. Jn 1,45 BOISMARD 1984 Bb115; GOULDER 1989; NEIRYNCK 1985	16,29.31; 24,27	26,22	0	0

Literature

BDAG 2000 890-891 [literature]; DENAUX 2009 Laⁿ [Μωϋσῆς καὶ προφῆται]; GERSDORF 1816 212 [προφήτης ὑψίστου]; HAUCK 1934 [Vorzugsverbindung: προφήτης τις]; JEREMIAS 1980 209 [πάντων τῶν προφητῶν: red.].

HAGENE, Sylvia, *Zeiten der Wiederherstellung*, 2003. Esp. 193-199: "Besonderheiten der Bezeichnung Jesu als 'Prophet'".

RESE, Martin, *Alttestamentliche Motive in der Christologie des Lukas*, 1969. Esp. 131-133: "Προφήτης, ἅγιος, δίκαιος, ἀρχηγός, σωτήρ und υἱὸς θεοῦ in der Apostelgeschichte"; 206: "Προφήτης im Lukasevangelium".

προφῆτις 1	prophetess (Lk 2,36)

Literature

GERSDORF 1816 258 [καὶ ἦν ῞Αννα προφῆτις - αὕτη προβεβηκυῖα].

πρωτοκαθεδρία 2 (Mt 1, Mk 1)	seat of honor (Lk 11,43; 20,46)

πρωτοκλισία 3 (Mt 1, Mk 1)	seat of honor (Lk 14,7.8; 20,46)

πρῶτον 10 + 5/6 (Mt 9/10, Mk 6[7])

before

Word groups	Lk	Acts	Mt	Mk
οὐ/οὐχὶ (+) πρῶτον (VKe)	11,38; 14,28.31		0	0
DENAUX 2009 L[n]				
πρῶτον δέ (VKf)	9,61; 17,25		0	0
DENAUX 2009 L[n]				
πρῶτον + δεῖ	17,25; 21,9			
DENAUX 2009 L[n]				
πρῶτον + δεύτερον (VKc) → πρῶτος + δεύτερος; cf.		7,12(-13)	0	0
πρῶτον + εἶτα Mk 4,28				
πρῶτόν τε καί (VKg)		26,20	0	0
πρῶτον … τότε (SCa; VKd)	6,42		3	1

Literature

JEREMIAS 1980 267-268 [πρῶτον δέ; πρῶτον + δεῖ: red.]; SCHÜRMANN 1957 85, n. 287.

πρῶτος 10 + 11/12 (Mt 16, Mk 9[10]/11)

1. first (Lk 12,1; Acts 26,23); 2. before; 3. prominent (Acts 17,4); 4. best (Lk 15,22); 5. most important

Word groups	Lk	Acts	Mt	Mk
πρώτη ἡμέρα (SCa; VKa)		20,18	0	1
οἱ πρῶτοι τοῦ λαοῦ → ἄρχων τοῦ λαοῦ; cf.	19,47		0	0
ἀρχιερεῖς τοῦ λαοῦ Mt 2,4; 21,23; 26,3.47;				
27,1; γραμματεῖς τοῦ λαοῦ Mt 2,4; πρεσ-				
βύτεροι τοῦ λαοῦ Mt 21,23; 26,3.47; 27,1				
πρῶτος + δεύτερος (SCb; VKd) → πρῶτον +	19,16(-18); 20,29(-30)	12,10	2/3	2/3
δεύτερον; cf. ἡ πρώτη Mt 26,17; Mk [16,9]				
πρῶτος + ἔσχατος (SCc; VKe)	11,26; 13,30[1.2]		8	3
πρῶτος + ἕτερος (SCb; VKd)	14,18(-19); 16,5(-7)		1	0

Characteristic of Luke	Lk	Acts	Mt	Mk
ὁ πρῶτος / οἱ πρῶτοι the most prominent men (SCd) → οἱ	19,47	13,50; 17,4;	0	1
πρῶτοι τοῦ λαοῦ		25,2; 28,7.17		
BOISMARD 1984 Bb51; HARNACK 1906 30; NEIRYNCK 1985;				
SCHÜRMANN 1957 77				

Literature

DENAUX 2009 lAn [ὁ πρῶτος / οἱ πρῶτοι the most prominent men]; RADL 1975 426 [πρῶτος "bezogen auf Personen, mit Genitiv"].

BURCHARD, Christoph, Fußnoten zum neutestamentlichen Griechisch, 1970. Esp. 160: "Lc 15,22 ταχὺ ἐξενέγκατε στολὴν τὴν πρώτην".

HAACKER, Klaus, Erst unter Quirinius? Ein Übersetzungsvorschlag zu Lk 2,2. — *BibNot* 38-39 (1987) 39-43.

MUÑOZ IGLESIAS, Salvador, El censo (anterior al) de Quirino. — *Miscelánea Comillas* 41 (1983) 159-166.
WOLTER, Michael, Erstmals unter Quirinius! Zum Verständnis von Lk 2,2. — *BibNot* 102 (2000) 35-41.

πρωτότοκος 1 (Mt 0/1)

1. firstborn (Lk 2,7); 2. existing before; 3. superior

Word groups	Lk	Acts	Mt	Mk
ὁ υἱὸς + ὁ πρωτότοκος (*VK*a)	2,7		0/1	0

πτερύγιον 1 (Mt 1) — pinnacle (Lk 4,9)

Literature

BDAG 2000 895 [literature].

SCHWARZ, Günther, τὸ πτερυγιον του ιερου. — *BibNot* 61 (1992) 33-35.

πτέρυξ 1 (Mt 1) — wing (Lk 13,34)

πτοέω 2/3 — πτοέομαι: be terrified (Lk 12,4*; 21,9; 24,37)

Literature

DENAUX 2009 L[n]; HAUCK 1934 [seltenes Alleinwort]; JEREMIAS 1980 320 [red.].

πτύον 1 (Mt 1) — Winnowing shovel (Lk 3,17)

πτύσσω 1* — roll up

Word groups	Lk	Acts	Mt	Mk
πτύσσω τὸ βιβλίον → **ἀναπτύσσω/ἀνοίγω** τὸ βιβλίον; **διανοίγω/συνίημι** τὰς γραφάς	4,20		0	0

Literature

HAUCK 1934 [seltenes Alleinwort].

πτῶσις 1 (Mt 1)

1. destruction; 2. falling (status) (Lk 2,34); 3. worsening

πτωχός 10 (Mt 5, Mk 5)

1. poor (Lk 6,20); 2. of little value

Word groups	Lk	Acts	Mt	Mk
(δια)δίδωμι πτωχοῖς	18,22; 19,8		2	2

(οἱ) πτωχοί (SCa; VKb) → (οἱ) πλούσιοι	4,18; 6,20; 7,22; 14,13.21; 18,22; 19,8		5	3
πτωχός attributive (VKa)	21,3		0	2

Characteristic of Luke

GOULDER 1989

	Lk	Acts	Mt	Mk
πτωχός + πλούσιος (SCb; VKc) DENAUX 2009 L*** (?)	6,20(-24); 14,(12-)13; 16,(19-)20.22		0	1

Literature

BDAG 2000 896 [literature]; HAUCK 1934 [Vorzugsverbindung: πτωχὸς δέ τις].

DUPONT, Jacques, *Les Béatitudes*, II, 1969. Esp. 19-34: "Le vocabulaire de la pauvreté".
—, *Les Béatitudes*, III, 1973. Esp. 42-43.
—, Gesù Messia dei poveri, Messia povero. — ID. – HAMMAN, A.G. – MICCOLI, G., *Seguire Gesù povero* (Parola e Storia). Magnano: Comunità di Bose, 1984, 9-87. Jésus, Messie des pauvres, Messie pauvre. — ID., *Études*, I, 1985, 86-130. Esp. 87-90: "Le vocabulaire de la pauvreté".
HATCH, Edwin, *Essays*, 1889. Esp. 73-77.
NÚÑEZ, Helio Mª., ΄Āni, πτωχός, pobre (Métodos para el entronque del vocabulario griego-hebreo). — *EstBíb* 25 (1966) 193-205.
ROTH, S. John, *The Blind, the Lame and the Poor. Character Types in Luke* (JSNT SS, 144). Sheffield: Academic Press, 1997, 253 p. Esp. 28-55, 112-134.
SECCOMBE, David Peter, *Possessions and the Poor in Luke-Acts* (SNTU, B6). Linz: SNTU, 1982, 298 p.
TOPEL, L. John, *Children of a Compassionate God: A Theological Exegesis of Luke 6:20-49*. Collegeville, MN: The Liturgical Press, 2001, XVII-340. Esp. 67-87.

πυκνός 1 + 1 (Mk 0/1)   often

Word groups	Lk	Acts	Mt	Mk
νηστεύω πυκνά; cf. νηστεύω πολλά Mt 9,14	5,33		0	0
πυκνότερος comparative (VKa)		24,26	0	0

Characteristic of Luke

PLUMMER 1922 lix

Literature

DENAUX 2009 LAⁿ.

πύλη 1/2 + 4 (Mt 4)   gate,door (Lk 7,12; 13,24*)

Word groups	Lk	Acts	Mt	Mk
ἀνοίγω τὴν πύλην → ἀνοίγω τὴν θύραν/τὸν πυλῶνα		12,10	0	0

πυλών 1 + 5 (Mt 1)

1. door, gate (Lk 16,20; Acts 14,13); 2. entrance (Acts 12,13)

Word groups	Lk	Acts	Mt	Mk
ἀνοίγω τὸν πυλῶνα →ἀνοίγω τὴν **θύραν**/τὴν **πύλην**		12,14	0	0
ἡ θύρα τοῦ πυλῶνος (VKa)		12,13	0	0

Characteristic of Luke
BOISMARD 1984 Eb30; NEIRYNCK 1985

Literature
DENAUX 2009 lAn.

πυνθάνομαι 2 + 7 (Mt 1)
1. inquire (Lk 15,26; 18,36); 2. learn about (Acts 23,34)

Word groups	Lk	Acts	Mt	Mk
πυνθάνομαι + direct discourse BOISMARD 1984 Aa105		4,7; 10,29; 23,19	0	0
πυνθάνομαι εἰ (VKa)		10,18	0	0
πυνθάνομαι ὅτι (VKb)		23,34	0	0
πυνθάνομαι + τι (VKc)		23,20	0	0

Characteristic of Luke
BOISMARD 1984 Eb91; DENAUX 2009 lA*†; HAWKINS 1909B; NEIRYNCK 1985

	Lk	Acts	Mt	Mk
πυνθάνομαι τίς/τί εἴη; cf. Jn 13,24 BOISMARD 1984 Ab144; NEIRYNCK 1985	15,26; 18,36	21,33		

Literature
VON BENDEMANN 2001 429; COLLISON 1977 98 [noteworthy phenomena]; DENAUX 2009 La[n] [πυνθάνομαι τίς/τί εἴη]; HAUCK 1934 [Vorzugswort]; JEREMIAS 1980 253 [red.]; RADL 1975 426.

πῦρ 7 + 4 (Mt 12, Mk 4/8)
1. fire (Lk 22,55); 2. bonfire

Word groups	Lk	Acts	Mt	Mk
ἀν/περιάπτω πῦρ →ἅπτω **πῦρ**; cf. ἅπτω πυράν Acts 28,2 DENAUX 2009 L[n]	12,49; 22,55		0	0
βαπτίζω ἐν + πυρί	3,16		1	0
εἰς (τὸ) πῦρ βάλλω (SCa; VKa); cf. βάλλω εἰς τὴν κάμινον τοῦ πυρός Mt 13,42.50; εἰς γέενναν Mt 5,29.30*; 18,9; Mk 9,45.47; εἰς ὕδατα Mk 9,22	3,9		3	1/2
πῦρ ἄσβεστον (SCd; VKd); cf. τὸ πῦρ οὐ σβέννυται Mk 9,48	3,17		1	1/2
πῦρ + βάλλω (LN: cause discord)	12,49		0	0
πῦρ + θεῖον (VKg)	17,29		0	0
πῦρ κατακαίω (SCb; VKb); cf. πῦρ + καίω Mt 13,40 v.l.	3,17		2	0
πῦρ + ὕδωρ →**φλόξ** + ὕδωρ	3,16		2	1
πῦρ φλόξ (VKh)		7,30	0	0

Characteristic of Luke	Lk	Acts	Mt	Mk
ἅπτω πῦρ/λύχνον→ ἀν/περιάπτω **πῦρ**; ἅπτω **λύχνον** BOISMARD 1984 Ab69; HARNACK 1906 39.54; NEIRYNCK 1985	22,55*	28,2	0	0

Literature

BDAG 2000 606; JEREMIAS 1980 204 [red.]

πύργος 2 (Mt 1, Mk 1)   (watch)tower (Lk 13,4; 14,28)

Literature

BDAG 2000 899 [literature ad Lk 14,28]; PAFFENROTH 1997 77.

DERRETT, J. Duncan M., Nisi dominus aedificaverit domum: Towers and Wars (Lk XIVK 28-32. — *NT* 19 (1977) 241-261. Esp. 251-254: "The tower"; = ID., *Studies in the New Testament*, III, 1982, 85-106. Esp. 95-98.

πυρετός 2 + 1 (Mt 1, Mk 1)   fever (Lk 4,38.39; Acts 28,8)

Word groups	Lk	Acts	Mt	Mk
συνέχω (+) πυρετός	4,38	28,8	0	0

Literature

HARNACK 1906 42 [συνέχομαι + πυρετός Lk 4,38; Acts 28,8 the whole expression is of a distinctly medical character]

CADBURY, Henri J., Lexical Notes on Luke-Acts, II, 1926. Esp. 194-195: "ἦν συνεχομένη πυρετῷ μεγάλῳ".

πωλέω 6 + 3 (Mt 6, Mk 3)   sell

Word groups	Lk	Acts	Mt	Mk
πωλέω (+) ἀγοράζω (SCa; VKa)	17,28; 19,45 *v.l.*; 22,36		3	1
πωλέω ὅσα ἔχεις + ἀκολουθέω	18,22		1	1

Literature

SCHÜRMANN 1957 123 [Lk 22,36 könnte luk R sein].

πῶλος 4 (Mt 3, Mk 4)   foal

Word groups	Lk	Acts	Mt	Mk
λύω (+) πῶλον → λύω βοῦν	19,30.33[1.2]		1	3

Literature

BDAG 2000 900 [literature].

MICHEL, Otto, Eine philologische Frage zur Einzugsgeschichte. — *NTS* 6 (1959) 81-82. Esp. 81: "Aus der Wortbedeutung als solcher lässt sich im Griechischen keineswegs die Tierart festlegen, eine bestimmte Spezifizierung muss im allgemeinen hinzutreten. Im Griechischen besteht aber die Neigung, wenn πῶλος gebraucht wird, an junge Pferde zu denken ... Tatsächlich scheint aber sowohl in Aegypten wie in Palästina bei πῶλος und den entsprechenden hebräischen und aramäischen Aequivalenten an den Esel gedacht zu sein, was ja auch das Natürlichste ist". [NTA 4, 367]

πώποτε 1	ever (Lk 19,30)

πῶς 16 + 9 (Mt 14, Mk 14/16)   how?

Word groups	Lk	Acts	Mt	Mk
διηγέομαι πῶς BOISMARD 1984 ca41		9,27; 12,17	0	1
ἢ πῶς	6,42 v.l.		2	0
καὶ πῶς → καὶ ὅτι/πόθεν	12,50; 20,44	2,8	0	2
πῶς + adjective or adverb (SCf; VKg)	18,24		0	2
πῶς in indirect questions (SCh)	8,36; 12,11.27; 14,7; 22,2.4	4,21; 9,27[1.2]; 11,13; 12,17; 15,36; 20,18	3	7
πῶς + optative (SCb; VKb)		8,31	0	0
πῶς + subjunctive (SCa; VKa)	12,11; 22,2.4	4,21	3	3/4
πῶς (+) οὐ/οὔτε (SCd; VKd)	12,27.56		1	0/2
πῶς … ὡς		20,18(-20)	0	1
πῶς in exclamations (SCg)	12,50; 18,24		0	2

Characteristic of Luke

GASTON 1973 66 [Lked?]

	Lk	Acts	Mt	Mk
τὸ πῶς (SCc; VKc) → τὸ τίς/τί; cf. 1 Thess 4,1 BOISMARD 1984 cb47; NEIRYNCK 1985	22,2.4	4,21	0	0

Literature

BDR § 436,3: "πῶς τί: Lk 8,18; 10,26; 13,18"; DENAUX 2009 La[n] [τὸ πῶς]; HAUCK 1934 [Vorzugsverbindung: τὸ πῶς]; RADL 1975 419 [τό vor interrogativem πῶς]; SCHÜRMANN 1957 12 [τό vor πῶς: Hand des redigierender Luk ist deutlich].

BAUER, Johannes, Πῶς in der griechischen Bibel. — NT 2 (1958) 81-91. [NTA 3, 317]; = ID., Scholia Biblica et Patristica, 1972, 29-39.

P

ῥάβδος 1 (Mt 1, Mk 1)	
1. stick (Lk 9,3); 2. governing	

Ῥαγαύ 1	Reu (Lk 3,35)

ῥῆγμα 1	destruction (Lk 6,49)

Literature
HAUCK 1934 [seltenes Alleinwort].

ῥήγνυμι 2 (Mt 2, Mk 2)
1. rip (Lk 5,37); 2. begin to shout; 3. break forth with; 4. throw into a fit (Lk 9,42)

ῥῆμα 19/20 + 14 (Mt 6/7, Mk 2)
1. word (Lk 2,17); 2. statement (Acts 28,25); 3. event

Word groups	Lk	Acts	Mt	Mk
ἀκούω ῥήματα → ἀκούω τὸν **λόγον** / τοὺς **λογούς** / τῶν **λόγων**		10,22	0	0
ἀπαγγέλλω + τὰ ῥήματα ταῦτα → ἀπαγγέλλω τοὺς **λόγους** τούτους		16,38	0	0
διαλαλέω + τὸ ῥῆμα (*SC*a; *VK*a) → λαλέω (τὸ) **ῥῆμα**; λαλέω τὸν **λόγον**	1,65		0	0
κατὰ τὸ ῥῆμα (*SC*h; *VK*h)	1,38; 2,29		0	0
πᾶν ῥῆμα (*SC*g; *VK*g) → πάντα τὰ **ῥήματα**	1,37; 4,4*		3/4	0
ῥῆμα ἀποφθέγγομαι (*SC*c; *VK*c)		26,25	0	0
ῥῆμα + attr. part. of γίνομαι DENAUX 2009 La[n]	2,15; 13,17	10,37	0	0
ῥῆμα + γίνομαι DENAUX 2009 La[n]	1,38; 2,15; 3,2	10,37	0	0
τὸ ῥῆμα τοῦ κυρίου with double article DENAUX 2009 LA[n]	22,61	11,16	0	0
ῥῆμα + λέγω/εἶπον (*SC*b; *VK*b); cf. διάλεκτος + λέγω Acts 21,40; 26,14	18,34; 22,61	11,16; 28,25	0/1	1
ῥῆμα + πληρόω → γεγραμμένα/γραφή/**λόγος** + πληρόω; cf. ῥηθέν + πληρόω Mt 1,22; 2,15.17.23; 4,14; 8,17; 12,17; 13,35; 21,4; 27,9.35*	7,1		0	0
τὰ ῥήματα ἅπαντα	2,51 *v.l.*		0	0
ῥῆμα (θεοῦ) the word of God (*SC*d; *VK*d) → **λόγος** τοῦ θεοῦ	1,38; 2,29; 3,2; 4,4*		1	0
ῥῆμα (Ἰησοῦ) the word of Jesus (*SC*f; *VK*f)	5,5; 7,1; 9,45[1.2]; 18,34; 24,8		1	2

Characteristic of Luke
DENAUX 2009 L***; GOULDER 1989*; HAWKINS 1909 L; HENDRIKS 1986 434; MORGENTHALER 1958LA

	Lk	Acts	Mt	Mk
πάντα τὰ ῥήματα (*SC*g; *VK*g) → πᾶν **ῥῆμα**; τὰ **ῥήματα** ἅπαντα BOISMARD 1984 Ab62; DENAUX 2009 L***; NEIRYNCK 1985	1,65; 2,19.51; 7,1	5,20	0	0
λαλέω (τὸ) ῥῆμα / (τὰ) ῥήματα (*SC*a; *VK*a) → διαλαλέω τὸ **ῥῆμα**; λαλέω τὸν **λόγον**; cf. Jn 3,34; 6,63; 8,20; 14,10 BOISMARD 1984 cb156; DENAUX 2009 lA*; NEIRYNCK 1985	2,17.50	5,20; 6,11.13; 10,44; 11,14; 13,42	1	0
ῥῆμα in the meaning of "thing" BOISMARD 1984 Ab41; DENAUX 2009 L***; HARNACK 1906 146-147; NEIRYNCK 1985; PLUMMER 1922 lxi	1,37; 2,15.19.51	5,32; 10,37	0	0
τὸ ῥῆμα τοῦτο → τὰ **ῥήματα** ταῦτα; **λόγος** οὗτος DENAUX 2009 L***; GOULDER 1989*; HARNACK 1906 147;	2,15; 9,45[1.2]; 18,34		0	0

τὰ ῥήματα = proclamation, preaching DENAUX 2009 IA*	2,51 v.l.; 7,1; 24,8	2,14; 5,20; 10,22.44; 11,14	0	0
τὰ ῥήματα ταῦτα → ῥῆμα τοῦτο BOISMARD 1984 Ab29; DENAUX 2009 IA*; GOULDER 1989*; NEIRYNCK 1985	1,65; 2,19; 24,11	5,32; 10,44; 13,42; 16,38	0	0

Literature

COLLISON 1977 176 [linguistic usage of Luke: certain]; 204 [οὗτος + ῥῆμα: linguistic usage of Luke: certain]; GERSDORF 1816 205 [πάντα τὰ ῥήματα ταῦτα]; 238 [καὶ ἴδωμεν τὸ ῥῆμα τοῦτο τὸ γεγονός]; 240 [πάντα συνετήρει τὰ ῥήματα ταῦτα συμβάλλουσα ἐν τῇ καρδίᾳ αὐτῆς]; 254-256 [νῦν ἀπολύεις τὸν δοῦλόν σου, δέσποτα, κατὰ τὸ ῥῆμά σου ἐν εἰρήνῃ]; 271 [τὸ ῥῆμα ὃ ἐλάλησεν αὐτοῖς]; 272 [διετήρει πάντα τὰ ῥήματα ταῦτα]; HAUCK 1934 [Vorzugswort]; JEREMIAS 1980 54: "lukanisches Vorzugswort ... So ist für den lukanischen Gebrauch von ῥῆμα kennzeichnend: a) die Wendung πάντα τὰ ῥήματα ..., b) τὸ ῥῆμα τοῦτο / τὰ ῥήματα ταῦτα, im NT nur Lk/Apg ..., c) τὸ ῥῆμα mit attributiv gebrauchtem Partizip von γίνομαι, im NT nur Lk/Apg ..., d] τὸ ῥῆμα τοῦ κυρίου (mit doppeltem Artikel) ..., e) der Hebraismus ῥῆμα = 'Sache', 'Angelegenheit', 'Gegenstand', 'Begebenheit' ..., f) schließlich ist charakteristisch für Lukas die missionstheologische Bedeutung von τὰ ῥήματα = 'die Verkündigung'".

BURCHARD, Christoph, A Note on ῥῆμα in JosAs 17:1f.; Luke 2:15,17; Acts 10:37. — NT 27 (1985) 281-295. [NTA 30, 624]
DELEBECQUE, Édouard, Études grecques, 1976. Esp. 42-47 [2,41-52]; 59-69.
JUNG, Chang-Wook, Infancy Narrative, 2004. Esp. 115.119-120 [Lk 1,37].
MAHFOUZ, Hady, La fonction littéraire et théologique de Lc 3,1-20, 2003. Esp. 55-57 [ῥῆμα θεοῦ].
REPO, Eero, Der Begriff "Rhēma" im biblisch-griechischen: Eine traditionsgeschichtliche und semasiologische Untersuchung. II: "Rhēma" im Neuen Testament, unter Berücksichtigung seines Gebrauchs in der übrigen altchristlichen Literatur (Annales Academiae Scientiarum Fennicae, 88/1). Helsinki: Suomalainen Tiedeakatemia, 1954, 214 p. Esp. 21-58: "Das Evangelium des Lukas und die Apostelgeschichte". (see critique by G. ZUNTZ, in L'Antiquité Classique 22 [1953] 106-112).
SWELLENGREBEL, J.L., Puzzles in Luke. — BTrans 17 (1966) 118-122. Esp. 118-119 [Lk 3,2: ῥῆμα θεοῦ].
VAN UNNIK, Willem C., Die rechte Bedeutung des Wortes treffen, Lukas 2,19. — Verbum: Essays on Some Aspects of the Religious Function of Words, Dedicated to Dr. H. W. Obbink (Studia Theologica Rheno-Traiectina, 6). Utrecht: Kemink en zoon, 1964, 129-147; = ID., Sparsa Collecta, I, 1973, 72-91.

Ῥησά 1   Rhesa (Lk 3,27)

ῥίζα 2 (Mt 3, Mk 3)
1. root (Lk 3,9; 8,13); 2. descendant; 3. cause

ῥίπτω 2 + 3 (Mt 3)
1. throw (Lk 4,35; 17,2; Acts 27,19.29); 2. put down; 3. wave (Acts 22,23); ῥίπτομαι: 1. be dejected

Characteristic of Luke
BOISMARD 1984 cb149; NEIRYNCK 1985

ῥομφαία 1
1. sword (Lk 2,35); 2. war

Word groups	Lk	Acts	Mt	Mk
τὴν ψυχὴν διέρχεται ῥομφαία (*LN*: feel pain and sorrow)	2,35		0	0

Literature
GERSDORF 1816 257 [διελεύσεται ῥομφαία].

BENOIT, Pierre, "Et toi-même, un glaive te transpercera l'âme!" (Luc 2,35). — *CBQ* 25 (1963) 251-261.

DERRETT, J. Duncan M., Ἀντιλεγόμενον, ῥομφαία, διαλογισμοί (Lk 2:34-35): The Hidden Context. — *FilolNT* 6 (1993) 207-218. ["the author examines the meaning and significance of the main terms used in Lk 2:34-35, by studying their double context, the obvious one and the one based on Genesis and Deuteronomy. The choice of vocabulary is part of a great scheme of Luke's to demonstrate the new religion as a renewal of the pristine worship of YHWH"]; = ID., *Studies in the New Testament*, VI, 1995, 64-75.

ῥύμη 1 + 2 (Mt 1)   narrow street (Lk 14,21; Acts 9,11; 12,10)

Characteristic of Luke
BOISMARD 1984 cb48; NEIRYNCK 1985; PLUMMER 1922 lx

ῥύομαι 1/2 (Mt 2)   rescue

Word groups	Lk	Acts	Mt	Mk
ῥύομαι ἀπό (*VK*b) → (ἀπο)λύω ἀπό	11,4*		1	0
ῥύομαι passive (*VK*d)	1,74		0	0

ῥύσις 2 (Mk 1)   flow

Word groups	Lk	Acts	Mt	Mk
ἅπτομαι + ῥύσις αἵματος; cf. Mk 5,27-28 ἅπτομαι + πηγὴ αἵματος	8,44		0	0
ῥύσις (τοῦ) αἵματος (*LN*: menstrual flow)	8,43.44		0	1

Literature
WEISSENRIEDER, Annette, The Plague of Uncleanness? The Ancient Illness Construct "Issue of Blood" in Luke 8:43-48. — STEGEMANN, Wolfgang – MALINA, Bruce J. – THEISSEN, Gerd (eds.), *The Social Setting of Jesus and the Gospels*. Minneapolis, MN: Fortress, 2002, 207-222.

—, *Images of Illness in the Gospel of Luke*, 2003. Esp. 229-256.

Σ

σάββατον 20 + 10 (Mt 11, Mk 11[12])
1. Sabbath (Lk 4,16); 2. week (Lk 18,12)

Word groups	Lk	Acts	Mt	Mk
δὶς τοῦ σαββάτου (VKe)	18,12		0	0
μία τῶν σαββάτων (SCg; VKg)	24,1	20,7	1	1
ἐν ἑτέρῳ σαββάτῳ / τῷ ἐρχομένῳ σαββάτῳ (SCb; VKd) DENAUX 2009 LAⁿ	6,6	13,44	0	0
ἐν (τῷ) σαββάτῳ (SCb; VKb)	6,1.7		1/2	0
ἐπὶ σάββατα τρία (VKk)		17,2	0	0
κατὰ πᾶν σάββατον (SCh; VKj)		13,27; 15,21; 18,4	0	0
κύριος + σαββάτου	6,5		1	1
σάββατον + συναγωγή DENAUX 2009 lAn	4,16; 6,6; 13,10	13,14.42 v.l.; 15,21; 17,(1-)2; 18,4	0	2
σαββάτου/ἡμέρας ὁδός (LN: Sabbath journey; VKm) → ἡμέρας ὁδός BOISMARD 1984 Ab187; NEIRYNCK 1985		1,12	0	0
(ἐν) τοῖς σάββασιν (SCc-d; VKc)	4,31; 6,2.9 v.l.;13,10		0	1
σάββατα plural	4,16.31; 6,2; 13,10; 24,1	13,14; 16,13; 17,2; 20,7	7	6

Characteristic of Luke	Lk	Acts	Mt	Mk
(ἐν) (τῇ) ἡμέρᾳ τοῦ σαββάτου / τῶν σαββάτων (SCe+f; VKf) DENAUX 2009 L***; GOULDER 1989; HARNACK 1906 31; HAWKINS 1909 187; PLUMMER 1922 lii; VOGEL 1899C	4,16; 13,14².16; 14,5	13,14; 16,13	0	0
σάββατον singular GOULDER 1989	6,1.5.6.7.9; 13,14¹·².15.16; 14,1.3.5; 18,12; 23,54.56	1,12; 13,27.42.44; 15,21; 18,4	4	5
(τῷ) σαββάτῳ (SCa; VKa); cf. Jn 5,16 BOISMARD 1984 cb49; DENAUX 2009 La*; NEIRYNCK 1985	6,9; 13,14¹.15; 14,1.3	13,44	1	0

Literature

BDAG 2000 909-910 [literature]; DENAUX 2009 Lan [σάββατον singular]; EASTON 1910 155 [ἡμέρα τοῦ σαββάτου: probably characteristic of L]; JEREMIAS 1980 120: "Die Wendung (ἐν) τῇ ἡμέρᾳ τῶν σαββάτων / τοῦ σαββάτου ist ein Septuagintismus, der im NT nur im lukanischen Doppelwerk vorkommt"; PAFFENROTH 1997 81 [ἡμέρα τοῦ σαββάτου (singular)]; RADL 1975 403 [ἐγένετο + σάββατον].412 [(ἐν) (τῇ) ἡμέρᾳ τῶν σαββάτων].

DELEBECQUE, Édouard, Études grecques, 1976. Esp. 71-83: "Les moissonneurs du sabbat (6,1)".
DODD, Charles H., New Testament Translation Problems. — BTrans 27 (1976) 301-311. Esp. 305-307: "τῇ μιᾷ τῶν σαββάτων"; 28 (1977) 101-116.
LABERGE, L., Sabbat: étymologie et origines. — Science et Esprit 44 (1992) 185-204.
MATEOS, Juan, Σάββατα, σάββατον, προσάββατον, παρασκευή. — FilolNT 3 (1990) 19-38. Esp. 26-28: "En el evangelio de Lucas"; 29-30: "En Hechos y en las cartas paulinas".

Σαδδουκαῖος 1 + 5 (Mt 7/8, Mk 1)   Sadducee (Lk 20,27)

Word groups	Lk	Acts	Mt	Mk
Φαρισαῖοι + Σαδδουκαῖοι (SCa; VKa)		23,6.7.8	5/6	0

Literature

BDAG 2000 910 [literature].

σάκκος 1 (Mt 1)	sackcloth (Lk 10,13)

Σαλά 2	Shelah			
Word groups	**Lk**	**Acts**	**Mt**	**Mk**
Σαλά son of Kainan (VKb)	3,35		0	0
Σαλά son of Naasson (VKa)	3,32		0	0

Σαλαθιήλ 1 (Mt 2)	Salathiel (Lk 3,27)

σαλεύω 4 + 4 (Mt 2, Mk 1)

1. shake (Lk 6,38.48; 7,24; 21,26); 2. cause riot (Acts 17,13); σαλεύομαι: 3. be distressed

Word groups	**Lk**	**Acts**	**Mt**	**Mk**
σαλεύω active (VKa)	6,48	17,13	0	0

Characteristic of Luke
GOULDER 1989; PLUMMER 1922 lx

Literature
DENAUX 2009 LAn; LA[n] [σαλεύω active].

JOÜON, Paul, "Les forces des cieux seront ébranlées" (Matthieu 24,29; Marc 13,25; Luc 21,26). — RechSR 29 (1939) 114-115.

σάλος 1	surging waves (Lk 21,25)

Literature
HAUCK 1934 [seltenes Alleinwort].

Σαμάρεια 1 + 7	Samaria (Lk 17,11)			
Word groups	**Lk**	**Acts**	**Mt**	**Mk**
πόλις τῆς Σαμαρείας (VKa)		8,5	0	0

Characteristic of Luke
BOISMARD 1984 cb65; NEIRYNCK 1985

Literature
DENAUX 2009 lA[n].

Σαμαρίτης 3 + 1 (Mt 1)	Samaritan person (Lk 9,52; 10,33; 17,16; Acts 8,25)			
Word groups	**Lk**	**Acts**	**Mt**	**Mk**
κώμη/πόλις (τῶν) Σαμαριτῶν (VKa)	9,52	8,25	1	0

Characteristic of Luke
DENAUX 2009 La*

Literature
BDAG 2000 912 [literature]; HAUCK 1934 [Vorzugsverbindung: Σαμαρίτης δέ τις].
ENSLIN, Morton S., Luke and the Samaritans. — *HTR* 36 (1943) 278-297.

σαπρός 2 (Mt 5)
  1. bad (vale) (Lk 6,43¹·²); 2. harmful

Σάρεπτα 1   Zarephath

Word groups	Lk	Acts	Mt	Mk
Σάρεπτα τῆς Σιδωνίας (Σιδῶνος Lk 4,26 *v.l.*)	4,26		0	0

σάρξ 2 + 3/4 (Mt 5, Mk 4)
  1. flesh (Lk 24,39); 2. body (Acts 2,26); 3. people (Lk 3,6; Acts 2,17); 4. human; 5. nation; 6. human nature; 7. physical nature; 8. life

Word groups	Lk	Acts	Mt	Mk
κατὰ σάρκα (*VK*a)		2,30*	0	0
πᾶσα σάρξ (*SC*a; *VK*b)	3,6	2,17	1	1
σάρκες plural (*VK*g)	24,39 *v.l.*		0	0
σάρξ (+) πνεῦμα (*VK*e)	24,39	2,17	1	1

σαρόω 2 (Mt 1)   sweep

Word groups	Lk	Acts	Mt	Mk
σαρόω + οἰκία/οἶκος	11,(24-)25; 15,8		1	0

Σατᾶνας 5/6 + 2 (Mt 4, Mk 6)
  1. Satan (title); 2. Satan (name) (Lk 10,18; 11,18; 13,16; 22,3.31; Acts 26,18)

Literature
COLLISON 1977 172 [noteworthy phenomena]; REHKOPF 1959 96 [vorlukanisch]; SCHÜRMANN 1957 102-103 [Lk 22,31 luk R weniger wahrscheinlich]; 1961 276.

σάτον 1 (Mt 1)   batch (measurement) (Lk 13,21)

σεαυτοῦ 6 + 3 (Mt 5/6, Mk 3)   yourself

Word groups	Lk	Acts	Mt	Mk
σεαυτοῦ (*VK*a)		26,1	0/1	0
σεαυτῷ (*VK*b)		9,34; 16,28	0	0

Literature

NOLLAND, John, Classical and Rabbinic Parallels to "Physician, Heal Yourself" (Lk. iv 23). — *NT* 21 (1979) 193-209.

σεισμός 1 + 1 (Mt 4, Mk 1)

1. earthquake (Lk 21,11; Acts 16,26); 2. storm on the sea

Word groups	Lk	Acts	Mt	Mk
σεισμοί plural (*VK*a)	21,11		1	1

σελήνη 1 + 1 (Mt 1, Mk 1)   moon

Word groups	Lk	Acts	Mt	Mk
σελήνη + ἥλιος → **ἄστρον** + ἥλιος	21,25	2,20	1	1

Σεμεΐν 1   Semein (Lk 3,26)

Σερούχ 1   Serug (Lk 3,35)

Σήθ 1   Seth (Lk 3,38)

Σήμ 1   Shem (Lk 3,36)

σημεῖον 11 + 13 (Mt 13, Mk 5[7])   sign

Word groups	Lk	Acts	Mt	Mk
δίδωμι (+) σημεῖον/σημεῖα; cf. Rev 13,14	11,29[2]	2,19; 14,3	4	2
(ἐπι)ζητέω + σημεῖον	11,16.29[1]		2	2
(ὁράω/)εἶδον σημεῖον	23,8		1	0
ποιέω σημεῖα καὶ τέρατα ἐν BOISMARD 1984 Aa64		2,22; 6,8; 7,36; 15,12	0	0
σημεῖα plural (*VK*c) (exc. *VK*b)	21,11.25	8,6.13	1	[2]
σημεῖον γίνεται διά + genitive BOISMARD 1984 Aa34		2,43; 4,16.30; 5,12; 14,3	0	0
σημεῖον + δύναμις		2,22; 6,8; 8,13	0	0
σημεῖον Ἰωνᾶ (*SC*a; *VK*a); cf. σημεῖον + Ἰωνᾶς Lk 11,30	11,29[3]		2	0
σημεῖον μέγα	21,11	6,8	1	0
σημεῖα + τέρατα (*SC*b; *VK*b); cf. Jn 4,48; Rom 15,19; 2 Cor 12,12; 2 Thess 2,9; Heb 2,4 BOISMARD 1984 Ca78		2,19.22.43; 4,30; 5,12; 6,8; 7,36; 14,3; 15,12	1	1

Literature

BDAG 2000 920-921 [literature]; GERSDORF 1816 257 [εἰς σημεῖον ἀντιλεγόμενον].

GERHARDSSON, Birger, Jesu maktgärningar: Om de urkrista berättarnas val av termer. — *SEÅ* 44 (1979) 122-133.
SCHMITT, Götz, Das Zeichen des Jona. — *ZNW* 69 (1978) 123-129.
WEIß, Wolfgang, *"Zeichen und Wunder": Eine Studie zu der Sprachtradition und ihrer Verwendung im Neuen Testament* (WMANT, 67). Neukirchen: Neukirchener Verlag, 1995, VIII-189 p.

σήμερον 11/12 + 9 (Mt 8, Mk 1) — today

Word groups	Lk	Acts	Mt	Mk
σήμερον καὶ αὔριον (*SC*a; *VK*a)	12,28; 13,32.33		1	0
ἡ σήμερον (ἡμέρα) (*SC*b; *VK*c)		19,40; 20,26	3	0

Characteristic of Luke
GOULDER 1989

Literature
VON BENDEMANN 2001 426: "lukanisches Signalwort"; COLLISON 1977 161 [linguistic usage of Luke's "other source-material": probable]; 162 [σήμερον + αὔριον: noteworthy phenomena]; SCHNEIDER 1969 94.164 [Vorzugswörter und -ausdrücke des Luk]; SCHÜRMANN 1957 24-25 [von Luk bevorzugt].

DEWAILLY, Louis-Marie, "Donne-nous notre pain": Quel pain? Note sur la quatrième demande du Pater. — *RSPT* 64 (1980) 561-588.
PRETE, Benedetto, Prospettive messianiche nell'espressione σήμερον (oggi) del Vangelo di Luca. — *Il Messianismo: Atti della XVIII Settimana Biblica*. Paideia: Brescia, 1966, 269-284; = ID., *L'opera di Luca*, 1986, 104-117.
SILVA, R.P., Análise lingüística do σήμερον em Lucas 23,43. — *Revista de Cultura Teológica* (São Paulo) 10 (2002) 95-112.

σής 1 (Mt 2) — moth (Lk 12,33)

σιαγών 1 (Mt 1) — cheek (Lk 6,29)

σιγάω 3 + 3 — keep quiet about (Lk 9,36; 18,39; 20,26; Acts 12,17; 15,12.13)

Characteristic of Luke
BOISMARD 1984 cb174; DENAUX 2009 LA*; GOULDER 1989; HAWKINS 1909B; NEIRYNCK 1985; PLUMMER 1922 lix; VOGEL 1899B

Literature
COLLISON 1977 64 [linguistic usage of Luke: probable]; HAUCK 1934 [Vorzugswort]; JEREMIAS 1980 44 [red.].

Σιδών 3/4 + 1 (Mt 3, Mk 2/3) — Sidon (Lk 4,26*; 6,17; 10,13.14; Acts 27,3)

Word groups	Lk	Acts	Mt	Mk
Σάρεπτα τῆς Σιδῶνος (VKa)	4,26*		0	0

Σιδώνιος 1 + 1 — Sidonian (Lk 4,26; Acts 12,20)

Word groups	Lk	Acts	Mt	Mk
ἡ Σιδωνία (VKa)	4,26		0	0

σίκερα*** 1 — beer

Word groups	Lk	Acts	Mt	Mk
οἶνος καὶ σίκερα	1,15		0	0

Literature
JUNG, Chang-Wook, *Infancy Narrative*, 2004. Esp. 93-95.

Σιλωάμ 1 — Siloam (Lk 13,4)

Σίμων 17 + 13 (Mt 9, Mk 11) — Simon

Word groups	Lk	Acts	Mt	Mk
Σίμων (+) βυρσεύς (SCh; VKh)		9,43; 10,6.17.32²	0	0
Σίμων (+) (ὁ καλούμενος/λεγόμενος and similar) Πέτρος (SCb)	5,8; 6,14	10,5.18.32¹; 11,13	3	2
Σίμων+ μαγεύων (SCj; VKj)		8,9.13.18.24	0	0
Simon of Cyrene (SCe; VKd)	23,26	9,43	1	1
Simon of Kanaan, the zelote (SCc; VKb)	6,15	1,13	1	1
Simon Peter, brother of Andrew (SCa; VKa)	4,38¹·²; 5,3.4.5.8.10¹·²; 6,14; 22,31¹·²; 24,34	10,5.18.32¹; 11,13	5	7
Simon the Pharisee (SCg; VKg)	7,40.43.44		0	0

Characteristic of Luke
CREDNER 1836 136

Literature
BDAG 2000 924 [literature]; HAUCK 1934 [Vorzugsverbindung: Σίμων τις]; SCHÜRMANN 1957 100-102 [luk R sehr unwahrscheinlich].

ELLIOTT, James K., Κ ῆφας: Σίμων Πέτρος: ὁ Πέτρος: An Examination of New Testament Usage. — NT 14 (1972) 241-256. [NTA 17, 836]

σίναπι 2 (Mt 2, Mk 1) — mustard plant (Lk 13,19; 17,6)

σινδών 1 (Mt 1, Mk 4) — linen cloth (Lk 23,53)

σινιάζω** 1 — sift (Lk 22,31)

Literature

HAUCK 1934 [seltenes Alleinwort]; SCHÜRMANN 1957 104-105 [luk R weniger wahrscheinlich].

FOERSTER, Werner, Lukas 22,31f. — *ZNW* 46 (1955) 129-133.

σιτευτός 3
1. fattened (Lk 15,27); 2. prized (Lk 15,27)

Word groups	Lk	Acts	Mt	Mk
μόσχος σιτευτός DENAUX 2009 L[n]	15,23.27.30		0	0

Characteristic of Luke

PLUMMER 1922 lii

Literature

VON BENDEMANN 2001 429: "μόσχος σιτευτός findet sich im Neuen Testamnet nur in Lk 15,23.27.30"; DENAUX 2009 L[n]; HAUCK 1934 [seltenes Alleinwort].

σιτομέτριον** 1 | food ration (Lk 12,42)

Literature

HAUCK 1934 [seltenes Alleinwort].

σῖτος 4 + 1/2 (Mt 4, Mk 1)
1. wheat (seed) (Lk 22,31); 2. wheat (plant) (Lk 3,17; 12,8; 16,7)

Word groups	Lk	Acts	Mt	Mk
σῖτα plural (*VK*b)		7,12*	0	0

σιωπάω 2/3 + 1 (Mt 2, Mk 5)
1. be silent (Lk 19,40; Acts 18,9); 2. not able to speak (Lk 1,20); 3. become calm

Word groups	Lk	Acts	Mt	Mk
σιωπάω + κράζω	19,40		1	1
σιωπῶν εἰμι (*VK*a)	1,20		0	0

Literature

EASTON 1910 165 [cited by Weiss as characteristic of L, and possibly corroborative]; JEREMIAS 1980 44 [trad.].

ANDERSON, Julian G., A New Translation of Luke 1:20. — *BTrans* 20 (1969) 21-24.

σκανδαλίζω 2 (Mt 14, Mk 8)
1. cause to no longer believe; 2. cause to sin (Lk 17,2); 3. give offense
σκανδαλίζομαι: 4. cease believing; 5. fall into sin; 6. take offense (Lk 7,23)

Word groups	Lk	Acts	Mt	Mk
σκανδαλίζομαι ἐν (SCa; VKa)	7,23		4	1/2

Literature

HUMBERT, Alphonse, Essai d'une théologie du scandale dans les Synoptiques; — *Bib* 35 (1954) 1-28. Esp. 1-11: "La sémantique du σκάνδαλον".
MATEOS, Juan, Análisis semántico de los lexemas σκανδαλίζω y σκάνδαλον. — *FilolNT* 2 (1989) 57-92. Esp. 57-58: "Σκανδαλίζω: datos de la concordancia"; 58-59: "Σκανδαλίζω: interpretación de los diccionarios"; 66-67: "Forma medio-pasiva: Mt 11,6 (par. Lc 7,23): 'escandalizarse'"; 70-71: "Forma activa: Mt 18,6: Mc 9,42; Lc 17,2: 'escandalizar', 'causar la defección'".

σκάνδαλον 1 (Mt 5)

1. trap; 2. sin; 3. offense (Lk 17,1)

Literature

HUMBERT, Alphonse, Essai d'une théologie du scandale dans les Synoptiques; — *Bib* 35 (1954) 1-28. Esp. 1-11: "La sémantique du σκάνδαλον".
MATEOS, Juan, Análisis semántico de los lexemas σκανδαλίζω y σκάνδαλον. — *FilolNT* 2 (1989) 57-92. Esp. 78-79: "Σκάνδαλον: concordancia y diccionarios"; 86: "Lc 17,1".

σκάπτω 3

1. dig (Lk 6,48; 16,3); 2. till ground (Lk 13,8; 16,3)

Characteristic of Luke

GOULDER 1989; PLUMMER 1922 lii

Literature

VON BENDEMANN 2001 430; DENAUX 2009 Lⁿ; HAUCK 1934 [seltenes Alleinwort]; REHKOPF 1959 96 [vorlukanisch]; SCHÜRMANN 1961 284 [protoluk R nicht beweisbar].

σκεῦος 2 + 5 (Mt 1, Mk 2)

1. object; 2. vessel (Lk 8,16); 3. belongings (Lk 17,31); 4. person; 5. body; 6. wife

Word groups	Lk	Acts	Mt	Mk
σκεῦος ἐκλογῆς (VKa)		9,15	0	0

Literature

JEREMIAS 1980 269 [red.].

σκηνή 2 + 3 (Mt 1, Mk 1)

1. tent (Lk 9,33; 16,9; Acts 15,16); 2. tabernacle tent (Acts 7,44)

Word groups	Lk	Acts	Mt	Mk
σκηνὴ Δαυίδ (VKb)		15,16	0	0
σκηνὴ τοῦ μαρτυρίου (SCa; VKa)		7,44	0	0

Literature
BDAG 2000 928 [literature].

σκιά 1 + 1 (Mt 1, Mk 1)
1. shade; 2. shadow (Lk 1,79; Acts 5,15); 3. foreshadow

Word groups	Lk	Acts	Mt	Mk
σκιὰ θανάτου (SCa; VKa)	1,79		1	0

σκιρτάω 3
1. jump for joy (Lk 1,41.44; 6,23); 2. be extremely joyful (Lk 6,23)

Word groups	Lk	Acts	Mt	Mk
σκιρτάω (+) τὸ βρέφος	1,41.44		0	0

Characteristic of Luke
HARNACK 1906 139; PLUMMER 1922 lii

Literature
COLLISON 1977 88 [noteworthy phenomena]; DENAUX 2009 L[n]; EASTON 1910 158 [probably characteristic of L]; GERSDORF 1816 198 [ἐσκίρτησεν τὸ βρέφος]; HAUCK 1934 [seltenes Alleinwort].

σκολιός 1 + 1
1. crooked (Lk 3,5); 2. unscrupulous (Acts 2,40)

Literature
DENAUX 2009 LA[n]

MAHFOUZ, Hady, *La fonction littéraire et théologique de Lc 3,1-20*, 2003. Esp. 151-152.

σκοπέω 1
1. notice carefully; 2. watch out for; 3. be concerned about (Lk 11,35); 4. keep thinking about

Word groups	Lk	Acts	Mt	Mk
σκοπέω + μή (VKa) → βλέπω/φοβέομαι μή; cf. ὁράω μή Mt 18,10; 24,6	11,35		0	0

Literature
HAUCK 1934 [seltenes Alleinwort].

σκορπίζω 1 (Mt 1)
1. scatter (Lk 11,23); 2. give generously

Word groups	Lk	Acts	Mt	Mk
συνάγω + σκορπίζω → συνάγω + διασκορπίζω	11,23		1	0

σκορπίος 2 — scorpion

Word groups	Lk	Acts	Mt	Mk
ὄφις + σκορπίος	10,19; 11,(11-)12		0	0

Literature
DENAUX 2009 L[n].

GRELOT, Pierre, Étude critique de Luc 10,19. — *RechSR* 69 (1981) 87-100. Esp. 92-96: "Pourquoi des serpents et des scorpions?".
PEGG, Herbert, "A Scorpion for an Egg" (Lk xi.12). — *ExpT* 38 (1926-27) 468-469.

σκοτεινός 2 (Mt 1) — dark

Word groups	Lk	Acts	Mt	Mk
σκοτεινός + φωτεινός → **σκοτία/σκότος** + φῶς	11,34.36		1	0

Literature
DELEBECQUE, Édouard, *Études grecques*, 1976. Esp. 85-88: "La lampe et l'œil (11,33-36)".

σκοτία 1 (Mt 1/2)
1. darkness (Lk 12,3); 2. evil world

Word groups	Lk	Acts	Mt	Mk
ἐν τῇ σκοτίᾳ (*LN*: secretly)	12,3		1	0
σκοτία + φῶς (*VK*a) → **σκοτεινός** + φωτεινός; **σκότος** + φῶς	12,3		1/2	0

σκότος 4 + 3 (Mt 7, Mk 1)
1. darkness (Lk 1,79; 11,35; 23,44); 2. evil world

Word groups	Lk	Acts	Mt	Mk
ἀχλὺς καὶ σκότος + πίπτει (*LN*: become blind)		13,11	0	0
ἥλιος + σκότος; cf. ἥλιος + σκοτίζω Mt 24,29; Mk 13,24 DENAUX 2009 lA[n]	23,44(-45)	2,20; 13,11	0	0
ἐπιφαίνω + σκότος	1,79		0	0
σκότος + φῶς (*SC*a; *VK*e) → **σκοτεινός** + φωτεινός; **σκοτία** + φῶς	11,35	26,18	2	0

Literature
DELEBECQUE, Édouard, *Études grecques*, 1976. Esp. 85-88: "La lampe et l'œil (11,33-36)".
GRÁNDEZ, Rufino María, Crítica textual de Lc 23,45a: καὶ ἐσκοτίσθη ὁ ἥλιος. — *Scriptorium Victoriense* (Vitoria) 44 (1997) 5-20.

σκυθρωπός 1 (Mt 1) — sad (Lk 24,17)

σκύλλω 2 (Mt 1, Mk 1)
1. trouble (Lk 8,49); σκύλλομαι: 2. be troubled (Lk 7,6)

σκῦλον 1	booty (Lk 11,22)

Literature
HAUCK 1934 [seltenes Alleinwort].

Σόδομα 2 (Mt 3, Mk 0/1)	Sodom (Lk 10,12; 17,29)

Σολομών 3 + 3 (Mt 5)	Solomon

Word groups	Lk	Acts	Mt	Mk
σοφία Σολομῶνος	11,31[1]		1	0
στοὰ (+) Σολομῶντος (VKa)		3,11; 5,12	0	0

σορός 1	bier (Lk 7,14)

Literature
HAUCK 1934 [seltenes Alleinwort].

GAFNER, Philippe, Le cercueil et la rosée: Le mot σορος en Luc 7.14. — *BibNot* 87 (1997) 13-16.

σός 4 + 3 (Mt 8, Mk 2)	your

Word groups	Lk	Acts	Mt	Mk
οἱ + σοί (SCc; VKd)	5,33		0	2
τὰ σά (SCb; VKc); cf. τὸ σόν Mt 20,14; 25,25	6,30; 15,31		0	0
DENAUX 2009 L[n]				

Literature
KILPATRICK, George D., The Possessive Pronouns in the New Testament. — *JTS* 42 (1941) 184-186; = ID., *Principles and Practice*, 1990, 161-162.

σουδάριον 1 + 1	face cloth (Lk 19,20; Acts 19,12)

Literature
DENAUX LA[n].

MARYKS, Robert A., Il latinismi del Nuovo testamento, 2000. Esp. 29.

Σουσάννα 1	Susanna (Lk 8,3)

σοφία 6 + 4 (Mt 3, Mk 1)	
	1. wisdom (Lk 2,40); 2. insight (Acts 7,22); 3. specialized knowledge; 4. Wisdom (title of a book) (Lk 11,49)

Word groups	Lk	Acts	Mt	Mk
[ἐν] πάσῃ σοφίᾳ (VKe)		7,22	0	0

σοφία τοῦ θεοῦ (VKa)	11,49		0	0
σοφία + πνεῦμα (VKh)	2,40 v.l.	6,3.10	0	0
σοφία + χάρις	2,52	7,10	0	0
DENAUX 2009 LAⁿ (?)				
σοφία Σολομῶνος (VKb)	11,31		1	0
σοφίαν + δίδωμι	21,15	7,10	0	1
στόμα καὶ σοφία	21,15		0	0

Characteristic of Luke
GOULDER 1989

Literature
JEREMIAS 1980 208-209 [ἡ σοφία τοῦ θεοῦ: red.].

CAMBE, Michel, La χάρις chez saint Luc: Remarques sur quelques textes, notamment le κεχαριτωμένη. — *RB* 70 (1963) 193-207. Esp. 198-199: "χάρις et σοφία".
FUCHS, Albert, *Sprachliche Untersuchungen zu Mattäus und Lukas*, 1971. Esp. 179-180.
LÖVESTAM, Evald, Till förståelsen av Luk. 7:35. — *SEÅ* 22-23 (1957-58) 47-63.
SWELLENGREBEL, J.L., Puzzles in Luke. — *BTrans* 17 (1966) 118-122. Esp. 121-122 [Lk 7,35 ἐδικαιώθη ἡ σοφία ἀπὸ πάντων τῶν τέκνων αὐτῆς].

σοφός 1 (Mt 2)
1. skilful; 2. wise (Lk 10,21)

Literature
KILPATRICK, George D., Φρόνιμος, σοφός and συνετός in Matthew and Luke. — *JTS* 48 (1947) 63-64.

σπαράσσω 1 (Mk 2/3)
throw into a fit (Lk 9,39)

σπαργανόω 2
clothe in swaddling cloth (Lk 2,7.12)

Characteristic of Luke
PLUMMER 1922 liii

Literature
DENAUX 2009 Lⁿ; HAUCK 1934 [seltenes Alleinwort].

KÜGLER, Joachim, Die Windeln Jesu als Zeichen: Religionsgeschichtliche Anmerkungen zu σπαργανοω in Lk 2. — *BibNot* 77 (1995) 20-28.
—, Die Windeln Jesu (Lk 2) – Nachtrag: Zum Gebrauch von σπαργανον bei Philo von Alexandrien. — *BibNot* 81 (1996) 8-14.

σπείρω 6 (Mt 17/18, Mk 12)
sow

Word groups	Lk	Acts	Mt	Mk
σπείρω + θερίζω	12,24; 19,21.22		3	0
σπείρω + σπόρος (SCf; VKk); cf. σπείρω + σπέρμα Mt 13,24.27.31.37; Mk 4,31	8,5²		0	0
ὁ σπείρων (used as a noun without object) (SCa; VKa)	8,5¹		2	2

σπέρμα 2 + 4 (Mt 7, Mk 5)

1. seed; 2. descendants (Lk 1,55; 20,28; Acts 3,25); 3. nature

Word groups	Lk	Acts	Mt	Mk
ἐξανίστημι σπέρμα (LN: beget); cf. ἀνίστημι σπέρμα Mt 22,24	20,28		0	1
σπέρμα + Ἀβραάμ (σου/αὐτοῦ) (SCa; VKa) → ϑυγατήρ/τέκνον/υἱός + Ἀβραάμ DENAUX 2009 1Aⁿ	1,55	3,25; 7,5.6	0	0
σπέρμα + Δαυίδ (VKb)		13,(22-)23	0	0

σπεύδω 3 + 2

1. do quickly (Lk 2,16; 19,5.6; Acts 20,16); 2. cause to happen soon; 3. be eager (Acts 20,16)

Characteristic of Luke

BOISMARD 1984 Bb79; HARNACK 1906 147; HAWKINS 1909add; NEIRYNCK 1985; PLUMMER 1922 lix

	Lk	Acts	Mt	Mk
σπεύδειν/σπουδή GOULDER 1989	2,16; 7,4; 19,5.6	20,16; 22,18	1	0

Literature

COLLISON 1977 98 [noteworthy phenomena]; DENAUX 2009 Laⁿ; EASTON 1910 165 [σπεύσας: cited by Weiss as characteristic of L, and possibly corroborative]; GERSDORF 1816 239 [καὶ ἦλθαν σπεύσαντες]; JEREMIAS 1980 85 [red.]; RADL 1975 426.

σπήλαιον 1 (Mt 1, Mk 1)   cave

Word groups	Lk	Acts	Mt	Mk
σπήλαιον λῃστῶν	19,46		1	1

σπλαγχνίζομαι 3 (Mt 5, Mk 4)   feel compassion for

Word groups	Lk	Acts	Mt	Mk
σπλαγχνίζομαι ἐπί + accusative (VKa)	7,13 v.l.		1/2	3
σπλαγχνίζομαι ἐπί + dative (VKb)	7,13		1	0/1
σπλαγχνίζομαι (+) (ὁράω/)εἶδον	7,13; 10,33; 15,20		2	1

Literature

COLLISON 1977 64 [linguistic usage of Luke's "other source-material": probable]; EASTON 1910 158 [probably characteristic of L]; PAFFENROTH 1997 77-78; REHKOPF 1959 97 [vorlukanisch]; SCHÜRMANN 1961 271.

ESTÉVEZ, Elisa, Significado de σπλαγχνίζομαι en el NT. — EstBíb 48 (1990) 511-541.
MENKEN, Maarten J.J., The Position of σπλαγχνίζεσθαι and σπλάγχνα in the Gospel of Luke. — NT 30 (1988) 107-114.

σπλάγχνον 1 + 1

σπλάγχνα: 1. intestines (Acts 1,18); 2. desires; 3. compassion (Lk 1,78); 4. object of affection

Characteristic of Luke

HARNACK 1906 74.145

Literature

DENAUX 2009 La[n].

MENKEN, Maarten J.J., The Position of σπλαγχνίζεσθαι and σπλάγχνα in the Gospel of Luke. — *NT* 30 (1988) 107-114.

MONTEVECCHI, Orsolina, "Viscere di misericordia". — *RivBib* 43 (1995) 125-133.

σποδός 1 (Mt 1)

ashes (Lk 10,13)

σπόριμος 1 (Mt 1, Mk 1)

σπόριμα: grain fields (Lk 6,1)

σπόρος 2 (Mk 2)

seed (Lk 8,5.11)

Word groups	Lk	Acts	Mt	Mk
σπόρος + σπείρω (*VK*a); cf. σπέρμα + σπείρω Mt 13,24.27.31.32.37; Mk 4,31	8,5		0	0

σπουδαίως 1

1. doing one's best (Lk 7,4); 2. eagerly

Literature

HAUCK 1934 [seltenes Alleinwort].

σπουδή 1 (Mk 1)

1. do quickly (Lk 1,39); 2. do one's best; 3. eagerness

Word groups	Lk	Acts	Mt	Mk
μετὰ σπουδῆς (*VK*a)	1,39		0	1

Characteristic of Luke	Lk	Acts	Mt	Mk
σπουδή/σπεύδειν DENAUX 2009***; GOULDER 1989	2,16; 7,4; 19,5.6	20,16; 22,18	1	0

στάδιον 1 (Mt 1)

arena (Lk 24,13)

στάσις 2 + 5 (Mk 1)

1. rebellion (Lk 23,19.25; Acts 19,40); 2. heated quarrel (Acts 23,7); 3. existence

Characteristic of Luke

BOISMARD 1984 cb11; DENAUX 2009 IA*; NEIRYNCK 1985; PLUMMER 1922 lx

	Lk	Acts	Mt	Mk
στάσις γίνεται/γενομένη BOISMARD 1984 Ab145; NEIRYNCK 1985	23,19	15,2; 23,7.10	0	0

Literature

DENAUX 2009 IAⁿ [στάσις γίνεται/γενομένη]; HAUCK 1934 [Vorzugsverbindung: στάσις τις]; JEREMIAS 1980 304 [red.]; RADL 1975 404 [γίνομαι + στάσις]; 426 [στάσις].

BORMANN, Lukas, *Recht, Gerechtigkeit und Religion*, 2001. Esp. 124.

σταυρός 3 (Mt 5, Mk 4) — cross

Word groups	Lk	Acts	Mt	Mk
αἴρω τὸν σταυρόν (*LN*: suffer unto death; *VK*a); cf. λαμβάνω τὸν σταυρόν Mt 10,38	9,23		2	2/3
βαστάζω τὸν σταυρόν (*LN*: suffer unto death; *VK*b)	14,27		0	0
φέρω τὸν σταυρόν (*VK*d)	23,26		0	0

Literature

BDAG 2000 941 [literature].

BRYAN, J. Davies, Cross-Bearing. — *ExpT* 38 (1926-27) 378-379.
MATHESON, Donald, Cross-Bearing. — *ExpT* 38 (1926-27) 188, 524-525.

σταυρόω 6 + 2 (Mt 10, Mk 8) — crucify

σταφυλή 1 (Mt 1) — grapes (Lk 6,44)

στάχυς 1 (Mt 1, Mk 3) — head of wheat (Lk 6,1)

Literature

DELEBECQUE, Édouard, *Études grecques*, 1976. Esp. 71-83: "Les moissonneurs du sabbat (6,1)".

στέγη 1 (Mt 1, Mk 1) — roof (Lk 7,6)

στεῖρα 3 — barren (Lk 1,7.36; 23,29)

Characteristic of Luke

PLUMMER 1922 lix

Literature

DENAUX 2009 Lⁿ; GERSDORF 1816 172 [καθότι ἦν ἡ Ἐλισάβετ στεῖρα].

WEISSENRIEDER, Annette, *Images of Illness in the Gospel of Luke*, 2003. Esp. 78-113.

στενός 1 (Mt 2)	narrow			
Word groups	**Lk**	**Acts**	**Mt**	**Mk**
στενὴ θυρά; cf. στενὴ πύλη Mt 7,13.14	13,24		0	0

στῆθος 2	chest			
Word groups	**Lk**	**Acts**	**Mt**	**Mk**
τύπτω τὸ στῆθος/τὰ στήθη DENAUX 2009 L[n]	18,13; 23,48		0	0

Literature
DENAUX 2009 L[n]; EASTON 1910 166 [τύπτω τὸ στῆθος: cited by Weiss as characteristic of L, and possibly corroborative].

στηρίζω 3 + 0/1				
1. strengthen (Lk 22,32; Acts 18,23*); 2. establish in a place (Lk 9,51; 16,26)				
Word groups	**Lk**	**Acts**	**Mt**	**Mk**
στηρίζω τὸ πρόσωπον (*LN*: decide firmly; *VK*b)	9,51		0	0
χάσμα + ἐστήρικται (*VK*c)	16,26		0	0

Characteristic of Luke; cf. ἐπιστηρίζω Acts 14,22; 15,32.41; 18,23
GOULDER 1989

Literature
VON BENDEMANN 2001 415; COLLISON 1977 98 [noteworthy phenomena]; DENAUX 2009 L[n]; EASTON 1910 158 [probably characteristic of L]; HAUCK 1934 [seltenes Alleinwort]; REHKOPF 1959 97 [vorlukanisch]; SCHÜRMANN 1957 110 [wahrscheinlich luk R]; 1961 271.

EVANS, Craig A., "He Set His Face": Luke 9,51 Once Again. — *Bib* 68 (1987) 80-84.

στιγμή 1	moment			
Word groups	**Lk**	**Acts**	**Mt**	**Mk**
ἐν στιγμῇ χρόνου	4,5		0	0

Literature
HAUCK 1934 [seltenes Alleinwort].

DAUBE, David, *The Sudden in the Scriptures*. Leiden: Brill, 1964, VII-86 p. Esp. 75-77:
"Stigme chronou and ripe ophthalmou".

στολή 2 (Mk 2)	long robe (Lk 15,22; 20,46)			
Word groups	**Lk**	**Acts**	**Mt**	**Mk**
ἐν στολαῖς περιπατέω (*VK*a)	20,46		0	1

Literature

BURCHARD, Christoph, Fußnoten zum neutestamentlichen Griechisch, 1970. Esp. 160: "Lc 15,22 ταχὺ ἐξενέγκατε στολὴν τὴν πρώτην".
RENGSTORF, Karl H., Die στολαί der Schriftgelehrten. Eine Erläuterung zu Mark. 12,38. — BETZ, O. – HENGEL, M. – SCHMIDT, P. (eds.), *Abraham unser Vater, Juden und Christen im Gespräch über die Bibel: Festschrift für Otto Michel zum 60. Geburtstag* (Arbeiten zur Geschichte des Spätjudentums und Urchristentums, 5). Leiden-Köln: Brill, 1963, 383-434.

στόμα 9 + 12 (Mt 11/12)

1. mouth (Acts 23,2); 2. speech (activity) (Acts 1,16); 3. speech (faculty) (Lk 1,64); 4. utterance (Lk 19,22); 5. sharp edge (Lk 21,24)

Word groups	Lk	Acts	Mt	Mk
δίδωμι + στόμα (*LN*: help to say)	21,15		0	0
ἐκ τοῦ στόματός τινος (*SC*b);cf. ἐκ στόματός τινος (*VK*b) Mt 21,16	4,22; 11,54; 19,22	22,14	2	0
στόμα (+) ἀνοίγω (*LN*: start speaking; *SC*e; *VK*k)	1,64	8,32.35; 10,34; 18,14	3	0
στόμα καὶ σοφία	21,15		0	0
στόμα + καρδία (*SC*d; *VK*h)	6,45		2/3	0
στόμα + λαλέω (*SC*f; *VK*l) DENAUX 2009 La* (?)	1,64.70; 6,45	3,21	1	0
στόμα μαχαίρης (*VK*f); cf. Heb 11,34	21,24		0	0

Characteristic of Luke	Lk	Acts	Mt	Mk
διὰ στόματός τινος (*SC*a; *VK*a); cf. διὰ τοῦ στόματός τινος Acts 15,7 BOISMARD 1984 Ab42; HARNACK 1906 144; NEIRYNCK 1985; PLUMMER 1922 lx	1,70	1,16; 3,18.21; 4,25 *v.l.*	1	0

Literature

DENAUX 2009 lAn [διὰ στόματός τινος]; GERSDORF 1816 207 [ἐλάλησεν διὰ στόματος τῶν ἁγίων ἀπ᾽ αἰῶνος προφητῶν αὐτοῦ]: "διὰ στόματος schreibt nur Lucas"; JEREMIAS 1980 73-74: "διὰ στόματός τινος ('durch'), vom Boten gesagt, durch den Gott sein Wort verkünden läßt, ist nicht geläufiger judengriechischer Sprachgebrauch"; PLUMMER 1922 lxi [διὰ στόματος: both the expression and the omission of the article seem to be Hebraistic].

FUCHS, Albert, *Sprachliche Untersuchungen zu Mattäus und Lukas*, 1971. Esp. 183-184.
LE ROUX, L.V., Style and Text of Acts 4:25(a). — *Neotestamentica* 25 (1991) 29-32.

στράτευμα 1 + 2 (Mt 1)

1. army; 2. soldiers (Lk 23,11; Acts 23,10)

Word groups	Lk	Acts	Mt	Mk
στράτευμα singular (*VK*a)		23,10.27	0	0

Literature

EASTON 1910 165 [στρατεύματα "soldiers": cited by Weiss as characteristic of L, and possibly corroborative].

στρατεύομαι 1

1. engage in war; 2. be a soldier (Lk 3,14)

στρατηγός 2 + 8

1. magistrate (Acts 16,20.22.35.38); 2. BDAG 2000: captain of the temple (Lk 22,4.52)

Word groups	Lk	Acts	Mt	Mk
στρατηγός/στρατηγοί (τοῦ ἱεροῦ) + ἀρχιερεῖς	22,4.52	4,1v.l.; 5,24	0	0
στρατηγοί + ἀρχιερεῖς + πρεσβύτεροι	22,52		0	0
στρατηγοί + ῥαβδοῦχοι		16,35.38	0	0

Characteristic of Luke

BOISMARD 1984 Ab10; DENAUX 2009 IA*; HAWKINS 1909LA.B; MORGENTHALER 1958*; NEIRYNCK 1985; VOGEL 1899A

	Lk	Acts	Mt	Mk
στρατηγὸς τοῦ ἱεροῦ (LN: commander of the Temple guard; SCa; VKa) PLUMMER 1922 lii	22,52	4,1; 5,24	0	0

Literature

DENAUX 2009 IAⁿ [στρατηγὸς τοῦ ἱεροῦ]; EASTON 1910 165 [στρατηγοί as Temple officials: cited by Weiss as characteristic of L, and possibly corroborative]; HAUCK 1934 [Vorzugswort]; JEREMIAS 1980 296: "Die Hauptleute (στρατηγοί) des Jerusalemer Tempels werden nur von Lukas erwähnt ... Ebenfalls nur bei ihm erscheint ὁ στρατηγός (τοῦ ἱεροῦ), der Jerusalemer Tempeloberst".

BACHMAN, Michael, Jerusalem und der Tempel, 1980. Esp. 194-200.
BORMANN, Lukas, Recht, Gerechtigkeit und Religion, 2001. Esp. 137-138.

στρατιά 1 + 1   heavenly army, host of heavens

Word groups	Lk	Acts	Mt	Mk
στρατιὰ οὐράνιος (LN: ranks of angels)	2,13		0	0

Characteristic of Luke

BOISMARD 1984 Ab10; HAWKINS 1909LA.B; MORGENTHALER 1958*; NEIRYNCK 1985; VOGEL 1899A

	Lk	Acts	Mt	Mk
στρατιὰ τοῦ οὐρανοῦ (LN: supernatural powers) VOGEL 1899C		7,42	0	0

Literature

DENAUX 2009 LAⁿ; JEREMIAS 1980 83: "Von 'der himmlischen Heerschar' ist im NT nur bei Lukas die Rede. Apg 7,42 redet er in Übereinstimmung mit LXX von ἡ στρατιὰ τοῦ οὐρανοῦ, Lk 2,13 sagt er στρατιὰ οὐράνιος".

JUNG, Chang-Wook, Infancy Narrative, 2004. Esp. 160-170 [πλῆθος στρατιᾶς οὐρανίου: Lk 2,13].

στρατιώτης 2 + 13 (Mt 3, Mk 1)   soldier (Lk 7,8; 23,36)

Word groups	Lk	Acts	Mt	Mk
στρατιώτης + ἑκατοντάρχης/ἑκατόνταρχος/χιλίαρχος (VKa)		21,32[T.2]; 27,31	0	0

Characteristic of Luke

MORGENTHALER 1958A

Literature

DENAUX 2009 lAn.

BORMANN, Lukas, *Recht, Gerechtigkeit und Religion*, 2001. Esp. 213-214.

στρατόπεδον 1   army (Lk 21,20)

Literature

HAUCK 1934 [seltenes Alleinwort].

στρέφω 7/8 + 3 (Mt 6)

1. turn (Lk 7,9); 2. change; 3. carry back; 4. pay back; 5. reject (Acts 7,4)
στρέφομαι: 6. turn around (Lk 7,44); 7. come to believe (Acts 7,39); 8. change one's ways; 9. establish a relation with (Acts 13,46)

Word groups	Lk	Acts	Mt	Mk
στραφείς (+) πρός DENAUX 2009 L[n]	7,44; 10,23; 23,28		0	0

Characteristic of Luke

PLUMMER 1922 lx [στρέφομαι]

	Lk	Acts	Mt	Mk
στραφείς; cf. Jn 1,38; 20,16; cf. ἐφιστραφείς Mk 5,30; 8,33; Jn 21,20 CREDNER 1836 139; DENAUX 2009 L***; GOULDER 1989*; HAWKINS 1909L; PLUMMER 1922 lxii	7,9.44; 9,55; 10,22*.23; 14,25; 22,61; 23,28		3	0
στραφείς (+) (λέγω/)εἶπεν DENAUX 2009 L***	7,9; 10,23; 14,25; 22,61; 23,28		2	0

Literature

VON BENDEMANN 2001 418: "Das verbum στρέφειν begegnet im dritten Evangelium stets im Partizip Aorist Passiv mit reflexivem Sinn. Davon sind die drei Belege in Apg nach Form und Sinn verschieden"; COLLISON 1977 65 [στραφείς: linguistic usage of Luke: likely; linguistic usage of Luke's "other source-material": also likely]; EASTON 1910 149 [στραφείς: especially characteristic of L]; HAUCK 1934 [Vorzugswort]; REHKOPF 1959 97 [στραφείς: vorlukanisch]; SCHNEIDER 1969 91-92.163 [καὶ στραφείς von Jesus: Vorzugswörter und -ausdrücke des Luk]; SCHÜRMANN 1961 284 [στραφείς: protoluk R weniger wahrscheinlich].

στρουθίον 2 (Mt 2)   sparrow (Lk 12,6.7)

στρώννυω 1 + 1 (Mt 2, Mk 2/3)

1. spread out; 2. furnish a room (Lk 22,12); 3. make one's bed (Acts 9,34)

Word groups	Lk	Acts	Mt	Mk
ἀνάγαιον + ἐστρωμένον (VKa)	22,12		0	1

σύ 226/233 + 139/145 (Mt 208/214, Mk 89/94) — you

Word groups				
σύ	**Lk**	**Acts**	**Mt**	**Mk**
σύ without copula (VKf) DENAUX 2009 LA[n]	1,28[2]*.42[1]	4,24	0	0
καὶ σύ (SCc; VKc) → καὶ σοῦ/σοί; καὶ ἐγώ/ἡμεῖς/ὑμεῖς	1,76; 10,15.37; 19,19.42[1]; 22,32.58	23,3[2]; 25,10	5	1
σύ + adjective (μόνος) (VKh)	24,18		0	0
σύ + vocative (SCd; VKd)	1,76; 10,15; 15,31	1,24; 4,24	2	0
σύ + ἐγώ (SCe; VKe)	22,32[1]	9,5; 22,8; 26,15	2	1
σὺ (+) εἶ (SCa; VKa) → ἐγώ εἰμι	3,22[1]; 4,41; 7,19.20[2]; 22,67.70; 23,3[1].37.39	13,33; 21,38; 22,27	6	5
σὺ λέγεις; cf. σὺ εἶπας Mt 26,25.64 → ὑμεῖς λέγετε	23,3[2]		1	2
σοῦ/σου	**Lk**	**Acts**	**Mt**	**Mk**
σοῦ after preposition (SCa; VKa)	1,28[1]; 4,10[1]; 7,27[3]; 10,21[2]; 12,20[2]; 13,26; 15,18.21[1]; 16,2[1]; 22,32[1].33	10,22[2]; 17,19; 18,10[1]; 21,21.24; 23,21[2].30[2]; 24,2.19; 25,26; 26,2; 27,24[3]; 28,21[1.2].22	16/17	0/2
σοῦ in the genitive absolute (SCd; VKe)		24,11	1	0
σοῦ governed by an adjective or adverb (VKc)	10,27[6]; 14,8		4	2/3
σοῦ governed by a verb (SCb; VKb)	8,28[2]; 9,38	8,34; 17,32; 21,39; 23,35[1]; 26,3*	3	2
σοῦ preceding a noun (SCc; VKd)	2,35; 6,29[2]; 7,44.48; 15,30[2]; 16,6.7[2]	10,31[1]; 22,18	8/10	2/3
καὶ σοῦ → καὶ σύ/σοί; καὶ ἡμῶν/ὑμῶν	2,35		1	0
πατήρ σου → πατήρ μου/ἡμῶν/ὑμῶν	2,48[1]; 15,27[2]; 18,20	7,32	5/7	2
σοῦ αὐτῆς (VKh) → ὑμῶν αὐτῶν	2,35		0	0
σοῦ δέ → σὺ δέ; ὑμῶν δέ	2,35v.l.?		1	0
σοῦ ἐστιν (SCe; VKf) → ὑμῶν ἐστιν	4,7[2]		0/1	0
→ λαός σου				
σοί/σοι	**Lk**	**Acts**	**Mt**	**Mk**
ἀμήν σοι λέγω → ἀμὴν λέγω ὑμῖν; cf. ἀμὴν λέγω σοι Mt 5,26; 26,34; Mk 14,30	23,43		0	0
καὶ σοί → καὶ σύ/σοῦ; καὶ ἐμοί/ἡμῖν/ὑμῖν	4,34[1]; 8,28[1]		2	2
τί ἐμοί/ἡμῖν καὶ σοί (SCb; VKb)	4,34[1]; 8,28[1]		1	2
(ἔστιν/γίνεται) τί σοι(VKc)	1,14; 8,30; 14,10[3].12[5]	8,21	3	1
οὐαί σοι (SCc; VKe) → οὐαὶ ὑμῖν	10,13[1.2]		2	0
σοί after preposition (SCa; VKa)	3,22[2]; 11,35; 19,44[3.4]	8,20	4	1
σοί governed by an adjective (VKd)		9,5*; 26,14	4	1/4
σοὶ λέγω / λέγω σοι introducing a speech (SCd) → ὑμῖν λέγω / λέγω ὑμῖν; λέγω ὑμῖν / σοι … οὐ μὴ … ἕως (ἄν); cf. ἐρεῖ σοι Lk 14,9.10; cf. ἔχω σοί τι εἰπεῖν Lk 7,40; λέγει σοι Lk 22,11	5,24[1]; 7,14.47; 12,59; 22,34; 23,43		4	3

σέ/σε	Lk	Acts	Mt	Mk
σέ after the verb	2,48²; 4,10².11¹.34²; 6,29¹.30; 7,50²; 8,20³.45.48²; 11,27.36²; 12,58²; 14,10¹.12⁴.18.19; 16,27; 17,19²; 18,42²; 19,21.22².43¹.44²; 22,64	4,30²; 5,3².9²; 7,34; 8,23; 9,34; 10,19.22¹; 13,33². 47¹·²;18,10³; 22,14.21; 23,3¹. 20; 24,4².10.25; 26,3. 16³.17¹·²	10	13
σέ before the verb	12,58³·⁴; 13,31; 14,9	7,27.35; 9,6; 23,11; 24,4¹; 26,24.29; 27,24¹	14/15	5
σέ following a preposition (SCa; VKa) → ὑμᾶς following a preposition	1,19¹.35¹; 7,7.20¹; 17,3*. 4¹·²; 19,43¹	10,33¹; 11,14¹; 13,11; 21,37; 22,19; 23,18¹.30²; 24,8*	4	1
σέ in a proleptic construction (VKb) → ὑμᾶς in a proleptic construction	4,34²		1	1

Characteristic of Luke	Lk	Acts	Mt	Mk
σὺ δέ/οὖν/τε (SCb; VKb) → σοῦ δέ; ἐγώ/ἡμεῖς/ὑμεῖς δέ/οὖν DENAUX 2009 L***	1,76; 4,7²; 9,60; 16,7¹.25³; 22,70	10,33²; 23,21¹	2	0
δέομαί σου BOISMARD 1984 Ab73; NEIRYNCK 1985	8,28²; 9,38	8,34; 21,39	0	0
σύ after a verb (VKg) DENAUX 2009 LA*; GOULDER 1989*	16,25*; 17,8; 19,42¹; 23,40	11,14²; 13,33¹; 16,31	0	0
σου … σοι DENAUX 2009 lA*; HARNACK 1906 72	1,13; 5,20.23	5,4; 8,20.21. 22²; 27,24	0	0
→ θεὸς τῶν πατέρων σου/ἡμῶν				

Literature

DENAUX 2009 LAⁿ [δέομαί σου]; SCHÜRMANN 1953 99 [λέγει σοι], 1955 [" das enklitische σου vor dem Wort: Verdacht auf luk R"], 1957 25 [Auslassung eines nicht emphrastisch gebrauchten Personalpronomens, speziell eine σύ]; 107-108 [καί σύ, σὺ δέ, σὺ οὖν; σύ τε; σύ vor Imperativ].

συγγένεια 1 + 2   relatives (Lk 1,61; Acts 7,3.14)

Characteristic of Luke

BOISMARD 1984 Ab204; HARNACK 1906 74; HAWKINS 1909LA; MORGENTHALER 1958*; NEIRYNCK 1985; PLUMMER 1922 lii; VOGEL 1899A

	Lk	Acts	Mt	Mk
συγγένεια/-ής/-ίς/-εύς DENAUX 2009 L***; GOULDER 1989*	1,36.58.61; 2,44; 14,12; 21,16	7,3.14; 10,24	1	0

Literature

DENAUX 2009 lAⁿ; EASTON 1910 158 [probably characteristic of L, not in Weiss]; HAUCK 1934 [Vorzugswort]; JEREMIAS 1980 67 [red.].

συγγενεύς 1 (Mk 1)   relative (Lk 2,44)

Characteristic of Luke	Lk	Acts	Mt	Mk
συγγενεύς/-εια/-ής/-ίς DENAUX 2009 L***; GOULDER 1989*	1,36.58.61; 2,44; 14,12; 21,16	7,3.14; 10,24	1	0

συγγενεύς/-ῆς/-ίς DENAUX 2009 L***; HAWKINS 1909 L	1,36.58; 2,44; 14,12; 21,16	10,24	1	0

Literature
EASTON 1910 158 [probably characteristic of L, not in Weiss]; GERSDORF 1816 265 [ἐν τοῖς συγγενεῦσιν καὶ τοῖς γνωστοῖς].

συγγενής 3/4 + 1
1. relative (Lk 1,58; 14,12; 21,16); 2. fellow countryman

Word groups	Lk	Acts	Mt	Mk
ἀδελφός + συγγενής DENAUX 2009 Lⁿ	14,12; 21,16		0	0
ἀδελφός + συγγενής + γείτων	14,12		0	0
συγγενής singular (VKb)	1,36*		0	0

Characteristic of Luke
BOISMARD 1984 Eb39; HARNACK 1906 149; NEIRYNCK 1985

	Lk	Acts	Mt	Mk
συγγενεύς/-εια/-ῆς/-ίς DENAUX 2009 L***; GOULDER 1989*	1,36.58.61; 2,44; 14,12; 21,16	7,3.14; 10,24	1	0
συγγενής/- εύς/-ίς DENAUX 2009 L***; HAWKINS 1909 L	1,36.58; 2,44; 14,12; 21,16	10,24	1	0

Literature
VON BENDEMANN 2001 427 [ἀδελφός + συγγενής]; COLLISON 1977 187-188 [linguistic usage of Luke's "other source-material": likely]; DENAUX 2009 Laⁿ; EASTON 1910 150 [ἀδελφοὶ καὶ συγγενεῖς καὶ γείτονες: probably characteristic of L]; 158 [probably characteristic of L, not in Weiss]; HAUCK 1934 [Vorzugswort].

συγγενίς* 1   relative (Lk 1,36)

Characteristic of Luke	Lk	Acts	Mt	Mk
συγγενίς/-εύς/-εια/-ής DENAUX 2009 L***; GOULDER 1989*	1,36.58.61; 2,44; 14,12; 21,16	7,3.14; 10,24	1	0
συγγενίς/-ῆς/- εύς DENAUX 2009 L***; HAWKINS 1909 L	1,36.58; 2,44; 14,12; 21,16	10,24	1	0

Literature
HAUCK 1934 [Vorzugswort].

συγκαθίζω 1
1. sit down with (Lk 22,55); 2. cause to sit down with

Word groups	Lk	Acts	Mt	Mk
συγκαθίσας → καθίσας	22,55		0	0

Literature
JEREMIAS 1980 296 [red.].

συγκαλέω 4 + 3 (Mk 1)   call together

Word groups	Lk	Acts	Mt	Mk
συγκαλέω + λέγω/εἶπον → (παρα/προσ)καλέω + λέγω/εἶπον/ἐρῶ; cf. ἐπικαλέω + λέγω Acts 7,59	15,6.9; 23,13(-14)		0	0
συγκαλέω active (VKa)	15,6.9	5,21	0	1

Characteristic of Luke

BOISMARD 1984 Bb35; CREDNER 1836 140; DENAUX 2009 L***; GOULDER 1989*; HAWKINS 1909 L; NEIRYNCK 1985; VOGEL 1899B.D [συγκαλέομαι]

	Lk	Acts	Mt	Mk
συγκαλέω τοὺς φίλους BOISMARD 1984 Ab150; NEIRYNCK 1985	15,6.9	10,24	0	0

Literature

VON BENDEMANN 2001 428; DENAUX 2009 Laⁿ [συγκαλέω τοὺς φίλους]; HAUCK 1934 [Vorzugswort]; JEREMIAS 1980 69 [συγκαλέω + λέγων: red.]; 246 [red.]; RADL 1975 426.

BORMANN, Lukas, *Recht, Gerechtigkeit und Religion*, 2001. Esp. 138.

συγκαλύπτω 1   conceal (Lk 12,2)

Literature
HAUCK 1934 [seltenes Alleinwort]; JEREMIAS 1980 211 [red.].

συγκατατίθεμαι 1   agree together (Lk 23,51)

Literature
HAUCK 1934 [seltenes Alleinwort]; JEREMIAS 1980 309 [red.].

συγκλείω 1

1. catch fish (Lk 5,6); 2. cause to happen

Literature
BUITENWERF, Rieuwerd, Vis vangen of insluiten? De vertaling van het woord *sunkleiô* in Lucas 5:6. — *Met* Andere *Woorden* (Haarlem) 22/2 (2003) 27-32.

συγκύπτω 1   be doubled up (Lk 13,11)

Literature
HAUCK 1934 [seltenes Alleinwort].

NEIRYNCK, Frans, Παρακύψας βλέπει: Lc 24,12 et Jn 20,5. — *ETL* 53 (1977) 113-152. Esp. 117-129: "Κύπτω et composés dans la LXX". [NTA 22, 130]; = Id., *Evangelica*, 1982, 401-440 (Appendix, *Evangelica II*, 1991, 799). Esp. 405-417.

RADL, Walter, Ein "doppeltes Leiden" in Lk 13,11? Zu einer Notiz von Günther Schwarz. — *BibNot* 31 (1986) 35-36.

SCHWARZ, Günther, και ην συγκυπτουσα. [Lk 13,11] — *BibNot* 20 (1983) 58.

| συγκυρία* 1 | by coincide (Lk 10,31) |

Literature
HAUCK 1934 [seltenes Alleinwort].

| συγχαίρω 3 | rejoice with (Lk 1,58; 15,6.9) |

Characteristic of Luke
HAWKINS 1909add

Literature
VON BENDEMANN 2001 428: "συγχαίρειν findet sich in den Synoptikern nur bei Lukas";
DENAUX 2009 Lⁿ; GERSDORF 1816 202 [καὶ συνέχαιρον αὐτῇ].

| συζητέω 2 + 2 (Mk 6) |
| 1. dispute (Lk 22,23); 2. talk with (Lk 24,15) |

Word groups	Lk	Acts	Mt	Mk
συζητέω + dative (VKa)		6,9	0	1/2

Characteristic of Luke	Lk	Acts	Mt	Mk
συζητέω πρός + accusative → verb of saying πρός + accusative CREDNER 1836 138	22,23	9,29	0	3

Literature
EASTON 1910 165 [cited by Weiss as characteristic of L, and possibly corroborative]; PLUMMER 1922 lxii [After verbs of speaking, answering, and the like he very often has πρός and the accusative instead of the simple dative. Thus, we have ... συζητεῖν πρός (xxii.23)]; SCHÜRMANN 1957 10-11.

| συκάμινος 1 | mulberry tree (Lk 17,6) |

| συκῆ 3 (Mt 5, Mk 4) | fig tree (Lk 13,6.7; 21,29) |

| συκομορέα** 1 | sycamore tree (Lk 19,4) |

| σῦκον 1 (Mt 1, Mk 1) | fig (Lk 6,44) |

| συκοφαντέω 2 | make false charges (Lk 3,14; 19,8) |

Characteristic of Luke
PLUMMER 1922 liii

Literature

VON BENDEMANN 2001 435: "συκοφαντεῖν im Neuen Testament nur bei Lukas"; DENAUX 2009 L[n]; EASTON 1910 165 [cited by Weiss as characteristic of L, and possibly corroborative]; HAUCK 1934 [seltenes Alleinwort]; PAFFENROTH 1997 78.

BORMANN, Lukas, *Recht, Gerechtigkeit und Religion*, 2001. Esp. 191.
HATCH, Edwin, *Essays*, 1889. Esp. 89-91.
SWELLENGREBEL, J.L., Puzzles in Luke. — *BTrans* 17 (1966) 118-122. Esp. 119-120 [Lk 3,14 διασείω, συκοφαντέω].

συλλαλέω 3 + 1 (Mt 1, Mk 1) — talk with (Lk 4,36; 9,30; 22,4; Acts 25,12)

Word groups	Lk	Acts	Mt	Mk
συλλαλέω + λέγω → **λαλέω/ὀνομάζω** + λέγω/εἶπον	4,36		0	0
συλλαλέω πρὸς ἀλλήλους → verb of saying **πρός** + acc.	4,36		0	0

Characteristic of Luke

BOISMARD 1984 cb53; NEIRYNCK 1985; VOGEL 1899B

Literature

HAUCK 1934 [Vorzugswort; Vorzugsverbindung: συλλαλέω πρός]; JEREMIAS 1980 69 [συλλαλέω + λέγων: red.]; 84 [συλλαλέω πρὸς ἀλλήλους: red.]; PLUMMER 1922 lxii [After verbs of speaking, answering, and the like he very often has πρός and the accusative instead of the simple dative. Thus, we have ... συλλαλεῖν πρός (iv.36)]; SCHÜRMANN 1957 10 [Lk 4,36 συλλαλεῖν instead of Mk 1,27 συζητεῖν].

συλλαμβάνω 7 + 4 (Mt 1, Mk 1)

1. seize (Lk 5,9; Acts 1,16); 2. become pregnant (Lk 1,24)

Word groups	Lk	Acts	Mt	Mk
συλλαμβάνω (ἐν γαστρί / ἐν γήρει / τῇ κοιλίᾳ) (*VK*b)	1,24.31.36; 2,21		0	0
συλλαμβάνομαι middle (*VK*a)	1,31; 5,7	26,21	0	0

Characteristic of Luke	Lk	Acts	Mt	Mk
συλλαμβάνω seize; cf. Jn 18,12	5,9;	1,16; 12,3;	1	1
BOISMARD 1984 cb50; NEIRYNCK 1985	22,54	23,27; 26,21		

Literature

COLLISON 1977 65 [linguistic usage of Luke's "other source-material": probable]; DENAUX 2009 L(***); lAn [συλλαμβάνω seize]; GERSDORF 1816 192 [συνέλαβεν Ἐλισάβετ]; 243 [πρὸ τοῦ συλλημφθῆναι αὐτόν]; HAUCK 1934 [Vorzugsverbindung: πρὸ τοῦ συλλημφθῆναι]; HAWKINS 1909 22; JEREMIAS 1980 46: "Die Vorliebe des Lukas für Verbkomposita mit συν-, vor allem aber die Statistik ... scheinen συλλαμβάνω der lukanischen Redaktion zuzuweisen. In Wahrheit ist die Vokabel auch in der Tradition eingebürgert, teils als Terminus für die Verhaftung Jesu ..., teils in der Kindheitsgeschichte als Terminus für die Empfängnis"; SCHNEIDER 1969 73-74.164 [Vorzugswörter und -ausdrücke des Luk].

JUNG, Chang-Wook, *Infancy Narrative*, 2004. Esp. 122-132 [συλλαμβάνω ἐν γαστρί].

συλλέγω 1 (Mt 7) — pick (Lk 6,44)

Word groups	Lk	Acts	Mt	Mk
συλλέγω + ἐκ (VKa); cf. συλλέγω ἀπό Mt 7,16; συλλέγω εἰς Mt 13,48	6,44		1	0

συλλογίζομαι 1   talk with

Word groups	Lk	Acts	Mt	Mk
συλλογίζομαι + λέγω → διαλογίζομαι + λέγω	20,5		0	0
συλλογίζομαι πρός + accusative → verb of saying πρός + acc.	20,5		0	0

Literature
HAUCK 1934 [seltenes Alleinwort]; JEREMIAS 1980 69 [συλλογίζομαι + λέγων: red.].

MUSSIES, G., The Sense of συλλογίζεσθαι at Luke XX 5. — BAARDA, T. – KLIJN, A.F.J. – VAN UNNIK, Willem C. (eds.), *Miscellanea Neotestamentica: Studia ad Novum Testamentum* ..., II (SupplNT, 48). Leiden: Brill, 1978, 59-76.

συμβαίνω 1 + 3 (Mk 1)   happen

Word groups	Lk	Acts	Mt	Mk
συνέβη + infinitive (VKa) → ἀναβαίνω + inf.		21,35	0	0

Characteristic of Luke
BOISMARD 1984 Eb50; NEIRYNCK 1985

	Lk	Acts	Mt	Mk
τὸ συμβεβηκός participle as a neuter noun (VKb) CREDNER 1836 134-135;	24,14	3,10	0	0

Literature
DENAUX 2009 LAⁿ [τὸ συμβεβηκός participle as a neuter noun]; JEREMIAS 1980 313 [τὸ συμβεβηκός: red.]; RADL 1975 427.

συμβάλλω 2 + 4
1. think about seriously (Lk 2,19); 2. confer (Acts 4,15); 3. debate (Acts 17,18); 4. meet (Lk 14,31; Acts 20,14); συμβάλλομαι: 1. help (Acts 18,27)

Word groups	Lk	Acts	Mt	Mk
συμβάλλω ἐν τῇ καρδίᾳ	2,19		0	0
συμβάλλω + λέγων		4,15(-16)	0	0
συμβάλλω + πρὸς ἀλλήλους → verb of saying πρός + acc.		4,15	0	0
συμβάλλομαι middle (VKa)		18,27	0	0

Characteristic of Luke
BOISMARD 1984 Ab43; CREDNER 1836 142; DENAUX 2009 IA*; HARNACK 1906 53.147; HAWKINS 1909LA.B; MORGENTHALER 1958*; NEIRYNCK 1985; PLUMMER 1922 lx; VOGEL 1899A.D

Literature
EASTON 1910 167 [classed by Weiss as characteristic of L on insufficient (?) evidence]; GERSDORF

1816 240 [πάντα συνετήρει τὰ ῥήματα ταῦτα συμβάλλουσα ἐν τῇ καρδίᾳ αὐτῆς]; HAUCK 1934 [Vorzugswort]; JEREMIAS 1980 69 [συμβάλλω + λέγων]; 87-88 [red.].

BELLIA, Giuseppe, "Confrontando nel suo cuore": Custodia sapienziale di Maria in Lc. 2,19b. — *BibOr* 25 (1983) 215-228.

MEYER, Ben F., "But Mary Kept All These Things..." (Lk 2,19.51). — *CBQ* 26 (1964) 31-49. Esp. 43-45: "Vocabulary of 2,19.51".

VAN UNNIK, Willem C., Die rechte Bedeutung des Wortes treffen, Lukas 2,19. — *Verbum: Essays on Some Aspects of the Religious Function of Words, Dedicated to Dr. H. W. Obbink* (Studia Theologica Rheno-Traiectina, 6). Utrecht: Kemink en zoon, 1964, 129-147; = ID., *Sparsa Collecta*, I, 1973, 72-91.

Συμεών 3 + 2 — Simeon

Word groups	Lk	Acts	Mt	Mk
Συμεών + ἄνθρωπος + δίκαιος καὶ εὐλαβής (*SC*b; *VK*c)	2,25.34		0	0
Συμεὼν ὁ καλούμενος Νίγερ (*SC*c; *VK*d)		13,1	0	0
Συμεὼν + Πέτρος (*SC*d; *VK*e)		15,14	0	0
Συμεών, son of Juda (*SC*a; *VK*b)	3,30		0	0

συμπαραγίνομαι 1 — come together

Word groups	Lk	Acts	Mt	Mk
συμπαραγίνομαι ὄχλος → **ἀκολουθέω/συμπνίγω**/ **συμπορεύομαι/συνάγω/συναντάω/σύνειμι/συνέρχομαι**/ **συνέχω** + ὄχλος/πλῆθος	23,48		0	0

Literature

HAUCK 1934 [seltenes Alleinwort].

συμπίπτω 1 — collapse

Word groups	Lk	Acts	Mt	Mk
συμπίπτω aorist → (**ἀνα/ἐμ/ἐπι/κατα/περι/προσ)πίπτω** aorist; cf. ἀποπίπτω Acts 9,18; ἐκπίπτω Acts 12,7; 27,17.26.29.32	6,49		0	0

Literature

HAUCK 1934 [seltenes Alleinwort].

συμπληρόω 2 + 1

συμπληρόομαι: 1. be swamped (Lk 8,23); 2. come to an end (Lk 9,51)

Word groups	Lk	Acts	Mt	Mk
συμπληροῦται ἡ ἡμέρα → **ἐπλήσθη/ἐπλήσθησαν/τελειόω** with reference to time DENAUX 2009 LA[n]	9,51	2,1	0	0

Characteristic of Luke

BOISMARD 1984 Ab146; CREDNER 1836 142; HAWKINS 1909LA; MORGENTHALER 1958*; NEIRYNCK 1985; PLUMMER 1922 lii; VOGEL 1899A

Literature

VON BENDEMANN 2001 415; DENAUX 2009 Laⁿ; HAUCK 1934 [seltenes Alleinwort]; JEREMIAS 1980 179 [red.]; SCHÜRMANN 1953 20 [nur in Luk und Apg].

DENAUX, Adelbert, The Delineation of the Lukan Travel Narrative within the Overall Structure of the Gospel of Luke. — FOCANT, C. (ed.), *The Synoptic Gospels. Source Criticism and the New Literary Criticism* (BETL, 110). Leuven: University Press – Peeters, 1993, 359-392. Esp. 374-375 [Lk 9,52 συμπληροῦσθαι: "were in the process of fulfilment"].

ROPES, James H., Three Papers on the Text of Acts. — *HTR* 16 (1923) 163-186. Esp. 168-175 [Acts 2,1 συμπληροῦσθαι: "was fully come"].

συμπνίγω 2 (Mt 1, Mk 2)

1. cause plants to die; 2. crowd around (Lk 8,42); 3. oppress (Lk 8,14)

Word groups	Lk	Acts	Mt	Mk
συμπνίγω ὄχλος → ἀκολουθέω/συμπαραγίνομαι/ συμπορεύομαι/συνάγω/συναντάω/σύνειμι/συνέρχομαι/ συνέχω + ὄχλος/πλῆθος	8,42		0	0

συμπορεύομαι 3 (Mk 1)

1. go with (Lk 7,11; 14,25; 24,15); 2. come together

Word groups	Lk	Acts	Mt	Mk
συμπορεύομαι + ὄχλος → ἀκολουθέω/συμπαραγίνομαι/ συμπνίγω/συνάγω/συναντάω/σύνειμι/συνέρχομαι/ συνέχω + ὄχλος/πλῆθος DENAUX 2009 Lⁿ (?)	7,11; 14,25		0	0

Characteristic of Luke

GOULDER 1989

Literature

COLLISON 1977 98 [noteworthy phenomena]; EASTON 1910 158 [probably characteristic of L]; HAUCK 1934 [Vorzugswort]; JEREMIAS 1980 157: "Sowohl πορεύομαι wie Verbkomposita mit συν- gebraucht Lukas bevorzugt. συμπορεύομαί τινι in der Bedeutung 'zusammen gehen, gemeinsam reisen mit jemandem' findet sich im NT nur im LkEv"; SCHÜRMANN 1953 90 [Vorliebe für πορεύεσθαι und einige seiner Komposita].

συμφύομαι 1   grow with (Lk 8,7)

Literature

HAUCK 1934 [seltenes Alleinwort].

συμφωνέω 1 + 2 (Mt 3)

1. agree (Acts 5,9); 2. match (Lk 5,36; Acts 15,15))

συμφωνία 1   music (Lk 15,25)

Literature

HAUCK 1934 [seltenes Alleinwort].

BARRY, Phillips, On Luke xv.25, συμφωνία: Bagpipe. — *JBL* 23 (1904) 180-190.
MOORE, George F., ΣυμφωνίαNot a Bagpipe. — *JBL* 24 (1905) 166-175.

σύν 23/26 + 51/53 (Mt 4, Mk 6)

1. with (association) (Lk 8,1); 2. with (addition) (Lk 5,19)

Word groups	Lk	Acts	Mt	Mk
σύν with composite verb συν- (*SC*b; *VK*c)		4,27; 21,16	1	1
σύν + ἐν; cf. παρέκτος + ἐν Acts 26,29		4,27; 21,29	0	0
σὺν χειρί (*LN*: with the help of)		7,35	0	0

→ εἰμι σύν; εἰς + σύν; ἐκ + σύν; ἔρχομαι σύν; καθίζω σύν; συνάγω σύν; συνέρχομαι σύν

Characteristic of Luke

BOISMARD 1984 Eb25; CADBURY 1920 202-203; CREDNER 1836 136; DENAUX 2009 L***;
GOULDER 1989*; HAWKINS 1909 22; HENDRIKS 1986 434.468; MORGENTHALER 1958LA;
NEIRYNCK 1985; PLUMMER 1922 lx

	Lk	Acts	Mt	Mk
ὁ/οἱ σύν τινι (ὤν, ὄντες) (*SC*a; *VK*a); cf. Gal 2,3 BOISMARD 1984 Bb52; DENAUX 2009 LA**; NEIRYNCK 1985	5,9; 8,45*; 9,32; 24,24.33	5,17.21; 19,38; 22,9	0	1
εἰμὶ σύν + dative; cf. Phil 1,1.23; Col 2,5; 1 Thess 4,17; 2 Pet 1,18 BOISMARD 1984 Cb150; DENAUX 2009 lA**; NEIRYNCK 1985	7,12; 8,38; 22,56; 24,44	4,13; 8,20; 13,7; 14,4; 22,9; 27,2	0	1
noun + σύν + noun; cf. 1 Cor 16,19; 2 Cor 1,2; Phil 1,1 BOISMARD 1984 Cb83; DENAUX 2009 lA*; NEIRYNCK 1985	20,1; 23,11	2,14; 3,4; 4,27; 5,1.26; 14,5; 15,22; 18,8; 23,15; 24,24	0	2
οἱ σὺν αὐτῷ/αὐτοῖς → οἱ μετ' αὐτοῦ DENAUX 2009 LA*; GOULDER 1989*	5,9; 8,45*; 9,32; 24,33	5,17.21; 19,38	0	1

→ ἐξέρχομαι σύν; μένω σύν; σὺν οἴκῳ; πορεύομαι σύν

Literature

VON BENDEMANN 2001 413: "lukanische Vorliebe für Komposita mit σύν"; COLLISON 1977 86
[verbs compound with συν-: linguistic usage of Luke: certain; linguistic usage of Luke's "other
source-material": also certain]; 145-146 [linguistic usage of Luke: certain; linguistic usage of Luke's
"other source-material": also probable]; HAUCK 1934 [Vorzugswort]; JEREMIAS 1980 63: "Lukas
hat eine ausgesprochene Vorliebe für diese Präposition"; 86-87 [Verbkomposita mit συν-: red.], n.25:
"Die 469 Belege verteilen sich wie folgt Mt 68, Mk 44, Lk 79/Apg 107, JohEv 20, sNT 151; die
relative hohe Zahl bei Mt verliert an Gewicht, wenn man beachtet, daß es sich dabei 24 mal um
συνάγω handelt"; 136: "Insbesondere ist die elliptische Wendung οἱ σύν τινι (ohne folgendes
ὄντες) typisch lukanisch"; RADL 1975 427; SCHNEIDER 1969 80-81.164 [Vorzugswörter und -
ausdrücke des Luk]; SCHÜRMANN 1953 95 [eine besondere Vorliebe für Zusammensetzungen mit
σύν]; 108 [σύν ist ein Vorzugswort des Luk].

συνάγω 6/7 + 11 (Mt 24, Mk 5)

1. gather together (Lk 3,17); 2. keep in a place (Lk 12,17); 3. turn into cash (Lk 15,13)
συνάγομαι: 4. come together (Lk 22,66)

Word groups	Lk	Acts	Mt	Mk
συνάγω + (τοῦ +) infinitive (SCg; VKk)		4,27; 13,44; 15,6; 20,7	0	0
συνάγω + ἀποθήκη	3,17; 12,18		3	0
συνάγω + εἰς + place (SCa; VKa) → (ἀν/ἀπ/εἰσ/ ἐξ/ἐπαν/κατ/προ/ὑπ)ἄγω εἰς + place	3,17	4,5 v.l.	4	0
συνάγω ἐν + place (SCc; VKc) → ἄγω ἐν + place BOISMARD 1984 Aa65		4,5.27.31; 11,26	0	0
συνάγω + ἐπί + accusative (person) (SCd; VKd) → (ἀπ/ὑπ)ἄγω ἐπί + acc. (person); (ἀν/κατ) ἄγω ἐπί + acc. (place); προάγω ἐπί + gen. (person)		4,27	1	0
συνάγω ἐπὶ τὸ αὐτό (VKe)		4,26	1	0
συνάγω + κατά + genitive (VKf)		4,26	0	0
συνάγω μετά + genitive (SCe; VKg)	11,23		2	0
συνάγω τὸ πλῆθος → ἀκολουθέω/ συμπαραγίνομαι/συμπνίγω/ συμπορεύομαι/συναντάω/σύνειμι/ συνέρχομαι/συνέχω + ὄχλος/πλῆθος		15,30	0	0
συνάγω + (δια)σκορπίζω	11,23; 15,13		3	0
συνάγω + σύν (VKj)		4,27	0	0
συνάγομαι passive → (ἀν/ἀπ/εἰσ/ἐπισυν/ κατ)ἄγομαι passive	22,66; 17,37*	4,5.26.27.31; 11,26; 13,44; 15,6; 20,7.8	11	5
συνάγω transitive → (ἀν/ἀπ/εἰσ/ἐξ/ἐπισυν/ κατ/προ/προσ)ἄγω transitive	3,17; 12,17.18; 15,13; 17,37*; 22,66	4,5.26.27.31; 11,26; 13,44; 14,27; 15,6.30; 20,7.8	19	5

Literature

RADL 1975 427 [συνάγω; συνήχθην].

LEE, John A.L., *A History of New Testament Lexicography*, 2003. Esp. 317-320.

συναγωγή 15 + 19/20 (Mt 9, Mk 8)

1. assembly (Acts 6,9); 2. congregation of Jews (Acts 9,2); 3. synagogue (Lk 7,5)

Word groups	Lk	Acts	Mt	Mk
ἄρχων τῆς συναγωγῆς (VKd)	8,41		0	0
διαλέγομαι + ἐν τῇ συναγωγῇ BOISMARD 1984 Aa81		17,17; 18,4; 24,12	0	0
εἰσέρχομαι εἰς τὴν συναγωγήν → ἀναβαίνω/ εἰσάγω/εἰσπορεύομαι/ (εἰσ)ἔρχομαι εἰς τὸ ἱερόν	4,16; 6,6	13,14; 14,1; 18,19; 19,8	0	2
συναγωγή + ἀγορά (VKg)	11,43; 20,46	17,17	1	1
συναγωγή + διδάσκω → συναγωγή + κηρύσσω	4,15; 6,6; 13,10		3	2
συναγωγή + ἱερόν (VKe)		24,12	0	0
συναγωγή (+) κηρύσσω → συναγωγή + διδάσκω	4,(19-)20.44	9,20; 15,21	2	1
συναγωγή + σάββατον (SCb; VKf) DENAUX 2009 IAⁿ	4,16; 6,6; 13,10	13,14.42*; 15,21; 17,1(-2); 18,4	0	2
συναγωγὴ τῆς Ἰουδαίας (SCa; VKa) → συναγωγὴ τῶν Ἰουδαίων	4,44			

συναγωγή τῶν Ἰουδαίων (*SC*a; *VK*a) → συναγωγή τῆς Ἰουδαίας BOISMARD 1984 Aa66		13,5.42*; 14,1; 17,1.10	0	0
συναγωγή + Λιβερτίνων (*VK*b)		6,9	0	0

Characteristic of Luke
BOISMARD 1984 cb140; MORGENTHALER 1958A; NEIRYNCK 1985

Literature
BDAG 2000 963 [literature].

CLAUSSEN, Carsten, *Versammlung, Gemeinde, Synagoge*, 2002. Esp. 120-127: "Συναγωγή".

συνακολουθέω 1 (Mk 2)   accompany (Lk 23,49)

συνανάκειμαι 3 (Mt 2, Mk 2/3)   associate in eating (Lk 7,49; 14,10.15)

Literature
COLLISON 1977 90 [noteworthy phenomena]; SCHÜRMANN 1953 107; 1957 81-82 [Luk schreibt (συν-)ἀνακεῖσθαι nirgends nachweisslich von sich aus, vermeidet dieses von Attizisten verpönte Wort].

συναντάω 2/3 + 2
1. happen (Acts 20,22); 2. BDAG 2000: meet (Lk 9,18*.37; 22,10; Acts 10,25)

Word groups	Lk	Acts	Mt	Mk
τὰ συναντήσοντα (*VK*a)		20,22	0	0
συναντάω + ὄχλος → ἀκολουθέω/συμπαραγίνομαι/ συμπνίγω/συμπορεύομαι/συνάγω/σύνειμι/συνέρχομαι/ συνέχω + ὄχλος/πλῆθος	9,37		0	0

Characteristic of Luke
BOISMARD 1984 cb124; NEIRYNCK 1985; PLUMMER 1922 lix; SCHÜRMANN 1953 95 [Luk scheint συναντᾶν immerhin näher zu liegen].

Literature
COLLISON 1977 98 [noteworthy phenomena]; DENAUX 2009 LAⁿ; RADL 1975 427 [συναντάω; συναντήσοντα].

συναντιλαμβάνομαι 1   join in helping (Lk 10,40)

Literature
HAUCK 1934 [seltenes Alleinwort].

συναρπάζω 1 + 3
1. seize (Lk 8,29; Acts 6,12; 27,15); 2. force off course (Acts 27,15)

Characteristic of Luke
BOISMARD 1984 Ab102; HARNACK 1906 52; HAWKINS 1909LA; MORGENTHALER 1958*; NEIRYNCK 1985; PLUMMER 1922 lii; VOGEL 1899A

Literature
DENAUX 2009 IA[n]; HAUCK 1934 [Vorzugswort].

συνέδριον 1 + 14 (Mt 3, Mk 3)
1. city council; 2. Sanhedrin (Lk 22,66; Acts 4,15)

Word groups	Lk	Acts	Mt	Mk
πᾶν τὸ συνέδριον		22,30	0	0
συνέδριον + ἀρχιερεύς/ἀρχιερεῖς (SCa; VKa)	22,66	5,21.27; 22,30	1	2

Characteristic of Luke
BOISMARD 1984 cb51; MORGENTHALER 1958A; NEIRYNCK 1985

Literature
BDAG 2000 967 [literature]; DENAUX 2009 IAn.

MEYER, Franz E., Einige Bemerkungen zur Bedeutung des Terminus 'Synhedrion' in den Schriften des Neuen Testaments. — NTS 14 (1968) 545-551. [NTA 13, 83]

σύνειμι 1 + 1
1. be with (Lk 9,18)

Characteristic of Luke
BOISMARD 1984 Ab205; HAWKINS 1909LA; MORGENTHALER 1958*; NEIRYNCK 1985; PLUMMER 1922 liii; VOGEL 1899A

Literature
DENAUX 2009 LA[n]; HAUCK 1934 [seltenes Alleinwort].

σύνειμι 1
1. come together (Lk 8,4); 2. be with

Word groups	Lk	Acts	Mt	Mk
σύνειμι + ὄχλος → ἀκολουθέω/συμπαραγίνομαι/συμπνίγω/ συμπορεύομαι/συνάγω/συναντάω/συνέρχομαι/ συνέχω + ὄχλος/πλῆθος	8,4		0	0

συνέρχομαι 2 + 16/17 (Mt 1, Mk 2/3)
1. come together (Lk 5,15; Acts 2,6); 2. go with (Lk 23,55); 3. have sexual intercourse

Word groups	Lk	Acts	Mt	Mk
(τὸ) πλῆθος συνέρχεται BOISMARD 1984 Aa158		2,6; 5,16	0	0
συνέρχομαι + dative (SCa; VKe) DENAUX 2009 IA[n]	23,55	1,21; 9,39; 10,23.45; 11,12; 15,38	0	0/1
συνέρχομαι + infinitive (VKg) → (ἀπ/εἰσ/ἐξ/προ/ προσ)ἔρχομαι + inf.	5,15		0	0
συνέρχομαι + εἰς (VKa)		5,16 v.l.; 15,38	0	0

συνέρχομαι (+) ὄχλος/πλῆθος → **ἀκολουθέω/** **συμπαραγίνομαι/συμπνίγω/συμπορεύομαι/** **συνάγω/συναντάω/σύνειμι/συνέχω** + ὄχλος/πλῆθος	5,15	2,6; 5,16	0	1
συνέρχομαι + σύν (*VKf*)		21,16	0	0

Characteristic of Luke

DENAUX 2009 IA*; MORGENTHALER 1958A; PLUMMER 1922 lx

	Lk	Acts	Mt	Mk
συνέρχομαι go with; cf. Jn 11,33 BOISMARD 1984 Bb23; NEIRYNCK 1985	23,55	1,21; 9,39; 10,23.45; 11,12; 15,38; 21,16; 25,17	0	0

Literature

DENAUX 2009 IA[n] [συνέρχομαι go with]; JEREMIAS 1980 310: "lk Vorzugswort"; RADL 1975 427.

συνεσθίω 1 + 2   eat together (Lk 15,2; Acts 10,41; 11,3)

Word groups	Lk	Acts	Mt	Mk
συνεσθίω + συμπίνω → **ἐσθίω/ἔσθω** + πίνω		10,41	0	0

Characteristic of Luke

BOISMARD 1984 cb175; NEIRYNCK 1985

Literature

COLLISON 1977 91 [noteworthy phenomena]; DENAUX 2009 IA[n]; JEREMIAS 1980 244 [συνεσθίω + dat. of person: "jmdm. Tischgemeinschaft gewähren"].

BARTOLOMÉ, Juan J., Comer en común: Una costumbre tipica de Jesús y su proprio comentario (Lc 15). — *Sal* 44 (1982) 669-712. Esp. 687-689: "Estudio del lenguaje y del estilo"; 701-702 [συνεσθίω].

—, Συνεσθίειν en la obra lucana: Lc 15,2; Hch 10,41; 11,3. A propósito de una tesis sobre la esencia del Cristianismo. — *Sal* 46 (1984) 269-288. [NTA 29, 569]

PARKIN, V., Συνεσθίειν in the New Testament. — *Studia Evangelica* 3 (1964) 250-253.

σύνεσις 1 (Mk 1)

1. what is understood; 2. intelligence (Lk 2,47)

συνετός 1 + 1 (Mt 1)   intelligent (Lk 10,21; Acts 13,7)

Literature

KILPATRICK, George D., Φρόνιμος, σοφός and συνετός in Matthew and Luke. — *JTS* 48 (1947) 63-64.

συνευδοκέω 1 + 2   agree (Lk 11,48; Acts 8,1; 22,20)

Characteristic of Luke

BOISMARD 1984 Db36; NEIRYNCK 1985

Literature

DENAUX 2009 lA[n]; HAUCK 1934 [seltenes Alleinwort].

συνέχω 6 + 3 (Mt 1)

1. restrain; 2. guard (Lk 22,63); 3. crowd around (Lk 8,45); συνέχομαι: 1.
experience (Acts 28,8); 4. be distressed (Lk 12,50); 5. continue (Acts 18,5)

Word groups	Lk	Acts	Mt	Mk
συνέχω ὄχλος → ἀκολουθέω/συμπαραγίνομαι/ συμπνίγω/συμπορεύομαι/συνάγω/συναντάω/ σύνειμι/συνέρχομαι + ὄχλος/πλῆθος	8,45		0	0
συνέχω πυρετός DENAUX 2009 LA[n]	4,38	28,8	0	0
συνέχω τινά (VKa) DENAUX 2009 L[n]		8,45; 19,43; 22,63		0	0
συνέχω τὰ ὦτα (LN: refuse to listen)		7,57	0	0

Characteristic of Luke

BOISMARD 1984 cb52; DENAUX 2009 L***; GOULDER 1989*; HARNACK 1906 42; HAWKINS 1909 L; NEIRYNCK 1985; PLUMMER 1922 lx; VOGEL 1899D

Literature

VON BENDEMANN 2001 414; COLLISON 1977 66 [linguistic usage of Luke: likely]; HAUCK 1934 [Vorzugswort]; JEREMIAS 1980 282 [red.].

HENSCHEL, Erich, Zu Apostelgeschichte 18,5. — *Theologia Viatorum* 2 (1950) 213-215.
[Acts 18,5 συνείχετο τῷ λόγῳ (Paul) was wholly absorbed in preaching].

συνθλάω 1 (Mt 1)   break into pieces (Lk 20,18)

συνίημι 4 + 4 (Mt 9, Mk 5)

1. understand (Lk 2,50; 8,10; 18,34; 24,45; Acts 7,25); 2. be intelligent

Word groups	Lk	Acts	Mt	Mk
συνίημι + ἀκούω (SCa; VKc) → βλέπω / θεωρέω / ὁράω/εἶδον + ἀκούω	8,10	28,26.27	6	2
συνίημι τὰς γραφάς → διανοίγω τὰς γραφάς; ἀνοίγω/(ἀνα)πτύσσω τὸ βιβλίον	24,45		0	0

Literature

GERSDORF 1816 271 [καὶ αὐτοὶ συνῆκαν τὸ ῥῆμα].

DANOVE, Paul, Verbs of Experience, 1999. Esp. 164-165.176.
DELEBECQUE, Édouard, *Études grecques*, 1976. Esp. 42-47 [2,41-52].

συνίστημι 1

1. recommend; 2. demonstrate; 3. hold together
συνίσταμαι: 4. stand with (Lk 9,32); 5. come into existence

Word groups	Lk	Acts		Mt	Mk
συνίστημι intransitive (*VK*b)	9,32			0	0

Characteristic of Luke	Lk	Acts		Mt	Mk
συνεστώς → (ἐφ/παρ)έστώς CREDNER 1836 140	9,32			0	0

συνοδία 1 — group of travellers (Lk 2,44)

Literature

HARNACK 1906 149 [hapax in NT, but see Acts 9,4 συνοδεύειν]; HAUCK 1934 [seltenes Alleinwort].

συνοχή 1 — distress (Lk 21,25)

Literature

HAUCK 1934 [seltenes Alleinwort].

συντελέω 2 + 1 (Mt 0/1, Mk 1)

1. complete (Lk 4,13); 2. cause to exist; 3. end (Lk 2,21*; 4,2; Acts 21,27)

Word groups	Lk	Acts	Mt	Mk
συντελέω with reference to time (*VK*a)	4,2	21,27	0	0

Characteristic of Luke

BOISMARD 1984 cb54; NEIRYNCK 1985

Literature

HAUCK 1934 [Vorzugswort]; JEREMIAS 1980 115 [red.]; RADL 1975 428 [συντελέω; συντελέω "bezogen auf ἡμέραι"].

συντηρέω 1/2 (Mt 1, Mk 1)

1. preserve (Lk 5,38*); 2. keep in mind (Lk 2,19)

Literature

GERSDORF 1816 240 [πάντα συνετήρει τὰ ῥήματα ταῦτα συμβάλλουσα ἐν τῇ καρδίᾳ αὐτῆς].

MEYER, Ben F., "But Mary Kept All These Things..." (Lk 2,19.51). — *CBQ* 26 (1964) 31-49. Esp. 43-45: "Vocabulary of 2,19.51".

συντίθημι 1 + 1/2 — agree together (Lk 22,5; Acts 23,20; 24,9*)

Characteristic of Luke

PLUMMER 1922 lx

Literature

DENAUX 2009 LAⁿ; HAUCK 1934 [seltenes Alleinwort].

BORMANN, Lukas, *Recht, Gerechtigkeit und Religion*, 2001. Esp. 162.

συντρίβω 1/2 (Mt 1, Mk 2)

1. break into pieces; 2. crush (Lk 9,39); 3. overcome completely

Word groups	Lk	Acts	Mt	Mk
οἱ συντετριμμένοι τὴν καρδίαν (*VK*a); cf. συνθρύπτοντες τὴν καρδίαν Acts 21,13	4,18*		0	0

συντυγχάνω 1

come near to (Lk 8,19; Acts 11,26*)

Literature

VON BENDEMANN 2001 415; HAUCK 1934 [seltenes Alleinwort].

Συρία 1 + 5 (Mt 1)

Syria (Lk 2,2)

Word groups	Lk	Acts	Mt	Mk
Συρία καὶ Κιλικία (*VK*a)		15,23.41	0	0

Σύρος 1

Syrian (Lk 4,27)

συσπαράσσω 1 (Mk 1)

throw into a fit (Lk 9,42)

σφόδρα 1 + 1 (Mt 7, Mk 1)

exceedingly (Lk 18,23; Acts 16,21)

Word groups	Lk	Acts	Mt	Mk
σφόδρα + adjective (*VK*a)	18,23		1	1

σχίζω 3 + 2 (Mt 2, Mk 2)

1. split (Lk 23,45); 2. divide (Lk 5,36$^{1.2}$; Acts 14,4; 23,7)

Word groups	Lk	Acts	Mt	Mk
ἐσχίσθη (+) τὸ πλῆθος BOISMARD 1984 Aa160		14,4; 23,7	0	0
σχίζω active (*VK*a)	5,36$^{1.2}$		0	0

Characteristic of Luke

PLUMMER 1922 lx

Literature

MEINERTZ, Max, Σχίσμα und αἵρεσις im Neuen Testament. — *BZ* NF 1 (1957) 114-118.

σῴζω 17/19 + 13 (Mt 15/16, Mk 14[15])
1. rescue; 2. save (Lk 6,9); 3. heal (Lk 8,48)

Word groups	Lk	Acts	Mt	Mk
σῴζω in the context of healings (SCf)	6,9; 7,50; 8,36.48.50; 18,42	4,9; 14,9	3	6
σῴζω ἀπό (VKd)		2,40	1	0
σῴζω + ἀπόλλυμι (SCb; VKl) → ζῳογονέω + ἀπόλλυμι	6,9; 9,24[1.2].56*; 17,33*; 19,10		2/3	2
σῴζω + δαιμονίζομαι	8,36		0	0
σῴζω + διά + genitive (VKe)		15,11	0	0
σῴζω ἐν + instrumental dative (SCd; VKh); cf. Rom 5,10 BOISMARD 1984 ca26		4,9.12; 11,14	0	0
σῴζω κατά + accusative (VKj)		15,11	0	0
σῴζω + πίστις/πιστεύω (SCe; VKm)	7,50; 8,12.48.50; 17,19; 18,42	14,9; 15,11; 16,31	1	2[3]
σῴζω (τὴν) ψυχήν (SCa; VKa) → ἀπόλλυμι/ ζητέω/ζῳογονέω τὴν ψυχήν; cf. εὑρίσκω τὴν ψυχήν Mt 10,39[1.2]; 16,25[2]	6,9; 9,24[1.2].56*; 17,33*		1	3
τὸ σωθῆναι/σῴζεσθαι (VKc)		14,9; 27,20	0	0

Characteristic of Luke	Lk	Acts	Mt	Mk
οἱ σῳζόμενοι (SCc; VKb) BOISMARD 1984 Db45; NEIRYNCK 1985	13,23	2,47	0	0

Literature

VON BENDEMANN 2001 425; DENAUX 2009 LA[n] [οἱ σῳζόμενοι].

COLON, Jean-Baptiste, La conception du salut d'après les évangiles synoptiques. — *Revue des Sciences Religieuses* 3 (1923) 62-92, 472-507; 10 (1930) 1-39, 189-217, 370-415; 11 (1932) 27-70, 193-223, 382-412.

DA SPINETOLI, Ortensio, Qualche rifessione su "la salvezza" nell'opera lucana (Vangelo e Atti). — LEONARDI, G. – TROLESE, F.G.B. (eds.), *San Luca Evangelista*, 2000, 265-281. Esp. 265-268: "Il vocabolario".

FOULKES, Irene W., Two Semantic Problems in the Translation of Acts 4.5-20. — *BTrans* 29 (1978) 121-125. Esp. 122-123: "ὄνομα 'name'"; 124-125: "σῴζειν 'save, heal', and σωτηρία 'salvation, healing'".

GEORGE, A., L'emploi chez Luc du vocabulaire de salut. — *NTS* 23 (1976-77) 308-320. Esp. 319-320: "Luc conserve le vocabulaire de salut de la tradition synoptique en deux domaines: pour l'accomplissement eschatologique de l'individu et pour le miracle, salut corporel présent (notion liée à celle du Règne présent en Jésus). Le langage de Luc présente aussi plusieurs caractéristiques originales: – Les Actes offrent un plus large emploi profane du vocabulaire de salut, du fait de leur genre narratif et de leur milieu païen. – Luc présente plusieurs cas de salut incorporel présent de l'individu: dans la foi et le pardon des péchés, l'expérience de l'Esprit, la vie en Église. Cette conception du salut trouve des analogies dans le langage de Paul et dans la pensée de Jean. – Cette perspective individuelle est complétée par une insistance caractéristique sur le salut du peuple de Dieu. Luc montre ce salut annoncé dans l'évangile de l'enfance; il le présente accompli dans le récit de la Pentecôte, où la communauté de Jérusalem, Israël des 'derniers jours', offre l'image idéale du peuple des 'sauvés', vivant par l'Esprit, dans la foi et la charité. La suite du livre des Actes rapporte l'effort apostolique pour la réalisation de ce peuple, par la proposition à Israël et aux païens du message du salut. Au terme de cette histoire, Luc entrevoit l'accomplissement final du salut, qu'il nomme de préférence 'le Règne de Dieu'". [NTA 21, 759]; = ID., *Études*, 1978, 307-320. Esp. 319-320.

MARROW, Stanley B., Principles for Interpreting the New Testament Soteriological Terms. — *NTS* 36 (1990) 268-280. Esp. 271-272: "Salvation".

MEYER, Ben F., The Initial Self-Understanding of the Church. — *CBQ* 27 (1965) 34-42. Esp. 37-38 [Acts 2,47: οἱ σῳζόμενοι].

THROCKMORTON, Burton H., σῴζειν, σωτηρία in Luke-Acts. — *Studia Evangelica* 6 (1973) 515-526.

VAN UNNIK, Willem C., L'usage de σῴζειν "sauver" et des dérivés dans les évangiles synoptiques. —*La formation des évangiles: problème synoptique et Formgeschichte* (Recherches bibliques, 2). Bruges: Desclée De Brouwer, 1957, 178-194; = ID., *Sparsa Collecta*, I, 1973, 16-34.

VOSS, Gerhard, *Die Christologie der lukanischen Schriften in Grundzügen*, 1965. Esp. 45-47: "Σῴζειν und εὐεργετεῖν".

WAGNER, Wilhelm, Über σῴζειν und seine Derivata im Neuen Testament. — *ZNW* 6 (1905) 205-235.

WELLS, Luise, *The Greek Language of Healing*, 1998. Esp. 180-191.

σῶμα 13 + 1 (Mt 14/16, Mk 4/5)

1. body (Lk 17,37; Acts 9,40); 2. physical being; 3. church; 4. slave; 5. reality

Word groups	Lk	Acts	Mt	Mk
ὅλον τὸ σῶμα (*SC*a; *VK*c) → ὅλη ἡ **ψυχή**	11,34^2.36		4	0
σῶμα + ἔνδυμα/ἐνδύω	12,22.23		2	0
σῶμα (+) (τοῦ) Ἰησοῦ (*VK*f)	23,52; 24,3		1	1
σῶμα (τοῦ) κυρίου (*VK*e)	24,3		0	0
σῶμα + ψυχή (*SC*b; *VK*j) → **καρδία/πνεῦμα** + ψυχή	12,22.23		4	0

Literature
JEREMIAS 1980 270 [red.].

LYS, D., L'arrière-plan et les connotations vétérotestamentaires de *sarx* et de *sōma* (étude préliminaire). — *Vetus Testamentum* 36 (1986) 163-204. [NTA 31, 57]

σωματικός 1   bodily (Lk 3,22)

Literature
HAUCK 1934 [seltenes Alleinwort].

σωτήρ 2 + 2

1. rescuer (Lk 1,47; 2,11); 2. Savior (Acts 13,23)

Word groups	Lk	Acts	Mt	Mk
ὁ θεὸς ὁ σωτήρ (*VK*a)	1,47		0	0
σωτήρ + θεός		5,31; 13,23	0	0
σωτὴρ Ἰησοῦς (*VK*b)		13,23	0	0
σωτήρ + κύριος	2,11		0	0

Characteristic of Luke
HARNACK 1906 140.151

	Lk	Acts	Mt	Mk
σωτήρ/-ρία/-ριον BOISMARD 1984 Eb19; CREDNER 1836 140; DENAUX 2009 L***; NEIRYNCK 1985	1,47.69.71.77 ; 2,11.30;3,6; 19,9	4,12; 5,31; 7,25; 13,23.26.47; 16,17; 27,43; 28,28	0	0

Literature

BDAG 2000 985 [literature]; COLLISON 1977 177 [linguistic usage of Luke's "other source-material": certain]; DENAUX 2009 LAⁿ; HAUCK 1934 [seltenes Alleinwort; Vorzugsverbindung: σωτήρ μου]; 39: "Exk 5: "Σωτήρ"; JEREMIAS 1980 81: "σωτήρ (von Christus aus gesagt, lukanisch)".

GEORGE, Augustin, La royauté de Jésus. — ID., *Études*, 1978, 257-282. Esp. 266-268: "Sauveur (Sôtèr)".

HAERENS, H., Σωτήρ and σωτηρία dans la religion grecque. — *Studia Hellenistica* 5 (1947) 57-68.

JUNG, Franz, ΣΩΤΗΡ. *Studien zur Rezeption erines hellenistischen Ehrentitels im Neuen Testament* (NTabh, NF, 39), Münster, 2002. XII + 404 pp.

KARRER, Martin, Jesus, der Retter (*Sôtêr*). Zur Aufnahme eines hellenistischen Prädikats im Neuen Testament. — *ZNW* 93 (2002) 153-176.

MARROW, Stanley B., Principles for Interpreting the New Testament Soteriological Terms. — *NTS* 36 (1990) 268-280. Esp. 271-272: "Salvation".

NOCK, Arthur D., Soter and Euergetes. — JOHNSON, Sherman Elbridge (ed.), *The Joy of Study: Papers on New Testament and Related Subjects Presented to Honor Frederick Clifton Grant*. New York: MacMillan Company, 1951, 127-148.

PRETE, Benedetto, "Oggi vi è nato ... il Salvatore che è il Cristo Signore" (*Lc* 2,11). — *RivBib* 34 (1986) 289-325. Esp. 309-313: "Salvatore (σωτήρ)".

POWELL, Mark A., Salvation in Luke-Acts. — *Word and World* 12 (1992) 5-10.

RESE, Martin, *Alttestamentliche Motive in der Christologie des Lukas*, 1969. Esp. 131-133: "Προφήτης, ἅγιος, δίκαιος, ἀρχηγός, σωτήρ und υἱὸς θεοῦ in der Apostelgeschichte"; 204-205: "Σωτήρ, Χριστός [υἱὸς Δαυίδ] im Lukasevangelium".

VOSS, Gerhard, *Die Christologie der lukanischen Schriften in Grundzügen*, 1965. Esp. 45-60: "Σωτήρ und κύριος als herrscherliche Jesusprädikate".

WENDLAND, Paul, Σωτήρ. Eine religionsgeschichtliche Untersuchung — *ZNW* 5 (1904) 335-353.

See also σῴζω.

σωτηρία 4 + 6 (Mk 0[1])

1. deliverance (Lk 1,71; Acts 7,25; 27,34); 2. salvation (state); 3. salvation (event) (Lk 1,69.77; 19,9; Acts 13,26)

Word groups	Lk	Acts	Mt	Mk
εἰς σωτηρίαν (VKa)		13,47	0	0
κέρας σωτηρίας	1,69		0	0
ὁδὸς σωτηρίας (VKc) HARNACK 1906 37		16,17	0	0

Characteristic of Luke

DENAUX 2009 L***; GOULDER 1989*; HARNACK 1906 144; HAWKINS 1909 22

	Lk	Acts	Mt	Mk
σωτηρία/-ριον/-ήρ BOISMARD 1984 Eb19; CREDNER 1836 140; DENAUX 2009 L***; NEIRYNCK 1985	1,47.69.71.77; 2,11.30;3,6; 19,9	4,12; 5,31; 7,25; 13,23.26.47; 16,17; 27,43; 28,28	0	0

Literature

GERSDORF 1816 206 [κέρας σωτηρίας]; HAUCK 1934 [seltenes Alleinwort]; JEREMIAS 1980 73: "Scheinbar beliebig wechselt das lukanische Doppelwerk zwischen σωτηρία (10mal) und σητήριον (3mal). Das Rätsel löst sich mit der Beobachtung, daß alle drei lukanischen Belege für σωτήριον LXX-Zitate sind (Lk 2,30; 3,6; Apg 28,28). So bleiben nur die 10 σωτηρία-Belege: von ihnen finden sich 3 im Benedictus (Lk 1,69.71.77, also traditionell), 6 in der Apostelgeschichte (4,12; 7,25; 13,26.47 cit.; 16,17; 27,34, also redaktionell), während die 10. Stelle, Lk 19,9, sich vom Inhalt her als traditionelles urkirchliches Gut zu erkennen gibt".

FOULKES, Irene W., Two Semantic Problems in the Translation of Acts 4.5-20. — *BTrans* 29 (1978) 121-125. Esp. 122-123: "ὄνομα 'name'"; 124-125: "σῴζειν 'save, heal', and σωτηρία 'salvation, healing'".

HAERENS, H., Σωτήρ and σωτηρία dans la religion grecque. — *Studia Hellenistica* 5 (1947) 57-68.

MARROW, Stanley B., Principles for Interpreting the New Testament Soteriological Terms. — *NTS* 36 (1990) 268-280. Esp. 271-272: "Salvation".

POWELL, Mark A., Salvation in Luke-Acts. — *Word and World* 12 (1992) 5-10.

THROCKMORTON, Burton H., σῴζειν, σωτηρία in Luke-Acts. — *Studia Evangelica* 6 (1973) 515-526.

See also σῴζω.

σωτήριον 2 + 1

1. salvation (means) (Lk 2,30; 3,6); 2. salvation (message) (Acts 28,28)

Word groups	Lk	Acts	Mt	Mk
σωτήριον τοῦ θεοῦ	2,30 (σου); 3,6	28,28	0	0

Characteristic of Luke	Lk	Acts	Mt	Mk
σωτήριον/-ήρ/-ία BOISMARD 1984 Eb19; CREDNER 1836 140; DENAUX 2009 L***; NEIRYNCK 1985	1,47.69.71.77; 2,11.30;3,6; 19,9	4,12; 5,31; 7,25; 13,23.26.47; 16,17; 27,43; 28,28	0	0

Literature

DENAUX 2009 La[n]; GERSDORF 1816 256 [σωτήριόν σου]; HAUCK 1934 [seltenes Alleinwort].

KILGALLEN, John J., Jesus, Savior, the Glory of Your People Israel. — *Bib* 75 (1994) 305-328.
POWELL, Mark A., Salvation in Luke-Acts. — *Word and World* 12 (1992) 5-10.
See also σῴζω.

σωφρονέω 1 (Mk 1)

1. be sane (Lk 8,35); 2. be sensible

T

ταμεῖον 2 (Mt 2)

1. inner room (Lk 12,3); 2. storeroom (Lk 12,24)

Literature

BORMANN, Lukas, *Recht, Gerechtigkeit und Religion*, 2001. Esp. 138.

τάξις 1

1. sequence (Lk 1,8); 2. good order; 3. kind

Literature

BORMANN, Lukas, *Recht, Gerechtigkeit und Religion*, 2001. Esp. 138-139.

ταπεινός 1 (Mt 1)

1. downhearted; 2. humble; 3. lowly (Lk 1,52); 4. gentle

Word groups	Lk	Acts	Mt	Mk
ταπεινός + ὑπερήφανος (VKa)	1,(51-)52		0	0
ταπεινός + ὑψόω → ταπεινόω + ὑψόω	1,52		0	0

Literature

HATCH, Edwin, *Essays*, 1889. Esp. 73-77.
LEIVESTAD, Ragnar, Ταπεινός – ταπεινόφρων. — *NT* 8 (1965) 36-47.

ταπεινόω 5 (Mt 3)

1. make low (special) (Lk 3,5); 2. level off (Lk 3,5); 3. make low (status) (Lk 14,11[1.2]; 18,14[1.2]); 4. make humble; 5. embarrass

Word groups	Lk	Acts	Mt	Mk
ταπεινόω + ὑψόω (VKa) → ταπεινός + ὑψόω DENAUX 2009 Ln	14,11[1.2]; 18,14[1.2]		2	0

Literature

MAHFOUZ, Hady, *La fonction littéraire et théologique de Lc 3,1-20*, 2003. Esp. 151-152.

ταπείνωσις 1 + 1

1. humiliation (Acts 8,33); 2. low status (Lk 1,48)

Characteristic of Luke

HARNACK 1906 74

Literature

DENAUX 2009 LA[n].

ταράσσω 2 + 3 (Mt 2, Mk 1)

1. stir up (Lk 1,12; 24,38; Acts 17,13); 2. cause great distress; 3. cause a riot (Acts 17,8)

Word groups	Lk	Acts	Mt	Mk
ταράσσω + φόβος (VKd)	1,12		1	0

Literature

HARNACK 1906 71 (ET 99) [ἐταράχθη ἰδών, Lukan]; RADL 1975 428.

RODRÍGUEZ, Isidoro, Consideración filologica sobre el mensaje de la anunciación, 1958.
Esp. 242-243: "ταράσσω".

τάσσω 1 + 4/5 (Mt 1/2)

1. assign (Acts 13,48); 2. cause to be (Lk 7,8); 3. command; 4. suggest (Acts 28,23); 5. give oneself to

Word groups	Lk	Acts	Mt	Mk
τασσόμενος ὑπὸ ἐξουσίαν (VKa)	7,8		0/1	0

Characteristic of Luke

BOISMARD 1984 cb151; NEIRYNCK 1985; PLUMMER 1922 lx

Literature

DENAUX 2009 lAn; HAUCK 1934 [häufiges Alleinwort].

MAKUJINA, John, Verbs Meaning "Command" in the New Testament: Determining the Factors Involved in the Choice of Command-Verbs. — EstBíb 56 (1998) 357-369. Esp. 358-359: "Παραγγέλλω"; 359-361: "Κελεύω"; 361-362: "'Εντέλλω"; 362-364: "Διαστέλλω"; 364-366: "-τάσσω complex"; 366-367: "Λέγω". [NTA 43, 57]

ταχέως 2 + 1

1. quickly (Lk 14,21; 16,6); 2. (very) soon (Acts 17,15)

Literature

DENAUX 2009 La^n.

τάχος 1 + 3   quickly

Characteristic of Luke	Lk	Acts	Mt	Mk
ἐν τάχει (LN: [very] soon)	18,8	12,7; 22,18; 25,4	0	0
BOISMARD 1984 db28; CREDNER 1836 138; NEIRYNCK 1985				

Literature

DENAUX 2009 lA^n; lA^n [ἐν τάχει]; JEREMIAS 1980 272 [red.]; RADL 1975 428.

ταχύ 1 (Mt 3, Mk 1/2)

1. soon; 2. quickly (Lk 15,22)

τε 9 + 151/174 (Mt 3/4; Mk 0/1)

1. and (Acts 10,22); 2. and then (Acts 2,37)

Word groups	Lk	Acts	Mt	Mk
ἔτι τε καί DENAUX 2009 LA^n	14,26	21,28	0	0
ὅς τε → ὅς καί		26,16$^{1.2}$.22	0	0
πᾶς τε → πᾶς οὖν		5,42; 8,1*; 21,18; 26,14.20	0	0

Characteristic of Luke

BOISMARD 1984 cb57; DENAUX 2009 L***; GOULDER 1989*; HAWKINS 1909 L; HENDRIKS 1986 468; MORGENTHALER 1958A; NEIRYNCK 1985

	Lk	Acts	Mt	Mk
ὅ τε + noun + καὶ ὁ + noun; cf. Heb 2,11 BOISMARD 1984 Bb21; DENAUX 2009 lA*; NEIRYNCK 1985	15,2; 23,12	5,24; 8,38; 17,10.14; 18,5; 26,23.30[1]	0	0
τε on its own; cf. Jn 2,15; 4,42; 6,18; Rom 7,7; 16,26; 1 Cor 4,21; Eph 3,19; Heb 1,3; 6,5; 9,1; 12,2; Jude 6 BOISMARD 1984 Bb80; NEIRYNCK 1985	24,20	1,15; 2,33.37.40; 4,13.14.33; 5,35; 6,7.13; 7,26; 8,3.13.25.31; 9,3; 10,22.28.33; 11,21; 12,6.12.17; 13,4.44.46.52; 14,11.12.13; 15,4.5. 6; 16,13.23.34; 17,26; 18,26; 19,11. 29; 20,3.7.35; 21,18.20.31.37; 22,8; 23,5.28; 24,10.27; 26,4.14; 27,3.5. 8.17.20.21.29.43; 28,2.23	1	0
τε καί (SCa; VKa) → γε καί DENAUX 2009 L***	12,45; 14,26; 21,11[2]; 22,66	1,1; 2.9.10.11; 4,27; 5,14; 8,12; 9,2.6*. 15[1].18.24.29; 14,1.5; 15,9.32; 19,10.17.27; 20,21; 21,12.28; 22,4; 24,3.15; 26,3.20[1].22[1]	1	0
τε ... καί (SCb; VKb) DENAUX 2009 L***	2,16; 15,2; 21,11[1]; 23,12	1,8.13; 5,24; 6,12; 8,38; 10,39; 13,1[1.2].2*; 15,3; 17,10. 14[2]; 18,5; 21,25.30; 22,23; 25,23.24; 26,10[1].23; 27,1; 28,23[2]	1	0
τε ... καὶ ... καί; cf. Phil 1,7; Heb 9,2 BOISMARD 1984 Bb81; DENAUX 2009 lA*; NEIRYNCK 1985	2,16; 21,11[1]	1,8.13; 6,12; 9,18(-19); 13,1[1]; 21,25; 22,23	0	0

→ ἄνδρες (τε) καὶ γυναῖκες; ἀπεκρίθη δέ/τε; εἶπόν/εἶπέν τε; Ἰουδαῖοί τε καὶ Ἕλληναι; πολύς τε

Literature

BDR § 443: "τε ist ein Vorzugswort in Apg"; COLLISON 1977 111 [linguistic usage of Luke: certain]; 112 [τε ... καί: certain]; DENAUX 2009 lAn [τε on its own];GERSDORF 1816 239 [καὶ ἀνεῦραν τήν τε Μαριάμ]; HAUCK 1934 [Vorzugswort]; JEREMIAS 1980 85: "Die enklitische Partikel τέ wird von Lukas in der Apg mit exzessiver Häufigkeit gebraucht"; RADL 1975 411 [ἔτι τε καί]; 428 [τε; τε ... καί; τε ... τε]; SCHNEIDER 1969 108-109.164 [τε (καί): Vorzugswörter und -ausdrücke des Luk]; SCHÜRMANN 1957 32 [ausgesprochene Vorliebe für τὲ ... καί und τὲ ... τέ].

ELLIOTT, James K., τέ in the New Testament. — *TZ* 46 (1990) 202-204.

LARSEN, I., Notes on the Function of γάρ, οὖν, μέν, δέ, καί, and τέ in the Greek New Testament. — *Notes on Translation* (Dallas) 5 (1991) 35-47.

LEVISOHN, Stephen H., *Textual Connections in Acts*, 1987. Esp. 121-136: "*te* solitarium".

MARSHALL, A., A Note on τε ... καί. — *BTrans* 5 (1954) 182-183.

READ-HEIMERDINGER, Jenny, *The Bezan Text of Acts*, 2002. Esp. 204-211: "δέ, καί and τε".

URBÁN, Angel, La coordinada modal en el Nuevo Testamento. — *FilolNT* 1 (1988) 193-208. Esp. 200-201 [Lk 12,46; 18,1; 20,1.31; Acts 8,25; 9,9; 10,42; 16,20-21; 20,2]; 207: "Summary: The article makes a detailed study of ... 'the modal coordinate sentence', found when of two verbal clauses, joined by the conjunction καί/τε or τε καί (also in the negative form), one indicates the *mode* of doing or taking place of the action/state expressed by the other".

τέκνον 14 + 5 (Mt 14/15, Mk 9)

1. child (own) (Lk 1,7); 2. descendant (Acts 2,39); 3. inhabitants (Lk 13,34); 4. child (endearment); 5. disciple; 6. kind of

Word groups	Lk	Acts	Mt	Mk
τὰ τέκνα + Ἰερουσαλήμ → τὰ **τέκνα** + πόλις	13,34; 23,28		1	0
τὰ τέκνα + πόλις → τὰ **τέκνα** + Ἰερουσαλήμ	19,(41-)44	21,5	3	0
τέκνον Ἀβραάμ (*VK*b) → **θυγάτηρ/σπέρμα/υἱός** + Ἀβραάμ	3,8; 16,25		1	0
τέκνον + γονεῖς (*SC*a; *VK*e) → **παιδίον** + γονεῖς	18,29		1	1
τέκνον + γυνή (*VK*f)	14,26; 18,29; 20,(29-)31	21,5	2/3	1/2
τέκνον + μήτηρ (*SC*a; *VK*d) → **παιδίον/παῖς** + μήτηρ	2,48; 14,26		1	2
τέκνον + πατήρ (*SC*a; *VK*c) → **παιδίον/παῖς** + πατήρ	1,17; 2,48; 11,13; 14,26	13,(32-)33	3	2

Characteristic of Luke	Lk	Acts	Mt	Mk
τέκνον (1st word, voc.) → **πάτερ** GOULDER 1989	2,48; 15,31; 16,25		1	1

Literature

JEREMIAS 1980 24-25: "οὐκ ἦν αὐτοῖς τέκνον: ist semitisierende Sprache der Quelle. Lukas selbst verwendet ἄτεκνος"; REHKOPF 1959 99 [τέκνον: "Substantiva in Anrede bei den Synoptikern"].

SWELLENGREBEL, J.L., Puzzles in Luke. — *BTrans* 17 (1966) 118-122. Esp. 121-122 [Lk 7,35 ἐδικαιώθη ἡ σοφία ἀπὸ πάντων τῶν τέκνων αὐτῆς].

τελειόω 2 + 1

1. make perfect; 2. make genuine; 3. complete (Lk 2,43; 13,32; Acts 20,24); 4. succeed fully; 5. initiate; 6. make happen; 7. become

Word groups	Lk	Acts	Mt	Mk
τελειόω with reference to time (*VK*d) → **ἐπλήσθη/ἐπλήσθησαν** with reference to time; **συμπληροῦται** ἡ ἡμέρα	2,43		0	0

Literature

DENAUX 2009 La[n]; RADL 1975 428; SCHÜRMANN 1957 125 [nur bei Lk: sehr wahrscheinlich luk R].

DENAUX, Adelbert, L'hypocrisie des pharisiens et le dessein de Dieu, [2]1989. Esp. 181-183.

DERRETT, J. Duncan M., The Lucan Christ and Jerusalem: τελειοῦμαι (Lk 13,32). — *ZNW* 75 (1984) 36-43. [NTA 29, 150]; = ID., *Studies in the New Testament*, V, 1989, 145-152.

DU PLESSIS, Paul Johannes, *Τέλειος: The Idea of Perfection in the New Testament.* Kampen: Kok, 1959, 255 p. — Diss. Kampen, 1959 (dir. H.N. Ridderbos). Esp. 173-174.

DUPONT, Jacques, *Le discours de Milet*, 1962. Esp. 107-110.

FERRARO, Giuseppe, "Oggi e domani e il terzo giorno" (osservazioni su *Luca* 13,32,33). — *RivBib* 16 (1968) 397-407. Esp. 401-407: "Considerazioni sul vocabolario di Luca 13.32.33" [ἐκβάλλειν δαιμόνια; ἰάσεις ἀποτελῶ; τελειοῦσθαι ε πορεύεσθαι; ἀπολέσθαι].

PRETE, Benedetto, Il testo di Luca 13,31-33: Unità letteraria e insegnamento cristologico. — *BibOr* 24 (1982) 59-79; = ID., *L'opera di Luca*, 1986, 80-103. Esp. 234.239-242.

τελείωσις 1

1. causing perfection; 2. fulfilment (Lk 1,45)

τελεσφορέω 1

bear ripe fruit

Literature

HAUCK 1934 [häufiges Alleinwort].

τελευτάω 1 + 2 (Mt 4, Mk 2/4)   die (Lk 7,2; Acts 2,29; 7,15)

τελέω 4 + 1 (Mt 7)

1. complete (Lk 12,50); 2. end; 3. make happen (Lk 18,31; 22,37); 4. obey (Lk 2,39); 5. pay taxes

Characteristic of Luke	Lk	Acts	Mt	Mk
τελεῖσθαι, passive GOULDER 1989	12,50; 18,31; 22,37		0	0
τελέω τὸ γεγραμμένον / τὰ γεγραμμένα BOISMARD 1984 Ab147; NEIRYNCK 1985	18,31; 22,37	13,29	0	0
ὡς (δὲ) ἐτέλεσαν ἅπαντα/πάντα VOGEL 1899C	2,39	13,29	0	0

Literature

DENAUX 2009 Lⁿ [τελεῖσθαι, passive], Laⁿ [τελέω τὸ γεγραμμένον / τὰ γεγραμμένα]; LAⁿ [ὡς (δὲ) ἐτέλεσαν ἅπαντα/πάντα]; EASTON 1910 166 [τελέω passive, aorist and future: cited by Weiss as characteristic of L, and possibly corroborative]; JEREMIAS 1980 99; SCHÜRMANN 1957 125 [τελεσθῆναι ἐν ἐμοί: sehr wahrscheinlich luk R].

τέλος 4 (Mt 6, Mk 3)

1. end (Lk 1,33; 21,9; 22,37); 2. result; 3. purpose; 4. completely (Lk 18,5); 5. tax

Word groups	Lk	Acts	Mt	Mk
εἰς τέλος (LN: completely; SCa; VKc)	18,5		2	1
τέλος ἔχω (VKb)	22,37		0	1

Literature

SCHÜRMANN 1957 129 [τέλος ἔχει: luk R weniger wahrscheinlich].

BARTSCH, Hans-Werner, Jesu Schwertwort, Lukas XXII. 35-38: Überlieferungsgeschichtliche Studie. — NTS 20 (1973-74) 190-203. Esp. 196-198: "Die Handschrift des Lukas".

DU PLESSIS, Paul Johannes, Τέλειος: The Idea of Perfection in the New Testament. Kampen: Kok, 1959, 255 p. — Diss. Kampen, 1959 (dir. H.N. Ridderbos). Esp. 122-168: "The N.T. significance of τέλος".

MATUJINGA, N., Τέλος dans l'eschatologie du Nouveau Testament. Diss. Genève, 1990 (dir. F. Bovon).

PRÜMM, Karl, Das neutestamentliche Sprach- und Begriffsproblem der Vollkommenheit. — Bib 44 (1963) 76-92.

τελώνης 10 (Mt 8/9, Mk 3)   tax collector

Word groups	Lk	Acts	Mt	Mk
τελώνης + proper name (VKc)	5,27		1	0

τελῶναι καὶ ἁμαρτωλοί (VKa); cf. τελώνης + ἁμαρτωλός Lk 18,13; ἀρχιτελώνης + ἁμαρτωλός Lk 19,2(-7)	5,30; 7,34; 15,1		3	3

Characteristic of Luke	Lk	Acts	Mt	Mk
τέλωνης, approvingly GOULDER 1989	3,12; 5,27.28.30; 7,29.34; 15,1; 18,10.11.13		6	2

Literature

BDAG 2000 989 [literature].

BARTELINK, Gerhardus J.M., Τελῶναι (Zöllner) als Dämonenbezeichnung. — Sacris Erudiri (Steenbrugge) 27 (1984) 5-18.
BORMANN, Lukas, Recht, Gerechtigkeit und Religion, 2001. Esp. 139.
MAHFOUZ, Hady, La fonction littéraire et théologique de Lc 3,1-20, 2003. Esp. 224-231.

τελώνιον 1 (Mt 1, Mk 1)	tax office (Lk 5,27)

τέσσαρες 1 + 6 (Mt 1, Mk 2)	four

Word groups	Lk	Acts	Mt	Mk
ὀγδοήκοντα τέσσαρες (VKb)	2,37		0	0

τεσσεράκοντα 1 + 8 (Mt 2, Mk 1)	forty (Lk 4,2)

Word groups	Lk	Acts	Mt	Mk
τεσσεράκοντα ἔτη (LN: very long time); cf. Heb 3,10.17; cf. τεσσερακονταετής Acts 7,23; 13,18 BOISMARD 1984 Ba14		4,22; 7,30.36.42; 13,21	0	0

τετρααρχέω** 3	be a tetrarch (Lk $3,1^{1.2.3}$)

Word groups	Lk	Acts	Mt	Mk
τετρααρχέω + Ἡρῴδης → Ἡρῴδης ὁ **τετραάρχης**; **Herodes** Antipas tetrarch	$3,1^{1}$		0	0

Literature

DENAUX 2009 L^{n}; HAUCK 1934 [seltenes Alleinwort]; JEREMIAS 1980 103 [red.].

BORMANN, Lukas, Recht, Gerechtigkeit und Religion, 2001. Esp. 124.

τετραάρχης 2 + 1 (Mt 1)	tetrarch

Word groups	Lk	Acts	Mt	Mk
Ἡρῴδης ὁ τετραάρχης → **τετρααρχέω** + Ἡρῴδης; **Herodes** Antipas tetrarch	3,19; 9,7	13,1	1	0

Characteristic of Luke
PLUMMER 1922 lx

Literature
JEREMIAS 1980 103 [red.].
BORMANN, Lukas, *Recht, Gerechtigkeit und Religion*, 2001. Esp. 124-125.

τετραπλοῦς* 1	four times (Lk 19,8)

Literature
HAUCK 1934 [seltenes Alleinwort].

Τιβέριος 1	Tiberius

Word groups	Lk	Acts	Mt	Mk
Τιβέριος Καῖσαρ	3,1		0	0

τίθημι 16 + 23 (Mt 5/6, Mk 11/12)

1. put (Lk 11,33); 2. appoint (Acts 13,47); 3. take off; 4. explain; 5. deposit (Lk 19,21); 6. cause to be (Acts 1,7); 7. cause to experience (Lk 20,43)

Word groups	Lk	Acts	Mt	Mk
αἴρω + τίθημι	19,21.22		0	1
θεμέλιον (+) τίθημι DENAUX 2009 L[n]	6,48; 14,29		0	0
τίθεμαι + εἰς τὰ ὦτα (*LN*: [a]listen carefully to; [b]remember well; *SC*b)	9,[b]44		0	0
τίθημι with double accusative (*VK*p) DENAUX 2009 IA[n]	20,43	2,35; 20,28	0/1	0/1
τίθημι βουλήν (*LN*: advise; *SC*b)		27,12	0	0
τίθημι (+) ἐν (*VK*c) → τίθημι ἐν **μνήματι**	1,66; 21,14; 23,53	1,7; 5,4.18.25; 7,16; 9,37; 19,21; 20,28	1/2	4
τίθημι (+) ἐν μνημείῳ / ἐν (τῷ) μνήματι / εἰς μνημεῖον and similar phrases (*SC*c)	23,53.55	7,16; 13,29	1	2
τίθεμαι (+) ἐν τῇ καρδίᾳ (*LN*: treasure up in mind; *SC*b) DENAUX 2009 LA[n]	1,66	5,4	0	0
τίθεμαι (+) ἐν τῷ πνεύματι (*LN*: make up mind; *SC*b)		19,21	0	0
τίθημι ἐν τῇ φυλακῇ / εἰς φυλακήν → **βάλλω/κατακλείω/παραδίδωμι** εἰς (τὴν) φυλακήν / ἐν (τῇ) φυλακῇ; cf. ἀποτίθεμαι ἐν φυλακῇ Mt 14,3		5,25; 12,4	0/1	0
τίθημι ἐνώπιον (*VK*d)	5,18		0	0
τίθημι + ἐπί + accusative (*VK*f)	6,48; 11,33	21,5	2	2/3
τίθημι (+) ἐπί + genitive (*VK*e) DENAUX 2009 LA[n]	8,16[2]	5,15	0	0
τίθημι (+) μετά + genitive (*VK*g)	12,46		1	0
τίθημι (+) παρά + accusative (*VK*j)		4,35.37 *v.l.*; 5,2	0	0
τίθημι (+) παρὰ/πρὸς τοὺς πόδας (*LN*: turn over to); cf. ἀποτίθεμαι παρὰ τοὺς πόδας Acts 7,58		4,35.37; 5,2	0	0
τίθημι (+) πρός + accusative (*VK*k)		3,2; 4,37	0	0
τίθημι ὑπό + accusative (*VK*l)	11,33v.l.?		1	0
τίθημι + ὑποκάτω + genitive (*VK*m)	8,16[1]		1	1

Characteristic of Luke	Lk	Acts	Mt	Mk
θεὶς τὰ γόνατα (*LN*: kneel down; *SC*a); cf. τιθεὶς τὰ γόνατα Mk 15,19; κάμπτω γόνυ Rom 11,4; 14,11; Eph 3,14; Phil 2,10 BOISMARD 1984 bb64; CREDNER 1836 139; HARNACK 1906 53; HAWKINS 1909 187; NEIRYNCK 1985; VOGEL 1899C	22,41	7,60; 9,40; 20,36; 21,5	0	0
τίθημι εἰς (*VK*b) DENAUX 2009 IA*	9,44; 11,33; 21,14 *v.l.*	4,3; 12,4; 13,29.47	0	0
τίθημι εἰς τὴν καρδίαν VOGEL 1899C	21,14 *v.l.*			
τίθημι ἐν τῇ καρδίᾳ BOISMARD 1984 Ab130; NEIRYNCK 1985; VOGEL 1899C	1,66; 21,14	5,4	0	0
τίθημι ἐν τῷ πνεύματι VOGEL 1899C		19,21	0	0

Literature

VON BENDEMANN 2001 415 [τίθεσθαι εἰς]; COLLISON 1977 66 [linguistic usage of Luke: certain; + ἐν καρδίᾳ; + οὓς: noteworthy phenomena]; DENAUX 2009 La^n [τίθημι ἐν τῇ καρδίᾳ, εἰς τὴν καρδίαν], IA^n [θεὶς τὰ γόνατα]; EASTON 1910 158 [τίθεσθαι ἐν ταῖς καρδίαις: probably characteristic of L]; 161 [θεμέλιον τίθημι: cited by Weiss as characteristic of L, and possibly corroborative]; GERSDORF 1816 205 [καὶ ἔθεντο - ἐν τῇ καρδίᾳ αὐτῶν]; HAUCK 1934 [Vorzugsverbindung: θεὶς τὰ γόνατα]; JEREMIAS 1980 71: "Wendungen mit übertragenem τίθημι + folgendem ἐν ('zu Herzen nehmen', 'sich vornehmen') schreibt im NT nur Lukas"; 294: "τιθέναι τὰ γόνατα ('die Knie beugen') ist eine fest eingebürgerte, jedoch nicht klassische Wendung, die sich im NT außer Mk 15,19 nur im lk Doppelwerk findet ..., gern mit προσεύχομαι verbunden"; RADL 1975 404 [θεὶς τὰ γόνατα + προσεύχομαι]; 428 [τίθημι; τίθεμαι ἐν καρδίᾳ].

CLAEREBOETS, Ch., In quo vos Spiritus Sanctus posuit episcopus regere ecclesiam Dei (Apg 20,28). — *Bib* 24 (1943) 370-387 [ἔθετο].

DUPONT, Jacques, *Le discours de Milet*, 1962. Esp. 107.159-162; 342-344 [τίθημι τὰ γόνατα].

FUCHS, Albert, *Sprachliche Untersuchungen zu Mattäus und Lukas*, 1971. Esp. 175-178 [θέτε οὖν ἐν ταῖς καρδίαις ὑμῶν].

τίκτω 5 (Mt 4)

1. give birth (Lk 1,31.57; 2,6.7.11); 2. grow

Literature

GERSDORF 1816 220 [ἔτεκεν τὸν υἱὸν αὐτῆς τὸν πρωτότοκον].

VICENT CERNUDA, Antonio, El paralelismo de γεννῶ y τίκτω en Lc 1–2. — *Bib* 55 (1974) 260-264.

τίλλω 1 (Mt 1, Mk 1)   pick (Lk 6,1)

Literature

DELEBECQUE, Édouard, *Études grecques*, 1976. Esp. 71-83: "Les moissonneurs du sabbat (6,1)".

τιμάω 1 + 1 (Mt 6, Mk 3)

1. honor (Lk 18,20); 2. set price on; 3. assist

Word groups	Lk	Acts	Mt	Mk
τιμάω τιμή (*VK*b) HARNACK 1906 43		28,10	1	0

τίς 114/120 + 55/58 (Mt 91, Mk 72/76)   who? what?

Word groups	Lk	Acts	Mt	Mk
διὰ τί (*SC*c; *VK*e)	5,30.33*; 19,23.31; 20,5; 24,38[2]	5,3	7	3
διὰ τί + ὅτι	19,31		1	0
εἰς τί (*SC*d; *VK*f) → εἰς αὐτό/οὐδέν/τοῦτο		19,3	2	2
ἢ τίς/τί/ἐν τίνι	12,11[1.2].29 *v.l.*; 14,31; 15,8; 20,2	3,12[2]; 7,49	4	2/3
κατὰ τί	1,18		0	0
τί + adjective (*VK*n)	23,22	26,8	5	2
τί + ἐμοὶ/ἡμῖν + καὶ σοί (*SC*l)	4,34[1]; 8,28		1	2
τί ἔτι (*VK*c)	22,71		2	2
τίνος ἕνεκα/ἕνεκεν → οὗ εἵνεκεν/ἕνεκεν		19,32	0	0
τί οὖν ἐστιν; (*VK*j)		21,22	0	0
τίς followed by a subjunctive (*VK*k)	3,10.12.14; 7,31[1]; 11,5; 12,5.11[1.2].17.22[1.2].29[1.2]; 13,18[2].20; 16,3; 19,48; 20,13; 23,31	2,37; 4,16; 22,10; 25,26	12	12/14
τίς + partitive genitive (*SC*a; *VK*a)	7,42; 10,36; 11,11 *v.l.*; 14,5; 20,33; 22,24	7,52; 19,35	1	1
(τὸ) τίς/τί + ἄν + optative; cf. Jn 13,24	1,62; 6,11; 9,46; 15,26; 18,36 *v.l.*	2,12 *v.l.*; 5,24; 10,17; 17,18.20 *v.l.*; 21,33[1] *v.l.*	0	0
τίς ἄρα / τί ἄρα (*SC*j)	1,66; 8,25; 12,42; 22,23	12,18	4	1
τίς (+) ἐκ (*SC*b; *VK*b) → εἷς/τις ἐκ; cf. τίς ἀπό Mt 27,21	11,5.11; 12,25; 14,28; 15,4; 17,7; 22,23		4	0
τίς ... ὅς	5,21[1]; 7,49; 9,9; 12,42; 17,7; 24,17	10,17.21; 19,35; 23,19	3	2
τίς (+) ὅτι → τί ὅτι	2,49; 4,36; 8,25; 12,17; 16,3	5,4.9	4	3/6
τίς οὖν	3,10; 7,31.42; 10,36*; 20,5*.15.17	19,3; 21,22	4	3
τίς as adjective in prepositive position (*SC*e)	11,11; 14,31; 15,4.8; 18,18; 23,22	10,29; 24,20	5	2
τί as adverb: how? (including exclamations) (*SC*h)	12,49		1	0
τί as adverb: why? (*SC*g)	2,48; 5,22; 6,2.41.46; 12,26.57; 18,19; 19,33; 22,46.71; 24,5.38[1]	1,11; 3,12[1.2]; 9,4; 14,15; 15,10; 21,13; 22,7.30; 26,8.14	11	15

→ ἐστιν/γίνεται τί σοι; ἔχω τί; τί κωλύει; τίς ὑμῶν

Characteristic of Luke	Lk	Acts	Mt	Mk
γινώσκω + τίς/τί DENAUX 2009 L***	1,18; 7,39; 10,22[1]; 16,4; 19,15	17,19.20	2	0
πυνθάνομαι τίς/τί εἴη; cf. Jn 13,24 BOISMARD 1984 Ab144; NEIRYNCK 1985	15,26; 18,36	21,23	0	0
τί ὅτι (*VK*d) → τίς + ὅτι BOISMARD 1984 Ab148; HARNACK 1906 149; NEIRYNCK 1985; VOGEL 1899C	2,49	5,4.9	0	0/1

τί ποιήσω DENAUX 2009 L***	12,17; 16,3.4; 20,13	22,10	0	1
τίς as adjective in postpositive position (SCf; VKm) DENAUX 2009 La*	14,31; 15,4.8	10,29	1	0
τίς + partitive genitive DENAUX 2009 L***; GOULDER 1989	7,42; 10,36; 11,11 v.l.; 14,5; 20,33; 22,24	7,52; 19,35	1	1
τίς followed by (ἄν +) optative (VKl) BOISMARD 1984 Bb12; DENAUX 2009 L***; GOULDER 1989*; HAWKINS 1909L; NEIRYNCK 1985	1,62; 6,11; 8,9; 9,46; 15,26; 18,36; 22,23	2,12; 5,24; 10,17; 17,18.20 v.l.; 21,33[1]	0	0
τίς ἐστιν οὗτος DENAUX 2009 L***; PLUMMER 1922 lxiii	5,21[1]; 7,49; 8,25; 9,9		1	1
τίς ἐξ ὑμῶν DENAUX 2009 L***; HAWKINS 1909L; PLUMMER 1922 lx	11,5; 11,11; 12,25; 14,5.28; 15,4; 17,7		2	0
τὸ τίς/τί (nominalized indirect question) (SCk) → τὸ πῶς; cf. Rom 8,26 BOISMARD 1984 Bb53; DENAUX 2009 L***; GOULDER 1989*; HAWKINS 1909L; NEIRYNCK 1985	1,62; 9,46; 19,48; 22,23.24	22,30	0	0

Literature

VON BENDEMANN 2001 414 [τίς ἀνήρ]; COLLISON 1977 111 [τίς οὖν: linguistic usage of Luke: likely]; 132 [τίς ἐξ ὑμῶν: linguistic usage of Luke's "other source-material": likely]; 209 [τίς + optative: linguistic usage of Luke: certain; τίς + subjunctive of ποιέω: linguistic usage of Luke's "other source-material": probable; τίς introducing parables: certain]; 210 [τίς + inferential particle: linguistic usage of Luke: likely]; DENAUX 2009 La[n] [πυνθάνομαι τίς/τί εἴη], LA[n] [τί ὅτι]; GERSDORF 1816 204 [τὸ τί ἂν θέλοι]; 205 [τί ἄρα τὸ παιδίον τοῦτο ἔσται]; 270 [τί ὅτι ἐζητεῖτέ με]; HAUCK 1934 [Vorzugsverbindung: τί ἄν + optative; τίς ἐξ ὑμῶν; Stileigentümlichkeit: τὸ τίς]; JEREMIAS 1980 67 [τὸ τί: red.]; 72 [τί ἄρα: red.]; 101 [τί ὅτι: trad.]; 173 [τίς οὗτος ἐστιν: red.]; 256 [τί ποιήσω: red.]; RADL 1975 419 [τό vor interrogativem τίς]; 428 [τίς + opt.]; REHKOPF 1959 97 [τίς/τί ἄρα: vorlukanisch]; SCHÜRMANN 1957 12-13.66 [τίς + gen. part. für Luk charakteristisch]; 81 [τίς für πότερος: luk R weniger wahrscheinlich]; 1961 273 [τίς/τί ἄρα].

BLACK, Matthew, *Aramaic Approach*, [3]1967. Esp. 121-124 [Lk 12,49].
DELEBECQUE, Éduoard, *Études grecques*, 1976. Esp. 41-42 [τί ὅτι].
WARD, Ronald A., St. Luke xii.49: καὶ τί θέλω εἰ ἤδη ἀνήφθη. — *ExpT* 63 (1951-52) 92-93.

τις 80/82 + 115/122 (Mt 21/24, Mk 32[33]/39)

1. someone, something (Lk 23,8); 2. someone important (Acts 5,36)

Word groups	Lk	Acts	Mt	Mk
number + τις	7,18; 22,50	23,23	0	1/2
ἐάν / καθότι ἄν + τις (SCg; VKk); cf. ἐὰν μή τις Acts 8,31; κἄν + τις Mk [16,18]	16,30.31; 19,31; 20,28	2,45; 4,35; 9,2; 13,41	5	3
εἴ (...) τις (SCf; VKj)	9,23; 14,26; 19,8[1.2]	13,15; 18,14; 19,38.39; 21,37; 24,19[2].20*; 25,5.11	2	7/8
εἰμί τις (LN: be important)		5,36; 8,9[2]	0	0
εἷς τις / δύο τινές (VKc)	7,18; 22,50	23,23	0	1/2
ἕτερός τις → ἄλλος τις		8,34; 27,1	0	0
μή/μηδὲ/μήτι ... τις (SCe; VKh)	11,36; 12,4	10,47	1/2	1/2

μή τις (SCd; VKg)	22,35	8,31; 27,42	1	1/3
οὐ/οὐδέ/οὐδείς/οὔτε ... τις (SCc; VKf) DENAUX 2009 lAn	8,51; 12,15	4,32.34; 17,25; 24,12; 25,8.16.26; 26,26v.l.?.31v.l.?; 28,21[1.2]	3	0/1
τις with partitive genitive (SCa; VKa)	6,2; 7,18.36; 9,8[2].19.27; 11,1[2].45; 14,1.15; 19,39; 20,27.39; 24,24	4,32; 5,15; 6,9; 10,23; 11,29; 12,1; 15,5; 17,5.18[1].28; 19,13.31; 23,9.12*.23; 26,26; 27,44; 28,21[1]	5	9
τις adjective + noun + ὀνόματι + proper name		5,34; 9,10.36; 16,14; 18,2; 20,9; 21,10	0	0
τις (+) ἐκ (SCb; VKb) → εἷς/τίς ἐκ, except εἷς τις / δύο τινές; ἄλλος/ἕτερός τις; cf. τίς ἀπό Acts 19,13 v.l.	11,15.54; 12,13	11,20; 15,2.24; 17,4	0	1
τις ἐκ τοῦ ὄχλου → ἀνήρ ἀπὸ τοῦ ὄχλου; γυνὴ ἐκ τοῦ ὄχλου	12,13		0	0

→ ἀνήρ τις; κριτής τις; τις τῶν μαθητῶν; τις ... ὅς; χρόνος τις

Characteristic of Luke

GOULDER 1989; HENDRIKS 1986 428.434.448.468; MORGENTHALER 1958LA

	Lk	Acts	Mt	Mk
noun + δέ τις BOISMARD 1984 Ab3; DENAUX 2009 L***; NEIRYNCK 1985	7,2; 10,33.38; 16,19.20	5,1; 8,9; 10,1; 18,24; 25,19; 27,16.26.39	0	0
noun + τις + adjective/participle BOISMARD 1984 Ab11; DENAUX 2009 L***; NEIRYNCK 1985	10,33; 11,36; 12,16; 19,12; 23,19.26	16,16; 17,5; 21,16; 27,8	0	0
noun + τις adjective + ὀνόματι + proper name; cf. ἀνὴρ δέ τις Ἀνανίας ὀνόματι Acts 5,1; Ἰουδαῖος δέ τις Ἀπολλῶς ὀνόματι Acts 18,24 DENAUX 2009 lA*	1,5; 10,38[2]; 16,20	8,9[1]; 9,33; 10,1; 16,1	0	0
participle + δέ τις BOISMARD 1984 Bb54; DENAUX 2009 LA*; NEIRYNCK 1985	14,15; 20,27.39	5,25.34; 20,9	0	1
ἄλλος τις / ἄλλο τι (VKd) → ἕτερός τις BOISMARD 1984 Db29; NEIRYNCK 1985	22,59	15,2; 19,32; 21,34	0	0
τι and epithet; cf. Jn 5,14 BOISMARD 1984 Eb18; NEIRYNCK 1985	12,4	17,21; 19,32; 21,34; 23,20; 25,11.26; 28,21	0	0
τις as adjective in postpositive position (SCh; VKl), except εἷς τις / δύο τινές; ἄλλος/ἕτερός τις; cf. Jn 12,20; Rom 15,26; 1 Cor 4,2; 5,1; 7,13; 11,18; 16,7; Col 2,23; James 1,18; 2 Pet 3,16 BOISMARD 1984 Bb58; DENAUX 2009 L***; HAWKINS 1909L, NEIRYNCK 1985	1,5; 7,2.41; 8,2.27; 9,8[2].19; 10,25.30.31.33.38[1.2]; 11,1[1].36.37*; 12,4.16; 14,2.16; 15,11; 16,1.19.20; 18,2[1].35; 19,12; 20,9; 22,56; 23,19.26; 24,22	4,34; 5,1.2.34*; 8,9[1]; 9,19.33; 10,1.5.11.48; 11,5; 13,6; 16,1.1*.9.12.16; 17,5.20; 18,14.23.24; 19,9*.24.32; 21,16.34; 22,12; 24,1[1.2].24; 25,11.13.14.19[1].26; 26,31; 27,8.16.26.39	0/2	1/2[3]
τις as adjective in prepositive position (SCj; VKm), except	11,27.36 v.l.; 12,4 v.l.; 13,31; 17,12;	3,2; 5,34; 8,9[2].36; 9,10.36.43; 10,6; 13,1*.6	1	1

εἷς τις / δύο τινές; ἄλλος/ἕτερός τις DENAUX 2009 L***;GOULDER 1989*; HAWKINS 1909L; PLUMMER 1922 lxiii	18,2².9.18; 21,2; 23,8; 24,41	v.l.15; 14,8; 15,2.36; 16,14; 17,5 v.l.6.21².34; 18,2.7; 19,1.14; 20,9; 21,10; 23,20; 24,19¹.20; 25,5.16.19²; 27,27; 28,3.21²		
τις + proper name BOISMARD 1984 Bb16; DENAUX 2009 IA*; NEIRYNCK 1985	10,33; 23,26	9,43; 10,5.6; 19,14.24; 21,16; 22,12; 24,1; 25,19	0	1
τις + ἐξ DENAUX 2009 IA*; GOULDER 1989	11,15; 22,50; 24,22	11,20; 15,2.24; 17,4	0	0
τις/τινες τῶν + preposition + noun/pronoun BOISMARD 1984 Bb63; NEIRYNCK 1985	24,24	6,9; 12,1; 15,5; 27,44	0	0
τις ... ὅς/ὅστις BOISMARD 1984 cb81; DENAUX 2009 IA*; NEIRYNCK 1985	8,2.27 v.l.; 9,27; 16,1.20 v.l.	3,2; 8,9¹(-10); 9,33; 10,5.6. 11(-12); 11,20; 13,6; 14,8; 15,24; 16,1(-2).14.16; 17,34; 18,7; 21,16; 24,1². 19¹; 24,14(-15).19²; 27,8. 39	1/2	1/3

→ ἄνθρωπός τις; τι ἄξιον θανάτου πράσσω; γυνή τις;; ἡμέραι τινες; ἱερεύς τις; οἵ/τινες ἀπό + place + Ἰουδαῖοι; οὐ + τις

Literature

COLLISON 1977 130 [τις ἐκ: noteworthy phenomena]; 210-211 [linguistic usage of Luke: certain; linguistic usage of Luke's "other source-material": also certain]; 211 [τις + noun: linguistic usage of Luke: certain. It may also have been a linguistic usage of Luke's "other source-material"; τις + noun beginning parable: linguistic usage of Luke's "other source-material": certain]; 212 [ἄνθρωπος = τις: linguistic usage of Luke: probable; ἄνθρωπός τις: linguistic usage of Luke's "other source-material": certain]; 213 [ἀνήρ = τις: linguistic usage of Luke's "other source-material": probable]; COLLISON 1977 64 [linguistic usage of Luke's "other source-material": probable]; DENAUX 2009 lAn, IAⁿ [ἄλλος τις / ἄλλο τι, τι and epithet, τις as adjective in postpositive position, τις/τινες τῶν + preposition + noun/pronoun]; HARNACK 1906 39 [Ad Acta 28,3: Zu diesem Gebrauch von τι vgl. Luk. 23,8; 24,41; Act. 5,2; 8,36; 11,5; 18,14; 25,19; es ist innerhalb des N.T. für Lukas charakteristisch]; HAUCK 1934 [Vorzugsverbindung: ἀνήρ / ἄνθρωπός / γυνή τις; ἱερεύς τις; κριτής τις; κώμη τις; παιδίσκη τις; προφήτης τις; πτωχός τις; Σίμων τις; Σαμαρίτης τις; στάσις τις; τόπος τις; τις χήρα; χρόνος τις]; JEREMIAS 1980 15: "Adjektivisches τις findet sich im NT gehäuft im lukanischen Doppelwerk ... Spezifisch lukanisch ist insbesondere die Wortfolge: Nomen + adjektivisches τις + ὀνόματι + Eigenname"; RADL 1975 398 [ἄλλο τι]; 399 [ἀνήρ τις]; 428-429 [τις "mit einem Nomen"; τις dem Substantiv nachgestellt; τις ὀνόματι]; REHKOPF 1959 91 [ἄνθρωπός τις: vorlukanisch]; SCHNEIDER 1969 79.87.164: "Dann aber ist das dem Substantivum nachgestellte τις dem Luk eigentümlich" [Vorzugswörter und -ausdrücke des Luk]; SCHÜRMANN 1957 8-9 [Luk ersetzt εἷς durch τις]; 13, n. 58 [τις + gen. part.]; 120 [μή τις (τι): luk R möglich, aber nicht beweisbar].

DICKERSON, Patrick L., The New Character Narrative in Luke-Acts, 1997. Esp. 293-298: "The elements of the Lukan new character narrative" [τις/ἰδοὺ ἀνὴρ/γυνὴ ὀνόματι]; 301-303: "The use of the word τις in the introduction".

HEIMERDINGER, Jenny, Word Order in Koine Greek, 1996. Esp. 164-167: "τις"; = READ-HEIMERDINGER, Jenny, The Bezan Text of Acts, 2002. Esp. 99-102.

NEIRYNCK, Frans, La matière marcienne dans l'évangile de Luc, 1973. Esp. 183 [τις + nouns]; ²1989. Esp. 93; = ID., Evangelica, 1982. Esp. 63.

τοίνυν 1 | therefore (Lk 20,25)

Literature

HAUCK 1934 [seltenes Alleinwort].

τοιοῦτος 2/3 + 4/5 (Mt 3, Mk 6/7)

1. like that (Lk 9,9; 13,2*); 2. of such a kind (Lk 18,16; Acts 22,22)

Word groups	Lk	Acts	Mt	Mk
τοιοῦτος ὁποῖος (*VK*c)		26,29	0	0
τοιοῦτος as adjective (*VK*a)		16,24	2	4/5

τόκος 1 (Mt 1) | interest (Lk 19,23)

τολμάω 1 + 2 (Mt 1, Mk 2) | dare (Lk 20,40; Acts 5,13; 7,32)

τόπος 19/20 + 18 (Mt 10, Mk 10)

1. place (Lk 2,7; 14,22); 2. passage (Lk 4,17); 3. task (Acts 1,25); 4. position (Acts 1,25); 5. possibility (Acts 25,16); 7. people

Word groups	Lk	Acts	Mt	Mk
γενόμενος ἐπὶ τοῦ τόπου / κατὰ τὸν τόπον DENAUX 2009 L[n]	10,32; 22,40		0	0
ἐπὶ τοῦ τόπου DENAUX 2009 L[n]	6,17; 22,40		0	0
κατὰ τοῦ τόπου → κατὰ τοῦ **νόμου** BOISMARD 1984 Aa145		6,13; 21,28[1]	0	0
κατὰ τόπους (*VK*d)	21,11		1	1
πᾶς + τόπος (*VK*c)	4,37; 10,1		0	0
τόπος + δίδωμι (*VK*e)	14,9[1]		0	0
τόπος with proper noun (*VK*f)	23,33	27,8	2	2
τόπος (+) ἅγιος (*VK*a) → **γῆ** ἁγία		6,13; 21,28[2]	1	0
τόπος διθάλασσος (*LN*: reef)		27,41	0	0
τόπος ἐκεῖνος		16,3; 28,7	0	0
τόπος ἔρημος (*LN*: lonely place; *VK*b)	4,42; 9,10*.12		2	5
τόπος (+) ἐστιν	2,7; 14,22		0	0
τόπος οὗ	4,17; 10,1		0	0
τόποι plural (except *VK*d) (*VK*g)	11,24		16,3; 27,2.29	1	1
τόπος = temple of Jerusalem; cf. Jn 11,48 BOISMARD 1984 Ba18		6,13.14; 21,28[1.2]	0	0

Characteristic of Luke				
GOULDER 1989				
	Lk	Acts	Mt	Mk
πορεύομαι εἰς (τὸν) τόπον BOISMARD 1984 Ab140; NEIRYNCK 1985	4,42; 14,10	1,25[2]; 12,17	0	0

Literature

DENAUX 2009 LAⁿ [πορεύομαι εἰς (τὸν) τόπον]; EASTON 1910 158 [τόπος after ἐπί: probably characteristic of L]; 165 [τόπος ἐστιν "there is room": cited by Weiss as characteristic of L, and possibly corroborative]; HARNACK 1906 41 [τόπος ἐκεῖνος]; HAUCK 1934 [Vorzugsverbindung: τόπος τις]; JEREMIAS 1980 293 [ἐπὶ τοῦ τόπου red.]; RADL 1975 429.

DELEBECQUE, Edouard, De la naissance de Jésus à la naissance d'une foi (sur un emploi "divin" du grec τόπος chez Luc et Jean). — *RBgPg* 63 (1985) 92-98.

τοσοῦτος 2 + 2 (Mt 3)

1. so many (Lk 15,29); 2. so much (Lk 7,9); 3. to the degree that

τότε 15 + 21 (Mt 90/91, Mk 6) — then

Word groups	Lk	Acts	Mt	Mk
ἀπὸ τότε (SCa; VKb)	16,16		3	0
εὐθέως δὲ τότε (VKj)		17,14	0	0
ὅταν ... τότε (SCc; VKd)	5,35; 11,24v.l.?; 21,20		3	2
πρῶτον ... τότε (SCd; VKf)	6,42		3	1

Literature

BDR § 459,2 [τότε as a connective particle: Lk 14,21; 21,10; 24,45; Acts 1,12; 4,8 etc.]; COLLISON 1977 162 [avoided: linguistic usage of Luke: nearly certain]; HARNACK 1906 38 [ad Acts 28,1, for this use see Lk 21,10; Acts 1,12; 6,11; 25,12; 26,1; 28,1]; RADL 1975 429.

LEVISOHN, Stephen H., *Textual Connections in Acts*, 1987. Esp. 151-153: "tote".
READ-HEIMERDINGER, Jenny, *The Bezan Text of Acts*, 2002. Esp. 211-225: "τότε".

τράπεζα 4 + 2 (Mt 2, Mk 2)

1. table (Lk 16,21; 22,1.30); 2. meal (Acts 16,34); 3. bank (Lk 19,23)

Word groups	Lk	Acts	Mt	Mk
διακονέω τραπέζαις (LN: handle finances)			6,2	0	0

Characteristic of Luke

GOULDER 1989

Literature

SCHÜRMANN 1957 18.48 [kein luk Vorzugswort].

τραῦμα 1 — wound (Lk 10,34)

Literature

HAUCK 1934 [seltenes Alleinwort].

τραυματίζω 1 + 1 — hurt, wound (Lk 20,12; Acts 19,16)

Characteristic of Luke
BOISMARD 1984 Ab206; HAWKINS 1909LA; MORGENTHALER 1958*; NEIRYNCK 1985;
PLUMMER 1922 liii; -VOGEL 1899A

Literature
DENAUX 2009 LAⁿ; HAUCK 1934 [seltenes Alleinwort].

τράχηλος 2 + 2 (Mt 1, Mk 1)   neck (Lk 15,20; 17,2)

Word groups	Lk	Acts	Mt	Mk
ἐπιπίπτω ἐπὶ τὸν τράχηλον (LN: embrace)	15,20	20,37	0	0
ἐπιτίθημι ζυγὸν ἐπὶ τὸν τράχηλον (LN: load down with obligations)		15,10	0	0

Characteristic of Luke	Lk	Acts	Mt	Mk
ἐπὶ τὸν τράχηλον BOISMARD 1984 Ab149; NEIRYNCK 1985	15,20	15,10; 20,37	0	0

Literature
DENAUX 2009 IAⁿ.

τραχύς 1 + 1   rough (Lk 3,5; Acts 27,29)

Characteristic of Luke
HARNACK 1906 54; HAWKINS 1909LA; MORGENTHALER 1958*; PLUMMER 1922 liii; VOGEL 1899A

Literature
DENAUX 2009 LAⁿ; HAUCK 1934 [seltenes Alleinwort].

Τραχωνῖτις 1   Trachonitis (Lk 3,1)

τρεῖς 10 + 14 (Mt 12, Mk 7)   three

Word groups	Lk	Acts	Mt	Mk
δύο + τρεῖς (VKc)	12,52[1.2]		2	0
εἷς + τρεῖς	9,33		3	3
τρεῖς with reference to time (ἡμέραι, ἔτη,...) (SCa)	1,56; 2,46; 4,25; 13,7	5,7; 7,20; 9,9; 17,2; 19,8; 20,3; 25,1; 28,7.11.12.17	8	6
τρεῖς following a substantive (VKe) DENAUX 2009 lAn	1,56; 2,46; 4,25; 9,33; 13,21	5,7; 7,20; 9,9; 10,19; 17,2; 19,8; 20,3; 28,7.12.17	2	2
Τρεῖς Ταβέρναι (VKd)		28,15	0	0
→ ἐπὶ **σαββάτα** τρία				

Literature
BDAG 2000 1014 [literature].

τρέμω 1 + 0/1 (Mk 1)

1. tremble (Lk 8,47; Acts 9,6*); 2. fear; 3. respect

τρέφω 3 + 1 (Mt 2)

1. provide food for (Lk 12,24; 23,29; Acts 12,20); 2. take care of; 3. rear (Lk 4,16)

Characteristic of Luke; cf. ἀνατρέφω Lk 4,16; Acts 7,20.21; 22,3
PLUMMER 1922 lx

τρέχω 2 (Mt 2, Mk 2)

1. run (Lk 15,20; 24,12); 2. try; 3. behave

Word groups	Lk	Acts	Mt	Mk
τρέχω ἐπί + accusative (VKc)	24,12		1	0

τρῆμα 1 (Mt 0/1)   eye of needle (Lk 18,25)

τριάκοντα 1 (Mt 5, Mk 2)   thirty (Lk 3,23)

τρίβος 1 (Mt 1, Mk 1)   path (Lk 3,4)

τρίς 2 + 2 (Mt 2, Mk 2)   three times (Lk 22,34.61; Acts 10,16; 11,10)

Word groups	Lk	Acts	Mt	Mk
ἐπὶ τρίς (VKa)		10,16; 11,10	0	0

τρίτος 10 + 4 (Mt 7, Mk 3/5)   third

Word groups	Lk	Acts	Mt	Mk
ἀνίστημι/ἐγείρω τῇ τρίτῃ ἡμέρᾳ; cf. ἀνίστημι/ἐγείρω μετὰ τρεῖς ἡμέρας Mt 27,63; Mk 8,31; 9,31; 10,34	9,22; 18,33; 24,7.46	10,40	3	0/1
τῇ τρίτῃ (VKb) DENAUX 2009 LAⁿ	13,32	27,19	0	0
τρίτη ἡμέρα → ὥρα τρίτη	9,22; 18,33; 24,7.21.46	10,40	4	0/2
(τὸ) τρίτον(VKc)	23,22		0	1
τρίτος with reference to time (SCa)	9,22; 12,38; 18,33; 24,7.21.46	2,15; 10,40; 23,23; 27,19	5	1/3
τρίτος + δεύτερος (VKe)	12,38; 20,30(-31)		2	1
τρίτος + ἕτερος (VKe)	20,11(-12)		0	0
ὥρα τρίτη → τρίτη ἡμέρα; ὥρα ἕκτη/ἐνάτη		2,15; 23,23	1	1

Literature

DE JONGE, Henk J., Sonship, Wisdom, Infancy: Luke II.41-51a. — *NTS* 24 (1977-78) 317-354. Esp. 324-327 "After three days".

PERRY, John M., The Three Days in the Synoptic Passion Predictions. — *CBQ* 48 (1986) 637-654. [τῇ τρίτῃ ἡμέρᾳ]

τρόπος 1 + 4 (Mt 1)

1. manner (Lk 13,34; Acts 7,28); 2. way of life

Word groups	Lk	Acts	Mt	Mk
οὕτως ... ὃν τρόπον BOISMARD 1984 AA149		1,11; 27,25	0	0
καθ' ὃν τρόπον BOISMARD 1984 Aa163; PLUMMER 1922 lx		15,11; 27,25	0	0

τροφή 1 + 7 (Mt 4)   food (Lk 12,23)

Word groups	Lk	Acts	Mt	Mk
λαμβάνω τροφήν / μεταλαμβάνω τροφῆς / προσλαμβάνομαι τροφῆς (VKa) BOISMARD 1984 Aa35		2,46; 9,19; 27,33.34.36	0	0

Characteristic of Luke

PLUMMER 1922 lx

τρυγάω 1   pick (Lk 6,44)

Literature

HAUCK 1934 [seltenes Alleinwort].

τρυγών 1   pigeon, dove (Lk 2,24)

Literature

HAUCK 1934 [seltenes Alleinwort].

JUNG, Chang-Wook, *Infancy Narrative*, 2004. Esp. 88-90.

τρυφή 1   revelling (Lk 7,25)

τυγχάνω 1/2 + 5   experience (Lk 10,30*; 20,35)

Word groups	Lk	Acts	Mt	Mk
οὐχ ὁ τυχών (VKc)		19,11; 28,2	0	0

Characteristic of Luke

BOISMARD 1984 Db14; HARNACK 1906 39.53; HAWKINS 1909 187; NEIRYNCK 1985

Literature

DENAUX 2009 1Aⁿ; HAUCK 1934 [seltenes Alleinwort]; RADL 1975 429.

CADBURY, Henry J., Litotes in Acts. — BARTH, E.H. – COCROFT, R.E. (eds.), *Festschrift to Honor F. Wilbur Gingrich*, 1972, 70-84. Esp. 63-36 [οὐχ ὁ τύχων].

τύπτω 4/5 + 5 (Mt 2, Mk 1)
1. strike (Lk 6,29; 12,45; 18,13; 23,48); 2. harm

Word groups	Lk	Acts	Mt	Mk
τύπτω + εἰς (VKa)	6,29 v.l.; 18,13		1	0
τύπτω + ἐπί + accusative (VKb)	6,29		0	0
τύπτω τὸ στῆθος/τὰ στήθη DENAUX 2009 Lⁿ	18,13; 23,48		0	0

Characteristic of Luke
BOISMARD 1984 cb66; GOULDER 1989; NEIRYNCK 1985

Literature
COLLISON 1977 92-93 [noteworthy phenomena]; DENAUX 2009 LAn; EASTON 1910 166 [τύπτω τὸ στῆθος: cited by Weiss as characteristic of L, and possibly corroborative]; HAUCK 1934 [Vorzugswort].

Τύρος 3 + 2 (Mt 3, Mk 3)
Tyre (Lk 6,17; 10,13.14; Acts 21,3.7)

τυφλός 8 + 1 (Mt 17/18, Mk 5)
1. blind (Lk 6,39); 2. not able to understand

Word groups	Lk	Acts	Mt	Mk
τυφλός + (ἀνα)βλέπω	7,21.22	13,11	3	2
τυφλός + κωφός (VKb)	7,22		4/5	0
τυφλός (+) χωλός (VKa)	7,22; 14,13.21		4	0
τυφλός in the context of healings (SCa)	4,18; 7,21.22; 18,35		8	5

Literature
ROTH, S. John, The Blind, the Lame and the Poor. Character Types in Luke (JSNT SS, 144). Sheffield: Academic Press, 1997, 253 p. Esp. 103-106.

Υ

ὑβρίζω 2 + 1 (Mt 1)
1. maltreat (Lk 18,32; Acts 14,5); 2. insult (Lk 11,45)

Characteristic of Luke
PLUMMER 1922 lx

BORMANN, Lukas, Recht, Gerechtigkeit und Religion, 2001. Esp. 191.

ὑγιαίνω 3
1. be healthy (Lk 5,31; 7,10; 15,27); 2. be accurate

Characteristic of Luke
GOULDER 1989; HAWKINS 1909add

Literature
VON BENDEMANN 2001 429: "ὑγιαίνειν in den Synoptikern nur bei Lukas"; COLLISON 1977 98 [noteworthy phenomena]; DENAUX 2009 L^n; HAUCK 1934 [seltenes Alleinwort]; JEREMIAS 1980 156 [red.].

WELLS, Luise, *The Greek Language of Healing*, 1998. Esp. 203-209.

ὑγρός 1	wet (Lk 23,31)

Literature
HAUCK 1934 [seltenes Alleinwort].

ὑδρωπικός* 1	suffering from dropsy (Lk 14,2)

Literature
HAUCK 1934 [seltenes Alleinwort].

CADBURY, Henry J., *Lexical Notes on Luke-Acts*, II, 1926. Esp. 205.

ὕδωρ 6 + 7 (Mt 7/8, Mk 5)	water

Word groups	Lk	Acts	Mt	Mk
βαπτίζω (ἐν) ὕδατι → βαπτίζω ἐν πνεύματι	3,16	1,5; 11,16	1	1
ὕδωρ + ἄνεμος	8,24.25		0	0
DENAUX 2009 L^n				
ὕδωρ (+) βαπτίζω (VKf)	3,16	1,5; 8,36^2.38; 10,47; 11,16	2	2
ὕδωρ + πνεῦμα (VKd)	3,16	1,5; 10,47; 11,16	1	1
ὕδωρ + πῦρ (VKe)	3,16		2	1
ὕδωρ + φλόξ	16,24		0	0

Literature
BÖCHER, Otto, Wasser und Geist. — BÖCHER, O. – HAACKER, K. (eds.), *Verborum Veritas*. FS G. Stählin, 1970, 197-209.

HOFIUS, Otfried, Fußwaschung als Erweis der Liebe: Sprachliche und sachliche Anmerkungen zu Lk 7,44b. — *ZNW* 81 (1990) 171-177.

υἱός 77/78 + 22 (Mt 89/91, Mk 35)	

1. son (own) (Lk 1,13); 2. son (endearment); 3. male descendant (human) (Acts 23,6); 4. male offspring (animal); 5. person of (Lk 16,8; Acts 13,10); 6. follower (Lk 11,19); 7. citizen; 8. kind of (Lk 16,8)

Word groups	Lk	Acts	Mt	Mk
μονογενὴς υἱός	7,12; 9,38		0	0
DENAUX 2009 L^n				
ὁ νεώτερος υἱός / ὁ υἱὸς ὁ πρεσβύτερος	15,13.25		0	0
DENAUX 2009 L^n				

	Lk	Acts	Mt	Mk
υἱοί + (τοῦ) θεοῦ (SCc)	20,36[1]		1	0
υἱοὶ τοῦ νυμφῶνος (LN: wedding guests)	5,34		1	1
υἱοὶ τοῦ φωτός (LN: people of God)	16,8[2]		0	0
υἱός + nomen parentis exc. c-g (VKf)	3,2.23; 4,22; 5,10	7,16; 13,21; 19,14	4	3
υἱὸς Ἀβραάμ (SCe; VKc) → θυγάτηρ/σπέρμα/τέκνον + Ἀβραάμ	19,9		1	0
υἱός + ὁ ἀγαπητός/ἐκλελεγμένος	3,22; 9,35; 20,13		2	3
ὁ υἱός (+) (τοῦ) ἀνθρώπου (LN: Son of Man; SCd; VKb)	5,24; 6,5.22; 7,34; 9,22.26. 44.56*.58; 11,30; 12,8.10.40; 17,22.24.26.30; 18,8. 31; 19,10; 21,27. 36; 22,22.48.69; 24,7	7,56	30/32	14
ὁ υἱὸς τοῦ ἀνθρώπου (+) ἔρχομαι	7,34; 9,56*; 12,40; 18,8; 19,10; 21,27		7/9	3
υἱὸς τοῦ ἀνθρώπου + κύριος	6,5		1	1
ὁ υἱὸς τοῦ ἀνθρώπου (+) παραδίδωμι	9,44; 18,31(-32); 22,22.48; 24,7		5	4
υἱός (+) Δαυίδ (SCf; VKd) → Ἰησοῦς υἱὸς Δαυίδ	18,38.39; 20,41.44		11	4
υἱός (+) θεός	1,16.32.35; 3,23(-38); 4,3.9.41; 8,28; 12,8; 20,36[1]; 22,69.70	3,25; 7,56; 8,37*; 9,20	10	4
υἱός + (τοῦ) θεοῦ (LN: Son of God; SCa; VKa) → Ἰησοῦς (ὁ) υἱὸς (τοῦ) θεοῦ	1,35; 4,3.9.41; 8,28; 22,70	8,37*; 9,20	10	4
υἱός (+) μου / τοῦ πατρός / ὑψίστου (= θεοῦ) (SCa)	1,32; 3,22; 6,35; 8,28; 9,35	13,33	5	3
υἱός + θυγάτηρ (VKj)		2,17; 7,21	1	0
υἱός + κύριος	6,5; 20,44		5	2
υἱός + μήτηρ (SCh; VKh) → θυγάτηρ + μήτηρ	7,12		3	0
υἱός + πατήρ (SCh; VKg)	9,26; 10,22[1.2]; 11,11; 12,53[1.2]; 15,11(-12).(18-)19.21[1.2]	3,25; 16,1	6	2
ὁ υἱός + ὁ πρωτότοκος	2,7		0/1	
υἱός (absolute) as a christological title (SCb)	10,22[1.2.3]		4	1

→ Ἰησοῦς (ὁ) υἱὸς (τοῦ) Ἰωσήφ

Characteristic of Luke	Lk	Acts	Mt	Mk
υἱοὶ Ἰσραήλ (LN: people of Israel; SCg; VKe) BOISMARD 1984 Db18; NEIRYNCK 1985	1,16	5,21; 7,23.37; 9,15; 10,36	1	0
υἱός (singular) τινος καλεῖται; cf. υἱοὶ θεοῦ κληθήσονται Mt 5,9 DENAUX 2009 L***	1,32.35; 15,19.21[2]		0	0

→ ἡμέρα + ὁ υἱὸς τοῦ ἀνθρώπου

Literature

BDAG 2000 1024-1027 [literature]; BDR § 162: "Genitiv der Herkunft und Zugehörigkeit. 1. Die Bezeichnung einer Person nach dem Vater ist klass. Nicht att., aber semitisch und lateinisch ist der öftere Zusatz von υἱός"; DENAUX 2009 lAn [υἱοὶ Ἰσραήλ]; GERSDORF 1816 195 [καὶ υἱὸς ὑψίστου κληθήσεται]; RADL 1975 413 [υἱοὶ Ἰσραήλ]; REHKOPF 1959 97 [υἱὸς τοῦ ἀνθρώπου: vorlukanisch]; 99 [υἱὲ Δαυίδ: "Substantiva in Anrede bei den Synoptikern"]; SCHÜRMANN 1961 276 [υἱὸς τοῦ ἀνθρώπου].

BAUCKHAM, Richard, The Son of Man: "A Man in My Position" or "Someone"? — *JSNT* 23 (1985) 23-33.

BOVER, José M., "Quod nascetur (ex te) sanctum vocabitur filius Dei" (Lc. 1,35). — *Bib* 1 (1920) 92-94.

—, "Quod nascetur (ex te) sanctum vocabitur filius Dei" (Lc., 1,35). — *EstE* 8 (1929) 381-392.

CASEY, P. Maurice, The Son of Man Problem. — *ZNW* 67 (1976) 147-154.

—, The Jackals and the Son of Man (Matt. 8.20 // Lk 9.58). — *JSNT* 23 (1985) 3-22.

DANKER, Frederick W., The υἱός Phrases in the New Testament. — *NTS* 7 (1960-61) 94. [Lk 10,6]

DAWSEY, James M., What's in a Name? Characterization in Luke. — *BTB* 16 (1986) 143-147. Esp. 143-144: "Luke's use of 'son of man'"; 146-147: "Luke's use of 'son of God'".

GEORGE, Augustin, Jésus Fils de Dieu dans l'Évangile selon saint Luc. — *RB* 72 (1965) 185-209; = ID., *Études*, 1978, 215-236.

—, La royauté de Jésus. — ID., *Études*, 1978, 257-282. Esp. 262-265: "Descendant de David".

HAHN, Ferdinand, *Christologische Hoheitstitel*, 1963. Esp. 13-23: "Menschensohn: Philologische und religionsgeschichtliche Probleme"; 242-279: "Davidssohn"; 280-346: "Gottessohn".

KUHNERT, E., Ὁ υἱὸς τοῦ ἀνθρώπου. — *ZNW* 18 (1917) 165-176.

MARTÍN DE VIVIÉS, Pierre de, *Jésus et le Fils de l'Homme. Emplois et significations de l'expression « Fils de l'homme » dans les Évangiles* (Exégèse), Lyon, 1995. 171 pp.

MUÑOZ IGLESIAS, Salvador, Lucas 1,35b. — *La idea de Dios en la Biblia. XXVIII Semana Biblica Española (Madrid 23-27 sept. 1968)*. Madrid: Consejo Superior de Investigaciones Cientificas, 1971, 303-324.

RESE, Martin, *Alttestamentliche Motive in der Christologie des Lukas*, 1969. Esp. 131-133: "Προφήτης, ἅγιος, δίκαιος, ἀρχηγός, σωτήρ und υἱὸς θεοῦ in der Apostelgeschichte"; 203-204: "υἱὸς ὑψίστου bzw. θεοῦ im Lukasevangelium"; 204-205: "Σωτήρ, Χριστός [υἱὸς Δαυίδ] im Lukasevangelium".

VOSS, Gerhard, *Die Christologie der lukanischen Schriften in Grundzügen*, 1965. Esp. 84-95: "Υἱὸς ἀγαπητός.

ὑμεῖς 221/231 + 124/132 (Mt 248/258, Mk 75/83) — you

Word groups

ὑμεῖς	Lk	Acts	Mt	Mk
καὶ ὑμεῖς (*VK*a) → καὶ **ὑμῖν/ὑμῶν**; καὶ **ἐγώ/ἡμεῖς/σύ**	6,31*; 12,29.36.40; 17,10[1]; 21,31	7,51[3]	10	2
πάντες ὑμεῖς (*SC*a; *VK*e) → πάντων **ὑμῶν**; πᾶσιν **ὑμῖν**; πάντες **ἡμεῖς**		20,25; 22,3	2	0
ὑμεῖς δέ (*VK*b) → **ὑμῶν** δέ; **ἐγώ/ἡμεῖς/σὺ** δέ	9,20; 11,48[2]; 19,46; 22,26[1].28; 24,49[2]	1,5; 3,14; 11,16; 19,15	5	4
ὑμεῖς (+) λέγετε → **σὺ** λέγεις	9,20; 22,70		2	2
ὑμεῖς οὖν/μέν (*VK*d) → **ἐγὼ/ἡμεῖς** μέν; **σὺ** οὖν	12,40 *v.l.*	3,13	1	0/1
ὑμῶν	**Lk**	**Acts**	**Mt**	**Mk**
ἐξ ὑμῶν (*SC*d)	11,5.11; 12,25; 14,28.33; 15,4; 17,7; 21,16	6,3; 20,30; 27,22	5	1
καὶ ὑμῶν (*VK*a) → καὶ **ὑμεῖς/ὑμῖν**; καὶ **σοῦ**	16,26[1]		0	0
πάντων ὑμῶν (*VK*e) → πάντες **ὑμεῖς**; πᾶσιν **ὑμῖν**; πάντων **ἡμῶν**		3,16	0	0
οἱ + πατέρες ὑμῶν (*SC*f) → πατήρ/πατέρες **ἡμῶν**	11,47[2].48[1]	3,25[2]; 7,51[2].52[1]; 28,25	1	0

			Mt	Mk
(ὁ) πατὴρ ὑμῶν (SCe) → πατήρ **μου/σου**	6,36; 12,30.32[1]		14	1/2
τίς/ἕκαστος/οὐδεὶς (+) ὑμῶν (VKf) → ἕκαστος **ἡμῶν** DENAUX 2009 La[n]	11,11; 13,15; 14,5	2,38[1]; 27,34	0	0
ὑμῶν in the genitive absolute (SCc; VKh)	22,10[1]		0	0
ὑμῶν as object of adjectives construed with genitive (VKk)	22,27		0	0
ὑμῶν as object of verbs construed with genitive (SCb; VKj)	9,41[2]; 10,16[1]	4,19; 18,14	1	2
ὑμῶν in prepositive position (SCa; VKl)	11,19[2]; 12,30.35; 21,34[1]; 22,53[2]	3,19	10	1
ὑμῶν αὐτῶν (VKg) → σοῦ **αὐτῆς**		20,30	0	0
ὑμῶν δέ (VKb) → **ὑμεῖς** δέ; **σοῦ** δέ	12,30		2	0
ὑμῶν ἐστιν (VKm) → **σοῦ** ἐστιν		1,7	0	0

ὑμῖν	Lk	Acts	Mt	Mk
δοκεῖτε ὅτι ...; οὐχί, λέγω ὑμῖν, ἀλλ'... DENAUX 2009 L[n]	12,51; 13,(2-)3.(4-)5		0	0
εἰρήνη ὑμῖν	24,36		0	0
ἐν ὑμῖν (SCc)	10,13; 22,26[2]	13,15.26; 15,7; 25,5	6	4
καὶ ὑμῖν (VKa) → καὶ **ὑμεῖς/ὑμῶν**; καὶ **ἐμοί/ἡμῖν/σοί**	11,46[1]	15,8*	2	0
οὐαὶ ὑμῖν (SCa) → οὐαί **σοι**	6,24[1].25; 11,42.43.44.47[1].52		6	
πᾶσιν ὑμῖν (VKe) → πάντες **ὑμεῖς**; πάντων **ὑμῶν** DENAUX 2009 LA[n]	9,48	4,10; 20,32*	0	0
ὑμῖν following a preposition (VKj)	9,48; 10,13; 22,26[2]; 24,44[2]	13,15.26; 15,7[2]; 25,5; 26,8	5	3
ὑμῖν as object of adjectives construed with dative (VKk)		14,15[1]	0	0
ὑμῖν γάρ (VKc)		2,39[1]	0	0
ὑμῖν λέγω / λέγω ὑμῖν (introducing a speech) (SCb) → **σοὶ** λέγω / λέγω **σοι**; **ἀληθῶς/ἀμὴν/ναὶ** λέγω ὑμῖν; **λέγω** ὑμῖν / **σοι** ... οὐ μὴ ... ἕως (ἄν); cf. ἐρεῖ ὑμῖν Lk 13,25[1]	3,8; 4,24.25; 6,27[1]; 7,9.26.28; 9,27; 10,12.24[1]; 11,8.9[1].51; 12,4.5[2].8.22.27.37.44.51; 13,3.5.24.35[2]; 14,24; 15,7.10; 16,9[1]; 17,34; 18,8.14.17.29; 19,26.40; 20,8; 21,3.32; 22,16.18.37	5,38	55	15/16

ὑμᾶς	Lk	Acts	Mt	Mk
ὑμᾶς in a proleptic construction (VKh) → **σε** in a proleptic construction DENAUX 2009 L[n]	13,25[2].27[2]		0	0
ὑμᾶς following a preposition (VKj) → **σε** following a preposition	9,41[1]; 10,6[2].9.11*; 11,20; 12,14; 16,26[2]; 21,12.34[2]; 24,44[1.2].49[1]	1,8; 2,22[1].29; 3,22[4]; 13,40*; 15,25; 17,28; 18,15.21; 20,29; 22,1; 23,15[2]; 24,22	7/8	2

→ **ἀληθῶς** λέγω ὑμῖν; **ἐφ'** ὑμᾶς; **οὐαὶ** ὑμῖν τοῖς; **τίς** ἐξ ὑμῶν

Literature

COLLISON 1977 57 [λέγω δὲ ὑμῖν: linguistic usage of Luke: probable]; 132 [τίς ἐξ ὑμῶν: linguistic usage of Luke's "other source-material": likely]; HAUCK 1934 [Vorzugsverbindung: τίς ἐξ ὑμῶν; (ἀληθῶς) λέγω ὑμῖν]; REHKOPF 1959 95 [λέγω γὰρ ὑμῖν; ναὶ λέγω ὑμῖν]; 97 [ὑμῖν λέγω: vorlukanisch]; SCHÜRMANN 1957 73 [ἡμεῖς δέ: Verdacht auf luk R]; 1961 276 [λέγω γὰρ ὑμῖν; ναὶ λέγω ὑμῖν]; 285 [ὑμῖν λέγω: protoluk R nicht beweisbar].

ARGYLE, A. W., Luke xxii.31f. — ExpT 64 (1952-53) 222.
BOTHA, F.J., ὑμᾶς in Luke xxii.31. — ExpT 64 (1952-53) 125.
For ἐντὸς ὑμῶν, see ἐντός.

ὑμέτερος 2 + 1 — your (Lk 6,20; 16,12; Acts 27,34)

Word groups	Lk	Acts	Mt	Mk
τὸ ὑμέτερον noun (VKb)	16,12		0	0

Literature
DENAUX 2009 La[n].

DUPONT, Jacques, Les Béatitudes, I, 1958. Esp. 282-283.
KILPATRICK, George D., The Possessive Pronouns in the New Testament. — JTS 42 (1941) 184-186; = ID., Principles and Practice, 1990, 161-162.

ὑπάγω 5/6 (Mt 19/20, Mk 15/16)
1. move along (Lk 8,42; 12,58); 2. depart (Lk 10,3; 17,14; 19,30); 3. leave; 4. die; 5. undergo

Word groups	Lk	Acts	Mt	Mk
ὑπάγω εἰς + place (VKa) → (ἀν/ἀπ/εἰσ/ἐξ/ἐπαν/κατ/προ/συν)ἄγω εἰς + place	19,30		4	4
ὑπάγω + ἐπί + accusative (person) (VKc) → (ἀπ/συν)ἄγω ἐπί + acc. (person); (ἀν/κατ)ἄγω ἐπί + acc. (place); προάγω ἐπί + gen. (person)	12,58		0	0
ὑπάγω μετά + genitive (VKd)	12,58		1	0
ὑπάγω ὀπίσω (VKe)	4,8*		1	1

Literature
COLLISON 1977 61-62 [noteworthy phenomena]; SCHÜRMANN 1953 93-94; 1957 5.

ὑπακούω 2 + 2 (Mt 1, Mk 2)
1. obey (Lk 8,25; 17,6); 2. answer door (Acts 12,13)

Word groups	Lk	Acts	Mt	Mk
verb of movement + ὑπακοῦσαι → verb of movement + ἀκούειν/ἀκοῦσαι		12,13	0	0
ὑπακούω technical term for a doorkeeper (VKa)		12,13	0	0
ὑπήκουεν/ὑπήκουον → ἤκουεν/ἤκουον		6,7	0	0

Literature
DANOVE, Paul, Verbs of Experience, 1999. Esp. 157.173.
MATEOS, Juan, Contribuciones al DGENT (Diccionario Griego-Español del Nuevo Testamento): Ὑπακούω y terminos afines en el Nuevo Testamento. — FilolNT 8 (1995) 209-226. Esp. 209-213.224: "ὑπακούω".

ὑπαντάω 2/3 + 1 (Mt 2, Mk 1)
1. draw near (Lk 8,27; 17,12*; Acts 16,16); 2. meet in battle (Lk 14,31)

ὑπάρχω 15 + 25/27 (Mt 3)

1. be (Lk 16,23; Acts 5,4; 19,40); 2. be identical (Lk 8,41); 3. exist (Acts 28,7); 4. belong to (Acts 28,7)

Word groups	Lk	Acts	Mt	Mk
ὑπάρχω + dative (VKf) DENAUX 2009 1A[n]	8,3; 12,15	3,6; 4,32.37; 28,7	0	0
ὑπάρχω οὐ μακρὰν ἀπό (VKb) → ἀπέχω οὐ μακρὰν ἀπό		17,27	0	0
ὑπάρχω πρός + accusative (VKe)		27,12	0	0
ὑπάρχω πρός + genitive (VKd)		27,34	0	0

Characteristic of Luke

CREDNER 1836 141; DENAUX 2009 L***; GOULDER 1989*; HARNACK 1906 41-42.53; HAWKINS 1908L; HENDRIKS 1986 468; MORGENTHALER 1958LA; PLUMMER 1922 lix; VOGEL 1899D

	Lk	Acts	Mt	Mk
τὰ ὑπάρχοντα (LN: possessions; SCa; VKa); cf. 1 Cor 13,3; Heb 10,34 BOISMARD 1984 cb157; DENAUX 2009 L***; GOULDER 1989*; HAWKINS 1909L; NEIRYNCK 1985; PLUMMER 1922 lx; VOGEL 1899D	8,3; 11,21; 12,15.33.44; 14,33; 16,1; 19,8	4,32	3	0
τὰ ὑπάρχοντα αὐτῷ → ἐστιν αὐτῷ/αὐτοῖς; cf. τὰ ὑπάρχοντα αὐταῖς Lk 8,3 PLUMMER 1922 lii	12,15	4,32	0	0
ὑπάρχω + attribute; cf. Rom 4,19; 1 Cor 11,7; 2 Cor 8,17; 12,16; Gal 1,14; 2,14; James 2,15; 2 Pet 2,19 BOISMARD 1984 cb84; DENAUX 2009 L***; NEIRYNCK 1985	8,41; 9,48; 11,13; 16,14; 23,50	2,30; 3,2; 4,34; 7,55; 8,16; 16,3.20. 37; 17,24; 19,40; 21,20; 22,3; 27,12. 21	0	0
ὑπάρχω for εἶναι DENAUX 2009 L***	7,25; 8,41; 9,48; 11,13; 16,14.23; 23,50	2,30; 3,2; 4,34; 5,4; 7,55; 8,16; 16,3.20.37; 17,24.29; 19,36; 21,20; 22,3; 27,12.34	0	0
ὑπάρχω ἐν (VKc) BOISMARD 1984 cb137; DENAUX 2009 1A*; NEIRYNCK 1985	7,25; 9,48; 16,23	4,34*; 5,4; 10,12; 28,7.18	0	0

Literature

COLLISON 1977 67 [ὑπάρχω for εἶναι: linguistic usage of Luke: certain; τὰ ὑπάρχοντα: likely. It may also have been a linguistic usage of Luke's "other source-material"]; DENAUX 2009 LA[n] [τὰ ὑπάρχοντα αὐτῷ]; HAUCK 1934 [Vorzugswort]; JEREMIAS 1980 163: "Lukas zeigt ... eine besondere Vorliebe für den Gebrauch von ὑπάρχειν als Ersatz für εἶναι mit Prädikatsnomen ... Ferner ist charakteristisch für ihn, daß er als einziger neutestamentlicher Autor τὰ ὑπάρχοντά τινι (also mit Dativ der Person) schreibt"; RADL 1975 429.

BORMANN, Lukas, Recht, Gerechtigkeit und Religion, 2001. Esp. 163 [ὑπάρχοντα].
LYGRE, John G., Of What Charges? (Luke 16:1-2). — BTB 32 (2002) 21-28. Esp. 24 [ὑπάρχοντα].

NEIRYNCK, Frans, La matière marcienne dans l'évangile de Luc, 1973. Esp. 183; [2]1989.
Esp. 93; = ID., *Evangelica*, 1982. Esp. 63.

ὑπέρ 5/6 + 7/9 (Mt 5, Mk 2)

1. on behalf of (benefaction) (Lk 6,28; 9,50; 22,19.20; Acts 21,26); 2. about (content);
3. beyond (degree) (Lk 16,8); 4. above (status) (Lk 6,40); 5. because of (reason) (Acts
5,41)

Word groups

ὑπέρ + genitive	Lk	Acts	Mt	Mk
ὑπέρ + κατά + genitive (*VK*d)	9,50		0	1
ὑπέρ + πρός (*VK*e)		8,24; 12,5*	0	0
ὑπέρ τοῦ ὀνόματος		5,41; 9,16; 15,26; 21,13	0	0
BOISMARD 1984 Aa59; NEIRYNCK 1985				
other instances with genitive (*SC*a)	22,19.20	5,41; 9,16; 15,26; 21,13.26	1	1
→ εἰμι ὑπέρ; **πάσχω** ὑπέρ; **προσεύχομαι** ὑπέρ				
ὑπέρ + accusative	Lk	Acts	Mt	Mk
ὑπέρ after comparative (*VK*g)	16,8		0	0
other instances with accusative (*SC*b; *VK*h)	6,40	26,13	4	0
→ εἰμι ὑπέρ				

Literature

BDR § 245: "Umschreibung der Steigerungsform durch den Positiv. 3. "Positiv statt Komparativ. a)
wenn die Vergleichung mit παρά oder ὑπέρ geschieht"; RADL 1975 419 [ὑπὲρ τοῦ ὀνόματος].

MARROW, Stanley B., Principles for Interpreting the New Testament Soteriological Terms.
— *NTS* 36 (1990) 268-280.
PETZER, Kobus H., Style and Text in the Lucan Narrative of the Institution of the Lord's
Supper, 1991. Esp. 115-116: "ὑπὲρ ὑμῶν".

ὑπερεκχύννομαι 1   overflow (Lk 6,38)

Literature

HAUCK 1934 [seltenes Alleinwort].

ὑπερήφανος 1   arrogant

Word groups	Lk	Acts	Mt	Mk
ὑπερήφανος + ταπεινός	1,51(-52)		0	0

Literature

GERSDORF 1816 200 [διεσκόρπισεν ὑπερηφάνους].

SCHOONHEIM, P.L., Der alttestamentliche Boden der Vokabel ὑπερήφανος Lukas I 51. —
NT 8 (1966) 235-246.

ὑπηρέτης 2 + 4 (Mt 2, Mk 2)   servant

Word groups	Lk	Acts	Mt	Mk
ὑπηρέτης + ἀρχιερεύς (*VK*d)		5,(21-)22	1	2

ὑπηρέτης τοῦ λόγου (VKb)	1,2		0	0
ὑπηρέτης καὶ μάρτυς (VKc)		26,16	0	0

Characteristic of Luke	Lk	Acts	Mt	Mk
ὑπηρέτης = servant of the word; cf. 1 Cor 4,1 BOISMARD 1984 cb55; NEIRYNCK 1985	1,2	13,5; 26,16	0	0

Literature

DENAUX 2009 IA[n] [ὑπηρέτης = servant of the word].

ALEXANDER, Loveday, *The Preface to Luke's Gospel*, 1993. Esp. 123 [Lk 1,2].

CADBURY, Henri J., Commentary on the Preface of Luke, 1922. Esp. 498-500 [Lk 1,2].

HOLMES, Benjamin T., Luke's Description of John Mark. — *JBL* 54 (1935) 63-72. Esp. 64-70.

KUHN, Karl A., Beginning the Witness: The αὐτόπται καὶ ὑπηρέται of Luke's Infancy Narrative. — *NTS* 49 (2003) 237-255.

MATHER, P. Boyd, Paul in Acts as "Servant" and "Witness". — *Biblical Research* 30 (1985) 23-44. Esp. 27-29.

ὕπνος 1 + 2 (Mt 1)	sleep

Word groups	Lk	Acts	Mt	Mk
βαρέομαι ὕπνῳ (*LN*: be sound asleep)	9,32		0	0
καταφέρομαι ἀπὸ τοῦ ὕπνου (*LN*: be sound asleep)		20,9[2]	0	0
καταφέρομαι ὕπνῳ (*LN*: get sleepier)		20,9[1]	0	0

ὑπό 31/35 + 41/45 (Mt 28/32, Mk 11[12]/13)
1. under (location) (Lk 7,6); 2. under (control) (Lk 7,8); 3. by (agent) (Lk 7,24); 4. because of (reason) (Lk 8,14); 5. at (time) (Acts 5,21)

Word groups				
ὑπό + genitive	**Lk**	**Acts**	**Mt**	**Mk**
ὑπό + genitive (*SCa*)	2,18.21.26; 3,7.19; 4,2.15; 7,24.30; 8,14.29; 9,7.7*.8; 10,22; 13,17; 14,8[1.2]; 16,22; 17,20; 21,16.17.20.24; 23,8	2,24; 4,11; 5,16; 8,6; 10,17.22[1.2]. 33.38.41.42; 12,5; 13,4.45; 15,3. 40; 16,2.4.6.14; 17,13.19.25; 20,3; 21,35; 22,11.12.30; 23,10. 27[1.2].30; 24,26; 25,14; 26,2.6.7; 27,11.41	23	9
ὑπό + accusative	**Lk**	**Acts**	**Mt**	**Mk**
ὑπό with reference to time (*VKc*)		5,21	0	0
ὑπό + ἐπί (*VKd*)	11,33v.l.		1	2
ἡ ὑπὸ τὸν οὐρανόν (*LN*: on earth)	17,24[1.2]		0	0
other instances with accusative (*SCb*; *VKe*)	7,6.8[1.2]; 13,34	2,5; 4,12	4	0

→ εἰμι ὑπό; εἰς + ὑπό; εἰσέρχομαι ὑπό; τασσόμενος ὑπὸ ἐξουσίαν; τίθημι ὑπό
→ βαπτίζω ὑπό; εἰς + ὑπό; ἐν + ὑπό

Characteristic of Luke				
GASTON 1973 66 [Lked?]				
	Lk	**Acts**	**Mt**	**Mk**
γίνομαι ὑπό + genitive (*VKa*); cf. Eph 5,12; εἰμι ὑπό + gen. Acts 23,30* BOISMARD 1984 Bb97; NEIRYNCK 1985	9,7*; 13,17; 23,8	12,5; 20,3; 26,6	0	0

λαλέομαι/λέγομαι ὑπό + genitive; cf. Eph 2,11; Heb 9,19 | 2,18; | 8,6; 13,45; 16,14; | 0 | 0
BOISMARD 1984 cb12; DENAUX 2009 IA*; HARNACK 1906 | 9,7 | 17,19; 27,11
33-34; NEIRYNCK 1985

→ μαρτυρέομαι ὑπό + gen.; ὑπὸ τὸν οὐρανόν

Literature

DENAUX 2009 IAⁿ [γίνομαι ὑπό + genitive].

READ-HEIMERDINGER, Jenny, *The Bezan Text of Acts*, 2002. Esp. 184-187: "ἀπό-ὑπό".

ὑποδείκνυμι 3 + 2 (Mt 1)

1. make known (Lk 3,7; Acts 20,35); 2. explain (Lk 6,47; 12,5)

Word groups	Lk	Acts	Mt	Mk
ὑποδείκνυμι + ὅτι (VKa)		20,35	0	0

Characteristic of Luke
BOISMARD 1984 Bb118; DENAUX 2009 La*; NEIRYNCK 1985; PLUMMER 1922 lx

	Lk	Acts	Mt	Mk
ὑποδείκνυμι ὑμῖν DENAUX 2009 La*; GOULDER 1989	3,7; 6,47; 12,5	20,35	1	0

Literature
HAUCK 1934 [Vorzugswort]; JEREMIAS 1980 149 [red.]; RADL 1975 429 [ὑποδείκνυμι; ὑποδείκνυμι "zur Einleitung eines indirekten Fragesatzes"].

ὑποδέχομαι 2 + 1 | welcome

Characteristic of Luke
BOISMARD 1984 cb56; NEIRYNCK 1985; PLUMMER 1922 lix

Literature
DENAUX 2009 Laⁿ; EASTON 1910 166 [cited by Weiss as characteristic of L, and possibly corroborative]; JEREMIAS 1980 193 [red.]; PAFFENROTH 1997 84 [pre-Lukan].

ὑπόδημα 4 + 2 (Mt 2, Mk 1) | shoe

Word groups	Lk	Acts	Mt	Mk
λύω τὸ ὑπόδημα → λύω τὸν ἱμάντα		7,33; 13,25	0	0
ὑπόδημα singular (VKa)		7,33; 13,25	0	0

Literature
BDAG 2000 1037 [literature]; REHKOPF 1959 97 [vorlukanisch]; SCHÜRMANN 1957 118 [Lk 22,35: luk R unwahrscheinlich]; 1961 276.

ὑποκάτω 1 (Mt 1, Mk 3)

1. under (Lk 8,16); 2. under surface

Word groups	Lk	Acts	Mt	Mk
τίθημι + ὑποκάτω + genitive	8,16		0	0

ὑποκρίνομαι 1 — pretend (Lk 20,20)

Literature

HAUCK 1934 [seltenes Alleinwort].

ὑπόκρισις 1 (Mt 1, Mk 1) — pretense (Lk 12,1)

ὑποκριτής 3/4 (Mt 13/15, Mk 1) — pretender

Word groups	Lk	Acts	Mt	Mk
γραμματεῖς καὶ Φαρισαῖοι ὑποκριταί (SCa; VKa)	11,44*		6/7	0
ὑποκριτά/ὑποκριταί vocative	6,42; 12,56; 13,15		9	0

Literature

BDAG 2000 1038 [literature]; HAUCK 1934 [Vorzugswort]; REHKOPF 1959 99 [ὑποκριτά: "Substantiva in Anrede bei den Synoptikern"].

AMORY, Frederic, Whited Sepulchres: The Semantic History of Hypocrisy to the High Middle Ages. — *Recherches de Théologie Ancienne et Médiévale* 53 (1986) 5-39.
MARSHALL, I. Howard, Who Is a Hypocrite? . — *Bibliotheca Sacra* 159 (2002) 131-150. [NTA 46, 1486]

ὑπολαμβάνω 2 + 2

1. take up (Acts 1,9); 2. reply (Lk 10,29-30); 3. help; 4. suppose (Lk 7,43; Acts 2,15)

Word groups	Lk	Acts	Mt	Mk
ὑπολαμβάνω of Christ → ἀνάλημψις; ἀναφέρω; cf. ἀναλαμβάνω Mk [16,9]; Acts 1,2.11.22		1,9	0	0

Characteristic of Luke

BOISMARD 1984 bb119; CREDNER 1836 142; NEIRYNCK 1985; PLUMMER 1922 lix; VOGEL 1899A

Literature

VON BENDEMANN 2001 418; DENAUX 2009 LAⁿ; EASTON 1910 166 [cited by Weiss as characteristic of L, and possibly corroborative]; HAUCK 1934 [seltenes Alleinwort]; JEREMIAS 1980 170-171 [red.].

ὑπομένω 1 + 1 (Mt 2, Mk 1)

1. resist; 2. stay behind (Lk 2,43; Acts 17,14); 3. continue; 4. endure

Literature

GERSDORF 1816 265 [ὑπέμεινεν Ἰησοῦς ὁ παῖς]; HARNACK 1906 148 [ὑπομένω in the sense of "to stay behind"]; SCHÜRMANN 1957 38 [ὑπομένω in der Bedeutung "zurückbleiben"].

ὑπομιμνῄσκω 1

1. remind; ὑπομιμνῄσκομαι: 2. remember (Lk 22,61)

ὑπομονή 2

endurance (Lk 8,15; 21,19)

Word groups	Lk	Acts	Mt	Mk
ἐν ὑπομονῇ (VKa)	8,15		0	0

Literature
DENAUX 2009 L[n].

CROATTO, J.S., Persecución y perseverancia en la teologia lucana. Un estudio sobre la 'hupomoné'. — RevistBib 42 (1980) 21-30.

ὑποπόδιον 1 + 2 (Mt 0/2, Mk 0/1)

footstool

Word groups	Lk	Acts	Mt	Mk
ὑποπόδιον τῶν ποδῶν (LN: be under someone's control); cf. Heb 1,13; 10,13 DENAUX 2009 1A[n]	20,43	2,35; 7,49	0/2	0/1

ὑποστρέφω 21/22 + 11 (Mk 0/1)

1. return (Lk 2,20); 2. turn back to belief; 3. be again (Acts 13,34)

Word groups	Lk	Acts	Mt	Mk
ὑποστρέφω + infinitive (VKe)	17,18		0	0
ὑποστρέφω + ἀπαγγέλλω/διηγέομαι → ἀποστέλλω / (ἀπ/δι/εἰσ/κατ/προσ) ἔρχομαι / (εἰσ)πορεύομαι / φεύγω + διαγγέλλω/κηρύσσω; cf. ἀναστρέφω + ἀπαγγέλλω Acts 5,22 DENAUX 2009 L[n]	8,39; 9,10; 24,9		0	0
ὑποστρέφω (+) ἀπό (VKa) → ἀνα/καταβαίνω /ἀποχωρέω/ (ἀπ/ἐξ/ ἐπ/κατ)ἔρχομαι/ πορεύομαι ἀπό DENAUX 2009 La[n]	4,1; 24,9	1,12	0	0
ὑποστρέφω διά + genitive (VKb)		20,3	0	0
ὑποστρέφω ἐκ (VKd)		12,25 v.l.	0	0
ὑποστρέψας → ἐπιστρέψας; cf. Jam 5,20; 2 Pet 2,22; Rev 1,12; cf. ἀναστρέψας Acts 5,22; συστρέψας Acts 28,3 DENAUX 2009 La	7,10; 9,10; 17,18; 23,56; 24,9	22,17	0	0

Characteristic of Luke
BOISMARD 1984 Bb13; CADBURY 1920 172; CREDNER 1836 140; DENAUX 2009 L***;
GOULDER 1989*; HARNACK 1906 53.143.148; HAWKINS 1909 L; HENDRIKS 1986 428.434.448;
MORGENTHALER 1958LA; NEIRYNCK 1985; PLUMMER 1922 lix; VOGEL 1899D

	Lk	Acts	Mt	Mk
ὑποστρέφω without complement BOISMARD 1984 Ab5; DENAUX 2009 L***; NEIRYNCK 1985	2,20.43; 8,34.40; 9,10; 10,17; 17,15.18; 19,12; 23,48.56	8,28	0	0

ὑποστρέφω εἰς (VKc) DENAUX 2009 L***	1,56; 2,39*.45; 4,14; 7,10; 8,39; 11,24; 24,33.52	1,12; 8,25; 12,25; 13,13.34; 14,21; 21,6; 22,17; 23,32	0	0
ὑποστρέφω εἰς Ἱεροσόλυμα/Ἱερουσαλήμ BOISMARD 1984 Ab22; DENAUX 2009 lA*; NEIRYNCK 1985	2,45; 24,33.52	1,12; 8,25; 12,25; 13,13; 22,17	0	0
ὑποστρέφω + εἰς τὸν οἶκον DENAUX 2009 L***; GOULDER 1989*	1,56; 7,10; 8,39; 11,24		0	0

Literature

VON BENDEMANN 2001 414: "ὑποστρέφειν gebraucht in den Synoptikern allein Lukas";
COLLISON 1977 67 [linguistic usage of Luke: certain]; 128 [ὑποστρέφω + εἰς: certain];
GERSDORF 1816 202 [ὑπέστρεψεν εἰς τὸν οἶκον αὐτῆς]; 240 [καὶ ὑπέστρεψαν]; HAUCK
1934 [häufiges Alleinwort]; JEREMIAS 1980 202: "ὑποστρέφω ist profiliertes lukanisches
Vorzugswort"; RADL 1975 429: "ὑποστρέφω steht bei Lukas etwa 20mal in typischen Abschluß-
oder Überleitungswendungen".

GARCÍA PÉREZ, José Miguel, El Endemoniado de Gerasa (Lc 8,26-39), 1986. Esp. 141-142.
NEIRYNCK, Frans, La matière marcienne dans l'évangile de Luc, 1973. Esp. 184; [2]1989.
Esp. 94; = ID., Evangelica, 1982. Esp. 64.
SCHENK, Wolfgang, Die makrosyntaktische Signalfunktion des lukanischen Textems
ὑποστρέφειν. — Studia Evangelica 7 (1982) 443-450.

ὑποστρωννύω 1	spread out underneath (Lk 19,36)

Literature
HAUCK 1934 [seltenes Alleinwort].

ὑποτάσσω 3	

1. bring under control; ὑποτάσσομαι: 2. obey (Lk 2,51; 10,17.20)

Literature
VON BENDEMANN 2001 417 [ὑποτάσσω + dat.]; DENAUX 2009 L[n]; GERSDORF 1816 271 [καὶ
ἦν ὑποτασσόμενος αὐτοῖς]; HARNACK 1906 149.

BORMANN, Lukas, Recht, Gerechtigkeit und Religion, 2001. Esp. 206.

ὑποχωρέω 2	withdraw (Lk 5,16; 9,10)

Characteristic of Luke
PLUMMER 1922 liii

Literature
DENAUX 2009 L[n]; HAUCK 1934 [seltenes Alleinwort].

ὑπωπιάζω 1	

1. annoy and wear out (Lk 18,5); 2. exercise self-control

Literature
DERRETT, J.D.M., Law in the New Testament. The Parable of the Unjust Judge. — NTS 18
(1971-72) 178-191. Esp. 189-191.

ὑστερέω 2 (Mt 1, Mk 1)

1. be in need (Lk 15,14; 22,5); 2. lack benefit; 3. be inferior; 4. fail to attain

Word groups	Lk	Acts	Mt	Mk
ὑστερέομαι passive (VKa)	15,14		0	0

Literature

SCHÜRMANN 1957 120 [luk R weniger wahrscheinlich].

DANOVE, Paul, Verbs of Experience, 1999. Esp. 170-171.178.

ὑστέρημα 1

1. need (Lk 21,4); 2. absence

Word groups	Lk	Acts	Mt	Mk
ὑστέρημα + περισσεύω (VKa); cf. 1 Cor 9,12; ὑστερέω + περισσεύω 1 Cor 8,8; Phil 4,12; ὑστέρημα + περίσσευμα 1 Cor 8,14$^{1.2}$; ὑστέρησις + περισσεύω Mk 12,44	21,4		0	0

Literature

HAUCK 1934 [seltenes Alleinwort]; SCHÜRMANN 1957 120.

ὕστερον 1/2 (Mt 7/8, Mk 0[1])

1. last; 2. later (Lk 4,2*; 20,32)

Word groups	Lk	Acts	Mt	Mk
ὕστερον δὲ πάντων (VKa)	20,32 v.l.		1	0

ὑψηλός 1/2 + 1 (Mt 2, Mk 1)

1. tall (Lk 4,5*); 2. world above; 3. very valuable (Lk 16,15); 4. arrogant (Lk 16,15)

Word groups	Lk	Acts	Mt	Mk
βραχίων ὑψηλός (LN: great power)		13,17	0	0

ὕψιστος 7 + 2 (Mt 1, Mk 2)

1. world above (Lk 19,38); 2. the Most High (Lk 1,32)

Word groups	Lk	Acts	Mt	Mk
δόξα ἐν ὑψίστοις; cf. ὡσαννὰ ἐν τοῖς ὑψίστοις Mt 21,9; Mk 11,10 DENAUX 2009 L^n	2,14; 19,38		0	0
δύναμις ὑψίστου	1,35		0	0
ἐν (τοῖς) ὑψίστοις (SCc; VKa)	2,14; 19,38		1	1
υἱός/υἱοὶ (τοῦ) ὑψίστου	1,32; 6,35; 8,28		0	1

Characteristic of Luke

CREDNER 1836 134; DENAUX 2009 L***; GOULDER 1989*; HAWKINS 1909 L; PLUMMER 1922 lii

	Lk	Acts	Mt	Mk
ὁ θεὸς ὁ ὕψιστος (SCa)	8,28	16,17	0	1
HARNACK 1906 36				
(ὁ) ὕψιστος absolute (= God) (SCb)	1,32.35.76;	7,48	0	0
BOISMARD 1984 Ab64; DENAUX 2009 L***; HARNACK 1906	6,35			
36.145; NEIRYNCK 1985; PLUMMER 1922 lxi				

Literature

BDAG 2000 1045 [literature]; COLLISON 1977 188 [noteworthy phenomena]; GERSDORF 1816 195 [καὶ υἱὸς ὑψίστου κληθήσεται]; 232 [δόξα ἐν ὑψίστοις θεῷ καὶ ἐπὶ γῆς εἰρήνη]; HAUCK 1934 [Vorzugswort].

BAARLING, Heinrich, Friede im Himmel: Die lukanische Redaktion von Lk 19,38 und ihre Deutung. — ZNW 76 (1985) 170-186. [ἐν οὐρανῷ εἰρήνη καὶ δόξα ἐν ὑψίστοις]

DAWSEY, James M., What's in a Name? Characterization in Luke. — BTB 16 (1986) 143-147. Esp. 146-147: "Luke's use of 'son of God'".

DELEBECQUE, Édouard, Études grecques, 1976. Esp. 25-38: "Le 'gloria' des anges (2,14)".

GUERRA GÓMEZ, Manuel, Análisis filológico-teológico y traducción del himno de los ángeles en Belén, 1989. Esp. 42-46: "ἐν ὑψίστοις θεῷ" = 'en las alturas a Dios' o 'al Dios Altísimo'".

RESE, Martin, Alttestamentliche Motive in der Christologie des Lukas, 1969. Esp. 203-204: "υἱὸς ὑψίστου bzw. θεοῦ im Lukasevangelium".

SCHNEIDER, Gerhard, Lk 1,34. 35 als redaktionelle Einheit. — BZ NF 15 (1971) 255-259. Esp. 256-257: "Lk 1,35 ist nach Wortschatz, Stil und Theologie 'lukanisch'".

—, Jesu geistgewirkte Empfängnis (Lk 1,34f): Zur Interpretation einer christologischen Aussage. — TPQ 119 (1971) 105-116. Esp. 110; = ID., Lukas, Theologe der Heilsgeschichte, 1985, 86-97. Esp. 91.

ὕψος 2
1. height (Lk 1,78); 2. world above (Lk 24,49); 3. high rank

Word groups	Lk	Acts	Mt	Mk
ἀνατολὴ ἐξ ὕψους (LN: the dawn from on high)	1,78		0	0
δύναμις ἐξ ὕψους	24,49		0	0

Literature

DENAUX 2009 Lⁿ; GERSDORF 1816 212 [ἐπισκέψεται ἡμᾶς ἀνατολὴ ἐξ ὕψους]; HARNACK 1906 145.

ὑψόω 6 + 3 (Mt 3)
1. lift up; 2. exalt (Lk 1,52; Acts 5,31)

Word groups	Lk	Acts	Mt	Mk
ὑψόομαι (+) τῇ δεξιᾷ (τοῦ θεοῦ)		2,33;	0	0
BOISMARD 1984 Aa164		5,31		

Characteristic of Luke

DENAUX 2009 L***†; HAWKINS 1909 L†

	Lk	Acts	Mt	Mk
ὑψόω + ταπεινόω/ταπεινός (VKa)	1,52; 14,11^{1.2};		2	0
DENAUX 2009 L*** (?)	18,14^{1.2}			

Literature

EPP, Eldon Jay, The Ascension in the Textual Tradition of Luke-Acts. — ID. – FEE, G.D. (eds.), *New Testament Textual Criticism.* FS B.M. Metzger, 1981, 131-145.

Φ

φάγος 1 (Mt 1)	glutton (Lk 7,34)

φαίνω 2 (Mt 13, Mk 1[2])

1. shine; φαίνομαι: 2. become visible (Lk 9,8); 3. make known; 4. appear to be (Lk 24,11)

Word groups	Lk	Acts	Mt	Mk
φαίνω ὡσεί (*VK*b)	24,11		0	0

Φάλεκ 1	Peleg (Lk 3,35)

φανερός 2 + 2 (Mt 1/4, Mk 3)

1. widely known (Lk 8,17²); 2. evident; 3. clearly seen (8,17¹)

Word groups	Lk	Acts	Mt	Mk
εἰς φανερὸν ἐλθεῖν (*VK*b)	8,17²		0	1

Φανουήλ 1	Phanuel (Lk 2,36)

φάραγξ 1	ravine (Lk 3,5)

Literature

HAUCK 1934 [seltenes Alleinwort].

Φάρες 1 (Mt 2)	Perez (Lk 3,33)

Φαρισαῖος 27/28 + 9 (Mt 29/31, Mk 12/13)   Pharisee

Word groups	Lk	Acts	Mt	Mk
ἄρχοντες [τῶν] Φαρισαίων	14,1		0	0
γραμματεῖς καὶ Φαρισαῖοι ὑποκριταί	11,44*		6/7	0
ζύμη + τῶν Φαρισαίων	12,1		3	1

Φαρισαῖοι + γραμματεῖς (SCb; VKb)	5,21.30; 6,7; 11,44*.53; 15,2	23,9	10/11	3/4
Φαρισαῖοι καὶ νομικοί/νομοδιδάσκαλοι (SCd; VKc)	5,17; 7,30; 14,3		1	0
Φαρισαῖοι + Σαδδουκαῖοι (SCe; VKd)		23,6^1.7.8	5/6	0

Characteristic of Luke	Lk	Acts	Mt	Mk
Φαρισαῖος singular; cf. Phil 3,5 BOISMARD 1984 Bb82; DENAUX 2009 L***; GOULDER 1989*; NEIRYNCK 1985	7,36.37.39; 11,37.38; 18,10.11	5,34; 23,6; 26,5	1	0

Literature

BDAG 2000 1049 [literature]; COLLISON 1977 171 [γραμματεῖς καὶ Φαρισαῖοι: linguistic usage of Lk: certain]; EASTON 1910 159-160 [Φαρισαῖοι καὶ γραμματεῖς: cited by Weiss as characteristic of L, and possibly corroborative]; HAUCK 1934 [Vorzugsverbindung: ἀρχόντων τῶν Φαρισαίων].

KLIJN, A.F.J., Scribes, Pharisees, Highpriests and Elders in the New Testament. — NT 3 (1959) 259-267.

φάτνη 4

1. feed box (Lk 2,7.12.16); 2. stall (Lk 13,15)

Word groups	Lk	Acts	Mt	Mk
φάτνη + βοῦς	13,15		0	0

Characteristic of Luke

PLUMMER 1922 lii

Literature

COLLISON 1977 182 [noteworthy phenomena]; DENAUX 2009 L(***); EASTON 1910 166 [cited by Weiss as characteristic of L, and possibly corroborative]; GERSDORF 1816 220-222 [ἀνέκλινεν αὐτὸν ἐν τῇ φάτνῃ]; 240 [ἐν τῇ φάτνῃ]; HARNACK 1906 147; HAUCK 1934 [seltenes Alleinwort]; HAWKINS 1909 23.

BENOIT, Pierre, "Non erat eis locus in diversorio" (Lk 2,7). — DESCAMPS, A. – DE HALLEUX, A. (eds.), Mélanges bibliques en hommage au R.P. Béda Rigaux, 1970, 173-186.
CADBURY, Henri J., Lexical Notes on Luke-Acts, III, 1926. Esp. 317-319.
—, Lexical Notes on Luke-Acts, V, 1933. Esp. 61-62.
DERRETT, J. Duncan M., Il significato della mangiatoia. — Conoscenza religiosa, 1973-74, 439-444; = ID., Studies in the New Testament, II, 54-59.

φέρω 4 + 10/11 (Mt 4/6, Mk 15)

1. carry (Lk 5,18; 23,26; Acts 4,34); 2. bring (Lk 15,23; 24,1); 3. drive along (Acts 27,17); 4. guide (Acts 15,29); 5. lead into (Acts 12,10); 6. bring about; 7. put; 8. experience; 9. sustain; 10. demonstrate reality of; 11. accept; 12. endure; 13. bear fruit φέρομαι: 14. move (Acts 10,3); 15. progress

Word groups	Lk	Acts	Mt	Mk
φέρω εἰς (VKb) → ἀναφέρω εἰς		12,10	0	0/1
φέρω + ἐπί + accusative (VKg)		14,13	0	1

			0	0
φέρω ἐπί + genitive (VKe)	5,18		0	0
φέρω κατά + genitive (VKh)		25,7*	0	0
φέρω τὸν σταυρόν	23,26		0	0
φέρω sick people to Jesus (SCa)	5,18		1	7

Literature

COLLISON 1977 36-38 [noteworthy phenomena].

BRYAN, J. Davies, Cross-Bearing. — ExpT 38 (1926-27) 378-379.
FITZMYER, Joseph A., The Use of agein and ferein in the Synoptic Gospels. — BARTH, E.H. – COCROFT, R.E. (eds.), Festschrift to Honor F. Wilbur Gingrich, 1972, 147-160.
MATHESON, Donald, Cross-Bearing. — ExpT 38 (1926-27) 188, 524-525.

φεύγω 3 + 2 (Mt 7/8, Mk 5)

1. flee (Lk 3,7; 8,34; 21,21); 2. escape (Acts 27,30); 3. disappear quickly; 4. avoid; 5. become invisible

Word groups	Lk	Acts	Mt	Mk
φεύγω + ἀπαγγέλλω → ἀποστέλλω/(ἀπ/δι/εἰσ/κατ/προσ) ἔρχομαι/(εἰσ)πορεύομαι/ὑποστρέφω + ἀπαγγέλλω/ διαγγέλλω/διηγέομαι/κηρύσσω	8,34		0	1
φεύγω ἀπό (VKb)	3,7		2	1/2
φεύγω εἰς (VKc)	21,21		3/4	1
φεύγω ἐκ (VKd)		27,30	0	0

φήμη 1 (Mt 1)   report (Lk 4,14)

φημί 8 + 25/28 (Mt 16/18, Mk 6)

1. tell (Lk 7,40); 2. imply

Word groups	Lk	Acts	Mt	Mk
ἀποκριθείς + ἔφη (VKd)	23,3.40		1	0/1
φημί + φωνή; cf. ἀποφθέγγομαι + φωνή Acts 2,14		26,24	0	0
φησίν (SCa)	7,40	2,38; 8,36; 10,31; 19,35; 22,2; 23,18; 25,5.22. 24; 26,24.25	2	0/1

Characteristic of Luke

MORGENTHALER 1958A

	Lk	Acts	Mt	Mk
φημί πρός + accusative (person) (VKa) BOISMARD 1984 Ab103; NEIRYNCK 1985	22,70	2,38*; 10,28; 16,37; 25,22*; 26,1.28*	0	0

Literature

COLLISON 1977 71 [imperfect form avoided: linguistic usage of Luke: probable]; DENAUX 2009 IAⁿ [φημί πρός + accusative (person)]; HAUCK 1934 [Vorzugsverbindung: πρὸς αὐτούς (ἔφη)]; RADL 1975 429-430 [φημί; ἔφη "am Ende der Phrase"]; SCHNEIDER 1969 84.163 [ἔφη "am Ende einer Phrase": Vorzugswörter und -ausdrücke des Luk]; 125.164: "Πρός in Verbindung mit ἔφη bei Erwähnung der Adressaten eines Wortes erscheint im NT nur in den lk Schriften" [Bei Luk beliebte Konstruktionen]; SCHÜRMANN 1957 27-28 [ἔφη + πρός].

φϑάνω 1 (Mt 1)

1. come to (Lk 11,20); 2. go prior to; 3. attain; 4. come upon

Word groups	Lk	Acts	Mt	Mk
φϑάνω + βασιλεία τοῦ ϑεοῦ → ἀναφαίνω/ἔρχομαι + βασιλεία τοῦ ϑεοῦ	11,20		1	0

Literature

BERKEY, Robert F., Ἐγγίζειν, φϑάνειν, and Realized Eschatology. — *JBL* 82 (1963) 177-187.

CLARK, Kenneth W., "Realized Eschatology". — *JBL* 59 (1940) 367-383. Esp. 374-381.

CARAGOUNIS, Chrys C., *The Development of Greek and the New Testament*, 2004. Esp. 261-278.

φιλάργυρος 1   loving money (Lk 16,14)

Literature

HAUCK 1934 [seltenes Alleinwort].

LOSS, Nicolò Maria, Amore d'amicizia nel Nuovo Testamento, 1977. Esp. 30.

φιλέω 2 (Mt 5, Mk 1)

1. love (Lk 20,46); 2. like to; 3. kiss (Lk 22,47)

Word groups	Lk	Acts	Mt	Mk
φιλέω τι (*VK*a)	20,46		1	0

Literature

BDAG 2000 1056 [literature]; COLLISON 1977 89 [noteworthy phenomena].

BROCK, Ann Graham, The Significance of φιλέω and φίλος in the Tradition of Jesus Sayings and in the Early Christian Communities. — *HarvTheolRev* 90 (1997) 393-409.

GREENLEE, J.Harold, "Love" in the New Testament. — *Notes on Translation* 14 (2000) 49-53. [NTA 46, 73]

JOLY, Robert, *Le vocabulaire chrétien de l'amour est-il original? Φιλεῖν et ἀγαπᾶν dans le grec antique* (Institut d'histoire du christianisme). Bruxelles: Presses universitaires de Bruxelles, 1968, 63 p.

LOSS, Nicolò Maria, Amore d'amicizia nel Nuovo Testamento, 1977. Esp. 7-20: "Breve esame comparativo della frequenza di ἀγαπάω e φιλέω e dei loro gruppi negli scritti del NT"; 20-54: "Analisi del significato di φιλέω e dei vocaboli desl suo gruppo".

MOFFATT, James, *Love in the New Testament*. London: Hodder and Stoughton, 1929, XV-333 p. Esp. 35-40: "Need for studying NT language about love"; 44-48: "The verbs ἀγαπᾶν and φιλεῖν".

SEGALLA, Giuseppe, La predicazione dell'amore nella tradizione presinottica. — *RivBib* 20 (1972) 481-528. Esp. 486: "Agapân e filein".

SÖDING, Thomas, Das Wortfeld der Liebe im paganen und biblischen Griechisch: Philologische Beobachtungen an der Wurzel ἀγαπ-. — *ETL* 68 (1992) 284-330. Esp. 327-328: "ἀγαπάω und φιλέω: ein Vergleich".

Spicq, Ceslaus, *Agapè dans le Nouveau Testament. Analyse des textes*, I (Études bibliques). Paris: Gabalda, 1958, 334 p. Esp. 175-179: "Le verbe φιλεῖν et ses dérivés".
—, *Agape in the New Testament*. III, trans. Marie Aquinas McNamara and Mary Honoria Richter. St. Louis, MO – London: B. Herder Book Co., 1963, ix-262 p. Esp. 197-200: "The verb *philein* and its derivatives in the Synoptics"; 224-246: "*Philein* and the other terms for love in the Acts and the Epistles of the New Testament".

φίλη 1	friend			
Word groups	Lk	Acts	Mt	Mk
φίλη + γείτων → φίλος + γείτων	15,9		0	0

φίλημα 2	kiss (Lk 7,45; 22,48)
Literature	
Denaux 2009 Lⁿ	

Φίλιππος 2/3 + 16/17 (Mt 3, Mk 3)		Philip		
Word groups	Lk	Acts	Mt	Mk
Φίλιππος the brother of Herod (*VK*b)	3,1.19*		1	1
Φίλιππος the evangelist (*SC*c; *VK*d)		6,5; 8,5.6.12.13.26.29.30. 31.34.35.37*.38.39.40; 21,8	0	0
Φίλιππος one of the twelve (*SC*b; *VK*c)	6,14	1,13	1	1
Φίλιππος the tetrarch (*SC*a; *VK*a)	3,1		1	1

φιλονεικία 1	desire to quarrel (Lk 22,24)
Literature	

Hauck 1934 [seltenes Alleinwort]; Schürmann 1957 66 [luk R kann nur vorsichtig vermutet werden].

Loss, Nicolò Maria, Amore d'amicizia nel Nuovo Testamento, 1977. Esp. 31.
Nelson, Peter K., The Flow of Thought in Luke 22.24-27. — *JSNT* 43 (1991) 113-123.

φίλος 14 + 2 (Mt 1/2)		friend		
Word groups	Lk	Acts	Mt	Mk
φίλος + γείτων → φίλη + γείτων	14,12; 15,6		0	0
φίλος γίνομαι/εἰμί (*VK*a)	11,8; 23,12		0	0
οἱ ἀναγκαῖοι φίλοι (*VK*c)		10,24	0	0
φίλος + ἀδελφός + συγγενής + γείτων/γονεῖς	14,12; 21,16		0	0
Characteristic of Luke				
Boismard 1984 cb161; Denaux 2009 L***; Goulder 1989*; Hawkins 1909 l; Hendriks 1986 428.433.448; Morgenthaler 1958l; Neirynck 1985				
	Lk	Acts	Mt	Mk
συγκαλέω τοὺς φίλους Boismard 1984 Ab150; Neirynck 1985	15,6.9	10,24	0	0

Literature

BDAG 2000 1059 [literature]; VON BENDEMANN 2001 427: "Die Verbindung von φίλος mit 'Verwandten' und 'Nachbarn' ist lukanisch'"; COLLISON 1977 177 [linguistic usage of Luke's "other source-material": certain]; DENAUX 2009 Laⁿ [συγκαλέω τοὺς φίλους]; HAUCK 1934 [Vorzugswort]; JEREMIAS 1980 153 [trad.]; REHKOPF 1959 97 [vorlukanisch]; 99 [φίλε: "Substantiva in Anrede bei den Synoptikern"]; SCHÜRMANN 1961 276.

BROCK, A.G., The Significance of φιλέω and φίλος in the Tradition of Jesus Sayings and in the Early Christian Communities. — HarvTheolRev 90 (1997) 393-409.

LOSS, Nicolò Maria, Amore d'amicizia nel Nuovo Testamento, 1977. Esp. 41-47: "L'aggettivo – sostantivo φίλος nel NT, eccetto Io".

φιμόω 1 (Mt 2, Mk 2)

1. muzzle; 2. put to silence (Lk 4,35); 3. cease to make sound

φλόξ 1 + 1   flame

Word groups	Lk	Acts	Mt	Mk
φλόξ + πῦρ		7,30	0	0
φλόξ + ὕδωρ → **πῦρ** + δωρ	16,24		0	0

Literature

DENAUX 2009 LAⁿ.

CADBURY, Henry J., Lexical Notes on Luke-Acts, II, 1926. Esp. 193-194.

φοβέομαι 23 + 14 (Mt 18, Mk 12)

1. be afraid (Acts 5,26); 2. respect (Lk 18,2); 3. worship (Lk 1,50)

Word groups	Lk	Acts	Mt	Mk
μὴ φοβοῦ / μὴ φοβεῖσθε and similar phrases (SCf) → **ἄγγελος** subject of λέγω/εἶπον + μὴ φοβοῦ/φοβεῖσθε	1,13.30; 2,10; 5,10; 8,50; 12,4.7.32	18,9; 27,24	8	2
φοβέομαι + infinitive (SCe; VKg)	9,45		2	1
φοβέομαι + participle BOISMARD 1984 ca27		9,26; 16,38; 22,29	0	1
φοβέομαι ἀπό (SCd; VKe)	12,4		1	0
φοβέομαι μή (VKf) → **βλέπω/σκοπέω** μή; cf. ὁράω μή Mt 18,10; 24,6 BOISMARD 1984 Da8		5,26; 23,10; 27,17.29	0	0
φοβέομαι τινά (except φοβέομαι τὸν θεόν) (SCc; VKc)	12,5¹; 19,21; 20,19; 22,2	5,26; 9,26	5	4
φοβέομαι φόβος (SCa; VKa)	2,9		0	1

Characteristic of Luke	Lk	Acts	Mt	Mk
μὴ φοβοῦ singular DENAUX 2009 L***; HARNACK 1906 71, GOULDER 1989	1,13.30; 5,10; 8,50; 12,32	18,9; 27,24	0	1
μὴ φοβοῦ + vocative HARNACK 1906 54	1,13.30; 12,32	27,24	0	0
φοβέομαι τὸν θεόν (SCb; VKb); cf. 1 Pet 2,17; Rev 14,7; 19,5; φοβέομαι αὐτόν Lk 1,50; 12,5²·³ BOISMARD 1984 cb67; DENAUX 2009 IA*; HARNACK 1906 141; NEIRYNCK 1985	18,2.4; 23,40	10,2.22.(34-)35; 13,16.26	0	0

φοβέομαι of (fearing) God	1,50; 12,51.2;	10,2.22.(34-)	1	0
DENAUX 2009***; GOULDER 1989*; HAWKINS 1909l	18,2.4; 23,40	35; 13,16.26		
φοβέομαι τὸν λαόν	20,19; 22,2	5,26	0	0
BOISMARD 1984 Ab151; NEIRYNCK 1985				

Literature

BDAG 2000 1061 ad 2 [literature]; COLLISON 1977 109 [μὴ φοβοῦ: linguistic usage of Luke's "other source-material": probable]; DENAUX 2009 Laⁿ [μὴ φοβοῦ + vocative, φοβέομαι τὸν λαόν]; GERSDORF 1816 181 [μὴ φοβοῦ, Ζαχαρία]; 195 [μὴ φοβοῦ, Μαριάμ]; RADL 1975 430 [φοβέομαι; φοβέομαι + μή; μὴ φοβοῦ]; PLUMMER 1922 lxiii [Lk "is fond om *combinations of cognate* words, e.g. ἐφοβήθησαν φόβον μέγαν (ii.9)]; REHKOPF 1959 95 [φοβεῖσθαι (Obj.: Gott): vorlukanisch]; SCHÜRMANN 1961 277 [φοβεῖσθαι (Obj.: Gott)].

WILCOX, Max, The "God-Fearers" in Acts – A Reconsideration. — *JSNT* 13 (1981) 102-122. [φοβούμενοι τὸν θεόν]

φόβητρον 1 | fearful thing (Lk 21,11)

Literature
HAUCK 1934 [seltenes Alleinwort].

φόβος 7 + 5/6 (Mt 3, Mk 1)
1. fear (Lk 1,12); 2. source of fear; 3. reverence (Acts 9,31)

Word groups	Lk	Acts	Mt	Mk
ἀπὸ (τοῦ) φόβου (*SC*b; *VK*e)	21,26		2	0
ἐπλήσθην φόβου → ἐγένετο **φόβος** ἐπί + acc.; ἐπέπεσεν **φόβος** ἐπί + acc.; **φόβος** λαμβάνει + acc.; ἐπλήσθην **θάμβους**	5,26		0	0
φόβος τοῦ κυρίου (*VK*c)		9,31	0	0
φόβος + λαμβάνει + accusative → ἐγένετο **φόβος** ἐπί + acc.; ἐπέπεσεν **φόβος** ἐπί + acc.; ἐπλήσθην **φόβου**; **θάμβος** περιέχει + acc.	7,16		0	0
φόβος + ταράσσω	1,12		1	0
φόβος φοβέομαι (*SC*a; *VK*a)	2,9		0	1

Characteristic of Luke
GOULDER 1989; HAWKINS 1909add

	Lk	Acts	Mt	Mk
ἐγένετο φόβος/θάμβος ἐπί + accusative → ἐπέπεσεν **φόβος** ἐπί + acc.; ἐπλήσθην **φόβου**; **φόβος** λαμβάνει + acc.; ἐγένετο **θάμβος** ἐπί + acc. BOISMARD 1984 Ab72; NEIRYNCK 1985	1,65; 4,36	5.5.11	0	0
ἐπέπεσεν φόβος ἐπί + accusative → ἐγένετο **φόβος** ἐπί + acc.; ἐπλήσθην **φόβου**; **φόβος** λαμβάνει + acc.; cf. Rev 11,11 BOISMARD 1984 cb126; HARNACK 1906 71.74; JEREMIAS 1980 32; NEIRYNCK 1985; VOGEL 1899c	1,12	19,17	0	0
φόβος μέγας (*SC*c; *VK*d); cf. Rev 11,11 BOISMARD 1984 cb125; CREDNER 1836 141; NEIRYNCK 1985; PLUMMER 1922 lx	2,9; 8,37	2,43*; 5.5.11	0	1

Literature
DENAUX 2009 IAⁿ [ἐγένετο φόβος ἐπί + accusative]; LAⁿ [ἐπέπεσεν φόβος ἐπί + accusative], LAn [φόβος μέγας]; EASTON 1910 166 [cited by Weiss as characteristic of L, and possibly corroborative]; GERSDORF 1816 180 [καὶ φόβος ἐπέπεσεν ἐπ' αὐτόν]; 204 [καὶ ἐγένετο ἐπὶ

πάντας φόβος τοὺς περιοικοῦντας]; JEREMIAS 1980 32: "φόβος ἐπέπεσεν ἐπ᾽ αὐτόν: Diese Wendung ist ein Septuagintismus"; 70: "Für lukanische Redaktion spricht ... der Gebrauch von φόβος als formelhafte Wendung des Chorschlusses nach Wundergeschichten"; 159 [ἔλαβεν δὲ φόβος: red.]; RADL 1975 416-417 [μέγας + φόβος].

φονεύω 1 (Mt 5, Mk 1)	murder (Lk 18,20)

φόνος 2 + 1 (Mt 1, Mk 2)	murder (Lk 23,19.25; Acts 9,1)

φόρος 2	tribute (Lk 20,22; 23,2)

Literature
DENAUX 2009 L[n]; EASTON 1910 166 [cited by Weiss as characteristic of L, and possibly corroborative].

BORMANN, Lukas, *Recht, Gerechtigkeit und Religion*, 2001. Esp. 163-164.

φορτίζω 1 (Mt 1)	cause to carry (Lk 11,46)

φορτίον 2 + 1 (Mt 2)	load (Lk $11,46^{1.2}$; Acts 27,10)

Word groups	Lk	Acts	Mt	Mk
φορτίον + πλοῖον; cf. ἀποφορτίζομαι γόμον + πλοῖον Acts 21,3		27,10	0	0

φραγμός 1 (Mt 1, Mk 1)
1. fence; 2. byway (Lk 14,23); 3. that which separates

φρέαρ 1
1. well (Lk 14,5); 2. deep pit

Literature
VON BENDEMANN 2001 426.

φρόνησις 1
1. thoughtful planning (Lk 1,17); 2. wisdom

φρόνιμος 2 (Mt 7)	wise

Word groups	Lk	Acts	Mt	Mk
οἰκονόμος + φρόνιμος DENAUX 2009 L[n]	12,42; 16,8		0	0
φρονιμώτερος comparative (VKb)	16,8		0	0

Literature
KILPATRICK, George D., Φρόνιμος, σοφός and συνετός in Matthew and Luke. — *JTS* 48 (1947) 63-64.

φρονίμως* 1	wisely

Literature

HAUCK 1934 [seltenes Alleinwort].

DU PLESSIS, Isak J., Philanthropy or Sarcasm? – Another Look at the Parable of the Dishonest Manager (Luke 16:1-13). — *Neotestamentica* 24 (1990) 1-20. Esp. 9-10: "A wrong translation?"; 10: "Should φρονίμως be understood ironically?".

SCHWARZ, Günther, "...lobte den betrügerischen Verwalter"? (Lukas 16,8a). — *BZ* NF 18 (1974) 94-95. Esp. 94: "..., wer in V. 8a (...) mit dem κύριος gemeint ist ... erledigt sich von selbst, wenn die Fehlübersetzung der entscheidenden Vokabeln (ἐπῄνεσεν und φρονίμως) korrigiert sein wird". [NTA 19, 588]

φυλακή 8/9 + 16 (Mt 10, Mk 3)

1. prison (Lk 3,20); 2. guard post (Acts 12,10); 3. period of night (Lk 12,38); 4. haunt

Word groups	Lk	Acts	Mt	Mk
βάλλω εἰς (τὴν) + φυλακήν / ἐν (τῇ) φυλακῇ (*SC*a; *VK*a)	12,58; 23,19.25	16,23.24.37	2	0
κατακλείω ἐν φυλακῇ DENAUX 2009 LAⁿ	3,20	26,10	0	0
τίθημι ἐν τῇ φυλακῇ / εἰς φυλακήν; cf. ἀποτίθεμαι ἐν φυλακῇ Mt 14,3		5,25; 12,4	0/1	0
φυλακαί plural (*VK*d)	2,8; 21,12	22,4; 26,10	0	0
φυλακή (τῆς νυκτός) watch of the night (*SC*b; *VK*b)	2,8; 12,38*.38		2	1

Characteristic of Luke

MORGENTHALER 1958A

	Lk	Acts	Mt	Mk
παραδίδωμι εἰς φυλακήν/τήρησιν BOISMARD 1984 cb126; NEIRYNCK 1985	21,12	8,3; 22,4	0	0
φυλακὰς φυλάσσω (*LN*: guard against;*VK*a) HARNACK 1906 43	2,8		0	0

Literature

DENAUX 2009 IAⁿ [παραδίδωμι εἰς φυλακήν]; GERSDORF 1816 226 [φυλάσσοντες φυλακάς]; PLUMMER 1922 lxiii [Lk "is fond of *combinations of cognate words*, e.g. φυλάσσοντες φυλακάς (ii.8)]; SCHÜRMANN 1957 33 [luk speziel im Sinn von "Gefängnis", "Heft"].

BORMANN, Lukas, *Recht, Gerechtigkeit und Religion*, 2001. Esp. 139-140.
MAHFOUZ, Hady, *La fonction littéraire et théologique de Lc 3,1-20*, 2003. Esp. 92-93 [κατακλείω ἐν φυλακῇ].

φυλάσσω 6 + 8 (Mt 1, Mk 1)

1. guard closely (Acts 12,4); 2. obey (Lk 11,28); φυλάσσομαι: 3. keep from

Word groups	Lk	Acts	Mt	Mk
φυλάσσω ἀπό (*VK*b) → **προσέχω** ἀπό	12,15		0	0
φυλάσσω τὸν νόμον; cf. Gal 6,13; νόμον τηρέω Acts 15,5.24* BOISMARD 1984 ca59		7,53; 21,24	0	0

φυλάσσομαι middle (*VKf*)	12,15; 18,21	21,25	0/1	1
φυλάσσομαι passive (*VKg*)	8,29	23,35	0	0
DENAUX 2009 LA^N				

Characteristic of Luke
DENAUX 2009 L***; GOULDER 1989*; HAWKINS 1909 L

	Lk	Acts	Mt	Mk
φυλακὰς φυλάσσω (*LN*: guard against;*VK*a)	2,8		0	0
HARNACK 1906 43				

Literature
VON BENDEMANN 2001 426: "φυλάσσειν ist lukanisches Vorzugsverb"; COLLISON 1977 99 [noteworthy phenomena]; GERSDORF 1816 226 [φυλάσσοντες φυλακάς]; HARNACK 1906 43 [φυλάσσοντες φυλακάς]; HAUCK 1934 [Vorzugswort]; JEREMIAS 1980 203 [red.]: "insbesondere die übertragende Bedeutung ('einhalten', 'befolgen' ist für seine Diktion kennzeichnend"; SCHÜRMANN 1957 33.

φυλή 2 + 1 (Mt 2)
1. tribe (Lk 2,36; 22,30); 2. nation

Word groups	Lk	Acts	Mt	Mk
αἱ δώδεκα φυλαί (*LN*: all God's people; *VK*a)	22,30		1	0
φυλὴ + τοῦ Ἰσραήλ → **λαὸς** Ἰσραήλ	22,30		1	0

φυτεύω 4 (Mt 2, Mk 1)   plant

Word groups	Lk	Acts	Mt	Mk
φυτεύω (+) ἀμπελών	13,6; 20,9		1	1

Characteristic of Luke
GOULDER 1989

Literature
COLLISON 1977 99 [noteworthy phenomena]; REHKOPF 1959 97 [vorlukanisch]; SCHÜRMANN 1961 285 [protoluk R weniger wahrscheinlich].

φύω 2   grow (Lk 8,6.8)

Literature
DENAUX 2009 L^n.

φωλεός 1 (Mt 1)   den (Lk 9,58)

φωνέω 10 + 4 (Mt 5, Mk 10/11)
1. call (Lk 16,2); 2. cry out (Lk 8,54); 3. name; 4. invite (Lk 14,12); 5. make a sound

Word groups	Lk	Acts	Mt	Mk
φωνέω (+) λέγω/εἶπον → **ἀνα/ἐπι/προσφωνέω** + λέγω/εἶπον	8.8.54; 16.2.24; 23,46	16,28	1	3
φωνέω of a rooster (*VK*b)	22,34.60.61		3	4

Characteristic of Luke

CADBURY 1920 172

	Lk	Acts	Mt	Mk
φωνήσας BOISMARD 1984 Ab44; DENAUX 2009 LA*; NEIRYNCK 1985	16,2.24; 23,46	9,41; 10,7.18	0	1
φωνέω = cry out DENAUX 2009 L***; GOULDER 1989*	8,8.54; 16,24; 23,46	16,28	0	0
φωνέω + φωνῇ μεγάλῃ (SCa; VKa) → ἀναφωνέω/ βοάω/(ἀνα)κράζω + φωνῇ μεγάλῃ HARNACK 1906 43	23,46	16,28	0	1

Literature

GERSDORF 1816 198-199 [φωνέω φωνῇ μεγαλῇ]; JEREMIAS 1980 57: "Lukas hat eine Vorliebe für Worte der Stammsilbe -φων"; 69 [φωνέω + λέγων: red.]; 307 [φωνήσας φωνῇ μεγάλῃ: red.].

φωνή 14/15 + 27 (Mt 7/8, Mk 7)

1. sound (Lk 1,44); 2. voice (Lk 9,35); 3. cry; 4. language

Word groups	Lk	Acts	Mt	Mk
φωνή + ἀποκρίνομαι (VKg)		11,9	0	0
φωνή + ἀποφθέγγομαι/φημί (VKl)		2,14; 26,24	0	0
φωνή βοάω (VKc); cf. φωνή + ἀναβοάω Mt 27,46	3,4	8,7	1/2	2
φωνή (+) (ἀνα)κράζω (VKf)	4,33; 8,28	7,57.60; 19,34; 24,21	1	1/2
φωνή + λαλέω (VKh)		22,9; 26,14 v.l.	0	0
φωνή (+) λέγω/εἶπον (VKj)	1,42*; 3,22 v.l.; 4,33 v.l.; 8,28; 9,35; 11,27; 17,13; 19,37(-38); 23,46	4,24; 9,4; 11,7; 14,10. 11; 16,28; 22,7.22; 26,14	3	1/3
φωνῇ μεγαλῇ + βοάω/(ἀνα)κράζω/(ἀνα)φωνέω → ἀναφωνέω κραυγῇ μεγάλῃ; cf. φωνῇ μεγαλῇ + ἀναβοάω Mt 27,46; Lk 1,42	1,42*; 4,33; 8,28; 23,46	7,57.60; 8,7; 16,28	1/2	3
φωναί plural (VKn) DENAUX 2009 Laⁿ	23,23[1.2]	13,27	0	0
φωνή divine voice (SCa)	3,22; 9,35.36	7,31; 9,4.7; 10,13.15; 11,7.9; 12,22; 22,7.9.14; 26,14	2	2

Characteristic of Luke

GOULDER 1989; MORGENTHALER 1958LA/A

	Lk	Acts	Mt	Mk
αἴρω/ἐπαίρω φωνήν (LN: speak loudly; SCc; VKb) → ἐπαίρω τοὺς ὀφθαλμούς BOISMARD 1984 Ab45; DENAUX 2009 1A*; NEIRYNCK 1985	11,27; 17,13	2,14; 4,24; 14,11; 22,22	0	0
ἐπαίρω φωνήν PLUMMER 1922 lii.lix; VOGEL 1899C	11,27	2,14; 14,11; 22,22	0	0
εἶπον φωνῇ μεγάλῃ BOISMARD 1984 Ab207; NEIRYNCK 1985	8,28	14,10	0	0

φωνή + (ἀνα)φωνέω (VKm) HARNACK 1906 43	1,42*; 23,46	16,28	0	1
φωνή + γίνομαι GOULDER 1989*; DENAUX 2009 L***; HARNACK 1906 139; HAWKINS 1909L;	1,44; 3,22; 9,35.36	2,6; 7,31; 10,13; 19,35	0	1
φωνὴ μεγάλη (SCb; VKa) → κραυγὴ μεγάλη CREDNER 1836 141; PLUMMER 1922 lx; VOGEL 1899C	1,42*; 4,33; 8,28; 17,15; 19,37; 23,23[1].46	7,57.60; 8,7; 14,10; 16,28; 26,24	2/3	4

Literature

COLLISON 1977 187 [φωνὴ μεγάλη: linguistic usage of Luke: probable]; DENAUX 2009 [lA[n]: ἐπαίρω φωνήν], [LA[n]: εἶπον φωνῇ μεγαλῇ]; EASTON 1910 166 [αἴρω φωνήν: cited by Weiss as characteristic of L, and possibly corroborative]; GERSDORF 1816 198-199 [φωνέω φωνῇ μεγαλῇ]; 199 [ἐγένετο ἡ φωνή - εἰς τὰ ὦτά μου]; HAUCK 1934 [Vorzugsverbindung: ἐγένετο ἡ φωνή]; JEREMIAS 1980 58 [φωνή singular + γίνομαι: red.]; 68 [αἴρω φωνήν + λέγων: red.]; 70 [φωνὴ ἐγένετο + λέγων: red.]; 203 [(ἐπ)αἴρω (τὴν) φωνήν (λέγων): red.]; 265 [φωνῇ μεγάλη: red.]; 307 [φωνήσας φωνῇ μεγάλη: red.]; RADL 1975 410 [ἐπαίρω τὴν φωνήν]; 416 [μέγας + φωνή].

STEUERNAGEL, Gert, Ἀκούοντες μὲν τῆς φωνῆς (Apg 9.7): Ein Genitiv in der Apostelgeschichte. — NTS 35 (1989) 625-627.
STRELAN, Rick, Recognizing the Gods (Acts 14.8-10). — NTS 46 (2000) 488-503. Esp. 490-493: "The stare"; 493-501: "The loud voice".

φῶς 7 + 10 (Mt 7, Mk 1)
1. light (Lk 2,32); 2. bonfire; 3. torch (Acts 16,29)

Word groups	Lk	Acts	Mt	Mk
υἱοὶ τοῦ φωτός (LN: people of God; VKb)	16,8		0	0
φῶς (+) (περι)λάμπω/περιαστράπτω (VKd)		9,3; 12,7; 22,6; 26,13	1	0
φῶς + σκοτία/σκότος (SCa; VKc) → σκοτεινός + φωτεινός	11,35; 12,3	26,18	3	0
φωτά plural (VKe)		16,29	0	0

Literature

GERSDORF 1816 256 [φῶς εἰς ἀποκάλυψιν ἐθνῶν].

DELEBECQUE, Édouard, Études grecques, 1976. Esp. 85-88: "La lampe et l'œil (11,33-36)".
HAHN, Ferdinand, Die Worte vom Licht Lk 11,33-36. — HOFFMANN, P. – BROX, N. – PESCH, W. (eds.), Orientierung an Christus. FS J. Schmid, 1973, 107-138.

φωτεινός 3 (Mt 2)
1. full of light (Lk 11,34.36[1.2]); 2. bright

Word groups	Lk	Acts	Mt	Mk
σκοτεινός + φωτεινός → σκοτία/σκότος + φῶς	11,34.36		1	0

Literature

DELEBECQUE, Édouard, Études grecques, 1976. Esp. 85-88: "La lampe et l'œil (11,33-36)".

φωτίζω 1
1. shine upon (Lk 11,36); 2. make known

X

χαίρω 12 + 7 (Mt 6, Mk 2)

1. rejoice (Lk 6,23); 2. greetings (Lk 1,28)

Word groups	Lk	Acts	Mt	Mk
χαῖρε/χαίρετε (formula of greeting) (SCa; VKa)	1,28		3	1
χαίρω αἰνέω → χαρά + εὐλογέω	19,37		0	0
χαίρω (+) ἐν (VKe)	6,23; 10,20[1]		0	0
χαίρω + χαρά (VKh)	1,14		1	0
χαίρειν at the beginning of a letter (SCb; VKb)		15,23; 23,26	0	0
χαίρων partic. of circumstance	15,5; 19,6.37	5,41; 8,39	0	0
DENAUX 2009 La[n]				

Characteristic of Luke

MORGENTHALER 1958L

	Lk	Acts	Mt	Mk
χαίρω, of rejoicing, not of greeting	1,14; 6,23; 10,20[1.2];	5,41; 8,39; 11,23;	3	1
DENAUX 2009 L***; GOULDER 1989*;	13,17; 15,5.32;	13,48; 15,31		
HAWKINS 1909L	19,6.37; 22,5; 23,8			
χαίρω at the end of a sentence	15,5; 19,6	8,39	0	0
BOISMARD 1984 Ab152; NEIRYNCK 1985;				
VOGEL 1899C				
χαίρω ἐπί + dative (VKf)	1,14; 13,17	15,31	1	0
HARNACK 1906 72				

Literature

VON BENDEMANN 2001 418; COLLISON 1977 68 [linguistic usage of Luke's "other source-material": probable; to rejoice: linguistic usage of Luke: also likely]; DENAUX 2009 La[n] [χαίρων at the end of a sentence]; HAUCK 1934 [Vorzugswort]; JEREMIAS 1980 246: "Das Partizip χαίρων als begleitende Zustandsbestimmung findet sich im NT nur im lk Doppelwerk"; REHKOPF 1959 97-98 [χαίρειν ('sich freuen'): vorlukanisch]; SCHÜRMANN 1961 276 [χαίρειν ('sich freuen')].

DELEBECQUE, Edouard, Sur la salutation de Gabriel à Marie (Lc 1,28). — Bib 65 (1984) 352-355.
DUPONT, Jacques, Les Béatitudes, II, 1969. Esp. 320-322: "'Se réjouir', 'exulter'".
LYONNET, Stanislas, Χαῖρε κεχαριτωμένη. — Bib 20 (1939) 131-141.
RODRÍGUEZ, Isidoro, Consideración filologica sobre el mensaje de la anunciación, 1958. Esp. 229-231: "χαῖρε".
STROBEL, August, Der Gruss an Maria (Lk 1 28). — ZNW 53 (1962) 86-110. Esp. 87-105.

χαλάω 2 + 3 (Mk 1)   let down (Lk 5,4.5; Acts 9,25; 27,17.30)

Characteristic of Luke

BOISMARD 1984 cb82; DENAUX 2009 lA*; NEIRYNCK 1985; PLUMMER 1922 lx

χαρά 8 + 4/5 (Mt 6, Mk 1)

1. gladness (Lk 1,14); 2. reason for gladness (Lk 2,10)

Word groups	Lk	Acts	Mt	Mk
ἀγαλλίασις + χαρά; cf. ἀγαλλιάω + χαρά/χαίρω Mt 5,12; Jn 8,56; 1 Pet 1,8; 4,13; Rev 19,7	1,14		0	0
μετὰ χαρᾶς (VKf)		8,13; 10,17; 24,52	20,24*	2	1
χαρά + εὐλογέω → χαίρω + αἰνέω	24,52(-53)		0	0
χαρά + χαίρω (VKg)	1,14		1	0

Characteristic of Luke	Lk	Acts	Mt	Mk
ἀπὸ τῆς χαρᾶς without determinative (VKc) BOISMARD 1984 Ab208; NEIRYNCK 1985	24,41	12,14	0	0
πολλὴ χαρά (VKa); cf. πᾶσα χαρά Rom 15,13; Phil 2,29; Jam 1,2 PLUMMER 1922 lx		8,8	0	0
χαρὰ μεγάλη (SCa; VKb) CREDNER 1936 141; PLUMMER 1922 lx	2,10; 24,52	8,8 v.l.; 15,3	2	0

Literature

VON BENDEMANN 2001 417: "χαρά ist ein lukanischer Schlüsselterminus"; DENAUX 2009 LAⁿ [ἀπὸ τῆς χαρᾶς]; GERSDORF 1816 182 [καὶ ἔσται χαρά σοι]; 227 [χαρὰν μεγάλην]; JEREMIAS 1980 81 [χαρὰν μεγάλην: red.]; RADL 1975 416-417 [μέγας + χαρά].

CAMBE, Michel, La χάρις chez saint Luc: Remarques sur quelques textes, notamment le κεχαριτωμένη. — RB 70 (1963) 193-207. Esp. 197-198: "χάρις et χάρα".

χάραξ 1

barricade (Lk 19,43)

χαρίζομαι 3 + 4

1. give generously (Lk 7,21; Acts 27,24); 2. forgive; 3. cancel a debt (Lk 7,42.43); 4. hand over to (Acts 25,16)

Characteristic of Luke

DENAUX 2009 1A*; HARNACK 1906 53; HAWKINS 1909B

Literature

HAUCK 1934 [Vorzugswort]; JEREMIAS 1980 162 [red.]; RADL 1975 430.

SCHULZ, Thomas, Charis nel Nuovo Testamento. — RicBibRel 5 (1970) 211-223. Esp. 211-213: "I verbi charitoo e charizomai".

See also χάρις

χάριν 1

1. because of (Lk 7,47); 2. for the purpose of

Word groups	Lk	Acts	Mt	Mk
οὗ χάριν → οὗ εἵνεκεν/ἕνεκεν	7,47		0	0

Literature

HAUCK 1934 [seltenes Alleinwort].

ANDERSEN, T. David, The Meaning of ἔχοντες χάριν πρός in Acts 2.47. — NTS 34 (1988) 604-610.

DUBLIN, John, οὗ χάριν. — *ExpT* 37 (1926-27) 525-526.
MEECHAM, H.G., Luke vii.47. — *ExpT* 38 (1926-27) 286. [οὗ χάριν]
SCHULZ, Thomas, Charis nel Nuovo Testamento. — *RicBibRel* 5 (1970) 211-223. Esp. 216-217: "La preposizione charin".

χάρις 8 + 17

1. kindness (Acts 15,40); 2. gift; 3. thanks (Lk 17,9); 4. good will (Lk 1,30; Acts 2,47)

Word groups	Lk	Acts	Mt	Mk
χάριν + δίδωμι (*VK*e)		7,10	0	0
χάρις (τοῦ) θεοῦ (*SC*a; *VK*b); cf. χάρις αὐτοῦ Acts 20,32 DENAUX 2009 IA[n]	2,40	11,23; 13,43; 14,26; 15,40 *v.l.*; 20,24	0	0
χάρις παρὰ τῷ θεῷ / ἐνώπιον τοῦ θεοῦ (*SC*b) DENAUX 2009 La[n]	1,30; 2,52	7,46	0	0
χάρις τοῦ κυρίου/(Ἰησοῦ)/Χριστοῦ (*SC*c; *VK*c); cf. χάρις αὐτοῦ Acts 14,3 BOISMARD 1984 Db9; NEIRYNCK 1985		15,11.40		
χάρις + σοφία DENAUX 2009 LA[n] (?)	2,40	7,10	0	0
χάριτα accusative (*VK*a)		24,27	0	0
χάριτες plural (*VK*m)		24,27	0	0

Characteristic of Luke

BOISMARD 1984 Eb15; CREDNER 1836 140; DENAUX 2009 L***; GOULDER 1989*; HARNACK 1906 150; HAWKINS 1909 L; MORGENTHALER 1958A; NEIRYNCK 1985; PLUMMER 1922 lx

	Lk	Acts	Mt	Mk
λόγος τῆς χάριτος (*SC*d; *VK*g) BOISMARD 1984 Ab134; NEIRYNCK 1985	4,22	14,3; 20,32	0	0
πλήρης χάριτος (without ὤν) → πλήρης πνεύματος VOGEL 1899C		6,8		
χάριν ἔχω (*VK*f) / εὑρίσκω; cf. Heb 4,16[2] BOISMARD 1984 Db30; NEIRYNCK 1985	1,30; 17,9	2,47; 7,46		

Literature

DENAUX 2009 IA[n] [λόγος τῆς χάριτος], LA[n] [χάριν ἔχω]; EASTON 1910 166 [cited by Weiss as characteristic of L, and possibly corroborative]; HAUCK 1934 [seltenes/häufiges Alleinwort]; JEREMIAS 1980 50: "Es bleibt dabei, daß Lukas das Wort χάρις gern gebraucht. Es darf jedoch nicht übersehen werden, daß Lukas im Evangelium vorgeprägte judenchristliche Formulierungen aufgreift, in der Apostelgeschichte dagegen die ihm selbst geläufige frühchristlich-hellenistische Terminologie bestimmend sein läßt"; RADL 1975 430 [χάρις; χάρις θεοῦ (κυρίου, Χριστοῦ)].

ARICHEA, Daniel C., Jr., Translating "Grace" (*Charis*) in the New Testament. — *BTrans* 29 (1978) 149-206.
CAMBE, Michel, La χάρις chez saint Luc: Remarques sur quelques textes, notamment le κεχαριτωμένη. — *RB* 70 (1963) 193-207.
GAMBA, Giuseppe Giov., Significato letterale e portata dottrinale dell'inciso participiale di Atti 2,47b: ἔχοντες χάριν πρὸς ὅλον τὸν λαόν. — *Sal* 43 (1981) 45-70.
KNOWLES, M.P., Reciprocity and "Favour" in the Parable of the Undeserving Servant (Luke 17.7-10). — *NTS* 49 (2003) 256-260.
NOLLAND, John L., Words of Grace (Luke 4,22). — *Bib* 65 (1984) 44-60.
—, Grace as Power. — *NT* 28 (1986) 26-31.

—, Luke's Use of χάρις. — *NTS* 32 (1986) 614-620.

Ó FEARGHAIL, Fearghus, Rejection in Nazareth: Lk 4,22. — *ZNW* 75 (1984) 60-72. Esp. 65-67 [μαρτυρέω]; 67 [θαυμάζω]; 67-69 [οἱ λόγοι τῆς χάριτος].

PANIMOLLE, Salvatore Alberto, La χάρις negli Atti e nel Quarto Vangelo. — *RivBib* 25 (1977) 143-158. Esp. 143-151: "La χάρις negli Atti degli Apostoli".

RIGGENBACH, Eduard, Ein Beitrag zum Verständnis der Parabel vom arbeitenden Knecht Luk. 17,7-10. — *Neue Kirchliche Zeitschrift* 34 (1923) 439-443 [Lk 17,9 χάριν ἔχειν = Dank wissen].

SCHULZ, Thomas, Charis nel Nuovo Testamento. — *RicBibRel* 5 (1970) 211-223. Esp. 211-213: "I verbi charitoo e charizomai"; 213-216: "Il nome charisma"; 216-217: "La preposizione charin".

STROBEL, August, Der Gruss an Maria (Lc 1,28). — *ZNW* 53 (1962) 86-110.

VAN UNNIK, Wilhelm C., Die Motivierung der Feindesliebe in Lukas VI 32-35. — *NT* 8 (1966) 284-300; = ID., *Sparsa Collecta*, I, 1973, 111-126.

χαριτόω 1	show kindness (Lk 1,28)

Literature

HAUCK 1934 [seltenes Alleinwort]; REHKOPF 1959 99 [κεχαριτωμένη: "Substantiva in Anrede bei den Synoptikern"].

BUZZETTI, Carlo, Kecharitōmēnē, "favoured" (Lk 1.28), and the Italian Common Language New Testament ("Parola del Signore"). — *BTrans* 33 (1982) 243.

—, Traducendo κεχαριτωμένη (Lc. 1,28). — *Testimonium Christi: Scritti in onore di Jacques Dupont*. Brescia: Paideia, 1985, 111-116.

CAMBE, Michel, La χάρις chez saint Luc: Remarques sur quelques textes, notamment le κεχαριτωμένη. — *RB* 70 (1963) 193-207.

CIMOSA, M., Il senso del titolo κεχαριτωμένη. — *Theotokos* 4 (1996) 589-597.

COLE, Eugene R., What Did Luke Mean by Kecharitomene? — *The American Ecclesiastical Review* 139 (July-Dec. 1958) 228-239. [Lk 1,28]

DE LA POTTERIE, Ignace, Κεχαριτωμένη en Lc 1,28. Étude philologique. — *Bib* 68 (1987) 357-382. [NTA 32, 643]

—, Κεχαριτωμένη en Lc 1,28. Étude exégétique et théologique. — *Bib* 68 (1987) 480-508.

DELEBECQUE, Edouard, Sur la salutation de Gabriel à Marie (Lc 1,28). — *Bib* 65 (1984) 352-355.

DELLA CORTE, Ernesto, Κεχαριτωμένη (Lc 1,28): *Crux interpretum*. — *Marianum* 52 (1990) 101-148. Esp. 103-105: "Analisi lessicografica"; 106-115: "Analisi filologica e contesto di Luca"; 115-122: "Κεχαριτωμένη nella storia dell'esegesi"; 122-133: "Κεχαριτωμένη nei vari commentari e articoli: le diverse traduzioni in alcune bibbie moderne"; 134-141: "Efesini 1,6 e il contesto lucano di κεχαριτωμένη".

LYONNET, Stanislas, Χαῖρε κεχαριτωμένη. — *Bib* 20 (1939) 131-141.

MOHRMANN, Christine, Ave gratificata. — *Rivista di Storia della Chiesa in Italia* 5 (1951) 1-6.

RODRÍGUEZ, Isidoro, Consideración filologica sobre el mensaje de la anunciación, 1958. Esp. 231-240: "κεχαριτωμένη".

SCHULZ, Thomas, Charis nel Nuovo Testamento. — *RicBibRel* 5 (1970) 211-223. Esp. 211-213: "I verbi charitoo e charizomai".

STROBEL, August, Der Gruss an Maria (Lc 1,28). — *ZNW* 53 (1962) 86-110. Esp. 106-107.

STUMMER, Friedrich, Beiträge zur Exegese der Vulgata. — *ZAW* 62 (1949-50) 152-167. Esp. 161-167 [Lk 1,28].

See also χάρις

χάσμα 1   chasm

Word groups	Lk	Acts	Mt	Mk
χάσμα + ἐστήρικται	16,26		0	0

Literature

HAUCK 1934 [seltenes Alleinwort].

χείρ 26 + 45/46 (Mt 24, Mk 24[26])

1. hand, finger (Lk 6,6); 2. person (Acts 7,50); 3. power (Acts 7,50); 4. be in control of (Acts 12,11)

Word groups	Lk	Acts	Mt	Mk
ἡ δεξιὰ χείρ / ἡ χείρ (...) ἡ δεξιά (SCa; VKa)	6,6	3,7	1	0
διὰ χειρός (SCg; VKk)		2,23; 7,25;	0	0
διὰ (τῶν) χειρῶν (SCg; VKl) BOISMARD 1984 Ba6		11,30; 15,23 2,23 v.l.; 5,12; 14,3; 19,11.26	0	1
εἰς (τὰς) χεῖρας (VKm)	9,44; 23,46; 24,7	21,11²; 28,17	2	2
ἐκ (τῆς) χειρός / τῶν χειρῶν others (VKn) → ἐκ τῆς χειρός (proper sense) DENAUX 2009 Laⁿ	1,71.74	12,11; 24,7*	0	0
ἐκ τῆς χειρός (proper sense) (VKp) → ἐκ (τῆς) χειρός / τῶν χειρῶν others		12,7; 28,4	0	0
ἐκτείνω τὴν χεῖρα (SCb; VKc)	5,13; 6,10¹	4,30; 26,1	5	2
ἐκτείνω τὰς χεῖρας ἐπί + accusative (LN: arrest)	22,53		0	0
ἐν/σὺν χειρί (LN: with the help of; VKr)	3,17	7,35	1	0
ἐπὶ χειρῶν (VKq)	4,11		1	0
ἐπιβάλλω τὴν χεῖρα ἐπ' ἄροτρον καὶ βλέπω εἰς τὰ ὀπίσω (LN: start to do and then hesitate)	9,62		0	0
ἐπίθεσις τῶν χειρῶν (SCd) → ἐπιτίθημι τὰς χεῖρας + dat./ἐπί + acc.		8,18	0	0
ἐπιτίθημι τὰς χεῖρας ἐπί + accusative (SCd; VKd) → ἐπιτίθημι τὰς χεῖρας + dat.; ἐπίθεσις τῶν χειρῶν; ἐπιβάλλω τὴν χεῖρα/τὰς χεῖρας + dat./ἐπί + acc.; cf. ἐπιτίθημι τὴν χεῖρα ἐπί + acc. Mt 9,18; τίθημι τὰς χεῖρας ἐπί + acc. Mk 10,16 BOISMARD 1984 ca46		8,17; 9,17	0	1[2]
ἐπιτίθημι (+) τὰς χεῖρας + dative (SCd; VKd) → ἐπιτίθημι τὰς χεῖρας ἐπί + acc.; ἐπίθεσις τῶν χειρῶν; ἐπιβάλλω τὴν χεῖρα/τὰς χεῖρας + dat./ἐπί + acc.; cf. ἐπιτίθημι τὴν χεῖρα + dat. Mk 7,32	4,40; 13,13	6,6; 8,19; 9,12; 13,3; 19,6; 28,8	2	3
ἔργα τῶν χειρῶν (VKh)		7,41	0	0
κατασείω τῇ χειρί CREDNER 1836 142		12,17; 13,16; 19,33; 21,40	0	0
κρατέω τῆς χειρός (SCe)	8,54		1	3
παραδίδωμι εἰς (τὰς) χεῖρας (LN: deliver to control of; SCh)	9,44; 24,7		21,11²; 28,17	2	2
χεὶρ ἀνθρωπίνη (LN: person)		17,25		
χείρ + πούς (VKg)	15,22; 24,39.40		21,11¹	3	2
χεῖρα + ἐπαίρω (VKf)	24,50		0	0
χεῖρες ἀνθρώπων	9,44; 24,7	17,25 v.l.	1	1

Characteristic of Luke
MORGENTHALER 1958A

	Lk	Acts	Mt	Mk
ἐπιβάλλω τὴν χεῖρα/τὰς χεῖρας + dative / ἐπί + accusative (LN: arrest; SCc; VKe) → ἐπιτίθημι τὰς χεῖρας + dat./ἐπί + acc.; cf. Jn 7,30.44 BOISMARD 1984 cb108; NEIRYNCK 1985	9,62; 20,19; 21,12	4,3; 5,18; 12,1; 21,27	1	1
χείρ + determinative (figurative sense); cf. Jn 3,35; 10,28.29; Heb 10,31; 1 Pet 5,6 BOISMARD 1984 cb127; DENAUX 2009 IA**; NEIRYNCK 1985	1,66.71.74; 9,44; 23,46; 24,7	2,23; 4,28.30; 7,25.35; 11,21; 13,11; 19,26; 21,11; 28,17	2	2
χεὶρ κυρίου (SCf; VKj) BOISMARD 1984 Ab153; NEIRYNCK 1985; PLUMMER 1922 lii	1,66	11,21; 13,11	0	0

Literature
BDAG 2000 1082-1083 [literature]; DENAUX 2009 IAn [ἐπιβάλλω τὴν χεῖρα/τὰς χεῖρας + dative / ἐπί + accusative], IAⁿ [χεὶρ κυρίου]; GERSDORF 1816 206 [καὶ γὰρ χεὶρ κυρίου ἦν μετ' αὐτοῦ]; 207 ἐκ χειρὸς πάντων τῶν μισούντων); JEREMIAS 1980 32 [χεὶρ κυρίου: trad.]; RADL 1975 410 [ἐπιβάλλω τὰς χεῖρας (τὴν χεῖρα) (ἐπί)].

χείρων 1 (Mt 3, Mk 2)
1. very bad; 2. worse (Lk 11,26)

χήρα 9 + 3 (Mt 0/1; Mk 3) — widow

Word groups	Lk	Acts	Mt	Mk
γυνὴ χήρα (VKa)	4,26		0	0
αἱ οἰκίαι τῶν χηρῶν (VKc)	20,47		0/1	1

Characteristic of Luke
BOISMARD 1984 Eb51; DENAUX 2009 L***; GOULDER 1989*; HAWKINS 1909 L; NEIRYNCK 1985

Literature
COLLISON 1977 177-178 [linguistic usage of Luke's "other source-material": certain]; GERSDORF 1816 260 [καὶ αὐτὴ χήρα]; HAUCK 1934 [Vorzugswort; Vorzugsverbindung: τις χήρα].

PRICE, Robert M., *The Widow Traditions in Luke-Acts. A Feminist-Critical Scrutiny* (SBL DS, 155). Atlanta, GA: Scholars Press, 1997.

SCHWARZ, Günther, "Die Häuser der Witwen verzehren"? (Markus 12,40 / Lk 20,47). — *BibNot* 88 (1997) 45-46.

χιλιάς 2 + 1 — group of a thousand

Word groups	Lk	Acts	Mt	Mk
δέκα χιλιάδες (VKc)	14,31[1]		0	0
εἴκοσι χιλιάδες (VKe)	14,31[2]		0	0
χιλιάδες πέντε (VKa)		4,4	0	0

χιτών 3 + 1 (Mt 2, Mk 2)

1. tunic (Lk 3,11; 6,29; 9,3); 2. clothing

Word groups	Lk	Acts	Mt	Mk
χιτών + ἱμάτιον (VKa) → ἱματισμός + ἱμάτιον	6,29	9,39	1	0

χοῖρος 4 (Mt 4/5, Mk 4/5)   pig

Word groups	Lk	Acts	Mt	Mk
ἀγέλη (τῶν) χοίρων (VKa)	8,32		3/4	1
χοῖρος (+) βόσκω	8,32.33(-34); 15,15		2	2

Literature
BDAG 2000 1086 [literature].

Χοραζίν 1 (Mt 1)   Chorazin (Lk 10,13)

χορός 1   dancing (Lk 15,25)

Literature
HAUCK 1934 [seltenes Alleinwort].

χορτάζω 4 (Mt 4, Mk 4)

1. cause to eat one's fill; χορτάζομαι: 2. eat one's fill (Lk 6,21; 9,17; 15,16; 16,21); 3. be content

Word groups	Lk	Acts	Mt	Mk
ἐσθίω + χορτάζομαι	9,17; 15,16		3	3
χορτάζομαι ἀπό VKc)	16,21		0	0
χορτάζομαι ἐκ (VKb)	15,16		0	0

Literature
PAFFENROTH 1997 83

χόρτος 1 (Mt 3, Mk 2)

1. grass (Lk 12,28); 2. sprout

Χουζᾶς 1   Chuza

χρεία 7 + 5 (Mt 6, Mk 4)

1. what is needed (Lk 10,42); 2. what should be; 3. needed task (Acts 6,3)

Word groups	Lk	Acts	Mt	Mk
χρεία ἐστιν	10,42		0	0

χρείαν ἔχω absolute (VKd)		2,45; 4,35	0	1
χρείαν ἔχω + genitive (VKa); cf. χρείαν ἔχω + inf. Mt 3,14; 14,16	5,31; 9,11; 15,7; 19,31.34; 22,71		4	3
χρείαι plural HARNACK 1906 43		20,34; 28,10	0	0

Literature

AUGSTEN, Monika, Lukanische Miszelle. — *NTS* 14 (1967-68) 581-583 [Lk 10,42].

BAKER, Aelred, One Thing Necessary. — *CBQ* 27 (1965) 127-137 [Lk 10,42].

FEE, Gordon D., "One Thing is Needful"?, Luke 10:42. — EPP, E.J. – FEE, G.D. (eds.), *New Testament Textual Criticism*. FS B.M. Metzger, 1981, 71-75.

NORTH, J. Lionel, ὀλίγων δέ ἐστιν χρεία ἢ ἑνός (Luke 10.42): Text, Subtext and Context. — *JSNT* 66 (1997) 3-13. [NTA 42, 266]

SUDBRACK, Josef, "Nur eines ist notwendig" (Lk 10,42). — *Geist und Leben* 37 (1964) 161-164.

χρεοφειλέτης 2   debtor (Lk 7,41; 16,5)

Characteristic of Luke
PLUMMER 1922 liii

Literature
DENAUX 2009 L[n]; HAUCK 1934 [seltenes Alleinwort]; PAFFENROTH 1997 78.82.

BORMANN, Lukas, *Recht, Gerechtigkeit und Religion*, 2001. Esp. 164.

χρῄζω 2 (Mt 1)   need (Lk 11,8; 12,30)

χρῆμα 1 + 4 (Mk 1/2)
1. riches (Lk 18,24); 2. money (Acts 4,37; 8,18; 20,24.26)

Characteristic of Luke
BOISMARD 1984 Bb83; NEIRYNCK 1985

Literature
DENAUX 2009 lA[n].

χρηματίζω 1 + 2 (Mt 2)
1. reveal divine message (Lk 2,26; Acts 10,22); 2. give a name to (Acts 11,26)

Word groups	Lk	Acts	Mt	Mk
χρηματίζω have the name of / be called (VKa); cf. Rom 7,3		11,26	0	0

Literature
HEINIGER, Bernhard, Hebr 11.7 und das Henochorakel am Ende der Welt. — *NTS* 44 (1998) 115-132.

χρηστός 2 (Mt 1)
1. good (value) (Lk 5,39); 2. good (moral); 3. kind (Lk 6,35); 4. easy

Word groups	Lk	Acts	Mt	Mk
χρηστότερος comparative (VKa)	5,39		0	0

Χριστός 12/13 + 25/33 (Mt 16/18, Mk 7/8)
1. Messiah; 2. Christ (Lk 2,11)

Word groups	Lk	Acts	Mt	Mk
ἀνάστασις τοῦ Χριστοῦ		2,31	0	0
διὰ Ἰησοῦ Χριστοῦ; cf. διὰ Χριστοῦ (VKh); 2 Cor 5,18 v.l.; Gal 4,7*		10,36	0	0
εἰς Χριστόν (VKj)		24,24	0	0
Ἰησοῦς Χριστός (SCa; VKa); cf. Ἰησοῦς ὁ λεγόμενος Χριστός Mt 1,16; 27,17.22		2,38; 3,6; 4,10.33*; 8,12. 37*; 9,34; 10,36.48; 11,17; 15,11*.26; 16,18.31*; 20,21*; 28,31	2/3	1
Ἰησοῦς ὁ Χριστός (VKb)		5,42 v.l.; 9,34 v.l.	0/1	0
Ἰησοῦς Χριστός + κύριος (SCb)		4,33*; 11,17; 15,11*.26; 16,31*; 20,21*; 28,31	0	0
κατὰ τοῦ Χριστοῦ; cf. κατὰ Χριστόν (VKl); cf. Kol 2,8		4,26		
ὄνομα (τοῦ) Ἰησοῦ Χριστοῦ → ὄνομα (τοῦ) Ἰησοῦ; ὄνομα (τοῦ) κυρίου		2,38; 3,6; 4,10; 8,12; 10,48; 16,18	0	0
Χριστὸς (ὁ) Ἰησοῦς (VKc)		3,20; 5,42; 17,3²; 18,5.28; 19,4*; 24,24	0	0

→ κηρύσσω τὸν Χριστόν

Characteristic of Luke	Lk	Acts	Mt	Mk
ὁ χριστὸς (τοῦ) θεοῦ/κυρίου BOISMARD 1984 Db37; NEIRYNCK 1985	2,26; 9,20; 23,35	3,18 (αὐτοῦ)	0	0
Χριστός + κύριος (SCc; VKe) DENAUX 2009 IA* (?)	2,11.26	2,36; 3,20; 4,26.33*; 11,17; 15,11*.26; 16,31*; 20,21*; 28,31	0	0

→ εὐαγγελίζομαι τὸν Χριστόν; πίστις εἰς (κύριον/Χριστὸν) Ἰησοῦν

Literature

BDAG 2000 1091 [literature]; DENAUX 2009 Laⁿ [ὁ χριστὸς (τοῦ) θεοῦ/κυρίου]; GERSDORF 1816 252 [τὸν χριστὸν κυρίου]; JEREMIAS 1980 208 [ὁ χριστὸς τοῦ θεοῦ: red.]; SCHÜRMANN 1955 55 [(ὁ) Χριστὸς κύριος bzw. κύριος Χριστός].

BOUSSET, Wilhelm, *Jesus der Herr: Nachträge und Auseinandersetzungen zu Kurios Christos*. Göttingen: Vandenhoeck & Ruprecht, 1916, 95 p.

DE JONGE, Marinus, The Use of ὁ Χριστός in the Passion Narratives. — DUPONT, J. (ed.), *Jésus aux origines de la christologie* (BETL, 40). Leuven: University Press; Gembloux: Duculot, 1975, 169-192; Leuven: University Press – Peeters, ²1989.

GEORGE, Augustin, La royauté de Jésus. — ID., *Études*, 1978, 257-282. Esp. 259-262: "Christ (Christos)".

HAGENE, Sylvia, *Zeiten der Wiederherstellung*, 2003. Esp. 178-188: "Textsemantische Beobachtungen zu χριστός".

HAHN, Ferdinand, *Christologische Hoheitstitel*, 1963. Esp. 133-225: "Christos".

KARRER, Martin, *Der Gesalbte: Die Grundlagen des Christustitels* (FRLANT, 151). Göttingen: Vandenhoeck & Ruprecht, 1991, 482 p.

MAHFOUZ, Hady, *La fonction littéraire et théologique de Lc 3,1-20*, 2003. Esp. 264-274.

PRETE, Benedetto, "Oggi vi è nato ... il Salvatore che è il Cristo Signore" (Lc 2,11). — *RivBib* 34 (1986) 289-325. Esp. 313-317: "Messia (χριστός)".

READ-HEIMERDINGER, Jenny, *The Bezan Text of Acts*, 2002. Esp. 254-274: "Titles of Jesus"
[(ὁ) Ἰησοῦς; Ἰησοῦς ὁ Ναζωραῖος; ὁ παῖς; ὁ ἅγιος παῖς σου Ἰησοῦς; (ὁ) Χριστός;
Χριστὸς Ἰησοῦς; Ἰησοῦς Χριστός; Ἰησοῦς Χριστὸς ὁ Ναζωραῖος; (ὁ) κύριος; (ὁ)
κύριος Ἰησοῦς; ὁ κύριος Ἰησοῦς Χριστός].
RESE, Martin, *Alttestamentliche Motive in der Christologie des Lukas*, 1969. Esp. 121-126:
"Χριστός in der Apostelgeschichte"; 204-205: "Σωτήρ, Χριστός [υἱὸς Δαυίδ] im
Lukasevangelium".
WINTER, Paul, Lukanische Miszellen. — *ZNW* 49 (1958) 65-77. Esp. 67-75: "Lc 2,11:
χριστὸς κύριος oder χριστὸς κυρίου"?

χρίω 1 + 2 | assign (Lk 4,18)

Word groups	Lk	Acts	Mt	Mk
χρίω said of Jesus BOISMARD 1984 Aa165		4,27; 10,38	0	0

Literature
DENAUX 2009 1A[n].

RAVENS, David A.S., The Setting of Luke's Account of the Anointing: Luke 7.2–8.3. —
NTS 34 (1988) 282-292.

χρονίζω 2 (Mt 2)
1. be late (Lk 12,45); 2. spend long time (Lk 1,21)

χρόνος 7 + 17 (Mt 3, Mk 2)
1. time (Acts 15,33); 2. occasion (Acts 7,17)

Word groups	Lk	Acts	Mt	Mk
ἐν στιγμῇ χρόνου	4,5		0	0
ἐπὶ χρόνον (VKj)	18,4	18,20	0	0
(ὁ) πᾶς χρόνος(VKd) BOISMARD 1984 Aa166		1,21; 20,18	0	0
ἐπλήσθη ὁ χρόνος → ἐπλήσθησαν αἱ **ἡμέραι**	1,57		0	0
πλείων χρόνος (VKf)		18,20	0	0
πολὺς (+) χρόνος (VKe)	8,29		1	0
χρόνοι καιροί (VKk); cf. 1 Thess 5,1		1,7	0	0
χρόνος οὐκ ὀλίγος (VKc)		14,28	0	0
χρόνος τις (VKg)		18,23	0	0

Characteristic of Luke				
DENAUX 2009 1A*; GOULDER 1989; MORGENTHALER 1958A				
	Lk	Acts	Mt	Mk
χρόνοι plural (VKl) BOISMARD 1984 Db15; DENAUX 2009 LA*; HAWKINS 1909B; NEIRYNCK 1985	8,27 v.l.29; 20,9; 23,8	1,7; 3,21; 17,30	0	0
χρόνος + ἱκανός (SCa; VKa) → **ἡμέρα** ἱκανή DENAUX 2009 LA*; HARNACK 1906 53	8,27; 20,9; 23,8	8,11; 14,3; 27,9	0	0

Literature
COLLISON 1977 178 [linguistic usage of Luke: probable]; HARNACK 1906 44 [dative of time Lk 8,29; cf. Acts 8,11; 13,20; 28,12]; HAUCK 1934 [Vorzugswort]; JEREMIAS 1980 64 [χρόνος ἱκανός; χρόνοι plural: red.].

BURNS, A.L., Two Words for "Time" in the New Testament. — *AusBibRev* 3 (1953) 7-22.
DAUBE, David, *The Sudden in the Scriptures*. Leiden: Brill, 1964, VII-86 p. Esp. 75-77:
"Stigme chronou and ripe ophthalmou".

χωλός 3 + 3/4 (Mt 5, Mk 1) | lame

Word groups	Lk	Acts	Mt	Mk
χωλὸς ἐκ κοιλίας μητρός		3,2; 14,8	0	0
χωλός + κωφός	7,22		1	0
χωλός (+) τυφλός (*VK*a)	7,22; 14,13.21		4	0

Literature
ROTH, S. John, *The Blind, the Lame and the Poor. Character Types in Luke* (JSNT SS, 144). Sheffield: Academic Press, 1997, 253 p. Esp. 107-108.

χώρα 9 + 8 (Mt 3, Mk 4)

1. land (Acts 27,27); 2. region (Acts 8,1); 3. countryside (Lk 21,21); 4. field (Lk 15,15); 5. inhabitants

Word groups	Lk	Acts	Mt	Mk
εἰς χώραν μακράν DENAUX 2009 L[n]	15,13; 19,12		0	0
χώρα + proper name (*SC*a; *VK*a) → χώρα τῆς Ἰου-δαίας/Ἰουδαίων; κώμη/πόλις + proper name	3,1; 8,26	8,1; 10,39; 16,6; 18,23; 26,20	1	2
χώραι plural (*VK*b) DENAUX 2009 LA[n]	21,21	8,1	0	0

Characteristic of Luke
BOISMARD 1984 Cb133; GOULDER 1989; NEIRYNCK 1985

	Lk	Acts	Mt	Mk
πόλις/κώμη/χώρα + determinative of region → πόλις/κώμη + determinative of region BOISMARD 1984 Bb34; IA*; NEIRYNCK 1985	1,26; 4,31; 5,17	8,1; 26,20	0	0

Literature
DENAUX 2009 La[n] [πόλις/κώμη/χώρα + determinative of region]; EASTON 1910 166 [εἰς χώραν μακράν: cited by Weiss as characteristic of L, and possibly corroborative]; GERSDORF 1816 225 [ἐν τῇ χώρᾳ αὐτῇ]; RADL 1975 424-425 [πόλις/κώμη/χώρα mit Landschaftsnamen im Genitiv] BORMANN, Lukas, *Recht, Gerechtigkeit und Religion*, 2001. Esp. 125.

χωρίς 1 (Mt 3, Mk 1)

1. without (Lk 6,49); 2. separately

Ψ

ψαλμός 2 + 2 | song of praise

Characteristic of Luke	Lk	Acts	Mt	Mk
ψαλμός in quotations BOISMARD 1984 Ab104; NEIRYNCK 1985	20,42; 24,44	1,20; 13,33	0	0

Literature
DENAUX 2009 LAⁿ [ψαλμός in quotations].

ψευδομαρτυρέω 1 (Mt 1, Mk 3)   give false witness (Lk 18,20)

Literature
TRITES, Allison A., *The New Testament Concept of Witness*, 1977. Esp. 75-76.

ψευδοπροφήτης 1 + 1 (Mt 3, Mk 1)   false prophet (Lk 6,26; Acts 13,6)

ψηλαφάω 1 + 1
1. touch (Lk 24,39); 2. try to find (Acts 17,27)

Characteristic of Luke
BOISMARD 1984 Db46; NEIRYNCK 1985

Literature
DENAUX 2009 LAⁿ.

ψηφίζω 1
1. calculate (Lk 14,28); 2. figure out

Literature
HAUCK 1934 [seltenes Alleinwort].

BORMANN, Lukas, *Recht, Gerechtigkeit und Religion*, 2001. Esp. 140.

ψυχή 14/15 + 15/16 (Mt 16, Mk 8/9)
1. inner self (Lk 1,46); 2. life (Lk 6,9; 9,24); 3. person (Acts 2,41)

Word groups	Lk	Acts	Mt	Mk
ἀπόλλυμι (+) τὴν ψυχήν (*LN*: die; *SC*a; *VK*a)	6,9; 9,24$^{1.2}$.56*; 17,33		5	2
ζητέω/σῴζω τὴν ψυχήν (*SC*b; *VK*a); cf. εὑρίσκω τὴν ψυχήν Mt 10,39$^{1.2}$; 16,25²	6,9; 9,24$^{1.2}$.56*; 17,33		2	3
κακόω τὴν ψυχὴν κατά + genitive (*LN*: cause to dislike)		14,2	0	0
κτάομαι τὴν ψυχήν (*LN*: protect oneself)	21,19		0	0
ὅλη ἡ ψυχή (*VK*h)	10,27		1	1/2
παραδίδωμι τὴν ψυχήν (*LN*: risk; *VK*b) → δίδωμι (τὸ) **πνεῦμα**; cf. δίδωμι τὴν ψυχήν Mt 20,28; Mk 10,45		15,26	0	0
πᾶσα ψυχή (*VK*g)		2,43; 3,23; 27,37	0	0

ψυχή + καρδία (VKk)	10,27	4,32	1	1/2
ψυχή + πνεῦμα (VKl)	1,46(-47)		1	0
ψυχή + σῶμα (SCc; VKm)	12,22.23		4	0
τὴν ψυχὴν αὐτοῦ περιποιέομαι (LN: save oneself)	17,33		0	0
τὴν ψυχὴν διέρχεται ῥομφαία (LN: feel pain and sorrow)	2,35		0	0
ψυχαί persons BOISMARD 1984 Da24		2,41; 27,37	0	0

Literature

BDAG 2000 1099-1100 [literature]; RADL 1975 430 [ψυχή; ψυχαί]; REHKOPF 1959 99 [ψυχή: "Substantiva in Anrede bei den Synoptikern"].

DAUTZENBERG, Gerhard, *Sein Leben bewahren: Ψυχή in den Herrenworten der Evangelien* (SANT, 14). München: Kösel, 1966, 181 p.
GREENLEE, J. Harold, Psuchê in the New Testament. — *BTrans* 2 (1951) 73-75.
SCHWARZ, Günther, ταυτη τη νυκτι την ψυχην σου απαιτουσιν απο σου? — *BibNot* 25 (1984) 36-41. [NTA 29, 983]

ψώχω 1*   rub (Lk 6,1)

Literature

HAUCK 1934 [seltenes Alleinwort].

DELEBECQUE, Édouard, *Études grecques*, 1976. Esp. 71-83: "Les moissonneurs du sabbat (6,1)".

Ω

ὦ 2 + 4 (Mt 2, Mk 1)   O! (Lk 9,41; 24,25)

Word groups	Lk	Acts	Mt	Mk
ὦ + name of a people (VKb) → ὦ Ἰουδαῖοι		18,14	0	0
ὦ + proper name (VKa)		1,1	0	0

ὧδε 15/17 + 2 (Mt 18, Mk 10)

1. here (Lk 4,23); 2. in this case

Word groups	Lk	Acts	Mt	Mk
ἕως ὧδε (VKb)	23,5		0	0
ὧδε + ἐκεῖ (VKd)	17,21.23		0	1
ὧδε (+) ἰδού (VKa) → ἰδοὺ ἐκεῖ	11,31.32; 17,21.23; 22,38		3	0/1

Literature

SCHÜRMANN 1957 130 [luk R nicht nachweisbar].

ὦμος 1 (Mt 1)   shoulder (Lk 15,5)

ᾠόν 1	egg (Lk 11,12)

Literature
HAUCK 1934 [seltenes Alleinwort].

ὥρα 17 + 11/12 (Mt 21/23, Mk 12)	
1. occasion; 2. a while; 3. hour (Lk 1,10)	

Word groups	Lk	Acts	Mt	Mk
ἐν ἐκείνῃ τῇ ὥρᾳ / τῇ ὥρᾳ ἐκείνῃ (SCf) → ὁ αἰὼν ἐκεῖνος; ἡ **ἡμέρα** ἐκείνη; αἱ **ἡμέραι** ἐκεῖναι; ὁ ἐκεῖνος **καιρός**; **νὺξ** ἐκείνη; cf. ἀπὸ τῆς ὥρας ἐκείνης Mt 9,22; 15,28; 17,18	7,21	16,33	4	1
μία ὥρα (cf. SCb; VKb)	22,59		2	1
ὥρα + numeral (except εἷς) (SCa; VKa)	23,44[1.2]	2,15; 3,1; 5,7; 10,3.9. 30*; 19,34; 23,23	6/7	4
ὥρα ἕκτη → **ὥρα** ἐνάτη/τρίτη	23,44[1]	10,9	2	1
ὥρα (+) ἐνάτη → **ὥρα** ἕκτη/τρίτη	23,44[2]	3,1; 10,3.30*	3	2
ὥρα + ἡμέρα (SCd; VKj)	12,46	2,15; 10,3.30	3	1
ὥρα τῆς νυκτός (VKk)		16,33; 23,23	0	0
ὥρα τρίτη → **ὥρα** ἕκτη/ἐνάτη		2,15; 23,23	1	1
ὥρα + ὁ υἱὸς τοῦ ἀνϑρώπου → **ἡμέρα** + ὁ υἱὸς τοῦ ἀνϑρώπου	12,40		2	1

Characteristic of Luke	Lk	Acts	Mt	Mk
αὐτὸς ὁ **καιρός**/**ἡμέρα**/**ὥρα** BOISMARD 1984 Ab4; DENAUX 2009 L***; NEIRYNCK 1985;	2,38; 10,21; 12,12; 13,1.31; 20,19; 23,12; 24,13.33	16,18; 22,13		
ἐν αὐτῇ τῇ ὥρᾳ (SCg) → ἐν αὐτῇ τῇ **ἡμέρᾳ**; ἐν αὐτῷ τῷ **καιρῷ** DENAUX 2009 L***; GOULDER 1989*; PLUMMER 1922 lii	2,38; 7,21 v.l.; 10,21; 12,12; 13,31; 20,19; 24,33	16,18; 22,13	0	0
ὥρα + determinative BOISMARD 1985 Cb87; DENAUX 2009 lA*; NEIRYNCK 1985	1,10; 14,17	2,15; 3,1; 10,3; 16,33; 23,23	0	0

Literature
COLLISON 1977 135 [ἐν αὐτῇ τῇ ὥρᾳ: linguistic usage of Luke: certain]; EASTON 1910 166 [ἡ ὥρα with genitive: cited by Weiss as characteristic of L, and possibly corroborative]; GERSDORF 1816 261 [αὐτῇ τῇ ὥρᾳ]; HAUCK 1934 [Vorzugsverbindung: ἐν αὐτῇ τῇ ὥρᾳ]; JEREMIAS 1980 31 [τῇ ὥρᾳ τοῦ ϑυμιάματος: trad.].

BURCHARD, Christoph, Fußnoten zum neutestamentlichen Griechisch, 1970. Esp. 167-168: "Act 19,34 ὡς ἐπὶ ὥρας δύο κράζοντες".

CADBURY, Henry J., Some Lukan Expressions of Time (Lexical Notes on Luke-Acts VII). — JBL 82 (1963) 272-278.

CRAGHAN, John F., A Redactional Study of Lk 7,21 in the Light of Dt 19,15. — CBQ 29 (1967) 353-367. Esp. 52-56: "The redactor's hand" [ἐν αὐτῇ/ἐκείνῃ τῇ ὥρᾳ].

DENAUX, Adelbert, L'hypocrisie des pharisiens et le dessein de Dieu, 1973. Esp. 258-259 [ἐν αὐτῇ τῇ ὥρᾳ]; [2]1989. Esp. 168-169.

FERRARO, Giuseppe, Il termine "ora" nei vangeli sinottici. — RivBib 21 (1973) 383-400.

JEREMIAS, Joachim, Ἐν ἐκείνῃ τῇ ὥρᾳ, (ἐν) αὐτῇ τῇ ὥρᾳ. — ZNW 42 (1949) 214-217.

ὡς 51/58 + 63/66 (Mt 40/43, Mk 22/26)	

1. like (Lk 3,22); 2. that (Lk 24,6); 3. how (Lk 24,35); 4. when (Lk 1,41); 5. while (Lk 12,58); 6. because (Acts 28,19); 7. in order to (Lk 9,52; Acts 20,24); 8. as a result; 9. approximately (Acts 4,4); 10. how great

Word groups	Lk	Acts	Mt	Mk
οὐχ ὡς (VKj)		28,19	2	1
πῶς ... ὡς (VKb)		20,(18-)20	0	1
ὡς causal: as, inasmuch as, since, seeing that (SCad) → **ὡς** γέγραπται		17,28; 22,5; 25,10	3	0
ὡς comparison with finite verb (SCaa) → **ὡς** γέγραπται	3,23; 9,54*; 11,36; 14,22*	2,15; 23,11	1	2
ὡς comparison without finite verb (SCb)	3,22; 6,22.40; 10,3.18; 11,2*.44; 12,27; 15,21*; 17,6; 18,11.17; 21,35; 22,26[1].31.52	3,22; 7,51; 8,32[1,2]; 9,18; 10,11.47; 11,5.17	22/23	8/10
ὡς + infinitive (final) (SCc; VKq) DENAUX 2009 LA[n]	9,52	20,24	0	0
ὡς + numerals (about, nearly) (SCbd; VKe)	1,56; 2,37*; 8,42	1,15*; 4,4; 5,7.36; 13,18.20; 19,34; 27,37*	0/1	2
ὡς + predicate: 2 acc. (SCbb)	10,27; 15,19.21*	7,37; 17,22	4	2
ὡς relative (SCaf)	14,22*		7	0
ὡς + subjunctive (VKp)		20,24	0	1
ὡς + superlative (SCbc; VKh)		17,15	0	0
ὡς γάρ (VKl) → **καθὼς/ὥσπερ** γάρ	12,58	23,11	1	0
ὡς (+) γέγραπται (SCae) → ὡς (causal/comparison); **καθὼς** γέγραπται	3,4	13,33	0	1/2
ὡς ἐτῶν ὀγδοήκοντα τεσσάρων	2,37*		0	0
ὡς + εὐθέως (VKd)		16,10	0	0
ὡς καί (VKk) → **καθὼς/ὁμοίως/ οὕτως/ὥσπερ** καί; cf. ὡς κἀγώ Mt 18,33	9,54*	10,47; 11,17; 13,33; 17,28; 22,5; 25,10	3/4	0
ὡς + καί (VKc) → **καθώς** + καί	2,15 v.l.; 7,12; 11,2*	1,10; 7,51; 10,17 v.l.	1/2	0
ὡς ὅταν (VKs); cf. ὡς ἐάν Mk 4,26 v.l.	11,36		0	0
ὡς + οὕτως (VKa) → **καθώς** + ὁμοίως/οὕτως; **ὥσπερ** + οὕτως		8,32[2]; 23,11	1	1
ὡς τάχιστα (LN: as soon as possible)		17,15	0	0
→ **μιμνήσκομαι** ὡς; **ποιέω** ὡς				

Characteristic of Luke	Lk	Acts	Mt	Mk
ἐγένετο ὡς temporal + finite verb (SCab) CREDNER 1836 133; DENAUX 2009 L***	1,23.41; 2,15; 19,29		0	0
καὶ ὡς → καὶ **καθώς/οὕτως**; cf. Heb 7,9 BOISMARD 1984 Bb17; DENAUX 2009 L***; NEIRYNCK 1985; PLUMMER 1922 lii	2,39; 8,47; 15,25; 17,28*; 18,11; 19,5. 41; 22,66; 23,26.55; 24,32 v.l.35	1,10; 8,32; 13,18	0	1
ὡς adverb + participle (SCba; VKg) BOISMARD 1984 Eb24; NEIRYNCK 1985	16,1; 22,26[2].27; 23,14	3,12; 23,15.20; 27,30; 28,19	1	2
ὡς = approximately HARNACK 1906 143	1,56; 8,42	4,4; 5,7.36; 13,18.20; 27,37*	0	2

ὡς conjunction; cf. Jn 2,9.23; 4,1. 40; 6,12.16; 7,10; 11,6.20.29.32. 33; 12,35.36; 18,6; 19,33; 20,11; 21,9; Rom 1,9; 15,24; 1 Cor 11,34; 2 Cor 5,19; 7,15; Phil 1,8; 2,23; Col 2,6; 1 Thess 2,10.11; 2 Thess 2,2; 2 Tim 1,3; Heb 7,9 BOISMARD 1984 Cb130; DENAUX 2009 L***; NEIRYNCK 1985	1,23.41.44; 2,15.39; 4,25; 5,4; 6,4; 7,12; 8,47; 9,52; 11,1; 12,58; 15,25; 19,5.29.41; 20,37; 22,61.66; 23,26.55; 24,6.32$^{1.2}$.35	1,10; 5,24; 7,23; 8,36; 9,23; 10,7.17.25.28.38; 11,16; 13,25.29; 14,5; 16,4.10.15; 17,13; 18,5; 19,9.21; 20,14.18.20.24; 21,1.12.27; 22,11.25; 25,14; 27,1.27; 28,4	0/1	2
ὡς indirect questions (SCag) DENAUX 2009 L***	6,4; 8,47; 22,61; 23,55; 24,6.35	10,28.38; 11,16; 20,20	0	1/2
ὡς temporal (SCac) DENAUX 2009 L***; GOULDER 1989*; HARNACK 1906 29.139; HAWKINS 1909L	1,44; 2,39; 4,25; 5,4; 7,12; 11,1; 12,58; 15,25; 17,28*; 19,5.41; 20,37; 22,66; 23,26; 24,32$^{1.2}$	1,10; 5,24; 7,23; 8,36; 9,23; 10,7.17.25; 13,25.29; 14,5; 16,4.10.15; 17,13; 18,5; 19,9.21; 20,14.18; 21,1.12.27; 22,11.25; 25,14; 27,1.27; 28,4	0/1	1
ὡς δέ (VKm) → καθὼς δέ; cf. Jn 2,9.23; 6,12.16; 7,10; 8,7 BOISMARD 1984 Bb55; DENAUX 2009 lA*; NEIRYNCK 1985	5,4; 7,12	5,24; 7,23; 8,36; 9,23; 10,7.17.25; 13,25.29; 14,5; 16,4.10.15; 17,13; 18,5; 19,9.21; 20,14.18; 21,1.12.27; 22,11.25; 25,14; 27,1.27; 28,4	0/1	0
ὡς (δὲ) ἐγένετο DENAUX 2009 LA*	1,44; 4,25; 17,28*; 22,66	10,25;14,5; 21,1	0	0
ὡς (δὲ) ἐτέλεσαν ἅπαντα/πάντα VOGEL 1899C	2,39	13,29	0	0
ὡς + ἤγγισεν DENAUX 2009 L***; PLUMMER 1922 lii	7,12; 15,25; 19,29.41		0	0

Literature

VON BENDEMANN 2001 419; 435 [καὶ ἐγένετο ὡς ἤγγισεν]; COLLISON 1977 117 [καὶ ὡς temporal/attendant circumstances: linguistic usage of Luke: likely]; 121 [temporal: certain. It may also be a linguistic usage of Luke's "other source-material"]; 122 [attendant circumstances: probable]; DENAUX 2009 lAn [ὡς adverb + participle, ὡς = approximately], LA^n [ὡς (δὲ) ἐτέλεσαν ἅπαντα/πάντα]; GERSDORF 1816 191-192 [καὶ ἐγένετο ὡς ἐπλήσθησαν]; 260 [ὡς ἐτῶν ὀγδοήκοντα τεσσάρων]; 261 [ὡς ἐτέλεσαν ἅπαντα]; JEREMIAS 1980 45: "Kennzeichnend für den lukanischen Gebrauch des ὡς temp. ist neben dieser beachtlichen Statistik: erstens die Beobachtung, daß von den 29 Belegen für ὡς temp., die die Apg aufweist, nicht weniger als 28 stereotyp auf ὡς ein δέ folgen lassen, während nur eine einzige Stelle καὶ ὡς bietet (1,10). Wendet man sich mit dieser Feststellung dem dritten Evangelium zu, so hat man die beiden ὡς δέ (5,4; 7,12) der Redaktion zuzuweisen, dagegen die 6 καὶ ὡς als vorlukanisch anzusprechen"; 103 [ὡς γέγραπται: red.]; 310: "Mit ὡς eingeleitete indirekte Fragesätze finden sich außer bei Paulus (Röm 11,2; 2 Kor 7,15) nur im lk Doppelwerk" [Lk 8,47; 23,55; 24,35; Acts 10,38; 20,20]; RADL 1975 403 [ὡς δὲ ἐγένετο]; 424 [πληρόω after ὡς δέ]; 430 [ὡς (= "wie") καί; ὡς "als Konjunktion"; ὡς δέ]; REHKOPF 1959 95 [καὶ ὡς (temporal); 98 [ὡς (εἶναι, γίνεσθαι ὡς): vorlukanisch]; SCHNEIDER 1969 94.164 [ὡς (conj.): Vorzugswörter und -ausdrücke des Luk]; 106.164: "καὶ ὡς (temporal) scheint luk Eigentümlichkeit zu sein" [Vorzugswörter und -ausdrücke des Luk]; SCHÜRMANN 1957 77 [γίνεσθαι ὡς]; 89 [ὡς c. part.; εἶναι ὡς]; 1961 271 [καὶ ὡς]; 277 [ὡς (εἶναι, γίνεσθαι ὡς)].

MURAOKA, Takamitsu, The Use of ὡς in the Greek Bible. — NT 7 (1964-65) 51-72.
NEIRYNCK, Frans, La matière marcienne dans l'évangile de Luc, 1973. Esp. 184 [ὡς time]; ^{2}1989. Esp. 94; = ID., Evangelica, 1982. Esp. 64.

ὡσαύτως 3/4 (Mt 4, Mk 2)   in the same way (Lk 13,5; 20,31; 22,20)

Word groups	Lk	Acts	Mt	Mk
ὡσαύτως (δὲ) καί (VKa)	20,31; 22,20 v.l.		0/1	1

Literature
PETZER, Kobus H., Style and Text in the Lucan Narrative of the Institution of the Lord's Supper, 1991. Esp. 117-118.

ὡσεί 9/11 + 6/10 (Mt 3/5, Mk 1/3)
1. like (Lk 22,44; 24,11); 2. approximately (Lk 22,41)

Word groups	Lk	Acts	Mt	Mk
φαίνω ὡσεί	24,11		0	0

Characteristic of Luke
BOISMARD 1984 cb70; CREDNER 1836 137; DENAUX 2009 L***; GASTON 1973 65 [Lked]; GOULDER 1989*; HAWKINS 1909L; NEIRYNCK 1985; PLUMMER 1922 lx; VOGEL 1899D

	Lk	Acts	Mt	Mk
ὡσεί + expression of time BOISMARD 1984 Ab65; NEIRYNCK 1985	9,28; 22,59; 23,44	10,3; 19,34*	0	0
ὡσεί + numeral (SCa; VKa) BOISMARD 1984 Bb24; CADBURY 1920 129; DENAUX 2009 L***; NEIRYNCK 1985	1,56*; 3,23; 9,14$^{1.2}$.28; 22,59; 23,44	1,15; 2,41; 4,4*; 5,36*; 10,3; 19,7.34*	1	0/1

Literature
COLLISON 1977 112 [linguistic usage of Luke: certain; with numerals: certain]; DENAUX 2009 La^n [ὡσεί + expression of time]; GERSDORF 1816 201 [ὡσεὶ μῆνας τρεῖς]; HAUCK 1934 [Vorzugswort]; JEREMIAS 1980 114 [red.]; SCHNEIDER 1969 86.164 [Vorzugswörter und - ausdrücke des Luk].

SCHNEIDER, Gerhard, Engel und Blutschweiß (Lk 22,43-44): "Redaktionsgeschichte" im Dienste der Textkritik. — BZ NF 20 (1976) 112-116. Esp. 113-115: "Vokabular und Stil von Lk 22,43.44"; = ID., Lukas, Theologe der Heilsgeschichte, 1985, 153-157. Esp. 154-156.
TUCKETT, Christopher M., Luke 22,43-44: The "Agony" in the Garden and Luke's Gospel. — DENAUX, Adelbert (ed.), New Testament Textual Criticism and Exegesis. FS J. Delobel, 2002, 131-144. Esp. 133-135: "Vocabulary and style".

ὥσπερ 2 + 3 (Mt 10/14)   just as

Word groups	Lk	Acts	Mt	Mk
ὥσπερ conjuction with finite verb (SCa)	17,24		7/9	0
ὥσπερ particle of comparsion without finite verb (SCb)	18,11	2,2; 3,17; 11,15	3/5	0
ὥσπερ γάρ (VKd) → καθὼς/ὡς γάρ	17,24		4/5	0
ὥσπερ καί (VKc) → καθὼς/ὁμοίως/οὕτως/ὡς καί BOISMARD 1984 Aa167		3,17; 11,15	0	0
ὥσπερ + οὕτως (SCc; VKa) → ὡς + οὕτως	17,24		4/5	0

Literature
ELLIOTT, James K., Καθώς and ὥσπερ in the New Testament. — FilolNT 4 (1991) 55-58. Esp. 55: "In Luke the καθώς clause usually follows the main clause: 1:2,55,70, 2:20,23, 5:14, 6:36, 11:1, 19:32, 22:13,29, 24:24,39. There are four exceptions (6:31, 11:30, 17:26,28) where

καθώς clause precedes. In each of these, the main clause is introduced by an expression which refers back to the καθώς]; 56: "In Acts 2:4,22, 7:42,44,48, 15:8,14,15, 22:3 the καθώς-clause follows the main clause. At 7:17, 11:29 it precedes but with no resumptive word following]; 58: "It [ὥσπερ] appears at Luke 17:24 also, but at Luke 18:11 we should read ὡς. At Acts 2:2, 3:17, 11:15 ὥσπερ follows. At 2:2 a noun has to be supplied from the main clause and ὥσπερ is equivalent to 'like,' but at 3:17, 11:15 a verb is wanted. ... Καθώς predominates in Luke (seventeen against one)".

ὥστε 4/5 + 8 (Mt 15, Mk 13)

1. as a result (Lk 5?7. 12,1); 2. in order to (Lk 4,29. 20?20)

Word groups	Lk	Acts	Mt	Mk
οὕτως + ὥστε (SCe; VKf)		14,1	0	0
ὥστε + infinitive (SCd)	4,29; 5,7; 9,52*; 12,1; 20,20	1,19; 5,15; 14,1; 15,39; 16,26; 19,10.12.16	12	11
ὥστε καί → ἕως καί; cf. ἵνα καί Mk 1,38; 11,25		5,15; 19,12	0	0

Literature

EASTON 1910 158 [ὥστε with infinitive of purpose: probably characteristic of L]; JEREMIAS 1980 127 ["ὥστε mit Inf. zum Ausdruck der beabsichtigten Folge": red.].

HIGGINS, Martin J., New Testament Result Clauses with Infinitive. — CBQ 23 (1961) 233-241.

MURAOKA, Takamitsu, Purpose of Result? Ὥστε in Biblical Greek. — NT 15 (1973) 205-219.

ὠτίον 1 (Mt 1, Mk 0/1)　　　ear (Lk 22,51)

Literature

ULRICHS, Karl Friedrich, Some Notes on Ears in Luke-Acts especially in Lk. 4.21. — BibNot 98 (1999) 28-31. [NTA 44, 975]

ὠφελέω 1 (Mt 3, Mk 3)

1. help (Lk 9,25); 2. accomplish